encyclopedia of
GENOCIDE *and* CRIMES AGAINST HUMANITY

editorial board

encyclopedia of
GENOCIDE *and* CRIMES AGAINST HUMANITY

Dinah L. Shelton [EDITOR IN CHIEF]

[A–H] 1

MACMILLAN REFERENCE USA
An imprint of Thomson Gale, a part of The Thomson Corporation

THOMSON
GALE

Detroit • New York • San Francisco • San Diego • New Haven, Conn. • Waterville, Maine • London • Munich

THOMSON

GALE

Encyclopedia of Genocide and Crimes Against Humanity
Dinah L. Shelton

Library of Congress Cataloging-in-Publication Data

Encyclopedia of genocide and crimes against humanity
Dinah L. Shelton, editor in chief.
    p. cm.
       Includes bibliographical references and index.
       ISBN 0-02-865847-7 (set hardcover : alk. paper)—
       ISBN 0-02-865848-5 (v. 1 : alk. paper)—ISBN 0-02-865849-3
       (v. 2 : alk. paper)—ISBN 0-02-865850-7 (v. 3 : alk. paper)—
       ISBN 0-02-865992-9 (ebook) 1. Genocide—History—
       Encyclopedias. I. Shelton, Dinah.
HV6322.7.E532 2004
304.66303—dc22   2004006587

This title is also available as an ebook.
ISBN 0-02-865992-9
Contact your Gale sales representative for ordering information.

Printed in the United States of America
10 9 8 7 6 5 4 3

contents

[VOLUME ONE] **1** Preface [vii]
Introduction [xi]
List of Articles [xix]
List of Contributors [xxv]
Outline of Contents [xxxiii]

*Encyclopedia of Genocide and Crimes
Against Humanity* [1]
A–H [1]

[VOLUME TWO] **2** I–S [483]

[VOLUME THREE] **3** T–Z [1017]
Glossary [1187]
Filmography [1191]
Primary Sources [1201]
Index [1395]

editorial and production staff

Project Editors	Justine Ciovacco Shawn Corridor
Additional Editing	Mark Drouillard Matthew May Kate Millson Wendy Morman Jenai Mynatt
Imaging	Randy Bassett Dean Dauphinais Lezlie Light Robyn Young
Cartography	XNR Productions (Madison, Wisconsin)
Copyeditors	Patti Brecht and Peter Rocheleau of BRECHT Nancy Gratton Gina Misiroglu Richard Rothschild Eleanor Stanford
Caption Writers	Patti Brecht and Peter Rocheleau of BRECHT
Proofreaders	Jane Brennan Shanna Weagle Ann Weller
Indexer	Laurie Andriot
Art Director	Michelle DiMercurio
Compositor	Datapage Technologies International (St. Peters, Missouri)
Permissions	Margaret A. Chamberlain Shalice Shah-Caldwell
Manager, Composition	Mary Beth Trimper
Assistant Manager, Composition	Evi Seoud
Manufacturing	Wendy Blurton
Editorial Director	Hélène Potter
Publisher	Frank Menchaca

preface

The *Encyclopedia of Genocide and Crimes Against Humanity* tackles a difficult and often horrific subject. It looks at the worst, but also the best, of human behavior. The set is designed to offer the reader information about the barbarous acts that humans have perpetrated against each other throughout history, but also at the many and sometimes heroic efforts that have been made to understand, prevent, combat, and respond to such acts through law, politics, education, the arts, and sciences. The *Encyclopedia* is intended for general readers with a high school or college level education, although many professionals working in humanitarian and human rights organizations will find much here of use and interest to them.

World War II's Holocaust brought a new language into the world, including the word genocide. In response to the horrors of that event and other crimes committed in Europe and Asia, the international community conducted trials to prosecute and punish crimes against peace, crimes against humanity, and war crimes. These terms garnered better understanding as a result, although war crimes trials had precedents from earlier conflicts. After the Nuremberg and Tokyo trials, the first half of the twentieth century ended with states adopting an international treaty, the Convention for the Prosecution and Punishment of the Crime of Genocide, which outlawed efforts to destroy a people. Subsequent agreements have further identified and defined *war crimes* and *crimes against humanity*.

Genocide and crimes against humanity are not merely historical phenomena. It is estimated that more than 250 armed conflicts have occurred since World War II, with casualties numbering upwards of 170 million people. Some of these conflicts have been genocidal or involved war crimes and crimes against humanity, such as so-called ethnic cleansing and the use of rape as an instrument of war. Indeed, nearly all uses of armed force have involved issues discussed in the *Encyclopedia*. Massive human rights abuses committed by repressive regimes, such as kidnapping and disappearance of political opponents, massacres of minorities and systematic torture also fall within the rubric of crimes against humanity and, sadly, exist in contemporary society.

Efforts to prevent and respond to genocide and crimes against humanity are evident in the development of international criminal courts, peacekeeping, and humanitarian intervention by the United Nations, and the many educational programs and cinematic representations intended to raise public awareness of the problem. In addition, those countries throughout the world that are recovering from internal conflict or repression face the tasks of understanding the past, making appropriate redress to survivors or victims of abuse, and ensuring the accountability of those responsible for the commission of violent acts.

The topic is thus of vital importance and requires the involvement of a wide array of intellectual disciplines, professions, and skills. Historians, archaeologists, and anthropologists explain its global and temporal dimensions, identifying the past events that often led to current conflicts. Psychologists, philosophers, and theologians attempt to grapple with the reasons why human beings commit atrocities and seek to understand the responsive behavior of others, from collaboration through silence to active opposition. Lawyers and political scientists seek to construct institutions and legal structures that can impact human behavior, deterring genocide and crimes against humanity by designing effective and appropriate laws and punishment. Those in the arts educate and raise public awareness through film, music, painting, and writing. All of these disciplines appear in the *Encyclopedia.*

There are more than 350 entries in the *Encyclopedia of Genocide and Crimes Against Humanity,* arranged in alphabetical order for easy reference. In addition, an outline of contents at the beginning of volume one groups the entries thematically. The entries range in length from five hundred to five thousand words and concern historical and contemporary examples of genocide and crimes against humanity, individuals, groups, international institutions and law, theories and philosophy, prevention, prosecution, and cultural representations.

The set covers the ancient world to the present day and looks at all regions of the world. The editorial board affirmatively decided to include any event that has been publicly and reasonably debated as falling within the subject matter broadly viewed. Groups that have been the target of genocide or crimes against humanity are separately discussed, as are the known perpetrators. The various forms of reparation and redress available to victims and survivors are included, as are the courts and tribunals where the accused may be tried for their alleged offenses. Some entries describe the means used to incite public opinion toward hatred and genocidal acts, such as through advertising, radio broadcasts, and film. Short entries provide biographical information about key historical and contemporary figures, from Genghis Kahn to Simon Wiesenthal, while others describe important places such as Auschwitz and Srebrenica. Discussions of national and international policies during periods of genocide and crimes against humanity aim to provide readers with a wider perspective on the events reported.

The entries were written by experts, authorities in their respective fields. Like the topics they address, the authors come from countries throughout the world. As much as possible, the authors have used language that should be easily accessible to the public at large. The authors and editors have also attempted to be responsive to the sensitive nature of the topic, avoiding terms that may be offensive and noting where respected opinion is divided on the events or persons they describe. The result is a set of entries reflecting solid scholarship. A glossary of terms with which the reader might be unfamiliar appears at the end of the third volume, and each entry contains a bibliography to guide readers to further sources of information. Cross-references at the end of each entry refer to related topics.

The *Encyclopedia* contains historical images and contemporary photographs to illustrate the entries. Particularly for this topic, it is often difficult to visualize the reality of the events described. The editors have chosen the images carefully, not to shock but to provide further information and representation of the events and persons included.

At the end of the set, further material is included to assist the reader. In addition to the glossary, the concluding matter includes a filmography, primary source documents, and a comprehensive subject index. The primary documents may be of particular interest to those undertaking research in this field. The documents consist of key legal instruments, such as the Convention for the Prosecution and Punishment of the Crime of Genocide and the Rome Statute of the International Criminal Court, as well as several important judicial decisions.

The editorial board and contributors have all benefited from the editorial assistance given by individuals at Macmillan Reference USA, in particular Hélène Potter, Justine Ciovacco, and Shawn Corridor. Their dedication to the project and infinite capacity for work inspired everyone. We express our thanks to them and to the others who contributed by suggesting authors, entries, and materials for the set.

Dinah L. Shelton

introduction

Human beings have committed atrocities against each other, showed compassion and altruism, and both perpetrated and combated oppression for at least as long as recorded history. The archaeological record as well as recent forensic evidence reveal the burning of cities, massacres, enslavement, and fearsome tortures inflicted on captives. The preamble to the 1948 Convention against Genocide says, "at all periods of history genocide has inflicted great losses on humanity." It is also true for crimes against humanity. At the same time, religious and philosophical texts from all parts of the world contain variations on the "Golden Rule": treat others as you would be treated.

It is perhaps impossible to understand or reach conclusions about these competing strands of human history to determine whether human nature is innately good or intrinsically driven to violence and power. If it is equally impossible to document in detail the innumerable incidents of good and evil. At the same time, it is crucial to remember the dark periods when the worst traits in human beings have flourished, in order to think about and put into place means to prevent future abuses and to remember and mourn the millions of victims. The resisters and rescuers must be celebrated and the role of institutions studied, especially those that seek accountability and deny impunity for perpetrators.

These volumes are intended to be used not only as a tool to look into particular acts as well as agents of and opponents to genocide and crimes against humanity, but to understand from various angles the modes of expressions through which such acts are anticipated or ignored, articulated and covered up, understood and memorialized.

Historical Overview

Many events, persons, places, and devices that make up the historical record are included in the following three volumes. The aim is to present as factual a record as possible, noting where respected scholarship differs about the responsibility for or characterization of events. The reader may evaluate the evidence and reach his or her own conclusions. The *Encyclopedia* focuses on those acts that may fall within the definitions developed over the past century of crimes under international law: war crimes, genocide, and crimes against humanity. These labels attach to the most serious violations of the dignity and worth of each human being. Genocide itself is both a crime against humanity and the greatest of such crimes. It is appropriate to include in one encyclopedia all crimes against humanity while featuring genocide as their most prominent and extreme expression. Further, by including all such crimes in the same encyclopedia, the understanding of their relationship becomes clearer.

At the time many of the events discussed herein took place, the protection of individuals from abuse had almost no role in international law and played little part in national or local law. Slavery was legal in most countries until the second half of the nineteenth century; colonial conquest and racial discrimination were prevalent and many indigenous groups were enslaved or annihilated by invaders. Torture and trial by ordeal were part of the criminal process by which it was assumed the truth would emerge. War was a means to gain wealth through looting and acquisition of territory. Rape, pillage, and destruction were the common features of armed conflict, with women and children considered a form of property to be taken along with works of art and other valuables.

Traditional international law regulated the international relations of states. Individuals or groups of individuals were only indirectly regulated in respect to specific matters having international consequence, like diplomatic immunities, asylum. In addition, only states could be responsible for violations of international law, except in the case of pirates who were deemed "enemies of all mankind" (*hostis humani*) and subject to prosecution by any state which captured them.

By the second half of the nineteenth century, international efforts to combat some of the worst abuses committed or tolerated by states had emerged, with anti-slavery societies and laws for the conduct of war becoming part of the national and international orders. Humanitarian law sought to protect various categories of persons not engaged in combat: prisoners of war, shipwrecked, sick or wounded, and civilian populations of occupied territories. Persons in these categories were automatically placed in a legal relationship with the foreign state having power over them, without necessarily involving any role for the state of which they were nationals.

By the beginning of the twentieth century, the development of more rapid means of communication, through invention of the telephone and telegraph, meant the public could be informed more quickly and take notice of events happening in distant parts of the world. Travel was also made easier with the use of steam and later gasoline engines. As the world grew smaller, information about massacres and other widespread abuses became harder to conceal. Public opinion emerged as a factor in law and politics. Still, the plight of the Hereros in 1904–1907 and the massacre of the Armenians somewhat later produced little concrete action, perhaps because not enough information was made available to the public to avoid a debate about whether or not genocide was taking place could not be avoided.

Atrocities at the beginning of the twentieth century paled in comparison with the Holocaust of World War II in which the deliberate and systematic effort to destroy entire groups of people because of their identity, rather than because of anything done by a particular individual, led to an unprecedented industrialization of murder. The postwar period vowed "Never Again" and took action to prosecute and punish those responsible for the worst abuses of the war. Yet, the national and international legal instruments designed to prevent genocide and crimes against humanity after World War II have not prevented these acts from continuing into the present. In 1994 in Rwanda, for example, an international military force was present and others available that might have stopped the genocide. Yet the atrocities continued without intervention until they had nearly run their course. In Cambodia (Kampuchea), as well, the world watched as mass killings gave rise to a new term: the *killing fields*. These events indicate that much greater understanding is necessary of the role of bystanders, as well as perpetrators and their victims.

Crimes and Punishment

Atrocities committed throughout history were rarely punished because the perpetrators acted with the authority and protection of governments. Only in the mid-twentieth century did the idea take hold that barbarous acts condoned by the governments where they took place could and should be punished by national or international courts.

Although the terms *genocide* and *crimes against humanity* are widely used in a colloquial sense to describe atrocities and mass killings, they also have a quite precise legal meaning. Indeed, fundamental principles of criminal law make it essential that the crimes be defined without ambiguity as a matter of fairness to all persons, who must be forewarned about the illegality of their behavior. The *Encyclopedia* retraces and explains, in depth, the evolution and terms of the body of laws in vigor now.

Many of the acts discussed in the *Encyclopedia* are considered to be crimes under international and national laws. Mechanisms of accountability seek to punish and deter perpetrators and provide redress for victims. While there are a few historical examples, accountability in both national and international law is relatively recent. Internationally, states could be held liable in some circumstances for the mistreatment of citizens of other states, but not of their own citizens. The laws of war allowed soldiers to be prosecuted for war crimes and examples of such trials date back to the late Middle Ages, but international law, generally, and treaties, specifically, demanded little in the way of accountability.

After World War I, the Allies created a commission which found that numerous acts had been committed in violation of established laws and customs of war and the elementary laws of humanity, but no international trials were held. A few individuals were tried by national courts.

At the end of World War II, the Allies brought before international tribunals the leaders and others involved in abuse of civilians and prisoners of war. Both crimes against humanity and genocide were first defined at this time, as Allied lawyers sought a basis for prosecutions of Nazi leaders. Because many of the Nazi atrocities, most specifically the persecution and extermination of the Jews and other groups within Germany, were carried out under cover of Nazi law in force at the time, it was necessary to root the war crimes in international law.

The creation of the courts at Nuremberg and Tokyo launched a half-century of advance in laws and procedures designed to restrain abuses of power. The trials emphasized that individuals, not the abstraction of states or governments, are responsible for violations of the law. The prosecutions of Nazi leaders provided the impetus for a more general recognition that such atrocities could be prosecuted by international courts, or by national courts operating on the basis of international law, even when they were condoned by the legal system of the country where they took place. It is presently widely accepted that those who order or commit such acts must be held accountable. The World War II trials helped ensure the development of the law and established the legitimacy of international criminal proceedings. The revelations about the Holocaust demanded invention of a new word to describe the scale and depth of what occurred: *genocide,* a term first proposed by Raphael Lemkin.

The Nuremberg Trial of the major Nazi war criminals established "crimes against humanity" as a general category of international offence, comprising forms of persecution, extermination, and deportation on racial, religious and political grounds. Following the trials, the newly created United Nations affirmed in 1946 the law and principles that formed the basis of the judgments and proceeded to draft the Convention to Prevent and Punish Genocide, adopted in 1948. The Convention defined genocide as the physical destruction of national, ethnic, racial, and religious groups, in whole or in part.

Genocide was in essence an aggravated form of crime against humanity. Whereas genocide involved the physical annihilation of the group, crimes against humanity covered a larger range of acts, subsumed under such terms as *persecution*. Genocide only covered groups defined by race, nationality, ethnicity or religion, whereas crimes against humanity extended to include political groups as well. But at the time they were devised in the mid-1940s, probably the most important difference was the fact that genocide could be committed in time of peace as well as during war. Crimes against humanity, though broader in scope in some respects, were also more limited, because they could only be carried out in time of armed conflict.

Another step in shifting the focus of international law from states to individuals came with the direct recognition of fundamental human rights and freedoms for all persons, independently of nationality or status under the jurisdiction of a given state. The United Nations and regional institutions in Europe, the Americas, and Africa proclaimed human rights and created international institutions and procedures where individuals claiming their rights had been violated could obtain a review of the matter. These were revolutionary developments in international law and relations, although they involved complaints brought against states and not against the individuals within the state responsible for the wrongs.

Immediately after the United Nations was founded, some members called for the establishment of a permanent international tribunal to try and punish those who commit international crimes. It took nearly half a century before the International Criminal Tribunal was in place. Indeed, for close to four decades from the 1950s, the idea was dormant. In the meantime, however, national courts became increasingly willing to prosecute crimes against humanity when committed in peacetime. In addition, when new atrocities appeared in various regions of the world—Cambodia, Yugoslavia and Rwanda—the UN responded by creating international criminal tribunals (for Yugoslavia and Rwanda) or trying to create such tribunals (Cambodia). Mixed national/international tribunals also have been created or foreseen for Sierra Leone, East Timor, and perhaps Cambodia. By the 1980s it became clear that impunity, that is, the failure to hold individuals responsible for committing atrocities, was not only encouraging further human rights violations, but that it was also a violation of the rights of the victims themselves to redress. The international community proceeded with efforts to establish a permanent international criminal court, adopting the statute of the court in 1998. The Court was formally created in 2002.

Although people still refer to war crimes trials, most international prosecutions address crimes that can be committed in peacetime. Genocide and crimes against humanity are in many ways the counterpart to the concept of gross and systematic violations of human rights, also prohibited by international law. The terms *genocide* and *crimes against humanity* are used by criminal courts to hold individuals accountable, while the phrase gross and systematic violations of human rights usually applies to acts of governments. In fact, because the acts of governments or states are committed by individuals, the terms are merely different ways to designate the same phenomenon: atrocities committed against vulnerable groups, usually racial or ethnic minorities.

Genocide and crimes against humanity often involve the participation of large numbers of individuals, making criminal prosecution difficult for political and practical reasons. A search for alternative approaches to provide accountability short of a full trial has led to the creation of truth and reconciliation commissions, before which victims and perpetrators can confront each other and attempt to find ways to coexist in post-conflict societies. Thus, South Africa in the 1990s decided not to prosecute most of those responsible for maintaining the apartheid regime, but their crimes were exposed in public and many perpetrators came forward to confess and seek forgiveness.

Presently, the law and procedures range from national to international in the fields of human rights, humanitarian law, and criminal law. The substance of the law determines the list of crimes and the definitional elements that serve to identify when a crime has been committed.

Trials that seek to bring to justice perpetrators must consider the goals of individual accountability. First, accountability can be significant to the victims and to society as a whole as a matter of justice and partial repairing of harm done. Second, accountability may deter future violations by making clear the prospect of punishment for perpetrators and more generally serving the rule of law and strengthening of institutions. Third, accountability is society's expression of moral condemnation and may contribute to rehabilitation of the perpetrator.

Accountability mechanisms often must confront efforts of perpetrators to evade justice through self-amnesties or other measures that afford immunity from prosecution. Even persons committed to the rule of law and human rights sometimes argue that the transition from repression to a democratic regime demands reconciliation and forgiveness rather than prosecution. The various goals of accountability may not always be congruent. In most instances, however, human rights tribunals have rejected amnesties because they are viewed as a violation of international obligations and the rights of victims to redress. These decisions rest on the doctrine that states have a duty to prosecute and punish the most serious violations of human rights and humanitarian law or at least to provide some mechanism of accountability.

Understanding

Efforts to understand and thus prevent genocide and crimes against humanity are not limited to laws and tribunals. Various disciplines have been used to gain some insight into the causes and interpretations of genocide and crimes against humanity. They all require documentation. All are used to educate the public on different facets of such crimes.

Modes of Memory, Commemoration, and Representation

Memorials, various modes of artistic expressions in a multiplicity of styles and media are used by witnesses and scholars to represent, re-experience, commemorate, question, and comment upon atrocities and their victims. Dance, film, music, literature, photography, drama, and paintings serve to express what cannot be transmitted solely or completely by historical documentation. The *Encyclopedia* includes entries and illustrations that indicate and reflect upon the importance of artistic expressions to convey the experience, character, and various other facets of genocide and crimes against humanity.

Those Involved

In looking at issues of genocide and crimes against humanity it is not enough to recount events. The individuals involved, whether perpetrators, resisters, victims, rescuers or scholars have been the agents. Their deeds, their motives to the extent known, and their backgrounds can perhaps shed some light on the mystery of otherwise inexplicable brutality. The *Encyclopedia* thus includes general entries covering various categories of actors, such as perpetrators, victims, survivors, and rescuers, as well as individual biographies of persons involved in or witness to the events described. In addition, the psychological and sociological theories that seek to understand, explain, or at least classify behavior are included, as they may be useful in the future.

The Editors

The composition of the board of editors reflects the necessity of an interdisciplinary and international approach to the complex subjects addressed.

Howard Adelman, a Visiting Professor at Princeton University, taught philosophy for over three decades at York University in Toronto, Canada, where he remains a Senior Scholar as well as a Senior Fellow of Massy College at the University of Toronto. He served as Director of the Center for Refugee Studies at York University between 1986 and 1993, and was editor of *Refuge,* Canada's periodical on refugees, for more than a decade. He has received numerous honors for his extensive scholarly work on conflict prevention, management, and resolution; refugees, humanitarian intervention, and genocide. His publications include *War and Peace in Zaire/Congo: Analyzing and Evaluating Intervention 1996–1997* (with Govind Rao, ed., 2003); *The Path of a Genocide: The Rwanda Crisis from Uganda to Zaire* (with Astri Suhrke, ed., 1999); and chapters in edited volumes including "Bystanders to the Genocide in Rwanda: Explanations and Descriptions" in *Genocide at the Turn of the Millenium* (Sam Totten, ed., 2004); "Cultures of Violence" in *Building Sustainable Peace* (Andy Knight, ed., 2004); and "Rwanda" (with Astri Suhrke) in the *UN Security Council: From the Cold War to the 21st Century* (David Malone, ed., 2004).

Frank Chalk is a history professor and the Co-Director of the Montreal Institute for Genocide and Human Rights Studies at Concordia University in Montreal, Quebec, where he teaches undergraduate and graduate courses on the history and sociology of genocide, the Holocaust, and the history of U.S. foreign relations. He has served as President of the International Association of Genocide Scholars and is a past president of the Canadian Association of African Studies. He has taught as a Fulbright Fellow at the University of Ibadan, Nigeria, and has been a Fellow of the Center for Advanced Holocaust Studies of the U.S. Holocaust Memorial Museum, Washington, D.C. He is the co-author (with Kurt Jonassohn) of *The History and Sociology of Genocide: Analyses and Case Studies* (1990). His most recent publications include chapters on "Hate Radio in Rwanda" (in *The Path of a Genocide,* ed. Howard Adelman and Astri Suhrke, 1999) and "Radio Broadcasting in the Incitement and Interdiction of Gross Violations of Human Rights, including Genocide" (in *Genocide: Essays toward Understanding, Early Warning, and Prevention,* ed. Roger Smith, 1999).

Alexandre Kiss is a citizen of France and Hungary. He is former director of the French National Center for Scientific Research and was a professor of law at the University of Strasbourg, France, where he was the director of the Center for Central and Eastern European Studies. He also served for ten years as the Secretary-General of the International Institute of Human Rights, and then became a Vice-President of the Institute. He is a member of the Hungarian Academy of Sciences and has been decorated by several governments and institutions. He has lectured throughout the world on issues of international law, litigated at the International Court of Justice, and is a member of the Permanent Court of Arbitration. His publications include the *Répertoire de la Pratique Française en Matière de Droit International* (7 volumes), *Abus de Droit en Droit International*, numerous works on international environmental law, and a seminal article on limitations in international human rights treaties.

William Schabas has been director of the Irish Centre for Human Rights at the National University of Ireland in Galway since 2000. For the decade before moving to Ireland he taught at the University of Quebec in Montreal, where he was Chair of the Department of Law for four years. He remains a member of the Quebec Bar. In 2002 Professor Schabas was appointed a member of the Truth and Reconciliation Commission of Sierra Leone. He has undertaken missions to investigate human rights violations and international crimes in Rwanda, Burundi, Sudan, Kosovo, and Chechnya and was a participant in the Rome Conference that drafted and adopted the Statute of the International Criminal Court. He has served with the Canadian delegation to international human rights bodies, including the UN Human Rights Commission. He has lectured extensively on humanitarian law and human rights law and is a renowned expert in international criminal law. His many publications include: *The Abolition of the*

Death Penalty in International Law (3rd edition, 2002), *Genocide in International Law* (2000), and *Introduction to the International Criminal Court* (2001). He is also editor of a two-volume set of essays on the Rome Statute of the International Criminal Court.

Dinah Shelton is professor of law at the George Washington University Law School in Washington D.C., where she teaches international law and the international protection of human rights. She has taught at other institutions in the United States and Europe, and lectured in Africa, Asia, and Latin America. She is a Counselor to the American Society of International Law and a member of the Board of Editors of the American Journal of International Law. She serves on the executive committees of numerous international human rights organizations and has been a consultant to most major international organizations concerned with human rights. Her publications on human rights include the prize-winning *Protecting Human Rights in the Americas* (with Thomas Buergenthal, 4th edition, 1995) as well as *Human Rights in a Nutshell* (with Thomas Buergenthal and David Stewart, 3rd edition, 2003), *Remedies in International Human Rights Law* (1999), and the edited volume *Peace, Human Rights and International Criminal Law* (2002). She has also published several books in the field of international environmental law with Alexandre Kiss, and is author of numerous articles on general international law.

Howard Adelman
Frank Chalk
Alexandre Kiss
William A. Schabas
Dinah L. Shelton

list of articles

Volume 1

[A]

Advertising
  Amy W. Leith

African Americans
  Roy L. Brooks

African Crisis Response Initiative
  Horace Campbell

Aggression
  Alfred de Zayas

Algeria
  Azzedine Layachi

Alien Tort Statute
  Beth Stephens

Almohads
  Maribel Fierro

Altruism, Biological
  Alexander J. Field

Altruism, Ethical
  David Miller

Amazon Region
  Alex Shoumatoff

Amnesty
  Michael P. Scharf

Ancient World
  Karin Solveig Bjornson

Anthropology, Cultural
  Alex Hinton

Anti-Semitism
  Frederick M. Schweitzer

Apartheid
  Johan D. van der Vyver

Arbour, Louise
  Carol Off

Archaeology
  Chris A. Robinson

Architecture
  Stephen C. Feinstein

Arendt, Hannah
  Stephen J. Whitfield

Argentina
  Juan E. Méndez

Argentina's Dirty Warriors
  James Brennan

Armenians in Ottoman Turkey
  and the Armenian Genocide
  Vahakn N. Dadrian

Armenians in Russia and the
  USSR
  Dennis R. Papazian

Art, Banned
  Stephen C. Feinstein

Art, Stolen
  Hector Feliciano

Art as Propaganda
  Anna M. Dempsey

Art as Representation
  Stephen C. Feinstein

Assassinations
  Brian K. Morgan

Atatürk, Mustafa Kemal Pasha
  Vahakn N. Dadrian

Athens and Melos
  A. B. Bosworth

Attempt
  Robert Cryer

Auschwitz
  Robert Jan van Pelt

Australia
  Russell McGregor

Aztecs
  Sarah Cline

[B]

Babi Yar
  Karel C. Berkhoff

Bagosora, Théoneste
  Howard Adelman

Bahā'īs
  Kit Bigelow
  Jerry K. Prince

Bangladesh/East Pakistan
  Craig Baxter

Barbie, Klaus
  Michael R. Marrus

Beothuk
  Sharon O'Brien

Biafra/Nigeria
  Kolawole Olaniyan

Biographies
  Mark C. Molesky

Bosnia and Herzegovina
  Christopher Michael Bennett

Burma/Myanmar
Josef Silverstein

Burundi
René Lemarchand

Bystanders
Douglas V. Porpora

[C]

Cambodia
Steve Heder

Canada
David King

Carthage
Michael P. Fronda

Cathars
Beverly Mayne Kienzle

Catholic Church
Joshua Castellino

Chechens
Christopher Swift

Cheyenne
Sharon O'Brien

Children
Nevena Vuckovic Sahovic

Chile
William F. Sater

China
Xiaorong Li

Chittagong Hill Tract, Peoples of
the
Sharon O'Brien

Chmielnicki, Bogdan
Paul Robert Magocsi

Christians, Roman Persecution of
Franziska E. Shlosser

Code of Crimes against the Peace
and Security of Mankind
M. Cherif Bassiouni

Collaboration
Wayne H. Bowen

Comics
Wolfgang K. Hünig

Commission on Responsibilities
M. Cherif Bassiouni

Comparative Genocide
Robert Melson

Compensation
John R. Crook

Complicity
Guénaël Mettraux

Concentration Camps
Joël Kotek

Conspiracy
William A. Schabas

Control Council Law No. 10
John Quigley

Convention on Apartheid
Garth Meintjes

Convention on the Prevention
and Punishment of Genocide
William A. Schabas

Conventions Against Torture and
Other Cruel, Inhuman, and
Degrading Treatment
Hans Christian Krüger
Alessia Sonaglioni

Cossacks
Shane P. O'Rourke

Crimes Against Humanity
Alexandre Kiss
William A. Schabas

Croatia, Independent State of
Robert M. Hayden

Crusades
Dawn Marie Hayes

[D]

Dance
Naomi Jackson

Death March
Joshua Castellino

Death Squads
Arthur D. Brenner

Deception, Perpetrators
Ralph Erber

Deception, Victims
Gunnar S. Paulsson

Defenses
Geert Jan Alexander Knoops

Del Ponte, Carla
Pierre Hazan

Demjanjuk Trial
Vinodh Jaichand

Denationalization
Vinodh Jaichand

Denial
Martin Imbleau

Der Stürmer
Martin Imbleau

Developmental Genocide
Wolfgang Mey

Diaries
Samuel Totten

Disabilities, People with
Janet E. Lord

Disappearances
Markus Schmidt

Documentation
Samuel Totten

Drama, Holocaust
Anat Feinberg

[E]

Early Warning
Gregory H. Stanton

East Timor
James Dunn

Economic Groups
Rebecca L. Barbisch

Education
Joyce A. Apsel

Eichmann Trial
Leora Bilsky

Einsatzgruppen
Benjamin B. Ferencz

El Salvador
Cynthia J. Arnson

Enlightenment
Robert Wokler

Ennals, Martin
Nigel S. Rodley

Enver, Ismail
Alfred de Zayas

Eritrea
John W. Harbeson

Ethiopia
Edward Kissi

Ethnic Cleansing
Norman M. Naimark

Ethnic Groups
Siegfried Wiessner

Ethnicity
Christian P. Scherrer

Ethnocide
Lyndel V. Prott

Eugenics
Lynne Fallwell

European Convention on the
Non-Application of Statutory
Limitations
Hans Christian Krüger
Alessia Sonaglioni

Euthanasia
Leslie C. Griffin

Evidence
Paul Seils
Marieke Wierda

Evil, Banality of Radical
  Robert Fine

Explanation
  Kristen Renwick Monroe

Extermination Centers
  Joël Kotek

Extradition
  Geoff Gilbert

[F]

Famine
  Asbjørn Eide

Female Infanticide and Fetal
  Murder
  Vineeta Gupta

Fiction
  Yvonne S. Unnold

Film as Propaganda
  Carolyn Patty Blum

Films, Armenian Documentary
  J. Michael Hagopian

Films, Armenian Feature
  Atom Egoyan

Films, Dramatizations in
  Marlene Shelton

Films, Eugenics
  John Michalczyk

Films, Holocaust Documentary
  John Michalczyk

Forcible Transfer
  Daniel D. Ntanda Nsereko

Forensics
  Luis Fondebrider
  Mercedes Doretti

France in Tropical Africa
  Benjamin Lawrance
  Richard Roberts

[G]

Gas
  Paulina Rudnicka

Geneva Conventions on the
  Protection of Victims of War
  Jiri Toman

Genghis Khan
  George Lane

Genocide
  Daniel Rothenberg

Germany
  Conan Fischer

Gestapo
  George C. Browder

Ghetto
  Joshua Castellino

Goebbels, Joseph
  Randall L. Bytwerk

Goldstone, Richard
  Garth Meintjes

Göring, Hermann
  Michael R. Marrus

Guatemala
  David Stoll

Gulag
  Edwin Bacon

[H]

Hague Conventions of 1907
  Alexandre Kiss

Harkis
  Géraldine D. Enjelvin

Hate Speech
  Marc Bossuyt
  Stefan Sottiaux

Herero
  Sidney L. Harring

Heydrich, Reinhard
  Francis R. Nicosia

Himmler, Heinrich
  George C. Browder

Hiroshima
  Paul S. Boyer

Historical Injustices
  Dinah L. Shelton

Historiography, Sources in
  Itai Nartzizenfield Sneh

Historiography as a Written Form
  Allan Megill

Hitler, Adolf
  Rudolph Binion

Holocaust
  Christian Gerlach

Homosexuals
  John Cerone
  Jason Bricker

Huguenots
  Raymond A. Mentzer

Humanitarian Intervention
  Sean D. Murphy

Humanitarian Law
  M. Cherif Bassiouni

Human Rights
  Hurst Hannum

Volume 2

[I]

Identification
  Diane Marie Amann

Immunity
  Marc Bossuyt
  Stef Vandeginste

Impunity
  Vahakn N. Dadrian

Incas
  Linda A. Newson

Incitement
  Robert Cryer

India, Ancient and Medieval
  Aloka Parasher-Sen

India, Modern
  Asghar Ali Engineer

Indigenous Peoples
  Erica-Irene A. Daes

Indonesia
  Robert Cribb

Inquisition
  Alexandra Guerson de Oliveira
  Dana Wessell

Intent
  Morten Bergsmo

International Committee of the
  Red Cross
  David P. Forsythe

International Court of Justice
  G. G. Herczegh

International Criminal Court
  Leila Sadat

International Criminal Tribunal
  for Rwanda
  Michelle S. Lyon
  Mark A. Drumbl

International Criminal Tribunal
  for the Former Yugoslavia
  Payam Akhavan
  Mora Johnson

International Law
  Alexandre Kiss

International Law Commission
  William A. Schabas

Investigation
  Xabier Agirre Aranburu

Iran
  Reza Afshari

Iraq
  Michael R. Fischbach

Irving, David, Libel Trial of
   Robert Jan van Pelt

Izetbegović, Alija
   Chris Bennett

[J]

Jackson, Robert
   Arieh Kochavi

Japan
   Franziska Seraphim

Jehovah's Witnesses
   Christine E. King

[K]

Kalimantan
   Jamie S. Davidson

Kalmyks
   Linda Kimball

Karadzic, Radovan
   Laura E. Bishop

Katyn
   Geoffrey Roberts

Khmer Rouge
   Ben Kiernan

Khmer Rouge Prisons and Mass
   Graves
   Craig Etcheson

Khmer Rouge Victim Numbers,
   Estimating
   Craig Etcheson

King Leopold II and the Congo
   Adam Hochschild

Kosovo
   Kathleen Z. Young

Kristallnacht
   Rita Thalmann

Kulaks
   Roman Serbyn

Kuper, Leo
   Bernard F. Hamilton

Kurds
   Amir Hassanpour

[L]

Labor Camps, Nazi
   Geoffrey P. Megargee

Language
   William Gay

Lemkin, Raphael
   Bernard F. Hamilton

Lenin, Vladimir
   Stephen Brown

Lepsius, Johannes
   Christopher Simpson

Liberia
   Daniel Elwood Dunn

Linguistic Genocide
   Tove Skutnabb-Kangas

London Charter
   John Quigley

[M]

Mandela, Nelson
   Alfred de Zayas

Mao Zedong
   Lorenz M. Lüthi

Massacres
   Jacques Semelin

Mass Graves
   William D. Haglund

Medical Experimentation
   Stephen P. Marks

Memoirs of Perpetrators
   Donald G. Schilling

Memoirs of Survivors
   Donald G. Schilling

Memorials and Monuments
   Harriet F. Senie

Memory
   Stephen C. Feinstein

Mengele, Josef
   William D. Haglund

Mercenaries
   Natalie Wagner

Milosevic, Slobodan
   Daniel L. Nadel

Minorities
   Péter Kovács

Mladic, Ratko
   Jaspreet K. Saini

Mongol Conquests
   George Lane

Morgenthau, Henry
   Arieh Kochavi

Moriscos
   Mercedes García-Arenal

Music, Holocaust Hidden and
   Protest
   Bret Werb

Music and Musicians Persecuted
   during the Holocaust
   Viktoria Hertling

Music at Theresienstadt
   Mark D. Ludwig

Music Based on the Armenian
   Genocide
   Jonathan McCollum

Music of Reconciliation
   Tania Krämer

Music of the Holocaust
   Joshua Jacobson

[N]

Namibia (German South West
   Africa and South West Africa)
   Jan-Bart Gewald

Nationalism
   Daniele Conversi

National Laws
   Luc Reydams

National Prosecutions
   John McManus
   Matthew McManus

Native Americans
   Stacie E. Martin

Nongovernmental Organizations
   Kathleen Cavanaugh

Nuclear Weapons
   Roger S. Clark

Nuremberg Laws
   James M. Glass

Nuremberg Trials
   David J. Scheffer

Nuremberg Trials, Subsequent
   Benjamin B. Ferencz

[O]

Organization for Security and
   Cooperation in Europe
   Emmanuel Decaux

[P]

Peacekeeping
   Christopher C. Joyner

Pequots
   Michael Freeman

Perpetrators
   Roger W. Smith

Persecution
   John Cerone

Peru
   Arturo Carrillo

Philosophy
   John K. Roth

Photography of Victims
   Teun Voeten

Physicians
   Lynne Fallwell

Pinochet, Augusto
   Peter Kornbluh

Pius XII, Pope
José M. Sánchez

Poetry
Peter Balakian

Pogroms, Pre-Soviet Russia
John Klier

Political Groups
Clémentine Olivier

Political Theory
Manus I. Midlarsky

Pol Pot
Ben Kiernan

Prevention
Rüdiger Wolfrum

Propaganda
Martin Imbleau

Prosecution
Kai Ambos

Proxmire, William
James T. Fussell

Psychology of Perpetrators
Dan Bar-On

Psychology of Survivors
Aaron Hass

Psychology of Victims
Aaron Hass

Punishment
Meg Penrose

[R]

Racial Groups
Péter Kovács

Racism
Timothy Longman

Radio
Jacques Semelin

Radio Télévision Libre Mille-
Collines
Martin Imbleau

Rape
Patricia Viseur Sellers

Reconciliation
Andrew Rigby

Refugee Camps
François Crépeau
Caroline Lantero

Refugees
François Crépeau
Delphine Nakache

Rehabilitation
Yael Danieli

Religion
T. Jeremy Gunn

Religious Groups
T. Jeremy Gunn

Reparations
Dinah L. Shelton

Reproduction
Patricia Viseur Sellers

Rescuers, Holocaust
Nechama Tec

Residential Schools
Vinodh Jaichand

Resistance
Mark Weitzman

Responsibility, State
James Crawford
Simon Olleson

Restitution
Pietro Sardaro
Paul Lemmens

Ríos Montt, Efraín
Jennifer Schirmer

Romania
Dennis Deletant

Romanis
Ian Hancock

Roosevelt, Eleanor
John F. Sears
Allida M. Black

Rosewood
Maxine D. Jones

Rwanda
Timothy Longman

[S]

Sabra and Shatila
Eyal Zisser

Saddam Hussein
Michael R. Fischbach

Safe Zones
John Cerone

Sand Creek Massacre
Stan Hoig

Satire and Humor
Viktoria Hertling

Shaka Zulu
Ian Knight

Sierra Leone
Paul Richards

Sierra Leone Special Court
Avril McDonald

Slavery, Historical
Patrick Manning

Slavery, Legal Aspects of
Renee C. Redman
Paul Finkelman

Social Darwinism
Peter Amato

Sociology of Perpetrators
Jack Nusan Porter

Sociology of Victims
Jack Nusan Porter

Somalia, Intervention in
Peter Ronayne

South Africa
Kanya Adam
Heribert Adam

Soviet Prisoners of War, 1941 to
1945
Christian Gerlach

Sparta
Ben Kiernan

Srebrenica
Jan Willem Honig

Sri Lanka
Bruce Kapferer

SS
Robert B. Bernheim

Stalin, Joseph
Elaine Mackinnon

Statistical Analysis
Patrick Ball

Statutory Limitations
Bruce Broomhall

Streicher, Julius
Randall L. Bytwerk

Sudan
Robert O. Collins

Superior (or Command)
Responsibility
Daryl A. Mundis

Volume 3

[T]

Taino (Arawak) Indians
Noble David Cook

Talaat
Vahakn N. Dadrian

Televison
Kelly Helen Fry

Terrorism, Psychology behind
Linda M. Woolf

Tibet
Robert A. F. Thurman

Tokyo Trial
R. John Pritchard

Torture
Fiona McKay

Trail of Tears
Stan Hoig

Transitional Justice
Louis Bickford

Truth Commissions
Priscilla B. Hayner

Tudjman, Franjo
Reneo Lukic

[U]

Uganda
A. B. Kasozi

Ukraine (Famine)
Roman Serbyn

Union of Soviet Socialist
Republics
Kevin McDermott

United Nations
Nigel S. Rodley

United Nations Commission on
Human Rights
Jean-Bernard Marie

United Nations General Assembly
Ray Murphy

United Nations Security Council
Linda Melvern

United Nations Sub-Commission
on Human Rights
Stephanie T. Kleine-Ahlbrandt

United Nations War Crimes
Commission
Arieh Kochavi

United States Foreign Policies
Toward Genocide and Crimes
Against Humanity
Lawrence J. LeBlanc

Universal Jurisdiction
Marc Henzelin

Utilitarian Genocide
Eric Markusen
Matthias Bjørnlund

Utopian Ideologies as Motives for
Genocide
Eric D. Weitz

[V]

Victims
Naomi Roht-Arriaza

Videotaped Testimonials
Karen Jungblut

[W]

Wallenberg, Raoul
Alfred de Zayas

Wannsee Conference
Mark Roseman

War
Ray Murphy

War Crimes
Jiri Toman

Weapons of Mass Destruction
Roger S. Clark

West Papua, Indonesia (Irian
Jaya)
Greg Poulgrain

Whitaker, Benjamin
Bernard F. Hamilton

Wiesel, Elie
Michael Berenbaum

Wiesenthal, Simon
Mark Weitzman

Women, Violence against
Catharine A. MacKinnon

World War I Peace Treaties
G. G. Herczegh

Wounded Knee
Jeffrey Ostler

[Y]

Yugoslavia
Mark Thompson

Yuki of Northern California
Virginia P. Miller

[Z]

Zulu Empire
Michael R. Mahoney

Zunghars
Richard Pilkington

list of contributors

Heribert Adam
Simon Fraser University
South Africa

Kanya Adam
Simon Fraser University
South Africa

Howard Adelman
Princeton University, Woodrow Wilson School, and York University, Canada
Bagosora, Théoneste

Reza Afshari
Pace University
Iran

Xabier Agirre Aranburu
International Criminal Tribunal for the Former Yugoslavia
Investigation

Payam Akhavan
Yale Law School
International Criminal Tribunal for the Former Yugoslavia

Diane Marie Amann
University of California, Davis
Identification

Peter Amato
Department of English and Philosophy, Drexel University
Social Darwinism

Kai Ambos
Universität Göttingen, Germany
Prosecution

Joyce A. Apsel
New York University
Education

Cynthia J. Arnson
Latin American Program, Woodrow Wilson International Center for Scholars
El Salvador

Edwin Bacon
University of Birmingham, England
Gulag

Peter Balakian
Colgate University
Poetry

Patrick Ball
Human Rights Programs, The Benetech Initiative
Statistical Analysis

Rebecca L. Barbisch
Economic Groups

Dan Bar-On
Department of Behavioral Sciences, Ben Gurion University of the Negev, Beer Sheva, Israel
Psychology of Perpetrators

M. Cherif Bassiouni
DePaul University
Code of Crimes against the Peace and Security of Mankind
Commission on Responsibilities
Humanitarian Law

Craig Baxter
Juniata College
Bangladesh/East Pakistan

Chris Bennett
NATO Review
Bosnia and Herzegovina
Izetbegović, Alija

Michael Berenbaum
University of Judaism, Los Angeles, California
Wiesel, Elie

Morten Bergsmo
International Criminal Court
Intent

Karel C. Berkhoff
Center for Holocaust and Genocide Studies, Netherlands
Babi Yar

Robert B. Bernheim
Department of History, Middlebury College
SS

Louis Bickford
Alliances and Capacity Development, International Center for Transitional Justice, New York
Transitional Justice

Kit Bigelow
Bahā'ís of the United States
Bahā'ís

Leora Bilsky
Tel-Aviv University
Eichmann Trial

Rudolph Binion
History Department, Brandeis University
　　Hitler, Adolf

Laura E. Bishop
George Washington University Law School
　　Karadzic, Radovan

Matthias Bjørnlund
Danish Institute for International Studies, Copenhagen
　　Utilitarian Genocide

Karin Solveig Bjornson
　　Ancient World

Allida M. Black
Eleanor Roosevelt Papers, George Washington University
　　Roosevelt, Eleanor

Carolyn Patty Blum
Boalt Hall Law School, University of California, Berkeley
　　Film as Propaganda

Marc Bossuyt
University of Antwerp, Belgium, and Constitutional Court, Belgium
　　Hate Speech
　　Immunity

A. B. Bosworth
University of Western Australia
　　Athens and Melos

Wayne H. Bowen
Ouachita Baptist University
　　Collaboration

Paul S. Boyer
Professor Emeritus, University of Wisconsin, Madison
　　Hiroshima

James Brennan
University of California, Riverside
　　Argentina's Dirty Warriors

Arthur D. Brenner
Siena College
　　Death Squads

Jason Bricker
American University's School of International Service
　　Homosexuals

Roy L. Brooks
University of San Diego School of Law
　　African Americans

Bruce Broomhall
Department of Judicial Studies, University of Quebec at Montreal
　　Statutory Limitations

George C. Browder
Professor Emeritus, Department of History, State University of New York, Fredonia
　　Gestapo
　　Himmler, Heinrich

Stephen Brown
University of Wollongong
　　Lenin, Vladimir

Randall L. Bytwerk
Calvin College
　　Goebbels, Joseph
　　Streicher, Julius

Horace Campbell
Syracuse University
　　African Crisis Response
　　　Initiative

Arturo Carrillo
George Washington University Law School
　　Peru

Joshua Castellino
Irish Centre for Human Rights, National University of Ireland, Galway
　　Catholic Church
　　Death March
　　Ghetto

Kathleen Cavanaugh
Irish Centre for Human Rights, National University of Ireland, Galway
　　Nongovernmental Organizations

John Cerone
Center for International Law & Policy, New England School of Law
　　Homosexuals
　　Persecution
　　Safe Zones

Roger S. Clark
Rutgers University School of Law
　　Nuclear Weapons
　　Weapons of Mass Destruction

Sarah Cline
University of California, Santa Barbara
　　Aztecs

Robert O. Collins
Professor Emeritus, History, University of California, Santa Barbara
　　Sudan

Daniele Conversi
University of Lincoln
　　Nationalism

Noble David Cook
Florida International University
　　Taino (Arawak) Indians

James Crawford
University of Cambridge
　　Responsibility, State

François Crépeau
University of Montreal
　　Refugee Camps
　　Refugees

Robert Cribb
Research School of Pacific and Asian Studies, Australian National University
　　Indonesia

John R. Crook
Multinational Force and Observers
　　Compensation

Robert Cryer
University of Nottingham
　　Attempt
　　Incitement

Vahakn N. Dadrian
State University of New York and Zoryan Institute, Cambridge, MA
　　Armenians in Ottoman Turkey
　　　and the Armenian Genocide
　　Atatürk, Mustafa Kemal Pasha
　　Impunity
　　Talaat

Erica-Irene A. Daes
Athens University School of Law
　　Indigenous Peoples

Yael Danieli
Group Project for Holocaust Survivors and Their Children, New York
　　Rehabilitation

Jamie S. Davidson
Van Vollenhoven Centre for Law, Governance, and Development, Leiden University, Netherlands
　　Kalimantan

Alfred de Zayas
Institut Universitaire de Hautes Etudes Internationales
　　Aggression
　　Enver, Ismail
　　Mandela, Nelson
　　Wallenberg, Raoul

Emmanuel Decaux
*University of Paris II and United
Nations Sub-Commission on Human
Rights*
　Organization for Security and
　　Cooperation in Europe

Dennis Deletant
*Romanian Studies, University
College, London and University of
Amsterdam, Netherlands*
　Romania

Anna M. Dempsey
*University of Massachusetts,
Dartmouth*
　Art as Propaganda

Mercedes Doretti
*Equipo Argentino de Antropologia
Forense (Argentine Forensic
Anthropology Team)*
　Forensics

Mark A. Drumbl
*School of Law, Washington
Lee University*
　International Criminal Tribunal
　　for Rwanda

James Dunn
Australia-East Timor Association
　East Timor

Daniel Elwood Dunn
*University of the South, Sewanee,
Tennessee*
　Liberia

Atom Egoyan
*Ego Film Arts, Toronto, Ontario,
Canada*
　Films, Armenian Feature

Asbøjrn Eide
Norwegian Centre for Human Rights
　Famine

Asghar Ali Engineer
*Centre for Study of Society and
Secularism, Santacruz, Mumbai*
　India, Modern

Géraldine D. Enjelvin
*University College Northampton,
England*
　Harkis

Ralph Erber
DePaul University
　Deception, Perpetrators

Craig Etcheson
*School of Advanced International
Studies, Johns Hopkins University*
　Khmer Rouge Prisons and Mass
　　Graves

Khmer Rouge Victim Numbers,
　Estimating

Lynne Fallwell
Pennsylvania State University
　Eugenics
　Physicians

Anat Feinberg
University of Heidelberg, Germany
　Drama, Holocaust

Stephen C. Feinstein
*Center for Holocaust and Genocide
Studies, University of Minnesota*
　Architecture
　Art, Banned
　Art as Representation
　Memory

Hector Feliciano
New York University
　Art, Stolen

Benjamin B. Ferencz
J.D. Harvard University
　Einsatzgruppen
　Nuremberg Trials, Subsequent

Alexander J. Field
Santa Clara University
　Altruism, Biological

Maribel Fierro
*Consejo Superior de Investigaciones
Cientificas, Madrid*
　Almohads

Robert Fine
*Department of Sociology, University
of Warwick, United Kingdom*
　Evil, Banality of Radical

Paul Finkelman
University of Tulsa College of Law
　Slavery, Legal Aspects of

Michael R. Fischbach
Randolph-Macon College
　Iraq
　Saddam Hussein

Conan Fischer
University of Strathclyde, Scotland
　Germany

Luis Fondebrider
*Equipo Argentino de Antropologia
Forense (Argentine Forensic
Anthropology Team)*
　Forensics

David P. Forsythe
University of Nebraska, Lincoln
　International Committee of the
　　Red Cross

Michael Freeman
University of Essex
　Pequots

Michael P. Fronda
McGill University
　Carthage

Kelly Helen Fry
*George Washington University Law
School*
　Televison

James T. Fussell
Prevent Genocide International
　Proxmire, William

Mercedes Garcìa-Arenal
*Consejo Superior de Investigaciones
Cientificas, Madrid, Spain*
　Moriscos

William Gay
*University of North Carolina,
Charlotte*
　Language

Christian Gerlach
University of Pittsburgh
　Holocaust
　Soviet Prisoners of War, 1941 to
　　1945

Jan-Bart Gewald
*African Studies Centre, Leiden,
Netherlands*
　Namibia (German South West
　　Africa and South West Africa)

Geoff Gilbert
*Department of Law/Human Rights
Centre, University of Essex*
　Extradition

James M. Glass
*Department of Government and
Politics, University of Maryland*
　Nuremberg Laws

Leslie C. Griffin
University of Houston Law Center
　Euthanasia

Alexandra Guerson de Oliveira
University of Toronto
　Inquisition

T. Jeremy Gunn
*Religion and Human Rights, Emory
University Law School*
　Religion
　Religious Groups

Vineeta Gupta
*Insaaf International and People's
Union for Civil Liberties, India*
　Female Infanticide and Fetal
　　Murder

William D. Haglund
International Forensic Program,
Physicians for Human Rights
    Mass Graves
    Mengele, Josef

J. Michael Hagopian
Atlantis Productions and Chairman of
the Armenian Film Foundation
    Films, Armenian Documentary

Bernard F. Hamilton
Leo Kuper Foundation and
International Campaign to End
Genocide
    Kuper, Leo
    Lemkin, Raphael
    Whitaker, Benjamin

Ian Hancock
Romanis Archives and Documentation
Center, University of Texas, Austin
    Romanis

Hurst Hannum
The Fletcher School of Law and
Diplomacy
    Human Rights

John W. Harbeson
City University of New York
    Eritrea

Sidney L. Harring
City University of New York Law
School
    Herero

Aaron Hass
Department of Psychology, California
State University, Dominguez Hills
    Psychology of Survivors
    Psychology of Victims

Amir Hassanpour
Department of Near and Middle
Eastern Civilizations, University of
Toronto
    Kurds

Robert M. Hayden
University of Pittsburgh
    Croatia, Independent State of

Dawn Marie Hayes
Department of History, Montclair
State University
    Crusades

Priscilla B. Hayner
International Center for Transitional
Justice, New York
    Truth Commissions

Pierre Hazan
Journalist, Paris and Geneva
    Del Ponte, Carla

Steve Heder
School of Oriental and African
Studies
    Cambodia

Marc Henzelin
University of Geneva
    Universal Jurisdiction

G. G. Herczegh
Budapest, Hungary
    International Court of Justice
    World War I Peace Treaties

Viktoria Hertling
Center for Holocaust, Genocide &
Peace Studies, University of Nevada,
Reno
    Music and Musicians Persecuted
      during the Holocaust
    Satire and Humor

Alex Hinton
Department of Sociology and
Anthropology, Rutgers University
    Anthropology, Cultural

Adam Hochschild
University of California, Berkeley
    King Leopold II and the Congo

Stan Hoig
Professor Emeritus, University of
Central Oklahoma
    Sand Creek Massacre
    Trail of Tears

Jan Willem Honig
King's College, London
    Srebrenica

Wolfgang K. Hünig
University of Dunisberg
    Comics

Martin Imbleau
Montreal, Canada
    Der Stürmer

Martin Imbleau
Montreal, Canada
    Radio Télévision Libre Mille-
      Collines

Martin Imbleau
Montreal, Canada
    Denial
    Propaganda

Naomi Jackson
Department of Dance, Arizona State
University
    Dance

Joshua Jacobson
Northeastern University Department
of Music
    Music of the Holocaust

Vinodh Jaichand
Irish Centre for Human Rights,
National University of Ireland,
Galway
    Demjanjuk Trial
    Denationalization
    Residential Schools

Mora Johnson
Irish Centre for Human Rights,
National University of Ireland, Galway
    International Criminal Tribunal
      for the Former Yugoslavia

Maxine D. Jones
Florida State University
    Rosewood

Christopher C. Joyner
Georgetown University
    Peacekeeping

Karen Jungblut
Survivors of the Shoah Visual History
Foundation
    Videotaped Testimonials

Bruce Kapferer
University of Bergen, Norway
    Sri Lanka

A. B. Kasozi
Kampala, Uganda
    Uganda

Beverly Mayne Kienzle
Harvard University, The Divinity
School
    Cathars

Ben Kiernan
Genocide Studies Program, Yale
University
    Khmer Rouge
    Pol Pot
    Sparta

Linda Kimball
Department of Anthropology, Western
Washington University
    Kalmyks

Christine E. King
Staffordshire University
    Jehovah's Witnesses

David King
Department of History, Concordia
College, Montreal, Quebec
    Canada

Alexandre Kiss
Director Emeritus, French National
Center for Scientific Research
    Crimes Against Humanity
    Hague Conventions of 1907
    International Law

Edward Kissi
*Department of Africana Studies,
University of South Florida, Tampa*
  Ethiopia

Stephanie Kleine-Ahlbrandt
*Office of the United Nations High
Commissioner for Human Rights,
Geneva, Switzerland*
  United Nations Sub-Commission
    on Human Rights

John Klier
University College London
  Pogroms, Pre-Soviet Russia

Ian Knight
Kwazulu-Natal Museum
  Shaka Zulu

Geert Jan Alexander Knoops
Amsterdam, Netherlands
  Defenses

Arieh J. Kochavi
University of Haifa, Israel
  Jackson, Robert
  Morgenthau, Henry
  United Nations War Crimes
    Commission

Peter Kornbluh
National Security Archive
  Pinochet, Augusto

Joël Kotek
Free University in Brussels
  Concentration Camps
  Extermination Centers

Péter Kovács
Miskolc University, Hungary
  Minorities
  Racial Groups

Tania Krämer
Berlin, Germany
  Music of Reconciliation

Hans Christian Krüger
Strasbourg, France
  Conventions Against Torture and
    Other Cruel, Inhuman, and
    Degrading Treatment
  European Convention on the
    Non-Application of Statutory
    Limitations

George Lane
*School of Oriental and African
Studies, University of London*
  Genghis Khan
  Mongol Conquests

Caroline Lantero
*Unviersity of Montreal and
University of Auvergne*
  Refugee Camps

Bejamin Lawrance
*Department of History, University of
California, Davis*
  France in Tropical Africa

Azzedine Layachi
St. John's University, New York
  Algeria

Lawrence J. LeBlanc
Marquette University
  United States Foreign Policies
    Toward Genocide and Crimes
    Against Humanity

Amy W. Leith
New York, NY
  Advertising

René Lemarchand
*Professor Emeritus, Political Science,
University of Florida*
  Burundi

Paul Lemmens
*Katholieke Universiteit, Leuven,
Belgium*
  Restitution

Xiaorong Li
*Institute for Philosophy and Public
Policy, University of Maryland*
  China

Timothy Longman
Vassar College
  Racism
  Rwanda

Janet E. Lord
*Landmine Survivors Network,
Washington, D.C.*
  Disabilities, People with

Mark D. Ludwig
Terezin Chamber Music Foundation
  Music at Theresienstadt

Reneo Lukic
Laval University, Canada
  Tudjman, Franjo

Lorenz M. Lüthi
*History Department, McGill
University*
  Mao Zedong

Michelle Lyon
*School of Law, Washington & Lee
University*
  International Criminal Tribunal
    for Rwanda

Catharine A. MacKinnon
University of Michigan Law School
  Women, Violence against

Elaine Mackinnon
University of West Georgia
  Stalin, Joseph

Paul Robert Magocsi
University of Toronto
  Chmielnicki, Bogdan

Michael R. Mahoney
*Department of History, Yale
University*
  Zulu Empire

Patrick Manning
Northeastern University
  Slavery, Historical

Jean-Bernard Marie
*National Center for Scientific
Research (CNRS), Strasbourg*
  United Nations Commission on
    Human Rights

Stephen P. Marks
Harvard School of Public Health
  Medical Experimentation

Eric Markusen
*Danish Institute for International
Studies, Copenhagen*
  Utilitarian Genocide

Michael R. Marrus
University of Toronto
  Barbie, Klaus
  Göring, Hermann

Stacie E. Martin
*George Washington University Law
School*
  Native Americans

Jonathan McCollum
University of Maryland
  Music Based on the Armenian
    Genocide

Kevin McDermott
*Sheffield Hallam University, United
Kingdom*
  Union of Soviet Socialist
    Republics

Avril McDonald
*TMC Asser Institute of International
Law, Netherlands*
  Sierra Leone Special Court

Russell McGregor
James Cook University
  Australia

Fiona McKay
Human Rights First
    Torture

John McManus
*Office of the Assistant Deputy
Attorney General, Department of
Justice, Canada*
    National Prosecutions

Matthew McManus
Ottawa, Ontario, Canada
    National Prosecutions

Geoffrey P. Megargee
*United States Holocaust Memorial
Museum, Washington, D.C.*
    Labor Camps, Nazi

Allan Megill
University of Virginia
    Historiography as a Written
    Form

Garth Meintjes
Notre Dame Law School
    Convention on Apartheid
    Goldstone, Richard

Robert Melson
*Purdue University and International
Association of Genocide Scholars*
    Comparative Genocide

Linda Melvern
*Department of International Politics,
University of Wales, Aberystwyth*
    United Nations Security Council

Juan E. Méndez
*Center for Civil and Human Rights,
Notre Dame Law School*
    Argentina

Raymond A. Mentzer
University of Iowa
    Huguenots

Guénaël Mettraux
*International Criminal Tribunal for
the Former Yugoslavia*
    Complicity

Wolfgang Mey
*Museum Service, Ministry of Cultural
Affairs of the Free and Hanseatic City
of Hamburg*
    Developmental Genocide

John Michalczyk
Boston College
    Films, Eugenics
    Films, Holocaust Documentary

Manus I. Midlarsky
Rutgers University
    Political Theory

David Miller
Nuffield College, University of Oxford
    Altruism, Ethical

Virginia P. Miller
*Martin's Brook, Luneneburg County,
Nova Scotia, Canada*
    Yuki of Northern California

Mark C. Molesky
*Department of History, Harvard
University*
    Biographies

Kristen Renwick Monroe
University of California, Irvine
    Explanation

Brian K. Morgan
*George Washington University Law
School*
    Assassinations

Daryl A. Mundis
*International Criminal Tribunal for
the former Yugoslavia*
    Superior (or Command)
    Responsibility

Ray Murphy
*Irish Centre for Human Rights,
National University of Ireland,
Galway, Ireland*
    United Nations General
    Assembly
    War

Sean D. Murphy
*George Washington University Law
School*
    Humanitarian Intervention

Daniel L. Nadel
*George Washington University Law
School*
    Milosevic, Slobodan

Norman M. Naimark
Stanford University
    Ethnic Cleansing

Delphine Nakache
University of Montreal
    Refugees

Linda A. Newson
*Department of Geography, King's
College, London*
    Incas

Francis R. Nicosia
St. Michael's College, Vermont
    Heydrich, Reinhard

Daniel D. Ntanda Nsereko
University of Botswana
    Forcible Transfer

Sharon O'Brien
University of Kansas
    Beothuk
    Cheyenne
    Chittagong Hill Tract, Peoples of
    the

Carol Off
Toronto, Ontario, Canada
    Arbour, Louise

Kolawole Olaniyan
Amnesty International
    Biafra/Nigeria

Clémentine Olivier
*Irish Centre for Human Rights,
National University of Ireland,
Galway*
    Political Groups

Simon Olleson
*Lauterpacht Research Centre for
International Law, University of
Cambridge*
    Responsibility, State

Shane P. O'Rourke
University of York
    Cossacks

Jeffrey Ostler
University of Oregon
    Wounded Knee

Dennis R. Papazian
*Armenian Research Center, University
of Michigan, Dearborn*
    Armenians in Russia and the
    USSR

Aloka Parasher-Sen
*Department of History, University of
Hyderabad*
    India, Ancient and Medieval

Gunnar S. Paulsson
Toronto, Ontario, Canada
    Deception, Victims

Meg Penrose
University of Oklahoma
    Punishment

Richard Pilkington
    Zunghars

Douglas V. Porpora
*Department of Culture and
Communication, Drexel University*
    Bystanders

Jack Nusan Porter
University of Massachusetts, Lowell
    Sociology of Perpetrators
    Sociology of Victims

Greg Poulgrain
Griffith University, Brisbane, Australia
    West Papua, Indonesia (Irian Jaya)

Jerry K. Prince
Bahā'ìs of the United States
    Bahā'ìs

R. John Pritchard
    Tokyo Trial

Lyndel V. Prott
Australian National University, Canberra
    Ethnocide

John Quigley
Moritz College of Law, Ohio State University
    Control Council Law No. 10
    London Charter

Renee C. Redman
International Institute of Connecticut
    Slavery, Legal Aspects of

Luc Reydams
University of Notre Dame
    National Laws

Paul Richards
Wageningen Universiteit, Netherlands
    Sierra Leone

Andrew Rigby
Centre for the Study of Forgiveness and Reconciliation, Coventry University
    Reconciliation

Geoffrey Roberts
Department of History, University College, Cork, Ireland
    Katyn

Richard Roberts
Department of History, University of California, Davis
    France in Tropical Africa

Chris A. Robinson
Department of Biology, Bronx Community College, City University of New York
    Archaeology

Nigel S. Rodley
University of Essex
    Ennals, Martin
    United Nations

Naomi Roht-Arriaza
University of California, Hastings College of Law
    Victims

Peter Ronayne
Federal Executive Institute, Charlottesville, VA
    Somalia, Intervention in

Mark Roseman
Indiana University
    Wannsee Conference

John K. Roth
Claremont McKenna College
    Philosophy

Daniel Rothenberg
International Human Rights Law Institute DePaul University College of Law
    Genocide

Paulina Rudnicka
George Washington University Law School
    Gas

Leila Sadat
Washington University School of Law
    International Criminal Court

Jaspreet K. Saini
George Washington University Law School
    Mladic, Ratko

José M. Sánchez
Saint Louis University
    Pius XII, Pope

Pietro Sardaro
Catholic University of Leuven, Belgium
    Restitution

William F. Sater
Professor Emeritus, History, California State University, Long Beach
    Chile

William A. Schabas
Irish Centre for Human Rights, National Unviersity of Ireland
    Conspiracy
    Convention on the Prevention and Punishment of Genocide
    Crimes Against Humanity
    International Law Commission

Michael P. Scharf
Frederick K. Cox International Law Center, Case Western Reserve University School of Law
    Amnesty

David J. Scheffer
Attorney, New York
    Nuremberg Trials

Christian P. Scherrer
Hiroshima Peace Institute (HPI) of Hiroshima City University, Japan
    Ethnicity

Donald G. Schilling
Department of History, Denison University
    Memoirs of Perpetrators
    Memoirs of Survivors

Jennifer Schirmer
Centre for Development and the Environment at the University of Oslo
    Rìos Montt, Efraín

Markus Schmidt
Office of the UN High Commissioner for Human Rights
    Disappearances

Frederick M. Schweitzer
Department of History, Manhattan College
    Anti-Semitism

John F. Sears
Eleanor Roosevelt Papers, George Washington University
    Roosevelt, Eleanor

Paul Seils
International Center for Transitional Justice
    Evidence

Patricia Viseur Sellers
International Criminal Tribunal for the Former Yugoslavia and Oxford University
    Rape
    Reproduction

Jacques Semelin
Centre for International Research and Studies and Institut D'Etudes Politiques de Paris
    Massacres
    Radio

Harriet F. Senie
City College and Graduate Center, City University of New York
    Memorials and Monuments

Franziska Seraphim
Boston College
    Japan

Roman Serbyn
University of Quebec
    Kulaks
    Ukraine (Famine)

Dinah L. Shelton
George Washington University Law School
  Historical Injustices
  Reparations

Marlene Shelton
University of California, Los Angeles
  Films, Dramatizations in

Franziska E. Shlosser
History Department, Concordia University
  Christians, Roman Persecution of

Alex Shoumatoff
Keene, New York
  Amazon Region

Josef Silverstein
Oxford University
  Burma/Myanmar

Christopher Simpson
American University
  Lepsius, Johannes

Tove Skutnabb-Kangas
University of Roskilde, Department of Languages and Culture, Denmark
  Linguistic Genocide

Roger W. Smith
College of William and Mary
  Perpetrators

Itai Nartzizenfield Sneh
History Department, John Jay College of Criminal Justice, City University of New York
  Historiography, Sources in

Alessia Sonaglioni
Council of Europe
  Conventions Against Torture and Other Cruel, Inhuman, and Degrading Treatment

Stefan Sottiaux
University of Antwerp, Belgium
  Hate Speech

Gregory H. Stanton
Genocide Watch, Washington, D.C. and Mary Washington College
  Early Warning

Beth Stephens
Rutgers University School of Law, Camden
  Alien Tort Statute

David Stoll
Middlebury College
  Guatemala

Christopher Swift
Center of International Studies, University of Cambridge
  Chechens

Nechama Tec
University of Connecticut, Stamford
  Rescuers, Holocaust

Rita Thalmann
Professor Emeritus, University of Paris
  Kristallnacht

Mark Thompson
  Yugoslavia

Robert A. F. Thurman
Department of Religion, Columbia University
  Tibet

Jiri Toman
Santa Clara University
  Geneva Conventions on the Protection of Victims of War
  War Crimes

Samuel Totten
University of Arkansas, and Institute on the Holocaust and Genocide, Jerusalem, Israel
  Diaries
  Documentation

Yvonne S. Unnold
University of Southern Mississippi
  Fiction

Stef Vandeginste
University of Antwerp, Belgium
  Immunity

Johan D. van der Vyver
Emory University School of Law
  Apartheid

Robert Jan van Pelt
School of Architecture, University of Waterloo, Canada
  Auschwitz
  Irving, David, Libel Trial of

Teun Voeten
Freelance journalist, Brussels, Belgium
  Photography of Victims

Nevena Vuckovic Sahovic
Child Rights Centre, Belgrade, Yugoslavia
  Children

Natalie Wagner
University of Ireland, Galway
  Mercenaries

Eric D. Weitz
University of Minnesota
  Utopian Ideologies as Motives for Genocide

Mark Weitzman
Simon Wiesenthal Center
  Resistance
  Wiesenthal, Simon

Bret Werb
United States Holocaust Memorial Museum, Washington, D.C.
  Music, Holocaust Hidden and Protest

Dana Wessell
University of Toronto
  Inquisition

Stephen J. Whitfield
Department of American Studies, Brandeis University
  Arendt, Hannah

Marieke Wierda
  Evidence

Siegfried Wiessner
Intercultural Human Rights, St. Thomas University School of Law
  Ethnic Groups

Robert Wokler
University of Exeter
  Enlightenment

Rüdiger Wolfrum
Max Planck Institute for Comparative Public Law and International Law, Heidelberg
  Prevention

Linda M. Woolf
Webster University
  Terrorism, Psychology behind

Kathleen Z. Young
Western Washington University
  Kosovo

Eyal Zisser
Department of Middle Eastern and African History, Tel Aviv University
  Sabra and Shatila

outline of contents

This topical outline was compiled by the editors to provide a general overview of the conceptual scheme of the *Encyclopedia of Genocide and Crimes Against Humanity.*

1. Biographies
2. Crime and Punishment
   Biographies
   Crimes
   Defenses
   Punishment
   Tribunals
3. Cultural Representations
4. History
   Biographies
   Early
   Middle Ages
   Rise of the Empires
   Modern Era
5. The Holocaust
   Biographies
6. Instruments
7. International and National Laws
8. International Institutions
9. Investigations and Evidence
10. People
    General Groups
    Perpetrators
    Specific Groups
11. Prevention and Reaction
    Biographies
    Prevention
    Reaction
12. Reparations
13. Theories and Explanations
    Biographies

1. [BIOGRAPHIES]

Arbour, Louise
Arendt, Hannah
Atatürk, Mustafa Kemal Pasha
Bagosora, Théoneste
Barbie, Klaus
Chmielnicki, Bogdan
Del Ponte, Carla
Ennals, Martin
Enver, Ismail
Genghis Khan
Goebbels, Joseph
Goldstone, Richard
Göring, Hermann
Heydrich, Reinhard
Himmler, Heinrich
Hitler, Adolf
Izetbegović, Alija
Jackson, Robert
Karadzic, Radovan
Kuper, Leo
Lemkin, Raphael
Lenin, Vladimir
Lepsius, Johannes
Mandela, Nelson
Mao Zedong
Mengele, Josef
Milosevic, Slobodan
Mladic, Ratko
Morgenthau, Henry
Pinochet, Augusto
Pius XII, Pope
Proxmire, William
Ríos Montt, Efraín
Roosevelt, Eleanor

Saddam Hussein
Shaka Zulu
Stalin, Joseph
Streicher, Julius
Talaat
Tudjman, Franjo
Wallenberg, Raoul
Whitaker, Benjamin
Wiesel, Elie
Wiesenthal, Simon

2. [CRIME AND PUNISHMENT]

Biographies
Arbour, Louise
Del Ponte, Carla
Goldstone, Richard
Jackson, Robert

Crimes
Aggression
Art, Stolen
Assassinations
Attempt
Complicity
Conspiracy
Crimes Against Humanity
Ethnocide
Female Infanticide and Fetal Murder
Forcible Transfer
Genocide
Incitement
Intent
Linguistic Genocide
Persecution
Torture
War Crimes

Defenses
Amnesty

Defenses
Immunity
Statutory Limitations
Superior (or Command)
   Responsibility

Punishment
Extradition
National Prosecutions
Prosecution
Punishment
Universal Jurisdiction

Tribunals
Demjanjuk Trial
Eichmann Trial
International Court of Justice
International Criminal Court
International Criminal Tribunal for
   Rwanda
International Criminal Tribunal for
   the Former Yugoslavia
Irving, David, Libel Trial of
Nuremberg Trials
Nuremberg Trials, Subsequent
Sierra Leone Special Court
Tokyo Trial

3. [CULTURAL REPRESENTATIONS]

Art, Banned
Art as Representation
Biographies
Comics
Dance
Diaries
Fiction
Film as Propaganda
Films, Armenian Documentary
Films, Armenian Feature
Films, Dramatizations in
Films, Eugenics
Films, Holocaust Documentary
Memoirs of Perpetrators
Memoirs of Survivors
Memorials and Monuments
Music Based on the Armenian
   Genocide
Music of Reconciliation
Music of the Holocaust
Photography of Victims
Poetry
Radio
Satire and Humor
Television

4. [HISTORY]

Historiography, Sources in
Historiography as a Written Form

Biographies
Genghis Khan
King Leopold II and the Congo
Shaka Zulu

Early
Ancient World
Athens and Melos
Carthage
Christians, Roman Persecution of
India, Ancient and Medieval
Sparta

Middle Ages
Almohads
Cathars
Crusades
Inquisition
Mongol Conquests

Rise of Empires
Amazon Region
American Indians
Aztecs
France in Tropical Africa
Incas
Namibia (German South West Africa
   and South West Africa)
Slavery, Historical
Slavery, Legal Aspects of

Modern Era
Africa
   Algeria
   Apartheid
   Biafra/Nigeria
   Burundi
   Eritrea
   Ethiopia
   Liberia
   Rwanda
   Sierra Leone
   Somalia, Intervention in
   South Africa
   Sudan
   Uganda
Asia and Oceana
   Australia
   Bangladesh/East Pakistan
   Burma/Myanmar
   Cambodia
   China
   East Timor
   Hiroshima
   India, Modern
   Indonesia
   Iran
   Iraq
   Japan
   Kalimantan
   Sabra and Shatila
   Sri Lanka
   Tibet
   West Papua, Indonesia (Irian Jaya)
Europe
   Babi Yar
   Bosnia and Herzegovina
   Croatia, Independent State of
   Katyn
   Kosovo
   Romania

Soviet Prisoners of War,
   1941–1942
Srebrenica
Ukraine (Famine)
Union of Soviet Socialist Republics
Yugoslavia
Latin America
   Argentina
   Chile
   El Salvador
   Guatemala
   Peru
North America
   African Americans
   Canada
   Cheyenne
   Sand Creek Massacre
   Trail of Tears
   Wounded Knee

5. [THE HOLOCAUST]

Art, Stolen
Auschwitz
Concentration Camps
Extermination Centers
Der Stürmer
Drama, Holocaust
Einsatzgruppen
Films, Dramatizations in
Films, Holocaust Documentary
Germany
Gestapo
Holocaust
Kristallnacht
Labor Camps, Nazi
Music at Theresienstadt
Music Banned during the Holocaust
Music of the Holocaust
Nuremburg Laws
SS
Wannsee Conference

Biographies
Barbie, Klaus
Goebbels, Joseph
Göring, Hermann
Heydrich, Reinhard
Himmler, Heinrich
Hitler, Adolf
Lemkin, Raphael
Mengele, Josef
Morgenthau, Henry
Streicher, Julius
Wiesel, Elie
Wiesenthal, Simon

6. [INSTRUMENTS]

Advertising
Architecture
Art as Propaganda
Concentration Camps
Death March
Deception, Perpetrators
Deception, Victims

Denationalization
Denial
Disappearances
Ethnic Cleansing
Eugenics
Euthanasia
Extermination Centers
Famine
Film as Propaganda
Gas
Ghetto
Gulag
Hate Speech
Khmer Rouge Prisons and Mass
    Graves
Massacres
Medical Experimentation
Nuclear Weapons
Pogroms, Pre-Soviet Russia
Propaganda
Radio
Reproduction
Residential Schools
Television
Weapons of Mass Destruction

7. [INTERNATIONAL AND
NATIONAL LAWS]

Code of Crimes against the Peace and
    Security of Mankind
Control Council Law No. 10
Convention against Apartheid
Convention on the Prevention and
    Punishment of Genocide
Convention against Torture and Other
    Cruel, Inhuman and Degrading
    Treatment
European Convention on the Non-
    Application of Statutory
    Limitations
Extradition
Geneva Conventions for the
    Protection of Victims of War
Hague Conventions of 1907
Human Rights
Humanitarian Law
International Law
London Charter
National Laws
Responsibility, State
World War I Peace Treaties

8. [INTERNATIONAL
INSTITUTIONS]

Catholic Church
International Committee of the Red
    Cross
International Law Commission
Nongovernmental Organizations
Organization for Security and
    Cooperation in Europe
Refugee Camps
United Nations

United Nations Commission on
    Human Rights
United Nations General Assembly
United Nations Security Council

9. [INVESTIGATIONS AND
EVIDENCE]

Archaeology
Commission on Responsibilities
Documentation
Evidence
Forensics
Identification
Investigation
Mass Graves
Videotaped Testimonials

10. [PEOPLE]

General Groups
Children
Disabled
Economic Groups
Ethnic groups
Homosexuals
Indigenous Peoples
Minorities
Physicians
Political Groups
Racial Groups
Refugees
Religious Groups
Victims
Women, Violence against

Perpetrators
Atatürk, Mustafa Kemal Pasha
Argentina's Dirty Warriors
Bagosora, Théoneste
Chmielnicki, Bogdan
Death Squads
Fujimori, Alberto
Izetbegović, Alija
Karadzic, Radovan
Khmer Rouge
Lenin, Vladimir
Mao Zedong
Mercenaries
Milosovic, Slobodan
Mladic, Ratko
Perpetrators
Pinochet, Augusto
Pol Pot
Ríos Montt, Efraín
Saddam Hussein
Stalin, Joseph
Taylor, Charles
Tudjman, Fanjo

Specific Groups
Armenians in Ottoman Turkey
Armenians in Russia and the USSR
Bahā'īs
Beothuk
Chechens

Cheyenne
Chittagong Hill Tract, Peoples of the
Cossacks
Harkis
Hereros
Huguenots
Jehovah's Witnesses
Kalmyks
Khmer Rouge Victim Numbers,
    Estimating
Kulaks
Kurds
Moriscos
Pequots
Romanis
Shaka Zulu
Taino (Arawak) Indians
Yuki of Northern California

11. [PREVENTION AND REACTION]

Biographies
Ennals, Martin
Kuper, Leo
Lepsius, Johannes
Mandela, Nelson
Pius XII, Pope
Proxmire, William
Roosevelt, Eleanor
Wallenberg, Raoul
Whitaker, Benjamin

Prevention
African Crisis Response Initiative
Early Warning
Education
Prevention
Safe Zones

Reaction
Altruism, Biological
Altruism, Ethical
Bystanders
Collaboration
Humanitarian Intervention
Impunity
Peacekeeping
Reconciliation
Rescuers, Holocaust
Resistance
United States Foreign Policies Toward
    Genocide and Crimes against
    Humanity

12. [REPARATIONS]

Alien Tort Statute
Compensation
Historical Injustices
Reconciliation
Rehabilitation
Reparations
Restitution
Rosewood
Transitional Justice
Truth Commissions

13. [THEORIES AND EXPLANATIONS]

Anthropology, Cultural
Anti-Semitism
Comparative Genocide
Denial
Developmental Genocide
Economics
Ethnicity
Evil, Banality of Radical
Explanation

Language
Memory
Nationalism
Philosophy
Political Theory
Psychology of Perpetrators
Psychology of Survivors
Psychology of Victims
Racism
Religion
Social Darwinism

Sociology of Perpetrators
Sociology of Victims
Statistical Analysis
Terrorism, Psychology behind
Utilitarian Genocide
Utopian Ideologies as Motives for
    Genocide
Victims
War

Biographies
Arendt, Hannah

Advertising

Advertising is a paid, persuasive form of communicating a message that attempts to influence the buying behavior or thought patterns of consumers. Advertisements are also a sign of the times, reflecting what consumers find attractive or influential. Throughout modern history advertising has played a role in idealizing favored groups, and dehumanizing or stereotyping disfavored groups.

The following advertisements ran in a special issue of a leading German weekly magazine (*Illustrierte Zeitung Leipzig: Sonderausgabe 1944, Der europäische Mensch*) during the height of World War II in Nazi Germany. Each advertisement depicts a Nazi ideal, or refers to a Nazi goal.

Focke-Wulf has been building airplanes for 20 years.

We join in the vastly increased use of labor and technology in the German aircraft industry. We are thus helping to solve the great tasks of the day, the fulfillment of which will bring about a New Order in Europe.

After the victorious end to this war for European self-determination, we will return to peacetime production. Using the knowledge we have gained, as well as our proven productivity, we will build better planes to meet the high expectations of coming European air traffic.

One of the main goals of the Nazi regime was to increase employment, but this text could also be interpreted as a reference to the slave labor provided by the concentration camp inmates. The text asserts that Germany would win the war and become the dominant economic power within Europe. The visual images used are the swastika and eagle symbol of the Third Reich.

Ford

On the roads of Europe, German Ford trucks testify to the work of German industry. The agile, reliable and easy to maintain Ford truck will be a welcome help in solving the major tasks that await our continent after the war.

The text of this ad assumes German domination of the continent of Europe and reflects the supposed superiority of German products and people. The ad also visually depicts Greek ruins—a theme consistent with Hitler's idealization of ancient, vast, and powerful empires.

UHU Glue

German children: Europe's future inventors!

While courageous men are fighting on the battlefields for the victory that will crown a happy and united Europe, the German home front is already working today on plans to benefit the freed peoples. German youth are preparing for the great tasks of reconstruction and peace. They tinker and build models, engaging in guided and creative learning. Whether it is in shop class at school, evenings at home, or while participating in youth organizations, UHU is everywhere. A special glue developed by the German firm Kunststoff-Chemie, it is in demand as a dependable product.

This ad reinforces the belief that the Germans were in fact liberating Europe, and that Germany would

"[T]he photographs taken by creative Germans during their vacations . . . are convincing evidence of peace! They demonstrate our desire to peacefully enjoy all that life has to offer, to see the world's marvels, and to meet the peoples of other nations. . . . Hauff film and Hauff plates, long-tested and improved during the war, will be ready to capture these coming happy memories of peace." [COURTESY OF RANDALL L. BYTWERK AND THE GERMAN PROPAGANDA ARCHIVE (WWW.CALVIN.EDU/CAS/GPA)]

emerge as the dominant force in a united Europe. It also encourages German children to join Nazi youth organizations. The ad visually depicts the Nazi ideal of a German child—male, blonde, productive, and loyal.

Lanz

A Picture of Peace

With their peaceful work, each LANZ-tractor, LANZ-thrasher, and LANZ-harvesting machine helps to guarantee the nutrition of Europe. Our agricultural technology is already showing the way to what will happen when peace comes.

This advertisement reflects the Nazi ideal of Germans nourishing themselves from the Fatherland, getting back to a basic way of life consisting of hard work. It also refers to the German domination of Europe and characterizes Germany as the provider for the rest of Europe. The ad visually depicts an idyllic German countryside, with two farmers diligently laboring.

Other examples of popular advertising that dehumanize disfavored groups can be seen throughout the

world. One familiar example is from the Jim Crow era in the United States, which extended from the mid-1870s to the mid-1960s. Many racist forms of advertising served to justify prejudice and discrimination against African Americans. The Aunt Jemima trademark, introduced in 1893 and based on an actual former slave, portrays a black "Mammy" in a kerchief as slow-witted, fat, and ugly. Childlike, subhuman portrayals such as this came to justify the denial of civil rights to blacks and supported the common misconception that blacks were intellectually inferior to whites.

SEE ALSO Art as Propaganda; Art as Representation; Deception, Perpetrators; Incitement; Propaganda; Television

BIBLIOGRAPHY

Advertising Age. "The Advertising Century." Available from http://www.adage.com/century/icon07.html.

Calvin University. "German Propaganda Archive." Available from http://www.calvin.edu/academic/cas/gpa/ads.html.

Davis, Ronald L. F. "Popular Art and Racism: Embedding Racial Stereotypes in the American Mindset—Jim Crow and Popular Culture." Ph.D. diss. Available from http://www.jimcrowhistory.org/resources/lessonplans/hs_es_popular_culture.html.

Greenspan, L., and C. Levitt, eds. (1993). *Under the Shadow of Weimar*. Westport, Conn.: Praeger Publishers.

Kressel, Neil J. (1996). *Mass Hate*. New York: Plenum Press.

Amy W. Leith

African Americans

Article 7 of the Rome Statute of the International Criminal Court (ICC) enumerates two crimes against humanity—enslavement and apartheid—whose delineation as crimes against humanity could have applied to the treatment of African Americans by the United States government, state governments within the United States, and the states' colonial predecessor regimes. Article 7 defines *enslavement* as "the exercise of any or all of the powers attaching to the right of ownership over a person and includes the exercise of such powers in the course of trafficking in persons, in particular women and children." The crime of *apartheid* refers to "inhumane acts . . . committed in the context of an institutionalized regime of systematic oppression and domination by one racial group over any other racial group or groups and committed with the intention of maintaining that regime." As set forth in Article 7, other crimes against humanity (e.g., murder, imprisonment, and torture) that have been committed against African Americans within the context of enslavement and/or apartheid are ancillary to the crimes of enslavement and apartheid.

Enslavement and apartheid (as well as other crimes against humanity) have long histories within the United States and North America. Slavery's tenure in the United States extended across roughly 225 years (c. 1640–1865), beginning in the colonial period and ending with the Civil War. Although some African Americans living in the South experienced a measure of racial equality during the brief period known as Reconstruction (1867–1877), most lived under an oppressive system of apartheid that defined racial relations for the next one hundred years (1877–1972). The duration of the two crimes against humanity suggests that they were not episodic in character, but, instead, were systemic. They were part of the "normal" way in which American society functioned, and were operative almost from the beginning of the colonial regime.

Slavery

The exercise of ownership and control over a human being by another human being—in other words, *chattel slavery*—has deep roots in Western civilization. Virtually every Western society has condoned slavery, and most have practiced it. Slavery, however, took on a unique form when it became established in the New World (the Americas and West Indies) by the Portuguese in the fifteenth century.

Most important, the element of "race" (i.e., skin color) was introduced into the master/slave relationship as slavery was practiced in the New World. For the first time in the history of slavery, dark skin became the marker that gave the slave his or her cultural status and identity. To rationalize the new face of slavery, the enslavers and their supporters created a race-specific ideology of white superiority and of black inferiority. It was argued that chattel slavery and, more generally, white hegemony were part of the natural order of things, that the white race was innately superior to all other races. It was further argued that this racial hierarchy was not the design of human beings but, rather, was ordained by God and/or nature. Similarly, it was part of the human condition—and something that mere mortals ought not to disturb. This racist rhetoric was not only devoid of empirical support or logic, but it also had an unprecedented effect on chattel slavery. Because skin color had become the sine qua non of bondage, the condition of the slave of the ancient Mediterranean world whereby a slave could become a senator, a teacher of the slaveholding class, or even his master's master was annulled. Nor was it possible for a slave to become related to his master by way of marriage or adoption—events unremarkable in the ancient Greek and Roman civilizations.

But what is perhaps most pernicious about the rhetoric that was used to justify chattel slavery in the New World is that it has outlasted slavery itself. Racism continued to make life perilous for African Americans long after 1865. In the early twenty-first century, components of U.S. culture (specifically, the belief that African Americans have a pathological values system) are often used as a proxy for racism. Whether it is old-fashioned racism (white supremacy) or the new form of racism (culture), the rhetoric has the same ring: it subordinates and stigmatizes African Americans, maintaining the system of race-based advantages (for whites) and disadvantages (for blacks) that began during slavery. To the extent that the ideas and concepts used to justify slavery have outlived slavery, it can be argued that slavery's rhetoric is in the final analysis more productive of harm than slavery itself.

Although reinforced by racist ideology, the enslavement of African Americans was initiated and sustained by quite a different motivation—profit. Indeed, if chattel slavery had been less profitable, it could not have endured nor would even have come into existence. But in fact slavery was enormously profitable; the demand for cheap labor needed to harvest the riches of the New World grew each decade. Chattel slavery, then, was part of an international economic network. That network, called the Atlantic Slave Trade, consisted of a triangular trade route that involved Africa, the New World, and Europe. The first leg of a typical trade route—commonly referred to as the Middle Passage—consisted of the passage from Africa to the New World; the second leg, from the New World to Europe; and the third, from Europe to Africa. Slaves were transported from the west coast of Africa to the Americas and West Indies, where they were auctioned off to the owners of plantations and small farms and other individuals. Sugar, tobacco, cotton, and other goods harvested and/or produced by slave labor were sent to Europe in exchange for cash and such items as textiles and hardware. Ships full of rum and iron would then set sail for Africa, where these goods would be used in the bartering for slaves.

Viewed from the perspective of the slave, the Atlantic slave trade was nothing less than a brutal, even diabolic process of human bondage that consisted of capture, the Middle Passage, the auction block, and plantation life (or the *peculiar institution*). Together, the four stages bring to light the contradictory nature of chattel slavery within a (putatively) free society.

Capture

Kindnapping and the taking of prisoners by the victors of intertribal wars were the primary methods used in the procurement of Africans for the Atlantic slave trade. Victorious African tribal chiefs used defeated enemies, traditionally regarded as the spoils of war, as currency for the acquisition of iron products (e.g., guns and ammunition), rum, and other goods. A tribal leader sometimes waged war for the sole purpose of taking possession of persons, who could then be commodified and sold for profit. Wars were sometimes waged against distant tribes even in instances in which the tribes posed no reasonable threat to the aggressors' security. As Charles Ball, the author of a slave narrative, recounted of his experience while still in Africa: "It was not the object of our enemies to kill; they wished to take us alive and sell us as slaves" (1854, p. 158).

There is some question as to whether the African chieftains understood that they were participating in a system of slavery very different from the one to which they were accustomed. Did they understand that their transactions with proprietors of the Atlantic slave trade were not "business as usual"? Did they have knowledge of the likely fates of their captives? Had they known what lay ahead for the Africans being put on ships, might they have banded together to resist the white slave traders? Could the system have operated for as long as it did without African complicity? These are perhaps unanswerable questions.

Captives were sometimes force-marched across interior regions of Africa to the villages of victorious tribes or armies. From there, they would continue on to the shores of the Atlantic Ocean. Some offered resistance by fleeing from slave forts on the West African coast. But most were less fortunate, and were forced to board ships to begin the infamous Middle Passage.

Middle Passage

The Middle Passage was, without a doubt, the most arduous part of the slave experience. Once on board sailing vessels, individual slaves were allotted spaces no larger than coffins. Some captives mutinied. It is estimated that as many as one-third of all slaves transported to the Americas and the West Indies died en route. Some died by suffocation; others from sickness that had been brought on by conditions on board ship and mistreatment by the slave traders. Babies who were thought to be incapable of surviving the passage were sometimes thrown overboard by ship captains. Mothers often leapt overboard in futile attempts to rescue their babies. It was not uncommon for a mother to hold her child to her bosom and cast herself into the ocean, choosing death over enslavement for herself and her child. It is estimated that from 14 to 21 million Africans endured the Middle Passage during the nearly four centuries of slavery in the New World.

Auction Block

At the conclusion of the Middle Passage, slaves faced the auction block. Before being put on display, slaves were cleaned up. These grooming gestures were not acts of kindness, but acts guided by self-interest, calculated toward the reaping of profit. The healthier a slave looked, the higher his or her selling price. Once spruced up, slaves were marched into a public square, put on display, inspected by prospective buyers as though they were livestock, and sold to the highest bidder. Families were often broken up on the auction block. Children were ripped from the arms of their parents, wives were taken away from husbands, and siblings were separated from each other—never to be rejoined.

Plantation

From the auction block, slaves were taken to the properties of their new masters—usually the plantations and farms of the American South. There they became slave laborers, forced to toil for the rest of their lives and for the aggrandizement of others. A child born into slavery remained a slave for life.

Southern states had precise laws that governed the freeing of slaves for fear of creating a large free black population. Free blacks in slaveholding states were regarded by whites living in those states as threats to the security of the white population. It was thought that the mere presence of free blacks would be an incitement to slave revolts. Some slaves did, however, succeed in gaining their freedom—in a variety of ways, such as reward for having provided "exceptional service" to their masters and, for those slaves who were allowed to hold assets, self-purchase. Slaves were sometimes freed upon the deaths of their masters, usually via provisions in their masters' wills. For example, George Washington, who predeceased his wife, stipulated in his will that his slaves were to be freed upon his wife's death.

Slaveholders would often give accounts of the peculiar institution that tended toward the purely fictional. They strove to portray themselves as benevolent slave masters in pursuit of the noble goal of bringing civilization and Christianity to the lives of savages. Southern historians, in their accounts, frequently added to this falsification during the nineteenth century and well into the twentieth century. In so doing they ignored concrete evidence of slave accomplishments, as well as of slave resistance—including evidence that showed that many slaves ran away to live among Native Americans and to live in free states or in Canada, as well as evidence that it was not uncommon for slaves to revolt openly, to feign sickness (in order to evade degradation), and to participate in work slowdowns.

In the second half of the twentieth century scholars were providing far more accurate accounts of the peculiar institution. Much of the new historiography was based on primary source materials that scholars had previously ignored—the *slave narratives,* which are autobiographical accounts of the slave experience. Slave narratives provide a vivid panorama of the horrors of human bondage. Although many slave narratives were committed to writing after slavery had ended in the United States, a good many of them came into existence during the period of slavery, often with the help of the abolitionists who wished to use the documents in their fight against slavery. Frederick Douglass's narrative, *Life and Times of Frederick Douglass: His Early Life as a Slave, His Escape from Bondage, and His Complete History,* is perhaps the best known of this genre.

The enslavement of Africans in America in all its cruel dimensions—capture, Middle Passage, auction block, and the peculiar institution—would not have been possible were it not for the imprimaturs given to

In the nineteenth century Frederick Douglass (c. 1818–1895) was the world's most famous African American. He remains the most influential orator and lecturer in U.S. history. Here, a head-and-shoulders drawing of Douglass adorns the cover of *Harper's Weekly,* November 24, 1883. *Harper's Weekly* was a progressive magazine, yet some of its former content (pertaining to African Americans) would be considered offensive by today's standards.

slavery by U.S. governments, both before and after the Revolutionary War. Laws that recognized or even made mention of the institution of slavery did not exist in 1619 when Africans first arrived in what was to become the United States. These Africans (all twenty of them) were put ashore at Jamestown, in the colony of Virginia, by the captain of a Dutch frigate. They had not entered his country (the Netherlands) as slaves, nor had they ever been treated as such. Most were indentured servants at the time of their arrival in Virginia (as were some of the white arrivals), and were listed as such in the Jamestown census counts of 1623 and 1624. After their periods of service had expired, the African settlers were "assigned land in much the same way that it was being assigned to whites who had completed their indenture" (Franklin and Moss, 1988, p. 53). Those African settlers who were not indentured were not slaves and were not treated as slaves by the colonists. Over time, however, slavery reared its head and became institutionalized in the North American colonies—first by custom, in the New England colonies in 1638, and then by law, in Massachusetts in 1641. From the vantage point of the slave owner, the enslavement of Africans was more cost-efficient than that of Native Americans or poor whites, because the Africans' general unfamiliarity with the land (and the skin color that was making them conspicuous) made it difficult for them to hide or to escape.

Once slavery had taken hold in colonial America, African Americans had no legal rights with which to protect themselves from enslavement. The U.S. Supreme Court made clear this vulnerability when, in 1857, it summarized (in the famous *Dred Scott* decision) the legal status of slaves and free blacks alike under colonial laws and the laws that existed at that time. Writing for the court, Chief Justice Roger B. Taney observed that African Americans were ". . . regarded as beings of an inferior order . . . unfit to associate with the white race" and, as such, ". . . they had no rights which the white man was bound to respect." Accordingly, "[T]he negro might justly and lawfully be reduced to slavery for his benefit" (*Dred Scott v. Sandford* [1857]).

This grim assessment of the U.S. Supreme Court has antecedents in the U.S. Constitution of 1787. No less than five provisions of the Constitution unambiguously sanction and protect slavery. Article I, Section 2, Paragraph 3 (the "three-fifths clause") ruled that a slave counted as three-fifths of a person in the calculation of a state's population for purposes of congressional representation and any "direct taxes." Article I, Section 9, Paragraph 1 (the "slave-trade clause") prohibited Congress from ending the slave trade before the year 1808, but did not require Congress to ban it after that date. Article I, Section 9, Paragraph 4, somewhat redundant of the three-fifths clause, ensured that a slave would be counted as three-fifths of a person if a head tax were to be levied. Article V, Section 2, Paragraph 3 (the "fugitive-slave clause") required the return of fugitive slaves to their owners "on demand, " and, finally, Article V prohibited Congress from amending the slave-trade clause before 1808.

These constitutional directives—plus about a dozen others that indirectly support slavery—made the Constitution of 1787 a slaveholder's constitution. William Lloyd Garrison, the nineteenth-century abolitionist, was not exaggerating when he referred to the Constitution as "a covenant with death," "an agreement with Hell," and "a pro-slavery" Constitution (Finkel-

man, 1996, p. 3). Modern historians, overwhelmingly, are in agreement with this view. Civil war scholar Don Fehrenbacher, for example, asserted, "prior to 1860, the United States was a slaveholding republic" (2001, p. 5). Similarly, historian David Brion Davis argues: "The U.S. Constitution was designed to protect the rights and security of slaveholders, and between 1792 and 1845 the American political system encouraged and rewarded the expansion of slavery into nine new states" (2001, p. 134).

Slavery ended on the battlefield rather than in the statehouse or the courthouse. The Union's defeat of the Confederate States of America in the Civil War brought down the peculiar institution. The U.S. Congress and the individual states then codified that victory with the ratification of the Thirteenth Amendment to the Constitution, which abolished slavery and involuntary servitude. President Abraham Lincoln's Emancipation Proclamation, signed on January 1, 1863, did not and could not free all slaves. It stated that "all persons held as slaves within any State or designated part of a State, the people whereof shall then be in rebellion against the United States, shall be then, thenceforward, and forever free." Thus, the Proclamation did not purport to free slaves in states that were not in rebellion against the United States, nor did it have the power to free the great majority of slaves who were under subjugation by the Confederacy. But the Emancipation Proclamation did have the effect of transforming the Civil War from a war to save the Union, which is how Lincoln and the North initially characterized the war, to a crusade to free the slaves, with Lincoln as the commander-in-chief of the liberation force.

After 1865

Following the Civil War, Congress passed a great many laws intended to reshape the South into a more democratic, racially inclusive society. These laws included the *Reconstruction Acts,* a series of acts that began with the Reconstruction Act of March 2, 1867. The purpose of these acts was to "provide for the more efficient government of the rebel states"—in other words, to facilitate restoration of the war-torn South. Congress also enacted legislation establishing the Freedmen's Bureau, a U.S. government bureau that helped the freed slaves adjust to a new life.

Early Civil Rights Gains and Losses

The Party of Lincoln spearheaded ratification of the Thirteenth (1865), Fourteenth (1868), and Fifteenth (1870) Amendments to the Constitution. These amendments abolished slavery and involuntary servitude; established citizenship for the freed slaves, plus guaranteed them due process and equal protection of

[1890 CONSTITUTION OF MISSISSIPPI. ADOPTED NOVEMBER 1, 1890]

ARTICLE 8—EDUCATION. Sec. 243. A uniform poll tax of two dollars, to be used in aid of the common schools, and for no other purpose, is hereby imposed on every male inhabitant of this State between the ages of twenty-one and sixty years, except persons who are deaf and dumb or blind, or who are maimed by loss of hand or foot; said tax to be a lien only upon taxable property. The board of supervisors of any county may, for the purpose of aiding the common schools in that county, increase the poll tax in said county, but in no case shall the entire poll tax exceed in any one year three dollars on each poll. No criminal proceedings shall be allowed to enforce the collection of the poll tax.

Sec. 244. On and after the first day of January, A. D., 1892, every elector shall, in addition to the foregoing qualifications, be able to read any section of the constitution of this State; or he shall be able to understand the same when read to him, or give a reasonable interpretation thereof. A new registration shall be made before the next ensuing election after January the first, A.D., 1892.

the laws; and granted them the right to vote, respectively. Federal troops were sent into the South to enforce these rights. A number of civil rights laws that protected the rights of the freed slaves were also passed by the Republican Congress. These laws were mainly a response to the "Black Codes" that had been enacted in most Southern states—laws that, like the Jim Crow laws that would come later, sought to return the newly freed slaves to a slavelike existence. The most important of the laws that were a response to the Black Codes were the Civil Rights Act of 1866 and the Civil Rights Act of 1871, the latter of which was enacted in response to the emergence of the Ku Klux Klan in 1868 (and thus is also known as the Ku Klux Klan Act of 1871). Congress also passed the Civil Rights Act of 1875, which the Supreme Court effectively overturned in a series of decisions it made in 1883 (the cases collectively known as the Civil Rights Cases).

As a result of this action, African Americans enjoyed degrees of freedom that were unprecedented, which they used to garner economic prosperity, not only for themselves but for the region as a whole. For the first time in U.S. history, African Americans were elected to Congress and state legislatures. But this era

of racial progress turned out to be short-lived, and abruptly ended with the Compromise of 1877.

The Compromise of 1877 decided the outcome of the disputed U.S. presidential election of 1876, which had been a contest between the Republican candidate, Rutherford B. Hayes, and the Democratic candidate, Samuel L. Tilden. The popular vote favored Tilden, but twenty Electoral College votes, representing four states, were in dispute. An ad hoc electoral commission, composed of Republican and Democratic leaders, decided, as a way of ending the stalemate, that the Republicans would be given the presidency and Southern Democrats would gain control of the South. In other words, it was agreed that the new president would remove all federal troops from the South. With the removal of federal troops, Southern whites were given free reign to re-establish white hegemony—marking the end of Reconstruction and the beginning of Jim Crow.

Lasting for approximately one hundred years, Jim Crow was America's age of apartheid. It was a time of legalized racial discrimination and segregation—a time in which African Americans lived under the yoke of white supremacy and were accorded second-class citizenship under the law. During the years of Jim Crow African Americans inhabited a world of limited opportunities and fear. They were vulnerable to beatings, maimings, lynchings, murders, and a constant stream of indignities.

African-American Disfranchisement

To lend legitimacy to this regime of racial repression, whites in positions of power devised stratagems to wrest from African Americans rights they had already been given, including the right to vote. Without this right, without political power, without access to the power of government, African Americans would then be powerless to prevent the erosion of other basic rights. To fulfill their agenda, Southern whites found ways to circumvent the Fifteenth Amendment (which had given African Americans the right to vote).

With African Americans constituting a majority of its population, Mississippi became the first state to move toward this disfranchisement. A state constitutional convention was convened in 1890. The delegates to the convention made their intentions clear: they had come together for the express purpose of disfranchising all African-American residents who had attained any measure of socioeconomic status. In the words of a delegate to the convention:

"I am just as opposed to Booker Washington [the leading African American figure of the day] as a voter, with all his Anglo-Saxon re-enforcements, as I am to the coconut-headed, chocolate-colored, typical little coon, Andy Dotson, who blacks my shoes every morning. Neither is fit to perform the supreme function of citizenship" (Brooks, 1999, p. 395).

Accordingly, the Mississippi constitution was amended to include the establishment of a $2 poll tax and a literacy test as preconditions to exercising the right to vote. The latter required the prospective voter to read a section of the state constitution selected by an election official (who was invariably white) and/or to answer questions in such a way as to prove to the official that he had understood what had been read. As a result of these constitutional amendments, scores of African Americans who had been eligible to vote during Reconstruction were suddenly ineligible.

Other states followed the lead of Mississippi. South Carolina disfranchised African Americans in 1895, by adopting amendments to its constitution that called for a two-year residence test, a $1 poll tax, a literacy test, and a property-ownership test. The property-ownership test established ownership of property in the state valued at $3000 (or greater) as another prerequisite to voting. Similarly, Louisiana amended its constitution in 1898 by adopting a new stratagem of disfranchisement called the grandfather clause. Under this clause, any male citizen whose father and grandfather had been qualified to vote on January 1, 1867 (just before the start of Reconstruction), was automatically eligible to vote, regardless of his ability to pass any of the new eligibility tests or to pay the poll tax. Prior to January 1, 1867, African Americans had not been eligible to vote in Louisiana. Thus, it was established that African Americans would be required to comply with the various eligibility tests and pay the poll tax in order to exercise their Fifteenth Amendment right to vote in Louisiana.

By 1910 African Americans were effectively disfranchised by constitutional amendments in North Carolina, Alabama, Virginia, Georgia, and Oklahoma, and other Southern states. The campaigns to reestablish white hegemony were often buttressed by violence. Race riots flared up—in Wilmington, North Carolina, in 1898; in Atlanta, Georgia, after an election in 1906; and in other cities. Dozens of African Americans died in their attempts to exercise their Fifteenth Amendment rights.

Effectiveness of Disfranchisement

The disfranchisement of African Americans yielded the sought-after results. For example, 130,344 African Americans were registered to vote in Louisiana in 1896 and constituted voting majorities in twenty-six parishes. But in 1900, just two years after the adoption of the new state constitution, only 5,320 African Americans were registered to vote. Similarly, of 181,471 African Americans of voting age in Alabama in 1900, only 3,000 were eligible to vote under that state's new constitution.

The disfranchisement of African Americans was hailed throughout the South as a furtherance of progressive statesmanship. African Americans were viewed as too ignorant, too poor, and/or too inferior to participate in their own self-governance. Those who were in basic agreement with this credo would have taken comfort in the 1910 edition of the *Encyclopedia Britannica*, which provided "scientific" justification for the systematic, government-sanctioned exclusion of African Americans from mainstream society. According to its editors: "[T]he negro would appear to stand on a lower evolutionary plane than the white man, and to be more closely related to the highest anthropoids." In response to such charges, African Americans pointed to the exemplary record of African-American achievement during Reconstruction, which included innovative achievements in public finance, building construction, and public education. Indeed, African Americans had been responsible for the establishment of the first public school systems in many Southern states. But no quantity of truth or logic was going to persuade white Southerners to abandon their designs.

Jim Crow Appears

The major push for the installment of Jim Crow laws in the South came after Reconstruction; especially after the state constitutions had been amended so as to remove the only obstruction to the creation of Jim Crow laws that had remained (the authority of politically powerful African Americans). These laws were established throughout the South. They mandated racial segregation in all public facilities, including hotels, restaurants, theaters, schools, vehicles of public transportation, and other places of public accommodation. Jim Crow laws denied African Americans employment and housing opportunities. Worse, African Americans were often arrested under local vagrancy and peonage laws, and subsequently hired out by sheriffs, who made tidy profits in the ventures. Thus, having enshrined white supremacy in new constitutions—the fundamental laws of the states—Southern states securely established the color line as the point at which African Americans and whites would be segregated.

The federal government was more than complicit in the apartheid system that became established in the South. In *Plessy v. Ferguson* (1896), the Supreme Court upheld the separate-but-equal doctrine as the federal constitutional underpinning of the Jim Crow laws. Despite passage of federal civil rights legislation, Congress continued to segregate Washington, D.C., and refused to pass an anti-lynching law—something that African-American activist Ida B. Wells had fought for so courageously. Wells had been galvanized into action by the ritualized lynching of African Americans (mostly male African Americans).

Lynchings began in the South shortly after the Civil War. They were an effort to terrorize the newly freed slaves—an attempt "to keep them in their place"—and continued well into the twentieth century. Indeed, at the start of the twentieth century, there were in the public record 214 lynchings from the first two years alone. Before the end of Jim Crow thousands of African-American males and females would die by lynching. So rampant and targeted were the lynchings (often taking place in carnival-like atmospheres) that a white poet and songwriter, Abel Meeropol (also known as Lewis Allan), was motivated to write a musical protest song entitled "Strange Fruit." Made famous in 1939 by Billie Holiday, an African-American blues singer, the ballad gives a mock-lyrical description of black bodies left hanging from trees for all to see. The lyrics include: "Southern trees bear a strange fruit / Blood on the leaves and blood on the root / Black body swinging in the Southern breeze / Strange fruit hanging from the poplar trees."

Although the Jim Crow ethos manifested itself in the form of rigid, racially repressive laws in the South, it reared its head in the North mainly in the form of social norms. Though the norms in many ways required less segregation than the laws, they were rigorously enforced and often just as racially repressive. Both the laws and the social customs denied opportunities to African Americans. As one white Southerner observed of his first visit to the North in the 1930s: "Proudly cosmopolitan New York was in most respects more thoroughly segregated than any Southern city: with the exception of a small coterie of intellectuals, musicians, and entertainers there was little traffic between the white world and the black enclave in upper Manhattan called Harlem" (Brooks, 1999, p. 396).

Death of Jim Crow

Jim Crow began its death march in 1954, when the Supreme Court handed down its decision in the case of *Brown v. Board of Education* (actually four similar cases that the court decided to hear simultaneously). This decision, quite simply, changed forever the course of race relations in the United States. In the *Brown* decision, Chief Justice Earl Warren, writing for a unanimous court, held that "in the field of public education the doctrine of separate but equal has no place." With

Jim Crow in bold relief. Dr. and Mrs. Charles Atkins and their sons Edmond and Charles Jr. wait inside a train depot in Oklahoma City, November 1955. [AP/WIDE WORLD PHOTOS]

those carefully chosen words a judicial decision that had to do with public education became the most important action of the U.S. government since the Emancipation Proclamation.

In banning racial segregation in public schools, the Supreme Court sought nothing less than to use society's most basic outpost of acculturation as the setting in which African Americans and whites (indeed all races, ethnic groups, and cultures) could be brought together for a lateral transmission of values. Hence, much more than school segregation was at stake in *Brown*. The court had been called upon to pass judgment on a morally corrupted way of life that the nation had known in one form or another since its inception—indeed a regime of racial domination and subjugation that predated the republic itself. The Supreme Court, thereby, placed itself in the vanguard of a third American revolution—the revolution that followed behind the Revolutionary War and the Civil War.

This third revolution was engineered by a team of lawyers from the National Association for the Advancement of Color People (NAACP). The lawyers included Charles Hamilton Houston, Thurgood Marshall (who would later become the first African American to sit on the Supreme Court), Constance Baker Motley, and Robert Carter. Carter, who along with Motley would later become a federal judge, summarized the significance of *Brown* when he observed that the case had transformed the legal status of African Americans from that of "mere supplicants seeking, pleading, [and] begging to be treated as full-fledged members of the human race" to persons entitled to equal treatment under the law.

Although *Brown* did not put an end to Jim Crow in 1954, it was a stimulus to the burgeoning civil rights movement of the 1950s and 1960s. Martin Luther King's famous "I Have A Dream" speech, which so galvanized the supporters of the civil rights movement who had gathered at the Lincoln Memorial in 1963, was a stab in the heart of Jim Crow—its norm of white supremacy—no less than was *Brown*. Both struck strong blows for racial equality. Certainly, the civil rights legislation enacted by Congress in the 1960s and early 1970s—beginning with the Civil Rights Act of 1964 and ending with the Equal Opportunity Act of 1972— would not have been possible without *Brown*. It is doubtful that, in the absence of the *Brown* decision, a racially skittish Congress would have passed civil rights statutes in contravention of the constitutional principle of separate but equal.

In the South and the North, African Americans were a subordinated people in the Jim Crow era. As during the period of slavery, African Americans during Jim Crow were targets for ill treatment and exploitation, singled out for invidious discrimination. They were abused physically and psychologically. They were the victims of a "crime against humanity." Neither *Brown*, the civil rights movement, nor the civil rights legislation of the 1960s and 1970s has fully repaired the damaged visited upon African Americans by three and a half centuries of criminal treatment.

SEE ALSO Racism; Rosewood; Slavery, Historical; Slavery, Legal Aspects of

BIBLIOGRAPHY

Ball, Charles (1854). *A Narrative of the Life and Adventures of Charles Ball, a Black Man,* 3rd edition. Pittsburgh, Pa.: John T. Shryock.

Brooks, Roy L. (1999). "Redress for Racism?" In *When Sorry Isn't Enough: The Controversy over Apologies and Reparations for Human Injustice,* ed. Roy L. Brooks. New York: New York University Press.

Davis, David Brion (2001). *In the Image of God: Religion, Moral Values, and Our Heritage of Slavery.* New Haven, Conn.: Yale University Press.

Douglass, Frederick (1892). *Life and Times of Frederick Douglass: His Early Life as a Slave, His Escape from Bondage, and His Complete History, Written by Himself.* New York: Collier Books, 1962.

Feagin, Joe R. (2000). *Racist America: Roots, Current Realities, and Future Reparations.* New York: Routledge.

Fehrenbacher, Don E. (2001). *The Slaveholding Republic: An Account of the United States Government's Relations to Slavery,* ed. Ward M. McAfee. New York: Oxford University Press.

Finkelman, Paul (1966). *Slavery and the Founders: Race and Liberty in the Age of Jefferson.* Armonk, N.Y.: M. E. Sharpe.

Franklin, John Hope, and Alfred A. Moss, Jr. (1988). *From Slavery to Freedom: A History of Negro Americans,* 6th edition. New York: Alfred A. Knopf.

Friedman, Leon, ed. (1965). *Southern Justice.* New York: Pantheon Books.

Higginbotham, A. Leon, Jr. (1978). *In the Matter of Color: The Colonial Period.* New York: Oxford University Press.

Johnson, Paul (1998). *A History of the American People.* New York: HarperCollins.

Klarman, Michael J. (2003). *From Jim Crow to Civil Rights: The Supreme Court and the Struggle for Racial Equality.* New York: Oxford University Press.

Kluger, Richard (1976). *Simple Justice: The History of Brown v. Board of Education and Black America's Struggle for Equality.* New York: Alfred A. Knopf.

Litwack, Leon (1961). *North of Slavery: The Negro in the Free States.* Chicago: University of Chicago Press.

Litwack, Leon (1979). *Been in the Storm So Long: The Aftermath of Slavery.* New York: Alfred A. Knopf.

Litwack, Leon (1999). *Trouble in Mind: Black Southerners in the Age of Jim Crow.* New York: Alfred A. Knopf.

McPherson, James M. (1997). *For Cause & Comrades: Why Men Fought in the Civil War.* New York: Oxford University Press.

Nichols, Charles H. (1963). *Many Thousand Gone: The Ex-Slaves' Account of Their Bondage and Freedom.* Leiden, Netherlands: Brill.

Roy L. Brooks

African Crisis Response Initiative

The history of mass murder in Central Africa has been traced to the colonial era when Belgian colonialists massacred more than ten million people during their occupation and pacification of the Congo in the 1890s. Adam Hochschild's *King Leopold's Ghost* documented this period of genocide, a central aspect of colonial expansion. The European powers defined their mission as the civilization of "uncivilized" peoples, elimination of slavery, redemption of souls through conversion to Christianity, and expansion of international commerce, all the while insisting that the key conflicts in the region related to tribal hostility.

The genocide and mass murder perpetrated within the Congo set the stage for a century of mass slaughter throughout Africa, with the killings in the German protectorate of Namibia in a sense serving as the rehearsal for the Holocaust during World War II. The Nazis' annihilation of some six million European Jews brought the issue of genocide to the center of international concern.

The U.S. government established the African Crisis Response Initiative (ACRI) force in September 1996, during the Clinton administration, to respond in a timely fashion to humanitarian crises and develop peacekeeping missions on the African continent. The possibility of a major genocide in Burundi, along the lines of what had occurred in Rwanda in 1994, was the principal reason for the creation of this force. However, after the ACRI was formed, these murders continued and the force never officially intervened. As of mid-2004, with the mass murders occurring in the Darfur province of the Sudan, the U.S. government had yet to deploy the ACRI force to put an end to genocide in Africa.

Episodes of ethnically organized and targeted massacres have been constant in Burundi since 1965, with large-scale massacres documented for 1969, 1988, 1991, 1993, 1996, and 1997, and an actual genocide in 1972. Throughout this period the United States continued to provide military assistance to the Burundi government, the agent of the genocide. In fact, while the African Union and Nyerere Foundation labored to establish peace and demilitarization in Burundi, the official U.S. government, despite its statements calling for humanitarian intervention in Africa as outlined in the ACRI's founding articles, did not actively support these efforts.

The formation of the ACRI was interpreted by some African leaders, such as South African Nelson Mandela, as a cynical attempt by the U.S. government to repair its image in the wake of the Rwandan genocide. Although the United States had been willing to mobilize the United Nations (UN) to stop mass murders in Bosnia, it aggressively intervened to ensure that the UN did not send troops to end the Rwandan genocide in 1994, often regarded as the "fastest" genocide in history as it took place over the course of several days. While graphic images of the genocide dominated the media, the U.S. government remained reluctant to even use the term *genocide* to characterize what was unfolding in Rwanda. It simply declared, "acts of genocide may have taken place."

The experience of the U.S. military in Somalia is directly relevant to the creation of the ACRI. After the fall of the Siad Barre regime in Somalia, the United States, in 1992, chose to send in military forces in a humanitarian operation called Restore Hope. However, the mission soon took on other dimensions when U.S. for-

eign policy began to move in the direction of restructuring Somalia's government. Before long tensions erupted between U.S. forces and local military entrepreneurs. In 1993 the Battle of Mogadishu resulted in the death of several U.S. troops and the dragging of their bodies through the city's streets. The humiliation of this incident led the U.S. State Department to pressure the UN against intervening in the 1994 genocide in Rwanda.

An international panel of experts assembled by the Organization of African Unity (OAU) investigated the genocide in Rwanda and concluded that during the period of civil war, genocide had indeed occurred, and a high degree of tolerance for genocidal violence committed by African leaders seemed to exist. In calling its report *Rwanda: The Preventable Genocide,* the panel drew attention to the possible culpability of the United States and UN in this tragedy.

Regional leaders such as Michel Micombero of Burundi, Emperor Bokassa of the Central African Republic, Idi Amin of Uganda, and Mobutu of Zaire (now the Democratic Republic of Congo) directly and indirectly contributed to the perpetuation of war and genocide by supporting, tolerating, or adopting a stance of indifference toward state-implemented criminal prescriptions originating from extremist political elements that exploited myths of Tutsi and Hutu origins.

SEE ALSO Burundi; Early Warning; Humanitarian Intervention; King Leopold II and the Congo; Prevention; Rwanda

BIBLIOGRAPHY

Campbell, Horace G. (2000). *The U.S. Security Doctrine and the Africa Crisis Response Initiative.* Pretoria: Africa Institute of South Africa.

Frazier, Jendayi (Summer/Fall 1997). "The African Crisis Response Initiative: Self-Interested Humanitarianism." *Brown Journal of World Affairs* IV (2).

Henk, Dan, and Steven Metz (1997). *The United States and the Transformation of African Security: The African Crisis Response Initiative and Beyond.* Carlisle Barracks, Pa.: Strategic Studies Institute.

McCallie, Marshall (April 1998). "ACRI: Positive U.S. Engagement with Africa." *USIA Electronic Journal* 3(2).

Horace Campbell

Aggression

Theologians and moralists have long attempted to restrict the use of force by states through elaborating the concept of just and unjust wars, condemning those deemed unjust. Legal efforts to outlaw recourse to war came much later, mostly dating from World War I.

December 6, 1939: The Nazi *Blitzkrieg* (lightning war), begun in September, continued in Warsaw, Poland. A section of the city was set afire by bombs dropped from Nazi planes. [BETTMANN/CORBIS]

Until that time, international law placed certain limitations on and pre-requisites to warfare, but did not prohibit it altogether. War was still perceived as a legitimate means of achieving political objectives.

From World War I to Nuremberg

World War I ("the war to end all wars") left ten million deaths in its wake, eliminating an entire generation of young men in Europe. This catastrophe led countries to seek ways to ban war as an exercise of State sovereignty. U.S. Secretary of State Frank Kellogg, the French Minister of Foreign Affairs Aristide Briand and the German Minister of Foreign Affairs Gustav Stresemann spearheaded negotiations to conclude a treaty that would achieve this aim. On August 27, 1928, in Paris the Kellogg-Briand Pact was signed and opened for adherence by states. By virtue of Article I of this short text, the forty-five State parties "condemn recourse to war for the solution of international controversies, and renounce it, as an instrument of national policy;" in Article II they "agree that the settlement or solution of all disputes or conflicts of whatever nature or of whatever origin they may be . . . shall never be sought except by pacific means."

As a corollary to the Pact, a subsequent American Secretary of State, Henry Stimson, enunciated the doctrine of non-recognition of international territorial changes effectuated by force. This doctrine was a response to Japan's unilateral seizure of Manchuria in September 1931. The Stimson doctrine was subsequently incorporated in several international declarations, including a League of Nations resolution of March 11, 1932; the Inter-American Pact of Rio de Janeiro of October 10, 1933; and the Budapest Articles of Interpretation (September 10, 1934) of the Kellogg-Briand Pact.

Germany and Italy were among the state parties to the Pact, but this did not prevent the outbreak of World War II, in which Hitler was the principal, but not the only aggressor. The Soviet Union, for instance, joined Germany in attacking Poland in September 1939, pursuant to a secret treaty signed by foreign Ministers Ribbentrop and Molotov, in which they divided Poland between the two countries. In October 1939 the Soviet Union occupied and annexed the three Baltic States of Estonia, Latvia and Lithuania. In November 1939, it took 18,000 square miles of Finnish territory and forced 450,000 Finns to resettle elsewhere. For the latter aggression the Soviet Union was formally expelled from the League of Nations in December 1939.

Following German capitulation in May 1945, the Allies adopted the London Agreement of August 8, 1945, which contained the Charter of the Nuremberg Tribunal. Article 6(a) of this charter provided for prosecution for crimes against peace: "namely, planning, preparation, initiation or waging of a war of aggression, or a war in violation of international treaties, agreements or assurances, or participation in a Common Plan or Conspiracy for the accomplishment of any of the foregoing." Many Nazis leaders were indicted and convicted of this offence, seven of whom were sentenced to death. Despite the adherence of Germany to the Kellogg-Briand Pact, controversy emerged over whether or not the inclusion of "crimes against peace" amounted to the enunciation of new law and made the prosecutions contrary to norms of justice prohibiting punishment for offenses *ex post facto*. It is clear that the Kellogg-Briand Pact prohibited recourse to war, but it did not include any reference to personal responsibility or international crimes, so the issue remains subject to debate.

Whatever the legal position before the London Charter, the illegality of aggression was settled in its aftermath. By virtue of General Assembly Resolution 95(1) of December 11, 1946, the Nuremberg judgment, including the condemnation of aggression, was recognized as binding international law. At the same time, the International Law Commission was entrusted with drafting what became known as the "Nuremberg Principles," which were adopted in July 1950, and included a definition of the crime against peace.

In General Assembly Resolution 177(II) of November 21, 1947, the International Law Commission was further mandated to prepare a code on offences against the peace and security of mankind. After nearly forty years of effort, the International Law Commission adopted in 1996 a "Draft Code on Crimes Against the Peace and Security of Mankind" (not yet approved by the UN General Assembly). Article 16 of the draft code contains the following statutory definition: "An individual who, as leader or organizer, actively participates in or orders the planning, preparation, initiation or waging of aggression committed by a State shall be responsible for a crime of aggression."

Defining Aggression

General Assembly Resolution 3314 (XXIX) of December 14, 1974, constitutes the most detailed statement of the United Nations on aggression. The resolution defines aggression in its first articles. Article 1 provides:

> Aggression is the use of armed force by a State against the sovereignty, territorial integrity or political independence of another State, or in any other manner inconsistent with the Charter of the United Nations.

Article 2 stipulates:

> The first use of armed force by a State in contravention of the Charter shall constitute prima facie evidence of an act of aggression although the Security Council may, in conformity with the Charter, conclude that a determination that an act of aggression has been committed would not be justified in the light of other relevant circumstances, including the fact that the acts concerned or their consequences are not of sufficient gravity.

Article 3 lists a series of acts which, regardless of a declaration of war, would constitute aggression, including the invasion or attack by the armed forces of a state of the territory of another state, bombardment by the armed forces of a state against the territory of another state, the blockade of the ports or coasts of a state, and the sending of armed bands, groups, irregulars, or mercenaries, which carry out acts of armed force against another state.

Article 5 warns that "no consideration of whatever nature, whether political, economic, military or otherwise may serve as a justification for aggression. A war of aggression is a crime against international peace. Aggression gives rise to international responsibility. No territorial acquisition or special advantage resulting from aggression is or shall be recognized as lawful."

Article 7 explains, however, that "nothing in this declaration . . . could in any way prejudice the right to self-determination, freedom and independence, as derived from the Charter, of persons forcibly deprived of that right and referred to in the Declaration on Principles of International Law concerning Friendly Relations and Cooperation among states in accordance with the Charter of the United Nations, particularly peoples under colonial and racist regimes or other forms of alien domination, nor the right of these peoples to struggle to that end and to seek and receive support, in accordance with the principles of the Charter and in conformity with the above-mentioned Declaration."

The UN General Assembly has reaffirmed the consensus definition in several declarations, including the Declaration on International Détente (Res.32/155 (1977)) the Declaration of Societies for Life in Peace (Res. 33/73 (1978)), the Declaration on the Non-Use of Force (Res. 42/22 (1988).

UN Efforts to Combat Aggression

The United Nations was founded "to save succeeding generations from the scourge of war" (preamble), and Article 1, paragraph 1 of the Charter establishes its mandate "to maintain international peace and security, and to that end: to take effective collective measures for the prevention and removal of threats to the peace, and for the suppression of acts of aggression. . ." Article 2, paragraph 3 imposes an obligation to resolve international disputes peacefully: "All members shall settle their international disputes by peaceful means." Finally, Article 2, paragraph 4 specifically engages States to "refrain in their international relations from the threat or use of force."

The Charter prohibition of force has been repeated in countless resolutions of the Security Council and of the General Assembly. It is detailed most importantly in GA Resolution 2625 (XXV) of October 24, 1970, *Resolution on Principles of International Law concerning Friendly Relations and Co-operation among States in accordance with the Charter of the United Nations*, which solemnly proclaims that

> Every State has the duty to refrain in its international relations from the threat or use of force against the territorial integrity or political independence of any State, or in any other manner inconsistent with the purposes of the United Nations. Such a threat or use of force constitutes a violation of international law and the Charter of the United Nations and shall never be employed as a means of settling international issues. A war of aggression constitutes a crime against the peace, for which there is responsibility under international law. In accordance with the purposes and principles of the United Nations, States have the duty to refrain from propaganda for wars of aggression.

The Security Council has, however, avoided labeling breaches of the peace as acts of aggression. Even in a case as clear as the 1990 aggression toward Kuwait by Iraq, the Security Council condemned it merely as an "invasion and illegal occupation" (Res. 674/1990), and decided that "the annexation of Kuwait by Iraq under any form and whatever pretext has no legal validity, and is considered null and void" (Res. 662 (1990)). However no reference was made to the application of Article 3(a) of the definition of aggression, or to the penal consequences pursuant to Article 5.

Other uses of force since World War II could be measured against the standards laid down by the UN Charter, the Nuremberg Principles and the Declaration on the Definition of Aggression. These incidents include Dutch "police actions" in Indonesia (1947–1950), the French Indochina wars (1952–1954), the French-Algerian conflict (1954–1963), the sinking of the Greenpeace vessel "Rainbow Warrior" in Auckland Harbour in New Zealand, the war over the Belgian Congo (1960–1962), the Indian-Pakistani war 1970–1971, the Warsaw Pact's invasion of Czechoslovakia in 1968, the Soviet Union's occupation of Afghanistan in 1980, the Iraq-Iran War (1980–1990), the Turkish invasion of Cyprus in 1974 and the Vietnam War.

Justifications for the Use of Force, Self-Defense

There are, of course, some justifications for the use of force which are legitimate according to international law. Article 51 of the UN Charter stipulates: "Nothing in the present Charter shall impair the inherent right of individual or collective self-defence if an armed attack occurs against a Member of the United Nations, until the Security Council has taken measures necessary to maintain international peace and security."

The application of this provision is, however, strictly limited by the over-all obligation to negotiate set forth in Article 2, paragraph 3, and the prohibition of the threat of or the use of force in Article 2, paragraph 4 of the UN Charter. In his address to the General Assembly on September 23, 2003, Secretary General Kofi Annan stated: "Article 51 of the Charter prescribes that all states, if attacked, retain the inherent right of self-defence. . .until now it has been understood that when states go beyond that, and decide to use force to deal with broader threats to international peace and security, they need the unique legitimacy provided by the United Nations." The International Court of Justice has specified the situations in which Article 51 can be invoked, most recently in an advisory opinion of July 9, 2004. The consensus of international law experts is that preventive or pre-emptive war is not compatible with article 51 of the charter, which requires an existing "armed attack" and places overall responsibility on the Security Council.

Humanitarian intervention is another possible justification for the use of force, and it remains the responsibility of the Security Council to legitimize or not a given military intervention. For example, approval was given in Resolution 688 of April 5, 1991, with respect to the necessity to create safety zones for Kurds and other minorities in Iraq. Humanitarian intervention would also have been possible in order to stop the genocide in Cambodia (1975–1979) or in Rwanda (1994).

While humanitarian intervention may be an international duty in order to stop genocide and crimes against humanity, it must not become a cloak or an excuse for military interventions responding to other political agendas. For instance, Human Rights Watch recently conducted a study of the arguments advanced by the United States as justification for the war on Iraq begun in 2003, and concluded that the U.S. intervention did not satisfy the constitutive elements of a humanitarian intervention.

Individual Responsibility
Aggression is not only an internationally wrongful act giving rise to State responsibility and the obligation to make reparation; it is also an international crime giving rise to personal criminal liability. The Diplomatic Conference of Rome adopted on July 18, 1998 the Statute of the International Criminal Court, which defines the jurisdiction of the Court in its Article 5, including with respect to the crime of aggression. Paragraph 2 of Article 5, however, stipulates: "The Court shall exercise jurisdiction over the crime of aggression once a provision is adopted in accordance with Articles 121 and 123 defining the crime and setting out the conditions under which the Court shall exercise jurisdiction with respect to this crime." This delay in the exercise of the Court's competence with regard to aggression is primarily attributable to the opposition of the United States. However, since the United States has indicated that it will not ratify the treaty, the assembly of States parties to the Rome Statute is now free to adopt a definition consistent with the judgment of the Nuremberg trials.

None of the Special Tribunals created since have jurisdiction over the crime of aggression, neither the International Tribunal for the Former Yugoslavia, nor the International Tribunal for Rwanda, nor the Iraqi Special Tribunal. Precisely because no international tribunal has been given competence to try aggressors for the crime of aggression, a number of representatives of civil society have organized "People's Tribunals."

Notable among these are the Russell Tribunal on the Vietnam War, organized by British pacifist Bertrand Russell and French philosopher Jean Paul Sartre (held 1967 in Sweden and Denmark) and the Brussels Tribunal on the Iraq War organized by former Attorney General Ramsey Clark (April 2004). The latter was conducted with the participation of two ex-United Nations humanitarian coordinators for Iraq, Dennis Halliday and Hans von Sponeck. Both tribunals condemned the United States as an aggressor in Vietnam and as an aggressor in Iraq. There is also a "Permanent People's Tribunal" (Fondation Internationale Lelio Basso), which has held more than 30 sessions, one of them in Paris in 1984, devoted to the genocide against the Armenians, and one held in Rome in 2002 devoted to international law and the new wars of aggression.

A Human Right to Peace
The international prohibition of aggression may also be viewed as asserting a human right to peace. On November 12, 1984 the United Nations General Assembly adopted Resolution 39/11, annexing the Declaration on the Right of Peoples to Peace. This declaration reaffirms that "the principal aim of the United Nations is the maintenance of international peace and security" and the "aspirations of all peoples to eradicate war from the life of mankind and, above all, to avert a world-wide nuclear catastrophe." By virtue of operative paragraph 2, the declaration proclaims that "the preservation of the right of peoples to peace and the promotion of its implementation constitute a fundamental obligation of each State." In paragraph 3, the declaration "demands that the policies of States be directed towards the elimination of the threat of war, particularly nuclear war, the renunciation of the use of force in international relations and the settlement of international disputes by peaceful means."

This declaration has been reaffirmed in resolutions of the General Assembly and of the United Nations Commission on Human Rights. In its Resolution 2002/71 of April 25, 2002, the Commission linked the right to peace with the right to development and affirmed that "all States should promote the establishment, maintenance and strengthening of international peace and security and, to that end, should do their utmost to achieve general and complete disarmament under effective international control, as well as to ensure that the resources released by effective disarmament measures are used for comprehensive development, in particular that of the developing countries." The resolution urged "the international community to devote part of the resources made available by the implementation of disarmament and arms limitation agreements to economic and social development, with a view to reducing the ever-widening gap between developed and developing countries."

In a world of weapons of mass destruction, it is imperative to strengthen the early warning and peaceful settlement mechanisms of the United Nations. In view of the human consequences of war, aggression must be prevented through international solidarity. The idea that has become the norm is that no country can take the law in its own hands. Force can only be used as a last resort and only with approval of the UN Security Council.

SEE ALSO Humanitarian Law; International
Criminal Court; Peacekeeping; United Nations
Security Council; War; War Crimes

BIBLIOGRAPHY

Bassiouni, M. Cherif (1998). *The Statute of the International
Criminal Court: A Documentary History.* New York:
Transnational Publishers.

Cassin V. et al. (1975). "The Definition of Aggression"
Harvard International Law Journal 16:598–613.

Dinstein, Yoram. *War, Aggression, and Self-Defence,* 2nd
edition. Cambridge, U.K.: Grotius.

Fastenrath, Ulrich (2002). "Definition of Aggression." In *A
Concise Encyclopedia of the United Nations,* ed. H.
Volger. Hague: Kluwer Law International.

Ferencz, Benjamin (1975). *Defining International Aggression,
the Search for World Peace: A Documentary Analysis,* 2
volumes. Dobbs Ferry, N.Y.: Oceana.

Roth, Kenneth (2004). "War in Iraq: Not a Humanitarian
Intervention." Available from http://www.hrw.org/
wr2k4/3.htm.

Alfred de Zayas

Algeria

Since the end of France's occupation of Algeria in 1962, there has been little debate about the French colonization campaign in North Africa and its subsequent efforts at maintaining the colony. Very few people have dared to re-examine the atrocities committed by colonizing states in many parts of the world in the last two centuries. Among the worst atrocities were those committed by France in Algeria between 1830 and 1962.

France invaded Algiers in June 1830 under the excuse of fighting piracy and avenging an affront caused by Hussein Dey's reprimand of the French ambassador over the failure to pay a long-standing debt owed to the Algiers regency, which was recognized as a sovereign state by the United States and most of Europe. According to many historians, the main reason for the military assault on Algiers was the need of French ruler Charles X to build up his weak popularity and power at home. After Algiers fell to the invading forces, it took more than forty years of violent and highly destructive military campaigns to control the rest of the country.

The French occupied Algeria for 132 years and imposed a series of policies which aimed at controlling the territory and its people by all means possible, opening the country to European settlers, and extracting substantial economic and geostrategic benefits. These policies, which were systematically and violently implemented, had devastating human, social and economic consequences.

The "Pacification" of Algeria: Massacres and Dispossession

In the late 1830s French rule in Algeria was entrusted to the military, which was ordered to pacify the country by all means and to facilitate the immigration of European settlers (mainly from France, Italy, and Spain). Command was given to General Thomas Bugeaud, who was named Governor General of Algeria in 1840. His army of 108,000 troops tracked down Algerians, tortured, humiliated, and killed them, or expelled them from their lands and villages. He conducted a long military campaign against the Algerian resistance, which was led by Emir Abdel-Qader. Bugeaud finally defeated this early resistance, but not without allowing and encouraging his troops to commit horrible crimes against the Algerians.

The crimes associated with this "pacification" campaign reached their peak in 1845, when hundreds of people were burned alive or asphyxiated in caves where they sought refuge from the advancing French troops that were conducting large scale *razzia* (systematic raids on villages). The raiding French troops burned, destroyed or stole property, food, and animal stocks; they also raped women and killed villagers in great numbers. The violent acts committed at that time against the indigenous population, and which today would constitute internationally recognized crimes, were documented in several witness accounts and reports such as the one issued by a royal commission in 1883.

> We tormented, at the slightest suspicion and without due process, people whose guilt still remains more than uncertain [. . .]. We massacred people who carried passes, cut the throats, on a simple suspicion, of entire populations which proved later to be innocent. . . . [Many innocent people were tried just because] they exposed themselves to our furor. Judges were available to condemn them and civilized people to have them executed. . . . In a word, our barbarism was worse than that of the barbarians we came to civilize, and we complain that we have not succeeded with them!

This policy of racism, wide-scale massacres, and scorched earth, enabled France to win the war of conquest by the end of 1847, and Algeria was annexed to France in 1848. In the years that followed, colonization increased the destruction of local social and economic structures and worsened the impoverishment of the indigenous population through property confiscation and forced mass migration from fertile lands. The worsening situation stimulated several attempts by the Algerians to end colonial rule. Some attempts were purely political, and aimed at achieving inclusion in the political process and changes in legislation. Others were mass actions, demanding independence.

In 1871 a mass rebellion led by El-Mokrani challenged the occupying forces in the Kabylie region, east of Algiers. This rural rebellion, the largest since the surrender of Emir Abdel-Qader, was crushed by the French and followed by the imposition of very heavy punishments on the entire indigenous population, including further land confiscations; new, onerous taxes, and a tighter control of the people. According to historian Charles Robert Ageron, in his book *Modern Algeria: A History from 1830 to the Present* (1991), this punishment "was intended to terrorize the natives into submission once and for all—also to procure lands and money for colonization" (p. 52).

In 1871 right after the ill-fated El-Mokrani rebellion, a group of notables published a text, *Colonisation de l'Algérie par le système de colonisation du Maréchal Bugeaud,* assessing the policy of Bugeaud. They declared that

> the empire has done in Algeria what it would never dare do in France. It has committed against the Arabs a crime against humanity and against the army, that of offering the elite of its officers to the monstrous appetite of the leaders (p. 13).

Alexis de Tocqueville, a member of the French Parliament who had just written his famous book *Democracy in America,* supported not only colonization itself, but also the means used by Bugeaud's army to achieve it:

> As for me, I often heard in France men, whom I respect but do not agree with, who found it bad that we burned crops, emptied stock silos, and took unarmed men, women, and children. For me, these are unfortunate necessities which any people that want to wage war against the Arabs is obliged to do (de Tocqueville, 1988, p. 77).

Although the 1871 rebellion did not succeed, it paved the way for the final assault on the colonial system, which occurred in 1954. Between these two dates, the Algerians made many peaceful demands for the end of colonial control, but to no avail.

The Massacres of May 1945

At the end of World War II in Europe, large-scale, peaceful demonstrations were organized, and on May 8 demonstrators throughout Algeria voiced their demands for independence. The most notable demonstrations took place in the northeastern cities of Setif, Guelma, Kherrata, Bejaia, Annaba, and Souk-Ahras. The demonstrators were met with hostile gun fire and physical attacks, both from settlers and from the French security forces. An Algerian carrying the then-prohibited Algerian flag was shot to death in Setif by a policeman, touching off riots. General Duval, commander of the military division of the province of Constantine, called in the air force and paratroopers, who responded to the demonstrators with such extreme violence that 45,000 Algerians were killed within a few days.

The Algerians began a well-coordinated push for independence, while France employed every means available to quell the uprising, including military repression, collective punishment, torture, and even concentration camps. The irony of the situation was not lost on some observers. Writing in *Le Monde Diplomatique,* Pascal Blanchard, Sandrine Lemaire, and Nicolas Bancel observe:

> Of course, one cannot compare colonialism to Nazism, but the contradiction was reinforced between a France that celebrates the victory of democratic nations over a genocidal state and its maintaining, by military means, the submission of a population that was subjugated for over a century (pp. 10–11).

State-Sanctioned Torture

In 1957 the International Red Cross disclosed the widespread use of torture by the French army and police against thousands of Algerians. After that, information about the French treatment of Algerians became available to the wider public. The torture techniques used by the French included electricity applied to the most sensitive parts of the body, near drowning in water, sodomy with glass and wood objects, hanging by the feet and hands, and burning with cigarettes.

It was not until the early 2000s, forty years after Algeria achieved independence, that some of the aging French colonels and generals who served in Algeria finally admitted the horrors that they, their colleagues, or their subordinates had committed in Algeria. Among them were Generals Marcel Bigeard, Jacques Massu, and Paul Aussaresses. In his book, *Services Spéciaux 1955–1957,* Aussaresses admits to a specific act of torture: "It was useless that day. That guy died without saying anything . . . I have no regrets for his death. If I regretted something, it was the fact that he did not speak before dying." He also tells of how he ordered and watched many cold-blooded killings of prisoners, just because he did not have enough room to keep them. The International Human Rights Federation indicated that the general should be charged with crimes against humanity, but the French government chose not to prosecute him and others like him because of a 1968 law that absolves everyone for acts committed during the war. This protection disregards the dispositions of Article 303 of the French penal code, which sanctions any person who engages in torture.

The Algerian War of Independence (1954–1962), a guerrilla-style struggle between the French army and pro-independence Algerians, left in its wake over a million Algerian citizens (both military and civilians) dead and the widespread destruction of the land. Here, a resting Harki soldier gazes on a devastated Algerian village, 1960. [MARC GARANGER/CORBIS]

According to most accounts, the political leaders of France were well aware of the crimes committed by the military they sent to quell the rebellion that began in November 1954. General Aussaresses admitted that Justice Minister Franìois Mitterand (who became France's president in 1981) knew about and approved the methods used by the Special Services of the army. In other words, the military were given *carte blanche* to do whatever they saw fit in combating the Algerian nationalists. In 1955, when evidence of torture in Algeria started becoming bothersome for France (which had just abandoned Vietnam), the government of Prime Minister Pierre Mendès France ordered an immediate study of the issue. However, that study was intended to dismiss the accusations rather than to confirm them. The ensuing Roger Willaume Report, which referred mostly to "violence" (*sévices*) rather than torture, did in fact find that the police used "violent methods that were 'old-established practice'" and that "in normal times they are only employed on persons against whom there is a considerable weight of evidence or guilt and for whom there are therefore no great feelings of pity"

(Maran, 1989, p. 48). Even though this report was not dismissed by the government, its findings had no effect on the use of torture by the French police and army in Algeria. As Rita Maran points out: "In the colonial milieu, the application of the ideology of the civilizing mission had failed a crucial test, through the barbarous behavior of the police trained by France. The 'rights of man' were not merely neutralized in the colonial situation, they were actively violated" (Maran, 1989, p. 51).

Violence against Algerians was not limited to Algeria proper. Immigrant workers in France were also punished for their sympathy for their embattled compatriots in the homeland. Beginning in August 1958, and using what he had learned during his service in Algeria, Parisian chief of police Maurice Papon rounded up more than 5,000 Algerian immigrants because of suspicion of support for the nationalists. In 1959 he created an internment (concentration) camp at Vincennes, just outside of Paris, where hundreds of Algerians were jailed without trial and were subjected to terrible treatment. On October 17, 1961, Algerian nationalist militants held a peaceful march in Paris to

encyclopedia of GENOCIDE *and* CRIMES AGAINST HUMANITY

demand the independence of Algeria. Unfortunately, that peaceful show of solidarity quickly turned into a bloodbath. The police charged the protesters with gunfire and night sticks, killing more than 200 immigrants, many of whom were thrown into the Seine river. Papon's culpability for crimes was not limited to his treatment of Algerians. He was tried in the year 2000 for having helped deport Jews to Nazi Germany during World War II.

Economic and Social Destruction

The horrific violence used by France against Algerians in the context of colonization did not limit itself to physical brutality and cruelty. It also came in the form of humiliation, economic dispossession, and social dislocation. After France decided to colonize Algeria and transform it into a French land, its military repression was complemented by a series of actions and policies that disrupted the lives and livelihoods of several generations of the indigenous population.

During the repressive "pacification" of Algeria's population, the colonization of the land also went forward, involving the destruction of the existing social structures and economic system. This was done by force and by passing laws, such as the *sénatus-consulte* and the Warnier law of 1873, which dispossessed rural families and communities of ancestral land that was not alienable under the existing Islamic and customary laws. General Bugeaud summed up France's interest in the land: "What is to take in [Algeria] is only one interest, the agricultural interest. . . . Oh, yes, I could not find another way to subdue the country other than take that interest" (Stora, 1991, p. 25). The expropriation of land was massive, and most Algerians found themselves deprived of their main mean of subsistence. Those who were lucky found insecure employment in the new large European-owned properties. Collective punishment was also used a regular means to take more land away from the local population. This happened after the El-Mokrani upheaval, in which 500,000 acres of land were confiscated. This punishment was accompanied by a total denial of due process and the 1881 imposition of harsh common law sanctions formulated in the Code de l'Indigénat (laws for the natives).

When France lost Alsace-Lorraine to Germany in 1871, thousands of residents of that region were resettled in Algeria and awarded land confiscated from the Algerians. By the end of the century, over half of Algeria's arable land was controlled by the Europeans. The few Algerians who had retained their land were so heavily taxed and victimized by so many natural and bureaucratic calamities that they could barely subsist. This condition led Alexis de Tocqueville—who wrote

a blueprint for colonization—to observe in 1847 "we have rendered the Muslim society a lot more miserable, more disorganized, more ignorant, and more barbarian than what it was before it knew us" (p. 170).

Between 1830 and 1860 there were 3 million Algerians, 3.5 million by 1891 and 5 million in 1921. In 1886 there were 219,000 French settlers and 211,000 other Europeans (Spaniards, Italians, and Maltese). The total European population reached 984,000 in 1954, while the Algerians numbered 6 million. Yet the European minority controlled not only most of the country's wealth, but also the fate of those they had subjugated in their own land.

Using the "divide and rule" principle, the French created through the 1870 Crémieux Decrees, which extended French citizenship to Algerian Jews and European settlers while excluding Muslim Algerians from citizenship. The French also created a distinction between Arab and Berber Algerians, and promoted Berber over the Arabic language because the latter was a unifying medium for Algerian nationalism. The social schisms thus created among Algeria's peoples continued to have a negative legacy into the twenty-first century, more than 40 years after Algeria's independence.

Violence at Independence and Beyond

The war of independence waged by the Algerians for more than 7 years (1954–1962) left 1.5 million Algerians dead and substantially weakened the already meagre economic and social infrastructure. Eighteen months after coming to power in 1958, retired General Charles de Gaulle understood that the war in Algeria no longer served France's interests. In 1960, negotiations with the Algerian nationalists (National Liberation Front) began for a "clean" and orderly exit of France from Algeria. A referendum in Algeria and France gave an overwhelming support to de Gaulle's policy with regard to Algeria. The Evian Accords between France and the Algerian nationalists sealed the final terms for Algeria's independence in July 1962. However, the hardliners among the French settlers in Algeria did everything possible to resist such an outcome. They disobeyed orders from Paris, and even threatened to invade the motherland and take control for the sake of maintaining Algeria as a French possession. In a last desperate attempt, they created the Organization of the Secret Army (OAS) which would use terror to try to stall the independence momentum. Led by General Raoul Salan, this organization engaged in terrorist actions not only against Algerians, but also against French individuals and public offices deemed sympathetic to Algeria's independence. A few months before Algeria regained its sovereignty, French radical settlers and disenchanted members of the military engaged in a systematic campaign of murder and destruction. Hundreds of people were killed in the midst of burning towns and cities.

In June 1962 French settlers began their exodus, returning to France by the thousands each day, leaving behind them death and destruction. France was exiting Algeria the same way it had entered, with a widespread terror and scorched earth policy. On July 1, 1962, a referendum in Algeria showed that 91.23 percent of voters supported independence.

The Harkis

In 1954, France managed to entice thousands of Algerians to collaborate with its forces with the promise of assimilation and better treatment by the colonial administration. They became known as the *harkis* and served mostly as self-defense groups aiding the colonial forces against the nationalists. According to a report sent the United Nations in 1961, there were 263,000 pro-France Algerians, of whom 58,000 were *harkis*.

When the French began to withdraw from Algeria, they knew that the *harkis* were in imminent danger of being slaughtered by fellow Algerians for treason. Nonetheless, French officials did not seem too concerned with the fate of their erstwhile allies. Thousands of *harkis* were left behind to die within the first weeks of independence. According to a 2003 book, *Un Mensonge Français* (A French Lie) by Georges-Marc Benamou, the government of Charles de Gaulle explicitly refused to repatriates the bulk of the *harki* population. Legal representative of thousands of *harkis* that managed to reach France in 1962 began a lawsuit in November 2003 against the surviving members of De Gaulle's government, accusing them of crime against humanity and ethnic cleansing.

The colonial venture in Algeria thus closed with yet another massacre that France could have avoided. Many of those responsible for the crimes committed in Algeria escaped persecution because of French amnesty laws protecting them and because of the resistance of French officials to open the files of colonization for an objective analysis and evaluation of that painful past.

Violence in Independent Algeria

After 132 years of colonial subjugation and a bloody seven-year war for independence, Algeria went through a period of relative peace and economic development that lasted almost three decades. However, the country entered into another troubled era in the 1990s. As one of the nationalist leaders, Larbi Ben M'Hidi was quoted as saying to his compatriots in the 1950s: "the easiest part was to regain independence and the toughest one comes after that." The economic and political systems that were established in independent Algeria failed. This led in the early 1990s to a social rebellion headed by Islamist groups, which, after having been denied a legitimate electoral victory in 1991, opted for armed rebellion against the state. However, the war they waged for a decade extended also to the civilian population and foreigners. Between 1992 and 2002, over 150,000 people were killed, entire villages were abandoned, and the economic infrastructure was badly damaged. While most of the violence is attributed to the Islamists, the government also committed repression and reprisals and is responsible for the disappearance of thousands of people. Many also accuse the Algerian security service of using French-style torture and of the summary execution of suspected Islamist rebels or their supporters. Because there has not been a full and independent inquiry of the massacres and other violations committed during this internal war, the whole truth about the ongoing tragedy in Algeria remains unknown.

SEE ALSO France in Tropical Africa; Harkis

BIBLIOGRAPHY

Ageron, Charles Robert (1991). *Modern Algeria: A History from 1830 to the Present*. Trenton, N.J.: Africa World Press.

Aussaresses, Paul (2001). *Services spéciaux: Algérie: 1955-1957*. Paris: Perrin.

Benamou, Georges-Marc (2003). *Un mensonge français, retours sur la guerre d'Algérie*. Paris: Robert Laffont.

Blanchard, Pascal, Sandrine Lemaire, and Nicolas Bancel (2001). "Les Impasses du débat sur la torture en Algérie: une histoire coloniale refoulée," *Le Monde Diplomatique* (June 2001):10–11.

Branche, Raphaëlle (1999–2002). "Entre droit humanitaire et intérêts politiques: les missions algériennes du CICR." *La Revue historique* 609:101–125.

Branche, Raphaëlle (2001). *La Torture et l'Armée Pendant la Guerre d'Algérie: 1954–1962*. Paris: Gallimard.

Duquesne, Jacques (2000). "Retour sur la torture en Algérie: un témoignage inédit." Available from www.lexpress.fr/Express/Info/France/Dossier/torture/dossier.asp?id=244949.

Harbi, Mohamed (2001). *Une Vie Debout: Mémoires Politiques, Vol. I, 1945-1962*. Paris: La Decouverte.

Maran, Rita (1989). *Torture: The Role of Ideology in the French-Algerian War*. New York: Praeger.

Mekhaled, Boucif (1995). *Chroniques d'un massacre: 8 mai 1945*. Paris: Syros.

Stora, Benjamin (1991). *Histoire de l'Algérie coloniale: 1830-1954*. Paris: La Découverte.

Stora, Benjamin (1995). *Histoire de l'Algérie coloniale: 1954-1962*. Paris: La Découverte.

De Tocqueville, Alexis (1988). *De la Colonisation en Algérie*. Paris: Complexe.

Vidal-Naquet, Pierre (1962). *Raison d'Etat*. Paris: Éditions Minuit.

Azzedine Layachi

Alien Tort Statute

Survivors of genocide and crimes against humanity often find it impossible to obtain compensation for the harms they have suffered and only rarely are the perpetrators punished for their crimes. In the United States victims and their families may be able to file civil lawsuits in federal court against those responsible, relying on a 200-year-old statute, the Alien Tort Statute (ATS) (codified as U.S. Code, vol. 28, sec. 1350). The ATS, enacted in the late eighteenth century, was one of the first laws approved by the newly established U.S. Congress. The Statute's use as a remedy for human rights abuses dates from a 1980 court decision recognizing that it authorizes civil lawsuits for violations of international law. In 2004 the U.S. Supreme Court upheld this use of the statute to seek redress for human rights violations. The ATS offers a potentially powerful tool to those seeking redress and accountability for gross human rights abuses, including genocide and crimes against humanity.

Criminal Prosecutions versus Civil Claims

In many countries efforts to seek justice for human rights abuses focus on criminal prosecution of the perpetrators. In the United States redress often involves a civil lawsuit filed by victims or family members. The line distinguishing criminal prosecutions and civil litigation varies among different countries and even among different U.S. states. Government prosecutors usually file criminal charges and generally seek to punish the defendant through a prison sentence or monetary fine. Civil lawsuits such as those authorized by the ATS are filed by private parties and cannot lead to imprisonment. Instead, they seek financial compensation for the injuries suffered by the plaintiffs along with punitive damages intended to sanction the defendant and deter others from similar misbehavior.

Civil litigation in the United States thus has certain advantages over criminal prosecutions: A civil lawsuit can be filed by a victim or family member, whereas a criminal case would depend on the government prosecutor's decision to take action. Moreover, any financial recovery in a civil lawsuit is paid to the plaintiff. Thus, although the defendant in a civil lawsuit does not face the possibility of a prison sentence or the moral sanction of a criminal conviction, some survivors and their families view civil litigation as an important means of seeking redress.

History of the ATS

The ATS, enacted by the first U.S. Congress in 1789, states that the federal courts have jurisdiction over a "civil action by an alien for a tort only, committed in violation of the law of nations." The goal of the statute seems to have been to strengthen the enforcement of international law by U.S. courts.

In the eighteenth century the founders of the United States recognized international law as a form of natural law that was binding on all governments. Moreover, violations of international rules often triggered reprisals, including war. During the early years after independence the European military powers repeatedly threatened retribution for violations of international law, particularly when the state courts refused to prosecute wrongdoers. Many commentators have concluded that the ATS was designed to ensure that foreigners could obtain redress for violations of international norms from federal courts, rather than being relegated to a less predictable fate in the state courts.

Although no early cases directly applied the ATS, mention of it in the writings of the period support the view that the ATS provided a remedy for foreigners complaining of violations of internationally protected rights. In 1795, for example, the U.S. attorney general stated that the ATS authorized a civil lawsuit by British citizens who were attacked in violation of international rules governing neutrality. Over the next two centuries, however, the statute was rarely mentioned.

Modern Revival

The ATS was revived by a case decided in 1980, *Filártiga v. Peña-Irala*. Joelito Filártiga, the son of a prominent opponent of the military regime in Paraguay, was tortured to death by a Paraguayan police officer. In the face of an international outcry the Paraguayan government spirited the officer out of the country; the Filártigas later discovered him living in New York City and filed a lawsuit against him under the ATS. Their claim was initially dismissed by a trial court judge who ruled that international law did not apply to the actions of a government against its own citizens. On appeal, however, a federal appellate court held that the "law of nations" in the statute refers to international law as that law has developed over time. Since international law had come to prohibit a government's torture of its own citizens, the court held that the ATS allows a federal court to judge a claim that a Paraguayan official tortured a Paraguayan citizen. Following this decision the lower court awarded over $10 million in damages to the Filártiga family, although they were unable to collect the judgment.

Over the next twenty-four years, federal courts applied the ATS to permit claims such as torture, execu-

Dolly Filartiga holds a photo of her brother, Joelito, who died after being tortured in 1976 in Paraguay. Filartiga won a $10.4 million judgment in U.S. courts against the man she blames for her brother's death. [AP/WIDE WORLD PHOTOS]

United States to face criminal prosecution, but later acquitted of the criminal charges against him. He won a lower court decision awarding him damages for arbitrary arrest and detention. On appeal, the Supreme Court held that the ATS permits private individuals to file claims for international law violations that satisfy a strict standard of international consensus and clear definition. The Court ruled against Alvarez-Machain, however, holding that his brief detention in Mexico, followed by an immediate transfer to lawful authorities in the United States, did not constitute a violation of a core international norm.

Current Applications

The Supreme Court decision validates post-*Filártiga* federal court decisions that applied the statute to permit aliens to sue for genocide and crimes against humanity, as well as for other egregious abuses such as war crimes, disappearance, torture, summary execution, and slavery. Each of these abuses meets the Supreme Court's requirement of international concensus and clarity of definition.

Lawsuits under the ATS may be filed in the U.S. courts even though the events took place entirely in another country: The statute does not require that the human rights violations have any connection to the United States. The U.S. Constitution, however, requires that the defendant have ties to the United States. Although most such cases have been filed against U.S. residents or United States–based corporations, several have involved defendants who were served while traveling in the United States, or foreign corporations subject to suit because of their U.S. business contacts.

Early court decisions made clear that the Statute permits a suit against commanders whose forces commit human rights abuses, as well as against the actual torturer, as in the *Filártiga* case. For example, a series of cases filed against an Argentine general held him liable for executions, torture, and disappearances committed under his command. Similarly, a Guatemalan general was held liable for the atrocities committed by his troops against indigenous Guatemalans. In both cases the plaintiffs demonstrated that the generals had planned and directed campaigns of violence against civilians.

A similar case filed in 1993 against Radovan Karadzic, the leader of the Bosnian-Serbs, sought damages for genocide and crimes against humanity committed against Bosnian Muslims following the break-up of the former Yugoslavia. Although Karadzic argued that he was not a government official and therefore could not violate international law, the court held that certain norms of international law apply to private par-

tion, genocide and slavery against a range of defendants, including commanders, government officials and corporations. Despite the virtual unanimity of the courts, a dispute developed among commentators about the validity of the *Filártiga* interpretation of the statute. Although the administrations of former presidents Jimmy Carter and Bill Clinton supported the *Filártiga* approach, president George W. Bush argued that the statute as applied infringed on the foreign affairs powers of the executive branch. The central point of contention was whether the ambiguous language of the eighteenth-century statute should be interpreted to permit individuals to sue for damages for violations of modern international law norms

The U.S. Supreme Court resolved the simmering debate in 2004, endorsing the *Filártiga* approach in the case of *Sosa v. Alvarez-Machain*. Humberto Alvarez-Machain was kidnapped in Mexico and taken to the ties as well as government officials. In particular, the United Nations Convention Against Genocide makes clear that genocide is a crime when committed by private persons. The court also ruled that Karadzic could be held liable as an accomplice to abuses committed in complicity with officials of other governments.

These holdings paved the way for lawsuits against private parties such as corporations. In the 1990s several civil claims were filed against banks, insurance companies, and other businesses for crimes committed during World War II. Most of these lawsuits ran into difficulties because of the years that had elapsed and because the U.S. government insisted that all outstanding claims had been resolved through negotiated diplomatic agreements. Despite these difficulties several such lawsuits were settled for significant amounts of money.

A claim filed in 2001 charged the Talisman Energy Corporation with responsibility for genocide and crimes against humanity committed by the government of Sudan. The case addressed widespread abuses committed against the non-Muslim inhabitants of southern Sudan as the government sought to extract oil from the region. Alleged abuses included killings, forced displacement, destruction of property, kidnapping, rape, and the enslavement of civilians, amounting to attempted genocide. The plaintiffs claimed that the company had helped to plan the government's campaign of ethnic cleansing and supplied the funds to finance it. In an initial decision filed in 2003 the court held that the corporation could be held liable for the abuses if it had knowingly provided "practical assistance, encouragement, or moral support that had a substantial effect on the perpetration" of the human rights abuses.

Benefits of Civil Litigation

In the case against Talisman and in similar cases against oil companies for abuses committed in Burma, Nigeria, and other countries, a victory for the plaintiffs would most likely result in a large monetary judgment that can be collected. Cases litigated against private individuals are less likely to produce enforceable judgments, yet plaintiffs continue to file such lawsuits despite the probability that they will not collect any money.

Carlos Mauricio, a survivor of torture in El Salvador and a successful plaintiff in a case against two Salvadoran generals, explained that part of his reason for suing was that the lawsuit gave him the opportunity to talk about his ordeal. Mauricio was a professor in El Salvador in 1983 when agents of the military government then ruling his country kidnapped him from his university office. He was detained and brutally tortured for two weeks. Upon his release he fled El Salvador and settled in the United States. For many years he told few people about his ordeal. "One of the facts from torture is that they make you not want to talk about it," Mauricio said in 2002. "It took me 15 years to be able to tell my story. I realized that telling my story to others is important, not only because it's important to know what happened in El Salvador, but also because in that way you are really out of prison" (Center for Justice and Accountability website).

Other survivors stress the value of a judicial forum in which they can obtain formal recognition of their suffering and of the culpability of the defendants. Many also see their litigation as contributing to the movement to enforce and strengthen international human rights norms in their home countries, in the United States, and around the world.

Related Statutes

Three other modern statutes offer a basis for civil lawsuits for human rights violations. The Torture Victim Protection Act, enacted in 1992, provides aliens or U.S. citizens a cause of action for torture or extrajudicial execution committed "under color of foreign law." The Anti-Terrorism Act, originally enacted in 1990, authorizes civil suits by U.S. nationals who are victims of terrorism. Finally, an exception to the Foreign Sovereign Immunities Act (FSIA) permits U.S. citizens to sue a handful of foreign governments for torture, extrajudicial killing, and other abuses; it applies only to governments on the U.S. State Department's list of "state sponsors of terrorism." Although none of these statutes specifically permits suits for genocide or crimes against humanity, a broad claim under the ATCA will often be joined with a specific claim under one of these statutes.

Conclusion

The Alien Tort Statute permits aliens to file civil lawsuits for genocide and crimes against humanity committed anywhere in the world, if the U.S. courts have jurisdiction over the defendants. Such civil litigation for human rights abuses permits survivors of egregious abuses to seek justice, through an award of damages as well as through a formal judicial process that enables them to obtain a judgment confirming the responsibility of the perpetrators.

SEE ALSO Compensation; Reparations

BIBLIOGRAPHY

The Alien Tort Claims Act. U.S. Code, vol. 28, sec. 1350.

Blum, Jeffrey M., and Ralph G. Steinhardt (1981). "Federal Jurisdiction over International Human Rights Claims: The Alien Tort Claims Act after Filártiga v. Peña-Irala." *Harvard International Law Journal* 22:53–113.

Bradley, Curtis A. (2002). "The Alien Tort Statute and Article III." *Virginia Journal of International Law* 42:587–647.

Burley, Anne-Marie (1989). "The Alien Tort Statute and the Judiciary Act of 1789: A Badge of Honor." *American Journal of International Law* 83:461–493.

Center for Justice and Accountability for Survivors. "Carlos Mauricio's Story." Available from http://www.cja.org/forSurvivors/CarlosforSurvivors.shtml.

Convention on the Prevention and Punishment of the Crime of Genocide. Art 4, 102 Stat. 3045, 78 U.N.T.S. 277, December 9, 1948.

Dodge, William S. (1996). "The Historical Origins of the Alien Tort Statute: A Response to the 'Originalists.'" *Hastings International and Comparative Law Review* 19:221–258.

Filártiga v. Peña-Irala. 630 F2d 876 (2d Cir 1980).

Kadic v. Karadzic. 70 F3d 232 (2d Cir 1995).

Sosa v. Alvarez-Machain. (2000). 124 SCt 2739.

Stephens, Beth (2002). "Translating Filártiga: A Comparative and International Law Analysis of Domestic Remedies for International Human Rights Violations." *Yale Journal of International Law* 27:1–57.

Stephens, Beth, and Michael Ratner (1996). *International Human Rights Litigation in U.S. Courts.* Irvington-on-Hudson, N.Y.: Transnational Publishers.

Beth Stephens

Almohads

The Almohad movement originated with the preaching of Ibn Tumart (died 1130 CE), a Berber religious reformer who was considered an Islamic messianic figure (*al-Mahdi*). Ibn Tumart found military support among his Masmuda tribesmen to fight Almoravid rule in the Maghreb (Morocco). One of his closest disciples (the so-called Ten) was ʿAbd al-Muʾmin (ruled 1130–1163), a Berber of the Zanata tribe who after Ibn Tumart's death became the political leader of the movement and defeated the Almoravids, establishing a new dynasty (the Muʾminids) and adopting the caliphal title (*khalifat Allah,* vicar of God).

The name of the movement, *al-muwahhidun* (Almohads), means "the Unitarians," that is, those who proclaim the absolute unity of God (*tawhid*). The name had a polemical overtone, as the Almohads legitimized their bid for power by accusing the previous dynasty, the Almoravids, of having indulged in anthropomorphism (*tajsim*) on the basis of the latter's doctrine on God's attributes. This accusation shed doubts on the Islamic belief of the Almoravids and opened the door to the possibility of declaring them unbelievers, thus encouraging their annihilation or subjugation as legal.

The establishment of the Almohad empire, covering what is now Morocco, Algeria, Tunisia, and the western part of Libya, as well as al-Andalus (the territory of the Iberian Peninsula under Muslim rule), involved armed conflict with the Almoravid rulers, lasting a period of some twenty years from the first attack against the Almoravid capital, Marrakech, until its capture in 1147. Internal purges among the followers of Ibn Tumart also occurred later at the directive of the first Muʾminid caliph.

Ibn Tumart's life is described by Almohad sources as closely resembling that of the Prophet Muhammad. Like him, Ibn Tumart emigrated or retreated (*hijra*) to escape Almoravid persecution, settling with his followers in Tinmal, about 75 kilometers south of Marrakech, in 1123. The original population in Tinmal was massacred, replaced by followers of the Mahdi. One of the Ten who protested the massacre was killed and crucified.

Some years later (c. 1128), the methodical elimination of real or suspected dissidents (*tamyiz*) within the Almohads themselves took place for reasons difficult to ascertain, given the nature of the sources, but which must have been related to internal tensions within the movement. As pointed out by J. F. P. Hopkins, the tamyiz was immediately followed by a campaign directed against the Almoravid capital, which indicates that the tamyiz could have consolidated the movement's strength or perhaps it aroused such resentment that a diversion of interest became necessary. This great purge was carried out by a close associate of Ibn Tumart, a man called al-Bashir who was alleged to be a soothsayer and dream interpreter, able to distinguish sincere believers from hypocrits.

The conquest of Morocco by ʿAbd al-Muʾmin was especially brutal. The famous scholar Ibn Taymiyya (died 1328) later condemned the massacres and persecutions of the civilian population carried out by the Almohads, accusing them of having killed thousands of good Muslims among the Almoravids and their supporters. The Almohads considered it legal to kill those who did not belong to their community of true believers, and this has been interpreted as reflecting a Kharijite influence among the Almohads, Kharijism having spread among the Berber population during the first centuries of Islamic rule in North Africa. However, the will to kill was probably just one aspect of the revolutionary character of the Almohad movement. The most famous episode was the "examination" (*iʿtiraf*) that took place between 1149 and 1150, when ʿAbd al-Muʾmin gave to the Almohad shaykhs lists of those who must be killed among the tribes that had previously rebelled. The number of those executed is said to have reached more than 32,000. Official Almohad chronicles state that, thanks to this great purge and the terror it entailed, peace was established and the divergence of opinion eliminated.

In regard to Almohad policies toward Jews and Christians, there were deportations of Christians from al-Andalus to North Africa, as well as forced conversions of Jews and Christians. ʿAbd al-Muʾmin, in fact, is said to have abolished the statute of *dhimma* that allowed the coexistence of Jewish and Christian communities in Muslim territory. Christian communities almost completely disappeared in the territory under Almohad rule. Many Jews emigrated to Christian territory or other regions of the Islamic world (the famous Jewish scholar Maimonides, who died in 1204, settled in Egypt). Forced Jewish converts were obliged by the Almohads to dress differently from Muslims. However, when the Almohad caliphate disappeared and the Marinids assumed power, Jewish communities again sprang up in the Islamic West.

SEE ALSO Forcible Transfer; Persecution; Religious Groups

BIBLIOGRAPHY

Hopkins, J. F. P. (1958). *Medieval Muslim Government in Barbary until the Sixth Century of the Hijra.* London: Luzac.

Huici Miranda, Ambrosio (1956–1957). *Historia política del imperio almohade* 2 volumes. Tetuán, Spain: Editora Marroquí.

Laoust, Henri (1960). "Une fetwa d'Ibn Taimiya sur Ibn Tumart." *B.I.F.A.O.* 59:157–184.

Merad, A. (1957)."ʿAbd al-Muʾmin et la conquête de l'Afrique du Nord, 1130–1163." *Annales de l'Institut d'Études Orientales d'Alger* XV:110–163.

Molénat, J.-P. (1997). "Sur le rôle des Almohades dans la fin du christianisme local au Maghreb et en al-Andalus." *Al-Qantara* XVIII:415–446.

Urvoy, Dominique (1974). "La pensée d'Ibn Tumart." *Bulletin d'Études Orientales* XXVII:19–44.

Shatzmiller, Maya "al-Muwahhidun." In *The Encyclopaedia of Islam,* 2nd edition, 11 volumes. Leiden, Netherlands: Brill.

Maribel Fierro

Altruism, Biological

In biology an altruistic act increases the reproductive fitness of a member of the same species (a conspecific) while reducing the reproductive fitness of the one committing the act. Reproductive fitness refers to the differential ability of an organism to influence gene frequencies in future generations. Altruism is distinguished from mutualistic behavior, which increases the reproductive fitness of others as well as the actor. Altruism also is distinguished from selfishness, which benefits the actor and either does not benefit or harms others' reproductive fitness.

In characterizing behavior as biologically altruistic, the issue of intention is not relevant as it is in the related but not identical meaning in moral philosophy, in contrast, an altruistic act is defined as one undertaken with the intention of helping another with the anticipation that it will incur or risk harm to the actor. In principle, the benefits rendered may be psychological or objectively beneficial in the sense that they prolong life or improve the material well-being of the beneficiary of the action. Similarly, the costs to the donor may be psychological or objectively verifiable as posing risk to life or limb. Altruistic acts can include affirmative acts of assistance as well as restraint where preemptively harming another might prevent or reduce the risk of attack from the individual harmed.

Humans are potentially dangerous to one another, and since they care about their own survival we might expect them to attack others when it is potentially beneficial for them to do so. Yet this is more the exception than the rule, a reality consistent with a wide range of experimental evidence showing that many humans are prepared to cooperate in one-shot or one-time prisoner's dilemma games. In such games, an actor has two choices: He or she can either defect or cooperate. Defecting can be understood here as engaging in preemptive attack, a strategy considered strictly dominant because if the other player cooperates, one is better off defecting, and if the other player defects, one is also better off defecting.

But to choose defect is to preclude any possibility of continuing mutually beneficial interaction. Cooperation, on the other hand, is altruistic in the biological sense, and arguably in a morally philosophical sense, because it provides a benefit to one's counterparty at potential cost to oneself. If both players cooperate, of course, the outcome that is most beneficial jointly results, and it is this strategy profile alone that opens the door to additional plays of the game.

Although it remains quite controversial, the most straightforward explanation of the origin of human predispositions to refrain from attacking nonkin (as well as our weaker inclination to provide affirmative assistance) is that human evolutionary history has been influenced by selection at multiple levels, including levels above the individual organism. Such an evolutionary account, which can be made completely consistent with the proposition that genes are the ultimate loci of selection could also explain our inclinations to devote disproportionate energy to detecting violators of social rules and engage in costly punishment against violators.

The complex of behavioral inclinations that enables human society to interact also has a dark side: in addition to underlying our ability to make peace, it also is behind our ability to wage organized war. In conjunction with the ease with which humans can define some as members of their own group and others as outsiders, altruistic behavior on behalf of other members of one's group may also entail preemptive violence against a feared other, thereby providing a biological underpinning for genocide. The fluidity with which the boundaries between the in group and out group can alter or be altered, however, gives hope that the frequency of genocide may be reduced. Genocide is not inevitable, and biology leaves intact our responsibility for all harms visited upon others.

SEE ALSO Altruism, Ethical; Rescuers, Holocaust

BIBLIOGRAPHY

Field, Alexander J. (2001). *Altruistically Inclined? The Behavioral Sciences, Evolutionary Theory, and the Origins of Reciprocity.* Ann Arbor, Mich.: University of Michigan Press.

Keller, Laurent, ed. (1999). *Levels of Selection in Evolution.* Princeton, N.J.: Princeton University Press.

Sober, Elliott, and David Sloan Wilson (1998). *Unto Others: The Evolution and Psychology of Unselfish Behavior.* Cambridge, Mass.: Harvard University Press.

Alexander J. Field

Altruism, Ethical

Altruism is sometimes defined very broadly so that it refers to all human behavior not motivated by the self-interest of the agent. In this use of the term, human actions are either egoistic or altruistic—there is no third alternative. However, such a broad definition may not be very useful. One reason is that many human actions have mixed motives—one acts in a way that benefits other people, but does so partly because one expects benefits in return, if not immediately, then at some time in the future. Such behavior is sometimes described as *reciprocal altruism*: It is not motivated just by self-interest, but neither is it pure altruism whereby the only concern is the interests or well-being of the recipient.

Another reason for narrowing the definition of altruism is that one may want to exclude actions that are motivated by respect for agreements, rules, social expectations, and so forth, even when their motivation is unselfish. One would not normally describe keeping a promise or fulfilling the requirements of a job as altruistic. This suggests that altruism is best understood as describing actions which are (1) intended to meet the needs or promote the welfare of people other than the agent and (2) not actions that the agent must perform by virtue of the rules and institutions to which he or she is subject.

Many everyday examples of altruism involve actions that deliver small benefits at little cost to the person who performs them—for example, helping an elderly person across the road, or taking time to give directions to a stranger who has lost his way. But more interesting issues arise when the benefit is much greater, but so, correspondingly, is the potential cost—for example, rescuing someone whose life is in peril, with the rescuer also running the risk of death or serious injury. Here, one encounters the paradox that the altruistic agent may believe and state that he had no choice but to carry out the rescue, whereas a third-party spectator would say that it was up to the agent whether to attempt the rescue or not—he was under no obligation to do so. How is one to understand this contrast between the agent's perspective and the spectator's?

A relevant observation here is that in many cases in which altruism is needed, a surplus of potential agents exists. Empirical studies have shown that when someone requires help, increasing the number of potential helpers diminishes the likelihood that any single person will intervene. No one is individually responsible for the plight of the victim, and so no one feels under an obligation to act. If some individuals do choose to intervene, however, then by the same token they have chosen to make themselves responsible, and will see the altruistic action as one that they are required to perform. But they will not blame others who made a different choice.

One might think that some people are simply altruistic by nature while others are not, and attempts have thus been made—for example, in the case of those who sheltered Jews from the Nazis, a paradigm example of an altruistic act with a potentially high cost—to identify the worldview of those who helped. But although personality must play some part in explaining altruistic behavior, the contingency of being selected as the responsible agent is also an important factor. A study of people who rescued Jews from the Holocaust highlighted the importance of being asked by an intermediary to shelter a Jew (Varese and Yaish, 2000). This takes one back to the idea of personal responsibility. Sometimes, people who behave altruistically do so because they are the only ones able to help—the responsibility is theirs by the very nature of the situation. But more often there are many potential helpers, and then what matters is whether someone is selected as the person to assume responsibility—either because she makes this choice herself, or because someone else, the person in need or a third party, asks her to act. Tragedies can occur when this mechanism breaks down: Many people would be willing to act if asked, but because responsibility is diffused, nobody in fact intervenes.

Altruism is a vital component of a good society precisely because one cannot anticipate all the occasions on which people may need to be helped, and therefore cannot formally assign duties to help. Examples of heroic altruism abound; so do cases in which altruism fails because people do not regard themselves as having responsibility for the problem they confront. Humans need to find better ways of sharing the burden of altruism so that everyone helps sometimes, and no one is required to sacrifice himself completely to altruistic causes.

SEE ALSO Altruism, Biological; Bystanders; Rescuers, Holocaust

BIBLIOGRAPHY

Latané, Bibb, and John M. Darley (1970). *The Unresponsive Bystander: Why Doesn't He Help?* Englewood Cliffs, N.J.: Prentice-Hall.

Miller, David (2002). "'Are They My Poor?' The Problem of Altruism in a World of Strangers." *Critical Review of International Social and Political Philosophy* 5(4):106–127.

Miller, Fred D., Ellen F. Paul, and Jeffrey Paul, eds. (1993). *Altruism.* Cambridge, U.K.: Cambridge University Press.

Monroe, Kristen R. (1996). *The Heart of Altruism: Perceptions of a Common Humanity.* Princeton, N.J.: Princeton University Press.

Varese, Frederico, and Meir Yaish (2000). "The Importance of Being Asked: The Rescue of Jews in Nazi Europe." *Rationality and Society* 12:307–334.

David Miller

Amazon Region

The decimation of the Amazon's native people over the past four centuries illustrates two patterns outlined in the seminal 1985 report by Benjamin Whitaker, the rapporteur on genocide for the United Nations Commission on Human Rights. Paragraph 41 (p. 20) states: "A conscious act or acts of advertent omission calculated neglect or negligence may be sufficient to destroy a designated group wholly or partially through, for instance, . . . disease [and] may be as culpable as an act of commission." Paragraph 33 (p. 17) discusses "the definition of genocide or 'ethnocide', the destruction of indigenous cultures," and "also 'ecocide'—adverse alterations, often irreparable, to the environment—for example . . . destruction of the rain forest—which threaten the existence of entire populations."

The Portuguese Colonization

The first Europeans to penetrate the Amazon basin were part of a Spanish expedition led by Francisco de Orellana in 1542. Hoping to find the fabled lands of El Dorado and La Canela, Orellana and his men set out from Quito, Ecuador, descended the Napo River to its confluence with the Solimões, the Amazon's upper region, and continued down the river for fifteen hundred miles to the Atlantic. At that time several million people were living in the Amazon Valley. They belonged to some two hundred tribes and ethnic groups in four linguistic families—the Gê, Tupi, Carib, and Arawak.

Starting with the Omagua, an intelligent, orderly people of the Solimões who farmed river turtles and wore cotton robes, the expedition passed one prosperous community after another. So rich were the resources of the *várzea,* or floodplain, that some of the close-packed lines of houses continued without interruption for days. The level of civilization of some of the riverine tribes was on a par with the Incas', although the materials they built and worked with were perishable, and few artifacts, besides their extraordinarily refined ceramics, survive.

Organized campaigns to exterminate the Indians, sponsored by the colonial administration and carried out by Portuguese colonists, had been taking place in northeastern Brazil, to the east, since 1500, and spread as colonists began settling the lower Amazon in 1620. So-called ransoming expeditions were in fact slave raids, initiated under the pretext of rescuing captives from tribes that were supposedly planning to eat them (in some cases they actually were). In the absence of gold, the colonists went after what was commonly referred to as red gold—the forced labor of Indians. The ransomed Indians were descended down the river and kept in tightly packed riverine pens called *caiçaras,* sometimes for months. Many died in battle, or in captivity, either losing the will to live and wasting way, or from European diseases that they had no genetic defenses against. Contagion, or smallpox, was the big killer, but influenza, pneumonia, the common cold virus, measles, chickenpox, and dysentery from the unhygienic conditions of their captivity also took a devastating toll. Malaria, syphilis, and tuberculosis reached the valley in the seventeenth century. In addition, many Indians became addicted to, and died as a result of their dependence on, *cachaça,* or rum.

The populous tribes of the Amazon were quickly extinguished, like the Tapajós or the Tocantins, who are simply remembered by the tributaries named after them; later, as the ransomers moved up river, the Manau followed them into oblivion, with only their name remaining, designating the largest city in the

The effects of gold mining in Venezuela's Amazon rain forest are shown in this 1997 photo of the Las Cristinas gold mine. [AP/WIDE WORLD PHOTOS]

middle Amazon. By 1750 the Native population had been reduced by two-thirds, and the *várzea* was almost completely depopulated. Those who had not been killed by "advertent omission" and "calculated neglect," in Whitaker's terms, melted into the forest and fled up north- and south-flowing tributaries, above the unnavigable rapids, to the Guyana and Brazilian shields, where they regressed into hunters and gatherers and lost the civilization they had developed on the várzea.

The Jesuits

The Indians' only champions were the Jesuits, who gathered them into missions that were organized along military lines to keep them from being dragged off into slavery. David Putnam's film, *The Mission,* portrays the heroic efforts of the Jesuits to protect the Guarani in the Paraná-Paraguay basin, south of the Amazon. The Jesuits in the Amazon were more exploitative, however, and the Indians in their *aldeias,* or mission villages, on Marajó Island, at the mouth of the river, became peons who took care of their vast herds of cattle. Indians were forcibly baptized and catechized, and became detribal-

ized "shirt Indians." With the colonists taking their most beautiful women, there were almost no pure-blooded Indians on the river by the time the Jesuits were expelled from Latin American in 1760; only *cablocos* or mestizos, remained. Miscegenation also played a major role in diluting and breaking down the cultural identity and physical distinctiveness of the Amazon's Natives. The offspring with Portuguese were known as *mamelucos,* and those produced with African slaves as *cafuzos.*

The Jesuits were replaced by directorates, and an imperial proclamation declared the end of the enslavement and forced labor of Indians. They were now free, but the pitiful remnants of once-proud peoples were open to other forms of exploitation. Unpacified and assimilated groups continued to be rounded up and massacred by the *bandeirantes,* or pioneers, who forged deep into the interior. Only a few tribes, such as the Kayapo in the upper Xingu Valley and Waimiri Atroari in Roraima, put up such fierce resistance that they managed to withstand the encroachment and invasion of their land until the late twentieth century.

encyclopedia of GENOCIDE *and* CRIMES AGAINST HUMANITY

The Rubber Boom

Starting in 1850 rubber became a hot new commodity in the industrializing countries of Europe and North America, and the Amazon's monopoly on the so-called black gold to be tapped from *Hevea brasiliensis* trees scattered throughout the rain forest spawned what contemporary Brazilian writer Euclides Da Cunha (*Amazon Frontier*, p. 293) called "the most criminal organization of labor ever devised." A Peruvian rubber baron named Julio Arana founded the Peruvian Amazon Rubber Company and grew fabulously wealthy by exploiting the Bora, Witoto, Andoke, and Ocaina on the Putumayo River, which forms the border between Peru and Colombia. Reports of systematic torture, an orgy of sadism, the perverted mutilation of men, women, and children; and women being kept as concubines by the Indian and Barbadian *muchachos,* or captains, of the rubber gangs reached Roger Casement, who had exposed similar atrocities ten years earlier in the Congo. By the time Casement reached the area, three-quarters of the population on the Putumayo had been wiped out in the previous six years, and there were only 8,000 to 10,000 left. Casement was knighted for his work as the main author of the 1912 *Blue Book on the Putumayo,* a precursor of present-day reports on human rights abuses, but later his journals revealed that he was a pedophile and had participated in the muchachos' orgies. In the early twenty-first century the culturally degraded descendants of Arana's Bora and Witoto rubber collectors live in villages above Iquitos, Peru, where they dance, usually drunk, for tourists from cruise ships and jungle safaris.

The Last Hundred Years

The same year that Casement's shocking report was published, the rubber boom abruptly collapsed, outcompeted by plantations in Malaya started from seeds smuggled out of the Amazon by the Englishman Henry Wickam. The exploitation of Indians for black gold did not end completely, however. In 1948 the newly contacted Kaxinawa in the state of Acre were forced into a brutal rubber-collection system. A genocidal massacre exterminated 75 to 80 percent of the group three years later, and by 1968 there were only 400 to 500 Kaxinawa left.

On the Amazon's southern frontier, colonists hired professional Indian killers, or *bugreiros,* who presented ears instead of scalps for payment, adorned their Winchester carbines with Indians' teeth, and poisoned the drinking pools in Indian villages with strychnine. By 1910 the remaining Indians had been reduced to a pathetic minority on the fringes of a burgeoning postcolonial society. Now that they were no longer a threat, they were embraced and romanticized by Brazilian urban intellectuals. An Indianist movement was born, and an extraordinary champion for the country's Native peoples surfaced, Colonel Cândido Rondon, who founded the Indian Protection Service, or SPI, in 1910. Rondon and the SPI's *sertanistas,* or field agents, contacted isolated tribes such as the Nambikwara and tried to protect them from the diseases, culture shock, invasion, and massacre to which their encounter with the national society would expose them. Their motto was "die, if necessary, but never kill." But by now the demographic catastrophe of the Native population was irreversible. It had plummeted from about 3.5 million in 1500 to 2 million by the expulsion of the Jesuits, and was approximately a million in the early twentieth century. By 1979 it would decline to 100,000. Of the 230 tribes that existed in 1900, the anthropologist Darcy Ribeiro could only count 143 in 1957, and half of them were represented by only a few hundred individuals.

The SPI's career was checkered. Although it undoubtedly saved the people, culture, and land of many tribes, it was dissolved in disgrace in 1969 after a 7,000-page report to the Brazilian congress documented the involvement of hundreds of SPI officials, ministers, governors, and generals in the homicide, machine-gunning, prostitution, and financial exploitation (to the tune of $60 million) of the people it was charged with protecting. A new agency, the Brazilian National Indian Foundation, or FUNAI, was created, and while many of its anthropologists and other employees were dedicated to the Indians' well-being, atrocities that the government turned a blind eye to or participated in continued to take place in the Amazon. The Brazilian Air Force bombed uncontacted villages of Waimiri Atroari; soldiers drove Macuxi out of their villages on the Brazil-Venezuela border.

In the early 1970s a network of highways pushed into the Amazon wilderness. A growing awareness of its untapped mineral wealth unleashed a new siege on the last remaining isolated Indians, and the innermost recesses of the valley where they lived were finally penetrated, with the usual lethal consequences. One of the most tragic stories was that of the Kreenakrore, a seminomadic group on the Iriri River, a tributary of the Xingu. For ten years during the 1960s the legendary *sertanistas* Claudio Villas Boas and Francisco Meirelles had made futile attempts to contact them. An expedition had been attacked and several of its members killed. Finally, as the new Cuiabá-Santarem Highway approached to within two kilometers of their village, several Kreenakrore, reduced by culture shock to eating dirt and the *urucu* seeds with which they painted their faces, appeared on the highway, begging for food from the road crews. Between 1969 and 1972 forty died of pneumonia contracted from the workers, and by 1974 the tribe was down to seventy-nine individuals. Villas Boas moved them to Xingu National Park, which had been set aside for other tribes. By 1976 the Kreenakrore numbered sixty-three, and only ten women could bear children who would be socially acceptable according to the tribe's rules of kinship and marriage. Nonetheless, the Kreenakrore slowly recovered and as of 2004 were holding their own.

The construction of the Perimetral Norte on the Brazil-Venezuela border had similar results for the Yanomami, who were still living in the Neolithic and are the only tribe, except for the Tukuna on the Solimões, with more than five thousand members. Gold was discovered and *garimpeiros,* wildcat prospectors from Brazil's huge marginalized poor population, poured into the Yanomami's homeland and massacred them, raped their women, and infected them with various diseases. AIDS is the latest disease with which the tribe must contend. An epidemic of measles also broke out when the Yanomami were made guinea pigs for a vaccine from a virulent strain of the microbe not appropriate for use in a population with no prior exposure to it.

Sixty-two percent of the tribes tested positive for a new strain of malaria introduced by the *garimpeiros.* By 1993 some two thousand Yanomami had been killed, but after a global outcry over the massacre of twenty-three tribe members in the upper Orinoco basin, a measure of protection was established for these Natives.

Similar horrors played out in the state of Rondônia (named for Rondon) during the 1980s. Some newly contacted Cintas Largas were massacred with the alleged complicity of the Summer Institute of Linguistics, an American evangelical group that placed missionaries with forty-three tribes in Brazil and was subsequently expelled because of suspected ties with the Central Intelligence Agency (CIA) and American oil and mineral interests.

That decade a monumental, incredibly misguided resettlement program for two million families of landless peasants, sponsored by the Brazilian government and financed by the World Bank, brought a lethal combination of ecocide, genocide, and ethnocide to Rondônia—massive deforestation and roadbuilding, the construction of *agrovilas,* vast agricultural communities laid out on grids, and massacres of isolated groups of Cintas Largas and Urueuwauwau. Satellite images of thousands of burning fires horrified the European and North American public, already apprehensive about the carbon dioxide and other greenhouse gases being released into the atmosphere. Anthropologists and other Western sympathizers rallied behind the Indians, se-

cured intellectual property rights for their knowledge of medicinal plants with possible pharmaceutical applications, and pushed for the demarcation and protection of their lands.

The last ten years have led to a huge, belated victory for the remaining Native peoples of Amazonia, even though during the 1990s Occidental and other companies drilling for oil brought ecocide and ethnocide to eight thousand U'wa on the Colombia-Venzuela border and the Huaroni, a nomadic people of the Ecuadoran Amazon who tried to drive off the drilling crews with spears. In general, the demarcation of Indian lands in the Brazilian and Peruvian Amazon is proceeding well. Twenty percent of of Brazilian Amazonia is now recognized by the government as indigenous territory. This is the largest area of protected rain forest in the world; when FUNAI replaced SPI in 1968, only a fraction of Native lands were protected. Small remnant groups remain at risk of being driven from their land or massacred for individual, political, or racial motives. The Yanomami homeland has been almost completely demarcated, but is still being invaded by *garimpeiros.* Efforts to complete demarcation for other tribes in Roraima are meeting with heavy resistance from local politicians.

Despite continuing difficulties the Native population in the Amazon region has rebounded to 325,000. A new generation of young, educated Brazilians realizes that their indigenous cultures and rain forest represent a unique and precious heritage. It can be said with some confidence that the tide has finally turned, although the future of the Amazon forest itself is not encouraging, with the Brazilian Congress's new law to open half of it to agriculture, cattle ranching, and multinational chip mills.

SEE ALSO Catholic Church; Developmental Genocide; Indigenous Peoples; Whitaker, Benjamin

BIBLIOGRAPHY

Brazilian Socio-Environmental Institute website. Available from http://www.socioambiental.org.

Cowell, Adrian (1977). *The Tribe That Hides from Man.* New York: Stein & Day.

Cowell, Adrian (1990). *Decade of Destruction: The Crusade to Save the Amazon Rain Forest.* New York: Henry Holt.

Hemming, John (1978). *Red Gold: The Conquest of the Brazilian Indians 1500–1760.* Cambridge, Mass.: Harvard University Press.

Hemming, John (1987). *Amazon Frontier: The Defeat of the Amazon Indians.* Cambridge, Mass.: Harvard University Press.

Roosevelt, Anna (1994). *Amazon Indians from Prehistory to the Present: Anthropological Perspectives.* Tucson, Ariz.: University of Arizona Press.

Tierney, Patrick (2002). *Darkness in El Dorado: How Scientists and Journalists Devastated the Amazon.* New York: W. W. Norton.

Alex Shoumatoff

Amnesty

In order to end an international or internal conflict, negotiations often must be held with the very leaders who are responsible for war crimes and crimes against humanity. When this is the case, some argue that insisting on criminal prosecutions can prolong the conflict, resulting in more deaths, destruction, and human suffering. Reflecting this view, peace arrangements reached over the past two decades in Argentina, Cambodia, Chile, El Salvador, Guatemala, Haiti, Sierra Leone, South Africa, and Uruguay have granted amnesty to members of former regimes who allegedly had committed international crimes. With respect to Cambodia, El Salvador, Haiti, and South Africa, the United Nations pushed for, helped negotiate, and/or endorsed the granting of amnesty as a means of restoring peace and democratic government.

The term *amnesty* is derived from the Greek word *amnestia,* meaning forgetfulness or oblivion. Legally, amnesty is an act of sovereign power immunizing persons from criminal prosecution for past offenses. The practical equivalent of amnesty occurs when asylum is granted to a former leader by a neighboring state, as in the case of former Ugandan ruler Idi Amin in Saudi Arabia, former Haitian leader Jean Claude "Baby Doc" Duvalier in France, former Ethiopian leader Megistu Haile Mariam in Zimbabwe, former Haitian leader General Raoul Cedras in Panama, and former Liberian leader Charles Taylor in Nigeria.

Interests Favoring Amnesty

The leaders of all parties to a conflict must agree to cooperate in order to end the fighting and halt violations of international humanitarian law. However, they have no incentive to agree to a peace settlement if, following the agreement, they could find themselves or their close associates facing potential life imprisonment. Three case studies—Haiti, South Africa, and Liberia—show that the offer of amnesty or asylum may induce human rights violators to agree to peace and to relinquish power.

Haiti

From 1990 to 1994 Haiti was ruled by a military regime, headed by General Raoul Cedras and Brigadier General Philippe Biamby that executed over three thousand civilian political opponents and tortured hundreds of others. The United Nations mediated negotiations at Governors Island in New York Harbor, during which Haiti's military leaders agreed to relinquish power and permit the return of democratically elected President Jean-Bertrand Aristide in exchange for a full amnesty for the members of the military regime and a lifting of the economic sanctions imposed by the UN Security Council. Under pressure from the UN mediators, Aristide agreed to the amnesty clause of the Governors Island Agreement. The UN Security Council approved the agreement, which it later said, "constitutes the only valid framework for resolving the crisis in Haiti." When the military leaders initially failed to comply with the Governors Island Agreement, on July 31, 1994, the Security Council took the extreme step of authorizing an invasion of Haiti by a multinational force. On the eve of the invasion, September 18, 1994, General Cedras agreed to retire his command "when a general amnesty will be voted into law by the Haitian parliament." The amnesty permitted Aristide to return to Haiti and reinstate a civilian government, the military leaders left the country, much of the military surrendered their arms, and most of the human rights abuses promptly, if temporarily, ended.

South Africa

Until 1994 black South Africans were routinely abused under the then-operative, segregationist system known as apartheid. Facing the prospect of civil war, the outgoing administration, then headed by F. W. de Klerk, made some form of amnesty a condition for the peaceful transition of power. The leaders of the majority black population decided that the commitment to afford amnesty was a fair price to pay for a relatively peaceful transition to full democracy. In accordance with the negotiated settlement between the major parties, on July 19, 1995, the South African Parliament created a Truth and Reconciliation Commission, consisting of a Committee on Human Rights Violations, a Committee on Amnesty, and a Committee on Reparation and Rehabilitation. Under this process, amnesty would be available only to individuals who personally applied for it and who fully disclosed the facts of their apartheid crimes. After conducting 140 public hearings and considering 20,000 written and oral submissions, the South African Truth Commission published a 2,739-page report of its findings on October 29, 1998. Most observers believe the amnesty in South Africa helped to defuse tensions and avoid a civil war. Others believe it was a means for both sides to cover up crimes they had committed.

Human rights activists around the world were jubilant when British law enforcement officers arrested Augusto Pinochet in 1998. A year later more than one thousand people attended this demonstration in London, calling for Pinochet's extradition to Spain, where he would face charges of genocide and torture. Pinochet's prosecution in Chile had been hampered by the Amnesty Law of 1978. [ALIANA/GAMMA]

Liberia

Beginning in 1980 Liberia experienced a series of bloody coups. Factional fighting repeatedly flared up during the 1990s. Conflict under the presidency of Charles Taylor left more than 100,000 Liberians dead between 1997 and 2002. In August of 2003, Taylor was indicted by the Special Court for Sierra Leone on the charge of "bearing the greatest responsibility" for war crimes and crimes against humanity in Sierra Leone, which shares a border with Liberia. With rebel troops on the verge of taking over the populous Liberian capitol of Monrovia, Taylor was induced to relinquish power and leave Liberia in return for a guarantee of asylum in Nigeria. This action immediately brought the fighting in Liberia to a halt, and thereby may have saved the lives of hundreds of thousands of civilians in Monrovia who otherwise would have been caught in the crossfire had Taylor and his supporters been forced to make a last stand against the rebels.

Amnesty with Accountability?

As in both Haiti and South Africa, the offering of amnesty may be tied to accountability mechanisms. Some-times the concerned governments have made monetary reparations to the victims and their families, established truth commissions to document the abuses (and sometimes identify perpetrators by name), or instituted employment bans and purges (referred to as "lustration") that keep such perpetrators from positions of public trust. While not the same as criminal prosecution, these mechanisms may encompass much of what justice is intended to accomplish: prevention, deterrence, punishment, and rehabilitation. Indeed, some experts believe that these mechanisms do not merely constitute "a second best approach" when prosecution is impracticable, but that in many situations they may be better suited to achieving the aims of justice.

The Benefits of Prosecution

Although providing amnesty or asylum to perpetrators may sometimes be seen as necessary to achieve peace, there are several important countervailing considerations favoring prosecution. In particular, prosecuting persons responsible for violations of international humanitarian law can serve to discourage future human rights abuses, deter vigilante justice, and reinforce respect for law and the new democratic government. Although such prosecutions might initially provoke resistance, many analysts believe that national reconciliation cannot take place as long as justice is foreclosed. Professor Cherif Bassiouni, chairman of the UN investigative Commission for Yugoslavia and author of *Searching for Peace and Achieving Justice: The Need for Accountability,* has said that "if peace is not intended to be a brief interlude between conflicts," then it must be accompanied by justice.

Failure to prosecute leaders responsible for human rights abuses may breed contempt for the law and encourage future violations. The UN Commission on Human Rights and its Sub-Commission issued a Report on the Consequences of Impunity, in which it concluded that impunity is one of the main reasons for the continuation of grave violations of human rights throughout the world. Fact-finding reports on Chile and El Salvador indicate that the granting of amnesty or impunity in those countries had led to an increase in abuses.

A new or reinstated democracy needs legitimacy, which in turn requires a fair, credible, and transparent accounting of what crimes may have taken place and who was responsible during the pre-democratic regime. Criminal trials, especially in cases involving widespread and systematic abuses, can generate just such a comprehensive record of the nature and extent of violations, how they were planned and executed, the fate of individual victims, who gave the orders, and who carried them out. While there are various means to develop the historic record of such abuses, the most authoritative rendering of the truth occurs through the crucible of a trial that accords full due process. United States Supreme Court Justice Robert Jackson, who served as Chief Prosecutor at the Nuremberg Trials, underscored the logic of this proposition in his Report to the President, in which he stated that the most important legacy of the Nuremberg trial was the documentation of Nazi atrocities "with such authenticity and in such detail that there can be no responsible denial of these crimes in the future." According to Jackson, the establishment of an authoritative record of abuses that would endure the test of time and withstand the challenge of revisionism required proof "of incredible events by credible evidence."

There is also a responsibility to provide justice to the victims and their families. Serious crimes against persons, including rape and murder, require holding the violators accountable for their acts. Prosecuting and punishing the violators gives significance to the victims' suffering and serve as partial remedy for their injuries. Moreover, prosecutions help restore the victims' dignity and prevent private acts of revenge by those who, in the absence of justice, might take it into their own hands.

Failure to punish former leaders who were responsible for widespread human rights abuses encourages cynicism about the rule of law and distrust toward the political system. To the victims of human rights crimes, amnesty represents the ultimate in hypocrisy. When those with power are seen to be above the law, the ordinary citizen will never come to believe in the principle of the rule of law as a fundamental necessity in a democratic country.

Finally, amnesty risks encouraging rogue regimes in other parts of the world to engage in gross abuses. Richard Goldstone, the former prosecutor of the International Criminal Tribunal for the Former Yugoslavia has concluded that the failure of the international community to prosecute Pol Pot, Idi Amin, Saddam Hussein, and Mohammed Aidid, among others, encouraged the Serbs to launch their policy of ethnic cleansing in the former Yugoslavia with the expectation that they would not be held accountable for their international crimes. When the international community encourages or endorses an amnesty for human rights abuses, it sends a signal to other regimes that they have nothing to lose by instituting repressive measures—if things start going badly, they can always bargain away their crimes by agreeing to peace.

Overriding the Grant of Amnesty

In a few narrowly defined situations there is an international legal obligation to prosecute and failure to prosecute can itself amount to an international wrong. An amnesty given to the members of a former regime could be invalidated in a proceeding before the state's domestic courts or an international forum. Moreover, it would be inappropriate for an international criminal court to defer to a national amnesty if the amnesty violates obligations contained in the very treaty that makes up the subject matter of the court's jurisdiction.

The prerogative of a state to issue an amnesty for an offense can be circumscribed by treaties to which the state is a party. Several international conventions clearly include a duty to prosecute the humanitarian or human rights crimes defined therein, including the grave-breaches provisions of the 1949 Geneva Conventions, the Genocide Convention, and the Torture Convention. When these Conventions are applicable, the granting of amnesty or asylum to persons responsible for committing the crimes defined therein would constitute a breach of a treaty obligation for which there can be no excuse or exception.

The 1949 Geneva Conventions

Each of the four Geneva Conventions negotiated in 1949 contains a specific enumeration of "grave breaches," which are war crimes for which there is individual criminal liability and for which states have a corresponding duty to prosecute or extradite. Grave breaches include willful killing, torture, or inhuman treatment, willfully causing great suffering or serious injury to body or health, extensive destruction of property not justified by military necessity, willfully depriving a civilian of the rights of fair and regular trial, and unlawful confinement of a civilian.

Parties to the Geneva Conventions have an obligation to search for, prosecute, and punish perpetrators of grave breaches of the Geneva Conventions, unless they choose to hand over such persons for trial by another state party. The Commentary to the Geneva Conventions, which is the official history of the negotiations leading to the adoption of these treaties, confirms that the obligation to prosecute grave breaches is "absolute," meaning that signatories to the conventions can under no circumstances grant perpetrators immunity or amnesty from prosecution for grave breaches of the conventions.

States or international tribunals may prosecute persons who commit war crimes in internal armed conflicts, whereas the duty to prosecute grave breaches under the Geneva Conventions is limited to the context of international armed conflict. There is a high threshold of violence necessary to constitute a genuine armed conflict, as distinct from lower level disturbances such as riots or isolated and sporadic acts of fighting. Moreover, to be an international armed conflict, the situation must constitute an armed conflict involving two or more nations, or a partial or total occupation of the territory of one nation by another.

The Genocide Convention

Most of the countries of the world are party to the Genocide Convention, which entered into force on January 12, 1952, and the International Court of Justice has determined that the substantive provisions of the Convention constitute customary international law that is binding on all states. Like the Geneva Conventions, the Genocide Convention imposes an obligation to prosecute persons responsible for genocide as defined in the Convention. It says that all persons who commit genocide shall be punished, irrespective of their official position. Furthermore, states are required to enact legislation and to provide effective penalties for criminal prosecutions of genocide.

The Torture Convention

Although the Torture Convention entered into force in 1987, it has not been widely ratified and currently has less than ninety state parties. The Torture Convention requires each state party to ensure that all acts of torture are offenses under its internal law, establish its jurisdiction over such offenses in cases where the alleged offender is present in a state's territory, and if such a state does not extradite the alleged offender, the convention requires it to submit the case to its competent authorities for the purpose of prosecution. Although there is no comparable treaty requiring states to prosecute crimes against humanity generally, where there are specific allegations that the crime against humanity included systematic acts of torture, and where the relevant states are parties to the Torture Convention, the granting of amnesty or asylum would violate the treaty's clear duty to prosecute or extradite.

General Human Rights Conventions

General human rights conventions include the International Covenant on Civil and Political Rights, the European Convention for the Protection of Human Rights and Fundamental Freedoms, and the American Convention on Human Rights. Although these treaties do not expressly require states to prosecute violators, they do obligate states to ensure the rights enumerated within the conventions. There is growing recognition in the jurisprudence of the treaty bodies responsible for monitoring enforcement of these conventions and the writings of respected commentators that the duty to ensure rights implies a duty to hold specific violators accountable for at least certain kinds of violations.

Yet, a careful examination of the jurisprudence of these bodies suggests that methods of obtaining specific accountability other than criminal prosecutions would meet the requirement of ensuring the rights enumerated in the various conventions. This jurisprudence indicates that a state must fulfill five obligations in confronting gross violations of human rights committed by a previous regime:

1. investigate the identity, fate and whereabouts of victims;

2. investigate the identity of major perpetrators;

3. provide reparation or compensation to victims;

4. take affirmative steps to ensure that human rights abuse does not recur; and

5. punish those guilty of human rights abuse.

Punishment can take many noncriminal forms, including imposition of fines, removal from office, reduction of rank, and forfeiture of government or military pensions and/or other assets.

Universal Jurisdiction

In the absence of a treaty containing the duty to extradite or prosecute, so-called universal jurisdiction is generally thought to be permissive, not mandatory. Yet, several commentators and human rights groups have recently taken the position that customary international law not only establishes permissive jurisdiction over perpetrators of crimes against humanity, but also requires their prosecution and conversely prohibits the granting of amnesty to such persons.

Commentators often cite the UN Declaration on Territorial Asylum (UN General Assembly Resolution 2312) as the earliest international recognition of a legal obligation to prosecute perpetrators of crimes against humanity. The declaration provides that "states shall not grant asylum to any person with respect to whom there are serious reasons for considering that he has committed a . . . crime against humanity." Yet, according to the negotiating record of this resolution, as discussed in the United Nations Year Book of 1967:

> [t]he majority of members stressed that the draft declaration under consideration was not intended to propound legal norms or to change existing rules of international law, but to lay down broad humanitarian and moral principles upon which States might rely in seeking to unify their practices relating to asylum (p. 759).

This evidences that, from the onset, the General Assembly resolutions concerning crimes against humanity were intended to be aspirational, not binding. To the extent any state practice in this area is widespread, it is the practice of granting amnesties or de facto impunity to those who commit crimes against humanity. That the United Nations itself has felt free of legal constraints in endorsing recent amnesty for peace deals in situations involving crimes against humanity confirms that customary international law has not yet crystallized in this area.

Amnesty and the International Criminal Court (ICC)

At the preparatory conference for the establishment of the permanent international criminal court in August 1997, the U.S. Delegation circulated an informal proposal (or "nonpaper") suggesting that the proposed permanent court should take into account amnesties in the interest of international peace and national reconciliation when deciding whether to exercise jurisdiction over a situation or to prosecute a particular offender. According to the U.S. text, the policies favoring prosecution of international offenders must be balanced against the need to close "a door on the conflict of a past era" and "to encourage the surrender or rein-

corporation of armed dissident groups," thereby facilitating the transition to democracy. While the U.S. proposal met with criticism from many quarters, the final text of the Rome Statute contains several ambiguously drafted provisions which, for better or worse, could potentially be interpreted as codifying the U.S. proposal.

The preamble of the Rome Statute suggests that deferring a prosecution because of the existence of a national amnesty would be incompatible with the purpose of the ICC, namely to ensure criminal prosecution of persons who commit serious international crimes. Yet, notwithstanding this preambular language, there are several articles of the Rome Statute that might be read as permitting the court under certain circumstances to recognize an amnesty exception to its jurisdiction. The apparent conflict between these articles and the preamble reflect the schizophrenic nature of the negotiations at Rome: The preambular language and the procedural provisions were negotiated by entirely different drafting groups, and in the rush of the closing days of the Rome Conference, the drafting committee never fully integrated and reconciled the separate portions of the Statute.

With respect to a potential amnesty exception, the most important provision of the Rome Statute is Article 16. Under that article, the international criminal court would be required to defer to a national amnesty if the Security Council adopts a resolution under Chapter VII of the United Nations Charter requesting the court not to commence an investigation or prosecution, or to defer any proceedings already in progress.

The Security Council has the legal authority to require the court to respect an amnesty if two requirements are met. First, the Security Council must have determined the existence of a threat to the peace, a breach of the peace, or an act of aggression under Article 39 of the UN Charter. Second, the resolution requesting the court's deferral must be consistent with the purposes and principles of the United Nations with respect to maintaining international peace and security, resolving threatening situations in conformity with principles of justice and international law, and promoting respect for human rights and fundamental freedoms under Article 24 of the UN Charter.

The decision of the Appeals Chamber of the Yugoslavia Tribunal in the case of Dusko Tadic suggests that the ICC could assert its authority to independently assess whether these two requirements were met as part of its incidental power to determine the propriety of its own jurisdiction. Jose Alvarez, a commentator writing of the Tadic appeal decision, has said that this decision "strongly support[s] those who see the UN Charter not as unblinkered license for police action but as an emerging constitution of enumerated, limited powers subject to the rule of law" (1969, p. 249). It is possible, then, that the international criminal court would not necessarily be compelled by the existence of a Security Council Resolution to terminate an investigation or prosecution, were it to find that an amnesty contravenes international law.

While an amnesty accompanied by the establishment of a truth commission, victim compensation, and lustration might be in the interests of justice in the broad sense, it would nonetheless be in contravention of international law where the grave breaches provisions of the 1949 Geneva Conventions or the Genocide Convention are applicable. It is especially noteworthy that the Geneva Conventions require parties "to provide effective penal sanctions for persons committing, or ordering to be committed, any of the grave breaches of the Convention," the Genocide Convention requires parties "to provide effective penalties for persons guilty of genocide," and the Torture Convention requires parties "to make these offenses punishable by appropriate penalties which take into account their grave nature."

This would suggest that the International Criminal Court might not defer to the UN Security Council under Article 16 of the Rome Statute where the accused is charged with grave breaches of the 1949 Geneva Conventions, the crime of genocide, or torture. Yet, a counter argument can be made that the Rome Statute codifies only the substantive provisions of the 1949 Geneva Conventions and the Genocide Convention, and does not incorporate those procedural aspects of the Conventions that require prosecution. Accordingly, the nature of the charges might constitute a factor to be considered, but would not necessarily be a bar to recognizing an amnesty.

Where the UN Security Council has not requested the international criminal court to respect an amnesty and thereby to terminate a prosecution, the court's prosecutor may choose to do so under Article 53 of the Rome Statute. That article permits the prosecutor to decline to initiate an investigation (even when a state has filed a complaint) if the prosecutor has concluded that there are "substantial reasons to believe that an investigation would not serve the interests of justice." However, the decision of the prosecutor under Article 53 is subject to review by the pre-trial chamber of the court. In reviewing whether respecting an amnesty and not prosecuting would better serve the interests of justice, the pre-trial chamber would have to evaluate the benefits of a particular amnesty and consider whether there is an international legal obligation to prosecute the offense.

When neither the UN Security Council nor the prosecutor have requested the International Criminal Court to defer to a national amnesty, the concerned state can attempt to raise the issue under Article 17(1)(a) of the Rome Statute. That article requires the court to dismiss a case where "the case is being investigated or prosecuted by a State which has jurisdiction over it, unless the State is unwilling or unable genuinely to carry out the investigation or prosecution." It is significant that the article requires an investigation, but does not specify that it be a criminal investigation. The concerned state could argue that a truth commission (especially one modeled on that of South Africa) constitutes a genuine investigation. On the other hand, subsection (2) of the article suggests that the standard for determining that an investigation is not genuine is whether the proceedings are "inconsistent with an intent to bring the person concerned to justice"—a phrase which, read together with the Preamble to the Treaty, might be interpreted as requiring criminal proceedings.

Conclusion

Nearly a decade ago, David J. Scheffer, then U.S. Ambassador-at-Large for War Crimes Issues publicly remarked: "[o]ne must understand that amnesty [and asylum] are always on the table in [peace] negotiations." In his view, there are frequently no legal constraints to the negotiation of an amnesty for peace deal. This is because the international procedural law imposing a duty to prosecute is far more limited than the substantive law establishing international offenses. But there are situations, such as the cases of Slobodan Milosevic of Serbia and Saddam Hussein of Iraq—each accused of grave breaches of the Geneva Conventions and genocide—where the international procedural law would rule out amnesty or asylum as a legitimate option for the peacemakers. Moreover, even in situations where amnesties do not contravene an applicable international obligation to prosecute, peacemakers must recognize that amnesties vary greatly. Some, as in South Africa, which are closely linked to mechanisms for providing accountability and redress, may be a legitimate diplomatic tool; others, as with the grant of asylum in 2003 for Charles Taylor in Nigeria, may be widely viewed as just another case of former leader "getting away with murder."

SEE ALSO Impunity; National Laws; Prosecution; Sierra Leone Special Court; Truth Commissions; Universal Jurisdiction

BIBLIOGRAPHY

Akhavan, Payam (1996). "The Yugoslavia Tribunal at a Crossroads: The Dayton Peace Agreement and Beyond." *Human Rights Quarterly* 19:259–282.

Alverez, Jose (1996). "Nuremberg Revisited: The Tadic Case." *European Journal of International Law* 7:245–255.

Bassiouni, M. Cherif (1996). "Searching for Peace and Achieving Justice: The Need for Accountability." *Law and Contemporary Problems* 59:9–22.

Minow, Martha (1998). *Between Vengeance and Forgiveness.* Boston: Beacon Press.

Morris, Virginia, and Michael P. Scharf (1995). *An Insider's Guide to the International Criminal Tribunal for the Former Yugoslavia.* Irving-on-Hudson, N.Y.: Transnational Publishers.

Orentlicher, Dianne (1991). "Settling Accounts: The Duty to Prosecute Human Rights Violations of a Prior Regime." *Yale Law Journal* 100:2537–2577.

Roht-Arriaza, Naomi (1990). "State Responsibility to Investigate and Prosecute Grave Human Rights Violations in International Law." *California Law Review* 78:451–481.

Roht-Arriaza, Naomi (1995). *Impunity and Human Rights in International Law and Practice.* New York: Oxford University Press.

Scharf, Michael P. (1996). "The Letter of the Law: The Scope of the International Legal Obligation to Prosecute Human Rights Crimes." *Law and Contemporary Problems* 59:41–61.

Scharf, Michael P. (1997). "The Case for a Permanent International Truth Commission." *Duke Journal of Comparative and International Law* 7:375–400.

Scharf, Michael P. (1999). "The Amnesty Exception to the Jurisdiction of the International Criminal Court." *Cornell International Law Journal* 32:507–527.

Simma, Bruno (1995). *International Human Rights and General International Law: A Comparative Analysis.* New York: Oxford University Press.

Weisman, Norman (1972). "A History and Discussion of Amnesty." *Columbia Human Rights Law Review* 4:520–540.

Williams, Paul and Michael P. Scharf (2002). *Peace with Justice?* Lanham, Md.: Rowman and Littlefield.

Michael P. Scharf

Ancient World

Genocides, one can surmise, may be as old as civilization itself. The many ancient cases of disappeared peoples and cultures may not always point to genocide, but the possibility that many of these peoples were the victims of genocide seems very likely. The reason for this is that awareness of genocide was widespread in antiquity and the frequent reports of its occurrence indicate that genocide was commonplace.

In Homer's *Iliad,* the Greek forces invading Troy have no qualms about planning the total destruction of its people. In Book IV, Agamemnon rouses Menelaus:

My dear Menelaus, why are you so chary of taking men's lives? Did the Trojans treat you as handsomely as that when they stayed in your house? No; we are not going to leave a single one of them alive, down to the babies in their mothers' wombs—not even they must live. The whole people must be wiped out of existence, and none be let to think of them and shed a tear.

Putting to one side the question of whether or not the inhabitants of Troy actually suffered this fate, what one finds in Agamemnon's words is the casual acceptance of genocidal warfare as legitimate and commonplace. In a world where the ruling elites exploited the lower classes to finance the building of great palaces and temples or to wage war against enemies (of the elites), the fate of an enemy city's inhabitants meant very little. Histories were written about kings, priests, and ruling elites, and heroic battles between the armies of kingdoms and/or empires. There were no histories written about ordinary men and women. As a result, we may never have enough information for a decisive analysis of many suspected cases of genocide.

From time to time, one does come across an account of a historical event in which the fate of common people is mentioned, giving us a rare glimpse, not only of the event itself, but also of patterns of thought that were prevalent at the time of the event. An example is the bloody battle of Kalinga (in India). Asoka (299–237 BCE) was the third emperor of the Mauryan dynasty of India and the best-known ruler of ancient India. In 260 BCE Asoka attacked Kalinga; the campaign was successful but resulted in a tremendous loss of life. Asoka's brutality in warfare and the slaughter of his enemies are legendary. But his brutality is cited in texts, not because the event of slaughtering hundreds of thousands of people was so egregiously horrific, but because Asoka came to regret his actions and converted to Buddhism. In these texts the fate of Asoka's victims is noteworthy only because his guilt at having committed genocidal crimes led to his religious conversion, not because of a sense of bereavement for the people he victimized.

Although we often lack information for many of the instances of suspected genocide, the accounts of mass killings for which we have relatively more information must still be called into question, as that information may be exaggerated. Sennacherib, king of Assyria (705–681 BCE) waged wars against Babylonia, Phoenicia, and Philistia, as well as several cities in Judea. In 689 BCE Sennacherib captured and destroyed Babylon, slaughtered all its inhabitants, and diverted rivers of water into the city.

Do we absorb this information as factual, in the absence of any other corroborating evidence? Obviously,

Pertaining to genocidal crimes of the ancient Mediterranean world, there is more speculation than hard evidence. The historical record is often slight. During the reign of Ramses II, the struggle between Egyptians (under Ramses) and Hittites for control of Syria culminated in a battle that was fought in Kadesh, Syria. Although Ramses claimed a great victory (and that version of events was much promulgated for centuries), in fact neither power was able to defeat the other. In this photo, the great temple of Ramses II (completed c. 1250 BCE) at Abu Simbel, Egypt. [**HULTON-DEUTSCH COLLECTION/CORBIS**]

there were surviving Babylonians after 689 BCE, as both historical and archaeological evidence suggests that the Babylonians subsequently took revenge on Assyria. This question aside, the interpretation of such data (coming out of antiquity) is inherently problematic, as much of the data was obtained from inscriptions that were not intended for mortal eyes and were sometimes far from truthful. Records of a king's "heroics" were inscribed on the peaks of mountains or the foundations of buildings—all for the gods to see. Moreover, a king would record only his accomplishments, and never his failures, and what he chose to record might bear little relation to actual events.

One such example (of the erratic and undependable character of ancient historiography) is the story of the victory of the Egyptian pharaoh Ramses II over the Hittites (a nation of Asia Minor). The story of the Egyptian victory was for centuries relied on as historically correct, until an archaeological discovery in the late nineteenth century proved that not only did the Hittites win this battle, they also signed a peace treaty with the Egyptians. An interesting feature of the Hittite society is the way they are alleged to have treated their enemies. Unlike the Assyrians, who had a reputation for widespread brutality, the Hittites apparently did not commit genocide. Once an enemy was defeated, the in-

encyclopedia of GENOCIDE *and* CRIMES AGAINST HUMANITY

habitants of the conquered nation would be taken into custody and distributed as slaves among the Hittite elites.

That the Hittites were at variance with the (presumed) general atmosphere of genocidal warfare in antiquity is subject to argument. In the ancient Mediterranean world, it was the reputation of Medes and Babylonians to have possessed no aversion to using exceptionally lethal techniques in warfare. There are several accounts of Medes and Babylonians (independently and jointly) slaughtering the inhabitants of enemy cities, but perhaps the most famous account would be that of the assault on Nineveh, the capital city of Assyria, in 612 BCE, wherein Medes and Babylonians united to destroy the city. After a two-month siege, the city was pillaged, severed heads were put on display at its main entrance, and the city itself was reduced to rubble.

A detailed source for accounts of warfare in antiquity would be the Old Testament. It is a record of many events that might be viewed as genocidal. In *Joshua* the Israelites are portrayed as annihilating towns in fulfillment of their divine providence; *Deuteronomy* and *1 Samuel* both prophesize the annihilation of the Amalekites. Egyptians and Assyrians alike professed to carry out the complete destruction of their foes. Yet there is little archaeological evidence to support Old Testament accounts of the widespread destruction of cities that took place during the Exodus period (1200–1100 BCE). It is helpful to examine these accounts, not because of any historical authenticity that they might possess, but because of the casual way in which acts of genocidal aggression are reported: a further argument that ancient peoples were not unacquainted with the concept of genocide.

Although the term *genocide* is a modern one that conjures up images of carnage in the aftermaths of twentieth-century conflicts, the slaughter of enemies has ancient roots—an examination of which is a necessary part of the quest to understand the historical development of genocide and the meaning of the term itself. All the instances of genocide or presumed genocide cited above have entailed the targeting of noncombatant men, women, and children for extermination. Regardless of whether the accounts of genocide are truthful, the manner in which they have been reported strongly suggests that genocide was widely practiced, and that awareness of its existence spanned many ancient cultures. A study of suspected genocides of antiquity is pivotal to an understanding of the development of genocide, what it is, and how it arises.

SEE ALSO Archaeology; Athens and Melos; Carthage; India, Ancient and Medieval; Sparta

BIBLIOGRAPHY

Gurney, O. R. (1975). *The Hittites*. London: Book Club Associates.

Homer. (1981). *The Iliad*, trans. A. Williamson. Middlesex, U.K.: Penguin Books.

Jastrow, Morris (1971). *The Civilization of Babylonia and Assyria*. New York: Benjamin Blom.

Mayor, Adrienne (1997). "Dirty Tricks in Ancient Warfare." *MHQ: Quarterly Journal of Military History* Autumn(2).

Saggs, H. W. F. (1984). *The Might That Was Assyria*. London: Sidgwick & Jackson.

Sircar, D. C. (1975). *Inscriptions of Asoka*. New Dehli: Publications Division, Ministry of Information and Broadcasting, Government of India.

Sircar, D. C. (1979). *Asokan Studies*. Calcutta: Indian Museum.

Karin Solveig Bjornson

Anthropology, Cultural

Anthropology, the study of human beings through time and across place, is characterized by the concept of culture, a particular set of methods (ranging from anatomical analysis to ethnographic fieldwork), and a holistic perspective. Most anthropologists also adhere to the principle of relativism, which holds that one must at least temporarily suspend judgment and comprehend behavior from the perspective of the people studied to combat human tendencies toward ethnocentrism and naive realism—the view that, at root, everyone views the world in a similar manner. Although a relativist stance might seem problematic in the face of genocidal horrors, few anthropologists adhere to a fanatical relativism, which argues that "anything goes." Relativism is nevertheless essential to the ethnographer's attempt, as one of the founding figures in anthropology put it, "to grasp the native's point of view, his relation to life, to realize *his* vision of *his* world" (Malinowski, 1984, p. 25). This anthropological perspective is of enormous importance to human attempts to understand genocide, which occurs in a variety of cultural contexts.

Given the broad scope of the discipline, it is not surprising that, particularly in recent years, anthropologists have engaged in a wide range of projects related to genocide, such as defending indigenous peoples, leading forensic investigations, consulting United Nations (UN) tribunals, assisting refugees, helping victims cope with trauma, promoting conflict resolution, participating in the reconstruction, and arguing against so-called primordialist explanations.

One key area in which anthropologists have contributed to human understanding of genocide is in helping to explain why people participate in mass murder. Perpetrator regimes—particularly those involved in "ideological genocides" (Fein, 1984, p. 1)—often rise to power as "revitalization movements" (Wallace, 1956, p. 1) that gain support in situations of rampant social, political, or environmental change which undermine local structures of meaning. Such upheaval provides a foundation for the emergence of radical ideologies and charismatic leaders whose blueprints for renewal require the elimination of those labeled as undesirable in the population.

To facilitate this project, genocidal regimes are centrally concerned with "manufacturing difference" (Hinton, 2004). As they reconstruct and crystallize boundaries of difference, for example, genocidal regimes set perpetrators and victims apart, marking the latter in dehumanizing discourses that facilitate their annihilation. Thus, Germans are split off from Jews, who are depicted as a disease that threatens to contaminate and even destroy the Aryan race. In a similar manner, Hutus have been divided from Tutsis, Bosnian Serbs from Muslims and Croats, Turks from Armenians, colonizers from indigenous peoples, and so forth.

Such genocidal ideologies are not constructed in a vacuum: They are located in particular places at a given moment in time. To motivate their minions to kill, genocidal ideologues forge their messages of hate out of a blend of the new and the old, thereby enabling them to tap into local knowledge that has deep ontological resonance for the actors. Examples range from the Hamitic hypothesis in Rwanda to the Khmer Rouge manipulation of local understandings of disproportionate revenge and Nazi invocations of anti-Semitism and the German Volk.

Besides revealing much about such boundary construction and ideology, anthropologists have also shown how violence is culturally patterned. In Rwanda, for instance, Hutu acts of violence, ranging from stuffing Tutsis into latrines to bodily mutilation, resonated with local understandings linking bodily health to proper blockage and flow. This "bodily inscription of violence" (Hinton, 2004) can be seen in a wide range of cases, from the torture chambers of the Khmer Rouge to the murder of so-called savage Putumayo in Colombia at the turn of the twentieth century.

Such violence always occurs in a social context. Anthropologists have examined a number of crucial group dynamics, such as kinship relations, liminality and rites of passage, socialization into microcultures of violence, ritual process, and local understandings of status, honor, face, and shame. Confronted with Putumayo who had been manufactured into beings classified as savage, ignorant, and wild, rubber traders engaged in ritualized murder, sometimes burning or crucifying the alleged infidels in a liminal locale where a microculture of brutal violence had emerged. Anthropology, of course, does not explain everything, but it provides a crucial level of analysis that may be fruitfully combined with insights garnered from other disciplines.

SEE ALSO Archaeology; Forensics; Sociology of Perpetrators; Sociology of Victims

BIBLIOGRAPHY

Hinton, Alexander Laban, ed. (2002). *Annihilating Difference: The Anthropology of Genocide.* Berkeley: University of California Press.

Hinton, Alexander Laban, ed. (2002). *Genocide: An Anthropological Reader.* Malden, Mass.: Blackwell.

Hinton, Alexander Laban (2004). *Why Did They Kill? Cambodia in the Shadow of Genocide.* Berkeley: University of California Press.

Malinowski, Bronislaw (1984). *Argonauts of the Western Pacific.* Prospect Heights, Ill.: Waveland.

Taussig, Michael (1987). *Shamanism, Colonialism, and the Wild Man: A Study in Terror and Healing.* Chicago: Chicago University Press.

Taylor, Christopher (1999). *Sacrifice as Terror: The Rwandan Genocide of 1994.* Oxford: Berg.

Alex Hinton

Anti-Semitism

Anti-Semitism is hatred, fear, and hostility that harms, has harmed, or has the potential to harm Jews. The term *anti-Semitism* was coined in 1879 by German anti-Semitic agitator Wilhelm Marr, who claimed that the term was based on "science," rather than religious concepts that would have justified antagonism toward Jews. Yet antipathy toward Jews (sometimes known as Jew-hatred, Judaeophobia, or "the longest hatred") is centuries old, and centuries ago became elaborated into an ideology. Anti-Semitic ideology, whose adherents have drawn and continue to draw on anti-Jewish myth and legend, has led to social and legal discrimination, demagogic political mobilization, and spontaneous or state-sponsored violence that has striven to isolate, expel, or annihilate Jews as Jews. That ideology considers the Jewish character as permanently and unreformably degenerate. And as per that ideology, Jews, no matter how few or assimilated, are perpetually engaged in conspiracies that seek to dominate, exploit, and destroy society or the world, and hence are menaces to society. Although some Greek and Roman authors (most notably Tacitus) expressed hostility toward Jews, no anti-Semitic ideology emerged in antiquity.

The New Testament and the Middle Ages

There are competing schools of thought as to the origins of anti-Semitism. One of these schools of thought holds that the roots of anti-Semitism are religious, that anti-Semitism derives from the narrative of the trial and crucifixion of Jesus Christ in the four New Testament gospels. Expressions of anti-Semitism that are essentially nonreligious (except perhaps racialist language) are transformations, secularizations, extensions, and "new" applications of the religious original.

Christianity is the only world religion that accuses another religion of murdering its god. Owing to Christian allegations that Jews are culpable for the crime of deicide, or Christ-killing, Jews are—in many settings—defined as criminals linked to the anti-Christ, a Jewish son of Satan who thwarts the Second Coming and will rule the world via a reign of terror that will mean affliction for all Christians. Also adumbrated in the New Testament is the myth of the Wandering or Eternal Jew. (See John 18:4–10, 20–22, parallels in Matthew 26:51, Mark 14:47, Luke 22:50–51) The Wandering Jew, supposed to be emblematic of the Jewish people, is doomed to wander to the end of time, homeless, alienated, unable to die, fated to live in misery, and suffering repentance for his unforgivable crime of having mocked Christ.

The medieval accusation of ritual murder is also adrumbrated in the gospels. In Matthew (27:23–26) the Jews of Jerusalem cry out to Pontius Pilate: "Crucify him. . . . His blood be upon us and our children." Thus are Jews made to pronounce an eternal curse on themselves. The most pernicious anti-Semitic motif in the gospels is the demonization of Jews. In John (8:44–47) Jesus excoriates the Pharisees (one of several Jewish parties or sects, and other Jews present):

> Your father is the devil and you choose to carry out your father's desires. He was a murderer from the beginning, and is not rooted in the truth; there is no truth in him. When he tells a lie he is speaking his own language, for he is a liar and the father of lies.

And so Jews became alleged to be pledged in allegiance to Satan's superhuman powers and to be devoted to his work of subversion and overturning God's plan, echoed (many centuries later) in Shakespeare's describing his character Shylock (in *The Merchant of Venice*) as a "fiend" and the "very devil incarnal." The putative capacity of Jews to lie, deceive, and manipulate is rooted in the same ideology as the image of the Jew as standing menace and arch-conspirator. That the origins of anti-Semitism are economics-related (a "doctrine" that tends toward the portrayal of Jews as greedy Judases, carnal, antispiritual, and rejected by God—and of the

"The Jew: The Inciter of War, the Prolonger of War." This poaster was released in late 1943/early 1944. [GERMAN PROPAGANDA ARCHIVE (WWW.CALVIN.EDU/CAS/GPA)]

Jew as Shylock, financial wizard, and huckster) finds its New Testament foundation in the story of Jesus expelling the moneychangers from the temple and Judas' betrayal of Jesus for thirty pieces of silver.

The Church Fathers (theologians, whose beliefs and writings are termed *patristic*) of the third to the seventh centuries wove anti-Semitic New Testament passages into an intellectually sophisticated ideology. For St. Augustine (354–430), Jews—as he stated some twenty times in his influential *Treatise against the Jews* and elsewhere—are the "witness people," fated to exist as suffering Cains (in collective punishment for the crime of deicide) until the Last Judgment. His writings strove to justify the degradations to which Jews were subject, but at the same time may have helped to shield them from genocidal aggression—by advocating that limits be set on their persecution. Augustine wrote in his *Reply to Faustus the Manichecan*: "The continued preservation of the Jews will be a proof [of the truth of Christianity] to believing Christians." St. John Chrysostom (c. 347–407), the most vituperatively anti-

Semitic of the Church Fathers, gave expression to almost every allegation that was part of the anti-Semitism of his day. In his writings Jews were devil-possessed, "impure, criminal, impious," their religion a "disease." And "Like an unruly draft animal, the Jews are fit for killing. And this is what happened to the Jews: while they were making themselves unfit for work [by rejecting Christianity], they grew fit for slaughter" (Perry and Schweitzer, 1994, 114–115). The need to shun Jews and to regard them as dangerous, polluting, and corrupting was a patristic teaching.

It was a staple of medieval Christian folklore that Jews suffered from terrible physical maladies and needed the blood of Christian children to carry out their medicinal and magical arts—or would simply exact that blood as revenge. According to the fable known as blood libel: Each spring a band of Jewish conspirators selected a town in which a Christian child was to be kidnapped. That child was sacrificed (a reprise of the crucifixion), and the child's blood was used in the making of matzohs and wine, to be consumed at Passover. As part of the aftermath of an accusation of ritual murder, Jews were expelled from cities and towns, their properties were expropriated, or they were massacred. Typically, a shrine to the "martyred saint" was erected. The first blood libel is supposed to have taken place in Norwich, England, in 1144; this species of slander became common all over Europe, and lived on into the twentieth century.

A parallel anti-Semitic fable is host desecration. As part of Christian dogma, a consecrated or "transubstantiated" host is the equivalent of the flesh of Christ. Mostly in Germany during the late Middle Ages, Jews were accused of stealing consecrated hosts, of "torturing Jesus again"—by stabbing, beating, boiling, or burning hosts, thereby causing hosts to "bleed" or cry out. Jews who had been accused of host desecration were made to confess and suffered the same consequences as the victims of blood libels. Unlike ritual murder accusations, which several medieval popes condemned, the host libel myths flourished with papal blessing. Almost all Protestant denominations condemned transubstantiation; hence, allegations of host desecration disappeared from Protestant countries, but lived on in Catholic areas until Vatican Council II (1962–1965).

Another expression of popular anti-Semitism was the passion play, a genre that originated in the church's liturgy of holy week. An early dramatization was the elaboration of the gospel narratives into an oratorio, combining singing and acting. There was clerical resistance to such developments on the grounds that dramatic performance is pagan and improper (the Latin for play, *ludes,* has the same root as lewd). But with the heightening of religious emotion that accompanied the Crusades, such inhibitions ended. There were also the precedents of liturgical plays (many included anti-Semitic motifs) dealing with the Nativity, Jesus' miracles, anti-Christ, the second coming, and the end of the world.

From the twelfth century, Christian art and drama dwelled on Jesus' suffering—mocked and pilloried, beaten and tortured, bleeding and tormented by the villainous Jews, with Judas and Caiphas prominent as Satan's evil-doing minions, and as greedy, bloodthirsty, power-hungry conspirators. The earliest manuscript of passion play dates from the mid-twelfth century. The first recorded performance occurred in Siena, Italy, c. 1200. By the fourteenth and fifteenth centuries, almost every town and hamlet in Europe—and many a local parish—put on its version of the story. The Protestant Reformation, except for the Calvinists and later Puritans, did not object to the performance of passion plays. They went on in England throughout the sixteenth and seventeenth centuries, as elsewhere in Europe and especially Germany (503 examples have been traced in southwest Germany alone in the early sixteenth century). Throughout all these centuries the fear and hatred unleashed by such productions meant that performances were often followed by Christian attacks on the community's Jewish ghetto, resulting in sack, arson, pillage, massacre, and expulsion. So often did such mayhem ensue that town ordinances required guards to be placed in defense at the ghetto gates, or performances were barred, as at Freiburg in 1338, Frankfurt in 1469, and Rome in 1539.

The most famous passion play, *Oberammergau,* dates from 1634, but that Bavarian village was the scene of similar performances centuries before; for all its elaboration and dramaturgical finesse, it closely resembles its medieval anti-Semitic archetypes and, notoriously, won the admiration of Adolf Hitler.

During later medieval centuries in Europe, Jews were isolated in ghettos and were required to wear badges and clothing that would identify them—indignities receiving the solemn sanction of church councils. Ordinances forbade Christians to associate with Jews, including marriage between Christians and Jews, eating with or buying food from Jews, or frequenting Jewish physicians (who were alleged to poison their patients). During the Black Plague (1347–1350) Jews were scapegoated and sometimes massacred; they were expelled from cities and towns for poisoning the air and water. In the theology of St. Thomas Aquinas (1225–1274), Jews were to be tolerated—however he went beyond the condemnations of the Church Fathers in his denunciations of "usury" and of Jews who were usurers. As part of that worldview Jews were "destined to absolute servitude" and rulers might confiscate their property—"treating Jewish goods as their own" (Perry and Schweitzer, 2002, p. 17). The Vatican cited Aquinas when it gave its approval to the anti-Semitic laws of Vichy France during World War II.

During the twelfth and thirteenth centuries Christian theologians discovered the great body of Jewish biblical commentary and interpretation known as the Talmud. Christian theologians and even some popes believed that Jews had replaced the Bible with the Talmud, and that Judaism had ceased to be biblical. In the view of these Christian scholars and ecclesiastics, Judaism was heretical and "of earth." Jews thus forfeited their right to be tolerated in Christendom and were a proper focus for the Inquisition courts (Roman Catholic courts set up in several European countries to punish heresy, most notably in Spain under royal auspices from 1378 on). For many Christian theologians, the Talmud and other Jewish texts affirmed Christ as the messiah. Accordingly, the lying Jews had concealed this revelation—which was justification for the involuntary progressions of Jews toward the baptismal fount. The Dominican and Franciscan friars were fanatical in their efforts to compel Jews to convert to Christianity, confiscating their books and forcing them to listen to conversionist sermons. The end result was forced conversions en masse, the best known of which occurred in the Spanish kingdoms in the century that followed 1391.

Many of these forced converts, known variously as crypto-Jews, New Christians, *Conversos* (converts), or *Marranos* (swine), and/or their descendants became steadfast Christians; others secretly remained steadfast Jews. *Conversos* became successful in all walks of life (as the laws that had discriminated against them were withdrawn). Before long, however, envied and under suspicion of "Judaizing," they were ruthlessly scrutinized and abused by Spanish and Portuguese Inquisition authorities for centuries. Anticipating the anti-Semitism of Nazi Germany, Spanish and Portuguese laws established "purity of blood" requirements for numerous kinds of employment, which had the intended effect of excluding *Conversos* from many occupations.

Other readers of the Talmud purported to find that its text enjoined Jews, as part of their religious duty, to malign, rob, maim, enslave, and kill Christians; to undermine Christian belief; to bankrupt and destroy the church. Copies of the Talmud were seized and burnt; consequently few copies of the Talmud survived into the more tolerant Renaissance period. By the end of the

Middle Ages, western Europe was essentially barren of Jews, who had either fled (mostly to Poland and the Ottoman Empire) or, fleeced of their property, been expelled—from England in 1290, France in 1306, Austria in 1421, and Spain in 1492. The *Summa Angelica* of the fifteenth-century Italian theologian Angelo di Chivasso epitomized the church's position: "To be a Jew is a crime, not, however, punishable by a Christian" (Poliakov, 1974–1985, vol. 3, p. 6). In practice, however, fifteenth-century Christian rulers, crusaders, ecclesiastics, and municipalities did punish Jews because they were Jews.

Economic Anti-Semitism

Jewish literacy and erudition (often acquired under the religious obligation to know Torah) long conferred economic advantages on Jews. However, their alleged mental and intellectual superiority—a weapon Satan reputedly bestowed on Jews—became an anti-Semitic stereotype: "Intelligence—that is the mortal sin of the Jews" (Weiss, 1996, p. 157). Because Jews in Christian Europe were normally excluded from owning land and barred from the crafts, their academic distinction and literacy would often enable them to become prominent in trade, and, later, finance, callings deemed disreputable and unprestigious by Christians during the Middle Ages and after. Socioeconomic standing enabled some Jews (most were poor) to play prominent roles in the commercial, financial, and industrial expansion of Europe.

Jewish emancipation, beginning in revolutionary France in 1790, and the more secular attitudes that obtained in Europe in the nineteenth century enabled many Western Jews to prosper as never before. Antisemitic explanations of Jewish prosperity abounded. Karl Marx equated Jews and Judaism with capitalism (so-called mammonism) and claimed that money-worshipping Jews had invented capitalism and had "Judaized" Western society because "Jewish" capitalism rose there and became the dominant economic system. Accordingly, capitalism would not end until Judaism, its source, ended. Marx pronounced this goal of Jewish annihilation in his essay of 1843, "The Jewish Question." The German economic historian and eventual Nazi Werner Sombart published an influential book, *The Jews and Modern Capitalism* (1911), which allegedly proved Marx's contentions.

Modern Period: Luther to Hitler

The acolytes of Reformation Calvinism were not obsessed with the strengthening of Christianity via the persecution of Jews and even tended toward philo-Semitism. In contrast, the Catholic Counter-Reformation and Lutheranism upheld the tradition of anti-Semitic persecution. Martin Luther, contemptuous of and dismissive of Judaism, was intent on converting Jews to Christianity. Frustrated by the failure of his attempts at conversion and fearful of accusations of "Judaizing," Luther vented his wrath against Jews in letters and pamphlets, in which age-old anti-Semitic calumnies were spewed. In his treatise *On the Jews and Their Lies* (1543), he delivered an edict: Burn their synagogues and homes, their prayer books, and Talmuds; on pain of death forbid rabbis to teach; outlaw Jews and exempt them from any protections afforded to travelers on highways; bar them from all financial and banking activity and confiscate their money; ostracize them; make them "earn their bread in the sweat of their brow"; treat them "as a physician treats gangrene—without mercy, to cut, saw, and burn flesh, veins, bones, and marrow" (Luther, 1971, pp. 268–274, 292). Much later German nationalists exploited Luther's hatred of Jews, and the Nazis reissued his diatribes as endorsements of their anti-Semitic ideology. In 1938 a Lutheran bishop published excerpts from the 1543 treatise and extolled Hitler and Martin Luther as Germany's "greatest anti-Semites" (Perry and Schweitzer, 2002, p. 83).

Voltaire was perhaps the most celebrated exemplar of the distinctly secular eighteenth-century Enlightenment philosophy (and its secular anti-Semitism). In his attacks on Christianity, he condemned Judaism as its source and denounced both religions as "superstitions." In his view Jews were avaricious and detestable. He informed his readers: "Still, we ought not to burn them." His instruction to Jews: "Renounce your sacred books" (Levy, 1991, pp. 41, 46). Thus, would Jews cease to be Jewish; Voltaire had proposed a form of cultural annihilation comparable to medieval forced conversions and later European nationalists' demands for Jewish assimilation. The nineteenth and twentieth centuries were periods of intense nationalism in Europe, and the particular forms of nationalism that had evolved fostered perceptions of Jews as foreigners and aliens who could never become true nationals.

As theories of "race" came to the fore, perceptions of Jews as inassimilable strangers and dangerous polluters grew in intensity, as racialist phobias and biological pseudoscience became conflated with hypernationalism. As distinct from Christian teaching, according to which baptism effaced Jewishness, "racial science" decreed that race (and separateness) could never be changed. The composer Richard Wagner expressed his own paranoia in this regard in his adoption of the neologism *Verjudung* ("Jewification," similar to Marx's "Judaizing"), which denoted the danger of "infection" by the Jewish spirit of German culture, German institutions, or the German soul. In his essay "Jewry in Music," he pronounced his verdict of annihilation in the form of a command: "Go under."

Adherents to the political anti-Semitism that emerged in Europe in the nineteenth century strove to curtail Jewish emancipation, to expel Jews from cities, towns, and neighborhoods on racialist grounds, and to require their conversion and assimilation—and, more generally, to combat political and social liberalism as a manifestation of Jewish influence. On the continent the ideologies and platforms of virtually all major political parties were tainted with anti-Semitism. For many years the members of left-leaning, socialist, and/or social democratic parties were prone to making an equation between Jews and "the capitalist enemy" (in the manner of Marx), and were slow to rid themselves of this bias. A pioneer of political anti-Semitism was the Lutheran pastor and German court preacher Adolf Stoecker, who founded the German Christian Social Workers' Party in 1878. In 1892 Germany's Conservative Party absorbed several anti-Semitic splinter parties by pledging itself "to battle against the manifold aggressive, decomposing, and arrogant Jewish influence" (Weiss, 1996, p. 116). In France in the 1890s and after, the Marquis de Morés and Édouard Drumont led the Anti-Semitic League, which elected a dozen or so deputies to the National Assembly and which was clamorously active during the Dreyfus Affair (centered on the 1895 treason conviction of Army captain Alfred Dreyfus, who was innocent but not acquitted until 1906—and whose accusers were motivated by anti-Semitism). In the late nineteenth century the governments of Romania and Russia were overtly anti-Semitic, and encouraged pogroms against their Jewish citizens. Although a short-lived organization called the International Anti-Jewish Congress held yearly conventions in the 1880s, a most negative portent was the coming to power of the Austrian Christian Social Party (the lone example of an anti-Semitic party winning elections and holding power over a span of several years). The party's leader was the demagogue Karl Lueger, who became mayor of Vienna in 1897 after gaining a clear majority in Vienna's city council elections; his anti-Semitic tactics and demagoguery were greatly admired by the young Hitler. In between the two world wars Europe's fascist parties (except Italy's before 1938), flourishing under the aegis of Adolf Hitler prior to and during World War II, were virulently anti-Semitic.

A noteworthy example of anti-Semitic hate literature is the Russian document *The Protocols of the Learned Elders of Zion*. Written in France in the 1890s at the behest of the Russian secret police, it sought to justify the tsarist regime's anti-Semitic policies and pogroms. Intended for the credulous, and recapitulating anti-Semitic mythology almost in its entirety, it is supposed to be the secret minutes of a conclave of Jewish elders meeting in the ancient Jewish cemetery of Prague and plotting to take over the world. To implement their plan, the Jewish conspirators employ every imaginable weapon. Acting like the evil god Vishnu with a hundred hands, they undermine religion; hatch revolutions (the French Revolution and all since); manipulate stock exchanges; ignite class warfare; set off economic crises; maneuver sources of power (judicial, parliamentary, the press, institutions of learning, and money—"over which [Jews] alone dispose"); dominate workers through socialism and trade unionism; promote alcoholism, prostitution, pornography, and humanism in order to befog the minds of non-Jews; and create anti-Semitism in order to bind the Jewish masses to their cause until the plot is fulfilled. Then the elders will eliminate all religions except Judaism and thus "shall determine the destiny of the earth." First published in Russia in 1903, the *Protocols* won the enthusiasm of Tsar Nicholas II at the time of the catastrophic Russo-Japanese war—a time when Russia was quaking with impending revolution. Nicholas blamed these catastrophes on the Jews, and joined with Kaiser Wilhelm II of Germany in signing the treaty of Björkö, in which they pledged to form a "continental league" to combat revolution and international Jewry. The next year Nicholas signed a secret agreement (which reads like the *Protocols* and was probably based on it). Nicholas envisioned a great alliance whereby combined powers would engage in "an active joint struggle" to avert "the impending general European revolution" and fight the "Judaeo-Masonic" conspiracy. No part of this plan materialized, but it is illustrative of how unconcealed anti-Semitic ideology could enter into the highest-level diplomatic exchanges and provide a basis for treaties and policy aims. Deploying the *Protocols* in the public arena for the first time, Nicholas exhibited the credulousness of most European minds and the willingness of those minds to believe bizarre myths about Jews, as well as his belief in the utility of anti-Semitism (as Hitler believed) in furthering the aims of foreign and domestic policy. Since 1918 the *Protocols* has remained a staple of anti-Semitic discourse worldwide—millions of copies in many languages continue to circulate in print and on the Internet—despite the fact that it was demonstrated to be a forgery and nothing other than paranoiac hate literature as early as 1921.

Hitler was immersed in the mental universe of the *Protocols* all his life. His speech before the German Parliament in January 1939 contained a prophecy: "If international Jewry . . . succeeds in plunging the peoples into another war, then the end result will not be the Bolshevization of the earth and the consequent victory of Jewry but the annihilation of the Jewish race in Europe" (Cohn, 1967, p. 190). His belief that Jews were menaces and a highly organized race of evil-doing supermen was a modern, secularized version of the medieval idea of the demonized Jew. He spoke in medieval accents when he declared: "The struggle for world domination will be fought between . . . Germans and Jews. We are God's people. Two worlds face one another: the men of God and the men of Satan." And: "The Jews . . . invented capitalism . . . an invention of genius, of the devil's own ingenuity" (Rauschning, 1940, p. 237–238). There is nothing original about Hitler's version of anti-Semitism except his political genius in promoting anti-Semitism. He feared Jews—they were "the people of Satan," people who conspired to enslave and rule the world through communism, socialism, capitalism, internationalism, democracy, pacifism, biological degeneration, and disarmament. In his eyes Jews were "culture-destroyers"; they embodied everything he feared, hated, and sought to destroy. Other high-ranking Nazis shared these views—an amalgamation of medieval, racial, and *Protocols* anti-Semitism. The demagogue Julius Streicher, publisher and editor of anti-Semitic newspapers and part of Hitler's inner circle, promulgated an anti-Semitism that was as much medieval and religious as it was modern and secular. He scoured specious texts such as J. A. Eisenmenger's *Judaism Uncovered* (1700), Theodor Fritsch's *Handbook of the Jewish Question* (1887), novels such as Gustav Freytag's *Debit and Credit* (1885), and forgeries such as *Protocols* (1903) as part of an attempt to prove (in his own words): "This satanic race really has no right to exist." He was perhaps the first Nazi to invoke and articulate the concept of a Final Solution, saying in a 1925 speech before a mass audience in Nuremberg: "[F]or thousands of years the Jew has been destroying the nations . . . [W]e can annihilate the Jews." Since the 1870s there had been many calls for the destruction of the Jews; until 1914 these calls had been more pervasive and vehement in France, Russia, Romania, and Austria-Hungary than in Germany, but it was Hitler's Germany that carried out what many in Europe believed to be history's mandate and science's dictate.

Contemporary Anti-Semitism

Holocaust denial is a new from of anti-Semitism, but one that hinges on age-old motifs. Another new form of anti-Semitism is that sponsored by the Nation of Islam (an anti-white supremacist movement founded in the United States in the 1930s) and its leader, Louis Farrakhan, who has employed a wide range of anti-Semitic propaganda weapons in his demagoguery. The Nation of Islam fabricated the myth that Jews originated and dominated the 400-year Atlantic slave trade, profited immensely from it, owned disproportionate numbers of slaves, and were the cruelest of slave masters. *The Secret Relationship between Blacks and Jews* (1991), with authorship attributed to the Historical Research Department of the Nation of Islam, purports to provide the evidence of Jewish culpability for "the black Holocaust." That some Jews were involved in slave trading is well-known, but their participation, when compared to that of many Muslims, Catholics, Protestants, freed blacks, and black Africans, was minuscule.

Since the 2001 terrorist attacks on the United States, there has been a media focus on Muslim anti-Semitism and on radical Islam or Islamism (distinct from Islam and characterized by deep antagonism toward non-Muslims and the West). Muslim hostility toward Jews has its origins in the Qur'an, in which several passages express hostility toward Jews and in which Jews are described, variously, as "the worst enemies of the Muslims," a "cursed people," "slayers of prophets," "perverters of scriptures," and "apes and swine" (Suras 2:73, 88; Qu'ran 5:60–65, 78–82). Jews lived for many centuries in Muslim lands as *dhimmis* (Jews or Christians living in Islamic countries as protected minorities), and were subject to governments that sought to degrade and humiliate them; there were pogroms and periodic forced conversions. Since the 1870s there has filtered into the Middle East the entire range of Christian/European/German/Nazi anti-Semitic beliefs, the principal intermediaries having been Christians who live in the Middle East. The principal literary sources for anti-Semitic ideologues living in the Middle East have been the *Protocols*, Hitler's *Mein Kampf*, Henry Ford's *International Jew,* and the churchman August Rohling's *Talmudic Jew* (which attempts to prove the myth of ritual murder; translated into Arabic by 1899). Some scholars have argued that Muslim anti-Semitism is essentially a byproduct of the Israeli-Palestinian struggle, and that when that struggle is concluded, Islamism will evaporate. Yet Islamism, which predates the founding of Israel by twenty years, contains a hatred so vile that Muslim anti-Semitism is unlikely to wane anytime soon. The "moderate" ex-president of Iran, Hashemi Rafsanjani, in a speech of December 2001 at Teheran University, urged Muslim countries to develop nuclear weapons: "It is theologically imperative. . . . Nothing will remain after one atom bomb is dropped on Israel. . . . The founding . . . of Israel is the worst event in all history." Islamism shares with mid-twentieth-century fascism ideological fanaticism, genocidal anti-Semitism, and terrorists' indifference to human life.

For half a century after 1945 anti-Semitism was disreputable in Western countries. Since 2000, however, exacerbations of the Israeli-Palestinian conflict have generated a resurgence of anti-Semitism in Europe. The Israeli military campaign in the West Bank in the spring of 2000, a response to suicide bombings in Israel, provoked a rash of anti-Semitic incidents in several parts of the world: Cemeteries were vandalized, Holocaust memorials defaced, synagogues torched, buses carrying Jewish children stoned, Jews beaten. Muslim fanatics were the main perpetrators of the violence. In protests against the military campaign, whether coming from the political right or the left, Israel was attacked as a belligerent, uncompromising, imperialistic state. At rallies and demonstrations in many cities of Europe, crowds shouted: "Death to the Jews!" Britain's *Guardian* proclaimed: "Israel has no right to exist." The Vatican's *L'Osservatore Romano* attacked Israeli "aggression that turns into extermination." A 2003 European Union poll reported that a majority of citizens believe that Israel is the greatest threat to world peace.

Communism and fascism have gone, but anti-Semitism remains and is again becoming socially and intellectually acceptable—although it often rears its head under the cover of anti-Zionism, or anticolonialism, or antiglobalism. In reportage on Israel, the European news media are biased to varying degrees against that nation and its people. They continue to rely on anti-Semitic stereotypes. These media, in their analyses of Israeli government actions (which include no comparisons to other bloody conflicts), dredge up ancient anti-Semitic *topoi,* a shared body of half-conscious, half-remembered motifs. All the European countries, despite some constructive efforts, remain shackled to age-old anti-Semitism. Almost all the European countries are burdened with the heritage of the Holocaust and a reluctance or unwillingness to face up to their collaborations with the Nazi regime. This is most clearly visible in France, where memory of the Vichy regime lingers on and recent anti-Semitic violence has been the worst.

SEE ALSO Catholic Church; Ethnic Groups; Hate Speech; Heydrich, Reinhard; Himmler, Heinrich; Hitler, Adolf; Holocaust; Inquisition

BIBLIOGRAPHY

Berman, Paul (2003). *Terror and Liberalism*. New York: Norton.

Cohn, Norman (1967). *Warrant for Genocide: The Myth of the Jewish World Conspiracy and the Protocols of the Elders of Zion*. New York: Harper & Row.

Curtis, Michael, ed. (1986). *Antisemitism in the Contemporary World*. London: Westview Press.

Flannery, Edward H. (1965). *The Anguish of the Jews: Twenty-Three Centuries of Antisemitism.* New York: Paulist Press, 1985.

Foxman, Abraham H. (2003). *Never Again? The Threat of the New Anti-Semitism.* New York: HarperCollins.

Katz, Jacob (1980). *From Prejudice to Destruction.* Cambridge, Mass.: Harvard University Press.

Langmuir, Gavin I. (1990). *History, Religion, and Antisemitism.* Berkeley: University of California Press.

Levy, Richard S., ed. (1991). *Antisemitism in the Modern World: An Anthology of Texts.* Toronto: D. C. Heath.

Luther, Martin. *On the Jews and their Lies,* vol. 47, ed. Franklin Sherman. Philadelphia: Fortress Press.

Perry, Marvin, and Frederick M. Schweitzer, eds. (1994). *Jewish-Christian Encounters over the Centuries: Symbiosis, Prejudice, Holocaust, Dialogue.* New York: Peter Lang.

Perry, Marvin, and Frederick M. Schweitzer (2002). *Antisemitism: Myth and Hate from Antiquity to the Present.* New York: Palgrave Macmillan.

Poliakov, Léon (1974). *The Aryan Myth: A History of Racist and Nationalist Ideas in Europe,* tran. Edmund Howard. New York: Basic Books.

Poliakov, Léon (1974–1985). *The History of Anti-Semitism.* 4 volumes. New York: Vanguard Press.

Rauschning, Herman (1940). *Voice of Destruction.* New York: Putnam's.

Rose, Paul Lawrence (1990). *German Question/Jewish Question: Revolutionary Antisemitism from Kant to Wagner.* Princeton, N.J.: Princeton University Press.

Trachtenberg, Joshua (1943). *The Devil and the Jews.* New Haven, Conn.: Yale University Press.

Wistrich, Robert (1991). *Antisemitism: The Longest Hatred.* New York: Pantheon Books.

Weiss, John (1996). *Ideology of Death: Why the Holocaust Happened in Germany.* Chicago: Ivan R. Dee.

Wolf, Lucien (1919). *Notes on the Diplomatic History of the Jewish Question.* London: Spottiswoode & Ballantyne.

Frederick M. Schweitzer

Apartheid

Apartheid, the Afrikaans word meaning separateness (literally, apartness), was coined during the 1930s by the Stellenbosch-based South African Bureau of Race Relations (SABRA) to denote the separate development of the races living in South Africa. It has subsequently come to be associated with the racial policy implemented by the National Party government of the Republic of South Africa during its rule in the period 1948 to 1994.

Concept of Apartheid

Perhaps the best synopsis of the policy of apartheid is to be found in the United Nations International Convention Against Apartheid in Sport of 1985:

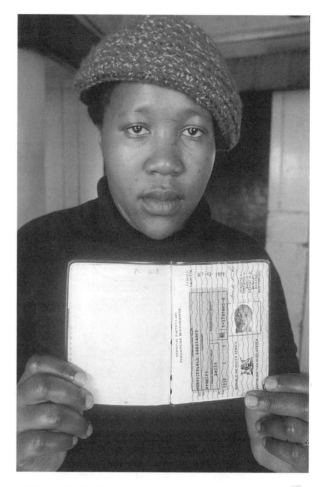

Under apartheid, black Africans had to have special permission to enter and remain within urban areas and were required to carry "interior passports" at all times. In this photo, a woman holds up the so-called dom pass. [ALAIN NOGUES/CORBIS SYGMA]

The expression "apartheid" shall mean a system of institutionalized racial segregation and discrimination for the purpose of establishing and maintaining domination by one racial group of persons over another racial group of persons and systematically oppressing them, such as pursued by South Africa.

Apartheid, as advocated and practiced in South Africa, was structured on three distinct bases:

- *separation* of sections of the population along racial lines (segregation);

- *exploitation* of persons of color for the benefit of a privileged white elite (discrimination); and

- *repression* of opposition to the policy seeking to implement the above (persecution);

Apartheid does not denote the racist sentiments and practices that linger in the hearts and minds and in the personal conduct of many people living in plural

When high-school students in Soweto demonstrated on June 16, 1976, against a government ruling that had named Afrikaans as the language of education, the police responded with tear gas and gunfire. Over the course of several days, the demonstrators were joined by angry Soweto residents who set fire to buildings. The government sent in more police and quelled the escalating violenceat the cost of several hundred black African lives. In this photo, demonstrators come up against soldiers and police. [**HULTON-DEUTSCH COLLECTION/ CORBIS**]

societies, but is confined to institutionalized racism—that is, racial discrimination imposed by the laws and enforced practices of a political community. Race is here the essential criterion of enforced differentiations in the social, economic, political, and legal structures within an apartheid society. Racial distinctions constitute a particular modality of social reality and must not be confused with those distinctions founded on national, ethnic, or religious grounds. A racial group is conventionally defined on the basis of "the hereditary physical traits often identified with a geographical region, irrespective of linguistic, cultural, national, or religious factors" (*Prosecutor v. Jean-Paul Akayesu*, Case No. ICTR-96-4-T, para. 513 [September 2, 1998]).

Historical Perspective

Of all pluralist communities, South African society is perhaps the most diverse. Segregation of the races has been part of the social structure of South Africa ever since the Dutch East India Company, seeking to establish an outpost that would provide the company's fleet with fresh produce while en route to its trading partners in the Far East, took possession of the Cape of Good Hope in 1652. In 1911 Lord Henry de Villiers (Chief Justice of the Union of South Africa) described the racial pattern within the social structures of the country in compelling terms:

As a matter of public history we know that the first civilized legislators in South Africa came from Holland and regarded the aboriginal natives of the country as belonging to an inferior race, whom the Dutch, as Europeans, were entitled to rule over, and whom they refused to admit to social or political equality. We know also that, while slavery existed, the slaves were blacks and that their descendants, who form a large proportion of the coloured races of South Africa, were never admitted to social equality with the so-called whites. Believing, as these whites did, that intimacy with the black or yellow races would lower the whites without raising the supposed inferior races in the scale of civilization, they condemned intermarriage or illicit intercourse between persons of the two races. . . . These pre-possessions, or, as many might term them, these prejudices, have never died out, and are not less deeply rooted at the present day among the Europeans in South Africa, whether of Dutch or English or French descent (*Moller v. Keimoes School Committee & Another,* 1911 A.D. 635, at 643).

During the mid-twentieth century two sets of circumstances were decisive in prompting the National Party of Dr. D. F. Malan (1874–1959) to select racial segregation as the political mandate it would seek from the predominantly white electorate in the forthcoming elections of 1948. General J. C. Smuts (1870–1950), Prime Minister in the United Party government, was a man of mature years, and it was rumored that he favored Jan Hofmeyr (1894–1948), an outspoken liberal known for his nonracist ideology, to become his successor. The second decisive circumstance derived from South Africa's resolve to incorporate South West Africa (Namibia) into the Union of South Africa. South West Africa was placed under South African control in 1919 as part of the mandate system of the League of Nations, and Smuts in 1946 informed the United Nations (UN) of his government's intention to bring the mandate to fruition by transforming South West Africa into a province of the Union. Within the UN India raised objections to this incorporation of South West Africa into South Africa based on South Africa's treatment of Indians and other people of color, under the prevailing laws of the country. The UN offered its good offices to secure a solution to the South African–Indian dispute. In order to gain the support of India for the incorporation of South West Africa, Smuts proposed to extend political rights to South African Indians (the Indians had been disfranchised by the British colonial authorities in 1896). The National Party therefore decided to exploit "the racial scare" as its election strategy and proposed apartheid as a feasible solution to the problem of race relations. To everyone's surprise, it won the 1948 elections, albeit by a narrow margin, and apartheid thus became the official policy of the newly elected government.

Implementation of the Apartheid Policy

In terms of the Population Registration Act of 1950, all South Africans were classified for legal purposes according to the racial categories of white, black, and colored, with the Indian population group constituting a distinct section within the colored community. The racist laws of apartheid South Africa never attempted to define race as such and applied different criteria so as to be able to allocate racial classifications to all its citizens. Being "white" depended on a person's appearance and general acceptance by other members of the white community, whereas being Native/Bantu/black/African depended on a person's belonging to an aboriginal race or tribe of Africa. A "colored person" was defined as someone who was neither white nor black. It is perhaps interesting to note that although Chinese persons were classified as colored, Japanese persons were classified as white.

Based on this classification, apartheid was particularly noted for the totalitarian interference of the state in the private sphere of peoples' day-to-day lives. In apartheid South Africa, the state prescribed, with race as the prime criterion, whom one could marry, where one could reside and own property, what schools and universities one would be allowed to attend, and which jobs were reserved for one. The state dictated to sports clubs whom they could admit as members, and against whom they were permitted to compete. The sick had to be conveyed in racially exclusive ambulances, could receive blood transfusions only from donors of their own racial groups, and could qualify for treatment only in racially defined hospitals. The state even regulated, with race as the prime criterion, who would be allowed to attend church services in some regions, and where one could be buried.

The implementation of segregation in pre-1994 South Africa was designed to secure the political dominance and the economic and social privileges of the white population group. When the Union of South Africa was established in 1910, political rights in the provinces of Natal, the Orange Free State, and Transvaal were almost exclusively confined to whites. Indians had been disfranchised by the British colonial authorities of Natal in 1896, but those who at that time were already registered voters retained their right to vote for life. When the 1948 elections were held, only two Indians were still on the voter rolls. In the Cape of Good Hope, Africans and coloreds had (qualified) franchise rights, and those rights were afforded entrenched protection in the Constitution of the Union of South Africa; however, Cape of Good Hope African voters were disfranchised by the legislature under United Party rule in 1936, and Cape coloreds were deprived of their voting rights by the legislature under National Party rule in 1956. The South African Constitution of 1983 reinstated political rights for coloreds and Indians, but did so on a racist basis. It created segregated legislative chambers for the colored and Indian population groups, elected by the colored and Indian voters (respectively). The constitution was carefully crafted to afford dominance to the white chamber of Parliament in all matters, including those over which the coloreds and Indians supposedly had primary jurisdiction. Because of the constitution's racist design and the political dominance of whites it upheld, only small percentages of the colored and Indian communities exercised their newly acquired political rights.

As prescribed by the Bantu Land Act of 1913 and the Bantu Trust and Land Act of 1936, portions of South Africa were demarcated for exclusive occupation by Africans. Although the African communities comprised approximately 80 percent of the South African population, the land allocated for their occupation constituted no more than 13 percent of the territory comprising the South African state. In 1951 the South African government appointed a commission instructed by the governor-general "to conduct an exhaustive enquiry into and report on a comprehensive scheme for the rehabilitation of the Native Areas with a view to developing within them a social structure in keeping with the culture of the Native, and based on effective socioeconomic planning." The commission, chaired by Frederick Tomlinson, professor of Agricultural Economy at the University of Pretoria, submitted its report to Parliament in 1954. It among other things calculated the costs of extending the African homelands and of creating economic incentives that might prompt Africans to remain in, return to, or settle in their respective ethnic homelands. The government rejected those recommendations as being too costly and instead embarked on a policy of separating the races by means of legal coercion. H. F. Verwoerd (1901–1966), commonly regarded as the architect of apartheid, transformed the Tomlinson recommendations into a policy that promoted the political "independence" of the black homelands, demarcated on an ethnic (tribal) basis. In due course eight black self-governing territories were proclaimed: Bophuthatswana, Ciskei, Lebowa, Transkei, Venda, Gazankulu, Qwaqwa, and kwaZulu. Four opted for independence: Transkei in 1976, Bophuthatswana in 1977, Venda in 1979, and Ciskei in 1981. In the UN, South Africa claimed that the policy of separate development was congruent with the right of its population groups to self-determination as proclaimed in international law. Not so, responded the UN: The right to self-determination presupposes participation of the people in the legislative and executive structures of the state that determine their fate, whereas the independence of the black homelands was imposed on the peoples of those territories without their consent. Further, the black homelands were never accepted as independent political entities by the international community of states.

The movement of Africans to and within the main employment centers of the country was regulated by the Blacks (Urban Areas) Consolidation Act of 1945. Africans required special permission to enter and to remain within an urban area and had to carry a reference book at all times that would indicate their right to be at a particular place within the country—the so-called dom pass (*dom* meaning stupid). As part of the Group Areas Act of 1966 (which consolidated earlier similar legislation), separate residential areas were designated for occupation by whites, Africans, coloreds, and Indians within the towns and cities of the country.

The South African exploitation of the African population group, and to a lesser extent the Indian and colored communities, was carried out in such a way as to preserve the privileged political, economic, and social status of white South Africans in a racially defined elitist oligarchy. Educational facilities, residential areas, and job opportunities reserved for persons of color were considerably inferior to those at the disposal of the dominant white community—both in quality and in degree of availability. The group areas reserved for occupation by members of a particular population groups other than whites were almost invariably far removed from the business districts and employment centers, and the residential areas reserved for Africans and coloreds were conspicuously inferior, as far as locality, infrastructure, and aesthetic appeal were concerned. When Verwoerd, Minister of Bantu Affairs at the time, introduced in Parliament the Bantu Education Act of 1953, he sought to justify the inferior education of blacks by invoking the system of job reservation imposed on the black community as part of the apartheid system:

> The school must equip the Bantu to meet the demands which the economic life . . . will impose on him. . . . What is the use of teaching a Bantu child mathematics when he cannot use it in practice? . . . Education must train and teach people in accordance with their opportunities in life.

Apartheid Enforcement and Apartheid Resistance

These racist accessories of a totalitarian and discriminatory regime did not reflect the "spirit" of those persons who were the victims of their practical impact, and who were a vast majority of the South African nation. Nor were these accessories supported by the moral convictions of the people, or of a majority of the people, or for that matter of any distinct section of the people. The state consequently had to resort to profoundly repressive measures—restrictions placed on freedom of speech and of assembly; erosions of the rule of law and the due process of law; and indifference to the prohibition of torture and of other forms of cruel, inhuman, or degrading treatment or punishment. Included in the security laws of South Africa were those that could be used to authorize the banning of organizations and the subjection of opponents of the system to severe restrictions that could practically amount to house arrest. As part of the Terrorism Act of 1967, persons suspected of having information that pertained to subversive activities could be detained indefinitely. The grounds of their detention could not be contested in a court of law.

Resistance toward the repressive and discriminatory laws of South Africa has a long history. Within the Indian community, Mohandas Karamchand (Mahatma) Gandhi (1869–1948), who lived in South Africa from 1893 to 1915, initiated a strategy of passive resistance in the furtherance of *satyagraha* (from *satya,* meaning truth, and *graha,* meaning grasping—that is, grasping the truth, or holding onto truth). The African National Congress (ANC) was founded on December 16, 1913, as an organization designed to mobilize the political aspirations of black South Africans. ANC-sponsored anti-apartheid protests were initially entirely peaceful. In 1961 the ANC president, Chief Albert Luthuli (1899–1967), became the first South African to be awarded the Nobel Peace Prize. The Pan-Africanist Congress (PAC) was formed in 1959 to promote a blacks-only policy for Africa and a more aggressive agenda of resistance. When the ANC and PAC were banned in 1960, many of their leaders and followers went into exile and embarked on an armed struggle against the South African apartheid regime. *Umkonto we Sizwe* (Spear of the Nation) was established as the armed wing of the ANC, and *Poqo* as that of the PAC. The African Resistance Movement (ARM), which at times engaged in acts of sabotage, consisted mainly of white intellectuals.

As aggressive opposition to apartheid escalated, the South African government enacted draconian security laws, and engaged in clandestine strategies that amounted to state-sponsored terror violence, in order to retain its illegitimate regime. The Truth and Reconciliation Commission that was established pursuant to the National Unity and Reconciliation Act 34 of 1995 to facilitate the political transition of South Africa to a democracy, and whose committee on human rights violations (chaired by Archbishop Desmond Tutu) was charged with investigating "gross violations of human rights" from 1961 to 1994, recorded the sordid details of overt and clandestine methods used by the security forces to suppress resistance under the headings of bannings and banishments; judicial executions; "public

order" policing; torture and deaths in custody; and killing, including many instances of abduction, interrogation and killing, ambushes, the killing of persons in the process of arrest or while pointing out arms, entrapment killing, killing of weak links within the security forces itself; and attempted killings, arson, and sabotage.

Violent confrontation between the South African authorities and groups of persons protesting the atrocities inherent in the policy of apartheid became part of everyday life in the black townships. On March 21, 1960, PAC organized a demonstration in Sharpeville, a black township sixty-five kilometers south of Johannesburg and just north of Vereeniging, in the Transvaal province, protesting the laws that required black citizens to carry passes at all times. The police opened fire on the demonstrators, killing sixty-nine people. On the twenty-fifth anniversary of Sharpeville (March 21, 1985), the police opened fire on a funeral procession in Uitenhage, killing nineteen people (the mourners had come from the black township of Llanga to bury comrades who had been killed while protesting unemployment). States of emergency were proclaimed by the government in 1985 and 1986.

Perhaps the turning point of white rule in South Africa was the Soweto riots of June 16, 1976, when black students staged massive demonstrations protesting the inferior system of Bantu education and a government decision to impose Afrikaans as the language of instruction in the teaching of at least one subject in black schools. The ensuing unrest swept through the entire country, had far-reaching repercussions, and prompted large numbers of young blacks of school-going age to leave the country and join the liberation forces in exile.

Among those who lost their lives in the struggle against apartheid was Black Consciousness activist Steve Biko (1946–1977), who died on September 11, 1977, of head injuries inflicted by those who held him captive while he was in police custody. Among the religious leaders subjected to profound humiliation because of their opposition to apartheid was Desmond Tutu (1931–), Anglican Archbishop of Cape Town and Secretary-General of the South African Council of Churches during the years 1979 to 1984. Perhaps the most celebrated person among the many incarcerated was Rolihlahla (Nelson) Mandela (1918–), who, after serving more than twenty-seven years of a sentence of life imprisonment (October 1962–February 1990), was released to become the first president of South Africa after its radical transition in 1994 to become a nonracist state.

The trials and tribulations of Mandela commenced with the infamous treason trial (1958–1961), at which he was among 156 political activists brought to trial following their arrest in December 1956. The accused were all members of a number of organizations comprising the Congress Alliance (the ANC, the Congress of Democrats, the South African Indian Congress, the South African Colored People's Organization, and the South African Congress of Trade Unions). In March 1961 a special criminal court in a unanimous decision acquitted all the accused, holding that the state had failed to prove that the Congress Alliance and its member organizations sought to overthrow the government by violent means or to replace it with a communist regime.

In July 1963 the police raided a house in Rivonia, a suburb on the outskirts of Johannesburg, and, using the newly enacted ninety-days detention law, detained seventeen persons found on the premises. Eleven of those detainees were subsequently brought to trial on charges of sabotage. The Transvaal Provincial Division of the Supreme Court (as it was then called) initially quashed the indictment owing to the state's failure to provide further particulars of the charges. The accused were then rearrested under the ninety-days detention law and thereafter charged with planning a violent revolution and with various acts of sabotage. On June 11, 1964, eight of the accused, including the leaders of *Umkonto we Sizwe* (Mandela, Walter Sisulu, and Govan Mbeki) were convicted and sentenced to life imprisonment. (At the time, Mandela was already serving a five-year sentence for incitement and leaving the country unlawfully, for both of which he was convicted in 1962.)

International Responses to Apartheid

Apartheid was being widely condemned throughout the world. In 1961 South Africa, on becoming a republic, was forced to withdraw its application to remain a member of the British Commonwealth because of apartheid (when the Union of South Africa acquired full sovereignty in 1931, it was constituted as a monarchy, with the king or queen of England its head of state). During the 1960s and 1970s many countries imposed economic, cultural, and sports events–related boycotts of South Africa. South Africa was forced out of the Olympic Games after the 1960 games and was formally expelled from the Olympic Games movement in 1970. Following the death of Biko, and in consequence of banning orders issued by the government against persons and organizations expected to be most vocal in their condemnation of his untimely death, the UN Security Council adopted Resolution 418 (1977). The Resolution proclaimed that the situation in South Africa constituted a threat to international peace and security and imposed a mandatory arms boycott against South Africa as a means of counteracting that threat.

It is not uncommon for persons who (quite rightly) condemn criminal conduct perpetrated by state action to (unjustifiably) attach a label to that action that would give it as bad a name as one could possibly conceive, even in instances in which the conduct or condition being condemned does not fit the essential elements of the label. The UN International Convention on the Suppression and Punishment of the Crime of Apartheid of 1973 contained in its circumscription of apartheid a passage that suggested that, as part of that policy, the South African government inflicted living conditions on one or more racial groups calculated to cause their physical destruction in whole or in part, which—if it were true—would amount to an act of genocide. In 1985 the UN established an ad hoc Working Group of Experts to investigate violations of human rights in South Africa. In its report, the working group proclaimed that apartheid was a special instance of genocide. However, such is not the case. Apartheid was not devised with special intent to destroy any racial group, in whole or in part, as required by the definition of genocide. Attempts to bring a state policy within the confines of practices that are likely to have an exceptionally strong emotional appeal (thereby distorting concepts that underlie that policy and those practices) may add emotional vigor to one's condemnation of the policy, but ought not to be taken as having literal meaning, for law enforcement purposes, by those charged with the administration of justice.

Apartheid does constitute a crime against humanity under customary international law. The 1965 UN Resolution, Implementation of the Declaration on the Granting of Independence to Colonial Countries and Peoples, thus proclaimed that "the practice of *apartheid* as well as all forms of racial discrimination threaten international peace and security and constitute a crime against humanity." Inhumane acts resulting from the policy of apartheid were also treated as a crime against humanity in the UN Convention of the Non-Applicability of Statutory Limitations to War Crimes and Crimes against Humanity (1968) and in the International Convention on the Suppression and Punishment of the Crime of Apartheid (1973). The latter convention listed a number of acts that would constitute the crime of apartheid.

> If committed for the purpose of establishing and maintaining domination by one racial group of persons over any other racial group of persons and systematically oppressing them, namely:

(a) Denial to a member or members of a racial group or groups of the right to life and liberty of person:

    i. By murder of members of a racial group or groups;

    ii. By the infliction upon the members of a racial group or groups of serious bodily or mental harm, by the infringement of their freedom or dignity, or by subjecting them to torture or to cruel, inhuman, or degrading treatment or punishment;

    iii. By arbitrary arrest and illegal imprisonment of members of a racial group or groups.

(b) Deliberate imposition on a racial group or groups of living conditions calculated to cause its or their physical destruction in whole or in part;

(c) Any legislative measures or other measures calculated to prevent a racial group or groups from participation in the political, social, economic, and cultural life of the country and the deliberate creation of conditions preventing the full development of such a group or groups, in particular by denying to members of a racial group or groups basic human rights and freedoms, including the right to work, the right to form recognized trade unions, the right to education, the right to leave and to return to their country, the right to a nationality, the right to freedom of movement and residence, the right to freedom of opinion and expression, and the right to freedom of peaceful assembly and association;

(d) Any measures, including legislative measures, designed to divide the population along racial lines by the creation of separate reserves and ghettos for the members of a racial group or groups, the prohibition of mixed marriages among members of various racial groups, the expropriation of landed property belonging to a racial group or groups or to members thereof;

(e) Exploitation of the labour of the members of a racial group or groups, in particular by submitting them to forced labour;

(f) Persecution of organizations and persons, by depriving them of fundamental rights and freedoms, because they oppose apartheid.

The task of delineating these "inhuman acts" as personal conduct that could attract criminal prosecution was initially delegated to the ad hoc Working Group of Experts under M. Cherif Bassiouni of De Paul University in Chicago. The draft statute (1980), prepared by the working group rather clumsily, confined criminal liability to "grave breaches of Article II of the Convention for the Prevention and Punishment of the Crime of Apartheid, namely, murder; torture; cruel, inhuman or degrading treatment or punishment; arbitrary arrest and detention." These breaches do not apply to the segregation and discrimination components of apartheid as such, but seemingly only to (some of) the repressive measures designed to counteract opposition to the policy of apartheid.

Apartheid is identified in the Statute of the International Criminal Court, adopted by the Rome Conference of Diplomatic Plenipotentiaries in 1998, as a crime against humanity. "The crime of apartheid" is defined in the statute as denoting:

> . . . inhumane acts of a character similar to those referred to in paragraph (1), committed in the context of an institutionalized regime of systematic oppression and domination by one racial group over any other racial group or groups and committed with the intention of maintaining that regime.

Paragraph (1) referred to in the statute's definition of apartheid makes mention of murder, extermination, enslavement, deportation or the forcible transfer of populations, imprisonment or other severe deprivation of physical liberty, torture, rape or other (specified) forms of sexual violence, persecution, and enforced disappearances. But, again, the essentials of apartheid are not encapsulated in the definition to be applied in order to found the jurisdiction of the International Criminal Court (ICC) the definition is confined to (state security) action that might be resorted to for purposes of maintaining the regime of segregation and racial discrimination. That is, the repression component of the apartheid system becomes the only prosecutable offense. The act of segregation and discrimination will not come within the jurisdiction of the ICC if a state system of racial segregation and discrimination can be maintained without the state's resorting to murder, extermination, enslavement, deportation or the forcible transfer of populations, imprisonment or other severe deprivation of physical liberty, torture, rape or other forms of sexual violence, persecution, or enforced disappearances.

The Demise of Apartheid

Over a two-decade period commencing in 1971, the South African government gradually abandoned some of its practices associated with apartheid, making "concessions" in that year in regard to segregation in sports, and then extending those concessions to the areas of trade union rights for Africans, political rights for coloreds and Indians, and the like. The final demise of apartheid in South Africa was formally announced by President de Klerk (1936–) in his opening-of-Parliament address of February 2, 1990. This initiative culminated in the radical transformation of South Africa, as defined in the Republic of South Africa Constitution Act of 1996, into "an open and democratic society based on human dignity, equality, and freedom."

Comparable Systems of Racial Discrimination

Racial discrimination has of course been practiced in many countries other than South Africa. In the United States, for example, the stratagems of racism were sanctioned in the 1895 judgment of the U.S. Supreme Court in the case of *Plessy v. Ferguson,* which decided that separate facilities for blacks and whites were constitutionally permissible provided the segregated facilities were equal. The U.S. doctrine of separate-but-equal received its death knell in the 1953 judgment of *Brown v. Board of Education,* wherein it was decided that "in the field of public education the doctrine of 'separate but equal' has no place." The principle enunciated in that case was subsequently extended to apply to all forms of segregation in public places.

In 1965, when Great Britain was contemplating the granting of independence to Southern Rhodesia under a one-person-one-vote dispensation, the minority white government of Prime Minister Ian Smith declared the country independent under a constitution that reserved political rights for whites only. The UN condemned the unilateral declaration of independence, and in Security Council Resolution 221 (1966) decided that the situation in Rhodesia constituted a threat to the peace. Security Council Resolution 232 (1966) imposed mandatory economic sanctions against Rhodesia with a view to bringing the racist regime of Smith to a speedy end. Following a bloody war between the Smith regime and internal resistance movements (with South Africa affording military support to the government forces of Rhodesia), the Lancaster House Agreement was concluded between Great Britain and the main political factions of Rhodesia. It culminated in the establishment of Zimbabwe as an independent state in 1980.

Although racial discrimination as practiced in the United States, Rhodesia, and elsewhere resembled apartheid, the policy as it existed in South Africa contained unique elements that one does not find in the history of any other country. It is perhaps fair to conclude that apartheid, as a special instance of racial discrimination that entails the exploitation of persons of a disadvantaged racial group for the purpose of retaining the privileged status of another, and requiring particularly stringent enforcement measure for its preservation, such as it existed in South Africa, has never found its equal in any other country.

SEE ALSO Convention on Apartheid; Mandela, Nelson; Namibia (German South West Africa and South West Africa); South Africa

BIBLIOGRAPHY

Alexander, Neville (2002). *An Ordinary Country: Issues in the Transition from Apartheid to Democracy in South Africa.* Pietermaritzburg, South Africa: University of Natal Press.

Ames, Frances (2002). *Mothering in an Apartheid Society.* Cape Town, South Africa: Department of Psychiatry and Mental Health, University of Cape Town.

Ballinger, Margaret (1969). *From Union to Apartheid.* Cape Town, South Africa: Juta & Company.

Brookes, Edgar H. (1968). *Apartheid: A Documentary Study of Modern South Africa.* London: Routledge & Kegan Paul.

Broun, Kenneth S. (2000). *Black Lawyers, White Courts: The Soul of South African Law.* Athens: Ohio University Press.

Carter, Gwendolen M. (1958). *The Politics of Inequality: South Africa since 1948.* New York: Praeger.

De Klerk, Willem (1991). *Die Man en Sy Tyd: F. W. de Klerk.* Cape Town, South Africa: Tafelberg Uitgewers.

Dugard, John (1978). *Human Rights and the South African Legal Order.* Princeton, N.J.: Princeton University Press.

Forsyth, C. F., and J. E. Schiller, eds. (1979). "Human Rights: The Cape Town Conference." In *Proceedings of the First International Conference on Human Rights in South Africa, January 22–26, 1979.* Cape Town, South Africa: Juta & Company.

Gready, Paul (2003). *Writing as Resistance: Life Stories of Imprisonment, Exile, and Homecoming from Apartheid South Africa.* Lanham, Md.: Lexington Books.

Heyns, Christof, Johann van der Westhuizen, and Tshidi Mayimele-Hashatse, eds. (1994). *Discrimination and the Law in South Africa: A Multi-Cultural Inquiry into De Facto Racial Discrimination.* Pretoria, South Africa: Centre for Human Rights.

Hoernlé, R. F. Alfred (1945). *Race and Reason, Being Mainly a Selection of Contributions to the Race Problem in South Africa.* Johannesburg, South Africa: Witwatersrand University.

Mathews, Anthony (1978). *The Darker Reaches of Government.* Cape Town, South Africa: Juta & Company.

Mathews, Anthony (1986). *Freedom, State Security and the Rule of Law: Dilemmas of the Apartheid Society.* Cape Town, South Africa: Juta & Company.

Mbeki, Govan (1964). *South Africa: The Peasant's Revolt.* Harmondsworth, U.K.: Penguin Books.

Moller v. Keimoes School Committee & Another. A.D. 635.

Prosecutor v. Jean-Paul Akayesu, Case No. ICTR-96-4-T. (September 2, 1998).

Punnell, MacDonald (1994). *Long Walk to Freedom: The Autobiography of Nelson Mandela.* Randburg, South Africa: MacDonald Punnell (Pty.) Ltd.

Randall, Peter, ed. (1972). *Law, Justice and Society: Report of the Legal Commission of the Study Project on Christianity in Apartheid Society.* Johannesburg, South Africa: South African Council of Churches.

Saunders, Christopher (1994). *Illustrated History of South Africa: The Real Story,* 3rd edition. Cape Town, South Africa: Readers Digest.

Serfontein, J. H. P. (1982). *Apartheid, Change and the NG Kerk.* Emmarentia, South Africa: Taurus.

Shimoni, Gideon (2003). *Community and Conscience: The Jews in Apartheid South Africa.* Hanover, N.H.: University Press of New England.

Uledi-Kamanga, Brighton J. (2002). *Cracks in the Wall: Nadine Godimer's Fiction and the Irony of Apartheid.* Trenton, N.J.: African World Press.

Van der Vyver, J. D. (1975). *Die Beskerming van Menseregte in Suid-Afrika.* Cape Town, South Africa: Juta & Company.

Yousaf, Nahem (2001). *Apartheid Narratives.* Amsterdam, Netherlands: Rodopi.

Johan D. van der Vyver

Arawak Indians see Taino (Arawak) Indians.

Arbour, Louise

[FEBRUARY 10, 1947–]
Chief Prosecutor for the International Criminal Tribunal for the Former Yugoslavia and the International Criminal Tribunal for Rwanda, 1996–1999

Louise Arbour was joint Chief Prosecutor for the International Criminal Tribunal for the Former Yugoslavia (ICTY) and the International Criminal Tribunal for Rwanda (ICTR) from October 1996 to September 1999. She was the second person to hold the position at the ad hoc tribunals, having replaced South African judge Richard Goldstone. The highlights of her term of office include the first indictment in history of a sitting head of state—Yugoslavian president Slobodan Milosevic—and the first prosecution of sexual assault and rape as crimes against humanity.

Background

Arbour was born in Montreal, Quebec, Canada. She studied law at the Université de Montreal, where, in the 1960s, she first encountered Quebec nationalism—an idea that appealed to her at that time, but one that she

revisited more critically in the late 1990s, during her investigations into the consequences of nationalism in the former Yugoslavia.

After being called to the Ontario bar, Arbour worked principally in Toronto, as a professor and then as associate dean at Osgoode Hall Law School. She was appointed to the Supreme Court of Ontario in 1987 and was then assigned to the appeals division of the same court in 1990.

Finta Decision

On the appeals bench, Arbour was one of three judges on a five-member panel who voted to uphold the controversial acquittal of Imre Finta, a former captain in the Hungarian gendarmerie who was charged with deporting 8,617 Jews to their deaths during World War II. The majority of the appeals court judges had upheld several rulings of the trial judge, among them the judge's decision to allow the trial jury to consider Finta's defense that he had been following orders.

The Finta trial was a landmark case in the history of Canada's response to Nazi war criminals who were residing in the country. Legal scholars and human rights activists argued that the courts had interpreted Canadian law too narrowly in acquitting Finta, and were setting such a high standard for conviction that it would become virtually impossible for anyone to successfully prosecute war criminals in the country.

Arbour's Controversial Appointment

Justice Goldstone recommended Arbour as his replacement at the international tribunals (ICTY and ICTR). Arbour's appointment was then guided through the United Nations (UN) Security Council approval process by Madeleine Albright, the U.S. ambassador to the UN, who favored the appointment of a woman and argued that a Canadian citizen with few affiliations would help to prevent politicization of the tribunals. But there was much international opposition to Arbour's candidacy, owing to her lack of profile in the field of international human rights and because of her role in the Finta decision. Tribunal activists were also alarmed that, in 1987, Arbour had been counsel in a successful legal challenge to Canada's rape shield law. The rape shield law had been introduced in Canada in order to prevent defense lawyers from challenging the credibility of a rape victim by presenting allegations on the subject of her past sexual history as evidence. Given the numbers of rape cases that were expected to come to the fore at the tribunals, Arbour was considered by some to be the wrong choice for Chief Prosecutor. But Arbour's consistent record of defending the rights of the accused appealed to members of the Security Council who wor-

Arbour announces the indictment of Yugoslav president Slobodan Milosevic for atrocities in Kosovo, at the international war crimes tribunal in The Hague, Netherlands. [AP/WIDE WORLD PHOTOS]

ried that the ad hoc tribunals were already balanced against the accused, specifically the Serbian suspects. The Arbour appointment was approved by the Security Council on February 29, 1996.

International Criminal Tribunal for the Former Yugoslavia

As Chief Prosecutor at the ICTY, Arbour faced a formidable obstacle. Goldstone had issued fifty-two indictments and had issued arrest warrants for the accused, including two wartime military and civilian leaders of the Bosnian Serbs, Ratko Mladic and Radovan Karadzic. But Goldstone was stymied by the absence of a practical way to serve the warrants. As part of the Dayton Agreement, the national leaders of Serbia, Croatia, and Bosnia had agreed to surrender anyone in their jurisdictions who had been indicted by the ICTY, but their commitment proved to be inadequate, particularly in the case of the Serbs, who considered the tribunal to be biased against them. The members of the North Atlantic Treaty Organisation (NATO)–led peacekeeping force that patrolled Bosnia and Herzegovina were also under an obligation to arrest suspects—if they found

them and if the arrests did not endanger their mission. Despite ample evidence that some of the "most-wanted" suspects, whose names and photographs had been distributed to NATO troops along with the warrants, were freely crossing checkpoints, the peacekeepers had not detained anyone prior to Arbour's appointment.

Arbour continued to issue indictments, but unlike Goldstone, who had made the indictments open and very public (in part to put pressure on the recalcitrant NATO leadership), Arbour took the privilege of sealing many of her indictments—allowing NATO soldiers the advantage of covert action. This, along with the added political incentive that was provided by the general awareness that the United States and the United Kingdom were monitoring changes in government in Bosnia and Herzegovina, allowed NATO forces to apprehend two men who were under secret indictment—Slavko Dokmanovic and Milan Kovacevic.

Dokmanovic had been the Serbian president of the municipality of Vukovar during the siege of that municipality in 1991. During the siege hundreds of civilians were killed and thousands driven from their homes by Serbian forces. Dokmanovic was arrested by NATO soldiers in eastern Slavonia and charged with crimes against humanity.

On July 10, 1997, British Special Air Service troops under NATO carried out a far more daring commando-style capture and arrest of Kovacevic, the commander of the Omarska camp in Prijedor where Muslim and Croat men had been tortured and murdered by Bosnian Serbs during the Bosnian war. For the first time, NATO had made an arrest in the former Yugoslavia without permission from the local authorities.

Both men would die in the UN compound at the Scheveningen Prison in the Hague before their cases could be concluded, but their captures represented a breakthrough in the "non-arrests" issue at the courts. More arrests, and many surrenders, followed. The UN was compelled to add two more courtrooms to the one that existed in order to accommodate the cases. A number of "big fish" (as the indictees were called in tribunal jargon) joined the ranks of the detained, but the two most-wanted Serbian suspects, Karadzic and Mladic, remained at large.

International Criminal Tribunal for Rwanda

The ICTR was a far more troubled organization than the ICTY. Arbour first visited the Rwandan tribunal in the fall of 1996 at its headquarters in Arusha, Tanzania. She came up against an organization in which the telephones and computers did not function, and in which the most common complaint was of a lack of basic sup-

encyclopedia of GENOCIDE *and* CRIMES AGAINST HUMANITY

plies. The ICTR had its own financial officers, but Arbour reported to the UN in New York that funds had been misspent and accounting procedures were nonexistent. (She had been warned of the possibility of gross corruption.)

A UN audit of the tribunal in the winter of 1997 averred that "not a single administrative area functioned effectively." Karl Paschke, the UN auditor, reported that much of the ICTR staff was incompetent and that funds had been misused, but he stopped short of making charges of criminal activities.

Arbour was also perturbed by the location of the Office of the Prosecutor (OTP). It was based, not in Arusha, but in Kigali, the capital of Rwanda. In Kigali, Arbour discovered that Paul Kagame, the president of Rwanda (who had been the commander of the Rwandan Patriotic Front [RPF] during the Rwandan civil war), would not allow her to investigate any criminal charges against the RPF. She reported to the UN that Kagame threatened to shut down the OTP whenever he was dissatisfied with its proceedings. Although the overwhelming bulk of the indictments of the ICTR were of the perpetrators of the Rwandan genocide and their slaughter of Tutsis, Arbour uncovered much evidence of atrocities committed by members of the RPF against Hutus. But the UN insisted that the OTP remain in Kigali (where the prosecution of former members of the RPF would be most difficult).

Despite privation and all manner of adversity, Arbour had the kinds of successes while presiding at the Rwandan tribunal that had evaded her at the tribunal for the former Yugoslavia. She was able to persuade Kenyan authorities to participate in an arrest sweep of suspected perpetrators of genocide who were hiding in Nairobi, Kenya. On July 18, 1997, ICTR prosecutors, along with Kenyan police, apprehended many who had been the heart of the Hutu leadership, including Jean Kambanda, the former Prime Minister of Rwanda; Hassan Ngeze, a newspaper editor accused of having incited genocide via his paper's inflammatory prose; and Pauline Nyiramasuhuko, the Rwandan government's Minister of Family and Women's Affairs—and the first female to be arrested by either tribunal. Also in custody was Theoneste Bagosora, the military leader of the *génocidaires,* who had been arrested under Goldstone and transferred to Arusha in January 1997. Guided by Arbour, the ICTR was able to gain custody of many of the highest-level planners of the genocide (who were, as well, former members of the Rwandan government).

The tribunal also set a number of precedents. On May 1, 1998, Kambanda became the first person in history to plead guilty to the crime of genocide. Despite allegations of irregularities in the evidence-gathering process, the conviction of Kambanda was considered a major breakthrough for the ICTR. Later, Jean-Paul Akayesu, the former mayor of the Rwandan village of Taba, became the first person ever to be convicted of rape and of inciting others to commit rape as crimes against humanity. Akayesu had directed a "rape camp" in his village, where women were sexually assaulted and killed. Arbour admitted in interviews that rape cases were not, for her, a priority, given the gravity of the genocide charges. She also stated that rape, as a crime against humanity, is extremely difficult to prosecute.

Arbour was celebrated for her successes at the tribunal, but she, herself, was dubious about the ongoing feasibility of the ICTR. She maintained that the tribunal was "a by-product of shame"—the collective shame of the international community—and an attempt by that community to make amends for its failure to intervene to stop the genocide. In an interview she stated that "there were too many fault lines" at the ICTR, principally consisting of the limitations that had been placed on her field investigations in Rwanda.

Slobodan Milosevic
In the fall of 1998, Slobodan Milosevic accelerated his ongoing military campaign against Albanians living in the Serbian province of Kosovo, where the Kosovo Liberation Army (KLA) was resisting his efforts at "ethnic cleansing" in the Albanian regions of the province. In January 1999 a massacre of forty-five people in the village of Racak caused an international outcry. Only nine of those murdered were KLA fighters. Up until that point the ICTY had been investigating crimes that were several years old. For the first time Arbour turned the focus of her prosecutors to war crimes happening in real time.

Two days after the Racak massacre Arbour was refused entry into Kosovo from Macedonia. She warned Milosevic that she was monitoring events in Kosovo for possible war crimes prosecutions. In February 1999 the United States opened talks with Milosevic in Rambouillet, France, where diplomats from many countries attempted to find a solution to the Kosovo conflict before it became another Balkan war. Milosevic refused to withdraw his troops. On March 24, 1999, thirteen NATO member countries began to bomb Yugoslavia, without permission from the UN or even much consultation with the Security Council.

Seven hundred thousand Albanians fled the country, under attack from Serbian forces who had accelerated the ethnic cleansing campaign, and from NATO bombing. Arbour gathered evidence from the field wherever possible and attempted to persuade foreign governments to give her the documents she needed to issue war crimes indictments. She did not tell these governments, until after the indictment was signed, that she was pursuing Slobodan Milosevic. World leaders were wary of any such indictment. It would mean that they would no longer be able to negotiate with Milosevic, something that seemed increasingly necessary as the NATO campaign stretched into weeks.

On May 22, 1999, Arbour signed an indictment against Milosevic for crimes against humanity, and against four other sitting members of the Yugoslavian government: Milan Milutinovic, Nikola Sainovic, Dragoljub Ojdanic, and Vlajko Stojiljkovic. The indictments were for the murder of 340 people in 16 villages, including Racak.

The following day, an ICTY judge also signed the indictment. Arbour offered the UN and NATO three days in which to state any reasons why the indictment should not be issued. The United States and the United Kingdom accepted the indictment, albeit with some reservations. France and Russia rejected it. Nonetheless, the indictment proceeded, making Milosevic the first sitting head of state to be charged with war crimes.

Milosevic became an international pariah overnight. Madeleine Albright, the U.S. Secretary of State and a major supporter of the ICTY at the UN, announced, "[W]e are not negotiating," when asked about the chances for a negotiated settlement to the NATO war. Three weeks after his indictment, Milosevic agreed to a ceasefire.

Just shortly after the Milosevic indictment, Arbour was asked by her government to return to Ottawa and join the bench of the Supreme Court of Canada, a position she accepted. On February 25, 2004, the UN General Assembly "approved by acclamation" the appointment of Arbour as the new UN High Commissioner for Human Rights. She replaced Brazil's Sergio Vieira de Mello, who, along with twenty-one others, was killed in a terrorist attack in Baghdad in August 2003.

SEE ALSO Del Ponte, Carla; Goldstone, Richard; International Criminal Tribunal for Rwanda; International Criminal Tribunal for the Former Yugoslavia

BIBLIOGRAPHY

Abella, Irving, and Harold Troper (1982). *None Is Too Many: Canada and the Jews of Europe, 1933–1948.* Toronto: Lester and Orpen Dennys Limited.

Cushman, Thomas, and Stjepan Mestrovic, eds. (1996). *This Time We Knew: Western Responses to Genocide in Bosnia.* New York: New York University Press.

Holbrooke, Richard (1998). *To End a War.* New York: Random House.

Morris, Virginia, and Michael P. Scharf (1995). *An Insider's Guide to the International Criminal Tribunal for the Former Yugoslavia.* Irving-on-Hudson, N.Y.: Transnational Publishers.

Off, Carol (2000). *The Lion, the Fox and the Eagle: A Story of Generals and Justice in Yugoslavia and Rwanda.* Toronto: Random House Canada.

Taylor, Telford (1992). *The Anatomy of the Nuremberg Trials.* Boston: Little, Brown.

Carol Off

Archaeology

Archaeology is the study of the remains of past cultures, both historic and prehistoric. In archaeological publications the term *genocide* is rarely encountered. Although it is often possible to determine the cause of death when skeletal remains are well preserved, the reasons why earlier peoples committed violent acts are not always clear. Consequently, interpretations of such actions are difficult and frequently controversial.

Damage to Skeletal Remains

Skeletal material provides the most useful source of information about acts of violence. An examination of skeletal remains first attempts to rule out reasons other than violence that could account for bone breakage. Interpretation of bone damage uses many of the same techniques as modern forensics, and comparative data from studies of present-day skeletal traumas aid archaeologists in determining the cause of death.

The skeletal material that archaeologists uncover may have been damaged postmortem (after death). Taphonomy is the study of the processes that modify bone between the death of the individual and the recovery of their remains. Taphonomic analyses help researchers determine whether an individual's bones were modified in any way postmortem due to, for example, crushing by shifting rocks, human intrusions into the grave, or trampling by large animals prior to burial. Postmortem and perimortem (around the time of death) bone fractures can usually be distinguished from those that occurred before death (antemortem), because antemortem fractures will exhibit evidence of healing. Differentiating perimortem injuries from postmortem damage is more challenging, particularly when the skeleton is not well preserved. In general, a perimortem break has the following features: (1) The bone at the break is of a similar color to that surrounding it, rather than lighter in color; (2) fracture lines radiate away from the break and; (3) the break angles acutely from the surface of the bone inward, rather than at a right angle.

Cause of Death

After deciding that the death of an individual was probably caused by some sort of perimortem trauma, archaeologists then attempt to determine how that injury was sustained. Fragments of weapons embedded within the skeleton provide the clearest evidence of violence against an individual. However, such findings are rare in the archaeological record. In most cases violence must be inferred based on the shape, size, location, and severity of skeletal injuries. For example, cranial (head) traumas caused by axes yield elongated and thin fractures. Most fatal skeletal injuries are located on the cranium, although when injuries result from projectile weapons, such as spears or arrows, they are more likely to be found on the postcranial (below the head) skeleton. Many deadly projectile wounds do not cause damage to the skeleton and, thus, there is no clear evidence of them in the archaeological record. Sometimes cause of death may be inferred when a projectile weapon is found at the burial site. The location of traumas can also provide information about the cause of death. For example, if most cranial injuries are on the frontal (forehead) bone, it is likely that they resulted from face-to-face combat.

In a case where archaeologists are investigating a site to determine if genocide was committed, multiple individuals are generally available for study. Consequently, researchers can search for patterns in the skeletal evidence to help them determine cause of death. If a series of skeletons exhibit injuries of a consistent size and shape, this provides evidence for a similar weapon having been used to kill all the individuals.

Demographic Profiles

A demographic profile of skeletal remains provides archaeologists with the age and sex of the individuals interred. The pelvis is the most accurate source of information; about 95 percent are correctly identified in determining the sex of an individual, with females having a broader, less muscular pelvis than males. When a pelvis is not found among the remains, features of the cranium (e.g., chin shape and muscle markings on the cranium) can be used with some confidence, to within 80 percent accuracy, to ascertain sex. DNA techniques have recently been developed that may provide a more useful means of establishing the sex of fragmentary specimens. An individual's age at death can be established using dental eruption patterns, the amount of wear on the teeth, and the extent to which sutures on the skull have closed. Social status can sometimes be inferred based on how the individual was buried. Burial context may also help in determining ethnic group affiliation, along with DNA data and skeletal information. Analyses of these data may demonstrate that a group

was overrepresented at the site (e.g., women or a particular social class) and, consequently, may have been the target of violence. However, the possibility must be considered that the individuals interred at the site were the only ones who were present when the group was massacred or that only they were afforded the privilege of burial.

Genocide in the Archaeological Record

In cases of possible genocide archaeologists must initially attempt to determine whether the population died at approximately the same time. When individuals are interred in the same grave, careful examination of the burial may show whether there was later intrusion at the site, resulting in the remains being buried together. When there is no mass grave, dating methods (e.g., carbon dating) may help resolve whether the death of the population occurred around the same time.

The motivation behind the violent actions of past cultures is difficult to determine. Historical records and ethnographic studies may be useful in suggesting the motives underlying violent behavior. However, these accounts of past events can be colored by cultural biases. Another possible source of data is the method of burial. For example, if individuals are found to be randomly positioned in a grave without the artifacts that usually accompany burials, this suggests that their bodies were dumped without thought to funerary rites. This evidence can be used in combination with data derived from skeletal material and demographic profiles to determine whether genocide was committed.

As of 2003 Ofnet and Schletz remain two of the earliest sites in the archaeological record with credible evidence of genocide. At the Schletz site in Austria, dating back approximately 7,500 years, 67 individuals with multiple traumas were recovered from the bottom of a trench. The demographic profile of the group showed that there were no young females among the dead, suggesting that they had been forcibly abducted by the attacking group. Based on these data, along with the finding that the remains from the site were unburied for many months, researchers argued that genocide was the most likely motive behind the deaths of the population. At the Ofnet site in Bavaria, dating to the same historical period as Schletz, archaeologists located two mass graves containing thirty-eight individuals who were probably buried during a single episode. Many of the skulls of these individuals have cranial fractures of a similar size and shape, indicating a similar type of weapon was used to kill the victims. A detailed analysis of the damage indicated that the injuries occurred perimortem. The demographic profile showed that most, but not all, of the individuals in the grave were females and subadults. David W. Frayer suggests that this indicates that most of the men were absent at the time of the massacre.

Archaeological material other than skeletal remains has occasionally been used to suggest that genocide took place at a particular site. Scorched layers of earth or burned structures may offer indirect evidence of genocide. A study of Roman camps in northern Britain provides an example of how nonskeletal data may be used as evidence of genocide. The placement and size of these camps, formed during the reign of the emperor Severus from 208 to 211 CE, indicated to researchers that the Romans attempted to control or destroy all agricultural products and, consequently, starve the local Caledonian population.

Human sacrifice and cannibalism are other methods by which particular groups have been singled out for violence in past cultures. Victims of human sacrifice can sometimes be identified by the artifacts buried with them, the location of their burial, or the nature of their wounds. To recognize when individuals were victims of cannibalism, remains are examined for evidence of postmortem corpse manipulation. Cut marks on bones may signify that the person was defleshed. The skull or postcranial bones may be broken in ways that indicate removal of the brain or extraction of bone marrow. The context in which the bones were found is also important. For example, discovering human material mixed with animal bones in trash heaps is strong evidence of cannibalism.

One of the more controversial cases of possible cannibalism involves the site of Cowboy Wash near the Anasazi dwellings at Mesa Verde in Colorado. Archeologists working at the site recovered human bones that exhibited signs of cannibalism. The evidence found at this site included: cut marks on bones; bones found in trash dumps; bones that were not discolored or pitted, indicating that flesh was removed prior to burial; a breakage pattern on bones, suggesting extraction of bone marrow; and color on some bones, indicating that they were cooked. Some have argued that this evidence does not necessarily imply cannibalism occurred because burial rituals may involve similar postmortem corpse manipulation. However, if the human bones were handled in the same manner as those of large animals, it seems logical to suggest that the humans were eaten. Archeologists have found that cut marks on the bones were similar in style and location to those made on bones of large game animals. Moreover, analysis of a coprolite (fossilized feces) from the site provided clear evidence that human flesh had been consumed there. Based on other data derived from the site, Brian R. Billman suggests that a population moved in and terrorized local communities by killing and eating their victims.

SEE ALSO Ancient World; Forensics

BIBLIOGRAPHY

Cox, Margaret, and Simon Mays (2000). *Human Osteology in Archaeology and Forensic Science.* London: Greenwich Medical Media.

Dold, Catherine (1998). "American Cannibal." *Discover* 19:64–69.

Frayer, David W. (1997). "Ofnet: Evidence for a Mesolithic Massacre." In *Troubled Times: Violence and Warfare in the Past,* ed. D. L. Martin and D. W. Frayer. Australia: Gordon and Breach.

Jurmain, Robert (1999). *Stories from the Skeleton: Behavioral Reconstruction in Human Osteology.* Australia: Gordon and Breach.

Marlar, Richard A., Banks L. Leonard, Brian R. Billman, Patricia M. Lambert, and Jennifer E. Marlar (2000). "Biochemical Evidence of Cannibalism at a Prehistoric Puebloan Site in Southwestern Colorado." *Nature* 407:74–78.

Martin, Colin (1995). "To Scotland Then They Came Burning." *British Archaeology* 6:12–14.

Martin, Debra L., and David W. Frayer, eds. (1997). *Troubled Times: Violence and Warfare in the Past.* Australia: Gordon and Breach.

Stone, Anne C., G. Milner, Svante Paabo, and Mark Stoneking (1996). "Sex Determination of Ancient Human Skeletons Using DNA." *American Journal of Physical Anthropology* 99:231–238.

Teschler-Nicola, M., F. Gerold, M. Bujatti-Narbeshuber, T. Prohaska, C. Latkoczy, G. Stingeder, and M. Watkins (1999). "Evidence of Genocide 7000 BP—Neolithic Paradigm and Geo-climatic Reality." *Colligium Antropologicum* 23(2):437–450.

Walker, Phillip L. (2001). "A Bioarchaeological Perspective on the History of Violence." *Annual Review of Anthropology* 30:573–596.

White, Tim D. (2000). *Human Osteology,* 2nd edition. San Diego, Calif.: Academic Press.

Willey, Patrick S. (1990). *Prehistoric Warfare on the Great Plains: Skeletal Analysis of the Crow Creek Massacre Victims.* New York: Garland Publishing.

Chris A. Robinson

Architecture

Architectural spaces designed for Holocaust museums and occasionally those to commemorate genocide have been instrumental in altering the design of the museum building, especially in advanced industrial societies where expense for museum space is an affordable luxury. Museums in the Western Hemisphere and Europe have changed from structures built simply to contain artifacts, art, and conceptual works to become memory forms in their own right. Because of the huge displacement of peoples in the twentieth century, which included many artists and architects who fled authoritarian regimes, the builders of museums to the crimes of genocidal regimes have felt the need to make the museum building itself a memorial space to the event.

Standing in contrast to the modern museum space, often built in a location where genocide itself did not occur, are the places of destruction themselves. The Auschwitz extermination camp, for example, became the Auschwitz State Museum. The same transition to a museum has occurred in other camps, such as Prison S-21 in Cambodia, which became the Tuol Sleng Museum of Genocide. The architecture of the killing sites often has a strong impact on museums built as memory spaces.

One of the best and first examples of the intersection of memory and the present was James Ingo Freed's design for the United States Holocaust Memorial Museum in Washington, D.C., Freed, himself a refugee from Germany, visited Auschwitz in October 1986. The powerful effect of the physical space of the camp and its industrial motif convinced him that the future United States Holocaust Memorial Museum could not be a traditional museum structure. It was this careful analysis of the Auschwitz camp that led Freed to develop plans for the Washington museum that would embody symbolic aspects of the concentration camp in the memory space. This included the well-known symbols of watchtowers, glass, and barbed wire, but also the red brick of Auschwitz I, and the use of steel and other elements. However, he did not wish these symbols to be overstated so as to create a narrative with a single conclusion.

The completed United States Holocaust Museum space has been called "a place of disorientation" (Linenthal, 1995, p. 89). Cantilevered walkways, exposed steel beams, doorways that recall the centers of annihilation at Auschwitz, all help to create a memory of the site of genocide. Within this is the space for the historical narrative. However, the exhibition space at the United States Holocaust Museum does not provide for a continuous chronological narrative of the history of the Holocaust. The story is broken up by the use of modern technologies to provide fragments of events and personal stories, plus an installation tower of photographs, sometimes called the "Tower of Life," designed by Yaffa Eliach to commemorate the memory of her hometown, Eishyshok.

Daniel Libeskind's extension of the Berlin Jewish Museum, renamed the Berlin Jewish Museum addition,

Interior of the U.S. Holocaust Memorial Museum, Washington, D.C., completed in 1993. The work of architect James Ingo Freed, the monumental structure is a space of exceptional impact, conveying grief, terror, and history in its innovative design. [KELLY-MOONEY PHOTOGRAPHY/CORBIS]

has prompted an important discourse about the role of architectural space in the twenty-first century. Libeskind's concept is based on a theory of absence, the absence of the Jews from Germany, which he converted into architectural "voids." The architect himself called the greater project "Between the Lines" because of what he perceived to be a complex web of connections and disconnections between Germans and Jews as a result of the Holocaust (Libeskind, 1992, p. 86). Technically, the result was not a Holocaust Museum, rather a Jewish Museum. But because the building was situated in a unified Berlin after the fall of both Nazism and communism, many refer to it as the Berlin Holocaust Museum.

From an aerial perspective Libeskind's design for the Berlin Museum appears to be a fractured Star of David. The inspiration for this came from Walter Benjamin's *One Way Street,* which provided a motif for the zig-zag and underground crisscrossing design that leaves the visitor disoriented. Within the space of the museum, the dominant features are the voids. These are empty spaces that literally go nowhere. Libeskind has written that in this space, "the invisible, the void, makes itself apparent as such" (1992, p. 87). In addition, the architect described the main spaces as:

> There are three underground "roads" which programmatically have three separate stories. The first and longest "road", leads to the main stair, to the continuation of Berlin's history, to the exhibition spaces in the Jewish Museum. The second road leads outdoors to the E.T.A. Hoffmann Garden and represents the exile and emigration of Jews from Germany. The third axis leads to the dead end—the Holocaust Void (Libeskind, 1992).

The zinc-clad Berlin Museum with its irregular windows was completed in 1998 and opened to visitors without any displays within. More than 400,000 people came to see the empty spaces until the museum's formal opening with a permanent exhibition on Jewish life in Germany on September 9, 1991.

For many years the Imperial War Museum in London has maintained a special museum space dedicated to the liberation of the concentration camp at Bergen-Belsen by British forces in April 1945. In deciding to establish a large and permanent exhibition about the Holocaust, which opened in June 2000, the curators focused on the role of the British as bystanders to genocide as well as liberators, and stressed the necessity of including original artifacts, something which the design for the United States Holocaust Museum chose to play down. Considerations about the building itself were moot, as the structure is a well-established museum that focuses on British military history. The result is perhaps a return to the essence of what a museum is supposed to be—more about what is displayed and how it is displayed, than the architectural features of the structure. Like other Holocaust museums, the Imperial War Museum exhibition features the extensive testimony of Holocaust survivors, in this case, those living in England.

Other Holocaust museums exist in North America (e.g., Vancouver, Los Angeles, Houston, El Paso, Detroit, St. Petersburg, Florida, and New York) that are smaller in size and often situated in remodeled, already existing structures. In some cases the museum buildings are new and overemphasize some of the symbols of the Holocaust, such as chimneys and barbed wire. Displays in these museums are remarkably similar and justified for their pedagogical role in local communities. Few Holocaust museums have concern for art except as a document from the victims.

In Milwaukee, Wisconsin, a museum has opened that chronicles the history of slavery; it is called America's Black Holocaust Museum. A museum initiated by the Armenian-American community is being developed in Washington, D.C.; located in a former bank building, it will serve as an educational center, library, and museum documenting the Armenian genocide of 1915 through 1922. In Rwanda the places of destruction have become both memorials and museums, while construction of a museum dedicated to telling the story of that country's genocide began in 2002 in Kigali. In Quebec architect Moshe Safdie designed the Museum of Civilization, which is "is committed to fostering in all Canadians a sense of their common identity and their shared past. At the same time, it hopes to promote understanding between the various cultural groups that are part of Canadian society" (Museum of Civilization website). However, this museum has started to discuss the possibility of including displays on the Holocaust, Armenian genocide, Cambodia, Rwanda, and genocide in the Ukraine. During 2002 a discussion and debate commenced in Ottawa, Canada, about the construction of a Canadian Museum of Genocide.

SEE ALSO Documentation; Memorials and Monuments; Memory

BIBLIOGRAPHY
Dannatt, Adrian (1995). *United States Holocaust Memorial Museum.* London: Phaidon.
Libeskind, Daniel (1992). *Countersign.* New York: Rizzoli.
Linenthal, Edward T. (1995). *Preserving Memory.* New York: Viking Press.
Young, James (2000). *At Memory's Edge: After-Images of the Holocaust in Contemporary Art and Architecture.* New Haven, Conn.: Yale University Press.

Stephen C. Feinstein

Arendt, Hannah
[OCTOBER 14, 1906–DECEMBER 4, 1975]
German political philosopher

A political theorist with a gift for grand historical generalization, Hannah Arendt focused contemporary thought, particularly in scholarly circles, on the experience of exile and in her most influential book, *The Origins of Totalitarianism,* confronted the worst horrors of European tyranny.

Arendt was born in Hanover, Germany, and died in New York City. She studied theology and philosophy at the University of Marburg, and then philosophy at the University of Heidelberg. As the National Socialists drew closer to power, she became a political activist and, beginning in 1933, helped German Zionists publicize the plight of the victims of Nazism. Arrested by the Gestapo, Arendt managed to escape to Paris, remaining there for the rest of the decade and aiding in the efforts to relocate German Jewish children to Palestine. In 1940 she married an ex-communist, Heinrich Blücher, but they were separated and interned in southern France along with other stateless Germans when the Wehrmacht invaded later that year. Arendt was sent to Gurs, a camp from which she escaped. She soon joined her husband, and the two reached the United States in May 1941. While living in New York during World War II, Arendt wrote *The Origins of Totalitarianism* (1951), published the year she secured U.S. citizenship.

No book was more reverberant in tracing the steps toward the distinctive twentieth-century tyrannies of Hitler and Stalin, or in measuring how grievously wounded Western civilization had become. Arendt demonstrated how embedded racism had become in central and western Europe by the end of the nineteenth century; by then imperialist governments had also succeeded in experimenting with the possibilities of cruelty and mass murder. The third section of her book exposed the operations of "radical evil," with the superfluity of life in the death camps marking an important discontinuity in the very notion of what it meant to be human. Totalitarianism put into practice what had only been imagined in medieval images of hell.

During the cold war of the 1950s, *The Origins of Totalitarianism* made its author an intellectual celebrity, but also engendered much doubt about her theories. Arendt's insistence on drawing parallels between Nazi Germany and Stalinist Russia—given their obvious ideological conflicts and the savage warfare between the two countries from 1941 to 1945—was especially criticized. When Arendt wrote her book, Soviet sources were barely available, nor could the author read Russian. But her emphasis on the plight of the Jews amid the decline of Enlightenment ideals of human rights, and her assertion that the Third Reich was conducting two wars—one against the Allies, the other against the Jewish people—have become commonplace in the historiography of the Holocaust. More than any other scholar, Arendt made meaningful the idea of totalitarianism as a novel form of autocracy, pushing to unprecedented extremes murderous fantasies of domination and revenge.

Arendt's most controversial work was published in 1963: *Eichmann in Jerusalem: A Report on the Banality of Evil*. This political and psychological portrait of the SS lieutenant-colonel who had directed the transportation of Jews to their deaths emphasized duty rather than fanaticism as his motivation. She believed that Israel had rightly hanged him in 1962. But Arendt's view that Eichmann had committed evil not because of a sadistic will to do so, or deep-rooted anti-Semitism, but because of thoughtlessness (a failure to think through what he was doing), led Arendt back in the final phase of her career to the formal philosophical approaches that had marked its beginning.

SEE ALSO Eichmann Trials; Evil, Banality of Radical; Psychology of Perpetrators

BIBLIOGRAPHY

Arendt, Hannah (1951). *The Origins of Totalitarianism.* New York: Harcourt, Brace.

Arendt, Hannah (1963). *Eichmann in Jerusalem: A Report on the Banality of Evil.* New York: Viking.

Whitfield, Stephen J. (1980). *Into the Dark: Hannah Arendt and Totalitarianism.* Philadelphia: Temple University Press.

Young-Bruehl, Elisabeth (1982). *Hannah Arendt: For Love of the World.* New Haven, Conn.: Yale University Press.

Stephen J. Whitfield

Argentina

In the 1970s political violence in Argentina resulted in thousands of deaths, prolonged arbitrary arrest, unfair trials, pervasive torture, and cruel, inhuman, and degrading treatment. The most salient feature of repression by the military dictatorship was the practice of disappearances: At least 15,000 (and possibly up to 25,000) were abducted by security forces, their detention unacknowledged. They were sent to one of 250 secret detention centers, where they were interrogated under barbaric methods of torture. Ultimately, the vast majority of the *desaparecidos* were systematically, but secretly, murdered. Their bodies were disposed of in clandestine gravesites or dumped from airplanes into the ocean. More than twenty-five years later at least 12,000 victims remain unaccounted for, despite efforts by their relatives and civil society to establish their fate and the whereabouts of their remains.

The repressive campaign was launched in March 1976, as the commanders-in-chief of Argentina's three armed forces ousted President Isabel Peron and proclaimed a de facto regime designed to eliminate once and for all what they called the Marxist subversive threat. Serious human rights violations had begun at least eighteen months earlier, and the military participated in them. Isabel Peron had been elected vice-president in 1973 and became president after the death of her husband, General Juan Domingo Peron, on July 1, 1974. Elements of her government organized secret death squads such as Triple A (*Alianza Anticomunista Argentina*) and *Comando Libertadores de America*. Years later it was established that some police and military officers were members of these squads, and that security forces and public institutions covered up their crimes. Their modus operandi included kidnappings, but within hours the victims' bodies would be found in visible places, often showing gruesome forms of mutilation. For this reason the regime of Isabel Peron was widely seen as increasing the insecurity felt by citizens, while making little progress in curbing the action of left-wing guerrilla movements. In that sense the coup d'etat of March 24, 1976, was an attempt to monopolize and intensify state violence and to expand its scope, while also hiding and denying it.

Unquestionably, official right-wing violence was a response to organized armed violence by several leftist revolutionary groups. As in other Latin American countries, Argentine guerrilla movements were organized shortly after the death of Ernesto Che Guevara in Bolivia in 1967. With some minor exceptions they employed urban guerrilla tactics; whether the violence reached the level of an internal armed conflict in terms of the laws of war remains an unanswered question. The largest of these groups was the Montoneros, formed by leaders emerging from student and working-class demonstrations in several cities in 1969. The Montoneros combined armed actions with political organization and mobilization, and considered themselves part of the Peronist movement. They had a commanding presence in the movement's large and actively mobilized student, rank-and-file labor, and grassroots wings. To the left of the Montoneros were several Marxist and Guevarist armed organizations, the most prominent of which was the *Ejército Revolucionario del Pueblo* (ERP). The Montoneros and ERP launched bold attacks on military and sometimes civilian targets, and occasionally engaged in terrorist actions. The aggregate effect of their actions provoked the police, the military, and right-wing death squads into a spiral of retaliatory violence.

On assuming control of the government, the military junta closed down Argentina's Congress, replaced members of its Supreme Court and most other judges, and intervened in all local and provincial (state) governments. Many prominent politicians and labor leaders were incarcerated for long prison terms without trial. In fact, the military utilized emergency powers to arrest nearly ten thousand persons and hold them indefinitely in administrative detention, pursuant to the state of siege provisions of Argentina's Constitution. The government refused to comply with the few judicial orders issued by its own judicial appointees, seek-

[ARGENTINA'S MUSEUM]

On March 24, 2004, exactly 28 years after the coup that launched the "dirty war," president Néstor Kirchner announced that the Escuela de Mecánica de la Armada (ESMA) naval base would be turned into a "Museum of Memory" to honor the thousands who disappeared after their capture by security forces between 1976 and 1983. The ESMA was only one of 340 camps used for these purposes. It was not the only camp in Buenos Aires, but the most notorious because it held an estimated 5,000 *desaparecidos*, of which perhaps 100 survived.

ing to release some detainees because of the authorities' failure to establish a clear rationale for their continued detention. Many state of siege detainees spent between four and six years in prison. Others were subjected to military trials without a semblance of due process. A larger number were tried in the federal courts under counterinsurgency legislation of a draconian nature and with evidence largely obtained through torture.

The most terrifying and pervasive practice of the military dictatorship, however, was that of forced disappearances described above. Investigations and prosecutions completed after the return of democracy established without a doubt that disappearances were conducted pursuant to official (albeit secret) policy, and implemented and executed under careful supervision along the chain of command. The National Commission on the Disappearance of Persons, one of the earliest truth commissions of recent vintage and set in motion by president Raúl Alfonsín as soon as the country reestablished democracy in 1983, determined this critical fact without dispute. It was further proven through rigorous court procedures in 1985, when the heads of the three military juntas that governed between 1976 and 1982 were prosecuted for planning, executing, and supervising the reign of terror. General Jorge Videla and Admiral Emilio Massera were sentenced to life in prison for their respective roles as commanders of Argentina's army and navy.

By Videla's own admission the targets were not only the armed guerrillas: They included also their lawyers, priests and professors who allegedly spread anti-Western and anti-Christian ideas, labor leaders, neighborhood organizers, human rights activists, and in general anyone who—as defined by the military—lent aid and comfort to the so-called subversive movement. Military leaders variously claimed that their war against subversion was a "dirty war." The deliberate, widespread, and systematic nature of the practice of disappearances, and the protection of its perpetrators from any investigation, qualifies the phenomenon, as implemented in Argentina, as a crime against humanity. To the extent that the targets were singled out because of ideology or political affiliation and did not belong to a racial or religious minority, the practice does not rise to the level of genocide as defined in international law. Nevertheless, many in Argentina, and significantly the courts of Spain exercising universal jurisdiction, consider it genocide insofar as it targets a distinct national group defined by its ideology and slated for extinction, in whole or in part, through mass murder.

Argentina's program to attain truth and justice about the crimes of the past was cut short when factions of the military staged four uprisings against the democratic regime. The laws of *Punto Final* (Full Stop) and *Obediencia Debida* (Due Obedience), enacted in 1986 and 1987 under the pressure of that military unrest, terminated the prosecution of an estimated four hundred identified perpetrators. Their legal effect was a blanket amnesty. Videla, Massera, and the other defendants in the only two cases to result in convictions were pardoned by Carlos Menem, who succeeded Alfonsín in 1989. In spite of these setbacks, Argentine nongovernmental organizations continued to press for accountability. They succeeded first in persuading federal courts to conduct truth trials designed to establish the fate and whereabouts of the disappeared for the purpose of relaying that information to their families and to society. Later, several courts found that the Full Stop and Due Obedience laws were unconstitutional for being incompatible with Argentina's international obligations under human rights treaties. In August 2003, at the initiative of president Néstor Kirchner, the Argentine Congress declared these laws null and void, and the prosecution of some cases has began again. In the matter of the abduction and illegal adoption of children of the disappeared, or of those born during the captivity of their mother, criminal prosecutions have been brought against Videla, Massera, and dozens of other defendants, because those crimes were specifically exempted from the pseudo-amnesty laws. Kirchner has lifted restrictions on processing extradition requests from Spain and other countries. He also expressed support for Mexico's decision to extradite an Argentine dirty warrior to Spain to stand trial there. In 2003 it seemed inevitable that Argentina would either prosecute the perpetrators of all dirty war crimes or extradite them to Spain or other countries exercising universal jurisdiction.

SEE ALSO Argentina's Dirty Warriors; Disappearances; Immunity; Torture

BIBLIOGRAPHY

Americas Watch (1991). *Truth and Partial Justice in Argentina—An Update.* New York: Human Rights Watch.

Centro de Estudios Legales y Sociales (CELS) (Argentina) (2000). *Derechos Humanos en Argentina: Informe Anual 2000, Eudeba.* Buenos Aires: University of Buenos Aires Press.

Fertlowitz, Marguerite (1998). *A Lexicon of Terror: Argentina and the Legacies of Torture.* New York: Oxford University Press.

Inter-American Commission on Human Rights (1980). *Report on the Situation of Human Rights in Argentina.* Washington, D.C.: Inter-American Commission on Human Rights.

Marchak, M. Patricia, and William Marchak (1999). *God's Assassins: State Terrorism in Argentina in the 1970s.* Montreal: McGill-Queen's University.

Nunca Más: Report of the Argentine National Commission on Disappearance of Persons (1985). New York: Farrar Strauss Giroux.

Mignone, Emilio F. (1988). *Witness to the Truth.* Maryknoll, N.Y.: Orbis Books.

Osiel, Mark (2001). *Mass Atrocity, Ordinary Evil, and Hannah Arendt: Criminal Consciousness in Argentina's Dirty War.* New Haven, Conn.: Yale University Press.

Juan E. Méndez

Argentina's Dirty Warriors

The so-called *guerra sucia* (dirty war), which took place in Argentina under the various military governments that ruled from 1976 through 1983, resulted in the disappearance of between 9,000 and 30,000 people, and many more victims of torture and prolonged imprisonment. It was one of the worst examples of state terrorism in twentieth-century Latin America. The demand for justice figured prominently in the electoral campaign of the winning candidate, Raúl Alfonsín, during the 1983 presidential elections that restored civilian rule. During Alfonsín's presidency (1983–1989) the human rights issue continued to occupy a prominent place in public discourse. The struggle to bring to justice the perpetrators of the crimes also generated controversy and sowed unrest within the ranks of the military. On assuming office, Alfonsín formed a truth commission, the National Commission on the Disappeared (*Comision Nacional sobre la Desparicion de Personas*, CONADEP), to investigate alleged human rights abuses by the military. The commission's final report was a damning indictment of the military's crimes and set the stage, as well as providing the body of evidence, for the trials of members of the military juntas that had ruled the country between 1976 and 1983.

The Mothers of Plaza de Mayo have become a symbol of human rights activism. For many years they have demonstrated every Thursday afternoon at this plaza in Buenos Aires, seeking information about the fate of their sons and daughters "disappeared" during Argentina's dirty war. [BETTMANN/CORBIS]

Alfsonsín's government always remained wary of provoking unrest in the military through its human rights policies. This explains the first halting steps taken by the administration on the promise of punishment for those guilty of crimes. Alfonsín initially attempted to reform the Code of Military Justice and establish military jurisdiction over the accused and sentencing by military courts, thereby keeping the trials within clearly prescribed institutional boundaries and placating the armed forces. Once it became clear that the military would assume no responsibility in recognizing the guilt of its former leaders and sanctioning punishment or even acknowledging that such commanders had committed crimes, Alfonsín transferred the cases to the civil courts. In April 1985 the public trials of the three military juntas that had ruled the country between 1976 and 1983 began. The trials were to last until the end of the year, and the lead prosecutor, Julio César Strasser, produced dramatic testimony that led to the conviction of former president General Jorge Videla, Admiral Emilio Massera, and other military commanders. The court rejected the defense's claims of

immunity from persecution because of an alleged "state of war" existing in the country, and the sentences handed down varied in severity according to the court's interpretation of the degree of involvement each commander had in the crimes.

The convictions, which elicited broad although not unanimous public support, unleashed great unrest within the ranks of the armed forces. Two abortive military uprisings threatened the country's fragile democracy, and Alfonsín faced the dilemma of fulfilling his campaign promise to deliver justice for human rights abuses while safeguarding democracy and civilian rule. He chose the safest path, restricting the scope of the trials through two highly controversial amnesty laws: the *Ley de Obediencia Debida* (Due Obedience Law) and *Ley de Punto Final* (Full Stop Law). The Due Obedience Law exempted lower-ranking officers and enlisted men from prosecution on the grounds that they were simply carrying out orders, whereas the Full Stop Law established a statute of limitations on further prosecutions for anyone accused of human rights crimes. The Full Stop Law did little to mollify the military because it triggered a wave of lawsuits to beat the deadline for filing stipulated by the law, although the cumulative effect of both laws was indeed to impose limits on criminal proceedings. The government of Carlos Menem (1989–1999) appeared to definitively seal the process when it issued a pardon in 1989 and released from prison the following year the incarcerated former junta commanders sentenced in 1985.

Though domestic politics had resulted in compromises and even a certain betrayal of human rights issue within Argentina, foreign governments and courts were not so constrained. There were periodic attempts to extradite accused perpetrators of human rights crimes against foreign nationals. Such demands intensified in 2002 and 2003. In January 2002 Sweden asked Argentina to extradite naval officer Alfredo Astiz. Astiz, who had worked as an undercover agent in the most notorious of the detention and torture centers, the Navy Mechanics School, and was sought for his involvement in the disappearance of Argentine-Swedish national Dagmar Hagelin. The French and German governments made similar extradition requests. Most dramatically, in August 2003, Spanish human rights judge Baltasar Garzón issued warrants for the extradition of forty-five former military officers accused of the torture and murder of Spanish nationals during the dictatorship of Argentina. The activities of foreign governments and judges helped to revitalize the human rights issue within Argentina and restored it to a central position in public debate.

The government of Peronist Néstor Kirchner, elected president in May 2003, has been as vigorous in pursuing accountability for the human rights abuses as Menem's Peronist government was indifferent. Kirchner persuaded a congress with Peronist majorities to repeal the two controversial amnesty laws from the Alfonsín years and received delegations from the Mothers of the Plaza de Mayo and other human rights organizations that demanded full accountability for the military's crimes. As of mid-2004, the pending decision of Argentina's Supreme Court on the legality of repealing the amnesty laws means the human rights situation in Argentina was rejuvinated, but remains a controversial and polarizing issue. Human rights organizations have reclaimed the initiative and are pressuring Kirchner to live up to his promises of justice and accountability for the crimes committed. It remains to be seen to what degree domestic political considerations will, as they did under Alfonsín, exercise pressures against a thorough investigation and exemplary justice. For example, although Kirchner annulled a decree preventing the extradition of Argentines to stand trial abroad for human rights crimes—an annulment that led the Spanish government to drop its extradition request—political considerations continued to complicate judicial proceedings. Indeed, Kirchner's decision to press forward with the repeal of the amnesty laws and proceed with trials within Argentina was partly intended to deflect criticisms of his annulment of the decree banning extraditions. Justice for human rights crimes of the last military government therefore continues to be complicated by Argentina's volatile domestic political situation.

SEE ALSO Amnesty; Argentina

BIBLIOGRAPHY

Brysk, Alison (1994). *The Politics of Human Rights in Argentina: Protest, Change, and Democratization.* Stanford, Calif.: Stanford University Press.

Feitlowitz, Marguerite (1998). *A Lexicon of Terror: Argentina and the Legacies of Torture.* Oxford, U.K.: Oxford University Press.

Human Rights Watch. "Yearly Reports, Argentina." Available from http://www.hrw.org.

Romero, Luis Alberto (2002). *A History of Argentina in the Twentieth Century.* State College: Penn State University Press.

James Brennan

Armenians in Ottoman Turkey and the Armenian Genocide

Armenia as a cultural, political, and geographical entity has existed for 2,700 years. The land, historically identified as Greater Armenia, lies east of the Euphrates River. It is bounded on the northwest by the river Choruh (Churuk or Tchorokh), on the north by the Kura River, on the east and southeast by the river Araks (also Araxes) and the Lake of Urmia, and on the south by the Tigris Valley.

Origins of the Armenian People

Described as Armenoi, the Armenians were first mentioned by the Greek historian Hecateus of Miletus around 550 BCE. Some thirty years later the inscription of Darius I, King of Persia, refers to Armina as the land of the Armenians. In the Bible itself, namely, in the Book of Jeremiah (Chap. 51, verse 27), there is also a reference to "the Kingdom of Ararat" denoting the timeframe of 594 BCE. Furthermore, according to the Greek historian Herodotus, the so-called father of history (fifth century BCE), the Armenians, an Indo-European people, migrated from the Balkan Peninsula to Asia Minor (Turkey), with the Phrygians whose colony they constituted, and spoke an Indo-European language. Following its later separation from them, however, this migrant colony over time amalgamated itself

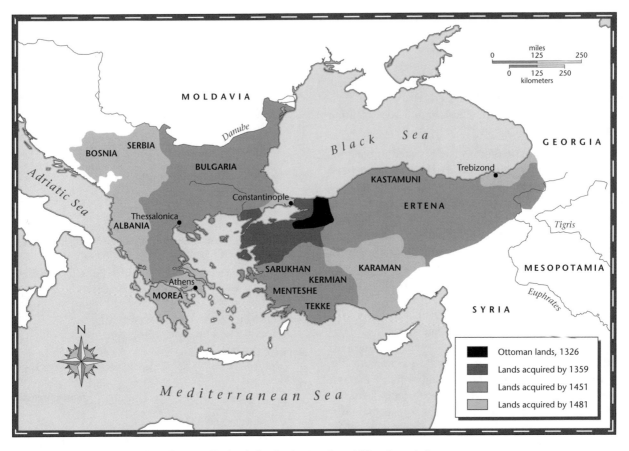

Map outlining the expansion of the Ottoman Empire during the fourteenth and fifteenth centuries. [XNR PRODUCTIONS/GALE GROUP]

with the indigenous population groups, especially the Hayasa-Azzi. It is worth noting in this respect that Armenians call themselves Hay and not Armenian. Moreover, in the annals of Assyria, the Armenian plateau is depicted as the land of Nairi, in and around which, toward the end of the eighth century BCE, the proto-Armenian migrant colony is seen evolving into the dominant population of the area historically known as Urartu (Ararat).

Sociocultural Evolution of the Armenian People: Historical Background

Hence, the region in eastern Turkey encompassing Mount Ararat and Lake Van does constitute the geographical matrix marking the birth and formation of the Armenian nation. During the successive centuries of this pre-Christian era, Armenia attained sufficient consolidation and strength to emerge as an imposing royal power. During the reign of King Artashes (190 BCE), for example, the kingdom extended from the Euphrates on the west, almost to the Caspian Sea, from the Caucasus in the north to the Taurus Mountains. The apogee of such power coincides with the reign of Tigran the Great (95–56 BCE) who through a series of

victorious military campaigns, created a vast Armenian empire. By 70 BCE it extended from the Caspian Sea to the Mediterranean Sea, from the Caucasus to Palestine, with him receiving as a result the title of King of Kings.

The subsequent decline of the Armenian Empire, power, and statehood coincides with the advent of Christianity. Its establishment during the first two decades of the fourth century in Armenia, as the first Christian state in history, was a defining moment for the formation of the Armenian nation in the centuries to follow. The Armenian Church consequently evolved as the single most important institution for Armenian national life. Its founders and leaders left their indelible imprint on Armenian religious literature, Armenian historiography, and linguistics, and provided the impetus for the cultivation of a distinct ethos relative to education and learning in general. The pillars of this initiative were Saint Sahag, the Catholicos, that is, the Supreme Patriarch of the Church, and Saint Mesrop, a polyglot and erudite monk, who, with the encouragement of the former and the help of others, set out to invent the Armenian alphabet. This effort yielded the intended result. In 414 a cultural milestone was achieved: The Bible was translated into Armenian, and thereby the fusion of religion and language in Armenian civilization became enshrined.

This religious immersion in Christianity was perilously tested some four decades later. In the epoch-making Battle of Avarair in 451, Armenians fought and died to protect and preserve their Christian faith while successfully resisting the pagan demands of the Persian King Yazdgard III. They resolutely refused to substitute the worship of sun and fire for their Christian faith.

Due to successive Muslim incursions from near and far, the Christian identity of the Armenians and their stubborn clinging to it resulted in an unending chain of national calamities. The historical unfolding of the fate of the Armenians is accordingly punctuated by constant tragedy, sorrow, and attrition in numbers. The incursions included that of the Arab rulers of the Abbasid Caliphate in the seventh century; that of the Selchuks, nomadic Turkic tribes from Central Asia, in the eleventh and twelfth centuries; Genghis Khan's Mongols in the thirteenth century, who, at the end of that century, converted to Islam; and finally the Turkish clans who under Osman, the son and successor of the original clan leader, established the Ottoman realm that was to grow and endure for some five centuries.

Ottoman Theocracy and Its Unsettling Impact on Armenians

The steady expansion of this incipient Ottoman realm and its eventual transformation over time into the Ottoman Empire had fateful consequences for the Armenian people, whose ancestral territories and major population centers had thus become incorporated into the territories of that empire. The overarching factor sealing the fate of Ottoman Armenians in this respect was the pervasive theocratic structure of that empire. The latter's multiethnic and multireligious character was a factor that drove the dominant Ottoman-Turkish element to rely heavily on the tenets and dogmas of the Islamic sacred law to govern the empire. The Ottoman sociopolitical system was dichotomized in terms of these antithetical entities: the ruling nation (*milleti hâkime*) and the subject nation (*milleti mahküme*). The underlying principle of this dichotomy was a religion that proclaimed the superordination of the faithful, that is, the Muslims, and accordingly assigned a subordinate status to the "infidel" and, therefore, "inferior" non-Muslims. The institutionalization of this Islamic dogma as a doctrine found expression in the practice of prejudice, discrimination, and exclusion directed against non-Muslims.

Nevertheless, the most debilitating liability structurally imposed on the Armenians, the preponderant

Abd-ul-hamid II (1842–1918), the last Sultan of the Ottoman Empire, known as the "Great Assassin." He refused to intervene on behalf of Armenians in the massacres of 1894 to 1896. [MICHAEL NICHOLSON/CORBIS]

non-Muslim minority in Asia Minor, was the categorical denial of their right to bear arms. This canonical prohibition was especially reconfirmed and reinforced in connection with the 1876 Constantinople Conference. The representatives of the six Great Powers of Europe, among other demands, urged the sultan to grant the Christian subjects of the empire the right to bear arms. But, after summoning and consulting the *Ulema*, the Islamic doctors of law, the Seyhulislam, their head, issued a *fetva*, a preemptory final opinion, declaring such a right to be a violation of Islamic sacred law. In an environment teeming with Turkish, Kurdish, and other Muslim overlords armed to their teeth, especially in the remote provinces of the interior of the empire, the defenseless Armenians were, by virtue of this theocratic fiat, consigned to a level of status involving ultimate vulnerability; they were, in fact, reduced to fair game, which served to invite all sorts of depredations, including murder, rape, exorbitant taxations, plunder, confiscations, and abductions. These conditions, endemic in the Ottoman imperial system of provincial administration not only persisted, but also during the reign of Sultan Abdul Hamit evolved into a portentous Turkish-Armenian political conflict.

Hamit and the Ensuing Series of Armenian Massacres (1894–1896)

The Turkish-Armenian conflict was but an integral part of a larger, evolving conflict between the Turkish-Muslim rulers of the empire on the one hand, and the empire's various Christian nationalities on the other. The Ottoman Empire's theocratic tenets, reinforced by the militant and imperial attitudes of these rulers, served to produce a regime unable to govern these subject nationalities. The resulting maladministration, marked by blight and ineptness, steadily aggravated the latter's plight. The interventionist response of the European powers, especially Russia, England, and France, not only further exacerbated the problem, but also in the process enabled these subject nationalities to jar themselves loose from the Ottoman yoke. Their ultimate success in emancipating themselves proved, however, contagious for the thus far docile Armenians, who, unlike these Balkan national groups, were not seeking independence, but rather local autonomy through administrative reforms. Their main concern was protection from the unabating depredations described above, within a broad scheme of reforms guaranteeing their overall security. The specific stipulation of Article 61 of the 1878 Berlin Peace Treaty, which followed the Russian military victory in the Turkish-Russian War of 1877 and 1878, had provided for such reforms; so did the 1895 Armenian Reform scheme that the European powers had negotiated with Hamit, who grudgingly signed it.

Determined to scuttle any program of Armenian Reforms, Hamit already in the years following the signing of the Berlin Treaty had begun to initiate a series of measures to this end. He solemnly swore to the German ambassador, Prince von Radolin, that he "would rather die than yield to unjust Armenian pressures and allow the introduction of large-scale Autonomy Reforms" (Lepsius et al., 1927, Document no. 2184). In two separate memoranda he composed as guidelines for his deputies, who were entrusted with handling the Armenian reforms issue, Hamit vented his wariness as he suspected ulterior motivations relative to the pursuit of these reforms. In one of these memoranda, he characterized such reforms as a device to strengthen the Armenians, who then would likely seek independence, and thereby cause the partition of the Ottoman realm. In the other, he expressed his anxiety that these reforms would eventually lead to the Armenians dominating the Muslims and establishing in eastern Turkey an Armenian principality. Hamit then instructed his

underling to emulate his standard policy, namely, "to put off [the Europeans] by advancing trumped-up excuses [oyalamak]" (Hocaoglu, 1989, pp. 170, 237). Namely, the Ottoman government would officially issue oral and written instructions on the Armenian reforms that, being contrary to the wishes of the monarch, were expected to be evaded by setting forth credible excuses.

In the meantime Hamit embarked on a multi-pronged campaign to nip the reforms advocated by the Great Powers in the bud. Having earlier prorogued the Ottoman Parliament, he then completely transferred the residual executive power to the palace, his seat and domain of power. Thus, the limited restraints attached to his constitutional monarchy largely dissolved themselves, paving the way for the onset of a more or less unfettered autocracy that soon degenerated into a regime of despotism (istibdad). Instead of normally functioning cabinet ministers taking charge of government, a despotic monarch, surrounded by a reckless palace camarilla (cabal), began to devise and implement a new Armenian policy that involved a new phase of anti-Armenian persecution through officially sanctioned terror.

In anticipation of the escalation of the conflict surrounding the projected Armenian reforms, in 1891 Hamit set up a new system of Kurdish tribal regiments of territorial cavalry (Hamidiye). By 1899 their numbers had grown from thirty-three to sixty-three. These quasi-official regiments received ranks, uniforms, regimental badges, and Martin rifles, and with them, the license to intensify the level of persecution of the unarmed and highly vulnerable Armenian population of the provinces. During the ensuing massacres of 1894 and 1896 these regiments would play a key role as instruments of widespread death and destruction.

Parallel to this undertaking, Hamit launched a comprehensive program of redistricting or "gerrymandering" to use colloquial parlance. By drastically altering the proportion of Armenian inhabitants of several provinces in eastern Turkey, whereby an Armenian majority was transformed into an Armenian minority, especially in the Van-Mus-Bitlis triangle, the heart of historic Armenia, the rationale for Armenian reforms was rendered untenable, thereby preempting the need for the entire scheme of Armenian reforms.

Meanwhile, the plight of the provincial Armenian population continued to deteriorate steadily. The gravity of this plight and the deliberate intent of Ottoman authorities to pursue such aggravation were cogently depicted by the veteran French ambassador to Turkey, Paul Cambon. On the eve of the 1894 to 1896 massacres "a high ranking Turkish official told me," reported

Cambon to Paris "that the Armenian Question does not exist, but we shall create it." Cambon went on to explain:

> Up until 1881, the idea of Armenian independence was non-existent. The masses simply yearned for reforms, dreaming only of a normal administration under Ottoman rule. . . . The reforms have not been carried out. The exaction of the officials remained scandalous. . . . [From] one end of the Empire to the other, there is rampant corruption of officials, denial of justice and insecurity of life. . . . [As] if it were not enough to provoke Armenian discontent, the Turks were glad to amplify it. . . . [The] maintenance in Armenia of a veritable regime of terror, arrests, murders, rapes, all this shows that Turkey is taking pleasure in precipitating the events [imperiling] an inoffensive population (Documents Diplomatiques Français, 1947, pp. 71–74).

It is against this backdrop that the Armenian reform movement lost its momentum and was replaced by the confrontational thrust of Armenian revolutionaries, who thus entered the arena of conflict with Ottoman provincial as well as central authorities. Unlike in the case of the Balkan nationalities, these revolutionaries, contrary to their fervent hopes, did not receive any support at all from any of the six European powers, thereby compounding the vulnerability endemic in the position of Ottoman Armenians. Alive to the advantages of this condition, Hamit, in total disregard, if not defiance, of the pro forma warnings and admonitions of these powers, set out to punish the Armenians on a massive and indiscriminate scale, by resorting to empire-wide massacres that lasted from August 1894 to September 1896 and claimed some 250,000 to 300,000 direct and indirect victims. And, as if to underscore his disdain for these powers, two in the series of these massacres were perpetrated in Constantinople, then the Ottoman capital, in broad daylight, and before the very eyes of the official representatives of the Great Powers.

These massacres are significant in several respects. First, they were perpetrated mostly with special cudgels or sticks that were fitted with a piece of iron that helped bludgeon their victims to death. According to a well-informed Turkish source, Hamit, in the aftermath of the massacres, gloatingly gave European diplomats a tour of the depots in which those cudgels were stored. Another method of massacre was immolation in houses, but especially churches. In the large cathedral of Urfa, for example, three thousand Armenians, mostly women and children, were burned alive in December 1895. There was massive popular participation in these atrocities incited by the haranguing of *Mullahs* at special religious services in the mosques on Fridays. Addi-

tionally, in some cities and towns convicts were released from prison for massacre duty.

The material desolation was no less significant. According to German investigator Johannes Lepsius, who immediately inspected the sites following the massacres, 2,500 towns and villages were ruined, 645 churches and monasteries were destroyed, and 328 churches were converted into mosques. Moreover, 508 churches and monasteries were completely plundered. Furthermore, the survivors of 559 villages and hundreds of families were forcibly converted to Islam; included in this toll were 15,000 Armenians from the provinces of Harput and Erzurum. Perhaps the most consequential feature of this era of massacres is the fact that the perpetrators almost in toto were deliberately spared from prosecution and punishment. This paramount aspect of impunity associated with the large-scale mass murder at issue here may well be regarded as the integral nexus, the inevitable connecting link, to the subsequent 1909 Adana massacre and, ultimately, the Armenian Genocide during World War I.

Advent of the Young Turk Regime and the 1909 Two-Tier Adana Massacre

The scope and intensity of the Hamit-era massacres had demonstrated the broad latitude that the monarch was domestically and internationally allowed in the exercise of his sanguinary tyranny. But, the tentacles of that tyranny reached beyond the confines of the Christian Armenians, deep into the community of his Muslim subjects as well—albeit not in the form of massacres, but through a variety of methods of individual persecution. Consequently, a select group of Armenian revolutionaries, *Dashnaks* in particular, joined hands with the emerging Young Turk revolutionaries to topple "the Red Sultan." Through jointly held public demonstrations and great fanfare heralding a new era of Muslim-Christian fraternity and solidarity, a new regime was ushered in. By reinstituting the 1876 Constitution, which the sultan had first expediently embraced only to prorogue it with equal expediency within a year, the constitutional form of monarchy was thereby restored. But the unfolding of some precipitous events culminating in a new major massacre against the Armenians underscored the tenuousness of this Muslim-Christian fraternity and the fragility of the guarantees of the newly restored constitution.

Unhappy with the secular and egalitarian aspects proclaimed by the founders of the new Young Turk Regime, the Committee of Union and Progress (CUP), the apostles of fundamentalist Islam, the advocates of *Sheri,* the canon law of Islam, staged an uprising that was suppressed in short order. Coincidentally, however, there erupted in the city of Adana and its environs a major conflagration, historically known as the 1909 Adana massacre, to which some 25,000 Armenians fell victim.

Several factors converged in the outbreak of this bloodbath, the levels of fiendishness and ferocity of which exceeded those of all other episodes of mass murder against the Armenians, including the World War I genocide. Foremost among these factors was a large number of disaffected partisans of the partly dethroned monarch, who, together with a host of Islamic religious leaders and local military officers who likewise identified with the monarch, gladly joined in precipitating and consummating the bloodbath. Another factor involved was the accumulated wealth of the region's Armenians who had been spared from the death and destruction of the 1894 to 1896 massacres because of the fear of the nearby, combative Armenian mountaineers of Zeitun. That wealth served as a magnet for the lethal cupidity of the perpetrators. An equally important factor concerned the aggressive nationalism of some Armenian community leaders. Intoxicated with the new spell of freedom, these Armenians, suddenly relieved of the centuries-old Ottoman-Turkish yoke, openly vented their spirit of defiant nationalism, thereby challenging their erstwhile Muslim overlords. However, the most potent factor in question was the clandestine, instigative role of the CUP, egged on by the CUP's Saloniki branch leaders, headed by Mehmet Nazim, one of the architects of the subsequent Armenian Genocide. Through coded messages they directed the local CUP members and their fellow perpetrators in the operations of the two-tier Adana massacre (April 1–14 and April 14–27, 1909).

Two postmassacre official investigations concluded that the massacre was premeditated and organized. One of them, which was issued by a CUP deputy of Armenian extraction (Hagop Babikian), placed the blame squarely on the CUP as the arch culprit. He had been dispatched by the Ottoman Parliament along with another Turkish deputy (Yusuf Kemal) to investigate the matter on the spot. The results of the other investigation were reported by Grand Vizier Hilmi Pasa during an address before the Ottoman Chamber of Deputies. In it he denounced "the criminal scoundrels who were bent on massacring and plundering the Armenians through a surprise attack." Notwithstanding, there was very little retribution as far as the arch organizers were concerned and hardly any significant restitution or rehabilitation as far as the survivors were concerned. The vulnerability of the victim population proved once more to be a warrant for the kind of mass murder that would again escape any meaningful punishment.

Armenian Reform Issue as a Prelude to Impending Genocide

In the continuum of the era of Armenian massacres spanning the regimes of Hamit and the Young Turks, there is discernible a pattern of centrally directed organization. Whereas a palace camarilla was involved in the former case, in the latter a conspiratorial clique holding sway in the upper echelons of the CUP stands out. In both cases, the organizers had managed to gain the upper hand in control of the state's key apparatuses. The steady deterioration of the plight of the Armenian population of the Ottoman Empire and the intensification of the attendant Turkish-Armenian conflict coincide with the onset of a new policy of Turkish nationalism this CUP regime adopted. Pursuant to this policy, the CUP initiated a series of steps. To expand its base and acquire new resources, Mehmet Talaat, the CUP's party boss and frequent interior minister, established new party cells and clubs throughout the length and breadth of the empire. Additionally, it acquired substantial power by co-opting a significant number of army officers, many of who actually enrolled in the ranks of the CUP as active party members. In the meantime, the CUP's Central Committee, a kind of politburo, underwent a major structural change. After increasing the number of its members from seven to twelve, the top party leaders allowed three men to forge and inexorably carry out a new policy on nationalities, whereby the empire would be purged of its non-Muslim elements by way of supplanting multiethnic Ottomanism with exclusionary Turkism. Most significant, these three men—the MDs Behaeddin Sakir and Mehmet Nazim, and party ideologue, Ziya Gökalp—within a few years, namely, during World War I, would prove the principal architects of the Armenian Genocide.

A new crisis in the Balkan Peninsula, one involving the explosion of war in a brewing conflict with Christian subjects on that peninsula, brought matters to a head. Responding to two ghastly massacres the Ottoman rulers had perpetrated in Macedonia in the summer of 1912, the Greeks, Serbs, and Bulgarians, former Ottoman subjects, set aside their disputes on Macedonia and jointly declared war. Within weeks the Ottoman armies were roundly defeated, and Ottoman dominion in the Balkans came to a devastating end as tens of thousands of destitute Muslims fled and took refuge in all corners of Constantinople, then the capital of the empire. It was under these bleak circumstances that the various leadership groups of the Armenian community decided to resuscitate once more the languishing Armenian reform issue. Delegations were sent to the European capitals; their pleas served to mobilize Great Powers to pressure Turkey for the adoption of a new reform scheme. Following arduous and exacting negotiations, the CUP leadership felt impelled to sign a new reform accord on February 8, 1914, which for the first time stipulated European supervision and control of the accord's implementation.

Having gained total control of the machinery of the Ottoman state through a second coup d'état on January 23, 1913, the CUP leaders in no time became monolithic dictatorial masters of the empire after having purged virtually all opposition groups. Vested with this enormous power, they set out to implement their plan of coercive Turkification, with the Armenians becoming the prime target. The CUP prepared themselves for this task and waited for a suitable opportunity, which eventually came with the outbreak of World War I.

The enormity of the crime of genocide accents the importance of contextualizing that crime. War in this sense provides a unique context in which opportunism and exculpatory self-righteousness dynamically converge to motivate and even embolden the arch perpetrators. While the optimal vulnerability of the targeted victim group is the source of the opportunity, the perils of defeat implicit in any war are often used as a rationale, if not justification, for resorting to draconian measures against such a group, which almost invariably is denounced as "the internal foe" by these perpetrators. This is the general framework within which the World War I Armenian Genocide must be understood.

Several major military defeats the Ottoman armies suffered in the winter and spring of 1915, including those of Sarikamis and Dilman, were conveniently attributed to the military role of Armenian volunteer units enrolled in the enemy Russian Caucasus Army; three units were comprised, in part, of soldiers who were former Ottoman citizens. The April 1915 Van uprising, which the Armenians mounted to resist the impending massacre of that province's Armenian population, further provided the needed ammunition to declare the Armenians an internal foe. The stage was set to embark on the plan of wholesale extermination.

Recourse to Genocide

More than any other form of capital crime, genocide, if undertaken by a state organization, requires detailed preparations in order not only to ensure optimal success, but also to conceal or camouflage intent and outcome. During post–World War I Turkish court-martials it was ascertained and recorded in the respective official judicial gazette that the wholesale destruction of Armenians was premeditated (*ta'ammüden*) and that deportations were but a vehicle toward that end. In his affidavit prepared for that court, Third Army Commander General Vehip, when attesting to this fact of premeditation, used the term (*kasden*

by prior deliberation). Moreover, the respective official documents of imperial Germany and imperial Austria-Hungary, the Ottoman Empire's wartime allies, confirm the incidence of such premeditation.

Within weeks after the outbreak of war, while Turkey was maintaining a position of "armed neutrality," the newly formed brigand units (*çete*) of the Special Organization (*Teskilat'i Mahsusa*) began a campaign of harassment and terror against the Armenian population in eastern Turkey. When plans to encircle and destroy the Russian Caucasus Army disastrously failed in the aftermath of Turkey's intervention in the war, these brigand cadres were assigned a new and definitive mission: They were to be redeployed as killing units to attack and massacre the countless Armenian deportee convoys. Behaeddin Sakir, the head of the Special Organization East, with headquarters in Erzurum, in eastern Turkey, undertook a special trip to the Ottoman capital, where he sought and obtained the sanction of the CUP's omnipotent Central Committee to proceed with this mission. By way of a sweeping and reckless generalization, the Armenians were hereby expediently vilified as traitors and accordingly targeted as the so-called internal foe. Sporadic Armenian acts of desertion, espionage, and sabotage, common among other Muslim groups, especially Kurds and also Turks, in the service of the enemy Russians, and the coincidental Armenian Van uprising, were treated as welcome opportunities. They were conveniently and adroitly exploited as justifiable excuses for indiscriminate massive and lethal retaliation.

In order to streamline the mechanisms for implementing the projected extermination mission, the CUP leadership first suspended the Parliament, thereby transferring all state authority from the legislative to the executive branch. In short order, the executive began to run the country through the enactment of temporary laws as provided under Article 36 of the Ottoman Constitution and Article 12 of the CUP's party statutes. Accordingly, on May 13 and 26, 1915, Interior Minister Talaat railroaded through the Ottoman Cabinet the Temporary Law on Deportation that entailed the wholesale uprooting and eventual destruction of the empire's Armenian population. The gradual liquidation of able-bodied Armenian males, who through the General Mobilization decree had been conscripted months earlier, was already in progress.

The organization of the genocidal field of operations was entrusted to a number of agencies and groups. Foremost among these was the military. The coordination of the dual tasks of marshalling the logistics of the deportee convoys on the one hand, and their subsequent massacre through ambushes by the Special

Among the trees, victims of the Armenian genocide of 1915. Although many American lawmakers and politicians have advocated for the United States' formal recognition of the genocide perpetrated by Turkey, as of mid-2004 no such action has been taken. [BETTMANN/ CORBIS]

Organization gangs on the other, was entrusted to Staff Colonel Seyfi, head of Department II in Ottoman General Headquarters. These gangs were largely comprised of bloodthirsty (*kanli katil*) convicts, who had been especially selected and released from the prisons of the empire for such massacre duty, and led by young active and reserve officers. Three army commanders likewise played key organizational roles. The military and civilian jurisdiction of General Mahmud Kâmil, Commander of the Third Army, encompassed the largest concentration of the Ottoman Armenian population identified with the provinces of Sivas, Trabzon, Harput, Diyarbekir, Erzurum, Bitlis, and Van. It was this general who, through a prearrangement with the CUP Central Committee, was appointed to that post and shortly thereafter demanded (*talep*) authorization from General Headquarters to order the wholesale forcible deportation of this huge block of Armenians. General Halil Kut, Commander of Army Groups East, and General Ali Ihsan Sabis, Commander of the Fourth Army, inexorably liquidated all Armenians belonging to their respective armies and ordered the wholesale massacre of the civilian Armenian populations of the regions under their command.

The details of the empire-wide deportations were handled by a special category of powerful party functionaries, mostly ex-army officers, who were carefully selected by the party leadership. Dubbed in ranking order as responsible secretary (*kâtibi mesul*), delegate (*murahhas*), and inspector (*müfettis*), they had superordinate authority, including veto power over the decisions of provincial governors. These omnipotent "commissars" were assisted in their task by members of local CUP party cells.

Beyond the levels of premeditation, decision making, organization, and supervision, the ultimate level involved the actual execution of death and destruction—the crux of the Armenian Genocide. The primary executioners in this respect were the tens of thousands of convicts of the Special Organization described above. They were assisted by a number of irregular units of the Ottoman Army that included several Kurdish cavalry formations, and squads of gendarmes and homefront militia, who served as convoy escort personnel. Frequently, large mobs were mobilized from surrounding areas to deal with bulky convoys; they willingly participated in the butcheries given the ever-present lure of plunder and spoils.

One of the most distinguishing, if not singular, features of the Armenian Genocide is the array of methods and instruments employed. To spare powder and shells, for example, the perpetrators mostly used daggers, swords, scimitars, bayonets, axes, saws, and cudgels, as attested to by wartime U.S. Ambassador Henry Morgenthau. Then, there were mass shootings primarily applied to thousands of disarmed Armenian Labor Battalion soldiers, who were always tied together with heavy ropes in fours and fives, before being executed. The inordinate gruesomeness of the Armenian Genocide is revealed most hauntingly, however, in the next two methods used. One of them involved massive drowning operations, whereby the tributaries of the Euphrates River, crisscrossing Turkey's eastern provinces, several lakes, and in particular, the Black Sea, covering the Samsun-Trabzon coastline stretch, became the fathomless graveyards of tens of thousands of women, children, and elderly men. The other concerns the fate of untold other multitudes, who were systematically burned alive in haylofts, stables, and large caves in such areas as Harput province, the deserts of Mesopotamia, but especially in Mus City and the Mus Plain in Bitlis province, where no less than sixty thousand Armenians were torched. In a rare act of condemnation, Turkish Army Commander Vehip, who during an inspection trip had observed the charred remains of women and children in Tchurig village, north of Mus City, one of those spots of that area's Armenian holocaust, decried what he called this evidence of "atrocity and savagery that has no parallel in the history of Islam" (Dadrian, 2002, pp. 84–85).

When warning Turkey of the dire consequences of the genocide then in progress, the entente powers—France, England, and Russia—on May 24, 1915, introduced the legal term *crimes against humanity,* which was later codified in Article 6c of the Nuremberg Charter and the Preamble of the 1948 United Nations Convention on the Prevention and Punishment of the Crime of Genocide. Even though no exact statistical figures are available, based on an average of German, British, Austrian, and U.S. estimates, about 1.2 million perished in the genocide, while another half-million dispersed to all corners of the world as refugee survivors. While "the dire consequences" trumpeted by the victorious Allies dismally failed to materialize, the crime of the Armenian Genocide not only still remains negatively rewarded by way of impunity, but also official Turkey, past and present, with little hesitation, still persists in denying that crime.

SEE ALSO Armenians in Russia and the USSR; Atatürk, Mustafa Kemal Pasha; Enver, Ismail; Talaat

BIBLIOGRAPHY

Adalin, Rouben P. (1994). *U.S. Archives: Guide to the Armenian Genocide 1915–1918.* London: Chadwyck-Healy.

Bryce, James (1896). *Transcaucasia and Ararat,* 4th edition. London: Macmillan.

Bryce, Viscount (1916). *The Treatment of the Armenians in the Ottoman Empire, 1915–1916,* ed. V. Bryce and A. Toynbee. London: His Majesty's Stationary Office.

Dadrian, Vahakn (1988). "The Circumstances Surrounding the 1909 Adana Holocaust." *Armenian Review* 41:1–16.

Dadrian, Vahakn (2002). "The Armenian Question and the Wartime Fate of the Armenians as Documented by the Officials of the Ottoman Empire's World War I Allies: Germany and Austria-Hungary." *International Journal of Middle East Studies* 34:59–85.

Dadrian, Vahakn (2003). *The History of the Armenian Genocide: Ethnic Conflict from the Balkans to Anatolia to the Caucasus,* 6th edition. New York: Berghahn Books.

Dadrian, Vahakn (2003). *Warrant for Genocide: Key Elements of Turko-Armenian Conflict,* 3rd edition. New Brunswick, N.J.: Transaction Publishers.

Davis, Leslie A. (1989). *The Slaughterhouse Province: An American Diplomat's Report on the Armenian Genocide, 1915–1917,* ed. Susan K. Blair. New Rochelle, N.Y.: A. Caratzas.

Documents Diplomatiques Français (1947). French Foreign Office Archives, 1871–1900. Vol. 11, Document no. 50, pp. 71–74.

Hartunian, Abraham H. (1986). *Neither to Laugh Nor to Weep: A Memoir of the Armenian Genocide,* 2nd edition, trans. V. Hartunian. Cambridge, Mass.: Armenian Heritage Press.

Hocaoglu, M. (1989). *Abdülhamid Han ve Muhtiralari* (Abdulhamit's memoranda). Istanbul: Türkiyat.

Hovannisian, Richard, ed. (1999). *Remembrance and Denial: The Case of the Armenian Genocide.* Detroit, Mich.: Wayne State University Press.

Kloian, Richard D. (1985). *The Armenian Genocide: News Accounts from the American Press, 1915–1922,* 3rd edition. Berkeley, Calif.: Anto Publishers.

Lepsius, J. (1897). *Armenia and Europe: An Indictment,* trans. J. Rendel Harris. London: Hodder and Stoughton.

Lepsius, J., A. M. Mendelssohn Bartholdy, and F. Thimme, eds. (1927). *Die Grosse Politik der Europäischen Kabinette, 1871–1914. Sammlung der Diplomatischen Akten des Auswärtigen Amtes. Vol. 9: Der Nahe und der ferne Osten.* Berlin: Deutsche Verlagsgessellschaft für Politik und Geschichte.

Nassibian, Akaby (1984). *Britain and the Armenian Question, 1915–1923.* New York: St. Martin's Press.

Pears, Sir Edwin (1916). *Forty Years in Constantinople.* New York: D. Appleton and Co.

Somakian, Manoog J. (1995). *Empires in Conflict: Armenia and the Great Powers, 1895–1920.* New York: I. B. Tauris Publishers.

United States Official Documents on the Armenian Genocide. Vol. 1: The Lower Euphrates (1993). *Armenian Review* (Special Edition): I–XXX, 1–186.

United States Official Documents on the Armenian Genocide. Vol. 2: The Peripheries (1994). *Armenian Review* (Special Edition): I–XIX, 1–174.

United States Official Documents on the Armenian Genocide. Vol. 3: The Central Lands (1995). *Armenian Review* (Special Edition): I–XXIV, 1–157.

Walker, Christopher J. (1990). *Armenia: The Survival of a Nation,* 2nd edition. New York: St. Martin's Press.

Winter, Jay, ed. (2003). *America and the Armenian Genocide of 1915.* Cambridge: Cambridge University Press.

Vahakn N. Dadrian

Armenians in Russia and the USSR

Armenian history can be traced back some three thousand years to a time when the Armenian people were clearly identifiable on what was traditionally called the Armenian plateau, which extended through present-day eastern Anatolia (or eastern Turkey) to the South Caucasus (or Transcaucasia). The Armenians were on the crossroads of international commerce and, accordingly, their land became a region fought over by contending empires and nomadic invaders.

Eastern Armenia, in the South Caucasus, was laid waste by centuries of warfare. Western Armenia, present-day eastern Turkey, was conquered by the Ottomans between 1514 and 1534. Many Armenians fled to other countries, so by the seventeenth century the Armenians experienced a large diaspora that extended from Poland in the west to India and the Far East. This diaspora was chiefly mercantile, and it enjoyed a high standard of living and education. It was from the Persian and Indian diasporas that the Armenian liberation movement originated in the seventeenth century.

Attempts were made by a wealthy, self-appointed adventurer to better Armenian security in the Caucasus by encouraging a forward movement of the nominally Christian Russian Empire. Nothing much came of these early appeals, but by the early 1800s the Russians of their own accord occupied South Caucasus and Eastern Armenia.

The Armenian peasants in Eastern Armenia, under the Russian Empire, remained serfs until 1870. Armenian peasants in Western Armenia, who were no better off than serfs, saw their condition deteriorate further in the nineteenth century as the Ottoman Empire, under pressures from the European powers, was forced to abandon, one after the other, its possessions in the Balkans and some territory in eastern Anatolia.

The Armenian Enlightenment

The Armenian enlightenment movement of the nineteenth century sought to better the condition of peasants both in the east and in the west by raising national consciousness. This movement arose in several quarters: the Russian Armenian intelligentsia, university graduates, who lived in the major cities of Russia and the Caucasus; the scions of the Armenian moneyed class, the *amiras,* of Constantinople and Smyrna, who were sent to Europe to study and adopted progressive European values; the American Protestant missionaries who established churches, schools, and medical clinics all over Anatolia, and who instilled in Armenians the American ideals of democracy; and, finally, there were Armenian rite Roman Catholic monks who revived Armenian scholarship.

Failure of Ottoman Reforms

The Ottoman liberal reform movement (the Tanzimat), which evolved at the same time as the Armenian enlightenment, failed chiefly because of the enmity of the fundamentalist Muslim clergy and conservative Muslim society that objected to the acceptance of Christians and Jews, the despised *gavours* (unbelievers), as the equals of Muslims.

Armenians in the Russian Empire

The Armenians of the former Russian Empire can be divided roughly into two groups: those living in Caucasian Armenia, the vast majority of whom were peasants, and those who lived in other parts of the empire as merchants/entrepreneurs, craftsmen, various professionals, and the like. In the Caucasus, for instance, the Armenian middle class dominated Tbilisi, the seat of the Transcaucasan viceroy and the capital of Georgia, and they enjoyed great financial success in Baku, which later became the capital of Azerbaijan.

Russian tsar Nicholas II continued his father's policy of repressing the domestic radical movement, which drove the revolutionaries into hiding or abroad, chiefly to Geneva and London. Native Armenian radicals made little headway domestically until 1903 through 1905, when Nicholas II closed down Armenian schools and attempted to deprive the Armenian Church of the income from its hereditary properties.

The Armenian radical intelligentsia followed the example of their Russian and Jewish compatriots. Armenian socialists established the Hunchak Party in Geneva in 1887, among the Russian radicals who had fled Russia, and patterned their party on the *Narodniks,* the Russian populists, who believed in "going to the people" to educate and radicalize them. For the Russian populists, "going to the people" meant going out to the oppressed Russian peasants of the Russian Empire, whereas for the Hunchaks, the people (they) were the oppressed Armenian peasants of the Ottoman Empire, among whom the Hunchaks eventually became active.

A lithograph depicting a group of Armenians, c. 1849. By the early 1800s the Russians had occupied South Caucasus and Eastern Armenia. Many Armenians became serfs living within the Russian Empire. [HISTORICAL PICTURE ARCHIVE/CORBIS]

Another Armenian political party, the *Dashnaktsutiun,* was founded by Russian Armenians in 1890 and spread then to the Ottoman Empire. Interestingly, this Armenian Revolutionary Federation, realizing that the Armenians were too few in number and too weak in strength to attempt to overthrow either of the powerful imperial governments or to establish themselves as an independent state, did not advocate Armenian independence. It was the *Dashnaktsutiun* that cooperated first with the Young Ottomans, an aristocratic liberal group of European-educated Turks, and then up to 1913 with the Young Turks (*Ittihad ve Terakke Jemieti,* the Committee for Union and Progress), mostly young army officers from the Turkish military academy in the Balkans.

Hamedian Massacres

Both the Armenians and Young Turks wanted to overthrow Sultan Abdul Hamid II (1876–1909) and reestablish the constitution that Abdul Hamid had arbitrarily suspended. Using the pretext of an Armenian revolt, Abdul Hamid turned viciously against the Armenians and instigated a series of massacres from 1894 to 1896 in the six "Armenian provinces" that resulted in the death of some 100,000 to 200,000 [to 300,000] Armenians and demoralized tens of thousands more.

Young Turk Revolution

In 1908 the Young Turks, encouraged by the Armenians and other minorities, carried out a revolution and reestablished the constitution. These early, heady days witnessed jubilation among enlightened Turkish and non-Turkish inhabitants of the empire, since the constitution now guaranteed all inhabitants—Muslim, Christians, and Jews alike—equality under the law. As before under the Tanzimat, traditional Muslim society and clergy refused to accept non-Muslims as equals.

The very next year, in 1909, the Armenians of Cilicia—among whom a wealthy and Westernized class existed—angered tradition-bound Turkish leaders, and a massacre resulted whereby some thirty thousand Armenians were slaughtered throughout the region.

The Armenian Genocide

In 1913 a radical group of Young Turks overthrew the Ottoman government and established a dictatorship. The ruling triumvirate led an ill-prepared Turkey into World War I on the side of Germany against Russia and the Allies. The ideology of exclusive nationalism became a policy sometime around the beginning of Word War I, when the central organ of the Committee for Union and Progress instituted a plan to empty Anatolia entirely of Armenian Christians by deportations and massacres under the cover of war.

A major Turkish argument for eliminating the Armenians is that it was a military necessity because Nicholas II had offered the Armenians a homeland if they supported Russia during the war, and that the Armenians were a potential fifth column. Such promises as the many made by Tsar Nicholas were part and parcel of wartime propaganda that few on any side intended to keep. Similarly, the Young Turks promised a "semi-autonomous" Armenia at the Erzerum (or Erzurum) Congress of the Dashnaktsutiun in July 1914, if the Armenians on both sides of the border would fight against the Russians. The Armenian delegates declined both offers.

Founding a Republic

In March of 1917 the Russian bourgeois revolution took place. The Russian armies in Turkey, losing clear direction, began to disintegrate. The Armenians who lived in the territories added to Russia in 1878 fled with the retreating Russian armies. The Armenians within Russian territory organized a federation with Georgia and Azerbaijan to bring order to South Caucasus. With the advance of the revitalized Turkish army into the Caucasus in 1918, however, the Transcaucasian Federation dissolved and Armenia, only some 4,000 square miles (or 11,000 sq. km.) in size, declared its independence on May 28, 1918, and was left to face the advancing Turkish armies alone. In acts of desperate self-defense, fearing a continuation of the massacres, the Armenian remnant repulsed the Turkish onslaught in three major encounters, thereby bringing it to a temporary halt.

U.S. President Wilson and the Armenian Mandate

Struggling with the problems of security, refugees, war, and famine, Armenia sought an American mandate to sustain the fledgling state and to assist in its reconstruction. President Woodrow Wilson made an appeal to the U.S. Senate and traveled throughout the United States seeking public support for his plan. The Senate, however, which had grown isolationist in the interim, rejected the proposal and left Armenia to survive as best as it could.

Bolshevik Takeover and the Armenian Soviet Republic

Meanwhile, the Bolsheviks carried out a coup d'etat against the provisional government in November of 1917 and created a Red Army to consolidate their power and recapture the territories of the defunct Russian Empire. Almost no Bolsheviks lived in Armenia, because Armenia at that time was an agricultural region. The Armenian Bolsheviks, later known as the Baku Commissars, were concentrated in Baku, which was the most industrialized part of South Caucasus.

Armenia at this juncture faced three enemies: the revitalized Turkish nationalist army that stood ready to attack Armenia once more and annihilate the remnant of Armenians; the Azerbaijani nationalist army that sought, successfully, to occupy Nakichevan and Nagorno-Karabakh, two districts inhabited by Armenians; and the Red Army that had struck a deal with Mustafa Kemal Pasha Ataturk not to lay claim to the areas of eastern Turkey (specifically Kars, Ardahan, and Batum) that had been captured by the tsar in 1877 and 1878 and abandoned in 1917.

The Bolshevik leaders in Moscow saw Ataturk's army as an anti-imperialist force and hoped to see the growth of communism in Turkey. Moscow also wanted to establish its power in Muslim Central Asia and did not want to antagonize the Muslims of Turkey. Lenin's hope for a communist revolution in Turkey was in vain. Once Ataturk assumed full control, he obliterated the Turkish Communist Party.

In 1920 the Armenian Republic, facing a Turkish army in the west and a Red army in the east, surrendered to the Bolsheviks as the lesser of two evils. The Bolsheviks then signed a draconian peace in Moscow with the Turkish nationalists that left Armenia bereft even of its traditional emblem, Mount Ararat, and its historic capital, Ani. Eventually, an Armenian Soviet Socialist Republic was established as one of the constituent republics of the USSR. The present-day independent Armenian Republic, with the same boundaries as the former Soviet Republic, occupies only the central eastern edge of historic Armenia.

Armenian Soviet Socialist Republic

The Baku Commissars having been killed, the young Armenian Bolsheviks who came under the leadership of the Red Army were inexperienced and ideologically narrow. They immediately conducted purges and in

A Turkey just coming into existence entered World War I on the side of Germany against Russia. Tsar Nicholas II promised Armenians a homeland on the condition that they support Russia during the conflict. This 1915 photo shows Armenian soldiers from Transcaucasia who have joined forces with the Russians. [UNDERWOOD & UNDERWOOD/CORBIS]

1921 the Armenians rebelled against Soviet power. The rebellion was but a brief interlude and was harshly vanquished.

The Armenians in the Soviet Union, except for being deprived of the eastern Armenian territory by Russia, Turkey, Azerbaijan, and Georgia, were treated as well or better than the other nationalities within the union. Lenin attempted to pacify the national minorities by a system of *khorenizatsya* (nativization), which encouraged the various nationalities to administer their local republics while at the same time remaining loyal to the Soviet central government. Due to Soviet policies, Armenian nationalism was preserved and strengthened during the Soviet period, even though Moscow continued to take harsh action against overt nationalists.

Armenian intellectuals living in Baku, Tiflis, or Moscow were encouraged to emigrate to Armenia in order to enrich Armenian life. State support was given to historians, linguists, composers, painters, sculptors, novelists, and poets. The state supported a university, a conservatory of music, a national theater and opera,

and a film studio. Religion and religious practices, however, were discouraged and the church was suppressed.

Stalinism

Once Joseph Stalin solidified his power and introduced rapid industrialization, the five-year plans, and collectivization of agriculture, political repression was applied against all those who resisted the new order. Furthermore, the great purges that began in the 1930s wiped out almost the entire cadre of top-ranking Armenian communists, as well as many intellectuals, who were either imprisoned, exiled, or executed. By 1939 the purges came to an end and Stalin had removed any real or possible opposition to his rule. He brought to an abrupt halt Lenin's policy of nativization and introduced a period of Soviet patriotism, which was thinly disguised Russian nationalism.

World War II and the Death of Stalin

Armenians fought gallantly during World War II and Armenian troops engaged in heavy fighting at the front, and produced sixty generals and four (out of ten) marshals of the Soviet Union. Toward the end of the war

Stalin allowed the Armenians to elect a new head of their church, the Catholicos, a post that had remained vacant since 1938 when the then Catholicos was apparently murdered by the KGB and Stalin denied permission to the Armenians to elect a new one.

Following the war Stalin ordered a "repatriation" campaign to bring Armenians from overseas to help rebuild their devastated country. Over 100,000 Armenians, chiefly from the Middle East and Greece, immigrated to Armenia. The local population, however, did not welcome the extra burden imposed on a country already beset by a shortage of food, housing, and decent working conditions. By 1948 the inability of the newcomers to adapt themselves to Soviet conditions made them suspect and many were exiled to Siberia. It was also around this time that Stalin raised the question of a return of the territories from Turkey that the Russian Empire held between 1878 and 1921, not with the intention of adding them to Armenia because there were no longer any Armenians living there, but to Georgia that already had a Muslim population in the area abutting Turkey.

Armenia and Georgia seemed to have been favored by Stalin economically, although he retained strong political control and viciously suppressed any signs of nationalism. Beginning in the 1950s Georgia and Armenia, because of their climates, topography, development, and facilities, became destinations for Soviet tourists, and Armenia attracted diasporan Armenians as well, advertising the "advantages of socialism." Otherwise, Armenia experienced the vissitudes of Soviet rule much as the other European republics did, contending with economic development and political repression. Armenian cultural and intellectual life, however, managed to grow exponentially.

The Free and Independent Armenian Republic
Armenia remained relatively prosperous for a Soviet republic until the period of Leonid Brezhnev's rule, when the economy was undermined by indifference and corruption at all levels. Furthermore, bad planning and unrestrained growth of industry led to degradation of the environment and an ecological disaster. A movement in the 1980s to save the ecology morphed into a political movement, the Armenian National Movement (ANM), which sought to unify Nagorno-Karabakh with Armenia. The ANM argued that the Azeris were engaging in cultural genocide by repression that undermined the Armenian nature of the province, which they likened to the Armenian Genocide of 1915, calling it a "white genocide," or slow death, as compared to a "red genocide," or outright massacres.

The Azeri leaders in Azerbaijan were incensed by Armenian demands. In February 1988 a massacre of Armenians occurred in Sumgait, a working-class suburb of Baku, and then, subsequently, in January 1990 another bloody pogrom took place in Baku. War broke out between Armenia and Azerbaijan. In 1991 the former Soviet Union imploded and Armenia, along with all the other Soviet republics, became independent. In the first free elections in Armenia since 1919, the ANM became predominant in the parliament and Levon Ter-Petrossian, its leader, was elected president. Since then presidential power has passed into the hands of Robert Kocharian, the former president of Nagorno-Karabakh, who had been appointed premier by Ter-Petrossian. The war with Azerbaijan ended with a truce, and as of mid-2004 the issue of the political future of Nagorno-Karabakh had yet to be settled. Although Armenia is once more growing economically, it is hindered by a blockade imposed by Azerbaijan in the east and the Republic of Turkey, in sympathy with Azerbaijan, in the west. Nevertheless, it remains the most stable of the three South Caucasus republics.

SEE ALSO Atatürk, Mustafa Kemal Pasha; Armenians in Ottoman Turkey and the Armenian Genocide; Enver, Ismail; Talaat

BIBLIOGRAPHY

HISTORICAL OVERVIEWS
Bournoutian, George (2002). *A Concise History of the Armenian People: From Ancient Times to the Present.* Costa Mesa, Calif.: Mazda Publishers.
Hovannisian, Richard G., ed. (1997). *The Armenian People from Ancient to Modern Times.* New York: St. Martin's Press.
Walker, Christopher J. (1990). *Armenia: The Survival of a Nation, Revised Second Edition.* New York: St. Martin's Press.

DOCUMENT COLLECTIONS
Bournoutian, George A., trans. (1998). *Russia and the Armenians of Transcaucasia, 1797–1889: A Documentary Record.* Costa Mesa, Calif.: Mazda Publishers.
Bournoutian, George A., trans. (2001). *Armenians and Russia, 1626–1979: A Documentary Record.* Costa Mesa, Calif.: Mazda Publishers.
Burdett, Anita L. P., ed. (1998). *Armenia: Political and Ethnic Boundaries, 1878–1948: Documents and Maps.* New York: Archive Editions.

MONOGRAPHS
Brook, Stephen (1992). *Claws of the Crab: Georgia and Armenia in Crisis.* London: Sinclair-Stevenson.
Hovannisian, Richard G. (1971–1996). *The Republic of Armenia,* 4 volumes. Berkeley: University of California Press.
Malkasian, Mark (1996). *"Gha-Ra-Bagh!": The Emergence of the National Democratic Movement in Armenia.* Detroit, Mich.: Wayne State University Press.

Matossian, Mary Kilbourne (1962). *The Impact of Soviet Policies in Armenia.* Leiden: E. J. Brill.

Somakian, Manoug Joseph (1995). *Empires in Conflict: Armenia and the Great Powers, 1895–1920.* London: I. B. Tauris and Company.

Dennis R. Papazian

Art, Banned

Art that is banned may be found in all types of regimes, ranging from democracies to those that are authoritarian and genocidal. On the one hand, there has been a consistent debate about the use of public funds for the arts, which always has had a low appeal with electorates. On the other, humankind's knowledge of many civilizations has developed through their artistic contributions, even if they are handed down through history in disfigured form. Ancient Egyptian rulers usually mutilated the images of their predecessors. Almost all religions have tried to ban one form of art or another because of the deity or belief depicted. In Christian art, especially the Byzantine variant, biblical images of Christ and the Holy Family had to follow axiomatic rules on the representation of icons. The work of artists and intellectuals that has criticized military policy or underscored political follies has often been banned and even destroyed in gallery settings. The critique of war and patriotism has always been considered bad form, and in the early twentieth century this viewpoint was best expressed in the German government of Kaiser Wilhelm II, which reacted to the extremism of the Dadaists and expressionist artists who painted the horrors of World War I's battlefields and sometimes created images of the ruling elite as soldiers with pig's heads.

From the modern perspective of authoritarian regimes, the former Soviet Union under Joseph Stalin was the first to ban large areas of artistic representation and numerous artists. By the end of the 1920s, after a long period of creative and experimental achievement by Russian artists, the Soviet Union declared that all art must follow socialist realism, meaning it be realist in form, socialist in content. Thus, art in the Soviet Union ceased to be free and became a means of propaganda to prop up the regime. Artists had to choose to conform, emigrate if possible, or opt for "inner exile," which meant avoiding controversial subjects altogether. Many artists died in Soviet prison camps, and it was not until the early 1960s, during a period of Soviet history known as "the thaw," that artists began to confront formerly taboo subjects. By the 1970s and through the end of the Soviet regime in 1991, a substantial unofficial art movement became rooted in many intellectual capitals of the Soviet Union. The critiques of these artists, which ranged from visual puns to pop art and reli-

Often, banned art is work deemed "morally deficient" by regimes. Other times, it is art targeted for the religious or political beliefs it conveys. Here, an ancient Buddha as obliterated by the Taliban, extreme Islamic fundamentalists who ruled Afghanistan up until the early twenty-first century. [REUTERS/CORBIS]

gious themes, were symptomatic of the failing political regime.

Nazi Germany was the only genocidal regime that made aesthetics and art an important component of regime ideology. This unique characteristic may be linked to the Nazi consolidation of power over a six-year period before mass murder and war began. The key word for Nazism was *degeneracy,* which came to include physical, genetic, and psychological deformations in human beings; abstract and expressionist art; modern forms of music like jazz; and various campaigns to purify the human body, as exemplified by campaigns against white bread, margarine, women wearing cosmetics, and smoking. Adolf Hitler, who had aspired to become an artist earlier in his career, always maintained a keen interest in the arts and future architecture of Germany. In 1933, under the jurisdiction of Joseph Goebbels, *Deutscher Kunstbericht* (The German

Art Report) published a five-point manifesto for purifying German art. The main points included: the removal of all "cosmopolitan" works that were Bolshevist or Marxist in nature, the removal of all museum directors who spent public funds on such works, the condemnation and prevention of construction of "boxlike" buildings (a specific attack on the Bauhaus School of Design), and the removal of all public sculptures not approved by the public. On November 26, 1936, Goebbels, by then Hitler's Minister of Propaganda, banned art criticism. This edict restricted the number of people allowed to write about art and gave the government a monopoly over artistic ideas. A fundamental aspect of this assault, subsequently used in Nazi propaganda, was the belief that Jews controlled the art market and reaped huge profits. Thus, the Weimar Republic was defined by Nazism as a period of Jewish takeover of the arts, with the Jews becoming the scapegoat of antimodernists.

In July 1937 six hundred works of art representing heroic Aryan themes were hung for the *Grosse Deutsche Kunstausstellung* (Great German Art Exhibition) that opened in Munich. Hitler himself used this occasion to spell out, in essence, his plan for extermination: "From now on we are going to wage a merciless war of destruction against the last remaining elements of cultural disintegration"(Barron, 1991, p. 17). The alternative to so-called degenerate art was a heroic form linking the body and politics to race. The same month in 1937 the first of many *Entartete Kunst* (degenerate) art shows opened. These shows, which may have drawn the largest crowds in museum history, juxtaposed degenerate art, as influenced by "Jews and Negroes," against the Aryan ideal, that expressed romanticized themes of German mythology, militarism, productive workers and docile women tending to families in painting and sculpture. Only a small number of the artists shown were, in fact, Jews. Most were German artists who had been part of the avant-garde movement: Ernst Nolde, himself a member of NSDAP—The Nazi Party; Max Beckmann; Willi Baumesiter; Otto Dix; Paul Klee; Max Pechstein; Ernst Barlach; Ernst Ludwig Kirchner; Oskar Kokoshka; Kathe Kollwitz; Max Lieberman; Mies Van der Rohe; and Ludwig Gies.

Nazi guidelines on the arts became part of the destruction and regulation of all cultural life in Germany. In a broader sense, a good deal of the Nazi attack on culture might be called a war against imagination and the vision of the other. This became the prelude to genocide on a larger scale. In Germany the misuse of art helped define the victim. The administration of the visual arts came to parallel treatment of the Jews. The military conquests of Nazi Germany during World War II were followed immediately by expropriation of artistic treasures from all over Europe on a scale that was unprecedented. A new German art failed to materialize, as the limited subject matter for artistic concerns—military heroism; a fit body; portraits of the Führer; and seductive, almost pornographic, images of women—became the style of the period. The two major German sculptors who have remained the subject of artistic investigation are Arno Breker and Josef Thorak because of their focus on the human body, considerations of classical form, and a type of slick modernism that crept into corporate commercials and advertising during the 1990s.

Communist regimes in Asia, beginning with Maoist China, also placed a ban on most art forms. Painting immediately after 1948 largely evolved into graphic design adaptable to huge posters that supported the regime's policies. Certain so-called bourgeois concepts, such as Western art, Western music, and the playing of the card game bridge, were prohibited. Once in power, Maoist ideology was instrumental in destroying many of the cultural legacies of the Chinese artistic past, especially when an intersection of the arts and religion occurred. This was especially true in Tibet, where countless Buddhist monasteries were destroyed. The destruction of Tibetan Buddhist art had strong impact on the decline of the religion there. The Taliban regime in Afghanistan went even further by destroying, with artillery fire, two of the largest statues of Buddha in the world in Bamiyan Province.

Denial of genocide by current regimes can also be the basis for a ban on art. Thus, as the Turkish Republic has a state-directed policy about acknowledging the genocide of Armenians under Ottoman rule in 1915, discourse about this subject takes place in Armenia and in the Armenian diaspora.

SEE ALSO Art, Stolen; Art as Propaganda; Art as Representation

BIBLIOGRAPHY

Barron, Stephanie (1991). *Degenerate Art: The Fate of the Avant-Garde in Nazi Germany.* New York: Harry Abrams.

Golomstock, Igor (1990). *Totalitarian Art in the Soviet Union, The Third Reich, Fascist Italy and the People's Republic of China.* New York: HarperCollins.

Petropoulos, Jonathan (1996). *Art as Politics in the Third Reich.* Chapel Hill: University of North Carolina Press.

Spotts, Frederic (2002). *Hitler and the Power of Aesthetics.* New York: Overlook Press.

Welch, David (1993). *The Third Reich: Politics and Propaganda.* London: Routledge.

Stephen C. Feinstein

Art, Stolen

The theft of art, or cultural looting, has almost always been one of the staple by-products of genocide and genocidal regimes. From ancient times to modern conflicts (e.g., the war in the former Yugoslavia), the plunder of artworks and the willful destruction of a cultural heritage have been used by the victor as a supplementary means to conquer, annihilate, and humiliate the enemy. Not only do conquerors try to obliterate their enemies physically, but they also try to take possession of their victims' precious art objects, including those that express their identity thereby simultaneously stealing the soul, meaning, and cultural values of a people.

Such stealing and destruction have occurred in many modern instances of genocide, including the Armenian genocide, the Khmer Rouges in Cambodia, Native Americans in the United States and Latin America, the wars in former Yugoslavia, but Adolf Hitler and the Nazis carried out what can be considered the most important systematic, methodical, and ideologically organized art theft in history.

Hitler's genocidal policies led to the extermination of millions of people and the eradication of long-established cultures in large areas of Europe. In addition, the Nazi policy of destruction of the enemy included the theft of the private and religious art collections and libraries of Jews, Freemasons, political opponents, and Gypsies in the German-occupied countries of Europe during World War II. To reach their goals, the Nazis used modern methods taken from industrial society: preliminary spying and research, renowned art historians and experts, and highly trained assistants, photographers, and administrative personnel. To safeguard their acquisitions, they employed double-entry accounting and coded inventories, and used land and air transport to carry off their stolen goods.

The well-planned Nazi theft, executed mostly under the guise of "legal confiscations," was also an integral part of the entire genocidal process known as the Final Solution and the Holocaust. From 1939 to 1945, Hitler and the Nazis, using a well-knit network of informers and collaborationist art dealers in Germany and the occupied countries, collected hundreds of thousands of works of art and millions of books confiscated or forcibly purchased from museums, private collections, libraries, and religious institutions. At a conservative estimate, the thefts in Western Europe reached an astounding total of about 300,000 artworks and antiques, and more than two million books and manuscripts confiscated by Hitler's looting staff. In Eastern Europe and the former Soviet Union, the Nazi

program of art theft was not as well-organized, but it was more destructive.

Art theft acquired its surprisingly central importance under Nazism, mainly due to Hitler's personal interest in art. A mediocre painter as a youth, Hitler had, as a student, twice tried and failed the entrance examination to the School of Fine Arts in Vienna. In time he became an avid, though unskilled, art collector. His personal artistic taste was rigid, and he favored the Old Masters of Northern Europe—Dürer, Cranach, Vermeer, Rembrandt and Rubens, among others—that strongly enhanced and fit into his own political views on the superiority of Germanic culture. He also coveted the words of the Italian Renaissance Masters, such as Michelangelo or Leonardo da Vinci.

On the other hand, Hitler despised Picasso, Matisse, and the whole modern art school. In *Mein Kampf*, his autobiography, he ferociously attacked the degeneracy of modern art, considering Cubism, Futurism, and Dadaism to be the product of decadent twentieth-century society. After taking power in 1933, Hitler sold or destroyed the modern paintings found in Germany's state museums. He did not allow looted modern or degenerate artworks into Germany; instead, these were returned to the European art market in exchange for pieces that met the approval of Nazi ideology.

Hitler intended his thousands of newly, ill-gotten Old Masters and realistic paintings to form the central collection of a European Art Museum to be built in the Austrian city of Linz, where he had spent his childhood years. Other Nazi dignitaries, including Reichsmarschall Hermann Goering and Foreign Affairs Minister von Ribbentrop, also took advantage of German conquests to increase their private art collections.

Among the wealthy occupied countries of Western Europe, France suffered the most from Nazi looting, not only because it was probably the richest in art, but also because French Jews were among the best and most important art dealers and collectors at the time. From 1940 to 1944, an astronomical 100,000 artworks—or one-third of all art in French private hands—were confiscated there.

Nazis understood art theft as a way to redress what they considered to be the wrongs of history against the German people. They perceived Jewish collectors as usurpers. The legal, moral, and political justifications for Nazi theft and looting are clearly explained in a statement of principles issued by the Berlin head of the Einsatzstab Reichsleiters Rosenberg (ERR), the organization in charge of the plunder of the cultural and artistic treasures of the Jews. This memorandum, published November 3, 1941, and written by Gerhard Utikal, the

In Germany, a U.S. soldier inspects stolen paintings inside what had been barracks for Luftwaffe officers. Priceless art was looted from all over Europe and transported to Germany at the directive of Hermann Göring (who adorned his own mansions with stolen art treasures).
[HULTON ARCHIVE/GETTY IMAGES]

head of the ERR in Berlin, provides the reasons behind cultural looting in France:

> The war against the Greater German Reich was incited by world Jewry and Freemasonry, which have provoked various states and European peoples into waging war against Germany. . . . The armistice with the French state and people does not extend to Jews in France . . . who are to be considered "a state within the state" and permanent enemies of the German Reich. . . . German reprisals against Jews are based on people's rights. . . . Jews have since ancient times, and following the dictates of Jewish law set forth in the Talmud, applied the principle that all non-Jews be considered cattle and therefore without rights, and that non-Jewish property be considered abandoned and ownerless.

The looting of cultural property was one of the main indictments introduced against Nazi dignitaries at the Nuremberg War Crimes Tribunal. It is also one of the war crimes under investigation at the International Criminal Tribunal for the Former Yugoslavia, particularly with regard to Bosnia and the planned destruction of cultural and religious monuments of Muslim and Croats by Bosnian Serbs.

One of the primary ideological goals of genocidal regimes is to change the course of history; and the Nazis, in this sense, were no exception. By stealing—illegitimately transferring ownership—or destroying the art of their enemies, they tried to impose a homogeneous and restrictive cultural view of the world. Recent investigative work had brought to the fore of international public opinion the presence of thousands of Nazi-looted artworks in museums, auction houses, art galleries, and private collections in Europe, the United States, and Canada. Even though an important segment of the art world and art market has set numerous legal and administrative obstacles, in a few years' time, thousands of looted artworks have been returned to their rightful owners and heirs, stirring a world-wide ethical

Around 1910 the poster became a respectable advertising medium. By World War II warring governments used it to solicit recruits, to raise money, and to urge the conservation of resources. Here, the British-born artist Albert Sterner paints a war poster in his studio in the United States, c. 1917. [CORBIS]

and juridical debate on the subject of the selling, acquisition, and possession of art stolen by the Nazis.

SEE ALSO Art, Banned; Art as Propaganda; Restitution

BIBLIOGRAPHY

Feliciano, Hector. (1997). *The Lost Museum: The Nazi Conspiracy to Steal the World's Greatest Works of Art.* New York: Basic Books.

Hilberg, R. (1961). *The Destruction of the European Jews.* Chicago: Quadrangle Books.

Nicholas, Lynn H. (1994). *The Rape of Europa: The Fate of Europes Treasures in the Third Reich and the Second World War.* New York: Knopf.

Hector Feliciano

Art as Propaganda

For genocide and crimes against humanity to occur, the dehumanization of the potential victims must first take place. Perpetrators of such crimes often use art as a tool to help them accomplish their goals. Indeed, without the intense propagandistic effort of the National Socialists to demonize Jews, Africans, Roma, the ill, and others they deemed "undesirable," the genocidal intentions of Hitler and the Nazi party may not have been realized. As historian David Welch suggests in his 1993 book, *The Third Reich: Politics and Propaganda,* Nazi propaganda was used to convince those who were not yet persuaded of the importance of the Hitler's racial policies, and to inspire those who already adhered to his views.

The Jews were one of the primary targets of Nazi smear campaigns. Hitler's propagandists employed newspaper caricatures, films, and posters in their attempt to dehumanize the Jews. Julius Streicher, the editor of the National Socialist *Der Stürmer,* printed a number of editorial cartoons that depicted Jews as either "children of the devil," or as rat-like vermin whose "claws" can stretch out and infect the entire globe. Film was also used to distill and disseminate the Nazis' racist values. For example, in the movie *Jud Süss,* the director Veit Hartlan distorted the story of an actual eighteenth century Jewish court financier who had been hanged for "Christian treachery and hypocrisy" (Welch, 1983, p. 285). Veit transformed him into a stereotypical cosmopolitan Jew. He portrayed him as someone willing to disguise his Jewishness so that he might rape the Aryan maiden Dorothea and satiate his reputedly monstrous sexual appetites. Although the rape of Dorothea incensed many in the German audience who viewed the film, it was, as one newspaper critic remarked, the scene of the Jews bringing "all their belongings into Stuttgart . . . [that] repeatedly prompted . . . shouts of . . . 'Throw the last of the Jews out of Germany!'" (Welch, 1983, p. 291). If films such as *Jud Süss* or editorial cartoons did not fully achieve the goals of the National Socialist Party, the party's propaganda minister, Goebbels, was willing to employ other tactics as well. Widely circulated posters such as *Der Ewige Jude* (The Eternal Jew) asserted that the Orthodox Jew was crooked, was concerned only with money, and was aligned with the forces of Bolshevism.

Like the Jews, African-Germans, homosexuals, Roma and others were rendered as racially undesirable by Nazi propaganda. On August 5, 1929, Hitler concluded that "If Germany was to get a million children a year and was to remove 700,000–800,000 of the weakest people, then the final result might be an increase in strength" (Burleigh and Wippermann, 1992, p. 142). African workers who stayed in Germany in order to remain with their Caucasian wives and interracial children represented a potential "corruption" of the Aryan blood line. As a result, many of the so-called *mischling* or mixed race children were forcibly sterilized. Indeed, the Nazis were so fearful of African and African-American culture (particularly jazz) that in 1930 a law was passed that was titled "Against Negro Culture." In other words, the Nazis were clearly aware of the potential for popular cultural forms to taint what they considered to be genuine Aryan culture—whether this taint was a result of marriage or of music. As a consequence, the Germans often conflated stereotypes of African-American musical performers with those of Jews and Africans into some of their most heinous propaganda pieces.

Two of the most infamous and well-known Nazi propaganda artworks were posters which advertised cultural events. In a poster advertising an exhibition of *entartete musik* (degenerate music), for example, the viewer is confronted with a dark-skinned man in a top hat with a large gold earring in his ear. This distorted caricature of an African homosexual male in black face playing a saxophone has a Star of David clearly emblazoned on his lapel. To the National Socialists, the most polluting elements of modern culture were represented

by this single individual. They were suggesting that anyone who listened to jazz (or enjoyed other forms of art that they judged to be degenerate) could be transformed into such a barbarous figure.

Toward the end of the war, the Nazis circulated posters in a somewhat desperate attempt to get their "white European brothers" to join their cause. In one infamous poster, the designer depicted a multi-armed monster clutching two white American women. Attached to his muscle-bound body are iconic references to the Ku Klux Klan, Judaism (the Star of David), boxing gloves, jazz dancing, and a lynching noose. At his middle is a sign that reads in English "Jitterbug—the Triumph of Civilization." This poster was directed at white European men, and it urged them to protect their wives and their culture against a coming invasion of primitive, inferior American men. As occurred in the poster that warned against jazz, this image conflated stereotypes of the Jew with that of the African in an attempt to frighten white (Aryan) Europe and America into joining their cause. The exaggerated racist stereotypes served to strengthen and amplify widely accepted attitudes regarding racial and ethnic superiority. With these images, the National Socialists were offering their justifications as to why certain groups should be feared and thus eliminated.

SEE ALSO Advertising; Architecture; Art, Banned; Art, Stolen; Film as Propaganda; Propaganda

BIBLIOGRAPHY

Burleigh, Michael, and Wolfgang Wipperman (1991). *The Racial State: Germany 1933–1945.* Cambridge: Cambridge University Press.

Lusane, Clarence (2003). *Hitler's Black Victims: The Historical Experiences of Afro-Germans, European Blacks, Africans, and African Americans in the Nazi Era.* New York: Routledge.

Petropoulos, Jonathan (1996). *Art as Politics in the Third Reich.* Chapel Hill: University of North Carolina Press.

Welch, David (1983). *Propaganda and the German Cinema: 1933–1945.* Oxford, U.K.: Oxford University Press.

Welch, David (1993). *The Third Reich: Politics and Propaganda.* London: Routledge.

Anna M. Dempsey

Art as Representation

The artistic legacy of genocide emanates from many quarters: outsiders and insiders warning about genocide or massacres in posters and paintings; images by survivors that include art created by children in the aftermath of genocide; imaginative, surrealistic, and what may be called postmodern art executed under the worst

Picasso's *Guernica,* depicting the horrors of war. A tapestry copy of *Guernica* is displayed at the entrance of the UN Security Council chamber in New York City. On January 27, 2003, a curtain was placed over the tapestry, so that it would not be visible when Colin Powell, John Negroponte, and others gave press conferences there. It was reported that television news crews had requested the curtain; however, some UN diplomats told journalists the United States had demanded that UN officials cover the tapestry. [**AP/WIDE WORLD PHOTOS**]

circumstances in order to convey a specific message about genocide via art. Artists, often seen as social outsiders, articulate various reasons for presenting genocidal subjects in art: witnessing; helping to commemorate or create an alternative form of memory to inform another generation of the event and its danger; use of fragmented, deconstructed visual forms instead of historical narratives as a means of telling the story; and warnings about lessons from the past that may bear on the future.

The styles of such critical artistic representation vary according to the chronological time of the genocidal event related to mainstream art movements. They have been expressionistic (George Grosz, Hannah Hoch, and Otto Dix's visual commentaries on the Jewish question from the early 1920s), photomontages (John Heartfield), surrealist (Max Ernst and Salvador Dali), realistic and satirical drawings (art from the concentration camps and ghettos, such as the work of Jozef Szajna and Eli Leskley, and Karl Stojko's images of the destruction of the Romani), and a vast array of media and forms of depiction in the aftermath of genocide, including sculpture, memorials, installation art, and large projects that often attempt a visual narrative. Key questions for such socially and politically directed art (and questions with illusive answers) are how specific it should be to the event, versus generalized human suffering, and what the balance between aesthetics and politics should be. The iconographic works that have

best stood the test of time are Francisco Goya's *Diasters of War* (early nineteenth century) and Pablo Picasso's *Guernica* (1937).

Depictions of the Armenian genocide contemporaneous with the event appeared largely in political posters and editorial cartoons in newspapers. The Holocaust took place over a longer time span and was connected to the chronic political and economic difficulties of the Weimar Republic. This event, therefore, as well as the fact that Jews are part of a larger religious story and have played an important role in modern art, produced a wider array of artistic responses than any other genocide. Second only in duration were the genocidal events in Bosnia during the 1990s, which led to the production of art ranging from simple painting by children that conveyed the horrific effects of events beyond their control, to sophisticated postmodern installations in galleries. Art about the Rwandan genocide appeared only after the event, particularly in the form of children's art completed with the help of psychologists attempting to treat post-traumatic stress disorders.

Issues in Artistic Representation of Genocide

Artists were keenly aware of the power of photography and film in the depiction of twentieth-century genocides. Many early-twenty-first-century photographic projects now focus on the often barren landscape of genocide. The most important question asked about photographs invariably is, "Who took the photographs?" Often the images were made by perpetrators or liberators, rarely by the victims themselves, and are thus documents. In the aftermath of such crimes photography also plays an important role as photojournalists often dwell on the images of remains and chaos. These scenes, in the hands of artists, often become the basis for other art such as collage, a form that includes well-known photographic images as part of larger canvases.

Artists who focus on genocidal events are concerned about the effect of their work. If the art is so visceral, many feel, it may alienate viewers. Controversies have also occurred over the inflammatory nature of their art, which has sometimes led to censorship. If the art and representation of genocide contain repetitive scenes of dead bodies, a characteristic of documentary-style photographs of genocide, the result might well repel viewers from the subject rather than maintain interest. Such work has the potential to be viewed as lowbrow or simply sensationalist. Furthermore, piles of human remains do not convey a sense of genocide, especially its source, except for being the most vivid representation of its aftermath. As genocides have occurred in different places, their artistic representations often contain images that convey a sense of geography, landscape, technology, and culture.

Themes of Absence

Still another subject found primarily in postmodern representations of genocide is the theme of absence, usually related to the aftermath of genocide. Loss can be conveyed by using old photographs of people and historic landmarks, and creating a visual sense of overall disturbance. Abstract artists Barnett Newman and Mark Rothko created a variation on absence in the late 1940s. Newman destroyed all of his art executed before 1945, insisting that a new form of visual representation was needed. The result was his *zip paintings,* large canvases with fields of color, or black and white, and vertical lines. The allusion of these works was the impossibility of adequately representing the Holocaust, as well as Newman's own retreat into the study of the kabbalah and the story of Creation from the Bible.

The British photographer Simon Norfolk produced an exhibition of the photos he had taken at many sites of genocide, from Namibia to Cambodia; that show was titled, *For Most of It, I have No Words.* Norfolk's ideological approach is related to the power of art to produce memory about atrocity, in both a kind and unkind way. He has written: "Forgetting is the final instrument of genocide" (Norfolk, 1998b). Installation artists also often deal with the theme of absence: French artist Christian Boltanski never depicts dead bodies or massacres, but does confront the viewer with mixed-media images of people who may be dead or alive, walls and metaphorical lakes filled with clothing, and haunting environments that suggest some sinister event. Chilean artist Alfredo Jaar produced a multi-room installation about Rwanda titled, *Let There Be Light* (1994–1998). A significant part of this exhibit stresses the impossibility of representing genocide and absence, all the while provoking viewers by sometimes perplexing devices. Jaar created eight different exhibits called *Real Pictures,* photos shown in an unexpected way: Groups of rectangular black boxes were arranged in patterns on the floor to form a series of monuments. No actual images were plainly visible, however. The photos were inside the black boxes, while the box lid, which could not be opened, recorded with white lettering a description of the images inside. But the viewer was not allowed to see the photos, as seeing, in the artist's vision, did not necessarily mean understanding.

In Bosnia such postmodernism was employed by some of the potential victims. *Witnesses to Existence* was a 1993 exhibition in Sarajevo conceived by Mirsad Purivatra, who invited a group of Sarajevo artists to install one-day solo shows in his ruined gallery. The exhibition was the official entry from the Republic of Bosnia and Herzegovina for the 45th Venice Biennale. As it turned out, however, the gallery was unable to ship the artists' works to Italy because of the Serbian blockade. Only a videotape of the exhibition found its way to Venice.

Art and Theodicy

Art also often relates to theological issues and a search for the spiritual. This is a difficult subject; one associated more closely with the Holocaust as a genocidal event because of its underlying race-religion question and Christianity's Jewish background. Spiritual themes and images are found in many artistic works about the Holocaust and occasionally in other genocide-related art. The idea of creating art from such extremely negative circumstances, thus affirming the value of human life and the existence of a Creator, is at best questionable, and suggests some of the difficult theological questions posed by the Holocaust: the presence and/or absence of God, the death of God, the use of mysticism as a way of understanding the immensity of the event and its purpose—for good to be understood, evil must perhaps exist. Paintings by Marc Chagall, Anselm Kiefer, Arie Galles, Alice Lok Cahana, Samuel Bak, Lea Grundig, Fritz Hirschberger, Mauricio Lasansky, Rico LeBrun, and others attempt to address some of these difficult questions. Armenian-American artist Robert Barsamiam has used images of the crucifixion in his room installations as a symbol of the fate of the Armenian people, but such a device does not invite theological questioning on the scale that a work about the Holocaust does. Artistic responses to the Bosnian war have not tried to deal with Christian or Muslim theological questions. Simon Norfolk's photographs of Rwanda after the genocide there have the power to raise questions about the failure of the Catholic Church in preventing genocide, or even witnessing the active participating in mass murder by a few priests and nuns.

One of the most successful painters of the Holocaust is a survivor from Vilna, Lithuania, Samuel Bak; he paints with a classical palette but after much experimentation with different forms of representation, Bak's painting settled into a kind of surrealism that revealed the artist's close ties with Renaissance paintings, the Jewish traditions as well as his feelings of estrangement from them. Bak does not describe this process as a long intellectual journey, rather a "responding to something that was pushing out from the inside, something visceral, something that takes a long time for the mind to comprehend." The result was a large body of paintings that focused on the themes of absence, the post-Holocaust landscape of Jewish existence, and the peoples of the technologically advanced modern age who are barely able to function, and made metaphorical use of specific objects such as chess pieces or pears for a discourse about the post-Holocaust world. Bak has described his vision as follows: "These representational paintings of mine depicted devastated landscapes of ancient cities, urban constructions that seemed to be made of a child's building blocks. In painted figures that were half-alive, and half-contrived of bizarre prostheses. I imagined helpless and abused angels. . . . My painting carried no answers, only questions."

Cambodia: Archive or Art?

A postgenocide art has materialized within Cambodia and in émigré Cambodian communities around the world that adds to an understanding of events there. One particularly important set of photographic images is *Facing Death: Portraits from the Killing Fields,* assembled by the Photo Archive Group at Boston University. The exhibition consists of photographs taken in S-21, a secret Cambodian prison operated by the Pol Pot regime in the capital city of Phnom Penh from mid-1975 through the end of 1978. As the text of the exhibition reads, "Individuals accused of treason, along with their families, were brought to S-21 where they were photographed upon arrival. They were tortured until they confessed to whatever crime their captors charged them with, and then executed" (University of Minnesota Center for Genocide and Holocaust Studies). Of the 14,200 people taken as prisoners, only 7 are known to have survived. After the Vietnamese army captured the

prison site in 1979, it was transformed into the Tuol Sleng Museum of Genocide. The photographic archive was catalogued and its contents published in 1994. One hundred negatives were selected for final printing, many of which are reproduced in the 1996 book *The Killing Fields.* Many of the photos, although documentary, have an artistic dimension. Some of the victims show fear, while others appear to laugh, as if they do not comprehend the horrible fate that awaits them. Viewers are left to ponder, at least for a second, if they would resist a similar fate or attempt to bargain for their lives.

Bunheang Ung, a prolific Cambodian artist and survivor of genocide, has created an important artistic chronicle of the Cambodian genocide. Ung was forced to flee Phnom Penh with his family in 1975. At the time he was twenty-three years old and a university student studying art. Assigned to work units in the rural economy, he witnessed the mass murder of thirty relatives. His black and white drawings, done in the late 1970s, possess a fascinating amount of detail. The energy of the artist's hand in drawing the images suggests his own agitation and need to fill every space on the drawn surface, as if there was too much to relate. His *Communal Dining* depicts resettlement camps where Cambodian life was realigned along collective lines. The drawings of torture, oppression, and murder share similarities with the images of the German painters Otto Dix and George Grosz, who recreated the horrors of World War I in their work. However, certain uniquely Cambodian symbols distinguish all art produced about this event, such as Ung's *Demolition of the Phum Andong Pagoda.*

Art about genocide is not in the public view as much as film, literature, and drama on the same subject. Since art needs appropriate gallery or museum space for display, it has certain constraints not encountered by other forms of representation. Therefore, the most frequent exhibitions that have included art about genocide have occurred in large European shows or historical commemorations, in galleries at colleges and universities, and only occasionally at large museums.

SEE ALSO Art as Propaganda

BIBLIOGRAPHY

Amishai-Maisels, Ziva (1993). *Depiction and Interpretation.* London: Pergammon Press.

Gambrell, Jamey. "Sarajevo: Art in Extremis." *Art in America* (May 1994).

Jaar, Alfredo (1998). *Let There Be Light: The Rwanda Project, 1994–1998.* Barcelona: Actar.

Norfolk, Simon (1998a). *For Most of It I Have No Words.* Stockport, U.K.: Dewi Leis.

Norfolk, Simon (1998b). "Remember the Killing Fields." *Peacematters* 23. Available from http://www.ppu.org.uk/peacematters/pre99/pm_autumn98b.html.

Riley, Chris, and Doug Niven (1996). *The Killing Fields*. Santa Fe, N.M.: Twin Palms.

Salem, Richard A., ed. (2000). *Witness to Genocide: The Children of Rwanda*. New York: Friendship Press.

Stuart-Fox, Martin, and Bunheang Ung (1988). *The Murderous Revolution*. Bangkok, Thailand: Orchid Press.

Taha, Khalid Ali. "Artistic Freedom." Available from http://www.reyum.org/media/misc-articles.

UNICEF (1993). *I Dream of Peace: Images of War by Children of Former Yugoslavia*. New York: HarperCollins.

University of Minnesota Center for Holocaust and Genocide Studies. "Facing Death: Portraits from Cambodia's Killing Fields." Available from http://www.chgs.umn.edu/Visual_Artistic_Resources/Cambodian_Genocide.

Witnesses of Existence (1993). Catalogue, La Biennale di Venezia, Galerija Obala Sarajevo.

Stephen C. Feinstein

Assassinations

Assassination is commonly defined as "political murder." While it is not necessary that the victim of an assassination be a political leader, assassinations are generally killings that target specific individuals for a political purpose, and are often accomplished by means of surprise or treachery. When ordered by a state against leaders of a foreign state, assassinations generally violate international law.

The word *assassination* first appeared in English in the play *Macbeth* by William Shakespeare. However, the root of the word, *assassin,* is much older. It originally comes from the Arabic word *hashshashin,* which means "eaters of hashish." This Arabic meaning derives from a certain Islamic sect whose members were known for murdering their political opponents after ingesting the drug hashish.

International law distinguishes between state-sponsored assassination and assassination that is not state-sponsored. When an assassination is committed by a group that is not affiliated with a government or by an individual acting alone, it is not state-sponsored. There have been many well-known assassinations of this type throughout history. For example, the Roman general and statesman Julius Caesar was assassinated by a group of conspirators in the Roman Senate in 44 BCE. The American Presidents Abraham Lincoln and John F. Kennedy were also assassinated by individuals who were not acting on behalf of any state, as was the civil rights leader Martin Luther King, whose killer was an escaped convict. Another example of this type of as-

sassination is the murder of Egyptian president Anwar al-Sadat, who was assassinated by Islamic extremists in his own army, while he was reviewing a military parade in 1981.

Assassinations that are not sponsored by states are usually treated as murders in the countries where they occur. Because no state is responsible, they usually do not violate international law. Except in the case of international criminal law, only states can be held responsible for violating international law.

State-Sponsored Assassination

Under most circumstances, international law prohibits state-sponsored assassination. The United Nations Charter prohibits the aggressive use of force by one state against another. The Charter also prohibits interfering in the territory or affairs of another state. Chapter I of the Charter requires that all states must "settle their international disputes by peaceful means" and must "refrain in their international relations from the threat or use of force". When a state sponsors the assassination of the leader of another state, it violates this basic rule of international law.

However, there are two important exceptions to this rule. First, state-sponsored "targeted killings" may sometimes be legal during times of war. Under the law of war, two states that are at war with each other may kill soldiers in the opposing army. The killing of enemy soldiers is not considered illegal assassination because during a war soldiers are said to have a legal "privilege" to kill their enemies. This privilege extends to military leaders, who are often considered fair game as "command-and-control" targets. In some cases, government officials may be fair targets if they are part of the military chain of command.

However, even during times of war a "targeted killing" can only be legal if it does not violate the law of war. A state that uses "treachery" to kill an enemy may be guilty of war crimes. Article 23 of the Hague Convention IV of 1907 provides that "it is especially forbidden . . . to kill or wound treacherously, individuals belonging to the hostile nation or army." *Treachery* is usually defined as a breach of confidence, such as an attack on an individual who believes that there is no need to fear the attacker. Examples of treachery include attacking while pretending to seek a truce or surrender, attacking while pretending to be injured or sick, or attacking while pretending to be a non-combatant civilian. However, the mere act of surprising an enemy or failing to meet the enemy face-to-face is not enough to constitute treachery. Treacherous assassinations are illegal under the law of war.

The second exception to the general prohibition against state-sponsored assassination is the exception for self-defense. Article 51 of the United Nations Charter grants states an "inherent right" to self-defense if an armed attack against them occurs. If assassination is used as self-defense it may be legal under international law. The self-defense exception does not require that the state be at war, but the assassination must meet the definition of a legitimate act of self-defense.

There are three main requirements for a legitimate act of self-defense. First, self-defense may only be used when the threat of aggression is imminent. This means that defensive force may only be used to defend against an act of aggression that is occurring or is about to occur. Second, force must be necessary in order to defend against the aggression. If there is any other way to defend against the threat, such as a diplomatic solution, it must be used first. Third, the defensive response must be proportionate to the threatened aggression. A state may not use more force than necessary to defend against the threat. Any extra force would be considered an illegal reprisal, and not a legal act of self-defense. Under these criteria, an assassination must be designed to defend against an immediate threat of aggression to be considered a legitimate form of self-defense. The assassination must be the only way to defend against the aggression. Furthermore, the assassination may not be used for reprisals against an attack that has already occurred.

Scholars have debated whether the right to self-defense permits the use of assassination to prevent or deter future attacks. This is generally called "anticipatory self-defense." The more restrictive view is that assassination can only be legal when used to defend against a specific attack that is occurring or is about to occur. Others argue that terrorism and weapons of mass destruction have created a new environment, in which states must be allowed to defend themselves by any means necessary, even before an attack has begun. Israel has frequently used assassination as a kind of anticipatory self-defense. In 1988 its agents killed Abu Jihad, the head of military strategy for the Palestinian Liberation Organization. In 1992 an Israeli helicopter gunship killed Sheik Abbas Musawi, the leader of the Islamic Resistance Movement. In 2004 an Israeli missile killed the spiritual leader of Hamas, Sheikh Ahmed Yassin. Israel has argued that these killings are necessary to prevent future terrorist attacks, but many international observers view them as reprisals for past acts and, therefore, as illegitimate forms of self-defense.

U.S. Law on State-Sponsored Assassination

The U.S. position on assassination has changed over time. As of the early twenty-first century, U.S. law prohibited the use of assassination. However, although as-

[DEATH OF YASSIN]

Returning from his morning prayers at a mosque in Gaza City on March 22, 2004, Sheikh Ahmed Yassin, the sixty-seven-year-old founder and "spiritual leader" of Hamas, was killed when a missile was fired by an Israeli helicopter.

Hamas is a loosely structured organization formed in 1987 that has used violent and political means to pursue the goal of replacing Israel with an Islamic Palestinian state. The organization had claimed responsibility for a wave of suicide bombings against Israeli civilians and was considered a terrorist organization by the United States.

The killing was viewed as an assassination that violated international law by much of the international community. Algeria introduced a United Nations Security Council resolution that would have condemned the killing as an "extrajudicial execution." However, the United States vetoed the resolution after Algeria refused to include language condemning previous acts of violence by Hamas.

sassination has been prohibited by the U.S. army as a technique of warfare since the Civil War, there have been periods where assassination has been used as an instrument of foreign policy. For example, during the cold war the CIA attempted to assassinate a number of foreign leaders who were thought to be sympathetic to communism. These assassination plots were made public in 1975. A congressional committee lead by Senator Frank Church found that successive U.S. presidents had authorized plans to assassinate five foreign leaders during the 1960s and early 1970s. The targeted leaders included Chilean President Salvador Allende and Cuban dictator Fidel Castro, against whom eight unsuccessful assassination plots were authorized.

The Church Committee made clear its disapproval of these tactics and concluded that: "short of war, assassination is incompatible with American principles, international order, and morality. It should be rejected as a tool of foreign policy." The Committee recommended that Congress pass a law to make assassination illegal. Congress, however, has never passed such a law. Instead, U.S. policy on assassination has been governed by a series of Executive Orders, beginning in 1976. These orders have prohibited employees of the United States from engaging in assassination during peacetime, but have not defined the exact meaning of assassination. The absence of a precise definition has given U.S. Presidents leeway to order missions that some observers have viewed as assassination attempts.

For example, in the 1980s and 1990s, the U.S. launched several military attacks that were most likely designed to kill specific individuals. In 1986, the Reagan administration launched air strikes against Libya and targeted the army barracks where Libyan leader Muammar Qaddafi was known to be sleeping. In 1998, in retaliation for the al-Qaeda attacks on U.S. embassies in East Africa, the Clinton administration launched cruise missiles against a training camp in Afghanistan with the hope of killing Osama bin Laden.

International Criminal Responsibility

Assassination is generally considered a violation of the international law against treachery in war or aggression in times of peace. In addition, it is possible, although less likely, that individuals or groups of individuals accused of assassination could be held accountable for committing genocide or crimes against humanity.

An assassination could rise to the level of a crime against humanity only if it was part of a systematic or widespread pattern of attacks against a civilian population. There would have to be a pattern of "extra-judicial killing" of civilians, of which the assassination formed one part. In general, assassinations do not fit this definition because they often occur as single isolated events and involve treachery, often against quasi-military targets, rather than systematic or widespread attacks against civilians.

An assassination could constitute genocide only if the killing was committed with the intention of destroying a national, ethnic, racial, or religious group in part or as a whole. Because assassinations generally target specific individuals for political purposes, they would not often meet this requirement. However, if an assassination that targeted a particular individual was a part of a broader plan to destroy the individual's entire group, it could be viewed as part of a genocide. This might have been the case during the early stages of the Rwandan genocide, when groups of Hutu used written lists to search out and murder specific Tutsi political leaders.

SEE ALSO Crimes Against Humanity; War Crimes

BIBLIOGRAPHY

Anderson, Chris A. (1992). "Assassination, Lawful Homicide, and the Butcher of Baghdad." *Journal of Public Law and Policy* 13:291.

Beres, Louis R. (1992). "The Permissibility of State Sponsored Assassination during Peace and War." *Temple International and Comparative Law Journal* 5: 231.

Ford, Franklin, L. (1985). *Political Murder: From Tyrannicide to Terrorism.* Cambridge, Mass.: Harvard University Press.

Godfrey, Brenda L. (2003). "Authorization to Kill Terrorist Leaders and Those Who Harbor Them: International Analysis of Defensive Assassination." *San Diego International Law Journal* 4:491.

Heaps, Willard A. (1969). *Assassination: A Special Kind of Murder.* New York: Meredith Press.

Pickard, Daniel B. (2001). "Legalizing Assassination? Terrorism, the Central Intelligence Agency, and International Law." *Georgia Journal International and Comparative Law* 30:1.

Raines, Joshua (2002). "Osama, Augustine, and Assassination: The Just War Doctrine and Targetted Killings." *Transnational Law and Contemporary Problems* 12:217.

Schmitt, Michael N. (1992). "State-Sponsored Assassination in International and Domestic Law." *Yale Journal of International Law* 17:609.

Wiebe, Mathew C. (2003). "Assassination in Domestic and International Law: The Central Intelligence Agency, State-Sponsored Terrorism, and the Right of Self-Defense." *Tulsa Journal of Comparative and International Law* 11:363.

Wingfield, Thomas C. (1989). "Taking Aim at Regime Elites: Assassination, Tyrannicide, and the Clancy Doctrine." *Maryland Journal of International Law and Trade* 22:287.

Zengel, Patricia (1992). "Assassination and the Law of Armed Conflict." *Mercer Law Revue* 43:615.

Brian K. Morgan

Atatürk, Mustafa Kemal Pasha

[1891–NOVEMBER 10, 1938]
Founder and first president of the Turkish Republic

There is no evidence that Atatürk was in any way involved in the enactment of the World War I Armenian Genocide, either directly or indirectly. However, there is ample evidence that, as the forceful founder of the modern Republic of Turkey, he played a decisive role in the handling of many problems arising from that genocide. Foremost among these problems was the demand of the victorious allies—France, Italy and Great Britain—to bring all Turks who were responsible for the genocide to trial, and to severely punish all who were found guilty. This was in line with the official and public pledge the Allies had made on May 24, 1915, when they denounced members of Turkey's leadership for crimes against humanity. The call for justice was the first time that the violation of human rights was integrally linked to the crime of genocide.

Of greater concern for Atatürk, however, was the Allied powers' plan to partition the territories of the former Ottoman Empire. As part of a package of compensation for the victims of the Armenian genocide, the Allies envisaged the creation of a new Armenia that would encompass several former Ottoman provinces in eastern Turkey. Prior to the genocide, these provinces had constituted part of historic Armenia. The Allied powers warned that, unless Turkey acquiesced to prosecuting the genocide's perpetrators and providing compensation to the victims, the terms of their impending peace treaty with Turkey would be even more severe. Trapped by a regime of occupation, the captive Sultan and a succession of subservient postwar Turkish governments agreed to cooperate. The result was the establishment of an extraordinary military tribunal with the mandate to prosecute the authors of the genocide and to make certain territorial concessions to the newly established Armenian Republic.

To mitigate, if not avert, what he regarded as ominous developments for Turkey, Atatürk embarked on a two-pronged campaign. First, he challenged the authority of the reigning Sultan and questioned the legitimacy of his tottering regime. Second, he launched a militant movement to liberate Turkey from the debilitating clutches of the occupying Allied powers, while repudiating their territorial designs for the benefit of the nascent Armenia. In an effort to facilitate the attainment of these strategic goals, Atatürk employed a series of tactics intended to assuage the Allies. On November 9, 1918, he published a major editorial in *Minber*, a Turkish daily newspaper that he had helped to found and finance. In his editorial he denounced the wartime regime of the Young Turks (Committee of Union and Progress, or CUP) for having attempted genocide against Turkey's Armenian population. When a more self-assertive government came to power in Istanbul in autumn of 1919, Atatürk co-signed the Amasya Protocol. Article 1 of the protocol declared both the CUP's policies and its ideology as anathema. Article 4 of the same document provided for "the criminal prosecution of the perpetrators of the Armenian deportations as a matter of justice and politics." In a companion but confidential protocol, Atatürk further promised to prosecute those CUP leaders who were principally implicated in the crime of Armenian deportations and massacres and who were being detained by the British in Malta, as soon as they were released from British custody. He also acknowledged to U.S. Major-General James Harbord the mass murder of 800,000 Armenians. In interviews with foreign correspondents he denounced the CUP perpetrators as "rascals who ought to be hanged" for "ruthlessly deporting and massacring" the Armenians.

As his national liberation movement began to gain momentum, however, Atatürk abandoned these tactics in order to accommodate a domestic audience that was animated with a new brand of nationalism. He not only tried to cover up the catastrophe of the genocide but, when occasionally forced to take a position, he proceeded to blame the Armenians for their own fate. Moreover, he welcomed many of the former Malta detainees into the ranks of his liberation movement, some of whom had been released by the British under prisoner exchange programs, others of whom had simply escaped custody. By openly embracing known perpetrators of the genocide, Atatürk was in violation of the Amasya Protocol that mandated their criminal prosecution and punishment.

These newly repatriated militants knew they had a high stake in Atatürk's ultimate success. Were his movement to fail, they would likely not only face criminal prosecution but also enormous losses of the property and financial assets that they had acquired from the murdered victims of the genocide. Atatürk also recruited a number of other perpetrators who had gone into hiding to avoid prosecution by the Istanbul government. All of these fugitives of justice substantially contributed to the ultimate triumph of Kemalism and its standard-bearer, Atatürk. They included several army commanders, cabinet ministers, presidents of the republic's Grand National Assembly, governors-general, deputies, and heads of the Special Organization, the main instrument of the Armenian genocide.

By an ironic twist, however, in 1926 a dozen of these organizers of the Armenian genocide were hanged following a series of trials in Izmir and Ankara. Their prosecution was based on charges of conspiracy to assassinate Atatürk and restore the CUP to power in the new Republic of Turkey.

BIBLIOGRAPHY

Akçam, Taner (1999). *Insan Haklari ve Ermeni Sorunu. Ittihat ve Terakki den Kurtulus Savasina.* Ankara, Turkey: Dün Bugün Yarin Publishers.

Armstrong, H. C. (1961). *Gray Wolf: The Life of Kemal Atatürk.* New York: Capricorn Books.

Atatürk, Mustafa Kemal (1961). *Gazi Mustafa Kemal: Founder of the Turkish Republic.* Ankara, Turkey: Turkish Ministry of Press.

Atatürk, Mustafa Kemal (1963). *Nutuk: Kemal Atatürk,* vol. 3: *Vesikalar* (Documents), 7th edition. Istanbul: Education Ministry Press.

Atatürk, Mustafa Kemal (1963). *A Speech Delivered by Mustafa Kemal Atatürk 1927.* Istanbul: Ministry of Education Press.

Dadrian, Vahakn (1991). "The Documentation of the World War I Armenian Massacres in the Proceedings of the Turkish Military Tribunal." *International Journal of Middle East Studies* 23:549–576.

Kinross, Lord (1965). *Atatürk: A Biography of Mustaya Kemal, Father of Modern Turkey*. New York: W. Morrow.
Vahakn N. Dadrian

Athens and Melos

In the summer of 416 BCE an Athenian naval force attacked the small island of Melos, with the intention of coercing it into their alliance. The Melian government refused to cooperate, and the city came under siege. It held out until the winter, when starvation and internal dissidence forced the defenders to unconditional surrender. Then, according to the contemporary historian Thucydides, the Athenians "killed all of the adult Melian men whom they had captured and enslaved the children and women. They settled the place themselves, subsequently sending out five hundred colonists" (Strassler, 1996, p. 357).

One can to some degree delve beneath this bald statement. In the first place Melos was a small community, even by Greek standards. The surface area of the island is a mere fifty-nine square miles. Its total population in antiquity could not have been much more than three thousand, and its military forces were insignificant. Against an expeditionary force of three thousand fighting men, more than its entire male population, Melos had no chance of survival, unless there was outside intervention. That was the nub. The Melians claimed to be related to the Spartans and, unlike the vast majority of Aegean islands, had held aloof from the Athenian alliance. For Thucydides that was the sole motivation for the Athenian aggression. Some modern commentators have argued that the attack was provoked by the Melians, in that the state had contributed money to the Spartan war fund some ten years previously, but the dating of the document in question is very uncertain and it probably dates to a much later period. The Athenians did claim suzerainty, and in 425 they demanded tribute from Melos (along with many other states that they did not, in fact, control). But Melos was not annexed or forced into alliance. A perfunctory operation occurred in 426, when the Athenians ravaged Melian land and quickly withdrew to another theater. At that time they were at war with Sparta and might reasonably have been uncomfortable with Melian neutrality. The invasion of 416, by contrast, took place within the context of a general peace, when Melian sympathies for Sparta were in no sense a threat to Athens, and there is every reason to believe that the motive for the attack was imperial expansion.

Thucydides considered that the Melians had no hope of survival and set on record the famous Melian Dialogue, in which the Athenians and the Melian government exchange views, and the Athenians attempt to coerce their interlocutors to surrender immediately. This is a very elaborate and difficult passage, and it is clearly not a verbatim report of proceedings. However, one cannot dispute that the Athenian generals made representations to the Melian government, and that Thucydides gives the substance of what he believes was said. At the very least, his writings reflect contemporary thinking. In the dialogue the Athenians justify their actions in the most brutal terms. The Melians' very weakness forces them to attack. Their own credibility would suffer if they allowed the Melians to remain neutral. They have no hope of assistance, for the Spartans would not jeopardize the peace they had signed with Athens only five years previously. The only sensible course was to surrender and avoid destruction. If the dialogue does represent the arguments that were actually voiced, then the Melians were threatened with extermination before the siege began, but chose to resist and placed their hopes in the Spartans and divine providence.

There can be no doubt that the Athenians were by any standards violating the norms of civilized behavior, as Thucydides makes them admit in the dialogue: They are not going to make specious claims of justice, for matters of justice are decided when the compulsion on both side is equal. Otherwise, the strong do what they can and the weak concede. Following this logic, the extermination of Melos was a guarantee against resistance elsewhere, and it was appropriate retribution for its government's obstinacy. Other mass killings had more justification. Scione, a city in the north of Greece, suffered the same fate as Melos, but it was already an ally of Athens and had revolted. Scione was explicitly excluded from the peace of 421, in which the Athenians were given a free hand to dispose of it. Similarly, the city of Mytilene in Lesbos had revolted against Athens and, like Melos, surrendered unconditionally after internal dissent. In this case the Athenian assembly voted to kill all males of military age, but retracted the decree the following day. Even so, over one thousand Mytileans were executed as instigators of the revolt. In contrast, the Melians were not in any sense in rebellion. They were attacked in peacetime and their crime was simply resistance, their punishment exemplary. The Athenians at first appear to have been indifferent. Shortly afterward the comic poet Aristophanes in the *Birds* made a callous joking reference to "Melian starvation." The Athenians may have treated it as a joke, but they recognized the enormity of their action. In 405, when it was apparent that they would be forced to capitulate, they felt they would suffer what they had inflicted on others; the treatment of the Melians is first on the list of atrocities that are mentioned. It was a repeated accusation against Athens throughout the next century, and the orator Isocrates can only echo Thucydides' dialogue and offer the lame excuse that other states would do the same and worse.

The killing did not result in extermination. It is clear that many Melians survived and lived elsewhere as exiles. One actually served as a commander in the Spartan navy that won the decisive victory over the Athenians, and there were enough Melians left to form a viable community on Melos after the Athenian colonists were expelled in 404. Thereafter Melos continued its history as a small independent state, and there is an epigraphic record that exists of the settlement of a land dispute that it had with its even smaller neighbor Cimolus. This leads one to question how systematic the killing had been. Thucydides himself notes that only those whom the Athenians had captured were put to death. Others presumably escaped during the course of the siege, which did witness a few localized Melian victories. Events at Mytilene may provide a parallel. There, once the city had surrendered unconditionally, its fate was decided by the Athenian assembly, as was that of the Melians, and an interval of a week or fortnight must have elapsed before the decree was received by the fighting force. During that time there would have been ample opportunity for Melian prisoners to escape. The commanders on the scene may well have felt some political sympathy for the democratic faction there, given that the city had been driven to resistance by what Thucydides regards as its pig-headed oligarchic government, and some Melians at least had made overtures to the Athenians before their surrender. Whether (as has been argued) they felt any affinity with imperial Athens is dubious, but they were not dogmatically set on resistance at any price. A number of them may have been allowed to disappear before the order for execution was given. That being said, Athens' actions fall squarely within the terms of Article 2 of the Genocide Convention, in that they were intended to destroy a national group (as the Melian city-state could be defined) "in whole or in part," and they were largely successful in achieving that end.

By any standards the treatment of the Melians was a crime against humanity. The crux is not the enslavement of women and children. However repugnant to modern sentiment that may be, it was acknowledged contemporary practice. According to Xenophon in *Cyropaedia* (7.5.73), "it is a universal and eternal law that in a city taken during a war everything, including persons and property, belongs to the victor." In his *Politics*, Aristotle was to agree, claiming that the "law" was in fact a convention, a general agreement. The Athenians themselves were threatened with collective en-

slavement when they surrendered in 404, but were saved by their reputation (and no doubt the logistics of justifying such vast numbers). There can have been little quarrel with the enslavement of captives after capitulation. However, the killing of combatants who had thrown themselves on the victor's mercy was a different matter. It amounted to violation of the rights of the suppliant. For Thucydides, admittedly in a tendentious passage (3.58.2), "it is law for the Greeks not to kill such people," (Thucydides 3.58.3) and it seems to have been a general principle as well as logical practice to spare the lives of opponents who surrendered unconditionally. Otherwise, there was nothing to gain by surrender. The killing of the Melians was compounded by the circumstances of the attack, which was an unashamed exercise in imperialism, and it is rightly seen as the most flagrant and unjustified act of repression carried out by the Athenians during the Peloponnesian War.

SEE ALSO Armenians in Ottoman Turkey and the Armenian Genocide; Enver, Ismail; Talaat

BIBLIOGRAPHY

Bosworth, A. B. (1993). "The Humanitarian Aspect of the Melian Dialogue." *Journal of Hellenic Studies* 113:30–44.

Crane, G. (1998). *Thucydides and the Ancient Simplicity. The Limits of Political Realism*. Berkeley: University of California Press.

de Ste. Croix, G. E. M. (1954). "The Character of the Athenian Empire." *Historia* 3 (Heft 1):1–41.

Gomme, A. W., A. Andrewes, and K. J. Dover (1970). *A Historical Commentary on Thucydides*. Vol. IV. Oxford: Oxford University Press.

Kagan, D. (1981). *The Peace of Nicias and the Sicilian Expedition*. Ithaca, N.Y.: Cornell University Press.

Loomis, W. T. (1992). *The Spartan War Fund: IG V1, 1 and a New Fragment. Historia Einzelschriften 74*. Stuttgart, Germany: Franz Steiner.

Macleod, C. (1983). "Form and Meaning in the Melian Dialogue." In *Collected Essays*. Oxford: Clarendon Press.

Strassler, R. B., ed. (1996). *The Landmark Thucydides: A Comprehensive Guide to the Peloponnesian War*. Trans. Richard Crawley. New York: The Free Press.

A. B. Bosworth

Attempt

An *attempt to commit a crime* is an unsuccessful effort to engage in conduct that is proscribed by criminal law. Attempts to commit both genocide and crimes against humanity are criminal under international criminal law. The criminality of attempts to commit genocide was made clear in 1948, in Article III(d) of the United

Nations Convention on the Prevention and Punishment of the Crime of Genocide (Genocide Convention). With respect to war crimes, crimes against humanity, and genocide, the criminality of attempt can be gleaned from Article 25(3)(f) of the Rome Statute of the International Criminal Court. It states that liability exists for "[a]ttempts to commit [one of these crimes] by taking action that commences its execution by means of a substantial step, but [wherein] the crime does not occur because of circumstances independent of the person's intentions." It goes on: "However a person who abandons the effort to commit the crime or otherwise prevents the completion of the crime shall not be liable for punishment . . . for the attempt to commit that crime if that person completely and voluntarily gave up the criminal purpose."

The justifications for criminalizing attempt are multiple. First, by attempting to bring about a crime, which does not occur only, In the words of Article 25, "because of circumstances independent of the person's intentions" the person is, in a moral sense, virtually identical to a person who succeeds in completing a crime. Both have tried to arrive at a result prohibited by law, but one is "lucky" enough to bring the crime to fruition. Second, the person attempting a crime has brought into being the risk of harm to others, which is itself wrongful. Finally, by criminalizing attempt, international criminal law allows those enforcing it to act at an earlier stage, not having to wait for a crime to occur. This should allow for more effective crime prevention.

An attempt to commit genocide is an attempt to engage in conduct prohibited by Article II of the Genocide Convention (e.g., an attempt to commit murder or serious bodily harm, with genocidal intent). It should not be confused with successful completion of conduct prohibited in Article II which, however, does not lead to the destruction, in whole or in part, of the protected group. That is an offence of genocide. A completed offence of genocide does not require that in fact the group is destroyed in whole or in part, merely that the perpetrator completed the conduct with genocidal intent.

The definition of attempt in the Rome Statute is not easy to apply to particular cases. The International Criminal Court will have to determine exactly when a person has "commence[d] . . . execution [of an international crime] by means of a substantial step." This formulation of the test for attempt is not clear. Attempt must be intentional; however, there is no liability for reckless or negligent attempt. A person may avoid liability if he or she abandons the attempt and "completely and voluntarily gives up the criminal purpose" he or she harbored. This is intended to provide an incentive to people to abandon attempts to commit crimes before

the crimes are complete, but it is unlikely that in practice people are encouraged to return to lawfulness by such provisions.

SEE ALSO Convention on the Prevention and Punishment of Genocide; War Crimes

BIBLIOGRAPHY

Ambos, Kai (1999). "Article 25." In *Commentary on the Rome Statute of the International Criminal Court,* ed. O. Triffterer. Baden-Baden, Germany: Nomos.

Eser, Albin (2002). "Individual Criminal Responsibility." In *The Rome Statute of the International Criminal Court: A Commentary,* ed. A. Cassese, P. Gaeta, and J. R. W. D. Jones. Oxford, U.K.: Oxford University Press.

Fletcher, George P. (1998). *Basic Concepts of Criminal Law.* Oxford, U.K.: Oxford University Press.

Schabas, William A. (2000). *Genocide in International Law: The Crime of Crimes.* Cambridge: Cambridge University Press.

United Nations Convention on the Prevention and Punishment of the Crime of Genocide (1948). Available from http://www.fletcher.tufts.edu/multi/texts/BH225.txt.

Robert Cryer

Auschwitz

Over the last few decades the term *Auschwitz* has become in common parlance a synecdoche for the Holocaust in general. Such a meaning has often overshadowed the alternate historical significance of the name. The town of Auschwitz, located on the border between Germany and Poland, was established by Germans in the thirteenth century and became a Polish fief known as Oswiecim in the fifteenth century. The Duchy of Auschwitz merged into the Hapsburg patrimony as part of Austrian Galicia in the First Polish Partition (1772). With the collapse of the Austro-Hungarian Empire in 1918 Oswiecim become a part of the Polish republic. In 1939, following its Polish campaign, Auschwitz was incorporated within the German Reich in the newly established province of Upper Silesia. After World War II ended in 1945 Oswiecim returned to Polish sovereignty.

Auschwitz's historical significance in the twentieth century relates to the massive concentration/extermination camp that the Germans established in a suburb of the town in the spring of 1940. The camp remained in operation until January 27, 1945, when it was liberated by the Red Army.

The nature and scope of the atrocities that took place at Auschwitz justify its identification as the symbolic center of the Holocaust. It was the site where the single largest group of Jews was murdered: over one

Beyond a front gate ironically proclaiming "Work Shall Set You Free" stood the elaborate death camp at Auschwitz, preserved as a monument to Nazi depravity and the victims of the Holocaust. [**CORBIS**]

million men, women, and children (or more than 90% of the 1.1 million Jews deported to the camp). Furthermore, Jewish citizens from at least twelve European countries were deported to Auschwitz, and as such, its history testifies to the pan-European character of the Holocaust. In addition, Auschwitz was a place where the Germans killed more than 100,000 non-Jews: 75,000 Poles (or some 50% of the 150,000 Poles deported to the camp), 21,000 Sinti and Romani (or more than 80% of the 23,000 Sinti and Romani registered at Auschwitz), 15,000 Soviet prisoners of war (almost all who were deported to the camp), and some 15,000 others (or 60% of that group). Auschwitz thus testifies to a historical circumstance too easily forgotten: The Holocaust of the Jews was part of a larger German fantasy about a new world order that also called for the genocide of other undesirable groups (select Slavic populations, undesirable Sinti and Romani, and the mentally ill, to name but a few).

Auschwitz is also worth focusing on because in its technology and organization it was thoroughly modern and a model of Nazi efficiency. Given its central location within the European railway infrastructure, its

business relationship with many larger and smaller industries that relied on the slave labor provided by the camp, its medical experiments conducted by highly qualified physicians in collaboration with distinguished research institutions, and its large and efficient crematoria—equipped with logically designed killing installations, including rooms for undressing and gas chambers, for those who were deemed "unfit for labor" on arrival—Auschwitz stands for industrial civilization. Auschwitz has also become the focus of moral and philosophical reflection because it created two new variations of the human species: the *Sonderkommando*, the slave laborer who kept the factory of death running, and the *Muselmann*, the living dead.

Establishing the German New Order in Poland

In light of the scale of the atrocities at Auschwitz, it is easy to overlook the complex historical evolution of the camp. When the Nazis annexed the town of Auschwitz to the Reich in 1939, they designated the region with the highest priority for political, social, and economic redevelopment. For the Germans Auschwitz signified a return to the pristine, lost past of medieval German

The main entrance at Birkenau. In the former Polish town of Oswiecim, the Nazis built Auschwitz I, the original concentration camp; Auschwitz II (Birkenau), an extermination center; and Auschwitz III (Monowice), essentially a labor camp for IG Farben.
[(C) RAYMOND DEPARDON/MAGNUM PHOTOS]

achievement and represented opportunity and promise to new generations. As Reich Commissioner for the Consolidation of the German Nation, SS chief Heinrich Himmler oversaw its redevelopment; he soon initiated a policy of ethnic cleansing by deporting Poles and Jews, and organizing the immigration of Germans into the area. This formula was not without its problems in Auschwitz, however. Some of the local Polish population could not be deported as they were employed in industry, and there were few skilled ethnic German workers to replace them. Himmler's response to this circumstance was to claim a former Polish military base located in the suburbs of Zasole as a concentration camp to terrorize the local population. In order to provide practical support to the new arrivals in establishing economically viable farms, Himmler made the concentration camp the center of a huge agricultural experiment, a scientific farm. The camp, headed by SS Sturmbannführer (Major) Rudolf Höss, claimed increasingly larger territories for this new function, and Himmler began to see that its future might be different from what he had originally envisioned: As a concentration camp Auschwitz was assumed to be a temporary

facility; as an agricultural estate, it would claim permanence.

Originally a small compound surrounded by a double barbed wire fence, the camp had grown by the beginning of 1941 into a 15-square-mile so-called zone of interests, an area that was under direct control of the SS and which was legally a municipality with all the rights that came with it. A huge influx of money and building materials was needed to develop this zone. Therefore, Himmler sought to generate income by attracting a major chemical manufacturer, IG Farben, to Auschwitz. The terms of the bargain were simple: The camp would supply the labor to construct Farben's synthetic rubber plant; and a new satellite camp, Birkenau, that was to be populated by Soviet prisoners of war, would provide labor to transform the town of Auschwitz into a place worthy of a Farben enterprise. In return, Farben agreed to finance and supply the building materials required for Himmler's Germanization project in the area, which included the expansion of the concentration camp and construction of an idyllic village for SS guards.

The SS expected many deaths due to endemic and epidemic disease in the Auschwitz camp, which was intended to house 125,000 Soviet prisoners of war in Birkenau and 30,000 Polish prisoners in the main camp at Zasole. The existing crematorium, constructed in 1940 in a former ammunition depot and equipped with three double-muffle ovens with the ability to process 340 corpses per day, was deemed too small. Thus, the SS commissioned in the fall of 1941 the design of a very large, state-of-the-art crematorium with the capacity to incinerate 1,440 corpses per day. Remarkably enough, this seemingly excessive capacity was considered appropriate to cope with the anticipated mortality of the 155,000 slave laborers to be worked to death in Auschwitz. The crematorium was not meant to provide execution facilities: Nothing in the original conceptual sketches of the crematorium, or in the blueprints dating from January 1942, suggests the presence of gas chambers, or their use in the Final Solution.

Auschwitz as a Center of the Holocaust

When the large-scale mass murder of Jews began in the summer and fall of 1941 in the wake of Operation Barbarossa, the SS in Auschwitz was still fully committed to Himmler's project to develop the town and region. However, the camp at Auschwitz soon became a center of genocide, with the SS sending to the camp not only Soviet prisoners of war (POWs) for forced labor, but also those considered officials of the Soviet Communist Party for execution. Initially, these men were executed

encyclopedia of GENOCIDE *and* CRIMES AGAINST HUMANITY

[GAS CHAMBER TECHNOLOGY]

A key innovation that distinguishes the Holocaust from other genocides is the widespread use of gas chambers. Of the 5 to 6.5 million Jewish victims, about half were killed in stationary gas chambers. The use of these gas chambers reveals the deliberate nature of the German genocide of the Jews. Gas chambers are designed and built to kill non-combatants. They allow for the anonymous execution of many people simultaneously. The victims can be killed out of sight by the simple opening of a valve, or by emptying a canister full of pellets through a trapdoor. A gas chamber can be operated with a total diffusion of responsibility.

The idea of using gas chambers originated in the British and American eugenics movements. In the two decades that preceded World War I, many people advocated the use of "lethal chambers" where degenerates, the mentally ill, and the physically handicapped could be killed "humanely." In the belief that gassing caused a quick and merciful death, the state of Nevada installed a gas chamber in 1924 to execute convicted criminals. By the end of the 1930s, eight states had followed Nevada's example. Gas chamber executions were popular with prison authorities because they were effective and above all clean.

In the Third Reich, official death sentences were executed by means of guillotines. In the autumn of 1939, German officials began to construct gas chambers in selected asylums, first to kill groups of mentally ill and handicapped patients (T-4 program) and, from 1941 on, to kill groups of selected concentration camp inmates (14f13 program). The gas used was bottled carbon monoxide. Apart from the secrecy and clearly illegal character of the operation, the T-4 program, which killed over 70,000 people, realized many of the policies advocated by the earlier eugenic theorists.

In late 1941, when German soldiers, the SS, and the police faced increasing stress from conducting mass executions of Jewish civilians in the East, the SS introduced the first mobile gas chambers ("gas vans") as a preferred, anonymous, and "clean" means of killing in occupied Russia. Later, in occupied Poland, stationary gas chambers were installed in specially built extermination camps. The gas vans on the Russian front and in Chelmno, and the stationary gas chambers of Belzec, Sobibor and Treblinka, used diesel engine exhaust which, when modified to run with a less efficient fuel-air ratio, produced an asphyxiating and toxic mix of carbon dioxide and carbon monoxide. In these gas chambers, some two million victims died a slow and agonizing death.

In 1941 the Auschwitz SS began to experiment with using Zyklon B as a killing agent. A commercially available delousing agent, Zyklon B consisted of small diatomite pellets soaked with cyanide and sealed in metal cans. Upon opening, the contents would "degas," expelling a lethal toxin for a continuous 24 hours. This was important in delousing or killing other vermin, which can last as much as 14 hours in a highly toxic environment. Zyklon B had proven its wider use in 1938, when the city of Vienna adopted it to kill pigeons. Three years later, in Auschwitz, Zyklon B was used on people. After the war, Auschwitz Kommandant Rudolf Höss claimed that he had adopted Zyklon B because it ensured a quick and easy death for the victims— a claim not supported by the evidence.

Höss first installed a gas chamber in the morgue of crematorium 1, and in early 1942 transformed two peasant cottages into gas chambers. These makeshift installations proved reliable and efficient, and in the summer and fall of 1942, SS architects modified the designs of four new crematoria to include sophisticated cyanide gas chambers, creating true factories of death. In the case of crematoria 2 and 3, which could hold up to 2,000 victims at one time, the large underground chambers were equipped with hollowed-out, wire-mesh columns, which allowed for an easy introduction of Zyklon pellets in the crowded room and the quick removal of the still degassing pellets after twenty minutes, when all the victims had died. With the pellets removed and the ventilators turned on, the cyanide gas could be removed from the room in half an hour, allowing corpse cremation to begin without delay in the chamber's fifteen large ovens. Thus, a consignment of victims could be killed and cremated within a 24 hour period, allowing for a regular daily schedule of arrivals, selections, and killings. In operation until the end of October 1944, the Auschwitz gas chambers killed 1.1 million people. For further reading, see Eugen Kogon, Hermann Langbein, and Adelbert Rückerl, eds. (1994). *Nazi Mass Murder: A Documentary History of the Use of Poison Gas*. New Haven, Conn., and London: Yale University Press. **ROBERT JAN VAN PELT**

by rifle and machine-gun fire. In August 1941 camp officials conducted a few experiments to determine if a more efficient and less psychologically jarring method of execution could be devised. Hydrogen cyanide, marketed under the brand name Zyklon (Cyclone) and sold in versions A, B, and C, was available in the camp in large quantities for delousing purposes. Zyklon B also proved effective in killing the Soviet prisoners.

In January 1942 Hermann Göring ordered the transfer of Soviet POWs from Auschwitz to German armament factories; it was at this point that Himmler began to consider the so-called Auschwitz Project as part of a systematic plan or Final Solution to address the Jewish question. This did not mean that Himmler wanted to solely use the camp as a site for the continuous mass murder of Jews. In early 1942 he remained intent on making Auschwitz the centerpiece of his racial utopia. Only now this would not be accomplished on the backs of Soviet POWs: Jewish slave laborers were to take their place. The Wannsee Conference gave Himmler (through Reinhard Heydrich) the power to negotiate with German and foreign civilian authorities for the transfer of Jews to his SS empire. The first transports carrying Jews fit for labor departed from Slovakia for Auschwitz-Birkenau soon thereafter.

When the Slovak government asked Himmler to also take Jews unfit for labor in exchange for a cash payment, he dispatched SS construction chief Hans Kammler to Auschwitz. Kammler toured the site and ordered the transformation of a cottage there into a Zyklon gas chamber. Two months later, on July 4, 1942, the first transports of Jews from Slovakia were submitted to selection. Those who could work were admitted to the camp; those who could not were killed in the cottage, known as Bunker I. The murder of select Jews at Auschwitz changed from an incidental practice to a continual one, although it had not yet become official Nazi policy. Bunker I and a second cottage outfitted with four gas chambers, Bunker II, were an outgrowth of Slovak unwillingness to provide for old and very young Jews, and German greed. The main purpose of Auschwitz at this time remained the creation of a city and a region, and not the annihilation of Jews.

In mid-July 1942 Himmler assumed responsibility for a German settlement in Russia—a position that he had coveted for more than a year. His view of Auschwitz and his plans for it changed rapidly and dramatically. The Auschwitz Project was no longer of interest to him. The camp could be used for the systematic killing of Jews. Practice became policy. In August camp architects received the order to construct a large crematorium in Birkenau, to be known as crematorium 2. The plan also called for the design and creation of a third crematorium and two smaller crematoria, each with an incineration capacity of 768 corpses per day and equipped from the outset with gas chambers. When under construction crematoria 2 and 3 were retroactively fitted with gas chambers. SS architect Walter Dejaco revised the design of each building's basement, changing one of the two underground morgues into a room for undressing and the other into a gas chamber.

As work crews busily constructed these factories of death, daily transports arrived in Auschwitz. In May 1942 regular transports from Poland began to arrive, in June transports from France, in July transports from Holland, and in August transports from Belgium and Yugoslavia. On average some one thousand deportees arrived every day at the *Judenrampe* located between the main camp and Birkenau; in a quick selection process most were declared to be unfit for work, loaded on trucks, and transported to Bunkers I and II, where they were forced to undress and then killed. Initially, their bodies were buried nearby, but in the late summer the SS changed this practice, instead incinerating the bodies on large pyres. Primitive as the method of corpse disposal may have been, it did not limit the rate of murder: In 1942 some 200,000 Jews were killed in Auschwitz.

In the late winter and early spring of 1943, with the killing continuing at the rate of eight hundred people per day, the first of the new crematoria in Birkenau came into operation. In their final form all the crematoria offered a relatively discrete method of murder and corpse disposal. People calmly entered the buildings, in many instances not suspecting their fate; their ashes either exited through the chimneys or were dumped in waterholes, or "lakes," that are still visible in Birkenau. The larger of these lakes is said to contain the ashes of 600,000 victims. Between entrance and exit the crematoria constructed by the Germans followed a well-conceived plan, which included ample rooms for undressing, gas chambers of different sizes, other rooms where workers could quickly shear off the hair of female victims for industrial use and extract golden crowns from their mouths, and fuel-efficient ovens that allowed for the high-rate incineration of multiple corpses. Thirty adjacent storehouses, nicknamed Canada because of the wealth they contained, provided an efficient sorting and storage facility for the deportees' belongings. Anything that was deemed usable was shipped back to the Reich as charity for the use of less fortunate Germans. Most importantly, the new crematoria offered the SS the opportunity to kill anonymously. The SS doctors selecting victims could justify their actions by claiming that because all Jews who arrived at Auschwitz were a priori condemned, they actually saved the lives of those whom they chose as slave laborers. Moreover, the SS medics who fed Zyklon B into the gas chambers crowded with those deemed unfit for labor never saw their victims. In the case of crematoria 2 and 3 they just opened vents at ground level, emptied a can of Zyklon into those openings, and then closed the vents. The killing below became invisible to them and everyone else. As for cleaning the gas chambers afterward and incinerating the corpses: Jewish *Sonder-kommandos* were forced to do this job.

Oddly enough, on their completion, the crematoria seemed superfluous. By the summer of 1943, when the SS had all four crematoria at their disposal, the Holocaust itself had peaked. The genocide had begun in 1941, with the Germans killing some 1.1 million Jews that year. In 1942 they murdered another 2.7 million Jews, of whom less than 10 percent died in Auschwitz. The year the crematoria of Auschwitz came into operation the number of victims dropped to 500,000, half of whom were killed in Auschwitz. Most of the Jews whom the Germans had been able to catch had already been successfully eliminated. In June and July 1943 average daily transports brought only 275 Jews to the camp. The crematoria ran on a mere 5 percent of their total capacity. This lull gave the Germans an opportunity to liquidate in August the nearby Sosnowiec ghetto—the place where, two years earlier, the Oswiecim Jewish community had been imprisoned to make room for German settlers and Farben personnel. The Jews from Sosnowiec, some 24,000 in number, were the bulk of the deportees in August. In the fall and winter the number of arrivals decreased again to 250 people per day.

At this time the major interest of the SS at Auschwitz was an increasingly lucrative collaboration between German industry in Upper Silesia and the camp. In 1942 three satellite camps providing slave labor to the Farben synthetic rubber and fuel plant in Monowitz, the coal mines in nearby Jawischowitz, and German industry in Chelmek were established; in 1943 five more satellite camps followed, and in 1944 another nineteen. In 1942, 4,600 prisoners (out of 24,000) worked for outside firms; in 1943 that number had increased to 15,000 (out of 88,000), and in 1944 some 37,000 (out of 105,000). When the camp was evacuated in early 1945, more than half its prisoners provided slave labor outside of the camp. The rest worked on the construction and maintenance of the camp and the 15-square-mile estate surrounding it, and for SS-owned companies. Working for outside firms or the SS, whether slaving in mines, factories, the camp, or the fields, all was lethal: Prisoners labored for long hours on starvation diets, with insufficient clothing in the winter, without adequate protection or shelter, and subject to the brutal treatment meted out by supervisors and guards. Regular selections ensured that any prisoner not able to work would be sent to the gas chambers.

By the end of 1943 the Germans closed the death camps built specifically to exterminate Jews: Kulmhof, Sobibor, Belzec, and Treblinka. Auschwitz remained to kill off the remnants of Jewish communities from Po-land, Italy, France, the Netherlands, and the rest of occupied Europe. In 1944 another 600,000 Jews would be killed in Auschwitz, most of them Hungarians. In the months of May and June almost 7,000 Hungarian Jews arrived in Auschwitz everyday, and most were killed on arrival. The crematoria could not keep up; Bunker II was brought back into operation, and once again many corpses were disposed of on large pyres. When the Hungarian transports stopped arriving in July, the Lodz ghetto provided in August another 65,000 victims, the last major group to arrive and succumb in Auschwitz. In October Himmler ordered the gas chambers to be closed, and their killing infrastructure was dismantled. The incinerators, with the rest of the crematoria, were blown up in January 1945, just before the arrival of the Red Army.

With more than 1.1 million victims, of whom 1 million were Jews, Auschwitz had become by the end of the war the most lethal death camp of all. But Auschwitz was also the camp with the greatest number of survivors because not all the victims deported to Auschwitz were killed on arrival; many more survived than any of the other death camps. Only a few people survived Belzec, and several hundred survived the hell of Sobibor and Treblinka. Of the 1.1 million Jews shipped to Auschwitz, some 100,000 Jews left the camp alive. Many of these survivors perished, however, during the death march to the West, or in 1945 in other concentration camps such as Buchenwald and Bergen-Belsen. Yet tens of thousands lived to see liberation and testify about their ordeal after the war. Of the 100,000 Gentile survivors of Auschwitz, with the Poles, at 75,000, being the largest group, all who could did bear witness to the use of the camp as an extermination center for Jews. This ensured that Auschwitz would figure forever prominently in the memory of the Holocaust. In addition, the survival of significant parts of the camp became another important witness to its importance. In Treblinka, Belzec, and Sobibor, which together hosted the murder of 1.5 million Jews, little of the original camps may be observed. In Auschwitz the SS dismantled the gas chambers and blew up the crematoria, but other sections of the camp remain largely intact. In 1947 the Polish parliament adopted a law titled Commemorating the Martyrdom of the Polish Nation and Other Nations in Oswiecim, and the minister of culture included both the main camp in Zasole and Birkenau in the new state museum at Auschwitz-Birkenau. But it was only until the early 1980s that the site mentioned the murder of Jews at Auschwitz.

SEE ALSO Concentration Camps; Extermination Centers; Gas; Holocaust; Medical Experimentation; Memory

BIBLIOGRAPHY

Agamben, G. (1999). *Remnants of Auschwitz: The Witness and the Archive.* New York: Zone Books.

Aly, G., and S. Heim (2003). *Architects of Annihilation: Auschwitz and the Logic of Destruction.* Princeton, N.J.: Princeton University Press.

Arad, Y. (1987). *Belzec, Sobibor, Treblinka: The Operation Reinhard Death Camps.* Bloomington: Indiana University Press.

Bartoszewski, W. (1991). *The Convent at Auschwitz.* New York: George Braziller.

Czech, D. (1990). *Auschwitz Chronicle.* New York: Henry Holt.

Des Pres, T. (1980). *The Survivor: The Anatomy of Life in the Death Camps.* New York: Oxford University Press.

Dlugoborski, W., and F. Piper (2000). *Auschwitz 1940–1945.* 5 volumes Oswiecim, Poland: Auschwitz-Birkenau State Museum.

Dwork, D., and Robert Jan van Pelt (1986). *Auschwitz: 1270 to the Present.* New York: W. W. Norton.

Galinski, J. (1975). *Fighting Auschwitz: The Resistance Movement in the Concentration Camp.* London: Julian Friedmann.

Gutman, Y., and M. Berenbaum (1994). *Anatomy of the Auschwitz Death Camp.* Bloomington: Indiana University Press.

Hayes, P. (1987). *Industry and Ideology: IG Farben in the Nazi Era.* Cambridge: Cambridge University Press.

Hoess, R. (1992). *Death Dealer: The Memoirs of the SS Kommandant at Auschwitz.* Buffalo, N.Y.: Prometheus Books.

Levi, P. (1958). *Survival in Auschwitz: The Nazi Assault on Humanity.* New York: Simon and Schuster.

Lifton, R. J. (1986). *The Nazi Doctors: Medical Killing and the Psychology of Genocide.* New York: Basic Books.

Neufeld, M. J., and M. Berenbaum (2000). *The Bombing of Auschwitz: Should the Allies Have Attempted It?* New York: St. Martin's Press.

Sofsky, W. (1997). *Order of Terror: The Concentration Camp.* Princeton, N.J.: Princeton University Press.

Todorov, T. (1996). *Facing the Extreme: Moral Life in the Concentration Camps.* New York: Metropolitan Books.

van Pelt, Robert Jan (2002). *The Case for Auschwitz: Evidence from the Irving Trial.* Bloomington: Indiana University Press.

Robert Jan van Pelt

Australia

Beginning in 1788 British colonization drastically diminished the indigenous or Aboriginal population of Australia. Precise enumeration of the decline is impossible. Estimates of the precolonial population range from 300,000 to 750,000 and statistics for the colonial period are unreliable, but the indigenous population probably reached its nadir, at around 75,000, in the 1920s. Disease, compounded by destitution, malnutrition, alcohol, and other drugs, accounted for most deaths. The numbers deliberately killed by colonists are disputed, although 20,000 is a plausible estimate. The uncertainties of body counts notwithstanding, it was by force and the threat of force that the lands of Australia passed from indigenous to European hands.

Early colonial governments sought to assimilate the Aborigines into British civilization. By the 1820s this ambition gave way to the belief that it was not possible to civilize Aborigines and they were thereby doomed to extinction. This racist assumption underpinned the protectionist legislation that was first enacted in Victoria in 1869 and subsequently in all other mainland colonies (states after 1901). Only full-blood Aborigines, however, were expected to die out; those of mixed descent were encouraged, even forced, to integrate into white society. Such ideas guided Aboriginal policy well into the 1930s. After World War II policy shifted toward the assimilation of all indigenous people, regardless of the degree of white descent, although much of the earlier protectionist apparatus, including restrictions on civil rights, remained in place until the 1960s. A consistent assumption throughout these changing policies was that indigenous peoples were too incompetent to realize their own best interests.

Indigenous peoples' varied responses to colonization belie that assumption. During the frontier period they not only fought against the invaders, but also forged alliances with them for motives both pragmatic and strategic. In the second half of the nineteenth century many Aborigines in southern Australia established themselves as self-sufficient farmers. Others, especially in the north, became skilled workers in the pastoral and pearling industries. Indigenous peoples responded creatively to changing circumstances, adopting and adapting elements of Western culture while simultaneously preserving much of their own heritage. Out of shared experiences of colonization, and to more effectively assert their interests, Aboriginal people fashioned a pan-Aboriginal identity and solidarity that surpassed (without completely displacing) traditional affinities to kin and language group. The growth of pan-Aboriginality was largely a phenomenon of the second half of the twentieth century. Alongside it the peoples of the Torres Strait Islands fashioned their own distinctive collective identity.

Genocide

Allegations that Australia has a genocidal past have provoked fierce disputes, with the public dichotomy

encyclopedia of GENOCIDE *and* CRIMES AGAINST HUMANITY

often being a clash between assertions of the intrinsically genocidal nature of colonization and flat denials of the possibility of genocide having been committed on the continent. Scholarship on Australian genocide has moved beyond such stark polarities. In an influential article published in 2000, Dirk Moses argued that although Australian history since 1788 is not ubiquitously genocidal, it has been punctuated by "genocidal moments." No consensus is emerging on the questions of whether, where, or when genocide was committed in Australia, but the debate has promoted public awareness of historical injustices to indigenous people, and encouraged a more internationally comparative approach to the study of Australian race relations.

In Tasmania a decade of violent conflict culminated in 1830 in a military sweep through the center of the island, followed by the deportation of the survivors to the islands of Bass Strait where the last full-blood Tasmanian Aborigine, Truganini, died in 1876. Although this is widely cited as an instance of genocide, Australia's leading historian of frontier conflict, Henry Reynolds, disagrees. He points out that while numerous Tasmanian settlers urged the extermination of the Aborigines, this was not the intent of the colonial government, which sought to segregate them from belligerent settlers and thereby ensure their survival. Similarly, on mainland Australia the disjunctions between intentions and consequences, together with the difficulty of discriminating between forcible subjugation and attempted eradication, complicate attempts to judge the actions of colonial governments as genocidal.

In 1997 the Human Rights and Equal Opportunities Commission (HREOC) report on the forcible separation of indigenous children from their families propelled the Stolen Generations into public prominence and frequently into bitter controversy. HREOC's claim that the removal of indigenous children throughout the period 1900 to 1970 was genocidal in intention has been criticized on several grounds, notably its presumption of consistent administrative intentions over a seventy-year span, and its supposition that cultural genocide (ethnocide) comes within the scope of the 1948 Genocide Convention. The number of children removed remains in dispute, although twenty to twenty-five thousand, or one in every ten indigenous children over seventy years, is a widely cited estimate. Whatever the numbers, and regardless of administrative intentions, the consequences of forced removal were traumatic, often tragic, both for the separated children and for the grieving family members and communities left behind.

The number of violent deaths of Aborigines at the hands of white colonizers is much contested and the subject of intense political debate. The figure is perhaps as high as 20,000. In this photo from 1976, an Aboriginal man, wearing traditional body paint, plays the didgeridoo—an Australian musical instrument that has been in use for thousands of years. [PENNY TWEEDIE/CORBIS]

Into the Twenty-First Century

When, in 1998, prime minister John Howard refused to offer an official apology to the Stolen Generations, concerned citizens instituted a national Sorry Day on May 26 to allow the Australian public an opportunity to convey their own collective apology. Although annual Sorry Days express contrition for the pain inflicted on indigenous peoples, they have also crystallized public disagreement over the remembrance of Australia's past. Conservative commentators have condemned Sorry Days as a manifestation of black-armband historiography, which allegedly caricatures the past as a mere litany of misdeeds inflicted on indigenous innocents. Their opponents, in turn, accuse them of a white-blindfold approach that seeks to expunge unpleasantries from the record. Such polemical labels may obscure the nuances of debate, but they highlight the political potency of historical representation.

In the last quarter of the twentieth century some indigenous groups regained ownership of their lands, a process facilitated by the 1992 *Mabo* judgment of the Australian High Court that determined native title, predating British sovereignty over Australia, still prevailed over much of the continent. However, many indigenous groups remain landless, and land rights have not always delivered the expected benefits. Compared to other Australian groups, indigenous people are severely disadvantaged in terms of all significant socioeconomic criteria, including income, health, housing, employment, and education; in many indigenous communities these problems are compounded by inordinately high rates of violence, suicide, alcoholism, and drug abuse. Indicative of the scale of disadvantage, in 2001 indigenous Australians had an average life expectancy almost twenty years less than that of other Australians, and the gap is not narrowing. Although some indigenous individuals have achieved success in the arts, media, sports, business, and politics, such successes have made little dent in aggregate disadvantage, and standards in certain areas, for example, literacy and health, may be deteriorating.

Since 1990 all major Australian political parties have proclaimed their commitment to a reconciliation between the indigenous population and other Australians, apparently with strong public support. What reconciliation means, however, is uncertain. Conservative interpretations tend to construe it as a strategy for attaining socioeconomic equality between indigenous and nonindigenous Australians through a common commitment to national and liberal-capitalist norms. More leftist commentators and most indigenous leaders, while equally committed to eliminating disadvantage, regard reconciliation as a process demanding the recognition of indigenous peoples as distinct groups, with special rights and entitlements. Behind the differing interpretations lie deeper disagreements over the extent and requirements of indigenous autonomy, and how sociocultural distinctiveness might be maintained in harmony with the demand for socioeconomic parity.

SEE ALSO Indigenous Peoples; Residential Schools

BIBLIOGRAPHY

Attwood, Bain, and Stephen Foster, eds. (2003). *Frontier Conflict: The Australian Experience*. Canberra, Australia: National Museum of Australia.

Haebich, Anna (2000). *Broken Circles: Fragmenting Indigenous Families 1800–2000*. Fremantle, Australia: Fremantle Arts Centre Press.

Human Rights and Equal Opportunities Commission (1997). *Bringing Them Home: National Inquiry into the Separation of Aboriginal and Torres Strait Islander Children from Their Families*. Sydney: Human Rights and Equal Opportunities Commission.

Manne, Robert (2001). "In Denial: The Stolen Generation and the Right."*Australian Quarterly Essay* 1.

McGregor, Russell (1997). *Imagined Destinies: Aboriginal Australians and the Doomed Race Theory, 1880–1939*. Melbourne: Melbourne University Press.

Moses, A. Dirk (2000). "An Antipodean Genocide? The Origins of the Genocidal Moment in the Colonization of Australia." *Journal of Genocide Research* 2:89-106.

Reynolds, Henry (2001). *An Indelible Stain? The Question of Genocide in Australia's History*. Melbourne: Penguin.

Russell McGregor

Aztecs

The Aztecs were the last major civilization to control central Mexico before their defeat by the Spaniards and their indigenous allies in 1521. Although commonly known as the Aztecs, a name derived from their supposed place of origin in Aztlan, they called themselves the Mexica. One of many groups speaking Nahuatl, the major language of central Mexico, the Mexica had humble beginnings. They were an obscure hunting and gathering people who migrated to the populous Nahua region of the Mexican central plateau sometime before 1325, when they established a settlement at Tenochtitlan, on the snake-infested island in the middle of an inland lake system. After serving as mercenaries for other city-states, they became a power in their own right, the dominant member of the Triple Alliance, a confederation composed of Tenochtitlan, Texcoco, and Tlacopan, which conquered other city-states in central and southern Mexico and Central America.

In 1519 Tenochtitlan had a population estimated at 150,000, making it one of the world's major cities. It boasted huge temples, palaces of rulers and nobles, an enormous daily market, and a dense artisan and warrior population. Long-distance and local trade, with both permanent and periodic markets, was already well established, and Tenochtitlan became a major hub. The Aztecs built on the achievements of prior civilizations, which were highly complex. Their accomplishments are even more impressive given that there were no beasts of burden to ease human labor and provide a steady source of animal protein.

Much of the Aztecs' imperial history is recorded in glyphic writing. The conquest of other city-states garnered them payment of tribute goods and labor service, as well as captive warriors who became ritual sacrifices to the Aztec deities. The Aztecs were not unique in practicing human sacrifice in Mesoamerican civilizations, but they practiced it on a huge scale. When the great temple was dedicated in 1487, thousands, perhaps tens of thousands, of captives had their hearts offered to the sun god. The capture of warriors on the battlefield was considered the optimal way to acquire victims; this greatly affected combat. Tenochtitlan conducted ritual warfare with the nearby independent city-state of Tlaxcala in so-called flowery wars (*xochiyaotl*) to acquire warriors for sacrifice. Weaker city-states realized that their quick capitulation would prevent large-scale battlefield capture of warriors so a quick surrender was in their interest. They then had no incentive to revolt because unsuccessful uprisings put them at risk again for sacrifice. The specter of being sacrificial victims thus aided the Aztecs as conquerors and facilitated their continued control of other city-states. Following the Spanish Conquest, human sacrifice ceased, likely not just because the Christian Spaniards aggressively suppressed it, but because sacrificial victims were from populations other than the Aztecs themselves.

The Aztec Triple Alliance was fragile and quickly disintegrated during the Spanish-led Conquest because it was a confederation and not an integrated, unitary state. Although one language group (Nahuatl) dominated on the central plateau, city-states sought autonomy. Spaniards did not expend much effort to divide and conquer because the potential for fragmentation already existed. At the Spaniards' arrival, a number of key city-states saw the opportunity to gain powerful allies to pursue their own political goals, particularly the independent, secondary state of Tlaxcala, which had been a long-standing enemy of the Aztecs. Tlaxcalans and the Spaniards' other indigenous allies provided tens of thousands of warriors to battle the Aztecs, so the Aztecs' defeat was not accomplished by a mere five hundred seasoned Spanish soldiers of fortune, but also their numerous indigenous allies fighting for their own reasons.

The Spaniards had several technological and tactical advantages over native warriors, including horses, cannons and guns, steel weapons, and ships, as well as training in battlefield conduct. Horses were Spanish imports to the New World and gave riders protected by armor and armed with steel weapons enormous advantages in open field engagement. Furthermore, the Spaniards were not interested in capturing their enemies alive on the battlefield, but fought a war to the death. The dissimilarity between Spanish and indigenous practices afforded Spaniards a tactical advantage. Cannons and a long gun, the harquebus, gave Spaniards both firepower and a psychological advantage over warriors who had never seen explosive weapons that killed at a distance. Furthermore, the Spaniards took control

A nineteenth-century drawing depicting the death of Moctezuma (or Montezuma), the ruler of the Aztec Empire of Mexico at the time of the Spanish invasion. [BETTMANN/CORBIS]

of the inland lake system by building shallow draft brigantines and mounting a cannon on them, bombarding the Aztecs' island capital and cutting them off from water, food, and contacts with allies on the mainland.

Also key to the European victory was the rapid spread of smallpox during the siege of Tenochtitlan, unintentionally introduced by one of the Spaniards' African slaves who had an active case. Spaniards were largely immune to the disease due to prior exposure. In 1520 smallpox killed the Aztec emperor Cuitlahuac, who had rallied his people to defeat the Spaniards, just months after his accession to the throne following the death of the vacillating emperor Moctezuma, held captive by the Spaniards. Cuitlahuac's successor, Cuauhtemoc, attempted to again rally the Mexica, but the Aztecs' situation was untenable. Tenochtitlan was in ruins, its population ravaged by smallpox and cut off from food and water; its allies had deserted to join the Spaniards. Cuauhtemoc was captured on August 13, 1521, marking the end of the Aztec empire.

The Spaniards' goals during the Conquest are often summarized as gold, glory, and God, that is, material wealth, personal aggrandizement through warfare, and the spread of Christianity as the exclusive religion. In central Mexico Spaniards recognized that the long-term

The Pyramid of the Sun at Tenochtitlan (or Teotihuacán), Mexico, was built between the first and second centuries CE.[JOSE FUSTE RAGA/ CORBIS]

exploitation of its population was in the Europeans' material and religious interests because prior to European contact these central Mexican Indians were sedentary farmers and skilled artisans, accustomed to paying taxes and rendering labor service to their overlords. The Spaniards incorporated cooperative indigenous rulers into the colonial system as nobles, turning dynastic lords into important mediators between Spanish rulers and indigenous commoners, who continued to render tribute and labor. The Aztec empire as such disappeared and epidemics reduced the Nahua population, but nonetheless a sizable indigenous population remained. The essential structures of their society and economy became the basis for Spanish colonial rule. Spaniards built their colonial capital on the site of Tenochtitlan, drawing on its symbolic power as an imperial center.

Central Mexican populations prior to European contact were quite dense, largely sedentary agriculturalists living in nucleated settlements, although the exact numbers are controversial, perhaps between fifteen and twenty-five million for the whole region. There were many cities of significant size, and a network of towns and villages. Rapid population decline in the first fifty years after European contact, perhaps as high as 90 percent, was due to epidemics that killed populations with no immunity, not homicidal Spaniards bent on the Indians' extermination. The Spaniards viewed population decline with alarm because these Indians were a source of tribute and labor. Their attitude was unlike the English in North America, who considered Indians an environmental hazard and viewed their demise as providential. Epidemics had a major impact on transforming the post-Conquest central Mexican economy from one based on traditional compelled labor and delivery of tribute goods to a colonial economy based on free labor on Spanish landed estates that produced goods for a Spanish market. Colonial Mexico City, the former Aztec capital of Tenochtitlan, continued to have a significant indigenous population, from natural increase and immigration from elsewhere. Although the imperial Aztecs were conquered in 1521, their descendants live in modern central Mexico, some still speaking Nahuatl.

SEE ALSO Indigenous Peoples

BIBLIOGRAPHY

Berdan, Frances F. (1982). *The Aztecs of Central Mexico: An Imperial Society.* New York: Holt, Rinehart, and Winston.

Carrasco, Pedro (1999). *The Tenochca Empire of Ancient Mexico: The Triple Alliance of Tenochtitlan, Tetzcoco, and Tlacopan.* Norman: University of Oklahoma Press.

Durán, Fray Diego (1994). *The History of the Indies of New Spain [1581],* trans. Doris Heyden. Norman: University of Oklahoma Press.

Léon-Portilla, Miguel (1963). *Aztec Thought and Culture.* Norman: University of Oklahoma Press.

Sahagún, Fray Bernardino (1950–1982). *Florentine Codex, General History of the Things of New Spain,* 13 vols., trans. Arthur J. O. Anderson and Charles Dibble. Santa Fe, N.M.: The School of American Research and the University of Utah.

Sarah Cline

Babi Yar

A ravine on the western outskirts of Kiev, the capital of Ukraine, Babi Yar was the site on September 29 and 30, 1941, of the single largest Nazi shooting of Jews in the occupied Soviet Union. The massacre at Babi Yar (in Ukrainian, *Babyn Yar*) also stands out as a vivid example of the German military's involvement in the Holocaust. German forces entered Kiev on September 19, 1941. Five days later mines laid by the retreating Soviet authorities started to explode and set off a fire that demolished much of the city's center. SS and police officials together with officers of the Sixth Army found this an acceptable rationale for taking vengeance on Kiev's Jews, whom they had already started persecuting. Some time between September 25 and 27 they decided to murder all the Jews. On Sunday, September 28, the newly installed Ukrainian auxiliary police posted an order in Russian, Ukrainian, and German addressed to the Jews of Kiev and the surrounding area. It ordered them to appear early the next morning at a specific intersection and to bring along their identity papers, money, valuables, and warm clothing. No reason was provided. "Yids" who disobeyed would be shot, the poster added.

Many thousands of Jews, most of them expecting to be deported, arrived at the intersection of Melnyk Street (today Melnykov Street) and Dehtiarivska Street, where at that time a freight train station stood nearby. They were directed to the entrance to the Jewish cemetery; there across Melnyk Street, Germans and Ukrainians controlled a checkpoint. After entering it, Jews had to surrender their documents and possessions and pass

a gauntlet of Germans with dogs. Ukrainian police then forced them to take off their clothes, and drove them into Babi Yar, where Germans shot them with rifles or machine guns. The killers were members of *Sonderkommando* 4a, a subunit of Security Police Task Force C (one of the four *Einsatzgruppen*). Reserve Police Battalion 45 and Police Battalion 303 assisted them in the massacre. All morning and afternoon Jewish men, women, and children, as well as non-Jewish husbands and wives, and others who wished to remain with them, arrived at the site. The massacre resumed the next day when more Jews arrived at Babi Yar. Thus, the ravine became a huge mass grave. According to the records of the Security Police, they shot 33,771 Jews in two days. Historians have generally considered this statistic reliable or at the very least close to reality.

Many Jews were shot at Babi Yar after September 1941, although wartime records that have been preserved do not mention figures for those later shootings. For instance, some three thousand Jewish Red Army prisoners of war (POWs) were executed at the site late in September and early in October 1941. Non-Jews, in particular non-Jewish POWs and Roma, were also killed at Babi Yar. In February 1942 Kiev's mayor and some members of the Organization of Ukrainian Nationalists were killed; if perhaps these crimes did not physically occur at Babi Yar, the Nazis still dumped the corpses there. Later the Nazis also used vehicles fitted with gas vents to murder other victims at the site. From August 1943, in a cover-up operation supervised by *Sonderkommando* 4a's former commander Paul Blobel (who was executed in 1951), Jewish inmates from a nearby camp had to dig up and incinerate all of the

Execution in progress at Babi Yar (just outside the city of Kiev). According to records maintained by the Nazis, 33,771 Jews were killed here on September 29 and 30, 1941. [HULTON ARCHIVE/GETTY IMAGES]

corpses at Babi Yar. Four survivors have estimated that over 100,000 corpses were burned, and this became the official Soviet (and now Ukrainian) figure for the total number of victims of Babi Yar from 1941 to 1943.

During the war the Soviet media reported the massacre of Kiev's Jews, and in March Soviet Ukrainian authorities decided to erect a monument at the site. But the design for the latter never evolved beyond the planning stage, and it soon became impossible to properly commemorate Babi Yar, for the increasingly anti-Semitic Communist Party prohibited any commemoration of the Holocaust. Nearby brick factories started pumping refuse into the ravine and officials made plans for a stadium and park. In 1959, in a sign that First Secretary Nikita Khrushchev wished to relax Soviet restrictions, Literaturnaya gazeta, a prominent Moscow weekly, published a letter from the Kiev writer Viktor Nekrasov that demanded a memorial to the victims of the Babi Yar massacre. On March 13, 1961, the factory refuse broke loose, wreaking havoc on Kiev's nearby Kurenivka district and killing an unknown number of people. In September 1961 Literaturnaya gazeta created another sensation by publishing a pro-Jewish poem, "Babi Yar," by the Russian writer Yevgeni Yevtushenko.

(Later, after intense pressure, he added a patriotic sentence about Russia.) The composer Dmitri Shostakovich set the story to music as part of his Thirteenth Symphony, which premiered in 1962.

In the mid-1960s there were two official design competitions for a memorial, but neither led to any changes on the grounds. On the twenty-fifth anniversary of the massacre a spontaneous commemoration occurred that included the remarks of Ukrainian writer Ivan Dziuba, who courageously condemned anti-Semitism. After that, as before 1966, commemorations were suppressed. In 1966 a Moscow monthly published installments of Anatoli Kuznetsov's novel Babi Yar, and one year later it was officially published as a book. This work, actually the author's memoirs, also included an account of the massacre by Dina Pronicheva, one of the handful of survivors. The Communist Party began to harass Kuznetsov, who escaped to the United Kingdom and published there a more complete version of Babi Yar, which included cases of wartime anti-Semitism.

The political climate of the 1970s resulted in some of the worst distortions of the massacre at Babi Yar. On March 12, 1970, Pravda, the official Soviet newspaper, carried a statement signed by fifty-one Jews from Ukraine that included this passage: "The tragedy of Babi Yar will forever remain the embodiment not only of the Hitlerites' cannibalism, but also of the indelible disgrace of their accomplices and followers: the Zionists" (p. 4). Although in 1976 a large, bronze sculpture commemorating the citizens and POWs shot there between 1941 and 1943 did finally appear at Babi Yar, in artificially sculpted terrain, it made no mention of Jews. Likewise, a 1981 Soviet television documentary about Babi Yar conveyed a message of anti-Zionism.

In September 1991, one month after the declaration of an independent Ukraine, the first state-sponsored commemoration of the Babi Yar massacre took place. Additional text was added to the Soviet monument, and at another location (far from the shooting site), local Jews placed a bronze menorah. Other new commemorative objects in or near the area include a wooden cross erected by the Organization of Ukrainian Nationalists in 1991; another cross erected in 2000 to honor two Russian Orthodox priests believed to have been shot at Babi Yar in November 1941; and a memorial built in 2001 devoted to the children of Babi Yar. The first stone for a Babi Yar museum was laid in 2001. In 2002 an emotional debate took place in Kiev, primarily among Jews, about the possibility that the museum and community center would rise atop human remains.

In the wider world an awareness of Babi Yar has evolved from sources as diverse as Leon Uris's bestselling novel *Exodus* (1958), which briefly mentions Babi Yar; war crimes trials in Nuremberg and elsewhere; Babi Yar Park in Denver (open since 1970); translations of Yevtushenko's and Kuznetsov's work; the TV mini-series *Holocaust* (1978), which included a scene of the massacre; and visits to the monument by former U.S. president George Bush (1991) and Pope John Paul II (2001).

SEE ALSO Anti-Semitism; Einsatzgruppen; Holocaust; Massacres; Mass Graves; Memorials and Monuments; Ukraine (Famine); Union of Soviet Socialist Republics

BIBLIOGRAPHY

Anatoli (Kuznetsov), A. (1970). *Babi Yar: A Document in the Form of a Novel.* Trans. David Floyd. New York: Farrar, Straus and Giroux.

Barenboym, I. Yu., et al. (1970). "'Obuzdat' Agressorov, Presech' Zlodeyania Sionistov." *Pravda* (March 12):4.

Berkhoff, Karel C. (2004). *Harvest of Despair: Life and Death in Ukraine under Nazi Rule.* Cambridge, Mass.: Belknap Press.

Sheldon, Richard (1988). "The Transformations of Babi Yar." *Soviet Society and Culture: Essays in Honor of Vera

The Babi Yar monument near the Ukranian capital of Kiev stands as a memorial to more than 100,000 Jews massacred by the Nazis at the site. [AP/WIDE WORLD PHOTOS]

S. Dunham, ed. Terry L. Thompson and Richard Sheldon. Boulder, Colo.: Westview Press.

Karel C. Berkhoff

Bagosora, Théoneste

[AUGUST 16, 1941–]
Rwandan defense minister who briefly assumed control of the country and was ultimately indicted for his role in the Rwandan genocide.

Théoneste Bagosora, known as "Colonel Death," was a cousin of President Juvenal Habyarimana's wife and a member of the "Clan de Madame," a group of Hutu political extremists opposed to sharing power with Tutsis in the Rwandan government. He was born on August 16, 1941, in the Gisenyi prefecture in Rwanda, the same region from which President Habyarimana came. After serving as Second in Command of the *École Supérieure Militaire* in Kigali and Commander of the military camp in Kanombe, he became *Chef de cabinet* (Director of the Cabinet) of the ministry of Defense in June of 1992. When Rwandan President Juvénal Habyarimana's plane crashed on April 6, 1994, he assumed de facto political and military control during the Rwandan genocide. The International Criminal Tribunal for Rwanda (ICTR) indicted him on August 9, 1996 for his responsibility in the Rwandan genocide. He was arrested in the Republic of Cameroon on September 3, 1996, and transferred to Arusha, Tanzania, for trial on January 23, 1997. He pled not guilty on March 7, 1997. His trial was still underway in 2004.

Colonel Bagosora was accused of being the "mastermind" of the genocide, as well as of performing crimes against humanity and war crimes. He and three other military officers were accused of being co-conspirators since late 1990 in planning to exterminate the civilian Tutsi population and eliminate members of the opposition. Bagosora was also charged in April 1995 by the Belgian legal authorities for murder and serious violations of the Geneva Conventions of August 12, 1949, and of Geneva Protocols I and II of June 8, 1977. Bagosora was a member of Akazu, the extremist network based in Ruhengeri and Gisenyi and centered around President Habyarimana's wife. Akazu was accused of smuggling arms and drug trafficking, and was believed to be responsible for the training of the militias from 1992. Akazu was also believed to be responsible for the incitement to ethnic violence that was conducted by local authorities, and for the massacres of the Tutsi minority in Kibilira (1990), Bagogwe (1991), and Bugesera (1992). In 1992 Bagosora instructed the two General Staffs to establish lists of people to be identified as the enemy and its accomplices. These lists were drawn up by the Intelligence Bureau (G-2) of the Rwandan Army and regularly updated. In 1993, following a traffic accident, a list of this type was found in the wreckage of the car of Chief of Staff, Déogratias Nsabimana.

Colonel Bagosora, as military adviser to the government delegation at the Arusha peace talks in the spring of 1993, openly expressed his opposition to the concessions made by the government representative, Boniface Ngulinzira, Minister of Foreign Affairs. (On April 11, 1994, Ngulinzira was assassinated.) When Bagosora left Arusha at the end of the talks, he declared that he was returning to Rwanda to "prepare the apocalypse." Subsequently, in the presence of senior officers on various occasions, he evidently reiterated that the implementation of the Arusha Accords would unleash war and that the solution to such a war would require plunging the country into an apocalypse that would eliminate all the Tutsis and thus ensure lasting peace.

Just before the final version of the Arusha Accords was signed on August 4, 1993, James Gasana, Minister of Defense in President Habyarimana's cabinet and a longtime MRND politician, attempted to recall weapons that were being transferred to the militias. In response, Bagosora, then Gasana's Chief of Staff, threatened Gasana's life. Gasana fled with his family to Italy. From July 1993 to July 1994, the Minister of Defense, Augustin Bizimana, who replaced James Gasana, encouraged and facilitated the acquisition of weapons for MRND militants by openly asserting that the Ministry of Defense was a Ministry of the MRND.

General Romeo Dallaire, the Force Commander of the United Nations Assistance Mission in Rwanda (UNAMIR), met Bagosora in August 1993 as the military liaison to UNAMIR; Dallaire described this bespectacled and pudgy military officer as "bemused by Arusha." Bagosora, according to Dallaire, made only rhetorical gestures at adhering to the arms agreement concerning heavy weapons and at maintaining the neutral corridor, and did nothing to stop the militia training.

Subsequently, in a letter dated December 3, 1993, FAR officers informed Dallaire of the "Machiavellian plan" of the Northerners to destroy the Arusha Accords by exterminating the Tutsis and their "accomplices." On January 10, 1994, a leader of the *Interahamwe* (Hutu militia group that carried out much of the genocide) gave Dallaire details of just such a plan. On January 11, 1994, Dallaire sent a cable to UN headquarters detailing the plan, which called for Hutus to kill Tutsis at the rate of 1,000 every 20 minutes, to kill 10 Belgian peacekeepers, and to restart the war. He wanted UN permission to investigate the potential for this plan to be carried out by seeking out hidden arms caches, of which he had been informed. However, his superiors, including Kofi Annan, then head of the United Nations Department of Peacekeeping, countermanded this suggestion.

Dallaire claimed that Bagosora was behind the training and arming of the militias and the youth gangs—the Interahamwe and *Impuzamugambi*. There was cooperation between the *Interahamwe* and military personnel in the Presidential Guard and the Para-Commando Battalion, contrary to the provisions of Arusha. On April 4, 1994, three days before the beginning of the genocide, Bagosora exclaimed before witnesses that the only solution to the political impasse was to eliminate all the Tutsis. On April 6, 1994, immediately after Habyarimana's plane was shot down, Dallaire found Bagosora at the center of a cadre of military officers. Bagosora was the spokesperson of the coup. In his trial testimony, Dallaire testified that Bagosora took control of the country. It was Bagosora who announced the curfew on April 7, and who, over the next two days, assembled the *Comité de Salut de Public* (Committee of Public Safety) to pick a provisional government. On April 9, Paul Kagame denounced Bagosora as the mastermind behind the coup.

A prosecution witness, testifying by video link from The Hague at Bagosora's trial, claimed that, between April 9 and 12, 1994, Bagosora possessed a list of Tutsis and businessmen to be killed, and that the people on the list were massacred a day later. On April 13, Bagosora demoted or pushed aside the army officers who signed a communiqué drawn up by moderate military officers in an attempt to stop the resumption of the war and the genocide. Further, it was Bagosora who, on May 1, 1994, arranged a meeting with the *Interahamwe*. On May 22, 1994, films were taken that showed Bagosora in control of genocidal militias (Dallaire, 2003, p. 386). On July 1, 1994, General Dallaire saw Bagosora for the last time before testifying against him from the witness box at his trial. During that July encounter, Bagosora threatened to kill Dallaire the next time he saw him.

SEE ALSO Geneva Conventions on the Protection of Victims of War; Incitement; Rwanda

BIBLIOGRAPHY

Dallaire, Roméo (2003). *Shake Hands with the Devil,* Toronto: Random House.

des Forges, Alison (1999). *Leave None to Tell the Story: Genocide in Rwanda.* New York: Human Rights Watch.

Jones, Bruce (2001). *Peacemaking in Rwanda: The Dynamics of Failure.* Boulder, Colo.: Lynne Rienner.

Mamdani, Mahmood (2001). *When Victims Become Killers: Colonialism, Nativism, and the Genocide in Rwanda.* Princeton, N.J.: Princeton University Press.

Prunier, Gérard (1995). *The Rwandese Crisis (1959–1994): From Cultural Mythology to Genocide.* New York: Columbia University Press.

Howard Adelman

Bahā'īs

The Bahā'ī Faith is an independent religion founded in Iran in the nineteenth century by Mīrzā Ḥusayn 'Ali Nūrī, whose religious appellation was Bahā' Allāh (Arabic for *glory of God*). The word Bahā'ī signifies a follower of Bahā' Allāh.

During the early 1800s there was a messianic expectation among Shi'ite Muslims that the Twelfth Imam, a descendant of the prophet Muhammed, would return to renew the religion of Islam and establish a just society. This belief was central to the teachings of the Shaykhī sect, named after Sheik Ahmad-i-Ahsā'ī.

On May 22, 1844, Mīrzā 'Ali Muhammad announced that he was the promised Twelfth Imam and took the name of the Bāb (Arabic for *gate*), indicating that he was the forerunner of yet another divine messenger to appear imminently. The Bāb's message spread throughout Persia (now Iran) and provoked the ire of powerful Shi'ite clergy. These clerics convinced government officials that the Bāb's rapidly growing influence posed a threat to ruling authorities. In 1848 the Bāb was arrested, beaten, imprisoned, and tried before the Muslim clerics of Tabriz. On July 9, 1850, the Bāb was executed by a firing squad.

After the Bāb's execution two followers of the Bāb attempted to kill the Shah of Persia, only confirming the Shah's fears of rebellion. This act led to the mass imprisonment of thousands of the Bāb's followers over the next few years. Bahā' Allāh was among those imprisoned for being a Bābī even though evidence demonstrated his innocence. After several months Bahā' Allāh was released and banished from Iran. He traveled to Baghdad, where he announced in 1863 that he was the messenger of God about whom the Bāb had spoken. Persian officials, concerned about the flow of pilgrims and foreign dignitaries seeking an audience with Bahā' Allāh, requested that Turkish officials move Bahā' Allāh further away from Persian territory. Bahā' Allāh was moved from Baghdad to Constantinople, then to Adrianople in an unsuccessful attempt to diminish his influence. Finally in 1868 Bahā' Allāh was banished to the distant prison city of 'Akká (Acco, Acre), Palestine.

Before Bahā' Allāh died on May 29, 1892, his teachings spread from Persia and the Ottoman Empire to the Caucasus, Turkistan, India, Burma, Egypt, and the Sudan. 'Abd al-Bahā, Bahā' Allāh's son, assumed leadership of the Bahā'ī community after his father's death and embarked on several journeys around the world, spreading the religion to regions of Africa, Europe, and America. When 'Abd al-Bahā died, his will designated his eldest grandson, Shoghi Effendi Rabbanī, as the new leader of the community. Shoghi Effendi continued to expand the Bahā'ī community and build up the administrative structures of the Bahā'ī Faith. By the time of his death in 1957, the foundation had been laid for the first international election of a governing body called the Universal House of Justice. The Universal House of Justice, located in Haifa, Israel, guides the administrative affairs of the Bahā'ī community.

In just over 150 years the Bahā'ī Faith has become the second-most geographically widespread religion in the world. It embraces people from all economic classes and more than two thousand ethnic, racial, and tribal groups. In 2003 there were approximately five million

Bahā'īs in more than two hundred countries and territories worldwide.

A central tenet of the Bahā'ī Faith is unity. Bahā'īs believe that there is only one unknowable God who has revealed himself to humanity through a series of messengers, including Moses, Zoroaster, Buddha, Krishna, Jesus, Muhammad, the Bāb, and Bahā' Allāh. Bahā'īs believe in the oneness of humanity, the unity of religious truth, the harmony of science and religion, the equality of women and men, independent investigation of truth, the elimination of all forms of prejudice, and a spiritual solution to extremes of wealth and poverty.

Persecution of the Bahā'īs in Iran

Since the founding of their religion the Bahā'īs of Iran have suffered torture, imprisonment, mob violence, and execution despite Bahā'ī beliefs of obedience to government and tolerance. Some twenty thousand Baha'is perished in the face of opposition from Islamic religious authorities during the nineteenth century. Persecutions continued intermittently throughout the twentieth century until the Islamic revolution in 1979, when clerics seized control of the government and embarked on a systematic campaign to eradicate the Iranian Bahā'ī community.

Between 1978 and 1998 the Iranian government executed more than two hundred Bahā'īs. The majority of these Bahā'īs were members of the community's democratically elected governing councils. During the 1980s hundreds of Bahā'īs were imprisoned and tens of thousands were deprived of jobs, pensions, businesses, and educational opportunities solely because of their religious beliefs.

International Responses

In response to intense international pressure in the late 1980s, including a series of country-specific United Nations (UN) resolutions, the Iranian government began to reduce the rate of executions and number of Bahā'īs held in prison. However, despite the apparent abatement of persecution in the late twentieth century, evidence revealed that the Islamic Republic of Iran continued its campaign to marginalize and eliminate the 300,000-member Bahā'ī community. Bahā'īs were arrested and released without documentation to confirm their freed status. Suspended sentences were used to threaten individuals who continued to participate in Bahā'ī activities. These practices were calculated to extinguish the life of the community without drawing the attention and ire of the international community.

Evidence of the government's altered tactics emerged in early 1993 with the discovery of a confidential government policy memorandum regarding the Bahā'ī question. Drafted by the Supreme Revolutionary Cultural Council and signed by former president Ali Khamenei, the document described the government's objective: to ensure that the "progress and development" of the Bahā'ī community remain "blocked." The memorandum declared that all Bahā'īs should be expelled from universities and prevented from obtaining positions of influence and employment. The memorandum further suggested that Bahā'ī youth should be sent to Islamic schools with "a strong and imposing [Islamic] religious ideology" and must be expelled from schools and universities if they identified themselves as Bahā'īs. It also discussed plans for reaching beyond the borders of Iran "to confront and destroy their [Bahā'ī] cultural roots outside the country."

Twenty-First Century Developments

International efforts to focus on Iran's human rights record faltered in April 2002. Iranian officials were able to convince other nations that the previous seventeen resolutions adopted by the UN Commission on Human Rights were not helpful in advancing human rights in Iran and other means would prove more effective in improving the status of Bahā'īs, and other groups, in that country.

After the Commission on Human Rights suspended its monitoring of Iran, arrests and short-term detentions of Bahā'īs increased. Bahā'ī teachers and students were constantly watched and harassed. Instances of confiscation increased, while attempts to obtain redress from the courts failed. The Bahā'ī community constitutes Iran's largest non-Muslim religious minority, yet it remains unrecognized by Iran's constitution.

Thousands of newspaper articles about the situation of the Bahā'īs in Iran have appeared around the world. Prominent international organizations, including the European Parliament and several national legislatures, have passed resolutions expressing serious concern for their situation.

SEE ALSO Iran; Religious Groups

BIBLIOGRAPHY

Bahā'ī International Community (1994). *The Bahā'īs: A Profile of the Bahā'ī Faith and Its Worldwide Community.* New York: Author.

Bahā'ī International Community (1999). *The Bahā'ī Question: Iran's Secret Blueprint for the Destruction of a Religious Community.* New York: Author.

U.S. Commission on International Religious Freedom (USCIRF). "The Annual Report of the United States Commission on International Religious Freedom." May 2003.

East Pakistanis were struggling for independence from Pakistan in 1971 when the Pakistani Army inaugurated a genocide there. Here, in a photo taken in Dhaka (or Dacca), corpses are transported for burial. [BETTMANN/CORBIS]

U.S. Department of State Bureau of Democracy, Human Rights and Labor. "The Fifth Annual Report on International Religious Freedom." December 18, 2003.

Kit Bigelow
Jerry K. Prince

Bangladesh/East Pakistan

India's independence from Great Britain in August 1947 resulted in the partition of British India into India and Pakistan. Pakistan was created out of the Muslim-majority provinces of British India, with no regard for geographical contiguity. The resulting state was formed into two physically separate wings, with the territory of India intervening between the two. The eastern wing was created by the partition of the British province of Bengal, and the principal language spoken there was Bengali. Although it was principally the language of those who fled India to Pakistan, the government of Pakistan decreed that Urdu would be the national language.

In the evening of March 25, 1971, the Pakistan army attacked East Pakistan, as the future Bangladesh was then known. The attack was an effort to put down East Pakistani protesters who demanded that the national government recognize the right of the elected majority party, the Awami (People's) League, to assume political office. The attacks by the Pakistanis, and resistance by the Bangladeshis, continued until December of that year, with the Bangladeshis seeing this as a war of independence, and the government forces viewing it as a civil war. Throughout the year, India provided support for the East Pakistani rebels, and received a large number of refugees. Early in December, Pakistan's internal conflict assumed international dimensions with the direct intervention of Indian troops. The violence ended on December 16, when the Pakistani commander at the time, General A. K. Niazi, surrendered to General Jagjeet Singh Arora, commander of the Indian forces.

The discontent of East Pakistanis in the united state of Pakistan had a long history before it finally culminated in war. The Muslim League government of Pakistan, led by Muhammad Ali Jinnah, had long ignored East Bengal. However, during his only visit to the east-

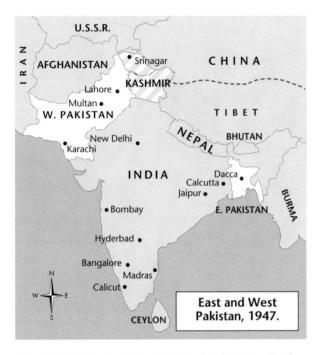

U.S.S.R.

AFGHANISTAN

IRAN

Srinagar

CHINA

KASHMIR

Lahore

Multan

W. PAKISTAN

TIBET

NEPAL

BHUTAN

New Delhi

Karachi

INDIA

Dacca

Calcutta

Jaipur

BURMA

Bombay

E. PAKISTAN

Hyderbad

Bangalore

Madras

Calicut

N

W   E

S

CEYLON

East and West Pakistan, 1947.

Map of India and to its east, Bangladesh/East Pakistan, site of the well-documented Hindu genocide. [EASTWORD PUBLICATIONS DEVELOPMENT/GALE GROUP]

ern province, in March 1948, Jinnah was confronted by Bengalis who demanded that their language be recognized along with Urdu as a co-official language of Pakistan. Jinnah stated that anyone who opposed the status of Urdu as the official language of Pakistan was a traitor to the country. This angered the Bengali faction, and in 1952 that anger gave rise to the "language movement" in East Pakistan.

After independence, the Pakistani government was constituted according to the Government of India Act (1935) as modified by the India Independence Act of 1947, both acts of the British Parliament. It was not until 1956 that a formal constitution was promulgated (India adopted its own constitution in 1950). The constitution of 1956 changed the name of the eastern wing of the country from East Bengal to East Pakistan and the four provinces of the west wing were consolidated into West Pakistan. The constitution also instituted the concept of parity between the eastern and western regions. This meant that representation in the National Assembly would be equal from each province, even though East Pakistan had about 54 percent of the total population of Pakistan. The Bengalis of East Pakistan viewed this as an affront.

This shortchanging of representation in the National Assembly was also seen in the military services. There were very few officers from East Pakistan in a military overwhelmingly dominated by West Paki-

stanis. There was a similar disparity in representation within the civil service. Although a quota system was later instituted, the disparity persisted at the higher levels throughout the 1960s.

In 1954 a major and violent strike occurred at the Adamjee Jute Mill in Narayanganj, a suburb of Dhaka. In addition to disputes over pay and labor practices, the East Pakistani workers felt that the company was showing favoritism to Urdu-speaking Biharis in employment. *Bihari* is a general term applied to those Urdu-speaking Muslims, most of them from the Indian state of Bihar, who fled east at the time of partition but who never learned to speak Bengali. In addition, the East Pakistani strikers were protesting the fact that the majority of East Pakistan's manufacturing and banking firms were owned by West Pakistanis, among whom the Adamjee family was prominent.

The leading Muslim political party in Bengal prior to Pakistan's independence had been the Muslim League, which dominated the Bengal Provincial Assembly. At the time of independence, the sitting members of the Bengal Provincial Assembly chose their future membership in either the assembly of West Bengal in India or the assembly of East Bengal in Pakistan. The Muslim League maintained control. Although elections were held in each of the provinces of the west wing as early as 1951, elections in East Bengal were delayed until 1954. The election, when it was finally held, resulted in an almost total rout of the Muslim League, which was looked upon locally as a proxy of the central government.

The winning coalition in East Pakistan was comprised of the Awami League and the Krishak Sramik (Farmers and Workers) Party. The principal founder of the Awami League was Husain Shahid Suhrawardy. The Krishak Sramik Party was led by Fazlul Haq. Haq had been a prime minister of united Bengal (i.e., prior to independence) when his party was known as the Krishak Praja (Farmers and Peoples) Party. For the 1954 election, the Awami League and the Krishak Sramik Party joined forces as the United Front and ran for office on a platform called "21 Points." Among the issues addressed by the coalition were the recognition of Bengali as an official language of Pakistan; autonomy for East Bengal in all matters except defense, foreign affairs, and currency; land reform; improved irrigation; nationalization of the jute industry; and other points that, if enacted into law, would give East Bengalis greater control of their own governance.

The demand that Bengali be recognized as an official language was an outgrowth of the language movement of 1952. Since the early days of independence, East Pakistanis had demanded that Pakistan recognize two official languages: Bengali (the most widely spoken language) and Urdu. An attempt by the central government to devise a means to write Bengali in the Urdu script was met with widespread opposition and rioting, mainly from academics and university students. On February 21, 1952, in an attempt to suppress the violence, the police fired on a crowd of demonstrators, and about twenty students were killed. Today, a monument stands at the site of the killings, and February 21 is celebrated annually as Martyrs' Day.

For its championing of this and other issues important to the majority of East Pakistanis, the Krishak Sramik–Awami League coalition won the 1954 election. Eventually, however, the Krishak Sramik Party withered away, and the Awami League became the most important party in the province. It would become the leader of the independence movement and dominate emerging Bangladeshi politics.

In October 1958 General Muhammad Ayub Khan proclaimed himself president of Pakistan following a military coup, declared martial law, and dissolved the National Assembly and the provincial legislatures. He then set up what he called "Basic Democracy," which he described as a more representative government. Elections at the local level would be direct, and those elected at this level would be designated Basic Democrats. Elections for the provincial and national assemblies and for the presidency would be indirect, with the Basic Democrats serving as the electoral college. He retained the principle of parity, however. This meant that each province was allocated an equal number of Basic Democrat electors, so that East Pakistanis continued to be underrepresented at the higher levels of government. Not unexpectedly, Ayub was elected president in 1962 and reelected president in 1967. Although he won majorities in each wing in each election, his majority in the east wing in 1967 was dramatically less than in 1962.

Nonetheless, Ayub's power began to slip after his reelection to office, as did his health. Opposition to his rule spread, even in West Pakistan. Ayub grew concerned about a growing secessionist movement in East Pakistan. The Awami League, now headed by Sheik Mujibur Rahman, demanded that changes be made in regard to East Pakistan. These changes were embodied in Mujib's Six Points Plan, which he presented at a meeting of opposition parties in Lahore in 1966. In brief, these Six Points called for:

(1) a federal and parliamentary government with free and fair elections;

(2) federal government to control only foreign affairs and defense;

(3) a separate currency or separate fiscal accounts for each province, to control movement of capital from east to west;

(4) all power of taxation to reside at the provincial level, with the federal government subsisting on grants from the provinces;

(5) enabling each federating unit to enter into foreign trade agreements on its own and to retain control over the foreign exchange earned; and

(6) allowing each unit to raise its own militia.

If these points had been adopted, it would have meant almost de facto independence for East Pakistan. Many observers saw point six, a separate militia, as the point most unacceptable to the central government, but they were wrong. The 1965 Indo-Pakistan War had demonstrated the lack of local defense forces in East Pakistan, which would have left the province defenseless had India attacked there. In fact, it was point four, regarding taxation, that proved to be the problem, because the enactment of this point would make it all but impossible for a central government to operate.

In 1968, in response to the Six Points Plan, the Ayub government charged Mujib and his supporters with treason. This later became known as the Agartala Conspiracy Case, so-called as it was alleged that Mujib had met with Indian agents in Agartala, the capital of the Indian state of Tripura, which borders on Bangladesh. Mujib and the Awami League denied that any such meeting had ever taken place. In early 1969, as hostility to Ayub increased in both East and West Pakistan, he invited opposition leaders to meet with him. Mujib, having been jailed awaiting his trial for treason, was not invited to this meeting. The opposition leaders refused to come to the meeting unless the charges against Mujib were withdrawn and demanded that he, too, be invited to attend. Ayub complied with these demands. The meeting, which Ayub hoped would work to his advantage, instead strengthened the opposition's position, which called for the end of the policy of Basic Democracy and the return to direct parliamentary elections.

The opposition movement expanded beyond the political sphere to the military, and Ayub was forced to resign on March 25, 1969. He was replaced by General Agha Muhammad Yahya Khan, who promised to reinstate direct elections. These were held in December 1970 in most of the country, but flooding in East Pakistan forced a few constituencies to delay their elections until January 1971. In addition to reinstating free and direct elections, Yahya also acted to restore the former provinces of West Pakistan, which had been united into a single unit by the 1956 constitution. More important for East Pakistan, he ended the principle of parity. In the 1970 election for the National Assembly, East Pakistan would have 162 general seats out of a total of 300, reflecting the 54 percent majority that Bengalis enjoyed according to the 1961 population census.

Yahya also introduced legislation that, in his view, would limit the changes that could be made to the constitution by the National Assembly. This legislation, called the Legal Framework Order, touched upon seven points:

(1) that Pakistan would be a federated state;

(2) Islamic principles would be paramount;

(3) direct and regular elections would be held;

(4) fundamental rights would be guaranteed;

(5) the judiciary would be independent;

(6) maximum provincial autonomy would be allowed, "but the federal government shall also have adequate powers, including legislative, administrative, and financial powers, to discharge its responsibilities"; and

(7) economic disparities among provinces would be removed.

The result of the election in East Pakistan startled outside observers, and even took some supporters of the Awami League by surprise. The party won 160 of the 162 seats in East Pakistan, thereby gaining a majority in the National Assembly without winning a single seat in West Pakistan, which had thrown its support behind the Pakistan People's Party, led by Zulfiqar Ali Bhutto. Neither Yahya, nor his military associates, nor Bhutto looked favorably on a government comprised solely of the Awami League and headed by the author of the Six Points Plan. Yahya began a series of negotiations, perhaps in the hope of creating a coalition government, but more in an effort to sideline Mujib. As the talks became more rancorous and compromise seemed impossible, the Pakistani government began to increase the strength of its rather small contingent of military forces stationed in East Pakistan.

Yahya negotiated with Bhutto and Mujib, the former declaring that there were "two majorities" in Pakistan, and the latter insisting on the full enactment of the Six Points, even where these were at variance with Yahya's Legal Framework Order (i.e., on the issues of taxation). Demonstrations supporting the Awami League's position spread across East Pakistan. Violence began to look more attractive than political activism as a means of protecting East Pakistan's interests. By this time, the term *Bangladeshi* was widely adopted by the Awami League and its supporters to replace the designation *East Pakistani*.

The army struck back on March 25, 1971. Its first move was to attack the faculty and students at Dhaka University and to take Mujib into custody. By one estimate, up to 35,000 Bangladeshis were killed at the university and elsewhere on the first few days. Mujib was transported to jail in West Pakistan. (There were fears that he would be executed, but these later proved unfounded when he was released at the end of the conflict.) A number of Mujib's associates fled, first to a village on the border with India, then to Calcutta. Major Ziaur Rahman, who would later become president of independent Bangladesh, issued a declaration of independence.

Bangladeshi police and border patrol forces organized a resistance force to oppose the Pakistani army, and they were later joined by several civilians, many of whom had been university students. It was, however, almost nine months before India intervened, triggering the December 16, 1971, surrender of the Pakistani army. India intervened both for strategic reasons (as weakening Pakistan) and for humanitarian reasons, to alleviate the suffering of Bangladeshis.

Pakistan complained about India's invasion of its sovereign territory to the UN Security Council in early December. In an often emotional speech, Bhutto argued, with reason, that this intervention was a violation of international law. The Security Council agreed, but the question soon became moot with the surrender of the Pakistani troops in Bangladesh.

The number of Bangladeshis killed, disabled, raped, or displaced by the violence of 1971 is not fully known. Estimates by Bangladeshi sources put the number killed at up to three million, and it is estimated that as many as ten million may have fled to India. Initially, the Pakistani army targeted educators, students, political leaders, and others who were generally considered to be prominent sympathizers of the Awami League. As the Bangladeshis formed military units, however, these units also became the targets. Some of these units were formed by Bangladeshis who had formerly served in the Pakistani army; others were recruited from the police and the East Pakistan (now Bangladesh) Rifles, a border security force. These units, based in rural and outlying areas of Bangladesh, were able to take advantage of the Pakistani army's initial focus on the student-led demonstrations in the Dhaka region. Survivor accounts, such as that by Jahanara Imam, suggest that much of the killing soon devolved into little more than indiscriminate slaughter.

The Pakistani surrender and the termination of conflict left several unsettled questions. Many Bangladeshis—mostly civil servants or military troops and their families—were still detained in Pakistan. In

Bangladesh, there were non-Bengalis—again, mostly civil servants or military troops, but also some business owners and professionals—who wished repatriation to Pakistan. In addition, the fate of de facto prisoners of war held by Bangladesh, and Pakistani prisoners of war held by India had yet to be decided. Bangladesh wanted to place 195 Pakistani military personnel on trial for war crimes and genocide. On August 9, 1975, a tripartite agreement between Bangladesh, India, and Pakistan was reached to create a panel that would attempt to settle these issues. Bangladesh also agreed to drop all charges against the 195 Pakistanis accused of war crimes and to permit their repatriation to Pakistan.

In the end, and at great cost, Bangladesh achieved its independence. Slowly, the two countries were able to establish diplomatic relations. Pakistan recognized Bangladesh as independent on February 22, 1974, primarily at the urging of the Organization of the Islamic Conference (OIC), which was meeting in Lahore at that time. The OIC insisted that Bangladesh, a Muslim state, be permitted to attend the conference. Bangladeshis, however, remained unsatisfied. They wanted an apology from the Pakistanis for the excesses committed during the war. They received one finally from the Pakistani president, Pervez Musharraf, when he visited Bangladesh in July 2002.

SEE ALSO Humanitarian Intervention; India, Modern; Rape; Refugees

BIBLIOGRAPHY

Ahmad, Moudud (1979). *Bangladesh: A Constitutional Quest for Autonomy.* Dhaka, Bangladesh: University Press.

Baxter, Craig (1997). *Bangladesh: From a Nation to a State.* Boulder, Colo.: Westview Press.

Chaudhri, Kalyan (1972). *Genocide in Bangladesh.* Bombay: Orient Longmans.

Imam, Jahanara (1989). *Of Blood and Fire: The Untold Story of Bangladesh's War of Independence,* tran. Mustafizur Rahman. New Delhi: Sterling Publishers.

Jahan, Rounaq (1982). *Pakistan: Failure in National Integration.* New York: Columbia University Press.

Sisson, Richard, and Leon Rose (1990). *War and Secession: Pakistan, India and the Emergence of Bangladesh.* Berkeley: University of California Press.

Zaheer, Hasan (1994). *The Separation of East Pakistan.* New York: Oxford University Press.

Craig Baxter

Barbie, Klaus
[OCTOBER 25, 1913–SEPTEMBER 25, 1991]
German Officer, Chief of the Gestapo in France

A German officer during World War II, Klaus Barbie was the chief of the Gestapo in Lyons, France, between November 1942, when the Germans assumed control of the previously unoccupied zone, and the occupation's collapse after the Allied D-Day landings in Normandy. Subsequently known as the Butcher of Lyons for his responsibility for the wartime arrest, deportation, torture, and death of thousands, Barbie finally appeared before a French court in 1987, after having lived for three decades in South America under the assumed name Klaus Altmann. His trial was the first in France to deal explicitly with crimes against humanity.

Barbie seems to have escaped justice in the postwar period because of his work on behalf of the United States as a counterintelligence agent. In 1951 he found his way to La Paz, Bolivia, and although tried in France and sentenced to death twice in absentia, in 1952 and 1954, he virtually disappeared until discovered by the French Nazi-hunters Beata and Serge Klarsfeld in 1971. Extradited to France in 1983, Barbie was charged with crimes against humanity committed against civilians, particularly Jews—charges that gained an independent status in French law in the mid-1960s, and for which the twenty-year statute of limitations for war crimes did not apply. In a controversial decision, the *Cour de cassation,* the highest appeals court in France, defined crimes against humanity as those perpetrated "in the name of a state practicing a hegemonic political ideology. . .not only against persons because they belong to a racial or religious group, but also against the adversaries of this [state] policy, whatever the form of their opposition."

The two-month trial of Klaus Barbie, which opened on May 11, 1987, was a cause célèbre in France and, it has been claimed, marked a turning point in the French memory of the Holocaust and wartime resistance. Specifically, Barbie was charged, among other crimes, with having led a raid on the headquarters of the Jewish council in Lyons, with the deportation to Auschwitz of forty-three Jewish children and five adults who were seized from a place of hiding in the village of Izieu, and with the deportation of various other victims, both Jews and members of the French Resistance. Despite the efforts of Barbie's brilliant defense lawyer, Jacques Vergès, to divert attention from his client's wrongdoings to allegations of misdeeds on the part of the Resistance, France's historic complicity in war crimes in Algeria, and even Israeli policies, the extensive publicity generated by the evidence highlighted the sufferings of Barbie's victims—both Jews and the wartime resistance. In the end Barbie was found guilty of crimes against humanity and sentenced to life imprisonment—the maximum sentence allowed by French law. Barbie died in prison in 1991. He was the last ranking Nazi to be tried by a tribunal of justice.

SEE ALSO Crimes Against Humanity; Gestapo; Prosecution; SS

BIBLIOGRAPHY

Douglas, Lawrence (2001). *The Memory of Judgement: Making Law and History in the Trials of the Holocaust.* New Haven, Conn.: Yale University Press.

Finkielkraut, Alain (1991). *Remembering in Vain: the Klaus Barbie Trial and Crimes against Humanity,* tran. Roxanne Lapidus with Sima Godfrey. New York: Columbia University Press.

Rousso, Henry (1991). *The Vichy Syndrome: History and Memory in France since 1944,* tran. Arthur Goldhammer. Cambridge, Mass.: Harvard University Press.

Michael R. Marrus

Beothuk

The Beothuk, speakers of a proto-Algonkian language, had lived in the area now known as Newfoundland and southern Labrador, Canada, for more than two thousand years before John Cabot's landing in 1647. Nomadic, they followed the coastlines, taking advantage of the rich migratory fisheries, shorebirds, and land and sea mammals. In winter they supplemented their diets with inland caribou, herded through specially constructed fences.

Estimates of the Beothuk population in 1500 vary widely, ranging from seven hundred to five thousand individuals, organized into bands of seven to ten families, comprising thirty-five to fifty people. Egalitarian in social organization with decision making by consensus, each band bestowed leadership positions on those men and women respected for their wisdom and experience. They called themselves Beothuk (red people) in reference to the red ochre paint mixed with fish oil or animal grease that coated their bodies, clothing, canoes, and personal goods. The coating, which served as a symbol of tribal identity and initiation, may be the basis for the later European term "redskins."

The Beothuk learned early on to mistrust European explorers, who captured dozens of their people between 1501 and 1510, transporting them to Europe as slaves. For the next 150 years Europeans fished off the Newfoundland coast, making few permanent settlements, but cutting off the Beothuk from their traditional fishing grounds during the important summer months. The Micmac, once allies but now armed by the British, further reduced the food supply by invading the Beothuk's territory and killing their game for the fur trade.

Unlike other tribes, the Beothuk refused to enter into relations with the Europeans, enforcing a penalty

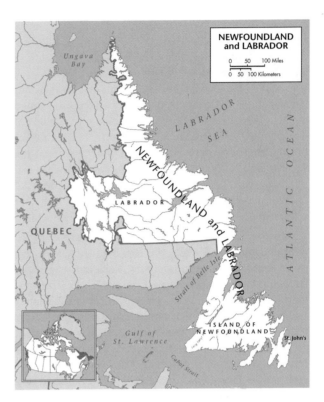

Map of present-day Newfoundland and Labrador, where the Beothuk flourished prior to the arrival of European traders in the seventeenth century. [EASTWARD PUBLICATIONS DEVELOPMENT/ GALE GROUP]

of death on those who did. By the 1720s Beothuk relations with European settlers and the Micmac had deteriorated beyond repair. The Europeans, angered by the Beothuk practice of stealing and scavenging iron implements, which the tribe then refashioned into various tools, responded by frequently killing Beothuk, who in turn exacted their own revenge. By 1768 the Micmac and European settlers had pushed the Beothuk further north, reducing their number to fewer than four hundred people attempting to subsist on the inadequate resources of the Exploits River system. Although some early efforts were made to protect the Beothuk, official intervention on the part of the Canadian government came too late. By 1823 starvation and disease, especially tuberculosis, had left only three female survivors. The last known Beothuk, Shanawdithit, a twenty-six-year-old young woman, died in 1829 from tuberculosis.

SEE ALSO Canada; Indigenous Peoples

BIBLIOGRAPHY

Assiniwi, Bernard (2002). *The Beothuk Saga,* tran. Wayne Grady. New York: Thomas Dunne Books.

Carignan, Paul (1955). "The Beothuks." Available from http://www.wordplay.com/tourism/beothuk.html.

Frederick, William (1977). *Extinction: The Beothuks of Newfoundland.* New York: McGraw-Hill Ryerson.

Marshall, Ingeborg (1989). *Reports and Letters by George Christopher Pulling Relating to the Beothuk Indians of Newfoundland.* St. John's, Newfoundland: Breakwater.

Marshall, Ingeborg (1996). *A History and Ethnography of the Beothuk.* Montreal: McGill-Queen's University Press.

Pastore, Ralph T. (1997). "The Beothuks." Available from http://www.heritage.nf.ca/aboriginal/beothuk.html.

Sharon O'Brien

Biafra/Nigeria

Agitation for secession among the more than 250 ethnic groups in Nigeria started almost immediately after the British-engineered amalgamation of January 1, 1914, which joined the southern and northern protectorates to form what is Nigeria. Vast distances, differences of history and traditions, and ethnological, racial, tribal, political, social, and religious barriers all hampered the creation of a unified state. Nigeria became a federation of three regions based on ethnic groupings upon independence on October 1, 1960, but pressure for secession continued even after that development.

In 1967 Biafra attempted to secede from the Nigerian federation. That effort culminated in a devastating, intense, and prolonged civil war. Scholars differ in their view of its history and consequences, but broad agreement exists on some pertinent issues.

The Nigerian Civil War, spanning a thirty-month period, from May 30, 1967, to January 12, 1970, was precipitated by a combination of factors. Among the many reasons advanced are growing interethnic rivalry and suspicion between the three major ethnic groups (Hausa/Fulani in the north, Yoruba in the west, and Igbo in the south); agitations over alleged domination by one ethnic group to the exclusion of the others; a controversial 1963 federal census; disputed postindependence elections in 1964 and volatile western regional elections in 1965, inevitably resulting in prolonged political crisis, anarchy, and uncertainty. These events triggered the first military coup on January 15, 1966, by predominantly young Igbo army officers led by Major Chukwuma "Kaduna" Nzeogwu, himself an Igbo from the eastern region.

Although prominent northern politicians such as the prime minister, Tafawa Balewa, and the Sarduana of Sokoto, Sir Ahmadu Bello, were killed in the process, there were no casualties in the east, reinforcing the belief in many quarters, especially in the northern region, that the coup was ethnically motivated to achieve domination by the Igbo over other ethnic groups. Nzeogwu's coup failed, but a countercoup, led by another Igbo, Major General Johnson Umunakwe Aguiyi-Ironsi, abolished the federal structure and introduced in its stead a unitary system of government.

Although the new government arrested the suspected plotters of the first coup, they were never tried. Consequently, on July 29, 1966, a "revenge coup" by largely northern officers led to the killing of the Nigerian head of state, Major-General Aguiyi-Ironsi at Ibadan, while he was making an official visit to the western region. During this same period several Igbo officers and civilians were also killed in the north, and their properties looted or destroyed.

By October 1966 over fifty thousand Igbos had lost their lives, several thousands more were maimed, and an estimated two million Igbos fled from other parts of Nigeria back to the east. In response, Lieutenant Colonel Chukumeka Odumegwu Ojukwu, Eastern Military Governor stated, "The brutal and planned annihilation of officers of Eastern Nigeria origin had cast serious doubt as to whether they could ever sincerely live together as members of a nation" (Ojiako, 1979, p. 48).

To reduce the political tensions that had engulfed the country, representatives of all concerned parties attended a summit of military leaders at Aburi, Ghana, beginning January 4, 1967, and agreed to a confederal system of government, but the agreement was never implemented. After several unsuccessful efforts to negotiate peace, Ojukwu unilaterally declared Biafra's independence from Nigeria on May 30, 1967, citing the Nigerian government's inability to protect the lives of easterners and suggesting its culpability in genocide. Biafra derived its name from the Bight of Biafra and comprised the East-Central, South-Eastern, and Rivers states of Nigeria. Biafra's independence was recognized by Gabon, Haiti, Ivory Coast, Tanzania, and Zambia. The federal government of Nigeria responded to Biafra's declaration of independence with its own declaration of war.

The Nigerian Civil War, fought almost entirely in the southeastern portion of that country, resulted in the death of millions of unarmed civilians and massive destruction of property. As the conflict progressed, the living conditions in Biafra deteriorated. The Biafrans, fighting against a numerically and materially superior force, were virtually encircled and isolated. The Biafran armed forces made sporadic strategic incursions into federal territories, but limited means of support frequently forced a retreat. A combination of military operations—by land, air, and sea—and an economic blockade against Biafra and the destruction of its agricultural life by the Nigerian federal government led to the starvation, mass death, and displacement of Igbos.

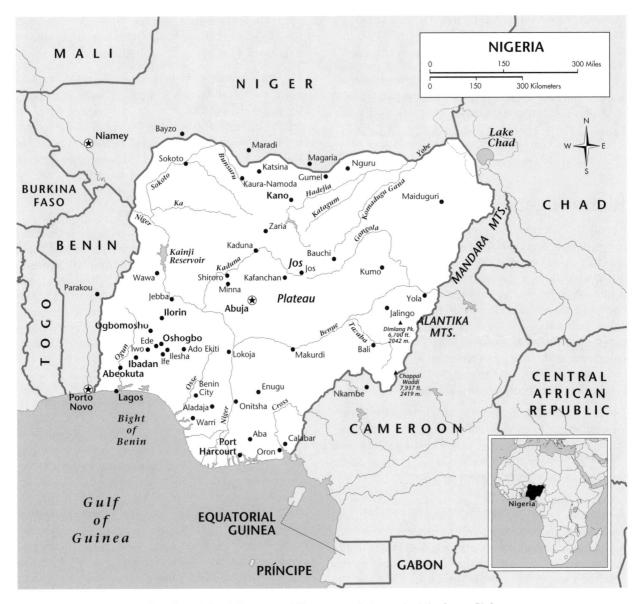

Map of Nigeria, including the East-Central, South-Eastern, and Rivers states that comprised the former Biafra. [MARYLAND CARTOGRAPHICS]

The Nigerian government blockaded the region from the sea, thus preventing the shipment of critical items and services to the east. Furthermore, the government recaptured the Rivers state, cutting off the oil revenue with which Biafra had expected to finance the war; suspended telephone, telegraph, and postal services; and cancelled all air flights to the region, except those cleared by Lagos. The enforcement of a comprehensive blockade led to severe shortages of food, medicine, clothing, and housing, precipitating heavy casualties among Biafran civilians. About three million Biafrans are believed to have lost their lives, an estimated one million of them as a result of severe malnutrition. More than three million Igbos became internally displaced persons or refugees. For a variety of reasons, including the national interests of most of its member states, the international community, except for limited humanitarian relief, left Biafrans to their fate.

Biafra alleged genocide, fueling international sympathy. Although a team of observers found considerable evidence of famine and death as a result of the war, it uncovered no proof of genocide or the systematic destruction of property. Furthermore, although claims of starvation and genocide secured military and political support from some members of the international community and international organizations, they also helped to lengthen the war, thereby furthering the suf-

Two British businessmen held prisoner, along with Biafrans, after being beaten by Nigerian federal troops during the civil war between the central government and the province of Biafra (1967–1970). [HULTON-DEUTSCH COLLECTION/CORBIS]

fering in Biafra. In December 1968 the International Committee of the Red Cross (ICRC) estimated that fourteen thousand people were dying each day in Biafra. Many civilians who had already survived the war reportedly died of starvation because the federal government obstructed direct access to relief agencies and ignored international pressure to allow mass relief operations entry into Biafra, accusing relief agencies of concealing arms shipments with supplies from their humanitarian flights.

It would appear that the implementation of the Geneva Conventions of 1949 and its Protocol II Relating to the Protection of Victims of Non-International Armed Conflicts, to which Nigeria is a party, was the exception rather than the rule. According to Additional Protocol II,

> [All] persons who do not take a direct part or who have ceased to take part in hostilities, whether or not their liberty has been restricted, are entitled to respect for their person, honor and convictions and religious practices. They shall in all circumstances be treated humanely, without any adverse distinction.

The fall of Owerri, one of Biafra's strongholds on January 6, 1970, signaled the collapse of the resistance, leading to the flight of its leader, Ojukwu, to the Ivory Coast. On January 12, 1970, the Biafran chief of army staff, Major General Phillip Effiong, surrendered to the federal government. According to Effiong, "We are firm, we are loyal Nigerian citizens and accept the authority of the Federal Military Government. We accept the existing administrative and political structure of the federation of Nigeria. The Republic of Biafra hereby ceases to exist" (Oko, 1998, p. 336).

The Nigerian head of state, Colonel Yakubu Gowon, accepted Biafra's unconditional surrender, declaring that there would be no victor and no vanquished. Although the civil war resulted in mass death, starvation, displacement, and destruction of property, its principal objective was to bring back the eastern state to the federation, not the destruction of the Igbos. In contrast to the policies of extinction underpinning the Holocaust and Rwandan genocide, those of the Nigerian government did not call for the extermination of the Igbos, but instead sought to address the threat of secession.

Thus, after the war, the government developed a Reconciliation, Reconstruction, and Rehabilitation program to resettle those who had been displaced from their homes and places of permanent residence; rehabilitate both troops and civilians alike; reconstruct damaged infrastructure and public institutions; and correct economic and social problems—poverty, preventable diseases, squalor, and ignorance. Furthermore, the federal government promised to provide food, shelter, and medicines for the affected population; hand over power to a civilian government on October 1, 1975; reorganize the armed forces; complete the establishment of the twelve states announced in 1967; conduct a national census; draft a new constitution; and hold elections. Although some of these commitments were fulfilled—new states were created, a new constitution was implemented, the armed forces were scaled down in size, and power was handed over to a civilian government—Nigeria's subsequent history of corruption and military coups has left many of its promises unfulfilled.

SEE ALSO Ethnic Groups; Geneva Conventions on the Protection of Victims of War; Minorities; Nationalism

BIBLIOGRAPHY

Adewale, Ademoyega (1981). *Why We Struck*. Ibadan, Nigeria: Evans Brothers Publishers.

Akinnola, Richard (2000). *History of Coup d'Etat in Nigeria*. Lagos: Rich Konsult.

Alexander, Madiebo (1980). *The Nigerian Revolution and the Biafran War*. Enugu, Nigeria: Fourth Dimensions Publishers.

De St. Jorre, John (1972). *The Nigerian Civil War*. London: Hodder & Stoughton.

Dudley, Billy (1973). *Instability and Political Order: Politics and Crisis in Nigeria*. Ibadan, Nigeria: Ibadan University Press.

Ijalaye, David (1971). "Was Biafra at Any Time a State in International Law?" *American Journal of International Law* 65:551.

Nayar, Kaladharan (1975). "Self-Determination Beyond the Colonial Context: Biafra in Retrospect." *International Law Journal* 10:321, 324.

Njoku, H. M. (1987). *A Tragedy Without Heroes: The Nigerian-Biafran War*. Enugu, Nigeria: Fourth Dimensions Publishers.

Nwankwo, Arthur Agwunch, et al. (1970). *Biafra: The Making of a Nation*. New York: Praeger Publishers.

Obasanjo, Olusegun (1980). *My Command: An Account of the Nigerian Civil War 1967–70*. London: Heinemann Publications.

Ojikao, James O. (1979). *13 Years of Military Rule*. Lagos: Daily Times of Nigeria.

Oko, Okechukwu (1998). "Partition or Perish: Restoring Social Equilibrium in Niagara through Reconstruction." *Indiana International and Comparative Law Review* 8:336.

Okpaku, Joseph, ed. (1972). *Nigeria: Dilemma of Nationhood*. New York: The Third Press.

Tamuno, Tekena (1970). "Separatist Agitations in Nigeria since 1914." *Journal of Modern Affairs Studies* 8:563, 565.

Kolawole Olaniyan

Biographies

Of all the individuals who have either participated in or been the victims of genocide, the majority of those who are the subject of biography have come from three relatively small and discrete groups: the perpetrators in the highest echelons of political and/or military power; victims (mostly survivors) who have distinguished themselves through their literary works; and the liberators, those who risked their lives to save or aid victims. Unsurprisingly, biographies emanating from each of these groups have been significantly different in tone as well as purpose.

The biographies of perpetrators have drawn the most attention from both scholars and the reading public. These works not only chart the rise to power and prominence of their relatively well-known subjects, they also invariably seek to explain the environmental, psychological, political, and ideological forces that motivated these infamous individuals to plan and organize mass killings. Although no biography of Adolf Hitler has achieved undisputed canonical status, several have provided satisfying and convincing portraits. Allan Bullock's *Hitler: A Study in Tyranny* (1962) still remains the most penetrating biography, although Joachim Fest's *Hitler* (the English translation was published in 1975) does an excellent job of exploring the German fascist dictator's early ideological development. A superb overview and analysis of the existing literature on Hitler may be found in John Lukacs's *The Hitler of History* (1998).

Although source material is less complete (and less available) for the communist mass murderers of the twentieth century, several fine biographies of Joseph Stalin do exist, including Dmitrii Volkogonov's *Stalin: Triumph and Tragedy* (1991) and Robert Conquest's *Stalin: Breaker of Nations* (1991). For Mao Zedong, Ross Terrill's *A Biography of Mao* (1999) and Stuart Schram's *Mao Tse-Tung* (1974) are excellent. As of 2004 several biographies of the enigmatic Khmer Rouge leader Pol Pot have been written—although the amount and overall quality of scholarship on Cambodian genocide remain inadequate.

Biographies of victims have primarily (although not exclusively) focused on writers who were also survivors, such as Primo Levi, Elie Wiesel, Nelly Sachs, and Paul Celan. These works provide insight into how these survivors' experiences affected their lives post-trauma as well as informed their writing. The finest examples examine the capacity of history and literature to convey both the horror of mass murder and the evil underlying it. In many cases biographies have furnished valuable added insight into the lives of acclaimed memoirists and diarists such as Anne Frank and Hannah Senesh. Two notable works that defy categorization are *Maus* (1986) and *Maus II* (1991), Art Spiegelman's comic book portrayals of his parents' experiences in pre-war Poland, Auschwitz, and post-war America. Blending biography and autobiography with self-conscious explorations of aesthetic representation, Spiegelman has created an original and individualized approach to Holocaust narration. In the realm of visual media many fine bio-documentaries have been made about individuals from all three groups. One example—*Chaim Rumkowski and the Lodz Ghetto* (1991)—paints a dramatic and unflinching portrait of the Jewish leader and Holocaust victim.

Biographies of liberators (or righteous Gentiles in the case of the Holocaust) have focused primarily on the reasons such individuals risked their lives to save others. As such, they tend to emphasize the heroic as well as the personal. Two prominent subjects include Raoul Wallenberg, the Swedish businessman and diplomat who saved tens of thousands of Jewish lives in wartime Budapest, and Oskar Schindler, the German businessman turned protector of Polish Jews. Both men have also been the subjects of widely acclaimed feature films—*Good Evening, Mr. Wallenberg* (1990) and *Schindler's List* (1993).

The biographies of perpetrators and victims (as well as liberators) of genocide have explored issues of wide scholarly and public interest. Combining the historical and the private, such biographies have provided valuable perspective on the incalculable human toll of mass murder in the twentieth century.

SEE ALSO Diaries; Memoirs of Perpetrators; Memoirs of Survivors

BIBLIOGRAPHY

Gilbert, Martin (2003). *The Righteous: The Unsung Heroes of the Holocaust.* New York: Henry Holt.

Lukacs, John (1997). *The Hitler of History.* New York: A. A. Knopf.

Mark C. Molesky

Bosnia and Herzegovina

At the beginning of April 1992, Serb forces swept through much of Bosnia and Herzegovina, systematically brutalizing and expelling non-Serbs and, in particular, Bosnian Muslims, in a campaign of terror. In the process, the term *etničko čiščenje* (ethnic cleansing) passed from Serbo-Croat into English to encapsulate the brutality of a conflict in which the principal aim was to erase all traces of a culture. Meanwhile, the name Bosnia and Herzegovina became synonymous with killing, cruelty, and human suffering on an almost unprecedented scale.

In response to the atrocities committed in Bosnia and Herzegovina, and to assist post-war reconciliation, the International Criminal Tribunal for the Former Yugoslavia (ICTY) was set up in The Hague to try perpetrators of war crimes, including genocide. The war itself lasted three years and nine months and only ended after NATO intervention, first with an air campaign in August and September 1995, and then with the deployment of a peacekeeping force in December of that year, following agreement on a peace plan negotiated in Dayton, Ohio.

The Bosnian question boils down to two issues: how 2.2 million Muslim Slavs could live amid 4.5 million Christian Croats and 8.5 million Christian Serbs in the wider region of the former Yugoslavia; and how 750,000 Christian Croats and 1.3 million Christian Serbs could live together with 1.9 million Bosnian Muslims within Bosnia and Herzegovina itself. Depending on where borders are drawn and whether they are respected, Muslims either form a minority squeezed between two more powerful ethnic groups, or they comprise a relative majority in a territory shared with two large minority communities, both of which generally consider the neighboring states of Croatia, Serbia, and Montenegro to be their mother countries.

Of Bosnia and Herzegovina's 109 pre-war municipalities, 37 had an absolute Muslim majority, 32 an absolute Serb majority, and 13 an absolute Croat majority. A further 15 municipalities had a simple Muslim majority, 5 had a simple Serb majority, and 13 had a simple Croat majority. With the exception of Croat-populated Western Herzegovina, an absolute majority rarely accounted for more than 70 percent of the population and, as often as not, neighboring municipalities had majorities of one of the republic's other peoples. Therefore, Bosnia and Herzegovina could not fragment neatly along ethnic lines, because there were no ethnic lines to fragment along. Dividing Bosnia and Herzegovina into ethnic territories would inevitably be messy and would require massive population transfers.

In the early 1990s, the fundamental cause of conflict in the former Yugoslavia was not simply the drive by the country's Serbs to forge their own national state at the expense of their neighbors. Structurally speak-

During the siege of Sarajevo (at the start of the Bosnian War), all roads leading in and out of the city were blockaded. Approximately 400,000 residents became trapped during the siege, cut off from food, water, medicine, and electricity. Here, a young woman transports water in a wheel barrow and a boy plays atop a burned-out car. [TEUN VOETEN]

ing, this was only a manifestation of a much deeper-rooted problem. As communism disintegrated, the gel that had held Yugoslavia together since World War II disappeared, and the country was institutionally ill equipped to deal with the transition to democracy. Nearly half a century of communism had failed to resolve the national question. Indeed, communist rule may even have exacerbated the potential for conflict within Yugoslavia because it had stifled open dialogue on ethnic issues. Moreover, the planned economy had failed to sustain prosperity and had been disintegrating throughout the 1980s.

Although Bosnians had lived together in apparent harmony before the war, ethnic identities formed over centuries of Ottoman rule—when each religious community was governed separately under its own spiritual rulers—remained strong. As a result, when elections took place in November 1990, the vote was divided along ethnic lines. Although the ethnically based parties ostensibly formed a coalition and governed together, they rapidly fell out with one another, and politics descended into a "zero-sum" game.

Western media generally portrayed the Bosnian War as a conflict between nationalists—in particular Serbs, but also Croats—seeking to destroy the multi-ethnic Bosnian state and the predominantly Muslim Sarajevo government, which formally espoused multi-ethnicity. This reflected the brutality of the siege of Sarajevo, witnessed by journalists, and the massive ethnic-cleansing campaign of the first months of fighting. However, most media failed to cover the disintegration of the former Yugoslavia, which was probably unstoppable in the absence of the preventive deployment of international forces. In the early 1990s, the key international institutions and the world's most powerful countries possessed neither the capabilities nor the mindset for such intervention, with the result that international diplomacy also contributed to the impending catastrophe.

In the 1990 elections, many Bosnians, especially those of mixed ethnic origins or from the cities, did vote for nonethnic parties, choosing instead one of two former communist options. These people were genuinely committed to a multinational state, but they rep-

encyclopedia of GENOCIDE *and* CRIMES AGAINST HUMANITY

resented an increasingly marginalized group and had no influence on the events leading to their country's disintegration. In many ways, Bosnia and Herzegovina was in an impossible and untenable position as soon as the rest of Yugoslavia broke apart. All three ethnically based parties behaved as if they believed that they were locked in a struggle for survival. The moderation of the Bosnian Muslim leadership and the extremism of their Serb counterparts reflected, in part, the reality of the situation that the rival leaders faced.

The debate over the future of the Yugoslav federation was effectively a question of life and death for Bosnia and Herzegovina. For this reason, the Bosnian Muslim leader, Alija Izetbegović, who was also Bosnia and Herzegovina's president, joined his Macedonian counterpart, Kiro Gligorov, in a failed eleventh hour initiative to save a "Yugoslav state community" in June 1991. Although Izetbegović supported the continued existence of some form of Yugoslavia, he was not prepared to see Bosnia and Herzegovina remain in a Serb-dominated country in the event of Slovene and Croatian secession. He opted instead for independence. In preparation, he and his party, the SDA, attempted to push a declaration of sovereignty through the Bosnian parliament in the first half of 1991. As war loomed and it became clear that Bosnia and Herzegovina's Serbs were well armed and willing to use force, Izetbegović saw the best way to advance his aims was by internationalizing the Bosnian question.

The Bosnian Serb leadership, under Radovan Karadzic, had made elaborate advance preparations for the disintegration of Bosnia and Herzegovina. A month before the 1990 elections, they formed a Serb National Council within Bosnia and Herzegovina, and by September 1991 they had set up four so-called Serb Autonomous Authorities, which were effectively self-governing Serb entities. In October 1991 a new, self-appointed Assembly of the Serb Nation of Bosnia and Herzegovina declared that the Bosnian Serbs would remain with other Serbs as part of Yugoslavia, and staged a referendum among Serbs to endorse this decision, which provided near unanimous support. On December 21, 1991, the Assembly proclaimed the creation of the Serb Republic of Bosnia and Herzegovina, and on January 9, 1992, they declared independence. Many Bosnian Serbs had been mobilized by the Yugoslav Peoples Army (YPA) to fight in Croatia and still retained their weapons. The YPA in Bosnia and Herzegovina effectively turned itself into a Bosnian Serb Army by deploying Bosnian Serbs in their home republic in place of Serbs from elsewhere. The Bosnian Serb leadership was in a position to fight to achieve its aims.

Bosnian Croats formed two of their own Autonomous Authorities in November 1991 and were equally adamant that they should not end up in a rump, Serb-dominated state. The community and its leadership were, however, internally divided. A moderate faction represented the two-thirds of Bosnian Croats who lived as a minority among Serbs and Muslims in Bosnia. An extreme faction represented the third who lived in western Herzegovina and formed a large majority of the population there. The Bosnian Croat faction was politically dominant until February 1992, and, like the Muslim leadership, generally pursued a cautious line because of the vulnerability of most Croats in the event of hostilities. That month, however, the moderate Croat leader, Stjepan Kljujic, was ousted at the wishes of Croatian president Franjo Tudjman and replaced by Mate Boban, a Herzegovinian radical. Many Herzegovinian Croats fought in Croatia during the Croatian War and had returned home armed and willing to continue the struggle.

In the course of the Croatian War, which ended after the Sarajevo Accord of January 1992, Bosnia and Herzegovina's communities effectively split into three hostile, armed camps, with the bulk of the weapons in Bosnian Serb hands. A United Nations (UN) arms embargo against the whole of the former Yugoslavia was imposed in September 1991, ensuring that the imbalance in weaponry became a permanent feature of the conflict. The best internal hope for avoiding conflict would probably have been agreement among the nationalist parties to create government mechanisms that would protect the interests of each ethnic community. A constitutional commission was formed early in 1991, but the parties failed to agree on whether the Bosnian state should be a republic of citizens or nations, let alone the manner in which power should be exercised by the central and provincial governments. A Council on National Equality, intended to ensure that no legislation undermined any of Bosnia and Herzegovina's nations, failed to come into operation, and each nationalist party sought to achieve its own aims, largely irrespective of the potential impact on the other two peoples.

The best external hope for avoiding conflict in Bosnia and Herzegovina was the European Community's Conference on Yugoslavia, headed by former North Atlantic Treaty Organisation (NATO) secretary-general Lord Peter Carrington. Although it sought an overarching solution to all conflicts then undermining the country, it failed to halt escalating fighting in Croatia and was unable to influence Serbian president Slobodan Milosevic. An arbitration commission set up within the Conference under the French jurist Robert Badinter determined in late November 1991 that Yugoslavia was in the process of dissolution. Against Carrington's (and for that matter Izetbegović's) wishes, Germany recognized Croatian independence on December 23, 1991, followed by the rest of the European Community on January 15, 1992. The Badinter Commission suggested the holding of a referendum to determine the popular will about independence for Bosnia and Herzegovina.

Although referenda are arguably the worst possible tool for resolving identity-related questions, both the European Community (EC) and the United States gave their support to the Bosnian vote. In his desperation to prevent Bosnia and Herzegovina ending up in a rump Yugoslavia, Izetbegović decided that the referendum should go ahead "even if the devil is knocking at our door." As expected, Serbs boycotted the vote and Muslims voted for independence. The swing vote was that of the Croats, most of whom would probably have preferred something other than Bosnian independence, but sided with the Muslims to avoid the risk of coming under Serb domination. Close to 63 percent of voters supported independence. On March 3, 1992, Izetbegović declared independence. The move was ratified by the parliament a day later, in the absence of the Serb deputies.

The international community refused to recognize Bosnia and Herzegovina, but a war did not break out after the referendum. War erupted only when irregulars from Serbia proper under General Zeljko Raznjatovic Arkan entered northeastern Bosnia and Herzegovina in Bijeljina on April 2, 1992, and carried out a premeditated massacre of Muslims. This triggered large-scale ethnic cleansing of both Muslims and Croats in areas earmarked for a Greater Serbia. The campaign entailed, above all, the systematic expulsion of non-Serbs and included large-scale rape, the creation of internment camps, and other well-publicized atrocities. Summary executions took place, but were not the rule. Selected killings, usually of leading Muslims and Croats, were designed to frighten their victims' ethnic kin into leaving of their own accord. The exercise was also a lucrative enterprise for the ethnic cleansers, who appropriated any valuables left behind. The EC and the United States recognized Bosnia and Herzegovina on April 6, 1992, hoping to dampen the flames of conflict, but achieving the opposite.

With the outbreak of war, international efforts to end the conflict intensified in the framework of the International Conference on the Former Yugoslavia, which was headed by both an EC and a UN representative. UN peacekeepers were deployed, but only to provide humanitarian aid. International efforts amounted to little more than persuading the Bosnian Serbs to make some territorial concessions and forcing the Bosnian Muslims to accept the resulting deal. It was almost a recipe for failure.

The Vance-Owen peace plan (named after its principal authors: former UK Foreign Secretary David Owen and former U.S. Secretary of State Cyrus Vance) attempted to devise a reasonably equitable solution after more than a year of fighting. It failed to win sufficient international backing, however, and was rejected by the belligerents. This contributed to the outbreak of a second war in Bosnia and Herzegovina, this time between Croats and Muslims. The Croat-Muslim alliance had always been one of convenience, and was exhibiting strains even during the initial Serb offensive in which Croats and Muslims fought on the same side. It broke down completely when Croats began unilaterally to implement elements of the Vance-Owen plan that effectively gave them control over contested territory in Herzegovina.

In 1995 the U.S. Congress pushed a policy of "Lift and Strike." It wished to lift the arms embargo against the region while striking the Bosnian Serbs from the air. To achieve this, an extraction force would have to be deployed to assist the withdrawal of the UN peacekeepers on the ground. Three events prevented the policy from being implemented: Croatian offensives of May and August 1995 changing the geographic balance on the ground, the taking of UN hostages by Bosnian Serbs in May 1995, and the Srebrenica massacre of July 1995. Some 8,000 Bosnian Muslim men and boys were summarily executed in the single greatest atrocity of the wars of Yugoslavia's dissolution. The massacre led to the first genocide ruling at the International Criminal Tribunal of the Former Yugoslavia (ICTY). In response to these three events, NATO launched the first air campaign of its history on August 31, 1995. The campaign lasted two weeks and succeeded in shattering Bosnian Serb communications, helped the Croats and Muslims reverse some of the Serb gains from the beginning of the war and, most importantly, paved the way for the peace negotiations in Dayton, Ohio, that eventually brought the Bosnian War to an end.

The Dayton Agreement came into force on December 20, 1995. It defined Bosnia and Herzegovina as a single state with three main constituent peoples—Croats, Muslims, and Serbs—but divided into two entities. One was the Federation of Bosnia and Herzegovina, comprising 51 percent of the territory; the other was the Republika Srpska, with 49 percent. Both entities have their own armed forces (the Federation army is effectively divided into Croat and Muslim forces), whose strength is regulated and related to that of the neighboring states. The country that emerged out of Dayton nevertheless inherited the political independence, territorial integrity, and sovereignty of the previous state, the republic of Bosnia and Herzegovina.

The Dayton Agreement contains eleven annexes. Only the first concerns the cease-fire and military matters; the remaining ten cover civilian aspects of the peace plan, including the right of displaced Bosnians to return to their homes or to be compensated for the loss of their property. The condition of the country has depended as much on the manner in which the civilian side of the peace plan has been implemented, as on the political structures contained within it.

Bosnia and Herzegovina's central institutions are weak and government is handled by complex, power-sharing mechanisms. This means that the system requires broad agreement and consensus to function. However, given enduring animosities and a lack of trust, such consensus has not existed. The Dayton Agreement, therefore, includes provision for international involvement in all aspects of the peace process, with overall coordination entrusted to a so-called High Representative, under the authority of the UN Security Council.

The scale of the international presence, although critical to the peace process, has in some ways been counterproductive for Bosnia and Herzegovina. Domestic institutions and politicians have given up much of the responsibility for governing their own country. Nonetheless, the massive international stake has led key players to declare the peace process a success, irrespective of how it is actually evolving, since failure would reflect badly on those states people, organizations, and countries responsible for the agreement. Unsurprisingly, the peace remains fragile. After all, the settlement was agreed to by the very individuals who were responsible for the war: Izetbegović, Milosevic, and Tudjman.

SEE ALSO Crimes Against Humanity; Ethnic Groups; Genocide; International Criminal Tribunal for the Former Yugoslavia; Izetbegović, Alija; Milosevic, Slobodan; Rape; Srebrenica; Tudjman, Franjo; Yugoslavia

BIBLIOGRAPHY

Burg, Steven L., and Paul S. Shoup (1999). *The War in Bosnia and Herzegovina: Ethnic Conflict and International Intervention.* New York: M. E. Sharpe.

Donia, Robert J., and John V. A. Fine (1994). *Bosnia-Hercegovina: A Tradition Betrayed.* London: Hurst.

Malcolm, Noel (1994). *Bosnia: A Short History.* London: Macmillan.

Christopher Michael Bennett

Burma/Myanmar

In the last half-century the peoples of Burma have experienced six different political transformations.

Constitutional Democracy, 1948 to 1958

In 1947 a partially elected constituent assembly wrote a new constitution, a mixture of liberal democratic and socialist principles; organized the nation into a federation of unequal states, two with the right of secession; created a parliamentary system and an independent judiciary; and guaranteed rights, freedom, and equality to all. During its deliberations the nation's leader, Aung San, was assassinated; his successor, U Nu, finished the constitution. Although flawed, incomplete, and hastily written against a backdrop of political unrest and incipient revolution, the basic document was approved unanimously and Burma became independent on January 4, 1948.

With independence came internal war and invasion. The Burma Communist Party (BCP) revolted in March 1948, as did the Karen National Defense Organization at year's end. In 1949 Nationalist Chinese soldiers fled China, took refuge in Burma, refused to disarm, and joined the local wars. By 1950 the Burmese army gradually began to recover political control and, with international help, removed nearly half the Chinese.

Throughout the worst days of war the government upheld the constitution, parliament met without interruption, courts functioned, people and press were free, schools remained open, and the economy grew. Two national elections were held in the 1950s; the independence party, the Anti-Fascist Peoples' Freedom League (AFPFL), won both while a parliamentary opposition gradually emerged.

Caretaker Government, 1958 to 1960

In 1958 the AFPFL split. Unable to govern, Nu urged parliament to utilize a constitutional provision and elect a nonmember, General Ne Win, his successor. Ne Win formed a Caretaker Government (CG) of military and nonparty members. The general governed Burma's heartland strictly and harshly, but within the letter of the law. In the Shan state, martial law was declared in combating indigenous and Chinese forces; the army used violence against accused civilians, made arbitrary personnel and institutional changes in the government, and was not held accountable. Ne Win, with parliamentary approval, pressed the Shan and Karenni states' rulers to surrender hereditary power and forced state governments to agree to replace civilian administrations in contested and border areas with new military-controlled administrations. The CG ended in April

1960, following a national election in which the public voted overwhelmingly against the party pledged to continue Ne Win's policies and returned Nu to power.

Second Constitutional Democracy, 1960 to 1962

Nu's government restored the letter and spirit of the constitution, strengthened democracy and human rights, and sought to end internal wars through negotiations. However, divisions among his fellow leaders emerged and threatened to split the party. Angry because Nu had reversed many CG decisions and appeared to support Shan and Karenni secession, Ne Win and a cabal of officers overthrew the government, set the constitution aside, dismissed parliament, and arrested members of the government and ethnic leaders.

Military Dictatorship, 1962 to 1974

On March 2, 1962, Ne Win and sixteen military officers formed a Revolutionary Council (RC) that ruled by decree and proclamation. It replaced the federal structure with a unitary hierarchy, the military-led Security and Administration Councils; abolished the two highest courts; established a Chief Court of Burma; and unified the administration of justice. Judges upheld the new "laws," the military and police acted with little restraint in arresting scores without warrants, the courts conducted judicial procedures in secret and extended sentences without notice, and prisoners were beaten, brutalized, and killed while in custody. To maintain its hold on the public and control the dissemination of information, the RC replaced the free press with a single government publication, created huge mass and class organizations, and formed a single political party, the Burma Socialist Program Party (BSPP). In essence, a police state was created—one that involved regular surveillance and required all of its citizens to inform the authorities of their own and their neighbors' movements, the presence of houseguests, and any contacts with outsiders. By 1970 the government had closed Burma to tourists and journalists and severely curtailed its citizens' right to travel.

Religions continued, but under strict state control. Western-based religions had to sever all foreign connections, whereas Buddhist orders were required to register with the government, with monks forced to carry identity cards.

In 1963 the RC began transforming Burma into a socialist state. Without preparation and placing untrained and inexperienced military officers in charge, it seized private property and nationalized most of the urban economy. Trade and distribution quickly broke down, leading to shortages, hoarding, inflation, corruption, and black markets. Although the government used force to root out illegal markets, it eventually gave up in this regard as it was incapable of providing needed goods and services.

By holding talks with insurgent groups in 1963 and offering a national amnesty in 1981, the RC tried, but failed, to solve peacefully the problems of national unity.

Constitutional Dictatorship, 1974 to 1988

In 1971 the RC ordered the BSPP to write a new constitution. It was approved by 90 percent of the country's voters. On January 3, 1974, the constitution came into effect and the nation was renamed the Socialist Republic of the Union of Burma. The new law created a unitary state with fourteen political divisions, a one-house legislature, and one recognized party. Two leadership bodies were formed, and judicial power rested with two councils. Three levels of government existed beneath the national level, and all four were governed under the principle of democratic centralism.

Rights were paired with duties and made conditional upon the completion of state goals. None were absolute. All citizens had to work toward the fulfillment of socialist objectives and surrender any right that interfered with them. Dissent was outlawed, and the military had no right to seize power and rule by decree.

Between 1974 and 1988 periods of serious social unrest developed, led by unemployed workers over rising prices and by students and monks over the internment of U Thant, former Secretary-General of the United Nations (UN). A coup by middle-grade officers to restore civilian rule and the 1947 constitution failed. In the early 1980s an improving economy proved short-lived. In 1987 new economic problems and social unrest contributed to Ne Win's acknowledgment of past mistakes, with his call for policy changes and his own resignation. The removal of currency from circulation without the substitution of a new form of currency provoked student demonstrations and national discontent.

On March 12, 1988, a riot between students and townspeople in a tea shop near the Rangoon Institute of Technology caused the death of one student and led to student clashes with the police that continued until September. The public largely supported the students, and some military units even marched with the demonstrators. On August 8, believing that the date, 8-8-88, had spiritual significance and would lead to the end of military rule, thousands of students and ordinary citizens gathered in Rangoon. Near midnight the military attacked, shooting anyone still on the streets. The crowds dispersed; no one, in fact, knows how many were killed, as the army seized and disposed of the bodies.

On September 18, 1988, the military struck again. General Saw Maung and senior officers seized all power, set the 1974 constitution aside, and established a new military dictatorship, the State Law and Order Restoration Council (SLORC)—later renamed the State Peace and Development Council (SPDC). Marching through the streets with rifles leveled, the soldiers fired at anyone in sight and the carnage lasted for three days. Again, the number murdered is unknown as the soldiers seized the bodies. Thousands were arrested and even more fled the country, seeking refuge in neighboring states.

Second Military Dictatorship since 1988

Since the SLORC was established, it has ruled with an iron hand. Arrest, imprisonment, execution, and long prison terms have intimidated and subjugated all peoples in Burma's heartland. Governing under martial law, the army expanded to over 400,000; it built hundreds of jails and filled them with political prisoners and ordinary criminals. It has remained in continuous conflict with the nation's minorities in its efforts to force an end to their actions against the state.

SLORC issued a new election law; 233 parties were formed, but only a few had national or regional support. Aung San Suu Kyi, daughter of Burma's first democratic leader, Aung San, helped form the National League for Democracy (NLD) and was named Secretary-General. Her party was committed to restoring democracy and freedom. In the May 27, 1990, national election the NLD won 60 percent of the vote and 392 of the 485 seats contested. It expected to form a new parliament and government, but on July 27 SLORC refused to step down, instead declaring (in Announcement 1/90) its intention to continue ruling under martial law, not bound by any constitution.

In 1992 General Than Shwe replaced Saw Maung as dictator. He announced that a National Convention (NC) of 702 delegates would be formed to write a new constitution. The NC was convened in January 1993 and met irregularly. In 1995 the NLD was expelled for its absence following criticism of Convention procedures and rules. Before the NC was suspended in 1996, it adopted 104 principles as the basis of a new constitution. Key provisions required that the military would hold one-fourth of parliamentary seats, the president must have long military experience, and in times of emergency, the Minister of Defense would take power.

In 1989 the BCP cadres revolted and created several nationalist ethnic organizations. The government quickly offered to end its war against them—allowing them to keep their weapons, control their areas, and continue their business activities without interfer-

An elderly Burmese woman tosses bricks at a construction site in Rangoon, Burma. Human-rights groups and several Western governments have condemned Burma's labor practices. [AP/WIDE WORLD PHOTOS]

ence—if they halted their activities against the state and broke all contact with other ethnic groups at war with the government. Offering the same terms to others, seventeen groups accepted. As of 2004 the last two large groups, the Karens and the Karenni, are discussing an end to their conflicts with the government.

Human Rights

During the last half-century of internal wars, military governments, a rapacious army, and predatory insurgent groups have plundered the Burmese peoples. The UN, International Labor Organization (ILO), Human Rights Watch, and other international bodies have reported the abuses and violations of human rights suffered. The UN General Assembly has passed several resolutions condemning the behavior of military governments, and several individual nations have adopted measures to pressure dictators to change, but the rulers of Burma have ignored all such directives.

Forced labor, bordering on slavery, is used by the military in battle zones and the hinterland. When confronted by international organizations, military rulers deny human rights violations, or claim that they have stopped. Women are victimized in the frontier areas through seizure, abuse, and sexual violation by soldiers. Civilians, too, prey on rural women, promising good jobs but instead passing them on to brothels. Peasants are forced to grow crops and give food to the army, and if they refuse or fail in their efforts, their crops and animals are seized, their houses are burned, and they are forced to serve the soldiers.

Citizens accused of political crimes are arrested without warrants, tried in courts without legal representation where decisions are predetermined, given long sentences, and incarcerated far from their families. Without new trials sentences often are extended and prisoners are held for indeterminate periods of time. Inside prison they are ill treated, badly housed, poorly fed, and denied adequate health care. Despite international protests against these violations and others, the government responds in two ways: It will not tolerate interference in its internal affairs and it is studying the problem. In May 2003 the UN Special Rapporteur on Human Rights reported there were thirteen hundred political prisoners in Burma's jails.

In fighting internal wars, the military uses a "Four Cuts" policy. It seeks to isolate its enemies from supporters by cutting off food, funds, intelligence, and recruiting. Women, children, and the elderly who help insurgents or hide in contested areas are beaten, imprisoned, raped, and murdered. In urban areas civilians are seized on city streets and forced to work as porters and lead soldiers through mine fields. There are no avenues of appeal against such demands.

Captured noncombatants in contested areas such as the Chittagong Hill Tracts are driven from their homes and made dependent on the army for food and shelter. Those who can escape to neighboring states face inhospitable governments; they are rounded up and are either placed in camps without adequate food, shelter, and medical support or forced to return to their own country and face certain imprisonment or death.

Isolated and alone, without real internal or external help, and with the international community divided on how to deal with Burma, no real change is on the horizon.

Daw Aung San Suu Kyi and the Depayin Massacre
Suu Kyi remains the leader of peaceful resistance to military rule. Born in Burma, schooled in Burma and India, graduated from Oxford, and the widow of an Oxford University distinguished professor, she returned to Burma in 1988 to care for her ailing mother.

On August 26, following an address at Shwedagon Pagoda, Suu Kyi emerged as the leader of the democratic movement. Although she was her party's leader, SLORC prohibited her from contesting a seat in the 1990 election. Despite government harassment and threats, she addressed ever-growing crowds, criticized military rule, and called for political change. On July 20, 1990, the army arrested and placed Suu Kyi under house arrest; without being charged or tried, she remained a prisoner until 1995. In 1991, while imprisoned, she won the Nobel Peace Prize.

Upon her release Suu Kyi's freedom was limited. When, in 1996, she withdrew her party from the NC because of its lack of democracy and freedom of speech, she came under constant verbal and occasional physical attacks. As she worked to strengthen the NLD, harassment continued. In 2000 she was once more placed under house arrest; following her release in 2002, she resumed her political work, traveling, and public speaking. She drew ever-larger crowds.

On the night of May 30, 2003, while Suu Kyi and NLD party members were driving home from the state of Kachin, they were intercepted, with their passage blocked at Depayin, and attacked by truckloads of government-sponsored Union Solidarity and Development Association (USDA) members and hired thugs. Suu Kyi was assaulted and injured, her automobile was damaged. Her driver managed to steer their vehicle away from the confrontation but was stopped by the military, and the NLD leader was placed in "protective custody." Officially, the government said that four were killed and 50 injured; the NLD claimed the totals were 70 and 200, respectively. After two months of detention and no communication with the outside world, Suu Kyi was returned home and, again, she remains under house arrest in 2004.

The Depayin massacre signaled a nationwide attack on the NLD; party offices were closed and leaders arrested. Despite international demands no official inquiry into or full explanation of the affair was made. Meanwhile, government leaders sought to divert world attention by naming the head of intelligence, General Khin Nyunt, as prime minister. He quickly introduced a seven-step road map to democracy and initiated the process by declaring that the NC would reconvene and continue its work writing a new constitution. Although some nations applaud this action, most do not as they have no faith that the military will surrender power freely.

SEE ALSO Chittagong Hill Tract, Peoples of the; United Nations Commission on Human Rights

BIBLIOGRAPHY

Fink, Christina (2001). *Living Silence: Burma under Military Rule.* London: Zed Books.

Kyi, Aung San Suu (1995). *Freedom from Fear and Other Writings,* revised edition. London: Penguin Books.

Kyi, Aung San Suu (1997). *The Voice of Hope.* London: Penguin Books.

Lehman, F. K., ed. (1981). *Military Rule in Burma since 1962.* Singapore: Maruzen Asia.

Maung, Mya (1992). *Totalitarianism in Burma: Prospects for Economic Development.* New York: Paragon House.

Silverstein, Josef (1977). *Burma: Military Rule and the Politics of Stagnation.* Ithaca, N.Y.: Cornell University Press.

Silverstein, Josef (1980). *Burmese Politics: The Dilemma of National Unity.* New Brunswick, N.J.: Rutgers University Press.

Silverstein, Josef (1997). "Fifty Years of Failure in Burma." In *Government Policies and Ethnic Relations in Asia and the Pacific,* ed. Michael E. Brown and Sumit Ganguly. Cambridge, Mass.: MIT Press.

Smith, Martin (1999). *Burma: Insurgency and the Politics of Ethnicity,* revised and updated. London: Zed Books.

Steinberg, David I. (2001). *Burma: The State of Myanmar.* Washington, D.C.: Georgetown University Press.

Josef Silverstein

Burundi

Burundi has the sad distinction of having experienced the first genocide recorded in the Great Lakes region of Central Africa. In the summer and spring of 1972 between 100,000 and 200,000 people were taken to their graves in the wake of a Hutu-led insurrection. Though largely overshadowed in public attention by the far more devastating bloodbath in Rwanda—a total genocide—the ghastly carnage in Burundi undoubtedly qualifies as genocide, or at least a selective genocide. The key difference is that in Burundi the Hutu, not the Tutsi, were targeted for extermination. In both cases, however, the killings were intentional and deliberately targeted a specific ethnic community.

The past and present histories of Burundi and Rwanda are inseparable from each other. Both were archaic kingdoms and shared roughly the same ethnic map, consisting of Hutu agriculturalists (85% of the total population), Tutsi pastoralists representing the ruling minority, and a numerically and socially marginal group of pygmoid people known as the Twa. Both were first colonized by Germany and incorporated into German East Africa. After World War I they were entrusted to Belgium as mandated territories and became United Nations trust territories after World War II. Both gained independence in 1962, but in contrast to Rwanda, where a Hutu revolution between 1959 and 1961 overthrew the monarchy and shifted power into Hutu hands, Burundi acceded to self-government as a constitutional monarchy ruled by a mixed assemblage of Hutu and Tutsi. On the eve of the 1972 genocide power was largely the monopoly of Tutsi elites.

Burundi and Rwanda's divergent trajectories are traceable in part to differences in their traditional political organization. Burundi differed from Rwanda in the greater complexity of its social hierarchies. Unlike Rwanda, where power was highly centralized in the hands of a small fraction of the Tutsi minority, in Burundi the real holders of power were a distinct social category, neither Hutu nor Tutsi, but a princely aristocracy known as *ganwa,* with the king reduced to *a primus inter partes* (first among equals). The Tutsi were divided into two groups: the lowly Tutsi-Hima and the more status-conscious Tutsi-Banyaruguru. Thus, because of its greater pluralism and social complexity, the Hutu-Tutsi cleavage in Burundi did not materialize until after independence and then largely as a result of the demonstrated effect of the Rwanda revolution.

Road to Genocide

Ethnic massacres did not begin in 1972, yet they set the stage for the cataclysm to come. A turning point in the escalation of Hutu-Tutsi tensions came in May 1965 with the first postindependence elections to the national assembly. Although Hutu candidates scored a landslide victory, capturing twenty-three seats out of a total of thirty-three, their victory proved illusory. Instead of appointing a Hutu as prime minister, the king turned to a princely figure and longtime protégé of the court, Leopold Bihumugani. On October 18, 1965, Hutu anger exploded in an abortive coup directed at the king's palace, followed by sporadic attacks against Tutsi elements in the countryside. Repression swiftly followed: Eighty-six leading Hutu politicians and army officers were immediately arrested and shot. After the discovery of an alleged Hutu plot in 1969, seventy Hutu tribesmen, both civilian and military, were arrested; of these twenty-five were sentenced to death and nineteen immediately executed. Thus, by the late 1960s the Hutu had been virtually excluded from political participation.

The polarization of ethnic feelings so soon after independence must be seen in the light of the enormous power of attraction of the Rwanda model among those aspiring Hutu politicians who saw in the republican ideology of their neighbor the promise of a better future. For most Tutsi identified with the ruling party, *Union pour le Progrès National* (Uprona), however, Rwanda stood as the dreaded symbol of the tyranny of the majority. The nightmarish possibility that Burundi might become another Rwanda seemed real enough to justify the brutality of the repression that befell the nascent Hutu elites in 1965 and 1969.

But if political exclusion was clearly the key factor behind the rise of Hutu extremism, the timing of the insurrection draws attention to the violent intra-Tutsi squabbles and maneuverings that preceded the Hutu uprising. By late 1971 the long-simmering struggle for power between the Tutsi-Hima from the south and the Tutsi-Banyaruguru from the north was threatening to escalate beyond control. The country was awash with rumors of plots and counterplots, in turn leading to the arrest and bogus trials of scores of Banyaruguru politicians, many of them accused of working hand in glove with the monarchists to overthrow the regime. The ruling clique, headed by President Michel Micombero, consisting principally of Tutsi-Hima from the Bururi province, saw its legitimacy plummet. The sudden eruption of bitter internecine rivalries among Tutsi is what prompted the insurgents to strike a decisive blow in hopes of capturing power. Instead, they triggered a bloodbath on a scale that none had anticipated.

Anatomy of Mass Murder

On April 29, 1972, Hutu-instigated violence suddenly engulfed the normally peaceful lakeside towns of Rumonge and Nyanza-Lac in the south. In a matter of hours terror was unleashed on the Tutsi population. Countless atrocities were reported by eyewitnesses, including the evisceration of pregnant women and the hacking off of limbs. In Bururi all military and civilian authorities were slain. After seizing the armories in Rumonge and Nyanza-Lac, the insurgents fanned out into several southern localities. In Vyanda, near Bururi, they proclaimed a mysterious *République de Martyazo*. A week later government troops brought the republican experiment to an end. What followed was not so much a repression as a hideous slaughter of Hutu civilians. The carnage went on unabated until August. By then almost every educated Hutu element was either dead or in exile.

Exactly how many died between May and August is impossible to say. Conservative estimates put the total number of Hutu victims somewhere between 100,000 and 200,000, whereas one Tutsi opponent of the regime (Boniface Kiraranganiya) speaks of 300,000. The same holds for Tutsi victims of the insurrection, with estimates ranging from 2,000 to 5,000. Nonetheless, however much one can disagree about the scale of the massacre, that it reflects a planned annihilation is hardly in doubt.

The standard argument advanced by Hutu intellectuals is that the killings were inscribed long before any action on the *plan Simbananiye,* the directives of Artémon Simbananiye, Minister of Foreign Affairs at the time of the slaughter. The aim, presumably, was to provoke the Hutu into staging an uprising so as to justify a devastating repression and thus cleanse the country once and for all of the Hutu peril. Although there is no evidence of such a provocation, little doubt exists that Simbananiye played a key role in organizing the killings. As the social profile of the victims suggests, there was an element of rationality behind the carnage: In killing all educated Hutu elements, including civil servants, university students, and schoolchildren, any serious threat of another Hutu rebellion would be ruled out for the foreseeable future. In this sense one can indeed speak of a Simbananiye plan.

Given these circumstances, it is easy to understand why some of the most gruesome atrocities occurred on the premises of the University of Bujumbura, and in secondary and technical schools. Scores of Hutu students were physically assaulted by their Tutsi classmates, and many beaten to death. In a scenario that would repeat itself again and again, groups of soldiers and members of the Uprona youth wing, the *Jeunesses Révolutionnaires Rwagasore* (JRR), would suddenly appear in classrooms, call Hutu students by name, and take them away. Few ever returned. Approximately one-third of Hutu students enrolled at the University of Bujumbura disappeared under such circumstances. A missionary source indicated that at least 1,450 secondary school students of Hutu origins were either killed or in hiding. Out of a total of 138 Hutu priests, 18 were massacred. The army was thoroughly purged of all Hutu elements, beginning with 700 troops massacred immediately after the outbreak of the rebellion. A total of 190 Hutu officers were shot and killed between May 22 and May 27. Meanwhile, the execution of the young King Ntare, in Gitega on May 1, effectively ruled out the resurrection of the monarchy.

The cables dispatched by Deputy Chief of Mission Michael Hoyt from the U.S. Embassy in Burundi to the State Department paint a gruesome picture of this hellish climate:

> No respite, no letup. What apparently is a genocide continues. Arrests going on around the clock. (May 26)

Tutsi reprisals unabated in the interior but have slackened somewhat in Bujumbura. In the north Hutu take cover upon arrival of any vehicle, reflecting pervasive fear. (July 11)

In two days following July 14 three new ditches filled with Hutu bodies near Bujumbura airport. Arrests have continued throughout the week in Bujumbura, in the hills around town, in Ngozi region and central Burundi. (July 21)

Repression against Hutu is not simply one of killing. It is also an attempt to remove them from access to employment, property, education and the general chance to improve themselves. (July 25)

Describing what he saw at the time, Tutsi observer Boniface Kiraranganiya wrote: "It is the paroxysm of dementia, the most perfect example of what men are capable of doing when their hold on power allows them to do anything they want, when there is no obligation for him to control his destructive instincts" (Kiraranganiya, 1985, p. 76). That these lines were penned by a Tutsi should disabuse us of the notion that the killings were universally endorsed by the Tutsi community. Many in fact did everything possible to save their Hutu neighbors (as in Rwanda in 1994 when many Tutsi owed their survival to the protection of their Hutu neighbors) but could do little else to stop the carnage. Nonetheless, from this orgy of genocidal violence emerged a state system entirely dominated by Tutsi elements from the south, and it would remain so for years to come.

Indifference of the International Community
In the official doctrine issued by the Micombero government in the wake of the killings, the so-called White Paper, the argument is made that the Hutu rebels were bent upon committing genocide against the "people of Burundi." Thus, in putting down the rebellion, the state allegedly prevented the insurgency from taking an even bigger toll. Surprisingly, this inversionary discourse was received with little more than polite indifference by international public opinion. The unwillingness of the international community to see through the humbug of official media is no less astonishing than its extraordinary passivity in the face of mass slaughter.

The most surreal of all international responses was that of the Organization of African Unity (OAU)—now the African Union (AU)—on May 22, 1972, during OAU secretary general Diallo Telli's visit to Bujumbura. "The OAU," said Telli, in a statement reported by the U.S. embassy deputy chief of mission, Michael Hoyt, "being essentially an organization based on solidarity, my presence here signifies the total solidarity of the Secretariat with the President of Burundi, with the government and the fraternal people of Burundi." Hardly more edifying were the comments of United Nations (UN) Secretary General Kurt Waldheim, who expressed his "fervent hopes that peace, harmony and stability can be brought about successfully and speedily, that Burundi will thereby achieve the goals of social progress, better standards of living and other ideals and

principles set forth in the UN Charter." In 1972, as in 1994, the UN sat on its hands as tens of thousands of human beings were being slaughtered.

Legacy of 1972
The bloodbath was intended to achieve several long-term objectives: (1) to insure the stability of the state by the wholesale destruction of all educated elites and potential elites; (2) to transform the instruments of force—the army, the police, and the gendarmerie—into a Tutsi monopoly; (3) to rule out the possibility of a restored monarchy accomplished with Hutu assistance (hence the killing of King Ntare on May 1); and (4) to create a new basis of legitimacy for the Hima-dominated state by projecting an image of the state as the benevolent protector of all Burundi against their domestic and external foes.

On each count the government of Micombero, a Tutsi-Hima, met with considerable success. For the next sixteen years Burundi experienced a period of unprecedented peace under Tutsi hegemony. This surface impression of a country at peace with itself was suddenly shattered by a new outburst of ethnic hatred in August 1988, in the northern communes of Ntega and Marangara. Triggered by the provocations of a local Tutsi notable, Hutu-instigated riots took the lives of hundreds of Tutsi civilians before the army moved in and unleashed another bloody repression that resulted in the deaths of an estimated 15,000 Hutu.

In sharp contrast to what happened in 1972, the international community responded to the 1988 killings with a sense of shock. Substantial press coverage of the events led to charges of gross human rights violations by the European Community. In the United States congressional hearings were held in September 1988, followed by a nonbinding resolution urging the Burundi government to conduct an impartial inquiry into the circumstance of the riots. All of these responses eventually persuaded the Burundi government to introduce major constitutional and political reforms.

A major breakthrough toward liberalization came in 1993 with the organization of multiparty presidential and legislative elections. Twenty-one years after the 1972 genocide, the clear victory scored by the predominantly Hutu *Front des Démocrates du Burundi* (Frodebu) effectively wrested power away from the Tutsi minority. The Frodebu victory proved short-lived: On October 21, 1993, the newly elected Hutu president, Melchior Ndadaye, was arrested and killed by units of the Tutsi-dominated army, thus unleashing yet another cycle of ethnic violence, from which the country has yet to recover. An estimated 300,000 people have died since 1993, and at least as many have joined the 1972 refugees in United Nations High Commission for Refugees (UNHCR) camps in Tanzania.

Ndadaye's assassination brought into sharp focus the enduring legacy of 1972. Having reaped for decades the benefits of political hegemony, Tutsi extremists within and outside the army were quick to grasp the economic and political implications of a transfer of power to representatives of the Hutu majority. None were more eager to challenge the verdict of the polls than those Tutsi who had seized the land and houses of the 1972 refugees: To this day the refusal of Tutsi claimants to return ill-gotten properties to their rightful owners remains a critical issue facing the implementation of the Arusha accords.

Perhaps the most threatening problem of all inherited from 1972 is the enduring vitality of Hutu radicalism. It is worth recalling that it was in the refugee camps of Tanzania that the *Parti de la Libération du Peuple Hutu* (Palipehutu), the principal vehicle of anti-Tutsi radicalism, emerged in 1973. Today the most vehemently anti-Tutsi of the half-dozen political parties identified with Hutu interests are the *Parti pour la Libération du Peuple Hutu-Forces Nationales de Libération* (Palipehutu-FNL), led by Agathon Rwasa, and the *Conseil National pour la Défense de la Démocratie-Forces pour la Défense de la Démocratie* (CNDD-FDD), headed by Pierre Nkurunziza: Both are heirs to Palipehutist ideology in their uncompromising anti-Tutsi stance and unwillingness to lay down their arms.

With the power-sharing agreement formalized by the Arusha accords of August 28, 2000, a major step forward in restoring a measure of stability to the country was made. For this much of the credit goes to the mediating efforts of former Tanzanian president Julius Nyerere and after, his death, South Africa's Nelson Mandela. Although often suspected of Hutu sympathies by Tutsi extremists, Mandela was able to achieve a broad consensus on the need to work out a constitutional formula for a genuine sharing of executive and legislative responsibilities between Hutu and Tutsi. Among other issues, and pending the holding of multiparty elections in 2004, agreement was reached on a rotating presidency and a fifty-fifty share of cabinet positions among Hutu and Tutsi parties. Thus, after serving as president from 2000 to 2002, Pierre Buyoya, a Tutsi, handed power over to Domitien Ndayizeye, a Hutu, and the Hutu vice-president who served under Buyoya was succeeded in office by a Tutsi.

Much remains to be done, however, to fully implement the Arusha accords, including the restructuring of the army on the basis of parity between Hutu and Tutsi. The country is still wracked by chronic eruptions of violence. To the loss of human lives caused by un-provoked attacks by Palipehutu-FNL and CNDD-FDD guerillas—neither of which were signatories to the Arusha accords—must be added the devastating retribution blindly visited by the Tutsi army against civilian populations suspected of harboring Hutu terrorists. Extremism at both ends of the ethnic spectrum poses the greatest threat to the sustainability of Arusha. Despite the presence on the ground of a two thousand–strong multinational African military force, under the auspices of the African Union, there is no cease-fire in sight as yet.

If time has yet to dim the memories of 1972, there is reason to wonder—short of a public acknowledgment of the atrocities committed since then by both Hutu and Tutsi—whether the power-sharing arrangement so painfully worked out at Arusha can once and for all exorcize the demons of Burundi's genocidal past and pave the way toward peace.

SEE ALSO Genocide; Mandela, Nelson; Peacekeeping; Rwanda

BIBLIOGRAPHY

Chrétien, Jean-Pierre (1997). *Le Défi de l'Ethnisme: Rwanda et Burundi: 1990–1996.* Paris: Karthala.

Chrétien, Jean-Pierre (2003). *The Great Lakes of Africa: Two Thousand Years of History,* tran. Scott Straus. New York: Zone Books.

Hoyt, Michael (1972). "U.S. Embassy Cables from Bujumbura to State Department." University of Florida at Gainesville Library Website. Available from http://www.uflib.ufl.edu/cm/africana.

Kiraranganiya, Boniface (1985). *La Vérité sur le Burundi.* Sherbrook, Canada: Editions Naaman.

Lemarchand, René (1970). *Rwanda and Burundi.* New York: Praeger.

Lemarchand, René (1995). *Burundi: Ethnic Conflict and Genocide,* 2nd edition. New York: Cambridge University Press.

Lemarchand, René (2002). "Le génocide de 1972 au Burundi: Les silences de l'histoire." *Cahiers d'Études Africaines* (XLII-3):551–567.

Malkki, Liisa (1995). *Purity and Exile: Transformations in Historical-National Consciousness among Hutu Refugees in Tanzania.* Chicago: University of Chicago Press.

Morris, Roger (1987). *Uncertain Greatness: Henry Kissinger and American Foreign Policy.* New York: Harper and Row.

Reyntjens, Filip (1994). *L'Afrique des Grands Lacs en Crise: Rwanda and Burundi, 1988–1994.* Paris: Karthala.

Teltsch, Kathleen (1972). "Killings go on in Burundi, U.N. Statement Suggests." *New York Times,* (July 29):1.

René Lemarchand

Bystanders

The *Oxford English Dictionary* defines a bystander as one standing by, one who is present without taking part in what is occurring. One may immediately think of the phrase *innocent bystander*. In this association what is occurring is a crime. In a crime a bystander is neither perpetrator nor victim and thus innocent of all active involvement. The bystander is present only as passive observer or witness.

Although all bystanders to crime initially find themselves passively observing, some abandon passivity to intervene. They actively seek to help the victim and, in so doing, move from bystander to rescuer. In contrast, other bystanders, remaining passive throughout, have come to be called *nonresponsive bystanders*.

Although there is a range of possible bystander behavior between all-out rescue and complete nonresponsiveness, many bystanders to crime do remain entirely nonresponsive. Why do so many people so frequently do nothing when others are in peril? Are not bystanders morally obliged to help somehow? These are important questions, especially when what is underway is genocide or some other crime against humanity. For crimes of this magnitude, it is unclear whether one can ever consider bystanders innocent.

Bystander is a complex category in crimes such as genocide. In a double sense genocide and crimes against humanity are collective crimes. In these crimes both the perpetrators and victims are collectives. Genocide, for example, is a crime an entire society commits. And genocide is committed not against an individual but against multiple individuals who themselves comprise a group or social category and thus also a collective.

Two distinctions need to be made about bystanders to collective crimes that do not generally need to be made when the perpetrator and victim are both individuals. Because collective crimes are crimes an entire society commits, a distinction must be made between internal and external bystanders. Whereas internal bystanders are individuals and organizations internal to a society committing a collective crime, external bystanders are individuals and organizations external to the society. Citizens of Nazi Germany, for example, who observed the Holocaust without contributing to it were internal bystanders to genocide. In contrast observers outside Nazi Germany were external bystanders.

In the case of collective crimes, it is also necessary to distinguish between individual and organizational bystanders. This distinction is ordinarily unnecessary in crimes involving only individuals. Crimes exclusively involving individuals are mostly episodic. In other words, they occur in one place at one moment, and the bystanders are those who were physically present at that place at that moment. Generally, the physically present bystanders also will all be individuals.

Some collective crimes are also episodic—massacres, for example. A massacre occurs suddenly in one place and is quickly over. The bystanders, if any, are those who are physically present at the time and place of the massacre, and these will generally all be individuals.

In contrast genocide and crimes against humanity exceed the limits of space and time that apply to crimes involving only individuals. First, because genocide and crimes against humanity are enormous social undertakings not confined to a single place and time, physical proximity is not necessary to observe them. Instead, genocidal efforts can be observed from afar. Thus, as noted, even people in other countries can be counted as bystanders.

Second, because genocide and crimes against humanity take place not in a moment but over an extended length of time, there is opportunity for reaction not just from observing individuals but also from observing organizations. Thus, in the case of collective crimes, bystanders include other collectives. These range from religious organizations and nongovernmental organizations such as the Red Cross to entire nations. Indeed, insofar as the signatories to the international Genocide Convention are actually nations, entire nations have now pledged themselves not to remain passive bystanders to genocide.

When people are endangered, bystanders presumably have an ethical obligation to help somehow. Yet from what does this ethical obligation derive and how much does it oblige bystanders to do? These questions have not been adequately addressed by professional philosophy. Most people would agree, however, that the greater the magnitude of the crime witnessed, the greater the obligation on bystanders to intervene somehow. Since genocide and crimes against humanity are the most enormous of crimes, bystanders to these crimes seemingly bear the greatest obligation to intercede.

However, it is not only the magnitude of the crimes witnessed that weighs on the shoulders of bystanders to genocide and other crimes against humanity. The collective nature of these crimes also morally complicates the position of bystander. Just as there is a positive range of bystander behavior between total nonresponsiveness and all-out rescue, a negative range of behavior also exists between total nonresponsiveness and active complicity in a crime.

A young girl, unsure of her next move, beyond the sight of a heavily armed soldier. Barrancabermeja, Colombia, March 2001. [TEUN VOETEN]

Generally, in crimes involving only individuals, the distinction between bystander and accomplice is clear. The accomplice is one who serves the perpetrator in some way such as lookout or driver of the getaway car. If one were only present at the time the crime was committed without having helped in any way the perpetrator, then one is not an accomplice but only an innocent bystander.

The moral complication in the case of collective crimes such as genocide and crimes against humanity is that even doing nothing abets the perpetrator; thus, arguably, even the totally passive bystander becomes something of an accomplice. If so, no bystanders to collective crimes ever remain totally innocent.

For bystanders to do nothing helps the perpetrator of a collective crime in two ways. First, arguably, while a society is committing a collective crime, anything that promotes normal social functioning also enables the society to continue the crime. Thus, as Henry David Thoreau famously argued, if the citizens of a society continue to conduct business as usual while their society is committing a collective crime, the citizens share complicity in that crime.

There is a second way in which doing nothing contributes to a collective crime. In contrast to the actions of an individual, when a society acts—especially in the absence of opposition—it establishes what is normal or legitimate for that society. Such is the case when a society engages in genocide or some other crime against humanity. To fail to challenge these acts is to condone them and thereby to make their continuation more possible. In her 1984 comparative study of Nazi-occupied Europe, Helen Fein found that when subjugated populations resisted the Nazis, more Jews escaped death. How bystanders behave is thus very important.

What explains bystander nonresponsiveness to genocide and other crimes against humanity? No one factor explains all cases. There are differences between individual and organizational bystanders and between bystanders who are inside and bystanders who are outside a society committing a collective crime. How important different factors are to each case requires specific historical study of that case.

Although they are intertwined, the general factors contributing to bystander nonresponsiveness can broadly be classified as rational, psychological, cultural, and social structural. First, for both individual and organizational bystanders, inaction may be a rational—although not necessarily morally legitimate—response. Individual bystanders, for example, must rationally weigh the benefits of action to protect victims against the costs of action to themselves and their families. These weights will vary depending on whether bystanders are inside or outside the criminal regime.

Organizations must rationally calculate, too. During the Holocaust, for example, the Red Cross kept silent about the atrocities it knew were occurring in Nazi concentration camps. Why? The Red Cross decided after rational consideration that the benefits of speaking out were outweighed by the possible costs to the people it could help if the Nazis were to consequently forbid Red Cross operations. Whether or not this decision was morally right, it was nonetheless rational.

The Red Cross ostensibly was at least evaluating moral weights. In contrast, if bystanders are morally indifferent to the victims, morality will not even enter their rational calculations. Consistently, for example, throughout the twentieth century the U.S. government did little to respond to the cases of genocide it knew about. Instead, successive U.S. administrations tended to weigh only the political costs of action against the political costs of inaction. As there seldom was much pressure to act from the American public, the costs of inaction were consistently small. Thus, with morality out of the equation, inaction generally became the government's rational response.

Why does the American public not put more pressure on its government to intervene in cases of genocide and crimes against humanity? A whole range of factors combine to produce in bystanders what can be called the social creation of moral indifference.

The crux of the matter is what Helen Fein terms the *universe of obligation,* the universe of people one feels obligated to help. How large is this universe? One's sense of obligation generally declines with physical and social distance. Physically, one feels most obliged to help people in need when their needs are observed firsthand. Social distance matters, too. In declining order one feels most obligated to help family, friends, community members, and compatriots. For many bystanders the universe of obligation ends abruptly with nationality.

Cultural factors can further constrict the universe of obligation, making bystanders indifferent to certain victims. Most examined in this regard is anti-Semitism during the Holocaust, which clearly contributed something to bystander nonresponsiveness. It also matters whether or not bystanders have been reared in a culture stressing care for others. Likewise important is whether

the culture is what is called *authoritarian,* that is, one that instills uncritical respect for and obedience to authority. Bystanders in an authoritarian culture will be apt not to question their government should it stand silently by as genocide unfolds or even be committing genocide itself.

Bystander nonresponsiveness is also produced by group effects deriving from the social structure of an emergency situation. It turns out that bystanders to an emergency are less likely to respond helpfully when other bystanders are present. When multiple bystanders are present, conditions arise that social psychologists call *pluralistic ignorance* and the *diffusion of responsibility.*

Pluralistic ignorance is a situation in which two or more heads are worse than one. When multiple bystanders witness an ambiguous event that may or may not be a crime or emergency, each bystander looks to the others for guidance. If all bystanders wait for others to respond, none reacts. Because no one seems to be reacting, all bystanders may mistakenly conclude that nothing urgent is occurring. This condition is pluralistic ignorance.

The diffusion of responsibility is similar. When a single bystander witnesses an emergency, he or she may feel the full responsibility to react. When multiple bystanders are present, the responsibility is diffused among all witnesses. Each bystander assumes someone else will take responsibility for action. If all bystanders make this assumption, once again, no one acts.

Pluralistic ignorance and the diffusion of responsibility are even more pronounced at a national level (Porpora, 1990), where they are also likely to be combined with authoritarianism and governmental efforts to obfuscate the situation. If, in addition, a citizenry feels it is politically disempowered, it may not pay enough attention even to notice that genocide is taking place.

Despite all barriers to action some bystanders do respond—even at great personal risk. What makes responders different? Psychological study of the so-called altruistic personality has not turned up anything remarkable: Gentiles who rescued Jews during the Holocaust possessed good, moral role models and a strong sense of right and wrong. It is unclear whether nonresponsive bystanders are without these qualities. Most individuals probably possess what is psychologically necessary to respond appropriately when others are endangered. Mainly required is that one muster what has been called the *courage to care.*

SEE ALSO Altruism, Ethical; Anti-Semitism; Collaboration; Perpetrators; Rescuers, Holocaust; Resistance; Sociology of Perpetrators

BIBLIOGRAPHY

Barnett, Victoria (2000). *Bystanders: Conscience and Complicity during the Holocaust.* Westport, Conn.: Greenwood Press.

Baum, Ranier (1981). *The Holocaust and the German Elite: Genocide and National Suicide in Germany, 1871–1945.* Totowa, N.J.: Rowman and Littlefield.

Fein, Helen (1984). *Accounting for Genocide: National Responses and Jewish Victimization during the Holocaust.* Chicago: University of Chicago Press.

Latane, Bibb, and John W. Darley (1970). *The Unresponsive Bystander: Why He Doesn't Help.* New York: Appleton-Century-Crofts.

Oliner, Samuel P., Pearl M. Oliner, and Harold Schulweiss (1992). *The Altruistic Personality.* New York: The Free Press.

Porpora, Douglas V. (1990). *How Holocausts Happen: The United States in Central America.* Philadelphia: Temple University Press.

Power, Samantha (2003). *A Problem from Hell: America and the Age of Genocide.* New York: HarperCollins.

Staub, Ervin (1992). *The Roots of Evil: The Psychological and Cultural Roots of Genocide.* New York: Cambridge University Press.

Thoreau, Henry David (1993). "Civil Disobedience." In *Walden.* New York: Barnes and Noble.

Wyman, David (1998). *The Abandonment of the Jews: America and the Holocaust, 1941–1945.* New York: New Press.

Douglas V. Porpora

Cambodia

The kingdom of Cambodia traces its heritage to the realm of Angkor Wat, the twelfth-century center of a network of principalities, including many where ancient Khmer was spoken. Angkor's political reach was large, and the Hindu-influenced Angkor temple complexes are among the greatest in Southeast Asia. In the thirteenth and fourteenth centuries, however, Khmer-dominated political networks—which gradually adopted Buddhism—shrank, becoming increasingly subordinate to Buddhist Siam (Thailand) and the Confucian Dai Nam (Vietnam). The Khmer court welcomed a mid-nineteenth-century French offer of protection against Siam and Dai Nam, although some princes rebelled unsuccessfully against French supremacy.

Colonialism, Nationalism, and Communism: 1863 to 1953

The French dominated Cambodia together with Vietnam and Laos as part of their creation, French Indochina. Colonialism profoundly transformed Vietnam, generating rich landlords, landless peasants, industrial workers, and a vibrant intelligentsia, but left Cambodia more or less intact, with the small farms of peasants predominant and a tiny educated elite. The great changes in Vietnam made it fertile ground for the communist take-over of a strong nationalist movement in the 1930s and 1940s, whereas in Cambodia a milder cultural nationalism stimulated by two related French views of Cambodian history dominated the relatively scarce political activity. One depicted Khmer as inheritors of lost Angkorian greatness, recoverable with French help; the other portrayed them as a decadent race doomed to extinction at the hands of the superior Vietnamese, whom the French imported as bureaucrats and laborers to help administer Cambodia and work its plantations. The French also promoted the immigration of Chinese, who engaged in trade and became Cambodia's biggest ethnic minority, more numerous than Islamic Cham garden farmers and merchants and forest-dwelling upland peoples, whose presence predated French colonialism.

During the anticolonial upsurge that swept Southeast Asia after World War II, senior Khmer aristocrats and bureaucrats argued that Cambodia's splendor could be restored if the French handed power over to them, but were challenged by younger and lower-status Cambodians who believed progress required political reform or even armed revolution. They established the Democrat Party, which won elections allowed by the French, and launched rural Khmer Issarak (emancipated Khmer) insurgencies to drive out the French and topple King Norodom Sihanouk. Some Issarak accepted guidance from Vietnamese communists who entered Cambodia to fight the French there, in support of their own struggle in Vietnam. After Sihanouk dissolved the parliament, a few youthful Democrat Party activists joined the Vietnamese-led Issarak, including Pol Pot, who had become a Marxist while a student in France. Another recruitment route was followed by Nuon Chea, a Cambodian originally enrolled as a communist by the Vietnamese following university studies in Thailand. Both, however, resented the Vietnamese argument—echoing French colonial views—that Cambodia was too backward to mount a revolution without Vietnamese direction.

Independence, Sihanouk, the Khmer Republic, and War: 1954 to 1975

Harboring such ill-feelings, Pol and Nuon emerged as leaders of the Cambodian communist movement (known as the Khmer Rouge) after the 1954 Geneva Agreements provided for the withdrawal of French and Vietnamese military forces, a ceasefire, and elections in which all political parties were allowed to run candidates. Sihanouk used elections as an opportunity to destroy the communist opposition, driving it underground and eventually back into armed insurrection. Under Sihanouk's autocratic regime—which lasted sixteen years—the economy stagnated amidst corruption, generating rising discontent among an impoverished peasantry and a restless urban intelligentsia, some of whom joined the communist underground. Internationally, Sihanouk refused to align with the United States in its war against the communists in Vietnam, allowing the Vietnamese to establish sanctuaries on Cambodian soil, thereby persuading them not to support the violent rebellion Pol and Nuon launched in 1968.

Although Sihanouk alleged his April 1970 overthrow by his army chief Lon Nol was a U.S. plot, it probably resulted from domestic factors, with Lon Nol initially enjoying urban support for abolishing the monarchy as an obstacle to progress, making Cambodia a Khmer republic. However, the coup precipitated cataclysmic changes. From exile Sihanouk called on Cambodians to rise up against Lon Nol as part of a front including Pol and Nuon's guerillas, to which the Vietnamese suddenly provided overwhelming support, attacking the Khmer Republic's army and recruiting peasants to form local revolutionary administrations. In May 1970 the United States invaded Cambodia, attacking Vietnamese sanctuaries, but withdrawing ground forces—while continuing bombing—without preventing the Vietnamese from conquering rural Cambodia, which Pol and Nuon demanded be turned over to their Communist Party of Kampuchea. The transfer was completed by 1973, after the Vietnamese withdrew most of their troops and as a final blitz of U.S. bombing devastated the countryside. Pol and Nuon meanwhile initiated forced collectivization of agriculture, brutal curtailment of Buddhism and Islam, the bloody deportation of the populations of captured towns, and escalating executions of supposed traitors, spies, and other enemies in the Party and general population, the victims often being opponents of their policies, which alienated many peasants. However, the military dictatorship Lon Nol had imposed was also unpopular, and his regime collapsed in the face of a Communist offensive as U.S. military aid ran out in April 1975.

Democratic Kampuchea: April 17, 1975, to January 7, 1979

Pol and Nuon pursued even more extreme and homicidal policies once in complete power over what they called Democratic Kampuchea. Their ambition was to restore Cambodian glory by developing a form of communism that combined the most radical aspects of the Soviet, Chinese, and Vietnamese revolutions, applying their nationalist logic to survive. Cambodia had to advance free of foreign—especially Western and Vietnamese—tutelage; they also believed that the more rapidly Cambodian backwardness was overcome via true and autonomous communism, the more quickly genuine independence would be guaranteed. Their vision of communism called for the expulsion of the entire urban population into agricultural cooperatives; the deportation of Vietnamese to Vietnam; the abolition of markets, money, religion, and ethnic identities; the construction of railroads, steel mills, and hydroelectric dams amidst the rice fields; and the annihilation of anyone in the general population or within the Party who got in the way. They set out to vastly increase agricultural productivity and industrialize the country by transforming the whole population into proletarianized, atheistic peasants working in economic and eventual political equality to create an agricultural surplus to finance industry. However, their policies soon caused catastrophic agricultural and industrial regression, ever-worsening mass starvation, and increasingly vicious social division, and they directly ordered or empowered their subordinates to carry out killings to preempt and repress opposition to their vision and its results.

Various estimates suggest that during the less than four years of communist rule, between 1.5 and 3 million Cambodians out of a population of 7 to 7.5 million died in excess of normal mortality, among whom one-third to one-half were executed, the remainder dying from famines and illnesses resulting from conditions created by the regime. Among the dead from all causes were one in seven of the country's rural Khmer, one-quarter of urban Khmer, half of ethnic Chinese, more than a third of Islamic Cham, and 15 percent of upland minorities, while Vietnamese who refused deportation were totally wiped out. Also, by the end of the regime, around 20,000 communists and troops in the Party's armed forces were executed for purported treason, among an overlapping membership of 40,000 in the Party and strength of 60,000 combatants in the army.

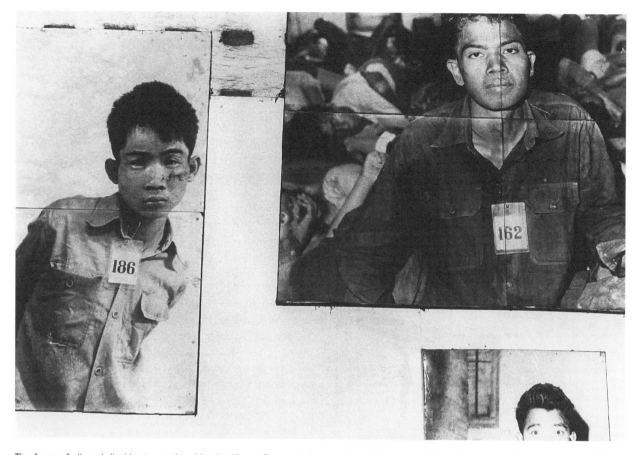

The faces of alleged dissidents murdered by the Khmer Rouge at the secret Tuol Sleng (S21) "security office" in Phnom Penh, c. 1978. Victims were photographed prior to interrogation and execution.[HOWARD DAVIES/CORBIS]

Several hundreds of thousands of the executions were carefully planned murder campaigns targeting well-defined categories of victims for complete elimination, carried out under specific and direct orders from Pol and Nuon. Victims included Khmer Republic military personnel and civil servants and religious and intellectual elites, with many having been killed by communist troops during the evacuation of towns, and the remainder hunted down by local security forces in the countryside, who also exterminated Vietnamese. With regard to deaths from starvation and disease, although Pol and Nuon's long-term policy was to create a prosperous rural society, they knew in advance that the effort to do so would involve temporary difficulties, during which some people would die. They then ignored mounting evidence that such sacrifices were occurring for a much longer period of time than anticipated and claiming many more lives than envisaged, insisting that the population march ahead, regardless of the cost. Finally, they authored a policy that anyone who opposed or failed to carry out their agricultural policies could be declared an enemy by local Party bosses and execut-

ed, a delegation of discretionary authority that was widely used and abused.

Many of the starvation and execution victims were so-called new people, urban Khmer, Chinese, and Cham deported in 1975 to the countryside then dispersed among the veteran people, the mostly Khmer peasants living in communist cooperatives since 1973. Pol and Nuon's policy was that the new people were to be welcomed, well-treated, properly fed with equal rations, and politically reeducated by veteran people and cadres who ran the cooperatives, but until their transformation into proletarianized peasants like veteran people was achieved, they had no right to participate in the running of the cooperatives. Worse yet, although Pol and Nuon asserted the new people, as such, were not enemies, they also said that new people were more likely to harbor enemies and be susceptible to enemy subversion than veteran people.

In fact, most veteran people did not share weal and woe—much less food—with the deportees. Amidst widespread famine, new people starved in droves as some veteran people gloated, verbally and physically

More photographs of prisoners of the Khmer Rouge, taken at the time of their admission to Tuol Sleng, prior to execution. The building is now preserved as the Tuol Sleng Museum. [HOWARD DAVIES/CORBIS]

abusing urbanites as previously privileged who deserved punishment for their supposedly luxurious and decadent lifestyles. Cadres often gave them the most difficult, unhealthy, and dangerous labor assignments, working many to death, while others perished in accidents and from ravaging illnesses. Those who protested their mistreatment, otherwise complained, or were accused of laziness were executed by cooperative militias or district security centers, with the extent of the killings decided by local Party members.

Although veteran people were deeply implicated in the mass death of evacuees, they were not the mainstay of Pol and Nuon's communism because they became more unhappy about a regime that increasingly also made them work harder and harder for less and less food, and insisted they accept a more and more alien communist political culture, totally renouncing Buddhism and many Khmer traditions. If they resisted or criticized any of this, they, too, were vulnerable to execution locally, and more and more were killed as the food situation worsened and dissatisfaction intensified.

Nevertheless, the death toll among new and veteran Khmer was far short of the 50 percent and 35 percent fatalities suffered by Chinese and Cham, figures suggesting that these minorities may have been targeted for progressive extermination as such. This conclusion seems supported by survivor testimony about rac-

ist remarks made by local Party bosses, encouraged by an official Party analysis stigmatizing them as belonging—like some Khmer groups—to special class strata with upper-class connections, and by an official policy requiring minorities to give up their language and other ethnic particularities and meld into a Khmer-speaking worker-peasantry. However, in contrast to the virulent demonization of Vietnamese in Party texts, these contain no anti-Chinese or anti-Cham racialist discourse, and victim testimony is inconsistent. Although many Chinese and Cham have reported their communities were sooner or later targeted for complete extermination, others have said they were treated no worse than Khmer, if they practiced assimilation and followed Party orders. It appears that—before 1978, at least—Chinese and Cham were targeted not for extermination, but suffered disproportionately from starvation and execution, the severity of this discriminatory ill-treatment depending on how local power-holders exercised their delegated powers. Chinese were mostly new people and many were upper-class, so they sometimes suffered doubly or triply. Originally, Cham were mostly rural veteran people, but after a few rebelled against renouncing Islam, almost all Cham were demoted to new-people status and dispersed throughout the country, like urban deportees. Both Chinese and Cham were killed for not speaking Khmer or for objecting to discrimination, the numbers again determined by on-the-spot decisions.

All of this points to variations and a paradox in killings by local cadres. Although some eliminated the Khmer Republic elite, Vietnamese, new people, Chinese, Cham, and dissident veteran people with gusto, others were not happy about all of the killing they were carrying out or about the regime they were protecting with murder. Moreover, at the same time that they starved to death and executed more people, there was an ever-growing malaise within the Party, reflecting the fact that many Party members who had been reformists before becoming revolutionaries retained liberal values. That even those who were dedicated communists had expected a milder form of communism; and that even those who had once shared Pol and Nuon's radical vision were disillusioned by the endless famine, epidemics, social strife, and escalating killings it was bringing about. Intra-Party dissidence was intensified by Pol and Nuon's policy of launching aggressive cross-border raids to force Vietnam to cede disputed territory to Cambodia. The Vietnamese counterattacked in 1977, routing Cambodian border units before withdrawing. Pol and Nuon blamed the defeats on traitors within the ranks, but the defenders realized that their policies were inviting military disaster by provoking the overwhelmingly superior Vietnamese forces.

Pol and Nuon reacted to the malaise with increasingly large-scale executions of dissident Party members falsely accused of being CIA, Soviet KGB, or Vietnamese communist spies plotting against the revolution. These purges were carried out under their direct supervision at the secret S21 (Tuol Sleng) security office, which tortured confessions from arrested cadres, forcing them to name scores or more of purported co-conspirators, who were then arrested and compelled to confess, naming still others. A massive purge in mid-1978 precipitated armed resistance from some cadres in eastern Cambodia who managed to escape, taking refuge with local veteran people, some of whom helped them fight back, unsuccessfully. Defeated peasants were subjected to large-scale execution, mass demotion to new-people status, and immediate deportation to other parts of Cambodia. As a few surviving insurgent cadres fled to Vietnam, Pol and Nuon pushed S21 to purge every last dissident inside the Party, with arrested cadres naming almost all leading figures except Pol and Nuon as traitors by late 1978. Meanwhile, local killings of all suspect population categories escalated to new heights, with Cham particularly targeted. There is some evidence that this reflected a change in Pol and Nuon's policies toward exterminating them completely, although definitive proof remains elusive.

What is certain is that Pol and Nuon continued to order the grossly depleted army to attack Vietnam. Each battle that was lost precipitated more arrests and executions of the enemy agents in the ranks supposedly responsible for the inevitable defeats. When the Vietnamese finally responded with a full-fledged invasion at the end of 1978, the Democratic Kampuchea regime disintegrated, the population welcoming the Vietnamese as liberators, while Pol and Nuon fled with part of their forces to Cambodia's border with Thailand. Their murderous quest for glory, prosperity, and independence thus ended in infamy, penury, and foreign occupation.

Regime Changes and Accountability since 1979

In January 1979 the Vietnamese installed the People's Republic of Kampuchea regime, in which Communist Party of Kampuchea defectors played prominent roles, but which the Vietnamese dominated. Pol and Nuon's remaining forces were treated by China, the United States, and the Association of Southeast Asian Nations (ASEAN) as still embodying Cambodian sovereignty. Therefore, Democratic Kampuchea retained its United Nations seat, and its army was supplied by China via Thailand to pursue guerrilla warfare against the Vietnamese and their clients, until the Paris Agreement of 1991. That internationally authored peace pact confirmed the withdrawal of Vietnamese and provided for United Nations–organized elections, which continuing Democratic Kampuchea supporters, former clients of the Vietnamese, and other Cambodian political organizations—including one founded by deposed King Sihanouk and headed by his son—were allowed to contest. No provision to determine accountability for Democratic Kampuchea crimes was made, but the United States, which backed the accord, declared it would support an effort by an elected government to bring perpetrators to justice. However, although the Democratic Kampuchea remnants refused to participate in elections and resumed insurgency, the coalition government of the restored kingdom of Cambodia that emerged from the ballot did not pursue the matter of accountability. The coalition included Sihanouk's organization, which had won the election, and the Cambodian People's Party (successor to the People's Republic of Kampuchea), which had lost but obtained a 50 percent share of power by threatening violence against the winners and the United Nations. The People's Party dominated the country under the leadership of Hun Sen, a one-time junior Communist Party of Kampuchea member, who preferred to respond to the Democratic Kampuchea insurgency through armed suppression and amnesties for insurgents who surrendered. In 1997 he asked for United Nations help to establish an International Tribunal, but later reversed himself, demanding instead cosmetic international participation in a domestic court trial of selected senior Democratic Kampuchea figures, Pol Pot having died in 1998. The United Nations resisted this move, convinced that Hun Sen's control of the judiciary would pervert the course of justice. From 1999 the United States attempted to broker a compromise, which the United Nations believed would still not guarantee a fair trial, but after bitter negotiations, the United Nations finally agreed to participate in a mixed tribunal in 2003. This court's personal jurisdiction was effectively limited to surviving Democratic Kampuchea senior leaders, thus shielding subordinate cadres, including Hun Sen and others who had defected before the Vietnamese invasion of 1978, from scrutiny.

SEE ALSO Khmer Rouge; Photography of Victims; Pol Pot; Statistical Analysis

BIBLIOGRAPHY

Becker, Elizabeth (1998). *When the War Was Over: Voices of Cambodia's Revolution and Its People,* 2nd edition. New York: Public Affairs Press.

Chandler, David P. (1991). *The Tragedy of Cambodian History: Politics, War and Revolution since 1945.* New Haven, Conn.: Yale University Press.

Chandler, David P. (1999). *Brother Number One,* revised edition. Boulder, Colo.: Westview Press.

Ea, Meng-Try, and Sorya Sim (2002). *Victims and Perpetrators? The Testimony of Young Khmer Rouge Comrades at S-21*. Phnom Penh: Documentation Center of Cambodia.

Englebert, Thomas, and Christopher E. Goscha (1995). *Falling Out of Touch: A Study of Vietnamese Communist Policy towards an Emerging Cambodian Communist Movement, 1930–1975*. Clayton, Australia: Monash University Center of Southeast Asian Studies.

Goscha, Christopher E. (1995). *Vietnam or Indochina: Contesting Concepts of Space in Vietnamese Nationalism, 1887–1954*. Copenhagen: Nordic Institute of Asian Studies.

Gottesman, Evan (2003). *Cambodia after the Khmer Rouge: Inside the Politics of Nation Building*. New Haven, Conn.: Yale University Press.

Heder, Steve (1997). "Racism, Marxism, Labeling and Genocide in Ben Kiernan's The Pol Pot Regime." *South East Asia Research* 5(2):101–153.

Heder, Steve (2002). "Hun Sen and Genocide Trials in Cambodia: International Impacts, Impunity, and Justice." In *Cambodia Emerges from the Past: Eight Essays*, ed. Judy Ledgerwood. De Kalb: Northern Illinois University Press.

Heder, Steve (2003). *Cambodian Communism and the Vietnamese Model: Imitation and Independence, 1930–1975*. Bangkok: White Lotus.

Heder, Stephen, and Brian Tittemore (2001). *Seven Candidates for Prosecution: Accountability for the Crimes of the Khmer Rouge*. Washington, D.C.: Washington College of Law War Crimes Research Office.

Heder, Stephen R. (2001). "Dealing with Crimes against Humanity: Progress or Illusion?" In *Southeast Asian Affairs 2001*. Singapore: Institute of Southeast Asian Studies.

Kiernan, Ben (2002). *The Pol Pot Regime: Race, Power, and Genocide in Cambodia Under the Khmer Rouge, 1975–1979*, 2nd edition. New Haven, Conn.: Yale University Press.

Metzl, Jamie F. (1996). *Western Responses to Human Rights Abuses in Cambodia, 1975–80*. Houndmills, U.K.: Macmillan Press.

Ponchaud, François (1978). *Cambodia Year Zero*, special edition. London: Penguin.

Steve Heder

Canada

In precontact Canada Amerindian societies were predominantly agrarian and hunter-gatherers. The two economies facilitated extensive trade routes and military alliances that were readily penetrated by European imperial rivals with the introduction of the fur trade.

Although neither Europeans or Amerindians needed lessons in the waging of armed conflict against an enemy, precontact hostilities were largely limited to blood feuds, which resulted in relatively few casualties when compared to European conventional warfare. Trade and alliances with European nations brought access to wealth and firearms that increased hostilities among Amerindian nations to unprecedented levels due to competition for furs and threats to sovereignty.

Trade in Furs and European Imperial Rivalries

Speculation that the Iroquois may have committed genocide against the Huron, who ceased to exist as a confederacy in 1649, is based on the hypothesis, first proposed by George T. Hunt in 1940, that the war between them was fought over the right to be the middlemen in the fur trade. Bruce Trigger, who dismissed Hunt's hypothesis as a "major dis-service" to scholarship argues that the Huron, because of their precontact allies and relationship with the French, represented a military threat to Iroquois sovereignty. The intent of the Iroquois was to break the Huron-French alliance. After the defeat of the Huron, the Iroquois made no attempt to replace them as middlemen. At the end of conflict the Iroquois compelled the Huron to join the Iroquois Confederacy. Many Iroquois were dispersed among the Onondaga and Mohawk, while one entire tribe and some of their allies were adopted by the Seneca Nation. This tribe was allowed to maintain its own language, culture, and customs.

A second possible case of genocide during the Huron-Iroquois conflict involves the Jesuits. In 1640 the Iroquois met with then Governor Montmagny of New France in an attempt to procure a treaty allowing them to kill Algonquin, allies of the Huron, without French interference. In return, Iroquois would no longer attack French or Huron furriers. Montmagny at first declined, but was persuaded by Jesuit priests to agree, provided the Iroquois promised to attack only non-Christian Algonquin. The Algonquin were never informed of the treaty. Trigger contends that the Jesuits, who were dependent on the fur trade, feared losing their missions if trade was cut off and recognized this as an opportunity to encourage Algonquin conversion. While the Iroquois' intent was to attack Algonquin randomly, Jesuit intent, inflicting conditions that aimed to annihilate non-Christian Algonquin, may have qualified as a genocide; however, Trigger points out that the treaty was only temporary.

Impact of European Infectious Diseases

Although there is a divergence of opinion as to the numbers of Aboriginal peoples who perished from the seventeenth century onward after contracting European infectious diseases, most notably smallpox, a consensus exists among historians that the spread of disease was one of the leading factors in the destruction of Amerindian societies. The primary debate centers on the issue of intent. Did the carriers of infectious disease deliberately facilitate its spread to Aboriginal peoples with the intent that Amerindians should die?

Jesuit missionaries, who first came into contact with the Huron Nation in the early 1600s, estimated the Huron population to be roughly 20,000 to 35,000. After a wave of epidemics, particularly smallpox, the Huron were reduced to about 10,000 by 1640. Many Huron observed that epidemics had occurred after visits from the black-robed missionaries. This led Huron to believe the Jesuits were practicing witchcraft. Jesuit ceremonies, such as the burning of incense and the priests' obsession with baptism (it did not go unnoticed that most Huron baptized while on their death bed with smallpox failed to survive), were interpreted as spell casting, or worse, soul stealing. Events culminated with a Huron attack on a Jesuit settlement in modern Midland Ontario, which resulted in the annihilation of its inhabitants.

While the Huron may not have understood the science behind the spread of European infectious diseases, in all probability they were likely correct in identifying the Jesuits as the carriers of disease. The Jesuits believed in the existence of two worlds after death. Heaven, which represented all they deemed holy, and hell, or purgatory, which represented all that was evil and feared. Better to risk the death of Amerindians after baptism, they reasoned, than not to baptize and risk eternal damnation for those unfortunate enough to die without having been baptized.

Intent and Implementation of British/Canadian Amerindian Policy

British Amerindian policy followed three discernible paths: protection, civilization, and finally assimilation. With the introduction of the Royal Proclamation of 1763, the British Crown recognized Amerindian land rights and forbade European settlement west of the Appalachian Mountains. Amerindian lands could only be surrendered to the Crown. The exception was the colony of British Columbia, where the colonial government favored what it called "peaceful penetration." However, after confederation, the Canadian government put an end to this policy and proceeded to invoke the tradition born out of the Royal proclamation where only the Crown could purchase land. The Crown, in turn, was the sole proprietor of land sales to settlers. Although this policy advanced British economic interests in the fur trade, it conflicted with the interests of American settlers, ultimately contributing to the American Revolution.

Between 1815 and 1841 Upper Canada accepted an influx of European settlers, creating demands on Amerindian lands. Sir Frances Bond Head, the lieutenant governor of Upper Canada, as U.S. President Thomas Jefferson before him, advocated the relocation of Amerindians. Bond Head proposed moving all Amerindians from central and southern Ontario to Manitoulin Island. While Bond Head's proposal was never actuated, all Indians were eventually isolated on reserves, opening land for settlement. Christian converts who originally built and maintained their own community of log houses, barns, and fields at the present-day site of Owen Sound, Ontario, were not spared. Bond Head told the Amerindians that they could not be protected from settlers unless they agreed to relocate and relinquish their lands.

In 1830 the Indian Department was transferred from military to civilian control. With this change, the Act for the Gradual Civilization of the Indian Tribes in the Canadas was introduced. Favored by white settlers and politicians, Governor George Simpson of the Hudson's Bay Company warned that policies undermining Amerindians societies would become a political issue in Britain. As J. R. Miller contends, "Assimilation through evangelization, education and agriculture would have to be the policy after 1830, because more coercive methods of achieving the 'Euthanasia of savage communities' were inimical, expensive and politically dangerous" (1996, p. 75). Miller appears to be correct in his estimations. From 1837 to 1861 Englishman Herman Merival, rejecting the notion of the physical extermination of Natives as unthinkable, openly advocated utilizing both the church and state to prepare Amerindians for assimilation, while isolating them from settlers until such time that they might be deemed "civilized." The Civilization Act of 1857 was precisely what Merival had advocated. The Crown went further in 1866, with the introduction of policies that "adjusted" reserves. Amerindians were expected to live on 10 acres per family, whereas whites were permitted to claim 160 acres and purchase an additional 480.

Recognition of a Nation

The introduction of the British North American (B.N.A.) Act of 1867 recognized Canada as a nation and entrenched Amerindians in Canadian law as wards of the Crown; however, Amerindians were encouraged under the act to pursue enfranchisement, which entailed full assimilation into white society.

In 1868 the Indian Act was passed into law. Its principles were once again protection, civilization, and assimilation. As Robert Surtees stresses, the "general framework" of policy was inherited from preconfederation:

It became increasingly legalistic in its orientation. Emphasis was directed toward enfranchisement, toward the meaning of Indian status, and toward eradicating all remnants, aspects, or symbols of tribal background or Indian heritage. The imposition of elected local governments on reserves and the proscription by federal statute of such customs as the Sun Dance and the potlatch were instances of the latter emphasis. And to promote the program, extended powers were accorded the Indian agents through an increase in the authority of the chief superintendent, who, after Confederation, was a minister of the federal government (Surtees, 1982, p. 44).

The creation of the Enfranchisement Act of 1869 authorized the federal government of Canada under the Indian Act to relinquish the status of anyone legally recognized as a "Status Indian" whom the government deemed fit for assimilation. The Indian Act was again amended in 1876 to clarify that Indians were minors, wards of the federal government, subjects, not citizens. Brian Titley explains, "It was designed to protect the Indians until they acquired the trappings of white civilization. At that point, they were supposed to abandon their reserves and their special status and disappear into the general population" (1986). John Milloy notes that it was tribal councils that first decided policies on agriculture, schools, and other forms of cultural change. Under the Indian Act of 1876 the Canadian government controlled the reserves.

After the collapse of the fur trade in western Canada, the Plains Cree made overtures to the federal government, aimed at the creation of a Cree homeland within the confederation. The Cree insisted on the inclusion of a commitment to providing schools and farm equipment in treaties. Federal promises either fell short or were neglected altogether. Successful farming operations were reduced in size after settlers complained of having to compete with Amerindians. Living conditions became deplorable, forcing some women into prostitution in order to acquire food. The government blamed the perceived immorality of Amerindian culture. Hostilities boiled over in the communities of Battleford and Frog Lake, at roughly the same time the Metis rebelled against federal subjugation. According to Robert Tobias, Edgar Dewdney, a senior bureaucrat with Indian Affairs, used the opportunity to publicly cover up the results of federal policy by claiming that Cree hostilities were part of the Metis Rebellion of 1885. Privately, Dewdney admitted the two were separate incidents. After 1885 Dewdney refused to honor treaties with the Cree. The Cree were eventually forced onto scattered reserves, their leaders wrongfully imprisoned, and the farming equipment promised in treaties never delivered.

In 1894 the Canadian Indian Act was amended to allow for the lease of so-called idle reserve lands to the growing numbers of settlers. Reserves were increasingly viewed as a hindrance to assimilation. In 1903 the Oliver Act became law. It was designed to make the seizure of allegedly surplus Indian lands for settlers easier. (At the beginning of the early twenty-first century Amerindians occupy less then 2% of the land in Canada below the 60th parallel.) Education also became compulsory under the Indian Act of 1894. The intent was to utilize day and residential schools to prepare Amerindian children for assimilation into Western society. Children were forbidden from practicing their own culture, language, and religion; the vacuum created was filled by Western culture, the English language, and Christianity. This policy remained unchallenged until the drafting of the United Nations (UN) Convention Against Genocide concluded in 1948. Canada, among other UN member nations, successfully lobbied for the removal of most of the references to cultural genocide in favor of limiting legislation to cases of "physical destruction." The Canadian government feared that the residential schools or forced education in its country might be seen as genocidal institutions.

Seven years after the ratification of the Genocide Convention, in response to external threats to her sovereignty in the high Arctic, Canada engaged both the Hudson's Bay Company and Royal Canadian Mounted Police to relocate Inuit, predominantly from Port Harrison, Quebec, to Grise Fiord and Resolute Bay. They were to select Inuit deemed "inefficient trappers." For the most part the Hudson's Bay Company ignored the fact that Inuit who were dependent on relief payments received this government assistance, in part, because some of the tribe's best hunters were too busy trapping for Hudson's Bay to hunt for their own people; furthermore, a number of self-sufficient hunters and at least one prominent carver who maintained a respectable income by southern standards were sent to the high Arctic.

In the 1960s Canadian policy toward its Native population underwent a radical change with the Supreme Court of Canada's ruling in Nishga, which confirmed the rights of Amerindians. This ruling legally quashed the 1969 White Paper that proposed the abolition of reserves and Amerindian rights as recognized by the Crown in earlier treaties. Although the 1960s bore witness to improved Canadian-Amerindian relations, Canada did not, as Micheal Asch asserts, shift policy from assimilation to negotiating Amerindians into the confederation. Contemporary land claims assert Crown sovereignty over unceded lands while recognizing some rights in return for the extinction of others and

Amerindian recognition of Canadian sovereignty. All modern treaties contain a clause stating that Amerindians must "cede surrender and extinguish all Aboriginal claims." The agreements offer Amerindians financial considerations on a per acre basis, generally well below market value, and an agreed upon percentage of royalties for resources.

Although there is general consensus among scholars that the Canadian government pursued an ethnocidal policy toward Amerindians, Miller underscores the frustration of this policy, as a result of Amerindian resistance, lack of government finances, and the overall failure of government agents to fully cooperate in the implementation of ethnocidal policies. However, Miller's work fails to take into account the agents who did cooperate or were overzealous, as demonstrated by Robin Brownlie and Mary-Ellen Kelm. Nor does Miller address the plight of Amerindians on the West Coast who were imprisoned if they participated in a potlatch or those who were released from prisons only after surrendering their religious regalia to museums. Brownlie and Kelm's findings are further validated by Chalk and Jonassohn, who state that few genocides are ever entirely successful. It is only logical that the same principle applies to ethnocide.

SEE ALSO Beothuk; Residential Schools

BIBLIOGRAPHY
Asch, Michael (1998). "To Negotiate into Confederation: Canadian Indian Policy." In *Readings in Canadian History Post-Confederation,* ed. R. D. Francis and D. B. Smith. Toronto: Harcourt Brace.

Brownlie, Robin, and Mary-Ellen Kelm (1994). "Desperately Seeking Absolution: Native Agency as Colonialist Alibi?" *Canadian Historical Review* 75(4):543–556.

Chalk, Frank, and Kurt Jonassohn (1990). *The History and Sociology of Genocide: Analyses and Case Studies.* New Haven, Conn.: Yale University Press.

Churchill, Ward (1998). *A Little Matter of Genocide.* Winnipeg: Arbeiter Ring Publishing.

Devreux, E. J. (1970). "The Beothuk Indians of Newfoundland in Fact and Fiction." *Dalhousie Review* 50:350–362.

Kulchyski, Peter, and Frank J. Tester (1994). *Tammarniit (Mistakes) Inuit Relocation in the Eastern Arctic 1939–63.* Vancouver: UBC Press.

Marshall, Ingeborg (1996). *A History and Ethnography of the Beothuk.* Montreal: McGill-Queens University Press.

McNeill, William H. (1976). *Plagues and Peoples.* Garden City, N.Y.: Doubleday.

Miller, J. R. (1996). *Shingwauk's Vision: A History of Native Residential Schools.* Toronto: University of Toronto Press.

Miller, J. R. (1998). "Owen Glendower, Hotspur, and Canadian Indian Policy." In *Readings in Canadian History Post-Confederation,* ed. R. D. Francis and D. B. Smith. Toronto: Harcourt Brace.

Milloy, John S. (1983). "The Early Indian Acts: Developmental Strategy and Constitutional Change." In *As Long as the Sun Shines and Water Flows,* ed. I. A. L. Getty and A. S. Lussier. Vancouver: University of British Columbia Press.

Milloy, John S. (1999). *A National Crime.* Winnipeg: University of Manitoba Press.

Surtees, Robert J. (1982). *Canadian Indian Policy: A Critical Bibliography.* Bloomington: Indiana University Press.

Titley, Brian A. (1986). *A Narrow Vision.* Vancouver: University of British Columbia Press.

Tobias, John L. (1983). "Canada's Subjugation of the Plains Cree, 1879–1885." *Canadian Historical Review* 64:519–548.

Trigger Bruce (1976). *The Children of Aataentsic: A History of the Huron People to 1660,* Vol. II. Montreal: McGill-Queens University Press.

David King

Carthage

The destruction of Carthage in 146 BCE ended the Third Punic War (149–146). It the violent anticlimax to more than a century of conflict between Rome and Carthage, the two most powerful states in the western Mediterranean. Rome's grim treatment of the Carthaginians and their city, while not entirely unprecedented as a postscript to Roman conquest, stands out as an extraordinary and calculated act of brutality.

Rome and Carthage had not always been enemies, but conflicting Roman and Carthaginian imperial interests resulted in the First Punic War (264–241) and the Second Punic War (218–201). In the latter war, the Carthaginian general Hannibal invaded Italy and brought Rome to the brink of defeat. However, Rome's ultimate victory left it the unrivalled power in the western Mediterranean. Carthage was forced to accept severe terms, including a large indemnity paid annually for fifty years and the loss of all overseas territories. Moreover, Carthage agreed not to wage war outside of Africa and, within Africa, only with Rome's permission.

Carthage also agreed to restore to Masinissa (the king of neighboring Numidia and a Roman ally since 206) all the territory that he or his ancestors had once possessed. Masinissa consistently raided or seized Carthaginian territory, claiming that the lands once belonged to his family. Each time, Carthage either acquiesced or dutifully sought Roman arbitration, and each time, the Romans sided with Masinissa.

Despite the loss of territory and military power, Carthage remained a prosperous city. A Roman embassy, which included the powerful senator, Cato the elder, visited Carthage in 153 and returned home impressed by the size and wealth of the city. After this visit, Cato reportedly began concluding all of his speeches in the Senate with the phrase "Carthage must be destroyed." In one speech Cato presented a number of Carthaginian figs to the senate. He warned his audience, amazed at the figs' size and freshness, that the country that produced them lay only a short distance from Rome. Cato's views probably reflected the popular Roman sentiment that Carthage was to be feared. This fear may have grown stronger after Carthage paid off its indemnity in 151.

Rome's justification for the Third Punic War came when the aging Masinissa again invaded Carthaginian territory in 150 and Carthage chose to resist the invasion without first seeking arbitration from Rome. The Carthaginians may have simply grown frustrated with Rome's consistent support of Masinissa over the previous half-century and decided to risk war rather than concede more territory to its enemy. Alternatively they may have believed the war indemnity stipulated by the treaty of 201 was paid, that they were no longer bound by the treaty and could pursue independent foreign policy. Whatever the case, the Numidians badly defeated the Carthaginian army, which fought under the command of Hasdrubal. The Carthaginians immediately condemned Hasdrubal to death, then sent an embassy to Rome to publicly disavow the actions of Hasdrubal and to seek arbitration over the dispute with Masinissa.

The Roman response was calculated and duplicitous. In fact, the Roman historian Appian claims that the Roman senate had had begun to seek a pretext to attack Carthage soon after Cato had returned from his visit to the city three years earlier, though the veracity of the statement is questionable. In any case, the Roman senate had already begun to prepare for an invasion of Africa by the time the Carthaginian embassy arrived. The senate blamed Carthage for the impending war and warned that it could be avoided only if Carthage "satisfied the Roman people" (Appian, 1972, p. 74). The next year (149), the Roman senate declared war and ordered a fleet and army to gather in Sicily, preparatory to invading Africa. The Carthaginians sent another embassy to the Roman senate in a desperate attempt to avoid conflict. The Romans responded that the Carthaginians could retain their lands in Africa and would be allowed to live under their own laws. To gain this concession, however, they were ordered to hand over 300 hostages—children from aristocratic families—within thirty days to the Roman generals in Sicily and obeyed Rome "in other ways" (Appian, 1972, p. 76).

The Carthaginians were suspicious, but they complied with this demand. The Roman generals then sent word that they would provide further conditions once the Roman army landed in Utica (a harbor town in north Africa). Carthage sent an embassy to meet the Roman generals in Utica, at which point the generals demanded that the Carthaginians turn over all stockpiled weapons and siege machines. Only after the Romans collected these weapons did they reveal their final conditions for peace: the Carthaginians must abandon their city and resettle at least ten miles from the sea. The city itself would be razed, except for its shrines and graves. Carthage rejected these terms, and the Romans began to prosecute the war.

The Third Punic War lasted longer than Rome expected, though there was little doubt as to the outcome. After a lengthy siege the Romans, under the command of Scipio Aemilianus, forced the city to surrender, but only after a great many women, children, and elderly had been killed or wounded when Scipio ordered residential buildings set on fire to clear a path to the citadel. Fifty thousand men, women, and children were sold into slavery. Roman soldiers looted the city for several days, after which a board of ten Roman senators oversaw the systematic destruction of the city. Carthage was burned to the ground and buildings were razed. The story that the Romans sowed salt on the fields to prevent crops from growing is a later invention.

What drove the Romans to extreme barbarity in this case is a matter of debate. Cato's speech about the wealth of Carthaginian territory, Carthage's economic resilience, and Rome's demand that the Carthaginians resettle away from the sea all suggest that commercial factors may have influenced Rome's policy toward Carthage. After the war, Carthaginian territory was reorganized as the province of Africa, and in 122 the Romans tried to establish a colony on the site of Carthage. However, this decision was reached long after the destruction of Carthage and was very controversial, suggesting that colonization had not been the foremost reason for Roman actions in 146.

Roman politics and the desire for glory certainly contributed to its treatment of Carthage. After the war, Scipio Aemilianus's popularity soared and he was awarded the title Africanus for defeating Rome's rival. Finally, one should not underestimate Roman hatred of Carthage, fear (even if unfounded), and desire to avenge the destruction wrought by Hannibal in the Second Punic War. According to Appian, the Romans who poured into the streets to celebrate the news of Carthage's destruction were still mindful of Hannibal's war.

Finally, it is worth considering to what degree the treatment of Carthage was typical of contemporary Roman military and diplomatic procedure. On the one hand, Roman brutality throughout the Mediterranean appears to have increased in the second century BCE. For example, in 146 Rome razed the city of Corinth and enslaved its population. On the other hand, Rome's apparent long-term policy of weakening Carthage and its calculated manipulation of the treaty of 201 are not typical of its treatment of other conquered rivals. This underscores the degree to which Roman fear, hatred, and desire for revenge may have been important motivating factors in the decision to wipe out Carthage both physically and symbolically.

SEE ALSO Ancient World

BIBLIOGRAPHY

Appian (1972). "Punic Wars." In *Appian's Roman History in Four Volumes*, Loeb Classical Library, tran. Horace White. Cambridge, Mass.: Harvard University Press.

Astin, A. E. (1967). *Scipio Aemilianus*. Oxford: Clarendon.

Caven, Brian (1980). *The Punic Wars*. New York: St. Martin's Press.

Goldsworthy, Adrian (2000). *The Punic Wars*. London: Cassell.

Lancel, Serge (1995). *Carthage: A History*, trans. Antonia Nevill. Cambridge, Mass.: Blackwell.

Polybius (1992). *The Histories in Six Volumes*. Loeb Classical Library, trans. W. R. Paton. Cambridge, Mass.: Harvard University Press.

Scullard, H. H. (1980). *A History of the Roman World*, 4th edition. London: Routledge.

Michael P. Fronda

Cathars

Catharism, a Christian heresy attested from approximately the tenth until the fifteenth century from France to Asia Minor, advocated a path to salvation through one sacrament, held that the material world was evil, and believed that salvation was available for all believers. The Cathars shared with the Bogomils (another, nearly contemporary Christian heresy) certain elements of belief, organization, and ritual, whose dissemination probably followed the trade routes from East to West. The Cathars, who called themselves simply "good Christians," constituted a real counter-church, consisting of believers, clergy, and bishops. The name "Cathar" was explained as referring to cat worshippers, because the Cathars were accused of holding diabolical rites, or as a derivative from the Greek word *katharos* (meaning "clean, pure") to describe the pure asceticism of the believers.

Origins and Development

In Bulgaria, the followers of a priest named Bogomil initiated a dissident movement in the tenth century, attested by various sources such as the sermon of Cosmas (c. 970). In the West, other heretical groups began to emerge around the year 1000, as lay apostolic movements reacted to the reforms initiated by Pope Gregory VII (1073–1085) and to the growth of monasticism. In the 1140s, when the trials and condemnations of the Bogomils were occurring in the East, Evervin, prior of Steinfeld (in Germany), wrote to Bernard, abbot of Clairvaux (in France), about heretics who claimed that their church originated with Christ and the apostles and had been existing secretly in and around Greece. Reports of heresy followed in the 1150s and 1160s. In 1163, five people were burned in Cologne by authority of a lay court. Eckbert of Schönau authored thirteen sermons against the heretics he termed Cathars. Eckbert's sister Elisabeth and Hildegard of Bingen both engaged in polemics against the dissidents. Popular heresy spread rapidly from the 1170s until the Fourth Lateran Council (1215). Among the various movements that arose, the Cathars attracted the greatest suspicion and were the primary targets of campaigns against heresy, from preaching missions to armed intervention.

Contacts between Eastern Bogomils and Western Cathars were not uncommon, especially in and through Italy because of its proximity to the Balkans. Sometime between 1167 and 1172, Pope Nicetas of Constantinople attended a synod in France at Saint-Félix-de-Caraman, north of Toulouse. A document from that council, the so-called Charter of Nicetas, gives the names of Cathar bishops who arrived at the conference from various parts of France and Italy. Nicetas reconsecrated bishops who already held office and consecrated newly elected bishops. Around 1190, Nazarius, the Cathar bishop of Concorezzo, brought the Bogomil text *Interrogatio Iohannis* from Bulgaria to Italy. Envoys carried letters between French and northern Italian Cathars, and leading French Cathars took refuge in Italy during periods of persecution in the thirteenth and fourteenth centuries.

Italian Cathars in cities such as Orvieto and Viterbo benefited from the protection of political leaders who opposed the papacy. Eventually, the Cathars in Italy emerged into three divisions according to their affiliation with different Bogomil churches: the Albanenses centered in Desenzano, near Lake Garda were affiliated with the church of Dragovitia; the Garatenses, located in Concorezzo, near Milan, observed ties to the church of Bulgaria; and the Bagnolenses from Bagnolo, near Mantua, maintained affiliation with the church of Sclavonia.

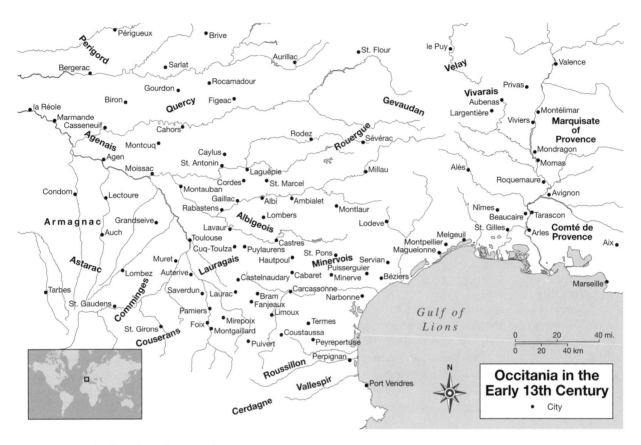

Map showing Occitania in the early thirteenth century. [MAP BY XNR PRODUCTIONS. THE GALE GROUP.]

Beliefs

Sources pertaining to the beliefs and existence of the Cathars consist primarily of polemical texts written against them, but also include three extant Cathar rituals, two in Occitan and one in Latin; an anonymous treatise for Cathar preachers; and the *Book of Two Principles*, a scholastic exposition written by John of Lugio, bishop of Desenzano.

Catharism differed from orthodox Christianity on several points, including beliefs regarding the nature of Christ, the role of the church hierarchy, the number and function of the sacraments, the source of evil in the world, and the possibility of salvation for all believers. The Cathars leaned toward docetism, which rejects the human nature of Christ. They practiced a single sacrament, the *consolamentum,* which was a laying-on-of-hands that served as baptism, confirmation, ordination, forgiveness of sins, and extreme unction. Through the *consolamentum,* human souls which had fallen away from God would return to God's realm. The Cathars rejected any necessity for a priest's absolution to forgive sins, any function for the saints' intercession, or any need of prayers for the dead. The Cathars shared a symbolic but non-sacramental breaking of bread. They

practiced a generally austere way of life, with special dietary restrictions. The women *perfectae* performed evangelical, pastoral, and sacramental functions. Cathars refused obedience to Rome and the local clerical hierarchy. With the Bogomils, they believed that matter was created by Satan and that the last fallen soul would be saved at the end of this world. Both Cathars and Bogomils rejected icons and practiced a simple, repetitive liturgy emphasizing the Lord's Prayer, an *Adoremus* formula, and multiple genuflections.

Social Location and Practices

Catharism included all social classes, perhaps having been introduced among the elites but later filtering down to the lower classes. Family ties represented an important force. Cathar houses played a religious and socio-economic role; people were welcomed there for instruction in trades as well as religion. Less prosperous and military than their northern counterparts, Occitan nobles engaged in some form of work, such as weaving or cobblery. They lived with members of other social classes in the *castrum*, a fortified village built around a castle. As the population of Occitan villages expanded, the Cathars developed a strong network.

Furthermore, Catharism placed no economic restrictions on believers and exacted no tithes.

Before their persecution, Cathar bishops preached widely, traveling with assistants who set forth their doctrines. Cathars also met and preached in the homes of their patrons. The Roman church responded first by expanding the scope and frequency of orthodox preaching to the people, mandated by the Fourth Lateran Council (1215) and implemented through the approval of the mendicant orders (Dominicans in 1216; Franciscans in 1220). Eventually, however, the ideology that justified the crusades to the Holy Land was extended to rationalize campaigns against heresy in Italy, France, and the Balkans.

The Albigensian Crusade: 1209 to 1229

Pope Innocent III launched the Albigensian Crusade in 1208/1209, after the murder of the papal legate, Peter of Castelanu. This decision followed decades of unsuccessful efforts at preaching conversion to the Cathars in Occitania and failed attempts to suppress their alliances with political enemies of the pope in Italian cities. It also rested on a gradual build-up of mechanisms for persecution. When teaching and preaching no longer proved effective in persuading dissenters to conform, church and secular leaders turned to coercion.

The third canon of Lateran IV (1215), which established the mechanisms for persecution, was preceded by a series of landmarks. These were:

1. Chapter 21 of the Assize of Clarendon in 1166, the first secular legislation against heresy;

2. Lateran III in 1179;

3. Ad abolendam in 1184, the first joint (secular and spiritual) condemnation of heresy since the Theodosian code;

4. Innocent III's 1199 decree *Vergentis in senium* equating heretics with traitors before the law.

Moreover, in 1207, just prior to the Albigensian Crusade, Innocent III issued *Cum ex officii*, which expressed the intent to "remove from the patrimony of St. Peter the defilement of heretics," and provided for the delivery of heretics to secular courts, the confiscation and sale of a heretic's possessions, destruction of his home, and penalties imposed on his followers or supporters. These papal measures, aimed at Cathars and political foes in Viterbo, equated the two groups and furthered the alliance of the ecclesiastical and secular forces that drove the Albigensian Crusade.

Historians divide the Albigensian crusade into six general phases, as follows:

1. 1209 to 1211, when the land belonging to the powerful Trencavel family was conquered;

2. 1211 to 1213, when Toulouse and the surrounding area were subdued;

3. 1213, the year of the decisive battle at Muret, when allied forces under Peter of Aragon were defeated by Simon of Montfort's armies;

4. 1213 to 1215, the period of Montfort's triumph and Lateran IV, where the disposition of conquered territory was debated and Count Raymond VI was deprived of his lands;

5. 1215 to 1225, a decade of counter-attack and reassertion of southern lords;

6. 1225 to 1229, when royal intervention conquered the southern forces and compelled Raymond VII's submission.

The first phase of the crusade included some of the most brutal massacres. On July 22, 1209, the city of Béziers was sacked and thousands were slaughtered. When asked whether to kill both Catholic Christians and heretics, the legate Arnaud Amaury supposedly replied: "Kill them all; God will recognize his own." Whether or not he uttered those infamous words, Amaury reported succinctly to Innocent III that "neither age, nor sex, nor status had been spared, and nearly twenty thousand people perished." The legate described the subsequent sack and burning of the city as "divine revenge raging wondrously against it," and he termed the event a "great miracle." In June of 1210, 140 Cathars were burned at Minerve. The following year, in April and May 1211, at Lavaur, about 80 *faidits*, Occitanian nobles who supported the Cathars, were executed, and 300 to 400 Cathars were burned. In May of the same year, at the siege of Cassès, 60 to 100 Cathars were burned.

The middle period of the crusade involved more victories for the French army, but those were followed by victories by southern (Occitanian) forces at Castelnaudary, Agen, Moissac (1221), and Carcassonne (1223 and 1224). The deaths of Raymond VI in 1222, Raymond-Roger of Foix in 1223, and King Philip Augustus in 1223 led to a reversal of southern victories. When Louis VIII acceded to the throne, full royal intervention in Occitania ensued. After negotiations with Raymond VII and his excommunication in 1226, the king's army moved southward. After Louis VIII's death in November of the same year, his cousin continued the campaign, under the urging of Blanche of Castille, who was serving as regent until her son, the future Louis IX, reached the age to assume the throne. Humbert de Beaujeau, the governor of Languedoc, directed the systematic devastation of the area around Toulouse, which along with pressure from Pope Gregory IX, forced the beginning of negotiations for peace, and culminated in the treaty of Paris/Meaux in 1229.

The brutality of the Albigensian crusade reflects the perception of heresy's threat to the social order, as expressed by Caesarius of Heisterbach, a Cistercian monk from the Rhineland, in his *Dialogus miraculorum*: "The Albigensian error was so strong that in a short period of time it would have infected as many as 1,000 cities, if it had not been repressed by the swords of the faithful. I think that it would have corrupted all of Europe."

Inquisition, Dissent, and Reform

After Innocent III's papacy, the legislative campaign to combat heresy was renewed by Honorius III (1216 to 1227). The migration of Occitan Cathars into northern Italy increased the presence of the counter-church there. The friars undertook influential preaching campaigns to swing public opinion toward enforcement of already existing legislation against heresy or toward the enactment of new laws. Attention to the crusade to the holy land eclipsed the effort against heresy again in 1221, but Gregory VIII, Honorius's successor, resumed the legal assault on heresy, establishing Dominicans as inquisitors first in Germany with *Ille humani generic* (1231).

The first permanent tribunal of inquisition functioned in Occitania in 1233 or 1234. In 1233 Gregory IX ordered friars sent to the archdioceses of Bourges, Bordeaux, Narbonne, and Auch to aid the bishops there in their fight against heresy. Accounts for inquisitorial proceedings in Toulouse and Albi during this period have survived. Local protests against the inquisitors began shortly thereafter, and the townspeople of Narbonne reacted violently during the years 1234 to 1237. Dominicans were expelled from Toulouse in 1235, but the people of the city continued to suffer persecution from 1237 to early 1238. Occitan nobles defied the French twice more, in 1240 and 1242, but were unsuccessful in both attempts. Meanwhile the inquisitors renewed their activities at various sites with fierce determination from 1241 onward. Acts of resistance to the inquisitors continued, and some were murdered at Avignonet in 1242. But the last strongholds of Cathar sympathizers were soon to fall: Montségur in 1244 and Quéribus in 1255.

Under Innocent IV's papacy (1243–1254), earlier procedures of inquisition were melded into the formalized office, the "inquisitor of heretical depravity." Pope Alexander IV granted inquisitors broader powers in 1256. Although heresy was waning, the inquisitorial commissions continued, examining earlier proceedings and opening posthumous investigations. The inquisition found new interrogants when a revival of Catharism took place in Occitania during the early four-teenth century, after the return from Italy of a Cathar preacher named Pierre Authié. Bernard Gui, a Dominican, was appointed inquisitor in Toulouse from 1307 to 1324. Jacques Fournier, a Cistercian who would become Pope Benedict XII (1334–1342) residing in Avignon, served as inquisitor from 1318 to 1325, and he left extensive registers recording interrogations. The year 1321 marked the burning of the last known Cathar perfect, William Bélibaste, in the town of Villerouge-Termenès.

However, medieval dissidence regained force during the fourteenth and fifteenth centuries. Some groups, such as the Lollards, claimed the right of all Christians to participate in the apostolic life. Others, like the Free Spirit heresy, rejected the hierarchical structure and domination of the Roman church. The Lollards, like the Cathars, rejected images; furthermore, they saw the propagation of the faith as the responsibility of all believers, as did the Hussites in fifteenth-century Bohemia.

Sixteenth-century reformers challenged some of the same issues argued by medieval dissident groups, notably the role of sacraments; the role of the saints and the dead; the role of and responsibility for evangelism; and issues of lay and clerical morality. During the Reformation, churches that held views espoused by some medieval dissidents, including the Cathars, were established, but not without considerable bloodshed.

SEE ALSO Crusades; Religion

BIBLIOGRAPHY

Arnold, John H. (2001). *Inquisition and Power: Catharism and the Confessing Subject in Medieval Languedoc*. Philadelphia: University of Pennsylvania Press.

Bernard of Clairvaux. *On the Song of Songs III* (1979), trans. K. Walsh and I. M. Edmonds. Kalamazoo, Mich.: Cistercian Publications.

Biller, Peter, and Anne Hudson, eds. (1994). *Heresy and Literacy, 1000–1530*. Cambridge: Cambridge University Press.

Cheyette, Fredric L. (2001). *Ermengard of Narbonne and the World of the Troubadours*. Ithaca, N.Y.: Cornell University Press.

Given, James Buchanan (1997). *Inquisition and Medieval Society: Power, Discipline, and Resistance in Languedoc*. Ithaca, N.Y.: Cornell University Press.

Kienzle, Beverly Mayne (2001). *Cistercians, Heresy and Crusade (1145–1229): Preaching in the Lord's Vineyard*. Woodbridge, U.K.: Boydell and Brewer.

Lambert, Malcolm D. (1998). *Cathars*. Oxford, U.K.: Oxford University Press.

Lansing, Carol (1998). *Power and Purity: Cathar Heresy in Medieval Italy*. Oxford, U.K.: Oxford University Press.

Moore, Robert I. (1987). *The Formation of a Persecuting Society. Power and Deviance in Western Europe, 950–1250.* Oxford, U.K.: Blackwell.

Moore, Robert I. (1994). *The Origins of European Dissent.* Toronto: University of Toronto Press.

Pegg, Mark Gregory (2001). *The Corruption of Angels: The Great Inquisition of 1245–1246.* Princeton, N.J.: Princeton University Press.

Wakefield, Walter L., and Austin P. Evans, eds. (1991) *Heresies of the High Middle Ages. Selected Sources Translated and Annotated.* 2nd edition. New York: Columbia University Press.

Beverly Mayne Kienzle

Catholic Church

Extreme controversy surrounds any discussion of the Catholic Church's role in genocide and crimes against humanity. Several issues need to be highlighted in seeking to unravel this controversy. First is the allegation that the Church was directly responsible for the drive toward colonialism in issuing papal bulls that commanded states such as Portugal to spread Catholicism. One might argue that these declarations led European nation-states to believe that it was their right to acquire territories abroad. The fact that crimes against humanity were committed during colonial conquest is uncontested. A second criticism often leveled against the Church is that it has failed in its moral duty to condemn or guide leaders and populations in curbing genocidal tendencies. Such an argument claims that the Church, by virtue of its proclaimed aim of spiritual guidance, ought to have played a more significant role in the prevention of crimes against humanity and genocide. The third and fiercest criticism of the Church, however, is that it has furthered genocidal tendencies. This remains the harshest criticism and goes beyond moral arguments to an examination of evidence suggesting that elements of the Church have colluded with forces perpetrating crimes against humanity and genocide.

The Papal Bulls

Many processes concurrent with colonization can be attributed to the Church and traced to a series of edicts issued by the Pope. These edicts, referred to as "bulls," were commands or grants the Church gave to its followers. One of the more well-known bulls was delivered by Pope Alexander III to the King of Portugal on May 21, 1179. In this edict the Pope declared:

> All the regions which you will have rescued from the hands of the Saracens, and where other neighboring Christian princes could not acquire any legal rights, are conceded by us to your Excellency (Consilia, 1547, p. 137).

As Bartolus points out in his treatise, although the papal bulls did not directly bestow territories on princes, they "legalized, recognized [and] sanctioned ex post facto territorial integrity which already existed in fact, or they gave assent, and thereby legal sanction *ex ante* to an intended occupancy, to a condition anticipated in the future" (p. 137).

Thus, it might be argued with some force of authority that an examination of the role of the Catholic Church within the context of genocide and crimes against humanity ought to take into account the Church's impact during the period of colonization, when European powers competed against each other for the pursuit of Christianity, civilization, and commerce. Again, the responsibility attributed to the Church may be characterized as direct and indirect: direct responsibility for the actions of people it directly commanded to pursue such ends, as in the case of the papal bulls, and indirect responsibility for its failure to condemn the immoral actions of others, including Church members, and its attempts to justify its own doctrine. Within this rubric the missionary work legitimized by the Catholic Church also needs to be assessed.

The Church and the Jews

The most significant issue in discussing the Church within the context of genocide concerns its role prior to and during the Holocaust. Once again, an analysis of the Church's role differentiates between acts of commission and acts of omission in the condemnation of activities directed toward the minority Jewish population. In many respects the tenuous relationship that existed between the Catholic Church and Jewish minorities who lived in various parts of Europe in the 1930s dated back to much earlier times. Many suggest it was the Church that in previous centuries had instigated, or at any rate fanned the flames of, the anti-Semitism which was to take such a high toll on the Jewish population in later years.

In terms of acts of commission, an argument may be made that anti-Semitism, to an extent, is linked to the teachings of the Catholic Church, one being the assignment of blame for the death of Jesus to the Jews. The ghettoization of the Jewish community all across Europe in the 1930s and 1940s can in some part be ascribed to the fervor with which Jewish lifestyles and beliefs were condemned by the Church. This is captured in the sentiments expressed by the Third Lateran Council (a gathering of 302 bishops under the aegis of the Pope to restore ecclesiastical discipline) in 1179—the same year that Pope Alexander III delivered his fa-

Heretics being burned at the stake, by order of Catholic Church authorities, in Piazza della Signoria, Florence, around 1400. Painting (artist unknown) from the Museo Firenze com'era.[DAVID LEES/CORBIS]

mous edict to the King of Portugal. The Fourth Lateran Council in 1215 went a step further in passing anti-Jewish decrees that included, among a host of other measures, the requirement for Jews to wear special badges clearly identifying them in the general population. The Church also encouraged monarchs to expel Jews from their states—a notable example being King Ferdinand and Queen Isabella's decision to expel Jews from Spain in 1492. In places such as Venice, the Church prevailed on city authorities to segregate Jews and prevent them from living among Christians. Although Venice did not undertake such measures to segregate its Jewish population until 1516, Jews at a much earlier period in the city's history regularly faced the wrath of Catholic clergy who actively advocated their removal and exclusion, especially during the Easter season.

Thus in terms of the Holocaust, the Church among other parties bears some moral responsibility for stoking anti-Semitism throughout European history, or at the very least, for failing to condemn such dangerous levels of antagonism on moral and spiritual grounds.

Much has been written about the Church and its role during the Holocaust. Great emphasis has been placed on the work of Pope Pius XII: described by many as a leading advocate of Jewish rights, and by others as having done too little during the Holocaust. A brief examination of this pontiff's views and actions casts significant light on the role of the Church during World War II.

Pope Pius XII

Many view Pope Pius XII (born Eugenio Pacelli) as a tireless defender of Jewish independence in the face of

encyclopedia of GENOCIDE *and* CRIMES AGAINST HUMANITY

the Nazi onslaught. He created the Pontifical Aid Commission whose mandate was the provision of relief to the victims of World War II on both sides. He is also believed to have opened the Holy See to Jewish refugees during the Nazi occupation of Rome in September 1943. Some estimate that Pius XII helped save as many as 1.5 million refugees, including Jews, by granting them Vatican citizenship. Many maintain that it was Pius XII who was responsible for organizing the network of priests who spirited Jews to safe havens at the height of the Nazi attack on this group. In addition, Jewish relief agencies who made large donations to the Catholic Church at the end of the war have formally acknowledged the pontiff's humanitarian role. There has also been official recognition of Pius XII's work: The Israeli government issued the "Righteous Gentile" award to him and, upon his death, Golda Meir (then Israeli ambassador) delivered a moving eulogy to the United Nations (UN) General Assembly.

Nevertheless, Pope Pius XII has also been criticized for failing to prevent genocide during World War II. Many contend that as the spiritual leader of the Catholic Church during this tumultuous period, he had a moral obligation to adopt strong public positions and explicitly condemn the events unfolding in Europe. Critics argue that such public statements would have unhinged support for the Nazis among Germany's large and influential Catholic population; in this sense the pontiff might have undermined the Nazi campaign for the genocide of the Jews. Two defenses are often proffered to explain the lack of a public statement by the Vatican during the Holocaust. The first suggests that the pontiff was unaware of the scale of the tragedy occurring; he believed the incidents of violence against Jews to be sporadic, rather than part of a deliberate state policy aimed at the organized annihilation of an ethnic and religious group. Historical information gathered in the later part of the twentieth century suggests that Pius XII was not only aware of the details of several horrific events, he was directly petitioned by several individuals and groups that implored him to intervene and make a public statement condemning the atrocities.

Notable among the direct pleas made to Pope Pius XII were those of Rabbi Isaac Herzog (chief rabbi of Palestine) in 1940, Theodor Innitzer (cardinal of Vienna) in 1941, Harold Tittman (assistant chief of the U.S. delegation to the Vatican) in 1941, Andrej Septyckyj (metropolitan of Ukraine) in 1942, Myron Taylor (U.S. representative to the Vatican) in 1942, and Wladislaw Raczkiewicz (president of the Polish government in exile) in 1943. On each occasion the request was either ignored or rebuffed, and on some occasions even the facts presented were disputed as lacking in evidence. In his 1942 Christmas Eve radio broadcast the pontiff acknowledged the "hundreds of thousands who through no fault of their own, and solely because of their nation or race, have been condemned to death or progressive extinction," but made no direct reference to the plight of Europe's Jews.

A second defense attributes Pope Pius XII's failure to openly condemn the genocide to the Catholic Church's perceived position of neutrality. Proponents of this argument suggest that any statement by the Church on the atrocities committed against the Jews might have compromised it, in the eyes of the international diplomatic community as well as its own followers, because the work of the Church was above that of governments. However, clear evidence of the Church's condemnation of other atrocities, notably those perpetrated by the former Soviet Union, exists, thereby suggesting that the Church did occasionally find it appropriate to make such statements.

Admissions of Culpability

The question of relations between Jews and the Catholic Church was the focus of much discussion in the closing years of the twentieth century. In seeking a reconciliation, the International Catholic-Jewish Historical Commission (ICJHC) was appointed in 2000, respectively, by the Holy See's commission for religious relations with the Jews and the International Jewish Committee for Interreligious Consultations (IJCIC). Its members (three Jewish and three Catholic scholars) undertook the study of Vatican archives, with a view toward understanding the true nature of the Church's relations with Jews and ways in which a reconciliation might be reached.

The commission's report entitled "The Vatican and the Holocaust" was intended to be an authoritative examination of that issue vis-à-vis general relations between the two religions, as well as an in-depth study of the Church's alleged complicity in the events of the genocide perpetrated during World War II.

One of the key findings of the panel's research was that Pope Pius XII was indeed fully aware of the extent and scale of Nazi atrocities during World War II. It is within this context that the Vatican's failure to respond to the situation and assume a significant public role is particularly troubling. The report also raises doubts about whether or not the Church did all it could to facilitate Jewish emigration to Palestine and South America.

The same scholars, in addition, examined the Church's claim of neutrality as a justification for its lack of condemnation. Drawing on evidence recently declassified by the U.S. National Archives, they suggested that within the context of other atrocities, notably those perpetrated by the Red Army against the German population, the Church adopted a strident tone of opposition, roundly condemning these events. This revealed that within the context of the Holocaust, the Church had selectively applied the notion of neutrality.

The same commission also requested access to Vatican archives to ascertain culpability for its role in the Holocaust. The request was denied, with the Vatican only willing to release documents prior to 1923, and as a result, the work of the ICJHC came to an end.

Road to Reconciliation

The attempt at reconciliation between the Catholic Church and Jewish communities has also taken other forms. In 1965 the Vatican issued a papal decree entitled Declaration on the Relation of the Church to Non-Christian Religions (*Nostra Aetate*). Proclaimed by Pope Paul VI on October 28, 1965, this declaration acknowledged the division that had existed between the Catholic Church and the Jewish community throughout history:

> True, the Jewish authorities and those who followed their lead pressed for the death of Christ; still, what happened in His passion cannot be charged against all the Jews, without distinction, then alive, nor against the Jews of today. Although the Church is the new people of God, the Jews should not be presented as rejected or accursed by God, as if this followed from the Holy Scriptures.

> Furthermore, in rejecting every persecution against any man, the Church, mindful of the patrimony it shares with the Jews and moved not by political reasons but by the Gospel's spiritual love, decries hatred, persecutions, displays of anti-Semitism, directed against Jews at any time and by anyone.

> Besides, as the Church has always held, Christ underwent His passion and death freely, because of the sins of men and out of infinite love, in order that all may reach salvation.

An effort was also made to mend relations between the Church and Jewish communities in 1974 when a Committee for Religious Relations with the Jews was established to formulate guidelines on religious relations with the Jews by December 1 of that same year. The declaration addressed the need for dialogue and an acknowledgment of the commonalities that exist between both communities in terms of liturgy, teaching, and education. It concluded by stressing the need for joint social action.

Similar attempts to examine relations between Jews and the Church were also conducted in 1982,

1996, and 1999, but rather than exploring the Church's culpability in genocide, they merely remain content to emphasize the importance of good relations in the future. Implicit in this is a focus on "ecumenical questions" that have formed the basis of the Church's view of Jews throughout history.

Rwanda

At the dawn of the twenty-first century the Catholic Church once more came to the fore within the context of genocide, that which took place in Rwanda. In determining the culpability of various parties in the Rwandan genocide, the International Criminal Tribunal for Rwanda (ICTR) has drawn attention to various horrific episodes meriting close examination. Allegations have been made suggesting that several members of the Catholic clergy incited hatred against the Tutsi and moderate Hutu. This claim is significant in that as many as 62 percent of the Rwandan population is Catholic, and the country's former president, the late Juvenal Habyarimana, himself enjoyed the patronage and support of the Catholic Church. The role of the Church in this particular genocide has not been fully determined.

The main allegation concerning the Church is that it switched its allegiance from the Tutsi elite to the creation of a Hutu-led revolution, thereby assisting in Habyarimana's subsequent rise to power in a majority Hutu state. In terms of the actual genocide, critics once again hold the Church directly responsible for inciting hatred, sheltering perpetrators, and failing to protect those who sought refuge within its walls. There are also those who believe that, as the spiritual leader of the majority population in Rwanda, the Church is morally responsible for failing to take all available measures to end the killing.

The discussion on remedies for atrocities has also reached international courtrooms, with the Church through its clergy being directly implicated. Belgium, in keeping with its stance on universal jurisdiction in cases concerning grave breaches of human rights, has sought to prosecute priests and nuns alleged to have played a significant role in the events leading up to the genocide. It handed down sentences of fifteen and twelve years to two nuns who were convicted for their involvement in the slaughter of approximately five thousand civilians who had sought refuge in their monastery at Sovu in Rwanda. Witnesses testified that the two nuns had directed the death squads to the civilians' place of refuge; some even stated that the nuns had assisted in the pouring of petroleum in a bid to burn down the monastery with civilians still inside.

Conclusion

When addressing the issue of the Catholic Church's responsibility for the perpetration of genocide and crimes against humanity, there are several subissues that need to be taken into account. Although one might insist that the Church has a particular moral responsibility to condemn genocide and crimes against humanity, and take all measures necessary to prevent and terminate such acts, this moral responsibility is not necessarily easily fulfilled. In addition, it might be argued that the Church did seek to protect thousands of Jews during the Holocaust: a fact recognized in different settings. Insisting that the Church adopt a particular strategy of public condemnation in the face of atrocities, rather than working behind the scenes for individual victims and families, would be unfair.

Defending other claims of direct action by the Church in the instigation and promotion of discrimination that later led to genocide is much less tenable. Thus, the policies of the Lateran Council and the sentiment expressed in the papal bulls need to be acknowledged for what they were: the legitimization of one particular religion over others. In this quest the rights of non-Catholics were ignored and considered to be of less value to the grand plan of proselytization. It can be further argued that the real responsibility of the Catholic Church in genocide and crimes against humanity may be traced to this aspect of its history, whether within the context of the Crusades, the quest for colonization, the incitement of discrimination, or the failure to condemn violations against non-Catholic communities.

Although some attempts at rapprochement and acceptance of culpability have been made within the context of the Church's role in modern-day episodes of genocide and grave breaches of human rights, the issue of violations perpetrated through colonialism remains neglected. This is especially true when evaluating the Church's missionary work, which sought to "civilize" communities far removed from European civilization. In this bid the Church has altered the fabric of many societies irrevocably, and while some might argue that this is a trend with positive aspects, from a human rights point of view this remains problematic because it gives greater credence to one particular religious belief over others; something at the very heart of much discrimination and upheaval in human history. Indeed, if the values of equality that are so fundamental to the human rights movement are to be more than mere lip service, then it is imperative that the Church's actions-be examined critically.

SEE ALSO Amazon Region; Christians, Roman Persecution of; Crusades; Ghetto; Pius XII, Pope; Religious Groups

BIBLIOGRAPHY

Carroll, J. (2001). *Constantine's Sword: The Church and the Jews—A History*. Boston: Houghton Mifflin.

Gourevitch, P. (1998). *We Wish to Inform You That Tomorrow We Will Be Killed with Our Families: Stories from Rwanda*. New York: Farrar, Straus, Giroux.

"Influence of the Roman Catholic Church in the Acquittal of Rwandan Bishop Debated" (2000). *Christianity Today*, June 19.

Kertzer, D. I. (2001). *The Pope against the Jews: The Vatican's Role in the Rise of Modern Anti-Semitism*. New York: Knopf.

Lapomarda, V. A. (1989). *The Jesuits and the Third Reich*. Lewiston, N.Y.: Edwin Mellen Press.

Lehmann, L. H. (1946). *Vatican Policy in the Second World War*. New York: Agora Press.

Manhattan, A. (1950). *The Catholic Church Against the Twentieth Century*. London: Watts.

Melvern, L. (2000). *A People Betrayed: The Role of the West in Rwanda's Genocide*. London: Zed Books.

Munro, D. C. (1927). "War & History." *The American Historical Review* 32:219–231.

Phayer, M. (1998). "Pope Pius XII, the Holocaust, and the Holy War." *Holocaust and Genocide Studies* 12:233–256.

Ramati, A. (1978). *While the Pope Kept Silent*. London: George Allen & Unwin.

Schwartz, S. B. (1991). "The Voyage of the Vassals: Royal Power, Noble Obligations, and Merchant Capital Before the Portuguese Restoration of Independence, 1624–1640." *The American Historical Review* 96:735–762.

Stehlin, S. A. (1983). *Weimar and the Vatican: 1919–1933*. Princeton, N.J.: Princeton University Press.

Straus, B. R. (1987). *The Catholic Church*. New York: Hippocrene Books.

Von der Heydte, F. A. F. (1935). "Discovery, Symbolic Annexation and Virtual Effectiveness in International Law." *American Journal of International Law* 29:448–471.

Zuccotti, S. (2001). *Under His Very Windows: The Vatican and the Holocaust in Italy*. New Haven, Conn.: Yale University Press.

Joshua Castellino

Chechens

Chechnya is a small mountainous region in the Russian Federation. Bordered by Georgia to the south and the Russian constituent republics of Ingushetia and Dagestan to the east and west, the Connecticut-sized enclave straddles the crossroads between Europe, the Middle

East, and Central Asia. Its indigenous people, known as Chechens, are an ethnically distinct national group with a language and culture predating the formation of the Russia state. Worldwide in the early 2000s, Chechens numbered around 1 million.

Although Chechens are Sunni Muslims, the practice of Islam in Chechnya is generally moderate and strongly influenced by Sufi teachings and various mystical orders. Equally important is the *adat*, a body of indigenous, pre-Islamic law resting on principles of family honor, deference to elders, and personal hospitality. While kinship, clan, and religious structures are strongly patriarchal, Chechen women nonetheless possess full social and political equality.

Prior to the Russian colonial, Chechnya was an independent nation but not a centralized state. Villages were largely autonomous, linked through mutual defense obligations and larger, multi-clan confederations. In 1858, however, Moscow consolidated its control of the Chechen lowlands and the neighboring regions of Ingushetia and Dagestan, eventually forcing the highland clans to capitulate after forty-six years of bloody conflict. Thousands of refugees left the Caucasus and resettled in Jordan and Turkey, where Chechen communities remain.

A History of Conflict

In 1918 Chechens and other peoples in the Northern Caucasus declared independence following the Bolshevik Revolution. Within four years, however, the Red Army had once again occupied the territory and began to impose communist rule. In 1944 Soviet leader Joseph Stalin departed the entire Chechen nation en masse to Kazakhstan and Siberia, killing at least one-quarter and as much as one-half of the entire population in transit. Though politically rehabilitated in 1956 and resettled in 1957, Chechens remained objects of both official and unofficial discrimination under both Soviet and post-Soviet governments.

In 1991 communist authorities in Chechnya supported the attempted military coup against Soviet President Mikhail Gorbachev. As the Soviet Union fell, Chechens deposed their hard-line leadership and declared independence. The following year, the newly formed Chechen Republic of Ichkeria (ChRI) adopted a constitution defining it as a secular democracy. In 1994 Russian troops invaded Chechnya to quash the independence movement. Some 100,000 people—most of them civilians—died before the conclusion of a ceasefire in the 1996 Khasavyurt Accords.

In August 1999, guerrillas led by Chechen warlord Shamyl Basayev launched a failed raid into neighboring Dagestan. Shortly thereafter, a string of unexplained

bombings rocked apartments in Moscow and Volgodonsk, killing 300 civilians. Though the ChRI condemned Basayev's actions, Prime Minister Vladimir Putin of Russia swiftly launched a second military campaign to end Chechnya's drive for independence.

The human cost of the Russian offensive proved severe. Between October 1999 and February 2000, no less than 200,000 Chechen noncombatants were displaced by aerial and artillery bombardment. Federal Army and Interior Ministry (MVD) troops failed to provide safe passage for many, ignoring key provisions of the 1949 Geneva Conventions. Thousands more were detained in filtration camps, where the MVD and the Federal Security Service (FSB) culled alleged terrorists from the general population.

Violations of basic norms governing warfare further exacerbated these derogations from international humanitarian law. Putin's decision to use SS-1 SCUD and SS-21 SCARAB rockets during the siege of Grozny, Chechnya's capitol, marked the first and only time (as of 2004) a modern head of state has used ballistic missiles against his own population. The strikes razed homes, schools, and hospitals, burying thousands of noncombatants seeking shelter below ground.

The Kremlin's offensive met with international condemnation. In February 2000, the U.S. Senate unanimously declared that "the people of Chechnya [were] exercising their legitimate right of self-defense" and demanded a negotiated settlement under the auspices of the Organization for Security and Cooperation in Europe (OSCE). Shortly thereafter, the Parliamentary Assembly of the Council of Europe (PACE) suspended the voting rights of its Russian delegation, citing egregious violations of the 1954 European Convention on Human Rights.

The diligent documentation of crimes against humanity and looming threat of genocide in Chechnya produced little more than rhetoric, however. Efforts by PACE and OSCE to monitor abuses met with hostility in Moscow and generated little support among Western governments. As the Russian offensive gradually became an armed occupation, the relevance of international institutions and enforcement of international conventions grew politically ambiguous.

Humanitarian Dimensions

Apart from ad hoc Russian consultative arrangements with PACE and the European Parliament, there were currently not any international or intra-governmental mechanisms for monitoring war crimes. With ethnic Chechens facing systematic discrimination within the Russian judicial system, many turned to civil suits before the European Court of Human Rights (ECHR) in

Grozny, Chechnya, after its destruction by Soviet bombing, April 1995. Here, two of the capital's survivors begin the grim task of rebuilding. [TEUN VOETEN]

order to hold Russian army and MVD troops accountable.

Left unchecked, the second Russo-Chechen conflict spawned a demographic crisis comparable, in relative terms, to the Balkan wars. Figures compiled by the U.S. Department of State estimate that at least 80,000 Chechens have died since 1999. Total deaths, including those from the first war, are believed to be around 180,000, though figures compiled by both Russian and international human rights monitors suggest that this number may be closer to 250,000.

Many of the survivors have been driven from their homes. The United Nations High Commissioner for Refugees (UNHCR) reports that approximately 350,000 Chechens were displaced between 1999 and 2002. Of that number, some 150,000 were believed to be sheltering in Ingushetia, with another 30,000 seeking refuge in regions throughout the Russian Federation. Thousands more joined growing diaspora communities in Central Asia, Europe, and North America. All told, half of Chechnya's pre-1989 population was either dead or displaced.

Those remaining in Chechnya are subject to arbitrary detention, beatings, lootings, and torture. Since the start of the war, more than 2,750 Chechen noncombatants have disappeared in Russian cleansing operations. Between 2003 and 2003, human rights organizations discovered some 49 mass burial sites, most near Russian military installations. Documents released in April 2003 by Kremlin-backed Chechen authorities revealed an average of 109 extrajudicial executions by Russian forces each month. Chechnya's per capita murder rate exceeds that recorded for the entire Soviet Union at the height of Stalin's purges.

This human calamity is compounded by an environmental and epidemiological catastrophe. In 2003 the Russian Health Ministry designated one-third of Chechnya as a "zone of ecological disaster" and another 40 percent as a "zone of extreme environmental distress." In 2003 Chechen infant mortality rates were nearly twice as high as those for Russians and almost four times greater than in the United States; and three percent of the Chechen population suffered from tuberculosis—an epidemic comparable to that present in the Russian penal system.

Yet despite documentation of widespread, systematic crimes against humanity, governments and nongovernmental organizations remain reluctant to frame the crisis in Chechnya using the rubric of genocide. Foremost among the relevant considerations is the fact that Chechen combatants have also committed egregious violations of international humanitarian law, though not on the scale perpetrated by their Russian counterparts. Those violations include abductions and extrajudicial executions of Russian loyalists, as well as the 2002 seizure of the Dubrovka Theater in Moscow by gunmen with ties to Chechen organized crime.

Also disturbing is the increasing frequency and intensity of suicide bombings by irregular elements along the radical fringe of Chechen society. Chief among them were the leveling of the pro-Moscow Chechen administration headquarters in December 2002 and the subsequent attacks on the Prokhladny Air Base in North Ossetia in 2003. Attacks against nonmilitary targets are also evident, with Chechen widows launching a series of reprisal bombings in Moscow during the summer and fall of 2003. Though these acts bore a striking similarity to the suicide campaigns by women in the Sri Lankan civil war, the means employed ultimately conflated the Russo-Chechen conflict with the global war on terrorism.

Further complicating efforts to discern ethnic or sectarian motives for the violence is the role of the numerically small but politically significant pro-Kremlin Chechen militia. Continued economic, political, and military cooperation between this armed faction and Russian forces belies suggestions that genocide, at least in the legal sense, is a motivating factor in the conflict. As such, the Russo-Chechen war is best understood as a postcolonial war, rather than an explicitly genocidal crisis.

SEE ALSO Cossacks; Union of Soviet Socialist Republics

BIBLIOGRAPHY

Dunlop, John (2002). *Chechnya Weekly* 3(8):1–4.

Estemirova, Natalya (2003). "Chechnya Stricken by TB." Caucasus Reporting Service. London: Institute for War and Peace Reporting.

Evangelista, Matthew (2002). *The Chechen War: Anti-Terrorist Operation or Human Rights Disaster?* Washington, D.C.: Woodrow Wilson International Center for Scholars.

Human Rights Watch (1998). *Russia/Chechnya: A Legacy of Abuse.* New York: Author.

Human Rights Watch (2001). *Russia/Chechnya: Burying the Evidence: The Botched Investigation into a Mass Grave in Chechnya.* New York: Author.

President Maskhadov Issues an Order Defining the Rules of Military Conduct of the Chechen Armed Forces (2003). Grozny, Russia: Chechen Ministry of Foreign Affairs.

"Testimony of Ambassador Steven Pifer" (2002). In *Developments in the Chechen Conflict.* Washington, D.C.: U.S. Commission on Security and Cooperation in Europe.

United Nations Children's Fund (2003). *The Official Summary of the State of the World's Children 2003.* Geneva: United Nations.

United Nations High Commissioner for Refugees (2002). *Paper on Asylum Seekers from the Russian Federation in the Context of the Situation in Chechnya.* Geneva: United Nations.

U.S. Congress, Commission on Security and Cooperation in Europe (2003). *The Critical Human Rights and Humanitarian Situation in Chechnya.* Washington, D.C.: Commission on Security and Cooperation in Europe.

U.S. Department of State (1999). *Ethnic Cleansing in Kosovo: An Accounting.* Washington, D.C.: Author.

Vazayeva, Asiyat (2003). *The Mental Scars of Chechnya's Children.* London: Institute for War and Peace Reporting.

Christopher Swift

Cherokees see Indigenous Peoples; Native Americans; Trail of Tears.

Cheyenne

The *Tse-tsehese-staestse* (the people) are an Algonquian-speaking tribe known to outsiders as the *Cheyenne*—a word possibly derived from their Sioux neighbors, meaning "people of a different language." The Cheyenne originally lived in permanent farming villages around the Great Lakes in Minnesota. Over the next two hundred years, the Cheyenne migrated one thousand miles westward to the Black Hills area, moving their camps, and adapting to a life dependent on the horse and buffalo. It was during this journey that Sweet Medicine, the Cheyenne prophet, appeared, bringing one of the two sacred covenants, their teachings, and their protection to his people. The Cheyenne developed a well-defined system of kinship, organized into bands and military societies, with a council of forty-four chiefs handling peace and trade relations.

The Cheyenne met their first Europeans in 1680 when visiting the French Fort Crevecoeur on the Illinois River. For decades they retained friendly, if distant, relations with the white settlers. The discovery of gold in Colorado in 1858 and the subsequent Sand Creek Massacre significantly altered this relationship. In 1864 Colonel John Chivington, a former Methodist minister with political aspirations, attacked Chief Black

Kettle's camp of five hundred Cheyenne at Sand Creek. Seeking peace with the white man, Black Kettle had surrendered under a promise of protection from Colorado's governor, John Evans. With Chivington reportedly stating, "I have come to kill Indians and believe it is right and honorable to use any means under God's heaven to kill Indians" (Brown, 1970, p. 86), seven hundred U.S. soldiers under his command brutally killed and mutilated nearly two hundred Cheyenne, mostly women and children. Four years later Lieutenant Colonel George Custer attacked Black Kettle's camp on the Washita River, killing the chief and sixty others, mostly women and children who, as before, had surrendered to the military before being slaughtered. In 1876 the Cheyenne, then fighting with the Sioux, defeated Custer at the Battle of the Little Big Horn. A year later several Northern Cheyenne bands surrendered. As retribution, the government sent them to Oklahoma Indian Territory, where they faced confinement and starvation. In January 1879, after the Cheyenne had mounted an unsuccessful escape attempt, the U.S. military brutally murdered their much-respected leader, Dull Knife, and seventy-three other men, women, and children at Fort Robinson.

Some of the Northern Cheyenne nevertheless managed to return to Montana, where, with other tribal members, they settled on a reservation established by executive order in 1884. In the early twenty-first century 6,500 members of the Northern Cheyenne Tribe control a 445,000-acre reservation in southeastern Montana that contains one of the largest coal deposits in the United States. Remembering the words of Sweet Medicine, who instructed them to take care of *Escehenan* (Mother Earth) above all else, they have, despite high unemployment rates, refused to open their lands to mining. Other bands of Cheyenne, who had traveled southward over the years and became known as the Southern Cheyenne, settled with the Southern Arapahoe on a reservation in Oklahoma. In preparation for Oklahoma's admission to the Union as a state, the federal government dissolved the Oklahoma reservations, allocating the majority of former reservation lands to individual tribe members. As of 2004, a combined Southern Cheyenne and South Arapahoe population of 7,300 reside on approximately 87,000 acres in northwestern Oklahoma.

SEE ALSO Indigenous Peoples; Native Americans; Sand Creek Massacre

BIBLIOGRAPHY

Berthrong, Donald J. (1963). *The Southern Cheyennes.* Norman: University of Oklahoma Press.

Berthrong, Donald J. (1976). *The Cheyenne and Arapaho Ordeal—Reservation and Agency Life in the Indian Territory, 1875–1907.* Norman: University of Oklahoma Press.

Brown, D. (1970). *Bury My Heart at Wounded Knee.* New York: Henry Holt.

Grinnell, George B. (1972). *The Cheyenne Indians: History and Society*, Vol. I. Lincoln: University of Nebraska Press.

Moore, John H. (1987). *The Cheyenne Nation—A Social and Demographic History.* Lincoln: University of Nebraska Press.

Moore, John H. (1996). *The Cheyenne.* Cambridge, Mass.: Blackwell Publishers.

Powell, Peter (1979). *People of the Sacred Mountain.* New York: Harper & Row.

Powell, Peter (1998). *Sweet Medicine.* Norman: University of Oklahoma Press.

Stands in Timber, John (1967). *Cheyenne Memories.* Lincoln: University of Nebraska Press.

Sharon O'Brien

Children

The rights of the child are human rights. What makes them so special, requiring separate legal treatment, is their link with the social category "childhood." Childhood is a human construct, not a natural phenomenon; its meaning has varied in different historical periods and social environments. An understanding of childhood is necessarily associated with culture, tradition, and social structure. For that reason, children are too often perceived as small adults; once physically ready, they engage in different life activities. That has at times included hard labor, marriages, armed conflict, and other activities now deemed only appropriate to adulthood. However, despite worldwide legal protection, in many places around the world children still engage in all sorts of such harmful activities and situations. Probably the worst of all is a situation of armed conflict.

There is great concern about and awareness of the vulnerability of children, particularly in special circumstances such as armed conflict. So as to be clear in mandating protection, international law, and primarily the 1989 Convention on the Rights of the Child, established an age limit and defined a child as a human being below the age of eighteen. This age limit also applies to situations where children must confront genocide and crimes against humanity. Therefore, the 2000 Optional Protocol to the Convention on the Rights of the Child on the Involvement of Children in Armed Conflicts forbids recruitment and participation of children younger than eighteen years in any armed conflicts. Only strict respect of those provisions could prevent children becoming either victims or perpetrators of crimes against humanity or genocide.

Bearing automatic weapons, two female adolescent "soldiers" await their perceived enemies. Ganta, Liberia, June 23, 2003. [TEUN VOETEN]

Children as Victims

Throughout history children have been victims of genocide and crimes against humanity. Such criminal acts have been committed against children in both times of peace and armed conflict. In the past, wars were officially announced and waged by armies, far away from the civilian population, on the battlefields. Civilians, including children, were victims of wars, but on a lesser scale than in the twentieth century, when the situation dramatically changed. In World War II, 47 percent of the victims were civilians, including children (compared to 5% in World War I). Children perished as a result of not only aerial bombardment, but also genocidal actions. They were not separated from adults nor spared in the Nazi concentration camps.

After World War II approximately 150 armed conflicts had occurred worldwide by 2004. The previous strict division between civilians and armed forces became weaker, and so did the division between children and adults. In the last two decades of the twentieth century such a development produced a period that was probably the most detrimental of all to the lives of children across the globe. The deaths of an estimated 1.5 million children in the 1980s were directly war-related. Within the timeframe of civil wars in Mozambique, Cambodia, Sierra Leone, the former Yugoslavia, Rwanda, El Salvador, Guatemala, the Middle East, and other locales, several million children died as a direct consequence of atrocities. Relentless warlords and their combatants, more frequently operating outside of the constraints of regular army forces, do not respect the established rules of conduct concerning civilian populations and children; they often commit genocide and crimes against humanity, organizing the campaigns and carrying out the orders to do so.

Being that such crimes should not be forgotten nor go unpunished, the United Nations (UN) established the International Criminal Tribunal for the Former Yugoslavia (ICTY) in 1993 and the International Criminal Tribunal for Rwanda (ICTR) in 1994, with the task of prosecuting, trying, and punishing individuals who are found guilty of committing genocide or crimes against humanity. In these two countries two terrible wars were waged, conflicts that left many children dead, displaced, abandoned, parentless, wounded, and sick. All who survived bear deep emotional scars.

Energetic prosecutions within both tribunals have resulted in numerous convictions. With regard to the crimes committed, the judgments of both courts have addressed different aspects of crimes against humanity and genocide. Many of them included the charge of atrocities committed against children. At the Rwandan tribunal the most well-known cases that included charges of genocide against children were those of Kayishema and Akayesy. At the tribunal for the former Yugoslavia a general of the army, Krstic, was tried and convicted of genocide, and sentenced to forty-six years in prison. He was found guilty of numerous crimes committed in the small town of Srebrenica in Bosnia and Herzegovina in July 1995. Those crimes included forcibly transferring children from their original place of residence that was considered an element of genocide.

The work of such tribunals, as well as that of national or combined courts (e.g., the Special Court for Sierra Leone), is very important because it deals with individuals who are responsible for genocide and crimes against humanity. By establishing such courts, the international community expresses its commitment to ending the impunity of warlords and criminals. A strong message is delivered to potential war criminals: Genocide and crimes against humanity will not be tolerated and perpetrators will face the consequences of their acts.

Child Soldiers as Perpetrators
As already noted, despite the high level of awareness and means of protection worldwide, children are still perceived as adults in some circumstances. Owing to such attitudes, children, sometimes as early as the age of five, are used as child soldiers. Several sources, including Save the Children UK (report 1989), claim that in the late 1980s children younger than sixteen participated in combat in twenty-five states and territories. In Mozambique, Sierra Leone, Iran, Rwanda, and many other places, children, mostly boys, have been brutally recruited, removed from their families, and forced to participate in all kinds of war activities. In some cases children joined military forces because of the absence of adult family members, and the only means of survival was joining some military group, whether legitimate or not. Child soldiers, usually under force, often perpetrate the most serious atrocities, including the crimes of genocide and those against humanity.

None other but national courts have dealt with children responsible for genocide and crimes against humanity. For example, thousands of children were recruited as soldiers in Rwanda. After the civil war ended, a significant number were arrested for being responsi-

ble, allegedly, for genocide against the moderate Hutu and Tutsi in that country. Since 1995 Rwandan authorities have arrested and detained some five thousand children under inhumane conditions for years without trial. In June 2002 four thousand children were still awaiting trial. A large number of the detainees are accused of having committed genocide. Rwandan cases indicate just how difficult it might be for a state to effectively try perpetrators, particularly when they are children.

The 1996 UN study on the impact of armed conflict on children notes: "The dilemma of dealing with children who are accused of committing acts of genocide illustrates the complexity of balancing culpability, a community's sense of justice and the best interest of the child." The severity of the crime involved, however, provides no justification for suspending or abridging the fundamental rights and legal safeguards accorded to children under the Convention on the Rights of the Child.

Only when the Statute of the International Criminal Court (ICC) was drafted in 1998 was the act of recruiting children as soldiers established as a war crime. That should, in the future, serve as a disincentive to the recruitment of children as soldiers and also prevent their participation in such terrible crimes.

International Law Protecting the Rights of Children in Armed Conflicts
The international legal protection of children facing genocide and crimes against humanity is provided through general provisions that apply to children in the situation of armed conflict. The Geneva Convention of 1949, and the two Additional Protocols of 1977, directly recognized such children as having special needs. The 1948 UN Convention on the Prevention and Punishment of the Crime of Genocide protects children by additionally defining the crime of genocide as the forcible transfer of children from one group to another. The 1989 Convention on the Rights of the Child of 1989 pays special attention to the protection of children in armed conflicts and also the prevention of recruitment of children for direct participation, as child soldiers. The same applies to a regional instrument: the African Charter on the Rights of the Child. The 2000 Optional Protocol to the Convention on the Rights of the Child, addressing the involvement of children in armed conflict, raises the standard of child recruitment by establishing an age limit of eighteen. The 1998 Rome Statute of the ICC characterizes as a war crime the conscription or enlistment of children under the age of fifteen into national armed forces, or their use as active participants in hostilities. The International Labor Organization's

Children, because they were too young to work, were often killed immediately upon arrival at Auschwitz. In this photo taken just after Allied forces liberated the camp on January 27, 1945, a group of survivors, Jewish children, stand behind a barbed wire fence.

(ILO's) 1999 Worst Forms of Child Labor Convention includes in its definition of the worst forms of child labor the forced or compulsory recruitment of children for use in armed conflict.

Besides the protection afforded by such binding international documents, there are numerous declarations, protocols, comments, and reports providing guidance to states in dealing with children in armed conflicts.

Key Roles in Protection

Several mechanisms exist whereby children are protected from such crimes. Some are legal, such as national and international courts. Besides legal actions, the numerous efforts of international organizations in the field can make a difference. The UN, United Nations Children's Fund (UNICEF), United Nations Educational, Scientific, and Cultural Organization (UNESCO), World Health Organization (WHO), United Nations High Commissioner for Refugees (UNHCR), and other intergovernmental organizations work actively to protect children. The International

Committee of the Red Cross (ICRC) orchestrates various sorts of interventions including, among others, the protection of children, visits to prisoners of war, and tracing family members. International nongovernmental organizations (NGOs), such as Medicines sans Frontier, Save the Children, Cooperative for American Relief to Everywhere (CARE), and other organizations, are also active protectors, particularly in the postwar recovery of children who have participated in armed conflicts, including those who were recruited to fight as soldiers, and the prevention of such activities.

SEE ALSO Guatemala; International Criminal Tribunal for Rwanda; International Criminal Tribunal for the Former Yugoslavia; Rwanda; United Nations; Yugoslavia

BIBLIOGRAPHY

Ackerman, John E. (2002). *Practice and Procedure of the International Tribunal for the Former Yugoslavia.* Sarajevo: Müller.

Archard, David (1993). *Children's Rights and Childhood.* London: Routledge.

Freeman, Michael (1995). "Morality of Cultural Pluralism." *The International Journal of Children's Rights* 3:7.

Hitch, Lisa M. (1989). "International Humanitarian Law and the Rights of the Child." *New York Law School Journal of Human Rights* 7(1):118.

Human Rights Watch (2003). "Lasting Wounds: Consequences of Genocide and War on Rwandan Children" *Human Rights Watch* 15(6).

Resler, Everett M., JoAnne Marie Tortorici, Alex Marcelino (1993). *Children in War—A Guide to the Provision in Services.* New York: UNICEF.

United Nations Security Council (2000). *Report of the Secretary-General on the Establishment of a Special Court for Sierra Leone.* UN Document S/2000/915.

Van Beuren, Geraldine (1995). *The International Law on the Rights of the Child.* Dodrecht, Netherlands: Martinus Nijhoff.

Vuckovic Sahovic, Nevena (2000). *The Rights of the Child and International Law.* Belgrade: Yugoslav Child Rights Centre.

Nevena Vuckovic Sahovic

Chile

With a promise to nationalize Chile's copper mines, banks, and largest industries, as well as break up its landed estates, Salvador Allende won less than 37 percent of the vote in a thee-way 1970 presidential race. Although opposed by almost two-thirds of the voters, he was still expected to occupy Chile's White House, the Moneda: Chilean law called for the Congress to select the president when no candidate had won a clear majority. And historically, the legislature always voted for the man who had garnered the most votes. Thus, Allende, leading a leftist coalition, the *Unidad Popular,* would win.

Fearing that Allende might convert Chile into a bastion of Marxism, the vehemently anticommunist U.S. president, Richard M. Nixon, ordered Secretary of State Henry Kissinger, to do something. Kissinger complied: Without informing Edward Korry, the U.S. ambassador to Chile, he encouraged the Central Intelligence Agency (CIA) to prevent Allende's inauguration. One plan called for the United States to bribe the Christian Democratic legislators into voting for Jorge Alessandri, the man who had placed second in the 1970 election. Alessandri had promised that if elected, he would resign, thus allowing the outgoing president, Eduardo Frei, to seek office again. Frei, fearing that Allende's followers might rebel if their candidate did not take office, refused. The CIA then tried another tact: It encouraged a putsch that would begin with the kidnapping of General René Schneider, the commander of the Chilean army. But Korry, noting that the pro-

posed coup's leader, General Roberto Viaux, was too unstable, insisted that Washington scuttle the plan. The CIA did withdraw, but Viaux's men persevered and in their attempt to capture Schneider, they mortally wounded the general. The military plot collapsed and the Christian Democrats voted for Allende, who then became president.

Allende's economic policies proved disastrous. He froze prices while increasing salaries, thus unleashing inflation. When his followers, in contravention of existing laws, seized farm and urban land in addition to factories, both agricultural and industrial productivity plummeted. After the U.S.-owned copper mines were nationalized, without compensation, the United States reduced its economic assistance while trying to prevent Chile from borrowing money from international banks. Allende, however, easily found other nations willing to lend him funds.

By 1973 inflation had reached 1 percent a day. Meanwhile, a series of strikes, as well as the leftist seizures of property and factories, paralyzed the economy. The opposition could do nothing: Allende's party possessed enough congressional seats to prevent his impeachment. Still, the collapse of the economy, a surge in violence, including assassinations, the armed resistance to the military's attempts to disarm worker groups, an abortive naval mutiny supported by an Allende ally, and the threat of creating armed militias convinced the normally apolitical military to rebel on September 11, 1973.

Pinochet Regime

The rebellious armed forces' intelligence services, particularly the army's *Dirección de Inteligencia Nacional* (DINA), arrested and sometimes tortured those whom they suspected of opposing the regime. Approximately 3,000 people, including 132 policemen and servicemen, died during the military's rule: About half of these, 1,205, perished in the last four months of 1973; another 1,216 died between 1974 and 1977. Some of these prisoners died from torture; some were executed. Various individuals fled, although exile, whether self-imposed or not, did not always guarantee safety: DINA agents tracked down and killed the army's former commander, General Carlos Prats, and his wife in Argentina. The government, sometimes in concert with foreign terrorist organizations, pursued others—such as the Christian Democratic politician Bernardo Leighton, whom they shot in Rome. To destroy or intimidate exiled foes, the Chilean authorities launched Operation Condor, under which Chile cooperated with the dictatorial regimes of Brazil, Argentina, Uruguay, and Paraguay to capture, kill, or in some cases repatriate suspected terrorists.

Suspected snipers are guarded by the Chilean army patrol in 1973. [AP/WIDE WORLD PHOTOS]

During the administration of President Jimmy Carter, elected in 1976, the United States ceased lending Chile money as well as providing it with either humanitarian or military assistance. It also pressured the Pinochet regime to become less repressive. In response, Pinochet promised to restore elected and constitutional government to Chile; he even abolished DINA, although he replaced it with another equally sinister organization, the *Centro Nacional de Informaciones* (CNI). In early 1978 he ended the state of siege, replacing it with a state of national emergency; a constitution, which the public supposedly ratified by plebiscite, was promulgated in 1980.

The September 1976 assassination of Orlando Letelier, former ambassador to the United States and a prominent left-wing critic of the Pinochet regime, as well as Ronni Moffit, an American, in Washington, D.C., dramatically altered U.S. policy vis-à-vis Chile. Infuriated by this blatant violation of its sovereignty, the United States ordered an investigation that soon proved Michael Townley, an American living in Santiago, together with Cuban exiles and Chilean army officers had murdered Letelier. Washington demanded that Chile extradite Townley who, receiving a lighter

sentence in return for his cooperation, implicated not only his Cuban accomplices but also explained his participation in the assassination of Prats and the attempted murder of Leighton. Townley and the Cubans would go to jail, but the Pinochet regime refused to extradite the Chilean army officers whom Townley named and an American court indicted. (One of the officers voluntarily came to the United States, where he stood trial and was incarcerated.) In retaliation, Carter reduced the American presence in Chile in addition to opposing loans to Santiago. A Chilean court subsequently sentenced General Manuel Contreras, the head of DINA, to jail. The Chilean government also awarded the families of Letelier and Moffit approximately $2.5 million to settle their wrongful death claims.

The Pinochet regime's economic policies, which produced enormous hardship, and its political repression eventually galvanized the opposition. Led by the Roman Catholic Church and their revived political parties, Chileans demanded that the government hold an election, as stipulated by the 1980 constitution, to determine if Pinochet could succeed himself in office. Aided by a clever public relations campaign, funded in part by U.S. human rights foundations, the anti-

Pinochet forces triumphed: A resounding 54 percent refused to give Pinochet another term of office. Under pressure from the armed forces, he resigned from office in 1989.

Return to Democracy

Patricio Aylwin, the newly elected president of Chile, convened the National Commission of Truth and Reconciliation to determine what precisely had occurred during the Pinochet regime. The commission, however, did not possess prosecutorial powers: A 1978 amnesty, which the armed forces and Pinochet regime had demanded and received in return for lifting the state of siege, pardoned the military and police for any illegal acts they might have committed between 1973 and 1978.

Obviously, the amnesty would not stop foreign governments from prosecuting any official who killed any Chilean holding dual citizenship. The first to fall afoul of a foreign court was Pinochet, whom British authorities detained in England when in 1998 a Spanish judge, Baltazar Garzón, demanded his extradition. Chile's foreign minister, José Miguel Insulza, himself an exile during the Pinochet regime, petitioned the British to release the general: Only Chile, he argued, had jurisdiction. Eventually, England's foreign minister overruled the courts that had voted to extradite Pinochet: The general, he stated, was too feeble to stand trial. Pinochet did return to Chile, but his arrest demonstrated his vulnerability. In increasingly declining health, he has become almost superfluous. The commission, however, continues to investigate the crimes committed under Pinochet's aegis and Chileans still have to accept and move beyond this heritage of abuse.

SEE ALSO Immunity; Pinochet, Augusto; Torture; United States Foreign Policies Toward Genocide and Crimes Against Humanity

BIBLIOGRAPHY

Collier, Simon, and William F. (1996). *A General History of Chile.* Cambridge: Cambridge University Press.

Report of the Chilean National Commission on Truth and Reconciliation (1993). 2 volumes. South Bend, Ind.: University of Notre Dame Press.

Sigmund, Paul E. (1977). *The Overthrow of Allende and the Politics of Chile: 1964–1976.* Pittsburgh: University of Pittsburgh Press.

Sigmund, Paul E. (1993). *The United States and Democracy in Chile.* Baltimore, Md.: Johns Hopkins Press.

William F. Sater

China

As China approached the end of the nineteenth century, it was ravaged by rebellions, warlords, and famines, while the Imperial government had done little to ease the suffering of the common folk. This ancient kingdom had collided with Western intruders and was plunged into wars with foreign powers as well as domestic political violence. In the coming century, hundreds of millions would be slaughtered, starved, tortured, raped, forced into slave labor, or persecuted on political and religious grounds. Crimes against humanity, including genocide and war crimes, accounted for many of the deaths and atrocities. Other than a few Japanese war criminals, culprits—including state and non-state forces, warlords, rebels, and foreign invaders—have not been scrutinized for their responsibility in such crimes.

The Boxer Rebellion: 1898–1901

Two deadly episodes preceded the Boxer Rebellion: the Opium Wars (1839–1842 and 1856–1860) and the Taiping Rebellion (1851–1864). The Opium Wars were skirmishes between the Imperial troops and the British army over British opium trafficking, which violated a Chinese ban on the trade. The wars ended in China's defeat and the imposition of treaties entirely to Britain's advantage. There were reports of British and French soldiers looting and burning, as well as the torture of prisoners by both sides. In addition, the opium trade resumed, leading to widespread drug use. As a result, many Chinese were debilitated and suffered both bodily and mental injury.

A further weakened Qing Dynasty, along with widespread discontent, and humiliation at the hands of foreign powers, spurred rebellions. One of the bloodiest of these insurgencies against the Qing government was the Taiping Rebellion, led by a failed scholar-official and Christian convert, Hong Xiuquan (1813–1864). Almost thirty million died in the 15-year conflict before the rebellion was crushed by the Qing army, with assistance from the British.

Toward the end of the nineteenth century, China had been defeated by Japan (1895) and had failed to realize the "self-strengthening reform" and the "Hundred Days' Reform" (June–September 1898). Western powers gained commercial privileges and demanded further concessions. The killing of two missionaries in Shandong in 1897 gave Germany an excuse to take Qingdao in the Northeast. Other European countries followed suit and carved up "spheres of interest" for themselves.

The Boxer Rebellion was an uprising against Westerners that took place in northeastern China. Thousands of Chinese, especially Christian converts, and 230 foreigners were killed before the rebellion was suppressed by foreign troops. Boxer was a secret martial art society in Shandong that had initially opposed both the Qing and Westerners. In early 1898, the Boxers first skirmished with Qing troops. In 1899, however, they reconciled with the government through the clandestine intervention of Empress Dowager Cixi, who saw secret societies a force against foreigners. The Boxers, with Cixi's backing, redirected their violence, attacking missionaries and Christian converts.

These targeted attacks on foreigners angered Western powers. In June 1900, when the Boxers and some Imperial forces attacked foreign compounds in Tianjin and Beijing, the uprising escalated into war. The swift international intervention of overwhelmingly powerful modern militaries and anti-Boxer Chinese provincial forces quickly defeated the rebels. The Imperial government signed the "Boxer Protocol" (1901), executed Chinese officials who had been blamed for the uprising, and had to pay $333 million in war reparations. Europeans gained the right to maintain troops in Beijing. The Boxer Protocol suspended the traditional civil service examination and banned arms imports into China.

The humiliation generated by successive defeats aroused a sense of nationalism, setting the stage for reforms. In 1902 girls were allowed to attend schools, and the school curriculum was expanded to include Western science and technology. The military was modernized under Yuan Shikai (1859–1916). In 1909–1910, provincial assemblies and an elected national Consultative Assembly were established. The 1911 revolution ended the Imperial Dynasty. This turbulent decade, according to historians, claimed as many as 100,000 lives.

The Civil War: 1926–1949

In 1913 Yuan became the first post-Imperial president. He gained office after making a deal with the reformers of Tongmenghui (which evolved into the Nationalist Party, or Kuomintang), which had won a majority in the National Assembly election. Yuan soon dissolved the Assembly, however, and declared himself Emperor in December 1915. He held that title until his death, three months later, in March 1916. Yuan's death began a period of divided rule by warlords, which lasted from 1916 to 1928. During that time, warlords fighting for territory killed more than 910,000 civilians.

The Kuomintang (KMT) was headquartered in Guangzhou and headed by President Sun Yat-sen (1866–1925). He pleaded for Western aid, but without success. Sun Yat-Sen then turned to the Soviet Union, which began supporting both the KMT and the Chinese Communist Party (CCP), which was founded in 1921. The struggle to reunite China became a power struggle between these two parties. The communists were in-

From left to right, Chinese Communist Party leaders Qin Bangxian, Zhou Enlai, Zhu De, and Mao Zedong, in Shaanxi Province, after the Red Army's retreat north in the Long March (1934–1935). The Long March—in which some 5,000 miles were traversed—later became an almost mythological event in Chinese revolutionary history. [BETTMANN/CORBIS]

structed by the Soviets to cooperate with the Kuomintang to create the "first united front" (1923–1926).

When Sun Yat-sen died in 1925 he was succeeded by Chiang Kai-shek, a young lieutenant who had been trained in the Soviet Union. Chiang Kai-shek soon broke with the CCP and ordered the arrest and execution of hundreds of communists and trade unionists in Shanghai in April 1927. This forced the CCP out of its urban base. It made abortive attempts to take control of other cities and rural areas. One such attempt was the Autumn Harvest Peasant Uprising in Hunan, led by Mao Zedong. The CCP was forced underground in rural areas in the south. Meanwhile, Chiang's northern expedition captured Beijing in 1928 and his Nanjing government received international recognition as the capital of unified China.

From 1927 to 1949, Chiang's troops used murder, torture, and other brutal tactics to wipe out the communists. In one campaign to destroy CCP–Soviet bases in central China in 1934, the KMT killed or starved to death as many as one million people, forcing the CCP to the brink of elimination. In October 1934, the CCP Red Army began its "Long March," retreating to northwest Shaanxi. Mao Zedong emerged from this strategic move as the top leader of the Chinese Communist Party.

The KMT troops reoccupied communist bases. They executed prisoners, communist sympathizers, and collaborators. They looted, raped women, and gunned down civilians as they passed through villages and towns. They were poorly fed, and were beaten or left to die when they fell sick or were wounded. The Nationalist government, corrupt and greedy, did little to ease the suffering from famine, drought, and war. It was responsible for perhaps as many as two million famine deaths during its rule. An estimated four million men died during forced conscription alone. In one battle, to deter advancing Japanese troops, the Nationalists opened the Yellow River dikes, drowning at least 440,000 people in the ensuing flood.

When Japan invaded China's northeast in 1932 and began moving southward in 1935, Chiang at first refused to form an alliance with the Communists to face the new, shared threat. In December 1936, however, KMT generals kidnapped Chiang in Xian and forced him to stop fighting the CCP. The "second united front" was thus formed against the Japanese, even if the unity between the CCP and the KMT was in name only. In December 1940, Chiang ordered the CCP's New Fourth Army to leave its base in Central China, then sent his own troops to ambush the retreating soldiers. This ended the second united front. The CCP and KMT then focused on fighting each other instead of the Japanese. Nonetheless, in 1945, Japan surrendered to the KMT. The United States attempted to broker a ceasefire between the KMT and the CCP, but failed. Civil war resumed.

Rampant corruption and postwar turmoil had weakened Chiang's government. Its troops were demoralized and repeatedly defeated by the more disciplined CCP Liberation Army, which had gained popularity for land reforms in northern China. KMT troops retreated rapidly, despite their advantages in size, weapons, and international support. Beijing fell to the communists peacefully in early 1949, followed by other major cities. The war ended when Mao Zedong proclaimed the birth of the People's Republic in Tiananmen on October 1, 1949. Chiang and his remaining troops fled to Taiwan, declaring Taipei the capital of the Republic of China, and vowing to reunite China. Before Chiang's death and Taiwan's democratization in the 1990s, the KMT ruled in authoritarian style, crushing dissidents and suppressing all indigenous Taiwanese movements for independence.

The communist "liberation" of mainland China provided no relief from the slaughtering and political violence. During the wars, the CCP also used terror in its campaigns. In areas under CCP control, communists executed "counterrevolutionaries," exterminated "bad landlords," and murdered members of the bourgeoisie as part of their program to eliminate "enemy classes," reform society, and redistribute land and property Nearly 3.5 million civilians died at their hands before the civil war ended in 1949. The civil war claimed a total of ten million civilian lives.

The Sino-Japanese War: 1937–1945

The Japanese fought furiously against local and military resistance in China, employing a degree of barbarity rarely seen in modern history. They slaughtered and tortured people indiscriminately, looted and burned whole villages and towns, conducted germ-warfare experiments, and used biochemical weapons. They forced prisoners of war and civilians into slave labor, and systematically raped women or forced them into prostitution.

During the "Rape of Nanking" in December 1937, 300,000 people, mostly civilians, were killed in that city. In northern China, the Japanese executed the "Loot, Kill, and Burn All" policy, designed to terrorize local population. As they took over villages and cities, Japanese soldiers murdered by firing squad, bayoneting, burning their victims alive, or beating them to death. They released flies infected with deadly plague germs during bombing raids over large cities, tossed disease-causing microbes into rivers and reservoirs, and mixed deadly germs with food distributed to the hungry population. Unit 731 of the Japanese Army conducted chemical warfare experiments on POWs and peasants, who were injected with a variety of lethal biochemicals and dumped into mass graves after death.

Studies estimate that about 3.5 million noncombatants were killed by Japanese troops, and as many as 15 million more died from bombing, starvation, and disease that resulted from the Japanese terror campaign. In August 1945, U.S. forces dropped two atomic bombs over the Japanese cities of Hiroshima and Nagasaki, killing many Japanese civilians. This forced Japan to surrender to the Allies, ending World War II, and forced the Japanese Army to retreat from its positions within China.

At the end of the war, a handful of Japanese were tried in Nanking (1946–1947) as war criminals, though not for genocide. Seven were convicted by the International Military Tribunal for the Far East in Tokyo. Many generals who perpetrated war crimes never faced prosecution. The Japanese repatriated their war criminals to Tokyo and systematically kept all mention of their atrocities out of the nation's history textbooks. Emperor Hirohito, whose controversial role in the war was obscured when the Japanese government destroyed many wartime documents, was given immunity from war-crime responsibility and was allowed to remain on the throne till his death in 1989.

Three-Year Famine: 1959–1961
Immediately after coming to power, the CCP mobilized political campaigns to purge "enemy classes" and fortify a "dictatorship of the proletariat" modeled after Stalin's Soviet Union. During the 1950s, there were several attempts at land reforms, as well as a series of movements to eliminate counterrevolutionaries and institute collectives. In addition, there were the "Anti-Rightist Struggle," and the "Great Leap Forward." These mass campaigns involved beating, torture, and execution, and were responsible for as many as 15 million deaths. One million "rightists" were punished for up to twenty years in internal exile or labor camps. The "Great Leap Forward" alone caused an estimated thirty million famine deaths, the highest number ever recorded in famine history.

The famine was the direct outcome of government policies, official cover-ups, and media censorship by the CCP. By 1957, land had been collectivized and peasants were organized into communes. Mao hoped to achieve rapid growth by doubling the pre-collectivization agricultural output and steel production. He exhorted the people to "leap forward," to "catch up with England and surpass America." This campaign coincided with a strained relationship with the Soviet Union and its withdraw of all aid.

The ailing economy nearly collapsed. The whole country, including 90 million peasants, was forced to recycle steel, even melting down the farm implements needed for food production. In the commune kitchens, food reserves were depleted. Local officials, fearing reprisal and competing for favor, systematically covered up their failures, reporting fabricated statistics of harvests instead. Leaders who spoke candidly, such as Marshal Peng Dehuai, and who tried to convince Mao to reverse the policy, were denounced and purged.

Encouraged by dazzling, but false, statistics, the government allocated food to cities and generously agreed to export the surplus to "socialist brother" countries. When local officials could not produce the food in the quantities that the false production statistics led them to expect, they accused peasants of concealing or stealing food. They tortured and killed thousands to extract confessions of hidden supplies.

The peasants, however, were starving. In some regions, after people had consumed all the mice, insects, and tree bark available, some resorted to cannibalism. The elderly and children especially suffered, starving to death in large numbers. Even more died from malnutrition in the years that followed. In 1957 half of all deaths

were under the age of 18; in 1963 half were under the age of 10.

Mao was eventually forced to reverse his policy and ally himself with pragmatists like President Liu Shaoqi and Vice-Premier Deng Xiaoping. Liu and Deng attempted to undo the damage by partially reversing the collectivization policy, but there was no public admission of policy errors before Mao's death. No efforts were made to seek accountability for the famine. In fact, the famine was a taboo subject, referred only as the "Three-Year Natural Disaster."

The Cultural Revolution: 1966–1976
Mao resented Liu and Deng for the popularity they garnered from reversing his policies. The Cultural Revolution was Mao's tactic to secure his power against the reforms offered by "capitalist roaders." He encouraged his Red Guards—students who had pledged personal loyalty to Mao—to challenge local Communist authorities. This quickly led to violent conflicts and anarchy. Historians estimate that a total of seven million were killed during the decade of the Cultural Revolution.

The establishment in 1996 of the "Cultural Revolution Committee" under Mao's wife, Jiang Qing, marked its official start. Jiang tried to root out sympathizers of "capitalist roaders" by building Mao's personality cult. Red Guards were organized under the aegis of the CCP's "Decisions on the Great Proletarian Cultural Revolution" to denounce and purge intellectuals and Mao's rivals. Millions of Red Guards converged on Beijing. Mao praised their actions and received their cheers in Tiananmen Square. Mao issued a public ordinance to suspend police interference in Red Guards activities. Mao even ordered that all transportation and accommodations be provided free of charge to all members of the Red Guards. Meanwhile, Mao ordered all government officials to participate in self-criticism sessions and denounce others for disloyalty. Those who refused would be purged. Such policies succeeded in turning everybody against everybody else.

The Red Guards were joined by workers and civil servants, but the different factions clashed, often violently. "Counterrevolutionaries" and other "bad elements," including prominent intellectuals and artists, were paraded in shame before the public, beaten, detained, or executed without any trial or judicial procedure. Looting was widespread, homes were searched, books were burned, and religious sites and ancient artifacts were destroyed. Many were sent to labor camps; some committed suicide or went insane. In many cities, Red Guards took control of the administrative authority. Lawlessness and anarchy ruled for months. In some areas, the rampage against "class enemies" degenerated into the worst possible atrocities, including mass cannibalism.

By 1967, Mao's rivals had been purged. In 1968 Mao decided to send the youth "Down to the Countryside." Perhaps Mao realized that the CCP was losing control, or perhaps he became alarmed by the Soviet military build-up along China's borders and its intervention in Czechoslovakia earlier in the year. During the next ten years, middle-school graduates were dispersed to communes or state-run farms to receive "re-education" from "poor, lower or middle class peasants."

The power struggle within the CCP did not stop, however. Mao even became suspicious of his hand-picked successor Lin Biao. Lin did attempt a military coup in 1971, but failed and was forced to flee with his family to the Soviet Union. His plane crashed over Mongolia, killing everyone aboard. Meanwhile, Mao's wife Jiang and her ultra-leftist cohorts ("the Gang of Four") helped Mao pick a new successor, the Shanghai official Wang Hongwen. This move was intended to undermine what they saw as Mao's leading rival from the right, Premier Zhou Enlai, who in 1973 had restored Deng Xiaoping to political favor. After Lin's coup attempt, Mao was weary of the leftists, yet he also distrusted the right. His ambivalence encouraged Jiang to start the absurd "Criticizing Lin, Criticizing Confucius" movement (where "Confucius" stood for the right). The campaign roused little enthusiasm from a population that was fatigued by years of purges: the economy had collapsed, strict rationing had been imposed, and people were struggling just to make ends meet.

In January 1976, Zhou died of bladder cancer. Mourners poured into Tiananmen Square, placing wreaths with messages criticizing the Gang of Four at the Monument of the People's Heroes. Deng, who took over Zhou's duties, became the Gang of Four's new target; they saw him as the only obstacle to their ascendance to power after Mao, who was also ill. Mao backed them and once again purged Deng. However, in choosing a new successor, Mao bypassed the Gang of Four and instead picked the little known Hua Guofeng for Premier.

On April 5, Memorial Day, the commemoration of Zhou turned into a rally of two million mourners, all protesting the Gang of Four. The Gang of Four ordered armed security to quell the incipient rebellion. Many protesters were beaten and detained. The protest, dubbed the "4.5 Tiananmen Incident," was labeled "counterrevolutionary." On September 9, 1976, Mao died. Hua became CCP chairman. With backing from revolutionary elders like General Ye Jianying, Hua put

In initiating the Cultural Revolution, Mao Zedong shut down China's schools and directed Red Guards (students and others pledging their loyalty to him) to attack "traditional" Chinese values and all things "bourgeois." Here, supporters, Chinese youth from the city of Changchun, march toward Beijing on January 14, 1967. [BETTMANN/CORBIS]

the Gang of Four under arrest, officially ending the Cultural Revolution. Hua allowed Deng back into running the State Council and named him vice-premier in July 1977.

Under Deng, a period known as the "liberation of thoughts" began. The reputations of many purged officials, including Liu, who had died in prison, were rehabilitated. Moderates Hu Yaobang and Zhao Ziyang became, respectively, CCP general-secretary and premier. Deng retired, but remained chairman of the Central Military Committee.

Tiananmen Massacre and Aftermath: Since 1989
On June 4, 1989, the People's Liberation Army, under order from Deng and Premier Li Peng, opened fire on pro-democracy protesters in and around Tiananmen Square in Beijing. The protest movement actually began on April 15, when students converged on Tiananmen to commemorate the death of Hu, who had been purged for sympathizing with earlier student protests in 1986. The April 15 protests, begun by students

and other intellectuals, were eventually joined by workers and ordinary citizens of Beijing. In huge rallies, demonstrators demanded freedom of association, expression, and the press; they called for the rule of law and denounced corruption. The protests quickly spread to other cities. Many traveled to Beijing to support the student leaders and their hunger strike.

Hardliners within the Politburo, such as Li and President Yang Shangkun, with backing from Deng, rejected the students' request for "dialogue." Instead, they imposed martial law and labeled the demonstrations "counterrevolutionary." Zhao and other moderates were willing to reach out to students, but they were overruled by the hardliners in the government. When demonstrators refused to leave Tiananmen Square, Deng and Li ordered the military to "clean up."

For days, the troops had been blocked from entering the square by Beijing's citizens. When the final order came, on the evening of June 3, soldiers advanced toward the Square along Chang-an Avenue, forcing their way through the crowds and firing automatic weapons at civilians. In shock and disbelief, the crowds charged back and skirmished with soldiers, which led to many deaths. Tanks and armored vehicles rolled to the square, and troops cleared the area of demonstrators in the early morning of June 4. Shootings and arrests continued in the surrounding streets, where citizens tried to rescue the wounded and hide the "counterrevolutionary rioters."

The immediate civilian death toll in Beijing was estimated to be around 2,600. The actual death total may never be known, and an unknown number of protesters died in other cities. The troops reportedly burnt many bodies. In Beijing, between 7,000 and 10,000 were wounded. In the aftermath, the government convicted and executed dozens of protesters, mostly workers. A nationwide manhunt began for other participants in the rally. Hundreds were arrested and sentenced to jail or sent to labor camps. Many more were forced to confess, demoted, or fired from their jobs. A few prominent leaders went into hiding and were eventually smuggled out of the country.

The government rolled back many of the reforms and personal liberties that they had introduced during the 1980s. The collapse of communism in Russia and Eastern Europe, combined with the Chinese government's desire to regain international prestige and domestic legitimacy, pressured Deng to speed up economic reform. Jiang Zeming, whose own bloody crackdown on protesters while he was mayor of Shanghai was less known at the time, was brought in Beijing to succeed Zhao.

Political reform remained a taboo subject throughout the 1990s. Since 1989, activists of pro-democracy organizations such as the Democratic Party, independent union organizers, liberal intellectuals broaching sensitive subjects, and religious groups have been relentlessly persecuted. Human rights organizations have documented the torture and arbitrary detention of hundreds of political prisoners who have been incarcerated without trial under harsh prison conditions, including forced labor in "re-education camps." It is impossible to estimate the general population that by 2004 was in Chinese prisons, labor camps, and local detention centers. In the early twenty-first century Tibetan Buddhists, Muslims in Xingjiang, and Catholics loyal to Rome continued to be subjected to persecution. In the crackdown on the quasi-Buddhist sect, Falun Gong, many practitioners were arrested, detained, persecuted, and tortured, and some died in police custody.

As of the mid-2000s, there was no program in place to investigate the war crimes, genocide, or crimes against humanity that have been committed by Chinese forces against their own people. Some activists have urged that the Tiananmen Massacre be investigated for violations of international law regarding genocide and crimes against humanity. They also have argued that other persecutions have been carried out for political and antireligious motivations and have cited instances of "bodily and mental harm" and "physical destruction" "with intent to destroy, in whole or in part" certain religious groups. On technical grounds, such demands have international law and UN conventions on their side. Despite forces within China pushing for political reform and the rule of law, the government has remained in the control of the same unchecked political power that for centuries has been responsible for atrocities against its citizenry.

SEE ALSO Japan; Mao Zedong

BIBLIOGRAPHY

Becker, Jasper (1997). *Hungry Ghosts*. New York: Free Press.

Brackman, Arnold C. (1987). *The Other Nuremberg: The Untold Story of the Tokyo War Crimes Trials*. New York: William Morrow.

Cell, Charles P. (1977). *Revolution at Work: Mobilization Campaigns in China*. New York: Academic Press.

Chang, Iris (1997). *The Rape of Nanking: The Forgotten Holocaust of World War II*. New York: Basic Books.

Griffin, Patricia E. (1976). *The Chinese Communist Treatment of Counterrevolutionaries: 1924–1949*. Princeton: Princeton University Press.

Liu, Binyan, Ruan Ming, and Xu gang (1989). *"Tell the World": What Happened in China and Why*, trans. Henry L. Epstein. New York: Pantheon.

Pepper, Suzanne (1978). *Civil War in China: The Political Struggle, 1945–1949.* Berkeley: University of California Press.

Rummel, R. J. (1991). *China's Bloody Century: Genocide and Mass Murder since 1900.* New Brunswick, N.J.: Transaction Publishers.

Seymour, James, and Richard Anderson (1998). *New Ghosts, Old Ghosts: Prisons and Labor Reform in China.* New York: M. E. Sharpe.

Tanaka, Yuki (1996). *Hidden Horrors: Japanese War Crimes in World War II.* Boulder, Colo.: Westview Press.

Wangyal, Phuntsog (1984). "Tibet: A Case of Eradication of Religion Leading to Genocide." In *Toward the Understanding and Prevention of Genocide: Proceedings of the International Conference on the Holocaust and Genocide,* ed. Israel W. Charny. Boulder, Colo.: Westview Press.

White, Lynn T. (1989). *Policies of Chaos: The Organizational Causes of Violence in China's Cultural Revolution.* Princeton, N.J.: Princeton University Press.

Yan Jiaqi, and Gao Gao (1986). *The Ten Year History of the Cultural Revolution.* (In Chinese.) Tianjin, China: Tianjin People's Publishing House.

Zhang, Liang (2001). *The Tiananmen Papers: The Chinese Leadership's Decision to Use Force against their Own People—In their Own Words,* ed. Zhang Liang, Andrew J. Nathan, and Perry Link. New York: Public Affairs.

Xiaorong Li

Chittagong Hill Tract, Peoples of the

The Chittagong Hill Tracts (CHT) constitute a geographically mountainous region in eastern Bangladesh, comprising approximately 5,000 square miles, or roughly 10 percent of the country's total land area. Originally populated by thirteen independent, indigenous groups, each with a distinct culture and language, the CHT strategically borders India, Burma, and the Bay of Bengal. The combined indigenous tribal population, currently estimated at 500,000, constitutes less than one percent of Bangladesh's total population. Historically organized into kinship groups who held their land in common, the CHT peoples employed a swidden, or slash-and-burn agricultural practice that required frequent moves to rotate their rice and other crops.

The Bengalis, a predominately Islamic people speaking an Indo-European language, inhabit the plains adjacent to the CHT. Their south Asian culture contrasts with that of the indigenous hill tribes, who, although possessing a variety of languages and religions, are historically tied to south East Asian cultures. In the mid-eighteenth century, the British assumed control over the entire Indian subcontinent, opening the CHT area for the first time to outside businesses and influences. By 1860 the British, in a move to protect their tea plantations and other economic interests, formally annexed the CHT. In 1900, the British extension of administrative control ended one thousand years of political and cultural autonomy for the indigenous tribes.

With Pakistan's independence from Great Britain in 1947, the CHT region became the southernmost district of East Pakistan. Adopting western notions of political integration and development, the Pakistani government moved to assimilate the CHT peoples into the national mainstream. In 1955, Pakistan ended all remnants of CHT's administrative autonomy, and in 1964 terminated its special political status. During this same period, the Pakistani government constructed the Kaptai Dam on the Karnafuli River, submerging 400 square miles of agricultural and culturally significant CHT lands. More than 100,000 CHT peoples were displaced by the dam, although 99 percent of the electricity generated by it is used to power development projects outside of the CHT. Other federal policies prohibited rice production, the basis of the tribal economies, leading to famines and starvation among the previously self-sufficient communities. Equally destructive was Pakistan's decision to end British immigration restrictions and to encourage Bangladeshi resettlement in the area.

In 1971 Bangladesh declared its independence from Pakistan. Cognizant of the CHT's strategic location, gas, coal, copper, and timber resources, and its lower population density, the new Bengali government quickly asserted its control over the region. The 1972 Constitution imposed Bengali as the state language, Islam as the state religion, and Bangladeshi as the national identity. A massive, government-sponsored movement of Bangladeshis into the CHT region altered the population ratio from 98 percent indigenous in 1971 to fifty percent by 2000. To secure its policies, the government sent one-third of the entire Bangladeshi military to the CHT region. Backed by Saudi financial aid, the military employed pressure tactics to force the peoples' conversion to Islam. The indigenous peoples had grown increasingly angry over federal policies and rage over the military's indiscriminate rape of indigenous women, 40 percent under eighteen years of age.

By 1972 that anger had progressed to armed conflict. For the next twenty-five years, the hill people fought a guerilla war against the Bangladesh Army. In 1997 the war-weary hill peoples agreed to a peace accord followed a year later by the Rangamati Declaration. The success of the accord and declaration's promised changes are mixed. Legally described as a "tribal inhabited region," a twenty-two-member, indigenously elected regional council administers the CHT region, with locally elected councils supervising community affairs. As of 2002, however, a Bangladeshi remained as head of the Ministry of CHT Affairs, the federal agency responsible for the region, and the agreement to withdraw Bangladeshi settlers continued to be unfulfilled. The state retained control over the region's natural resources, and state policies preventing communal land ownership and swidden agricultural practices have persisted.

SEE ALSO Indigenous Peoples

BIBLIOGRAPHY

International Institute of Social History Archives. "Organizing Committee Chittagong Hill Tracts Campaign". Available from http://www.iisg.nl/archives/gias/o/10803695.html.

Khan, Adilur Rahman. "Crisis in the Chittagong Hill Tracts: Bangladesh." Available from http://www.hurights.or.jp/asia-pacific/no_07/02crisisin.htm.

Mey, Wolfgang, ed. (1984). *Genocide in the Chittagong Hill Tracts, Bangladesh.* Copenhagen: International Work Group for Indigenous Affairs (IWGIA).

Moshin, A. (2003). *The Chittagong Hill Tracts, Bangladesh: On the Difficult Road to Peace.* Boulder, Colo.: Lynne Rienner Publishers.

Murthy, Vasudev. *Chittagong Hill Tracts: A History of Repression.* Available from http://ww.nativenet.uthscsa.edu/archive/nl/91c/0289.html.

Roy, Rajkumari (2000). *Land Rights of the Indigenous Peoples of the Chittagong Hill Tracts, Bangladesh.* Copenhagen: International Work Group for Indigenous Affairs.

Sustainable Development Networking Programme (SDNP). "Chittagong Hill Tracts." Available from http:www.sdnpbd.org/sdi/international_day/Indigenous-people/chittagong-hill-tracts.htm.

Sharon O'Brien

Chmielnicki, Bogdan
[1595–AUGUST 6, 1657]
Seventeenth-century Cossack ruler

Frequently identified by the Polish translation of his name, Bogdan (or Bohdan) Chmielnicki was hetman (supreme head) of the Cossacks based in southcentral Ukraine from 1648 until his death. He is also widely known by the Ukrainian form of his name, Bohdan Khmel'nyts'kyi. During the decade of his rule, Chmielnicki was responsible for leading a successful revolt against the Polish-Lithuanian Commonwealth, which dominated Ukraine at the time, and for bringing the lands he controlled under the authority of the tsardom of Muscovy in 1654.

During the first half of the seventeenth century much of Ukraine was a borderland region of southeastern Poland-Lithuania, beyond which a no-man's land separated it from the Ottoman Empire and its client state, the Crimean Tatar Khanate. Until 1648 Chmielnicki was what is known as a registered Cossack, that is, a kind of landowning petty gentryman of Orthodox Christian faith in the service of the Polish kingdom, as opposed to the Zaporozhian Cossacks, that is, military freebooters who lived in the no-man's borderland and opposed any kind of government control. In 1647 Chmielnicki clashed with a local Polish official over financial and personal matters, and finding no legal satisfaction, he fled in early 1648 to join the Zaporozhian Cossacks, who then elected him as their leader or hetman.

In his new role, Chmielnicki formed an alliance with the Crimean Tatars and within a few months he defeated the Polish army in several battles. He then pressed the government to grant further privileges to both the registered and Zaporozhian Cossacks as well as a large degree of autonomy for Ukraine. With the breakdown of Polish authority, spontaneous peasant revolts broke out in central Ukraine in the summer of 1648; the peasants were later joined by Zaporozhian Cossack forces, who expanded the scope of the revolts. The objective of the peasant and Zaporozhian marauders was to remove from Ukraine those who were perceived as their oppressor, first and foremost the Polish noble landlords, Jewish estate managers, Roman Catholic clergy and town dwellers, and fellow Christians known as Uniates (i.e., former Orthodox adherents who recognized the Roman pope as head of their church).

As for Chmielnicki himself, he and his armies did not participate in such revolts nor in the accompanying atrocities against civilians. As a petty gentryman, he hoped to remain under Poland-Lithuania provided that the state granted to the registered Cossacks the privileges that effectively would have amounted to their status as nobles. Chmielnicki was only partially successful, although he did manage to establish a Cossack state in 1649. Conflict with Poland persisted, however, and the civilian population, in particular Poles and Jews, continued to suffer losses until at least 1652.

Polish sources have traditionally depicted Chmielnicki in a very negative light, accusing him of having precipitated the steady decline of Poland's power in eastern Europe until eventually the state completely disappeared in the late eighteenth century. This image of Chmielnicki as a destroyer was preserved in the Polish psyche through the nineteenth-century novels of the Nobel Prize-winning author Henryk Sienkiewicz.

encyclopedia of GENOCIDE *and* CRIMES AGAINST HUMANITY

Jewish authors have been even more critical of Chmielnicki, in some cases characterizing him as the government official responsible for the first Holocaust perpetrated against Jews. Seventeenth-century Jewish chronicles, in particular, those of Nathan Hannover and Sabbatai Cohen, reported alleged Jewish losses ranging from 60,000 to 100,000 deaths and the destruction of 300 communities. Present-day Israeli scholars (Shaul Stampfer and Bernard D. Weinryb among them) have pointed out that these figures are grossly exaggerated and speak instead of the annihilation of 18,000 to 20,000 lives. Yet despite the fact that Chmielnicki's "control of events was rather limited," as conceded by the *Encyclopedia Judaica*, that same source also notes he is depicted in Jewish annals as "Chmiel the Wicked, one of the most sinister oppressors of Jews of all generations" (1972, p. 481).

In stark contrast to Polish and Jewish sources, traditional Russian historiography, in part repeated by later Soviet authors, considers Chmielnicki in a positive light as the leader who brought the Orthodox "Little Russians" (i.e., Ukrainians) into the political fold of Muscovy and its successor state, the Russian Empire. Most interesting is the Ukrainian image, which is decidedly mixed. The nineteenth-century national bard of Ukraine, Taras Shevchenko, consistently rejected any notion of Chmielnicki as a hero and portrayed him instead as a treacherous leader who sold out his country to the Muscovites (Russians). Last, general histories of Ukraine depict, and the popular image is, a Chmielnicki who single-handedly created an independent "Ukrainian" state. The strongly contrasting historical memories of Chmielnicki have contributed to the persisting negative stereotypes that Poles and Jews, on the one hand, and Ukrainians, on the other, have of each other.

SEE ALSO Anti-Semitism; Cossacks

BIBLIOGRAPHY

Hanover, Nathan (1983). *Abyss of Despair/Yeven Metzulah: The Famous 17th-Century Chronicle Depicting Jewish Life in Russia and Poland during the Chmielnicki Massacres of 1648–1649.* New Brunswick, N.J.: Transaction Books.

Hrushevsky, Mykhailo (2002). *History of Ukraine-Rus.* Vol. 8: *The Cossack Age, 1626–1650.* Edmonton, Canada: Canadian Institute of Ukrainian Studies Press.

Sysyn, Frank E. (1988). "The Jewish Factor in the Khmelnytsky Uprising." In *Ukrainian-Jewish Relations in Historical Perspective*, ed. Peter J. Potichnyj and Howard Aster. Edmonton, Canada: Canadian Institute of Ukrainian Studies

Sysyn, Frank E., and Shaul Stampfer (2003). "Jews, Cossacks, Poles, and Peasants in 1648 Ukraine." *Jewish History* 17(2):115–139, 207–227.

Vernadsky, George (1941). *Bohdan, Hetman of Ukraine.* New Haven, Conn.: Yale University Press.

Paul Robert Magocsi

Christians, Roman Persecution of

On November 20, 284 CE, Diocles, an Illyrian officer who had risen to high command in the Roman army, was elevated to the purple by the soldiers at Nicomedia. The new emperor took the name of Gaius Aurelius Valerius Diocletianus (284–305) and is known as Diocletian. Having been acclaimed by the military, Diocletian was the first emperor to disregard the Senate in Rome by not seeking its customary confirmation. Going a step further, he also pronounced that his elevation to the throne of Rome enjoyed divine sanction, having come about through the will of Jupiter Optimus Maximus, Rome's highest deity.

After defeating Carinus, the son of the former Emperor Carus, and warding off several attempts by would-be usurpers to seize power, the emperor implemented a program to restore the tottering empire. Diocletian was a superb administrator, but he was also an autocratic ruler. He expanded the army in order to better defend Rome's imperial borders; provinces were divided and grouped into new administrative units called dioceses. Most important, however, he separated military from civilian power and deprived the Senate of its right to govern provinces. In the economic sphere he legislated to stop rampant inflation by issuing his Edict of Prices that, being impossible to enforce, failed.

In order to govern the vast Roman Empire of late antiquity, he devised the tetrarchy, meaning rule by four men. To guarantee a trouble-free succession, the tetrarchs were bound in an artificial family relationship. A former comrade of Diocletian, Maximian, became Augustus in the West with Diocletian holding the senior position as Augustus in the East. Each man then adopted a "son," who bearing the title of Caesar, was designated as heir to move into the senior position when the first set of Augusti retired or died. Maximian took Constantius (the father of Constantine the Great), and Diocletian chose Galerius as Caesar. Diocletian subsequently placed his dynasty under the protection of Jupiter, while Maximian sought the favor of Hercules. Divine protection by the gods of Rome seemed to contemporaries a necessity if the Roman Empire was to survive. This belief remained constant throughout the reign of Diocletian, as attested to by imperial propaganda, and especially by the images on his coinage.

Besides the many military challenges and economic problems of the era, another source of concern was

Marble bust of Diocletian (245–313 CE), the Roman Emperor who became known for his brutal persecution of Christians. Although initially tolerant of Christianity, he issued a fourth and final edict in 304, whereby all Christians were ordered to worship Roman gods. Mass executions and the widespread destruction of churches and other property followed. [BETTMANN/CORBIS]

the growth of Christianity. By then, many Christians belonged to influential circles, including the army and the bureaucracy. This little understood religion had been first noticed, and persecuted briefly, during the time of Nero (54–68). There had also been a short-lived persecution under Maximinus the Thracian (235–238), which attempted to stop proselytizing and was mostly directed at the higher clergy. The Emperor Decius (249–251) tried to root out the Christian religion by issuing an edict ordering all citizens to worship the state gods or face dire consequences. This persecution had a measure of success, with many well-to-do Christians renouncing their beliefs to save themselves. It ended with the death of Decius in 251.

A more intense attempt to rid the empire of Christians in 257 under Valerian (253–260) renewed the policies of Decius. Meetings between Christians were prohibited, and the clergy was persecuted with much vigor. This effort to eliminate Christianity was once again foiled by the death of the emperor. Valerian's son and successor, Gallienus (253–268), had little sympathy for his father's policy, and under his rule the Christians enjoyed a period of toleration that lasted for forty years.

Diocletian ordered the last and cruelest persecution of the Christians in 305 after he had ruled the empire for twenty years. Why so late in his reign did he try to bring the Christians to heel? Some people have attempted to exonerate Diocletian by blaming the fanatical Galerius for the persecutions, whereas others proposed that the old and ailing emperor was no longer in command. Neither explanation is convincing to explain the final, great persecution of the Christians. There is a hint of Diocletian's attitute toward religions other than the accepted Roman pantheon in an edict of 297 against the Manichaeans. He considered them to be a danger to the state and viewed these followers of the Persian Mani as enemy agents. The first of three edicts against the Christians, issued in 304, aimed to destroy sacred books and churches. The second and third edicts ordered all Christian priests imprisoned unless they worshipped the gods of the Roman state by making appropriate sacrifices. The forth and last edict ordered all Christians to perform these sacrifices under pain of death.

What this meant to condemned Christians is mainly known from hagiographical texts that are by their very nature suspect. By Roman law the death penalty was rarely applied to members of the upper classes (honestiores); they were deported or exiled unless convicted of either treason or sacrilege. In the case of the lower classes (humiliores), a conviction could result in the prisoner being either burned alive or thrown to wild beasts in the amphitheaters of Roman cities, such as the Coliseum in Rome. In many cases, however, the prisoners would be sent to the mines or public works, which was essentially the same as being executed. Slaves found guilty of a crime faced death by crucifixion. The application of Roman law may have varied from region to region, from governor to governor.

There was no uniform enforcement of the law, but Africa and the eastern provinces, where Christians were numerous, seem to have suffered most. Provinces such as Bythinia, Syria, Egypt, Palestine, and Phrygia experienced great cruelties. In the western provinces, where Constantius held sway, the persecutions were light, giving rise to rumors that the father of Constantine I had been a secret Christian. Diocletian abdicated in 305 and retired to the fortress palace he had built for himself on the Adriatic. He forced an unwilling Maximian to do the same. Diocletian's tetrarchy did not last much beyond the abdication of its founder. The persecutions, too, did not produce the expected results. In 311, Galerius (305–311), who had succeeded Diocletian in the East and become mortally ill, was forced to issue an edict of toleration that granted the Christians freedom of worship but only as long as "they did not disturb or offend public order."

SEE ALSO Carthage

BIBLIOGRAPHY

Barnes, T. D. (1981). *The New Empire of Diocletian and Constantine.* Cambridge, Mass.: Harvard University Press.

Drake, H. A. (2000). *Constantine and the Bishops: The Politics of Intolerance.* Baltimore, Md.: John Hopkins University Press.

Eusebius (1989). *The History of the Church from Christ to Constantine,* revised edition, tran. G. A. Williamson. London: Penguin Books.

Jones, A. H. M. (1972). *Constantine and the Conversion of Europe.* Harmondsworth, U.K.: Penguin Books.

Lane Fox, R. (1987). *Pagans and Christians.* New York: Alfred A. Knopf.

Williams, S. (1985). *Diocletian and the Roman Recovery.* New York: Methuin.

Franziska E. Shlosser

Code of Crimes against the Peace and Security of Mankind

The establishment of the International Military Tribunal (IMT) and the International Military Tribunal of the Far East (IMTFE), respectively, in 1945 and 1946, evidences the problem of enforcing international criminal law without having an international criminal code or norms contained in positive international law.

The IMT charter and IMTFE statute provide for three crimes, namely, "crimes against peace," "war crimes," and "crimes against humanity." The first of these was not reflected in positive international law, the second was reflected in conventions embodying customary international law, and the third was an emerging international custom but without precedent in the practice of states. Furthermore, the charter and statute, as well as the jurisprudence, of these two tribunals brought about significant changes in the areas of immunity of heads of state, command responsibility, the defense of obedience to superior orders, and the defense or mitigation arguments of *tu quoque.*

These new developments in the international law of criminal responsibility challenged the "principles of legality," which are well established in the "general principles of law recognized in civilized nations" (Article 38 of the Statute of the International Court of Justice). These principles require that there be no crime without a criminal law, that there be no penalty without law, and that both the crime and the penalty not apply retroactively. To remedy the situation, the General Assembly (G.A.) of the United Nations adopted a resolution in 1946 affirming the "Nuremberg Principles," and in 1947 it adopted a resolution requesting that the International Law Commission (ILC) codify international crimes. That task was given to the ILC in a mandate for the preparation of a Draft Code of Offences Against the Peace and Security of Mankind. At the time, the mandate was envisaged as including the four major international crimes, namely, "crimes against peace," "war crimes," "crimes against humanity," and "genocide," which was embodied in a convention adopted by the G.A. in 1948. The mandate was broad enough to encompass other international crimes that might affect peace and security and to elaborate a draft statute for an international criminal court that would apply the Codes of Offences.

In the early 1950s the cold war and Realpolitik thwarted these efforts. However, because the international community was at that time still under the sway of the Nuremberg and Tokyo trials, as well as other Allied and national proceedings, an abrupt ending or modification of the ILC's 1947 mandate was not politically feasible. Instead, a more subtle approach was developed to hamper progress on the codification of international crimes, paradoxically, by the leading powers of the Eastern and Western blocks. This was done through bureaucratic techniques. Between 1950 and 1952 the ILC's 1947 mandate was curtailed by removing from it "crimes against the peace," which by then had become known as "aggression," and the establishment of an international criminal court. Both of these questions were attributed to two separate committees. The G.A. established a committee of states to define aggression, which was completed in 1974. It also established a committee of experts nominated by governments to prepare a draft statute for an international criminal court that produced a first text in 1951, amended in 1953.

The ILC's work on the Draft Code of Offences was completed in 1954 but did not include aggression, which was still being debated by a special committee. As a result, the 1954 Draft Code of Offences was tabled by the G.A. until such time as the special committee on aggression had completed its definition of that crime. In the meantime, the 1953 Draft Statute for an International Criminal Court had been tabled by the G.A. because the 1954 Draft Code of Offences had not been ready in 1953. The cascading effect of tabling each initiative because another one was still pending was a political work of art.

The 1954 Draft Code of Offences should have procedurally been taken up again in 1974, when the G.A. adopted by consensus, but not by a vote, the definition of aggression as established by the Special Committee appointed in 1952. But it was not until 1978 that the G.A. gave the ILC a new mandate, which it renamed in 1988 as the Draft Code of Crimes Against the Peace and Security of Mankind. Once again, because of the existing conditions of the cold war, the undertaking that had been delayed for thirty-eight years was not allowed to move at a rapid pace. But the ILC, wittingly or unwittingly, abetted this situation by deciding that precisely because of the passage of all these years, the 1954 Draft Code of Offences and the definition of aggression needed to be reexamined and a new rapporteur was appointed who, after an initial period of some years, came up with an ambitious plan to expand the number of crimes contained in the 1954 Draft Code. From 1978 to 1991 the ILC worked, obviously without great haste, at the development of a new Draft Code of Crimes, which by then contained twenty-six categories of crimes, as opposed to only four, namely, aggression, genocide, crimes against humanity, and war crimes.

The newly proposed crimes were, with respect to some of them, farfetched, and drafted in a manner that contravened accepted practices in most legal systems with respect to codification of crimes. In short, the 1991 Draft Code of Crimes used ambiguous, and more political than legal terminology. For example, the new 1991 Draft Code of Crimes considered among the new international crimes what it vaguely defined as "colonialism," "mercenarism," and "crimes against the environment." As a result of this overreaching and legal imprecision in the definition of these supposed new international crimes, the G.A.'s reaction was to send the project back to the ILC for further consideration. The technical legal flaws of the 1991 Draft Code served the purposes of those who opposed the codification effort.

In 1993 and 1994, the Security Council adopted, respectively, the statutes of the International Criminal Tribunals for former Yugoslavia (ICTY) and International Criminal Tribunal for Rwanda (ICTR), which included genocide (as defined in the 1948 convention), war crimes (as defined in the grave breeches of the Geneva Convention and as contained in the Laws and Customs of War), and crimes against humanity (approximately as defined in the Nuremberg Charter). As a result of these developments, as well as the clearly perceived rejection by most states of the 1991 Draft

Code of Crimes, the ILC produced a revised and shortened text in 1996 that eliminated most of the crimes contained in the 1991 draft, leaving only aggression (as defined in the 1974 G.A. resolution), genocide (as defined in the 1948 convention), war crimes (as defined in the grave breeches of the Geneva Convention, and as contained in the Laws and Customs of War, but without defining them), and crimes against humanity (as defined in the statutes of the ICTY and ICTR, though there are slight differences between the two definitions).

Notwithstanding this modified and shortened text, as of 2004 the G.A. had failed to adopt the Draft Code of Crimes Against the Peace and Security of Mankind as proposed by the ILC. The long-awaited codification of international criminal law has not materialized, even though it has been in the making for more than a half century. At first, the reasons were the cold war and Realpolitik; more recently, it was opposition by the United States that assumed in the early 2000s a hegemonic role in world affairs, coupled with an aversion for international criminal justice norms and institutions to which its nationals, particularly its senior political and military leaders, could be subjected. The laudable efforts that began in the wake of the IMT and IMTFE withered away, and no official contemporary efforts to codify international crimes have developed, even though the need for it is more dire in the early years of the twenty-first century than it was fifty years ago.

SEE ALSO Crimes Against Humanity; International Law; International Law Commission

BIBLIOGRAPHY

Bassiouni, M. Cherif. (1987). *A Draft International Criminal Code and Draft Statute for an International Criminal Tribunal*. Boston: Martinus Nijhoff.

Ferencz, Benjamin (1975). *Defining International Aggression*. Dobbs Ferry, NY: Oceana.

Johnson, D. H. N. (1955). "The Draft Code of Offences Against the Peace." *International & Comparative Law Quarterly* 4:462–463.

M. Cherif Bassiouni

Collaboration

Genocide in the twentieth century occurred with increasing frequency, from the Armenian catastrophe of World War I, to the Nazi extermination of six million European Jews, to the massacres of their own people by Soviet and Chinese communist leaders. In each of these cases government policies encouraged participation by local populations in the killing, as informants, auxiliary security forces, or even executioners.

Terms and Definitions

The term *collaboration* is often associated with the betrayal of one's nation to serve a foreign power, and many of those who did so believed they were serving the interests of their country, as well as themselves, by participating in actions at the behest of an outside force, usually the political leadership of another state. Collaboration is also the active participation in genocide by groups or individuals. Collaborators differ from perpetrators in that they are not the initiators of mass murder, but instead provide assistance out of opportunism, ideology, religious hatred, or psychological conditioning. For example, although members of the Nazi SS Action Groups (SS *Einsatzgruppen*) on the Eastern Front were the primary perpetrators of the Holocaust, especially in 1941 and 1942, Ukrainian peasants who reported hidden Jews were collaborators. Similarly, while many SS officials in occupied France were perpetrators with the primary task of deporting Jews to death camps, the Vichy French police who aided in the location and arrest of Jews were collaborators.

Genocide

The same terms hold true with other cases of genocide over the past century. In the Armenian genocide of World War I the perpetrators were primarily Ottoman military forces concerned about Armenian identification with the Russian enemy. In the commission of this genocide, however, local Turkish villagers in Eastern Anatolia and other provinces collaborated with the forces of the state, denying refuge and aid to those attempting to escape, and protecting only those Armenian women willing to convert to Islam and abandon their Christian heritage. The genocide of 1.5 million Armenians was made possible by collaboration.

The wars in the former Yugoslavia, from 1991 to 1999, involved not just the Serbian military and police forces of Slobodan Milosevic, but also Serbian vigilante groups recruited from peasants and workers throughout Serbia, Croatia, Kosovo, Bosnia, and other regions. These collaborators, although often not formed into organizations of the Yugoslav government, or given any clear guidance from the regime in Belgrade, nonetheless assisted in attacks on other ethnic groups—principally Croatians and Muslim Bosnians—or took opportunistic advantage by occupying the homes and land of those who had been ethnically cleansed. The result was over 200,000 killed and two million refugees, many murdered or uprooted by their neighbors.

The Holocaust

Even in areas not directly occupied by the perpetrating regime, collaborators can exist among the political

Wartime collaborator Maurice Papon was convicted in 1998 of complicity in crimes against humanity for his role in the persecution of French Jews during World War II. He is shown here leaving La Santé prison in Paris in 2002, after an appeals court ordered his release for medical reasons. [AP/WIDE WORLD PHOTOS]

leadership and security forces of other states. As the most widespread case of genocide in the twentieth century, the Holocaust of European Jews and other minorities provides examples of every kind of approach to collaboration: coperpetrators, collaborators, bystanders, and resisters.

Among the Axis nations, which were allies of Nazi Germany, some states joined in its enthusiastic persecution and destruction of Jews, Romani, and others. In Slovakia and Romanian-occupied territory in the former Soviet Union, the Holocaust took on significant similarities to that practiced by the Third Reich. The Hlinka Guard in Slovakia, a clerical fascist party, killed or aided in the deportation of nearly the entire Jewish Slovak population. Romania was unique, in that while the pro-German government refused to exterminate Jewish citizens on its own soil, its forces murdered tens of thousands of Jews in southwestern Ukraine, which it occupied from 1941 to 1944, even Romanian Jews who had been deported to the area.

The Nazis also found collaborators in the territories they occupied, even when their policies were harsh toward the non-Jewish civilian population. In the USSR local militias in the Baltic states of Estonia, Lithuania, and Latvia welcomed the German invasion as liberation from Communism, an ideology they identified with Jews. Nationalistic Baltic citizens created militia groups in response to the collapse of Soviet authority in the summer of 1941 and actively collaborated in the extermination of Jewish communities, in some cases even before the arrival of the first German military or SS forces. The same held true in the Ukraine, where thousands volunteered to assist in the murder of Jews, or reported on hidden Jews or their protectors.

Even some neutral states aided in Nazi efforts to exterminate the Jews of Europe. Switzerland, for example, routinely returned Jewish refugees to Nazi control, and others, including Turkey and Spain, refused to allow Jews to cross their borders unless they had visas allowing them to transit to a third nation, thereby in effect condemning these victims to a terrible fate.

Vichy France, the rump state left after France's defeat in 1940, is a distinct case. Although never officially a member of the Axis and occupied by Nazi Germany after the November 1942 Allied landings in North Africa, it nonetheless played an important role in extending the Holocaust to France. Although the regime of Marshall Henri Pétain and Pierre Laval never officially joined the Axis, it did provide indispensable support to the Nazi extermination of Jews. Vichy police participated in the round-ups of French and foreign Jews in France, and were very effective collaborators even after the Nazi occupation of 1942.

Some states in the Axis, most notably Bulgaria and Italy, before Benito Mussolini's overthrow in 1943, were less collaborationist. Bulgaria's leadership, despite strong German pressure, refused to surrender Bulgarian Jews to the Holocaust, supported in this decision by the local population, Orthodox clergy, and nearly all political organizations. Even Mussolini, so loyal in his devotion to Hitler in other matters, refused to deport Italian Jews to their deaths in Nazi-occupied territory. Some Jews had even been active in the initial leadership of the Fascist Party, although the anti-Semitic measures introduced by Mussolini's government in 1938 put an end to this involvement. In the two cases it seems to have been national pride, rather than any particular identification with Jews, that protected both communities.

Motivations

What motivates collaboration? Why do some chose to participate in genocide? There are a variety of motives, but one sobering truth remains: No twentieth-century regime bent on committing mass murder or genocide

has lacked collaborators. Four major factors have been most important in motivating collaboration in genocide: political ideology, opportunism, religious hatred, and psychological conditioning.

Collaboration based on political ideology occurs when there is a convergence of political objectives between the primary perpetrators and others. An example would be the Arrow Cross movement in Hungary during World War II. Even though a German ally, Hungarian dictator Miklós Horthy opposed the Holocaust and gave sanctuary to Jews until 1944. The Hungarian Arrow Cross movement, however, was enthusiastically pro-Nazi anti-Semitic and willingly assisted in the deportation and execution of Jews, eventually arresting Horthy when he tried to stop the killings. The political identification of the Arrow Cross with Nazi Germany was nearly complete, making collaboration an imperative for party members.

Collaboration also arises from opportunistic motives. In occupied Poland the German Order Police and SS offered bribes to peasants who would inform on hidden Jews or act as guides in leading Nazi forces to their locations. While in some cases the Germans offered direct payments of salt, sugar, or alcohol, in other cases they merely held out the opportunity to plunder the possessions of captured Jews. Other Poles blackmailed Jews to provide money or other treasures rather than reporting them to the occupation authorities, but often did so anyway once the savings of such desperate Jews were exhausted.

In addition, collaboration frequently stems from religious hatred or indifference. Catholic priests and members of religious orders collaborated with genocide perpetrated by the Nazis and the Croatian Ustasha satellite regime, including sanctioning the forced conversions of Serbian Orthodox believers and deportations of Jews, Serbs, and Romani to concentration camps. Although some priests opposed the exterminations that followed, few dissented from the Croatian program to remove the Serbian and Jewish populations, resulting in the deaths of over 200,000 Serbs and 50,000 Yugoslav Jews.

Psychological conditioning was also an important factor in promoting collaboration. On the Eastern Front soldiers received lessons in anti-Semitism and Nazi racial theory from educational officers attached to the German army. This, coupled with years of Nazi propaganda in German schools, entertainment, and military training facilities encouraged German soldiers to regard Jews, Russians, and Poles as subhuman, and unworthy of living. Although regular German military forces in World War II did not initially participate in genocide, soon after the invasion of the USSR in June

1941 their forces did provide support to SS actions, and later participated in atrocities against the civilian population and Soviet prisoners of war.

Collaboration was a widespread response to Nazi occupation policies and military victories, and was more common than direct resistance. Given the dominance of Hitler's Germany on the European continent and the benefits to be derived from cooperation, the question is perhaps not why so many collaborated with the Third Reich, but why more did not.

SEE ALSO Bystanders; Perpetrators

BIBLIOGRAPHY

Balakian, Peter (1997). *Black Dog of Fate*. New York: Broadway Books.

Bartov, Omer (1992). *Hitler's Army: Soldiers, Nazis and War in the Third Reich*. Oxford, U.K.: Oxford University Press.

Bowen, Wayne H. (2000). *Spaniards and Nazi Germany: Collaboration in the New Order*. Columbia, Mo.: University of Missouri Press.

Browning, Christopher (1992). *Ordinary Men: Reserve Police Battalion 101 and the Final Solution in Poland*. New York: HarperCollins.

Conway, Martin (1993). *Collaboration in Belgium: Léon Degrelle and the Rexist Movement, 1940–1944*. New Haven, Conn.: Yale University Press.

Hilberg, Raul (1992). *Perpetrators, Victims, Bystanders: The Jewish Catastrophe, 1933–1945*. New York: HarperCollins.

Piotrowski, Tadeusz (1998). *Poland's Holocaust: Ethnic Strife, Collaboration with Occupying Forces and Genocide*. Jefferson, N.C.: McFarland.

Sweets, John F. (1986). *Choices in Vichy France: The French under Nazi Occupation*. Oxford, U.K.: Oxford University Press.

Tomasevich, Jozo (2001). *War and Revolution in Yugoslavia, 1941–1945: Occupation and Collaboration*. Stanford, Calif.: Stanford University Press.

Wayne H. Bowen

Comics

In his two volumes *Maus: A Survivor's Tale* and *Maus: A Survivor's Tale II*, Art Spiegelman narrates the fate of his parents, a Polish Jewish couple who survive Auschwitz and the Holocaust. The most striking feature of the books is the trivial fact that they are comic strips in which the Jews are represented as mice and the Germans as cats. This metaphorical depiction of Nazi-Jewish relations is not a genuine animal fable, because it is much too complex. Various aspects of meaning are given in the cartoons, and there are different ways of

conveying those meanings. They entail, for instance, the narratives of Vladek, the narrator's (Artie's) father, as a single male and how he and his wife Anna are separated and reunited. The narration follows the increasing severity of Nazi persecution and also describes the inner conflict a member of the post-Holocaust generation faces. The flexibility of the comic strip as a medium facilitates a reflective manipulation of the different events in time.

The presentation of a human being as an animal or with some animal features is adopted in political cartoons in order to denigrate, for instance, a political opponent or social group. Its traditional intention is to transfer some negative animal characteristic, such as laziness or stupidity, to the victim of the cartoonist and thus create and/or emphasize a negative stereotypical trait. This, however, is not the case in *Maus*. In this cartoon, on the contrary, two separate mental spaces, that is, the space of human beings and the space of animals (mice, cats, dogs), are blended, creating anthropomorphic creatures who represent real people, for example, Artie, the protagonist and narrator, Vladek, his father, and Anna, his mother. They are drawn with human bodies and appropriately sized mouse heads. The faces are drawn in a neutral way and show very few expressive and distinguishing features.

This creation and blending of two separate mental spaces are everyday features of verbal language. In statements such as "If I were in your shoes, I would quit my job," the speaker takes over the role of the listener and states how he would act in that hypothetical space. Such a blending process activates at least four mental spaces: a generic space, the source space, the target space, and the resulting blended space. The generic space contains a skeletal structure, which reflects the commonalities of the two input spaces.

In the above example, the generic space would be represented by a sentence such as "An agent takes a decision." The first input space would read: "The speaker quits his job" and the second input space would read, "The listener quits his job." The blended space integrates selected parts of the structure from the input spaces and would read: "The speaker quits the job of the listener."

As is seen, the blended space integrates selected parts of the structure from the input spaces. The effect of alienation (*Verfremdungseffekt*) has two causes: Even if readers are familiar with anthropomorphic creatures in comic strips such as Spiderman, combining Spiegelman's hybrid creatures with Nazi terror and the Holocaust may seem strange and the meaning of such a blend is open to interpretation. The meaning potential of this pictorial blending can be described as follows:

the generic space contains a relative assessment of human beings together with other mammals. Depending on people's convictions, mammals do or do not have a distinct personality, dignity, a right to live, and they are or are not regarded as vermin. The first input space allots the positive qualities and rights to human beings and the second input space denies mice these qualities and rights. In the blended space the anthropomorphic mice, who represent the Jews, are denied these qualities and rights.

Because the readers of *Maus* know that Spiegelman is a Jew himself, it is very unlikely that they will interpret the blending in this way. It is clearly an ironic pictorial of Hitler's statement that Jews are vermin. When it is obvious that someone slips into the role of another person and acts in that role, irony is created. Thus, readers are constantly reminded of the ironic stance that the author adopts. He does so because the genocidal atrocities of the Nazis are beyond comprehension and, what is more, beyond description.

SEE ALSO Art as Propaganda; Art as Representation

BIBLIOGRAPHY

Fauconnier, G., *Mental Spaces*. Cambridge: Cambridge University Press.

Hünig, Wolfgang K. (1974). *Strukturen des comic strip*. Hildesheim: Olms.

Hünig, Wolfgang K. (2002). *British and German Cartoons as Weapons in World War I*. Frankfurt: Lang.

Rohrer, T. (2001). "Even the Interface Is For Sale: Metaphors, Visual Blends and the Hidden Ideology of the Internet." In *Language and Ideology*, ed. R. Dirven, R. M. Frank, and C. Ilie. Amsterdam: John Benjamins.

Turner, M., and G. Fauconnier (1995). "Conceptual Integration and Formal Expression". *Metaphor and Symbolic Activity* 10:183-203.

Turner, M., and G. Fauconnier (2002). "Metaphor, Metonymy, and Binding". In *Metaphor and Metonymy in Contrast and Comparison*, ed. R. Dirven and R. Pörings. Berlin: Mouton de Gruyter.

Wolfgang K. Hünig

Commission on Responsibilities

World War I was started by the Austro-Hungarian Empire over the assassination of Archduke Ferdinand by a Serb nationalist in Sarajevo. The event gave Germany an opportunity to declare war on August 2, 1914. Two days later it invaded Belgium and France, bringing the British Empire, tsarist Russia, Italy, and later the United States into the conflict. These allies and Japan, Greece, Poland, Romania, and Serbia were called the Entente Powers, but France, the British Empire, Italy, Japan,

and the United States referred to themselves as the Great Powers. Germany's allies, called the Central Powers, were the Austro-Hungarian Empire, the Turkish Ottoman Empire, and Bulgaria. The conflict was, until then, the bloodiest in history, resulting in more than 21 million casualties, with 8.5 million dead in slightly more than four years. During the conflict chemical weapons were used for the first time, and as a result of the harm they caused, their use was banned in 1925. Both sides committed violations of the laws and customs of war, particularly the Central Powers, and the Germans and Turks.

The hostilities ended with the signing of an armistice in a railroad car at Compiegnes, France, on November 11, 1918 (a date still celebrated in the United States as Veterans Day), and a formal peace conference and treaty soon ensued. On January 25, 1919, the Preliminary Peace Conference in Paris established the Commission on the Responsibility of the Authors of War and on the Enforcement of Penalties, which would deliberate on just punishment for the Germans and their allies. The Commission's mandate was to investigate individual criminal responsibility for the "authors of the war" and for violations of the laws and customs of war. The mandate included drawing up a list of persons to be prosecuted for such crimes, irrespective of how "highly placed" they were, and establishing procedures for "a tribunal appropriate for the trials of these offenders." The mandate also included what it referred to as a "cognate or ancillary to the above." It was the first time in modern history that such an investigatory commission was established on an international scale and with such a broad mandate.

The Commission consisted of fifteen representatives from the ten Entente Powers who were for the most part senior governmental officials from ministries of foreign affairs, many with a legal background and senior military officers. Each delegation had a support staff of military and legal experts.

The Commission's establishment preceded the signing of the official peace treaty that occurred on June 28, 1919, at the Versailles Palace. The Treaty of Versailles did not come into force until January 1920, a year after the Commission was established. The Commission's work, however, was based on the assumption that the peace treaty would contain provisions for the prosecution of those whom it was able to identify as criminally responsible for the conflict. This was the understanding of the Entente Powers after the Preliminary Peace Conference in Paris and as reflected in the Commission's mandate. The Central Powers, however, had other expectations, arising from the actual language of the earlier 1918 armistice, namely, immunity.

The Treaty of Versailles contained four articles relating to the Commission's work: Article 227 on the criminal responsibility of Kaiser Wilhelm, Articles 228 and 229 on the prosecution of those who violated the laws and customs of war contained in the 1907 Hague Convention No. IV and its Annexed Regulations, and Article 230, which obligated all the Central Powers to surrender for trial those persons wanted for prosecution pursuant to Articles 228 through 229.

The peace treaty, however, did not contain an explicit provision on the prosecution of Turkish officials with respect to the large-scale killing of Armenian civilians during World War I. The Commission nevertheless considered the matter "cognate or ancillary" to other aspects of its mandate, namely violations of the laws and customs of war by the Germans. Accordingly, it examined the responsibility of Turkish officials for what it called "crimes against the laws of humanity."

The Commission's work, which commenced shortly after its establishment, resulted in a preliminary report on March 29, 1919, and a final report on May 18, 1919.

The Commission's work had three legal tracks. The first was determining if the Kaiser bore responsibility for initiating war in Europe. Because no legal prohibition existed against the resort to war as an instrument of national policy, the decision to address the Kaiser's responsibility in the Treaty of Versailles (Article 227) was essentially a political one. This provision was drafted by a member of the British Empire's delegation to the peace conference whose political astuteness is reflected in the language of Article 227. The alleged crime was defined as "the supreme offence against international morality and sanctity of treaties." Because no such defined crime existed in international law, or for that matter in the national laws of almost all countries in the world, it was easy for The Netherlands to give the Kaiser political asylum and he was never prosecuted. This outcome did not displease Europe's monarchies, many of which were related to Germany's. Other than Belgium and France, there were few governments that did not support the preservation of the customary international principle of law granting immunity to a head of state. This is why the Commission's chairman, Secretary of State Robert Lansing, had originally opposed the prosecution of the German head of state, but he was overruled by the Commission's majority.

The U.S. position subsequently changed. American support for the Kaiser's prosecution was the result of a political quid pro quo—the peace conference's recognition of the Monroe Doctrine, thus giving the United States hegemony over the Southern Hemisphere. As a result of this political deal, a new historic development occurred, namely the personal criminal responsibility of a head of state for the newly established international crime contained in Article 227. The precedent paved the way for the Nuremberg Charter to unequivocally deny immunity to a head of state for the three crimes within its jurisdiction—a position followed by the later International Criminal Tribunal for the Former Yugoslavia (ICTY), the International Criminal Tribunal for Rwanda (ICTR), and the International Criminal Court (ICC).

The second track was more conventional and in better keeping with the Commission's mandate and expertise. It related to assessing the violations of the laws and customs of war by Germany and its allies, and preparing a list of persons who would be prosecuted in accordance with Articles 228 and 229. Government delegates on the Commission submitted their own lists of alleged war crimes and their accused perpetrators. The Commission as a whole reviewed these submissions and issued findings as to the facts alleged and the charges against the alleged perpetrators. In doing this, it asked governments to submit documentation to support their allegations. The Commission did not, however, independently investigate the facts; it merely reviewed the allegations and evidence presented by delegates and, when necessary, requested additional evidence. Consequently, it acted more as a gatherer and reviewer of allegations by the governments represented on the Commission than as an investigative organ, as these bodies are known in national criminal justice systems.

In the relatively short period between February and May 1919, the Commission drew up a list of situations in which war crimes were alleged to have been committed by Germans, and named or identified the alleged perpetrators. The categories of crimes charged included: systematic terrorizing of civilian populations, mass and individual murders of civilians, mistreatment of the civilian population, the use of civilians as human shields for the military, torture, rape, displacement of the civilian population, collective punishment, looting of private and public property, pillaging of private property, and the killing and mistreatment of prisoners of war (POWs). The Commission's list of alleged perpetrators, all Germans, exceeded twenty thousand. The Commission did not take into account any similar acts allegedly committed by the Entente Powers against the Central Powers. Also, Articles 228 and 229 of the Treaty of Versailles applied only to the defeated Central Powers. After World War II the Allies, who included all but two of the Great Powers' allies from World War I, adopted this same one-sided approach, thus leading to the label "victors' vengeance" with respect to post-conflict judicial proceedings.

Although the allegations of war crimes committed by German forces were for the most part substantially accurate, the large number of persons alleged to have committed war crimes was probably exaggerated. This may be why the Commission subsequently reconsidered the original number and lowered it to 895. This significant reduction also occurred for political reasons, as well as careful consideration of the time, effort, and costs associated with prosecuting such a large number of individuals.

The Allies' political will to carry out the prosecutions of 895 war criminals based on the findings of the Commission was, however, short-lived. Three years later no tribunals had been established and no prosecutions conducted. In 1922 the Commission abandoned the prospects of such action and asked Germany to assume responsibility for prosecuting its own war criminals. Germany agreed to this scenario and passed a special law for that purpose; in 1923 it prosecuted some 22 individuals on the Commission's scaled down list of 895. Belgium and France expressed outrage, as did the British public, but as time passed, support for postconflict justice waned. Then, as in the twenty-first century, public outrage over crimes of war is short-lived.

The Commission's files on the twenty-two individuals accused of war crimes constituted the basis of the prosecution conducted in Leipzig before the German Supreme Court. Because the work of the Commission was, by nature, more focused on preliminary findings rather than a thorough and complete investigation of the facts, it was easy for the defense at the Leipzig trials to argue against the charges and, at times, even ridicule them. The German public considered those prosecuted to be scapegoats for a defeated Germany and some viewed them as heroes. The German *Reichsgericht* (Supreme Court) nevertheless conducted its proceedings with fairness, and the judges were not partial to the accused, in fact convicting nineteen of them.

The third track was an extension of the second one, namely the prosecution of Turkish officials for crimes against the laws of humanity for the annihilation of its Armenian population. From a legal positivist's perspective, it was as much of a stretch as was the idea of prosecuting the Kaiser for the crime of violating the "sanctity of international treaties." But, in support of the concept of crimes against the laws of humanity, it must be said that the facts warranted the extension of the then existing law of armed conflict on the protection of the civilian population in a state at war, to apply to the same depredation when committed by a state against its own population during time of war. Because the 1907 Hague Convention and its Annexed Regulations prohibited killing the enemy's civilian population, it was reasonable to extend these prohibitions to a state committing the same violations against its own civilian population, provided that such actions were war-related. The gap in protecting civilians during time of war needed to be filled, particularly because the killing of the Armenians was done in such an egregious manner and on such a large scale that it could not be ignored (the estimated numbers of those killed range from 200,000 to 1,000,000). For the Commission, as for the drafters of the Nuremberg Charter some twenty-five years later, the facts drove the law.

The Commission wished to include what was then called "the Armenian massacre" among its list of crimes for which Turkish officials were to be prosecuted. However, there was no legal basis to do so pursuant to the 1907 Hague Convention and its Annexed Regulations because the victims were Turkish nationals and not the nationals of another state with which the Turkish Ottoman Empire was at war. The Commission developed an appropriate, although artful, legal argument based on both the language and spirit of the 1907 Hague Convention's Preamble. The Preamble had been drafted by a Russian diplomat, Fyodor Martens; the portion of it that the Commission cited was named "Martens' clause."

The premise of the Preamble of the 1907 Hague Convention is that international law reflects the human values that have emerged from civilization, and that this is what the term "laws of humanity" refers to. It thus follows that not everything falling under the category of laws of humanity could have been agreed on by state parties for inclusion in the 1907 Hague Convention and its Annexed Regulations. Therefore, the Preamble affirms that what is included in the specific provisions of the Hague Convention is only a portion of the laws of humanity, namely that portion which the signing nations had agreed to. Consequently, when other wartime practices emerge that constitute a violation of the laws of humanity, they would be considered part of the prohibited conduct contained in the original Convention. This represented a new development.

On the basis of such reasoning, the Commission concluded that the widespread and systematic killing of Armenian civilians in 1915 as part of a policy of persecution against the civilian population of a certain ethnic/religious background constituted a crime against the laws of humanity by analogy to war crimes. The assumption was that, if one of the purposes of the Law of Armed Conflict was to protect innocent civilians during time of war, then no distinction should be made based on the nationality of the victims. This was a humanistic perspective ahead of its time. In fact, it has continued opposed by those who believe that power and not law should control international affairs.

The Commission's majority agreed that Turkish officials, whether military or political, should be prosecuted for crimes against the laws of humanity on the same basis as Germans were to be prosecuted for war crimes. However, two delegations strongly dissented, namely the United States and Japan, insisting that their minority opinions be published as part of the Commission's final report. The legal argument presented by these two delegations was the notion that crimes against the laws of humanity was predicated on natural law and not positive law and therefore could not be recognized as a valid interpretation of existing international law.

Despite this opposition, the recommendation of the majority could have been carried out, but the western allies of the Entente Powers subsequently struck a political deal with Turkey, as reflected in the 1923 Treaty of Lausanne, which granted amnesty to Turkish officials for the period from 1914 to 1922. For political reasons, the Entente's western allies needed Turkey to be on their side: to serve as a buffer with the newly established Union of the Soviet Socialist Republics (USSR) that had come about as a result of the 1917 communist revolution against tsarist Russia. The about-face of the western allies concerning the criminal responsibility of Turkish officials is reflected in the 1923 peace treaty between the Entente Powers and Turkey, the Treaty of Lausanne, which replaced the 1920 Treaty of Sèvres that was not ratified. The latter contained a provision establishing the criminal accountability of Turkish officials before the Entente Powers' tribunals pursuant to Articles 228 and 229 of the Treaty of Versailles. The 1923 Treaty of Lausanne, the agreement that entered into force, did not however contain such a provision. Instead, it included a special protocol that gave amnesty to all Turkish officials for the time period of the Armenian massacre. At the signing of the Treaty of Lausanne, 118 Turkish officials were in British custody, with most of them held in Malta; they were subsequently released.

On August 8, 1945, the four major Allies (France, the United Kingdom, the United States, and the USSR) signed the London Agreement that established the International Military Tribunal (IMT) at Nuremberg; its Article 6(c) defines crimes against humanity. Although unstated in the London Agreement, Article 6(c) was based on the legal reasoning developed by the 1919 Commission with respect to crimes against the laws of humanity. This conclusion is supported by the fact that the definition of crimes against humanity in Article 6(c) requires the need for a connection between these crimes and other crimes within the jurisdiction of the IMT, including war crimes as defined in Article 6(b). The 1919 Commission had posited that crimes against the laws of humanity were an extension of war crimes arising from the laws and customs of war, and in 1945 that concept became part of international law.

The work of the 1919 Commission thus resulted in (1) reversing the customary rule of immunity for heads of state for international crimes, later referred to as "crimes against peace" in the IMT and Tokyo War Crimes Tribunal (or IMTFE) and as "aggression" in the UN Charter; (2) establishing the principle of international criminal responsibility for internationally proscribed crimes (with enforcement before international or national judicial bodies and, in this case, through the prosecution of twenty-two German military personnel before the Supreme Court of Germany sitting at Leipzig); and (3) providing the legal foundation for a new international crime, "crimes against the laws of humanity" (though the Commission failed to prosecute anyone for this crime, its efforts gave rise to the emergence of a customary rule of international law that was more clearly and fully defined in the Charter of the IMT and the Statute of the IMTFE).

All these developments can be traced back to the historic efforts of the 1919 Commission in formulating the concept of crimes against the laws of humanity. In addition, the establishment of international criminal investigatory commissions can be traced to the 1919 Commission. Both the 1943 UN War Crimes Commission established to document the Axis Powers' war crimes in Europe and the 1945 Far East Commission established to document Japanese war crimes in the Far East were, in large part, modeled on the 1919 Commission. In 1992 the Security Council followed a different model when it established, in Resolution 780, the Commission of Experts to Investigate Violations of International Humanitarian Law. The Security Council Commission on Yugoslavia was the only international body mandated to investigate violations by all parties to a conflict.

The work of the 1919 Commission, Articles 227 through 230 of the Treaty of Versailles, and the subsequent 1923 Leipzig trials did not perhaps fulfill the international community's expectations, but they made history and established precedents on which the international community built new advances in international criminal justice.

SEE ALSO Hague Conventions of 1907; Tokyo Trial; War Crimes; World War I Peace Treaties

BIBLIOGRAPHY

Bassiouni, M. Cherif (1987). *A Draft International Criminal Code and Draft Statute for an International Criminal Tribunal,* 2nd edition. Dordrecht: M. Nijhoff.

Bassiouni M. Cherif, and Benjamin B. Ferencz (1999). "The Crime against Peace." In *International Criminal Law,* 2nd edition, ed. M. Cherif Bassiouni. Ardsley, N.Y.: Transnational Publishers.

Ferencz, Benjamin B. (1975). *Defining International Aggression.* Dobbs Ferry, N.Y.: Oceana.

Gross, Leo (1983). "Some Observations on the Draft Code of Offences against the Peace and Security of Mankind." *Israel Yearbook on Human Rights* 13(9):10.

Johnson, D. H. N. (1955). "Draft Code of Offences against the Peace." *International Comparative Law Quarterly* 4(4):445.

M. Cherif Bassiouni

Comparative Genocide

Some of the central questions attending the analysis of any genocide, such as the Holocaust or the Armenian genocide, are: Why did it happen? How did it happen? How similar or different is it from other instances? And, what can be learned to prevent such occurrences in the future? A comparative approach may be helpful in providing some answers because the principle aim of scholarly comparison is to identify essential similarities and underlying patterns in order to arrive at credible explanations or theories for some types of genocide. Such explanations should be able to shed light on particular instances of genocide as well as on the process itself. The juxtaposition and comparison of a number of cases do not imply that they are identical or even similar. Indeed, differences from an underlying pattern, such as the Holocaust or the Armenian genocide, can be instructive in demonstrating the range of variation among cases or in challenging theories that claim to account for similarities.

Theories

Following the United Nations (UN) definition, which distinguishes between genocide in whole or "total genocide," and genocide in part or "partial genocide," and introducing a distinction first suggested by Leo Kuper, between genocide that is domestic and foreign with respect to the geographical and social boundaries of the state, it is possible to distinguish among four basic types of genocide: (1) *total domestic,* for example, German Jews in the Third Reich, Armenians under the Young Turks, the Tutsi in Rwanda; (2) *total foreign,* for example, Polish Jews under Nazi occupation, Native Tasmanians in the nineteenth century, and Herero under German colonialism; (3) *partial domestic,* for example, Bosnian Muslims during the Yugoslav war, gas-

sing of the Kurds in Iraq under the regime of Saddam Hussein; and (4) *partial foreign,* for example, Poles and others under Nazi occupation, destruction without extermination of a number of Native peoples in Africa and the Americas.

Except for noting that genocide entails the dehumanization of its victims, there is no general theory for the phenomenon, nor does space permit discussing in detail theories for the four types of genocide listed above. However, there are a number of key variables that writers have singled out for each type.

For total domestic genocides—even when, as in the case of the Holocaust, these mutate into total foreign genocides—nearly all writers have emphasized the ideology of the perpetrators as causal. This would include Nazi biological racism, the Pan-Turkism and organic nationalism of the Young Turks, the radical Maoism of the Khmer Rouge, and the "Hamitic hypothesis" of Hutu power in the Rwandan genocide. Others have pointed to political, social, cultural, and economic crises for the perpetrator regime. Well-known examples are the many crises of the Weimar Republic following Germany's defeat in World War I, and the defeats and crises that confronted the Young Turks following their coup in 1908. Touching on genocide in Africa, Biafra, in particular, Kuper has emphasized the tensions and contradictions between a sovereign state and the culturally plural society over which it rules. Other writers have stressed social or national revolutions within the context of general war and the dynamics of totalitarianism.

For partial domestic and foreign genocides, especially when, as in Yugoslavia, genocide took the form of ethnic cleansing, writers have emphasized the ideology of integral nationalism and the context of war or civil war. For foreign genocides, both partial and total, especially against indigenous peoples, writers have stressed an attitude of dehumanization of the "savage Other" within a context of imperialism, modernity, and capitalist development.

Fallacies

Most scholars would concur that there are both distinctive and comparative aspects to most genocides, including the Holocaust; however, a comparison may also be misleading and fallacious. This can be most clearly observed in the comparative treatment of the Holocaust wherein two fallacies often occur.

The first, the "equivalence" fallacy, suggests that because the Holocaust may be similar to another instance of genocide, it is therefore equivalent to it. The second, the "uniqueness" fallacy, claims that because it was unique, the Holocaust is incomparable. The first is a fallacy, because a thing or an instance can be similar in some dimensions without being equivalent in all. The second is a fallacy because a thing or an instance can be distinctive in one or more important ways without being distinctive in all dimensions.

Perhaps because they wish to undermine the significance of the Holocaust, some writers have drawn a false equivalence between it and other seemingly similar events. They discover Holocaust-like events throughout history and the world, not to understand them or even to exaggerate their import but to relativize and therefore make less exceptional the enormity of the Shoah. The recent controversy among German historians, the *Historikerstreit,* is one case in point.

It may be that in order to combat the trivializers and the relativizers, some scholars have insisted on the uniqueness of the Holocaust. Indeed, one writer, Steven Katz, plainly argues that only the Holocaust fits his narrow definition of genocide. He defines genocide as "the actualization of the intent, however, successfully carried out, to murder in its totality any national, ethnic, racial, religious, political, social, gender, or economic group, as these groups are defined by the perpetrator by whatever means" (1994, p. 131). He observes that only the Holocaust fits his definition, and he comes to the conclusion that the Holocaust is unique and incomparable.

It is apparent that Katz departs from the widely accepted UN definition by excluding the partial destruction of groups (genocide in part); these are seen as "tragedies" not genocides. And in his work he claims that in no other cases was there an actual attempt to exterminate a group. Why scholars of genocide should be limited only to the intended extermination of groups is never convincingly explained. Moreover, other scholars have demonstrated that the Armenian, Rwandan, as well as a number of Native-American and African genocides were instances of attempted extermination. These may not have been equivalent in intent or ideology to the Final Solution, but they were similar enough in other dimensions to prompt comparative research.

By reducing it to the ideologically driven intentions of the Nazis, Katz's definition prevents him and other scholars who would rely on his formulation from making valid comparisons to other aspects of the Holocaust. Thus, studies that have demonstrated that the Holocaust and other total genocides have occurred following revolutionary situations and during war-time conditions could not have been conducted had the authors followed the Katz definition. In effect, a misplaced emphasis on the uniqueness of the Holocaust prevents meaningful comparisons that can shed light on the Holocaust itself.

SEE ALSO Genocide; Sociology of Perpetrators; Sociology of Victims

BIBLIOGRAPHY

Fein, Helen (1990). "Genocide: A Sociological Perspective." *Current Sociology* 38:1–126.

Harff, Barbara (2003). "No Lessons Learned from the Holocaust?" *American Political Science Review* 91(1):57–74.

Hinton, Alexander L. (2002). *Annihilating Difference: The Anthropology of Genocide.* Berkeley: University of California Press.

Katz, Steven T. (1994). *The Holocaust in Historical Context,* vol. I. New York: Oxford University Press.

Kuper, Leo (1981). *Genocide: Its Political Uses in the Twentieth Century.* New Haven, Conn.: Yale University Press.

Melson, Robert (1992). *Revolution and Genocide: On the Origins of the Armenian Genocide and the Holocaust.* Chicago: University of Chicago Press, 1996.

Naimark, Norman M. (2001). *Fires of Hatred: Ethnic Cleansing in Twentieth Century Europe.* Cambridge, Mass.: Harvard University Press.

Staub, Ervin (1989). *The Roots of Evil.* Cambridge: Cambridge University Press.

Tatz, Colin (2003). *With Intent to Destroy: Reflecting on Genocide.* London: Verso.

Ternon, Yves (1995). *L'État criminel: Les Génocides au XXᵉ Siècle.* Paris: Seuil.

Weitz, Eric (2003). *A Century of Genocide.* Princeton, N.J.: Princeton University Press.

Robert Melson

Compensation

As used here, *compensation* means providing money or items of economic value to a person or group that has suffered an injury caused by another. Compensation is different from *restitution,* meaning the return of specific property to a previous owner, and *reparations,* usually applied to compensation a defeated country pays to the victors for damages or losses suffered during war.

Compensation has long been a familiar principle in law, business, and everyday life in many societies. Many legal systems provide procedures (e.g., lawsuits in U.S. courts) for determining an amount of compensation that the law regards as equivalent to certain types of injuries. Such compensation is not necessarily intended to punish the party causing the injury, but instead to try to relieve the injury; paying it generally relieves the offending party of further financial obligations.

President Ronald Reagan after signing the Civil Liberties Act of 1988, which provided a payment of $20,000 to every Japanese American who had been either interned or relocated by the U.S. government during World War II.[WALLY MCNAMEE/CORBIS]

Various justifications are offered for these ideas. Some identify their foundations in religious or ethical teachings; authorities ranging from Aristotle to the Qu'ran instruct that those causing harm should repair it. Although starting from different premises, many economists would urge the same result: Parties, even those engaging in lawful behavior, should bear the costs of their actions, including injuries inflicted on others. Whatever their ultimate sanction, these concepts are deeply woven into international law and most national legal systems.

Limitations and Possibilities

The idea of compensation as the equivalent of injury suffered may be accepted in many settings, but is certainly insufficient within the context of genocide or crimes against humanity. These offenses involve profound attacks on human life and dignity. Their enormity and brutality make it impossible to truly restore the situation that existed beforehand. The dead cannot be restored; injuries and traumas cannot be erased; lost communities are lost, except perhaps in memory. Viewing transfers of funds or property as the equivalent of victims' experiences obscures the offenses' gravity and to many seems to trivialize victims' suffering. Further, the notion that providing full compensation relieves the paying party of further responsibility is inadequate for addressing the personal responsibilities of perpetrators of genocide or crimes against humanity.

Nevertheless, survivors of such crimes have needs that must be met, including food, clothing, shelter, medical care, and the physical means to build new lives. Historically, such support often has been absent, leaving survivors in deplorable conditions. However, several innovative mass claims programs have shown that properly conceived compensation programs can ease survivors' material burdens. In addition, such programs provide individuals with validation and recognition. They also may clarify and enlarge the historical record, increasing the broader community's understanding of past crimes.

Relevant International and Domestic Norms

Until recent decades neither international law nor domestic legal systems allowed most individuals or groups injured by genocide or other large-scale abuses to claim and obtain compensation. Before World War II international law placed few restrictions on what states did to their own peoples. It required that states correct or compensate for certain economic injuries they inflicted on aliens, but these rules did not limit a state's abuse of its own people. The rules protecting aliens also included procedural limitations that often limited their effectiveness. For example, they generally required an injured alien to exhaust all remedies under the offending state's domestic law. The procedures for making international claims were likewise restrictive. A state could bring international claims against other states for mistreating the claimant's nationals, but individuals could not make an international claim against a state.

The situation was little better under national law. National legal systems generally applied the principle of sovereign immunity to bar suits against the state unless the authorities consented to such suits and waived immunity. Finally, neither international law nor domestic legal systems generally recognized or protected the rights of communities or groups.

New Norms, New Procedures

The decades after World War II witnessed important changes. The 1945 United Nations (UN) Charter identified the protection of human rights as a key purpose of the organization. There was growing international acceptance of human rights principles expressed in such documents as the Universal Declaration of Human Rights adopted by the UN General Assembly in 1948, international human rights covenants, and other global and regional treaties. These often included provisions like Article 2(3) of the International Covenant on Civil and Political Rights adopted by the UN General Assembly in 1966, which required countries to ensure effective domestic remedies for rights violations. Many states also adopted constitutional provisions or laws requiring both remedies and compensation for such violations. UN human rights bodies studied the right to compensation for rights violations and developed statements of principles elaborating on this. Human rights treaty bodies called for states committing specific violations to compensate victims.

Several large-scale programs to compensate victims paralleled these doctrine-related developments. With varying success these substituted administrative compensation procedures involving simplified procedures and evidence requirements for slow, expensive, and uncertain individual suits in national courts. This development recognized the fact that survivors of mass rights violations rarely have the time, stamina, or resources for long and elaborate individual legal proceedings, nor do they have the documents or other evidence normally required in such proceedings.

A key early precedent arose in 1952, when the Federal Republic of Germany (FRG or West Germany) and the new Jewish State of Israel agreed that West Germany would pay Israel 3.45 billion deutsche marks, most of it directed to the resettlement and rehabilitation of Jewish victims of Nazi persecution. Although fiercely attacked by some as debasing the memory of the Holocaust or as a cynical exercise in Realpolitik, the agreement resulted in the transfer of badly needed resources to Israel and to individual survivors. It also set an important precedent for later large-scale compensation programs. In 1953 West Germany passed an individual indemnification law eventually resulting in the payment of many more billions to victims of Nazi persecution. However, geographic and substantive limitations of the law led to the conclusion of additional compensation agreements between West Germany and several European countries.

Other efforts to compensate victims for large-scale state misconduct followed. The United States adopted the Civil Liberties Act of 1988, authorizing the compensation of Japanese Americans forcibly interned during World War II and formally apologizing for their mistreatment. At least 81,000 former internees each received $20,000 and—more important for many—official recognition of their unfair treatment and affirmation of their American identity. Australia, Canada, New Zealand, and the United States all wrestled in varying ways and with varying success on how to fairly compensate indigenous communities displaced and deeply wounded during the course of national development.

In Europe during the 1990s charges that Swiss banks had pocketed the accounts of Holocaust victims and that neutral Switzerland had benefited through financial transactions with the Nazi regime led to other compensation programs. Responding to such criticisms, major Swiss banks created an international committee to identify accounts dormant since the war and potentially owned by victims, as well as a process to resolve claims to those accounts. To settle class action lawsuits against them in the United States, Swiss banks also agreed to provide $1.25 billion for Holocaust claimants—$800 million to pay claims of deposited assets and $450 million to compensate some victims of Nazi slave labor. The Swiss government additionally proposed the establishment of a significant fund to assist victims and refugees worldwide, but a 2002 referendum to finance it by selling Swiss National Bank gold failed.

In the late 1990s, following settlement of the Swiss bank litigation in the United States, major German companies and the German government established a fund of 10 billion deutsche marks and related mechanisms to compensate the victims of Nazi slave and forced labor programs. Further mass claims programs aimed at redressing past injustices were undertaken with varying success in Eastern European countries and Russia after the fall of the Berlin Wall in 1989. Other programs sought to address tangled claims to real property in Bosnia and Kosovo after the Balkan Wars of the 1990s.

Following September 11, 2001, the U.S. government implemented an extensive program to provide compensation to those who lost family members in the terrorist attacks where the actual perpetrators could not be held liable.

UN Compensation Commission
All of the programs cited thus far rested on the voluntary acceptance of financial responsibility by the state or large private entities. In contrast, in 1991, the UN Security Council created an extensive compensation program funded by the compulsory transfer of Iraqi resources. The United Nations Compensation Commission (UNCC), an agency based in Geneva, has collected and processed more than 2.5 million claims for injuries to non-Iraqis directly caused by Iraq's 1990 invasion of Kuwait. By July 2003 the UNCC completed work on all but a few thousand of its timely filed claims, providing compensation of almost $17.8 billion to injured parties, including full payment to over 1.5 million injured individuals and families, most from developing countries.

The UNCC is the largest international compensation program and has been a laboratory for new techniques to implement large-scale programs intended to compensate rights violations. Although most claims were collected by states, the UNCC also developed procedures for Palestinians and others unable to file a claim through a state. It sought to provide compensation for valid claims when it was most needed, even if this required some approximation or crude estimate of justice. Given its huge caseload, the UNCC determined early on that it generally could not utilize traditional claim-by-claim adversarial legal processes. It instead developed more administrative procedures for collecting and assessing claims, particularly small claims of individuals and families. Initially, the UNCC's procedures, especially for individual and family claims, allowed only limited participation by Iraq, a feature

much criticized by some governments and scholars. Iraq was subsequently authorized to present evidence and participate in hearings on many large claims.

To manage 2.5 million claims, the UNCC developed and applied computer-based claims collection and management techniques that since have been modified and applied in other mass claims programs. It identified various subgroups of claims presenting common fact patterns and legal issues, allowing hundreds or even thousands of individual claims to be grouped, analyzed, and checked together.

The largest such group involved more than one million individuals and families, most from developing countries, forced to abandon jobs and property and flee Kuwait or Iraq following the invasion. To check and verify their claims of wrongful departure, the UNCC developed a massive database of official and nongovernmental organization records listing persons who crossed borders after Iraq invaded Kuwait. Powerful software permitted the checking and verification of sample claims using this database and other evidence. Individuals or families received fixed amounts of compensation calculated to approximate the economic injuries suffered by most people who fled. Persons with evidence of more significant injuries could file claims for larger amounts, but those claims were considered somewhat later in the process.

Conclusion
The various innovations introduced by the UNCC and other recent mass claims processes are available for application in other future settings. Nevertheless, one ingredient is essential for any mass compensation program to succeed—money, both to pay claims and to run the program. These programs require sizable financial resources; the few successful efforts to compensate large numbers of rights victims have involved the participation of a state or other significant organization able to supply substantial funding.

In contrast, many contemporary situations of genocide or crimes against humanity involve offenses by fragile and impoverished states or by nonstate players without significant financial resources. The situation involving Iraq's 1990 invasion of Kuwait represented an unusual blending of resources and political will in the international community. This may not be repeated often. Even in cases of significant abuses involving a wealthy state, national policymakers may resist accepting financial responsibility for past wrongs, as attested by the Japanese government's unwillingness to address claims of enforced sexual slavery during World War II.

SEE ALSO Rehabilitation; Reparations; Restitution

BIBLIOGRAPHY

Barkan, Elazar (2000). *The Guilt of Nations. Restitution and Negotiating Historical Injustices.* Baltimore, Md.: Johns Hopkins University Press.

Bassiouni, Cherif (2000). *The Right to Restitution, Compensation and Rehabilitation for Victims of Grave Violations of Human Rights and Fundamental Freedoms, Final Report of the Special Rapporteur.* UN Document E/CN.4/2000/62 (January 18). Available from http://www.unhchr.ch/huridocda/huridoca.nsf.

Eizenstat, Stuart (2003). *Imperfect Justice: Looted Assets, Slave Labor, and the Unfinished Business of World War II.* New York: Public Affairs.

Lillich, Richard, ed. (1995). *The United Nations Compensation Commission: Thirteenth Sokol Colloquium.* Irvington, N.Y.: Transnational Publishers.

Randelzhofer, Albrecht, and Christian Tomuschat, eds. (1999). *State Responsibility and the Individual: Reparation in Instances of Grave Violations of Human Rights.* The Hague: Martinus Nijhoff

Shelton, Dinah (1999). *Remedies and International Human Rights Law.* New York: Oxford University Press.

Van Boven, Theo (1993). *Study Concerning the Right to Restitution, Compensation and Rehabilitation for Victims of Gross Violations of Human Rights and Fundamental Freedoms.* UN Document E/CN/4/Sub.2/1993/8 (July 2). Available from http://www.unhchr.ch/Huridocda/Huridoca.nsf.

John R. Crook

Complicity

Historically, the commission of genocidal offenses has involved large numbers of perpetrators, whose contributions varied greatly with respect to both form and intensity. From a legal perspective, attributions of criminal responsibility to the involved parties does not mean that the overall responsibility for genocidal acts is somehow divided among them. Each individual involved in genocidal conduct bears responsibility for his or her conduct, and the attribution of individual guilt is organized pursuant to a set of recognized forms of participation. Those who participate in the commission of a genocidal act in accordance with one of those prescribed forms incur responsibility for their conduct.

One form of participation is "complicity" in genocide, pursuant to Article III(e) of the United Nations (UN) Convention on the Prevention and Punishment of the Crime of Genocide (Genocide Convention). Due in part to the word's terminological ambiguity and its slightly different connotation in several legal environments, the exact meaning of the word in the context of genocide is still subject to much debate, notably that taking place in the ad hoc tribunals for the former Yugoslavia and for Rwanda, and this ambiguity has yielded contradictory interpretations in existing case law.

What is certain is that an individual may be regarded as an accomplice in genocide if it is established that he or she deliberately provided practical assistance, encouragement, or moral support that had a substantial effect on the perpetration of the crime. This forms the minimum standard that a person who has contributed to the commission of the crime must meet if he is to be held responsible for complicity in genocide. His or her acts may take many forms, and the contribution of each accomplice may differ vastly in terms of its gravity. His contribution need not be an indispensable condition to the commission of the crime by the principal offender, but neither can it be entirely innocuous, in that it must have "substantially affected" the commission of the crime. Such complicity may in principle take place before, during, or after the time of the actions of the principal offender. Mere presence at the scene of the crime may, under certain circumstances, be sufficient to qualify as complicity (as, for instance, when such presence may be shown to provide encouragement to the principal offender, or when the individual present had a duty to intervene and failed to do so). So could acts of encouragement or assistance such as transporting executioners to killing sites, identifying members of the targeted group, providing forces and ammunition for the killings, and other forms of aiding and abetting the commission of the crime. The only form of complicity in the context of genocide that appears to have been criminalized, however, is complicity in genocide itself. Complicity in other acts that are related to genocide, such as "conspiracy to commit genocide" or "direct and public incitement to commit genocide," is not regarded as a discrete basis for criminal liability.

It has been suggested in a number of legal decisions that accomplice liability is limited to individuals who, from a hierarchical point of view, are lesser participants, whereas liability for genocide proper is reserved for high-level officials, which reasoning would create a division between the "planners," who would generally be principals to genocide, and "executioners," who would generally be mere accomplices to such crimes. Such a view does not appear to be supported in international criminal law. Anyone, regardless of rank or status, could in principle be found guilty of complicity in genocide, as well as of genocide itself. The law of genocide, as it stands, does not support any suggestion that different forms of liability have been assigned according to the different hierarchical levels of accused persons. What matters in respect of accomplice liability is the nature of the actions or omissions of an accused person, not his or her position within a hierarchy.

It is yet unclear whether, in order to be held responsible as an accomplice to genocide, an individual must possess the requisite genocidal mens rea (intent), or whether it is sufficient that he or she knows of the genocidal intent of those whom he or she assists. It would appear that the pivotal element of the crime of genocide is this very element of intent, and that genocidal intent should be required of each and every participant (in the establishment of his or her guilt) in a genocidal offense, including accomplices. One would therefore be found responsible for complicity in genocide only if the prosecution were able to establish that the accused possessed the requisite special intent (as opposed to his or her mere knowing of the principal offender's intent). In the absence of genocidal intent on the part of the accomplice, *actus reus* (action) of that accomplice, whatever its degree of atrocity and however similar it might be to the acts described in the Genocide Convention, could not be regarded as genocidal. The distinction between one who commits a genocidal crime and one who is merely an accomplice to it would thus depend on the motivational aspects of their respective contributions to the crime. It is important to note that, in that respect, the sentence imposed on an individual involved in a genocide would not be based primarily, if at all, on the legal classification of his conduct as commission rather than complicity, but would depend on the gravity of his conduct—so that an accomplice could theoretically receive a heavier sentence than a principle.

Complicity in genocide as a form of participation is not freestanding, in that it can only exist when there is a punishable principal act in which the accomplice could be complicit. Consequently, it must be proven that the crime of genocide has indeed been committed before liability for complicity may attach to a lesser participant in this crime. However, the principal offender need not have been prosecuted or convicted, and he need not even have been identified.

Complicity in genocide is sometimes understood in a broader, less technical, sense than the one expounded above, whereby one may be regarded as an accomplice to genocide if one has participated in the commission of a genocidal act in a form criminalized under international law but not explicitly under the Genocide Convention. The ad hoc tribunals for the former Yugoslavia and for Rwanda have recognized, for instance, that criminal liability for genocidal actions is not limited to those who have participated in the commission of these actions in one of the forms provided for under the Genocide Convention, but that other forms of participation are criminalized under customary international law. Two such forms of criminal participation deserve particular attention here: command, or superior, responsibility and joint criminal enterprise or common purpose doctrine.

Command, or Superior, Responsibility and Genocide

A superior—civilian or military—may under certain circumstances be held criminally responsible for the acts of his subordinates, or, to be more precise, for failing to prevent or punish his crimes. Drawing on the jurisprudence of court decisions that date back to World War II (and of later court decisions), the ad hoc tribunals for the former Yugoslavia and for Rwanda have determined that three conditions must be met before a superior can be held responsible for the criminal acts of his subordinates: (1) the existence of a superior-subordinate relationship; (2) the superior knew or had reason to know that the subordinate was about to commit criminal acts or had done so; and (3) the superior failed to take necessary and reasonable measures to prevent such acts, or to punish the offenders thereof. The first condition, the existence of a superior-subordinate relationship, requires that a hierarchical relationship between superior and subordinate exist, which may be demonstrated to exist (or to have existed) by virtue of an accused party's de facto or de jure position of superiority. What must be demonstrated is that the superior had "effective control" over the persons committing the alleged offenses, that is, that he had the material ability to prevent the offenses or to punish the offenders. Second, the superior must be shown to have known or have had reason to know that his or her subordinate was about to commit or had committed a crime. It must be proven that the superior had actual knowledge, established through either direct or circumstantial evidence, that subordinates were planning to commit or had committed crimes within the jurisdiction of the tribunal, or that he possessed information that would have at least put him on notice of the risk of such crimes—such information thereby alerting him to the need for additional investigation to determine whether crimes were about to be committed or had been committed by the subordinates. Third, it must be established that the superior failed to take necessary and reasonable measures to prevent or punish the crimes of his subordinates. The measures required of the superior are limited to those that are feasible in the relevant circumstances and are "within his or her power" to enact. A superior is not obliged to perform "the impossible," but he has a duty to exercise the powers he does have within the confines of these limitations.

A commander would almost be in a position to prevent the development of genocidal intent on the part of his subordinates, nor should the law expect him to do so. What the individual of superior rank is required to do, however, is to prevent acts such as killing and the inflicting of serious physical harm when he knew or had reason to know that these acts were about to be committed, or to punish the acts when they had already taken place. The measures (to prevent or punish) that the superior is obligated to enact are dictated, in part, by the nature of the crimes committed or about to be committed by subordinates. Because of the seriousness of the offenses that may constitute genocide, a superior is obligated to implement those measures to prevent or punish with some urgency.

The chief difficulty that attaches to the criminal liability of a commanding officer when applied to genocide (as with complicity in genocide) relates to the mental state that the commanding officer must be shown to possess or to have possessed in order that he be held responsible for the acts of subordinates. Although knowledge of the relevant acts (as defined above) is sufficient, in principle, for a superior to be held responsible for the acts of his subordinates, the crime of genocide must take in a specific intent to destroy in whole or in part a group as such. How can these two standards be reconciled? Is it sufficient for a commanding officer to know or to have had reason to know that his subordinates were committing genocidal acts in order that he be held responsible for genocide, as a commanding officer? Or must the commander himself possess the intent to destroy the group in whole or in part? Existing case law on this point is inconsistent, and arguments have been advanced in support of both positions. As was found previously, it seems more appropriate to require that the commanding officer be shown to have possessed the genocidal intent *himself*. The fact that a commander may have known of his subordinates' genocidal mens rea has evidential relevance to the extent that it may serve to establish *his own* genocidal mindset, but it is not in itself sufficient to establish his responsibility, as commander, for genocidal activities.

Joint Criminal Enterprise and Genocide

Joint criminal enterprise or common purpose doctrine is a concept that international law has borrowed from common law. Because this form of liability has the potential to lead to the excessive criminalization of behaviors and has created some legitimate concerns from the perspective of defendants, it has become a very contentious issue indeed.

Three forms of joint criminal enterprise have been recognized under customary international law. One is the instance in which all participants share the same criminal intent. The second is essentially similar to the first in that it too requires the shared intent of participants, but is limited, for all intends and purposes, to cases that involve criminal actions that took place in concentration camps. The third relates to the situation in which all participants share a common intention to carry out particular criminal acts, but in which one of the participants commits an act that falls outside of the intended joint criminal enterprise. If the act were nevertheless a "natural and foreseeable consequence" of the carrying out of the agreed joint criminal enterprise, all participants incur criminal liability for that act.

Joint criminal enterprise liability is different from membership in a criminal organization, which was criminalized as a separate offense in the Nuremberg Trials, and in subsequent trials that came under the sway of Control Council Law No. 10 (where it was determined that knowing and voluntary membership in one such organization was sufficient to entail criminal responsibility). Criminal liability pursuant to a joint criminal enterprise is not a liability for mere membership in an organization or for conspiring to commit crimes, but a form of liability concerned with participation in the commission of a crime as part of a joint criminal enterprise—a different matter.

Joint criminal enterprise is also different from the crime of "conspiracy." Although a judgment of conspiracy requires a showing that several individuals agreed to commit a crime or a number of crimes, proof of a joint criminal enterprise requires, in addition to such a showing, that the parties to an agreement took action in the furtherance of that agreement. For all three forms of joint criminal enterprise, the prosecution must establish the existence of that criminal enterprise and the part therein of the accused. A joint criminal enterprise may be said to exist where there is an understanding or arrangement amounting to an agreement between two or more individuals that they will commit a criminal offense. A person may participate in such a joint criminal enterprise in any of the following ways: (1) by participating directly in the commission of the agreed upon crime itself (as a principal offender); (2) by being a part of the criminal proceedings at the time the crime is committed, and (with knowledge that the crime is being committed or is to be committed) by intentionally assisting or encouraging another participant in the joint criminal enterprise to commit that crime; or (3) by acting in the furtherance of a particular scheme according to which the crime is committed (as evidenced by the position of authority or function of the accused), and with knowledge of the nature of that scheme and intent to further that scheme. If the agreed upon crime is committed by one or other of the participants in that joint criminal enterprise, all of the participants in that enterprise are guilty of the crime, regardless of the part played by each in its commission.

As far as the element of mens rea is concerned, proof of the existence of the first and second types of joint criminal enterprise requires that the prosecution establish that each of the persons charged and (even if not one of those charged) the principal offender or offenders shared a common state of mind, which is required for the crime's being pursued. Concerning the third type of joint criminal enterprise, the prosecution must show that the accused possessed the intention to participate in and further the criminal activity or criminal purpose of a group and contributed to the joint criminal enterprise or at least to the commission of a crime by the group. Responsibility for a crime or crimes that had not been agreed upon would be incurred by an accused person only when it was foreseeable that such a crime or crimes might be perpetrated by one or more members of the group and the accused willingly embraced the risk that would inevitably attach to a crime's being committed. What then is the mens rea that must be shown to have existed for an individual charged for his or her part in a joint criminal enterprise, the purpose of which was to commit genocide or a genocide-related offense? Would the participant's knowledge of the fact that such a crime or crimes were being envisioned by others be sufficient to establish his or her guilt, or would the participant have to have shared the genocidal intent of the principal offender? In parallel with what has been argued above in relation to "complicity" and "command responsibility," it seems that the most logical, and most sensible, conclusion would be that, regardless of the form of criminal participation, a finding of guilt for any sort of participation in a genocidal offense requires that the accused possess a genocidal intent. The matter, however, is not settled.

SEE ALSO Attempt; Bystanders; Conspiracy; Incitement; Superior (or Command) Responsibility

BIBLIOGRAPHY

Cassese, A. (2002). "Genocide." In *The Rome Statute of the International Criminal Court: A Commentary*, ed. A. Cassese, P. Gaeta, and J. R. W. D. Jones. Oxford: Oxford University Press.

Schabas, William A. (2000). Genocide in International Law. Cambridge, U.K.: Cambridge University Press.

Guénaël Mettraux

I am setting forth the above in my personal capacity. This article represents neither the policies of the Office of the Prosecutor of the International Criminal Tribunal for the Former Yugoslavia nor the United Nations.

Concentration Camps

Although monstrous for most observers, totalitarianism and concentration camps belong to the same family, forming a coherent and in some sense logical entity. Concentration camps were not created *ex nihilo* by totalitarianism. They appeared for the first time in 1896 in Cuba, at the time of an armed insurrection against the Spanish Crown. Valeriano Wyler y Nicolau, the *capitan general* of the island, decided to lock up a large portion of the peasant population in so-called camps of reconcentration, in order to isolate the guerrillas totally. Four years later, Lord Horatio Kitchener would take this as his model during the Boer War in South Africa.

The first camps were temporary, but all the ingredients of what would become the scandal of the concentration camp were nonetheless present: the notion of collectively punishing an entire group; the idea of preemption (with most of the interned being innocent); administrative detention (whereby no court has judged the internees); and bad health conditions (with mortality high from the start). Such a camp is most often hermetically sealed from its surroundings, and rapidly and summarily consigned, to mass together supposedly dangerous or threatening individuals or groups of individuals.

Why did colonial rulers decide, around the beginning of the twentieth century, to intern civilians en masse? The answer lies in the advent of mass politicization, when even the humblest citizen was portrayed as an active subject of the nation, and therefore in time of conflict imagined as a potential enemy. Until 1880 political life was largely restricted to the elite(s), but the early 1880s witnessed a significant change in political conditions, which resulted in the masses acquiring a much stronger sense of political consciousness.

Origins of the Concentration Camp

Two great passions of modern political life—Nation and Revolution—arouse the masses, and through conscription, which began with the Napoleonic Wars, have become enormously important in modern wars. With the confrontation of gigantic armies and each side determined to prevail, major conflicts have given rise to the problem of what to do with captured enemies. The problem is immense, because not only are there many prisoners, but it makes no sense to liberate them, whether shortly after capture, or thereafter. This is because a captured soldier is, and will remain for the duration of the conflict, a potential enemy and thus a distinct threat. From this comes the necessity of neutralizing him for as long as the war lasts. In fact, it was the U.S. Civil War that inaugurated the practice of interning great masses of people. Camps were created urgently and with necessarily scant regard for health factors—to receive on both sides huge populations of prisoners. These camps consisted of canvas tents sur-

The main entrance to Dachau, the first Nazi concentration camp, in 1945. The camp, site of a former gunpowder factory, had been established in February 1933 as a detention center for "enemies of the people." [BETTMANN/CORBIS]

rounded by metal wire fences. Barbed wire was not invented until 1867, two years after the South's capitulation, for the purpose of management and surveillance of the great herds of cattle in the American West. Barbed wire would become an enormous success, because it is cheap and easy to make and install. By 1896 the Spanish began using these "metal thorns" to surround the camps where they reconcentrated Cuban peasants and their families.

By 1900 it was the British who resorted to the practice in South Africa, followed by the Germans in 1904 in Hereroland (now Namibia). The Herero were the first victims of genocide in the twentieth century, but also of the policy of concentration camp elimination through work. The few survivors of the 1904 genocide found themselves penned in forced work camps and/or hired for the day by private enterprises.

The dehumanizing process was unleashed, and nothing henceforward would stop this instrument par

excellence of social control. It would spread even to the very heart of the European continent. It is impossible to understand the concentration camp system (from Soviet Russia to Nazi Germany, by way of France during the Third Republic) without considering World War I (1914–1918) and its consequences. The concentration camp universe can be seen as a product of the extreme violence of this war and a result of the brutalization of European society, especially in Germany and Russia, within the context of an increasing scorn for so-called civil society. Soon the detention camp for external enemies (civilian or military) would be destined for the internment of internal enemies; on August 8, 1918, Russian communist leader Leon Trotsky ordained the establishment of two camps, at Mourom and Arzamas, for "'suspicious agitators, counterrevolutionary officers, saboteurs, parasites, speculators' who will be interned until the end of the civil war" (Werth, 1997, p. 85). Soviet writer Alexander Solzhenitsyn correctly points out that for the first time "the word [camp] is applied to citizens of the country itself" (1974). From this moment on the enemy was seen as internal, and the function of the camp was to render innocuous such subjectively guilty individuals. Adolf Hitler's Germany copied Soviet Russia in this regard—witness the twelve thousand people arrested on February 28, 1933, the morning after the Reichstag fire. A decree promulgated for "the protection of the people and the State" (*Schutz von Volk und Staat, decree of the Reich President for the protection of the state*) aimed to isolate behind barbed wire any person who was or might be opposed to the regime. The detention of people known to be innocent of any crimes was deemed preventive (*Schutzhaft*).

A result of improvisation, the concentration camp system was imposed in the former Soviet Union as well as in Nazi Germany, and quickly became a permanent feature. The will to transform fundamentally an existing order in pursuit of an ideology, whether social or racial, leads to this system. It arises out of deep necessity, as something that is integral to totalitarian regimes, indicated by the fact that all such regimes have been endowed with powerful concentration camp systems: from the former popular democracies of Eastern Europe to communist China, by way of North Korea. Totalitarianism is anti-individualist, a kind of group religion that aspires to remodel the individual, adapting its method as necessary, from positive influences (propaganda) to negative education (brutality). Totalitarian concentration camp experiences are marked by this double perspective; they are terrorist but also "pedagogical."

The creation of Dachau can be very well understood from this point of view, as well as its infamous motto, "*Arbeit macht frei*," which means "Our own labor makes us free." Inaugurated March 21, 1933, by Heinrich Himmler, Dachau was a camp of preventive detention (*Schuzthaftlager*), aimed at both isolating enemies of the people and setting them on the right road. Dachau is often mentioned as the first of the Nazi concentration camps, but the initial camp dates from February 1933, or less than a month after the accession of Hitler to the Chancellery. Something like seventy camps, all told, would spring up just about everywhere in Germany before the end of World War II.

At Dachau an offer was held out to Aryan ideological "deviants," including a few dozen communists, who freshly converted to Nazism, were liberated from the camp. Economic functionality, that is to say productive work, was not necessarily linked to camp life. In the British camps of South Africa (1900), as in the French camps of the Third Republic, there was no work, no more than in the camps of the Algerian War. Work was not a component of nontotalitarian concentration camp

institutions. At the beginning even the Nazi camps had no productive goal, nor did they serve any economic purpose. Their essential function was to tame wayward minds, and break the rebels and any other opposition.

Progressively, the notion of profit emerged, to the point of transforming the camps into veritable factories, because it appeared as though the concentration camps would remain permanent institutions. Being that the camps were going to exist, they might as well yield an economic return. The idea of having the cost of the institution borne by the detained themselves arose at the same time in Germany and the former Soviet Union, where the principle of "cash autonomy" would come into use. Confirmed by the testimony Tzvetan Todorov gathered about work in the communist camps, huge profits were sometimes made from unpaid labor. Detainees were unable to refuse any arduous task, no matter how backbreaking. The Nazi camps became guided by the economic needs of the SS in 1937 and 1938, when camps were constructed near quarries and SS factories; not until 1942 were they integrated into the war effort of the Nazi state. By mid-September 1942 Himmler would invent the notion of "extermination through work" for Jews and other victims. Germany's great war machine needed replenishment, so the concentration camp supply of workers started growing exponentially. In 1941 the camps accounted for only 60,000 individuals, mostly Germans or Austrians. In August 1942 this number grew to 115,000. In August 1944 it reached 524,268. By mid-January 1945 a peak of 714,211 detainees was achieved. Hundreds of thousands of people would be sold to German industrial enterprises (Siemens, Daimler-Benz, Krupp, Volkswagen, Knorr, IG Farben, Dynamit Nobel, Dresdner Bank, BMW, AEG).

A Complex Reality

Unquestionably, the camps are creatures of modernity created by various kinds of political regimes, but all camps were not the same. Bloemfontain (the Boer camp in South Africa), Manzanar (in the United States), and Gurs (in France) cannot be compared to Nazi Germany's Buchenwald or the former Soviet Union's Magadan, nor even to Belene (in communist Bulgaria). Using the same term, *concentration camp*, to designate detention centers, work camps, even extermination centers is the source of much confusion and far too much relativism. The Manzanar camp that served to intern Americans of Japanese ancestry during World War II cannot really be compared to a Nazi, Soviet, or Chinese camp. There are at least two kinds of camp, if not three, if the six Nazi centers of extermination are (mistakenly) included:

The Auschwitz concentration camp in a 1995 photograph. A former Polish cavalry barracks, the camp was remodeled in 1940 as part of the plans for the Nazis' Final Solution. It is the site of the largest mass murder in the history of humanity. [DAVE G. HOUSER/CORBIS]

1. *Detention and/or internment camps* whose purpose is to isolate temporarily suspected or dangerous individuals. In this category are camps created during conflicts to imprison national "enemies" (as in August 1914 and September 1939), or those perceived as such (e.g., Japanese Americans in the United States). In most of these camps slave labor is unknown; their function is prophylactic, not productive. Living conditions in them can be harsh and sometimes atrocious whatever the regime and its purpose: colonial (Herero), security (Gurs), or dictatorial (Franco).

2. *Concentration camps.* These are the camps that constitute the most significant category, and are at the heart of the totalitarian concentration camp phenomenon, whether one is speaking of the Nazi KZ, the Soviet gulag, or communist European and Asian (*laogai*) camps. These camps, which are characterized by a quadruple logic of humiliation, reeducation, work, and annihilation, are essential to the regimes that created them. They are usually veritable extermination camps, where the mortality rate could approach 50 percent.

The four Nazi centers of immediate execution (Belzec, Chelmno, Sobibor, and Treblinka) should be excluded from this list, as well as Auschwitz-Birkenau and Majdanek. Technically speaking, these could not be called camps, even of extermination; they were not destined to receive internees, but to immediately exterminate those rounded up from the four corners of Europe.

SEE ALSO Auschwitz

BIBLIOGRAPHY

Applebaum, Anne (2003). Gulag. *A History of the Soviet Camps.* London: Allen Lane.

Commission on Wartime Relocation and Internment of Civilians (1997). *Personal Justice Denied: Report of the Commission on Wartime Relocation and Internment of Civilians.* Seattle: University of Washington Press.

Kaminski Andrjez J. (1982). *Konzentrationslager 1986 bis heute, Eine Analyse* (Concentration camps 1986 to today, an analysis). Munich: Piper Valag, 1996.

Kogon, Eugen (1960). *The Theory and Practice of Hell: The German Concentration Camps and the System Behind Them.* Trans. Heinz Norden. New York: Berkley.

Kotek, Joël and Pierre Rigoulot (2004). *Century of Concentration Camps: 100 Years of Radical Evil.* London: Orion/Weidenfeld.

Sofsky, Wolfgang (1997). *The Order of Terror: The Concentration Camp.* Princeton, N.J.: Princeton University Press.

Joël Kotek

Conspiracy

Conspiracy is one of the four "punishable acts" of genocide, in addition to the crime of genocide itself, declared punishable in Article III of the 1948 United Nations Convention on the Prevention and Punishment of the Crime of Genocide. The other three acts are direct and public incitement, attempt, and complicity. Subsequent instruments of international criminal law, such as the statutes of the ad hoc tribunals for the former Yugoslavia and Rwanda, have maintained this distinction between genocide itself and the four other punishable acts. The distinction reflects similar provisions in many domestic criminal law codes that define a crime, such as murder or rape, and then set out various forms by which an individual may participate in the crime other than as the primary or principal perpetrator.

The word *conspiracy* is derived from Latin and means, literally, to breathe together. By its very nature, therefore, conspiracy is a crime that must be committed collectively, involving a minimum of two offenders. The reference to conspiracy to commit the crime of genocide in Article III of the Genocide Convention is somewhat enigmatic, and there is nothing further in the text to suggest exactly what is meant. It is not necessarily helpful to look at national legal provisions for guidance, because the term *conspiracy* means different things in different criminal codes. In some, notably those based on continental European models like the Napoleonic penal code, *conspiracy* refers to a form of conspiracy. It entails collective planning or organization of a crime that is actually committed. Under the common-law system, on the other hand, conspiracy is a crime that can be committed once two or more persons meet and agree to commit a crime, even if it is not committed. It is thus an "inchoate" or incomplete crime.

Two factors suggest that the common-law approach should be followed in defining the crime of conspiracy to commit genocide. First, the published record of the General Assembly and the other United Nations (UN) bodies involved in drafting the Genocide Convention make it quite clear that this is what was intended. To an extent, it is acceptable under international law to refer to the debates surrounding adoption of a text as a way to interpret it. Second, if the rival interpretation is adopted, whereby conspiracy is treated as a form of complicity, then there is no need for the provision at all. Complicity to commit the crime of genocide is also a punishable act recognized by Article III of the Convention. Because the common-law concept of conspiracy was unfamiliar to lawyers from the continental tradition, there was difficulty finding an appropriate term for the French version of the Convention. Ultimately, the drafters opted for *entente* instead of *complot,* but they admitted there was no entirely appropriate term.

In a late 1990s ruling, the International Criminal Tribunal for Rwanda confirmed that conspiracy to commit genocide is an inchoate or incomplete offense, committed even when there is no evidence that the underlying crime of genocide has actually taken place. In the *Musema* case, the Trial Chamber said it was "of the view that the crime of conspiracy to commit genocide is punishable even if it fails to produce a result, that is to say, even if the substantive offense, in this case genocide, has not actually been perpetrated." Musema had been the director of a Rwandese tea factory during the 1994 genocide. He was convicted by the international criminal tribunal for his role in the killings.

The tension between the two major criminal law systems with respect to the concept of conspiracy had emerged at Nuremberg, three years before the Genocide Convention was adopted. The Charter of the Nuremberg Tribunal had recognized conspiracy as a distinct crime with respect to aggression, referring to "participation in a common plan or conspiracy for the accomplishment" of "a war of aggression, or a war in violation of international treaties, agreements or assurances." At the London conference, where the charter was adopted, the French and Soviet delegations agreed with the British and Americans that conspiracy was a common-law concept, because this was appropriate to the type of crimes being prosecuted. However, the intent of the drafters was not fully grasped by the judges at Nuremberg, who ruled that conspiracy could not stand alone as an autonomous crime and that, instead, it was a form of participation in a crime that had actually been committed. The prosecutor at Nuremberg had indicted Nazi leaders for conspiracy with respect to war crimes and crimes against humanity, as well as aggression, but this was rejected by the judges as being inconsistent with the Charter of the Nuremberg Tribunal.

Difficulty on the issue still persists. The much more recent Rome Statute of the International Criminal Court, adopted in 1998, does not entirely succeed in incorporating the common-law approach to conspiracy to commit genocide. Instead of listing the four other punishable acts together with the definition of genocide, as is the approach in the statutes of the ad hoc tribunals for the former Yugoslavia and Rwanda, the Rome Statute presents the definitions of three categories of crime—genocide, crimes against humanity, and war crimes—together in a series of provisions, Articles 6 through 8. In a totally separate section of the Rome Statute, Article 25, the various ways in which a person other than the principal offender may actually participate in the crime are enumerated.

The problem with the Rome Statute is that although conspiracy, at least in its inchoate or common-law formulation, was already recognized in international law with respect to the commission of genocide, there is nothing similar for crimes against humanity or war crimes. The same situation exists with respect to another of the punishable acts, direct and public incitement. In the latter case, Article 25 of the Rome Statute resolves this with a separate paragraph, making direct and public incitement to commit genocide a distinct form of the offense, but does not do the same for crimes against humanity and war crimes. It does not, however, do the same with respect to conspiracy to commit genocide. Nowhere does Article 25 actually use the word conspiracy. This is the best example of a failure in the Rome Statute to translate faithfully the terms of the Genocide Convention. Thus, the crime of conspiracy to commit genocide, while a punishable act under the 1948 Convention, cannot be prosecuted before the International Criminal Court.

Although it may be rather exceptional to prosecute crimes that do not actually occur, but that are only discussed and planned, the listing of conspiracy to commit genocide as a punishable act is a way of underscoring the seriousness of the crime and the intention of the world community to prevent it. After all, the 1948 Convention includes the word prevention as well as punishment in its title. Making punishment of conspiracy a distinct offense also provides criminal justice with a tool that can strike at criminal organizations, especially their leaders. Similar approaches are used in various domestic legal systems in order to deal with other particular forms of criminal behavior that elude prosecution, such as organized crime and gangsterism.

It would probably not be acceptable to convict an individual of genocide simply because that person was a member of an organization which had been involved in genocidal activity, such as the Nazi SS or Rwandan *interahamwe*. The Nuremberg Tribunal acquitted some Nazi leaders of conspiracy—Wilhelm Frick, Martin Bormann, and Karl Dönitz—because there was no evidence that they had actual knowledge of planning to commit crimes. But once it can be established that an individual participated in a meeting with others at which the crime was organized, then the crime of conspiracy to commit genocide is committed, and this is as it should be if prevention is to be truly effective. In one case before the International Criminal Tribunal for Rwanda, the Trial Chamber warned the prosecutor that indictments for conspiracy to commit genocide must mention names or other identifying information on co-conspirators (*Prosecutor v. Nsengiyumuva,* May 12, 2000).

There has only been one conviction for conspiracy to commit genocide before the International Criminal Tribunal for Rwanda, and none before the International Criminal Tribunal for the Former Yugoslavia, where it has not even been charged in indictments. On September 4, 1998, the man who had been prime minister of Rwanda during the weeks in 1994 in which genocide took place, Jean Kambanda, was found guilty of conspiracy to commit genocide and sentenced to life imprisonment. Kambanda pleaded guilty to the charge and conceded evidence that he had been part of the conspiracy. He was also convicted for the underlying crime of genocide, and to this extent the conviction for conspiracy was really redundant and should not have been imposed. But in a contested case, that of Elizaphan and Gérard Ntakirutimana, the same tribunal acquitted the accused for lack of any evidence that they had been part of meetings at which the crimes were planned, although they were both found guilty of genocide as such.

This has always been the great problem in proving conspiracy. Evidence of the meetings at which the crime is planned is difficult to obtain. Usually, this will require the cooperation of an insider who agrees to inform on his coconspirators. Sometimes international prosecutors will offer an individual immunity and other benefits in exchange for such insider evidence, but this raises other problems. The evidence of such insiders may be dismissed as lacking credibility, because it has in effect been purchased from them in exchange for favorable treatment.

The record of the ad hoc tribunals, and the effective exclusion of conspiracy to commit genocide from the Rome Statute of the International Criminal Court, may simply attest to the practical difficulties involved in such prosecutions. The idea of those who drafted the Genocide Convention in 1948 was a good one, namely to nip genocide in the bud and prosecute its organizers before the crime actually takes place. In practice, regrettably, the international community waits for the crime to occur before intervening. International criminal courts have enough of a burden dealing with genocide that has been committed. In practice, then, the criminalization of a stand-alone crime of conspiracy to commit genocide, despite the fact that it is not actually committed, has been of no real significance.

SEE ALSO Collaboration; Complicity

BIBLIOGRAPHY

Barrett, Richard P., and Laura E. Little (2003). "Lessons of Yugoslav Rape Trials: A Role for Conspiracy Law in International Tribunals." *Minnesota Law Review* 88:30.

Fletcher, George P. (2002). "Liberals and Romantics at War: The Problem of Collective Guilt." *Yale Law Journal* 111:1499.

Jorgensen, Nina (2001). "A Reappraisal of the Abandoned Nuremberg Concept of Criminal Organisations in the Context of Justice in Rwanda." *Criminal Law Forum* 12:371.

Schabas, William (2000). *Genocide in International Law, the Crime of Crimes.* Cambridge, U.K.: Cambridge University Press.

William A. Schabas

Control Council Law No. 10

Entered into force on December 20, 1945, Control Council Law No. 10 created a framework for the post–World War II trials of German military and civilian personnel. Commanders of the four zones of occupation in postwar Germany made up the Allied Control Council. Major war criminals were to be tried, under the London Charter, by the International Military Tribunal (IMT). Control Council Law No. 10 applied to those individuals not considered major war criminals.

Control Council Law No. 10 provided definitions for specific offenses, so that all the Allied powers would be using the same legal standard. These definitions were taken from the London Charter, with minor adjustments, and included crimes against peace, war crimes, and crimes against humanity. Control Council Law No. 10 did not ascribe particular penalties to offenses; rather, it named penalties that a court could apply to any person convicted of an offense falling into one of the three categories named above. These penalties included life imprisonment, imprisonment for a term of years, and capital punishment.

As it referred to and incorporated the terms of the London Charter, Control Council Law No. 10 did not permit superior orders as a form of defense, but allowed their consideration as a mitigating factor in determining punishment. Further, no one was immune from prosecution by virtue of a governmental position.

Control Council Law No. 10 also referred to the right of the IMT to declare as criminal a particular organization. It provided for the conviction of members of such organizations. The IMT declared as criminal certain categories of leadership within the Nazi Party, Gestapo, and SD, and most members of the SS.

Although Control Council Law No. 10 did not create courts to conduct trials, it assumed that each of the Allied powers would establish appropriate courts for this purpose in its zone of occupation. Each zone commander would then determine the rules of trial.

The Union of Soviet Socialist Republics (USSR) did not hold such trials in its zone of occupation, but did try Nazi military personnel in the USSR for atrocities committed against civilians during Germany's occupation of the former Soviet Union. France held a small number of trials in its zone of occupation and a larger number in France for atrocities committed during Germany's occupation of France. Great Britain conducted numerous trials in its zone of occupation before military courts, a number of them involving the killings of prisoners of war.

In implementing Control Council Law No. 10, the U.S. military government issued Ordinance No. 7, dated October 18, 1946, that provided for three-judge courts. Judges were to be drawn from a pool of attorneys in the United States. A listing of the rights of the accused was included. Judgments would enumerate the reasons behind the justices' decisions; they were final and not subject to appeal.

The United States established six such courts, all at Nuremberg. They heard a total of twelve cases between 1946 and 1948, all but one involving multiple defendants. Charges related to medical experiments performed on concentration camp inmates, the killing of the mentally ill in German hospitals and nursing homes (via the Nazis' euthanasia program), the persecution of Jews and political opponents in Germany, and the killing of Jews and political opponents in occupied countries of the Eastern Front.

German industrialists were tried in these courts for employing forced foreign laborers, concentration camp inmates, and prisoners of war in war industry plants. Military figures were tried for killing civilians in Yugoslavia and Greece as reprisal for partisan attacks on German troops. Some defendants were charged with membership in an organization declared criminal by the IMT, typically in conjunction with other charges.

The U.S. command additionally established military courts at Dachau to focus on violations of the rights of prisoners of war and atrocities committed in the concentration camps. German courts also conducted trials of Germans accused of offenses during World War II.

Even though the International Military Tribunal at Nuremberg, trying, as it did, top Nazi leadership, gained more notoriety, a much larger number of trials were held before the courts created under Control Council Law No. 10. These trials involved thousands of defendants. They were important not only for the penalties imposed on particular defendants, but also for the body of law they developed. The United States published the proceedings of its Nuremberg cases in fifteen volumes: *Trials of War Criminals before the Nuremberg Military Tribunals under Control Council Law No. 10.*

SEE ALSO London Charter; Nuremberg Trials; Nuremberg Trials, Subsequent

BIBLIOGRAPHY

Levie, Howard S. (1993). *Terrorism in War: The Law of War Crimes.* Dobbs Ferry, N.Y.: Oceana Publications.

Maugham, Viscount (1951). *U.N.O. and War Crimes.* London: John Murray.

Trials of War Criminals before the Nuremberg Military Tribunals under Control Council Law No. 10 (1946–1949). 15 volumes. Washington, D.C.: U.S. Government Printing Office.

John Quigley

Convention on Apartheid

The International Convention on the Suppression and Punishment of Apartheid was adopted by the United Nations (UN) General Assembly in November 1973. The treaty was an attempt to criminalize racial separation and segregation policies such as those that had been imposed by South Africa's white minority government. Under the Convention, which now has more than one hundred states parties, the crime of apartheid refers to a series of inhuman acts—including murder, torture, arbitrary arrest, illegal imprisonment, exploitation, marginalization, and persecution—committed for the purpose of establishing and maintaining the domination of one racial group by another. The Convention is particularly notable for its departure from the traditional rule of state sovereignty in that it authorizes the national courts of states parties to attribute individual criminal responsibility for the crime to both government leaders and their supporters in certain instances.

Although the UN Security Council and General Assembly had already condemned the apartheid policies of South Africa's national party government previously, the General Assembly's adoption of the Apartheid Convention provided the first formal legal framework within which UN member states could impose individual and collective sanctions aimed at pressing the South African government to change its racist policies. Impor-

tantly, the drafters of the Convention chose to formulate it in general terms, so that, in addition to the Convention's direct bearing on the "apartheid government," it would deter and prohibit any other states from adopting similar policies. In doing so, they gave added impetus to the continued development of a general prohibition against crimes against humanity.

Notwithstanding the Convention's stated or ostensible general and specific purposes, the fact that its criminal provisions are so broadly defined as to be practically unworkable raises doubts as to whether the states that adopted it ever really intended to make good on their forewarnings of individual prosecutions. In fact, since its adoption in 1973, no one has been charged under the Convention and, given the negotiated nature of South Africa's democratic transition, it has become very unlikely that anyone from the former regime will ever be prosecuted for the crime of apartheid. Arguably, therefore, the Convention's real significance lies not in individual criminal accountability (which it failed to bring about), but rather in its authoritative condemnation of the policy of apartheid as a crime against humanity—a conclusion also recognized by the majority of the members of South Africa's Truth and Reconciliation Commission.

The future of the Apartheid Convention itself as a legal instrument within the emerging international criminal justice framework is uncertain. Since 1993 only Yugoslavia (which, effectively, did not have a choice in the matter) has bothered to ratify the Convention. Even South Africa's new democratic government has not ratified the Convention. Nevertheless, future perpetrators of apartheid-like policies are on notice as to their potential international criminal liability, thanks less to the Convention itself than to the inclusion of a more precise definition of the crime of apartheid within the Rome Statute of the International Criminal Court (ICC). Within the latter's criminal jurisdiction, the crime of apartheid is a crime against humanity when it is knowingly committed as part of a widespread or systematic attack directed against any civilian population. More specifically, the crime of apartheid refers to inhumane acts (i.e., murder, extermination, enslavement, deportation, imprisonment, torture, rape, persecution, and the enforced disappearance of persons) committed in the context of an institutionalized regime of systematic oppression and domination of one racial group by another.

SEE ALSO Apartheid; International Law; Namibia (German South West Africa and South West Africa); South Africa

BIBLIOGRAPHY

Butcher, Goler Teal (1986). "Legal Consequences for States of the Illegality of Apartheid." *Human Rights Quarterly* 8:404–442.

United Nations Department of Public Information (1994). *The United Nations and Apartheid, 1948–1994.* New York: Author.

United Nations Special Committee Against Apartheid (1988). *Twenty-Five Years of Commitment to the Elimination of "Apartheid" in South Africa.* New York: Author.

Weissbrodt, David, and Georgina Mahoney (1986). "International Legal Action Against Apartheid." *Law & Inequality Journal* 4:485–508.

Garth Meintjes

Convention on the Prevention and Punishment of Genocide

The Convention on the Prevention and Punishment of the Crime of Genocide was adopted by the United Nations (UN) General Assembly on December 9, 1948. Within three years the Convention obtained the twenty ratifications required for entry into force. By 2003 some 130 states had ratified or acceded to the Convention. Accordingly, they are bound as a matter of international law to respect the obligations that it enumerates. But even for those states who have not, the key provisions of the Convention are widely accepted as a codification of customary legal norms that bind all states.

In his 1944 book *Axis Rule in Occupied Europe*, the inventor of the term *genocide*, Raphael Lemkin, deplored the shortcomings in the international legal protection of national minorities. He called for the development within international criminal law of an express prohibition on the destruction of minorities, which he named the crime of genocide. The Nuremberg Trial addressed the Nazi attacks on minorities, especially European Jews, but under the heading "crimes against humanity." The Nuremberg precedent was limited, because it applied only to atrocities committed during international armed conflict.

Within days of the Nuremberg judgment, in October 1946, India, Cuba, and Panama asked that the question of genocide be put on the agenda of the first meeting of the General Assembly, which was then in session. Critical of the failure of the Nuremberg Trial to condemn pre-1939 acts of the Nazi regime, they called on the General Assembly to condemn the crime of genocide, even when committed in peacetime. Also, noting that certain crimes of "relatively lesser importance," such as piracy and trafficking in drugs or pornography, were declared as international crimes, they

submitted the same should be the case for genocide. This would authorize the courts of any country to punish the crime, even acts not committed on the territory or by the nationals of such a state, a concept known as universal jurisdiction. In December 1946 the General Assembly adopted a resolution condemning genocide as a crime under international law, and calling for the preparation of a treaty on the subject.

Over the next two years various specialized bodies within the UN labored over the text of the draft convention. The finished text contained a definition of the crime of genocide and made clear that no one—not even a head of state—was exempt. It specified that the crime could be committed in time of peace, and it imposed on states a duty to include the offense in their own national legislation. However, the original hope that the Convention would also recognize universal jurisdiction for genocide failed to obtain sufficient support. It specified that genocide should be punished before the courts of the country where the crime was committed or, alternatively, by an international criminal court. But an international court did not yet exist, and it was only in 2002 when the Rome Statute of the International Criminal Court came into force that the Convention became fully operational in this respect. The text also specified that disputes between states about their obligations under the Convention could be litigated before the International Court of Justice.

The terms of the Convention were a difficult compromise. At the time it was drafted, states were still extremely uncomfortable with the idea that serious violations of human rights, especially those directed against national, ethnic, racial, or religious minorities, committed within their own borders in peacetime might be deemed of concern to the international community. Most of the great powers still held substantial colonial empires, while in the United States racist laws enforced a form of apartheid on the descendants of African slaves, especially in the southern states.

The most important consequence of these issues was an exceedingly narrow definition of the crime of genocide. The General Assembly intended to confine the crime of genocide to intentional acts aimed at the physical destruction of a national, racial, ethnic, or religious group. Acts of cultural genocide, including what might be called ethnic cleansing, were quite intentionally excluded from the Convention. Efforts to include political, economic, and social groups within the Convention were also voted down.

Despite these shortcomings, the Convention on the Prevention and Punishment of the Crime of Genocide remained the preeminent treaty in international criminal law for more than half a decade. By comparison, no similar treaty was ever adopted with respect to the related offense of crimes against humanity. At Nuremberg the scope of crimes against humanity had been restricted by the requirement that they be committed within the context of a war. But the acts that they punished were much broader, including such broad concepts as "persecution" and "inhumane acts" that meant they could extend to a wide range of human rights abuses.

As a result, states were willing to accept a treaty like the Genocide Convention, with its narrow definition, but resisted any similar obligation with respect to crimes against humanity. Over the decades that followed adoption of the Convention, there were many attempts to stretch the definition of genocide so as to include human rights abuses that it did not, on a literal reading of the text, appear to cover.

By the 1990s the distinction between genocide and crimes against humanity became less significant. The Rome Statute, which applies to both genocide and crimes against humanity, imposed many of the same obligations on states that they had assumed under the Genocide Convention. This evolution was largely the result of developments in international human rights law. But although it had become less important in a legal sense to establish that an atrocity met the definition of genocide as set forth in the Convention, the word itself retained a terrible stigma and it remains important for many groups that are victims of human rights violations to claim that genocide has been committed.

The definition of genocide in the 1948 Convention has stood the test of time. In contrast with definitions of crimes against humanity and war crimes in various international legal texts, which have changed and, in a general sense, expanded over the decades, attempts to amend the text adopted by the General Assembly in 1948 have met with resistance. The statutes of the ad hoc tribunals for the former Yugoslavia and Rwanda, as well as the International Criminal Court, reproduce the 1948 definition without any change. This argues strongly for the definition being a statement of customary international law, generally accepted by the international community. However, some of the other provisions of the 1948 Convention, such as the rejection of universal jurisdiction and the establishment of the compulsory jurisdiction of the International Criminal Court, cannot be said to correspond to international custom.

The Convention found little concrete application for many decades after its adoption. By the 1990s, however, it found a new dynamism. There were important prosecutions for the crime before the ad hoc tribunals for the former Yugoslavia and Rwanda, as well as several cases alleging genocide before the International Court of Justice. There has also been an increasing tendency to prosecute the crime before national courts. On the fine points of interpretation of the definition and of the Convention as a whole, considerable uncertainty remains. As long as violent ethnic conflict persists, the Genocide Convention will remain an important component of the international legal protection of human rights.

SEE ALSO Genocide; International Law

BIBLIOGRAPHY

Drost, Pieter Nicolaas (1959). *Genocide, United Nations Legislation on International Criminal Law.* Leyden: A.W. Sythoff.

Lemkin, Raphael (1944). *Axis Rule in Occupied Europe.* Washington, D.C.: Carnegie Endowment for World Peace.

Lippman, Matthew (1999). "Genocide." In *International Criminal Law*, volume 1, ed. M. Cherif Bassiouni. Ardsley, N.Y.: Transnational Publishers.

Robinson, Nehemiah (1960). *The Genocide Convention: A Commentary.* New York: Institute of Jewish Affairs.

Schabas, William (2000). *Genocide in International Law, the Crime of Crimes.* Cambridge: Cambridge University Press.

William A. Schabas

Conventions Against Torture and Other Cruel, Inhuman, and Degrading Treatment

Torture is an evil that cannot and will not be tolerated in our times. Since the end of World War II, international human rights treaties (both global and regional) that protect the individual against acts of torture committed by state authorities have come into being. Following the adoption of these treaties, there were calls to strengthen the protections provided for in the treaties, which led to the creation of law enforcement bodies designed to punish and prevent the crime of torture. The United Nations (UN) Convention Against Torture and Other Cruel, Inhuman, or Degrading Treatment or Punishment, a global treaty, was adopted in 1984. In the Americas the Inter-American Convention for the Prevention and Punishment of Torture was adopted in 1987. In Europe the European Convention for the Prevention of Torture and Inhuman or Degrading Treatment or Punishment entered into force in 1989. These three treaties, each applicable within specific regions and having an emphasis of its own, constitute the fundamental protection of individuals against acts of torture.

The UN Convention Against Torture and Other Cruel, Inhuman, or Degrading Treatment or Punishment

The Convention Against Torture and Other Cruel, Inhuman, or Degrading Treatment or Punishment (Convention Against Torture) was adopted by the UN General Assembly on December 10, 1984, and entered into force on June 28, 1987. By August 2003, 133 states had ratified the treaty and a further twelve states had signed it. The convention is based on a UN General Assembly declaration that was issued on December 9, 1975.

The Obligations Undertaken

Article 1 defines *torture* as "any act by which severe pain or suffering, whether physical or mental, is intentionally inflicted on a person for such purposes as [obtaining information or a confession, intimidation or coercion, or discrimination]." The convention takes in torture inflicted by state officials, and by private individuals who act with the consent or acquiescence of state officials.

State parties are invested with obligations that appertain to both the national and the international domains. At the national level states are obliged to take measures to prevent acts of torture. No exceptional circumstances, or commands from persons of superior rank, may be invoked as a justification of torture. All acts of torture must be made criminal offenses under national law and must be censured by penalties that take into account the grave nature of the crime. Individuals who complain of having been victims of torture shall have their cases examined promptly and impartially, and they shall be protected against all reprisals. Victims of torture shall be compensated. Confessions obtained under torture shall not be used as evidence in a court of law. Law enforcement personnel shall be educated and informed with regard to the punishment of torture. Rules, instructions, methods, and practices relating to interrogations shall remain under systematic review.

At the international level the convention entrenches the principle of universal jurisdiction. Thus, a state party shall have jurisdiction over persons suspected of having committed acts of torture, irrespective of their nationalities and of the places where the alleged crimes were committed. Acts of torture are to be classified as extraditable offenses in any extradition treaty existing between contracting states, but "no State Party shall expel, return, or extradite a person to another State where there are substantial grounds for believing that he would be in danger of being subjected to torture." If suspected persons are not extradited, they shall be tried in the state in which they were found.

Measures of Implementation

Article 17 establishes a Committee Against Torture (CAT). It is composed of "ten experts of high moral standing and recognized competence in the field of human rights who shall serve in their personal capacity." They are elected by state parties for periods of four years and may be reelected.

State parties must report periodically on the measures they have taken to fulfill the obligations with which they have been endowed. These reports are transmitted to all state parties. They are not public, but an individual report will often be made public by the relevant state party. CAT may make general comments on the reports. CAT may also include such comments and any replies it has received from state parties in its Annual Report, as provided for in Article 24. The convention does not provide for any other measure or action on the part of CAT with regard to state reports.

Options for the filing of complaints (by individuals or states who allege severe human rights violations) were modeled after those that pertain to the UN Covenant for Civil and Political Rights. All proceedings that refer to complaints filed by one state against another state are wholly confidential. If no solution to a dispute involving states is found, CAT prepares a report in which it summarizes the available facts, and the report is then transmitted to the relevant state parties.

Complaints may be filed by individuals who claim to be victims of violation by the state party under whose jurisdiction they reside. The claimant must have exhausted domestic pathways for the redress of grievances and must not have submitted a claim to another international body of investigation or settlement. The CAT meetings at which testimonies and available evidence are examined are closed meetings. The conclusions of CAT are forwarded to the claimant and to the relevant state party. A written summary of the argument is put into the CAT's Annual Report to the General Assembly.

Article 20 of the convention allows for a CAT inquiry into an allegation of torture in the absence of a complaint. If CAT receives reliable information that torture is being practiced systematically in the territory of a state party, it must ask that state to respond to the allegation. This kind of discourse can take place only if there is complete cooperation on the part of the state party in question. It is wholly confidential. The findings of CAT are communicated to the state party, together with the committee's recommendations and/or warnings. A state can opt out of this practice at the time of its ratification of the convention (Article 28).

The Inter-American Convention for the Prevention and Punishment of Torture

The Inter-American Convention for the Prevention and Punishment of Torture is the first treaty to come out of the Organization of American States (OAS) whose purpose is to strengthen the systems for the protection of human rights in the Americas, which were introduced under the 1948 OAS Charter and the American Convention on Human Rights of 1969. The Inter-American Convention entered into force on January 29, 1987, and presently binds sixteen states in the Americas. The obligations incumbent on state parties, as well as the methods of the convention's implementation, are very similar to those set forth in the UN Convention Against Torture.

The European Convention for the Prevention of Torture and Inhuman or Degrading Treatment or Punishment

The efforts of several states to amend the Convention Against Torture by adding a provision for the rights of experts to make regular visits to places of detention have so far failed. In March 1980 Costa Rica presented to the UN Commission on Human Rights a Draft Optional Protocol to that effect. The text of the protocol was based on a proposal made in 1976 by the Swiss banker and lawyer Jean-Jacques Gautier, founder of the Swiss Committee Against Torture. Because the efforts to amend the Convention Against Torture were unsuccessful, the Parliamentary Assembly of the Council of Europe (CoE), in 1983, submitted Gautier's proposal to the member states of the CoE. On November 26, 1987, the European Convention for the Prevention of Torture and Inhuman or Degrading Treatment or Punishment (European Anti-Torture Convention) was opened for signature. It entered into force on February 1, 1989. It is ratified by all forty-five member states of the CoE. Ratification of the European Anti-Torture Convention in fact constitutes a condition for membership in the CoE. The convention is nonjudicial and preventive in nature. The European Committee for the Prevention of Torture (CPT), a committee of independent and impartial experts, makes periodic ad hoc visits to places of detention of virtually any kind and submits its findings to the authorities of the state in question. The convention is based on the principle of cooperation, and its work is carried out in strict confidence. The CPT's reports are published only if the state in question fails to cooperate with the committee or refuses to make the improvements that the committee has recommended. Contracting states agree to grant the CPT unlimited access to places of detention, including the right of its inspectors to move freely inside such places and to interview in private any person whom they believe can provide relevant information.

The European Anti-Torture Convention in conjunction with the European Convention on Human Rights are an effective means to combat the crime of torture. It is hoped that a similar protective system will be adopted by the UN.

SEE ALSO International Law; Torture

BIBLIOGRAPHY

Buergenthal, T., and D. Shelton (1995). *Protecting Human Rights in the Americas, Cases and Materials*, 4th revised edition. Strasbourg, France: N. P. Engel.

Burgers, J. H., and H. Danelius (1988). *The United Nations Convention Against Torture: A Handbook on the Convention Against Torture and Other Cruel, Inhuman, or Degrading Treatment or Punishment*. Dordrecht, Netherlands: Martinus Nijhoff.

Morgan, R., and M. Evans (2001). *Combating Torture in Europe: The Work and Standards of the European Committee for the Prevention of Torture*. Strasbourg, France: Council of Europe Publishing.

Nagan, W. P., and L. Atkins (2001). "The International Law of Torture: From Universal Proscription to Effective Application and Enforcement." *Harvard Human Rights Journal* (Spring) 14:87–122.

Nowak, M. (1985). "Die UNO-Konvention gegen die Folter vom 10 Dezember 1984." *Europäische Grundrechte Zeitschrift (EuGRZ)* 1985: 109–116.

Hans Christian Krüger
Alessia Sonaglioni

Cossacks

On January 24, 1919, the Orgburo, the administrative body subordinate to the Politburo, issued a secret order for the immediate genocide of the Cossacks; local officials were ordered to carry out the policy with the utmost ruthlessness. The categories of those selected for extermination were broad and loosely defined, and within the space of twelve weeks more than ten thousand Don Cossack men, women, and children were executed by revolutionary tribunals. The policy was abruptly abandoned in March 1919 when the Cossacks revolted, driving the Bolsheviks from the Don territory and setting the stage for the climactic phase of the Russian civil war. The policy of genocide against the Cossacks was unique and arose from a complex matrix of Cossack history, Bolshevik beliefs, and the course of the civil war.

In 1914 the Cossacks numbered approximately 4.5 million people scattered across the whole of the Eurasian from the River Don in the west to the River Ussuri in the Far East. The Cossacks had originated in the steppe lands of Russia in the sixteenth century when Slavic frontiersmen and fugitives joined with nomadic

Cossacks wore dark blue uniforms and black fur hats. In this photo from 1910, Cossacks stand in formation in St. Petersburg. Their corps would be liquidated in 1919. [BETTMANN/CORBIS]

peoples of the steppe to form distinct and autonomous communities. For the first two hundred years of their existence, the Cossacks and their way of life had been the incarnation of freedom for the enserfed masses of Russia. From the late eighteenth century, however, the tsarist state succeeded in harnessing the Cossacks' military skills for its own ends, enlisting them to serve either as soldiers or as a form of paramilitary police. By the twentieth century the Cossacks were the most feared defenders of the tsarist state and widely loathed, particularly by the revolutionary movement and the Jews. Cossack attitudes toward the throne and the revolutionary movement were actually far more complex and ambiguous than the popular stereotype suggested. But the perception that all Cossacks were inveterate reactionaries remained an instinctive prejudice for all those opposed to the tsarist regime.

With the Bolsheviks' seizure of power in October 1917 came the civil war. The rapid descent into barbarism by all sides formed the immediate context for the genocide of 1919. But it was the combination of prejudice, the habit of violence, and Cossack behavior during the civil war that coalesced to trigger the policy of genocide. Although divided in their attitudes toward the October Revolution, most Cossacks were much less hostile to the Bolshevik regime than is generally recognized. Nevertheless, the experience of Bolshevik rule in early 1918 led to large-scale rebellions against it in many Cossack territories. These rebellions were not an endorsement of the wider anti-Bolshevik movement; rather, they had the much more limited aim of removing the Bolsheviks from Cossack territories. For the Bolsheviks, however, the rebellions during the spring of 1918 were ample proof of the counterrevolutionary nature of the Cossacks as a whole. Rebellion against Bolshevik rule was seen not as the action of individual Cossacks making choices, but as something inherent in being a Cossack. Already accustomed to using violence and terror on an unprecedented scale, the Bolsheviks took this policy to its logical conclusion with the order for genocide.

Compared to earlier and subsequent genocides and even by the standards of the Russian civil war, the killing of ten thousand Cossacks in the Don region over a three-month period can easily be overlooked. Yet there is no doubt that the genocide which occurred was a state-driven policy. It was devised at the highest level of the Bolshevik state, it targeted a specific community on the basis of who they were, not what they had done, and it was carried out by officials and organizations of that state. It stopped not because the leadership had qualms about the morality of the genocide, but because the Cossacks successfully rebelled and expelled the Bolsheviks. Later the Bolsheviks modified their treatment of the Cossacks, still regarding them suspiciously but acting more circumspect in their dealings with them. By this point, however, the civil war had eviscerated the Cossacks, destroying their communities and way of life. Collectivization was the final catastrophe for the Cossacks, irrevocably ending any possibility of their continued existence as a distinct community.

During World War II many Cossacks fought with the Nazis against the Stalinist regime at whose hands they had suffered so much. The Cossacks retreated with the German army and many thousands of Cossacks ended up in Austria at the war's end. In May 1945 they surrendered to the British. Although many of the Cossacks had never been Soviet citizens, the British decided to comply with a Soviet request for their repatriation. With a great deal of brutality, British soldiers forced the Cossacks onto trains and then to the NKVD. The leaders of the Cossack armies were executed in Moscow, while the rank and file were sent to the Gulag. The regime of Nikita Khrushchev later released any survivors.

SEE ALSO Chechens; Ethnic Cleansing; Famine; Gulag; Kalmyks; Kulaks; Lenin, Vladimir; Pogroms, Pre-Soviet Russia; Stalin, Joseph; Ukraine (Famine)

BIBLIOGRAPHY

Holquist, Peter (2002). *Making War, Forging Revolution: Russia's Continuum of Crisis 1914–1921.* Cambridge, Mass.: Harvard University Press.

McNeal, Robert Hatch (1987). *Tsar and Cossack 1855–1914.* New York: St. Martin's Press

O'Rourke, Shane (2000). *Warriors and Peasants: The Don Cossacks in Late Imperial Russia.* New York: St. Martin's Press.

Shane P. O'Rourke

Crimes Against Humanity

Crimes against humanity is a category of international crime usually associated with the related concepts of genocide and war crimes. Although international law contains several different definitions of crimes against humanity, they generally involve acts of physical violence or persecution committed against vulnerable groups of civilians. The Tel-Aviv District Court, in a 1952 judgment, said a crime against humanity "must be one of serious character and likely to embitter the life of a human person, to degrade him and cause him great physical or moral suffering." The United Nations (UN) Secretary-General has described them as "inhumane acts of a very serious nature."

Crimes against humanity are closely related to the crime of genocide, yet broader in scope, in that they encompass attacks on a wide range of civilian populations, whereas the crime of genocide is confined to national, ethnic, racial, or religious groups. Moreover, they do not require the physical destruction of the victims. Unlike war crimes, crimes against humanity may be committed in time of peace. It may be convenient to view crimes against humanity as being broadly analogous to serious violations of human rights. In the case of breaches of international human rights law, it is the state that is held responsible, whereas in the case of crimes against humanity, individuals are the perpetrators and they are the ones who are held criminally responsible. The consequence of a serious violation of human rights may be an order to cease the impugned act or to compensate the victim, whereas the consequence of a crime against humanity will generally be a significant term of imprisonment.

Because crimes against humanity are designated as an international crime, they are viewed as an exception to the general rule that it is the sovereign right of states to prosecute crimes committed within their own borders or by their own citizens. Crimes against humanity may be punished by courts of countries other than where the crime took place, and by international courts, such as the International Criminal Tribunals for the Former Yugoslavia (ICTY) and Rwanda (ICTR) or the International Criminal Court (ICC).

History of the Term *Crimes Against Humanity*

Perhaps the first use of the expression *crimes against humanity* was by the French revolutionary Maximilien Robespierre, who described the deposed King Louis XVI as a *criminel envers l'humanité* (criminal against humanity). He argued that for this reason King Louis XVI should be executed, although Robespierre had earlier fought for the abolition of capital punishment in the French National Assembly. A century later journalist George Washington Williams wrote to the U.S. Secretary of State, informing him that King Leopold's regime in the Congo Free States was responsible for "crimes against humanity."

A torture room at the Tuol Sleng Prison (the infamous S21), now a museum in Phnom Penh, Cambodia. In the late 1970s the interrogation, torture, and murder of dissident Cambodian Communist Party members were carried out under the direct supervision of Khmer Rouge leaders. [WOLFGANG KAEHLER/CORBIS]

The preamble to the important Hague Conventions of 1899 and 1907, in what is known as the Martens clause, spoke of "the usages established between civilized nations, from the laws." But the concept of crimes against humanity in international law made its first formal appearance in the declaration made by the governments of France, Great Britain, and Russia, dated May 24, 1915, directed at the Turkish massacres of the minority Armenian population, that "[i]n the presence of these new crimes of Turkey against humanity and civilization, the allied Governments publicly inform the Sublime Porte that they will hold personally responsible for the said crimes all members of the Ottoman Government as well as those of its agents who are found to be involved in such massacres." The United States did not joint in the denunciation, with U.S. Secretary of State Robert Lansing explaining this by referring to what he called the "more or less justifiable" right of the Turkish government to deport the Armenians to the extent that they lived "within the zone of military operations."

After the war the victorious Allies attempted to prosecute Turkish officials for what were called "depor-

tations and massacres" of the Armenians. The Turkish authorities actually arrested and detained scores of their leaders, later releasing many as a result of public demonstrations and other pressure. But Turkey refused to ratify the Treaty of Sèvres, signed on August 10, 1920, which imposed an obligation to surrender those who were deemed responsible for the persecutions of the Armenians. It also contemplated the establishment of a tribunal by the League of Nations with jurisdiction to punish those charged. The Treaty of Sèvres was eventually replaced by the Treaty of Lausanne of July 24, 1923. Rather than call for prosecution, it included a "declaration of amnesty" for all offenses committed between August 1, 1914, and November 20, 1922.

The essence of the controversy surrounding the Turkish prosecutions was whether or not atrocities, persecution, and deportations committed by a sovereign government against its own civilian population, including ethnic or national minorities established on its territory, should be subject to international law at all. As outrageous as the crimes against the Armenian minority were, the major victorious powers were nervous about a principle that might return to challenge their own treatment of vulnerable minorities within their own territories and especially their colonial empires. The debate resurfaced in the early 1940s, as work began to prepare the post-World War II Nazi prosecutions.

As early as 1943 the Allies proclaimed their intention to hold Nazi leaders accountable for war crimes. The United Nations War Crimes Commission was established to prepare the groundwork for postwar prosecutions. Meeting in London, it initially agreed to use the list of offenses that had been drafted by the Responsibilities Commission of the Paris Peace Conference in 1919 as the basis for its prosecutions. The enumeration consisted of a variety of war crimes, already recognized for the purposes of international prosecution, which had been agreed to by Italy and Japan and, at least, tacitly accepted without objection by Germany. These crimes addressed the means and methods of the conduct of warfare, and various acts of persecution committed against civilians in occupied territories.

Nevertheless, from an early stage in its work, efforts were made to extend the jurisdiction of the Commission to civilian atrocities committed against ethnic groups not only within occupied territories but also those within Germany itself. Serving on the Legal Committee of the Commission, the U.S. representative Herbert C. Pell used the term *crimes against humanity* to describe offenses "committed against stateless persons or against any persons because of their race or religion." But the idea that international criminal law extended to atrocities perpetrated against civilians by their own governments remained controversial, and there was ongoing resistance from the British and American governments because of the implications this might have for their own treatment of minorities. Jewish groups and other nongovernmental organizations (NGOs) lobbied members of the Commission to ensure that the postwar trials would not be confined to traditional war crimes, one of the first examples of the influence of NGOs and contributions to law-making in this area.

Within weeks of the end of the war in Europe, the four victorious major powers, the United Kingdom, France, the Soviet Union, and the United States, convened the London Conference, whose purpose was the organization of the postwar trials. In addition to war crimes, the draft treaty on which they worked included a category with as yet no generic name, which was labeled "atrocities, persecutions, and deportations on political, racial or religious grounds." As the Conference concluded, the U.S. delegate, Robert Jackson, suggested the category be given the title "crimes against humanity." Article VI of the Charter of the Nuremberg Tribu-

nal, adopted by the London Conference on August 8, 1945, defined three categories of crimes over which the Tribunal would exercise jurisdiction: war crimes, crimes against peace, and crimes against humanity. Crimes against humanity were defined as follows:

> Murder, extermination, enslavement, deportation, and other inhumane acts committed against any civilian population, before or during the war, or persecutions on political, racial or religious grounds in execution of or in connection with any crime within the jurisdiction of the Tribunal, whether or not in violation of the domestic law of the court where perpetrated.

Crimes against humanity are comprised of two categories of specific punishable behavior. The first, such as murder, extermination, enslavement, and inhumane acts, correspond generally to crimes under virtually all domestic criminal law systems, and cover such offenses as killing, assault, rape, and kidnapping or forcible confinement. The second, persecutions on discriminatory grounds, run afoul of antidiscrimination laws in many countries but fall short of criminal behavior. What elevates these acts to crimes against humanity, as held by the courts, is their commission as part of a widespread or systematic attack on a civilian population, although this is not stated explicitly in the Nuremberg Tribunal's definition.

In late 1945, acting in their role as the occupying government of Germany, the Allies enacted criminal legislation that made crimes against humanity a crime within German law. Although similar to the Nuremberg Charter definition, it was somewhat broader:

> Atrocities and offenses, including but not limited to murder, extermination, enslavement, deportation, imprisonment, torture, rape, or other inhumane acts committed against any civilian population, or persecutions on political, racial or religious grounds whether or not in violation of the domestic laws of the country where perpetrated.

Known as Control Council Law No. 10, it extended to all atrocities and offenses. Moreover, unlike the Nuremberg Charter, it did not require that crimes against humanity be committed "in execution of or in connection with any crime within the jurisdiction of the Tribunal."

Nexus with Aggressive War

The condition in the Nuremberg Charter that crimes against humanity be committed "in execution of or in connection with any crime within the jurisdiction of the Tribunal" is often referred to as the nexus. The Nuremberg Tribunal interpreted this phrase to mean that atrocities and persecution committed prior to the outbreak of the war, in September 1939, were not punishable as an international crime. It acknowledged that "political opponents were murdered in Germany before the war, and that many of them were kept in concentration camps in circumstances of great horror and cruelty. . . . The persecution of Jews during the same period is established beyond all doubt."

According to the judges at Nuremberg, to constitute a crime against humanity the acts had to be committed in pursuit of an aggressive war. This interpretation would appear to be consistent with what was intended by those who established the Nuremberg Tribunal. At the London Conference, the U.S. delegate, Jackson, spoke of "some regrettable circumstances at times in our own country in which minorities are unfairly treated," and of the concern of his government that such acts might now fall within the scope of crimes against humanity. The way to deal with his concern was to include, as an element of crimes against humanity, this nexus with aggressive war.

There was controversy about the nexus virtually from the day the Nuremberg judgment was issued. Frustrated by this limitation, other countries seized the occasion of the first session of the UN General Assembly to propose that the UN recognize and codify yet another international crime, to be named "genocide," that would not be confined to a link with aggressive war. The Convention on the Prevention and Punishment of the Crime of Genocide, adopted by the General Assembly on December 9, 1948, affirmed that genocide could be committed "in time of peace or in time of war" precisely in order to distinguish it from crimes against humanity. The price of this important concession was a definition of genocide that was confined to the destruction of a national, ethnic, racial, or religious group, in other words, to a much narrower class of atrocities than what was covered by the existing definition of crimes against humanity.

Over the years much debate and lingering uncertainty surrounded the link or nexus between crimes against humanity and aggressive war. In 1968 the Convention on the Non-Applicability of Statutory Limitations to War Crimes and Crimes Against Humanity referred to crimes against humanity "whether committed in time of war or in time of peace." Five years later the International Convention on the Suppression and Punishment of the Crime of Apartheid defined apartheid, which was clearly a practice not limited to wartime, as a crime against humanity. But confusion persisted when the Security Council, in establishing the ICTY in May 1993, reaffirmed that crimes against humanity should be punishable only when committed "in armed conflict." In the first major judgment of the ICTY, issued in October 1995, the Appeals Chamber dismissed the significance of these words, saying they were incompatible with customary international law. The issue was rather definitively resolved in 1998, in the Rome Statute of the ICC, which imposes no requirement of a nexus between crimes against humanity and aggressive war, although it does not explicitly state that crimes against humanity may be committed in time of peace as well as in time of war. Thus, for the future, little doubt can exist about this matter, although to the extent that there are prosecutions for crimes against humanity committed between 1945 and 1998, lawyers will continue to argue both sides of the question.

Contextual Elements of Crimes Against Humanity
Because the punishable acts falling within the rubric of crimes against humanity are either punishable as ordinary crimes under national laws or, in the case of persecution-type acts, often not punishable at all, it is fundamental that crimes against humanity be committed within a context of widespread or systematic attacks on a civilian population. If there were no such limitation on the scope of crimes against humanity, states would never accept the right of the courts of other states, or of international tribunals, to prosecute such acts when committed on their own territory. In other words, it is only when murder, extermination, and persecution reach a threshold of great seriousness and broad scale that states are prepared to let down the curtain of sovereignty that traditionally gives them the sole right to criminalize behavior committed within their borders. These additional constraints on the definition of *crimes against humanity* lie at the core of the entire concept, and are often referred to as the "contextual elements."

Crimes against humanity originally derived from a need to prosecute Nazis for acts committed against German nationals within Germany itself. Until 1945 international law clearly protected Jewish civilians within the occupied lands of Europe, such as Poland, Russia, Hungary, France, and the Netherlands, but the same could not be said of the German Jews. To some extent, the acts of persecution committed against the Germany Jews were legal under national legislation and even mandated by German laws. This explains the section of the Nuremberg Charter that states crimes against humanity were punishable "whether or not in violation of the domestic law of the court where perpetrated."

As a result, it may be said that crimes against humanity involve organized persecution that is either directed by a state and carried out in pursuance of its laws, or tolerated by the state and tacitly condoned or encouraged. Although this is probably an accurate statement of the law in a historical sense, a marked evolution has occurred over the years to weaken the requirement of state policy or plan in the commission of crimes against humanity. One authoritative body, the International Law Commission, stated in 1996 that crimes against humanity are inhumane acts "instigated or directed by a Government or by any organization or group." This matter was the subject of considerable debate when the Rome Statute of the ICC was being adopted in the 1990s. The Rome Statute's definition of *crimes against humanity* requires that they be committed as part of a "widespread or systematic attack on a civilian population," and that this attack be "pursuant to or in furtherance of a State or organizational policy to commit such attack." This definition is large enough to encompass what are sometimes called "non-State actors," and it certainly applies to statelike entities that exercise de facto control over a given territory and fulfill the functions of government.

It is somewhat less clear whether crimes against humanity may also be committed pursuant to a plan or policy of a terrorist organization, which operates without any formal link to a state and often with no obvious ambition to take power. The terrorist attacks of September 11, 2001, were described by many observers, including the United Nations High Commissioner for Human Rights, as crimes against humanity. But in extending the scope of crimes against humanity to terrorist organizations, it becomes increasingly difficult to distinguish them from ordinary crimes punishable under domestic law. While it may seem only logical and proportionate to describe acts such as those committed on September 11 as crimes against humanity, because of their sheer scale and horror, the choice of terminology is far less evident when the crimes are committed on a smaller scale. Indeed, if terrorist groups responsible for atrocities can be held accountable for crimes against humanity, why not organized crime families, motorcycle gangs, and individual serial killers? The distinctions become increasingly difficult to make once the context of a plan or policy of a state or statelike organization is removed from the definition of crimes against humanity. Yet this is precisely what the ICTY has done in its judgments subsequent to adoption of the Rome Statute, suggesting that it considers the Rome Statute requirements to be narrower than what should apply as a matter of customary international law.

The other factor serving to distinguish crimes against humanity as an international crime from ordinary crimes that fall within the scope of national laws is the element of discrimination. The definition in the Nuremberg Charter refers to "persecutions on political,

racial or religious grounds," although it does not seem to make the same requirement with respect to other acts, such as murder and extermination. This aspect of crimes against humanity is even more explicit in the definition found in the ICTR Statute, adopted by the Security Council in November 1994:

> The International Tribunal for Rwanda shall have the power to prosecute persons responsible for the following crimes when committed as part of a widespread or systematic attack against any civilian population on *national, political, ethnic, racial or religious grounds.*

This requirement suggests that a racist or otherwise discriminatory motive must exist for the crime. Therefore, when a defendant charged with crimes against humanity can suggest that a widespread or systematic attack was conducted on grounds that did not involve racial discrimination and that the motive was, for example, to achieve a military victory, the act might not qualify as a crime against humanity. This argument might be submitted, for instance, to counter claims that the atomic bombing of Hiroshima and Nagasaki in August 1945 was a crime against humanity.

Recent case law from the ICTY and ICTR has established that a discriminatory motive is not generally an element of crimes against humanity. This is a relief to prosecutors, for whom proof of motive is a daunting challenge. Exceptionally, discriminatory motive remains an element of the crime against humanity of persecution. This is because persecution-type crimes against humanity may involve acts that are actually authorized by national laws, such as measures preventing intermarriage with persons from specific ethnic groups, as was the case in Nazi Germany.

Punishable Acts

The lists of punishable acts of crimes against humanity are not the same in the various definitions of crimes against humanity. They have at their core the enumeration found in the Nuremberg Charter: murder, extermination, enslavement, deportation, other inhumane acts and persecution. The definition in Control Council Law No. 10, adopted in December 1945, added imprisonment, torture, and rape to the list. The definition was updated to take account of recent developments in international law when the Rome Statute of the ICC added apartheid and the forced disappearance of persons. But the Rome Conference rejected attempts to recognize other new acts of crimes against humanity, such as economic embargo, terrorism, and mass starvation.

The crime of murder is well defined in national legal systems and poses little difficulty within the con-

The 1994 genocide in Rwanda was marked by its savagery. In this photo, a neat row of human skulls, all that remains of some victims. [LANGEVIN JACQUES/CORBIS SYGMA]

text of crimes against humanity. Although there has been some disagreement about this in cases, it is now well established that the murder need not be premeditated.

Extermination as a crime against humanity refers to acts intended to bring about the death of a large number of victims. Evidence must exist that a particular population was targeted and that its members were killed or otherwise subjected to conditions of life calculated to bring about the destruction of a numerically significant part of the population.

Enslavement was widely practiced by the Nazis, who took hundreds of thousands of Jews, other minorities, and foreign nationals conscripted in various parts of their conquered territories, and forced them to work in factories making munitions and rockets and meeting other needs of their military machine. As the Nuremberg judgment pointed out, one of the perverse features of the Nazi slave labor policy was that "useless eaters"—the elderly and infirm, and the disabled—were systematically murdered precisely because they could not be enslaved. In the early twenty-first century international law recognizes various contemporary forms of slavery. The related practice of trafficking in persons,

particularly women and children, is associated with modern crimes against humanity of slavery.

The act of deportation involves the forcible expulsion of populations across international borders. The Rome Statute of the ICC added the words "forcible transfer of population" to deportation, thereby recognizing in its condemnation what in recent years has been known as "ethnic cleansing," particularly when this has occurred within a country's own borders. It should be borne in mind that the Allies themselves, following their victory in 1945, indulged in the forced transfer of ethnic Germans from parts of Eastern Europe. To this day some policy makers still entertain the suggestion that population transfer is an effective technique for dealing with ethnic conflict.

Imprisonment is, of course, a normal act of states carried out in the enforcement of criminal justice. For it to rise to the level of a crime against humanity, imprisonment must amount to the deprivation of physical liberty that is in violation of the fundamental rules of international law. Holding captured prisoners indefinitely, while denying them access to ordinary legal remedies, could fit within the parameters of this crime against humanity.

Torture was not explicitly listed in the Nuremberg Charter as a crime against humanity, although it clearly falls within the catch-all term *other inhumane acts*. A substantial body of international law now exists that addresses the issue of torture, including the UN Convention Against Torture and Other Cruel, Inhuman and Degrading Treatment or Punishment. According to the Rome Statute, *torture* means "the intentional infliction of severe pain or suffering, whether physical or mental, upon a person in the custody or under the control of the accused; except that torture shall not include pain or suffering arising only from, inherent in or incidental to, lawful sanctions." Human rights law requires that state officials perpetrate torture, but this is because human rights law governs the relationship between the individual and the state. In the case of crimes against humanity, there is no such requirement.

The most dramatic enlargement of the scope of crimes against humanity in recent years has taken place in the now very significant list of gender crimes that complement the more traditional reference to rape. In fact, the Nuremberg Charter did not even recognize rape as a form of crime against humanity, although it would have fallen under "other inhumane acts." In any event, the oversight was corrected some months later in Control Council Law No. 10. Building on the word *rape,* the 1998 Rome Statute enumerates several other related acts, namely "sexual slavery, enforced prostitution, forced pregnancy, enforced sterilization, or any other form of sexual violence of comparable gravity." Forced pregnancy means the unlawful confinement of a woman forcibly made pregnant, with the intent of affecting the ethnic composition of any population or carrying out other grave violations of international law.

The crime of apartheid was first defined to describe the racist regime in South Africa during much of the second half of the twentieth century. According to the Rome Statute, it refers to inhumane acts "of a character similar to" other crimes against humanity, when "committed in the context of an institutionalized regime of systematic oppression and domination by one racial group over any other racial group or groups and committed with the intention of maintaining that regime." Here, then, the involvement of a state in the commission of crimes against humanity is quite explicit.

Enforced disappearance of persons is a phenomenon that became widespread under repressive regimes in Latin America during the 1970s and 1980s. It was first recognized as a crime against humanity by the General Assembly in a 1992 resolution. In the ICC's Rome Statute, the term refers to the

> Arrest, detention or abduction of persons by, or with the authorization, support or acquiescence of, a State or a political organization, followed by a refusal to acknowledge that deprivation of freedom or to give information on the fate or whereabouts of those persons, with the intention of removing them from the protection of the law for a prolonged period of time.

Most of the lists of crimes against humanity conclude with the term *other inhumane acts*. Its scope is quite obviously vague, and for this reason some national attempts to introduce crimes against humanity have eliminated the reference. Even judges of international criminal tribunals have indicated their discomfort with applying criminal law whose meaning is not sufficiently certain. Reflecting these concerns, the Rome Statute declares that such "other inhumane acts" must not only be similar to those in the list of acts qualifying as crimes against humanity, but must also intentionally cause great suffering, or serious injury to body or to mental or physical health.

Finally, the crime against humanity of persecution comprises acts that are motivated by discrimination against an identifiable group. In the Nuremberg Charter, discrimination was limited to political, racial, or religious grounds, but more recent definitions, such as that of the Rome Statute, enlarge the concept to include nationality, ethnicity, culture, and gender as prohibited forms of discrimination. Moreover, they also extend the definition to "other grounds that are universally recognized as impermissible under international law," there-

by allowing for the further evolution of this concept. Perhaps sometime in the near future, it will be unquestioned that the crime against humanity of persecution may also be committed against the disabled, or against persons identified by their sexual orientation.

The case law of international criminal tribunals provides several examples of the crime against humanity of persecution: in general, destruction of property or means of subsistence, destruction and damage of religious or educational institutions, unlawful detention of civilians, harassment, humiliation and psychological abuse, violations of political, social, and economic rights violations. At the same time, these tribunals have rejected the argument that acts such as encouraging and promoting hatred on political grounds, or dismissing and removing members of a specific ethnic group from government, amount to persecution.

Statutory Limitations

Many legal systems provide that after a certain period of time has expired, offenses may no longer be prosecuted. This is known as statutory limitation or, sometimes, "prescription." It reflects a number of concerns, including the fact that with the passage of time prosecution becomes much more difficult because of the unavailability of witnesses and other evidence, as well as the interest of the state in prompt repression of crime, in order to deter the individual offender as well as others. Although these concerns may be relevant for many crimes, they are highly questionable in the context of the seriousness and horror of international crimes.

In the 1960s, when it appeared that some Nazi war criminals who had not yet been caught and prosecuted might escape justice, international law was extended to prohibit statutory limitations for crimes against humanity as well as war crimes. Countries whose laws contained statutory limitations were required to make amendments. Before an international criminal tribunal, no defendant can invoke the passage of time as a defense to a charge. This is stated explicitly in the Rome Statute of the ICC.

There are many examples of prosecutions of persons alleged to be responsible for crimes against humanity many decades after the acts transpired. In the late 1990s French courts convicted Maurice Papon for atrocities committed in occupied France during World War II. Papon was almost ninety years old at the time, but he was found guilty and sentenced to a term of imprisonment.

Prosecution of Crimes Against Humanity

The first prosecutions for crimes against humanity were held at the Nuremberg Tribunal. Most of the leading Nazi defendants were convicted of crimes against humanity, as well as other crimes punishable by the Tribunal. One of the defendants, Julius Streicher, was convicted only of crimes against humanity. He was executed for his role as propagandist in the Nazi persecution of Jews within Germany.

Crimes against humanity were also very much part of the prosecution at the other international tribunal, in Tokyo, and in a range of other postwar trials held by national military tribunals. After the late 1940s no international prosecutions for crimes against humanity occurred until the establishment of the ICTY and ICTR in 1993 and 1994, respectively.

Many national legal systems have introduced the concept of crimes against humanity into their own criminal legislation. Although neither required nor authorized by any international treaties, these jurisdictions have established that prosecution for crimes against humanity may be conducted even if the crime was committed outside the territory of the state and by a noncitizen. Although this principle of "universal jurisdiction" is increasingly recognized in national laws, it is in practice used rather rarely. Two such important trials were held in Israel: those of former Nazi mastermind Adolf Eichmann and John Demjanjuk, purported to have been a sadistic guard at the Treblinka death camp. In the late 1980s Canada prosecuted a Hungarian Nazi official, Imre Finta, for crimes against humanity committed forty-five years earlier. Of these three prosecutions, two led to acquittals. The difficulties in prosecuting crimes committed elsewhere, and usually many years earlier, pose great challenges to national justice systems and largely explain the reluctance to use the principle of universal jurisdiction on a large scale.

Distinguishing Genocide and Crimes Against Humanity

Two categories of international crime, genocide and crimes against humanity, both emerged in the 1940s as a response to the Nazi atrocities committed before and during World War II. Nervous about the implications that a broad concept of crimes against humanity might have for their own administrations, the great powers confined crimes against humanity to acts committed in the context of aggressive war. Unhappy with such a restriction, other states pushed for recognition of a cognate, genocide, which would require no such connection with armed conflict. As a result, for many decades, in their efforts to condemn and prosecute atrocities, international human rights lawyers attempted to rely on genocide rather than the considerably broader notion of crimes against humanity out of concerns that the acts were perpetrated in peacetime.

The nexus between crimes against humanity and aggressive war no longer exists. As a result, aside from some minor and insignificant technical distinctions, all acts of genocide are subsumed within the definition of crimes against humanity. Genocide can be usefully viewed as the most extreme form of crimes against humanity. The ad hoc tribunals for the former Yugoslavia and Rwanda have christened it "the crime of crimes." But if the distinction is no longer particularly consequential with respect to criminal prosecution, it remains important because there is no real equivalent to the Genocide Convention for crimes against humanity. The Genocide Convention imposes obligations on states to prevent the commission of genocide. It might be argued that this duty also exists with respect to crimes against humanity. However, the Convention, in addition, recognizes the jurisdiction of the International Court of Justice (ICJ) to adjudicate disputes between states with respect to their treaty obligations concerning genocide, and several such lawsuits have in fact been filed. No similar right to litigate crimes against humanity before the ICJ exists.

SEE ALSO Aggression; Genocide; International Court of Justice; International Criminal Tribunal for Rwanda; International Criminal Tribunal for the Former Yugoslavia; International Law; Khmer Rouge Prisons and Mass Graves; Massacres; Nuremberg Trials; Rape; Universal Jurisdiction; War Crimes

BIBLIOGRAPHY

Cherif Bassiouni, M. (1999). *Crimes Against Humanity*, 2nd edition. Dordrecht, Netherlands: Kluwer.

Clark, Roger S. (1990). "Crimes Against Humanity at Nuremberg." In *The Nuremberg Trial and International Law*, ed. G. Ginsburgs and V. N. Kudriavstsev. Dordrecht, Netherlands: Martinus Nijhoff.

Robinson, Darryl (1999). "Defining 'Crimes Against Humanity' at the Rome Conference." *American Journal of International Law* 93:43.

Schwelb, Egon (1946). "Crimes Against Humanity." *British Yearbook of International Law* 23:178.

William A. Schabas

Croatia, Independent State of

The Independent State of Croatia, generally known as the NDH (the acronym for its Croatian name, Nezavisna Drava Hrvatska), was created with the support of the Axis powers following Adolf Hitler's conquest of Yugoslavia in April 1941, and lasted until the defeat of Germany in May 1945. The NDH incorporated most of Croatia and Bosnia and Herzegovina. It called for the

Yugoslavia before the break-up. [MAP BY XNR PRODUCTIONS. THE GALE GROUP.]

extermination of Jews and Romani, and the elimination of Serbs through physical extermination (one-third), expulsion into Serbia (one-third), and forced conversion to Roman Catholicism (one-third). About 32,000 of 40,000 Jews living in the NDH, and almost all the Romani in the state, about 26,000, were killed. Figures on Serb victims are more controversial, as noted below, but the United States Holocaust Memorial Museum estimates that between 330,000 and 390,000 Serbs were killed by the Ustasha regime of the NDH.

Ethnic and Political Background

The peoples of the western Balkans (Bosnia and Herzegovina, Croatia, Montenegro, and Serbia) speak mutually understandable dialects although they have separate literatures and some differences in their vocabularies, and Serbs and Montenegrins traditionally have preferred to use Cyrillic script while the others employ Latin letters. These groups differ mainly by religion: Serbs and Montenegrins are Orthodox Christians, Croats are Roman Catholics, and Bosniacs are Muslims.

Until the end of World War I they were divided by political borders. Croatia belonged to the Austro-Hungarian Empire, while Bosnia had been part of the Ottoman Empire from the fifteenth century until 1878, when it came under Austro-Hungarian control. Serbia was also part of the Ottoman Empire before winning its independence in the middle of the nineteenth century. The assassination in Sarajevo that sparked World War I was carried out by a group that wanted to unify Bosnia with Serbia.

Following World War I Yugoslavia was created as a state for these South Slavic (*jugoslav*) peoples (along with Slovenians and Slavic Macedonians), in the belief that despite their differences in religion and history, they could form one nation on the grounds of their common language. However, by the end of the nineteenth century all the peoples involved had already developed their own separate national identities and separatist politics. Most Croats regarded inclusion in Yugoslavia, ruled by a Serbian king, as a denial of their own right to self-determination. From its founding in

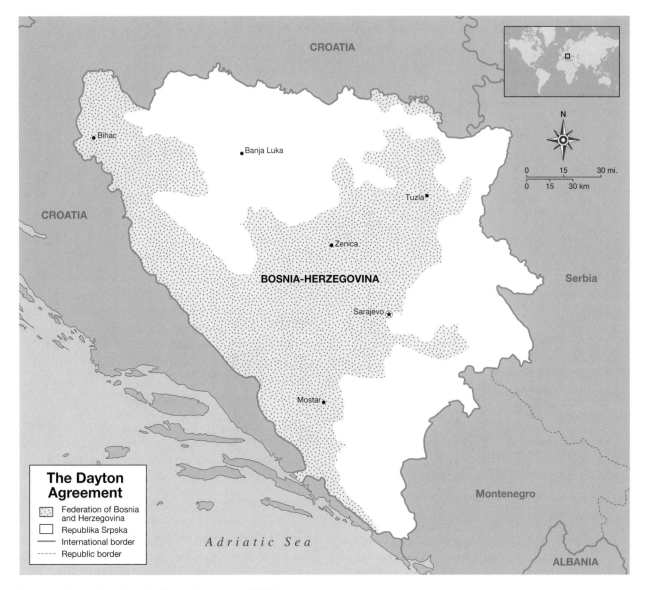

The map that resulted from the Dayton Agreement (1995). [MAP BY XNR PRODUCTIONS. THE GALE GROUP.]

1919 until the start of World War II, Yugoslavia was an unstable state, proclaimed a dictatorship in 1929 in large part to counter the demands of the leading Croatian political parties for independence.

Serbs, Croats, and Bosniaks lived intermingled in parts of Croatia and Bosnia and thus no clean separation was possible. On April 6, 1941, when the Axis powers invaded Yugoslavia and defeated the Yugoslav Army in less than a week, most Croats welcomed what they thought would be liberation from Serb dominance, and there was general support for the proclamation of the NDH on April 10, 1941. The leading Croatian politicians did not agree to form a puppet government dominated by Nazi Germany, so the Axis powers created a government run by the Ustasha, a fanatical group of Croatian nationalists who had been living in exile for more than a decade and who had previously been involved in terrorist actions against Yugoslavia. The Ustasha enjoyed little popular support within Croatia, but initially the local hierarchy of the Roman Catholic Church strongly supported them; they also faced little opposition when they assumed power.

Ustasha Ideology

Like the Nazis who put them in power, the Ustasha placed strong emphasis on the state as the tool that the nation must use to achieve its historical destiny, seeing the nation in racial terms and as engaged in a struggle for biological survival with other nations. Within the context of this ideology, members of minority groups were perceived as inherently threatening foreign bodies in the state. Within weeks of ascending to power, the Ustasha issued racial laws defining Aryan and non-Aryan and prohibiting marriages between Jews and Croats, and adopted the legal system of Nazi Germany. Jews were required to wear yellow stars and deprived of their rights of citizenship and their property. The Cyrillic script was banned. By August 1941 the Ustasha had established concentration camps for political prisoners and so-called racially undesirable peoples: Jews, Romani, and Serbs.

Ustasha ideology, however, seems to have been less consistently racist than that of the Nazis. Jews who supported the Ustasha could become "honorary Aryans." Although Serbs were considered non-Aryan, they were not slated for mass extermination. Serbs were to be eliminated by expulsion and conversion, and when necessary murder, because otherwise, their large numbers (1.9 million, about one-third of the entire population) would prevent the NDH from becoming an exclusively Croat state. The provision for conversion was not so much a racist principle, as a recognition that what distinguished Serbs from Croats was, primarily, religion. However, the Ustasha did not try to convert the Muslims of Bosnia, claiming that they were racially pure Croats whose ancestors had converted to Islam.

Genocide

What the Ustasha lacked in ideological consistency they made up in brutality. They created a number of concentration camps throughout Croatia and Bosnia, the largest of which was a series of five camps on the River Sava, collectively known as Jasenovac. The United States Holocaust Memorial Museum estimates that between 56,000 and 97,000 people were murdered in Jasenovac alone, including some 45,000 to 52,000 Serbs. Estimates of the Jews killed in Jasenovac run from 8,000 to 20,000. From 8,000 to 15,000 Romani were also killed there. In addition, the Ustasha deported another 7,000 Jews to Nazi concentration camps.

Most of the killing in the NDH, however, did not occur in camps, but rather in villages and without the use of sophisticated weapons or technology. Ustasha attacks on villages were not driven by military necessity, but propelled by the desire to drive Serbs out of Croatia by murder, rape, and terror, the same tactics that in Yugoslavia during the 1990s came to be known as "ethnic cleansing." An Ustasha attack would customarily involve the slaughter of anyone remaining in a village, including women, children, and the elderly. The purpose of such a campaign of terror was to convince other Serbs to leave, or convert to Catholicism. The extent of the violence is reflected in the high percentage of Serbs

killed in the NDH. Even using the lower estimate suggested by the United States Holocaust Memorial Museum, 330,000, about one-sixth of the Serb population residing in the NDH, were killed between 1941 and 1945, a percentage of deaths exceeded only by those of Jews and Romani during World War II in Europe.

End of the NDH

The brutality of the NDH and its failed policies produced increasing opposition among the Croats whom the state was meant to serve and covert opposition among many Roman Catholic leaders. By mid-1942 increasing numbers of Croats began to join Marshal Tito's partisans, the communist army that had as its goal the reconstitution of a Yugoslav state. With the defeat of the Third Reich, the NDH also collapsed, and Croatia became a republic in the new Yugoslavia. Most of the leaders of the NDH escaped and went into exile in Argentina, Spain, the United States, and Canada. However, the partisans did massacre somewhere between 45,000 to 55,000 NDH soldiers in May 1945.

Politics and the NDH Genocide

As communism weakened in the late 1980s, politicians in Yugoslavia found that the separate (and separatist) nationalism of each major group was an effective message for garnering the votes of members of that group. In Croatia, Franjo Tudjman led a new nationalist movement; he was a former army general who had faced political disgrace in 1971 for claiming that only sixty thousand people had been killed in NDH concentration camps. Tudjman, in fact, published a book in 1990 that referred to the "myth of Jasenovac" and attempted to minimize the genocide perpetrated by the NDH. Yet Tudjman had some legitimate points, being that there was a tendency among Serbs to inflate the numbers of those killed in the NDH, just as there had been a tendency among Croat authors to minimize them. The issue was especially divisive because Tudjman sought and received funding from Croatian émigrés (including many who viewed the NDH as having been a legitimate manifestation of the Croat nation's desire for self-determination) for his movement to gain Croatian independence from Yugoslavia, and he was elected president of Croatia in 1990. Most Serbs in Croatia felt threatened by Tudjman's nationalist project, a feeling that was shared by Serb politicians who themselves stressed the appeals that Tudjman made to supporters of the NDH. Serb resistance to Tudjman's nationalist movement led them to revolt against Croatian independence, a resistance ended militarily by the Croatian army and the North Atlantic Treaty Organization (NATO) intervention in 1995, and through the expulsion of most Serbs from Croatia.

The politicization of the NDH has seen many Serbs exaggerate the crimes of the Ustasha while many Croats have sought to minimize them. In both cases this politicization has been intentionally used to provoke great hostility on either side. Thus, many in the former Yugoslavia have remembered the history of the NDH not in order to avoid tragedy, but rather to provoke it anew.

SEE ALSO Bosnia and Herzegovina; Tudjman, Franjo; Yugoslavia

BIBLIOGRAPHY

Bogosavljevic, Srdjan (2000). "The Unresolved Genocide." In *The Road to War in Serbia*, ed. N. Popov. New York: Central European University Press.

Djilas, Aleksa (1991). *The Contested Country: Yugoslav Unity and Communist Revolution, 1919–1953*. Cambridge, Mass.: Harvard University Press.

Goldstein, Ivo (1999). *Croatia: A History*. London: C. Hurst.

Tanner, Marcus (1997). *Croatia: A Nation Forged in War*. New Haven, Conn.: Yale University Press.

Tomasevich, Jozo (2001). *War and Revolution in Yugoslavia, 1941–1945: Occupation and Collaboration*. Stanford, Calif.: Stanford University Press.

United States Holocaust Memorial Museum. "Holocaust Era in Croatia 1941–1945: Jasenovac." Available from http://www.ushmm.org/museum/exhibit/online/jasenovac/index.html.

Robert M. Hayden

Crusades

Among the best-known events of the Middle Ages, the Crusades were a series of armed expeditions by European Christians to conquer Muslim-controlled territory in the Holy Land. Historians have traditionally bracketed these campaigns between the years 1095, when Pope Urban II preached the First Crusade, and 1291, when the Mamelukes, a caste of Muslim slave soldiers, conquered the city of Acre (Israel), bringing to an end any significant European Christian presence in the Holy Land. Historians disagree over the exact number of crusades, though most agree that there were either seven or eight in total.

Like many historical events, the Crusades are difficult to define. The crusading spirit experienced in Europe also was expressed against Muslims in Spain, pagans in northern Europe, heretics in southern France, and even orthodox Christians in the Byzantine Empire. In addition, just as the geographic boundaries of the Crusades are unstable, so too are their chronological parameters. Although Western European Christians lost for good their last significant base in the Middle East in the late thirteenth century, they continued to make minor attempts to recover territory for centuries.

Background

The Crusades were military campaigns waged between two very different cultures that had developed separately but along paths that eventually brought them into violent contact. The Muslims of the Middle East were believers in an energetic religion of conquest and considered themselves the successors to the covenants God had established first with Jews and, later, with Christians. In the twenty-first century, Muslim-Christian relations in the Middle Ages were complicated. At times, believers in the two faiths lived comfortably side by side; at others, relations between them were difficult at best.

Messages in the *Qur'an*, the sacred book of Islam, about Christians are mixed. While there is hostility toward Christians on account of some of their beliefs, there is also a sense that Jesus's followers are to be respected because they, like Jews, are "people of the Book." Most European Christians, however, failed to realize that Muslims considered themselves successors to a covenant that they (Christians) had once enjoyed. Instead, most Christians considered Muslims to be pagans, and were unaware of Islam's monotheism and its perceived connection between Islam, Judaism, and Christianity.

It is difficult to determine what role these beliefs played in Muslim-Christian relations during the Crusades. It seems likely, though, that the catalyst that channeled European energy into armed pilgrimages to the Holy Land is to be found in developments occurring simultaneously in the Muslim world. The most significant of these was the advent of the Seljuk Turks. Since 1066 the Seljuks had been attacking the Byzantine Empire, a Christian state, and in 1071, under the command of Sultan Alp Arslan, they defeated the armies of Byzantine emperor Romanus IV at the Battle of Manzikert (in present-day Turkey). The victory was significant, a major defeat that wrested Asia Minor (Turkey) from Byzantine control and placed it under Turkish rule. Soon after, Arslan captured Jerusalem from the Fatimids, an Islamic dynasty whose power base was located in Egypt. Under Seljuk rule, Jerusalem became less accessible to Christian pilgrims, who at times were barred from holy sites, attacked, and even murdered.

For the next two decades, the Byzantine Empire continued to lose territory to the Turks. By 1095 the situation was grave and the Seljuks were poised to strike the Byzantine capital city, Constantinople. Seriously threatened, Emperor Alexius I Comnenus turned to the western Church for help. It was a timely appeal. On the eve of the Crusades, Western Europe was entering a period of cultural creativity, economic revival, political stability, and increased religious devotion. It was a time of energy and confidence, during which many men were willing to take up the cross and travel long distances in search of opportunity and adventure. Pope Urban II, and the nobility of France were willing to indulge this request, believing that it was their duty to help their fellow Christians in the East.

Many also saw the vast potential in such a campaign. Pope Urban called the First Crusade at the Council of Clermont in 1095. His speech played on the pride of the Franks, noted the opportunities available to those who participated, drew attention to the plight of Christian pilgrims to the Holy Land, emphasized the conquests of the Muslim Turks, cast Muslims as the enemies of Christ, and offered those who joined the protection of property as well as indulgences. The speech met with great success, including cries of "Deus vult!" ("God wills it!"), and by the following year the First Crusade was mobilized. In 1099, after a bitter siege followed by a bloody massacre that cost the lives of many women and children as well as combatants, the city of Jerusalem fell to the crusaders. As one Christian writer put it "the slaughter was so great that our men waded in blood up to their ankles."

History

The success of the First Crusade astonished many, including the crusaders themselves. Indeed, it is easily arguable that, from a Western European perspective, the first was the most successful of all the Crusades. The successive campaigns, by and large, were called to help Christians who were already in the Holy Land. For example, when the city of Edessa (Turkey), reverted to Muslim control in 1144, Pope Eugenius III called the Second Crusade, which was preached by no less a person than Bernard of Clairvaux, one of the most influential personalities of the twelfth century. Although backed by the churchman's clout and by the participation of King Louis VII of France and Emperor Conrad III of Germany, the crusade was a miserable failure for Western Europeans. In 1147, the same year the crusade began, Conrad's army was defeated by the Turks at Dorylaeum (Turkey). The remaining soldiers joined with the army of Louis VII, which had left for the field of battle later than the German forces. Both contingents traveled through the Balkans to reach their destination and, while doing so, had pillaged territories of the Byzantine Empire. Like the Byzantine emperor Alexius, who greeted the armies of the First Crusade, Emperor Manuel I was nervous about having an unruly army in his kingdom. He, again like Alexius, provided transportation for the crusaders to Asia Minor as soon as he could. The crusaders never did recapture Edessa; instead they targeted the city of Damascus (Syria), the unsuccessful siege of which signaled the end of the campaign in 1148.

The Third Crusade was also called as a defensive response, this time in reaction to the military conquests of the Muslim warrior Saladin, who in 1187 recaptured Jerusalem. Although Pope Gregory VII's appeal motivated numerous European leaders, including Kings Richard I and Henry II of England (who died before the crusade left), Philip II of France and Emperor Frederick Barbarossa (who drowned en route in June 1190), the crusade achieved little for those who participated. It came to an end when King Richard signed the Treaty of Jaffa with Saladin in 1192.

The infamous Fourth Crusade followed ten years later, when Pope Innocent III called for a crusade to Egypt. The crusaders arrived in Venice with insufficient money for their passage. In lieu of payment, the Venetians redirected the crusade to the city of Zara, which they wanted recaptured from the Hungarians. The city fell in 1202, and no sooner did it succumb than the army was again redirected—this time by Alexius IV, son of the recently blinded and deposed Emperor Isaac II. Alexius offered the crusaders 200,000 marks, reunification of the Orthodox and Roman churches, and a large army for a crusade if the crusaders would help restore his father to the throne.

The majority of the crusaders agreed to the proposition and in 1203 headed toward Constantinople. They attacked the city in July, and their successful campaign resulted in the co-coronation of Isaac and his son. Within months, however, the clergy and the people of the city, led by the future Alexius V, rioted against the monarchs. Isaac and his son were murdered in January 1204. In response, the crusaders took Constantinople by force. In May, Count Baldwin of Flanders was crowned the first Latin Emperor of Constantinople, an empire that would last until Emperor Michael VIII reclaimed the throne in 1261.

After the Fourth Crusade's failure to reach Egypt, Pope Innocent called another in 1213. The Fifth Crusade left Europe under the direction of Duke Leopold of Austria in 1217, and within two years the crusaders had captured the city of Damietta. However, the crusaders soon became bogged down by internal conflicts, and the Egyptians took advantage of the delay to fortify their positions. With their supply lines cut and facing considerable flooding due to deliberately broken dykes, this first wave of crusaders retreated from Egypt in 1221. There was a hiatus in the crusade until 1228, when Holy Roman Emperor Frederick II took up the cross. The emperor spent the next year peacefully negotiating a treaty that restored a section of Palestine (which included Jerusalem) to Christian control.

The two final crusades, the Six and Seventh, were led by King Louis IX of France. The army departed in August 1248, and by the following June the crusaders retook the city of Damietta and within a few months began marching toward Cairo. In 1250, Louis's army suffered a disastrous defeat at Mansurah (Egypt), which ultimately forced the crusaders to retreat. By April 6, Louis's forces were surrounded and the king was captured; he was ransomed one month later. Louis remained in the Holy Land until 1254 to negotiate various truces and fortify the cities of Acre, Jaffa, Caesarea, and Sidon. He returned to France in April, where he remained until 1270 when, energized by a report that Emir Muhammad I wanted to convert to Christianity, he departed for Tunis. However, immediately upon arrival in Tunis, Louis became gravely ill and died on August 25. Although the leadership of the crusade passed to the king's brother, Charles of Anjou, Louis's death brought an effective end to the crusade. In some ways the end of this crusade sounded the death knell of the movement. Within twenty years there would no longer be any significant Western European presence in the Holy Land.

Consequences for Muslims, Jews, and Orthodox Christians

From the Muslim perspective, the lasting effects of the Crusades on the Islamic Middle East were fairly negligible. To many Muslims, they were just episodes in a long running clash with Christians. In fact, as Carole Hillenbrand notes, it is only in the recent past that Muslims have taken an interest in the Crusades as a discreet set of historical events: modern Arabic terms for "the Cross wars" (*al-salibiyya*) or "the war of the Cross" (*harb al-salib*) were not introduced into the language until the nineteenth century. However, as Thomas Madden points out, the crusading movement did have some negative effects on the Muslim world, including slowing the conquest of Islam. The mere presence of European Christians in the region distracted Muslims and prevented the local populations from forming into a unified Islamic state. It is possible that by diverting Muslim energy and material resources, the Crusades may have bought Europe time to prepare itself for the threats that the Turks would pose to the continent in the fifteenth, sixteenth, and seventeenth centuries.

The consequences of the early crusades for the Jews of Western Europe were dramatic. As Robert Chazan notes, a great paradox of the Crusades is that, although numerous high churchmen condemned violence against Jews, they also initiated undertakings that led to the persecutions that some later tried to suppress. Long embedded in the European psyche was the notion of Jews as the enemies of Christ. The year 1096

was a notably devastating one for German Jews. Whereas John, bishop of the German city of Speyer, was willing and able to protect the Jews of his diocese, the Jews of Worms were not as lucky. Turned on by their neighbors and unable to be protected effectively by the town's bishop, many in this city were massacred or forced to convert. The Jews of Mainz also fell prey to violence, and many chose to die by their own hands rather than succumb to the crusaders. Suddenly and tragically, the once renowned Jewish community of Mainz was decimated.

The Second Crusade brought more attacks upon the Jews of Europe, although none were as severe as those of 1096. The Jews, the Church, and secular governments took precautions as the crusade was called. Indeed, one of the most vocal protectors of the Jews was the preacher of the crusade, Bernard of Clairvaux. The Third Crusade, which came on the heels of the coronation of King Richard I of England, inflamed anti-Jewish passions once again. Riots broke out in London in 1189, followed by others in the kingdom which destroyed a number of Jewish communities. Clearly, then, the Crusades had disastrous social and cultural consequences for Europe's Jews. They had highly negative economic consequences as well, because anti-Jewish violence was not only a religious instrument, it was also a financial one that could be used to force Jews to forgive the debts of the Christian populace.

The consequences of the Crusades for the orthodox Christians of the Byzantine Empire were also devastating. As George Dennis states in *The Crusades from the Perspective of Byzantium and the Muslim World*:

> Muslims believed force might be used to bring all people under the sway of Islam; Western knights believed that they were called not only to defend but "exalt" Christianity and that attacks on its enemies could be holy and meritorious. The Byzantines believed that war was neither good nor holy, but was evil and could be justified only in certain conditions that centered on the defense of the empire and its faith. They were convinced that they were defending Christianity itself and the Christian people, as indeed they were (Laiou and Mottahedeh, 2001, p. 39).

The defense came at a great cost. The pillage and desecration of the holy city of Constantinople in 1204 by their fellow Christians ripped wounds into the communal Orthodox memory that have yet to be healed. The empire lost many of its cultural and sacred treasures, which were carried off to western Europe in general and to Venice in particular. In addition, as the Latin Empire of Constantinople reigned, the outlying territories broke apart into separate independent states, striking a great and lasting blow to the unity of the empire. After the reassertion of Greek political authority in 1261, the politically fragmented state was unable to withstand the military blows it continued to sustain. Its strength would continue to be weakened for the next two hundred and fifty years by attacks from Charles of Anjou, the Venetians, the kingdoms of Serbia and Bulgaria and, most notably, the Ottoman Turks. The Turks would ultimately bring the once great empire to an inglorious end during a siege led by the founder of the Ottoman Empire, Sultan Mehmet II, on May 29, 1453.

SEE ALSO Catholic Church; Religion; Religious Groups

BIBLIOGRAPHY

Chazan, Robert (1980). *Church, State and Jew in the Middle Ages.* New York: Behrman House.

Chomates, Niketas (1984). *O City of Byzantium: Annals of Niketas Choniates,* trans. Harry J. Magoulias. Detroit, Mich.: Wayne State University Press.

Commena, Anna (1969). *The Alexiad of Anna Comnena,* tran. E. R. A. Sewter. Baltimore, Md.: Penguin Books.

The Crusades. (2003). Available from Internet Medieval Sourcebook at http://www.fordham.edu/halsall/sbook1k.html#The%20First%20Crusade.

Gabrielli, Francisco, ed. (1969). *Arab Historians of the Crusades,* tran. E. J. Costello. London: Routledge and Kegan Paul.

Hallam, Elizabeth, ed. (1989). *Chronicles of the Crusades: Nine Crusades and Two Hundred Years of Bitter Conflict Brought to Life through the Words of Those Who Were Actually There.* New York: Weidenfeld and Nicolson.

Joinville and Villehardouin (1963). *Chronicles of the Crusades,* tran. M. R. B. Shaw. Harmondsworth, U.K.: Penguin Books.

Odo of Deuil (1948). *De profectione Ludovici VII in orientem* (The Journey of Louis VII to the East), ed. and tran. Virginia Gingerick Berry. New York: Norton.

Dawn Marie Hayes

Cultural Genocide see Ethnocide.

Dance

Dance, in its vernacular, theatrical, and sacred forms, has been used by societies throughout history to incite violence and celebrate victory, as well as express resistance to repressive regimes and heal victims of injustice. Traditional war dances and victory dances may be found in many African cultures and among aboriginal peoples; as such, descriptions of dancing appear in human rights reports of the genocide in Rwanda and human rights abuses in Angola. Forms of folk dance are often promoted by states as a means of propaganda to further the cause of ruling powers. Examples include the widespread popularizing of Bavarian and Austrian folk dancing by the Nazis, and the promotion of Serbian folk dancing and *turbo folk* during Slobodan Milosevic's regime. Forcing people to dance and sing political slogans is not uncommon in such contexts, as is using dance as a means of humiliating those from opposing groups—for example, when men, and especially women, are forced to dance (and possibly strip naked) in front of their captors, as reported in Sierra Leone and Chechnya. The trafficking of women and children also may involve dancing as a means of humiliation, with victims forced to perform as nightclub dancers in addition to working as sex slaves.

As a creative, expressive, communal activity, however, dance is also a central means of resisting crimes against humanity. Historically, slaves from Africa employed dancing as a means of communication when they were denied other basic rights. During the Holocaust groups of German youth danced swing and listened to jazz as a form of resistance to Hitler's regime.

The individuality and syncopation characteristic of swing embodied their refusal to follow the lock-step mass psychology of the Nazis. More recent examples reveal the important role of dance in preserving the memory of genocide. Youth from the Northern Marianas Islands still perform a jig as a reminder of a massacre that occurred in the 1860s and as a symbol that their race will never be exterminated. In Chile women who are members of the *Asociación de Familiares de los Detenidos y Desaparecidos* (Association of the Relatives of the Detained and Disappeared) have chosen to perform a traditional couples dance as a solo, the *Cueca Solo,* as a living reminder of their missing partners.

In theatrical venues choreographers have long created works that represent and recreate a sense of the horror, suffering, and courage of the victims of genocide, as well as the brutality of the victimizers. They achieve this by using a variety of techniques, including parody and satire, metaphor and allegory, and perhaps most important, the somatic experience of trauma, from uncontrollable shaking to severe immobility, that can be recreated on stage to powerful effect. Of these pieces, the most celebrated include *The Green Table* by Kurt Jooss (1932) about the horrors of war; *Dreams* (1961) by Anna Sokolow about the Nazi concentration camps; *Soweto* (1977) by Mats Ek about apartheid in South Africa; and *Ghost Dances* (1983) by Christopher Bruce about the Chilean military coup. Some dance companies, such as Barro Rojo Arte Escénico (BRAE) in Mexico, have made it their mission to concentrate on human rights issues. This company's specific focus has been the horrors perpetuated in Latin America, with pieces like Arturo Garrido's *El Camino* (The path,

1982), which addressed the people of El Salvador's fight for liberty, and Laura Rocha's *Crujía H* (Ward H, 1987), which explores the theme of political prisoners.

Of special note are the many stage pieces and dances created for film and video that focus on the Holocaust. Examining these works sheds light on the more literal to abstract ways that the subject of genocide may be approached through the medium of dance. Tamar Rogoff's *Ivye Project* (1994), for instance, is set in the woods of Belarus at the actual site where 2,500 Jews were massacred in 1942. In this piece the audience is transported back through time to watch various life events, such as the dance of an elderly couple, a father and daughter preparing for bedtime, and an intensely moving scene at a cemetery where the performers appear and disappear behind the gravestones. However, in Danial Shapiro's *What Dark/Falling Into Light* (1996), emphasis is placed more on universal symbolism: A dancer sits and shakes, a young woman repeatedly hurls herself through the air toward her lover, and a man is supported by a group of prone dancers, as if being comforted by his dead ancestors. Allen Kaeja's trilogy of dance films, *Witnessed* (1997), *Sarah* (1999), and *Zummel* (1999), codirected with Mark Adam, combines these approaches by drawing on familiar Holocaust imagery such as train stations and people running through a forest, as well as metaphorical imagery that is more unique and general in its associations, as when a group of alternately desperate and hopeful dancers performs on a deserted raft in the middle of the ocean.

Finally, dance plays a major therapeutic role in recovery programs for the victims of genocide and crimes against humanity. Seen as a central means of bridging the mind/body gap and linking explicit and implicit memories through nonverbal expression, dance/movement therapy (d/mt) is common in trauma centers for refugees and torture survivors in Germany (Düsseldorf, Cologne, and Munich) and the United States (Boulder, Colorado), a community center in Tuzla, Bosnia, and the Trauma Clinic at the Centre for the Study of Violence and Reconciliation (CSVR) in Johannesburg, South Africa. In these settings dance is regarded as a treatment modality especially beneficial to victims of torture because it restores patients' sense of safety in their own bodies and rebuilds their capacity to experience joy and well-being. Related dance groups especially designed for children, include the "War Child's Ethiopian Dance Project," "Alive Kids" located in South Africa, and "Children of Uganda."

SEE ALSO Music, Holocaust Hidden and Protest; Music and Musicians Persecuted during the Holocaust; Music at Theresienstadt; Music Based on the Armenian Genocide; Music of Reconciliation; Music of the Holocaust

BIBLIOGRAPHY

DeFrantz, Thomas F., ed. (2002). *Dancing Many Drums: Excavations in African American Dance.* Madison: University of Wisconsin Press.

Gray, Amber (2001). "The Body Remembers: Dance/Movement Therapy with an Adult Survivor of Torture." *American Journal of Dance Therapy* 23(1):29–43.

Karina, Lillian, and Marion Kant (2002). *Hitler's Dancers: German Modern Dance and the Third Reich,* tran. Jonathan Steinberg. New York: Berghahn Books.

Shay, Anthony (2002). *Choreographic Politics: State Folk Dance Companies, Representation and Power.* Middletown, Conn.: Wesleyan University Press.

Naomi Jackson

Death Camps *see* Extermination Centers; Holocaust.

Death March

Death march is another of the horrific terms that have sprung up in the context of genocide. It signifies the process by which a regime, usually a government or an occupying power, begins to summon members of a particular nation, group, or subgroup—on the basis of their ethnicity, religion, language, or culture—with a view to their elimination. The term death march signifies the physical action by which the gathered persons are then lined up and marched to certain mass death.

Perhaps the most "classical" example of the death march was the one that occurred as part of the Armenian genocide in Ottoman Turkey (part of the fading Ottoman Empire) in 1915. The events leading up to that death march were paradigmatic of the experience of genocide victims in other places.

The death march of the Armenian population of the Ottoman Empire took place against the backdrop of the hostilities of World War I. In the spring of 1915 Ottoman rulers ordered that all Armenians be expelled from their homes in areas outside of war zones. The Armenians—men, women, and children—were then lined up and made to walk in convoys of tens of thousands toward the Syrian desert. Although the expulsions resembled deportations, the treatment of the people making the march by Turkish "guards" made it clear that a more sinister agenda was driving the march: a planned elimination of the Armenian population through a process of starvation and exhaustion. The death march was a culmination of decades of Turkish discrimination against Armenians, which had long con-

The Japanese force-marched 70,000 American and Filipino prisoners of war from the Bataan peninsula to transport trains fifty-five miles inland. The prisoners were often bound, beaten, or killed by their captors; some were bayoneted when they fell from exhaustion. Only 56,000 prisoners reached the internment camps alive. [CORBIS]

sisted of the barring of Armenians from serving in the Turkish army, executions of small groups of Armenians, and mass killings by special forces known as *Teshkilâti Mahsusa*—gangs of violent ex-convicts ordered by the Ottoman/Turkish government to commit murders of Armenians.

During the march many Armenians were killed indiscriminately by Ottoman forces, which left a trail of corpses along the route of the march. To break the will of the marchers, the killings were performed with swords, resulting in great bloodshed. Marchers who survived these attacks faced starvation, as no provisions for food were made; many elderly and infirm marchers died in this way during the march. The significantly reduced numbers of marchers who finally made it to the Syrian desert were put into concentration camps located between the towns of Jerablus and Deir ez-Zor, and then released into the scorching desert (with no food or water) to certain death.

The historical record suggests that the death march was methodically orchestrated, carried out in a system-

atized manner, clearly intended as genocide, and calculated to achieve this through a host of measures, including outright brutal killings, slow starvation and dehydration, death through trauma and exhaustion. It is estimated that this genocide was responsible for the deaths of up to half a million Armenians. While it is hard to estimate the exact number of those who perished in the march, the ways in which the expelled Armenians met their deaths make this episode of human history stand out, even among other death marches, as singularly brutal and horrifying.

The death march was one means used by the Ottoman government to wage an unofficial war against the Armenians, with the prime goals of eradicating them and furthering the creation of a pan-Turkish empire.

In many respects, the death march can be compared to the *death row phenomenon*. In both cases, the victims await elimination through a process dictated by the government in power. Both involve the slow march of time toward certain death. However, the death row

These American prisoners of war surrendered to the Japanese Imperial Army and were forced to march for six days without food or water in what is known as the Bataan Death March.

phenomenon applies to individuals and usually occurs within the context of due legal process, whereas death marches consist of an entire mass of people marched between fully armed soldiers to the place of their final execution. The length of such death marches varies tremendously, but they are characterized by starvation, exhaustion, and brutality.

The Armenian genocide is not the only death march whose details are part of the historical record. The phenomenon was also repeated in World War II by the Nazi regime and Japan. In Germany Nazi forces, under siege from the advancing Allies in the winter of 1944 and 1945, began to frantically move Jewish populations that they had imprisoned in concentration camps outside the camps. Although many of the inmates were marched to nearby labor camps, others were made to walk long distances, to labor camps much further away, in bitter cold, with little or no food, water, or rest. Those who fell behind the main column

were summarily shot by Nazi soldiers, while numerous others died of exhaustion, starvation, or exposure to the elements.

The largest death marches in World War II are recorded as having occurred that same final winter of the war, when the Red Army (armed forces of the Soviet Union) had begun its liberation of Poland. Sensing defeat, Nazi forces marched 60,000 prisoners out of the concentration camp at Auschwitz (a small town in Poland) toward another small town 35 miles away, where they were put on trains bound for other camps. As much as 25 percent of that group is calculated to have died en route. Many were killed during the march or immediately prior to the end of the march.

In another episode, in January 1945, SS officers ordered the further evacuation of prisoners from camps inside Germany in the face of the advancing Red Army. These marches were a continuation of the genocidal policies of the Nazi regime, but were also designed to keep the prisoners out of Allied hands, in fear of the evidence of Nazi atrocities that they would unquestionably find.

According to the United States Holocaust Memorial Museum, "[T]he term *death march* was probably coined by concentration camp prisoners. It referred to forced marches of prisoners over long distances under heavy guard in extremely harsh winter conditions. . . . Thousands . . . died of exposure, starvation and exhaustion." It is clear, in the context of the death marches perpetrated by the Nazi regime, that they were intended to accomplish the destruction of a particular group; at the same time, the Nazis sought to disguise their agenda of destruction and to make it look as though the mass killings were fallout of the attacks on Germany by the Allied forces.

Another World War II death march, occurring in the Pacific Theater, was that perpetrated by Japanese forces against U.S. and Filipino servicemen captured during the course of battles in the Philippine Islands, at Bataan and Corregidor. Stripped of their possessions, the prisoners who surrendered to the Japanese Imperial Army were made to march for six days along the road from Bataan to San Fernando in Pampanga province with no food and water—and to certain death. This particular death march can be differentiated from the marches perpetrated against the Armenians and European Jews in that it targeted military prisoners rather than civilians, but the results were similar.

Although the Armenian genocide is often described as the first death march, the term has been used to refer to events that took place prior to 1915. In 1830 the U.S. Congress passed the Indian Removal Act, despite the objection of Senator Davy Crockett of Tennessee and attempts to challenge it through the courts. The U.S. government wanted to remove the Cherokee from the state of Georgia, in part because of the demand for land coming from the non-Native population of Georgia. U.S. government policy led to the *Nunna dual Tsuny*, or Trail of Tears, in which, in 1838, several thousand Cherokee were forced off their lands and marched into the wilderness. Although the net effect of this action was the deaths of significant numbers of Cherokee, it should be distinguished from the Armenian and European concentration camp prisoner death marches, which had clear intents of the elimination of races. In the case of the Cherokee nation, the action of the U.S. Congress was aimed more at securing the lands on which Cherokee lived. Of course, for the victims of this death march and surviving family members, such a technical difference provides little succor.

SEE ALSO Armenians in Ottoman Turkey and the Armenian Genocide; Auschwitz; Famine; Japan; Trail of Tears

BIBLIOGRAPHY

About North Georgia. "Trail of Tears." Available from http://ngeorgia.com/history/nghisttt.html.

Battling Bastards of Bataan. "Bataan, Corregidor, and the Death March: In Retrospect." Available from http://home.pacbell.net/fbaldie/In_Retrospect.html.

Hovannisian, R. G. (1992). *The Armenian Genocide: History, Politics, Ethics.* New York: St. Martin's Press.

Knox, D. (1981). *Death March: The Survivors of Bataan.* New York: Harcourt Brace Jovanovich.

Oganesian, N. O. (2002). *The Armenian Genocide: Armenocide.* Yerevan, Armenia: Institute of Oriental Studies.

Slater, J. (1966). *Death March.* London: Horowitz Publishers.

United States Holocaust Memorial Museum. "Death Marches." Available from http://www.ushmm.org.

Joshua Castellino

Death Squads

In many civil and regional conflicts in the world since the 1950s, states, state agencies (most often the military or police), or semiprivate groups have formed special death squads in an effort to eliminate unwanted ideological, ethnic, or religious opponents. Death squads have been responsible for tens of thousands of deaths, and perhaps more, during this time. The phenomenon has been most commonly associated in the public mind with Latin American countries such as Argentina, Brazil, Colombia, Chile, El Salvador, Guatemala, and Honduras, but in fact, death squads have surfaced in many other countries and most parts of the world, including Indonesia, the Philippines, India, Turkey, Algeria, Uganda, apartheid South Africa, and Northern Ireland.

Death squads are clandestine and usually irregular organizations, often paramilitary in nature, that carry out extrajudicial executions and other violent acts (i.e., torture, rape, arson, bombing) against clearly defined individuals or groups of people. Murder is their primary or even sole activity. Except in the rare case where an insurgent group forms them, death squads operate with the support, complicity, or acquiescence of a government, or at least some parts of it. In many cases government security forces have participated directly. However, at the same time death squads may be privately constituted, almost always involve the support and participation of elements outside of government, and develop considerable independence from their backers. Except in unusual circumstances, organizations or units involved in the killing of combatants in the context of war between sovereign states, even when irregular forces of resistance are involved, do not fall under this definition, although the killing of noncombatants may indeed be so described.

A key element of the definition—that death squads are clandestine—helps explain why government agencies and sometimes private entities resort to their formation and use. Death squads give no visible indication that they exercise the legitimate use of force and they make no public acknowledgment of whose orders they follow. This makes it possible for the state and other backers of death squads to claim no knowledge of or influence over them, and therefore to deny any responsibility for their actions. This "plausible deniability" is vital to many states that want to appear to be upholding international norms of justice and human rights so they can qualify for foreign aid and be accepted as legitimate partners for foreign trade, or, conversely, so that they do not attain the pariah status that openly oppressive states acquire. For example, in the Bosnian war of the early to mid-1990s the government of Slobodan Milosevic materially supported ethnic cleansing by Serbian paramilitaries, but denied that it exercised any control over them. Later, while on trial at the International Criminal Tribunal for the Former Yugoslavia in the Hague in 2002 and 2003, Milosevic cited this alleged lack of control over the paramilitaries in his defense against charges of crimes against humanity.

The work of death squads is usually intended to spread terror, which can multiply their repressive effect, so their acts are not kept completely secret. For this reason most (but not all) death squads make sure that their actions are very public: They discard their victims in public places; they torture and mutilate them in horrific ways that will long be remembered; and they sometimes leave notes or visible signs that the tortured or killed were victims of a particular unit. In some cases lists of intended victims are even published in advance in the public media.

The irregular, informal organization of death squads and the demands of covert action make the exercise of control over them very difficult. They exist outside the law, which practically requires that their members be granted the widest possible exemption from prosecution and interference. The independence of death squads may also mean that they develop their own political agendas, while as appendages of a bureaucratic system (no matter how informal their organization), they often act according to organizational imperatives stemming from competition with other agencies.

The involvement of private or nonstate actors in death squads usually arises from a confluence of interests between private groups and governments: The government's need for deniability may induce it to have extrajudicial killing funded, organized, and committed by people who are not formally or officially associated with the state and who in some way share the government's ideological, economic, political, or religious ambitions. In El Salvador in the 1970s and 1980s, for example, death squads benefited from the considerable support and influence of large landowners and were often directed by a political movement (the Nationalist Republican Alliance), even though some arose organizationally within state agencies, such as the national guard, and all worked in some form of cooperation with state forces to stamp out an internal insurgency.

SEE ALSO Argentina; Chile; Einsatzgruppen; El Salvador; Guatemala

BIBLIOGRAPHY

Campbell, Bruce B., and Arthur D. Brenner, eds. (2000). *Death Squads in Global Perspective: Murder with Deniability*. New York: St. Martin's Press.

Mason, T. David, and Dale A. Krane (1989). "The Political Economy of Death Squads: Toward a Theory of the Impact of State-Sanctioned Terror." *International Studies Quarterly* 33:175–198.

Sluka, Jeffrey A., ed. (2000). *Death Squad: The Anthropology of State Terror*. Philadelphia: University of Pennsylvania Press.

Arthur D. Brenner

Deception, Perpetrators

The Nazi Holocaust, the extermination of Armenians in Turkey between 1915 and 1917, and the killings in Rwanda in 1994 are prime examples of genocide during the twentieth century. In each case, the initial victim group lived within the political boundaries of the countries that carried out the genocide, thus necessitating the establishment of an extermination system that maximized willful participation from the executioners, minimized resistance from the victims, and encouraged passive complicity from external and internal bystanders.

Perhaps the greatest obstacles that instigators of genocide face are inhibitions against killing on the part of those whose participation and complicity are required. The Nazi Holocaust is perhaps unsurpassed in terms of the sheer number of killings. Yet the monstrous efficiency with which they were carried out over a long period of time cannot be explained easily by references to bloodlust on the part of the executioners or coercion from leaders. Rather, participation and complicity were at least partly enabled through the widespread use of deception that began early on with propaganda. In the three genocides of the twentieth century, Armenians were marked as enemies of the Turkish Republic, the Jews as enemies of the German people, and the Tutsi as enemies of the Hutu. During the Holocaust the Nazi bureaucracy created very stringent rules on the use of language that specifically discouraged the use of terms such as *killing, liquidation,* and *extermination,* at least in official documents and written orders. In the Rwandan genocide euphemisms were employed—weapons were called tools, Tutsi were referred to as "infiltrators" and *inyenzi* (cockroaches), organizing for murder was described as *umuganda* (communal work). The Turks' forced deportations and marches of the Armenians (called "resettlements") through rural regions and rugged mountains allowed an area emptied of Armenians to become a wasteland of skeletons. In Nazi Germany most death camps were built in the occupied countries to the east of Germany, particularly in Poland. In Rwanda the Tutsi population was driven toward schools and churches where they sought sanctuary, but which turned out to be places to concentrate the slaughter. These efforts removed the killing from the larger populace both physically and psychologically, and in Turkey and Germany, it enabled the large-scale deception that those who were rounded up and transported to the death camps were instead marked for resettlement and "labor duty in the East."

In Nazi Germany the rules on language were entirely consistent with the outcome of the infamous Wannsee Conference of 1942, which provided the blueprint for "The Final Solution to the Jewish Problem in Europe." The resulting document contained no references to actual killing or extermination, yet it made the Holocaust part of another lie, namely that of "the battle of destiny for the German people," just as the resettlement of the Armenians was a battle for the soul of Turkey, and the extermination of Tutsi was intended to reverse the so-called victimhood of the Hutu. These lies suggested that the war against a part of the civilian population was not a choice, but a war forced on the perpetrators by destiny, and that in each case it was a matter of life and death for a dominant population who must annihilate its enemies or be annihilated.

Deception of this sort helps produce compliance because it ultimately allows for self-deception, especially if the lie is repeated over time. It allows perpetrators, bystanders, and victims alike to construe events in alternate and less threatening ways that elicit inhibition to a lesser degree, conceal the crime, and sew confusion. Knowing that a trainload of people will be killed may trigger more inhibition than believing that they are merely being resettled. This kind of self-deception not only helps to soothe one's conscience, it also takes responsibility away from all but those relatively few who do the actual killing. Even the concentration camp guard who dropped the cyanide into a gas chamber could deceive himself about the nature of his actions by identifying them with an abstract concept on a higher level. Rather than putting people to death, he was contributing to "the battle of destiny."

How important these types of self-deception are for the execution of genocide is underscored by the actions of bystanders who did not adopt the official deception. They did not remain passive, but instead influenced other bystanders and in some cases even perpetrators into taking actions aimed at rescuing those marked for death. Prime examples are the rescue of seven thousand Jews from Denmark with the help of small boats and delayed deportation orders from German officials, Bulgaria's refusal to surrender its Jewish population to the Germans in light of public demonstrations, the heroic efforts in the French village of La Chambon that saved thousands of refugees yet escaped reprisals from German officials, and the actions of a few lightly armed peacekeepers under General Romeo Dallaire who rounded up Tutsi and secreted them in a stadium where they remained under their protectors' guard. In all of these cases, deception did not lead to self-deception, but instead inspired individuals into taking responsibility for pro-social action.

SEE ALSO Bystanders; Complicity; Deception, Victims; Propaganda; Sociology of Perpetrators

BIBLIOGRAPHY

Arendt, Hannah (1965). *Eichmann in Jerusalem: A Report on the Banality of Evil.* New York: Viking.

Balakian, Peter (2003). *The Burning Tigris: The Armenian Genocide and America's Response.* New York: HarperCollins.

Browning, C. R. (1998). *Ordinary Men: Reserve Battalion 101 and the Final Solution in Poland.* New York: HarperCollins.

des Forges, Alison (1999). *Leave None to Tell the Story.* New York: Human Rights Watch.

Erber, R. (2002). "Perpetrators with a Clear Conscience: Lying Self-Deception and Belief Change." In *Understanding Genocide: The Social Psychology of the Holocaust,* ed. L. S. Newman and R. Erber. New York: Oxford University Press.

Staub, E. (2002). "The Psychology of Bystanders, Perpetrators, and Heroic Helpers." In *Understanding Genocide: The Social Psychology of the Holocaust,* ed. L. S. Newman and R. Erber. New York: Oxford University Press.

Vallacher, R. R., and D. M. Wegner (1987). "What Do People Think They Are Doing? Action Identification and Human Behavior." *Psychological Review* 94:3–15.

Ralph Erber

Deception, Victims

Deception is a key element of genocide. The perpetrators, always a government or other organized group, are able to operate in secrecy, whereas the victims, usually dispersed or leaderless, find it difficult to coordinate their knowledge and actions, and are also hampered by psychological barriers to belief and action. For these reasons victims can not only be easily deceived, but can be co-opted or coerced into helping to deceive outsiders. On the other hand, victims are sometimes able to evade genocide by hiding, fleeing, or assuming false identities, and to the extent that groups of victims are able to discover the truth and organize themselves, armed resistance may also be possible. All these responses require concealment both in preparation and execution, and hence are possible only if the victims in turn are able to deceive the perpetrators.

Ironically, past patterns of persecution short of genocide can help the perpetrators deceive the victims. Perpetrators and victims have typically lived side by side for many years, often in conflict but with long periods of peaceful coexistence. When violence begins to escalate, the victims tend to expect a repetition of previously experienced events and may fail to respond as decisively as they might if they knew what was coming. Perpetrators can thus deceive their victims by approaching genocide by degrees, recapitulating past persecutions. The Nazis, for example, started off by stripping Jews of property and civil rights, introducing discriminatory measures, expelling many of them, forcing them to wear identifying symbols, and confining them to ghettos: The Jews had experienced all these forms of persecution in the past and expected to be able to survive them, but this time they set the stage for genocide.

Either flight or some form of counter-deception, such as forging protective documents, or living under assumed identities or in concealed hiding places, usually provides the best chance of survival. In Cambodia individuals survived by such expedients as throwing away eyeglasses that could mark them as "intellectuals." In the case of pogroms or massacres of short duration, victims can also occasionally survive by feigning death. The very few eyewitnesses to the Cambodian Killing Fields survived in this way and played an important role in unmasking the genocide of the Khmer Rouge.

Totalitarian regimes have complete control of the media and are able to lie and mislead at will. A typical early move is to shut down all information channels but the official ones: For example, immediately after taking Phnom Penh, the Khmer Rouge confiscated all radios and televisions. Killing is usually not done in full view (Rwanda was an exception); victims may instead be transported to camps or remote locations, ostensibly for "resettlement." The Nazis went so far as to disguise gas chambers as shower rooms, with false showerheads, so as to continue the deception until the last moment.

The Holocaust was exceptional in that it allowed its victims many opportunities to practice counter-deception. Within some of the Nazi ghettos a political underground developed that published clandestine newspapers and was able to maintain a surprising degree of contact with the outside world. It was even able to smuggle out news of atrocities to the West and eventually organized a number of armed revolts. Deception within the ghettos took several other forms as well, for example, a thriving smuggling enterprise, which in the Warsaw ghetto was estimated to account for 80 percent of the ghetto's food and export income. Smuggling partly defeated the Nazis' intention of reducing the Jewish population through starvation. Once deportations to the death camps started, in 1942, the Jewish underground was able to track the deportation trains to their destinations and ascertain the true meaning of resettlement. But the Nazis continued to deceive the Jews by offering apparent exemptions from deportation and "amnesties" for those who had escaped from the ghettos. These deceptions persuaded some Jews to stay in the ghettos even after they knew what deportation entailed. Other Jews tried to evade the deportations by building hideouts in the ghettos, or by escaping and going into hiding "on the Aryan side."

The Nazis and the Jews thus played a cat-and-mouse game of deception and counter-deception. Victory went to the perpetrators, who killed nearly six million Jews; but some 200,000 Jews survived in hiding across Europe and more than a million managed to flee across borders to the Soviet Union, Sweden, Switzerland, and other countries of refuge.

Perpetrators often used Potemkin villages, and staged events to deceive outside observers, forcing the victims to cooperate in the deception. During the Anfal campaign against the Kurds in Iraq, reporters were given a guided tour of selected Kurdish areas and then attended a festive Kurdish wedding. In June 1944 a delegation of the International Red Cross visited the Nazi *Paradeisghetto* of Theresienstadt (in Czech Terezín), which had been spruced up for the occasion. The delegation was allowed to speak with a few prisoners who had been told what to say. The Nazis also forced Jews to take part in propaganda films depicting life at Theresienstadt and in the Warsaw ghetto.

Although most books that deal with genocide contain some discussion of deception by the perpetrators, the subject of evasion and deception by the victims has not been well served by the scholarly literature. There are a great many studies of victimization and its consequences (such as posttraumatic stress disorder), and many also of resistance and rescue, but the efforts of victims to save themselves by deceiving the perpetrators have only recently begun to draw the attention of scholars. Such experiences are described in memoirs and diaries too numerous to mention. The Bibliography here includes a small sample of these.

SEE ALSO Cambodia; Deception, Perpetrators; Ghetto; Propaganda

BIBLIOGRAPHY

Klemperer, Victor (1998). *I Will Bear Witness: A Diary of the Nazi Years 1933–1945.* London: Weidenfeld & Nicolson.

Paulsson, Gunnar S. (2001). "Evading the Holocaust: The Unexplored Continent of Holocaust Historiography." In *Remembering for the Future: The Holocaust in an Age of Genocide,* Vol. I. London: Palgrave.

Paulsson, Gunnar S. (2003). *Secret City: The Hidden Jews of Warsaw, 1940–1945.* New Haven, Conn.: Yale University Press.

Roseman, Mark (2001). *A Past in Hiding: Memory and Survival in Nazi Germany.* New York: Henry Holt.

Szpilman, Wladyslaw (1999). *The Pianist: The Extraordinary Story of One Man's Survival in Warsaw, 1939–45.* New York: Picador.

Welaratna, Usha (1993). *Beyond the Killing Fields: Voices of Nine Cambodian Survivors in America.* Stanford, Calif.: Stanford University Press.

Gunnar S. Paulsson

Defenses

A legal defense is the offering of substantive and procedural obstacles to the prosecution of a crime in a court of law. Regarding crimes of genocide, war crimes, and crimes against humanity, the first issue to consider is whether a particular defense or defense strategy can be sustained according to the general principles of international criminal law. Article 31 of the Rome Statute of the International Criminal Court (ICC) is significant in this regard. This statute is based on a mixture of common and civil law principles, as well as provisions drawn from comparative criminal law, and refers to "grounds for excluding criminal responsibility." However, Article 31 of the ICC statute accentuates the civil law dimension of this concept by refraining from the common law practice of distinguishing between certain types of defenses.

Significantly, the ICC statute does not differentiate between justifications and excuses offered in regard to the commission of a crime. A justification is a defense to the extent that the defendant argues that he is not to be punished for breaking a law, because certain special (justifying) circumstances exist that legitimize the particular action. An excuse, on the other hand, does not legitimize the criminal act. Rather, it amounts to the claim that the defendant cannot be held personally responsible for his act at the time of the crime. In the case of excuses, the act remains criminal, and therefore punishable—it is the perpetrator who is excused from culpability.

Many legal systems do differentiate between a defense based on justification and one that offers an excuse. This distinction seems relevant when seeking an exoneration for a charge of genocide and crimes against humanity. A justification emerges when a particular act is deemed to be morally just, whereas an excuse only exonerates the accused—not his or her act. An excuse, therefore, identifies the blameworthiness of the perpetrator. At its most fundamental level, therefore, the qualification of a defense to a charge of genocide or crimes against humanity may be perceived as a personal excuse, offered on a purely personal level, on the presumption that the accused cannot be held personally responsible for the particular genocidal act, since any ordinary person would have behaved in the same way.

Contrary to the 1948 Genocide Convention, which only addresses the issue of defenses in Article IV (which deals with the defense of heads of state), the ICC Statute (in Article 31) codifies a potentially wider scope of defenses that, at first sight, embraces the crime of genocide. Article 33(2) of the ICC Statute, however, places certain limits on defenses, declaring that orders to commit genocide or crimes against humanity are manifestly unlawful, which raises an obstacle for mounting a defense based on claims that the accused was following the orders of his or her superior.

The Status of Defenses to Genocide and Crimes against Humanity

The International Law Commission Draft Code of Crimes against the Peace and Security of Mankind, in its report of July 26, 1996, mentions that a competent court shall determine the admissibility of defenses "in accordance with the general principles of law, in the light of the character of each crime." These general principles of law include the contents of the Genocide Convention and the jurisprudence, which evolved from the Nuremberg Trials. This jurisprudence, as well as international legal instruments, have focused primarily on the defense of duress in connection with superior orders; and on defense claims of insanity, diminished responsibility, and intoxication, as well as self-defense, which did not feature in the Nuremberg Trials.

The law of the International Criminal Tribunals is informed by the fact that nearly every major legal system in the world recognizes a similar collection of defenses as admissible. However, the ICC at times employs somewhat different criteria in assessing the admissibility of some of these defenses.

The Head-of-State Immunity Defense

Claims of immunity for heads of states were not found admissible at the Nuremberg Trials or in other post–World War II international legal proceedings. Article IV of the Genocide Convention provides that a head of state's defense based on claims of immunity from prosecution cannot be invoked in case of a genocide charge. The inadmissibility of this defense therefore expresses a general principle within the meaning of Article 38(1)(c) of the International Court of Justice (ICJ) Statute.

Article 7 of the International Criminal Tribunal for the Former Yugoslavia (ICTY) Statute and Article 6 of the International Criminal Tribunal for Rwanda (ICTR) Statute also disallow a defense based on the claim of head-of-state immunity from prosecution. Specifically, the official position of any accused person, including the position of head of state, does not relieve such person of criminal responsibility, nor can it be used to mitigate punishment. Article 27 of the ICC Statute thus reaffirms the existing customary international law. In fact, it goes further, by specifically excluding this defense in the realm of genocide and crimes against humanity.

A case illustrating the inadmissibility of a head-of-state immunity defense is found in the ruling of the British House of Lords on March 24, 1999, in *R. v. Bow Street Stipendiary Magistrate and others, ex parte Pinochet Ugarte (Amnesty International and others intervening)*. In this ruling, Lord Phillips of Worth Matravers held that it was superfluous to invoke Article IV of the Genocide Convention to exclude the head-of-state defense, because both customary international law and conventional codification already achieved this aim. Furthermore, Article 13 of the 1991 Draft Code of Crimes of the International Law Commission reaffirmed this position. He noted that Article 13 declares that heads of state should be held accountable for their crimes against the peace and security of mankind.

The "Superior Orders" Defense

The perpetration of an international crime as the result of an order of a superior appears to be excusable only if it is clear that the accused did not know the order was manifestly illegal. Accordingly, the defense of superior orders does not appear in the Genocide Convention, because any order to commit genocidal acts is considered to be manifestly illegal. The Apartheid Convention also does not address this defense directly, for similar reasons, whereas Article 2 of the 1984 Torture Convention explicitly excludes the use of this defense as a justification of torture. Furthermore, Article 8 of the Charter of the International Military Tribunal at Nuremberg also explicitly excludes any defense based on claims that the perpetrator was obeying superior orders. The Allied Control Council Law No. 10, which came into force on December 20, 1945, did not contain a similar provision. Nonetheless, several judicial pronouncements of the post–World War II U.S. military tribunals, including *United States v. Von Leeb* (the German High Command Trial) and *United States v. Ohlendorf et al* (the Einsatzgruppen Trial), did explicitly exclude this defense.

A review of scholarly opinions and judgments of post–World War II tribunals and international instruments leads to the conclusion that "obedience to superior orders" is not a defense under customary international law to an international crime when the order is manifestly illegal, even when the subordinate has no moral choice with respect to either obeying or refusing to obey the order. This reasoning also applies to charges of genocide or crimes against humanity. In cases where the subordinate is mentally compelled to fulfil the order, the claim of duress, as a personal excuse, is the applicable defense.

By contrast, Article 7(4) of the ICTY Statute and Article 6(4) of the ICTR Statute exclude the defense of superior orders as a means of claiming nonculpability, and offers no exceptions. They do, however, allow the invocation of this defense for a defendant who seeks a potential mitigation of punishment. Article 33 of the ICC Statute, however, follows a different approach by allowing this defense, but imposes certain conditions upon its use. Still, the practical effect of the various articles of the ICC Statute, when taken as a whole, is to limit the use of this defense to the punishment phase of a trial, where it may be introduced as a mitigating factor.

Self-Defense

The claim of self-defense can be advanced when the individual charged with committing a crime has resorted to the use of force specifically in order to defend himself (or herself) from the imminent threat of illegitimate force, and when the force used is proportionate to the threat that occasioned it. Self-defense can also be invoked when the force was used in defense of a third party. In principle, the plea of self-defense can be invoked in the context of any crime, even in the case of genocide and crimes against humanity. What matters in this defense is the specific intent of a person. He or she must have acted with the intent to protect his or her life or the life of another. This raises problems when the defense is used to answer a charge of genocide, which by definition requires its own specific intentionality: the intent to destroy a national, racial, ethnic, or religious group as such.

The concept of self-defense can be invoked at either the state or the individual level. Several major legal instruments recognize the right of an individual to use proportionate force when acting in legitimate self-defense. Article 2(2) of the European Convention on Human Rights refers to self-defense as an exception to the principle of respect for the right of life. During the Nuremberg Trials, however, self-defense was not accorded any status as an international criminal law defense. In *U.S. v. Krupp et al.*, the claim of self-defense by individuals was assessed in connection with necessity. In one of the post–World War II cases (*Tressmann et al.*), this defense was accepted as "last resort." In several other post–World War II cases, this defense was invoked by individuals, and it was sometimes permitted, but not as a plea to genocide or crimes against humanity. Therefore it does not represent a rule of customary international law.

Self-defense is not explicitly mentioned in the ICTR and ICTY Statutes, but ICTY case law did refer to it. In the case of *Kordic and Cerkez,* the defense held that the Bosnian Croats acted in self-defense. The ICTY Trial Chamber, referring to Article 31(1)(c) of the ICC (Rome) Statute, ruled that military defensive operations in self-defense do not provide a justification for serious violations of international humanitarian law. This reasoning seems also relevant to the crime of genocide and crimes against humanity.

Article 31(1)(c) of the Rome Statute expressly codifies the admissibility of self-defense in the event of the crime of genocide and crimes against humanity, as well as in the case of war crimes, if the defensive act is done to defend property that is essential for survival or property that is essential for accomplishing a military mission. However, defense of property is not admissible with respect to a charge of genocide or crimes against humanity.

Duress

The defense of duress is offered as an excuse (as opposed to a justification), and is based on an external circumstance that causes an extreme mental pressure that the accused cannot reasonably be expected to have resisted. This defense was referred to in the Nuremberg judgments, albeit in conjunction with necessity. However, despite the fact that the defense of duress to charges of war crimes was assessed by the United States Military Tribunal in the German High Command Trials (in the *Krupp* and *Einsatzgruppen* cases), it did not exempt the particular accused in these cases, nor did it exonerate Adolf Eichmann during his trial in Israel in 1961, because he was shown to have willingly volunteered and never to have protested against the heinous crimes.

The Genocide Convention is silent on the defense of duress. The special rapporteur of the International Law Commission, Doudou Thiam, argued that this defense was admissible as a plea to genocide in the event of "an imminent and grave peril to life or physical well-being," whereby this peril is irremediable and otherwise inescapable. The final report of the International Law Commission concluded that there exist different views as to whether even the most extreme duress can ever constitute a valid defense or extenuating circumstance with respect with a particularly heinous crime, such as the killing of an innocent human being.

A close reading of the judgment of the U.S. Military Tribunal in the mentioned *Einsatzgruppen* case discloses that a defense of superior orders was refused because there was no evidence of compulsion or duress. Therefore, it follows that the use of "following a superior's orders" is, in fact admissible, but only if it results in causing duress. The difference between a plea based on superior orders and one based on duress is that the former defense may be invoked without the presence of any threats to life or limb, whereas the latter defense can only be raised when someone is compelled to commit a crime by a threat of his or her life, or to the life of another person. A person acting in duress has no realistic moral choice. Only in such a situation is the plea of superior orders admissible as a defense against the charge of genocide or crimes against humanity.

This view was accepted by the ICTY Trial Chamber decision of November 29, 1996, in *Prosecutor v. Erdemovic*. However, the ICTY Appeals Chamber, in its decision of October 7, 1997, held that duress was not admissible as a defense to genocide or crimes against humanity. In contrast, Article 31(1)(d) of the ICC Statute allows for the defense of duress, even when it concerns a genocide charge, under certain specific conditions. The accused must have acted to avoid a threat of imminent death or of continuing or imminent serious bodily harm against that person or another person, and the accused must not intend to cause a greater harm than the one sought to be avoided. In other words, the accused's acts must have been necessary, reasonable, and proportionate to the threat. In the event of a genocide charge, it is questionable whether these conditions—and especially the condition of proportionality—can ever be met. According to Judge Cassese, in his dissenting opinion to the ICTY decision in *Prosecutor v. Erdemovic,* it may be possible to meet the conditions allowing for a defense of duress even in the case of genocide, if the innocent civilians would be killed no matter what the defendant might have done.

Article 31(1)(d) of the ICC Statute strongly suggests that only physical threats can result in the kind of overwhelming mental pressure required to justify the defense of duress. When duress is invoked because the imminent threat of harm was presented not to the accused but to a third party, there seems to be no requirement of any special relationship between the person threatened and the person accused. However, it is reasonable to assume that assessments of the mental pressure suffered by the accused might be valued differently in the event the person threatened is a relative of the accused.

It does not seem unreasonable to suggest that extreme duress might be admissible as a defense against a charge of war crimes, crimes against humanity, and genocide. It must be remembered, however, that duress qualifies as an excuse, unlike the defense of necessity, which can be offered as a justification. In case of necessity, the accused is faced with a choice of evils, which leads to a decision in favor of the lesser evil—the incriminating qualification of the act is superseded by the fact that the accused intended to protect a higher legal norm. A further distinction between the two defenses is that, in duress, the external pressure stems from an individual, whereas in the event of necessity, the pressure arises from natural causes. Duress only exonerates an accused from his or her criminal responsibility, while leaving the unlawfulness of the act intact.

Military Necessity

The defense of military necessity relates to a choice of evils, similar to necessity as a criminal law defense. The choice is between military and humanitarian interests, and implies a deliberate choice to negate a norm of international humanitarian law. It appears to be admissible, even when it concerns a war crime charge. The distinguishing characteristic of military necessity is that it is affiliated with the furtherance of a specific interest of the state in the context of a particular armed conflict,

so that this defense can only be used to exonerate an individual in his or her capacity as an instrument of the state.

The ICC Statute does not mention this defense explicitly in Article 31(1). However, Article 8(2)(e)(xii) defines destruction of property as a war crime when it is not justified by military necessity. Furthermore, close reading of the documents generated during the preparation of the ICC Statute discloses that the drafters believed that this defense could be admitted as one of the special defenses referred to in Article 31(3). Nonetheless, it is unlikely that a defense based on the claim of military necessity could encompass the killing of innocent civilians. Such a defense is therefore not likely to be admissible against a charge of genocide or crimes against humanity.

Insanity, Mental Defect, and Diminished Responsibility

The defense of insanity or mental incapacity as such has no origin in international law. Instead, it was developed based on national criminal law, especially framed on the famous M'Naghten case of 1843, which was tried in a common law system. This defense played a modest role during the later Nuremberg Trials. For instance, the trial against Rudolf Hess suggests that insanity can indeed be of relevance in establishing criminal responsibility for international crimes.

It is better to speak of mental disease or defect, rather than insanity, and in fact this terminology has been adopted in Article 31 paragraph 1(a) of the ICC Statute, which article reflects the M'Naghten jurisprudence. Although the M'Naghten case was based on common law, the civil law systems generally follow the same reasoning with regard to the defense of mental disease or defect.

The M'Naghten rules are based on the concept of a disease of mind which produces such a defect of reason that the accused does not know the nature of his or her act, or, if he or she does, then the accused does not know that the act was wrong. Proof of either of these matters entails that the accused is legally insane.

The mental defect defense should be distinguished from the defense of diminished mental capacity. To claim mental defect requires the destruction—and not merely the impairment—of the defendant's mental condition. Such a claim, if proven, may lead to an acquittal. From a common law point of view, the defense of diminished mental capacity, when offered in response to a murder charge, eliminates the requirement of special intent, namely the elements of premeditation and deliberation, and is therefore not only relevant to the sentencing. Similarly, this defense could affect the special intent required for a charge of genocide as well as the intent required for crimes against humanity.

The ICTY and ICTR refer to this defense only in its Rules of Procedure and Evidence (RPE). The rules require that the prosecution must be informed of the intent to invoke this defense prior to the start of the trial, and must be provided with details regarding potential expert witnesses whom the accused intends to rely on for his or her defense.

In *Prosecutor v. Delalic et al.* (November 16, 1998), the ICTY Trial Chamber rejected the defense of diminished responsibility as put forward by the accused, noting that the defense did not establish the fact that the accused was unable to distinguish between right and wrong. The ICTY relied on the expert opinions offered by three forensic psychiatrists who were called by the accused to testify on his behalf, and a fourth who was called upon by the prosecution to offer a rebuttal. All of the defense expert witnesses agreed that the accused suffered from a personality disorder. The Trial Chamber opined that the burden of proof was not met by establishing a disorder as such, making a distinction between suffering from a personality disorder on the one hand, and being unable to control one's physical acts on account of abnormality of mind, on the other hand. Only the latter situation may justify this defense, which may be invoked in defense against a charge of genocide or crimes against humanity.

In *Prosecutor v. Vasiljevic,* Mitar Vasiljevic was charged with ten counts of crimes against humanity under Article 5 of the ICTY Statute, as well as with violations of the laws on customs of war (Article 3). In its judgment of November 29, 2002, the ICTY found Vasiljevic guilty of persecution and murder—he allegedly participated in leading seven Bosnian Muslim men to the bank of the Drina River, where five of them were shot to death (the other two managed to escape). As an alternative defense, the accused claimed that his sentence should be mitigated because during the incident he had suffered from diminished responsibility as a result of chronic alcoholism, and backed up his claim with testimony from three expert witnesses.

The Trial Chamber held that the accused bears the onus of establishing the defense of mental disease or diminished mental responsibility. This standard means that the accused must show that more probably than not, his impaired condition existed at the time of the commission of the crime. It also opined that the defense of mental disease or diminished responsibility is only admissible in two (alternative) events: either the accused must have been unable to appreciate the unlawfulness of or the nature of his conduct; or he must

have been unable to control his conduct in order to conform to the requirements of the law.

The ICC Statute, in Article 31(1)(a) and (b), sets the standard for the defense of mental disease (and for the related defense of intoxication). The article is in general agreement with the findings of the ICTY Trial Chambers, but does not touch upon the requirement that the defendant bear the burden of proof to establish the defense. In practical terms, this could lead to a situation where mere reasonable doubt concerning the existence of sufficient mental capacity is sufficient to meet the requirements for mounting this type of defense.

Intoxication

A defense based on claims of intoxication is closely related to one based on mental defect or diminished responsibility. Most criminal law systems do not recognize a separate statutory exception in the case of intoxication. Furthermore, at the level of international criminal litigation, the defense of intoxication has played almost no role. There are no precedents for this defense at the level of genocide and crimes against humanity. One of the rare occasions in which this defense was invoked concerned the case of *Yamamoto Chusaburo,* tried in 1946 by the British Military Court in Kuala Lumpur. In this case, the defense of intoxication was actually tried on the basis of British legal doctrine regarding voluntary drunkenness.

This defense lacks a foundation in international criminal law, but, it evolves at the international level from comparative criminal law. Its international status emerged for the first time within the Draft International Criminal Code and the ILA Model Draft Statute for the ICC. It is reasonable to conclude, therefore, that the defense of voluntary intoxication is not considered to be part of any rule of international customary law. Generally the defense of intoxication may be qualified as a derivative of the mental disease exception. It is important to note, however, that the ICC Statute codifies the defense of intoxication in its Article 31, paragraph 1, subparagraph (b).

The drafters of the Rome Statute followed the same approach as that taken by the British Military Court in the *Yamamoto Chusaburo* case. In practical terms, however, this defense as a plea to a genocide charge will be restricted to low-ranking officers and soldiers. Furthermore, the fact that acts of genocide generally take place over protracted periods of time, which further militates against the admissibility of an intoxication defense, due to an exception provided in Article 31(1)(b): "the person has become voluntarily intoxicated under such circumstances that the person knew, or disregarded the risk that, as a result of the intoxication, he or she was likely to engage in conduct constituted a crime (. . .)." In contrast, it may be argued that an intoxication defense could erase the special knowledge element required for bringing a charge of crimes against humanity.

A defendant invokes the defense of intoxication in order to advance the claim that he or she lacked the requisite mental element of intentionality. It is, therefore, a claim to exoneration, not mitigation. However, any such claim must meet specific criteria if it is to be successful.

Article 31(1)(b) of the ICC Statute sets forth just such criteria. It allows for the defense of intoxication if that intoxication has destroyed the accused's capacity to control his or her conduct to conform to the requirements of law. The intoxication need not be caused by alcohol, but may have derived from the use of drugs or medication. This condition is treated as the equivalent of a mental defect.

The intoxication defense fails if it can be shown that the accused became intoxicated voluntarily, knowing the risk of indulging in criminal behavior but disregarding it. This provision raised two questions that the ICC Statute leaves unanswered. First, it fails to define the term *voluntary*. Can an addict be considered to have voluntarily become intoxicated when the addiction is beyond his or her mental control? Second, does this defense also potentially apply to military commanders, or is its use restricted to cases involving individual soldiers? The ICC was founded with the intention to prosecute mainly political and military leaders and policymakers. If the intoxication defense can only be admitted for lower-ranking individuals, why would it be specifically included within the ICC Statute? Apparently, the ICC drafters did not exclude this defense at the latter prominent level and even not with regard to heinous crimes.

SEE ALSO Crimes Against Humanity; International Court of Justice; International Criminal Court; International Criminal Tribunal for Rwanda; International Criminal Tribunal for the Former Yugoslavia; Nuremberg Trials; Tokyo Trial; War Crimes

BIBLIOGRAPHY

A-G Israel v. Eichmann (1968). *International Law Reports* 36, nos. 18, 277. (District Court and Israeli Supreme Court)

Ambos, Kai (2002). "Other Grounds for Excluding Criminal Responsibility." In *The Rome Statute of the International Criminal Courts, A Commentary*, Volume I, ed. Antonio Cassese, Paola Gaeta, and John R. W. D. Jones. Oxford: Oxford University Press.

Bassiouni, M. Cherif (1999). *Crimes against Humanity in International Criminal Law*. The Hague: Kluwer Law International.

Dinstein, Y. (1965). *The Defense of Obedience to Superior Orders in International Law*. Leiden: A.W. Sijthoff.

Eser, A. (1987). "Justification and Excuse." In *Justification and Excuse,* ed. A. Eser and G. P. Fletcher. Vol. I: *Comparative Perspectives*. Freiburg: Eigenverlang Max-Plank-Instituit für Ausländisches und Internationales Strafrecht.

Gillies, Peter (1993). *Criminal Law 218*. Sydney, Australia: The Law Book Company.

Knoops, Geert-Jan Alexander (2001). *Defenses in Contemporary International Criminal Law*. New York: Transnational Publishers.

Knoops, Geert-Jan Alexander (2003). *An Introduction to the Law of International Criminal Tribunals*. New York: Transnational Publishers.

Prosecutor v. Delalic et al. Case No. IT-96-21-T; Judgment 16 November 1998.

Prosecutor v. Vasiljevic, Case No. IT-98-32-T; Judgment 29 November 2002.

Schabas, William A. (2000). *Genocide in International Law,* Cambridge, U.K.: Cambridge University Press.

Schabas, William A. (2001). *An Introduction to the International Criminal Tribunals*. Cambridge, U.K.: Cambridge University Press.

van Sliedregt, E. (2003). *The Criminal Responsisbility of Individuals for Violation of International Humanitarian Law*. The Hague: T.M.C. Asser Press.

United Nations. Report of the Preparatory Committee on the Establishment of an International Criminal Court, Volume I, UN Doc A/51/10.

United States v. Krupp (1948). *Trials of the War Criminals.* 9:1438.

United States v. Ohlendorf et al. (Einzatzgruppen Trial) (1948). *Law Reports of the Trials of the War Criminals* 4:411.

United States v. Von Leeb (German High Command Trial) (1949). *Law Reports of the Trials of the War Criminals* 11:1.

Geert Jan Alexander Knoops

Del Ponte, Carla

[FEBRUARY 9, 1947–]
Swiss attorney, named as prosecutor for the International Criminal Tribunals of the Former Yugoslavia and Rwanda.

Carla Del Ponte was born on February 9, 1947, in Lugano, Tessin, the sole Italian-speaking Swiss canton. After studying law in Bern and Geneva, Switzerland, she began her legal career in 1972, where she quickly gained a reputation as an independent and controversial figure. She worked closely with Judge Giovanni

Falcone, who enlisted her aid in his campaign against Italian mafia crime bosses. With Falcone, she escaped an assassination attempt (by underworld figures) in 1989. (Falcone was later assassinated in 1992.) She was appointed attorney general in 1994 and spent the next several years prosecuting the presumed godfathers of the Russia mafia, drug traffickers, and money launderers.

Although a member of the Swiss Radical Party, which has close ties to Switzerland's business interests, Del Ponte has nonetheless earned the enmity of much of the Swiss financial community for having focused international attention on banking scandals. In the summer of 1999, she was selected by UN Secretary-General Kofi Annan to assume the position of prosecutor for the International Criminal Tribunals for the Former Yugoslavia and Rwanda (ICTY and ICTR). She assumed the post the following autumn, replacing Louise Arbour.

On May 25, 1999, then-prosecutor Arbour indicted Serbian president Slobodan Milosevic for war crimes and crimes against humanity, alleged to have occurred before and during the North Atlantic Treaty Organisation (NATO) aerial bombardment of Kosovo. Because of political considerations, several UN member states began to criticize the ICTY as being the puppet of the NATO states. Russia, in particular, demanded that the prosecutor for the ICTY not be a national of any of the NATO members. Switzerland is not a member of NATO, making Del Ponte an acceptable choice for prosecutor.

Del Ponte's first challenge was to decide whether or not to open an inquiry into allegations that NATO's military intervention involved serious violations of the Geneva Conventions. In June 2000 she addressed this option before the UN Security Council in the following terms:

> I am very satisfied there was no deliberate targeting of civilians or of unlawful military targets by NATO during the bombing campaign. I am now able to announce my conclusion, following a full consideration of my team's assessment of all complaints and allegations, that there is no basis for opening an investigation into any of those allegations or into other incidents related to the NATO bombing.

Del Ponte's decision set off an international uproar that forced her to make public the Final Report to the Prosecutor, produced by a committee established to review the NATO bombing campaign against the Federal Republic of Yugoslavia. This degree of public disclosure by a UN prosecutor was unprecedented, but the move succeeded in disarming her critics and settling the issue.

Carla Del Ponte at the trial of former Yugoslav president Slobodan Milosevic in February 2002. At that time Del Ponte was chief prosecutor for both the ICTY and ICTR. Thus, she was responsible for bringing Milosevic to trial and for prosecuting an entire government for genocide in Rwanda. [REUTERS/CORBIS]

Her second challenge at the ICTY was the prosecution of Slobodan Milosevic. Thanks to pressure from the United States and the member states of NATO, she obtained Milosevic's arrest and transfer to The Hague, where he would stand trial. This was an historic first—never before had a head of state been brought to judgment for international crimes. At the end of 2001, Del Ponte expanded Louise Arbour's initial indictment to cover allegations of genocide and crimes against humanity that occurred during the wars in Bosnia and Croatia. Milosevic now stands accused of genocide for his responsibility in the massacres of Srebrenica in July 1995.

On February 12, 2002, the trial opened against Milosevic. A lawyer by training, he invoked the right to defend himself and launched into an attack on the legitimacy of the tribunal itself. Del Ponte crafted her prosecution to show that Milosevic was the main architect of a plan to create an ethnically cleansed Greater

Serbia. Throughout the trial, Serbian public opinion was hostile to the tribunal and the authorities had balked at cooperating with the prosecutor. After two years, Del Ponte finally brought the prosecutorial phase to a close on February 25, 2004. Her presentation relied on the testimony of 296 witnesses and thousands of pages of evidentiary documents. The defense phase of the trial was expected to last another two years, without counting the likelihood of an appeal.

Del Ponte has been under extreme pressure to bring her work for the ICTY to a close. She publicly denounced Serbia's lack of cooperation with the tribunal and criticized the delay in arresting another Serbian leader implicated in the ethnic cleansing policies in Bosnia: Radovan Karadzic.

As of 2004, fifteen perpetrators have entered guilty pleas to reduced charges. Some have criticized the use of plea bargains such as these in the context of crimes against humanity. This prosecutorial strategy has led to judgments that appear unequal, even arbitrary. For instance, Milomir Stakic, the unrepentant ex-mayor of Prijedor, was sentenced to life imprisonment for crimes committed locally, but his superior, Bijlana Plavsic, a member of the government of the Srpska Republic and, as such, a leading figure in ethnic cleansing, received a much lighter sentence of eleven years in prison, solely because he was willing to admit his guilt.

Del Ponte's work with the ICTY is only half of her prosecutorial responsibility. She also serves as prosecutor of the International Criminal Tribunal for Rwanda. The ICTR has been accused of inefficiency and disorder from its very inception. During the first ten years of its existence, the tribunal has succeeded in passing sentence on only about twenty accused, at a cumulative cost of $700 million. Del Ponte has been hindered in her Rwanda prosecutions by political obstacles. The Rwandan government has been resolutely hostile to the work of the tribunal. Over time, relations deteriorated so badly between Del Ponte and the Rwandan government that, on September 4, 2003, the UN Security Council decided to split the post of prosecutor of the two tribunals and to replace Del Ponte as prosecutor of the ICTR, allowing her to concentrate her attention and energies on the ICTY.

SEE ALSO Arbour, Louise; Goldstone, Richard; International Criminal Tribunal for Rwanda; International Criminal Tribunal for the Former Yugoslavia; Milosevic, Slobodan; Rwanda; Yugoslavia

BIBLIOGRAPHY

Ball, Howard (1999). *Prosecuting War Crimes and Genocide: The Twentieth-Century Experience.* Lawrence: University Press of Kansas.

Bass, Gary Jonathan (2000). *Stay the Hand of Vengeance: The Politics of War Crimes Tribunals.* Princeton, N.J.: Princeton University Press.

Beigbeder, Yves (1999). *Judging War Criminals: The Politics of International Justice.* New York: St Martin's Press.

Hazan, Pierre (2000). *La justice face à la guerre: de Nuremberg à la Haye.* Paris: Stock.

Moore, Jonathan, ed. (1998). *Hard choices, Moral Dilemmas in Humanitarian Intervention.* Lanham, Md.: Rowman and Littlefield.

Robertson, Geoffrey (1999). *Crimes Against Humanity: The Struggle for Global Justice.* New York: The New Press.

Scharf, Michael P. (1997). *Balkan Justice: The Story Behind the First International War Crimes Trial Since Nuremberg.* Durham, N.C.: Carolina Academic Press.

Pierre Hazan

Demjanjuk Trial

John Demjanjuk was a Ukrainian national born in the village of Dub Macharenzi on April 3, 1920. He was a tractor driver on the collective farm of his native village. In 1940, the Red Army conscripted Demjanjuk. After the Nazi invasion, he served in the artillery in the Crimea until being captured by the Germans in May 1942. After the war ended he immigrated to the United States, becoming a naturalized citizen in 1952. Little is known about the intervening ten years of his life.

In 1977 Demjanjuk was accused of being "Ivan the Terrible," a Nazi war criminal from the infamous Treblinka death camp. It was alleged that he ran the gas chamber there, and that he earned his nickname as a result of his brutal treatment of the camp's inmates. The accusation triggered a court action, filed by the U.S. Immigration and Naturalization Service, to strip Demjanjuk of his U.S. citizenship. He lost this court case and his citizenship in 1981. The United States then faced two options: Demjanjuk could be deported to the Ukraine, or he could be extradited to Israel, which wanted to put him on trial. The United States chose the second option, and, in 1987, Demjanjuk was extradited to Israel to face criminal prosecution for the crime of genocide. Israel was chosen as the venue for the trial because its laws permit prosecution of Nazi war criminals on the basis of universal jurisdiction.

Demjanjuk's trial commenced on November 26, 1986. He was found guilty of committing genocide by the District Court of Jerusalem on April 18, 1988, and was sentenced to death on April 25. While his lawyers appealed the court's decision, new evidence surfaced

John Demjanjuk on trial in Israel, March 18, 1987. Extradited from the United States where he had resided as a naturalized citizen for over thirty years, Demjanjuk faced charges of war crimes he allegedly committed at Treblinka, a Nazi death camp. [REUTERS/CORBIS]

that cast doubt on the original verdict. Newly discovered documents, primarily recovered from the archives of the former Soviet Union, supported the defense's claim that "Ivan the Terrible" was not Ivan Demjanjuk after all, but rather referred to a man named Ivan Marchenko. Consequently the Israeli Supreme Court granted an appeal. As the identification of Demjanjuk as "Ivan the Terrible" was no longer proved beyond reasonable doubt, the Supreme Court acquitted him. The Attorney General of Israel "refused to proceed with new charges, despite compelling evidence that Demjanjuk had in fact served as a guard in the Trawniki camp" (Schabas, 2000, p. 388).

The court held that Demjanjuk did not have "a reasonable opportunity to defend himself against the new charge" (Kremnitzer, 1996, p. 327), which had not been the focus of the original trial in the lower court. Further, U.S. extradition laws would not permit Demjanjuk to be prosecuted on charges that had not been cited in the original extradition order. Even the High Court of Justice of Israel declined to intervene in favor of a new trial.

Some observers remain very critical of the Demjanjuk trial. Geoffrey Robertson wrote: "The trial stands not only as a warning of the unreliability of eye-witness evidence and of justice miscarrying when it is too long delayed, but more importantly of the danger that some states will exploit universal jurisdiction for political ends" (Robertson, 1999, p. 233). The establishment of the International Criminal Court could ensure that there is less partisanship in the future, but it must be recalled that the ICC does not have jurisdiction over alleged offenses that occurred before its establishment in 2002.

SEE ALSO Concentration Camps; Prosecution

BIBLIOGRAPHY
Heath, John William (1999). "Journey over 'Strange Ground': From Demjanjuk to the International Criminal Court Regime." *Georgetown Immigration Law Journal* 13:393–407.
Kremnitzer, Mordechai (1996). "The Demjanjuk Case." In *War Crimes in International Law*, ed. Y. Dinstan and M. Tabory. The Hague: Martinus Nijhoff Publishers.
Lemkin, Raphael (1944). *Axis Rule in Occupied Europe.* Washington, D.C.: Carnegie Endowment for International Peace.
Robertson, Geoffrey (1999). *Crimes Against Humanity.* London: Penguin Press.

Schabas, William A. (2000). *Genocide in International Law.* Cambridge, U.K.: Cambridge University Press.

Vinodh Jaichand

Denationalization

The Commission on the Responsibility of the Authors of War and on Enforcement of Penalties first used the term *denationalization* in 1919 in an early effort to describe crimes similar to genocide that were committed during World War I. It cited many examples of Bulgarian, German, and Austrian official attempts to "denationalize the inhabitants of the occupied territory" in Serbia. Among the specific violations mentioned were the prohibition of the Serb language; the destruction of archives, churches, monasteries, and law courts; and the closure of schools.

Genocide was first described as the destruction of the national pattern or character of the victimized group and replacing it with the national pattern or character of the oppressor. Therefore, genocide involved a two-stage process. It was the first stage, which entailed the destruction of the national pattern of the victimized group, for which the word denationalization was used. The national pattern or character would include the political and social institutions; the culture, language, national feelings, religion, and economic existence; and the personal security of national groups, as well as such basic concepts as life, liberty, health, and dignity. The destruction of these was tantamount to the destruction of a nation, or of an ethnic group, through a coordinated plan of different actions aiming at the destruction of essential foundations of life within the group, with the aim of destroying the group itself.

There are many features of the concept of denationalization that are also evident in the crime of genocide, war crimes, or crimes against humanity as they are defined today. One distinction, however, is that even these shared features are, in denationalization, specifically related to the treatment of national groups rather than groups in general. Another distinction between denationalization and genocide in particular is that genocide is seen in more explicitly physical terms—the killing of groups of people—whereas denationalization includes the destruction of the foundations of national groups, such as the group's culture.

An example of denationalization can be found in the 1947 Nuremburg trial of *Ulrich Greifelt and Others.* During the proceedings, reference was made to the war crime of denationalization, citing the policy of forcibly "Germanizing" some groups within the local population of occupied Poland. Among the groups so treated were Poles, Alsace-Lorrainers, and Slovenes, as well as others deemed eligible for Germanization under the German People's List.

History

Over the years and in numerous international documents, various attempts have been made to define genocide. In many instances, what is now known as the international crime of genocide overlaps with other war crimes and crimes against humanity. Recognition of denationalization as a war crime had its origins in the Hague Convention IV of 1907, which attempted to create proper divisions between the responsibility of the state at war and the treatment of innocent civilian in occupied territories. This Convention now forms a part of established international humanitarian law, and applies only in times of armed conflict. Legal scholar William A. Schabas has noted that Section III of the Hague Convention might serve as a legal basis for acts related to denationalization as a war crime. This section deals with military authority over the territory of the hostile state, and includes a provision that makes it illegal to "compel the inhabitants of an occupied territory to swear allegiance to the hostile power" and another which exhorts respect for "the lives of persons and private property, as well as religious convictions and practice."

The preamble of the Hague Conventions of 1907 further promises broad protection under international humanitarian law, stating that "the inhabitants and the belligerents remain under the protection and the principles of the law of nations, derived from the usages established among civilized peoples from the laws of humanity and the dictates of public conscience."

The governments of France, Great Britain, and Russia declared on May 24, 1915, that they would hold all members of the Turkish government personally responsible for "crimes against humanity" for the massacre of Armenians that was ongoing at the time. Earlier, the International Commission to Inquire into the Causes and Conduct of the Balkan Wars (1912–1913) had enumerated thirty-two broad categories of violations committed during that conflict, among them: "Attempts to denationalize the inhabitants of occupied territory."

At the second plenary session of the Paris Peace Conference, on January 25, 1919, the Commission on the Responsibility of the Authors of the War and on Enforcement of Penalties was established. The task of this Commission was to inquire into and report upon the violations of international law committed by Germany and its allies during World War I. At this time, however, there was no mention of individual prosecutions for atrocities against civilians, because the Commission's members were more preoccupied with developing offenses against the laws of war and felt that the principle of sovereignty required them to focus their examination on the atrocities committed by a government against peoples within its own borders.

In 1941 Nazi Germany passed a decree that denationalized German Jews, stripping them of their property and, later, their lives. It was not until 1945, however, after the atrocities committed against the Jews by the Nazis, that the Nuremberg Charter defined crimes against humanity to include acts against a civilian population whether they occurred before or during the war. The offenses included murder, extermination, enslavement, deportation, imprisonment, torture, and persecution. Subsequent international legislation has further refined and extended the definition of war crimes and crimes against humanity, including protections not only for national groups but to all groups at risk of victimization.

Recent Uses of Denationalization

Another legal scholar, John Dugard, has maintained that the South African apartheid government's official plan to assign all blacks to homelands effectively constituted an act of denationalization. The apartheid laws meant that blacks ceased to be nationals of South Africa, thus depriving them of political and civil rights in the land of their birth. Instead, blacks were reassigned to fictitious nationalities, of Transkei, Bophuthutswana, Venda, and Ciskei, ostensibly because of their association by birth, language, or culture with one or another of those territories. This was contrary to the prohibition on denationalization on grounds of race that has been confirmed by the Universal Declaration of Human Rights, the Convention on the Reduction of Statelessness, and the International Convention on the Elimination of All Forms of Racial Discrimination. Apartheid, including its denationalizing aspects, is a crime against humanity and is now recognised as such by the Rome Statute.

Current Status of Denationalization

Denationalization is presently listed in the Ethiopian Criminal Code in Article 282 (e). Both Australia and the Netherlands also make it a specific offense to attempt "to denationalize the inhabitants of occupied territory" within their respective borders. Whether or not a state's domestic law recognizes the offense, however, that state may still be charged with war crimes in cases of denationalization. The *United States Department of Army Field Manual,* in section 27–10, "The Law of Land Warfare," recognizes the Nuremberg principles of non-immunity for government officials and disallows any defense based on domestic law "for an act which consti-

tutes a crime under international law." The List of War Crimes prepared by the Responsibilities Commission of the Paris Peace Conference of 1919, as a schedule attached to the Manual, contains the crime of denationalization.

Nationality and Statelessness

Under international law, a state has the discretion to withdraw nationality from its citizens. However, this discretion has limitations, largely limiting such withdrawals to a case-by-case basis. The wholesale deprivation of nationality from an entire group or denationalization on grounds of race, as occurred in Nazi Germany and apartheid South Africa, is prohibited by the Convention on the Reduction of Statelessness of 1961. Yet the problem still persists. Events in the Middle East have led to the denationalization of 3.7 million Palestinians and the confiscation of their property. At the start of the twenty-first century, it remained as yet unclear whether there would be any political will within the international community to resolve this situation.

SEE ALSO Commission on Responsibilities; Hague Conventions of 1907

BIBLIOGRAPHY

Avalon Project. "Laws of War: Laws and Customs of War on Land (Hague IV); October 18, 1907." Available from http://www.yale.edu/lawweb/avalon/lawofwar/hague04.htm.

Commission on Responsibilities (1920). "Commission on the Responsibility of the Authors of the War and on Enforcement of Penalties. Report presented to the Preliminary Peace Conference, March 29, 1919." *American Journal of International Law* 14:95–154.

Dugard, John (2001). *International Law: A South African Perspective.* Cape Town: Juta Law.

Lemkin, Raphael (1944). *Axis Rule in Occupied Europe.* Washington D.C.: Carnegie Endowment for International Peace.

Lemkin, Raphael (1947). "Genocide as a Crime under International Law." *American Journal of International Law* 41:145–151.

Schabas, William A. (2000). *Genocide in International Law.* Cambridge: Cambridge University Press.

Vinodh Jaichand

Denial

Deniers of genocide and other massive human rights violations are engaged in obsessive quests to demonstrate, via fallacious arguments, erroneous facts, and historical distortions, that the events never occurred or are grossly exaggerated. The denial speech, notwithstanding its effort to be perceived as an historical debate, is about contemporary political motivation, racism, and anti-Semitism. It is an ideology, not an historical endeavor. Deniers' conclusions precede their research and analyses. They aim, not to destroy the truth, which is indestructible, but to eradicate the awareness of the truth that prevents the resurgence of past criminal ideologies.

Denial of the Armenian Genocide

Denial of the Armenian genocide is the most patent example of a state's denial of its past. In this case, the state of Turkey officially denies the genocide committed against its Armenian population. Turkey has tried for decades to deny the burden of guilt that the genocide represents for an emerging nation trying to build itself a different past. The debate created by the Turkish state centers on the definition of genocide and its application to the crimes committed against the Armenians, rather than on whether the massacres ever actually occurred. Thus, the spurious debate about the Armenian genocide is more political than the one invoked in Holocaust denial, which is racially motivated. The international community, for the most part, acknowledges the existence of the Armenian genocide, but Turkey still threatens other states with diplomatic reprisals when the question of such recognition is debated.

Denial of Japan's Atrocities

Historical revisionism controversies are becoming frequent in Japan. Radicals from the Japanese political right reject historical accounts in which Japan is portrayed as guilty of crimes against the Chinese population. They deny or outrageously minimize the aggression and atrocities committed by the Imperial Army in the first half of the twentieth century. An example of the massive human rights abuses that the Japanese right minimizes or denies is the Rape of Nanking, during which Chinese women were held in confinement to be used as sex slaves and tortured. Similar to Turkey in its intent, the Japanese denial movement aims, not at perpetuating discriminatory behavior toward Chinese, but to exonerate Japan for atrocities committed on behalf of the state. Denial of events such as the Rape of Nanking has recently even found its way into schoolbooks. The books were later withdrawn, however. South Korea and China protested the introduction of the books in the classrooms, and most public schools rejected them. Denial also recently found its way into Japanese comic-book novels called *manga*.

Denial of the Rwandan Genocide

The denial movement of the 1994 Genocide in Rwanda is still limited in size and influence. The proximity in time of the killings of approximately 800,000 Tutsis and moderate Hutus makes it more difficult for deniers to claim that Tutsis were not targeted and killed. In this context, deniers focus more on the notion of "double genocide" than on the nonexistence per se of the genocide of the Tutsis. Extremist Hutus, both from the diaspora and within Rwanda, plead that a genocide was committed against them by Tutsis and the Front Patriotique Rwandais (FPR). By doing so, they put the two events—the genocidal violence against Tutsis and the killing of Hutus—on an equal footing. The difference between the concepts of genocide and killings, or even slaughter, is not only etymological, however. By assimilating the concepts, Hutu deniers downplay the importance of the crime and the intent behind the genocide. It removes the stigma of killers from the Hutu extremists. It suggests that, since genocide was committed on both sides, there are no victims and no perpetrators; and that all are equal in the scale of crimes. Some Rwandans, working primarily through survivors' associations, are lobbying for legislation in the Rwanda legal corpus prohibiting the denial and the minimization of the 1994 genocide.

Denial of the Holocaust

Holocaust denial has, over the last couple of decades, become an important and active anti-Semitic movement. It consists of the denial or minimization of all aspects of the Nazi genocidal enterprise—its intent, its means, as well as its results. It aims at reshaping history in order to rehabilitate the reputation of the Nazis. The movement focuses on denying the existence of the gas chambers and challenging the validity of the claim that six million Jews were killed, because these are the Holocaust's most vivid and most frequently used symbols. It is mainly active in Canada, in the United States, and in Western Europe. Deniers are also becoming active in some Arab countries.

France is considered the cradle of the movement. Maurice Bardèche and, even more so, Paul Rasinnier are considered by many to be the fathers of the movement, but Robert Faurisson, a literature professor at the University of Lyons, has been its true leader. *La Vieille Taupe*, a publishing house, has played a significant role throughout the years in the promotion and distribution of Holocaust denial materials. Henri Roques, Roger Garaudy, and Jean-Marie LePen, who brought Holocaust denial into politics, are other prominent members of the movement.

The origin of a structured Holocaust denial movement in the United States goes back to the creation of the Institute for Historical Review (IHR), a so-called academic organization, in the late seventies. The IHR uses its *Journal of Historical Review* and conferences to disseminate its propaganda. Contrary to what its name seems to suggest, the IHR is not engaged in good-faith historical research, but serves instead as a platform for racist publications and speeches. Members of the IHR include anti-Semite propagandists such as Ernst Zündel, David Irving, Roques, Faurisson, and Bradley Smith. They can also count on the support of self-proclaimed scholars such as Arthur Butz. Bradley Smith, under the guise of the Committee for Open Debate on the Holocaust, was active in the 1990s, placing paid advertisements in college newspapers inviting students to engage in "open debate" on the Holocaust, thereby implying that its very occurrence is subject to legitimate controversy.

Deniers' Arsenal

Holocaust deniers question what is indisputable, volunteer false evidence while denying historical evidence detrimental to their thesis, dwell on details to reject all testimonies of survivors, and hide behind claims of scientific or scholarly status without having any relevant scholarly background. Deniers plead the absence of specific written orders emanating from Hitler proving the genocidal intent. For deniers, the gas chamber is a myth. On that point, they rely heavily on a false report produced by Arthur Butz, who claims to prove that the Nazis lacked the technical capability to build the chambers. Having dismissed the technical feasibility of the killing centers, deniers move on to claim that places such as Treblinka, Chelmo, and Sobidor, but even more importantly for deniers, Auschwitz-Birkenau, are propagandist fantasies created by Jews. From this, they argue that the figure of six million Jewish victims also cannot be true. Finally, they claim that the International Military Tribunal was a fraud, set up by the Allies to make Germans feel guilty in order to obtain financial compensation for Jews.

By denying the Holocaust's most outstanding features, deniers achieve three goals. First, they remove the status and significance of the Holocaust as a point of reference. The deniers want to erase the teaching of the event, its prophylactic role. In other words, by eliminating the event from conscience and history, deniers hope to influence the present. This is why they disavow the existence of the gas chambers and the genocidal function of Auschwitz. Their agenda is the rehabilitation of the reputation of the Nazis: If such a crime was never committed, then there is nothing wrong with pursuing Nazi policies again. Finally, if the Holocaust is itself a propagandist fraud, deniers can confirm the basis of their racist rationale, which is that the Jews manipulated the world before World War II and still do. The evidence of this ongoing manipulation, claim the

deniers, is their ability to impose a lie of such magnitude—the Holocaust, in other words—for so long. In all cases, Jews are the targets.

When they do not simply deny that it occurred, deniers argue the Holocaust was only one event in a long list of similar crimes committed in the past. By putting aside the unique aspects of the Shoah and by minimizing the suffering of the Jews, deniers disavow the specific racist intent of the Nazis. But it is pointless to indulge in claims of comparative pain suffering, nor is it useful to enter into a competition over the head count of victims. To attempt to say, as deniers do, that all crimes are equivalent is to engage in historical distortion. For example, the use of the gas chambers is not just a different kind of technology employed in war—it has wider implications. The chambers were built with the specific intent of killing a mass of people, and were used with the goal of total annihilation of a group. When deniers seek to expunge the gas chambers from history, they are denying not just a detail of the larger event but one of that event's defining concepts.

Debate, Censorship, and the Prosecution of Deniers

Those who wish to confront the deniers of genocide face a dilemma. Should they engage in refuting deniers' allegations? Should the state forbid the publication of denial literature and depict it as "hate propaganda"? Should the state prosecute deniers, or does freedom of expression protect deniers' rights to promulgate their propaganda? Solutions have varied considerably from one region to another, but the issue is always the same: balancing the deniers' rights to freedom of speech against the protection of the rights of the people targeted, who are mainly minorities.

Freedom of speech is a basic element of any democratic society. Fundamental international, regional, and national laws protect it. Most of those laws, however, reject the idea that freedom of speech is absolute and not subject to certain restrictions. In most countries, Holocaust denial exceeds the limit of freedom of speech and is considered an act of racism. Countries facing active and influential denier movements, such as France and Germany, have specifically adopted and adapted legislation penalizing the denial of gross human rights violations. Other countries, for instance Canada, have relied on the prohibition of hate speech. In the United States, the First Amendment guarantee of the freedom of speech is sacrosanct and, it is argued, cannot be subject to much limitation. For this reason, there is a relative absence of jurisprudence against Holocaust deniers in the United States.

In Europe, where most Holocaust denial jurisprudence originates, the European Commission of Human

Rights has generally ruled that deniers' complaints about limitation of their freedoms were manifestly ill founded. It has also determined that deniers' speeches and writings are aimed at the destruction of the other rights and freedoms as set forth in the European Convention for Human Rights, and that they are engaged in a campaign against peace and justice, the values on which the Convention is based. For the European Court of Human Rights, the protection of the interests of the victims of the Nazi regime outweighs the freedom to impart views denying the existence of gas chambers. Thus, in the opinion of the Commission, Holocaust denial exceeds the freedom of speech.

The Gayssot Act, adopted in 1990 in France, makes it a punishable offense to engage in the denial of any of the crimes mentioned in the Charter of the International Military Tribunal of August 8, 1945. It was on the basis of this charter that Nazis were tried in Nuremberg. The prominent Holocaust denier, Robert Faurisson, was convicted in 1992 by the French court, but challenged the legitimacy of the Gayssot Act before the United Nations Human Rights Committee, charging that it violated his freedom of speech according to section 19 of the International Covenant on Civil and Political Rights. The Committee dismissed Faurisson's claim.

In Canada, where no specifically adapted legislation exists, Ernst Zündel was unsuccessfully prosecuted for spreading false news. Zündel's pamphlet, entitled *Did Six Million Really Die?*, suggested that the Holocaust was a myth perpetrated by a worldwide Jewish conspiracy. The Supreme Court of Canada found the scope of the provision (i.e., the statute prohibiting the spread of false news) to be too broad and, thus, that the limitation of freedom of speech was in this context unjustifiable. Other cases brought against deniers in Canada were prosecuted under laws prohibiting hate propaganda. In the case of *Q. v. Keegstra* (1990), the Canadian Supreme Court held that the defendant's expressive activity (denial propaganda) was only tenuously connected with the values underlying the guarantee of freedom of expression, that is the quest for truth and the promotion of individual self-development. Thus, the court went on to rule, the prohibition of such propaganda does not unduly impair freedom of expression. More recently, Canadian courts found Zündel, who hosted a web site dedicated to Holocaust denial, guilty of using telecommunication devices to spread heinous messages against minorities.

In Great Britain, the High Court rejected David Irving's claim that Professor Deborah Lipstadt and Penguin Books had slandered him when she named him as a Holocaust denier in one of her books. In court, Irving persistently and deliberately misrepresented and manipulated historical evidence to portray Hitler in an unwarrantedly favorable light, principally in relation to his attitude toward and responsibility for the treatment of the Jews. The court agreed with Lipstadt that Irving was indeed an anti-Semite, a racist, and an active Holocaust denier.

It is worth mentioning that not all legislation prohibiting denial of gross human rights violation applies to all such events. The Gayssot Act, for instance, leaves outside its scope the Armenian genocide, in part because an independent judicial body did not establish the genocide. In Switzerland, to the contrary, section 261*bis* of the Criminal Code, prohibits the denial or the gross minimization of any genocide or other crimes against humanity.

An increasing body of international legislation condemning the denial of crimes against humanity and the Holocaust has contributed to the formation of a soft-law corpus, or multilateral non-treaty agreements, on the issue. Some legal authorities have recommended combating the dissemination of negationist (denial) theories by introducing or strengthening penalties and improving the opportunities for prosecution. Those who still oppose the prosecution of deniers argue that that everything can and should be debated and that truth ought not to be imposed by governments or the law. This utopian belief assumes that lies are always revealed when they are freely debated, and that this would benefit everyone in a free society. This is the "light-of-day" argument taken to its extreme. But the deniers' debate exists only because of such utopian protections.

History vs. Pseudo-History

Deniers aim to confound history. By their denials, they aim to confound history. They pretend to be engaged in a legitimate and credible scholarly effort, a genuine attempt at presenting alternative historical interpretation. But denial propaganda is not interpretation; instead, it is a tissue of lies and distortions. Denial literature and other forms of denial propaganda oppose truth with lies. Historians may engage in historical revision of past events when new evidence supports a rethinking of earlier interpretations, but no such new evidence exists to raise serious questions about the fact that the Holocaust occurred. The deniers' only true goal is a racist one: to attack genocide targets for a second time.

Some fear that prosecuting deniers will lead to the imposition of state-sponsored versions of historical truth. Such fears seem unjustified. The prosecution of deniers is not done with the intent to impose a state-sponsored version of historical truth, but rather to protect the historical record. The fact that the Third Reich is responsible for the Holocaust has been established in trials around the world, but none of the fraudulent allegations of the deniers has ever been established on the strength of verifiable evidence. In addition, legislation such as the Gayssot Act does not preclude research on the historical facts. It only sets aside one historical fact—the very existence of the Holocaust—on the basis of authoritative evidence, such as that which was presented at the Nuremberg Trials, that the Holocaust did, indeed, occur. Postmodernists argue that history is subjective, pointing out that it is an intellectual reconstruction of events that the historians themselves have not lived through or witnessed. History may indeed contain subjective elements, but this does not mean that a good-faith reconstruction of the past is impossible, or that interpretations can be based solely on ideology and still make a claim to legitimacy. Even historians of the postmodern school cannot escape the supremacy of evidence—including physical evidence and eyewitness accounts—and therefore must concede that the Holocaust did, in fact, occur, or they cease to be historians.

SEE ALSO Holocaust; Propaganda

BIBLIOGRAPHY

Akcam, Taner (2001). "Le tabou du génocide arménien hante la société turque." *Le Monde Diplomatique* 568:20.

Bihr, Alain (1997). "Les mésaventures du sectarisme révolutionnaire." In *Négationnistes: Les chiffonniers de l'histoire*. Paris: Golias and Syllepse.

Edeiken, Yale F. (2000). "Irving's War." Available from http://www.holocaust-history.org/irvings-war/.

Guttenplan, D. D. (2001). *The Holocaust on Trial*. New York: W. W. Norton.

Hobsbawm, Eric (1997). *On History*. London: Abacus.

Lipstadt, Deborah (1994). *Denying the Holocaust: The Growing Assault on Truth and Memory*. New York: Plume, Penguin.

Pons, Philippe (2001). "Controverses sur l'histoire en Asie." *Le Monde Diplomatique* 571:16–17.

Rousso, Henry (1990). *Le syndrome de Vichy, de 1944 à nos jours*, 2d ed. Paris: Seuil.

Shermer, Michael and Alex Grobman (2000). *Denying the Holocaust: Who Says the Holocaust Never Happened and Why Do They Say It*. Berkeley: University of California Press.

Ternon, Yves (1999). *Du négationnisme: Memoire et Tabou*. Paris: Desclee de Brouwer.

Vidal-Naquet, Pierre (1991). *Les assassins de la mémoire: "Un Eichmann de papier" et autres essais sur le révisionnisme*. Paris: La Découverte.

Martin Imbleau

Der Stürmer

Julius Streicher has been known as the "Jew-Baiter Number One." He was not a career politician, but saw political parties as an efficient tool through which his racist propaganda could reach a larger audience. Streicher's initial political attempt was with the German socialist party (DSP), in which he was responsible for the publication of the *Deutsche Sozialist,* the DSP's journal. The DSP was not radical enough for his tastes, however. It would not let him use the party for mass propaganda against the Jews. This incited Streicher to join a new radical movement, the *Deutsche Werkgemeinschaft* (the first group to adopt the swastika), and to publish a new paper, the *Deutscher Volkswille,* to disseminate its propaganda. Three thousand copies of the *Deutscher Volkswille* were sold each week. Once again, however, Streicher's anti-Semitism was too strong for his ostensible allies. He lost influence among the movement's leaders, was forced to quit the movement, and abandoned control of the *Volkswille*. In the Nazi party, however, he finally found the ultimate vehicle for his racist sentiments.

Streicher took part in the Munich putsch of November 1923. From 1925 to 1940 he held the rank of *Gauleiter* (local party leader) of Franconia. Elected to the Reichstag in 1933, he was granted an honorary commission in the SA, with the rank of general. His duties, however, were only marginally military in nature. Streicher was above all the publisher of the notorious anti-Semitic newspaper *Der Stürmer* from 1923 to 1945, and served as its editor in chief for the first ten years of the paper's existence. The aim of *Der Stürmer* was to attack, denounce, and promote discrimination against Jews in every way possible. In the 1920s, Streicher's anti-Semitic publication elicited many charges of libel and slander, for which he, as publisher, editor, and author, served a total of eight months in prison. Other anti-Semitic Nazis may be more notorious, but Julius Streicher was by far the most vicious and prolific of them. As chairman of the Central Committee for the Defense against Jewish Atrocities and Boycott Propaganda, Streicher was responsible for the boycotts against Jewish businesses.

Originally, *Der Stürmer* had a fairly limited circulation, contained only a few pages, and even temporarily ceased publication. By the mid-1920s, however, the paper was growing in size, and the number of copies printed each issue began to increase. In 1927, approximately 15,000 copies were sold weekly, and by 1935, circulation had attained 500,000. At that time, *Der Stürmer* was widely distributed in Germany and was read by German citizens from all social classes, including Hitler himself. Members of the Nazi party were

In a front-page illustration of a May 1934 issue of Julius Streicher's *Der Stürmer,* the blood of an innocent Germany flows to awaiting Jews. In later convicting Streicher of crimes against humanity, the Nuremberg Tribunal referred to the publication as a "poison injected into the minds of thousands of Germans."
[HULTON-DEUTSCH COLLECTION/CORBIS]

strongly encouraged to subscribe to *Der Stürmer.* In addition to distribution through subscription, *Der Stürmer* was displayed in public places throughout Germany, where passersby could stop to read the propagandist titles or look at the racist cartoons of Philippe Rupprecht. Rupprecht, known as Fips, regularly drew anti-Semitic cartoons that employed all the popular stereotypes of the time to portray the physical characteristics of Jews. Streicher and *Der Stürmer* also published many special editions dedicated to anti-Jewish propaganda, including children's books. With the beginning of the war, the paper's circulation dropped significantly. One reason was the wartime shortage of paper, but the other was far more ironic: the absence of Jews in Germany. To boost circulation, *Der Stürmer* added more cartoons and used doctored photographs to further its propagandist aims.

The first issue of *Der Stürmer,* published in 1923, promoted the view that Germans were under the control of Jewish people and that Jews must be forced to leave Germany. Following a policy of gradual develop-

ment, Streicher initially limited himself to vague expressions, such as "the black shadow of foreign blood," to describe the alleged omnipresence of Jews in German society. Subsequently, however, *Der Stürmer* became more specific. In his articles, Streicher began targeting specific Jewish individuals, or claiming bluntly that Jews were deadly vermin. The paper frequently provided lists of names of Jews toward whom a boycott was to be initiated or who were to be physically assaulted.

For *Der Stürmer,* racial differences explained everything, and repeating this idea in different forms, again and again, was the paper's most effective technique. It did not seek to convince its readers with strong and sound arguments, but instead used an inflammatory style to further its anti-Semitic agenda. Its primary technique was the use of short articles and very simple language to explain in a direct way the so-called reality of the Germans vis-à-vis the Jews. For its racist propaganda to remain effective, and in order to reach the broadest possible readership, *Der Stürmer* repeated the same stories in different ways without bothering to supply new evidence, and used examples to which the general, non-Jewish public could relate. *Der Stürmer* both reported on scandals and initiated them. It created anti-Jewish stories, often relying on old stereotypes, such as the accusation that Jews were responsible for ritual murder and that they kept the blood of their victims, reporting on them as if they were ongoing events. Then, again in the guise of reporting, it publicized the stories far and wide.

Before the International Military Tribunal (IMT) in Nuremberg, Streicher was indicted for crimes against peace and for crimes against humanity, specifically because of his involvement with *Der Stürmer.* The prosecution filed dozens of his published articles, in which Streicher incited people to annihilate the Jews. On the charge of crimes against peace, the IMT concluded that, notwithstanding Streicher's unequivocal support of Hitler's policies, there was no evidence that Streicher was actually responsible for originating the policies that led to war, or that he even knew of such policies. The IMT thus found him not guilty of the crime of conspiracy to wage aggressive war.

On the charge of crimes against humanity, however, Streicher was less fortunate. In his defense, Streicher argued that he promoted his solution to the Jewish question not with the intent of annihilating the Jewish population, but to further the classification of Jews as aliens and to promote the adoption of discriminatory legislation such as the Nuremberg Laws. He even claimed his ultimate goal was the creation of a separate

Jewish state. The IMT rejected this defense, found him guilty, and sentenced him to death.

The IMT's conclusions focused more on Streicher's anti-Jewish incitements during the war, at the very moment that massive crimes were being perpetrated against the Jews, than on Streicher's role in creating a climate favorable to anti-Jewish policies. The tribunal concluded that Streicher's incitements to murder and extermination, even as Jews were being killed in great numbers, constituted persecution on political and racial grounds in connection with war crimes and thus qualified as a crime against humanity. He was sentenced to death on October 1, 1946, and was hanged on October 16, 1946. Among those convicted by the IMT, Streicher was the only one who shouted "Heil Hitler" before he was hanged.

SEE ALSO Incitement; Propaganda

BIBLIOGRAPHY

Bytwerk, Randall L. (2001). *Julius Streicher: Nazi Editor of the Notorious Anti-Semitic Newspaper Der Stürmer.* New York: Cooper Square Press.

Nuremberg International Military Tribunal Judgment (1947). *Nazi Conspiracy and Aggression, Opinion and Judgment.* Office of the U.S Chief of Counsel for Prosecution of the Axis Criminality, 56.

Martin Imbleau

Developmental Genocide

In many parts of the world, the view of indigenous peoples has been informed by the overarching European view of "others." This has resulted in expectations regarding tribal or native peoples that have less to do with the reality of these populations and more to do with the preconceived notions of Europeans. This phenomenon has had a powerful impact on the development of European political philosophy regarding emancipation and history of thought. It infused the project of colonial intervention and colonial ideology, and has persevered in postcolonial times to infuse the concepts of modernization, nation-building, and, particularly, the concept of development. The effect was something that came to be called developmental genocide. *Developmental genocide* can be defined as the destruction of the culture and way of life of a people, usually accompanied by massive dislocation, as a result of economic development in the name of progress and modernization.

Examples of developmental genocide can be found throughout the world. One striking example of the unbroken relation of colonial intervention, the project of development, and the resultant developmental genocide occurred in the Chittagong Hill Tracts after Bangladesh achieved independence in 1971. Europeans initially perceived the people of the Chittagong Hill Tracts as noble savages who were masters of their life. They were considered rich by the very existence of their sense of freedom, independence, and reciprocity. However, they were considered poor in terms of the so-called higher values of Western civilization—for instance, in terms of their religious practice or material wealth. This perception of indigenous poverty legitimated certain other attitudes that were highly convenient for development planners. It became possible to rationalize development practices as a way to "uplift" the indigenous people, who were now viewed as ignorant, poor, and downtrodden primitives.

Colonial intervention had intended the substitution of indigenous concepts of economy by introducing capitalist notions of accumulation, production, and distribution. This process was only partially successful, and did not endanger the lives of the hill people. However, the nation-building approach adopted after Pakistan achieved independence (in 1947) had somewhat greater impact. It made the hill people's economies the target of a structural change: The Chittagong Hill Tracts region, hitherto a restricted area, was opened for settlement by Bengali peasants. Shifting cultivation, as practiced by the indigenous peoples, was to be suppressed and substituted by cash crop farming for the national market. Hydroelectric resources had to be developed.

In 1964 a dam and a hydroelectric power plant were completed in the hills. The lake destroyed the backbone of the hill people's economy. An estimated 100,000 persons lost their lands, fields, and homesteads. Resistance to the project was widespread, but political pressure on the indigenous peasants was severe; 40 000 felt forced to migrate to India.

After the war of independence against West Pakistan (1971), the Hill Tracts were once again made the target of authoritarian, top-down development planning. At this point, a number of issues emerged: Oversettlement and exploitation of land in the plains of Bengal created a demand for new areas for settlement. The hill peoples' region, which was largely covered in tropical rainforest, seemed an ideal solution, especially because the area was believed to shelter an abundance of natural resources.

The long-term repercussions of the hydroelectric project, the ongoing process of destruction of the indigenous economy, and rising poverty in the region led to an increasing awareness among the hill people of a shared ethnicity. As more and more Bengali farmers migrated into the hill peoples' lands, another step was taken in the process of the planned destruction of indigenous cultures by the state. For more than ten years, the government turned a blind eye to raids on hill peoples' villages, looting, arson, rape, large-scale killings, eviction, and the destruction of holy sites, and even authorized military participation in these actions. The violence drove a large part of the hill people from their lands and forced them to take refuge in India. Bengali peasants were then settled on the newly vacated lands. A guerrilla force consisting of members of different hill peoples tried, with varying success, to resist the advancement of the army and Bengali settlers. By the mid-1980s, however, Bengali settlers outnumbered the hill people.

The military occupation of the hills set a frame for the change of the indigenous structures of proprietorship. Indigenous peasants were evicted from their legally occupied lands and were driven into wage labor, in the name of development. Such projects were partly supported by international agencies. When, in 1997, the government of Bangladesh and the representatives of the hill peoples signed a peace accord, there was no change the parameters of state intervention. The government's political aim (to force "backward tribes" into the national mainstream) and economic aims (to settle landless Bengali peasants and to gain undisputed command over and monopolize the natural resources of the hills) are legitimated by the state's notion of progress and development. Projects launched after the peace accord have repeated earlier strategies: In the name of the development, new projects, often funded by international agencies, have continued to alienate hill peasants from their land, evict indigenous farmers, deprive them of their property, and transform private and communal land of the hill peoples into state or private property of immigrant settlers.

The Chittagong Hill Tracts example is but one instance of genocidal development policies. In other parts of the world, the damming of rivers has led to a similar wider-scale loss of land and peasant evictions, and the sale of rainforest territories to international logging companies in South- and Southeast Asia are equally profound examples of the destruction of minority peoples legitimated by the imposition of development policies.

SEE ALSO Bangladesh/East Pakistan; Chittagong Hill Tract, Peoples of the; Genocide; Indigenous Peoples; Sri Lanka

BIBLIOGRAPHY

Bodley, J. H. (1982). *Victims of Progress,* 2nd edition. Palo Alto, Calif.: Mayfield Publishing Company.

Burger, Julian, and Alan Whittaker, eds. (1984). *The Chittagong Hill Tracts. Militarization, Oppression and the Hill Tribes.* Indigenous Peoples and Development Series, vol. 2. London: Anti-Slavery Society.

Gain, Philip, ed. (2000). *The Chittagong Hill Tracts: Life and Nature at Risk.* Dhaka, Bangladesh: Society for Environment and Human Development (SEHD).

IWGIA (1999). "Dams, Indigenous Peoples, and Ethnic Minorities." *Indigenous Affairs* 3(4).

Jomo, K. S. (2003). *Deforesting Malaysia. The Political Economy and Social Ecology of Agricultural Expansion and Commercial Logging.* London: Zed Books.

Lang, Charles (2002). *The Pulp Invasion, The International Pulp and Paper Industry in the Mekong Region (Thailand, Laos, Vietnam, Cambodia).* Montevideo, Uruguay: World Rainforest Movement.

McCully, P. (2001). *Silenced Rivers: The Ecology and Politics of Large Dams.* London: Zed Books.

Peterson, N., and W. Sanders, eds. (1998). *Citizenship and Indigenous Australians. Changing Conceptions and Possibilities.* Cambridge: Cambridge University Press.

World Dams Commission (2000). *Dams and Development.* Washington, D.C.: Author.

Zarsky, L. (2002). *Human Rights and the Environment.* London: Earthscan.

Wolfgang Mey

Diaries

Diaries about genocide are works that provide the contemporaneous perspective and invaluable first-hand observations of individuals living under regimes that are either heading toward or overtly planning, even actively pursuing, genocide. They are a record of the experiences, sights, sounds, rumors, and insights into the daily life of such individuals, and sometimes even detail the actual events of the genocide. By their very nature, diaries offer one person's limited but on-the-spot observations, commentary, and questions regarding his or her own fate, and the lives of family, friends, and colleagues—and perhaps even the fates of people whom the diarist does not know personally. The most powerful and most valuable diaries often reveal the diarist's self-inquiry into his or her own beliefs, the facts surrounding his or her own existence, and the circumstances of the government and of those carrying out genocidal polices. They can also disclose the diarist's assessment of the possibilities, for good or ill, available in the face of approaching or ongoing genocide. For historians, diaries are of inestimable value for they, in most cases, constitute "authentic and reliable sources of information" (Gutman, 1985, p. 371).

Every genocide is the result of specific and unique antecedents, causes, decisions, and the enactment of such decisions. Nonetheless, the diaries written by individuals who suffered through it, survived it, or witnessed it (such as the missionaries from various nations serving in the Ottoman Empire during the course of the Armenian genocide) may share common themes. These may include propaganda issued by perpetrators against a victim group, the fear instilled by perpetrators in the general populace, the call for the removal of certain groups from society, the incipient incitement of violence against a particular group of people, the "disappearance" of people, or the outright mass killing of targeted victims. Diarists focus on those experiences, issues, concerns, anxieties, fears, and hardships that they personally suspect, witness, or experience.

What must be understood and appreciated is that each diary provides but a single piece—as significant as that is—of the larger "puzzle" of a specific genocide. Many genocidal acts last several years, take place over enormous expanses of land, and involve hundreds of thousands—if not millions—of people. For example, between 1915 and 1919, the Armenian people were persecuted in their villages. Many were driven out into the desert of Syria and Mesopotamia from all across the Ottoman Empire, the primary exceptions being those who lived in Constantinople and Smyrna, where there was a heavy foreign presence. The Soviet manmade famine in Ukraine, which took place between 1932 and 1933, claimed an estimated three to eight million Ukrainians living in an area of some 232,000 square miles. The Holocaust encompassed all of continental Europe, from which Jews, Romani, and others were rounded up, forced into ghettos, and deported to concentration, slave labor, or death camps, where, ultimately, approximately 5.8 million Jews were starved, worked to death, or outright murdered. In 1994, within a period of three short but chaotic months, some 800,000 Tutsi and moderate Hutu were slain by Hutu extremists in Rwanda. The point is that no individual can possibly provide a comprehensive picture of a genocidal act based solely on his or her observations and experiences. Instead, diaries provide uniquely personal views of specific acts occurring within the context of the larger genocidal crimes.

Understandably, diaries written during actual periods of genocide are relatively rare. More common are such first-person accounts as memoirs, interviews, oral histories, and autobiographies that are written or provided in the aftermath of a particular genocidal period. The rarity of on-the-spot, contemporaneous accounts is a result of numerous factors. During an ongoing genocide, individuals are understandably more concerned about securing their own welfare and that of their immediate family than maintaining a record of events; in many cases. During the deportations of entire Armenian communities by the Ottoman authorities, the withering work and horrific conditions in Nazi slave labor camps, and the chaos of the 1994 Rwandan genocide, few of the victims had the opportunity or means to keep such records. In numerous instances of genocide—the Nazi genocide of the Romani being a classic case—the local populace may not be literate, and thus may not be capable of maintaining diaries.

During the 1990s and the early years of the twenty-first century, an ever-increasing number of diaries concerning genocides have been translated and published in English, dramatically adding to the store of such first-hand accounts that have accumulated over the years since World War I. The vast majority of the more recently discovered diaries are being uncovered in different repositories across the globe, such as the Armenian Genocide Museum-Institute in Yerevan, Armenia, and Yad Vashem Martyrs and Heroes Remembrance Authority in Jerusalem. To a lesser extent, some are being discovered by the families of victims or survivors. Such a phenomenon is a direct result of increased scholarly appreciation of the value of such diaries, and the efforts of researchers and victim's advocacy groups to make such works available to other academics and the general public.

A notable diary by a survivor of the Armenian genocide is Vahakn Dadrian's *To the Desert: Pages from My Diary*. Reportedly, Dadrian began his diary on May 24, 1915, in order to document the Ottoman Turks' ill-treatment of the Armenians and to keep track of the rumors then afloat regarding the fate of the Armenians. The members of Dadrian's community, Chorum, were deported to Aleppo and then to Jeresh (Jordan), where they struggled to survive. By the conclusion of World War I, half of Dadrian's family had perished or was murdered as a result of the genocide. In 1919 the surviving members of the family moved to Constantinople, where Dadrian assembled his diary notes for publication. Written in Armenian, the book was first published in 1945 and has only recently been published in English.

Some of the earliest diaries of a genocide were written not by victims or survivors, but by missionaries working in the Ottoman Empire during the Armenian genocide. One of the most informative diaries is *Diaries of a Danish Missionary: Harpoot, 1907–1919*, by Maria Jacobsen. Jacobsen remained in the area thoughout the period of genocide and World War I, and her diary is considered to be one of the more complete records of the Armenian genocide in Turkey. She observed the persecution of Armenians first hand, and attempted to save as many Armenian women and children as she could by pleading with the Ottoman authorities to release them and by providing clandestine assistance.

Another major diary of the Armenian genocide is entitled *Marsovan 1915: The Diaries of Bertha Morely*. Bertha Morely was an American music teacher who resided and worked in Marsovan, and who witnessed the Armenian genocide perpetrated in Marsovan between April and September 1915. In her diary, Morley comments on the arrest of Armenian community leaders and intellectuals in Marsovan, the subsequent deportation of the town's entire Armenian population, and the ultimate death of countless Armenians. She also describes how Armenian property was ransacked and stolen by Ottoman officials, and how Armenian women and children were forced, on the threat of death, to convert to Islam and then taken in by Muslim families, whom they served as anything from slave labor to concubines.

It is worth nothing that the officials of various governments, including the United States, maintained important documentation of the Armenian genocide, but these works were do not qualify as diaries, strictly speaking. Rather, they are narratives that reflect their own experiences, mediated by their role as representatives of other nations. A classic example of this type of work latter is *Ambassador Morgenthau's Story* by Henry Morgenthau, originally published in 1918. This volume is considered by many scholars to be one of the key sources on the Armenian genocide. Another significant work is Viscount Bryce's *The Treatment of the Armenians in the Ottoman Empire, 1915–1916*. This book, although not a diary, provides a massive collection of eyewitness accounts, and was written and published during the period in which the Armenian genocide was still in progress.

The Ukraine famine, is far less documented by diaries. Nonetheless, many first-person testimonies have been collected by the U.S. Commission on the Ukraine Famine, under the directorship of Dr. James Mace. In 1998, commenting in an article for the newspaper, The Day, Mace stated that

[A]s early as 1927 Serhiy Yefremov wrote in his diaries about hundreds of thousands of hungry in Kyiv, about the terrible lines for bread, about over 200,000 Kyivans who had been denied the right to buy bread at all, and about peasant unrest provoked by state grain seizures.

In an article for the Encyclopedia of the Holocaust (1995), Israel Gutman observes that diaries of the Holocaust can be classified into four distinct categories: day-by day records of public events; public diaries; private diaries; and diaries written by teenagers and children. He notes the relative abundance of such records, explaining it as follows:

[E]verybody was writing—journalists, writers, teachers, public figures, the teenagers, and even the children. Mostly they kept diaries, in which they described the tragic events unfolding before their eyes as the personal experiences that they indeed were [experiencing]. . . . Many of the diarists were Jews who were hiding among the Christian population or under their protection (as was the case of Anne Frank).

Many of the diaries and other writings composed during the Holocaust have been lost Even so, a tremendous amount of material has been preserved. In the Warsaw Jewish Historical Institute, which has a large collection of diaries, 272 of them are listed under "diaries," 65 of them from the Warsaw ghetto, in Polish and Yiddish. . . . A relatively large number of important diaries were rescued as part of the Ringelblum Archive. . . . So rich is the Warsaw diary collection in both quantity and quality, regarding the life of the Jews in the ghetto, the structure of the ghetto with its various institutions, and a range of details, that a day-by-day history of the Warsaw ghetto can be reconstructed based on this material alone (p. 272).

Among some of the most remarkable diaries kept during the Holocaust period were those of the *Sonderkommando* who were forced to work in the Auschwitz-Birkenau crematorium. The diaries provide extensive, vivid, and significant commentary on the horror of the death camps and the fate of the Jewish population and others. In addition, they provide significant information about the planning and execution of the *Sonderkommando* uprising in Birkenau. Although *The Diary of Anne Frank* is certainly the most famous diary related to the Holocaust, there are many diaries in English that supply much more in-depth and detailed commentary about a wide variety of issues and concerns, such as Nazi decrees and legislation in Germany, Nazi roundups and murders, and tales of life and death in the ghettos and death camps in Poland. They offer invaluable information to historians and others who seek to understand what transpired during the Holocaust and why it happened. Some of the notable diaries available in English are *A Cup of Tears: A Diary of the Wars Ghetto* by Abraham Lewin; *In the Beginning Was the Ghetto: Notebooks from Lódz* by Oskar Rosenfeld; *The Last Days of the Jerusalem of Lithuania: Chronicles from the Vilna Ghetto and the Camps, 1939–1944* by Herman Kurk; *I Will Bear Witness: A Diary of the Nazi Years* (2 volumes, 1933–1941 and 1942–1945) by Victor Klemperer; *In Those Terrible Days: Notes from the Lódz Ghetto* by Josef Zelkowicz; *The Diary of Dawid Sierakowiak: Five Notebooks from the Lódz Ghetto* edited by Alan Adleson, and *Salvaged Pages: Young Writers' Diaries of the Holocaust* compiled and edited by Alexandra Zapruder. Also worthy of mention is *Lódz Ghetto: Inside a Community under Siege*, a compilation of diaries and notes, assembled and edited by Alan Adelson and Robert Lapides, and *Children in the Holocaust and World War II: Their Secret Diaries*, which contains, in part, excerpts from diaries by children who endured the Holocaust, edited by Laurel Holliday.

Most of the genocides perpetrated in the aftermath of the Holocaust and following the establishment of the United Nations (UN) Convention on the Prevention and Punishment of the Crime of Genocide have not been addressed in diaries, but rather in first-person accounts by journalists, collections of interviews and oral histories by interested historians or survivor groups, and some major autobiographies (especially those related to the Cambodian genocide). Nonetheless, one book, *Zlata's Diary: A Child's Life in Sarajevo*, derives from the 1990s, when genocide was being perpetrated in the former Yugoslavia. Although the diary is not about any specific genocide, it does describe the conflict and war that eventually degenerated, in part, into genocide. Whether any diaries were written during the genocide of the Kurds residing in northern Iraq in 1988, the genocide in Rwanda in 1994, or the genocide perpetrated by the Serbs against the Muslim population in Srebrenica in 1995, is, as yet, unknown.

SEE ALSO Biographies; Memoirs of Perpetrators; Memoirs of Survivors

BIBLIOGRAPHY

Gutman, Israel (1995). "Diaries, Holocaust." In *Encyclopedia of the Holocaust*, ed. Israel Gutman. New York: Macmillan.

Mace, James (1998). "Ukrainian Scholarship." *The Day* November 24:1–9.

Totten, Samuel, ed. (1991). *First-Person Accounts of Genocidal Acts Committed in the Twentieth Century: An Annotated Bibliography*. Westport, Conn.: Greenwood Press.

Samuel Totten

Disabilities, People with

People with disabilities share the experience of stigma, discrimination, and segregation and, as a result, often find themselves denied the basic human rights and fundamental freedoms to work, pursue an education, live where they wish, move freely about society, and generally participate in the lives of their communities. Beyond these human rights infringements, however, lies a darker side to the reality of discrimination against people with disabilities. This includes egregious human

rights abuses such as forced abortion and sterilization, coercive medical intervention and experimentation, selective euthanasia (often excused as "mercy killing") and, finally, in the case of Nazi Germany, massive extermination. The twenty-first century offers some hope for the human rights promise that has thus far gone unfulfilled for people with disabilities, as an international movement of disabled advocates gains momentum and international disability rights standards progressively develop.

Over the last two decades, the global community of people with disabilities has combated the perception that disabled people are objects of pity and charity, or that they are sick people in need of a cure by medical professionals. The goal has been to redefine people with disabilities as full members of society, with important contributions to make to their families and communities. This revised thinking, often called the social model of disability, emphasizes that disabled people are prevented from reaching their full potential not by their disabilities, but rather by the unhealthy and disempowering attitudes and actions of their society. This social perspective is concerned principally with identifying, exposing, and examining the limitations imposed on people with disabilities by the physical and social environments in which they live.

People with Disabilities in Historical Context
Historically, societies have held competing attitudes about disability, making generalizations on the subject difficult. Still, it can be said that pejorative attitudes toward people with disabilities appear across cultures and historical periods.

Evidence supports the contention that children born with disabilities in ancient Greece and Rome were killed (infanticide), although perhaps not as extensively as was once assumed. Spartan law specifically mandated that children born with visible physical disabilities be put to death. During the Middle Ages, there was a pronounced tendency to credit certain disabilities—particularly deafness, epilepsy and mental disabilities—with demonological origin. Attempts to treat disabilities in medieval times reflected then-current beliefs in the curative power of magic and religious rites. At the same time, disability was also viewed as part of the natural order, an expected manifestation of human variation.

After the seventeenth century, developments in the medical sciences and the proliferation of custodial institutions to house people with disabilities led to the segregation and isolation of disabled people from their families, communities, and, more generally, from society. Science was invoked to justify social, economic,

Group portrait of T-4 Euthanasia program personnel at a social gathering. The euthanasia program began by killing disabled infants and toddlers. More facilities had to be created when the program was expanded to include older children and adults in institutions, resulting in six killing centers by 1940.[USHMM, COURTESY OF NATIONAL ARCHIVES.]

and educational barriers that prevented people with disabilities from fully participating in community life. This social segregation reinforced generally held negative attitudes toward disabled people. In the mid-nineteenth century, a highly popular form of entertainment was the freak shows, in which people with disabilities were put on display at circuses, fairs, and exhibitions. In addition to reinforcing notions of disability as abnormal and deviant, such displays constituted a largely untold story of extreme abuse and assaults to human dignity. Indeed, such displays were very often enabled by contractual arrangements granting show organizers the right to display disabled people for the duration of their lives, in according to terms closely akin to slavery. From the social attitudes of this

time came the eugenic agendas that were pursued with enthusiastic abandon by the early twentieth century.

People with Disabilities and the Eugenics Movement

The rise of the eugenics movement in America and Europe during the late nineteenth century led to the specific and widespread targeting of people with disabilities for abuses, and ultimately, to mass murder in Nazi Germany. Theories of race were couched in a biological framework, and appeals to science lent legitimacy to decidedly racist ideologies. Eugenicists warned that the birthrate of the "fit" and "talented" members of society had declined to an alarming extent, whereas less desirable members of society continued to multiply. There was a perception of racial degeneration, and it was feared that medical care for weak or unfit members of the population might compromise optimal human evolution.

In the United States, eugenic theories were applied with vigor, and populations of people with disabilities were primary targets. The infamous Eugenics Record Office (ERO), founded in 1910 at Cold Spring Harbor, New York, furthered eugenicists' goals through flawed and fraudulent research programs. The ERO received a steady stream of funding from notable philanthropists of the time, including John D. Rockefeller, Jr. and Mary Harriman. In 1914, one of the ERO's advisory committees concluded that 10 percent of the American population was defective and should be sterilized. In 1926 the American Eugenics Society (AES) was founded to build broad public support for eugenics, and forced sterilization in particular, and was financed by the Rockefeller Foundation, the Carnegie Institution, and George Eastman of Eastman Kodak, among others. In conjunction with this movement, many doctors began refusing treatment to infants born with disabilities.

The AES campaign largely succeeded in its mission. Among the world's nations, the United States stood at the forefront of forced sterilizations imposed upon disabled persons, particularly people with intellectual disabilities, as bogus studies linked this community to criminality, immoral behavior, and pauperism. Between 1907 and 1939, more than thirty thousand people in twenty-nine states were sterilized during incarceration in prisons or mental institutions. In 1927 the United States Supreme Court placed its imprimatur on forced sterilization in *Buck v. Bell,* where an eight to one majority upheld the constitutionality of the 1924 Virginia Eugenical Sterilization Act. Writing for the majority, Justice Oliver Wendell Holmes, Jr. stated:

> We have seen more than once that the public welfare may call upon the best citizens for their lives. It would be strange if it could not call upon those who already sap the strength of the State for these lesser sacrifices, often not felt to be such by those concerned, in order to prevent our being swamped with incompetence. It is better for all the world, if instead of waiting to execute degenerate offspring for crime, or to let them starve for their imbecility, society can prevent those who are manifestly unfit from continuing their kind. Three generations of imbeciles are enough.

"Racial Hygiene" in Nazi Germany

The appointment of Adolf Hitler as German chancellor in 1933 created the political context for the rapid implementation of eugenic and racial policies. Legal enactments affecting the lives of disabled people and responsive to the eugenics movement were swiftly introduced. The Law for the Prevention of Offspring with Hereditary Diseases was adopted in July 1933, and served as the foundation for successive eugenic and racial policies against Jewish and Roma populations, among others, throughout the Nazi era. This legislation authorized compulsory sterilization for persons found to have any of a broad range of physical and mental disabilities. Estimates suggest that at least 300,000 disabled persons were sterilized under the law prior to the outset of World War II, with an additional 75,000 sterilized soon thereafter.

In October 1935 the Marriage Health Law was introduced to prevent marriage by disabled persons. The law introduced mandatory screening of the entire population, and the issuance of a marriage license required proof that any offspring from the proposed union would not be affected with a disabling hereditary disease. This legislation paved the way for the enactment of similar laws barring marriage between Jews and Germans.

Nazi Targeting of Disabled Children for Extermination

Children with disabilities were targeted for systematic killing under a separate Nazi program that was implemented before the state began the mass murder of disabled adults. The origins of the program have been linked by historians to a 1938 request, by a father, that doctors perform a "mercy killing" on a child born with multiple disabilities—the request was granted by Hitler himself.

In August 1939 Hitler instructed his physicians to appoint a committee to oversee the killing of disabled children in a more systematic fashion. The Reich Committee for Scientific Research of Serious Illness of Hereditary and Protonic Origin was established, and it issued a decree mandating that all newborns and infants under three years of age born with suspected "hereditary diseases" (including, among others, Down's syndrome, deafness, blindness, paralysis, and congenital physical disabilities) be reported to a committee. Doctors were required to answer detailed questionnaires about quality of life and submit their results to the committee. Those selected by the committee for killing were transferred to one of twenty-eight official institutions, usually the wing of a regular hospital and among them some of Germany's finest hospitals.

A variety of particularly horrific killing methods were used to eliminate these patients, including mas-

In 1933 the German Ministry of Justice proposed legislation authorizing physicians to grant "mercy deaths" in order to "end the tortures of incurable patients, upon request, in the interests of true humanity." The legislation was never formally enacted, yet its objectives—not euthanasia but the mass killing of people with mental and physical disabilities—were implemented in the form of a program known as Operation T-4, a reference to the address of its headquarters in Berlin: Tiergartenstrasse 4.

Under the top-secret T-4 program, patients in all government- and church-run sanatoria or nursing homes with a wide range of physical, sensory, and mental disabilities perceived to be hereditary in nature were targeted for extermination. Included were those with blindness, deafness, epilepsy, intellectual disabilities, autism, depression, bipolar disorder, mobility impairments, or congenital disabilities. The pool of victims later expanded to include sick residents of poorhouses and old-age homes.

Under the T-4 program by mandate, the Interior Ministry collected data from institutions about the health and capacity for work of all patients. Expert assessors, including psychiatrists, served in review commissions that evaluated completed forms. Forms were marked "+" in red for those designated for death, "−" in blue for those designated to live, and "?" for cases requiring additional review.

Six major sites existed where people with disabilities were killed under the T-4 program, of which Hadamar was the most notorious. At the Hadamar euthanasia center, authorities would issue death notices following mass executions of people with disabilities, with newspaper obituary columns stating the date and place of death. After the killing of its ten thousandth victim in 1941, the hospital staff at Hadamar held a celebration complete with a polka band, words of praise for the important work accomplished under the program, and a celebratory corpse burning, garnished with fresh flowers and small flags emblazoned with swastikas.

The T-4 program served as a testing ground for the Nazi killing machine. At the outset T-4 victims were killed by lethal injection, but they soon became the first victims of an experimental gas chamber at Brandenberg Prison. In a test run in January 1940, patients diagnosed with mental disabilities were gassed to death in an experiment intended to show the effectiveness of poison gas over other methods of killing. Nazi techniques of outfitting killing chambers with false showerheads and bathroom tiling were developed under the T-4 program.

The secrecy of the program became compromised on account of mistakes made by officials and because of the sheer scope of the program, which made it impossible to conceal from the public. The Third Reich officially halted T-4 in August 1941, after some seventy thousand disabled people had been killed. This halt related only to the official operation of killing centers and use of poison gas. The mass killing of people with disabilities continued through the end of World War II, in institutions as well as concentration camps.

In October 1945 the U.S. Military Commission considered the case of seven former staff members at Hadamar. They were tried for violations of international law for their role in the killing of over four hundred mentally disabled Polish and Soviet nationals. All accused in the Hadamar case were found guilty: Three were sentenced to death and summarily executed, one was sentenced to life imprisonment, and three served lengthy prison terms.

sive lethal injection to the heart, poison administrated over an extended period of time, gassing with cyanide or chemical warfare agents, starvation, and exposure. The latter two methods were sometimes selected so that doctors could attribute the death to natural causes or to routine illness such as pneumonia. The program soon expanded, in the manner of other Nazi killing programs. In time, medical officials were asked to register all minor children with disabilities up to the age of seventeen. Estimates suggest that at least 5,000 disabled children were killed under the euthanasia program during World War II.

Forced Labor Programs and Medical Experimentation

Although the Nazis characterized people with disabilities as a burden on society without productive use, large numbers of disabled people were nonetheless subjected to forced labor in concentration camps, institutions, and elsewhere. Survivors were interviewed for a 2000 report by Disability Advocates, an American disability rights organization, as a part of a project to uncover and expose human rights abuses against disabled people during World War II. These witnesses described a wide array of abuses, including the threat made to factory laborers who sewed uniforms, that they would be sent to a concentration camp if they broke five needles. One such survivor, whose disability was a degree of hearing loss, reported the fierce pressure of enduring many more months of labor after having already broken four needles.

Disabled people were also subjected to horrific medical experiments during the Nazi era. On December 9, 1946, an American military tribunal opened criminal proceedings against twenty-three leading German physicians and administrators for their willing participation in these experiments, which were classified by the tribunal as war crimes and crimes against humanity. Sixteen of the accused were found guilty, and seven were sentenced to death.

Legal Implications of Nazi Persecution against People with Disabilities

In order to assess whether abuses against disabled people in Nazi Germany constituted the modern crime of genocide, it is first necessary to determine whether that law applies to disabled people as a protected group. A cursory examination of the definition of genocide suggests that it does not. Genocide, as defined in Article 2 of the Genocide Convention, is premised upon the intent to destroy, in whole or in part, a national, ethnic, racial, or religious group. Disabled persons would not fall within the parameters of a national or religious group, defined under international law, respectively as a group with a legal bond grounded in citizenship, or as a group sharing a common religious denomination or mode of worship. Nor would the majority of the disabled community appear to fall within the meaning of the term *ethnic group*, whose members share a common language or culture, although the German deaf community could indeed be considered an ethnic group so defined.

Significantly, in 1998, in the *Akayesu* case, the International Tribunal for Rwanda defined *racial group* as a stable and permanent group "based on the hereditary and physical traits often identified with a geographical region, irrespective of linguistics, cultural, national, or religious factors." The racial hygiene policies of Nazi Germany that targeted people with disabilities were based explicitly on an imagined threat to the national "germ plasm." Physical traits—whether real or perceived—were employed as distinguishing factors for the Nazi policy. The thinking, grounded in bogus scientific findings by some of the most respected scientists of the time, assumed that hereditary deafness and blindness, congenital physical disabilities, and mental disability represented direct threats to the racial health of the nation and to the mythic construction of a racial-

ly pure and strong people. The "intent to destroy in whole or in part," which is a core component of the legal definition of genocide, was made explicit in Nazi policies.

Forced sterilization and extermination programs targeting people with disabilities were thus directly related to the racist Nazi effort to "purify" and "cleanse" the nation. Accordingly, the Nazi "racial" policies would indeed appear to fall within the definition of racial group as understood in the *Akayesu* case. Significantly, the court in that case approached the definition of *ethnic group* not by reference to any universally accepted understanding, rather, it relied upon the usage of the term by the Rwandan people.

Even assuming that people with disabilities cannot be considered a "racial group" under the law of genocide, the tribunal recognized in the *Akayesu* case that genocide can indeed occur without meeting the definition of any of the four groups expressly protected, provided the group in question is a "permanent and stable group." This would appear to apply in relation to the atrocities against disabled persons in Nazi Germany. Notably, the Nazis had an array of classifications and registrations according to which disabled people were subjected. While the classification systems were ever expanding under the system, the subjective test remained constant—a group defined by a real or imagined hereditary characteristic linked to a mental, physical, or sensory disability—and was tied to the relentless pursuit of racial hygiene.

Linking the specific acts carried out against disabled people by the Nazis to genocidal acts as defined by the law of genocide is relatively straightforward. The systematic mass sterilizations of disabled people fall within one of the specifically prohibited acts under the Genocide Convention: "[i]mposing measures intended to prevent births within the group." The mass exterminations of disabled children and adults under the euthanasia programs clearly constitute killing members of the group. Medical experimentation, exploitative labor practices, and the appalling conditions in institutions, among other abuses, constitute "causing serious bodily or mental harm."

Finally, separate and distinct contraventions of international law apply to the atrocities against disabled people in Nazi Germany, including crimes against humanity. As defined in Article 7 of the Statute of the International Criminal Court, certain acts committed as part of a widespread, systematic attack directed against any civilian population, with knowledge of the attack, constitute crimes against humanity, including, among others, murder, extermination, severe deprivation of physical liberty, and enforced sterilization.

Modern Manifestations

Widespread abuses against people with disabilities are by no means confined to the Nazi era. Indeed, many of the attitudes and prejudices that fueled the Nazi mass murder against the disabled persist today, reflected in laws and policies that reinforce stereotypical perceptions of people with disabilities as passive, sick, dependent, in need of medical cure and charity, and, in the case of people with mental disabilities, dangerous. Such attitudes, while they have not led to the large-scale genocidal persecutions of the Nazis, have nonetheless supported a devaluing of the lives of people with disabilities that has real currency in an age of genetic engineering and renewed debate surrounding the "mercy killings" of disabled people.

While international humanitarian law and international human rights law are fully applicable to people with disabilities, massive human rights abuses experienced by this community remain largely unaddressed. People with disabilities are subjected to a variety of abuses, including forced abortion and sterilization. The February 2000 U.S. State Department Human Rights Report indicates that in 1997, the government of Japan acknowledged that some 16,500 disabled women were sterilized without their consent between 1949 and 1992. (Japan has denied compensation to the victims.) In *Mad in America*, Robert Whitaker details decades of electroshock "treatment," forced brain damaging surgery, and the coercive drugging of people with mental disabilities. In institutional settings, physical and mental abuses and gross neglect endangering the lives of people with disabilities are widespread. Reports issued by Mental Disability Rights International on conditions for people with mental disabilities warehoused in dismal and dangerous institutions detail unhygienic conditions of detention; excessive use of physical restraints; lack of adequate food, water, clothing, and medical care; and other life-threatening conditions, including instances of patients freezing to death.

Genocidal policies pursued relentlessly against people with disabilities in Nazi Germany are part of a long and persistent pattern of human rights abuses. Efforts by disability advocates to expose continuing discrimination and abuse, some of which may indeed amount to crimes against humanity, along with improved awareness about people with disabilities and law and policy reform at the national, regional, and international level, are of critical importance to the lives of some 600,000 disabled persons worldwide.

SEE ALSO Eugenics; Euthanasia; Germany; Medical Experimentation

BIBLIOGRAPHY

Biesold, Horst (1999). *Crying Hands: Eugenics and Deaf People in Nazi Germany.* Washington, D.C.: Gallaudet University Press.

Braddock, David L., and Susan L. Parish (2001). "An Institutional History of Disability." In *Handbook of Disability Studies,* eds. Gary L. Albrecht, Katherine D. Seelman, and Michael Bury. Thousand Oaks, Calif.: Sage Publications.

Burleigh, Michael (1994). *Death and Deliverance: "Euthanasia" in Germany c. 1900–1945.* Cambridge: Cambridge University Press.

Disability Rights Advocates. (2000). *Forgotten Crimes: The Holocaust and People with Disabilties.* Oakland, Calif.: Disability Rights Advocates. Available from: http://www.dralegal.org/publications.

Gallagher, Hugh Gregory (1995). *By Trust Betrayed: Patients, Physicians, and the License to Kill in the Third Reich.* Arlington, Va.: Vandamere Press.

Hinton, Alexander Laban, ed. (2002). *Annihilating Difference: The Anthropology of Genocide.* Berkeley: University of California Press.

Lord, Janet E. (2002). *A White Paper: Understanding the Role of an International Convention on the Human Rights of People with Disabilities,* Washington, D.C.: National Council on Disability.

The Medical Case, Trials of War Criminals before the Nuremberg Military Tribunals, Vol. 1, Nuremberg, October 1946–April 1949. Washington D.C.: U.S. G.P.O, 1949–1953.

Mental Disability Rights International (1997). *Human Rights and Mental Health: Hungary.* Washington, D.C: MDRI. Available from: http://www.mdri.org.

Mental Disability Rights International (1999). *Children in Russia's Institutions: Human Rights and Opportunities for Reform.* Washington, D.C.: MDRI. Available from: http://www.mdri.org.

Mental Disability Rights International (2000). *Human Rights & Mental Health: Mexico.* Washington, D.C.: MDRI. Available from: http://www.mdri.org.

Proctor, Robert (1988). *Racial Hygiene: Medicine under the Nazis.* Cambridge, Mass: Harvard University Press.

Whitaker, Robert (2002). *Mad in America: Bad Science, Bad Medicine and the Enduring Mistretament of the Mentally Ill.* Cambridge, Mass.: Perseus Publishing.

CASE LAW

Buck v. Bell 274 U.S. 200 (1927).

Prosecutor v. Jean-Paul Akayesu. 1998. Case No. ICTR 96-4-T (September 2).

Trial of Alfons Klein and Six Others (Hadamar Trial), Trials of War Criminals before the Nuremberg Military Tribunals under Control Council Law No. 10. Vol. 1, Nuremberg, October 1946–April 1949. Washington D.C.: U.S. G.P.O, 1949–1953.

Janet E. Lord

Mothers and other relatives of the missing stage a demonstration near the Plaza de Mayo in Buenos Aires, 1982. A 1976 coup in Argentina resulted in a seven-year military dictatorship, during which an estimated 30,000 people "disappeared." [HORACIO VILLALOBOS/ CORBIS]

Disappearances

Enforced disappearances constitute a set of particularly invidious violations of human rights, not only for the victims, who are deprived of their liberty, frequently tortured, and in fear for their lives, but also for their families and friends, who are left in ignorance regarding the fate of their disappeared loved one. The Universal Declaration of Human Rights outlaws the practice, as do the two UN Covenants: the Covenant on Civil and Political Rights and the Covenant on Economic, Social, and Cultural Rights. Other international human rights instruments take up the issue of enforced disappearances, as well.

Historical Background and International and Regional Reaction

Human rights groups are said to have first coined the term "disappeared" ("desaparecido") in 1966, referring to the victims of secret governmental crackdowns on political dissidents in Guatemala. Thousands of cases of disappearances were reported in the 1970s, primarily but by no means only from Central and Latin American

countries. In response, the UN General Assembly adopted Resolution 33/173, entitled "disappeared persons," on December 20, 1978. In it, the General Assembly voiced concern over reports of enforced or involuntary disappearances from many countries. The disappearances were alleged to be the a result of unlawful actions and violence, and of excesses committed by law enforcement officials or security forces, and it was claimed that they often occurred while the persons were detained or imprisoned. The resolution further expressed concern over reports of difficulties in obtaining reliable information from the competent authorities about the situation of such persons, including reports of the persistent refusal of such authorities or organizations to account for such persons or even to acknowledge that they held such persons in their custody.

Regional organizations were similarly faced with the issue of disappearances. In October 1979 the General Assembly of the Organization of American States (OAS), at its ninth regular session, declared that the phenomenon of disappearances was a stain on the conscience of the hemisphere and contrary to traditional

A forensic anthropologist exhumes the remains of one victim of Argentina's dirty war. [HORACIO VILLALOBOS/CORBIS]

values and the declarations and agreements signed by the American States. A similar resolution was passed by the OAS General Assembly in November 1980.

In Europe, the Committee of Ministers of the Council of Europe adopted Recommendation No. R(79)6 on April 20, 1979, concerning the search for missing persons. On July 11, 1980, the European Parliament adopted a resolution on a report of enforced or involuntary disappearances in which the Parliament made an urgent appeal that everything possible be done to trace all persons reported as missing.

Definitional Issues and Rights Violated by the Practice of Disappearances

By resolution No.43/133 of December 18, 1992, the UN General Assembly adopted the Declaration on the Protection of All Persons From Enforced Disappearance. The preamble of the declaration sets forth the conditions defining an enforced disappearance:

> [P]ersons are arrested, detained, and abducted against their will or otherwise deprived of their liberty by officials or different branches or levels of Government, or by organized groups, or private individuals acting on behalf of, or with the

support, direct or indirect, consent, or acquiescence of the Government, followed by a refusal to disclose the fate or whereabouts of the person concerned or a refusal to acknowledge the deprivation of their liberty, which places such persons outside the protection of the law.

Article 7 of the Rome Statute of the International Criminal Court (ICC) reiterates these definitional elements and adds to them by specifically referring to the intention of the perpetrators to remove the disappeared persons from the protection of the law for a prolonged period of time. Article 2 of the Inter-American Convention on Forced Disappearance of Persons, adopted in Brazil in September 1994 and in force since March 28, 1996, adds the further stipulation that the disappearance of a person impedes the victim's "recourse to the applicable legal remedies and procedural guarantees."

Pursuant to article 1, paragraph 2, of the UN Declaration, any act of disappearance constitutes a violation of the rules of international law which guarantee, among other things, the individual's right to recognition as a person before the law, his or her right to liberty and security of their person, and the right not to be subjected to torture and other cruel, inhuman, or degrading treatment or punishment. It further frequently violates or constitutes a grave threat to the right to life. Some of the most fundamental principles enshrined in the Universal Declaration of Human Rights have been further spelled out in General Comments, which were adopted by the UN Working Group on Enforced and Involuntary Disappearances.

In addition, the preamble of the UN Declaration also notes that disappearances may entail violations of the UN Standard Minimum Rules for the Treatment of Prisoners (adopted in 1957), the Code of Conduct for Law Enforcement Officials (1979), and the Body of Principles for the Protection of All Persons under Any Form of Detention or Imprisonment (1988).

Characterizing Disappearances as a Crime against Humanity

The fourth preambular paragraph of the Declaration on the Protection of All Persons from Enforced Disappearance clearly states that the systematic practice of disappearances "is of the nature of a crime against humanity." The Rome Statute of the International Criminal Court (ICC), also expressly states that the practice of enforced disappearances constitutes a crime against humanity. Because of this, when disappearances occur on a large scale, such as in Argentina under military rule until 1983, in Sri Lanka during the armed conflict between the government and the Liberation Tigers of Tamil Eelam (LTTE) during the 1980s and 1990s, or in the former Yugoslavia in the early 1990s, it is in principle possible to prosecute the principal perpetrators on charges of crimes against humanity.

A Belgian law adopted in June 1993 established universal jurisdiction for the prosecution of war crimes and crimes against humanity. Prosecutors in Spain have invoked this law to initiate judicial investigations against several individuals, including former Chilean president Augusto Pinochet and other heads of state. Four individuals were convicted under this law by the Brussels Assises Court in April 2001 for their participation in the genocide in Rwanda. This conviction has prompted others to attempt to bring charges against acting or former heads of state. Even though this law was replaced in August 2003 with new legislation that severely limited the instances in which Belgian tribunals may assert universal jurisdiction, forced disappearances is nonetheless still recognized as a crime against humanity.

In contrast, a case brought against former Chadian president, Hissène Habré, was dismissed by the Senegalese Court of Cassation in a judgment dated March 20, 2001. The court held that no procedure confers universal jurisdiction upon Senegalese tribunals that would allow them to prosecute and judge foreigners under Senegalese jurisdiction for acts committed outside Senegal. The ICC, however, may be expected to prosecute disappearances where such acts are committed as part of a widespread or systematic attack against a civilian population.

Monitoring Mechanisms and Bodies

In Resolution No. 33/173, the General Assembly requested the UN Commission on Human Rights to consider the issue of disappearances. On February 29, 1980, the Commission passed Resolution 20 (XXXVI) and established a working group "consisting of five of its members, to serve as experts in their individual capacities, to examine questions relevant to enforced or involuntary disappearances of persons." The group was given a five-year mandate, and was the first mechanism established within the UN human rights program to specifically deal with flagrant and consistent human rights violations occurring on a global scale. Since 1980, the mandate of the Working Group has been renewed consistently every three years.

Since its creation, the Working Group has dealt with over 50,000 cases reported from more than seventy countries, but despite the group's best efforts, some 42,000 cases remain outstanding. The mandate of the group is primarily humanitarian in nature, and its working methods are designed to help it meet its main objective: to assist families in ascertaining the fate and the location of missing relatives who have been deprived of the protection of the law. The group seeks to establish channels of communication between the families and the governments concerned. Whenever appropriately documented and clearly identified cases are brought to the group's attention, it tries to ensure that these cases are investigated by the relevant government, with the ultimate goal of discovering the location of the missing person.

The group meets three times annually and reports on its activities to the Commission on Human Rights. For its part, the Commission has urged governments to take steps to protect the families of disappeared persons against any intimidation or ill-treatment to which they might be subjected. It has also asked these governments to give serious consideration to inviting the Working Group into their country for a visit. Since 1982, the working group has conducted a total of thirteen missions to ten countries.

The Human Rights Committee was established under Article 28 of the International Covenant on Civil and Political Rights (ICCPR). Among its other duties it regularly examines issues pertaining to disappearances. These may take the form of individual complaints that have been submitted for consideration, or they may arise from reports submitted by member states. If it determines that a country may have failed to thoroughly investigate charges of disappearances, or that it has neglected its duty to bring the responsible parties to justice, the Committee makes reference to these concerns. It has done so on several occasions in recent years, for example in its concluding observations on the periodic reports of Guatemala and Sri Lanka. In addition, it has held that the prohibitions against unacknowledged detentions (one of the principal root causes for disappearances), hostage taking, and abductions are absolute and cannot be annulled, not even during a state of emergency. The Inter-American Convention similarly outlaws the practice of forced disappearances in all circumstances, even during an emergency.

In addition to the UN Working Group and the Human Rights Committee, there is one other agency that is authorized to deal with and monitor cases of missing and disappeared persons. This is the International Committee of the Red Cross, which is granted such authority in situations of international armed conflict, by the Geneva Conventions of 1949 and their 1977 Protocols.

Selected Jurisprudence

The Human Rights Committee has dealt with a number of complaints involving enforced disappearances. In the 1981 case of *Elena Quinteros v. Uruguay*, the complainant's daughter was arrested by members of the military and held incommunicado. Later, she managed to elude her captors and to enter the grounds of the Venezuelan embassy in Montevideo, but was abducted from there by Uruguayan police officers. Although the Committee failed to determine her subsequent whereabouts, it did find that the Uruguayan authorities were in violation of the ICCPR on several counts, although the specific definition of forced disappearance was not invoked.

The 1991 case of *Barbarin Mojica v. Dominican Republic* provides another example of the Committee's work. In this case the son of a well-known Dominican labor leader was last seen by his family on May 5, 1990. The missing man had been receiving death threats in the weeks prior to his disappearance. Witnesses testified that they had seen him board a taxi in which other unidentified men were traveling. His father repeatedly asked the authorities to open an investigation into his son's disappearance, but his requests were ignored. The Committee found that the Dominican authorities were in violation of the ICCPR. What is interesting in this case is that although there was no specific allegation of torture of the disappeared, the Committee nonetheless felt justified in concluding that "the disappearance of persons is inseparably linked to" such treatment.

In 1996 the Committee decided the case of *Ana Celis Laureano v. Peru.* Here, the petitioner reported that his granddaughter had been abducted in Huaura province by unknown armed men, presumed to be members of the Shining Path movement. Several months later, the granddaughter was released, only to be picked up by the Peruvian military on suspicion of collaboration with the Shining Path. The military held the young woman incommunicado. A a judge ordered her release on the ground that she was a minor, and she was returned to the care of her grandfather. She was abducted again, and this time her grandfather could not discover where she was being kept. Upon investigating her disappearance, a civil court judge concluded that military or special police units were responsible for her disappearance, and found these bodies to be in violation of several articles of the Covenant on Civil and Political Rights. Once again, however, the specific definitional language of forced disappearances was not invoked.

The case of *Sarma v. Sri Lanka,* decided in 2003, is the first in which the specific legal definition of forced disappearance was explicitly invoked by the Committee. In this case the complainant, his son, and other individuals were taken from their family home by army officers in the presence of several witnesses. The complainant's son, suspected of membership in the Tamil Tigers, was later transferred to an army camp, while the complainant (Sarma) and others were released. Sarma then made several attempts to locate his son and to secure his release, but was frustrated on both counts. Upon investigation of the case, the Committee found the Sri Lankan authorities guilty of several violations contained under the general rubric of forced disappearances.

Over the years, the Committee has become more and more specific in its recommendations on appropriate remedies in disappearance cases. Thus, in the last-mentioned case, the Committee urges Sri Lanka to "expedite the current criminal proceedings and ensure the prompt trial of all persons responsible for the abduction of the [complainant's] son under Section 365 of the Sri Lankan Penal Code." This tendency toward greater specificity indicates the Committee's determination that all countries party to the ICCPR recognize the need for rigorous investigation whenever disappearance has been formally alleged, and that they honor their obligation to provide effective remedies to the victims.

The Inter-American Court of Human Rights has also dealt with the issue of unacknowledged and incommunicado detention. In January 1987, it delivered an Advisory Opinion on the right to habeas corpus in Emergency Situations, in which it held that the legal remedies guaranteed under to victims of forced disappearance—including the right to habeas corpus—are absolute and may not be suspended. The court was prompted to render this decision at the request of the Inter-American Commission, which was troubled by the tendency of several Latin American countries to enact special laws in order to provide legal cover for their practice of holding detainees in incommunicado custody for prolonged period of times. The court's opinion rendered such all such special laws invalid, so that they could no longer be asserted as a defense against a charge of forced disappearance.

Duty to Investigate and to Provide Effective Judicial Remedies

In resolution 33/173, the UN General Assembly calls upon member states to conduct rapid and impartial investigations into cases of enforced or involuntary disappearances, and to ensure that law enforcement and security authorities are held fully accountable in the discharge of their functions. Article 3 of the Disappearances Declaration further stipulates that each state "shall take effective legislative, administrative, judicial, or other measures to prevent and terminate acts of enforced disappearance in any territory under its jurisdiction." The declaration asserts that acts of enforced disappearance "shall be offenses under criminal law punishable by appropriate penalties." Similarly the Human Rights Committee notes that "States should establish effective facilities and procedures to investigate thoroughly cases of missing and disappeared persons in circumstances which may involve a violation of the right to life." It is unfortunately the case that few countries have taken steps to incorporate the principles embodied in the Disappearances Declaration into their domestic legislation. The Working Group on Enforced or Involuntary Disappearances has consistently emphasized that the obligation to implement the Declaration applies to all states, not only to those in which disappearances actually have occurred or continue to occur.

The Working Group has noted that the presumption of impunity has been the major reason behind the continued practice of forced disappearance. In its report to the Commission on Human Rights in 2002, the Group stressed the importance of bringing perpetrators to justice. This is a difficult challenge to meet, for in many countries with a high incidence of cases of disappearances, such as Iraq, Algeria, and Guatemala, the absence of specific legislation and/or the unwillingness or inability of the authorities to properly investigate disappearances or prosecute the perpetrators remains a serious problem. So does the tendency of some countries to grant amnesty to the perpetrators of acts of disappearance and torture, in the name of national reconciliation, because such amnesty helps to reinforce the idea that perpetrators can commit these crimes with impunity.

Several countries have passed specific legislation to assist national authorities in successfully investigating and prosecuting acts of disappearances. Among these success stories is Argentina. In October 2000 the Human Rights Committee welcomed the criminal prosecution and conviction of several former high-ranking Argentinian military officers who had been accused of acts of disappearance and torture.

Argentina has taken a number of other steps to ameliorate the damage done by the practice of forced disappearances. It has set up a mechanism to facilitate the identification of children who had been taken by force from their parents, when it became clear that the parents had disappeared. It has passed legislation that gives constitutional rank to the Inter-American Convention on Forced Disappearance of Persons. The Argentinian Constitution of 1994 introduces forced disappearance as a ground for habeas corpus proceedings. Mindful of the disappearances that occurred during the military regime in the 1970s and 1980s, the government signed into law an act that offers compensation to the survivors of certain victims of forced disappearance and of those who had died as a result of action by the armed forces, security forces, or any paramilitary group prior to December 1983. The law was passed in 1994, and in June 1995 a second law was passed that extended the time limit for submitting benefit applications by five years.

The government of Sri Lanka has also attempted to come to grips with the large number of disappearances resulting from the armed conflict. Three regional Presidential Commissions of Inquiry into Involuntary Removal or Disappearance of Persons were set up in November 1994. Over the next three years they investigated more than 27,500 complaints and found evidence of forced disappearance in 16,742 of them. On September 3, 1997, they submitted their reports to the Sri Lankan president.

While the commissions conducted their investigations, the Sri Lankan Parliament enacted the Human Rights Commission of Sri Lanka Act of August 1996. The National Human Rights Commission is entrusted with many human rights tasks. It investigates complaints about disappearances and conducts surprise visits to police stations and detention centers. In May 1999, the government established a special unit charged with computerizing lists of all reported cases of disappearances, in an effort to facilitate investigations. These computerized lists, together with the enactment of new legislation, have greatly expedited the process of issuing death certificates in respect to missing persons who are presumed dead. Between 1995 and 1999, some 15,000 death certificates were issued, permitting more than 12,000 families to receive compensation from the government for their loss.

The Sri Lanka Criminal Code includes the abduction of persons as a criminal offense. However, the Human Rights Committee has noted after examining a report submitted by Sri Lanka that this is a difficult charge to prove. The majority of prosecutions initiated against members of the armed forces on charges of abduction and unlawful confinement have been inconclusive because of the lack of satisfactory evidence and unavailability of witnesses, and only very few police or army officers have been found guilty and punished.

Toward a Binding New Instrument

In spite of the existing international instruments and mechanisms in place to deal with the practice of disappearances, the UN Sub-Commission on Protection and Promotion of Human Rights submitted a Draft Convention on Disappearance to its parent body, the Commission on Human Rights, in 1999. The aim of the drafters was to further strengthen legal protections for all persons threatened with enforced disappearance. Comments on the draft were solicited from member nations, intergovernmental institutions, and nongovernmental institutions operating in the international arena. These comments were published in 2001.

Publication of the draft and its comments was followed in January 2003 by the formation of a working group of the Commission on Human Rights. The group was charged with the task of determining what new legal instrument might be needed, what provisions should be included in it, and how to best monitor its application. In January of 2004, the group held its second meeting, during which a number of unresolved and contentious issues emerged.

For instance, many states wanted to entrust the monitoring functions to the Human Rights Committee or a special chamber thereof. Discussion also centered on the mechanics of monitoring, with some states recommending that the monitoring agency be granted fact-finding capabilities and perhaps periodic country visits by the Committee's special chamber. Participants in the meeting were clear that the new monitoring agency should not adversely affect the role of the UN Working Group on Enforced and Involuntary Disappearances.

The inclusion of enforced disappearances as a crime against humanity was another well-debated issue. Many states favor a prominent reference in the Preamble of the new instrument to enforced disappearances that occur on a massive or systematic scale as a crime against humanity, using the definition of such crimes that has been established by the Rome Statute of the International Criminal Court. Other states prefer a separate provision stipulating that disappearances committed in a massive or systematic manner constitute a crime against humanity and carry consequences in accordance with international law. The specific wording of the definition of enforced disappearances was also subject to debate, as was the question as to whether there should be any statute of limitations applied to the crime. Also unresolved was the exact nature of the obligations of each state to enact domestic legislation that incorporates the crime of enforced disappearance, the propriety of granting amnesty or pardons to perpetrators of this crime, and the designation of jurisdictions in which crimes of force disappearances might most competently be prosecuted. Finally, the group debated what might be appropriate preventive measures that could be taken by states to reduce the incidence of this crime.

SEE ALSO Argentina; Chile; United Nations Commission on Human Rights; United Nations General Assembly

BIBLIOGRAPHY

Buerganthal, Thomas, and Dinah Shelton (1995). *Protecting Human Rights in the Americas: Cases and Materials,* 4th revised edition. Arlington, Va.: N.P. Engel.

Commission on Human Rights, 57th session (2001). *Question of enforced or involuntary disappearances: Note by the Secretariat.* Document E/CN.4/2001/69 and Add.1.

Guest, Iain (1990). *Behind the Disappearances.* Philadelphia: University of Pennsylvania Press.

Nowak, Manfred (2000). "Individual Complaints before the Human Rights Commission for Bosnia and Herzegovina." In *International Human Rights Monitoring Mechanisms, Essays in Honour of Jakob Th. Möller,* ed. Gudmundur Alfredsson. Cambridge, Mass: Martinus Nijhoff Publishers.

Office of the UN High Commissioner for Human Rights (1997). *Enforced or Involuntary Disappearances.* Fact Sheet No.6 (Second Revision).

La historia oficial (The Official Story) (1985). Directed by Luis Pvenzo. Distributed by Fox Lorber.

UN Working Group on Enforced or Involuntary Disappearances (January 26, 1981). *Question of Human Rights of All Persons subjected to any form of Detention or Imprisonment, in Particular: Question of Missing and Disappeared Persons.* Document E/CN.4/1435.

UN Working Group on Enforced or Involuntary Disapearances (December 21, 1999). Report on the visit to Sri Lanka, October 1999. Document E/CN.4/2000/64/Add.1.

Markus Schmidt

Doctors see Disabilities, People with; Eugenics; Euthanasia; Physicians.

Documentation

Genocide is not created or perpetrated in a vacuum. It is generally preceded by key decisions and acts and the plan for its conduct is usually mapped out ahead of time, whether in fits or starts or as a well-orchestrated process. Many perpetrators have left revealing and detailed documents that delineate—some extremely clearly, others not so clearly or under the cover of euphemism—the genesis and evolution of a genocidal process.

German Genocide of Hereros in Southwest Africa

In 1904 German military and government officials documented all aspects of the uprising of the Hereros of southwestern Africa and the colonial reaction to the uprising, including genocidal actions against the Hereros. *Die Kämpfe der deutschen Truppen in Südwesafrika,* published in 1907, is considered to be the "major source for the military operations of the Germans. [It] is based on official materials and was written by the Ministry History Section of the German General Staff" (Bridgman, 1981, p. 175). The General Staff produced and submitted fairly regular reports on the war to the German government, which were printed as appendices to the Reichstag debates over actions in Southwest Africa. The German Colonial Office also published a weekly magazine, *Deutsches Koloniablatt,* which included an overview of what was taking place under German rule, particularly as it pertained to the Hereros and other oppressed groups.

Ottoman Turk Genocide of the Armenians

The Ottoman Turks produced ample records (primarily directives, memoranda, and telegrams) of their plans and actions vis-à-vis the Armenian genocide. Most of the documents were riddled with intentional euphemisms (e.g., the use of the term *deportation* served as a code for "massacre" or "destruction"). Telegrams containing specifics about the genocide were burned immediately after they were read, by direct orders from the Central Committee of the Young Turks' Ittihad party government. Furthermore, fearful of prosecution and "drastic retributive justice" at the conclusion of World War I, the perpetrators destroyed "batches of state and party documents" (Dadrian, 1991, p. 86, 87). The obliteration of the vast bulk of the records produced and maintained by the Young Turks Central Committee, destruction of personal documents by the three key leaders of the Ittihad (Talat, Enver, and Cemal), and "the burning of all the evidence of the activities of the Special Organization," gutted the invaluable paper trail (Dadrian, 1999, p. 93).

Vahakn N. Dadrian, an expert on the Armenian genocide and the documentation of the Armenian genocide in Turkish sources, reported in 1999 that:

> Nevertheless, a host of high-ranking officials supplied first-hand evidence in the course of a series of court-martial proceedings instituted in the 1918–1920 Armistice period by successive Ottoman governments anxious to exact punishment from the perpetrators involved. However exercised and reluctant, these officials in various forms of testimony grudgingly admitted to a scheme of deportation, the covert intent and end-result of which was the actual destruction of the masses of the deportees. Another group of Turks, most former military commanders and civil officials, recounted their relevant observations and knowledge through memoirs (p. 87).

Key information was gleaned from various Turkish documents that survived, and is now contained in the archives of the Turkish Military Tribunal, among other sources. The documents were used in the few prosecutions that took place. The Fifth Committee of the Ottoman Chapter of Deputies interrogated and deposed ministers who had served in the wartime government, and among those interrogated were two *Seyhulislams* (highest ranking religious official in the Ottoman Empire). During the months from October to December of 1918, the subject of the genocide was taken up in debates within the Turkish parliament.

The most voluminous and accurate information available on the Ottoman Turk genocide of the Armenians is located in the reports and archives of the German and United States governments. Dadrian asserts, "In terms of reliability and verifiability, no other single source may compare to the critical importance of official German records on the Armenian Genocide in documenting the capital crime of the genocide" (1999, p. 90). Beginning in mid-June 1915, reports of German consuls throughout the Ottoman Empire began to awaken the German government to the reality of what was taking place on the ground. A mountainous pile of German reports detailed the deportations, the looting of Armenian property, and the killing of Armenian civilians.

As for the information and documentation collected by the U.S. government within and during the Armenian genocide, the United States National Archives and Library of Congress now contains a microfiche set of 37,000 pages of documentation. Compiled and edited in the 1990s by Rouben Adalian, Director of the Armenian National Institute in Washington, D.C., the collection contains approximately 4,500 documents that were located in official U.S. archives. The collection is accompanied by a 475-page *Guide* that Adalian developed.

Nazi-Perpetrated Genocide of Mentally and Physically Handicapped, Jews, and Gypsies

The German leaders of the Third Reich and the perpetrators of the Holocaust kept meticulously detailed and voluminous records of all aspects of the events leading up to and culminating in the Holocaust (1933–1945). The records and pages, numbering in the tens of millions, are now held in various documentation centers. These include but are not limited to the Berlin Documents Center; the Centre de Documentation Juive Contemporaine in Paris, France; the Centro di Documentazione Ebraica Contemporanea in Milan, Italy; the Main Commission for Investigation of Nazi Crimes in Poland; the Rijksinstituut voor Oorlogsdocumentatie (Netherlands State Institute for War Documentation); the Wiener Library in London; Yad Vashem in Jerusalem; and the Zydowski Instytut Historyczny in Warsaw).

The collection housed in the Berlin Documents Center is extensive, and features detailed information regarding major government officials in the Third Reich, including Joseph Goebbels, Herman Göring, Julius Streicher, and Joachim von Ribbentrop, as well as voluminous data on lower-ranking individuals. The documentation also includes correspondence carried out within the Nazi party and government offices, "ranging from the *Gaue* (the territorial units into which the Reich was divided for Nazi party purposes) all the way up to the Reich chancellery—and papers produced and used by the People's court and the Reich's supreme court" (Mushkat, 1995, p. 391).

The Centre de Documentation Juive Contemporaine was secretly established in 1943 in Grenoble. It contains key records on the Nazi occupation of France, the actions of the Vichy French collaborators, and the fate of the Jews captured, incarcerated, or deported by the Nazis.

The Centro di Documentazione Ebraica Contemporanea contains important records regarding the fate of the Italian Jews at the hands of the Fascists and Nazis, with a particular emphasis on the period from 1938 to 1945. The records include information on the persecution of the Jews as well as the role of Jews in the Italian resistance movement.

The Rijksinstituut voor Oorlogsdocumentatie holds hundreds of archives and collections of documents related to a wide variety of issues and events that deal directly with the impact of the Holocaust on the Jews of the Netherlands. Among the specific records housed here are documents collected by the Committee for Jewish Refugees (Comité voor Joodsche Vluchtelingen) and the Jewish Council (Joodse Raad), as well as documents pertaining to the Westerbork transit camp and the Vught concentration camp. Further collections include records of the Reichssicherheitshauptamt (RSHA; Reich Security Main Office) branch in The Hague, and particularly those records that pertain to the RSHA's IV B 4 section, which dealt specifically with Jews. The institute also houses papers from The Hague branch of the Omnia Treuhandgesellschaft (Trust Company), which dealt with the policy of "aryanization" of Dutch-Jewish enterprises, as well as numerous German propaganda materials.

A particularly valuable set of captured German documents recorded the plans and actions of the *Einsatzgruppen*. These were the mobile killing units that operated in certain German-occupied territories during World War II and resulted in the murder of approximately 1.25 million Jews and hundreds of thousands of Soviet citizens, including both Soviet and Jewish prisoners of war.

Following the end of World War II, a series of trials were held, during which defendants were tried on charges of conspiracy, crimes against peace, crimes against humanity, and war crimes. The most famous of the trials was conducted by the International Military Tribunal (IMT) and later came to be known as the Nuremberg Trial. Subsequent trials were also held, for example, by Great Britain (two of which were the Bergen-Belsen Trial and the Zyklon B Trial), West Germany, Hungary, the Netherlands, Norway, and Romania. There was also the Eichmann Trial, held by Israel in 1961. Not only did such trials make use of Nazi-produced documentation, they also produced invaluable records of the charges and the evidence for such and detailed documentation of the cross-examination of the witnesses. Equally important is the record of the defendants' own words, and that is true even when the latter consisted of disclaimers, deceit, and outright denial of their involvement or guilt in the crimes of which they were accused.

The transcripts of the first Nuremburg Trial were published under the official title: *Trial of the Major War Criminals Before the International Military Tribunal, Nuremberg, 14, November 1945-October 1946*. It ultimately filled forty-two volumes, and came to be known as the "Blue Series." These transcripts constitute the official text of the proceedings in the English, French, and German languages. The set contains the transcripts of testimony given by the defendants, the witnesses for the prosecution and defense, and tens of thousands of documents of incriminating documentary evidence.

Cambodian Genocide

The Khmer Rouge, the communist leaders of Democratic Kampuchea (Cambodia) and the perpetrators of the Cambodian genocide from 1975 to 1979, produced and maintained extensive documentation of its genocidal activities. The main repository of the various documents produced by the Khmer Rouge is housed at two major centers: Yale University's Cambodian Genocide Program and the Documentation Center of Cambodia, in Phnom Penh, Cambodia. Yale's Cambodian Genocide Program is developing a computer database that will contain all of the primary and secondary source material directly related to the Khmer Rouge overthrow of the Cambodian government and the Khmer Rouge's rule and activities between 1975 and 1979. The Documentation Center of Cambodia is an autonomous research institute, containing copies of all of Yale's documentation and research of the genocide.

The Khmer Rouge documents comprise two major sets: the archive of material maintained, produced, and collected by the Tuol Sleng prison, where the Khmer

Rouge incarcerated, interrogated, tortured, and, ultimately, murdered suspected dissidents or enemies of the revolution; and the archive maintained by the Khmer Rouge's national security force, the Santebal, which was responsible for carrying out surveillance on and repression of its own people throughout Cambodia during the Khmer Rouge's rule.

When the Vietnamese invaded Kampuchea in 1979, the chief of Tuol Sleng Prison attempted to destroy the documents in his possession, but in his rush to escape he left over 100,000 pages behind. These documents provide detailed accounts of the Khmer Rouge's "security activities" beginning in 1974. Likewise, approximately 100,000 Santebal documents were discovered in a house that is thought to have been the residence of Son Sen, Democratic Kampuchea's Deputy Prime Minister for Defense.

Iraq Genocide of the Iraqi Kurds

In May 1992 and August of 1993, eighteen tons of official Iraqi state documents captured by Kurdish parties during the course of the March 1991 uprising were shipped to the United States for safekeeping and analysis. The human rights group Middle East Watch led a team that began researching the documents in 1992. The materials provide an in-depth view of Iraq's 1988 Anfal campaign of extermination against its northern Kurdish population.

The materials include "memoranda, correspondence, arrest warrants, background information on suspects, official decrees, activity and investigation reports, logbooks, minutes of meetings, membership rosters, lists of names, census forms and salary tables" (Human Rights Watch, 1994, pp. 1–2). Among the many documents included in the tons of materials are the Ali Hassan al-Majid tapes. These are more than a dozen audiotapes of meetings between Ali Hassan al-Majid, the Secretary General of the Ba'ath party's Northern Bureau, and senior Ba'ath officials in 1988 and 1989, during which he specifically commented on the chemical attacks he had carried out against the Kurds.

1994 Rwandan Genocide

A wide variety of documents—some produced or disseminated by high government officials, others by local leaders and perpetrators of the Rwandan genocide, and still others by radio announcers—were discovered in the aftermath of the genocide. Such records are being used by scholars in an attempt to understand the reasons for and process of the genocide, and are also being used in the trials of alleged perpetrators being held in Rwanda and at the International Criminal Tribunal for

Rwanda (ICTR) in Arusha, Tanzania. Among the documents that have been unearthed, catalogued, analyzed, or used in one or both of the two court settings are examples of virulent anti-Tutsi propaganda, much of which was disseminated by hand or posted on local bulletin boards. Also included are speeches and directives issued by high governmental officials on *Radio Télévision Libre des Mille Collines* (RTLM) that were aimed at inciting members of the Hutu general public to seek out and kill Tutsis in general as well as specific, named individuals. The RTLM was jointly owned by members of Hutu Power, or the *génocidaires*, and virtually became the "voice" of the genocide.

In addition to these records, there are speeches by the Rwandan president and prime minister to the general Hutu populace urging them to continue to seek "security" for the nation, in which the term "seeking security" was a euphemism for "continue the killing." The documentation also includes letters from leading perpetrators seeking to instill fear in the Hutu masses and calling on the Tutsis to carry out "wartime security" measures (another euphemism for the mass killings of Tutsis). There are administrative records from governmental meetings and from communes and prefectures throughout Rwanda; government reports (disseminated throughout the country) falsely accusing the Tutsis of planning an armed insurrection; and "minutes of local meetings where operations against Tutsi were planned and correspondence in which administrators congratulated their subordinates for successfully destroying 'the enemy'" (Des Forges, 1999, p. 3). Equally important among these documents are the censuses carried out prior to the genocide for the express purpose of ascertaining how many Tutsis lived in each village; and carefully detailed records that tallied the number of people killed and "not just of overall numbers of dead, but also of the elimination of those persons named as priority targets for their communes" (Des Forges, 1999, p. 241). Two major sources for locating such documentation are the reports issued by Human Rights Watch and the trial records issued by the International Criminal Tribunal for Rwanda (ICTR).

Yugoslavia

Many of the former leaders who are now alleged suspects in the commission of genocide in the former Yugoslavia were careful not to leave a paper trial of their true intentions. Nonetheless, many alleged perpetrators of genocide—including the leaders of the various factions—did make a plethora of assertions, announcements, and propaganda statements on both radio and televisions during the genocide, and both the transcripts and tapes of such broadcasts are still available.

These clearly indicate the actual intent and motivation of the Serbian government, including its contempt and disregard for the safely and welfare of its foes and the desire to "cleanse" the area of groups it considered hostile. The intent and motivation come through clearly, despite the purposeful use of euphemistic words and phrases.

Over and above the broadcasts, other forms of documentation (including minutes of meetings, correspondence, reports, and internal governmental documents) have been collected and are being used by the prosecutors, defense attorneys, and accused at the trials being conducted by the International Criminal Tribunal for the Former Yugoslavia (ICTY). Much of this documentation is available for use by scholars and students, but to obtain information about or access to actual governmental documentation or documents produced by paramilitary groups that have been introduced during the course of a trial, a researcher must provide the press and public information personnel with the specific case name and exhibit number of the document.

Conclusion

While not all who perpetrate genocide meticulously document their plans and actions, many do. The minutes of meetings, memoranda, records of debates in governmental councils, legislation, mandates, and even records of the killing process and "body counts," among other types of information, all provide scholars with invaluable information and insights into the thinking, motives, decisions, and actions of the perpetrators of genocide.

SEE ALSO Evidence; Videotaped Testimonials

REFERENCES

Adalian, Rouben (1999). "Documentation of Armenian Genocide in U.S. Archives." In *Encyclopedia of Genocide,* Vol. 1, ed. Israel W. Charny. Santa Barbara, Calif.: ABC CLIO.

Ali Hassan al-Majid Tapes. Available from http://www.hrw. org/reports/1994/iraq/TEXT.htm.

Bridgman, Jon (1981). *The Revolt of the Hereros.* Los Angeles: University of California Press.

Dadrian, Vahakn N. (1991). "Documentation of the Armenian Genocide in Turkish Sources." In *Genocide: A Critical Bibliographical Review,* vol. 2, ed. Israel W. Charny. New York: Facts on File.

Dadrian, Vahakn N. (1999). "Documentation of Armenian Genocide in German Sources." In *Encyclopedia of Genocide,* vol. 1, ed. Israel W. Charny. Santa Barbara, Calif: ABC CLIO Inc.

des Forges, Alison (1999). *Leave None to Tell the Story: Genocide in Rwanda.* New York: Human Rights Watch.

The Documentation Center of Cambodia. Available from http://www.bigpond.com.kh/users/dccam.genocide.

Human Rights Watch (1994). "Bureaucracy of Repression: The Iraqi Government in Its Own Words." Available from: http://www.hrw.org/reports/1994/iraq/TEXT.htm

The International Criminal Tribunal for Rwanda. Available at http://www.ictr.org.

Mushkat, Marian (1995). "Berlin Documents Center." In *Encyclopedia of the Holocaust,* ed. Israel Gutman. New York: Macmillan Publishing.

Paape, Harry (1995). "Rijksinstituut voor Oorlogsdocumntatie." In *Encyclopedia of the Holocaust,* ed. Israel Gutman. New York: Macmillan Publishing.

Yale University's Cambodian Genocide Program. Available from www.yale.edu/cgp.

Samuel Totten

Drama, Holocaust

Notwithstanding reservations on moral and artistic ground, plays and performances addressing the Holocaust and its repercussions are gaining in number the more time passes since the actual event. Can and should the Holocaust be staged in the first place? Is a representation of the horror appropriate and commendable? What happens to the actor who takes on the part of a Nazi perpetrator, or, alternatively, the role of the victim, and how can a play affect spectators without being overtly didactic?

In his 1988 seminal book *The Darkness We Carry: The Drama of the Holocaust,* Robert Skloot notes five objectives that underscore serious dramas dealing with the Holocaust: "honouring the victims, teaching history to audiences, evoking emotional responses, discussing ethical issues, and suggesting solutions to universal, contemporary problems" (p. 10).

Instances of drama depicting the agonies of the victims of the Nazi ascent to power can be traced back to the early 1930s. Ferdinand Bruckner's *Rassen* (Races, 1933) shows the effect of Germany's new racial laws on students, whereas Friedrich Wolf's *Professor Mamlock* (1934) stages the tragedy of a prominent physician. Written in 1941 during his internment in a camp, Rudolf Leonhard's *Geiseln* (Hostages) depicts the plight of Jews and communists who were brutally executed on charges of plotting against Hitler's regime. All of these plays were designed to open people's eyes to the infamous crimes perpetrated by the Nazis and to warn of possible greater evil. *Eli* is a surrealistic, poetic drama depicting martyrdom and redemption, a modern mystery written by Nelly Sachs in 1943 while she was in Swedish exile.

Most of the plays written soon after the war follow a realistic style. In Germany attempts were made to confront German collective guilt through the character of a Nazi who came to acknowledge his mistake or make amends as an act of atonement. Ingeborg Drewitz's *Alle Tore waren bewacht* (All gates were watched, 1955) is one example of such an approach. Other plays tried to lend the anonymous suffering a concrete form in the figure of a single representative victim. Best known among these plays is the stage adaptation (by Frances Goodrich and Albert Hackett) of the world-famous *Diary of Anne Frank*, a melodrama that has enjoyed great success since its premiere in 1956. The East German writer Hedda Zinner sets her *Ravensbrücker Ballade* (1961) in an internment center for women; in *Playing for Time* (1985), Arthur Miller explores the fate of singer Fania Fénelon, from her arrest in Paris to Auschwitz, where she was forced to join the camp's all-women orchestra; Martin Sherman devotes his attention in *Bent* (1979) to the sufferings of homosexuals during the Third Reich. Special mention should also be made of Thomas Strittmatter, a German who enjoyed the *Gnade der späten Geburt*—the grace of belated birth, having been born in 1961—and the author of a number of plays (e.g., *Viehjud Levi*, 1983) that delineate the fate of outcasts under the Nazis.

A fairly large group of plays address the guilt and agonies of Holocaust survivors. Charlotte Delbo, a survivor of Auschwitz, creates in *Et toi, comment as-tu fait?* (Crawling from the Wreckage, 1978) a semidocumentary montage of interviews with other survivors; Hans Joachim Haecker in *Dreht Euch nicht um* (Don't Turn Around, 1961) and René Kalisky in *Jim the Lionhearted* (1972), concentrate on the continued aftereffects of victims' traumatic experiences. The survivors are often shown as mentally and physically broken people, such as in Yoram Kaniuk's *Adam's Purim Party* (1981). Questions of nemesis and justice figure in Franz Theodor Csokor's *Das Zeichen an der Wand* (The Writing on the Wall, 1962), and in Heinar Kipphardt's controversial play about Adolf Eichmann, *Bruder Eichmann* (Brother Eichmann, 1983).

Dissatisfied with psychological realism, some authors have sought other dramatic venues to stage that which cannot be grasped, imagined, or represented. Erwin Sylvanus offered a Pirandellian staging of the final journey of *Dr. Korczak and the Children* (1957). Other German playwrights sought to present the bare facts, relying on documents (Rolf Hochhuth, *Der Stellvertreter*, The Representative, 1963) and the testimony of witnesses (Peter Weiss, *Die Ermittlung*, The investigation, 1965). *The Cannibals* (1968) was George Tabori's first experiment with the theater as a locus of remembrance; it was followed, among other works, by *My Mother's Courage* (1979), *Jubilee* (1983), and *Mein Kampf* (1987). The Israeli playwright Joshua Sobol created a trilogy about everyday life in Vilna (*Ghetto*, 1983, *Adam*, 1989, and *The Underground*, 1991), focusing on life in the ghetto, in which the lines demarcating theater and reality, past and present, are deliberately blurred. Liliane Atlan combined pageantry and modern techniques in *Les Messies ou le mal de terre* (The Messiahs, 1969), while her fellow-countryman, Armand Gatti, depicted his Holocaust images in a surrealistic (*Chroniques d'une planète provisoire*, Chronicles of a provisional planet, 1963) or avant-garde context (*Le Cinécadre de l'Esplanade Loreto*, 1990). Other experimental productions include *Akropolis* (1962) by Jerzy Grotowski, an innovator in the Polish theater, and *Arbeit macht frei from Toitland Europa* by the Israelis David Maayan and Smadar Yaron, a performance in which the audience joins the actors in various spaces connected to the Holocaust (such as the Holocaust Museum in a kibbutz founded by Holocaust survivors). Most of these experimental performances shun sentimental pity and sanctimonious judgment, calling instead for the audience's immersion in memory, in survivors' traumatic pain, and for genuine reflection.

SEE ALSO Films, Holocaust Documentary; Holocaust

BIBLIOGRAPHY

Feinberg, Anat (1999). *Embodied Memory: The Theatre of George Tabori*. Iowa City: University of Iowa Press.

Feingold, Ben-Ami (1989). *The Theme of the Holocaust in Hebrew Drama*. Tel Aviv: Hakibbutz Hameuchad.

Schumacher, Claude, ed. (1998). *Staging the Holocaust: The Shoah in Drama and Performance*. Cambridge, U.K.: Cambridge University Press.

Skloot, Robert (1982). *The Theater of the Holocaust: Four Plays*. Madison: University of Wisconsin Press.

Skloot, Robert (1988). *The Darkness We Carry: The Drama of the Holocaust*. Madison: University of Wisconsin Press.

Anat Feinberg

Early Warning

The genocides in Rwanda (in 1994) and in Bosnia (during the period between 1992 and 1995) were alarming evidence of the failure of the United Nations (UN) Security Council and its member states to prevent genocides and other crimes against humanity. Studies by the UN Commissions of Inquiry concluded that reform in four areas is needed to prevent such crimes: institutions for early warning, programs for prevention, capacity for rapid response, and courts for punishment. Willingness to use these institutions on the part of political leaders is necessary to render reform measures effective. Public pressure is needed to motivate leaders to act.

One of the most common false assumptions about genocide is that it is the result of conflict—the resolution of which would be a preventive to genocide. Most genocide does not result from conflict. Genocide is one-sided mass murder. Empirical research by Helen Fein, Matthew Krain, Barbara Harff, Benjamin Valentino, and others has shown that genocide is most often committed by elites that are attempting to stay in power in the face of perceived threats to their dominance. Fein and Harff have found that six factors enhance the likelihood of genocide: prior genocide in the same polity, autocracy, ethnic minority rule, political upheaval during war or revolution, exclusionary ideology, and closure of borders to international trade.

Wishing to complement these statistical models, Gregory H. Stanton has devised a developmental model of the stages of genocide. The eight stages of genocide are classification ("us vs. them"), symbolization, dehumanization, organization (the formation of hate groups), polarization, preparation (the identification, expropriation, rounding up, and transportation of victims), extermination, and denial. Stanton's model is designed so that policy makers can recognize early warning signs and implement specific countermeasures to prevent genocide.

Who should be warned of the likelihood of impending genocide? Members of the victim group should surely come first, so that they can prepare to flee or defend themselves. Others who should receive this warning are political moderates, the members of religious and human rights groups, and the members of antigovernment opposition forces (who would be likely to oppose the impending genocide). If the government is not party to an impending genocide, it should be called upon to intervene and to protect its citizens. (This approach has halted ethnic and religious massacres in Kalimantan, Sulawesi, and the Moluccas [all part of Indonesia], and in Nigeria.) But because most genocides are committed by governments (either directly or indirectly through militias), regional and international leaders must be warned as well—with the idea that they will be able to bring pressure to bear on the government planning the genocide. In democracies, leaders seldom act without the stimulus of public pressure, so early warning must get through to the media and groups that can organize campaigns for action.

How early must warning come if it is to trigger action that will contribute to the prevention of genocide? The answer depends on the action that is being sought. In the context of long-term efforts to prevent genocide, the warning should be given as early as possible. Because structural factors such as totalitarian or autocratic government and minority rule correlate substantially with the incidence of genocide, long-term policies for genocide prevention should promote democracy, freedom, and pluralist tolerance. Rudy Rummel's meticulously documented conclusion that democracies do not commit genocide against their own enfranchised populations has often been challenged, but never refuted. The protection of democracies requires that, in the face of threats by extremist, military, or totalitarian movements to overthrow those democracies, the warning be communicated as early as possible.

Freedom House, which tracks information pertaining to the relative freedoms of many countries and publishes an annual report on the subject, in its 2003 report counted 121 electoral democracies out of the 192 countries it evaluated (leaving 71 nondemocracies). Ted Robert Gurr has pointed out that periods of transition (from autocratic governments to democratic ones) can be particularly dangerous periods—at which times minority elites attempt to hold onto their power and are sometimes willing to commit mass murder to do so. The foreign policies of other nations should promote the peaceful transition to democracy, but must avoid the enunciation of mortal threats that would set off the undertaking of genocide by elites determined to maintain their power.

Rwanda was a case in which early warning failed. In 1992 the Belgian Ambassador to Rwanda warned the Belgian government that Hutu Power advocates were "planning the extermination of the Tutsi of Rwanda." In April 1993 the UN Special Rapporteur on Summary, Arbitrary, and Extrajudicial Executions issued a statement that the massacres of Tutsi in Rwanda already constituted genocide. General Roméo Dallaire, Commander of the UN Assistance Mission in Rwanda, in a cable sent on January 11, 1994, warned the UN Department of Peacekeeping Operations, headed by Kofi Annan, of the plan of extremist Hutu to exterminate Tutsis. The UN denied Dallaire permission to confiscate the cache of 500,000 machetes that had been shipped to Rwanda for the Hutu militias (the existence of which had come to his attention). Both early and late warnings of the Rwandan genocide were ignored by UN and other policy makers who denied the facts, who resisted calling the genocide by its proper name, and who refused to consider options for intervention—and who refused to risk the lives of any of their own soldiers. Instead they withdrew 2,000 UN Assistance Mission for Rwanda (UNAMIR) troops and sacrificed the lives of over 500,000 defenseless Rwandans.

There had been a similar failure of early warning in Cambodia in 1975, at which time reporters and diplomats were predicting a Khmer Rouge bloodbath. Political leftists in other countries refused to believe the warnings, and denied the mass killing while it was underway. Worn out by the wars in Indochina, the United States and western European nations were unwilling to intervene to overthrow the murderous Khmer Rouge. The UN General Assembly even condemned Vietnam for its intervention.

Instances of early warning that were successful in generating courses of action to prevent or frustrate genocidal massacres and the commission of crimes against humanity include Macedonia (in 1992 and 2001, when several hundred UN peacekeepers prevented the Balkan wars from widening); East Timor (in 1999, when, after East Timor had voted for independence, coordinated warnings coming from human rights groups and the intervention of Australian troops brought to a halt the massacre of East Timorese by Indonesian troops and militias); and Côte d'Ivoire (in 2002, when warnings by the Belgian organization *Prévention Génocides,* followed by French military and diplomatic intervention, helped to avert massacres).

What steps have been taken to develop early warning systems? The early warning of threats to national interests has long been a job of the intelligence agencies that inform government policy makers. Threats of genocide were added to that task by the U.S. Central Intelligence Agency (CIA) in 1994, when that organization inaugurated its "State Failure Task Force," whose mission includes the analysis of factors that predispose states to genocide. Efforts to develop systems of early warning on the part of think tanks and university officers have also been funded by governments—in the United Kingdom, the Netherlands, Denmark, Sweden, and Germany.

At the UN, the Framework for Coordination was established within the Department of Political Affairs to convene high-level planners from UN departments and agencies to discuss and plan responses to crises that are judged to be capable of generating genocical aggression. On April 7, 2004, Annan announced that he would appoint a Special Adviser on the Prevention of Genocide. In July Juan Mendez was named to the post.

Nongovernmental organizations (NGOs) and university-based organizations in Europe and the United States have also focused on early warning—notably the International Crisis Group, the Forum on Early Warning and Early Response (FEWER), Genocide Watch, and the International Campaign to End Genocide (a global coalition of organizations dedicated to preventing genocide).

Early warning is meaningless without early response. But early warning is the necessary first step toward prevention.

SEE ALSO Prevention; Rwanda

BIBLIOGRAPHY
Fein, Helen (1993). "Accounting for Genocide after 1945: Theories and Some Findings." *International Journal on Group Rights* 1(1):79–106.

Gurr, Ted Robert (2000). *Peoples Versus States: Minorities at Risk in the New Century.* Washington, D.C.: U.S. Institute of Peace Press.

Harff, Barbara (1998). "Early Warning of Humanitarian Crises: Sequential Models and the Role of Accelerators." In *Preventive Measures: Building Risk Assessment and Crisis Early Warning Systems*, ed. L. Davies and Ted Robert Gurr. Lanham, Md.: Rowman & Littlefield.

Harff, Barbara (2003). "No Lessons Learned from the Holocaust? Assessing Risks of Genocide and Political Mass Murder since 1955." *American Political Science Review* (February) 97(1):57–73.

Krain, Matthew (1997). "State-Sponsored Mass Murder: The Onset and Severity of Genocides and Politicides." *Journal of Conflict Resolution* 41:331–360.

Rummel, Rudolph J. (1995). "Democracy, Power, Genocide, and Mass Murder." *Journal of Conflict Resolution* 39:3–26.

Stanton, Gregory H. (2004). "Could the Rwandan Genocide Have Been Prevented?" *Journal of Genocide Research* 6(2):211–228.

Valentino, Benjamin A. (2004). *Final Solutions: Mass Killing and Genocide in the Twentieth Century.* Ithaca, N.Y.: Cornell University Press.

Gregory H. Stanton

East Timor

In 1975 Indonesian military forces (the TNI) invaded the Portuguese colony of East Timor, then under the administration of the pro-independence Fretilin Party (the Revolutionary Front for the Independent East Timor), which had just unilaterally declared independence. From the outset, the invasion was strongly resisted by the heavily out-gunned and outnumbered Fretilin armed forces. The invaders treated the local population harshly, indiscriminately killing hundreds of mostly civilian Dili residents in the first two weeks of the occupation.

The Indonesian occupation lasted twenty-four years, until the intervention of the UN authorized Interfet force in September 1999. The UN intervention followed a plebicite in which 78.5 percent of the population rejected integration with Indonesia. In the first decade of the occupation, the treatment of the population at large by the occupying forces displayed genocidal characteristics. The worst period was between December 1975 and 1980, when intense military operations were carried out across the island. Then East Timor was closed to the outside world, and even the International Red Cross was denied access until some four years after the invasion. According to East Timorese sources, including the Catholic Church which traditionally maintained population statistics and monitored the humanitarian situation, as many as 200,000 East Timorese died. Tens of thousands were killed by troops, while many others died from disease and starvation, conditions resulting directly or indirectly from occupation policies. A study of the population decline supports these charges. East Timor's population was estimated at 688,000 in the months before the invasion, and was growing at about 2 percent per year. According to Indonesia's census assessment in 1980, the population had fallen to 550,000.

Following visits to the territory by the International Red Cross and foreign diplomats in 1979, the human rights situation began to improve, but major atrocities continued. One of the worst of these was the massacre at Creras in 1983, where more than a thousand East Timorese, including women and children, were massacred in reprisal for the killing of several Indonesian soldiers in an engagement with resistance forces of the Falintil (the Armed Forces of National Liberation of East Timor). Summary executions and disappearances continued to feature in the annual reports of Amnesty International and Human Rights Watch. In 1991 the massacre of more than 200 East Timorese by TNI troops at a peaceful demonstration in Santa Cruz cemetary attracted world condemnation. This atrocity had a systematic character, reflecting a determination on the part of the Indonesian authorities to eliminate opponents of integration. However, in the case of the Santa Cruz massacre the Suharto government bowed to international pressure, and a number of soldiers were tried by a military court. The few who were found guilty were given only short sentences, ranging from six to eighteen months. This punishment was in stark contrast to the long terms of imprisonment handed out to surviving demonstrators in a separate trial, where they were sentenced to periods of imprisonment ranging from six to more than twenty years.

Since Indonesia's withdrawal in 1999, UN agencies and other humanitarian organizations have had free access to East Timor, and revelations of past events reveals beyond doubt that the humanitarian costs of this act of forced integration reached genocidal proportions. The East Timor case is manifestly one of the most serious of its kind in modern history. Indonesia's education policy banned the teaching of Tetum, East Timor's lingua franca, and Portuguese. This was a clear effort to eradicate a portion of East Timorian culture. Indonesia's policy of sending thousands of Indonesian settlers into the province also seemed designed to achieve the destruction of the distinctive culture of East Timor.

The international response to Indonesia's serious violation of international law was at first characterized by indifference and irresolution. As a result, the Suharto government, despite its heavy dependence on Western economic aid, did not feel the need to respond to international concerns in a positive way. The expressions of international concern at the deteriorating humanitarian situation in the years following the invasion were so weak that Indonesian authorities became openly defiant of world opinion. In the 1980s, however, East Timor's Bishop Carlos Belo, began to expose the situation to the international media and visiting foreign dignitaries. The Santa Cruz massacre in November 1991 forced the Indonesian authorities onto the defensive. The Suharto government's concessions were nevertheless of little real significance, falling well short of popular demands by East Timor's leaders for the removal of the Indonesian military, and for the right of self-determination.

Indonesia agreed to hold a plebiscite under UN auspices, in August 1999. This concession was attributable less to international pressures than to the fall of Suharto following the Asian economic collapse. The flexible stance adopted by President Habibie and the determined efforts of Kofi Annan, the newly appointed UN Secretary-General, were the key elements in the fortuitous sequence of events that led to East Timor's liberation in September 1999, after twenty-four years of occupation. As it happened, the Indonesian military maintained its oppression until the very end. TNI generals formed a militia force with the aim of preventing the loss of the province. When the results of the plebiscite were announced, a large-scale TNI operation swung into action. Pro-independence supporters, now representing the majority opinion, were the subject of violence and intimidation. In the space of a few weeks, more than 1,500 were killed. An estimated 250,000 were deported to West Timor, and 73 percent of all building and houses were destroyed. This spate of killing and destruction was interrupted by the Interfet intervention, and by President Habibie's decision to withdraw from East Timor in the face of strong international protests.

The pattern of the atrocities carried out by Indonesian troops reveals a systemic character. Until Santa Cruz, no TNI troops or commanders were ever placed on trial for these crimes against humanity. In the case of the events of 1999, the tribunal set up by the Indonesian government was apparently designed to prevent disclosure of TNI command responsibility. The few TNI commanders placed on trial were charged not with their role in organizing the violence, but with having failed to stop it. Even so, most were acquitted, while the few who were found guilty won their appeals to a higher court.

SEE ALSO Indonesia; Peacekeeping; West Papua, Indonesia (Irian Jaya)

BIBLIOGRAPHY

Aditjondro, George J. (1999). *Is Oil Thicker Than Blood? A Study of Oil Companies' Interests and Western Complicity in Indonesia's Annexation of East Timor.* Commack, N.Y.: Nova Science.

Archer, Robert (1995). "The Catholic Church in East Timor." In *East Timor at the Crossroads: The Forging of a Nation*, ed. Peter Carey and G. Carter Bentley. Honolulu: University of Hawaii Press.

Ball, Desmond (2001). "Silent Witness: Australian Intelligence and East Timor." *Pacific Review* 14:35–62.

Boxer, C. R. (1960). "Portuguese Timor: A Rough Island Story: 1515–1960." *History Today* 10:349–355.

Breen, Bob (2000). *Mission Accomplished, East Timor: The Australian Defence Force Participation in the International Forces East Timor (INTERFET).* St. Leonards, New South Wales, Australia: Allen and Unwin.

Budiardjo, Carmel, and Liem Soei Liong (1984). *The War Against East Timor.* London: Zed.

Carey, Peter, and Steve Cox (1995). *Generations of Resistance: East Timor.* London: Cassell.

Dunn, James (1996). *Timor: A People Betrayed*, new edition. Milton, Queensland: Jacaranda.

Martin, Ian (2001). *Self-Determination in East Timor: The United Nations, the Ballot, and International Intervention.* Boulder, Colo: Lynne Rienner.

Tanter, Richard, Mark Selden, and Stephen R. Shalom, eds. (2001). *Bitter Flowers, Sweet Flowers: East Timor, Indonesia, and the World Community.* Lanham, Md.: Rowman and Littlefield.

Taylor, John G. (1995). "East Timor: Contemporary History: A Chronology of the Main Events since 1974." In *East Timor at the Crossroads: The Forging of a Nation*, ed. Peter Carey and G. Carter Bentley. Honolulu: University of Hawaii.

James Dunn

Economic Groups

Protection has traditionally been offered to those groups whose defining characteristics are as inflexible as their race. Amorphous qualities such as monetary wealth or property ownership can change. For this reason economic status alone probably is insufficient to qualify for protection under the laws concerning genocide or crimes against humanity, despite the fact that economic groups have been the target of persecution throughout history. Slaves, serfs, wage laborers, Africans in the trans-Atlantic slave trade, Native Americans, wealthy Jewish money lenders, the Chinese in southeast Asia, East Indians in Uganda, and caste members in Asia and Africa—all have at various times been the target of persecution. In almost all these situations, the desire for wealth and greed motivated the persecutors, but the economic status of the victims often was not the sole means of identifying them, because their economic status was coupled with race, religion, or nationality.

Situations have arisen in which persecution was based purely on economics, such as the struggles confronting serfs, peasants, wage laborers, labor unions, and communist class warfare. Classes within feudalistic societies were clearly defined by law. During both the Bolshevik Revolution in Russia and the French Revolution lower economic classes targeted wealthy landowners. In the nineteenth and twentieth centuries labor union leaders in the United States were imprisoned, deported, and executed for their role in organizing and directing the actions of the labor movement.

In the majority of instances, however, economic status was not the sole criterion for persecution. Slaves have traditionally been regarded as property, and in most cases that status is transmitted from one generation to the next. Slaves were frequently branded or marked in order to more easily identify them, but the origins of enslavement can often be traced to racial, ethnic, or religious groups. The Chinese minority in Indonesia has been persecuted for their wealth, but their ethnicity and religion also set them apart from the Muslim majority. They have been forced to give up their Chinese names, their language, their schools, and their traditions. In addition, repression reaches down to the entire Chinese minority in Indonesia and does not target only the wealthy.

Indians in East Africa also have been persecuted for their perceived wealth. In the 1970s Idi Amin threatened to imprison nearly 55,000 Asians (Indians and Pakistanis who made up the majority of the merchant class) if they did not leave Uganda. Upon their departure, he nationalized their shops. In 1980 Tanzania nationalized Asian-owned businesses. In 1982 following an unsuccessful coup in Kenya, Asian-owned shops and homes were looted and Asian women raped.

The International Convention on the Elimination of All Forms of Racial Discrimination protects caste members based on their descent. The notion of caste may have originated as an economic concept, or it may have had racial or ethnic connotations. The lowest caste, the untouchables, were given the dirtiest jobs and persecuted as "subhuman." Some theories suggest that Aryans initiated the caste system following their invasion of India and categorized those with the darkest skin as untouchables.

Economic status can thus factor into genocide and crimes against humanity. At a post-World War II war crimes tribunal, the court, with a U.S.–led prosecution team, found executives at a German firm guilty of crimes against humanity for the economic sanctions and political pressures they had imposed on the Jewish owners of industrial businesses that they later seized with Nazi support. In Rwanda Belgian colonists were unable to differentiate between the Hutu and Tutsi so they used the number of cattle a family might own to determine its ethnic origin and legal status. Tutsi were generally wealthier and more powerful than the Hutu. This simplistic system of ethnic determination was the foundation for the genocide that later occurred in the 1990s.

The 1948 United Nations (UN) Convention for the Prevention and Punishment of the Crime of Genocide protects "national, ethnical, racial, and religious" groups. Political groups had been included in the draft of the Convention, but last-minute negotiations ended in the deletion of that reference in order to get more member nation-states to sign the treaty. The Universal Declaration of Human Rights calls for the individual freedom to change one's nationality and religion if so desired. But if peoples worldwide freely change their nationality and religion, then groups become mutable. Domestic legislatures have thus expanded the definition of genocide without reference to the permanence of group membership. France legally defines genocide as the intentional destruction of any group.

If economic groups constitute a subgroup of one of the protected groups, they would fall under the protection of the Genocide Convention. The Convention clearly defines genocide as the intent to destroy a group even in part. If only the wealthy Chinese were targeted in Southeast Asia, for example, it would still be considered a case of genocide.

The International Criminal Court (ICC), in its Rome Statute, defines crimes against humanity as actions committed as part of a widespread or systematic attack directed against any civilian population. The statute includes the persecution of identifiable groups based on grounds that are universally recognized as impermissible under international law. The phrase "any civilian population" could be interpreted to include the targeting of economic groups, even those groups that are more loosely defined.

Historical instances of persecution based on economic status have often led to the persecution of a larger ethnic group, but if persecutors stopped short and merely targeted an economic group, using no other basis in their selection, such persecution may not rise to the level of genocide or crimes against humanity.

SEE ALSO Slavery, Historical

BIBLIOGRAPHY

Berberoglu, Berch, ed. (2002). *Labor and Capital in the Age of Globalization.* Boulder, Colo.: Rowman and Littlefield.

Fitzpatrick, Sheila (2001). *Russian Revolution*, 2nd edition. New York: Oxford University Press.

Human Rights Watch Asia (1999). "Broken People: Caste Violence Against India's 'Untouchables.'" Available from http://www.hrw.org/reports/1999/india/.

James, Harold (2001). *The Deutsche Bank and the Nazi Economic War Against the Jews: The Expropriation of Jewish-Owned Property.* New York: Cambridge University Press.

Schabas, William A. (2000). "Groups Protected by the Convention." In *Genocide in International Law.* Cambridge, U.K.: Cambridge University Press.

Stallbaumer, L. M. (1999). "Big Business and the Persecution of the Jews: The Flick Concern and the 'Aryanization' of Jewish Property before the War." *Holocaust and Genocide Studies* (Spring):1–27.

Rebecca L. Barbisch

Economics see Economic Groups.

Education

In the U.S. educational system, courses focusing on genocide and other gross human rights violations developed in the early 1970s as part of a larger response to rewriting the curriculum by including subjects and issues traditionally ignored or silenced. University courses introduced issues of gender, class, race, and ethnicity, including histories of slavery, colonialism, and other atrocities perpetrated against individuals because they were members of targeted civilian groups. From the destruction of indigenous peoples of the Americas to the Great Famine in Ireland to the Armenian Genocide, new scholarship and courses emphasized the intentional patterns, brutality, range of accomplices, and ongoing denial by alleged perpetrator-states of these events. In the following decades, an increasing number of courses have been developed to deal with comparative genocide and other crimes against humanity, human rights issues, and connections with state policy and international affairs.

The majority of courses have focused on the Holocaust, in particular the Nazi destruction of European Jewry. Interest in World War II, liberation of the concentration camps, and the Nuremberg Trials, all contributed to interest in the subject. Popular representation and misrepresentation, such as the Pulitzer Prize winning play *Diary of Anne Frank* and the television mini-series *The Holocaust*, as well as literary works by Elie Weisel, Andre Schwartz-Bart, Primo Levi and others have generated further interest in the subject. Writings by Hannah Arendt as well as Raul Hilberg's *Destruction of European Jewry*, Lucy Dawidowicz' *War Against the Jews*, Zygmunt Baumann's *Holocaust and Modernity*, and Christopher Browning's *Ordinary Men* are among texts used in classrooms. Scholarship in the field is substantial and controversies and debates about interpretation continue among scholars, worldwide. Popular classroom resources include Art Spiegelman's *Maus* and films such as Claude Lanzmann's *Shoah* and Steven Spielberg's *Schindler's List*.

A small sample of the range of courses include: *Sociology of the Holocaust, History of Anti-Semitism, Dutch Holocaust Literature, The Holocaust Theme in Western Drama, The Holocaust: Historical, and Philosophical and Literary Aspects*, and *The Holocaust and Law*. This last course includes coverage of issues of reparations and restitution. The establishment of museums and memorials, worldwide, as well as the funding of university chairs and Holocaust Centers provide institutional support for study of the Holocaust. Most notable among these institutions is the U.S. Holocaust Memorial Museum in Washington, D.C., which supports research and teacher training, as well as offering public exhibits and programs.

In the United States, primary and secondary Holocaust education has been mandated in some states. For example, the Florida school system focuses on the Holocaust, and the state of New Jersey mandates the study of other genocides as well. Peter Novick's *The Holocaust in American Life* provides a useful critique of the politics of U.S. Holocaust education. While many courses reinforce the Holocaust as "uniquely unique" and subscribe to the hegemonic model of understanding the phenomenon, some courses also include the study of Roma Gypsies and other groups that were targeted by the Nazis for elimination, and raise the issue of other genocides, particularly the Armenian Genocide, as possible precursors of the Holocaust.

Leo Kuper's work on genocide from the 1970s on (for instance, *Genocide and Genocide: Its Political Uses in the Twentieth Century*, 1981) was influential in the emergence of a small but growing number of international researchers and academics who were developing scholarship and multidisciplinary courses that emphasized a comparative approach to studying mass destruction. Definitions, content, classifications, and interpretations varied across this emergent discipline. Some relied on the definition developed by the U.N. Genocide Convention. Others added political and other categories. Rudolph Rummel coined the term "democide," which is a broad category that includes the murder of any individual or people by a government, including genocide, politicide and mass murder. An example of the analytic utility of Rummel's concepts can be found in his *Statistics of Democide: Genocide and Mass Murder since 1900*. The pedagogical goal of such courses was to demystify genocide and move away from its depiction as irrational, as well as to counter an academic trend toward the "ghettoization" of genocide studies and the creation of hierachies of victimization. It was hoped that this could be accomplished by examining recurrent patterns of genocidal behavior in order to better understand it and to work toward prevention. Mass destruction in Cambodia (1974–1979) and Rwanda (1994), and targeted killings from Guatemala to Indonesia, as well as ethnic cleansing in the former Yugoslavia, ironically have provided ongoing course materials that have helped to prove how widespread such crimes are.

In 1980, for example, Kurt Jonassohn and Frank Chalk, on the faculty at Concordia University in Montreal, developed a two semester multidisciplinary model called *A History and Sociology of Genocide* (their book, published a decade later with the same title, is used as an introductory course text). Their course traces genocidal events from ancient to modern times. Most courses on genocide and ethnic cleansing last a single semester and concentrate on events in the twentieth century. Many such courses employ the text *Century of Genocide: Eyewitness Accounts and Critical Views*, edited by Samuel Totten, William S. Parsons and W. Charny. This is a collection of specific genocidal events that occurred throughout the twentieth century, along with eyewitness testimony. African specialist Rene Lemarchand has taught a course entitled *Comparative Genocide* in the United States, Canada, and Denmark, and his presentation reflects the major themes generally touched upon in one semester courses. Lemarchand begins with conceptual and theoretical issues and follows with case studies divided into categories: Ideological Genocides (The Holocaust, Armenia, Cambodia); Colonial Genocide (Herreros), and Retrib-

utive Genocides (Burundi and Rwanda). A third section of the course discusses intervention and prevention strategies, including international tribunals, truth commissions, and the politics of denial.

Denial has become an increasing theme in genocide courses from the Turkish government's ongoing, official denial campaign of the Armenian Genocide to the trial of Holocaust denier Clifford Irving and including the continued denial by the United States of its complicity in different stages of genocide in settings ranging from Cambodia to Guatemala. The publication of the multi-volume *Encyclopedia of Genocide* (1999) and the *Journal of Genocide Research* (2002), as well as Samantha Power's Pulitzer Prize and Lemkin Award winning *"A Problem from Hell" America and the Age of Genocide* (2002) reflect growing scholarship and interest in the field. A text aimed specifically at educators is *Teaching about Genocide* (2002) coedited by Joyce Apsel and Helen Fein, providing resources, essays, centers (such as the Cambodian Genocide Project at Yale University), and syllabi devoted to genocide studies.

In 1995 the International Association of Genocide Scholars (www.iags-isg.org) was founded by Israel Charny, Helen Fein, Robert Melson, and Roger Smith, and in 2002 more than 200 members participated in the fifth biennial conference on *Genocide and the World Community* at the Irish Human Rights Center, University of Ireland, Galway. The last decade has seen a shift in the study of genocide and other life-integrity violations, another rewriting of history that places greater emphasis on human rights, international law, and foreign policy. From truth commissions in Central America and South Africa to release of documents on state terror and mass killings in the Soviet Union, to debate on "just humanitarian military intervention," from Kosovo to Iraq to the AIDS pandemic, new undergraduate and graduate courses have multiplied. The establishment and rulings of the international criminal tribunals, the proceedings against Chilean dictator Augusto Pinochet, the establishment of the International Criminal Court, new national constitutions from South Africa to Russia, transnational terrorism, and military interventions throughout the world have all contributed to the increase in human rights clinics in law schools and courses in international human rights law, including international criminal justice, refugee law, and comparative constitutional law.

Jack Donnelly's *International Human Rights* (1997) is one of the widely used introductory undergraduate texts on the subject, and contains a valuable essay on further suggested readings by topics and areas. A growing interest in legal studies, politics, and history as they relate to genocide and human rights issues is reflected in courses such as *Women and Rights in Africa, Health and Human Rights, Anatomy of War Crime Trials, The Culture of Human Rights in Latin America, China and Human Rights*, and *Truth and Reconciliation or Justice and Vengeance*. These courses reflect a cross-disciplinary interest in crimes against humanity and other forms of violence as an integral part of modernity, from state building to foreign policy and globalization. In addition to academic courses, the establishment of human rights centers around the world has contributed to the process of documenting past and present abuses and attempted to address the ongoing challenges of war, humanitarian crises, recovery, and prevention. Legal and other scholarly journals such as the *Human Rights Quarterly* provide forums for the burgeoning research in the field. Growing on-line scholarship and internet sources provide access to ongoing resources and reports. For example, www.umn.edu/humanrts/center/hronline connects to the University of Minnesota Human Rights Library, which contains over 14,000 documents on treaties and other international instruments, U.N. documents, and other resources. Internet websites provide links to monitoring agencies such as Human Rights Watch and Freedom House. The trend is toward the development of more undergraduate and graduate curricula that include multidisciplinary courses on human rights, crimes against humanity, and related subjects.

SEE ALSO Biographies; Films, Dramatizations in

BIBLIOGRAPHY

Andreopoulos, George, ed. (1994). *Genocide: Conceptual and Historical Dimensions*. Philadelphia: University of Pennsylvania Press.

Apsel, Joyce, and Helen Fein, eds. (2002). *Teaching about Genocide: An Interdisciplinary Guidebook with Syllabi for College and University Teachers*, revised edition. Washington, D.C.: American Sociological Association.

Chalk, Frank, and Kurt Jonassohn, eds. (1990). *The History and Sociology of Genocide: Analyses and Case Studies*. New Haven, Conn.: Yale University Press.

Donnelly, Jack (1997). *Human Rights and International Relations*, 2nd edition. Boulder, Colo.: Westview Press.

Gellately, Robert, and Ben Kiernan, eds. (2003). *The Specter of Genocide: Mass Murder in Historical Perspective*. Cambridge: Cambridge University Press.

Kuper, Leo (1981). *Genocide: Its Political Use in the Twentieth Century*. New Haven, Conn.: Yale University Press.

Novick, Peter (1999). *The Holocaust in American Life*. Boston: Houghton Mifflin.

Power, Samantha (2002). *'A Problem from Hell': America and the Age of Genocide*. New York: Basic Books.

Terry, Fiona (2002). *Condemned to Repeat? The Paradox of Humanitarian Action*. Ithaca, N.Y.: Cornell University Press.

Totten, Samuel, William S. Parsons, and Israel W. Charny, eds. (1997). *Century of Genocide; Eyewitness Accounts and Critical Views*. New York: Garland Press.

Totten, Samuel, and Steven Leonard Jacobs, eds. (2002). *Pioneers of Genocide Studies*. New Brunswick, N.J.: Transaction Press.

Weiss, Thomas G., and Cindy Collins (2000). *Humanitarian Challenges & Intervention, 2nd edition*. Boulder, Colo.: Westview Press.

Joyce A. Apsel

Eichmann Trial

The Eichmann trial began on April 11, 1961, in the theater house Beit-Ha'am (in Hebrew, "House of the People") in Jerusalem. Adolf, the son of Karl Eichmann, was charged with crimes against Jews, Gypsies, and others during the years of Nazi reign in Germany and in the Nazi-occupied areas. He was tried under a special Israeli law, the Nazis and Nazi Collaborators (Punishment) Law of 1950. The trial was viewed from the outset as a historical event of great importance. In a dramatic announcement before the Knesset (the Israeli parliament) David Ben-Gurion, then Prime Minister of Israel, declared that Eichmann had been captured by Israeli security services in Argentina, where he was hiding under a false identity. Eichmann's kidnapping was a violation of Argentina's sovereignty. The Security Council intervened, but Argentina did not press the matter, and Eichmann failed when he attempted to raise this as an objection to his trial. He was brought to Israel in a special plane in May 1960. A special panel of judges—which included Supreme Court Justice Moshe Landau, who headed the bench, and District Court judges Benjamin Halevy and Isaac Raveh—was appointed. The auditorium was packed with representatives of the international media as well as interested members of the Israeli public, Holocaust survivors were alongside native Israelis. The prosecution was headed by Gideon Hausner, Israel's attorney general, and the defense was conducted by a German attorney, Robert Servatius, who had previously defended Nazis at the Nuremberg trials.

During World War II, Eichmann was in charge of the Nazi security police's Jewish Department. In September 1939 he became head of the Jewish Section in the Gestapo. It was his job to oversee the transfer of Jews from the countries conquered and annexed by the Nazis and from Germany itself to concentration and extermination camps in the east. In this role he became responsible for the deaths of millions. From his early days in the service of the Nazi apparatus Eichmann specialized in questions relating to Jews and Zionism, and in 1937 he even visited Palestine incognito. His first noteworthy role was to organize the enforced emigration of Jews from Austria after the Anschluss (the annexation of Austria by Germany in March 1938), where in a short time he and his team managed to force more than 50,000 Jews to emigrate by stripping them of their property. By the end of 1940 Eichmann's office had the authority over all the Jews within the Reich. Later, he personally directed the 1944 deportations from Hungary while negotiating with Jewish representatives over a deal to exchange Jewish lives for goods or money. This deal never materialized and about 400,000 Hungarian Jews were sent to their deaths. His importance for the implementation of the Final Solution, however, did not derive from his formal rank in Nazi bureaucracy, as he had never attained a rank higher than the equivalent of a lieutenant colonel (*Oberstleutnant*) and was thus separated from Interior Minister Himmler by at least two ranks. Instead, the main source of his influence was his expertise in connection with Jewish affairs and his having dealt with them throughout the Nazi period.

At the Jerusalem District Court Eichmann was indicted on fifteen counts, including crimes against the Jewish people, crimes against humanity, war crimes, and membership in various criminal organizations, including the SS, the Security Service (SD), and the Gestapo. Trying Eichmann in a domestic criminal court raised some very difficult questions. First, there was the problem of judging him according to an extra-territorial and retroactive law. Second, the connection of the judges to the community of the victims seemed to undermine the objectivity of the court. Third, the focus of the trial on victims' testimonies and on their suffering was unprecedented. Aside from these legalistic problems, the judges had to resort to doctrines of domestic criminal law to adjudicate the novel category of crimes against humanity that were committed over an extended period of time, in different places, and by numerous actors. The court refused to rely on the law of conspiracy that was used in the Nuremberg trial, because of its overreach, and its tendency to blur important distinctions of the criminal law. Thus, although the Anglo-American doctrine of conspiracy offered a simple solution to adjudicating collective crimes, it also threatened to undermine the age-old distinction between the principal agent and the accessories to the crime. Instead, the Israeli court developed a unique interpretation of the Final Solution as a crime that implicated different agents in its various stages of implementation and was able in this way to attribute responsibility to Eichmann as a principal agent. Eichmann relied on the defense of "obeying superior orders," but

Former SS Lieutenant Colonel Adolf Eichmann, the "Man in the Glass Booth," on trial for his crimes against the Jewish people committed some two decades earlier. Israeli officials built the booth for his protection because they feared his assassination before a verdict was reached. [CORBIS]

the court rejected it on the basis of the doctrine of "manifest illegality" that was previously recognized by the Nuremberg tribunal. The task of the court was not simple. It had to find a way to adjust its jurisdiction rules and to interpret domestic criminal law so that it could address the novel categories of Nazi crimes without undermining the procedural guarantees of a fair trial.

The special significance of the Eichmann trial both to the international community and to the national community in Israel can be understood in light of two earlier trials: the Nuremberg trial, conducted after World War II, and the Gruenwald libel trial (better known by its popular name the Kastner trial), which took place in Israel during 1954 and 1955. Many of the prosecution's decisions regarding the way in which to structure the Eichmann trial were undertaken to avoid the risks that had materialized in those two earlier trials. Eichmann was not tried by the international military tribunal at Nuremberg, together with other Nazi criminals, because he had managed to escape to Argentina. Not only was Eichmann absent from Nuremberg but the full story of the Holocaust of European Jewry was absent as well, as Ben-Gurion emphasized in press interviews. Among the reasons for this were the jurisdictional limitations imposed by the charter of the International Military Tribunal, which held the great Nuremberg trial. The charter authorized the court to adjudicate only those actions falling under the category of "crimes against the peace" and "war crimes" that took place after 1939. These limitations stemmed from the novelty of the legal category of "crimes against humanity" and from the fear that the precedent might unduly serve to undermine the sovereignty of states later on. By contrast, the Jerusalem court, which derived its authority from the Israeli law, was able to consider the whole range of Eichmann's actions throughout the prewar and wartime period (1933–1945), because the law did not impose a similar time limitation. In addition, the court was called to focus on crimes against the Jews, alongside crimes against humanity.

The prosecution used the platform of the trial to tell the missing story of the Jewish Holocaust. For this purpose it brought 112 witnesses who testified about the events of the Holocaust and Eichmann's involvement in coordinating and carrying out the Final Solution. In addition, it submitted 1,600 documents that described the systematic persecution of European Jewry in all its phases. This evidence helped the prosecution draw a picture of the full extent of the Holocaust, even though some of the facts it sought to establish were not controversial, since the defendant did not contest the facts about the "extermination" of Jews, or the authenticity of the documents. The main line of defense was of "obeying orders" and it therefore called for a much narrower scope of factual examination in the trial. Accordingly, the defense decided not to cross-examine witnesses whose testimony did not relate directly to the actions of Eichmann. Although the court did not adopt this view of the defense, it noted in its verdict the undue extension of the trial's scope, saying that the attorney general "occasionally deviated to a small extent from the path which the court had deemed correct to delineate."

Relying solely on Israeli law, however, raised other concerns, because it was an ex post facto legislation that extended the jurisdiction of the Israeli court to adjudicate crimes that occurred outside the state of Israel, and before its establishment. For this reason the appellate court advanced an alternative basis for the court's jurisdiction, known as the doctrine of universal jurisdiction for trying crimes against humanity. The doctrine of universal jurisdiction remained dormant for forty years, because the international community viewed with suspicion the political aspects of the Eichmann trial. However, during the 1990s, when the international community was struggling to establish a permanent criminal international court, the ruling in the Eichmann trial came to serve as one of the main precedents for national courts that were beginning to adjudicate crimes against humanity that had taken place outside their territorial borders.

The second trial that Eichmann's prosecutors had in mind and that had a crucial impact on their approach was the Kastner trial, as noted earlier. During the 1950s the Israeli law for trying the Nazis and their collaborators was used mainly to try "their collaborators" among the Jews in Israel. One trial that caught much of the public attention and gave rise to an intense controversy within Israel dealt with the failed negotiations that the Zionist leader Rudolph Kastner had conducted with Adolf Eichmann. Israeli public opinion divided over the appropriate course of action taken by Jews to the Nazi oppressor. Some favored armed resistance, whereas others upheld the course of negotiations and cooperation. This debate reached a tragic climax when Kastner was assassinated a short time after the trial court reached its verdict, in which it strongly condemned Kastner for collaborating with the "devil." The prosecution in the Eichmann trial, aware of this traumatic event, attempted to change the atmosphere of blaming the victims' leaders by focusing on the guilt of the Nazi perpetrator—the defendant Adolf Eichmann. The Eichmann trial was to play a crucial role in unifying the ranks in Israel and in helping to construct a collective Israeli memory of the Holocaust. The prosecution asked key witnesses to avoid the debate over the cooperation of the *Judenrate* (Jewish leaders) with the Nazis and instead focused on the suffering of the victims. This decision to rely on the victims' testimonies had an enormous symbolic significance in legitimizing their words and lifting the taboo on discussing the Holocaust from the point of view of the victims, both for legal and for historical purposes.

These decisions of the prosecution—turning the trial into a platform for telling the story of the Jewish Holocaust by the victims, as well as avoiding the issue of Jewish cooperation with the Nazis—were sharply criticized by philosopher Hannah Arendt. Arendt, a German Jew, was living in France at the start of World War II. Interned in southern France along with other stateless Germans in 1940, she escaped and reached America in 1941. She made her name in 1951 with *The Origins of Totalitarianism,* a thorough account of the historical and philosophical origins of the totalitarian state that drew parallels between Nazi Germany and Stalinist Russia. In 1961 *The New Yorker* sent Arendt to Jerusalem to cover the Eichmann trial. Her reports, which harshly criticized the Israeli prosecution, were later published in expanded form in the book *Eichmann in Jerusalem.* She disagreed especially with the prosecution's decision to cast the trial's spotlight on the Jewish Holocaust and its victims. Arendt believed that instead of employing a category created by Israeli law, "crimes against the Jewish people," the prosecution should have based its case solely on "crimes against humanity." However, unlike many in the international community, she did not doubt the wisdom of using a legal process against Eichmann, or the right of Israel to judge him. In her opinion the systematic plan of the Nazis to annihilate the Jewish people justified the trial of Eichmann by a tribunal belonging to the victims' new political community. She praised the judges, especially Justice Landau, for resisting the temptation to allow politics into the court.

The parts of Arendt's narrative that stirred much controversy discussed the complicity of the Jewish leaders in the destruction of their own communities, and the depiction of Eichmann's state of mind as "banal." Jacob Robinson, who served as an advisor on international law to the prosecution team, devoted a book, *And the Crooked Shall Be Made Straight*, to refuting the inaccuracies in Arendt's report. Gershom Scholem, an eminent scholar and public intellectual, published a letter questioning Arendt's unforgiving condemnation of the *Judenrate*. The report sparked a furor and an intense debate that was waged primarily in the American press. Notwithstanding the controversy, Arendt's book remained one of the classic sources addressing the philosophical and jurisprudential aspects of the Eichmann trial. Ironically, it was Arendt's book that kept the trial from losing its pertinence some forty years later. The book was belatedly translated into Hebrew in the year 2000, stirring a new public debate, this time, regarding historical representations of the period.

In its verdict, the district court rejected Eichmann's arguments, both those challenging the jurisdiction of the court and those raising the substantive defense of obeying superiors' orders. Eichmann was found guilty on all counts and on December 15, 1961, was sentenced to death. He appealed, but the Supreme Court upheld the district court's decision. His appeal for clemency was also denied by Israel's president, notwithstanding the pleas of several public intellectuals on his behalf. Eichmann was hanged on the night of May 31, 1962. His body was cremated, and the ashes were scattered at sea. It was the only death sentence to be carried out in the history of the state of Israel.

Above all, the Eichmann trial is symbolized by the bulletproof glass booth in which Adolf Eichmann had been seated to protect his life. Abba Kovner, a leader of a Jewish Resistance group and a witness in the trial, proposed seeing the glass booth as a symbol of the predicament of the Jews themselves under Nazi rule. Today, after the publication of numerous historical studies of the crimes of the Nazis, we may understand the glass booth as a symbol of the Nazi criminals themselves. By resorting to "clean language" and by distancing the higher members of the Nazi apparatus from the daily murder and brutality that was the fate of the victims, the Nazis succeeded in introducing to the world a new form of crime that threatens to pervert the technological achievements of civilization into the instruments of its destruction. In this regard, the Eichmann trial stands as a warning sign to humanity.

SEE ALSO Arendt, Hannah; Nuremberg Trials; Universal Jurisdiction; War Crimes

BIBLIOGRAPHY

Arendt, Hannah (1964). *Eichmann in Jerusalem: A Report on the Banality of Evil*. New York: Viking Press.

Lippman, Matthew (2002). "Genocide: The Trial of Adolf Eichmann and the Quest for Global Justice." *Buffalo Human Rights Law Review* 8:45–121.

Papadatos, Peter (1964). *The Eichmann Trial*. New York: Praeger.

Leora Bilsky

Einsatzgruppen

No satisfactory English translation has been found for the German term *Einsatzgruppen* (EG). An accurate description might be "special extermination groups." Their primary assignment was to kill every Jewish man, woman, or child they could lay their hands on. Romani (pejoratively called "gypsies") were to suffer the same fate. Communist leaders or others suspected of any future threat to Adolf Hitler's conquests would also be targets for annihilation. Security Chief Reinhard Heydrich issued the order on September 21, 1939: "The total measures planned are to be kept strictly secret" (1949, p.120).

In May 1941, with Germany's assault against the Soviet Union imminent, four Einsatz groups were assembled. Each encompassed 500 to 800 men commanded by leading Nazis. The German army provided help and logistic support. On orders from Hitler, the EG were to break all possible civilian resistance behind the fighting front by ruthlessly destroying those deemed undesirable by the Führer or his supporters.

Einsatz units issued daily top secret reports that were consolidated in Berlin. These captured records revealed the full depravity of their deeds, despite euphemisms that sought to conceal their criminality. Victims were "given special treatment," "rendered harmless," or "resettled." EG A reported that it had liquidated 118,430 Jews and 3,398 communists. EG D reported 90,000 Jews eliminated. On September 29 and 30, 1941, one unit of EG C dispatched 33,771 Jews into a ravine that became known as Babi Yar. It has been min-

The SS Einsatzgruppen, the mobile killing units of the Third Reich, rounded up their victims (who were overwhelmingly Jewish) and transported them to secluded sites. They were shot and buried in ditches, gorges, quarries, and the like. In this photo, a Ukrainian Jew is summarily executed before a mass grave.[USHMM]

imally estimated that between one and two million innocent and helpless civilians were murdered in cold blood by these Nazi killing squads.

The procedures for mass murder were basically similar. Jews and Romani, who were earmarked for total annihilation, were ordered to assemble under penalty of death. They were transported by trucks to a hidden site where their clothing and possessions were seized. The helpless were directed to stand or kneel near the edge of a large pit that had been prepared. An EG firing squad of about ten men would shoot for about an hour before being rotated. Each row of victims fell into the pit on top of the corpses that lay dead or dying below.

In the spring of 1942 some EG units were equipped with gas vans for the easier "resettlement" of women, children, the old and infirm. Exhaust fumes were piped back into the camouflaged van. By the time the van reached its destination, the passengers were asphyxiated.

Upon conviction for their crimes against humanity at Nuremberg, EG leaders showed no remorse. They argued that Hitler had declared Germany was fighting a defensive war and they were bound to follow his orders. In a "total war" against Bolshevism, they contended, all potential enemies had to be eliminated by every possible means. Secret killing squads were a military necessity. They left no doubt that they would do it again.

In delivering his judgment, Presiding Judge Michael Musmanno noted: ". . . Mankind pleads for an understanding which will prevent anything like this happening again" (1949, p. 509). Nazi Einsatzgruppen wrote the blackest page in human history. Their cruel deeds illustrate the dangers of blind obedience to an authoritarian leader who defies the rule of law.

SEE ALSO Death Squads; SS

BIBLIOGRAPHY

Trials of War Criminals before the Nuremberg Military Tribunals under Control Council Law No. 10 (1946–1949). Vol. IV: "The Einsatzgruppen Case." Washington, D.C.: U.S. Government Printing Office.

Benjamin B. Ferencz

El Salvador

Between 1980 and 1992, the tiny Central American republic of El Salvador was engulfed in a brutal civil war. The Salvadoran armed forces, internal security forces such as the National Guard and National Police, and death squads allied with them killed tens of thousands of Salvadoran civilians in an effort to wipe out the guerrilla insurgency of the Farabundo Martí National Liberation Front (FMLN). Throughout the conflict, but most particularly in its early years, state forces committed grave and systematic abuses of human rights, including massacres, murders, disappearance, and torture. The FMLN carried out a smaller but nonetheless serious number of violations of international humanitarian law, including targeted assassinations of prominent public figures, kidnappings for ransom, and harming civilians in violation of the rule of proportionality of the laws of war. A United Nations-sponsored Commission on the Truth for El Salvador, created in 1992 as part of a UN-brokered peace accord, concluded that 85 percent of the human rights cases brought to its attention involved state agents, paramilitary groups, or death squads allied with official forces. Five percent of cases brought to the Truth Commission were attributed to the FMLN.

Political factors that led to the outbreak of war included decades of military rule, blatant fraud when civilians won the 1972 and 1977 presidential elections, and increasingly violent suppression of the regime's opponents. These political factors were coupled with the domination of the economic life of the country by a small landed elite that was opposed to reforms, especially agrarian reform, and who derived their control from the economic transformation of the country in the late nineteenth century. That period saw the rapid expansion of coffee cultivation, the abolition of indigenous tribal lands, and the creation of rural police forces for the explicit purpose of evicting peasants from communally held properties.

A landmark event in El Salvador's modern history was the 1932 peasant revolt, which was prompted by worldwide depression and plunging coffee prices. In December 1931, Minister of War General Maximiliano Hernández Martínez seized power in a military coup. Poorly armed and poorly organized peasants staged an uprising, led by communist organizer Farabundo Martí (from whom the latter-day guerrillas took their name). In quelling the rebellion, Hernández Martínez and his troops massacred between 10,000 and 30,000 people in a matter of weeks. According to the U.S. Central Intelligence Agency (CIA), in a 1985 assessment, "the resulting endemic national paranoia over the Communist threat reinforced authoritarian rule by the armed forces and its affluent civilian backers for the next half century. The chain of military regimes provided order and stability, and largely gave the plantation owners and monopolist businessmen a free hand over the economic life of the country."

Political violence dramatically increased in 1979, following a reformist military coup aimed at staving off a violent revolution like the one that had begun in 1978 in neighboring Nicaragua. Efforts by military officers and progressive civilians to promote reforms, including an end to human rights abuses, were blocked by a wave of violence unleashed by the army and security forces. Through mass demonstrations and sit-ins, grassroots organizations, some with direct or indirect links to guerrilla groups that had emerged in the early 1970s, challenged the junta to rapidly fulfill its promises. Targeted killings by state forces and increasing confrontations between government troops and demonstrators brought the civilian death toll to a record 9,000 to 10,000 in 1980. High-profile victims included El Salvador's Archbishop, Oscar Romero, who was shot by a death squad as he celebrated mass. Six leaders of the leftist political opposition were kidnapped by security forces from a press conference and then tortured and murdered, and four U.S. churchwomen were abducted,

San Salvador's Archbishop Oscar Arnulfo Romero, a well-known critic of violence and injustice, was assassinated while celebrating mass on March 24, 1980. The UN Truth Commission later determined that Major Robert D'Aubuisson had ordered his death. [BETTMANN/CORBIS]

raped, and killed by troops of the National Guard. Amid the escalating repression, guerrilla groups coalesced to form the Farabundo Martí National Liberation Front (FMLN). Their failed "final offensive" in January 1981 effectively launched the country into full-scale civil war.

The years 1980 to 1983 witnessed the heaviest repression. Massacres in rural areas, gruesome murders by death squads, and the killing or disappearance of teachers, trade unionists, students, religious and humanitarian workers, journalists, and members of opposition political parties were the products of a military mindset that equated opposition with subversion and that viewed civilians in combat zones as legitimate targets of attack. The scale of the killings in rural as well as urban areas subsided in the second half of the decade, largely as the result of pressure from the United States, which provided approximately $6 billion in military and economic assistance to the Salvadoran government over the course of the war. El Salvador became

Funeral mass for six Jesuit priests gunned down in San Salvador. When several army officers were directly linked to their murder, it became a human rights case with international repercussions and was one of several factors that led to a negotiated peace in late 1989. [REUTERS/CORBIS]

one of the most contentious U.S. foreign policy issues of the cold war. Pressure for improvements in human rights originating in the U.S. Congress was coupled with the persistent downplaying or outright denial of abuses by senior U.S. authorities who were concerned with maintaining a flow of aid to defeat the insurgency.

The December 1981 massacre in El Mozote and surrounding villages epitomized both Salvadoran army practices and the pattern of U.S. denial. According to the Truth Commission, the army's elite Atlacatl Battalion "deliberately and systematically" executed more than 500 men, women, and children over a period of several days, torturing some victims and setting fire to buildings. Exhumations in and around El Mozote after the war revealed that, in one parish house alone, 131 of the 143 victims were children whose average age was six. The Truth Commission found "no evidence" to support arguments made publicly by the U.S. government at the time of the massacre that the victims had participated in combat or had been trapped in crossfire between combatant forces.

Other large-scale massacres of civilians in rural areas took place at the Sumpul River (1980), San Fran-

cisco Guajoyo (1980), El Junquillo (1981), the Lempa River (1981), El Calabozo (1982), Las Hojas (1983), the Gualsinga River (1984), Los Llanitos (1984), and San Sebastián (1988). While the death toll in massacres subsided as the decade wore on, hundreds of civilians were killed and many more thousands were displaced or forced to flee the country by indiscriminate aerial bombing campaigns conducted by the Salvadoran Air Force from 1983 to 1986. The goal was to drive civilians out of zones where the guerrillas were active. Bombing attacks subsided after 1986, a result of international pressure and a change in FMLN tactic, which emphasized small unit operations over the massing of large numbers of fighters.

Guerrilla abuses against the civilian population took place mainly but not exclusively in the context of the conflict. Before the outbreak of war, the guerrillas kidnapped prominent individuals for ransom, including the Salvadoran foreign minister in 1978 (he was subsequently executed). Beginning in the 1970s and continuing throughout the conflict, the FMLN summarily executed civilians suspected of being government informants. Such individuals were known as *orejas*, or "ears."

Targeted killings and disappearances of civilians by the FMLN were smaller in number than those of state forces, but constituted serious violations of international humanitarian law, nonetheless. Victims included more than eleven mayors, who were executed between 1985 and 1988 in areas the guerrillas considered their zones of control. Also killed were four off-duty U.S. Marines, who were machine-gunned at an outdoor café in 1985; and conservative public figures such as Attorney General José Roberto García Alvarado and intellectual Francisco Peccorini, both assassinated in 1989. Other episodes of FMLN abuse included the mass execution of a group of captured civilians in Morazán (1984), the kidnapping of the daughter of President José Napoleón Duarte (1985), and the killing of civilians who refused to stop at guerrilla roadblocks. Scores of civilians were killed and hundreds were wounded by the guerrillas' indiscriminate use of land mines. On numerous occasions, the use of crude and inaccurate homemade weapons and explosives resulted in civilian deaths.

Nothing so epitomized the terror of the Salvadoran war as the activities of the death squads. According to the Truth Commission, the squads' share of abuses was relatively small (just over 10% of documented cases), but they "gained such control that they ceased to be an isolated or marginal phenomenon and became an instrument of terror used systematically for the physical elimination of political opponents." The Truth Commission reported that civilian as well as military authorities during the 1980s participated in, encouraged, and tolerated death squad activities, offering "complete impunity" for those who worked in them.

Official U.S. documents that were declassified after the end of the war contain a wealth of information on death squad operations, structure, and personnel. For instance, Roberto D'Aubuisson, a cashiered National Guard officer, was a key figure in death squad violence. According to the U.S. Embassy in San Salvador, one of his most notorious crimes was overseeing the drawing of lots for the "privilege" of assassinating Archbishop Romero. According to a 1981 CIA memo, D'Aubuisson was funded by members of the "extreme right-wing Salvadoran elite" who "have reportedly spent millions of dollars" in an effort to return the country to right-wing military rule. Another 1981 CIA report said that D'Aubuisson favored the "physical elimination" of leftists, whom he defined as "anyone not supportive of the traditional status quo." According to the Truth Commission, D'Aubuisson maintained close contact with the intelligence sections of the security forces, combining "two elements in a strategic relationship": money (and weapons, vehicles, and safehouses) provided by

the extreme right, and ideology, providing "the definition of a political line," for the intelligence units of the security forces.

To give a political front to the death squads, D'Aubuisson organized the *Frente Amplio Nacional* (Broad National Front), which later became the Nationalist Republican Alliance (*Alianza Republicana Nacionalista*, or ARENA) party. As ARENA's candidate, D'Aubuisson was elected to the Constituent Assembly in 1982, later becoming its president. From that post, according to the CIA in 1984, he directed a team that engaged in "political intimidation, including abduction, torture, and murder." In 1985, the CIA identified the notorious Secret Anticommunist Army (*Ejército Secreto Anticomunista*, or ESA) as the public face of the ARENA death squad.

Other death squads operated out of the military and security forces, occasionally conducting joint operations. These included death squads organized out of the intelligence sections of the National Guard and National Police. The army's First Brigade, Signal Corps, Second Brigade, and cavalry, artillery, engineer, and infantry detachments throughout the country also participated in death-squad killings. A death squad operating out of an intelligence unit of the Air Force in the early 1990s threw bound but living prisoners out of aircraft over the Pacific Ocean, a practice referred to as "night free-fall training."

Negotiations to end the Salvadoran conflict began in late 1989, the result of a military stalemate, the end of the cold war, and the international disrepute of the armed forces following the army's murder of six prominent Jesuit priests. This atrocity led to a human rights case with broad international repercussions. The sweeping accord signed in 1992 under UN auspices established a Truth Commission composed of non-Salvadorans to investigate grave acts of violence, and an Ad Hoc Commission of Salvadoran citizens to review the records of military officers with an eye to purging those who had violated human rights. Those recommended for dismissal eventually included the minister and vice-minister of defense. The accord also abolished the security forces, established a new National Civilian Police, and reduced the role of the military in postwar society. While most of the provisions of the peace accord were implemented, the majority of the recommendations of the Truth Commission remained unfulfilled. In 1993, amid death threats and high-profile killings of demobilized FMLN leaders, the Salvadoran government created a Joint Group (*Grupo Conjunto*) for the Investigation of Politically Motivated Illegal Armed Groups. It found that politically motivated violence was linked to "the broad network of organized crime" operating in El Salvador, and raised questions about the ties between earlier death squad participants and the "highly organized criminal structures" engaged in a host of illegal activities, including drug trafficking.

SEE ALSO Death Squads; Truth Commissions

BIBLIOGRAPHY

Americas Watch (1991). *El Salvador's Decade of Terror: Human Rights since the Assassination of Archbishop Romero.* New Haven, Conn.: Yale University Press.

Americas Watch and American Civil Liberties Union (1982). *Report on Human Rights in El Salvador.* New York: Vintage Books.

Anderson, Thomas (1971). *Matanza: El Salvador's Communist Revolt of 1932.* Lincoln: University of Nebraska Press.

Arnson, Cynthia J. (2000). "Window on the Past: A Declassified History of Death Squads in El Salvador." In *Death Squads in Global Perspective: Murder With Deniability*, ed. B. Campbell and A. Brenner. New York: St. Martin's Press.

Danner, Mark (1994). *The Massacre at El Mozote.* New York: Vintage Books.

Human Rights Watch/Americas (1993). "El Salvador. Accountability and Human Rights: The Report of the United Nations Commission on the Truth for El Salvador." 5(7). New York: Human Rights Watch.

National Security Archive (1996). *El Salvador: War, Peace, and Human Rights 1980-1994.* Alexandria, Va.: Chadwyck Healey. Available from http://nsarchive.chadwyk.com/cgi-bin/cqcgi.

Popkin, Margaret (2000). *Peace Without Justice: Obstacles to Building the Rule of Law in El Salvador.* University Park: Pennsylvania State University Press.

United Nations Commission on the Truth for El Salvador (1993). *From Madness to Hope: The 12-Year War in El Salvador*, UNDoc. S/25500. New York: United Nations.

United Nations (1995). *The United Nations in El Salvador 1990–1995.* The United Nations Blue Book Series, Volume IV. New York: United Nations Department of Public Information.

Cynthia J. Arnson

Enlightenment

To mount concerted opposition to mankind's inhumanity was one of the central objectives of the Enlightenment, an intellectual movement prevalent in Europe and some European colonies for around one hundred years from the late seventeenth century. Progressive ideas of toleration and of civil and human rights such as came to be realized in the American and French revolutions were largely inspired by Enlightenment princi-ples. Religious intolerance, especially in England and France, offered many Enlightenment thinkers their main focus of criticism, as they resisted, in the first case, the efforts of King James II to debar Protestants from the monarchy and public office and defied, in the second, the revocation of the Edict of Nantes, which in 1685 abruptly terminated the long truce that had followed the ravages of sectarian wars associated with the Reformation and the Counterreformation.

Understood in this way the Enlightenment was committed to humanitarian ideals, cosmopolitan notions of citizenship, and a spirit of toleration. Its principles were to come to fruition in England's so-called Glorious Revolution of 1688. On the Continent these principles were mobilized against political and theological institutions that had driven French Huguenots in particular into exile, until a century later, when the *ancien régime* itself was overthrown. William and Mary's Act of Toleration and John Locke's *Letter Concerning Toleration,* both dating from 1689, as well as many of the chief writings of Spinoza, Bayle, Montesquieu, Rousseau, and Diderot, were designed to combat religious bigotry and sectarian violence. Voltaire was perhaps the eighteenth century's preeminent campaigner for toleration, rallying other luminaries of his age around his battlecry, *Ecrasez l'infâme.* It was in the mid-eighteenth century that the term *civilization* came to acquire its modern meaning as opposition to barbarism, which, in addition to primitive morals, arbitrary power, and ruthless violence, was now deemed also to embrace religious fundamentalism, such as had plunged Europe into darkness during the time of the Crusades and the Inquisition. From this point of view the French Revolutionary Declaration of the Rights of Man and the Citizen in 1789—one of the principal sources for twentieth-century charters of human rights—may be seen as marking the Enlightenment's triumph, in heralding, at least in principle, a new and secular age of toleration.

Following the rise of totalitarianism and the advent of the Holocaust in the twentieth century, an altogether different image of the Enlightenment has sometimes been preferred, concentrating instead on its commitment to the advancement of science and reason as the main vehicles of human progress. When conceived as providing a philosophical foundation for the scientific revolution through the contributions of Bacon, Descartes, Newton, and French materialists, the Enlightenment's origins are characteristically dated from around sixty or seventy years earlier in the seventeenth century, and critics have sugggested that this intelletual movement did not so much abandon Christianity as turn Christianity inside out, substituting the pursuit of earthly happiness for the unworldly salvation of our souls, replacing one form of absolutism with another, dogmatic reason for dogmatic faith.

Three major implications with respect to the problem of genocide and crimes against humanity have been drawn from that assessment of the Enlightenment, each of which trades on the facts that modern barbarism embraced science rather than rejected it and that the Holocaust was perpetrated through the use of scientifically enlightened practices. The first is that by way of the Enlightenment, Western civilization itself became barbarous, in implementing strategic plans for moral and social reconstruction that encapsulated an Enlightenment faith in the unity of all the sciences. The second is that the Enlightenment's blind devotion to science and reason destroyed the ethical moorings of classical and Christian values alike, replacing them with merely instrumental notions of rationality by virtue of which a program of genocide could be scientifically organized. The third is that the Enlightenment's trust in the idea of scientific progress made it particularly hostile to Judaism as a mystical religion more primitive even than the Christianity it engendered, so that the attainment of cosmopolitan human rights implied the creation of a world without Jews.

Insofar as some Enlightenment thinkers, including Voltaire, showed little interest in preserving Jewish rituals, they in fact subscribed not to the Jews' annihilation but to their assimilation and enjoyment of rights belonging to all citizens. The contention that genocide is characterized by unrestrained rationality turns around ideas of reason peculiar to a German tradition of discourse over the past three hundred years rather than to mainstream English or French contributors to Enlightenment thought. And the truth of the proposition that crimes against humanity are evidence of civilization's own barbarism has been obscured by the religious fundamentalism that inspires much of terrorism today. The survival and current resurgence of crimes against humanity perhaps demonstrate how limited has been the Enlightenment's success in marshalling support for its objectives.

SEE ALSO Philosophy

BIBLIOGRAPHY

Arendt, Hannah (1958). *The Origins of Totalitarianism*, 2nd edition. London: Allen and Unwin.

Wokler, Robert (2000). "The Enlightenment Project on the Eve of the Holocaust." In *Enlightenment and Genocide: Contradictions of Modernity*, ed. B. Sträth and J. Kaye. Brussels: Presses Universitaires Européennes.

Wokler, Robert (2000). "Multiculturalism and Ethnic Cleansing in the Enlightenment." In *Toleration in Enlightenment Europe*, ed. O. P. Grell and R. Porter. New York: Cambridge University Press.

Robert Wokler

Ennals, Martin
[JULY 27, 1927–1991]
Human rights activist

Charismatic but modest, Martin Ennals was one of a handful of figures who catapulted human rights from the fringes of transnational political relevance into the center of international relations in the second half of the twentieth century. This he did primarily by transforming a small, recently formed body, Amnesty International (AI), into the premier human rights organization.

Educated at Walsall Grammar School (in England, 1935–1945) and the London School of Economics (where he pursued a B.S. in international relations, 1945–1949), Ennals was present at the 1948 United Nations (UN) General Assembly when it adopted the Universal Declaration of Human Rights. Not long afterward he began working at the United Nations Educational, Scientific, and Cultural Organization (UNESCO) in Paris (1951–1959), where he found himself prominently involved in a historic human rights issue. As secretary and then president of the UNESCO staff association, he defended U.S. citizens, members of the international civil service, who risked dismissal because they, in his words, "refused to break the UNESCO and UN staff rules by completing political questionnaires demanded of them by the U.S. State Department during the McCarthy period."

Ennals left UNESCO to become general secretary (1960–1966) of the prominent human rights activist group in the United Kingdom, the National Council for Civil Liberties (NCCL, now known as Liberty). Among the issues NCCL concentrated on during his tenure (with some success) was the need for legislation against racial discrimination and the incitement of racial hatred. Ennals continued working on race relations after departing from the NCCL, and in 1968, appalled by the adoption of the Commonwealth Immigration Act, which deprived nonresident British passport holders without British ancestry of the right to live in the United Kingdom, he undertook a study on the predicaments of the East African Asians with UK passports who were affected by the act.

That same year Ennals began his twelve-year tenure as secretary general of AI (1968–1980). At the inception of his tenure, the organization's international secretariat had a staff of seven and an annual budget of £17,000. By the time Ennals resigned, AI had a staff

Martin Ennals was behind the creation of at least ten human rights organizations, which together span the full spectrum of human rights. From left to right, Lord Gardiner, Sean MacBride (a founding member of Amnesty International), and Martin Ennals, at the start of Amnesty International's first worldwide campaign for the abolition of torture, 1972.[HULTON ARCHIVE/GETTY IMAGES]

of 150 and an annual budget of approximately £2,000,000; AI also received the Nobel Peace Price in 1977. For Ennals, effectiveness demanded professionalism. His special skill was mobilizing a truly international movement of activists through the leadership of a professional core. The work of AI ranges from grassroots work on behalf of imprisoned individuals, to the development of international standards and implementation mechanisms at the highest intergovernmental levels. Ennals led all this with a pervasive institutional commitment to factual accuracy and political impartiality.

After his tenure at AI, Ennals was associated with various nongovernmental organizations (NGOs), several of which he helped found. These included the International Human Rights Information and Documentation System (HURIDOCS), Article 19 (the freedom of expression and information organization) and International Alert (IA). The latter was the merged result of two initiatives: the Standing International Forum on Ethnic Conflict, and International Alert on Genocide and Massacres, and Ennals was its first secretary general (1985–1990). Not shirking the greatest challenges, IA started to promote cross-community contacts in Sri Lanka.

Ennals died of cancer on October 15, 1991, in Saskatoon, Canada, where he had recently begun a year's residency at the University of Saskatchewan as the Ariel Fellows Chair of Human Rights.

SEE ALSO Nongovernmental Organizations

BIBLIOGRAPHY

Martin Ennals Foundation "Martin Ennals: A Giant Human Rights Defender." Available from http://www.martinennalsaward.org/en/martinennals/index.html.

Nigel S. Rodley

Enver, Ismail

[NOVEMBER 22, 1881–AUGUST 4, 1922]
Turkish Minister of War in the Ottoman Empire during
World War I; better known as Enver Pasha

Ismail Enver was born on November 22, 1881, into a well-to-do family in Istanbul. His father was a civil servant. Enver studied in Germany, where he was particularly influenced by German military theory and organization, which he tried to emulate upon his return to the Ottoman Empire. He was quickly promoted in the army, attaining the title of Pasha (Bashaw) in 1913, when he was but thirty-two years old. He married Naciye Sultana, the Sultan's daughter. He was one of the leaders of the Committee for Union and Progress, also known as Ittihadists or Young Turks, together with Talaat Pasha and Cemal Pasha. He was a vocal supporter of a pan-Turkish Empire extending deep into the Caucasus, Iran, India, and Central Asia.

A bloodless revolution in July 1908 deposed Sultan Abdul Hamit and led the Ittihadists to power. At their 1910 congress in Saloniki, the Ittihadists discussed a plan for the "complete Ottomanization of all Turkish subjects." Their aggressive nationalist policies contributed to the outbreak of the Balkan war of 1912, where ethnic cleansing was practiced on all sides. In 1912 the loss of Libya to Italy eroded the Ittihadists power and drove them into a coalition with the Liberal Union. However, on January 23, 1913, the Three Pashas putsched and established a military dictatorship. This eventually drew the Ottoman Empire into World War I on the side of the Central Powers.

Enver's Third Army suffered a disastrous defeat at Sarikamish during the December 1914 offensive against Russia, in which some 80,000 Turkish soldiers perished. This diminished Enver's prestige, but he blamed the Armenians for his defeat, unjustly accusing them of connivance with the Russians. Together with Talaat Pasha, then serving as Minister of the Interior, he conceived the plan to physically eliminate all Christian minorities—including the Armenians, Assyrians, and Orthodox Greeks—that, theoretically, might have sympathies with the enemy. The genocide against the Armenians was begun on April 24, 1915, with the arrest and murder of Armenian leaders and intellectuals in Istanbul. The Armenian civilian population in Eastern Anatolia was then subjected to massacres and deportations that cost 1 to 1.5 million lives. Within the Ministry of War, Enver gave responsibility to a Special Organization (*Teshkilâti Mahsusa*); one of its assignments was the liquidation of the Armenians.

Pursuant to Article 230 of the Treaty of Sèvres between the Allies and the Ottoman Empire, Turkish officers and politicians responsible for the genocide of non-Turkish populations were to be tried by an international tribunal. On November 23, 1918, an Ottoman Parliamentary Commission started an inquiry into the massacres, which led to the indictment of Enver, Talaat, and former Minister of Justice Ibrahim Bey. They were tried in absentia before a Turkish court martial in Istanbul, found guilty pursuant to Articles 45 and 170 of the Ottoman Penal Code, and sentenced to death. The sentences were not carried out, however, because the Young Turk cabinet had resigned and gone into exile shortly before capitulation.

Enver fled to Germany in October 1918 and established contacts with German communists, including Karl Radek. In 1920 he went to Moscow and eventually traveled to Asia, where he supported an anti-Bolshevik revolt. He was killed in battle on August 4, 1922, near Baldzhuan in Turkestan (present-day Tajikistan).

SEE ALSO Armenians in Ottoman Turkey and the Armenian Genocide; Atatürk, Mustafa Kemal Pasha; Talaat

BIBLIOGRAPHY

Ahmad, F. (1969). *The Young Turks.* Oxford: Oxford University Press.

Dadrian, Vahakn (1999). *Warrant for Genocide: Key Elements of Turko-Armenian Conflict.* New Brunswick, N.J.: Transaction Publishers.

Morgenthau, Henry (2000). *Ambassador Morgenthau's Story.* Ann Arbor, Mich.: Gomidas Institute.

Shaw, S. J., and E. K. Shaw (1977). *History of the Ottoman Empire and Modern Turkey.* Cambridge, U.K.: Cambidge University Press.

Vardy, Steven, and Hunt Tooley, eds. (2003). *Ethnic Cleansing in Twentieth Century Europe.* New York: Columbia University Press.

Alfred de Zayas

Eritrea

Eritrea is one of the world's newest states, having been created in 1993 at the conclusion of a thirty-year war of independence waged against Ethiopia. The territory that is Eritrea was first associated with Ethiopia as part of its precursor kingdom, Aksum, which flourished in the fourth century CE. Eritrea's present-day population is almost equally divided today between Christian and Muslim faiths, but the nation began a history distinct from Ethiopia with its incorporation in the Ottoman empire prior to becoming an Italian colony in 1890. Italy briefly joined Eritrea with Ethiopia, which it conquered in 1936 and occupied until 1941, when British armies liberated the entire region. Discouraged from

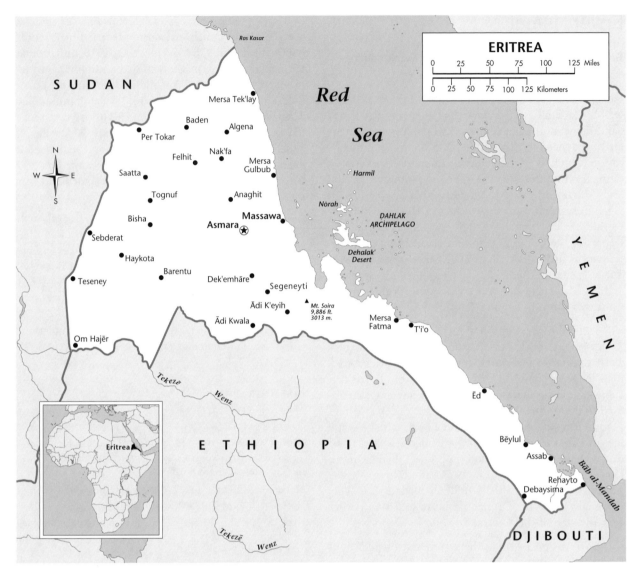

One of the newer countries in the world, Eritrea won its indepedence from Ethiopia in 1993.[MARYLAND CARTOGRAPHICS]

contemplating post–World War II colonization of Ethiopia, Britain administered Eritrea until 1949 as a trust territory on behalf of the United Nations.

As an early and important accomplishment, the United Nations rejected both Eritrea's bid for independence and its incorporation within Ethiopia, opting instead for federating it with Ethiopia in 1951. Ethiopian emperor Haile Selassie I then systematically undermined this agreement, eventually co-opting the Eritrean parliament to vote for full union with Ethiopia. This prompted the birth of the Eritrean Liberation Front (ELF). The ELF was later rivaled and then supplanted by the Eritrean People's Liberation Front (EPLF), which led the war against Ethiopia, achieved victory in 1991, and successfully gained formal independence in

1993. The EPLF has since renamed itself the People's Front for Democracy and Justice (PFDJ).

An independent commission named by the Eritrean government produced a thoroughly democratic constitution developed through extensive and exemplary consultations with all Eritrean communities, including citizens residing outside the country. The government, however, comprehensively failed to implement its constitutional provisions for the protection of human rights and democratic elections. In the estimation of Freedom House, a respected pro-democracy and human rights watch group, Eritrea's record on human rights has become one of the poorest in sub-Saharan Africa. Renewed war with Ethiopia from 1998 to 2000, prompted by a border dispute, caused incalculable suffering in both countries and seems to have been a factor in Eritrea's increasingly severe abuse of basic human rights.

Eritrea has, however, been severely victimized by Ethiopian abuses of human rights, both during its war of liberation and in the recent border war. Under its military dictator, Mengistu Haile Mariam (1974–1991), Ethiopia indiscriminately bombed Eritrean civilians in both urban and rural areas, in a futile effort to stamp out the guerrilla-based liberation movement by conventional military means. No formal international tribunal was subsequently proposed or convened to investigate war crimes committed during this conflict, although for more than a decade, Ethiopia's Special Prosecutor has brought former Mengistu regime officials to trial for egregious crimes now prosecuted under the Rome Statute of the International Criminal Court regarding genocide, war crimes, and crimes against humanity. Had he been brought before an international criminal tribunal, Mengistu would no doubt have claimed that his government was seeking to restore and preserve the unity of the Ethiopian state, which constitutes a mitigating factor within the meaning of the applicable Rome Statute's provisions. The statute is less clear on how the outlawing of war crimes applies to a liberation movement such as Eritrea's, which functioned entirely within the borders of what it regarded as its own territory. The statute distinguishes between international and non-international conflicts, but Eritrea's long history in relation to Ethiopia makes it unclear as to which category (international or internal) applies.

The Liberation War, 1962–1991

That war crimes were committed on a massive scale, at least by Ethiopian troops during the liberation war, is beyond dispute. These crimes included, inter alia, willful killing and willful causing of great suffering. Ethiopian armies inevitably directed attacks against civilian populations given the difficulty in guerrilla warfare of distinguishing between military and civilian personnel.

Mengistu insisted throughout his rule that the only acceptable end to the conflict would be an Ethiopian military victory. In a region where the average age of the population is under the age of twenty, it is all but certain that "children" participated in this conflict and in the subsequent border war, which automatically qualifies as a violation of international laws regarding war crimes as established by the Rome Statute.

Domestic Human Rights Performance, 1993–2004

To an observer not schooled in international law, Eritrea's very poor human rights record, especially since the border war, appears not to include genocide, since

its transgressions have not been directed against any ethnic, religious, national, or racial community within its borders. Indeed, the PFDJ regime has gone to some lengths to try to protect each of its two major and nine distinct ethnic communities and to insure their equitable representation within the government. Pervasive abuse of the civil and political rights that are generally understood as essential to democracy does conflict with the Rome Statute's proscription of crimes against humanity, however, in so far as these include torture and imprisonment or other severe deprivation of physical liberty in violation of fundamental rules of international law. Assessments of Eritrea's poor human rights record by Amnesty International, Freedom House, Human Rights Watch, and the U.S. Department of State have found these abuses to be widespread and comprehensive.

Eritrea does not appear to have been guilty in any major way of violating the other major categories of crimes against humanity identified by the Rome Statute. By contrast, Eritrea has consistently and flagrantly violated political and civil rights normally deemed essential to democracy but that are not, however, considered genocide or crimes against humanity. These violations have included pervasive denial of freedom of speech and association, blocking the emergence of a free and independent press, and arrests, trials, and incarcerations that are in direct violation of due process as it is understood by judiciaries in democratic countries. Eritrea has indefinitely postponed the holding of the free and fair multiparty national elections that are mandated by its draft constitution. Jehovah's Witnesses have been persecuted because of their refusal to accept compulsory military service.

The Border War, 1998–2000

Eritrea's border war with Ethiopia has profoundly victimized hundreds of thousands of people in both countries. The most easily identifiable war crime, of which both countries were guilty, was unlawful deportation within the meaning of the Rome Statute. Each country identified citizens with heritage traceable to its opponent, and then forcibly deported them to their putative "home" country. Numerically, Ethiopia's transgression was far greater than that of Eritrea. The United Nations-sponsored agreement ending the war contained provisions for the repatriation of such involuntary deportees.

The Rome Statute appears implicitly to presume a distinction between soldiers and citizens that the border war blurred. It was a war between peoples notwithstanding their important ties of consanguinity and their historically intertwined economies, politics, and cultures. Both countries mobilized hastily trained "civilian soldiers" as well as their professional military personnel. As one consequence there was no clear empirical distinction between military targets and civilian enterprises, which were destroyed in the thousands. Nor was there a clear delineation between military personnel and civilians, whom the Rome Statute seeks to protect. Hundreds of thousands of people were killed, maimed, and rendered destitute, whether or not they were unarmed civilians or professional soldiers.

The Rome Statute's focus on "intent" is similarly problematic in the case of Eritrea and Ethiopia. Given their historic interdependence, neither side has fully come to terms with Eritrea's still new independence. Each has felt—and continues to feel—betrayed, violated, and threatened by the other's "unilateral" and contrary courses of political and economic action.

Both the liberation war and the subsequent border war, and their aftermath, have greatly exacerbated longstanding environmental degradation in both countries. Eritrea and Ethiopia face "natural" disasters that have their roots in the damage of the war years and which have strained the capacities of humanitarian relief agencies, and deepened some of the worst, most comprehensive, and most pervasive poverty anywhere in the world.

SEE ALSO Ethiopia

BIBLIOGRAPHY

Iyob, Ruth (1995). *The Eritrean Struggle for Independence: Domination, Resistance, Nationalism, 1941–1993.* New York: Cambridge University Press.

Medhana, Tesfatsion (1986). *Eritrea: Dynamics of a National Question.* Amsterdam: G.Gruner.

Negash, Tegash, and Kjietil Tronvoll (2000). *Brothers at War: Making Sense of the Eritrean-Ethiopian War.* Athens: Ohio University Press.

Sherman, Richard (1980). *Eritrea: The Unfinished Revolution.* New York: Praeger.

John W. Harbeson

Ethiopia

Ethiopia is a large, multi-ethnic country located in the eastern part of Africa. It covers 437,600 square miles of land, as much as California, Oregon, Missouri and Idaho combined. Ethiopia's population in 2004 is estimated at approximately 68 million and includes about seventy different ethnic groups. The largest group is the Oromo. They live mainly in the central and southwestern parts of the country and constitute about 40 percent of the national population. The Amhara and Tigre

ethnic groups are found in the central and northern highland regions of Ethiopia, and together make up 32 percent of the country's population. Minority ethnic groups such as the Anywaa, popularly called Anuak (less than 1%), Afar (4%), Somali (6%) and Gumuz (6%) make up the remaining 28 percent of the national population. Amharinya, the language of the Amhara ethnic group, is the official language of the country.

Ethiopia is one of only two African territories that were never European colonies. (The other is Liberia.) Italy's attempt to conquer and colonize Ethiopia in the late nineteenth century ended in disaster and humiliation when Italian forces were crushed in the northern Tigrean town of Adwa, on March 1, 1896. Ethiopia thus became "an insulting symbol" of Italy's failure to achieve its imperial ambitions in Africa (Bahru, 1996, p. 151).

Ethiopia's most popular and well known ruler was Ras Tafari Makonnen, popularly known as Haile Selassie I. He ruled Ethiopia as Emperor from 1930 to 1974. He was regarded as the 225th Emperor in a line of Ethiopian monarchs who claimed to be descendants of a legendary marriage between King Solomon of Israel and the Ethiopian "Queen of Sheba" in the tenth century BC (Bahru, 1996, pp 7–9).

The Italian Invasion of 1935-36

Italy invaded Ethiopia for a second time on October 3, 1935 with a hundred thousand troops and two hundred and fifty airplanes equipped with mechanisms for spraying poison gas. Many historians agree that this invasion was undertaken in part to vindicate Italy's national honor, which had been bruised by the Ethiopians in 1896. Another reason for the invasion was that Italy's fascist dictator, Benito Mussolini, had promised to give Italy's poor large tracts of Ethiopian land for cultivation.

The Italians launched a well-planned attack, bombarding defenseless civilians. Since Italy had ratified the Geneva Protocol of 1925 on April 3, 1928, banning the use of poison gas in warfare, the actions of Italian troops in Ethiopia clearly violated international law.

The Office of Chemical Warfare of the Italian Ministry of War had long admired Germany's use of poison gas warfare. Between 1930 and 1932, the Office of Chemical Warfare produced tons of mustard gas bombs and secretly shipped one thousand of them closer to the Ethiopian heartland. In these same years, the Italian Ministry of War authorized the shipment of "56,000 artillery shells loaded with arsine gas" to Eritrea, then the northern province of Ethiopia that Italy had controlled as a protectorate or informal colony, with the consent of Ethiopia, since the 1880s.

Map of Ethiopia showing locations of Sudan, Somalia, Uganda, Kenya, Saudi Arabia, Red Sea, and Eritrea, 1994. [EASTWORD **PUBLICATIONS DEVELOPMENT**]

The shipment of chemical weapons close to Ethiopia suggests that Italy's military plans to use poison gas in Ethiopia began five years before the actual invasion. By the time the invasion began, 45 tons of C-500T lethal mustard gas, 265 tons of other poison gas as well as 7,483 gas bombs were ready for use at the Eritrean seaport of Massawa.

Mussolini's troops first used gas on October 10 and 29, 1935. Afterwards, the use of poison gas in aerial bombardment of Ethiopia became routine policy. In November, 1935 Marshall Pietro Badoglio, then High Commander of all Italian forces in East Africa, ordered Italian military planes to spray villages, livestock, pas-

tures and all water sources with mustard gas. Badoglio prevented Ethiopian soldiers and civilians gasping for breath, under suffocating mustard and arsine gas, from fleeing to safety. Badoglio ordered Italian military pilots to bombard any fleeing or retreating Ethiopians with mustard gas.

On June 5, 1936, one month after Ethiopian forces surrendered, and Italian troops occupied Addis Ababa, Mussolini ordered his Viceroy in Ethiopia, Marshall Rodolfo Graziani, to impose a reign of terror on the country. Under these orders, Graziani waged a campaign of total destruction. About 250 Italian planes dropped poison gases in all regions of Ethiopia and tar-

In the 1990s, as the decades-long conflict between Ethiopia and Eritrea raged on, severe drought threatened a catastrophic famine. The government of Ethiopia was severely criticized for its continual spending on war as thousands of its citizens were dying of starvation. In this photo, taken June 14, 1998, Ethiopians displaced by the war wait for food distribution in the Ethiopian town of Adi Gudom, near Makelle. [AP/WIDE WORLD PHOTOS]

geted not only the kingdom's peasant volunteer army, but also noncombatant civilians in nonmilitary villages. Sbacchi has estimated that for the entire length of the military campaign (October 3, 1935–June 10, 1940), the Italian Royal Air Force dropped 2,100 poison gas bombs, containing about 500 tons of poison gas, on Ethiopia.

Effects of Poison Gas in Ethiopia

Poison gas had a devastating effect on military morale and civilian life in Ethiopia. The mustard gas bombs contained a corrosive liquid. When they exploded, they emitted lethal vapors that penetrated the human skin and produced both internal and external lesions that ultimately killed some victims. Others were blinded by the toxic gases. Many of those who escaped the deadly rain of mustard gas on the battlefield finally succumbed to its lethal effects when they drank water from the rivers and lakes contaminated by the gas.

Even the comparatively nonlethal C 100 P bombs filled with the chemical arsine had devastating results. Exploding C 100 P bombs filled the air with thick va-

pors and infected the respiratory tracts of people who inhaled them. The result was instant suffocation.

Fumes from phosgene bombs were just as deadly. Their vapors choked the lungs of their victims and killed them instantly. The Italian Southern Air Command used such bombs in Southeastern Ethiopia, on December 24, 1936, to kill Ethiopian troops in desert trenches who had not yet surrendered.

Related Italian Atrocities in Ethiopia

Italy committed other atrocities in its colonial war in Ethiopia. Italian soldiers bombed Red Cross ambulances and hospitals, and targeted Ethiopian intellectuals and priests. On February 19, 1937, two Ethiopians, Abraha Daboch and Mogas Asgadom, tried but failed to assassinate the Italian Viceroy of Ethiopia, Rudolfo Graziani. After this, the Blackshirts, the Italian fascist occupation army, unleashed a ferocious terror on Ethiopia, with official backing from Rome. The atrocities included beheadings, burning down houses, and disembowelling pregnant women. The Blackshirts also targeted educated Ethiopians, especially those who occupied administrative positions, and other religious figures. The massacre of February, 19–21, 1937, robbed Ethiopia of one of the kingdom's finest generation of intellectuals. Some monks and priests of the Ethiopian Orthodox Church were also murdered on Graziani's orders. In one private telegram to Mussolini, Graziani proclaimed that "nothing anymore remained" of the priesthood of the medieval Debra Libanos monastery, in northeastern Ethiopia (Imani, 2003, p.18).

International Reaction

Ethiopian protest at the League of Nations for recognition of the crimes against humanity that they suffered at the hands of the Italians bore little fruit. On June 30, 1936, Emperor Haile Selassie gave a high profile, and now famous speech to the League, asking for international protection of small nations against the designs of the powerful. Even this, however, drew little international sympathy and brought no condemnation of Italy.

Rome worked successfully to divert attention from its aggression and crimes. It sought to direct any international condemnation toward alleged Ethiopian war crimes against Italian troops. The Italian government produced questionable pictures and eyewitness reports of alleged Ethiopian atrocities against captured Italian soldiers from the Greek Consulate at Dire-Dawa, in southeastern Ethiopia, and three members of the Egyptian Red Cross operating in Ethiopia. Their accounts claimed that the Ethiopians had tortured, crucified, and decapitated captured Italian pilots and tank drivers in violation of the Geneva Accords. In this way Rome sought to quash international condemnation of its own violations of the same accords, which banned the use of poison gas. The supposed Ethiopian barbarities turned out, upon serious investigation, to be trumped-up allegations that bore no comparison to the Italian atrocities.

Revamping Ethiopia's Military: 1941–1970

Unfortunately, Italy's justification of its crimes by portraying Ethiopia as a kingdom that showed no respect for international humanitarian law seemed to have worked. No serious condemnation of Italy came from any European capital. Thus, the Italian invasion of Ethiopia and its aerial bombardment with poison gas had little or no consequence internationally. Italian troops occupied the Ethiopian capital on May 5, 1936. Four days later, on May 9, Mussolini formally proclaimed Ethiopia a colony, and therefore part of Italy's East African Empire.

But the occupation was to last for only five years, the shortest European colonial experience on the African continent. On May 5, 1941, the Italians were defeated by a British-led combined force of Ethiopians

and other Africans from British and French colonies under the command of Major Orde Wingate. In June 1941 Haile Selassie returned to Ethiopia from exile in London to resume his rule as Emperor. However many Ethiopians who stayed at home to resist the Italians, as well as the post–World War II generation of educated Ethiopians were not pleased to see an Emperor who had abandoned his subjects at such a critical moment in their history return to power.

The entire Italian campaign taught Haile Selassie an important lesson about military power, modern warfare and international relations. In the post-1941 period, Haile Selassie made a strong modern national army, equipped with the latest weaponry, the centerpiece of Ethiopia's foreign policy. Through various military agreements with the United States and the former Soviet Union, during the cold war period, Haile Selassie built the fourth largest armed forces on the African continent (after Egypt, South Africa, and Nigeria). The Ethiopian defense forces increased threefold in the 1970s and 1980s.

Famine in Ethiopia: 1970–1974

Unfortunately Ethiopia's peasant agricultural economy was not modernized at the same rate as the kingdom's military. Peasants in the central and highlands regions of Ethiopia continued to depend upon rainfall for the cultivation of their crops. Inadequate rainfall in February and March 1972 not only delayed the planting season, but also caused sprouting crops to wither. Had the June and September rains been adequate, many peasants could have grown enough food or revived withering crops, but drought in June through September caused food shortages in the northern regions.

By June 1973, as many as two million people in northern Ethiopia were in desperate need of food. The conditions of peasants in Wollo, in northeastern Ethiopia had been worsened by the outbreak of cholera. Large numbers of the nomadic Afar ethnic group, who live in the remote semi-desert areas of northeastern Ethiopia, died when drought or lack of rain killed the cattle upon which they depended for their milk diets.

The scope of the disaster was equally overwhelming in other parts of the country. More than two million people are estimated to have died of famine-induced starvation and epidemics in Ethiopia between 1972 and 1973.

In hindsight, many lives could have been saved had the Imperial Government acknowledged the famine, and imported large quantities of food, or publicly and vigorously sought international relief assistance. The Emperor's cavalier response to the famine added to the famine-related deaths in the early 1970s. The tepid official response has also raised questions about the extent of the Emperor's knowledge of the famine.

There are several plausible reasons for the failure of the Haile Selassie government to publicly acknowledge the famine and openly seek help. Acknowledging famine and seeking relief aid would have embarrassed a government that had since the 1940s spent huge public funds on military security and denied that famine was a serious problem in Ethiopia. Many Ethiopians accepted as fact the Emperor's claims, in his annual televised speeches, that theirs was a rich and fertile kingdom.

Because Ethiopians construed famines as normal occurences in a prosperous empire, this distorted the ways state officials responded to famine. Moreover, any worldwide publicity about famine and starvation in Ethiopia hurt the Emperor's personal image and Ethiopia's international prestige.

Famine and the Rise of the *Dergue*

Haile Selassie's indifference to famine set in motion a series of developments that eventually led to his deposition and the overthrow of his government. The famine of 1972–1973 provided an opportunity for discontented groups in the kingdom to rise up against the Imperial Government and to promote their quest for change in the name of protecting peasants and preserving the human rights of oppressed ethnic groups.

The conduct of some parliamentarians, between January and September 1974, highlighted a new attitude in Ethiopia that famine could no longer be accepted as natural disasters, as the Emperor often asserted. These politicians, and students, began to view famine in Ethiopia as not only a product of government indifference, but also as a crime against humanity that should be prosecuted by the courts.

On March 1, 1973, Mohammed Madawa, the Member of Parliament for Elkerre, in Bale province in southeastern Ethiopia, called for the indictment and trial of the Ministers of Agriculture, Finance and Interior for failing to respond to his January 16, 1973, appeal for immediate state famine-relief assistance to save the dying in his constituency. The lukewarm attitude of the officials, Madawa alleged, had resulted in the needless death of 50 people in Elkerre. The representatives of the pastoral Afars and Issas, in northeastern Ethiopia, joined this new spirit of parliamentary militancy.

In May 1973 the Haile Selassie I University Famine Relief and Rehabilitation Organization (UFFRO) launched the first large-scale domestic relief operation in Ethiopian history with money it had collected from students and faculty. The students and soldiers used their relief operations as a framework to voice their grievances against the Emporer's government. Encouraged by the relief efforts of the University, the Army and other organizations bypassed the state and took their contributions directly to the victims of famine in northeastern Ethiopia.

On June 28, 1974, a group of junior officers of the Ethiopian military established their own committee (*Dergue*, in Amharinya) to coordinate the grievances of the army, police, and air force. In keeping with the new militancy induced by the lukewarm official response to the famine, some of the *Dergue*'s junior officers arrested government officials alleged to have concealed the famine, and delivered them to the Emperor as "enemies of Ethiopia" be prosecuted for crimes against humanity (Kissi, 1997, pp. 176–177). By September 1974, these junior officers had concluded that deposing the Emperor and overthrowing his government would be the best way to address the problem of famine in Ethiopia.

On September 12, 1974, under the instigation of Majors Mengistu Haile Mariam and Atnafu Abate, some members of the *Dergue* entered Haile Selassie's palace, read out a proclamation of deposition to the Emperor, and whisked him away in a Volkswagen vehicle. He was later murdered in the presence of Mengistu and Atnafu, and then secretly buried in the capital city. The *Dergue* elevated itself, by proclamation, into a Provisional Military Administrative Council (PMAC) to take over the reins of government. Many Ethiopians saw the deposition of Haile Selassie as a necessary ending of that era in national politics in which government overlooked the plight of the famine-stricken. But a government led by soldiers, who had propped up the Emperor's regime since his return from exile, drew mixed responses throughout the country.

In its early years in power, the *Dergue* military government actually showed more eagerness to deal with the intractable problem of famine in Ethiopia than the civilian Imperial Government had. The soldiers reformed the semi-feudal land tenure system and improved the mechanisms for delivering state famine-relief assistance. But like its predecessor, the military government could not reconcile its political interests with public welfare. Failure to deal with famine, therefore, became a pattern in Ethiopian history that did not change with the change of government. The *Dergue* and its many armed opponents used famine and the control of relief supplies as weapons in their prolonged struggle for power from September 12, 1974, to May, 28, 1991.

The *Dergue*'s most determined armed opponents included the Eritrean People's Liberation Front (EPLF), Ethiopian People's Revolutionary Party

(EPRP), Tigrayan People's Liberation Front (TPLF) and the Oromo Liberation Front (OLF). Each group had a substantial, independent and organized military machinery and controlled particular regions of the country. Ultimately, it was the TPLF's and EPRP's objective of overthrowing the *Dergue*, and the EPLF's and OLF's ethnic self-determination and secessionist ideology, that resulted in a protracted and violent power struggle between these insurgent groups and the military regime that advocated absolute national unity. This struggle was characterized by terror and extrajudicial killings.

The White and Red Terror Campaigns

In September 1976 the EPRP, a multi-ethnic political group with Amhara leadership, initiated a systematic rural and urban campaign of assassination of supporters and sympathizers of the military regime.

The EPRP called its extrajudicial killing campaign the White Terror. That provoked the *Dergue*'s infamous counter-campaign of assassination of EPRP members and supporters. Between February 1977 and March 1979, the *Dergue* ordered state security forces and the government's own trained civilian death squads to eliminate EPRP leaders and members. The military government in turn called its extrajudicial murderous campaign, the Red Terror. Thus the competitors for power in Ethiopia after Haile Selassie, sought to emulate the political murders that characterized the Bolshevik revolution and the Stalinist period in Russian history.

In its Red Terror campaign, the *Dergue* targeted anyone who opposed the military regime or was suspected of having any link with or sympathy for the EPRP regardless of age, religion, gender or ethnicity. To intimidate its political opponents, the *Dergue*'s killing squads left the corpses of their victims on public streets for many hours often with notices around their necks labeling them as counter-revolutionaries. Worse still, the *Dergue* prevented bereaved families from mourning these so-called "counter-revolutionaries." In some cases, the families were required to participate in state-organized public demonstrations supporting these extra-judicial killings.

Both the White and Red Terror campaigns claimed between 20,000 and 30,000 lives. The terror campaigns went beyond extra-judicial killings. They also included arbitrary arrests, imprisonments without trial and torture of political opponents.

It was fashionable for the *Dergue*, in the face of protests from Western human rights organizations such as Amnesty International, to describe its Red Terror crimes as necessary for national security and political

Mengistu Haile Mariam, an army officer who participated in Haile Selassie's overthrow in 1974, as military ruler and then president of Ethiopia was responsible for human rights violations on a truly massive scale. Tens of thousands were murdered or "disappeared." Forced to flee in 1991, Mengistu currently lives on his private ranch in Zimbabwe. [CAMPBELL WILLIAM/CORBIS SYGMA]

stability. But forcing political opponents to dig their own graves before being executed, mutilating the bodies of murdered political opponents, and compelling surviving family members to pay money for the bullets used to kill their relatives were, indeed, inhumane: they constituted crimes against humanity, possibly involving genocide.

However, Jean-Claude Guillebaud, and others have accurately noted the extrajudicial killing of political opponents in Ethiopia, in the mid-1970s, was "not all the work of one side" (Guillebaud, 1978, pp. 11, 13). Members and sympathizers of the EPRP and the TPLF, for instance, demonized one another and settled their ideological scores by murder. Kiflu Tadesse, a former EPRP member, has added that hundreds of EPRP members were killed by the TPLF and vice-versa, all in the name of ridding the new Ethiopia of "counter-revolutionaries," "narrow nationalists," "booklickers," and "traitors" (Kiflu, 1998, p. 259). Indeed, while the crimes of the Dergue are well documented, the comparable deeds of anti-government groups such as the EPRP and TPLF are not well-known because they have yet to be researched.

Famine and Food Relief As Weapons

While the White and Red terror campaigns continued, the famine of the early 1970s reared its head again. Unlike the Emperor's government, the military administration did not suppress information about famine during its tenure in office. In fact the *Dergue* publicly and vigorously sought and received international relief aid.

However, the *Dergue* regulated the operations of foreign relief workers, tightened visa regulations, and charged exorbitant fees for discharging relief cargo at Ethiopia's ports.

Anti-government groups also used relief aid as a military tool. The TPLF and EPLF concluded that international relief assistance provided the military government with a source of food and international legitimacy that prolonged its existence and enabled it to target its opponents. Therefore, by attacking relief convoys heading for zones under government control, as the EPLF did on October 23, 1987, the armed movement heightened starvation conditions in areas outside its control. Acute starvation in government-held areas forced many of the starving to move to rebel-held areas where their loyalties and military services were enlisted in the war against the *Dergue*.

Also, by providing food, shelter and medicine to many famine victims, as the TPLF did, and by encouraging and helping peasants who could not get food from the RRC to cross the Ethiopian border to the Sudan, where the relief organizations of the TPLF and EPLF operated, these two antigovernment groups successfully integrated public welfare into their military strategies. As a result, they broadened their political support, gained new recruits and kept the war going.

It is fair to state that mass death from famine and starvation in Ethiopia under the *Dergue* was mainly the result of war and politically motivated use of famine, starvation and relief food as weapons of war. Again, as in the White and Red terror campaigns of the mid-1970s, all sides in the Ethiopian civil war stand guilty of committing crimes against humanity. By pursuing military strategies that accentuated starvation, the *Dergue*, the EPRP, TPLF, and indeed all antigovernment groups violated the Geneva Conventions prohibiting the intentional use of starvation of civilians as a weapon of war.

Fall of the *Dergue* and the Ethiopian Genocide Trial

Ethiopia's oppressive military junta was overthrown on May 28, 1991, by the Ethiopian Peoples Revolutionary Democratic Front (EPRDF), a coalition of anti-government groups organized and led by the TPLF. In 1994, the EPRDF established a Central High Court to try Ethiopia's former head of state Mengistu Haile Mariam, who fled into exile in Zimbabwe, thirty-seven of his top officials, and many supporters and mid-level bureaucrats of the ousted regime, for "genocide" and "crimes against humanity."

Ethiopia was the first nation to ratify the UN Genocide Convention of December 9, 1948, on July 1, 1949. Eight years after ratifying the Genocide Convention, Ethiopia incorporated the basic ideas of the Convention into its national laws. In fact, Ethiopia went further and became, arguably, the first country to redefine the legal concept of genocide broadly to include protection of political groups—an important and vulnerable group that the framers of the Genocide Convention, for political reasons, left out of the list of protected groups in the international law on genocide.

The Genocide Convention obliges its signatories to prevent and punish genocide. But the Ethiopian High Court trying Mengistu and his officials for genocide and crimes against humanity is not doing so under international law, but rather under Ethiopia's own domestic laws on genocide. Under Ethiopian law, genocide and crimes against humanity are defined as acts committed "with intent to destroy, in whole or in part, a national, ethnic, racial, religious or political group." Individual perpetrators or groups acting as such are guilty of genocide or crimes against humanity if, "in time of war or in time of peace," they organize, order or engage directly, in:

(a) killings, [or causing] bodily harm or serious injury to the physical or mental health of members of the [protected] group, in any way whatsoever; or

(b) measures to prevent the propagation or continued survival of its members or their progeny; or

(c) the compulsory movement or dispersion of peoples or children, or . . . placing [them] under living conditions calculated to result in their death or disappearance (Ethiopian Penal Code, 1957, p. 87).

The charges against the *Dergue* are contained in eight thousand pages of legal documents. In them, the Ethiopian Court alleges that the *Dergue* jailed, tortured and ordered the killing of members of opposition political groups and caused "bodily harm or serious [physical and mental] injury" to their leaders and supporters (Transitional Government of Ethiopia, 1994, p. 8).

Ethiopian domestic law on genocide and crimes against humanity also holds criminally responsible for genocide several categories of people. First among these are higher government officials who authorize extra-judicial killings. Second are low-level bureaucrats who implement criminal orders or commit such killing on their own without state authority. Third are ordinary people who support extra-judicial killings even if they did not directly or actively participate in them.

As of June 2004, nearly 6,426 defendants—including Ethiopia's ousted head of state, Mengistu Haile Mariam, now exiled in Zimbabwe, thirty-seven of Mengistu's higher government officials and a large number of ordinary citizens—have been charged with genocide and crimes against humanity.

Mengistu and nearly 3,000 indictees are being tried in absentia. All the defendants are answering charges that they ordered, participated in or supported the *Dergue*'s infamous Red Terror campaign of the mid-1970s against opposition political groups. The Ethiopian genocide trial is a significant test case, in international and domestic Ethiopian law, of the prosecution of extra-judicial killing of political opponents of an ousted regime as a crime of genocide. In Ethiopia, the crime of genocide is punishable by death or imprisonment from five years to life.

Approximately 1,569 decisions have been handed down so far. Nearly 1,017 of them have resulted in convictions to various prison terms. Six death sentences have been passed. However, the trial has stirred up emotions domestically and internationally. In the course of the ten years of the trial, forty-three of the accused persons have died in prison. The trial has also proceeded at an erratic pace. It was suspended from 2002 to November 2003. The prosecutors attributed the suspension and the slower pace of the trial to the arduous task of gathering evidence on crimes committed nearly thirty years ago.

In February, 2004, thirty-three of the surviving members of the *Dergue* in detention and awaiting trial wrote to Ethiopia's Prime Minister Meles Zenawi, a former leader of the TPLF, requesting state funds to prepare their defense. The accused former officials pointed to the thirty-year time lapse of their alleged crimes, the deaths of some of their witnesses and the unjust fact that only "the few surviving . . . supporters of one side" in a power struggle are facing prosecution as reasons for the entire trial to be canceled (IRINnews.org, 2003; Amnesty International, 2004).

Human Rights in Ethiopia, 1998–2004

Since the overthrow of the *Dergue*, and despite the genocide trial, human rights abuses have continued in Ethiopia under the EPRDF. Three consistent patterns of violations of human rights can be discerned. One violation is in the treatment of the Oromo people. Some analysts and human rights groups have gone as far as

to suggest that there is an "unfolding genocide" against the Oromo people of Ethiopia, under the EPRDF (Trueman, 2000). Second, since June 1998, the Ethiopian government has implemented a systematic policy of expulsion of Eritreans living in Ethiopia. The government has also committed or overlooked persecution of the Anuak people. Third, journalists in Ethiopia are today the targets of organized and systematic state repression.

Oromos

The Ethiopian government continues to face armed opposition from the Oromo Liberation Front (OLF). Since the 1970s, the OLF has waged an armed struggle for an autonomous state of Orominya, within Ethiopia, for the Oromo people as the Eritreans had achieved. In July 2000, the Oromia Support Group, a human rights organization with its headquarters in England, recorded many instances of grave abuses of people of Oromo ethnicity by the Ethiopian government. These abuses included 2,555 extrajudicial killings, 824 disappearances of Oromo people, banning of Oromo organizations as well as "opposition to the use of the Oromo language." Though the latter may be an exaggeration of state repression by the OLF and its external supporters, it is clear, from other sources, that members and supporters of the OLF have been the main victims of state-sanctioned torture and arbitrary arrests in Ethiopia.

Eritreans

Eritrea, a former northern province of Ethiopia, became an independent state in April 1993. Members of the defunct Tigray Peoples Liberation Front (TPLF), now in power in Ethiopia, assisted the defunct Eritrean Peoples Liberation Front (EPLF), during the period of the *Dergue*, to achieve the EPLF's ultimate objective, which was Eritrea's independence.

But the war that broke out between Ethiopia and Eritrea in May 1999, over unresolved border issues, has damaged relations between the two countries which were former political allies. What is worse, between June 1998 and April 2002, the Ethiopian government expelled about 75,000 people of Eritrean nationality living in Ethiopia in what Natalie S. Klein, Solicitor of the Supreme Court of South Australia, has described as a "deliberate" and "inhumane" state-organized "program of mass expulsion" of an ethnic and national group (Klein, 1998, p. 1).

Anuaks

It is not only Oromo and Eritrean residents in Ethiopia who have borne or continue to bear the brunt of human rights abuses. The latest victims have been the Anywaa (also known as Anuak) people. They live in the Gambella region, in southwestern Ethiopia, and number about 100,000, in population. On December 13, 2003 eight people, all Ethiopian government and UNHCR officials traveling by car, were ambushed and killed near Gambella. Their bodies were mutilated. The Ethiopian government reportedly blamed the attacks on the Anuak who live in that region. On that day government soldiers and settlers from the Amhara, Oromo and Tigray ethnic groups living in the Gambella region descended on the Anuaks and exacted retribution in a manner characteristic of the Italian atrocities in Ethiopia in the 1930s.

Not only did the soldiers and the accompanying mobs kill 424 unarmed Anuak civilians, they also set Anuak straw-roofed homes on fire in a manner that resembles the atrocities committed by the Italians in February 1937. The perpetrators also stabbed and dismembered their Anuak victims with machetes, knives, spears, axes, clubs, and hoes, and dumped some of the dead in a nearby river in a fashion similar to what extremist Hutus did to Tutsis in Rwanda in 1994. As they sought and killed their victims, they chanted: "Erase the trouble makers!"; "There will be no Anuak land!"; "Let's kill them all"; and "Today is the day of killing Anuaks." Under strong international pressure, the Ethiopian government apologized for not preventing the killings. It remains to be seen if its apology betokens a changed policy on the ground.

Journalists

Journalists join Oromos, Eritreans and Anuaks on the list of victims of the most egregious violations of human rights by government in Ethiopia today. Muzzling of the press is not new in Ethiopia. But the Meles government appears to have taken it to new heights. The Meles government insists on censoring news reporting in Ethiopia. A Press Law which the government passed in October 1992 makes the failure of journalists to report accurately on every issue in the country a criminal offense. Under the law, the government retains the power "to withhold or withdraw registration and publication" of the newspapers of libelous journalists. The government has also reserved the right to censor articles that accuse government officials of abuses and/or any other article that the government regards as endangering "peace," "security," or "patriotism." Ironically, the press laws that the Meles government has instituted are the same oppressive press laws that the Dergue used, and are based on the same arguments the military junta made, in its era, to muzzle press freedom and restrict the voices of members of opposition political groups who are now in power.

Conclusion

The use of poison gas in Ethiopia by the Italian Royal Air Force in 1935–1936 and the massacre of Ethiopia's educated elite and monks in February 1937, represent an important benchmark in the history of crimes against humanity and possible genocide in Ethiopian history. In the mid-1970s the human corpses that littered the streets of Addis Ababa constituted incontestable evidence of state and insurgent terror. That terror mirrored the massacre of Ethiopians on the orders of Marshall Graziani in 1937. The difference was that in the 1970s Ethiopians themselves did the killing and the victims were their own kith and kin. The cause was not colonial occupation by an outside power, but rather a power struggle between the Ethiopian government and its armed domestic opponents.

These crimes against humanity, some verging on genocide, have not stopped. Today human rights abuses in Ethiopia go beyond extrajudicial killings and mass expulsions of people on the basis of their ethnic background and nationality. Those abuses also involve suppression of press freedom. Their most visible manifestation is the arbitrary arrests and jailing of journalists. Historically, Ethiopia has been the first to sign international legal treaties on human rights. Ironically, though, the country has often been the last to adhere to them. Crimes against humanity, possibly involving genocide, continue in Ethiopia.

SEE ALSO Eritrea; Gas

BIBLIOGRAPHY

Amnesty International (2004). "Report 2004: Ethiopia." Available from http://web.amnesty.org/report2004/eth-summary-eng.

Bahru, Zewde (1996). *A History of Modern Ethiopia, 1855-1974*. London: James Currey.

Clay, J., and Bonnie Holcomb (1986). *Politics and the Ethiopian Famine, 1984-1986*. 2nd edition. Cambridge, Mass.: Cultural Survival.

Dawit, Wolde-Giorgis (1989). *Red Tears: War, Famine and Revolution in Ethiopia*. Trenton, N.J.: The Red Sea Press.

Empire of Ethiopia (1957). *Penal Code of the Empire of Ethiopia*. Addis Ababa: Ministry of the Pen.

Gellatelly, R. G., and Ben Kiernan, eds. (2003). *The Specter of Genocide: Mass Murder in Historical Perspective*. Cambridge: Cambridge University Press.

Greenfield, Richard (1967). *Ethiopia: A New Political History*. London: Pall Mall Press.

Guillebaud, J. C. (1978). "Dergue's Red Terror." *The Guardian Weekly* 118(8).

Human Rights Watch (2003a). "Report 2003, Africa: Ethiopia." Available from http://www.hrw.org/wr2k3/africa5.html.

Human Rights Watch (2003b). "Eritrea and Ethiopia, The Horn of Africa War: Mass Expulsions and the

Nationality Issue (June 1998–April 2002)." 15(3). Available from http://hrw.org/reports/2003/ethioerit0103.

Human Rights Watch (2004) "Ethiopia: Stop Harassing Journalists' Group." New York. February 13. Available from http://hrw.org/english/docs/2004/02/ethiop7347.htm.

IRINnews.org (2003). "Ethiopia: Defence Trial of ex-president begins." Addis Ababa, November. Available from http://www.irinnews.org/report.asp?ReportID=37617&SelectRegion=Horn-of-Africa.

Kali-Nyah, Imani (2000). *Italy's War Crimes in Ethiopia, 1935–41: Evidence for the War Crimes Commission.* Special Year 2000 edition. Chicago: The Ethiopian Holocaust Remembrance Committee

Kiflu, T. (1998). *The Generation, Part II: Ethiopia: Transformation and Conflict.* New York: University Press of America.

Kissi, Edward (1997). "Famine and the Politics of Food Relief in United States' Relations with Ethiopia: 1950–1991." Ph.D. diss. Montreal, Canada: Concordia University.

Klein, N. S. (1998). *Mass Expulsion from Ethiopia: Report on the Deportation of Eritreans and Ethiopians of Eritrean Origin from Ethiopia, June–August, 1998.* New York: United Nations.

Kuper, Leo, (1981). *Genocide: Its Political Use in the Twentieth Century.* New Haven, Conn.: Yale University Press.

Mesfin, W. (1986). *Rural Vulnerability to Famine, 1958–77.* London: Intermediate Technology Publications.

Mockler, A. (2003). *Haile Selassie's War.* New York: Olive Branch Press.

Niggli, P. (1986). *Ethiopia: Deportations and Forced Labor Camps: A Study by Peter Niggli on Behalf of the Berliner Missionswerk.* Berlin: Berliner Missionswerk

Okbazghi, Y. (1997). *The United States and the Horn of Africa: An Analytical study of Pattern and Process.* Boulder, Colo.: Westview Press.

Paulos, M. (1994). "Mengistu Haile Mariam: Profile of a Dictator." *Ethiopian Review* February:46–56.

Sbacchi, Alberto (1997). *Legacy of Bitterness: Ethiopia and Fascist Italy, 1935–1941.* Lawrenceville, N.J.: The Red Sea Press.

Schabas, William A. (2000). *Genocide in International Law.* Cambridge: Cambridge University Press.

"Statement by Mr. Obang Metho, The Representative of The Anywaa Survival Organization to the UN Commission on Human Rights, 60th Session, Item 15, Indigenous Issues." (April 8, 2004). Available from http://www.genocidewatch.org/ethiopiastatement-obang.htm.

Trueman, T. (2000). *Gadado, The Agony of the Oromo: Unfolding Genocide in Ethiopia.* Worcestershire, U.K.: Oromia Support Groups.

Edward Kissi

Ethnic Cleansing

The term *ethnic cleansing* came into common parlance during the war in Bosnia in the spring of 1992. It was initially used to describe the attacks by Serbs on Bosnian Muslims, which were undertaken for the purposes of driving the Muslims out of targeted Bosnian territory that was claimed by the Serbs. Eventually, the term was also applied to similar attacks by Croats against Bosnian Muslims, as well as, retroactively, the attacks of Serbs and Croats against each other during the fighting of the late summer and fall of 1991. In the winter of 1998–1999, ethnic cleansing was similarly used to describe the assaults of Serbian forces against Kosovar Albanians, which prompted an enormous refugee crisis and, subsequently, NATO military intervention. In 2004, Kosovar Albanians were accused of the ethnic cleansing of Serbs living in Kosovo. Beyond the Balkans, ethnic cleansing has also been used to describe attacks on native populations. In the Sudan, for example, the deadly fate of the people of Darfur at the hands of government-supported Arab militia has been documented as a contemporary case of ethnic cleansing.

From the outset of the war in Bosnia, some analysts challenged the validity of using the term "ethnic cleansing" as a euphemism for genocide. However, the term remains in use precisely to distinguish ethnic cleansing, which is considered both as a crime against humanity and a war crime, from genocide. The definition of genocide, codified in the UN Convention of December 9, 1948, and upheld in the International Courts formed for the purposes of trying criminals from the wars in former Yugoslavia and in Rwanda, focuses on the intentional murder of part or all of a particular ethnic, religious, or national group. The purpose of ethnic cleansing, by contrast, is the forced removal of a population from a designated piece of territory. Although campaigns of ethnic cleansing can lead to genocide or have genocidal effects, they constitute a different kind of criminal action against an ethnic, religious, or national group than genocide. The transcripts of the International Criminal Tribunal for Former Yugoslavia frequently mention ethnic cleansing, but subsume it under the category of forced deportation, a crime against humanity that was widespread particularly in Bosnia. Genocide, on the other hand, has been much more difficult to prove in court, since it involves the intent to murder a part or all of a population. However, the mass murder of roughly 7,300 Bosnian Muslim men and boys in Srebrenica in July 1995 has been designated by the court as genocide.

Genocide and ethnic cleansing occupy adjacent positions on a spectrum of attacks on national, religious, and ethnic groups. At one extreme, ethnic

In 2004 Human Rights Watch issued statements that the government of Sudan was, indisputably, participating in ethnic cleansing in Darfur (in western Sudan), and that it was operating jointly with the Arab Janjaweed militias in their attacks on the villages and people of Darfur. This photo, taken April 29, 2004, shows the remains of huts, destroyed by militia groups, in the Sudanese village of Bandago.
[AP/WIDE WORLD PHOTOS]

cleansing is close to forced deportation or what has been called "population transfer;" the idea is to get people to move, and the means are meant to be legal and semi-legal. At the other extreme, ethnic cleansing and genocide are distinguishable only by the ultimate intent. Here, both literally and figuratively, ethnic cleansing bleeds into genocide, as mass murder is committed in order to rid the land of a people. Further complicating the distinctions between ethnic cleansing and genocide is the fact that forced deportation often takes place in the violent context of war, civil war, or aggression. At the same time, people do not leave their homes peacefully. They often have deep roots in the locales; their families are buried in local graveyards. The result is that forced deportation, even in times of peace, quickly turns to violence, as local peoples are forcibly evicted from their native towns and villages and killed when they try to stay.

Ethnic cleansing takes on genocidal overtones not only at the initial point of violence. Victims often die in transit or in refugee camps at their destinations. The history of ethnic cleansing is replete with cases where transportation on foot in long treks, in rail cars, in the holds of ships, or in crowded buses causes severe deprivation, hunger, starvation, and death by disease. Disease-ridden refugee camps similarly contribute to the high mortality of people forced not just from their normal homes, but from their work places, their land, and their traditional sources of food and medicine. When international or state organizations are allowed to step in to help, they are often late and erratic with relief. As a consequence, the victimization of the ethnically cleansed cannot be said to cease once they have been chased from their homes.

Scholars argue about the modernity of ethnic cleansing, whether it is something that can be traced back to the origins of human history or whether it, like genocide, constitutes the kind of attacks of one nation, religious, or ethnic group on another that belong to the twentieth century. There are abundant examples from the ancient world, documented in Homer, as well as the Bible, where nations attack others for the purposes of expulsion. The medieval and early modern world saw countless examples of such expulsions—of the Incas and Aztecs of South America, of the Jews of Spain, the Albigensians, and the Huguenots. Settler and government attacks on the North American Indians, the Australian aborigines, and the African peoples by their colonial oppressors also could be classified in this way. In this sense, ethnic cleansing can be seen as a constant feature of human history.

Yet the twentieth century brought with it a number of aspects of modernity that made ethnic cleansing more virulent, more complete, and more pervasive. The development of the nation state and the end of empires gave the state unprecedented power, the ostensible mandate, and the means for attacking and transferring large, allegedly alien populations. The drive of the modern state to categorize and homogenize its populations has contributed to this phenomenon, as has its intolerance for economic or political anomalies within its society. Modern ethnic entrepreneurs, politicians ready to exploit ethnic and national distinctions through the media, have also played an important role. The development of integral nationalism at the end of the nineteenth century emphasized the racial essence of national groups, thus serving as a convenient ideological motivation for ethnic cleansing. The origins of industrial murder during World War I serves as the backdrop for a century of ethnic cleansing, as well as for the horrors of genocide.

Prominent cases of ethnic cleansing in the twentieth century underline its modern character. The modernist Young Turk government attacked its Armenian population in 1915, forcing the vast majority on fearsome treks through the Anatolian highlands to Mesopotamia. These death marches were at the heart of the first widely recognized case of genocide in the twentieth century. At the end of the Greco-Turkish war of 1921–1922, Mustafa Kemal (Ataturk), at the head of the infant Turkish Republic, engaged in an ethnic-cleansing campaign against the country's Greeks. The Lausanne Treaty of 1923 completed the process of the forcible transfer of the Greeks by confirming a "population transfer" between the remaining Greeks in Anatolia and the Turks in Greece. Hitler is known to have said on the eve of his murderous attack against Poland, August 22, 1939, "Who, after all, speaks today about the annihilation of the Armenians?" Certainly, the indifference of the world to the fate of the Armenians and Greeks gave Hitler every confidence that his planned attack on the Jews would rouse little opposition. Like the mutation of the Young Turk campaign of ethnic cleansing into genocide, one could argue that what started as a Nazi campaign of ethnic cleansing in the 1930s—the expulsion of Jews from Germany and Europe—ended in the genocidal mass murder of the Jews.

Other prominent cases of ethnic cleansing in the twentieth century underline its murderous character. When Stalin and Beria decided to deport entire nations, such as the Chechen-Ingush and Crimean Tatars, from their homelands to Soviet Central Asia during World War II, there was no discernable intent to kill large numbers of these peoples. Yet the brutal processes of transfer and resettlement to barren and hostile lands served as the source of substantial mortality, perhaps as much as 40 percent of some of the peoples involved. Similarly, when the Polish and Czechoslovak governments decided at the end of World War II to forcibly deport their respective German populations, totaling more than 11.5 million people, as many as 2 million died, mostly from disease, exposure, and hunger. In both sets of cases, the modernity of the operations was evident in the completeness of the transfers, the nationalism that drove them, the state-defined legality that supported them, and the means of moving people from their homes. The transfer of the Germans should be seen as a case of ethnic cleansing, one that was given an international imprimatur by the Potsdam Treaty of July–August 1945.

Many of the characteristics common to ethnic cleansing over the course of the twentieth century are exemplified by the wars in former Yugoslavia in the 1990s. War itself serves as a cover for ethnic cleansing, offering the means and the strategic justification for its perpetrators. Yet the violence of ethnic cleansing goes beyond the rules of war and involves the brutalization, humiliation, and torture of victims. In the campaigns to drive out all Bosnian Muslims (Serbs, Croats, or Kosovar Albanians), the authors of ethnic cleansing in the Balkans also mimic the totalist preoccupations of earlier perpetrators. Attacks on women and mass rape, most notable in the case of the Serbian assault on Bosnian Muslims, similarly is often part of the general process of ethnic cleansing. Instances of robbery, theft, the killing of animals, the burning of homes, and extortion accompany ethnic cleansing, whether in the Balkans or elsewhere. The Yugoslav cases demonstrate, as do the others, that ethnic cleansing involves not just the driving out of a people, but the eradication of their culture, architectural monuments, and artifacts. The idea is to eliminate entire civilizations from targeted territories, along with the peoples who represent them.

SEE ALSO Bosnia and Herzegovina; Cossacks; Ethnicity; Ethnocide; Holocaust; Karadzic,

Radovan; Kosovo; Massacres; Mladic, Ratko; Nationalism; Sri Lanka; Sudan; United States Foreign Policies Toward Genocide and Crimes Against Humanity; Yugoslavia

BIBLIOGRAPHY

Bell-Fialkoff, A. (1996). *Ethnic Cleansing*. New York: St. Martin's Press.

Cigar, N. (1995). *Genocide in Bosnia: The Policy of 'Ethnic Cleansing'*. College Station: Texas A&M Press.

Gellately, R., and Ben Kiernen, eds. (2003). *The Specter of Genocide: Mass Murder in Historical Perspective*. Cambridge: Cambridge University Press.

Hayden, R. M. (1996). "Schindler's Fate: Genocide, Ethnic Cleansing, and Population Transfers." *The Slavic Review* 55(4):727–749.

Martin, T. (1998). "The Origins of Soviet Ethnic Cleansing." *The Journal of Modern History* 70(4):813–861.

Melson, R. (1992). *Revolution and Genocide: On the Origins of the Armenian Genocide and the Holocaust*. Chicago: University of Chicago Press.

Naimark, Norman (2001). *Fires of Hatred: Ethnic Cleansing in Twentieth Century Europe*. Cambridge, Mass.: Harvard University Press.

Ther, P., and A. Siljak, eds. (2001). *Redrawing Nations: Ethnic Cleansing in East-Central Europe, 1944-1948*, Boulder, Colo.: Rowman and Littlefield.

Norman M. Naimark

Ethnic Groups

Ethnicity is difficult to define. Its close analog, race, has been discarded by some as a useful subject of scientific research. Common ethnicity as a psychosocial reality constituting a community is now understood as a cultural attribute that links individual human beings, such as a common language, religion, social rituals and routines, and a feeling of togetherness. Donald L. Horowitz attributes this feeling of togetherness to a "strong sense of similarity, with roots in perceived genetic affinity, or early socialization, or both" (Horowitz, 2001, p. 47). The common bond of an ethnic group may have been intensified through a shared history of being victimized by others, as exemplified by the social pathology of anti-Semitism or the persecution suffered by the Roma and the Sinti.

Conflict is an essential part of human existence, be it inter-individual or inter-group. Although a large part of the twentieth century was dominated by the struggle of political ideologies, expressed in both hot and cold wars, the 1990s and the early part of the twenty-first century saw a resurgence of ethnic rationalizations for the outbreak of hostilities. The atrocities in disintegrat-

ing Yugoslavia, fuelled by policies of ethnic cleansing and culminating in the slaughter of Srebrenica, as well as the genocide in Rwanda and continuing bloody feuds in Africa, are two examples of major outbreaks of inter-ethnic violence.

Ethnicity as a perceived social bond is a fact of human life, and can be used to good or insidious effects. It is often at the root of a social group's quest for political, economic, and cultural self-determination. Self-assertion of an ethnic group may yield socially positive outcomes, such as its economic flourishing and political integration. It can lead to linguistic as well as cultural diversity and the development of distinctive styles of art and cuisines. It can thus be, and often is, an important reference point for building a nation. Tensions between groups may be seen as natural, even beneficial, to the extent that they promote healthy competition and a quest for common rules limiting the contest itself.

When self-assertion of an ethnic group turns from creative into destructive tension, brooding hostility, and ultimately violence against outsiders, however, ethnic conflict becomes pathological and destructive of the values of human dignity. Still, in many of the conflicts occurring in recent years, the phenomenon of ethnic difference may only partially explain the actions on the ground. In Rwanda, for example, the colonial regime's perceived preferences for the Tutsis, and political power differentials in the post-independence years may have contributed as much to the mass slaughter as the ethnic difference itself. The presence of an economically dominant minority ethnic group (e.g., the Chinese in Malaysia and Indonesia) may also play a role in the emergence of ethnic hostilities, as do religious differences (as seen in the Catholic-Protestant conflict in Northern Ireland or the riots between Hindus and Muslims in India).

Social and political solutions to the issues raised by ethnic self-assertion can be categorized according to effect. If the self-assertion is positive, functioning as the glue of a nation, it can be used to create a common engine in the quest for achievement of all the things that humans value. The group's claim to self-determination, recognized for "peoples" essentially self-defined, would allow for the establishment of confident units of self-government, be they nation-states or autonomous units within a political structure in which power is shared vertically (federalism) or horizontally (with provisions for minority rights) or a mixture of both. An order of human dignity would aspire to ensure that such self-assertion of the group will not infringe on the rights of outsider individuals and groups.

Several international legal prescriptions have been designed to protect ethnic groups as such. The 1948 Convention on the Prevention and Punishment of the Crime of Genocide defined this international crime as any of a number of acts "committed with intent to destroy, in whole or in part, a national, ethnical, racial or religious group." This definition is repeated verbatim in the 1998 Rome Statute establishing the International Criminal Court. More generally, the 1948 Universal Declaration of Human Rights, as well as the two United Nations human rights covenants of 1966, mandate equality before the law and specifically prohibit discrimination on account of "race," or "national or social origin." Article 27 of the International Covenant on Civil and Political Rights provides a positive guarantee for "ethnic minorities" "not [to] be denied the right, in community with the other members of their group, to enjoy their own culture, to profess and practice their own religion, or to use their own language." The 1992 UN Declaration on the Rights of Persons Belonging to National or Ethnic, Religious, and Linguistic Minorities defines those rights in greater detail, adding a people's right to participate in decisions that affect it, as well as the right to establish and maintain its own institutions, as well as positive and negative obligations of states to foster minorities. The Council of Europe's 1995 Framework Convention for the Protection of National Minorities obligates member states to detailed standards of treatment and requires them to report periodically on their performance to an advisory committee composed of eighteen independent experts in the field. Indigenous peoples have received their own level of international legal protection, as reflected in the 1989 International Labor Organization's Convention No. 169; the 1993 Draft United Nations Declaration on the Rights of Indigenous Peoples; the creation, in 2000, of a Permanent Forum on Indigenous Issues; and customary international law rights to their culture and their traditional lands.

As far as the dark side of ethnic self-assertion is concerned, the international system has often been less than diligent in preventing outbreaks of ethnic violence, or in stopping it, sanctioning it, and preventing it from reoccurring. A model for effective monitoring and prevention could be the High Commissioner on National Minorities of the Organization for Security and Cooperation in Europe (OSCE). This office fulfills a dual mandate of "early warning" and "early action": it is duty-bound to alert the OSCE when tensions involving national minorities that have an international character threaten to escalate to a level where they cannot be contained. To arrest inter-ethnic violence once it has broken out, mechanisms such as humanitarian intervention (e.g., in Kosovo) have been developed that would appear to allow the use of force from the outside, at least in the case of genocide and other massive violations of fundamental human rights. Humanitarian law would put limits on the conduct of hostilities and thus would protect civilians, even though the line between civilians and combatants in this type of conflict has often been blurred. Domestic and, increasingly, international criminal sanctions are being put in place to punish conduct such as genocide, crimes against humanity, and violations of the laws of war. The International Military Tribunals of Nuremberg and Tokyo set precedents for sanctioning forums such as the International Criminal Tribunal for the former Yugoslavia, the International Criminal Tribunal for Rwanda, and the International Criminal Court, as well as hybrid domestic-international tribunals such as those established for East Timor and Sierra Leone. Also, systems of civil liability, such as the Alien Tort Claims Act in the United States, are designed to redress the wrongs involved. Beyond those immediate reactions and restorations of the social order, societies torn apart by ethnic conflict face the need to be healed over a long period of time. Institutions searching for the truth and society-wide sharing of pertinent information have helped in this quest for ultimate reconciliation.

SEE ALSO Cossacks; Ethnic Cleansing; Ethnicity; Kosovo; Minorities; Racial Groups; Sri Lanka

BIBLIOGRAPHY

Alston, Philip, ed. (2001). *Peoples' Rights.* New York: Oxford University Press.

Chua, Amy (2003). *World on Fire.* New York: Doubleday.

Horowitz, Donald L. (1985). *Ethnic Groups in Conflict.* Berkeley: University of California Press.

Horowitz, Donald L. (2001). *The Deadly Ethnic Riot.* Berkeley: University of California Press.

Kymlicka, Will, ed. (1995). *The Rights of Minority Cultures.* New York: Oxford University Press.

McDougal, Myres S., W. Michael Reisman, and Andrew R. Willard (1988). "The World Community: A Planetary Social Process." *University of California at Davis Law Review* 21:807–972.

Morris, H. S. (1966). "Ethnic Groups." In *International Encyclopedia of the Social Sciences*, vol. 5, ed. David L. Sills. New York: Macmillan.

Power, Samantha (2002). *A Problem from Hell: America and the Age of Genocide.* New York: Basic Books.

Ratner, Steven R. (2000). "Does International Law Matter in Preventing Ethnic Conflict?" *New York University Journal of International Law and Politics* 32:591–698.

Rossie, Ino, ed. (1980). *People in Culture: A Survey of Cultural Anthropology.* Brooklyn N.Y.: J. F. Bergin Publishers, Inc.

Wiessner, Siegfried (1996). "Faces of Vulnerability: Protecting Individuals in Organic and Non-Organic

Groups." In *The Living Law of Nations*, ed. Gudmundur Alfredsson and Peter Macalister-Smith. Kehl, Strasbourg: N.P. Engel.

Wiessner, Siegfried (1999). "Rights and Status of Indigenous Peoples: A Global Comparative and International Legal Analysis," *Harvard Human Rights Journal* 12:57–128.

Wiessner, Siegfried, and Andrew R. Willard (1999). "Policy-Oriented Jurisprudence and Human Rights Abuses in Internal Conflict: Toward A World Public Order of Human Dignity." *American Journal of International Law* 93:316–334.

Siegfried Wiessner

Ethnicity

The term *ethnicity* was coined by American sociologists in the 1920s to describe the phenomena and the politicization of the basic concept of an ethnic group. It derives from the Greek word *ethnos*, meaning "peoples." The problem is that ethnic groups are almost always seen as minorities, not as peoples.

Ethnicity has been the dominant motif in most modern genocides and acts of mass violence in the twentieth century, particularly in the deadliest "genocides-in-whole" (according to the UN Convention of 1948), which were all committed by perpetrators from ruling national majorities against members of ethnic and religious minority groups. Examples are the large-scale genocides committed by the regime of the Young Turks against the Armenians (AGHET), Pontian Greeks, and Assyrians in the 1920s; the Holocaust committed by the German Nazis and their allies and vassal regimes between 1939 and 1945 throughout most of Europe against the Jews (SHOA), Roma (PORRAJMOS), Soviet POWs, Slavic peoples, and twenty other groups; and the widespread slaughter committed in 1994 between April 6 and mid-July by the Hutu power regime in Rwanda against the Tutsi. Colonial genocides begun in the fifteenth century but in some cases continued into the twentieth century. One of the most devastating was committed by the Belgian colonizers in the Congo Free State, the later Belgian Congo, from the 1870s to the 1920s against the indigenous African peoples of the Great Congo Basin (taking 12 to 18 million victims), as well as the smaller but almost total genocide by the German colonialists against the Herero and Nama in Namibia (that time German Southwest Africa) from 1904 to 1907.

Ethnic category killing was predominant in genocide as well as in violent conflict. In the 20th century, genocide directed against ethnic and religious groups has been the dominant form of both extermination-in-whole and in-part. Additionally, the ethnic factor has been predominant in two thirds of some 300 intra-state violent conflicts since World War II—more precisely, since the period of decolonization that started in 1948—as well as in a number of inter-state conflicts.

The ethnic factor also plays a leading role in what has been termed *ethnic cleansing*, which is more accurately termed expulsions or deportations. Another euphemistic expression for ethnic cleansing is "population transfer," although atrocities may be included as a part of such activities. Contrary to genocide and violent ethnic conflict, the aim of ethnic cleansing is not to kill all the members of an ethnic group in a territory, but to drive that ethnic group from their ancestral lands and settlement area. Ethnocide or cultural genocide, on the other hand, is an attempt to wipe out the culture of a particular group and replace it with the majority "national" culture by means of repression and assimilation, not by killing the members of a distinct ethnic or cultural group.

The ethnic factor is delimited, but contentiously, within certain boundaries, in the older social science disciplines of ethnology and social/cultural anthropology. There are quite a variety and number of categorizations offered by the different ethnological and anthropological schools, but any combination of the more accessible definitions is not really possible, given the differing approaches and standards used by various scholars. The most frequently mentioned elements of ethnicity are shared origin and similar culture, religion, class, and language. However, two of these (class and religion) are not apposite. Language is seen as the most objective attribute for an ethnically distinct group and, thus, questions have been raised about whether Hutus and Tutsis can be referred to as different ethnic groups, since both groups share the same language and cultural practices as well as religious affiliations.

The ethnic form of socialization must be distinguished from socialization into social classes. The extent and boundaries of the two are often congruent, but they can also merely overlap, as can be seen in more complex societies, or exclude one another entirely, as occurs in egalitarian societies. Religion must be rejected as a criterion for ethnicity, since it is an ideological domain that within the framework of colonialism, was mostly externally imposed and fortuitously selected. Imported, colonially induced religions and syncretistic variants are more common and dominant than indigenous religions.

Whereas there are less than 200 formally constituted states in the world, there are between 2,500 to 6,500 ethnic groups as defined according to linguistic criteria. Lately the figure of 10,000 or more ethnic groups has been mentioned. The variation in figures is due to the differences in the criteria or attributes used to define an ethnos. One of several possible approaches to identifying distinct ethnicities focuses on attributes other than language, for instance on clusters of "special features" or social specializations, which are both seen as contributing to the defining characteristics of a particular ethnos. Such clusters are called "ethnic markers," and are only relevant within the framework of inter-ethnic relations. Often they only become a major focus of perception when situations of conflict arise.

Understanding ethnicity and the ethnic factor can best be done by considering key attributes of an ethnic community:

1. a historically generated or (in some cases) rediscovered community of people that largely reproduces itself;

2. a distinct name, which often simply signifies 'person' or 'people' in the ethnic community's language;

3. a specific, heterogeneous culture, including, particularly, a distinct language;

4. a collective memory or historical remembrance, including community myths (myths of foundation or emergence relating to shared ancestry); and

5. solidarity between members of the community, generating a feeling of belonging.

Attributes of ethnic community by no means constitute a definitive checklist. They are, rather, an attempt to get closer to an appropriate understanding of ethnicity, the individual elements of which can be examined more closely for each concrete instance. Maintaining ethnic borders—and thus also being able to delimit different ethnic groups—has its problems. Most peoples live closely and intermingled with other groups. (There is no such thing as ethnically homogeneous or pure "areas," if not as a result of violence and ethnic cleansing.) Over-emphasizing certain elements, such as participation in a shared culture or the social dimension (which sees ethnic groups as a particular form of social organization), would also appear to be problematic. Ethnic communities may be imagined, but as imagined entities they are significantly more concrete and more tangible than that of the nation.

Perspective—that is, whether or not one views ethnicity from inside or outside the group in question—seems crucial to understanding ethnicity. The point of view of group insiders is called an *emic* perspective, as opposed to the *etic* view of the outsiders. Emically speaking, most ethnic group members see themselves as a people or as a nation, and the idea of shared origin is crucial. This shared origin does not have to be based on historical fact, and is usually putative, mythical, or fictitious in nature. Emically speaking, however, ethnic affinity is generally not perceived in any way as ideologically generated or as primordial.

In the anthropological literature, theories of ethnicity vary widely depending on the scholarly framework employed, be it primordialism, constructivism, situationism or other orientation. Vastly different statements about group affinity and personal identity can be generated depending on the terms of reference used in the underlying context. In modern societies, for instance, very different conditions of group affinity obtain than in traditional societies. The ethnic and sociocultural identity of an individual also varies according to the location or standpoint of the observer; and the terms by which the Other and the Self (i.e., outgroup and ingroup characteristics) can also vary.

Conflict brings about fundamental changes in frames of reference. In a situation of threat, individual elements of personal and collective identity become enhanced. Alternatively, the political instrumentalization of mechanisms of demarcation is often done for the purposes of exclusion of certain groups. Exclusion marks the crucial step which leads from simple discrimination to more profound instances of ethnic conflict and genocide. Ethnic identity constitutes itself via processes of demarcation that do not occur within a nonauthoritarian space and whose modalities cannot be determined freely and independently. The abstract difference of others poses no problem, but the experience of real threat from others, or a construed feeling of superiority *vis-à-vis* others, are, in contrast, results of processes of exclusion and polarization. Constant injury to central elements of the shared ethnic identity, either from within or from without the group, elicits specific forms of resistance in each particular case, ranging from withdrawal to armed rebellion.

Since World War II, more than 300 wars and instances of mass murder have taken place worldwide—most of them, until the end of the 1980s, in the less-developed nations. Among the possible conflict types, the most deadly are genocides and certain forms of nonwar mass violence. (Genocide is often committed behind a smoke-screen of war and crisis.) Claims by the governments (usually despotic governments) of a number of nation-states in regard to the national groups, which happen to live on the territory of the respective state (often unwanted) and in regard to ethnic minorities and indigenous peoples, seem to become increasingly aggressive in times of change. In empirical and historical terms, this state of affairs has the most dangerous potential, and has been the source of real conflicts and wars both in the underdeveloped world and, since 1989–90, in Eastern Europe, within the former socialist multinational states.

Almost two-thirds of current violent conflicts are susceptible to ethnic interpretation. It was only when the Janus-like countenance of nationalism reappeared in Europe (after the dissolution of the Soviet Socialist Republics) that the media and broad sections of the public in the West became aware of this global trend towards ethnic nationalism, of which there had been evidence since the period of decolonization. It was a long-established fact that this belated nationalism represented a renegotiation of the situation left behind by the colonial world-order. It involved a fundamental struggle between liberation and oppression, between emancipation and barbarity.

The global trend toward an increase of intra-state conflicts and a decrease—if not near disappearance—of the classic Clausewitzean "war between states" has grown steadily greater over the second half of the twentieth century. The trend reflects the increasing importance of intra-state conditions in the generation of conflict, but the violence that ultimately erupts often spills over borders. There is a multiplication of actors in some complex new conflicts, with the Congo and Sudan being the best examples.

In empirical research, different types of contemporary conflicts can be observed. Their dominant character is either anti-regime or ethno-nationalistic, followed by interethnic wars, often without state actors being involved, and gang wars and warlordism, which have been named "post-modern wars" despite the fact that this type of conflict has a long history. There are some decolonization conflicts, as well. A recent example of this type of conflict occurred in East Timor, which was brought under Indonesian occupation by a genocide that reduced the Timorese population by one-third from 1975 to the 1980s. Terrorist conflicts, which in the form of international gang wars gained much attention since September 11, 2001, are neither a new phenomenon nor a particular deadly form of mass violence. Their death toll is relatively low—in 2001 such conflicts may have caused 0.2 percent of all conflict-related fatalities worldwide.

Conflict types suited to ethnic interpretation—with ethnicity as the mobilizing force—seem to be rapidly increasing in incidence and ferocity, although they have been prominent for quite some time. Increases in violent ethno-nationalist conflicts have been observed in the wake of a number of phases of decolonization. Ethnic conflicts of a violent kind are both products and causes of colonial creation and of the inherent instability of newly formed states. Thus, ethno-nationalism appears to be a response to serious ongoing crises. Its primary cause, the struggle against the neo-colonial state, has strong structural aspects and, therefore, a truly global spread. However, the level of conflict varies considerably in the different regions of the world. As the example of the Community of Independent States (CIS) shows, the structure and dynamics of the process of fragmentation in the recently emerged states of Eastern Europe followed its own rules and differed significantly from the situation in the nations of Africa and other less developed, formerly colonized regions of the world.

Attempts to clarify or resolve sub-national conflicts must be preceded by the realization that existential questions relating to the survival of an ethnic group are not factors that are open to negotiation but essential prerequisites to dialogue. There are a number of highly destructive forms of interaction between states, nations, and nationalities that have resulted in the exclusion and persecution of national groups but that have not yet been subject to systematic investigation and for which the international community has not yet developed any consistent policy. This was demonstrated with devastating clarity in the case of the genocide in Rwanda in 1994.

The crime of genocide not only calls for prevention but for its elimination. Genocide prevention requires different means than the prevention of ethnic violence in general and ethno-nationalism in particular. The political and humanitarian concern to find ways of avoiding violent forms of ethno-nationalism from below and ethnicization from above leads to the questions of (1) how ethnic and cultural difference can be understood and acknowledged; (2) how destructive forms of interaction between states and nations or nationalities can be prevented; and (3) which institutions, legal measures, and policies are most appropriate for that purpose.

Procedures aimed at the "structural prevention" of violence are required. Structural prevention seeks to end repression and injustice, which is ingrained in state policies and underdevelopment, and which is also inherent in the cultural attitudes held by many dominant groups. "Structural" means that new political frameworks and institutions are created to avert the possibility of direct and indirect violence such as discrimination against non-dominant groups. Johan Galtung developed the concept of structural violence in the 1970s, based on his path-breaking distinction between direct personal violence (massacres or war) and structural violence (e.g., impoverishment of a group to the point of lethality). Galtung also reflected on cultural violence, noting, for example, the values that promote and/or justify violence and superiority complexes that result into aggressive attitudes. Here the contribution of systemic peace research can be crucial.

Preventive activities range from initiatives by popular local and regional movements to the elaboration of norms and legal instruments for the protection of minorities and vulnerable groups within the framework of international and universal organizations. Efforts to change violence-promoting conditions through disarmament, controls and bans on arms production and trade, demobilization, and the strengthening of civil society are often neglected in the debate about how to deal with or prevent violent conflicts. Political and institutional consultancy in peaceful dispute-settlement is often carried out by third party go-betweens in the case of protracted ethnic conflicts. Mediation and facilitation in such conflicts can undoubtedly be successful as an instrument of international politics and should not be left solely to state and interstate actors. Efforts at go-between mediation by civil actors and initiatives for preventing and transforming violent ethnic conflicts are arduous, however, and generally hold little attraction for the media.

SEE ALSO Ethnic Cleansing; Ethnic Groups; Ethnocide; Nationalism

BIBLIOGRAPHY

Anderson, Benedict (1991). *Imagined Communities. Reflections on the Origin and Spread of Nationalism.* Rev. Edition. London: Verso.

Barth, Frederik, ed. (1969). *Ethnic Groups and Boundaries.* Boston: Little, Brown.

Dadrian, Vahakn N. (1997). *The History of the Armenian Genocide. Ethnic Conflict from the Balkans to Anatolia to the Caucuses.* Providence, R.I.: Berghahn Books.

Galtung, Johan (1996). *Peace by Peaceful Means: Peace and Conflict, Development and Civilization.* London: Sage Publications.

Isajiw, Wsevolod (1980). "Definitions of Ethnicity." In *Ethnicity and Ethnic Relations in Canada*, ed. Rita M. Bienvenue and Jay E. Goldstein. Toronto: Butterworth.

Melson, Robert (1996). *Revolution and Genocide. On the Origins of the Armenian Genocide and the Holocaust.* Chicago: University of Chicago Press.

Sherrer, Christian P. (2001). *Genocide and Crisis in Central Africa.* Westport, Conn.: Príger.

Scherrer, Christian P. (2002). *Ethnicity, Nationalism, and Violence.* Aldershot, U.K.: Ashgate.

Scherrer, Christian P. (2002). *Structural Prevention of Ethnic Violence.* New York: Palgrave Macmillan.

Smith, Anthony D. (1991). *National Identity.* London: Penguin Books.

Smith, Paul, ed. (1991). *Ethnic Groups in International Relations.* Aldershot, U.K.: Dartmouth Publishing.

Christian P. Sherrer

Ethnocide

Ethnocide concerns policies and processes designed to destroy the separate identity of a group, with or without the physical destruction of its members. This concept was developed by Raphael Lemkin as part of the definition of genocide:

> Generally speaking, genocide does not necessarily mean the immediate destruction of a nation, except when accomplished by mass killings. It is intended rather to signify a coordinated plan of different actions aimed at the destruction of the essential foundations of the life of national groups, with the aim of annihilating the groups themselves. The objectives of such a plan would be a disintegration of political and social institutions—of culture, language, national feelings, religion, and the economic existence of national groups, and the destruction of personal security, liberty, health, dignity, and even the lives of the individuals belonging to such groups. Genocide is directed at the national group as an entity, and the actions involved are directed at individuals, not in their individual capacity, but as members of the national group (1944, p. 79).

For Lemkin genocide had two phases: "one, destruction of the national pattern of the oppressed group; the other, the imposition of the national pattern of the oppressor." If these two conditions are met, a genocide has, according to Lemkin's view, occurred, even if every member of the targeted group has survived the process in a physical sense. Such actions may include the destruction or removal of tangible heritage (monuments, sites, artifacts, etc.) or obliteration of intangible heritage by prohibiting cultural manifestations that do not leave physical evidence. It may also include gross abuses of human rights designed to ensure the disappearance of a group as a separate entity, such as the removal of children.

The existence of cultural remnants, such as monuments, writings, or movable objects of a type unique to that culture, may enable it to be identified and, perhaps, revived, even when all its members have apparently been annihilated or so assimilated into another culture that they no longer identify with it. Scholars have developed a spoken language from written texts (modern Hebrew) and unique basket-making techniques from a study of museum objects.

Definition

The original draft of the 1948 Convention on the Prevention and Punishment of the Crime of Genocide, prepared by the United Nations (UN) Secretariat and based on the work of Lemkin, included definitions of physical genocide, biological genocide, and cultural genocide. The latter was defined as follows:

The destroyed interior of the Bosnian National Library at Sarajevo, where thousands of rare books and manuscripts burned after Bosnian Serb gunners fired incendiary shells at the building. The ultimate goal of the Bosnian War of 1992–1995: the complete annihilation of the non-Serb population. [TEUN VOETEN]

Destroying the specific characteristics of the group by:

(a) forcible transfer of children to another human group; or

(b) forced and systematic exile of individuals representing the culture of a group; or

(c) prohibition of the use of the national language even in private intercourse; or

(d) systematic destruction of books printed in the national language or of religious works or prohibition of new publications; or

(e) systematic destruction of historical or religious monuments or their diversion to alien uses, destruction or dispersion of documents and objects of historical, artistic, or religious value and of objects used in religious worship.

The only provisions in the Convention as finally adopted that can be used against ethnocide are Article 2(d) (on the prevention of births) and (e) (the forcible transfer of children). Because the inclusion of cultural genocide in the Convention proved controversial and was finally rejected, some have taken the view that the present text of the Genocide Convention excludes the concept of cultural genocide. However, there is now much more awareness of both the frequent interpenetration of physical and cultural genocide, as well as the need to preserve threatened cultures. Canada and the United Kingdom were the most active in eliminating the stronger references to cultural genocide in the definition, perhaps because of assimilation policies toward Native Americans, since abandoned, still employed by Canada at the time of the Convention's drafting.

Although the courts will, in criminal prosecutions, apply the legal definition of genocide included in the Convention or in one of the other international instruments granting them such jurisdiction, as the undisputed minimum content of that crime, this does not exclude the use of Lemkin's explicit definition of cultural genocide in other contexts. It is nonetheless helpful to have a separate term for this, since popular usage has followed the limited definition in the Genocide Convention as referring only to the physical destruction of persons. Several theorists have suggested the use of eth-

Book-burning in Berlin, the evening of May 10, 1933. German students, inspired by a speech that had just been given by Minister of Propaganda Joseph Goebbels, gather around a bonfire. On that same evening, in towns all over Germany, students marched, burned books, and participated in the "Action against the UnGerman Spirit." Works considered "unGerman" (including the works of many Jewish authors) were burned. [AP/WIDE WORLD PHOTOS]

nocide to describe the intentional destruction of social, racial, religious, ethnic, and linguistic groups. Ethnocide in that sense would include compulsory exogamy, forced pregnancy, prevention of births, removal of children, insistence on mainstream education without education in their own culture, prohibition of the use of a mother tongue, distortion of history, and discrimination in access to cultural resources. Planned compulsory assimilation, often making use of such activities, would fall within that concept. The deleterious effect of all such policies, even if thought at the time to represent enlightened humanitarianism, is the loss of creative diversity.

Historical Examples

The removal of cultural property from a defeated people and destruction of their heritage were practiced from the earliest times (e.g., the Romans' total destruc-tion of Carthage in 146 BCE) especially in conquest and as an action against minorities. Because cultural heritage has been seen as a rallying point for the self-confidence, aggressiveness, and revival of enemy communities, its destruction was used as part of successful warfare and domination (e.g., destruction of Khmer sites by Thai and Burmese forces in the thirteenth century, of the Inca and Aztec cultures by the Spanish invaders, of Korean and Chinese culture by Japan during its colonial and wartime occupations of territory in the Asian arena, of Jewish culture in Nazi Germany, of Tibetan culture by the Chinese authorities since 1951, of Croat, Muslim, and Serbian monuments during the conflicts among the former states of the Federal Republic of Yugoslavia).

Policies of "assimilation" of a minority, often indigenous, people into the majority population were often applied. The methods employed included the suppression of a mother tongue, the schooling of children in the majority culture, and prohibiting the use of a Native language (e.g., the banning of Welsh, Irish, and Scots Gaelic at various periods, and forced education of Native American children in English-speaking schools in Canada and the United States). Other examples are the removal of children from their own cultural group for rearing in another (e.g., the stolen generations of children taken from their Australian Aboriginal communities for adoption by white families or placement in institutions, a practice that continued until the 1970s) and a ban on the publication and distribution of materials representing a minority culture (e.g., the burning of Armenian manuscripts in Turkey). Policies of suppression of intangible heritage have included rigorous application of the family law of the ruling majority, which has severely changed pre-existing social structures, and suppression of indigenous religious practices.

Legal Restraints

Current international laws (excluding regional agreements) in force against ethnocide include Conventions IV and IX on the laws of war adopted by the Hague peace conference in 1907. These advanced the protection of civilian property generally, but also specifically provided for the protection of buildings with religious, scientific, or charitable purposes, and historic monuments (Regulations 1907 annexed to Convention IV, especially Articles 27 and 56). The 1954 Hague Convention for the Protection of Cultural Property in the Event of Armed Conflict greatly expanded the provisions of earlier Hague conventions, whereas its Protocol, also adopted in 1954, covered the return of movable cultural property removed from occupied territory. This Convention and Protocol have been supplemented by Protocols added to the Geneva Conventions of August 12, 1949, and related to the Convention for the Protection of Victims of International and Non-international Armed Conflicts of June 8, 1977 (Articles 53 and 85(d), Protocol I; Article 16, Protocol II). They have also been updated by a Second Protocol to the 1954 Hague Convention, adopted at the Hague in 1999.

The United Nations Educational, Scientific, and Cultural Organization (UNESCO) has developed a code of protective international legislation for cultural heritage in general. In addition to the 1954 Hague Convention protecting all tangible heritage in times of conflict, the following conventions have been adopted: the 1970 Convention on the Means of Prohibiting and Preventing the Illicit Import, Export and Transfer of Ownership of Cultural Property, concerned with movables in peacetime; the 1972 Convention for the Protection of World Cultural and National Heritage, addressing

the protection of sites with cultural and national importance during peacetime; the 2001 Convention on the Protection of Underwater Cultural Heritage, which deals with all underwater heritage over one hundred years old, including warships; and the 2003 Convention for the Safeguarding of Intangible Cultural Heritage. There is also a universal convention concerned with the return of cultural heritage, whether taken during peace or war: the 1995 UNIDROIT Convention on Stolen or Illicitly Exported Cultural Objects. Returns of cultural property, some of which may relate to ethnocide, may be sought under the 1970 and 1995 Conventions, but neither is retrospective. In the Netherlands an unsuccessful claim was made under the 1954 Protocol for the recovery of icons looted from a church in Northern Cyprus (*Greek Autocephalous Orthodox Church of Cyprus v. Lans*). Of the conventions administered by UNESCO, only the Hague Convention and its Second Protocol provide for punitive provisions, which state parties are responsible for implementing.

The International Criminal Tribunal for the Former Yugoslavia (ICTY; its Statute dated May 25, 1993) and the International Criminal Court (ICC; the Rome Statute dated July 17, 1998) have the jurisdiction to prosecute certain acts of ethnocide. The ICTY has filed a suit based on offenses against cultural heritage (Dubrovnik and Mostar Bridge), although the accused have not yet been handed over to the authorities. The case of the International Criminal Tribunal for Rwanda (ICTR; its Statute dated November 8, 1994) is more problematic because Rwanda was in civil, not international, conflict when ethnocide occurrred. Thus, the protection of cultural property remains a difficult task; it is usually only addressed through the law on human rights or the norms and standards of cultural heritage law established by UNESCO.

Importance of Cultural Heritage

The importance of preservation of cultures, of whatever origin, was stressed in the Preamble to the 1954 Hague Convention (paras. 2 and 3), where it is stated that "damage to cultural property belonging to any people whatsoever means damage to the cultural heritage of all mankind, since each people makes its contribution to the culture of the world." An egregious example was the Taliban's destruction of important Buddhist art in Afghanistan in March 2001. This religious art was of great importance to Buddhist communities outside that country (no Buddhists had lived in Afghanistan for centuries), and to art lovers and historians everywhere. Destruction of cultural heritage removes from the body of human knowledge unique responses to the environment that are not only culturally enriching but also may be of considerable use to future human groups.

[BANDA]

In 1621 forces of the Dutch East Indies Company (VOC) conquered the small Banda archipelago in present-day eastern Indonesia and largely exterminated its people. The archipelago was the only site for the cultivation of nutmeg, *Myristica fragrans*, that grew in groves on the lower parts of the volcanic slopes of the archipelago's five main islands. Nutmeg was enormously valued in India, the Middle East, and the West. The Banda Islands were thus at the beginning of a trade route extending halfway around the world.

Bandanese society was dominated by a wealthy commercial elite that kept slaves from neighboring islands and maintained tight control of the sale of nutmeg to foreign traders. The population of the islands numbered perhaps fifteen thousand in 1621 and for food depended on rice imported from distant Java. Although the archipelago was tiny, its steep volcanic slopes provided a refuge for the Bandanese when they were attacked from the sea. During the sixteenth century the Portuguese joined other traders at Banda, but they were never able to establish a fort on the islands and many quarrels erupted between Bandanese and Portuguese over the prices and quality of goods supplied by either side and over Portugal's efforts to gain a military foothold in the islands.

So vexatious were the Portuguese that the Bandanese welcomed rival Dutch ships in 1599. VOC troops, however, forced their way ashore, built a fort, and compelled the Bandanese to sign a treaty granting the company a monopoly on nutmeg purchases. Nevertheless, the Bandanese never submitted to the inequitable Dutch monopoly. They traded with English and other merchants and in 1609 massacred forty-six VOC employees. In 1621 the VOC Governor-General Jan Pieterszoon Coen arrived with a fleet to conquer the islands. After an initial Dutch show of force, the Bandanese elite tried to negotiate with Coen, but he ordered forty-eight of them executed and shipped their families into slavery in Batavia (now Jakarta). The Bandanese then fled to the uplands, where Dutch troops undertook a sustained campaign of extermination for several months. Many Bandanese were killed; others starved to death or cast themselves from the cliffs near Selamma rather than surrender. A few managed to escape by boat to the Kai Islands, where a small community still remained as of 2004. Bandanese on the English-occupied island of Run were not slaughtered, but captured and enslaved. The population of the archipelago declined from 15,000 to about 1,000. The VOC directors in Amsterdam later concluded that Coen should have acted with greater moderation, but awarded him 3,000 guilders for his services.

As well as ensuring control of the nutmeg trade, the genocide perpetrated by Coen's troops cleared the way for European settlement, with which Coen hoped to consolidate Dutch power in the archipelago. The nutmeg groves were divided into *perken* (parks), each with about fifty trees, and allocated to European settlers as VOC tenants, while labor was supplied by slaves introduced from other parts of the archipelago. For further reading, see Hanna, Willard A. (1978). *Indonesian Banda: Colonialism and Its Aftermath in the Nutmeg Islands*. Philadelphia: Institute for the Study of Human Issues and Loth, Vincent C. (1995). "Pioneers and Perkeniers: The Banda Islands in the 17th Century." *Cakalele* 6:13–35. **ROBERT CRIBB**

Destruction or suppression of the culture of a group no longer present in a territory, or indeed no longer extant anywhere, should be punished even when the group no longer exists, since it distorts history and limits the access of all of humanity to certain cultural resources. Ethnocide also renders the rehabilitation of traumatized communities especially difficult, since the loss of landmarks that helped the community establish its identity induces alienation and despair.

The need to identify and prevent ethnocide has greatly increased with the international community's recent recognition of the importance of cultural diversity within the context of globalization, especially in the areas of communication and culture (UNESCO's 2001 Universal Declaration on Cultural Diversity; as of 2003, its convention was still being drafted). The development of a parallel new instrument to specifically address ethnocide should now be considered.

Means of Prevention

Because ethnocide often follows centuries of discrimination, the latter should be regarded as an early warning system. Abuse of rights such as the rights to one's religious beliefs, to freedom of association, to control the education of children, and to use one's own language indicates the threat of ethnocide (e.g., discrimination against Albanian pupils and teachers, and the closing of Albanian educational, cultural, and scientific institutions, as well as the virtual elimination of the Albanian language, preceded violence in Kosovo). Societal pressures leading toward ethnocide should be immediately addressed, especially when enmity has historically existed between communities.

The first step is publicizing a breach of human rights and requiring compliance. A program of tolerance, based on UNESCO's 1995 Declaration of Principles on Tolerance, and encouragement of cultural diversity should also be put in place. Appreciation, particularly of traditional cultures under threat, can be engendered by programs encouraging respect for the practitioners of older cultural values and traditions, such as UNESCO's Living Human Treasures program (instituted in 2002). Programs that encourage the survival of threatened languages can also play an important role, as can language-teaching programs. Multilingualism is an important aspect of intercultural appreciation, since it enables better understanding of unfamiliar value systems. In addition, cultural exchanges should be encouraged.

Polices of multiculturalism, similar to those that have been officially adopted in countries such as Australia and Canada, promote the value of cultural diversity within states by various means: the promotion of multicultural and multilinguistic media, the provision of at least some government services in minority languages, the recognition of religious and other important holidays celebrated by all communities in a state, and the provision of education, at least at the primary school level and in the communities most affected, in a mother language. Including the representatives of many cultures in official and other public ceremonies, and representatives of all groups in public committees and other official activities, also raises awareness of these groups and their contribution to the culture of the state as a whole.

The acknowledgment of former ethnocidal policies and the groups responsible for them is also important in preventing their recurrence. The Truth and Reconciliation Commission of South Africa has sought, by admission of the evils perpetrated and a purposeful confrontation with its former opponents, to defuse intercommunal hatreds. Rwanda has taken similar action.

Another reaction to threatened or actual genocide, including ethnocide, has historically been armed intervention (e.g., the UN's intervention in the Belgian Congo from 1960 to 1964 following the violence after that country gained its independence). However, interventions by individual states have very often been associated with other motives, such as the protection of economic interests or the pursuit of political ends. And such interventions have also generally been regarded as perilous; especially after the loss of eighteen U.S. soldiers in Somalia in 1993, states remained reluctant to intervene in Rwanda in 1994, despite the clear threat and later evidence of genocide. Subsequent interventions, such as that in Kosovo, have shown the limited success of such efforts once violence has broken out. Many of these efforts have been made without sufficient force—the example of Srebrenica being the most obvious—and the preservation of culture has been abandoned in favor of rescuing human lives. What peacekeepers can do to save endangered heritage is therefore limited, and in the current international context ethnocide is unlikely to be substantially deterred by the threat of intervention by force.

Finally, the prosecution of offenders comes long after the event of ethnocide and is dependent on states' handing over the perpetrators. It is very important that the international community as a whole not tolerate such behavior and ensure its punishment, but thus far the deterrent effect of this more frequently held approach has proven small.

SEE ALSO Ethnic Cleansing; Ethnic Groups; Genocide; Lemkin, Raphael

BIBLIOGRAPHY

Charny, Israel W., ed. (1999). *Encyclopedia of Genocide*, 2 volumes. New York: ABC-CLIO.

Hitchcock, Robert K. (2003). "Genocide, Ethnocide, Ecocide, with Special Reference to Indigenous Peoples: A Bibliography." Available from http://www.aaanet.org/committees/cfhr/bib_hitchcock_genocide.htm.

Hitchcock, Robert K., and Tara M. Twedt (1997). "Physical and Cultural Genocide of Various Peoples." In *Century of Genocide, Eyewitness Accounts and Critical Views*, ed. Samuel Totten, Israel W. Charny, and William S. Parsons. New York: Garland Publishing.

Kuper, Leo (1981). *Genocide: Its Political Use in the Twentieth Century*. Harmondsworth, U.K.: Penguin Books.

Lemkin, Raphael (1944). "Axis Rule in Occupied Europe." Available from http://www.preventgenocide.org/lemkin/AxisRule1944-1.htm.

Prosecutor v. Krstic. ICTY Judgment (August 2, 2001). Available from http://www.un.org/icty/krstic/TrialC1/judgement/krs-tj010802e-3.htm.

Schabas, William A. (1999). "The Genocide Convention at Fifty." Special Report 41, United States Institute of Peace. Available from http://www.usip.org/pubs/specialreports/sr990107.html.

Schabas, William A. (2000). *Genocide in International Law: The Crime of Crimes*. New York: Cambridge University Press.

UNESCO (1995). *Our Creative Diversity*. New York: UNESCO.

UNESCO (1996). Guidelines for the Establishment of "Living Human Treasures" Systems. New York: UNESCO.

Lyndel V. Prott

Eugenics

The term *eugenics* (from the Greek *eugenes*, meaning well-born) was coined by Englishman Francis Galton in 1883. Galton, a cousin of Charles Darwin, used Darwin's ideas of evolutionary fitness in the animal kingdom to forge a concept of selective breeding for humans. Proposing to produce superior citizenries, eugenics encompasses two interconnected philosophies: (1) restricting the reproduction capabilities of so-called undesirable segments of a population (negative eugenics); and (2) encouraging so-called desirable segments to reproduce (positive eugenics). At the turn of the twentieth century a eugenics movement gained widespread international support, particularly in Great Britain, the United States, and Germany. In 1895 German physician Alfred Ploetz created the related science of *Rassenhygiene* (racial hygiene), and in 1907 he founded the International Society for Racial Hygiene. That same year Indiana passed laws making it the first U.S. state to permit involuntary sterilization of individuals considered criminally insane or genetically inferior. By 1932 similar laws existed in twenty-seven other U.S. states. Other countries issued comparable legislation, including Denmark (1929), Sweden and Norway (1934), Finland (1935), and Estonia (1936).

In Germany eugenics underwent a transformation from scientific theory to state policy when the Nazis (National Socialists) assumed power in 1933. Propaganda Minister Joseph Goebbels declared that all facets of German life were to be informed by a "eugenic way of thinking." Doctors and midwives became "guardians of the nation," responsible for ensuring proper racial health. The Office for Racial Policy disseminated printed materials that strove to indoctrinate the general public on the importance of marrying "correctly." A series of laws aimed at guaranteeing racial purity were introduced. The Law for the Prevention of Genetically Diseased Offspring (July 1933) allowed for the sterilization of individuals suffering from any of a cluster of hereditary disabilities, including feeblemindedness, schizophrenia, insanity, genetic epilepsy, Huntington's chorea, genetic blindness or deafness, and chronic alcoholism. The Nuremberg Laws on Citizenship and Race (1935) were focused on "Aryanizing" German blood, redefining citizenship to exclude Jews, and preventing marriage or any sexual contact between Christians and Jews.

The Nazis did not restrict their eugenic agenda to preventing the birth of undesired offspring, but went a step further to formalize the killing of those deemed "lives unworthy of living," targeting first children and later adults with mental and/or physical disabilities. At the heart of this agenda was Operation T-4 (named

> **[THE MODEL EUGENICAL STERILIZATION LAW]**
>
> Harry Hamilton Laughlin (1880–1943) served as superintendent in charge of the Eugenics Record Office (ERR) in Cold Spring Harbor, New York, from the office's origin in 1910 until 1921; he later acted as ERO director, from 1921 to 1940. At the time of Laughlin's appointment, at least two states—Indiana and Connecticut—had enacted laws allowing for sterilization on eugenic grounds. In 1914 Laughlin drafted his Model Eugenical Sterilization Law. The statute proposed sterilization of the "socially inadequate," targeting those persons who were institutionalized or "maintained in whole or part at public expense." Factors influencing "social inadequacy" were determined to include alcoholism; epilepsy; blindness; deafness; and "orphans, ne'er-do-wells, tramps, the homeless and paupers."
>
> In 1922 Laughlin's Model Law was published in *Eugenical Sterilization in the United States*. The book presented various documentation, including legal materials, tables, and charts, to support eugenic education and legislation. By 1924, approximately 3,000 people had been involuntarily sterilized in the United States as a result of state sterilization statues, many modeled directly on the Laughlin's model.

after its Berlin headquarters, at Tiergartenstrasse 4), headed by Philip Bouhler and Karl Brandt. From December 1939 to August 1941, under the sponsorship of Operation T-4, some 70,000 psychiatric patients, asylum inmates, and concentration camp internees deemed nonproductive were transported to six killing institutions (Bernburg, Brandenburg, Grafeneck, Hadamar, Hartheim, and Sonnenstein), where they died, primarily by gas asphyxiation. Although offshoots of Operation T-4 continued to operate after August 1941, killing another estimated 130,000 people by 1945, many T-4 doctors had transferred to extermination camps, where they continued to help to actualize the Holocaust.

It was Nazi Germany's shift from an agenda of mass sterilization to one of mass killing and its efforts to annihilate the world's Jewish population (and the eventual reportage of these calamities) that brought an end to widespread social acceptance of eugenics as a means to create a better race. However, the collapse of the Third Reich did not mean the corresponding collapse of eugenic practices elsewhere. For example, it was not until

1972 that the western Canadian province of Alberta repealed its sterilization act, originally passed in 1928. In 1996 the National Film Board of Canada released a film, *The Sterilization of Leilani Muir*, that documented the history of the province's eugenic practices. The film tells the story of Muir, the first woman to win a wrongful sterilization suit against the province. In the 1990s other countries began recognizing and compensating victims of involuntary or coerced sterilization. In 1997 news stories revealed that, between 1936 and 1976, some 63,000 people in Sweden had undergone sterilization. Although most of these people had signed consent forms, the ten percent who had not were suddenly entitled to compensation. In 2002 the state of Virginia issued a formal apology to the approximately seven thousand victims of its eugenics program, which had operated until 1979, and erected a memorial to commemorate them.

Not all countries, however, have chosen to recognize the victims of or even suspend eugenic practices. In the 1970s and 1980s the government of Czechoslovakia sponsored a policy that strove to reduce the nation's Romani population through involuntary sterilization. The Czech successor state of Slovakia, formed in 1993, has sustained the sterilization practices. Still other countries promote programs that are reminiscent (to varying degrees) of earlier Nazi legislation. For example, in China, couples seeking to marry must undergo medical tests that screen for hereditary diseases and related conditions. Finally, for many countries, eugenics-related issues continue to hover at the periphery of national debate as new scientific and medical discoveries raise related moral and ethical questions: Should governments permit physician-assisted suicide with consent of the patient? Should parents be allowed to select the sex of their unborn child? How far should medical scientists pursue human cloning?

SEE ALSO Euthanasia; Films, Eugenics; Racism

BIBLIOGRAPHY

Aly, Götz, Peter Choust, and Christian Pross (1994). *Cleansing the Fatherland: Nazi Medicine and Racial Hygiene.* Trans. Belinda Cooper. Baltimore, Md.: Johns Hopkins University Press.

Commission on Security and Cooperation in Europe. "Coerced Sterilization of Romani Women in Slovakia." Available from http://www.csce.gov/pdf/ Coerced%20sterilization.pdf.

Hesketh, Therese (2003). "Getting Married in China: Pass the Medical First." Available from http://bmj. bmjjournals.com/cgi/content/full/326/7383/277.

Kater, Michael H. (1989). *Doctors under Hitler.* Chapel Hill: University of North Carolina Press.

Kühl, Stefan (1994). *The Nazi Connection: Eugenics, American Racism, and German National Socialism.* Oxford, U.K.: Oxford University Press.

People and Politics: The People behind the Process/ Government of Canada Digital Collections. "Eugenics in Alberta." Available from http://collections.ic.gc.ca/ abpolitics/people/influ_eugenics.html.

Lynne Fallwell

European Convention on the Non-Application of Statutory Limitations

Criminal law normally permits the prosecution of accused offenders only for prescribed periods of time, outside of which no legal actions are possible—this kind of restriction known as statutory limitation. In January 1965 the Parliamentary Assembly of the Council of Europe (PACE) recommended that the Committee of Ministers of the Council of Europe (CM) draw up a Convention on the Non-Application of Statutory Limitations to Crimes Against Humanity and War Crimes. It was the position of PACE that member states of the Council of Europe (CoE) should take appropriate measures to disallow that crimes that had been committed with political, racial, and religious motives before and during World War II (and more generally crimes against humanity) could remain unpunished simply by virtue of the application of statutory limitation.

Finding that several CoE member states had already adopted, as part of their domestic laws, measures that tended toward the nullification of statutory limitation with respect to crimes against humanity, and taking into account that United Nations (UN) organs were dealing with the same matter, the CM proposed that the negotiations for an international convention should take place within the wider framework of the UN.

In December 1968 the UN General Assembly adopted a draft Convention on the nonapplicability of statutory limitation to war crimes and crimes against humanity. However, of the member states of the CoE, only one (Cyprus) voted in favor of the Convention.

In January 1969, attentive to the fact that most CoE member states had voted not to accept the UN Convention, PACE adopted a recommendation that reiterated the invitation it had extended to the CM in January 1965. Also in January 1969 the CM decided to include the subject of statutory limitation in its intergovernmental work program for examination by the European Committee on Crime Problems (ECCP). In May 1973 the CM adopted the draft European Convention on the Non-Applicability of Statutory Limitation to Crimes against Humanity and War Crimes, which was opened for signature in January 1974. It entered into force on June 26, 2003, following its ratification by Belgium. It had previously been ratified by the Netherlands (1981) and Romania (2000). France became a signatory to the Convention in 1974.

The Convention requires that the contracting states undertake to adopt any and all measures as are necessary to secure that statutory limitation shall not apply to the imposition of or enforcement of sentences for: (1) crimes against humanity, as specified in the 1948 UN Convention on the Prevention and Punishment of the Crime of Genocide; (2) war crimes, as specified in the 1949 Geneva Conventions, or any comparable violations of the laws of war and/or customs of war existing at the time of the Convention's entry into force (in 2003); and (3) any other crimes of a comparable nature that the contracting states believe may be established as such in future international law. The Convention stipulates that crimes for which statutory limitation does not apply should be of a particularly grave character, by virtue of either their factual elements and premeditated nature or the extent of their foreseeable consequences (Article 1). The Convention applies to crimes committed by a state after the document's entry into force in that state, as well as to crimes committed before its entry into force, provided that the statutory periods of limitation from that time are not yet expired (Article 2).

The Convention was not a great success with the CoE member states. The domestic laws of most states already provided for the nonapplication of statutory limitation to the crimes referred to in the Convention.

SEE ALSO Crimes Against Humanity; Genocide; International Law

BIBLIOGRAPHY

Fawcett, J. E. S. (1965). "A Time Limit for Punishment of War Crimes." *The International and Comparative Law Quarterly* 14(part 2):327–632.

Kreicker, H. (2002). "Die völkerrechtliche Unverjährbarkeit und die Regelung im Völkerstrafgesetzbuch." *Neue Justiz* 6:281–286.

Trifterer, Otto, ed. (1999). *Commentary on the Rome Statute of the International Criminal Court.* Baden Baden, Germany: Nomos.

Hans Christian Krüger
Alessia Sonaglioni

Euthanasia

Literally meaning a "good death" (from the Greek *eu* and *thanatos*), and frequently defined as a gentle or easy death, euthanasia ordinarily refers to intentional death in a medical setting or achieved by medical means. The noun is usually modified by adjectives—active, passive, voluntary, nonvoluntary, and involuntary—that identify the moral and legal concerns surrounding death by euthanasia. By definition, euthanasia is distinct from, although often confused with, physician-assisted suicide. The morality and legality of euthanasia are a central subject of health law and medical ethics, where the major arguments involve the individual's right to die and the doctor's ability to hasten the death of ill or suffering patients. Distinguishing the different types of euthanasia is central to understanding the moral and legal debate about its practice and legalization.

During the 1930s, Germany developed state-sponsored euthanasia programs to end lives that the government deemed "unworthy of living," and these programs became the source of the Final Solution and the medicalized killing that was later conducted in the concentration camps. Hence, the specter of genocide haunts more recent discussions about any death by medical means. Analogies to Nazi practice and concerns about unrestricted killing under the German euthanasia programs continue to influence moral and legal arguments about the need for limits to death by euthanasia.

Types of Euthanasia

Euthanasia hastens death. It may do so by active or passive means employed by a doctor or other agent. Active euthanasia occurs by an affirmative act that intentionally causes death, for instance, by a lethal injection by a doctor upon a patient that ends the patient's life. Passive euthanasia occurs when medical treatment is withheld or withdrawn, with awareness that death will result from the omission of care. For example, a doctor or other individual may decide not to place or keep a patient on a respirator or feeding tube. Active refers to "causing death," while passive means "letting die."

"Causing death," namely killing another human person, is usually prohibited by the criminal law of homicide. Hence, active euthanasia is illegal in most Western nations, except the Netherlands and Belgium. In contrast, passive euthanasia has not been subject to the same criminal sanction, although some nations punish it as the crime of not helping someone in danger. Many writers have challenged the moral distinction between active and passive upon which these legal conclusions are based, arguing that intentionally causing a patient's death and intentionally letting an individual die are morally equivalent and should face similar legal bans. Moreover, active and passive may be words too simple to deal with complex clinical situations that have aspects of both causing death as well as omitting necessary care to sustain life (e.g., by withholding nutrition and hydration in some circumstances). Nonetheless, the difference between causing death and letting die remains the basis for many legal and ethical prohibitions against active but not passive euthanasia.

The adjectives *active* and *passive* focus on the nature of the actions of the medical professional (or family member or friend) who hastens death. By contrast, the words *voluntary*, *nonvoluntary*, and *involuntary* refer to the level of the patient's consent to euthanasia. Voluntary euthanasia occurs at the patients' request or with their consent. The nonvoluntary patients' consent is absent because these individuals are unable to give consent—they may be unconscious or otherwise incapacitated. Involuntary euthanasia is imposed against the patient's wishes or will.

The patient's level of participation in euthanasia, whether voluntary, nonvoluntary, or involuntary, is significant because a patient's informed consent to medical care became a primary concern after the revelations arising from the Nuremberg trials. Nonvoluntary and involuntary actions are unsatisfactory forms of consent. The level of patient participation also explains the distinction between euthanasia and physician-assisted suicide. In physician-assisted suicide, the medical professional provides the means of death to the patient, who uses them to commit suicide. Euthanasia, however, is done to the patient by another person. Recent legal debates about medicalized death have argued the advantages and disadvantages of physician-assisted suicide over voluntary, active euthanasia. In both cases, the patient consents to death, but only in physician-assisted suicide is the patient the agent of death. One is suicide, whereas the other is killing, or mercy killing, or murder.

Medical ethics codes have disfavored both voluntary, active euthanasia and physician-assisted suicide, both of which are distinguished from the common medical practice of providing pain-relieving medication to patients with the knowledge that it will hasten death. In such cases, deaths are foreseen but not intended, and so, according to the principle of double effect, do not qualify as either physician-assisted suicide or euthanasia. Because death is not intended, such provision of death-hastening therapeutic drugs is not ordinarily grounds for prosecution even in nations that criminalize voluntary, active euthanasia. In practice, some doctors who are prosecuted for euthanasia insist that they were just providing pain relief. Critics have argued that the moral and medical distinction between foreseeing and intending death is too slim a reed to support the legal difference.

Death with Dignity

Debate about euthanasia intensifies when patients and doctors request death with dignity and defend the right to die. Supporters of a right to die argue that hastening the death of suffering or terminally-ill patients who request death is not unjustified killing but instead promotes human dignity and patient autonomy. Advocates of a right to die have challenged traditional legal bans on euthanasia and suicide.

The voluntary aspect of voluntary, active euthanasia raises the question whether the law should permit euthanasia to which patients consent. In 1984, the Dutch Supreme Court recognized a defense against murder for doctors who commit voluntary, active euthanasia. In 2001, the Netherlands promulgated substantive standards to guide the legal practice of euthanasia in cases where certain safeguards are met. The Netherlands has provided the world a laboratory for observing the practice of euthanasia for over twenty years, but its legacy and lessons remain disputed.

In other Western nations, euthanasia remains illegal, while physician-assisted suicide is widely debated. During the 1990s in the United States, the state of Oregon passed legislation allowing physician-assisted suicide, and two federal appeals courts ruled that state laws banning assisted suicide are unconstitutional. In these instances, physician-assisted suicide was viewed as promoting death with dignity. The U.S. Supreme Court, however, upheld state laws against assisted suicide. The Supreme Court recognized a strong state interest in criminalizing physician-assisted suicide because the practice of legally assisted suicide may lead to episodes of nonvoluntary and even involuntary euthanasia. The Supreme Court invoked the popular "slippery-slope" argument that once assisted suicide is legalized, all forms of euthanasia may follow without restraint. Several justices cited the experience of the Netherlands, where some data suggest that euthanasia now occurs without patient consent, that is, involuntarily. The recurrent fear is that human lives, especially the lives of the vulnerable or unwanted, will be ended against their will, that patients will be pressured into requesting a death that they do not desire, and that depressed patients will choose easy death rather than receive appropriate medical care.

Ending the Lives of the Unwanted

The slippery-slope argument resonates with many individuals because of the legacy of Nazi Germany. The roots of the Nazi euthanasia program lay in the eugenics movement that was popular in both Germany and the United States in the late nineteenth and early twentieth centuries. Eugenics, literally "good genes," identified bad genes as the source of disease, mental retardation, and illness, as well as criminality. The medical or scientific solution to the problems of health and crime was to limit the heredity of bad genes. In Germany, the eugenics movement went beyond the sterilization of "defectives" to killing. German authors defended the state's right to end unhealthy or defective lives. State-sponsored sterilization and euthanasia were justified as protecting the state against those individuals it deemed unworthy of life.

With Hitler's commitment to racial purity and anti-Semitism, the Nazi government developed a systematic euthanasia program that culminated in the concentration camps and the Final Solution. Hitler ordered his physician, Karl Brandt, to develop a euthanasia program in 1939. The first to be killed were mentally retarded children, followed by mentally ill adults and the handicapped. Then the war expanded, and, among others, the Gypsies, Jews, and other concentration camp prisoners were subjected to medicalized killing. The medical apparatus was moved from the mental institutions to the concentration camps and, as Robert J. Lifton put it in his 1986 book, *The Nazi Doctors: Medical Killing and the Psychology of Genocide*, the doctors' euthanasia programs provided the "medical bridge to unrestrained genocide" by the Nazis.

At war's end, Brandt and other doctors were prosecuted at Nuremberg in the Medical Trials; Brandt was hanged for his crimes. Among numerous counts involving crimes of medical experimentation on unconsenting victims, Brandt and three others were charged with a war crime and crime against humanity for the euthanasia program. In *The Nazi Doctors and the Nuremberg Code*, edited by George Annas and Michael A. Grodin, these crimes are specified as follows:

> [The] systematic and secret execution of the aged, insane, incurably ill, of deformed children, and other persons, by gas, lethal injections, and diverse other means in nursing homes, hospitals and asylums. . . . German doctors involved in the "euthanasia" program were also sent to the eastern occupied countries to assist in the mass extermination of Jews (1992, p. 101).

As Matthew Lippman notes in a 1998 article appearing in the *Arizona Journal of International and Comparative Law*, the Nuremberg Medical Trials set the precedent that state-sponsored euthanasia against non-nationals is a war crime and a crime against humanity.

In discussions about the morality and legality of euthanasia, analogies are frequently drawn to the Nazi doctors. Today's comatose patient may be the equivalent of yesterday's mentally retarded person, whose life is deemed unworthy of living. On the other hand, advocates of a right to die contrast Nazi state-sponsored killing with an individual's choice to die with dignity. On all sides, the moral and legal arguments about euthanasia are nuanced and contested.

SEE ALSO Eugenics; Germany; Medical Experimentation; Nuremberg Laws; Physicians

BIBLIOGRAPHY

American Medical Association, Council on Ethical and Judicial Affairs (2002). *Code of Medical Ethics: Current Opinions with Annotations*. Chicago: AMA Press, 2002.

Annas, George and Michael A. Grodin, ed. (1992). *The Nazi Doctors and the Nuremberg Code: Human Rights in Human Experimentation*. New York: Oxford University Press.

Brock, Dan W. (1997). "Death and Dying." In *Medical Ethics*, 2nd edition, ed. Robert M. Veatch. Boston: Jones and Bartlett.

Browning, Christopher R., and Jurgen Matthaus (2004). *The Origins of the Final Solution: The Evolution of Nazi Jewish Policy, September 1939–March 1942*. Lincoln: University of Nebraska.

Burleigh, Michael (1994). *Death and Deliverance: 'Euthanasia' in Germany c. 1900–1945*. Cambridge: Cambridge University Press.

Caplan, Arthur L. (1992). "The Doctors' Trial and Analogies to the Holocaust in Contemporary Bioethical Debates." In *The Nazi Doctors and the Nuremberg Code: Human Rights in Human Experimentation*, ed. G. Annas and M. A. Grodin. New York: Oxford University Press.

Cohen-Almagor, Raphael (2003). "Euthanasia and Physician-Assisted Suicide in the Democratic World: A Legal Overview." *New York International Law Review* 16:1–42.

Kamisar, Yale (1991). "When Is There a Constitutional 'Right to Die'? When is There No Constitutional 'Right to Live'?" *Georgia Law Review* 25:1203–1242.

Keown, John (2002). *Euthanasia, Ethics and Public Policy*. Cambridge: Cambridge University Press.

Lifton, Robert J. (1986). *The Nazi Doctors: Medical Killing and the Psychology of Genocide*. New York: Basic Books.

Lippman, Matthew (1998). "The Convention on the Prevention and Punishment of the Crime of Genocide: Fifty Years Later." *Arizona Journal of International and Comparative Law* 15:415–514.

Magnusson, Roger S. (2002). *Angels of Death: Exploring the Euthanasia Underground*. New Haven, Conn.: Yale University Press.

Paust, Jordan (1995). "The Human Right to Die with Dignity: A Policy-Oriented Essay." *Human Rights Quarterly* 17:463–487.

Singer, Peter (1994). *Rethinking Life and Death: The Collapse of Our Traditional Ethics*. New York: St. Martin's Press.

Washington v. Glucksberg (1997). *United States Reports* 521:702–789.

Leslie C. Griffin

Evidence

Genocide and crimes against humanity are the same as almost every other crime, in that a conviction requires proof beyond a reasonable doubt (or similar standard in the relevant lexicon of the jurisdiction) that a prohibited act (*actus reus* or "objective element") was carried out by the accused with the appropriate degree of fault (*mens rea* or "subjective element"). The international crime of genocide specifies five prohibited acts committed against a national, racial, ethnic, or religious group that need to be proved. The fault element requires proof that the act was committed with the intention of destroying the particular group in whole or in part. Crimes against humanity require proof that certain acts were carried out in the context of a widespread or systematic attack against the civilian population. The fault element requires proof that the accused participated in the act in the knowledge that it formed part of the context of the attack. No discriminatory intent is required.

Challenges of Evidence Collection and Investigations

Genocide and crimes against humanity can be referred to as "system crimes." These are a type of organized crime that will generally require a significant degree of planning, and a probable division of labor between those planning and those executing the plan. The key challenge is not normally in proving that the facts occurred, but in relation to the nature of the participation and the knowledge and intentions of those "behind the scenes." While it is generally the case that proving the facts is the least of the evidential problems in these crimes, there remain nonetheless significant matters to be considered regarding problems of evidence preservation, timing, scale, security, and appropriate treatment of witnesses. Proving the "crime base" presents its own challenges. Essentially, crime base is the proof that the criminal act has taken place. In general terms, this is done through traditional investigation techniques: the testimony of witnesses who are sufficiently proximate to the facts to be deemed credible and reliable, and the analysis of physical evidence from the crime scene, including ballistic and other forensic investigation.

The Issue of Timing and Preservation

The delay between the commission and investigation of a crime can have two key prejudicial effects on evi-

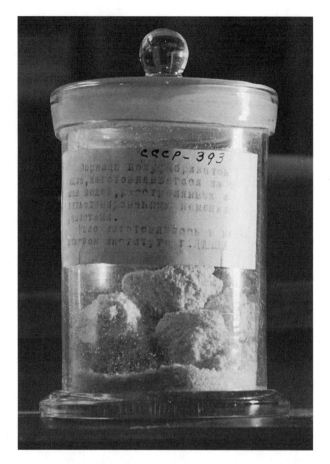

Some of the physical evidence offered at the Nuremberg trials was incendiary, such as this jar of soap manufactured from the body fat of camp inmates. It was the prosecution's hope that a symbol of such horror would prevent atrocities of this magnitude from ever occurring again. [HULTON-DEUTSCH COLLECTION/CORBIS]

dence: degradation and contamination. When investigating the crime base of genocide and crimes against humanity, contamination presents the more significant risk. Clandestine graves may be interfered with, either by relatives looking for remains of loved ones, or by those seeking to pervert the course of investigations. Any indications that this might have occurred could create serious difficulties for the admissibility of any evidence from a particular site.

The nature and context of the crimes makes it much less likely that witnesses will forget their experiences than might be the case in more mundane crimes. Similarly, the degradation of physical evidence such as human remains, while clearly undesirable, is not usually significantly damaging to its use as evidence. Exhumations are generally not required in order to clearly identify victims of genocide and crimes against humanity, but rather are needed to show with sufficient clarity the immediate circumstances of the victims' deaths and credible indications (in the case of genocide) that they belonged to a particular group. Several years between the event and the investigation will generally not degrade the remains so much that this kind of evidence cannot be obtained.

Scale

The fact that these are massive and complex crimes means that more evidence regarding the crime base will be required than in common and simple cases. However, evidence pertaining to the dimensions of the crime base has frequently been facilitated by the judicious use of experts and reliable objective observers. In the case of Jean-Paul Akayesu, for instance, the International Criminal Tribunal for Rwanda (ICTR) was satisfied that at least two thousand people had been killed between April and July 1994 primarily, though not exclusively, on the basis of experienced journalists and researchers (*Akayesu*, paras. 115–122, 181). This approach was much more swift and efficient than taking testimony from affected relatives in order to prove the loss of each individual.

In prosecutions arising from the Yugoslav and Rwandan conflicts, significant attention has been paid to the issue of rape and sexual abuse. Such crimes, and evidence of other serious physical or mental injury, do not have to be proved to the same degree of specificity that might be expected in an ordinary case of sexual assault. There is generally no requirement of medical evidence of the specific sexual attack, for instance. Instead, credible testimony from victims and witnesses has proved sufficient, as can be seen in the case of *Stakic* (*Stakic*, para. 229–236), which was prosecuted before the International Criminal Tribunal for the former Yugoslavia in connection with serial sexual assault in various prison camps, including Omarska. Similarly, the psychological impact of certain acts has not been addressed by seeking evidence from each victim as to specific consequences of their treatment, but instead has been sought on a broader level, with various kinds of experts (medical as well as anthropological) explaining the impact that certain treatment will have on individuals as well as on larger numbers of people.

The nature of the evidence presented in such trials is profoundly disturbing, not only for the witnesses, but also for the judges. Prosecutors have to strike the balance between providing sufficient proof and respecting the emotional capability of all concerned to absorb large quantities of distressing information.

Security and Sensitivity to Witness Needs

The biggest challenge to securing crime base evidence is encouraging witnesses to testify. The costs of effective witness protection over sustained periods are generally prohibitive except in a very limited number of cases. Even where trials take place far from the homes of such witnesses, they still have to return, and when they do, they may find themselves endangered. Significant strides have been made in understanding that protection is only one of a spectrum of issues that have to be dealt with, if witnesses are to be encouraged to cooperate with investigations. There is both an ethical imperative and strategic advantage in being absolutely honest with witnesses regarding the risk they may face should they agree to testify. No prosecutor should ever try to mislead witnesses in this regard. This is never acceptable, but it is even more reprehensible when the witnesses are survivors of horrendous crimes such as genocide.

Strategically, as well, prosecutors should understand that witnesses will provide more compelling testimony if they feel engaged and valued in the process as a whole. Sensitivity to the needs of such witnesses must be expressed through effective and regular communication, treatment that respects cultural and social influences that may govern the ability and speed with which certain matters can be spoken about, and, generally, the creation of a relationship of trust and respect. Such efforts may often prove sufficient to convince at-risk witnesses to accept danger in the interest of serving the cause of justice.

Proving Participation

In the case of Jelisić, the ICTY has confirmed that genocide does not necessarily require the prior existence of a plan or the participation of more than one person. Nonetheless, it is generally accepted that most cases will normally involve some form of organization and a division of labor. As with any form of organized crime, proving the participation of behind-the-scene actors requires an investigative approach that is quite different from crime base investigations. It requires a multidisciplinary investigation that is capable of understanding policy, strategy, and tactics, emphasizing especially the analysis of command structures, communications, disciplinary practices, logistics, and munitions. It is generally unlikely that those who work behind the scenes will leave unambiguous indications of their involvement, so proving the overall circumstances of the events allows the court to understand the context in which policy and operational decisions were made.

One important element in such investigations is the recovery of documentary evidence. Such evidence has several key advantages. For one thing, it is less susceptible to challenges from the defense and may be more directly incriminating than personal testimony. Human testimony will always carry the potential of being undermined in ways that are much less likely in

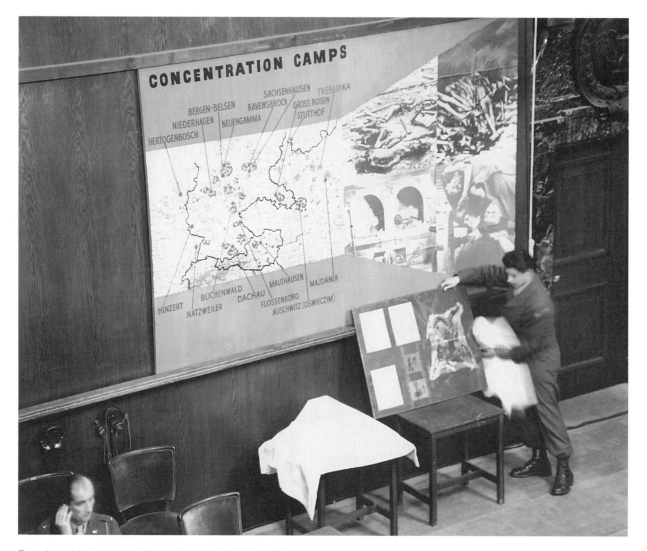

Extensive evidence presented at the International Military Tribunal in Nuremberg documented the Third Reich's massive concentration camp system, including its well-organized extermination centers, and innumerable crimes against humanity. On its strength, 21 of the original 24 defendants, all high-ranking Nazis, were convicted and sentenced to death or long prison terms.[CORBIS]

relation to documentary evidence. The recovery of documentary evidence is susceptible to contamination, however. It is true that much documentary evidence may be destroyed, but it is surprising how often even apparently insignificant documents may be useful. The investigations between 1984 and 1987 into the torture and disappearances of thousands during Argentina's "dirty war" benefited considerably from the study of official military plans that explained political and strategic goals, even though they did not specify any treatment of individuals.

Improved technology also makes proving some aspects of participation more feasible. In the ICTY case of *Kordic*, the accused was convicted in relation to some matters (specifically, the attacks on Busovaca) based on the evidence of intercepted radio messages

that indicated his direct role in ordering and facilitating the crimes that were committed (see also *Krstic*, paragraphs 105-117). However, an important aspect in proving the involvement of others who worked behind the scenes may be the ability to persuade people with inside knowledge to testify. This is always a difficult exercise, both psychologically and ethically, but it has proved key in some trials where high-ranking officials have been convicted. The conviction of General Krstic before the ICTY on charges of aiding and abetting genocide in Srebrenica depended partially upon the testimony of subordinate sources. The cooperation of Drazen Endemovic has proved important in the investigation of the Srebrenica genocide (*Krstic*, para. 234). His assistance in investigations was also important in the "Rule 61" hearings, which dealt with the culpability of

Radovan Karadzic and Ratko Mladic. Some forms of plea-bargaining may offer a valuable way to secure this type of evidence.

Evidence at Trial

Admissibility of evidence at trial in domestic systems is regulated by the system governing the conduct of the trials, be it common or civil law. In general, common law systems take a more technical approach to admissibility than do civil law systems. On occasion, however, these rules have been relaxed, particularly when dealing with cases of crimes against humanity and genocide. Civil law systems tend to be liberal in their admission of evidence, and are guided mainly by criteria of relevance.

The approach to admissibility before international criminal courts, from the Nuremberg and Tokyo Tribunals to the ad hoc International Criminal Tribunals for the former Yugoslavia and Rwanda, and most recently the Special Court for Sierra Leone, has resembled that of civil law systems, in that the general approach to admissibility is flexible. Thus, probative evidence is admitted regardless of its format, unless the rights of the accused are deemed to be prejudiced by admission. This flexibility is justified by the fact that evidence on these crimes can be difficult to secure. There may be few surviving witnesses, and physical evidence may have been destroyed. Because the international criminal courts are composed of professional judges, they are deemed capable of according a particular piece of evidence its appropriate weight, and of disregarding any evidence that is unreliable. For instance, hearsay evidence—that is, a statement, other than one made by the declarant while testifying at the trail or hearing, offered in evidence to prove the truth of the matter asserted—is readily available in such trials.

To date, the presentation of evidence at trial before international criminal courts has generally been adversarial, where each side presents its own evidence, and where witnesses are subjected to both direct and cross examination. It is not clear yet to what extent this trend will be followed by the International Criminal Court. According to the principle of equality of arms, the prosecution and defense have an equal opportunity before the court both to call witnesses and to submit facts into evidence. International courts have the power to call their own witnesses, but this has usually been used to supplement the witnesses called by the prosecution and the defense.

The ICTY and ICTR have also developed an extensive system of rules of disclosure by which evidence is shown ahead of time to the other side in the trial. Similar rules were not applied at Nuremberg and Tokyo, where rules of disclosure were far more rudimentary. In those earlier tribunals, documents were often disclosed twenty-four hours in advance as a matter of course, and they were sometimes purposely used to surprise witnesses during cross-examination.

Such "trial by ambush" is not permissible before the modern tribunals. The duty to disclose is greater for the prosecution than for the defense. As a general rule, the prosecutor has specified time limits within which he or she must disclose material supporting the indictment, prior statements by the accused, and copies of witness statements. Of particular significance is Rule 68, shared by both the ICTY and ICTR, which establishes the duty to disclose the "existence of material known to the prosecutor which in any way tends to suggest the innocence or mitigate the guilt of the accused or may affect the credibility of prosecution evidence." This rule has given rise to much litigation at the ICTY, including litigation on appeal charging that the prosecutor did not adequately meet this burden during trial.

Depending on the nature of the trial, the prosecution (and defense) may rely more heavily on live testimony or on documentary evidence. Assessing the credibility of witnesses may be particularly challenging when, as occurs with some frequency in international trials, the judge does not speak the same language and has no intimate knowledge of the cultural context. Many witnesses to genocide or other grave crimes may suffer from post-traumatic stress disorder, but judges have held that this does not necessarily affect their credibility. Many witnesses request protection, including measures to conceal their identity before and during trial. Such requests must be balanced against the right of an accused to a public trial.

Victims of sexual offenses benefit from additional rules that seek to protect them, including rules relating to the inadmissibility of their prior sexual conduct. This is the case for the International Criminal Court and both the Rwandan and Former Yugoslavian tribunals, which also recognize the principle that consent may not be inferred in certain coercive circumstances, and gives the courts the latitude to hear evidence in camera—that is, in private, excluding the public. Children are rarely called as witnesses in such trials, but when their testimony is required, they are able to give testimony via closed circuit television from a remote location. Witnesses may also be granted safe conduct, which confers on them a temporary immunity from arrest and prosecution.

Evidence from experts is common in trials of genocide and crimes against humanity. There are a variety of evidentiary categories that call for the testimony of experts including historical, ballistics, medical, regional, and anthropological evidence. An expert can be challenged on his or her qualifications and methodology, and does not testify directly on the matters which the court is called upon to decide. The court may choose to hear the evidence and simply disregard certain conclusions and not rely on them for conviction. At ICTY, a special regime governs the reception of expert evidence, aimed at expediting the trial. An expert's statement must be disclosed ahead of time and the opposing party must decide whether it wishes to cross-examine.

The ICTY and ICTR can generally compel individuals to testify, unless an individual benefits from a privilege or immunity. One exception to the principle of compellability is the lawyer-client privilege, which prohibits a witness from being compelled to divulge conversations occurring between a lawyer and his or her client. Another recognized exception is the privilege against self-incrimination, which holds that a witness cannot be forced to testify against his or her own interests. Other privileges have been recognized in the jurisprudence, where there is a public interest to keep certain information confidential. This includes, for instance, the official duties of court functionaries. In one case, the ICTY Appeals Chamber decided to extend a privilege to a war correspondent, except for evidence of direct and important value in determining a core issue in the case that cannot reasonably be obtained elsewhere. The ability of the ICC to compel individuals to testify is less clear than it is for the ICTY and the ICTR. The ICC's statute and rules state that requests for witnesses to appear must be directed through state parties.

The ad hoc tribunals have broad enforcement powers by virtue of their establishment by Security Council Resolution under Chapter VII of the UN Charter. They have the power to issue a binding order to a state to produce information, even if the information concerns national security. In such cases, certain measures can be put in place to safeguard the confidentiality of that information. This differs from the ICC, where states are able to deny requests for assistance on national security grounds. It also differs from the Special Court for Sierra Leone, which lacks such powers, as it was created by Agreement between the UN and government for Sierra Leone and not by a Security Council Resolution. International organizations do not have the same obligation as nations do when it comes to providing the ad hoc tribunals with information. For instance, in the case of *Simic et al*, the ICTY has recognized that the International Committee for the Red Cross benefits from a privilege and that its former employees cannot be forced to testify. A similar privilege is recognized in Rule 73 of the ICC.

Documentary evidence is particularly prevalent in cases where the defense is based on a claim of superior responsibility (being ordered to commit an act by a superior officer) or other forms of indirect participation. Documents are admissible depending on their relevance and probative value, but questions may arise as to their authenticity. With this type of evidence, as with others, the chain of custody may have to be demonstrated, to show that the evidence could not have been tampered with after the fact. Diaries and videos have proved a particularly powerful source of evidence in international criminal trials.

Documentary evidence may also be used in the place of live testimony. A particular challenge in trials of genocide and crimes against humanity has been the volume of the evidence, in part resulting from the adversarial nature of the proceedings. This constitutes a threat to the right of the accused to an expeditious trial. Live testimony is time-consuming, and many of the procedural developments in evidence at ICTY have sought to limit its scope. At Nuremberg and Tokyo, affidavit evidence was freely admissible, but rules on affidavits before the modern tribunals have proved difficult in practice. Instead, the ad hoc Tribunals allow for the admission of other forms of written statements in certain circumstances, bearing in mind the right of the accused to cross-examine witnesses against him or her. The jurisprudence on the admissibility of statements from deceased witnesses has been particularly inconsistent. Such statements are currently not admissible before the Sierra Leone Special Court.

An additional way to save time is by submitting a compilation of evidence. Unlike civil law systems, international criminal courts have not ordinarily allowed for the submission of "dossiers" or case-files, but they do allow for the production of compiled materials, as long as these do not contain analysis of the evidence. Transcripts from other trials may also be admitted into evidence as a way to save time, subject to certain rights to cross-examination. Judicial notice may be another way to save time, but before the ad hoc tribunals it has been limited to facts of common knowledge or facts adjudicated by the appeals chamber.

The absence of forensic evidence in killings is not decisive if there is convincing eyewitness testimony of the crimes. The rules of some national systems, requiring the production of a body as proof of death, therefore do not apply. The same holds true for torture or rape, neither of which require forensic or medical evidence. At the same time, forensic evidence often does play an important part in the trials.

According to rule ninety-five of the ICTY, evidence before the ad hoc tribunal may be excluded "if obtained by methods that cast substantial doubt on its reliability or if its admission is antithetical to, and would seriously damage, the integrity of the proceedings." If the rights of the accused are infringed to a certain threshold, so as to cause irreparable damage to the integrity of the proceedings, this may result in a discontinuance of the proceedings against the accused.

An appeal should not amount to a retrial, and the tribunals have strict rules on which new or additional evidence shall be permitted to be heard. For instance, the evidence on which an appeal is based cannot have been available at trial, or it must be in the interests of justice to admit it. Nonetheless, applications for additional evidence are very frequent. Also, the appeals chamber for both the ICTY and the ICTR may be called upon to review a judgment where a new fact has been discovered.

SEE ALSO Forensics; International Criminal Court; International Criminal Tribunal for Rwanda; International Criminal Tribunal for the Former Yugoslavia; Nuremberg Trials; Rape; War Crimes

BIBLIOGRAPHY

Kniriem, A. von (1959). *The Nuremberg Trials*. Chicago, Il.: Regnery.

Lee, Roy S., ed. (2001). *The International Criminal Court: Elements of Crimes and Rules of Procedure and Evidence.* Ardsley, N.Y.: Transnational Publishers, Inc.

Röling, B. V. A., and C. F. Rüter eds. (1977). *The Tokyo Judgment: The International Military Tribunal for the Far East*. Amsterdam: APA-University Press Amsterdam.

Paul Seils
Marieke Wierda

Evil, Banality of Radical

The evil that German philosopher Hannah Arendt confronted was the phenomenon of totalitarian terror, vividly, but by no means exclusively, exemplified by the mass slaughter of Jews. She saw this phenomenon as marking not only a rupture with civilization that shattered all previously engraved images of Europe as a civilized community, but also an assault on human categories of thought and standards of judgment. She argued that it created particular difficulties of understanding for the social sciences because it contradicted all ways of thinking that presuppose an element of rational choice or a means/ends calculation on the part of social players. The frenzy of destruction that was the hallmark of totalitarian terror seemed to exceed all political, economic, or military utility. Arendt did not sug-

gest that the death camps and other institutions of totalitarian terror were, therefore, beyond human understanding, but rather that if we assume "most of our actions are of a utilitarian nature and that our evil deeds spring from some 'exaggeration' of self-interest" (1994, p. 233), then we would be forced to conclude that such institutions are within human understanding. The difficult path she took was to not accept this conclusion, but on the contrary to try to make sense of the senselessness of genocide. In so doing, she defended the activity of understanding as such, as a sign of humankind's humanity and resistance to totalitarian ideology.

In the section on total domination in *Origins of Totalitarianism*, Arendt wrote that the death camps had "the appearance of some radical evil previously unknown to us" (1951, p. 443). The idea of evil, let alone radical evil, is not commonly used in modern political thought, so implicit in Arendt's use of the term was an opposition to certain modernist presuppositions. Among these the following might be mentioned. First, the tendency to *relativize* moral standards exists, as if conformity to a contingent normative order is all that defines what is moral or not. Second, there is the tendency to *subjectivize* moral standards, as if what is right and wrong are reducible to subjective opinions (individual or collective) of what is right or wrong. Third is humankind's inclination to *dissolve* the very idea of evil, as if neither its concept nor its existence is any longer pertinent to the modern world. Arendt characterized all three of these tendencies as the origins of totalitarianism prevalent within normal bourgeois society. The first allowed Germans to move effortlessly from democracy to Nazism and then back to democracy after World War II, as though moral standards were no more than a set of table manners that could be exchanged without trouble for another. The second allowed the question of what is right and wrong to be reduced to mere subjective feeling, so that any crime could be justified as long as it was committed with conviction or in good conscience. The third allowed the idea of good and evil to be abandoned in favor of some notion of historical or natural necessity. It was within this context that Arendt turned to Immanuel Kant's concept of *radical evil*.

More explicitly stated in Arendt's use of the term radical evil is its reference to the sheer nonutility of the death camps and mass killings. The conventional approach to understanding evil is recognizing it as a product of human self-interest in the form of greed, vanity, lust, prejudice, spitefulness, sadism, and other such vices. Ordinary evil is easily understandable in these terms. The idea of radical evil, however, indicated to Arendt that something else was at stake in the institu-

Hannah Arendt in 1954. While living in Argentina in 1960, Nazi leader Adolf Eichmann was kidnapped and taken to Israel, where he was put on trial for crimes against humanity. Arendt's *Eichmann in Jerusalem* probes the unsettling fact that Eichmann was a "little man" who was just following orders. In her controversial book, she maintains that he was an average guy, a petty bureaucrat interested in furthering his career—and not that different from all the rest of us. [AP/WIDE WORLD PHOTOS]

tions of totalitarian terror: a form of evil that ordinary people could commit quite easily in a spirit more of selflessness than selfishness, people for whom ordinary human vices were secondary to their sense of duty on behalf of the movement. In this form of evil the sheer *superfluousness* of the victims is mirrored in that of the perpetrators themselves. The radicalism of evil, then, may be found in its surpassing the bounds of what Kant recognized as the normal sources of evil given the freedoms and frailties of the human will.

A further implication of Arendt's use of this term is that the radicalism of evil lies in its hostility to the very idea of humanity. Normally, the idea of evil makes sense against a backdrop of what it is to be human: I am evil when I satisfy my own cravings without regard for what makes me or someone else a human being. However, the peculiarity of radical evil—the peculiarity that makes it radical—is that the crimes committed are in the most literal sense crimes against humanity. As

Arendt put it in *Origins*, in the case of totalitarian terror "individual human beings did not kill other individual human beings for human reasons," but rather an organized attempt was made to "eradicate the concept of the human being" (1992, p. 69). If the idea of universal humanity is the achievement of the modern age, at issue here was a politics whose aim was the destruction of all human spontaneity, plurality, and differentiation. This was the extremely radical nature Arendt detected in totalitarian movements whatever pretexts they advanced for their actions (e.g., the achievement of "a thousand year peace"). It also led her to ask why the idea of humanity caused such offense as to incite modern political movements attempting to destroy it? One answer she offered in a chapter titled, ironically, "The Classless Society," takes us back to the growth of European nihilism that emerged when, as Friedrich Nietzsche suggested, the values and beliefs taken as the highest manifestation of the spirit of the West lost their validity and in their place was born a spiritless radicalism, full of hostility to culture and consumed by images of destruction. Arendt located a source of modern nihilism in the rise of imperialism, when violence became the aim of the body politic, power could achieve nothing but more power, moral inhibitions were superseded, and nihilism became the practical spirit of the age.

Arendt may not have known precisely why she used the term *radical evil*. Her precise words were that totalitarian terror had "the appearance of radical evil" (1951, p. 443)—an indicator perhaps of a certain equivocation on the subject. In his correspondence with Arendt about the Nuremberg trials German psychiatrist and philosopher Karl Jaspers highlighted a risk involved in the use of the term: It might endow perpetrators with a "streak of satanic greatness" and mystify their deeds in "myth and legend." Against this danger Jaspers emphasised the "prosaic triviality" of the perpetrators and coined the phrase "the banality of evil" to make his point. In reply Arendt acknowledged that there was truth to his observation and her own use of the term radical evil did come close to "mythologising the horrible" (Arendt and Jaspers, 1992, p. 69).

Writing some fifteen years later on the Eichmann trial, Arendt reintroduced the term banality of evil (seemingly without memory of Jaspers's earlier comments) to address the fact that the perpetrators were "men like ourselves" (1962). It was a rejoinder to conventional images of the so-called Nazi monster, according to which the world was portrayed in terms of the dichotomy between what Alain Finkielkraut has called "our own absolute innocence and the unspeakable Nazi beast" (1992, p. 61). One lesson Arendt took from the

Eichmann case was that the perpetrators of the most radical evil could be pedestrian, bourgeois individuals, mired in an everyday existence that made them incapable of critical reflection or serious moral judgment. They were marked more by "thoughtlessness" and "remoteness from reality" than by any streak of Satanic greatness: "The deeds were monstrous but the doer . . . was quite ordinary, commonplace, and neither demonic nor monstrous" (1962, p. 54). The Eichmann trial was the trigger for Arendt's reaffirmation of a humanist tradition. According to it, only the good is radical; evil is never radical, only extreme. There is no meaning in destruction.

It is well known that Arendt's use of the term banality of evil was challenged, or denounced, by many critics, including her friend Gershom Scholem, on the grounds that she thereby trivialized the Holocaust. Arendt had been a relatively lonely voice in the 1940s and 1950s when calling for social and political thought to recognize the significance of the Jews' massacre during World War II. She celebrated the fact that the Eichmann trial helped to break a long silence, and that the survivors of the camps might now find an audience for their writings and memories. What, then, lay behind the uproar that greeted the use of banality of evil within this context. How can one make sense of it except as an aberration?

Perhaps the charges leveled against Arendt expressed the advent of a new kind of discourse: one that made use of theological terms such as Holocaust and Shoah to name the unnameable event; eschewed generic political terms such as totalitarian terror, crimes against humanity, or genocide; and underscored the singular uniqueness of the Shoah and its inability to be understood in human terms. As Elie Wiesel has put it: "The Holocaust? The ultimate event, the ultimate mystery, never to be comprehended or transmitted" (Roth and Berenbaum, 1989, p. 2). Arendt was the target of criticism because she represented an old humanistic tradition that emphasised a secular analysis of totalitarian terror, even if it required a major rethinking of the premises of existing social and political theory. The revision from radical evil to the banality of evil confirmed her secular stance. Banality of evil was her way of saying that the Final Solution—like all phenomena of totalitarian terror—was "human, all too human" and needed to be understood as such.

In any event, Kant's more original use of the concept of radical evil, to be found in *Religion Within the Bounds of Mere Reason*, conveyed a meaning that throws no clear light on the phenomenon of totalitarian terror, inasmuch as it had to do with the omnipresent ability of human beings to choose self-love and self-interest over and above the moral law. This is not at all what Arendt had in mind or wished to convey in her analysis of evil in the modern age.

SEE ALSO Arendt, Hannah; Eichmann, Adolf

BIBLIOGRAPHY

Arendt, Hannah (1951). *The Origins of Totalitarianism.* New York: Harvest, 1976.

Arendt, Hannah (1978). *The Jew as Pariah,* ed. Ron Feldman. New York: Grove Press.

Arendt, Hannah (1962). *Eichmann in Jerusalem: A Report on the Banality of Evil.* New York: Penguin, 1994.

Arendt, Hannah (1994). *Essays in Understanding 1930–1954.* New York: Harcourt Brace.

Arendt, Hannah and Karl Jaspers (1992). *Correspondence 1926–1969,* ed. Lotte Kohler and Hans Saner, tran. Robert Kimber and Rita Kimber. New York: Harcourt Brace.

Bauman, Zygmunt (1990). *Modernity and the Holocaust.* Oxford, U.K.: Polity.

Bernstein, Richard (1996). *Hannah Arendt and the Jewish Question.* Cambridge, U.K.: Polity.

Fackenheim, Emil Ludwig (1996). *The God Within: Kant, Schelling, and Historicity,* ed. John Burbidge. Toronto: University of Toronto Press.

Fine, Robert (2001). *Political Investigations: Hegel, Marx, Arendt.* London: Routledge.

Fine, Robert and Charles Turner (2000). *Social Theory after the Holocaust.* Liverpool: University of Liverpool Press.

Finkielkraut, Alain (1992). *Remembering in Vain.* New York: Columbia University Press.

Kant, Immanuel (1998). *Religion Within the Bounds of Mere Reason,* tran. and ed. Allen Wood and George di Giovanni. Cambridge: Cambridge University Press.

Lara, Maria Pia, ed. (2001). *Rethinking Evil: Contemporary Perspectives.* Berkeley: University of California Press.

Rose, Gillian (1996). *Mourning Becomes the Law: Philosophy and Representation.* Cambridge: Cambridge University Press.

Roth, J., and Michael Berenbaum (1989). *Holocaust: Religious and Philosophical Implications.* New York: Paragon House.

Villa, Dana (1999). *Politics, Philosophy, Terror: Essays on the Thought of Hannah Arendt.* Princeton, N.J.: Princeton University Press.

Robert Fine

Explanation

What causes one human being to kill another, not for anything the victim has done but simply because the victim belongs to a particular religion, ethnic or communal group? Such behavior confounds rationality, and analysts are forced to focus on either identifying the broad macrophenomena and the structural-cultural factors that correlate with genocide or on specifying the psychological processes that might contribute to genocide.

The most frequently cited precipitating factors or facilitating conditions that correlate with genocide and ethnic violence are political unrest and economic upheavals. The Holocaust—certainly the best known genocide—is usually "explained" by reference to the political dislocations resulting from World War I, especially the ensuing breakup of political empires, the punitive Versailles Treaty, a weak Weimar Republic, and the economic depression that gripped the world but which was particularly acute in Germany. The breakup of the Ottoman Empire (which gave rise to the Armenian genocide) and the disintegration of Yugoslavia and the USSR (which was followed by ethnic cleansing in Bosnia) provide further illustrations of macro-events contributing to genocide.

Beyond this, genocide occurs most frequently in plural societies in which there are diverse racial, ethnic, and/or religious groups that exhibit persistent and pervasive communal cleavages. A strong overlap between such cleavages and political and socio-economic inequities, plus a history of conflict between the diverse groups, also encourages genocide and ethnic violence. Genocide rarely occurs in political regimes that are not totalitarian or authoritarian. This was evident during the Holocaust and in the recent genocides in the Balkans and Africa (Rwanda-Burundi, the Sudan). The isolation and secrecy that accompany totalitarian regimes that lack a free press are major contributors, enabling elites to manipulate internal tensions and turn them toward violence. Such structural-cultural factors form the foundation for another category of explanation.

Psychological Factors

The richest and most varied explanations of genocide are found at a more personal level, all focusing on the psychology of the genocidalist. The psychoanalysis of genocidal leaders such as Hitler has led some scholars, such as Alan Bullock, to focus attention on their tendency toward neurotic-psychopathic personalities. The argument here is that certain people have a deep-seated and psycho-pathological need that leads them toward genocide, either through the elite manipulation of masses or the actual, personal commission of genocide. Other scholars, including Theodor Adorno and Bob Altemeyer, focus on the extent to which an entire society can exhibit patterns of behavior, such as child-rearing or authority relations in school, that result in certain kinds of psychodynamics, such as the authoritarian personality, that encourage genocide.

The work of scholars such as Daniel J. Goldhagen still accept explanations of genocide that are painted in such broad cultural terms, but most social psychologists and historians, including Stanley Milgram and Christopher Browning, find the situation more complex, arguing that situational factors can turn even an ordinary person into a genocidalist. The fundamental assumption for these scholars is a median personality around which a great deal of variance occurs. Analysts in this school focus on external stimuli and understanding how situational or contextual effects can trigger genocide in ordinary people.

Studies of social cognition find all political behavior strongly influenced by how people think about themselves and the social world, especially how people select, remember, interpret, and use social information to make judgments and decisions. Attitudes, schemas and social representations all offer ways in which the definition of social identities of self and others might be conceptualized, and provide the building blocks upon which more detailed theories of socio-political identity and prejudice are built. Such approaches include social role theories focusing on the "internalized role designations corresponding to the social location of persons" (Stryker, 1987, p. 84) and stress the shared behavioral expectations that become salient. Such explanations have been offered to explain the traditional "I was just following orders" excuse for genocide. Robert Jay Lipton's intriguing 1986 study of Nazi doctors turned the concept of social roles upside down by asking: How could doctors and health officials, dedicated to saving lives, utilize their knowledge to perfect killing? The answer—a desire to protect the German body politic from infestation by inferior and diseased *untermenschen*—suggests how traditional social roles can be utilized to lead people to genocide.

Other social psychologists focus more on the cognitive process of drawing boundaries and categorizing individuals in conflict situations. Social-identity theory and self-categorization literature suggest that perceptions of competition for scarce resources reinforce ingroup/out-group distinctions but are not necessary conditions for in-group favoritism and inter-group discrimination to occur. The social identity theory employed by Michael A. Hogg and Dominic Abrams and based on Henri Tajfel's "minimal group paradigm" has found that in situations of group decision making, people tend to favor their own membership group over out-groups, even when these groups are artificial laboratory constructs and competition for resources between groups is absent. Previous perspectives in group psychology, exemplified by the work of Muzafer Sherif, explained group differentiation in terms of real or perceived competition between in-group and out-groups, but Tajfel's research suggests that the mere formation of otherwise meaningless groups may produce in-group favoritism. Tajfel argues that groups provide their members with positive self-esteem, and that group-members are therefore motivated to enhance their image of the in-group in relation to relevant out-groups.

The Self-Categorization Theory of Group Formation

A 1987 study by John C. Turner and Michael Hogg suggests that the formation of psychological groups is driven by the cognitive elaboration of one's self-identity in comparison with others and implies mechanisms for the formation of political preferences. The salient level of self-categorization and the determination of which schemas and categories are evoked by a given political object or objects will interact to shape a person's political preferences in relation to that political object. The key assumptions of Turner's self-categorization theory of group formation suggest that self-categorizations are hierarchical. In other words, the category of "human being" functions as the most inclusive and superordinate group level, below which in-group/out-group categories based on social comparisons of gender and ethnicity or other dimensions form an intermediate level categorization, and there are subordinate level categories that distinguish individuals as unique.

Turner's framework assumes that the cognitive representation of the self is a multi-faceted affair, and that different portions of that self become salient in different contexts. The theory hypothesizes that factors enhancing the relevance of in-group/out-group categorizations increase the perceived identity between self and in-group members, thus depersonalizing individual self-perception on the stereotypical dimensions that define the relevant in-group membership. This makes the depersonalization of self-perceptions the critical process underlying group behavior, such as stereotyping, ethnocentrism, cooperation and altruism, emotional contagion, collective action, shared norms, and social influence processes.

Members of groups who are perceived as different from the self will tend to be seen in terms of stereotypes. Self-categorization theory builds upon social identity theory by arguing that the self-categorization with a cognitive representation of the group results in the depersonalization of self and the homogenization of both the in-group and the out-group, based on dimensions that reflect the prototypicality or stereotypicality of members of each group. Thousands of experiments underlying social identity theory—for instance,

those conducted by A. Gagnon and R. Y. Bourhis—have consistently shown that individuals will identify with the in-group, support group norms, and derogate out-group members along stereotypical lines, even when there is no individual gain at stake. The introduction of "superordinate goals," which is posited as a solution by some realistic conflict theorists, can be seen instead as the cognitive reclassification of social identity by individuals into another social identity category.

This cognitive reclassification of groups may provide the key to ending genocide, prejudice, and ethnic violence; Serbs and Croats can think of themselves as Yugoslavs. Preliminary empirical work suggests cognitive categorization may affect all participants in genocide, not just genocidalists. Kristen Renwick Monroe's work on rescuers, published in 1996 and 2004, and James Glass's 1997 study of genocidalists have noted the importance of cognitive classifications during the Holocaust. A 1997 study by Lina Haddad Kreidie and Kristen Monroe found similar categorization and dehumanization in communal violence in the Middle East. Historical literature on slaves within United States also points to the process of declassification and recategorization as critical before people feel justified in the mistreating and eventual killing of other human beings. This comparative work suggests that if we can declassify people, we also can reclassify them in an upward manner. The process, in other words, works both ways. Further work to determine how this recategorization process works may provide an answer to the implicit question underlying most analyses of genocide: How can it be stopped?

SEE ALSO Genocide; Philosophy

BIBLIOGRAPHY

Adorno, Theodor, et al. (1950). *The Authoritarian Personality*. New York: Harper and Row.

Altmeyer, Robert (1988). *Enemies of Freedom: Understanding Right Wing Authoritarianism*. San Francisco, Calif.: Jossey-Bass.

Browning, Christopher (1992). *Ordinary Men: Reserve Police Battalion 101 and the Final Solution in Poland*. New York: Aaron Asher/HarperCollins.

Bullock, Alan (1991). *Hitler and Stalin*. London: HarperCollins.

Gagnon A., and Bourhis R Y. (1996). "Discrimination in the Minimal Group Paradigm: Social Identity or Self-Interest." *Personality and Social Psychology Bulletin* 22, no. 12:1289–1301.

Glass, James (1997). *Life Unworthy of Life: Racial Phobia and Mass Murder in Hitler's Germany*. New York: Basic Books.

Hogg, Michael A. (1992). *The Social Psychology of Group Cohesiveness: From Attraction to Social Identity*. New York: New York University Press.

Hogg, Michael A., and Dominic Abrams (1988). *Social Identifications: A Social Psychology of Intergroup Relationships and Group Processes*. New York: Routledge.

Kreidie, Lina Haddad, and Kristen Monroe (1997). "The Perspectives of Islamic Fundamentalists and the Limits of Rational Choice Theory." *Political Psychology* 18(1):19–43.

Lipton, Robert Jay (1986). *The Nazi Doctors: Medical Killings and the Psychology of Genocide*. New York: Basic Books.

Milgram, Stanley (1974). *Obedience to Authority: An Experimental View*. New York: Harper and Row.

Monroe, Kristen Renwick (1996). *The Heart of Altruism: Perceptions of a Common Humanity*. Princeton, N.J.: Princeton University Press.

Monroe, Kristen Renwick (2004). *The Hand of Compassion: Portraits of Moral Choice during the Holocaust*. Princeton, N.J.: Princeton University Press.

Sherif, Muzafer (1973). *Groups in Harmony and Tension: An Integration of Studies on Intergroup Relations*. New York: Octagon Books.

Stryker, Sheldon (1987). "Identity Theory: Developments and Extensions." In *Society and Identity: Psychosocial Perspectives*, ed. Krysia Yardley and Terry Honess. New York: Wiley.

Tajfel, Henri (1981). "Human Groups and Social Categories." *Studies in Social Psychology*. New York: Cambridge University Press.

Tajfel, Henri and John C. Turner (1979). "An Integrative Theory of Intergroup Conflict." In *The Social Psychology of Intergroup Relations*, ed. W. G. Austin and S. Worchel. Monterey, Calif.: Brooks/Cole.

Turner, John C., and Michael A. Hogg (1987). *Rediscovering the Social Group: A Self-Categorization Theory*. Oxford, U.K.: Basil Blackwell.

Kristen Renwick Monroe

Extermination Centers

Were Belzec, Chelmno, Sobibor, Birkenau (Auschwitz II), and Treblinka concentration camps? Can they be mentioned or studied in the same terms as Dachau or Mauthausen? No. In order to distinguish them from "classic" concentration camps and define their dreadful uniqueness, it is not enough to substitute one simple descriptive word for another—designating them as "extermination camps" or simply "death camps". At Dachau, Buchenwald, or even Ravensbrück, human beings considered dangerous to the larger society, but nevertheless "recyclable," were confined for more or less lengthy periods. At Treblinka, however, the men, women, and children arriving there constituted an ontologically irrecoverable set of "subhumans" that, according to the Nazi perspective, encumbered the world and prevented its proper functioning. They were gassed as soon as they arrived. Not infrequently, nine thousand Jews were deported to Treblinka on a single day, with no provisions made to shelter them, or to feed them for even twenty-four hours. Treblinka performed a single, unique function: the extermination of Jews.

These different functions—on the one hand quarantine, on the other immediate death—require that a clear distinction be made between these two types of places, one that uses two sets of concepts and two vocabularies. Although the practice has been to refer to sites where German inmates were maintained alive, more or less alive (since hope remained to reintegrate them into the national community), as well as to sites where Jews were exterminated as soon as they descended from the cattle cars, as *concentration camps*, this is an abusive catch-all concept. The conception of homogeneous and generic units became disseminated largely as a result of the Nuremberg Trials, whose judges considered the horrendous images of the mass graves of the Bergen-Belsen camp at liberation as proof of the German extermination of the Jews. The discovery of Bergen-Belsen, writes Walter Laqueur in *The Terrible Secret*, "unleashed a violent wave of anger, although paradoxically it wasn't at all a camp of extermination, nor even a concentration camp, but rather a *Krankenlager*, a camp for sick people, where, true enough, the only treatment offered to patients . . . was death" (1981, p. 8).

Some historians, and not minor ones, try to deal with this quandary by distinguishing between extermination camps and concentration camps. They are nevertheless on the wrong track, for in respect to the *Shoah* (Hebrew term for the Holocaust), the very notion of "camp," whatever the word used to qualify it (death camp or extermination camp), should be proscribed. It is historically inaccurate to define Dachau and Treblinka identically through the use of a common expression when the Nazis themselves insisted on making a clear distinction between the two types of establishment. They designated Dachau, and the places modeled after it, by the term *Konzentrationslager* (KL), literally concentration camp. In contrast they referred to places such as Treblinka as *SS Sonderkommando* (SK), or "special commando of the police and the SS." There was no concern in these latter places with quartering or warehousing human beings; what concern there was involved exterminating all who were delivered methodically and systematically, on the very day of arrival and without delay. The SK were only places of transit to immediate death. Jews were led, without detour or loss of time, straight from the ghetto to the slaughterhouse.

The very notion of "camp" must be rejected in consideration of the four centers of immediate death (Bel-

A monument in Sobibor, Poland. Sobibor was not a concentration camp, but an extermination center. During its first two months of operation, from early May until the end of June 1942, approximately 100,000 Jews were murdered there. Even at that, in 1942 the Nazis looked for ways to make the murder factories even more efficient. **[IRA NOWINSKI/CORBIS]**

zec, Chelmno, Sobibor, and Treblinka) and the two "mixed centers" (having the double function of concentration and extermination) that were Auschwitz-Birkenau and Majdanek. Situated near railroad terminals, these places must be designated as *extermination centers*, or, to use the expression of Raul Hilberg, "immediate death centers," operated with the unique purpose of systematically, immediately implementing the complete destruction of European Jews. Existing apart from the Nazi concentration camp system, these centers escaped its inspection body (IKL) situated in Oranienburg, with the exception of Auschwitz and Majdanek, which had been "simple" concentration camps before they became mixed.

The Execution Centers

Starting in the summer of 1941, four Einsatzgruppen methodically carried out massacres. On September 29 and 30 alone, Group D shot 33,771 Jewish men, women, and children. The executions took place at Babi Yar, on the outskirts of Kiev. This first phase of the genocide, which cost more than 1.3 million Jews

their lives, was efficient, but also crude. Even the SS killers had a hard time getting used to what was required of them. Inside the SS the idea of exterminating Jews at fixed locations, following procedures more "humane" (for the killers), took hold.

The first solution proposed to Heinrich Himmler was that of the gas truck. The idea of extermination by gas is not new. From 1939 to 1941, the Nazis gassed about seventy thousand terminally ill, handicapped, or mental patients to death with carbon monoxide, in what was called Operation T-4 since the operation center was situated in Tiergartenstrasse number four Berlin. In November 1941 the Central Office of Reich Security (RSHA) made its first killing trials, and when they were successful, gas trucks were dispatched to the occupied territories of the Soviet Union. The method was then "perfected," first in Serbia, then in the Chelmno (Kulmhoff) camp, near Lodz (in Poland).

The First Execution Center: Chelmno

Chelmno in December 1941 marked the transition between the two types of extermination (firing squad and death by asphyxiation). Chelmno was not a camp but a former chateau, where Jews were assembled, undressed, and directly gassed. The rudimentary complex killed up to a thousand people a day, with the help of three trucks transformed into mobile gas chambers. Every afternoon the Jews of Lodz and its environs were brought to the site and physically thrust, first into the cellars, then toward the so-called shower rooms, where they would be forced to descend a ramp that would lead them directly inside the gas trucks. Those who delayed or refused to enter the trucks were beaten by the guards. When approximately fifty to seventy people were inside, the doors of the truck were shut, and the chauffeur, often a member of the *schutzpolizei*, drove through the Rzuchow forest toward the Waldlager pits. About ten minutes were required for the deadly gas to take effect. At the Waldlager pits Jewish prisoners, under the surveillance of the SS, prepared pyres and common graves. A team of around forty to fifty prisoners unloaded the cadavers and threw them into the mass graves. It is estimated that at least 150,000 Jews and 2,500 Romani were exterminated at Chelmno. Another team in the "chateau" sorted through the clothes and objects of value, selecting items that would be sent to the Reich. Almost 370 railroad cars of clothing would be filled in this way.

The Belzec, Sobibor, and Treblinka Centers

After Chelmno, three other SK centers were created: Belzec, Sobibor, and Treblinka. The sites were chosen for their isolation as well as their proximity to important railroads. More than 1.5 million human beings were exterminated in these places. Belzec opened its doors in March 1942, Sobibor in April 1942, and Treblinka in July of the same year. Belzec served as a model for Sobibor and Treblinka, both of them constructed, like Belzec, within the framework of the *Einsatz Reinhard (Action Reinhard)*.

Action Reinhard was the code name for the extermination of Polish Jewry. It's possible that this term was coined in remembrance of Reinhard Heydrich of the SS and coordinator of the *Endlösung der Judenfrage* (Final Solution of the Jewish question)—the extermination of the Jews living in the European countries occupied by German troops during World War II. Agents of the Czech government-in-exile fatally shot Heydrich on May 27, 1942.

Those three extermination centers were constructed to "accommodate" the populations of adjacent ghettos and other victims from surrounding areas: first Belzec, then Sobibor, and finally Treblinka.

The Belzec execution center was located in the Lublin district, the heart of a region rich in Jewish cities,

villages, and communities. Christian Wirth, an ex-police officer who played a major role in the T-4 killing program was named to head it. Under his command were 20 to 30 SS officers, helped by 120 specially trained Ukrainian guards. Belzec, just like Sobibor and Treblinka, was an establishment of modest dimensions, equipped rather summarily. It was divided into two sections, each one encircled by a barbed wire fence, with control towers along the main perimeter. The first section was also divided into two parts: The smaller contained administrative buildings and barracks for the Ukranian guards; the larger was where the railroad line unloaded the deported prisoners, separated into two groups—men on one side, women and children on the other. In the larger part were also the buildings where prisoners were stripped and shaved, the depots where personal objects were stocked, and finally the barracks for the Jewish prisoners in charge of burning the cadavers and sorting through the baggage.

The gas chambers and pyres were located in the second section of the center, connected to the first by a long passage (which the Germans called "the tube"), flanked by high barbed wire. The extermination site proper was separated from the main camp by trees and greenery. Camouflage was one of the essential elements of the extermination procedure perfected at Belzec.

The process was simple: A convoy of forty to sixty cars, containing around 2,500 persons, entered the station. The convoy was immediately divided in such a manner that the wagons arrived at the quay in groups of ten or fifteen. The prisoners were unloaded and told that they were in a transit camp and that, for reasons of hygiene, they had to shower and have a haircut. Men were separated from women and children. After passing through the places where they undressed and their heads were shaved, the prisoners were pushed into "the tube" leading to the gas chambers. The carbon monoxide necessary to cause asphyxiation was produced by a diesel motor set up outside the chamber. Once the chamber was filled with gas, it took around thirty minutes for death to occur. Various "cleaning" crews of prisoners then entered. More or less three hours elapsed between the moment the convoy stopped in the Belzec station and conclusion of the last sorting operations.

As the second camp constructed according to plans of the Einsatz Reinhard, Sobibor was entrusted to veteran officers of the T-4 program. In less than eighteen months, 250,000 Jewish men, women, and children perished there.

The third center was Treblinka, situated about 80 kilometers northeast of Warsaw. It was reserved for Jews of the Polish capital or of nearby Central Europe.

Around 700 to 1,000 Jews performed various "service functions" for their Nazi masters. A minimum of 750,000 Jews were gassed with carbon monoxide at Treblinka.

The Two Mixed Camps: Lublin-Majdanek and Auschwitz

In 1942 two new extermination centers, both outfitted with gas chambers, were added to the death machinery of the SS. They were not constructed in isolated places, but in close proximity to concentration camps: the first in the area of Lublin-Majdanek, the second nearby in the vast complex of Auschwitz, at Birkenau. The Majdanek center was equipped in September and October 1942 with three gas chambers. The gassing began forthwith and concluded November 3, 1943, with the simultaneous extermination of all Jewish prisoners in the course of an operation "poetically" baptized "harvest festival." Thereby, the last 17,000 Jews of Madjanek died, in a center that had seen between 50,000 and 200,000 victims perish.

A little after the Wannsee Conference, the conference held in January 1942 that coordinated, not decided the extermination of the European Jewry, the Birkenau site was designated as the "principal execution center." The extension of the Final Solution to the whole of Europe made Birkenau the epicenter of the extermination effort. There, on the initiative of Rudolf Hess, its ambitious ruler, a new gas was used, one much more efficient than carbon monoxide: Zyklon B. This gas, which included the rapid-acting gas hydrogen cyanide, was first used (in December 1941 in the basement of Block 11 of Auschwitz I) on two hundred and fifty tubercular detainees and around three hundred Soviet prisoners of war. Following Wirth (the promoter of carbon monoxide gassing), Hess may be regarded as one of the inventors of this method of mass execution. Patched together at first, the method transformed Auschwitz II into a very efficient death factory. During 1943, structures that coordinated and integrated the diverse phases of execution, from undressing to cremation, were put in place. Two thousand bodies could be piled into each of the *Leichenkeller* (cadaver rooms); the daily incineration capacity reached 4,756 bodies. By 1944 the Auschwitz equipment was complete.

The Nazi ideology found here its ultimate realization: an efficient, orderly, and clean extermination via the gas chambers, the Final Solution to the Jewish question, which shielded the Germans from having to get their hands dirty, and avoided the embarrassment of the Einsatzgruppen and their crude methods. This was a triumph of intelligence and method in service of the great plan.

In contrast to the four other extermination centers, Auschwitz-Birkenau, and to a lesser measure Lublin-Majdanek, were not authorized to carry out the asphyxiation of all arriving Jews. The scarcity of labor forced the authorities to "select" varying quantities of them to serve the war economy. The SS divided the arrivals into two categories: the suitable and the unsuitable. The former, after having been registered and given tattoos on their left forearms, were integrated into the camp and channeled into the work force. The Central Office of the Management of the Economy of the SS and its camp inspection section, under the supervision of Himmler, submitted them, like the non-Jewish detainees, to a process of "extermination by work." The others (the unsuitable) were gassed as soon as they arrived. Statistics on the Jewish population of Western Europe show that 150,511 Jews of France, Belgium, and the Lowlands were deported toward the East as part of the Final Solution. Three-quarters of these went to Auschwitz, most of the remainder to the Sobibor extermination center. In all, 93,736 were gassed as soon as they descended from the train; 55,126 were put to work. When the camps were liberated, scarcely 4,000 of these 55,126 were still alive, or less than 3 percent.

At the end of November 1944, after the appearance in English newspapers of accounts of the extermination of Jews at Auschwitz-Birkenau, Himmler ordered the destruction of active crematoria.

Nazi Camps and Extermination Centers

There is little basis for comparison between concentration camps and extermination centers. In the former there was always a slight chance of survival; in the latter such a possibility was statistically nil.

From 540,000 to 720,000 people of all persuasions perished within the framework of the concentration camp system, representing 30 to 45 percent of the 1.65 million who were deported there. In contrast, nearly all of the 2.7 million Jews deported to the six extermination centers died, most as soon as they arrived.

The recent German attempt to compare the Nazi KL system to the Soviet concentration camp system (which predated it) through affirming that "the Gulag precedes Auschwitz" is not false. It is nonetheless purposeless, for two fundamental reasons. First, the Shoah, the process of extermination of the Jews, strictly speaking stands as a thing apart from the Nazi concentration camp system; and, second, the Gulag produced nothing equivalent to the Nazi execution centers.

SEE ALSO Auschwitz; Gas; Genocide

BIBLIOGRAPHY

Arad, Yitzhak (1987). *Belzec, Sobibor, Treblinka: The Operation Reinhard Extermination Camps.* Bloomington, Ind.: Indiana University Press.

Dwork, Deborah and Robert Jan van Pelt (1996). *Auschwitz: 1270 to the Present.* New York: Norton.

Gutman, Israel and Michael Berenbaum, eds. (1994). *Anatomy of the Auschwitz Death Camp.* Bloomington, Ind.: Indiana University Press.

Hilberg, Raul (1973). *The Destruction of the European Jews.* New York: Watts.

Kotek, Joël, and Pierre Rigoulot (2000). *Le siècle des camps, 100 ans de mal radical.* Paris: Lattès.

Laqueur, Walter (1981). *Le Terrifiant secret, la solution finale et l'information étouffée (The Terrible Secret: Suppression of the Truth About Hitler's "Final Solution"),* trans. Antoinette Robichaud-Stretz. Boston: Little Brown.

Piper, Franciszek and Teresa Swiebocka, eds. (1996). *Auschwitz Nazi Death Camp,* trans. Douglas Selvage. Oswiecim, Poland: The AuschwitzBirkenau State Museum.

Pressac, Jean-Claude (1989). *Auschwitz : Technique and Operation of the Gas Chambers.* New York: Beate Klarsfeld Foundation.

Vrba, Rudolf and Alan Bestic (1964). *I Cannot Forgive.* New York: Bantam.

Joël Kotek

Extradition

Criminal law is particular to each state. What is unlawful in one state may well be lawful in another. Even when the same actions are criminal in two states, the specific elements of the crime may well differ. Jurisdiction to prosecute a crime is principally based on that crime having occurred within the territory of the state seeking to try the alleged offender. In addressing offenses against individuals or property, such restrictions pose few if any problems. Nevertheless, for centuries states have had to respond when an alleged offender has committed a crime in one state and then fled to another. The law of extradition provides the traditional solution. Extradition is the legal method by which one state surrenders an alleged offender to another state so that the latter can prosecute him or her. It is a discreet and specialized area of law that needs to be explored in a general context before looking at the aspects specific to those accused of genocide or crimes against humanity.

Extradition is more than a method for removing undesirable persons from the territory of a state. Such removal for aliens can be accomplished through deportation, which allows the state to remove those deemed inimical to the public interest. The state has no interest in where a person goes after he or she is deported, although sometimes states use deportation as a form of disguised extradition. Extradition, in contrast to deportation, is based on an agreement between at least two states to surrender suspects to face prosecution. The destination of the individual is fundamental to the process. Furthermore, being based on an agreement between at least two states, it is their interests that determine the nature of the process; the individual concerned is simply an element, although not completely powerless, in that interstate agreement. Originally, extradition agreements were bilateral (meaning they existed between two states), so differences in practice can be found within international extradition law. Most common law states, that is, those with an Anglo-American tradition, for example, require a certain degree of evidence against the alleged fugitive offender, while states adopting the continental European model only look for a warrant, proof of identity, statement of the law, and a brief outline of the facts.

There are two matters that are intrinsic to extradition law. First, the agreement may be bilateral, multilateral, formal, informal, or ad hoc, but it is an interstate mechanism. Thus, surrender to some other entity, such as the International Criminal Tribunals for the Former Yugoslavia (ICTY) and Rwanda (ICTR) or to the International Criminal Court (ICC), is not based on extradition but some other mechanism for surrendering the accused. Second, the state making a request must have jurisdiction to prosecute the alleged offender for the crimes that form the basis of the request. This second matter is called the requirement of double criminality and is found in nearly all extradition arrangements. Double criminality provides that extradition shall not take place unless the actions of the accused would constitute a crime within the jurisdiction of both the courts of both the requested and requesting states. The premise for the rule is that states should only surrender someone to another state for behavior that both of them have criminalized, recognizing that criminal law reflects the mores and customs of each state. Although the criminalization of genocide and crimes against humanity may be assumed to be universal, such an assumption needs to be examined in slightly closer detail. Genocide was very precisely defined in the 1948 United Nations (UN) Convention on the Prevention and Punishment of the Crime of Genocide in terms of *actus reus* (act or omission) and *mens rea* (mental element of the crime). Some states have adopted a broader definition in their domestic legislation, however, and it is only when some convergence exists that one could assume double criminality.

With respect to crimes against humanity, the situation is even less clear because there is, as yet, no universally accepted definition. This is not to suggest that acts commonly described as crimes against humanity would not be criminalized in most states; rather, double criminality is not based on the simple identity of terms. One should look to see if the activities listed in an extradition request are criminalized by the requested state. The difficult cases involve requests made by a state asserting a form of extraterritorial jurisdiction. Not only must the activity be criminalized by both states, but both states must be able to prosecute in regard to the extraterritorial elements of the crime—common law states have a much more restricted capacity to prosecute crimes that did not take place within their territory. Civil law states have jurisdiction over their own citizens for crimes committed anywhere in the world, as well as a much more developed understanding of crimes that threaten the state and universal jurisdiction. Moreover, several have adopted the "passive personality" principle giving a state jurisdiction when the victim is a citizen of the state. The consequence is that the requesting state may well have jurisdiction over acts criminalized in both states, but the requested state would lack jurisdiction because of an extraterritorial element to the crime based on the facts.

Genocide and Crimes Against Humanity

Genocide and crimes against humanity present some particular issues for extradition law. The Genocide Convention states in its Article VI:

> Persons charged with genocide or any of the other acts enumerated in article III shall be tried by a competent tribunal of the State in the territory of which the act was committed, or by such international penal tribunal as may have jurisdiction with respect to those Contracting Parties which shall have accepted its jurisdiction.

On the basis of Article VI, until the establishment of the ICC, one could argue that only the territorial state had the authority to prosecute. Custom, however, provides that universal jurisdiction exists over genocide—see the International Court of Justice (ICJ) Advisory Opinion in the *Reservations to the Genocide Convention* case (1951) and Randall (1988).

Crimes against humanity are more problematic in a legal sense because no universally accepted definition exists. Even the statutes of the ad hoc international criminal tribunals and the ICC do not have uniform definitions. Article 5 of the statute for the International Tribunal for the former Yugoslavia requires that the crime occurred during an armed conflict, but persecution is simply a freestanding crime within crimes

Businessman Ricardo Miguel Cavallo behind bars in Mexico City, August 26, 2000. Detained in flight after a local newspaper had exposed his previous identity, Cavallo was formally charged days later by Madrid Judge Baltazar Garzon with genocide, torture, and terrorism for his role in the "enforced disappearances" that occurred in Argentina during the 1976–1983 military junta. On June 28, 2003, in an unprecedented act of international cooperation, Mexico's highest court ruled that Cavallo could be extradited to Spain to stand trial for crimes committed in Argentina. [REUTERS/CORBIS]

against humanity; Article 3 of the statute of the International Tribunal for Rwanda does not require there to be an armed conflict, but the crime has to be committed as part of a widespread or systematic attack and with a persecutory intent; the most recent definition of the crime in an international instrument, Article 7 of the Statute of the International Criminal Court, does not require an armed conflict, the crime, on the other hand, does have to be part of a widespread or systematic attack, but there is no need for persecutory intent, although persecution is a separate crime as long as it is associated with another crime within Articles 6, 7, or 8 of the Statute. The only element on which all definitions agree is that the crime has to be directed against a civilian population. Given such divergence, the requirement of double criminality in extradition law could be problematic if the requesting and requested states have adopted definitions of crimes against humanity from different statutes.

One might argue that crimes against humanity are subject to universal jurisdiction, rendering part of the double criminality requirement easier to satisfy. It is clear that some of the crimes listed as crimes against humanity, such as torture and possibly enslavement, if committed in the appropriate context (in an armed conflict or as part of a widespread or systematic attack) would be subject to permissive universal jurisdiction, but it has not been established that all crimes against humanity enumerated in the Rome Statute would provide domestic courts with the jurisdiction to prosecute, regardless of the place where the crime occurred or the nationality of the alleged perpetrator or victim. For instance, Article 7.1(i) lists the enforced disappearance of persons as one crime that could constitute a crime against humanity. Paragraph 2(i) of the same article provides as follows:

> "Enforced disappearance of persons" means the arrest, detention or abduction of persons by, or with the authorization, support or acquiescence of, a State or a political organization, followed by a refusal to acknowledge that deprivation of freedom or to give information on the fate or whereabouts of those persons, with the intention of removing them from the protection of the law for a prolonged period of time.

Although such actions ought to be criminalized, it is not certain that prior to 1998 enforced disappearance was recognized by states as a crime attracting universal jurisdiction, unless seen as a form of torture (see *Sarma v. Sri Lanka*, 2003, para. 9.5). Its adoption in the Rome Statute does not of itself accord such a status.

Defenses to Extradition

Extradition law includes a series of specific defenses that prohibit surrender and, additionally, international human rights law provides its own safeguards for alleged transnational fugitive offenders. These defenses have been interpreted by various domestic courts in different states, so while they are recognized as part of state practice in the field of extradition law, no uniform definition exists and they may indeed have been omitted from particular treaties and therefore be irrelevant with respect to a particular request.

Military Offenses

Although it might appear to be contrary to the fundamental objective of prosecuting those who commit genocide or other crimes against humanity to exempt from extradition those committing military offenses, extradition law has applied a very specific and limited definition to what constitutes an offense of a military character. It is not every offense committed by a member of the military forces that constitutes a military offense. To result in protection at an extradition hearing, the offense must be purely military in character, such as going absent without leave or refusing to perform military service.

Specialty

"Specialty" is peculiar to extradition law. It provides that the requesting state can only prosecute the transnational fugitive offender after surrender for the crimes stipulated in the request and for no others. Indeed, since extradition law also extends to requesting the return of a convicted fugitive, if a request fails to include previous convictions after the fugitive absconds, he or she cannot be reincarcerated for those convictions on surrender, so strong is the principle of specialty (*R v. Uxbridge Justices, ex parte Davies*, 1981). Although one might initially deduce that specialty has little to do with extradition in cases of genocide or crimes against humanity, the case of John Demjanjuk suggests that it could prove problematic in certain instances.

The Political Offense Exemption

The political offense exemption provides that surrender shall not take place when the offense is of a political character. The nonextradition of persons accused of political offenses might even be accepted as a norm of customary international law when it is not expressed in the international agreement between two states. However, Article VII of the Genocide Convention explicitly states that "genocide and the other acts enumerated in article III shall not be considered as political crimes for the purpose of extradition." Such clauses rejecting the political offense exemption are extremely rare in international treaties (see the 1973 International Convention on the Suppression and Punishment of the Crime of Apartheid, the 1998 International Convention for the Suppression of Terrorist Bombings, and the 2000 International Convention for the Suppression of the Financing of Terrorism).

Although extradition law is part of international law, it is nevertheless implemented in domestic courts and therefore there is no one accepted definition of a political offense. Certain crimes are seen as purely political, such as treason, but ordinarily a political offense is a common crime whose political character predominates, such as murdering a tyrant with the intent of overthrowing the government. It is not sufficient that the crime was committed by a politically motivated offender. The exemption applies to offenses of a political character, not politically motivated offenders—on the other hand, the offender must have a political rather than a personal motive. Four main approaches have developed to the political offense exemption (with three being very similar), and, depending on which one is followed, crimes against humanity could be deemed as political, no matter how appalling that idea may seem.

The first approach is contained in the law of the United Kingdom. For an offense to be of a political character under this approach, it had to be part of, and in furtherance of, a political disturbance, and not too remote from the ultimate goal of an organization attempting to change the government or its policies. In addition, the request has to be made by the state that was the target of the fugitive offender's crime. Imagining crimes against humanity that would satisfy the remoteness element of that test is difficult: How could a crime against humanity be sufficiently proximate to overthrowing a government or changing its policies when it involves an "attack on a civilian population"? The Swiss approach, now also adopted in the United Kingdom, includes elements of the U.K. approach, but adds proportionality to its predominance test. Even if the crime would have been political under the traditional U.K. approach, if it were determined to be disproportionate, then the Swiss approach would find it to be nonpolitical:

> Homicide, assassination and murder, is one of the most heinous crimes. It can only be justified where no other method exists of protecting the final rights or humanity (*In re Pavan*, 1928).

The Swiss test would deem crimes against humanity to be nonpolitical as they are disproportionate. The third approach may be found in the decisions of the Irish courts. They have followed the Swiss approach since 1982:

> The offenses set forth in the two warrants . . . cannot be regarded as political offenses . . . as they contemplate and involve indiscriminate violence and can be correctly characterized as terrorism (*Ellis v. O'Dea* [No. 2], 1991).

In addition, the Irish courts demand that the crime not threaten the democratic nature of the requested state. If the transnational fugitive offender is as much of a threat to the requested state as he or she was to the requesting state, then the alleged offender forfeits the protection of the political offense exemption.

The final approach derives from U.S. court decisions. The basic test is that an offense will be deemed political if it is part of, or in furtherance of, a political uprising. Although an uprising requires a greater degree of violence and instability than a disturbance, an offense which is part of that uprising is prima facie political—there is no requirement of proximity to the ultimate goal or proportionality. As such, crimes against humanity might be deemed political. In the *Artukovic* case the breadth of the U.S. approach was made apparent. Yugoslavia requested the extradition of Andrija Artukovic in 1956 with respect to war crimes. He had served as Minister of the Interior under the Axis-controlled Croatian government of World War II. In that position he had allegedly ordered the death of

1,293 named individuals and approximately 30,000 unidentified persons. The District Court for the Southern District of California held that these were political offenses because they had been committed in a political uprising, namely the power struggle that occurred in Croatia during World War II. The U.S. Court of Appeals for the Ninth Circuit upheld the district court's refusal to extradite Artukovic to Yugoslavia, rejecting the asserted principle that war crimes were automatically nonpolitical.

Even if one accepts that stance by the U.S. courts, it is difficult to see how the murder of 30,000 people, principally civilians, could be part of, or incidental to, a political uprising. The Supreme Court vacated the Court of Appeals decision and remanded the case to the District Court. The District Court in its second attempt at interpreting existing law again decided to refuse extradition, partly because of lack of evidence. However, it did find that the offenses alleged were of a political character as well. The 1959 decision in the series of *Artukovic* cases would seem to be a most disturbing misinterpretation of the exemption. Not only should war crimes and, by analogy, crimes against humanity be excluded from the ambit of political offenses like genocide, but the offenses charged here were of a type and nature that the scope of the accepted political incidence test might be stretched beyond rational limits. Artukovic was eventually extradited, but only in 1986 after the Court of Appeals for the Ninth Circuit recognized the error of the earlier 1959 decision.

A sounder approach to crimes against humanity and the political offense exemption may be seen in the reasoning of *Kroeger v. The Swiss Federal Prosecutor's Office* (1966):

> The offense must have been committed in the course of a struggle for power in the State and must also be in appropriate proportion to the object pursued, in other words suitable to the attainment of that object. The extinction of human life, one of the most reprehensible crimes, can only appear excusable if it constitutes a last resort in the pursuit of a political objective. On the facts, . . . such a situation does not come into question. The accused was acting at a time when the nationalist socialist regime stood at the pinnacle of its power. He acted against helpless women, children and sick persons who could not possibly have threatened German dominion.

In the words of the Argentinian Supreme Court:

> Extradition will not be denied on grounds of the political or military character of the charges where we are dealing with cruel or immoral acts which clearly shock the conscience of civilized people (*In re Bohne*, 1968).

Although the political offense exemption is fundamental to extradition law, the UN Genocide Convention excludes it in relation to Article III crimes and crimes against humanity are non-political by their very nature.

Death Penalty

When the state requesting extradition retains the death penalty for crimes that the requested state does not apply capital punishment to, then most modern extradition treaties provide that the latter shall seek assurances from the former that it will not impose the death penalty on the transnational fugitive offender if he or she is surrendered. Although such a rule is not customary international law at this time, death penalty clauses are becoming more prevalent in extradition arrangements. States that have ratified the second optional protocol to the International Covenant on Civil and Political Rights (ICCPR), other abolitionist states that are parties to the ICCPR, and states party to Protocol 6 of the European Convention for the Protection of Human Rights and Fundamental Freedoms (ECHR) cannot extradite without gaining such assurances from the requesting state (*Judge v. Canada*, 2003; *Soering v. United Kingdom*, 1989). In addition, returning someone to face the death penalty may, in certain cases, amount to torture, inhuman or degrading treatment, or punishment contrary to Article 3 of the United Nations Convention Against Torture 1984 (torture only) or the ECHR's Article 3.

Nationality

Given that most recent examples of genocide and crimes against humanity have occurred in noninternational armed conflicts, the rules in extradition law pertaining to nationals ought to have little impact. Most civil law states will not extradite their nationals. By way of corollary, they assert jurisdiction over crimes committed by their nationals anywhere in the world. Furthermore, their rules of evidence in criminal trials more readily permit the admission of documentary evidence so witnesses to genocide or crimes against humanity do not have to appear at the trial in person. Nevertheless, if a trial for genocide or crimes against humanity is seen as a form of postconflict justice, allowing a previously divided state to face up to gross human rights violations of the past, then a remote trial in a third state may not satisfy that objective.

Immunity

Extradition law does recognize immunity as a defense, as is clear from the *Pinochet* cases. Former heads of state and their equivalents, however, ought not to have immunity for genocide or crimes against humanity

committed during their terms of office, although it is not as simple as saying that they cannot have immunity for any criminal acts perpetrated during that time. In *Pinochet No. 3* (1999), the English House of Lords held that former Chilean President Augusto Pinochet's immunity for torture committed while he was head of state ceased on the date that Spain, the United Kingdom, and Chile (respectively, the requesting state, the requested state, and the state where the crimes occurred) became parties to the 1984 UN Torture Convention. By analogy Article IV of the Genocide Convention stipulates no immunity for former heads of state for Article III crimes committed during their tenure in office. No equivalent provision exists for crimes against humanity, but given that they have been accepted as international crimes since the Nuremberg tribunals, the reasoning of *Pinochet 3* is that former heads of state do not enjoy immunity.

Existing heads of state and their equivalents, on the other hand, receive a much broader immunity, even for serious international crimes. In *Congo v. Belgium* (2002), the ICJ held that domestic courts had no jurisdiction to prosecute under principles of universal jurisdiction acting high officials (in this case the Congolese foreign minister). While Article IV of the Genocide Convention holds that even "constitutionally responsible rulers" shall be punished, this directive has to be interpreted in light of Article VI, which gives jurisdiction to the territorial state and an international penal tribunal. The ICJ accepted the notion that an international tribunal could prosecute an acting head of state.

Irregular or de facto Extradition

As can be seen, there are a variety of reasons why an extradition request may fail, if one assumes that the request has been properly made in the first place. Given the desire to bring persons accused of genocide or crimes against humanity to trial, irregular methods have been used to obtain jurisdiction: "collusive" deportation and abduction. When extradition would be impossible because an international agreement does not exist between the requesting and requested states and there is no option of trying a transnational fugitive offender before an international tribunal or a domestic court on the basis of universal jurisdiction, then alternative methods of surrendering the accused, with due regard for his or her human rights, may be justified. However, given the existence of the ICC and the burgeoning acceptance of universal jurisdiction as well as the seriousness of genocide and crimes against humanity, one might hope that such alternative methods will need to be used rarely.

Collusive deportation involves the prosecuting state and the state where the transnational fugitive offender is seeking refuge. The latter uses its power to deport aliens in order to return the transnational fugitive offender to the state seeking to prosecute him or her. As such, a legal process is initiated. Nevertheless, following the decision of the European Court of Human Rights in *Bozano v. France* (1986), Council of Europe (CoE) member states should not deport a transnational fugitive offender, with extradition being the appropriate means of surrendering that individual to the requesting state. The opposite perspective emerged when Bolivia expelled Klaus Barbie (the former Nazi referred to as the "Butcher of Lyon") to France to face trial for crimes against humanity. Barbie's legal team alleged that France violated international law in obtaining jurisdiction through expulsion rather than extradition. The French high court, the Cour de Cassation, held that:

> "All necessary measures" are to be taken by the Member States of the United Nations to ensure that war crimes, crimes against peace and crimes against humanity are punished and that those persons suspected of being responsible for such crimes are sent back "to the countries in which their abominable deeds were done in order that they may be judged and punished according to the laws of those countries."

The English House of Lords, on the other hand, has divested itself of jurisdiction with respect to the return of a transnational fugitive offender to face charges for financial crimes when extradition would have been possible. Canadian, South African, and Zimbabwean courts have decided similarly. However, the First Section of the European Court of Human Rights was prepared to sanction collusive deportation in *Ócalan v. Turkey* (2003). Abdullah Ócalan was the leader of the Workers Party of Kurdistan (PKK), a Kurdish separatist group. Turkish authorities took him into custody at Nairobi Airport with the collusion of Kenyan authorities. Given that there was no extradition treaty between the two states, the European Court of Human Rights was prepared to hold that the detention was lawful under Article 5.1 of the ECHR. The decision of the First Section raises many questions, the most fundamental of which relates to its function. Domestic courts deciding whether they should divest themselves of jurisdiction to prosecute need to take into account the availability of extradition, but the European Court of Human Rights ought to focus on the rights of the applicant, particularly those relating to the lawful deprivation of liberty—if bundling Lorenzo Bozano across the Swiss border on his way to Italy was contrary to Article 5.1, accepting Ócalan after he had been whisked onto a waiting plane by Kenyan authorities must also be unlawful. The situation might have been different if Ke-

nyan authorities had used their ordinary laws relating to deportation with a right to judicial review.

If collusive deportation raises questions of legality, abduction from a third state, violating the latter's sovereign status, should never be adopted—it is, in the words of Ivan Shearer, "manifestly extra-legal" (1971, p. 75). The leading authority in this area is *Eichmann* (1960). Former Nazi Adolf Eichmann was abducted from Argentina by agents acting for Israel. He was tried and convicted, but only after the UN Security Council addressed the violation of Argentina's sovereignty. Nevertheless, the ICTY later determined that it would prosecute an individual snatched by Nato troops from Bosnia and Herzegovina (*Prosecutor v. Dragan Nikolic*, 2003, para. 33).

Duty to Prosecute and Universal Jurisdiction
Grave breaches of the Geneva Conventions for the protection of victims of war and the First Additional Protocol relating to international armed conflicts impose a duty on all signatories to investigate and prosecute. Extradition is a secondary response. Mandatory universal jurisdiction, however, is limited to grave breaches. All other crimes, including genocide and crimes against humanity, have, at best, permissive universal jurisdiction, except when the alleged genocide or crimes against humanity also qualify as grave breaches—there is a degree of overlap in the appropriate circumstances. Nevertheless, even though no mandatory universal jurisdiction exists, a duty to prosecute does arise when an alleged offender is found in the territory of the state and is not extradited—*aut dedere, aut judicare*, that is, the state must either surrender the fugitive to another state with jurisdiction or prosecute him or her itself (Bassiouni and Wise, 1995). Article V of the Genocide Convention provides as follows:

> The Contracting Parties undertake to enact, in accordance with their respective Constitutions, the necessary legislation to give effect to the provisions of the present Convention, and, in particular, to provide effective penalties for persons guilty of genocide or any of the other acts enumerated in article III.

Although it might be argued that Article V should be read in conjunction with Article VI, only requiring states to enact legislation to prosecute individuals for genocide committed within the territory of that state, customary international law gives states universal jurisdiction over genocide, particularly since Article IV stipulates that persons committing genocide shall be punished.

As for crimes against humanity, one again has to rely on customary international law that, as might be expected, is not expounded in a single document. Nevertheless, the writings of scholars and the decisions of several international tribunals suggest that if evidence exists that a person has committed crimes against humanity and this person is found within the territory of a state, that state would have a duty to prosecute if it does not extradite the alleged offender to the state where the crimes against humanity occurred.

The ICC and Rendition

The ICC was established by means of an interstate treaty. As such, the rules about surrender are laid down in the 1998 Rome Statute (Part 9, Articles 86–102). Although the Statute provides the framework, individual states party will establish their own mechanisms for surrender (Article 88); states that are not party to the Statute can agree to surrender on an ad hoc basis. Such systems will be similar to the extradition process, but noticeable differences will exist. Extradition is based on a request by a coequal sovereign state, whereas surrender to the ICC will follow a request made by the Office of the Prosecutor. It will, however, be much like an extradition request under the extradition law of the requested state (Article 91): proof of identity and evidence of location; a copy of the arrest warrant; and

> Such documents, statements or information as may be necessary to meet the requirements for the surrender process in the requested State, except that those requirements should not be more burdensome than those applicable to requests for extradition pursuant to treaties or arrangements between the requested State and other States and should, if possible, be less burdensome, taking into account the distinct nature of the Court.

The Rome Statute foresees only three reasons why a requested state that is a state party might refuse surrender: *ne bis in idem* (double jeopardy, Article 20); a competing request from another state (Article 90); and a contrary obligation under international law (Article 98). It is the latter ground that is giving rise to controversy. Article 27 provides that official capacity, even as a head of state, is not a defense to any of the Article 5 crimes. Article 98, however, provides:

> The Court may not proceed with a request for surrender or assistance which would require the requested State to act inconsistently with its obligations under international law with respect to the State or diplomatic immunity of a person or property of a third State, unless the Court can first obtain the cooperation of that third State for the waiver of the immunity.

The interplay of the two articles is complex, but one likely interpretation is that Article 98 protects those with immunity, with the immunity stemming from a nonstate party. A person with immunity from a state party to the Rome Statute cannot rely on Article 98—ratification of the statute gives rise to a waiver not only with respect to the ICC, but also in relation to all other states party (Akande, 2003).

SEE ALSO International Criminal Court; International Criminal Tribunal for Rwanda; International Criminal Tribunal for the Former Yugoslavia; Prosecution; Universal Jurisdiction

BIBLIOGRAPHY

Akande, D. (2003). "The Jurisdiction of the International Criminal Court Over Nationals of Non-Parties: Legal Basis and Limits." *Journal of International and Criminal Justice* 1:618–650.

Bassiouni, M. C., and E. Wise (1995). Aut Dedere, Aut Judicare: *The Duty to Extradite or Prosecute in International Law*. Dordrecht: Martinus Nijhoff.

Gilbert, G. (1998). *Transnational Fugitive Offenders in International Law*. Dordrecht: Martinus Nijhoff.

Randall, K. (1988). "Universal Jurisdiction Under International Law." *Texas Law Review* 66:785–841.

Shearer, I. (1971). *Extradition in International Law*. Manchester, U.K.: Manchester Uiversity Press.

INTERNATIONAL INSTRUMENTS

European Convention for the Protection of Human Rights and Fundamental Freedoms. ETS 5 (1950). Also available from http://www.echr.coe.int.

Genocide Convention, 1948. 78 UNTS 277 (1951).

Geneva Conventions, 1949. 75 UNTS 31-417 (1950). Additional Protocols, 1977. 1125 UNTS 3-608 (1979) and 16 ILM1391 (1977).

International Covenant on Civil and Political Rights. UNGA Resolution 2200A(XXI), UNGAOR, 21st Session, Suppl. No. 16, 52 (1966); 999 UNTS 171; 6 ILM 368 (1967); 61 AJIL 870 (1967).

International Criminal Court Statute, July 17, 1998. 37 ILM 999 (1998).

International Criminal Tribunal for the Former Yugoslavia Statute. UNSC Resolution 827 (1993) and 32 ILM 1192 (1993).

International Criminal Tribunal for Rwanda Statute. UNSC Resolutions 935 and 955 (1994).

United Nations Convention Against Torture. 23 ILM 1027 (1984) and 24 ILM 535 (1985).

CASES

Artukovic v. Boyle. 140 F Suppl. 245 (1956); *Karadzole v. Artukovic*. 247 F2d 198 (1957); *US ex rel. Karadzole. Karadzole v. Artukovic*. 355 U.S. 393 (1958); *US ex rel Karadzole*. 170 F Suppl. 383 (1959); *In re Extradition of Artukovic*. 628 F Suppl.1370 (1985); *Artukovic v. Rison*. 784 F2d 1354 (1986).

Banegas, In re Banegas. Supreme Federal Court of Brazil, 15 ILR 300 (1948).

Bohne, In re Bohne. Argentinian Supreme Court, 62 AJIL 784 (1968).

Bozano v. France. European Court of Human Rights, Series A, Vol. 111 (1986).

Congo v. Belgium. International Court of Justice (February 14, 2002). Available from http://www.icj cij.org/icjwww/ idocket/iCOBE/iCOBEframe.htm.

Davies, R v. Uxbridge Justices, ex parte Davies. English High Court, 1 WLR 1080 (1981).

Demjanjuk, In re Extradition of Demjanjuk. 612 F Suppl. 544 at 571 (1985).

Demjanjuk v. Petrovsky. 776 F2d 571 (1985); cert.den.106 Supreme Court 1198 (1986).

Attorney-General of the government of Israel v. Adolf Eichmann. District Court of Jerusalem, Israeli Supreme Court, 36 ILR 5 (1960).

Ellis v. O'Dea (No. 2). Irish High Court, confirmed by Supreme Court, ILRM 346 (1991).

Fédération Nationale des Déportés et Internés Résistants et Patriotes et al. v. Barbie. Cour de Cassation, 78 ILR 125 (1985).

Judge v. Canada. Human Rights Committee, CCPR/C/78/D/ 829/1998 (August 13, 2003).

Kroeger v. The Swiss Federal Prosecutor's Office. Swiss Federal Tribunal, 72 ILR 606 (1966).

Ôcalan v. Turkey. European Court of Human Rights (First Section), 46621/99 (March 12, 2003). Available from http://hudoc.echr.coe.int/hudoc/ default.asp?Language=en&Advanced=1.

Pavan, In re Pavan. Swiss Federal Tribunal, Annual Digest 347 (1928).

Pinochet, In re Pinochet. 2 WLR 272 (1999).

Pinochet, R (No. 2) v. Bartle and the Commissioner of Police for the Metropolis and Others, ex parte Pinochet; R v. Evans and Another and the Commissioner of Police for the Metropolis and Others, ex parte Pinochet. 3 WLR 1456 (1998).

Pinochet, R v. Bartle and the Commissioner of Police for the Metropolis and Others, ex parte Pinochet; R v. Evans and Another and the Commissioner of Police for the Metropolis and Others, ex parte Pinochet. On Appeal from a Divisional Court of the Queen's Bench Division, 2 WLR 827 (1999).

Prosecutor v. Dragan Nikolic. Decision on Interlocutory Appeal Concerning Legality of Arrest. ICTY Appeals Chamber, IT-94-2-AR73 (June 5, 2003).

Reservations to the Genocide Convention. International Court of Justice Reports, 15 (1951).

Sarma v. Sri Lanka. Human Rights Committee, CCPR/C/78/ D/950/2000 (July 31, 2003).

Soering v. United Kingdom. European Court of Human Rights, Series A, Vol. 161 (1989).

Geoff Gilbert

Famine

Human history is replete with occurrences of famine causing death by starvation of hundreds of thousands or even millions. Some famines have had their origin in environmental problems such as long periods of drought or exceptional floods; other were provoked by human action. Whatever the causes of origin, however, in the modern world famine can be prevented, which may not always have been possible in the past. When famine still occurs, it is either a result of deliberate action intended to cause starvation, serious mismanagement, bad or nonresponsive government failing to respond adequately to natural disasters, or lack of sufficient international cooperation in redressing a threatening situation. Some provoked famines may legally be characterized as genocide or crime against humanity, but the problem of famine goes far beyond such cases.

Concept of Famine

The term *famine* is usually reserved to describe a condition that is temporary and extreme. It is temporary in that it constitutes a departure from the normal conditions in the area or for the particular group affected, and it is extreme in the sense that the number of persons affected by starvation is much higher than normal.

Most famines affect mainly the poorer and most vulnerable population, often those who for a variety of reasons are "food insecure" in advance. Some of the provoked famines, particularly those that can be classified as genocide, are targeted at persons belonging to one or more particular national, racial, or ethnic groups.

Famine is therefore distinguished from conditions of chronic hunger. In the past there have always been, and there continue to be, large groups of people who suffer from severe undernutrition due to insufficient access to adequate food. The percentage of the world population suffering from chronic hunger has undoubtedly been significantly reduced over the centuries, but the number is still staggeringly high. The Food and Agriculture Organization of the United Nations (FAO) estimates that in 2003 the number of food insecure (undernourished) was 798 million, and the number of undernourished people continues to steadily increase in South Asia and Central Africa.

Causes of Famine

Even when conditions of famine exist, the problem in the contemporary world is not an overall lack of food. Famine emerges when a significant number of persons are physically or economically barred from access to food. They may be physically barred through deliberate action by some who have the power to do so, such as during the existence of the Warsaw ghetto (1941–1942) or the siege of Leningrad (1941–1944), or because of the unavailability of transport, which makes it impossible to bring the food to those who need it. They may be economically barred because they do not have the means to purchase food that is available on the market, either because they live from subsistence agriculture and have no income to purchase food when their own production fails, or because their other sources of income have failed or the prices have skyrocketed so they are no longer able to purchase what they need. Amartya Sen, awarded the Nobel Prize in

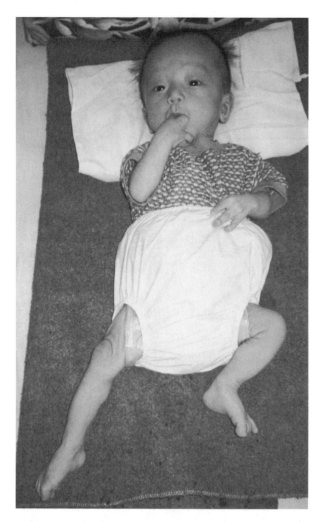

North Korea's famine resulted in high rates of not only infant mortality, but also deformities among children who survived. This young boy, born with only four fingers on each hand as a result of his mother's malnutrition, lies bedridden at an orphanage in Hyesan City. [REUTERS/CORBIS]

economics, has effectively demonstrated that famines, apart from deliberate policies of starvation, affect mainly those who lose their productive assets or entitlements in the market.

In discussions of the causes of famine, it has been common to classify them as either natural or manmade. The famines considered to be caused by natural events are those originating from an extreme or long spell of drought, or excessive floods, or a disease on the staple food plant (i.e., the Irish famine). Manmade famines are, primarily, those that have been deliberately provoked, or caused by war or conflict even if the starvation was not intended, or those resulting from extreme mismanagement, such as the Chinese famine of 1958 through 1962. At closer inspection, however, one recognizes that every famine transpiring in modern times

has had a manmade element (or elements). This is important to recognize, because it implies that conditions of famine can be prevented or stopped in their infancy, provided appropriate rules of responsibility and accountability are in place. Neither droughts nor floods nor plant diseases can always be prevented, but their consequences in terms of famine can.

The ability to prevent famines has not always existed in the past. Although many records of preventive and relief measures date far back in history, conditions were not such that widespread starvation could be prevented when there were major spells of drought or floods. In times or areas where subsistence agriculture dominated, general food insecurity was widespread and little surplus was available to help those affected by major natural disasters; nor were there transport possibilities to bring food from afar, if stocks did exist. Provoked famines were also common, including the use of siege to starve the defendants of stronghold in feudal times. Frequent and extensive wars ravaging vast areas, such as the Thirty Years' War, also brought starvation to many as a consequence of both the disruption of production and extensive pillage of cattle or food produced.

Famines in History

Provoked famines were part of the European conquest and settlement of the Americas. The ethnic cleansing of Native Americans to seize land for the colonizers and settlers included wars, the destruction of their sources of livelihood such as the deliberate encouragement of hunting to decimate the bison on the American plains, and death marches such as the Trail of Tears. In South America the use of slave labor under famine conditions led to the massive death and decimation of the indigenous population.

One of the worst famines in modern times in the Western world was the Irish famine of 1846 through 1849. It started as the result of a prolonged potato blight that over several years caused the nation's potatoes to rot. While this occurred not only in Ireland but also in other parts of Europe, it had a devastating impact in Ireland. Four factors caused the disease to become a tragedy of enormous proportions: As a result of the British occupation and Cromwell's wars, most of the Irish were peasants engaged in subsistence agriculture. The potato was their staple food. They had little income beyond whatever minuscule incomes they could make from the sale of the potato and other farm products. Second, they did not own their farmsteads, but were tied to Protestant or British landlords who insisted that they should continue to pay their rent even when no income could be obtained. As they could not

Widespread famine struck North Korea in 1995, but it was some time before a secretive government acknowledged the crisis and permitted relief efforts. In this August 10, 1997, photo, Red Cross workers unload bags of corn from a truck. [CORBIS]

pay, hundreds of thousands were evicted. Third, Ireland was not an independent country with its own government, which might have recognized its responsibility to take remedial action; Ireland was under British rule. The fourth and most serious obstacle to the prevention of the famine was the stubborn belief, in British political circles of the time, in the laissez-faire ideology, the ultraliberalistic theory that government should not interfere in economic activity. In his book on the history of the Irish famine, Cecil Woodham-Smith writes:

> Not only were the rights of property sacred; private enterprise was revered and respected and given almost complete liberty, and on this theory, which incidentally gave the employer and the landlord freedom to exploit his fellow man, the prosperity of nineteenth-century England had been unquestioningly based.

The influence of laissez-faire on the treatment of Ireland during the famine is impossible to exaggerate. Almost without exception the high officials and politicians responsible for Ireland were fervent believers in non-interference by Government, and the behavior of the British authorities only becomes explicable when their fanatic belief in private enterprise and their suspicions of any action which might be considered Government intervention are borne in mind (1961, p. 54).

Subjected to absentee landlords and this fervent ideology espoused by the government controlling them, the Irish were doomed. Governmental inaction in the face of certain economic dynamics, coupled with marginal and misplaced efforts to give some relief, caused one million persons to die from starvation and related illnesses; nearly two million emigrated, a large part of them to the United States. Ireland's population dropped from eight million people before the famine to five million in the years following it.

Severe famines originating in droughts or floods occurred in India under British rule, during the eighteenth and nineteenth century. Although some modest remedial action was taken by the British through measures required under the Famine Codes previously established by them, hundreds of thousands starved to death. Once again, one of the main problems was the ruling government's strong faith in the laissez-faire principle. The export of grain from India was fully permitted even when famines raged.

The last major famine during British rule was the Bengal famine in 1943. It was not a result of any environmental or other natural disaster, but of policies and measures adopted due to the ongoing war and the advance of the Japanese armies. A war boom had emerged in Calcutta due to the high military presence and various military preparations, from which a part of the population profited. On the other hand, a scarcity of food emerged as a consequence of several factors, including Japan's occupation of Burma, one of the traditional sources of rice imports. While food existed in other Indian provinces, self-regulating food control powers given to the provinces in 1941 hindered supplies to Bengal at affordable prices. As a consequence of the increased purchasing power in Calcutta at a time of scarcity, the price of rice increased significantly. The losers were the landless rural workers and many of the traditional fishermen population who lost the ability to fish due to restrictions related to wartime conditions. The Famine Codes, which had been adopted by the British in the previous century, were never invoked during the Bengal famine in 1943; they were, in fact, deliberately ignored. It has been estimated that some three to five million people perished during the famine. To a large extent this could have been prevented by appropriate and resolute government action, had a responsive government, democratically accountable to those affected by the threatening famine, been in place.

The Armenian genocide perpetrated by the Young Turk regime in the final years of the Ottoman Empire from 1915 to 1918 included death marches with massive starvation on the way. In a 1999 review of other manmade or provoked famines of the twentieth century, Fiona Watson describes the allied blockade of Germany during World War I, the Soviet (mainly Ukrainian) famine from 1932 to 1934, conditions in the Warsaw ghetto from November 1940 to July 1942, the siege of Leningrad from September 1941 to January 1944, the Chinese famine from 1958 to 1962, and the Sudan famine of 1998. The Soviet famine of 1932 and 1933, which hit Ukraine the hardest, resulted from the enforced collectivization of agricultural production as part of the five-year plan launched by Joseph Stalin. The plan met intense opposition particularly from the self-owning farmers (kulaks) in Ukraine, some of whom engaged in armed resistance in response. The response by Stalin was ruthless; a combination of massive, outright killing and extensive food deprivation en-

sued. Agricultural production plummeted and fell by 40 percent, and most of the food produced was forcibly seized. The Soviet Union doubled its grain exports to raise currency for equipment for industrialization, while famine ravaged rural Ukraine. Stalin prohibited relief grain to be delivered to Ukraine in order to break the backbone of his opposition. The conditions were horrible and even cannibalism is reported to have occurred. It is estimated that somewhere between five and eight million people died during the famine.

Starvation was also extensively used by both German and Japanese forces during World War II, partly as a deliberate component of the Holocaust, partly by taking the food resources of the civilian population in occupied territories to feed the occupying army.

From 1940 to 1942 the Warsaw ghetto was an early measure in the Holocaust conducted by Hitler's Germany against the Jews. Following the invasion of Poland in September 1939, the German occupants confined some 380,000 Jews in a small section of the city of Warsaw. Others were soon relocated there, and the population subsequently increased to 445,000. A wall was then built around the ghetto. The Jews were prohibited from leaving the ghetto at risk of being shot on sight. By 1941 the official Nazi ration allowed 2,613 kilocalories (kcal) per day for Germans in Poland, 699 kcal for Poles, and 184 kcal for Jews in the ghetto. The German intention was to destroy the ghetto's inhabitants through mass starvation and related infectious illnesses. Mortality increased steeply. Nevertheless, the Germans did not succeed in starving all the ghetto's residents, partly because outside groups were able to smuggle in some food. In July 1942 the Germans took the next step in the Holocaust by deporting the Jews to the gas chambers of Treblinka and Auschwitz.

The siege of Leningrad by German forces from September 1941 to January 1944 lasted for nine hundred days. The siege made supplying food extremely difficult. The German Luftwaffe prevented airlifts, and transport over land was highly precarious and severely limited. During the period of the siege the city was incessantly bombarded from the air and by artillery. The bombardment also destroyed many food storehouses. It is estimated that deaths due to starvation numbered somewhere between 630,000 and 1 million people. The prewar population of Leningrad (now St. Petersburg) had been some 2.5 million persons.

The famine causing the greatest number of deaths during the twentieth century was the catastrophic Great Leap Forward of Mao Zedong's China, from 1958 to 1962. It had some similarities with Stalin's provoked famine in Ukraine in 1932, but was not pursued with the same targeted brutality. The number of deaths, however, was much higher. Like Stalin, Mao wanted to achieve industrialization through a vast increase in steel production, while at the same time "modernizing" agriculture for grain export and feeding the workers of the expanding industrialization. Peoples' communes were established, private plots were abolished, and obligatory state procurement of grain at low prices was institutionalized. In the midst of the enforced transformation of agriculture, several natural disasters occurred. Coupled with the disarray resulting from the enforced transformation, this caused grain output to fall dramatically. The local representatives of the authorities did not dare to report the truth, but falsely insisted that harvests had increased substantially. The state procurement was set at 40 percent of the alleged output, which meant that in some places the whole harvest was seized. As a result, large parts of the rural population had little or no access to food. Famine soared in the countryside, but Mao and other leaders appear to have been misled by their own propaganda and by fabricated reports submitted by local party officials, making the Chinese authorities believe that they had many millions of tons of grain more than what was actually on hand.

During the final decades of the twentieth century and the early years of the twenty-first century, Central and Southern Africa have been the regions of the world most affected by, and most likely to experience, famine. Many of these famines were caused or influenced by armed conflict: Biafra in 1969, Ethiopia in 1984, Angola from 1995 to the present, Democratic Republic of the Congo from 2000 to 2003. Others were the result of droughts or floods combined with severe mismanagement and political manipulation, such as the famine that occurred in Zimbabwe from 2001 to 2003, when food was used as a weapon by preventing the access of food relief to persons who do not support the incumbent government. In Southern Africa the HIV-AIDS epidemic has emerged as a new factor seriously increasing food insecurity and the famine risk in the region.

Responsibility and Accountability under International Law

Famines and starvation are often manmade—by intent, mismanagement, or bad governance. Even when the origin is a severe environmental deterioration or other natural phenomena, it is possible to prevent its evolution into a famine. This section examines the issue of responsibility under international law for acts or omissions causing famine.

States have the primary responsibility for compliance with international law. Part of that responsibility is to criminalize acts and omissions where required by

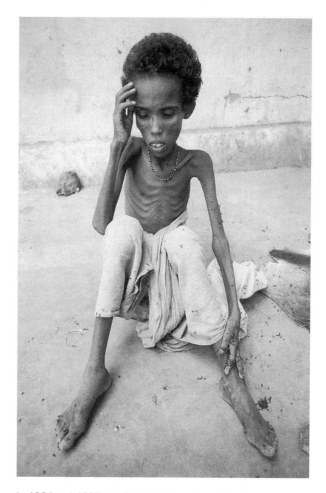

In 1984 and 1985 sub-Saharan Africa, drought-induced crop failure and armed conflict coalesced, resulting in massive famine, with an estimated one million victims. Here, an emaciated child rests at a Red Cross refugee camp in Ethiopia. [CHRIS RAINIER/ CORBIS]

international law. Individuals can also to an increasing extent be held responsible directly under international law.

War Crimes

Humanitarian law in armed conflict is primarily based on the four Geneva Conventions adopted in 1949 and the two Additional Protocols adopted in 1977. The main function of this law is to ensure that the parties to international conflicts, and to a somewhat lesser extent in internal conflicts, respect the civilian population, prisoners of war, the sick and wounded, and other military personnel who are no longer taking part in the hostilities.

Additional Protocol I, Article 54, deals with protection of objects indispensable to the survival of the civilian population. Its paragraph 1 prohibits starvation of civilians as a method of warfare, whereas paragraph 2 states that it is a crime to attack, destroy, remove, or render useless objects indispensable to the survival of the civilian population, such as foodstuffs, agricultural areas for the production of foodstuffs, crops, livestock, drinking water installations and supplies and irrigation works, for the specific purpose of denying them for their sustenance value to the civilian population or to the adverse party, whatever the motive, whether in order to starve civilians, to cause them to move away, or for any other motive.

It is quite obvious that many of the measures adopted in past wars would fall under this provision, had it then existed. The German siege of Leningrad, including the shelling and bombardment destroying the food supplies, the extensive confiscation of food resources in the occupied territories, and the scorched earth policies applied by retreating German forces in northern Norway due to the advance of Soviet forces in 1944 and 1945, would all have constituted violations of Article 54.

The rule did not exist during World War II, however. The Additional Protocols were adopted only in 1977, while a first beginning had been made with the Fourth Geneva Convention adopted in 1949, which addressed the protection of the civilian population in occupied territories. Article 23 of that convention provides for assistance to be given to the most vulnerable categories of the civilian population, particularly in the form of foodstuffs. During the Nuremberg Trials, the destruction or removal of foodstuffs on a large scale, leading to starvation of the affected population, was held to be a crime against humanity and was included among the offenses for which several of the Nazi and Japanese leaders were found guilty. Examples may be found in Gabrielle Kirk McDonald and Olivia Swaak-Goldman's *Substantive and Procedural Aspects of International Criminal Law,* Volume II.

Additional Protocol II, regarding noninternational armed conflicts, contains in its Article 14 a similar prohibition of the starvation of civilians as a method of combat and the same type of acts as described above. This can also be considered a specific application of common Article 3 to the four Geneva Conventions of 1949, which imposes on parties to the conflict the obligation to guarantee humane treatment for all persons not participating in hostilities and, in particular, prohibits violence toward life.

Genocide

Among the acts constituting genocide is the deliberate infliction of conditions of life on a national, ethnical, racial, or religious group calculated to bring about the destruction, in whole or in part, of the group. Under this heading fall measures such as denying members of a group food, water, shelter, health care, and other necessities of life. Provoked famine that targeted in a systematic way the members of a group would clearly constitute genocide, as was extensively done during the Third Reich Germany. The creation of, and conditions in, the Warsaw ghetto would be one such obvious case.

The Charter of the International Military Tribunal (IMT), on which the Nuremberg Trials was based, did not include the category of genocide, but used the terms *crimes against peace, war crimes,* and *crimes against humanity.* Many of the actions committed by those defendants convicted under crimes against humanity would now more properly fall under the category of genocide.

There are strong reasons to argue that the lack of access to food resulting from the death marches perpetrated against the Armenian population by the Young Turk regime toward the end of the Ottoman Empire was also an intended genocide, even though this claim is hotly contested by the Turkish government (Charny, 1999). Representatives of indigenous peoples also consider many of the measures of ethnic cleansing perpetrated against Native Americans, including famines, to have constituted genocidal action.

In addition, the severe deprivation of food has a devastating impact on the mental capacity of persons, in particular children. Such acts, directed against a group as defined in the 1948 United Nations (UN) Convention on the Prevention and Punishment of the Crime of Genocide, would therefore also be held to cause serious bodily or mental harm to members of a group.

Crimes against Humanity

The term *crimes against humanity* was first used in a codified way as basis for the jurisdiction of the IMT in its prosecution of major Nazi war criminals (the Nuremberg Trials) and has since been elaborated through the statutes of the International Criminal Tribunals for the Former Yugoslavia (ICTY) and Rwanda (ICTR) and particularly the statute of the International Criminal Court (ICC). Under the ICC Statute, Article 7, crimes against humanity includes any of the acts listed there when committed as part of a widespread or systematic attack directed against any civilian population, with knowledge of the attack. As distinct from genocide, it is not limited to cases where a particular group is targeted. No discriminatory intent is required. As an example, the extermination policies of the Khmer Rouge in Cambodia were directed at all groups, including the majority Khmer population. Even if the action to that extent could not have been defined as genocide, it is clearly a case of crimes against humanity. Second, in contrast to the Nuremberg Trials, to bring measures within the ambit of crimes against humanity under the ICC Statute, they do not have to be committed during an armed conflict.

Among the acts listed in ICC Statute, Article 7, constituting a crime against humanity are "extermination," "deportation or forcible transfer of population," and "other inhuman acts of a similar character intentionally causing great suffering, or serious injury to body or to mental or to physical health." But in order to be held as a crime against humanity, the act must be part of a widespread or systematic attack directed against a civilian population. It must be an active attack, thus not only the neglect of a country's duty to take remedial action when a significant number of people lose their access to food as a result of a natural disaster or economic developments. Although the Soviet famine of 1932 in Ukraine today would be labeled as genocide or a crime against humanity, the Chinese famine from 1958 to 1962 would not be so labeled, because it was clearly not an intended attack on the civilian population. Similarly, neither the Irish famine from 1846 to 1849 nor the Bengal famine from 1943 to 1944 could, even under present international law, be labeled as genocide or crimes against humanity.

Human Rights Law

State obligations under conventional international human rights law exist on three levels: the obligation to respect, protect, and fulfill the rights concerned. All these levels are relevant in regard to the prevention of famine. State parties to the International Covenant on Economic, Social and Cultural Rights have recognized under Article 11 of that covenant the right of everyone to adequate food and the fundamental right of freedom from hunger. This establishes a set of obligations on states that, if fully implemented, would prevent famines from arising. These obligations have been clarified in General Comment No. 12 of the UN Committee on Economic, Social and Cultural Rights. (The General Comment can be found at the website of the UN High Commissioner for Human Rights, under Documents, Charter-based bodies, Committee on Economic, Social and Cultural Rights.)

Amartya Sen, probably the leading expert on the study of famines, argues in his 1999 *Development as Freedom* that "appropriate policies and actions can indeed eradicate the terrible problems of hunger in the modern world. Based on recent economic, political and social analysis, it is, I believe, possible to identify the measures that can bring about the elimination of famines and a radical reduction in chronic undernourishment" (p. 160).

It should be added that this would require a general recognition of the responsibility by governments and the international community to ensure the fundamental right of everyone to be free from hunger. This will not only require responsive governments at the national level, making full use of the economic, political, and social insight referred to by Sen, but also a corollary duty of outside states and international organizations to assist the affected states in meeting their responsibility, in line with their commitment under the UN Charter, Articles 55 and 56. This international responsibility is gradually being recognized, although still imperfectly. The World Food Programme and a host of humanitarian organizations, including the Red Cross and Red Crescent, play a major role, but more commitment and coordination will be required to make famines truly a problem of the past.

SEE ALSO Armenians in Ottoman Turkey and the Armenian Genocide; Armenians in Russia and the USSR; Death March; Kulaks; Ukraine (Famine); Union of Soviet Socialist Republics

BIBLIOGRAPHY

Charny, Israel W., ed. (1999). *Encyclopedia of Genocide,* Vols. 1 and 2. Denver, Colo.: ABC-CLIO.

Drèze, Jean, and Amartya Sen, eds. (1989). *Hunger and Public Action.* Oxford: Clarendon Press.

Drèze, Jean, and Amartya Sen, eds. (1991). *The Political Economy of Hunger.* Vol. I: *Entitlement and Well-Being,* Vol. II: *Famine Prevention,* and Vol. III: *Endemic Hunger.* Oxford, U.K.: Clarendon Press.

McDonald, Gabrielle Kirk, and Olivia Swaak-Goldman, eds. (2000). *Substantive and Procedural Aspects of International Criminal Law,* Vols. I–III. The Hague: Kluwer Law International.

Newman, Lucile, ed. (1995). *Hunger in History.* Cambridge, Mass.: Blackwell Publishers.

Ratner, S. S., and Jason S. Abrams, eds. (2001). *Accountability for Human Rights Atrocities in International Law,* 2nd edition. Oxford: Oxford University Press.

Sen, Amartya (1981). *Poverty and Famines.* Oxford: Clarendon Press.

Sen, Amartya (1999). *Development as Freedom.* Oxford: Oxford University Press.

Standing Commitee on Nutrition (2004). *Fifth Report on the World Nutrition Situation.* Geneva: World Health Organization.

Watson, Fiona (November 1999). "Millenium Special: One Hundred Years of Famine." *Field Exchange Online* 6. Available from http://www.ennonline.net/fex/08/index.html.

Woodham-Smith, Cecil (1961). *The Great Hunger: Ireland 1845–1849.* London: Penguin Books.

World Food Programme (2001). *Enabling Development: Food Assistance in South Asia*. Oxford: Oxford University Press.

Asbjørn Eide

Female Infanticide and Fetal Murder

Female infanticide is the intentional killing of an infant, and female feticide (or fetal murder) is the intentional destruction of a fetus for the sole reason that it is female. Historically, female infanticide has occurred on a global scale. Various studies have reported its practice among Arabian tribes, among the Yanomani in Brazil, and in ancient Rome. In nineteenth-century India it was common practice to bury a female child alive by placing her in an earthen pitcher, with cane sugar in her mouth and cotton in her hands. Burying the pitcher in the ground, women would chant, "*Gur kaayeen punee kateen, aap na ayeen bhayee nuu khaleen*" (Eat sugar, weave cotton, don't come back, send your brother). There were many other methods used to kill a female baby: starving her to death, suffocating her by wrapping her tightly in a quilt, poisoning her, strangling her, drowning her, or breaking her spinal cord by snapping it. These methods continue to be used.

In the twenty-first century such practices remain predominant in many Asian and Middle Eastern countries, in sub-Saharan Africa, and within the Asian diaspora in Great Britain, the United States, and Canada. Female infanticide is particularly widespread in India, Nepal, Bangladesh, Pakistan, China, South Korea, Singapore, and Taiwan. In China its origins may be traced back to the first millennium.

Incidence of Practice

Female infanticide and feticide are extreme forms of gender discrimination that occur systematically and threaten to eliminate females in the communities where they are practiced. There are unfortunately no specific or reliable data available on female infanticide or feticide. Both practices happen in a clandestine manner, and no specific provision for documenting them exists in most states' usual statistical mechanisms. In general, the sex ratio imbalance worldwide, with a decreasing number of females for every 1,000 males, may be regarded as an indicator of the prevalence and increase of female infanticide and feticide. The missing status of innumerable women (more than 100 million women are reported to be missing worldwide) points toward female feticide, infanticide, and other forms of gender discrimination as resulting in the high mortality of females at most stages of life. On average 105 women exist for every 100 men, but that number is lower in certain countries: 93 in India and Pakistan, 94 in China, 97 in Egypt and Iran, and 95 in Bangladesh.

Feticide

Female feticide is a recent phenomenon made possible by advances in genetic and information technology. Technology without regulation gives society unlimited access to intrauterine life. Three principal methods have been used for the intrauterine sex determination of the fetus—amniocentesis, chorionic villus sampling, and ultrasound scanning. Ultrasound scanning has become the most common method of fetal sex determination because it is quicker, cheaper, easily available, and noninvasive. It results in no recognized side effects or complications for the fetus or mother. It is often misused in countries with a sociocultural preference for male children.

Feticide is fast becoming a socially acceptable means of dispensing with a female child. A significant change in social attitudes developed in the 1980s and 1990s, with determination tests frequently occurring and subsequent abortions in the case of many female fetuses. The request process for these services is more open, with a decreasing sense of moral crisis attached to it. The arguments for seeking testing and female feticide became a matter of choice rather than of circumstantial compulsion. Ironically, more widespread approval of female feticide now exists in many societies due to the acceptance of monetary arguments, the easy availability and willingness of service providers, the pressures most normally small families face, changing standards and ethics, easier methods of abortion, and the relatively simple killing and disposal of the fetus.

At the start of the twenty-first century many remote areas could claim mobile ultrasound clinics (consisting of portable ultrasound machines installed in a van) that visited periodically to offer their services. Since the identification of a fetus's sex is possible with little training and experience, as compared to other methods, both medical and nonmedical personnel may provide ultrasound services. Quacks and untrained midwives perform the often subsequent abortions in most of these rural areas and within low socioeconomic groups, with enormous health hazards to the mothers.

India, South Korea, China, and most European countries have laws banning fetal sex determination. In most Asian countries, however, such laws are flagrantly ignored, and they have become an instrument of corruption, thereby increasing the costs of safe services.

Explanations for Gender Preference

Traditionally, the major causes of discrimination against the female child have been the son preference rooted in a patriarchal society and the prevalence of dowry. Their lack of education, low financial productivity, and negligible presence in high-profile professions and positions have only added to the devaluation of females. There has been significant improvement in most of these factors except dowry. The escalating pace of globalization in developing countries has coincided with the increase in female feticide and suggests a link that merits critical examination.

In addition to the small family norm, the growing cost of raising a child has contributed to the increased intolerance of female children. Starting from birth, the costs of child rearing are affected by those associated with health care and education, marriage and dowry, and consumerism. When a society with a sociocultural preference for sons finds itself facing conditions that require limiting the family size for various reasons in the absence of preparatory and regulatory mechanisms and policies, then an increase in female infanticide and feticide may be predicted. The female child is increasingly seen as a high input and no output investment, reducing the child to little more than a commodity in the eyes of society.

In India the dowry is one of the major reasons why a female child is often unwanted. The amount and nature of a dowry have changed enormously in the contemporary world. There appears to be a direct link between consumerism, competitive expansion of capitalism, and the increasing economic aspirations brought about by globalization and the escalation in dowry demands and related offenses such as harassment of the bride's family, the acid burning of a bride, and even her murder. The advertisements for sex determination in the 1980s bore slogans like, "Pay five hundred now to save fifty thousand later." The gender-based oppression of women in India starts at birth in the form of infanticide and feticide, and continues to their death in the form of sati (or suttee), a Hindu ritual whereby a wife self-immolates at the funeral pyre of her husband.

The number of female babies killed by feticide is greater than the number killed by infanticide. A debate has emerged as to why an increase in female feticide has occurred despite laws prohibiting it, policies that are supposed to promote the female child and global efforts toward women's empowerment. It gives rise to a discussion of whether the causes thus far identified as making female children unwanted are inclusive of all the factors associated with female infanticide and feticide in the present-day situation. The causes routinely attributed to the increase in female feticide, and the policies adopted by states and civil society, do not address its connection to escalating globalization, thus leaving a large gap between the goals of and actual measures for abolishing female infanticide and feticide.

Consequences

This grave human rights violation of denying birth to a female child or not allowing her to live because she is a female has had a far-reaching impact on society as a whole. It not only affects the communities in which such practices flourish; it also impacts in many ways on the national and international communities where female infanticide and feticide may not occur. Social unrest as a result of the disproportionate female and male gender ratio may manifest itself as crime in these societies, for example, the kidnapping of young women, forced marriages, sex crimes, wife purchasing, frustration-related psychological problems, and an increase in prostitution. Some of these effects have already been reported in China. Increasing female feticide and the continuation of infanticide also pose serious challenges to the international community and its obligation toward women's empowerment and elimination of all forms of discrimination based on sex.

Crime against Humanity

There is emerging debate on addressing female feticide as the murder of female fetuses and acknowledging female feticide and infanticide as crimes against humanity. The pro-choice point of view opposes the consideration of feticide as the murder of a fetus, thus giving rise to the question of fetal "personhood." The condition that differentiates female feticide from abortion is its gender-discriminatory nature. Therefore, female feticide deserves to be treated as a separate category and not viewed in a simplistic way, in terms of the abortion of an unwanted pregnancy.

Female feticide and infanticide are widespread and systematic. Although mothers aborting female fetuses appear to be the perpetrator of the attack, they are actually the victims. Families may seem to choose female feticide and infanticide voluntarily, but it is the onslaught of government policies, sociocultural compulsions, and the effects of globalization directed against the population that often leaves them with no choice and amounts to a systematic attack against the female gender. Government policies that promote female feticide include the small family norm, unregulated genetic technology, an uncontrolled market economy, and unofficial acceptance of female feticide as a means of population control. Knowledge of the fast decreasing numbers of the female population due to feticide and infanticide and corresponding concerns, including threats to the female gender's survival as a result of these practices, continues to grow.

SEE ALSO Children; China; Women, Violence against

BIBLIOGRAPHY

Center for Enquiry into Health and Allied Themes (CEHAT) et al. v. Union of India et al. Petition No. 301, Supreme Court of India (April 4, 2001).

Gu, Baochang, and Krishna Roy (1995). "Sex Ratio at Birth in China, with Reference to Other Areas in East Asia: What We Know." *Asia-Pacific Population Journal* 10(3):17–42.

Maithreyi, Krishnaraj, Ratna M. Sudarshan, and Abusaleh Shariff, eds. (1998). *Gender, Population, and Development.* New York: Oxford University Press.

United Nations. "Harmful Traditional Practices Affecting the Health of Women and Children." Fact Sheet No. 23. Available from http://www.unhchr.ch/html/menu6/2/fs23.htm.

U.S. Department of State (2002). "China (Includes Hong Kong and Macau) Country Reports on Human Rights Practices—2001." Available from http://www.state.gov/g/drl/rls/hrrpt/2001/eap/8289.htm.

Vineeta Gupta

Fiction

Genocide fiction is written for a reason and with an agenda in mind. Motivations for genocide fiction include the search for meaning of an actuality that is not accessible, and the search for a personal and collective identity of first or later generation survivors as part of an effort of coming to terms with or working through the past. Genocide fiction is informed by an effort to promote remembrance, to give voice, to raise awareness, and to deepen a public's understanding of atrocities. Temporal distance from the historical events has been seen to affect the decision to undertake historical fiction rather than memoirs or autobiographical representation as a medium for communication and reflection about atrocities. Survivor authors may write memoirs and histories before turning to fiction in an effort "to establish the historicity of the subject before admitting it to the imagination" (Dekoven, 1980, p. 59) while the memory is still fresh, and decide on more creative storytelling as atrocities move further into the past. Holocaust survivors Anna Langfus, Piotr Rawicz, and Elie Wiesel opted for fiction because it facilitates detachment from suffering and allows for the creation of a new personal and collective identity. Empowered by an agenda to come to terms with the "unmasterable past," to search for meaning, and to reveal "something truthful—about the fragmented self under siege, about memory, about trauma—that may otherwise elude expression" (Horowitz, 1997, p. 24), genocide fiction bridges history, memory, and imagination.

Ida Fink, recipient of the Anne Frank Prize for Literature in 1985 and the Yad Vashem Prize in 1995, is the author of *A Scrap of Time and Other Stories* (1987), *The Journey* (1992), and *Traces* (1997), among other works. She shows in her fictional rendering "A Spring Morning" that fiction can serve to deliver multiple perspectives: Her work renders, on the one hand, a surviving eyewitness report, and on the other, the perspective of its murdered victim. By providing the latter a voice and enabling it to echo throughout the pages of the narrative, the extensive "imaginative intercession into historical reality—the murdered man's life, fate, and feelings, the tragic indignity and the superfluous cruelty of his suffering" counteracts the victim's "radical muteness" consigned to him by his assassins (Horowitz, 1997, p. 14). Genocide fiction gives voice to mute victims; muteness also emerges as an essential behavioral element aimed at enunciating the use of silence as a method of resistance, and serves to vocalize the speechlessness with which atrocities are remembered. In the case of Philip Roth, representation of the void takes the form of ghosts who embody fantastic revivifications of genocide victims and give the writer an opportunity to return to Bruno Schulz and Anne Frank's thoughts, voice, and vision. The inability to heal the wound increases with time, and second or later generations who inherit trauma without personal memory cannot fill the void with knowledge and experience. Second generation Holocaust writers David Grossman (*See Under: Love,* 1986; English translation, 1989) and Spiegelman (*Maus,* 1986) enunciate in their writings the fragmentation of self-identity, and the acknowledgement that complete answers will be found. Holocaust author Henri Raczymow writes empty spaces into the narrative, reinforcing the idea that, although the lack of memory cannot be reconstituted, forgetting is not an option.

It lies within the power of literature to complement, enhance, and affect the memory and understanding of history. In the words of distinguished Latin American writer Mario Vargas Llosa, author of *Conversación en La Catedral* (1969), and *La fiesta del Chivo* (2000), among other works, "The originality of a narrative lies not in what it portrays of the real world but rather in what it reforms or adds to it. . .a reality that, without being reality, being distinct and alternative, asserts itself, in the case of successful narratives, due to its power of persuasion, as the real reality, the authentic, secret reality, reflected in literature" (Rebasa-Soraluz and Chaddick, 1997). A postgenocide generation can access history only through representation and their and others' imaginations; hence, as those generations then take on the task of further enhancing the representation, the question arises of how their representations affect a new memory and enhance or over-power the history closest to the event. As Neil R. Davison emphasizes in 1995, narrative determines history in the present as well as in the past; at the same time, narrative depends on history and literary form.

Each work adds a new perspective, and influences the concept of history as well as the outlook on the future. Julia Alvarez, author of *In the Time of the Butterflies,* found motivation for writing a work of fiction about the Trujillo dictatorship through her interest in understanding the special courage that gave the persecuted the strength to stand up to the terror of the time. Alvarez opted for fictional discourse because neither fact nor legend were within her reach or sufficed to reach her goal of raising consciousness and understanding:

> What you find in these pages are not the Mirabal sisters of fact, or even the Mirabal sisters of legend. The actual sisters I never knew, nor did I have access to enough information. . . . As for the sisters of legend, wrapped in superlatives and ascended into myth, they were finally also inaccessible to me. . . . To Dominicans separated by language from the world I have created, I hope this book deepens North Americans' understanding of the nightmare you endured and the heavy losses you suffered—of which this story tells only a few (1995, p. 324).

With emphasis on the implication of understanding history for the creation of a better future, Jane Yolen in *Devil's Arithmetic* (1988) enables her protagonist to travel back through time to gain an understanding of the experiences of Jewish enslavement and her grandfather's associated peculiar behavior. African American writer Nalo Hopkinson turns to science fiction and fantasy writing about slavery in the hope that African Americans find motivation to fight for a better world. She perceives that African Americans as still straitjacketed by the history of slavery and thus contends: "If black people can imagine our futures, imagine—among other things—cultures in which we aren't alienated; then we can begin to see our way clear to creating them" (Davison, 1995, p. 589). Some critics nevertheless caution against such a positivistic approach, although it is reflected in many writings. As Efraim Sicher states,

> There is thus both awesome responsibility and ironic ambivalence in imagining the past in order to remember the future. There can indeed be no future without the past, but, when remembrance relies on imagination to give it meaning, one must be aware of the risks that are involved (2000, p. 84).

Despite the strong affirmation that genocide is indeed unrepresentable, representing the unrepresentable may be attempted through fiction. The fictional representation of genocide history, according to Sicher, enunciates the "fragmentation of the self, to the relativity of truth, to the fluidity of memory and to the impossibility of ever fully knowing. . . . Narrative recreates different identities and acts out in fantasy form repressed stories which test the freedom or dependence of the individual vis-à-vis the past" suggesting a relationship with the victim or survivor (2000, p. 81). Fictional renderings of genocide have been considered especially successful in eliciting imaginative responses from readers and in serving as a bridge between the Holocaust and the contemporary reader, affirming the event's historical import. Genocide fiction can compel reader response to pain and suffering and summon the imaginative empathy of affinity with the other. In the words of John Hersey, author of the 1950 book *The Wall* (1950), "Imagination would not serve; only memory could serve. To salvage anything that would be worthy of the subject, I had to invent a memory" (Hartman, 1999, p. 66). The combination of emotional and imaginative engagement of the reader coupled with factual consistency, such as that achieved in Charlotte Delbo's *None of Us Will Return,* Susan Schaeffer's *Anya,* and Livia Jackson's *Elli,* capture the experience of victimization through the lyrical use of prose that enhances the presentation of emotions and thereby serves to augment the reader's involvement with the novel. Fictional poetic discourse, sustained by historical facts and data, may facilitate a meaningful and imaginative personal memory that approaches genocide memory and provides the latter an opportunity to endure in spite of time and place.

Techniques in genocide fiction are multifold and often contest previous fictional conventions as these texts "make imagination serve fact rather than the reverse. . .to provide a narrative perspective and to make the facts. . .more accessible to the senses" (Heinemann, 1986, p. 118). Perhaps in direct correlation to the notion that "too much fiction can make a fool of history" (Kearney, 2002, p. 57), genocide fiction is marked by authenticating devices such as imitation of a memoir through first-person narrators, authorial voice attributes in prefaces or introductions, as well as the incorporation of documentation, reportage, and diaries, similar persons, patterns, or incidents to suggest that the information is drawn primarily from survivor and historical evidence. Nevertheless, the recurrence of statements attesting to an essential truthfulness in fiction on atrocities in history, which suggests that the achievement of historical discourse is ultimately a condition aspired to even within the context of genocide fiction, does not necessarily signify apprehension about this choice of discourse by writers of fiction.

Many works of fiction specifically identify themselves as fiction and request to be read as such, regardless of the historical accuracy of events, and circumstances, or the similarity between the experiences of the survivor author and those of the fictional protagonist. Wiesel's novel *Night* is by some referred to as a light fiction due to the apparent connection between Wiesel's own sufferings as a five-year-old boy in Buchenwald and his fictional account of the five-year-old protagonist's struggles in the Nazi death camp. The author negates testimonial validity of the work because, despite the influences of the personal experience on the narrative, it remains a result of his creative imagination. Fictionality provides the author with more control over the representation and message; in genocide fiction, imagination may serve fact in presenting a particular perspective of the event and incorporating testimonial conventions. To give voice to experiences in the Warsaw ghetto, Raczymow incorporates a fictional diary into his narrative that transposes autobiographical information with that of other fictional as well as historical characters, and interweaves actual and fictional events and personal experiences. However, to emphasize the fictionality of the work and to undermine the effect of authenticity rendered through the incorporation of certain devices, Raczymow disrupts the consideration of unmediated testimonial function by signaling the mimetic distance of the diary he incorporates as twice removed from anyone's actual experience (Zeitlin, 1998, p. 9). Because genocide fiction does not pretend to serve as a historical document, Alvarez confirms,

> I sometimes took liberties—by changing dates, by reconstructing events, and by collapsing characters or incidents. For I wanted to immerse my readers in an epoch in the life of the Dominican Republic that I believe can only finally be understood by fiction, only finally be redeemed by the imagination. A novel is not, after all, a historical document; but a way to travel through the human heart (1995, p. 324).

In genocide fiction the protagonist's fate is handcrafted by a writer who integrates elements from history to enhance and shape the plot, yet manipulates circumstances, folds events, merges characters, and manipulates circumstances to reinforce a particular reading of the interrelationship between people, time, place, as well as fate. An author's decision on how to end a novel involves consideration of resolution and closure; generally, it also involves a question of hope. However, in most genocide fiction, hope, like the protagonist, is inexorably tied to a final demise. Echoing an absolute lack of hope, Pierre Gascar's "The Seasons of the Dead" evokes "a haze of fearfulness and disbe-

lief," facing "death without coffins, without reasons, without rituals, without witnesses," and culminates in the realization passed on to the reader that the pain and grief will find no closure (Howe, 1988, pp. 191, 196). Nevertheless, a contrasting image is advanced in some children's and junior literature with the tendency to overwrite the impossibility of hope through an open ending, thereby inviting the thought that a particular protagonist might possibly have escaped the claws of the very event that earned it the name of genocide. Novels with open or optimistic endings have become more frequent with the increased publication of escape, rescue, and survival accounts involving children, such as Antonio Skármeta's *Nothing Happened* (1980), Christa Laird's *But Can the Phoenix Sing?* (1993); Malka Drucker and Michael Halperin's *Jacob's Rescue* (1993), Vivian Vande Velde's *A Coming Evil* (1998), and Julia Alvarez's *Before We Were Free* (2002).

Sidra DeKoven Ezrahi confirms that

> the distorted image of the human form which the artist might present as but a mirror of nature transformed can hardly be contained within the traditional perimeters of mimetic art, because, although Holocaust literature is a reflection of recent history, it cannot draw upon the timeless archetypes of human experience and human behavior which can render unlived events familiar through the medium of the imagination (1980, p. 9).

Schwarz-Bart's *The Last of the Just* echoes this notion that within the context of genocide, legend, myth, and folktale do not suffice to establish an authenticity effect. His novel depends on authenticity devices for the "cohesiveness and historiographical implications of its story-telling" until the novel's timeline approaches the Holocaust and the narrative is overtaken by, initially rather general and later specific, significant Holocaust phenomena and events (Davison, 1995, p. 294). Genocide fiction can extend beyond the traditional concept of fiction and attain the status of a cultural and social document by providing an insight into genocide horrors and dimensions by creating a literary memory "whose meaning will endure" through "a narrating consciousness who makes sense out of the confusion of history and makes the reader imagine being there" (Sicher, 2000, p. 66). In that respect genocide fiction can contribute toward a postmemory that is connected to the atrocities of the past, perhaps primarily through imagination and literary creativity rather than remembrance.

Unlike authoritarian regimes "that attempt to impose a singular 'reading' of the human condition," literature through its "multifarious coherence" is "always provisional and never final" (Tierney-Tello, 1996, p. 4); at the same time, literature also provides voice to multi-faceted interpretations and agendas. Consequently, many scholars, historians, victims, witnesses of atrocities, and others, who seek to remember history as it was and to ensure that certain events will never occur again, caution against free-ranging representation of these horrors, as with each representation one may indeed move further and further away from historical fact. Genocide fiction enables people to represent the past as they visualize it or to "reinvent it as it might have been" (Kearney, 2002, p. 69), to inform others about their interpretation as well as to help others remember. However, the very fact that revisionists and fascists in many instances of genocide have sought to rewrite history in an effort to deny or downplay its significance and horrors keeps critics and readers on the lookout for distorted representation. Argumentation against employing fiction as a means of representing the Holocaust and, in extension, any genocide, includes Lanzmann's affirmation of the impossibility to communicate absolute horror. However, the unrepresentability per se of genocide is not contradicted by genocide fiction and its intent to present what was or might have been and to facilitate remembrance. Genocide fiction requires a delicate balance between "a historical fidelity to truth (respecting the distance of the past as it was in the past) and an aesthetic fidelity to imaginative vivacity and credibility (presenting the past as if it were the present)" in order to serve genocide by "an aesthetic" that matches historical triumph in terms of intensity and impact and that may even require exceeding the latter in an effort to "compete for the attention of the public at large" (Kearney, 2002, p. 60). Due to genocide fiction's particular strength in engaging the reader and eliciting imaginative responses by serving as a bridge between the historical event and experience and the present, genocide fiction may serve to affirm rather than erase the historical import.

SEE ALSO Biographies; Diaries; Memoirs of Survivors; Wiesel, Elie

BIBLIOGRAPHY

Alvarez, Julia (1995). *In the Time of the Butterflies.* New York: Penguin Books.

Davison, Neil R. (1995). "Inside the 'Shoah': Narrative, Documentation, and Schwarz-Bart's 'The Last of the Just.'" *CLIO* 24(3):291–322.

Dekoven, Ezrahi Sidra (1980). *By Words Alone: The Holocaust in Literature.* Chicago: University of Chicago Press.

Fine, Ellen S. (1988). "The Absent Memory: The Act of Writing in Post-Holocaust French Literature." In *Writing and the Holocaust,* ed. Berel Lang. New York: Holmes & Meier.

Hartman, Geoffrey H. (1999). "Public Memory and Modern Experience." In *A Critic's Journey. Literary Reflections, 1958–1998,* ed. Geoffrey H. Hartman. New Haven, Conn.: Yale University Press.

Heinemann, Marlene E. (1986). *Gender and Destiny: Women Writers and the Holocaust.* New York: Greenwood Press.

Hirsch, Marianne (1997). *Family Frames: Photography, Narrative, and Postmemory.* Cambridge, Mass.: Harvard University Press.

Horowitz, Sara R. (1997). *Voicing the Void: Muteness and Memory in Holocaust Fiction.* Albany: State University of New York Press.

Howe, Irving (1988). "Writing and the Holocaust." In *Writing and the Holocaust,* ed. Berel Lang. New York: Holmes & Meier.

Kearney, Richard (2002). *On Stories, Thinking in Action.* New York: Routledge.

Lang, Berel, ed. (1988). *Writing and the Holocaust.* New York: Holmes & Meier.

Lehmann, Sophia (1998). "'And Here [Their] Troubles Began': The Legacy of the Holocaust in the Writing of Cynthia Ozick, Art Spiegelman, and Philip Roth." *CLIO* 28(1):29–52.

Rebasa-Soraluz, Luis, and Larisa Chaddick (1997). "Demons and Lies: Motivation and Form in Mario Vargas Llosa." *The Review of Contemporary Fiction* 17(1):15–24.

Rutledge, Gregory E. (1999). "Speaking in Tongues: An Interview with Science Fiction Writer Nalo Hopkinson." *African American Review* 33(4):589–601.

Sicher, Efraim (2000). "The Future of the Past: Countermemory and Postmemory in Contemporary American Post-Holocaust Narratives." *History and Memory* 12(2):56–91.

Tierney-Tello, Mary Beth (1996). *Allegories of Transgression and Transformation: Experimental Fiction by Women Writing Under Dictatorship.* Albany: State University of New York Press.

Unnold, Yvonne S. (2002). *Representing the Unrepresentable: Literature of Trauma in Chile.* New York: Peter Lang.

Zeitlin, Froma I. (1998). "The Vicarious Witness: Belated Memory and Authorial Presence in Recent Holocaust Literature." *History and Memory* 10(2):5–42.

Yvonne S. Unnold

Film as Propaganda

Visual media have been exploited to serve genocide and crimes against humanity. They have perpetuated racial and ethnic hatreds, targeted political opponents, aggrandized the national image of regimes, and portrayed the nation as a victim of evil, outside forces. The Nazis were the penultimate masters in this regard—usurping the German film industry, creating a ministry to assure that films served the Reich, and recruiting film directors to enhance Hitler's power and present frightening images of Germany's perceived enemies. Similarly, other nations have employed visual media to support the political values of genocidal and criminal regimes. They also routinely use censorship to guarantee the absence of countervailing visual images.

Nazi control of the German film industry is the most extreme example of the use of film in the service of a fascist national program. Prior to Hitler's rise to power, Germany had a lively, creative film community in which many Jewish actors, directors, and producers were active participants. However, in 1933 Hitler created the Reich Ministry for People's Enlightenment and Propaganda and appointed the youthful Joseph Goebbels as its head. He had the authority to decide which films could be produced; the ministry reviewed scripts, decided which actors, directors, and screenwriters worked, and controlled the content and imagery of films. Film criticism was banned, and Jews were forbidden to work in the film industry. In the Nazi's media dictatorship film was its most important tool.

Early films promoted the consolidation of the German people in the service of the Nazi state. One of the first productions in 1933, *Hitler Youth Quex,* depicted a young man's transformation from a communist sympathizer to a servant of the Hitler Youth movement and the "new" Germany. In a visceral sense he became the political property of the state, no longer needing to be an autonomous individual.

Triumph of the Will, the 1935 documentary by Leni Riefenstahl, was created in the same vein. The film eschews references to Jews, Romani, homosexuals, or political opponents that the Nazis would be jailing and murdering in the coming years. Instead, the film focuses on visual imagery of a united, joyful German people and the powerful control of public space exerted by the Third Reich. The film, utilizing thirty-six cinematographers, captured the drama and triumph of the 1934 Nazi Party meetings in Nuremberg. In its repetitive images of smiling, young Aryan men, perfectly aligned marching German soldiers, fluttering swastika flags, and Adolf Hitler, alighting from the sky as a godlike figure, *Triumph* conveys a powerful, seductive message on the sacrifice of the individual for the good of the revitalized, collective whole, as represented in the person of Hitler.

In the years that followed Nazi film production shifted its focus to overt propaganda against perceived enemies. Perhaps the most profound exemplar was the 1940 production of *Jud Suss,* a viciously anti-Semitic film, directed by Viet Harlan. It was screened for SS commandos before missions against the Jews and for concentration camp guards; over twenty million people are said to have seen the film. Its story—set in the eighteenth century—was billed as history. The protagonist, Joseph Suss Oppenheimer, is portrayed as a deceitful, treacherous Jew, who lusts after power, money, and sex. At the film's finale Oppenheimer's final defeat and public execution are a prelude to the film's cautionary message, urging its audience to heed the film's lessons in order to spare future generations from exploitation by the Jews. The documentary *The Eternal Jew* mirrored similar themes of Jews as duplicitous and toxic. At the end of World War II Harlan was the only German film director to be charged with crimes against humanity. Although the film was condemned, the director was exonerated, his defense successfully arguing that in making such a film, he was only following Goebbels's orders.

Since the Nazi period other abusive regimes have utilized visual media in the service of criminal ends. In Yugoslavia the 1989 film *The Battle of Kosovo,* commemorating the battle's six hundredth anniversary, portrayed a Serbian hero sacrificing his own life, but simultaneously taking that of the Turkish sultan. Dark, scary images of Muslim invaders are pervasive. The Bulgarian film *Time of Violence* traded on similar violent, cruel images of the Turkish invasion and the suffering of the Slavs. Documentaries, such as the 1994 *The Truth Is a Victim in Croatia,* were thinly disguised propaganda films on Croatian victimization of the Serbs. Television also was utilized to these ends by masters of media manipulation and control, such as Slobodan Milosevic. In regular television appearances Milosevic and other Serbian leaders usurped and inverted the language of genocide—decrying that their kinsfolk in Kosovo were the victims—even as they covertly planned their own genocidal campaign in Bosnia.

In El Salvador, under military control in the 1980s, the lack of a film industry made television the medium of choice for labeling regime opponents. Roberto D'Aubuisson, a former major in the Salvadoran military, procured the dossiers of hundreds of political activists subject to government surveillance. In early 1980 he staged a series of dramatic television appearances in which he denounced these academics, clergymen, trade unionists, and others as guerrilla sympathizers, subversives, and communists. He used these appearances to launch his own political career as the demagogic voice of the extreme right wing. And in the weeks following his appearances, many of those named were assassinated.

Though she later tried to minimize her collaboration with the Nazis, an ebullient Leni Riefenstahl is received by Adolf Hitler and Joseph Goebbels, April 29, 1938. Riefenstahl, who first heard Hitler speak in 1932 and was dazzled, made propaganda films at his behest.
[BETTMANN/CORBIS]

Censorship has also assisted such regimes in obscuring truthful histories, objective realities, and the genocidal actions of the government. For example, soon after the 1973 military coup in Chile, a censorship decree led to the banning of hundreds of films. In his documentary *The Battle of Chile,* Patricio Guzman, the Chilean filmmaker, realistically captured the increasing violence of right-wing opposition to Salvador Allende, the military takeover, and the final words of the democratically elected president. But Guzman was forced to smuggle the film out of the country, and it was not shown until after Augusto Pinochet's dictatorship ended.

The precise impact of propagandistic imagery on the popular imagination can never be fully measured. Nevertheless, there is no question that the media play an important role in sustaining criminal regimes and fostering cultures that support the commission of crimes against humanity and genocide.

SEE ALSO Advertising; Art as Propaganda; Deception, Perpetrators; Goebbels, Joseph; Propaganda; Television

BIBLIOGRAPHY

"Chile: End to Film Censorship." Available from http://www.indexonline.org/indexindes20021104_chile.shtml.

Gow, James, Richard Paterson, and Alison Preston, eds. (1996). *Bosnia by Television.* London: British Film Institute.

Iordanova, Dina (2001). *Cinema of Flames: Balkan Film, Culture and the Media.* London: British Film Institute.

Nairn, Allan (1984). "Behind the Death Squads." *The Progressive* May: 20–29.

Rentschler, Eric (1996). *The Ministry of Illusion Nazi Cinema and Its Afterlife.* Cambridge, Mass.: Harvard University Press.

Riefenstahl, Leni (1935). *The Triumph of the Will.* Connoisseur Video Collection.

Thompson, Mark (1999). *Forging War: The Media in Serbia, Croatia, Bosnia and Hercegovina.* Luton, England: University of Luton (England) Press.

"The Battle of Chile (Part 1 & 2). A Film by Patricio Guzman." Available from http://www.frif.com/new98/boc.html.

Carolyn Patty Blum

Films, Armenian Documentary

Seventeen films that document the Armenian genocide of 1915—all of them in English—have been made. This paucity of films about the Armenian genocide is owing to a paucity of certain types of documenting materials, which may be ascribed to several factors: the strict censorship in Ottoman Turkey at the time of the genocide, which prohibited the photographing of expulsions and death marches; the general absence of investigative reporters in war zones (which included parts of the Ottoman Turkish Empire) during World War I; and the scarcity of foreign consular agents and officials (who might have served as witnesses).

Nonetheless, a limited number of still photographs (of genocidal events in the making) managed to reach the outside world, owing to the efforts of Christian missionaries living in Turkey—and those of German civilians and soldiers who photographed events clandestinely. Two sources of photographic documentation were Armin T. Wegner, a German Red Cross official, and Leslie A. Davis, a U.S. consular agent in the interior of the Armenian provinces of Turkey. No motion picture footage of the deportations or the slaughters has ever been located.

Despite these handicaps the first documentary film on the genocidal events of 1915 and 1916 was produced in 1965. *Where Are My People?* is a vehicle for the expression of a plaintive voice, a voice of bereavement and sorrow—over the extermination of a people and the loss of nationhood. The film relies heavily on still photographs, lithographs, paintings, and excerpts from books about the genocide. The potency of the film derives from the strength and poetry of its narrative and its use of Armenian musical themes. A Turkish scholar, Sedat Laciner (who denies the genocide), writing in 2003 described *Where Are My People?* as a "classic film."

The Republic of Turkey (established 1923), in keeping with its policy of denial vis-à-vis the Armenian genocide, responded immediately to the release of the film and assigned persona non grata status to the producer of *Where Are My People?* From its inception the Republic of Turkey has maintained that there was no mass murder of Armenians—only incidental suffering and death among both Turks and Armenians, the results of a civil war. Owing to political and economic pressure placed on the United States by the Turkish government, the United States has not yet recognized the Armenian genocide, and until the late 1990s, members of the U.S. media often used the term "alleged" to describe the catastrophic events of 1915 and 1916. As evidence of the pressure that has been placed on the United States by the Turkish government, no Hollywood-type feature film on the subject of the Armenian genocide has ever been produced in the United States. *Ararat* (2003), a film by Atom Egoyan, was a Canadian-sponsored (fictional) dramatic film.

Where Are My People?—coming as it did on the fiftieth anniversary of the Armenian genocide—launched an era of political activism and awareness of the enormous calamity that had befallen Armenian people. The anger felt by descendants of Armenians of the Armenian diaspora—at the Turks, at the world, and even at parents who had remained timid and voiceless for five decades—produced demonstrations at major Turk embassies and assassinations of Turkish diplomats in Southern California. Armenian study programs and endowed chairs and professorships in Armenian studies sprang up at major U.S. universities; Armenian studies research institutes came into being, and by the late 1980s scholarly monographs on the subject of the Armenian genocide began to be published.

The year 1976 ushered in the production of the companion films *The Forgotten Genocide* and *The Armenian Case* (which contains a seventeen-minute epilogue about post–World War I events). *The Forgotten Genocide* is a highly acclaimed film and has won film festival awards and two Emmy nominations. It is perhaps the definitive film on the Armenian genocide. Both films employ the traditional documentary film elements of comments and testimony by scholars and witnesses, still photographs, film footage of events related to the Armenian diaspora following the genocide, and maps. Both films use an expository mode of presentation to lay out the "anatomy" of the Armenian genocide; both films call on the Turkish nation to accept responsibility, and on the wider world to recognize that genocide and crimes against humanity were committed.

The Armenian Genocide, commissioned in 1990 by the California Board of Education, is the first film of its kind intended for use in school curricula. The target audience of the twenty-five-minute film is tenth-grade students. The film includes dramatic reenactment of historic events; it also uses historical cartoons, diagrams, and segments of filmed student discussions.

Five films that appeared at the turn of the twenty-first century (all of them by non-Armenian filmmakers) are worth noting. *I Will Not Be Sad in This World* (2001) follows the daily life of a ninety-four-year-old survivor of the Armenian genocide; its setting is present-day, but there is some use of old photographs in the film. *A Wall of Silence* (1997) traces out the passionate involvement of two scholars—one Armenian and one Turkish—in historical investigation of the Armenian genocide, and focuses on their quest to attain recognition of the genocide by the Turkish government. *The Armenians: A Story of Survival* (2001) and *The Great War and the Shaping of the Twentieth Century* (1997), documentary films about Armenian history and World War I, respectively, both have short sequences about the Armenian genocide. *The Hidden Holocaust* (1992) is perhaps the most impressive of this cluster of films. It resembles *The Forgotten Genocide* (1976) in respect to methods of research used, content, and tone. An advantage that these films have enjoyed over their forerunners is that they have reached larger audiences.

In 2000 another advance was made in the collective effort to document the Armenian genocide. The film *Voices from the Lake* was innovative in that it focused on a small pocket of the Armenian genocide, and examined this small pocket from a multitude of vantage points—through the eyes and via the reports of several witnesses. *Germany and the Secret Genocide* (2003) was similarly innovative; the film focused on the Berlin-Baghdad Railway and specific historical German documents as it sought to emphasize the closeness of the Armenian genocide to other genocides.

SEE ALSO Films, Armenian Feature; Films, Dramatizations in; Films, Holocaust Documentary

BIBLIOGRAPHY

The Armenian Case (1976). Atlantis Productions, Inc. Directed and produced by J. Michael Hagopian. Distributed by Atlantis Productions.

The Armenian Genocide (1991). Atlantis Productions, Inc. Directed and produced by J. Michael Hagopian. Distributed by Atlantis Productions.

An Armenian Journey (1997). WGBH Boston. Directed by Theodore Bogosian.

Back to the Ararat (1988). HB Peá Holmquist. Produced by Peá Holmquist. Distributed by First Run/Icarus Films. Available from http://www.lib.Berkeley.edu/MRC/BacktoArarat.html.

Bryce, James, and Arnold Toynbee (2000). *The Treatment of the Armenians in the Ottoman Empire, 1915-1916.* London: Gomidas Institute.

Dadrian, Vahakn N. (1995). *The History of the Armenian Genocide.* Providence, R.I.: Berghan Books.

Dadrian, Vahakn N. (1996). *German Responsibility in the Armenian Genocide.* Watertown, Mass.: Blue Crane Books.

Dadrian, Vahakn N. (1999). *Warrant for Genocide: Key Elements of the Turko-Armenian Conflict.* New Brunswick, N.J.: Transaction Publishers.

Destination Nowhere (1997). Gruppo BL and Forum Pictures. Directed by Carlos Massa.

Everyone's Not Here: Families of the Armenian Genocide (1988). Armenian Assembly of America. Executive producers John McGannon and William Parson. Distributed by Intersection Association.

Forgotten Genocide (1976). Atlantis Productions, Inc. Directed and produced by J. Michael Hagopian. Distributed by Atlantis Productions.

Germany and the Secret Genocide (2003). Armenian Film Foundation. Directed and produced by J. Michael Hagopian. Distributed by the Armenian Film Foundation.

The Great War and the Shaping of the Twentieth Century (1997). KCET/BBC with the Imperial War Museum. Directed by Lyn Goldfarb and Carl Byker. Produced by Lyn Goldfarb and David Mrazek.

The Hidden Holocaust (1992). Panoptic Productions, Ltd. Directed and produced by Michael Jones.

Hovannisian, Richard, ed. (1999). *Remembrance and Denial, The Case of the Armenian Genocide.* Detroit, Mich.: Wayne State University Press.

Laciner, Sedat (2003). "Identity, Art and Propaganda: The Armenian Film Industry as a Case Study." *Review of Armenian Studies* 1(2).

Morgenthau, Henry (2000). *Ambassador Morgenthau's Story.* London: Gomidas Institute.

Voices from the Lake (2000). Armenian Film Foundation. Directed and produced by J. Michael Hagopian. Distributed by the Armenian Film Foundation.

A Wall of Silence: The Unspoken Fate of the Armenians (1997). Humanist Broadcasting Foundation, The Netherlands. Produced and directed by Dorothée Forma. Distributed by the Humanist Broadcasting Foundation. Available from http://www.omroep.nl/human/tv/muur/welcome.htm.

Where Are My People? (1965). Atlantis Productions, Inc. Distributed by Atlantis Productions.

J. Michael Hagopian

Films, Armenian Feature

Any act of tyranny or terror involves a dehumanizing of the "other"—the individual or group upon which the act is perpetrated. Can a work of art that depicts an act

The novel *Mayrig* and the film of the same name, both by Henri Verneuil, are semifictional and autobiographical. The story is about Armenian refugees struggling to build lives in France in the wake of the genocide of 1915. The Armenian word *mayrig means* "mother."
[RIEN/CORBIS SYGMA]

of terror ever serve to counter this effect? If an act of genocide is only made possible by the abstraction of other human beings, can a film about genocide serve to rectify this violence? While it is certainly clear that there is a disparity between the horror of man's inhumanity to man and the uneasy alchemy that occurs when one combines elements of cinema and atrocity, it is also obvious that we live in a world where the currency of images is crucial to our understanding of any historic event. Who has the authority—be it moral, spiritual, or artistic—to tell a story of horror? And who decides if this story of horror can even be told?

The best-known novel to deal with the Armenian Genocide was written by an Austrian Jew, Franz Werfel, in 1933. *The Forty Days of the Musa Dagh* was translated into over twenty languages and became an international best-seller. The novel is about the siege of the mountain village of Musa Dagh, where a group of exhausted and poorly armed Armenians were able to resist a Turkish attack for forty days before being rescued by French warships. Its potential as a Hollywood epic was immediately seized upon, yet despite repeated attempts by Metro-Goldwyn-Mayer (MGM) to translate

this important story to the screen, Turkish pressure on the U.S. State Department prevented the film from ever being made.

Besides some scenes dealing with the Armenian Genocide in Elia Kazan's 1963 classic *America, America*, the historic event was not really touched upon again until the French-Armenian director Henri Verneuil (born Ashot Malakian, the son of genocide survivors), told his autobiographical version of the event in his 1991 film *Mayrig*, starring Omar Sharif and Claudia Cardinale. Despite the presence of these stars and a substantial production budget, *Mayrig* failed to find international theatrical exposure. Indeed, the only other dramatic feature films that have dealt with the aftereffects of this trauma—Don Askarian's *Komitas* and Henrik Malian's *Nahapet*—have received only limited distribution, despite their artistic merits.

In both these later films, the viewer is engaged by the eponymous survivors as they try to deal with the burning memories of the genocide. *Nahapet* (the very name means the head of a large family group) is seen at the beginning of the film as he crosses the border from historic Western Armenia into the fledgling Cau-

It is this very denial of the genocide which was to become the central theme of my film, *Ararat*, which was produced in 2002. In this film, an aging French-Armenian film director (a reference to Henri Verneuil, played by the legendary French-Armenian singer Charles Aznavour) arrives in Canada to shoot his old-fashioned interpretation of another heroic event in Armenian genocide history—the siege of the city of Van. Intercut with staged scenes from this film-within-a-film, various contemporary characters interact in relation to their roots, their family problems, and the lingering effects of ancient history on their modern lives.

The structure of the film is multi-layered and complex, showing how history is often created from the effort to accommodate differing accounts of the same event. By interweaving the stories of different families and different generations, I wanted to show how the stories of the survivors passed onto children and grandchildren create a collective human linkage of experience. *Ararat* is a film about the trans-mission of trauma, and is the first film dealing with the Armenian Genocide that has been internationally distributed, having been theatrically released in over thirty countries around the world since its premiere at the Cannes Film Festival.

In making *Ararat* I was aware that any film dealing with this historic event would be accused, from a Turkish point of view of perpetrating stereotypes. Indeed—as of this printing—the film has been prevented from screening in Turkey, despite the efforts of a Turkish distributor who bought the film for release in that country in 2003. While *Ararat* certainly shows scenes of extreme cruelty and torture, these stories—from an Armenian perspective—are part of any upbringing. The barbaric and vicious imagery is very real. In this context, the challenge of telling the story of *Ararat* was threefold: First of all I had to find a way of presenting the strongest and most persistent of cultural beliefs with which I had been raised. Secondly, I needed to examine and question the drives and sources that determined those beliefs. And finally, I had to show the emotional foundations of those beliefs as they persist in our culture today.

Like many in my community, I await a traditional large-budget film that will set the record straight. But it is important to stress that the mere production of this film will not assure its distribution, as evidenced by Verneuil's *Mayrig*. I believe that the success of *Ararat* is based on its ability to find a compelling way of dramatically presenting the most distinct aspect of the Armenian Genocide: its complete denial by the Turkish perpetrator. This, undoubtedly, is the most painful source of continuing confusion and trauma.

---

casian state. His memories come flooding back throughout the film, most poetically in a flashback where hundreds of red apples fall off a gigantic tree (or family tree) into the banks of a river, where they rot, turning the sky-blue water into blood. Eye-witness accounts tell of thousands of bodies floating down the river Euphrates during the genocide, and Malian's cinematic interpretation of this horror is stunning in its beauty and restraint.

Askarian's *Komitas* is a highly charged and visually impressive piece of filmmaking. Highly influenced by the transcendent style of the Russian master Andrei Tarkovsky, it tells the true story of an Armenian priest and musicologist who survives the genocide, only to spend the later part of his life in an asylum, unable to overcome his deep psychic wounds. It is interesting to note that in both these later films the references to the perpetrators of these crimes, the Ottoman Government of Turkey, are muted and vague. In the case of *Nahapet*, which was produced by the Soviet regime, this may have been a calculated attempt not to offend subsequent Turkish governments, none of which have ac-cepted the guilt of this crime against humanity. At no point in Malian's film is the word "Turkish" ever mentioned, thought the murderers are visually identified.

SEE ALSO Film as Propaganda; Films, Armenian Documentary; Films, Dramatizations in; Films, Holocaust Documentary

BIBLIOGRAPHY

Egoyan, Atom (2002). *Ararat. The Shooting Script.* New York: Newmarket Press.

Werfel, Franz (1934). *The Forty Days of Musa Dagh.* New York: Viking.

Atom Egoyan

Films, Dramatizations in

Ever since Thomas A. Edison said, "I am experimenting upon an instrument which does for the eye what the phonograph does for the ear which is the recording and reproduction of things in motion," the human race has remained fascinated with its portrayal in film. This wonderful pairing of sight and sound has allowed the chronicalling of the events of the past century. However, the images a person sees has everything to do with the eye of the beholder. Film is a director's medium and every frame shot overtly or covertly represents his or her personal prejudices, values, and esthetics. Every camera angle, every light and shadow, every word whispered or screamed, every close-up or long shot, every note of music occurs at the discretion of the director.

How then does a director set about making a film based on historic events so horrific that to avert one's eyes is the natural response? It is an enormous challenge, especially because in reproducing these images, there is something inherently false in acting out such brutality. One can only imagine what an actual survivor of the Holocaust must feel to see what looks like blood on disinterested extras waiting to perform the next scene. How does one show the darkest side of humanity and respect its victims? What is the appropriate response? How does one make a film that is palatable to a mass audience yet expose the severity of the crimes of its perpetrators? There is no template, no perfect film. To assume documentary filmmakers make a more authentic film is to forget that they are also peering through the eyepiece of the camera seeking the best shot to tell their story. Here, is an examination of several films on the Holocaust, many of them made by U.S. directors, and other genocides. Each film is an expression of the cinematic artist, the director, who fills a darkened room with images that become his or her signature on celluloid. These films speak for the silent, the dead, and those that lived, to tell their stories in the hope that moviegoers in viewing these images, however disturbing and shocking, will cling more tightly to that which is good and moral and just.

The Great Dictator

Charlie Chaplin and Adolf Hitler were born four days apart, with the "Little Tramp" arriving on April 16 and Hitler on April 20 in 1889. Chaplin, although British by birth, was a pioneer in the American film industry. Hitler admired Chaplin until the director satirized him in his 1940s masterpiece, *The Great Dictator*. It is worthy of note that when this film was made, the United States stood neutral as France and Belgium fell to the Nazis, and Hollywood, in turn, remained neutral too. In the more than five hundred films made during World War II, only *The Great Dictator* specifically addressed events in Europe. Why would Chaplin, best known for his silent films, make such a movie? Why did he choose to invest over $1 million of his own money to make this, his first talking picture? One may speculate that Chaplin's Jewish wife, Paulette Goddard

(born Goddard Levy), might have had something to do with his decision. *The Great Dictator* was written and directed by Chaplin; the movie starred Chaplin and his wife.

There is no doubt that Chaplin, ever the genius, saw the potential for satire in the highly influential Nazi propaganda film, *The Triumph of Will* (1934), directed by Leni Rienfenstahl. Shot during the Sixth Party Congress in Nuremberg, with powerful black-and-white images of marching troops foreshadowing the coming war, the film shows all the Nazi archetypes in attendance: Hitler, Hermann Göring, Joseph Goebbels, Heinrich Himmler, and Rudolf Hess, to name but a few.

With their matching mustaches, Chaplin and Hitler become cinematic doppelgängers, and this makes Chaplin's performance as the tyrannical dictator inspired. Chaplin also carries the look-alike further by playing a Jewish barber. In one of the more unforgettable scenes in the film, Chaplin as Hynkel the dictator plays with a globe, tossing it up and down; in a demented and almost balletlike sequence of steps, he bounces the globe from his rear until it bursts. In the film a double cross takes the place of the Nazi swastika, and Hynkel spares no one, including Mussolini who is reborn as Benzini Napaloni of "Bacteria."

Chaplin's film addressed the events of the day, showing the displacement of the Jews, the burning of ghettos, and resistance attempts. Mistaken identity as a vehicle for comedy is as old as the Greeks, and it works once again as Chaplin, as the Jewish barber, is mistaken for Hynkel. At the film's end in a moment of solemnity Chaplin seems to urge brotherhood, triumph over fascism, and world peace. Some critics dismissed the ending as it contrasted so starkly with the film's preceding lunacy, but given the subject matter, Chaplin obviously felt compelled to speak his mind. Chaplin later stated that had he known the extent of the Jews' persecution, he would have never satirized it. As for Hitler, a record of his having seen the film does exist; not surprisingly, he had it banned, as did two other dictators, Mussolini and Francisco Franco.

Life Is Beautiful

Life Is Beautiful (1997, in Italian *La Vita è Bella*) takes its cue from Chaplin. Roberto Benigni plays the clownlike character who tries to protect his son from the horrors of the Nazis. Benigni, like Chaplin, wrote, directed, and costarred with his wife (in Benigni's case, Nicoletta Braschi). Benigni has the same wiry frame as Chaplin and makes comic use of his body. The first half of the film is extremely humorous, depicting the madcap adventures of the loving and lovable Benigni as Guido Orefice, a man with a beautiful wife and adorable son.

Some critics have complained that the film makes light of a serious situation. However, Orefice's zany antics become his method to survive the madness and to keep his young son alive and hopeful when they are sent to a concentration camp.

In the remarkable 2003 *Indelible Shadows, Film and the Holocaust,* Annette Insdorf makes the point that "the extraordinary international popularity of *Life Is Beautiful* means that audiences—which might otherwise not have been aware of the Nazi persecution of Italian Jewry—embraced an appealing Jewish hero who inspires respect rather than merely pity" (Insdorf, 2003, p. 292). Benigni, like Chaplin, was motivated by personal need to make this film. His (non-Jewish) father Luigi Benigni spent two years in the Bergen-Belsen labor camp, from 1943 to 1945, and weighed just seventy-seven pounds when liberated. Roberto grew up listening to his father's stories and, drawing inspiration from Chaplin, created a film that celebrates a man's love and devotion to his family. Although it is understandable that survivors would find little to laugh at in viewing "cartoonlike" behavior of the Nazis, both Chaplin and Benigni use the tradition of the hapless clown, the buffoon of *commedia dell'arte,* to lampoon the absurdities of fascism and render the jester triumphant over his tyrant.

Sophie's Choice and The Pawnbroker

Sophie's Choice (1982) and *The Pawnbroker* (1964), both award-winning films produced by major Hollywood studios, deal with a subject that has to some extent created a false stereotype, the guilt-ridden Holocaust survivor. In *Sophie's Choice,* based on the book by William Styron, Meryl Streep plays Sophie Zawistowska, a Polish Catholic who is sent to Auschwitz for her collaboration with the Polish resistance. Having barely survived the Holocaust, she finds herself in postwar Brooklyn, where she becomes friends with Nathan, a New York Jew, and Stingo, a Southern Gentile beguiled by her beauty. It is Stingo who narrates the story and to whom Sophie reveals the impossible choice she was forced to make at Auschwitz.

Alan J. Pakula, the son of Polish immigrants, wrote the adapted screenplay and directed the film. He makes use of color and setting to create a dichotomy between the two worlds of Sophie's experience: The scenes in postwar Coney Island have an energetic and dizzying feel to them, in stark contrast to the listless and lifeless haze of Auschwitz. Coney Island is a perfect visual metaphor for the relationship between Sophie and Nathan, which is an emotional rollercoaster. Sophie is physically and emotionally fragile, and one expects her, like an egg resting on a spoon, to fall and crack at any moment.

Her face in close-up resembles an eggshell; there is great authenticity in Streep's performance when she speaks in broken English, Polish, and German. Sophie's love affair with Nathan, a Nazi-obsessed, cocaine-addicted manic depressive (played by Kevin Kline), reinforces the notion that the troubled survivor welcomes terror and chaos because it is familiar and therefore strangely comforting. Such guilt will only permit the most fleeting moments of joy. At the film's end Sophie chooses to commit suicide with Nathan in what feels like an emotional release from a life haunted by memories too difficult to face.

In *The Pawnbroker* Sidney Lumet directs Rod Steiger in a masterful performance as a Holocaust survivor working in a Harlem pawnshop owned by an African American. Lumet, who began his career performing in the Yiddish theater, uses black-and-white cinematography to illustrate the fact that even in daylight, Steiger's character, Sol Nazerman, is a man living in a dark world. The audience becomes privy to Nazerman's interior thoughts as present events trigger recollections that are seen in flashbacks. A ride on a subway car allows us to observe Nazerman as a face in the crowd, but one emotionally alone and isolated from his fellow passengers. It is as if the only feeling he can resurrect is pain, and his wretched memories at least provide him with abundant material for that. As Nazerman rides the subway, he is jolted by the memory of a fateful train ride, as he and other Jews traveled on their way to certain death at the hands of the Nazis.

Lumet effectively uses the cagelike surroundings of the pawnshop, showing the shadow of crisscrossed bars across Nazerman's face and body to convey the image of a man imprisoned. The tragedy of Nazerman's past continues into the present when a young Hispanic coworker named Jesús (played by Jaime Sanchez) attempts to befriend him, only to be rebuffed. When Jesús is killed during an attempted robbery, once again Nazerman is the survivor left to mourn the dead. But his emotions have completely shut down, and his stifled cry at the film's end symbolizes his inability to articulate his loss.

There are numerous other testaments to the fortitude and courage of many Holocaust survivors. Perhaps for some, the Hollywood image of emotionally scarred and haunted characters perpetuates the myth of Jewish victimization or, worse, cowardice. It is hoped that the ongoing efforts to commit to film the many stories of survivors and their achievements will serve as a counterpoint to films they feel may distort the truth.

Night and Fog

It is important to mention the film *Night and Fog* (1955, in French *Nuit et Brouillard*) by director Alain Resnais.

Although not an American film, it is nevertheless the first documentary film made about the Holocaust and it influenced many subsequent films. This film was made only ten years after the end of the war; it uses stills and newsreel to expose the horror and depravity that was Auschwitz. The title *Night and Fog* is the term used by Hitler on December 7, 1941, when he issued his Night and Fog Decree. The intent of this edict was to replace the practice of taking hostages with the total disappearance of those suspected of resistance. They would disappear into the "night and fog." To quote Himmler's memo to the Gestapo, "An effective and lasting deterrent can be achieved only by the death penalty or by taking measures which will leave the family and the population uncertain as to the fate of the offender. Deportation to Germany serves this purpose."

Renais's film is remarkable in its understated tone and almost monotone narration. The images need no heightened emotional soundtrack for they are shocking enough and invite quiet introspection. The film begins in color narrated by survivor Jean Cayrol, and postwar Auschwitz looks like a travel poster, inviting one to spend a day in the country. This sylvan scene cuts away to freight cars and images of human cargo. As the camera enters the camp, the past replaces the present, and scenes of inconceivable atrocities soon fill the now empty spaces of the rooms. The collection of human hair, bones, and skin used as raw materials in the production of German goods are a still-life testament to the lives lost. In its detachment this film is most effective. There is no need for embellishment: *Night and Fog* stands on its own as witness to humankind's capacity for pure evil.

Missing

The 1982 film *Missing,* directed by Constantin Costa-Gavras, deals with the "night and fog" disappearance of Charles Horman (played by John Shea) during the 1973 military coup led by Augusto Pinochet in Chile. It is the true story of businessman Ed Horman (played by Jack Lemmon) who along with Charles's wife (played by Sissy Spacek) attempt to determine what happened to the missing son and husband. The story unfolds in flashbacks, and Costa-Gavras seamlessly draws us into the plight of the anguished father and distraught wife. U.S. involvement in the coup is acknowledged, although a viewer would do well to read the now declassified documents detailing the true extent of this involvement. This film along with *The Official Story* and others provides chilling evidence that Hitler's 1941 decree found favor with the military governments of South America. It is estimated that more than fifty thousand young men were tortured or killed during the Pinochet takeover, and throughout Argentina's dirty

war an estimated thirty thousand disappeared. Such numbers are difficult to comprehend, and by following the story of one missing person, the audience is able to put a face on the rest.

Schindler's List

Schindler's List (1993) is considered to be director Stephen Spielberg's greatest achievement. The film, based on Thomas Keneally's book, tells the story of Polish Catholic Oskar Schindler (portrayed by Liam Neeson) who ultimately saved the lives of more than a thousand Polish Jews. The film, shot in black-and-white in Poland, has an air of authenticity as Spielberg's attention to detail—from the characters' distinctly Polish appearance to Hebrew prayers—sets this film apart from the usual Hollywood fare. The audience is introduced to an ensemble of Polish Jews, and as the story unfolds, Schindler's efforts to save them from extermination becomes the focal point.

Spielberg's experiences in creating this film led him to establish the Shoah Foundation, an institution devoted to chronicling on film the testimonies of Holocaust survivors. *Shoah* is the Hebrew word for "destruction"; it has come into prominence as a preferred word to Holocaust, which means "sacrifice consumed by fire" (from the Greek word *holos-kaustos*). According to the Shoah Foundation website, over 52,000 visual testimonies from 56 countries in 32 languages have been recorded. Although Spielberg did not personally experience World War II, he chose to use his recognized filmmaking skills to create a moving pictorial archive of the Holocaust's survivors.

The Pianist

One of the most recent films to dramatize the true story of a Holocaust survivor is *The Pianist* (2002), directed by Roman Polanski. Polanski, born Raimund Liebling, the son of Polish Jews, was initially approached to film *Schindler's List,* but he declined the offer, insisting that making such a movie would be too personally wrenching for him as a survivor of the Kraków ghetto. *The Pianist* is based on Wladyslaw Szpilman's biography written in 1946. Szpilman (played by Adrien Brody) was a classically trained pianist who narrowly escaped deportation to a concentration camp and survived the war through the help of Polish Catholics and the Jewish resistance.

Polanksi drew on his own experiences of survival in making the film. As a ten-year-old, he had escaped the Kraków ghetto when his father took him to a barbed-wire fence near the SS guardhouse and, cutting the wire, pushed his son through the opening, with strict instructions to go to the home of a nearby family.

Oskar Schindler was a real-life German entrepreneur who outmaneuvered the Nazis and saved the lives of over 1,000 Polish Jews during the Holocaust. Here, director Steven Spielberg, on the set of *Schindler's List,* watches two actors. [JAMES DAVID/CORBIS SYGMA]

When the frightened Polanski found no one at home, he returned to the guardhouse area, only to see his father being led away by the SS. The father implores the young Polanski to "get away," a moment frequently mirrored in *The Pianist* as Szpilman repeatedly gets away from the Nazis. After the war Polanksi learned that his pregnant mother had been killed in the Auschwitz gas chamber. He was later reunited with his father, who survived a labor camp. According to Szpilman's son, his father had once claimed, "No other director could make this film." Szpilman died before seeing the finished product.

Conclusion

A motion picture has the power to impose its version of factual events on one's conscience. It is conceivable that the director who has an emotional investment in a film's message will not be as likely swayed by the demands of the box office. However, the film industry is one area of "show business," and often to fund "the show," it is necessary to bend to the demands of "the business." This is a heavy burden for any filmmaker wishing to tell the story of mass murder and human rights violations. Although the majority of filmgoers are unlikely to attend documentaries on this subject, any student of history would be wise to see archival footage of these events. To some extent, the admonition of survivors, that to make these stories "artistic" is to betray those that perished, is reasonable. But human nature being what it is, to look away would be an even greater evil. Thus, the courageous artists who seek to portray genocide and crimes against humanity are to be admired for their attempts to speak the unspeakable, to shed light on the darkness in hope that such atrocities will never be repeated.

SEE ALSO Drama, Holocaust; Films, Armenian Documentary; Films, Armenian Feature; Films, Eugenics; Films, Holocaust Documentary

BIBLIOGRAPHY

"Charlie Chaplin." Available from http://www.nationmaster.com/encyclopedia/Charlie-Chaplin.

"Edison Motion Pictures." Available from http://Icweb2.loc.gov/ammem/edhtml/edmvhm.html.

"The Great Dictator." Available from http://www.imdb.com/title/tt0032553/.

"Holocaust." Available from http://www.fact-index.com/h/ho/holcaust.html.

Insdorf, Annette (2003). *Indelible Shadows, Film and the Holocaust.* Cambridge, U.K.: Cambridge University Press.

La Vita è Bella (Life Is Beautiful). Available from http://www.imdb.com/title/tt0118799/.

Lownes, Marilyn Coles. "*Pianist* Interview." Available from http://minadream.com/romanpolanksi/ThePianistInterview.htm.

Missing. Available from http://www.imdb.com/title/tt0084335/.

"The Night and Fog Decree." Available from http://www.historyplace.com/worldwar2/timeline/nacht.htm.

Nuit et Brouillard (Night and Fog). Available from http://www.imdb.com/title/tt00484434/.

Owino, Peres. "Roberto Benigni, Actor and Director." Available fromhttp://www.uwgb.edu/galta/333/BIOS98/BENIGNI.HTM.

The Pawnbroker. Available from http://www.imdb.com/title/tt0059575/.

The Pianist. Available from http://www.imdb.com/title/tt0253474/.

"Roman Polanksi." Available from http://www.eonline.com/Facts/People/Bio/0,128,239,00.html?celfact1.

Schindler's List. Available from http://www.imdb.com/title/tt0108052/.

Sophie's Choice. Available from http://www.imdb.com/title/tt0084707/.

Survivors of the Shoah. Available from http://www.vhf.org/vhf-new/0-Splash.htm.

Marlene Shelton

Films, Eugenics

Eugenics, "the wellborn science," was a staple of sociologic and intellectual inquiry during the late nineteenth century. Springing from social Darwinism and the social theories of Sir Francis Galton in England, eugenics became first a philosophy and then a movement. One of its foundations was a belief in human perfectablity. As a discipline, eugenics overlapped with many other disciplines. Eugenics-related discourse took in discussion of criminal behavior, anthropology, immigration policy, IQ testing, and racial theory. In approximately thirty countries in which a burgeoning eugenics movement took root, government policy came under the sway of the movement's basic principles of racial superiority, which in turn would provide a philosophic rationale for genocide. Clarence Darrow, Helen Keller, John D. Rockfeller, Andrew Carnegie, and E. H. Harriman were unable to see the implications of eugenics principles and to recognize the slippery slope onto which they had climbed when they espoused some of these principles.

Films that strove to indoctrinate audiences with a eugenics way of thinking would document and reinforce—but eventually expose as pseudoscience—eugenics ideologies and practices. In the United States the films of this kind that were produced during the height of that country's eugenics movement (the first two decades of the twentieth century) brought to the national fore the controversial issues of mandatory sterilization and euthanasia. In Germany the Third Reich, building on the eugenics-related research and new legislation that were happening in the United States, would use the medium of film to propagate the claim of Aryan superiority and biological perfectability and to advocate that the infirm and the disabled were a burden on societies. In the 1980s and 1990s in the United States, a new focus on eugenics history was becoming evident, and eugenics history became popularized; during that period several documentary films that delineated this history were made.

One of the first U.S. films to promote a eugenics philosophy and to advocate "euthanasia" for disabled persons was *The Black Stork* (1917), written by Hearst Corporation reporter Jack Lait. The film was aggressively promoted by Chicago surgeon Dr. Harry Haiselden (who plays a eugenics-oriented doctor much like himself in the film), one of the most ardent advocates of eugenics in the United States at that time. Prior to the making of the film Haiselden had gained notoriety when he refused to operate on a sick child who had been classified as "defective." Although Haiselden was never found guilty of charges of homicide that had been brought against him for his medical "euthanizing" of infants with disabilities, he was expelled from the Chicago Medical Society.

In the film that is based on Lait's "photoplay," Dr. Dickey (Haiselden) counsels Claude and his wife Anne. Claude has "tainted blood" (a sexually transmitted disease). Anne has just given birth to a severely disabled child. Dr. Dickey advises euthanasia for the child. The child's mother has a dream in which the child grows up, becomes a criminal, and kills the doctor who allowed him to live. The couple allows the child to die. The unequivocal message of *The Black Stork* (which ends with the child's soul being welcomed into heaven by Jesus Christ) is stated in the film by Dr. Dickey: "There are times when saving a life is a greater crime than taking one."

The Black Stork was a popular sensation in 1917 and played in movie houses throughout the United States. It is perhaps worth noting that the film was released almost on the heels of the appearance in theaters of D. W. Griffith's racist *Birth of a Nation* (1915). Martin Pernick, in his volume *The Black Stork: Eugenics and the Death of "Defective" Babies in American Medicine and Motion Pictures Since 1915,* expounds on the historical and moral climates in which this eugenics film (which is both fiction and documentary) was created.

An unusual film made in the United States in the 1930s (a time when the eugenics movement was waning in that country) is producer Brian Foy's *Tomorrow's Children* (1934). In the film the Mason family is composed of mental and physical "misfits"—with its alcoholic, club-footed, and retarded members (as judged by society and the law). Alice, one of the healthier members of the Mason family, wishes to marry Jeff, but a court rules that she must first be sterilized. Advocates for Alice's sterilization cite the infamous phrase, "Three generations of imbeciles are enough"—part of the U.S. Supreme Court decision (delivered by Justice Oliver Wendell Holmes) in *Buck v. Bell* (1927), in which the decision by another judge that "feebleminded" Carrie Buck was required to undergo surgical sterilization was upheld. At the last minute Alice is spared sterilization because Mrs. Mason confesses that Alice is not her biological daughter. The film dealt with the topic of involuntary sterilization at a time when twenty-seven U.S. states had passed laws permitting the involuntary sterilization of individuals deemed "socially unfit." Although Alice is saved from sterilization, the film asserts that sterilization is morally acceptable and legal because of the threats to society that sterilization eliminates.

Selling Murder: The Killing Films of the Third Reich (1991) is a documentary film, written by Michael Burleigh, on the Nazi euthanasia programs of the 1930s; it opens and closes with tributes to the victims of those programs. The film was inspired by the then-recent discovery of a cache of Nazi propaganda films of the 1930s—films that strove to be didactic about the racial and biological rationales that the Nazis had used to justify the elimination of the "unfit," the disabled, and others who had received the classification "life unworthy of life." *Was du Erbst* (What You Inherit), *Erb Krank* (The Hereditarily Ill), *Opfer der Vergangenheit* (Victims of the Past), and *Das Erbe* (The Inheritance) were films that showed actual images of disabled persons and promoted the thesis that the disabled are economic burdens to societies. In the United States Harry Laughlin, a biologist and a powerful figure in the U.S. eugenics movement (and for twenty years the director of the Cold Spring Harbor Eugenics Center) would take these German eugenics films on the road, showing them to the American public (including high school audiences)—among whom he found great support and admiration for the ideas contained therein.

Included in the film *Selling Murder* is a segment on two German films that were commissioned in 1939 as part of the Reich's pursuit of euthanasia practices at six extermination centers. *Dasein ohne Leben* (Existence without Life) and *Geisterkrank* (The Mentally Ill) advocate for euthanasia and attempt to provide justification for euthanasia policy. Also included in *Selling Murder* is a discussion of the sentimentally propagandistic *Ich klage an* (I Accuse). A German feature film, it was made in 1941 by German actor and director Wolfang Liebeneiner. It is about the decision of an established pianist to be euthanized at a time when her physical condition is rapidly deteriorating. The film, however, did not distinguish between voluntary euthanasia and euthanasia mandated by state policy.

With film clips and on-site visits by survivors, *Selling Murder* provides many insights into the pseudoscience and eugenics-related policies of the Third Reich. The leaders of the Reich, having installed their programs of sterilization, forced euthanasia, and genocide (many of which were under the sponsorship of Operation T-4), hoped to create a biocentric state in which the disabled would have no recourse to any kind of protection and no inherent value.

Stephen Trombley's film *The Lynchburg Story* (1994) was in part a product of the aforementioned interest in eugenics history that came into being in the United States in the 1980s and 1990s. The film tells the story of the Lynchburg Colony for the Epileptic and the Feebleminded in Lynchburg, Virginia. From 1927 to 1972 more than 70,000 Americans were sterilized in the 27 U.S. states in which forcible sterilization was permitted. Of these, more than 8,000 persons (deemed "unfit to reproduce") were sterilized at the Lynchburg Colony. The film makes clear that it was the United States (and not Germany) which devised the original blueprint of eugenics-related policy in the Third Reich. In Trombley's film, which includes testimony from survivors, the tragic stories of the victims of the Lynchburg Colony unfold.

A documentary film by the author of this entry, *In the Shadow of the Reich: Nazi Medicine* (1996), describes the many connections between the eugenics movement in the United States and the Third Reich's campaign against "undesirables." As German medical scientists and bureaucrats built on U.S. eugenicist theory and practice, scientists and intellectuals of both nations praised one another for the "advances" each country was making for the betterment of their respective societies.

Peter Cohen's documentary film *Architecture of Doom* (1991) provides a striking account of how subjective standards of physical beauty became a criterion of the selection process that was part of the German agenda of "cleansing" society of those whom German political leaders judged to be alien to their utopian vision. His *Homo Sapiens 1900* (2000), another documentary film, is an indictment of the Nazi concept of racial purity—and of similar concepts that were once present in the United States, Sweden, and Russia. Cohen's historical and sociological analyses of concepts of racial superiority are most insightful, as is his argument that modern science can sometimes become science in the service of state policy, which is no longer science.

The documentary film *After Darwin: Genetics, Eugenics, and the Human Genome* (1999), produced by Arnie Gelbert of Mundo Vision, exposes the dark side of many scientific and technological advances. The film delves into the history of the collective fascination with eugenics principles, and then brings the viewer up to date as it raises ethical concerns that attach to contemporary advances in science and technology.

These films dealing with eugenics not only provide a window into the all too inglorious past, but also provoke one to raise a cautious eye when technology may advance more rapidly than morality.

SEE ALSO Film as Propaganda; Films, Dramatizations in; Films, Eugenics; Films, Holocaust Documentary

BIBLIOGRAPHY

Adams, Paul (1990). *The Wellborn Science.* New York: Oxford University Press.

Black, Edwin (2003). *War against the Weak: Eugenics and America's Campaign to Create A Master Race.* New York: Four Walls Eight Windows.

Burleigh, Michael (1994). *Death and Deliverance: "Euthanasia" in Germany 1900–1945.* Cambridge: Cambridge University Press.

Michalczyk, John J. (1994). *Medicine, Ethics, and the Third Reich: Historical and Contemporary Issues.* Kansas City, Mo.: Sheed & Ward.

Pernick, Martin S. (1996). *The Black Stork: Eugenics and the Death of "Defective" Babies in American Medicine and Motion Pictures since 1915.* New York: Oxford University Press.

Proctor, Robert (1998). *Racial Hygiene: Medicine Under the Nazis.* Cambridge, Mass.: Harvard University Press.

Smith, J. David (1993). *The Eugenic Assault on America: Scenes in Red, White, and Black.* Fairfax, Va.: George Mason University Press.

John J. Michalczyk

Films, Holocaust Documentary

Documentary films about the Holocaust are generally well-researched and precise chronicles of the inordinately tragic events in Europe from 1933 through 1945. They include films of the Ministry of Propaganda of the Third Reich, made at the time these tragic events were taking place, and documentary studies of these events that appeared years afterward. Each film has its own historical context, values, and sociopolitical and moral impact.

Origins of Genocide

One can trace the sources of some of the Third Reich's anti-Semitic and genocidal policies to eugenics, the early twentieth-century pseudo-science and international social movement. That some "races" are superior to others was a doctrinal element of this movement. *Selling Murder: The Killing Films of the Third Reich* (1991), a film written by Michael Burleigh and directed by Joanna Mack, chronicles Nazi propaganda films of the 1930s. It has unsettling clips from *Erb Krank* (The hereditarily ill, 1935), which provide a basis for understanding Germany's efforts to create a biological new world order—an agenda that included the elimination of persons with disabilities. Peter Cohen's documentary films *Architecture of Doom* (1991) and *Homo Sapiens 1990* (2000) both delineate how, in Germany, "aesthetic" cleansing both in art and human form, as well as "racial purity," would become rationales for the mass murder of the weak and marginalized. *In the Shadow of the Reich: Nazi Medicine* (1996), a documentary film by the author of this article, places the origins of eugenics-related medical practices used by the Nazis and experimentation with human subjects in the involuntary sterilization laws that were passed in the United States in the 1920s.

Third Reich Propaganda

Joseph Goebbels became the Reich Minister of Propaganda and Enlightenment in 1933, and subsequently all German-made films were scrupulously censored by his office—as part of the effort to promote a collective vision of an "Aryan" Germany and its great destiny. Leni Riefenstahl's *Triumph of the Will* (1935) and *Olympia* (1938), the most well known of the Nazi propaganda films, are about the Nazi party rally in Nuremberg in 1934 and the 1936 Olympics in Berlin, respectively. Merging propaganda and art, the films—as propaganda pieces—have few rivals. Less well known is Riefenstahl's *Victory of Faith* (1933), about the (more seminal) 1933 Nazi party rally in Nuremberg. Providing direct evidence of the propaganda campaigns of the Third Reich are *Die Deutsche Wochenschau* (weekly newsreels produced in Nazi Germany) and the large number of films about these campaigns that have been made in Great Britain and the United States. Among films that document the Nazi rise to power, two stand out: *Campaign in Poland* (1939), a Nazi-produced propaganda film that strove to justify the German invasion of Poland, and *For Us* (1937), a film about the sixteen German demonstrators who died during the failed Munich Beer Hall Putsch of 1923 (Hitler's first attempt to gain power in Germany). More pernicious is the viscerally anti-Semitic film *The Eternal Jew* (1940), which compares Jews to rodents that have infested civilized society. In general, the Nazi documentaries portray Hitler and the Third Reich as saviors of the German people—a superior race destined for eternal glory.

Overview of the Holocaust

Several films provide an overview of the Nazi Holocaust. One of the earliest of these is Alain Resnais's *Night and Fog* (1955), filmed within a decade of the events and two decades before the U.S. production *Holocaust* (1978), the made-for-television miniseries. *Night and Fog,* which shows footage of abandoned concentration camps (such as they were in 1955) mixed with wartime footage of the camps, chronicles the cruelties of the Holocaust. It documents the rise of the Nazi Party and the horrors of the concentration camps—from the round-ups of prisoners to the camp experiences. The film's closing sequence consists of footage from the 1946 Nuremberg Trials.

"Genocide," written by Michael Barlow, was an episode within the British made-for-television series *World at War* (1975), narrated by Laurence Olivier. It furnishes a basic understanding of the forces that produced the Holocaust.

Claude Lanzmann's nine-hour documentary epic *Shoah* (1986) is a provocative study of the Holocaust that includes interviews with eyewitnesses of many nationalities. The film, which does not use archival footage, blends heartrending testimony from interviewees, who represent a wide array of perspectives that divulge the horrors of the camps.

The Cross and the Star: Jews, Christians, and the Holocaust (1992), a film by the author of this article, examines how religious, political, and cultural anti-Semitism can be traced from the Gospels, through Crusades and Inquisition courts, to Auschwitz.

Resistance

By the time the brutal Nazi war machine was fully in operation, resistance forces in several European nations had come into being. Resistance took many shapes—spiritual, political, and military. Marcel Ophuls's controversial documentary *The Sorrow and the Pity* (1970) tells the story of France under Nazi occupation, at times confronting what some historians considered the "myth" of the resistance. Interviewed in the film are French men and women who found themselves performing heroic acts for the Free French movement, as well as those who collaborated with the Nazis. Aviva Kemner's *Partisans of Vilna* (1986) is an account of the lesser-known Jewish resistance movement in Eastern Europe; it shows Jews in an active role, taking on their enemies, and challenges the more prevalent view of Jewish victimization and passivity during the Holocaust. Haim Gouri's *Flames in the Ashes* (1985), the Israeli educational film *Forests of Valor* (1989), and Chuck Olin's *In Our Own Hands* (1998) poignantly document the generally underrecognized Jewish resistance.

Rescue

The Foundation for Moral Courage (formerly Documentaries International) produces educational films and teachers' guides. It has produced a series of films about rescue efforts during the Holocaust; the films include *The Other Side of Faith* (1990) and *Zegota* (1991), both dealing with rescue efforts that took place in Poland; *Rescue in Scandinavia* (1994); and *It Was Nothing—It Was Everything* (1998), about the rescue of Jews in Greece during the Holocaust.

Two of the better-known films about rescue efforts during the Holocaust are Alexander Ramati's *The Assisi Underground* (1985) and Pierre Suavage's *Weapons of the Spirit* (1988). Both films illustrate how the altruism of private individuals saved lives. *The Assisi Underground* is about rescue efforts by Italian priests. *Weapons of the Spirit* is the story of a small town in France, Le Chambon-sur-Lignon, inhabited mostly by French Protestants (descendants of Huguenots), in which villagers risked their lives to shelter and hide approximately five thousand Jews.

Two films that focus on the rescue of children are Mark Jonathan Harris's *Into the Arms of Strangers* (2001) and Melissa Hacker's *My Knees Were Jumping: Remembering the Kindertransports* (1998).

The Ghetto Experience

Roman Polanski's Oscar-winning feature film *The Pianist* (2003) and Jon Avnet's television miniseries *Uprising* (2001), both fictional accounts of historical events, brought about a renewed interest in the Warsaw Ghetto and its resistance movement. A documentary film entitled *The Warsaw Ghetto* (1969), a BBC production, studies the daily life and the struggle to survive within the Warsaw Ghetto during World War II. David Kaufman's documentary film *From Despair to Defiance: The Warsaw Ghetto Uprising* (2002) tells the story of that uprising via the personal accounts of veterans of the Warsaw Jewish Fighting Organization. A related documentary film is Alan Adelson and Kathryn Taverna's *Lodz Ghetto* (1989), about the Nazi occupation of the Polish city of Lodz.

Concentration Camps

Produced by the Nazi Ministry of Propaganda of the Third Reich, *Theresienstadt* was shot in 1944—a film that (the Nazis presumed) would be used to prove to the International Red Cross and the world that Jews were being well treated in "relocation camps." The film purports to show the wholesome daily life of Jews in Theresienstadt (in Czech, Terezín), a "city" established by the Nazis in the former Czechoslovakia. The film was an elaborate hoax. Every scene in the film is staged. Upon completion of the film, most of its cast of prisoners were shipped to Auschwitz. *The Führer Gives the Jews a City* is a 1991 reconstruction of the film. Malcolm Clarke and Stuart Sender's *Prisoner of Paradise* (2002) tells the tragic story of Kurt Gerron, a German-Jewish cabaret and film star—and the director of *Theresienstadt*.

The Memory of the Camps was filmed by the British Army in 1945 (and stored in London's Imperial War Museum until 1984); it is a compilation of original documentary footage taken inside the concentration camps immediately following Germany's surrender and the liberation of the camps. Alfred Hitchcock served as one of the consultants. The film was never shown until 1985, when it was broadcast by PBS Frontline.

A camera crew accompanying the Russian Army filmed the liberation of Auschwitz in January 1945; the Russians excepted, the armies of the United States and Great Britain (with their camera crews) were the first to document the horrors of the camps. In the wake of liberation, the U.S. government sponsored several films about the camps and the freeing of prisoners, including *Nazi Concentration Camps* (1945), *Death Mills* (1945), and Henri-Cartier Bresson's *The Reunion* (1946). Bresson, a prisoner of war, made the film for the U.S. Information Service.

Among the films that are about the experiences of other (non-Jewish) prisoners in concentration camps, two stand out. The Watch Tower Society's *Jehovah's Witnesses Stand Firm Against Nazi Assault* (1996) deals with the persecution of Witnesses in the camps, and Rob Epstein and Jeffrey Freidman's *Paragraph 175* (1999) recounts the persecution of homosexuals.

Postwar Narratives

In the wake of the Nuremberg Trials, the U.S. government produced *Nuremberg* (1946), an account of the actual trials, which includes the footage of the camps at liberation that was shown at the trials, as evidence of German crimes against humanity. Marcel Ophuls's film diptych about the Nazi crimes examines the phenomenon of sadism. The films that make up this diptych, *The Memory of Justice* (1976) and *Hotel Terminus:*

The Life and Times of Klaus Barbie (1988), uncover some aspects of the psychology of human barbarism.

Displaced: Miracle at St. Ottilien (2002), another film by the author of this article, and Mark Jonathan Harris's *Long Road Home* (2002) show evidence that, immediately following the war, the world's populations became rapidly disinterested in the plight of persons displaced by the war. The films illustrate how the survivors of the Nazi genocide were able to begin life anew in the state of Israel, a reluctantly welcoming America, or a postwar Nazi-free Europe.

SEE ALSO Films, Dramatizations in; Films, Eugenics

BIBLIOGRAPHY

Avaisar, Ilan (1988). *Screening the Holocaust: Cinema's Images of the Unimaginable.* Bloomington: Indiana University Press.

Doneson, Judith (1987). *The Holocaust in American Film.* Philadelphia: Jewish Publication Society.

Hull, David Stewart (1973). *Film in the Third Reich.* New York: Simon & Schuster.

Insdorf, Annette (1989). *Indelible Shadows: Film and the Holocaust.* New York: Cambridge University Press.

Lansmann, Claude (1985). *Shoah: An Oral History.* New York: Pantheon Press.

Leiser, Erwin (1974). *Nazi Cinema.* New York: Collier Books.

Schwarz, Dan (1999). *Imagining the Holocaust.* New York: St. Martin's Press.

Taylor, Richard (1998). *Film Propaganda: Soviet Russia and Nazi Germany.* New York: St. Martin's Press.

Totten, Samuel, and Stephen Feiberg, eds. (2001). *Teaching and Studying the Holocaust.* Needham, Mass.: Allyn and Bacon.

John Michalczyk

Final Solution see Explanation; Historiography, Sources in; Hitler, Adolf; Holocaust.

Forced Labor see France in Tropical Africa; Gulag; King Leopold II and the Congo; Labor Camps, Nazi; Slavery, Historical; Slavery, Legal Aspects of.

Forcible Transfer

The forcible transfer of children of a protected group to another group is the fifth punishable act of genocide. It originally formed part of the definition of cultural genocide. The definition was contained in a draft by the UN Secretariat, submitted as a first step in creating the Genocide Convention that was adopted in 1948. The definition reads as follows:

> Destroying the specific characteristics of the group by (a) forced transfer of children to another human group; or (b) forced and systematic exile of individuals representing the culture of the group; or (c) prohibition of the use of the national language even in private intercourse; or (d) systematic destruction of books printed in the national language or of religious works or prohibition of new publications; or (e) systematic destruction of historical or religious monuments or their diversion to alien uses, destruction or dispersal of documents and objects of historical, artistic, or religious value and objects used in religious worship.

The UN General Assembly rejected the concept of cultural genocide, holding that it was not consonant with the principal aim of the law of genocide. The aim of that law is to protect the right of national, ethnic, racial, and religious groups to physical existence as such. The acts that are listed in the Genocide Convention as acts of genocide are: killing members of the group; causing serious bodily or mental harm to members of the group; deliberately inflicting on the group conditions of life calculated to bring about its physical destruction in whole or in part; imposing measures intended to prevent births within the group; and forcibly transferring children of the group to another group. The list is exhaustive and, with the exception of the forcible transfer of children, all the acts contained therein are physical. Generally speaking, therefore, the law of genocide is not concerned with cultural, economic, educational, linguistic, and political or social continuity. These concerns are protected elsewhere, by laws pertaining to human rights and minority rights.

The forcible transfer of children was added to the list of acts of genocide at the insistence of Greece after the UN General Assembly had rejected the inclusion of cultural genocide in the Convention. Its inclusion was achieved by a minority vote. Only twenty-five member states voted for its inclusion, whereas thirteen opposed it and thirteen abstained from voting.

The lukewarm support for including the forcible transfer of children among the acts of genocide may be explained by the fact that it is out of harmony with the other listed acts, whose common denominator is the physical destruction of the protected groups. Forcibly transferring children from one group to another results in the dispersal of the original group's members. It weakens their cohesion as a group, but it does not take away their physical characteristics. An African or Chinese remains African or Chinese, wherever he or she may be. The transfer, however, does make the transferred members of the group lose their cultural or linguistic identity by forcibly assimilating them into other groups. If those other groups speak different languages, practice different religions, or possess different cultures, transferred children will be forced to do likewise. Strictly speaking, this would constitute genocide only if the purpose of the transfer were to subject the children to slave labor or other forms of physical or mental harm. Such treatment would weaken them physically and would amount to subjecting them to conditions of life calculated to bring about their physical destruction, in whole or in part.

It must, however, be conceded that the forcible transfer and isolation of children from their original group frequently makes it difficult for them when they become of age to marry people of their original group, for they may no longer share the linguistic, religious, cultural, or social traditions with that group. They are thus unable to reproduce their own kind and to perpetuate their group. As a direct result, the group itself will gradually dwindle in number and ultimately become extinct. The inclusion of the forcible transfer of children as an act of genocide is designed to prevent this eventuality.

Key Concepts

There are several key conceptual elements that underpin the assignment of forcible transfer to the broader category of genocidal acts. These concepts include the definition of "child," the characteristics that define an act as forcible transfer, the definition of "protected groups," and the broader issue of the intent behind the transfer of children from their group of origin to another group.

Definition of Children

Neither the Genocide Convention nor the statutes of ad hoc tribunals or the International Criminal Court defines who a child is. The statute of the International Criminal Court that outlaws the conscription or the enlisting of children into armed forces confined the crime to "children under the age of fifteen years" (Article 8(2), paragraph (e) (viii)). The U.S. proposal to adopt the age of fifteen as the defining criterion of children within the Genocide Convention was rejected, possibly because the UN Convention on the Rights of the Child, to which most states were already party, used the criterion of "every human being *below* the age of 18 years" in defining who qualified as a child. State representatives therefore took the view that the definition of what constituted a child was already settled and did not want to reopen it. In keeping with that understanding states that were party to the Rome Statute subsequently accepted the age of eighteen as the cut-off point in the definition of "child" and incorporated it as one of the elements defining the crime of genocide (Article 6(e)).

The Genocide Convention and the statutes of ad hoc tribunals and the International Criminal Court specifically refer to the forcible transfer of *children*. Does this mean that more than one child must be transferred for such transfer to qualify as an act of genocide? Not necessarily so. The transfer of even one child qualifies as an act of genocide if it is shown to be manifestly part of a master plan to destroy in whole or in part a protected group. It would be even more so if it were coupled with other acts of genocide. However, before a person who is charged with genocide on account of the forcible transfer of children can be found guilty of the crime, the prosecution must prove that the defendant knew or ought to have known that the persons being transferred were children as defined above. Such proof may not always be easy, particularly when large numbers of children are involved. For that reason it would be sufficient for the prosecution to prove that the accused knew or ought to have known that at least some of the people transferred were under eighteen years of age.

Forcible Transfer

Transfer means removing children from their parents or guardians and placing them in the custody of persons belonging to groups other than the one in which they had been raised up to the time of the transfer. It also includes removing the children from their physical place of residence, such as a neighborhood, village, district, or community inhabited by members of the child's group and sending them to another location that is inhabited by members of different groups. During the meetings of the Preparatory Committee for the International Criminal Court. the United States proposed that forcible transfer be restricted to children in "lawful residence." The Preparatory Committee rejected the proposal, contending that it is immaterial that the place of residence from which the children are transferred is unlawful, for the children are not responsible for their place of residence. Accepting the U.S. proposal would have denied legal protection to children of illegal immigrants, for example. Instead, the committee held that what is material is that the children are uprooted from the custody of their parents or guardians or from their actual place of residence.

Not only must there be a transfer, the transfer must be forcible. "Forcible" transfer means transfer by force or by compulsion, without the consent of the parents or guardians of the affected children. It is no defense to say that the children consented for, in law, children lack the capacity to give such consent. It must also be stressed that the term "forcible" is not restricted to physical force. It also includes the threat of force and coercion caused by fear of harm or oppression to the children or to their parents, guardians, or others. It also includes artifice and trickery, as well as psychological force exerted on the children, parents, guardians, or others connected with them.

Protected Groups

For purposes of the genocide law the children who are forcibly transferred must belong to a particular national, ethnic, racial. or religious group. These are the only groups that are protected under the law of genocide. One reason for restricting protection to these groups is that membership in the groups is involuntary. It is inherited, not opted for by an individual. Another reason is that such groups are relatively stable and easily identifiable. The only group that does not meet these criteria and is therefore out of place is the religious group. Membership in this group, as is the case with respect to cultural, social, or political groups, is voluntary. One may join or abandon the group as his or her conscience dictates. It is true that a child may be born into a religion, but on reaching the age of discretion, he or she may repudiate that religion and embrace another, or give up belief altogether. In the modern era of religious liberty, it can no longer be assumed that children will necessarily cling to their parents' or ancestors' religious beliefs.

The Concept of Intent

It is not enough to show that there was a forcible transfer of children from their group to another. Such transfer, in itself, is only what is known in law as the *actus reus*. To prove a charge of genocide, it must simultaneously be shown that the transfer was done with the specific intent of destroying the group, in whole or in part, and that the transfer was part of that plan. This aspect of intent is known in law as the *dolus specialis*. This point is well illustrated by the Australian case of *Alec Kruger & Ors; George Ernest Bray & Ors v. Commonwealth of Australia*. The plaintiffs in the case were aboriginal Australians, members of the so-called "lost generation." They alleged that, when they were children, they were forcibly removed from their home communities in the Northern Territory and forcibly transferred into the custody of the Chief Protector of Aborigines (or of his successor in function, the Director of Native Affairs). Thereafter they were denied contact with their families and kept in aboriginal reserves. Section 6 of the 1918 Aboriginals Ordinance under which they were so removed provided as follows:

Miskito, forcibly relocated to refugee camps during the U.S.–led Contra War in the 1980s, prepare for the return to their remote homeland along Nicaragua's northern coast. [**BILL GENTILE/CORBIS**]

1. The Chief Protector shall be entitled at any time to undertake the care, custody, or control of any aboriginal or half-caste, if, in his opinion, it is necessary or desirable in the interests of the aboriginal or half-caste for him to do so, and for that purpose may enter any premises where the aboriginal or half-caste is or is supposed to be, and may take him into his custody.

2. Any person on whose premises any aboriginal or half-caste is, shall, on demand by the Chief Protector, or by any one acting on behalf of the Chief Protector on production of his authority, facilitate by all reasonable means in his power the taking into custody of the aboriginal or half-caste.

3. The powers of the Chief Protector under this section may be exercised whether the aboriginal or half-caste is under a contract of employment or not.

These provisions were supported by further conditions set forth in Section 7 of the same Ordinance, which read:

1. The Chief Protector shall be the legal guardian of every aboriginal and of every half-caste child, notwithstanding that the child has a parent or other relative living, until the child attains the age of eighteen years, except while the child is a State child within the meaning of the Act of the State of South Australia in force in the Northern Territory entitled The State Children Act 1895, or any Act of that State or Ordinance amending or substituted for that Act.

2. Every Protector shall, within his district, be the local guardian of every such child within his district, and as such shall have and may exercise such powers and duties as are prescribed.

Under the Ordinance it was an offense for an aboriginal or half-caste child to refuse to be removed. Only in certain specific circumstances could a child be exempted from compulsory removal to the reserves or other state-run institutions. These circumstances included children who were lawfully employed, who held permits that authorized them to be absent from aboriginal reserves or institutions, or females lawfully married to and residing with a husband who was *substantially* of European origin or descent.

Alec Kurger & Ors; George Ernest Bra & Ors v. Commonwealth of Australia

In the case of *Alec Kruger & Ors; George Ernest Bray & Ors v. Commonwealth of Australia,* the plaintiffs sought, among other things, a declaration that the provisions of the 1918 Aboriginals Ordinance were invalid. They contended that the ordinance was contrary to an implied constitutional right to freedom from any law or executive act that, among other things, constituted or authorized the crime of genocide. In support of their case they cited several provisions contained within the Genocide Convention, which they argued were violated by the Aboriginals Ordinance. These included:

1. The removal and transfer of children of a racial or ethnic group in a manner which was calculated to bring about the group's physical destruction in whole or in part;

2. Actions which had the effect or likely effect of causing serious mental harm to members of a racial or ethnic group;

3. The deliberate infliction on a racial or ethnic group conditions of life calculated to bring about its physical destruction in whole or in part.

The Australian Parliament had passed the Genocide Convention Act in 1949, which had authorized the government to ratify the UN Convention. However, by as late as 1997 the Australian Parliament had not gotten around to enacting legislation to implement the Convention. In the case of *Alec Kruger & Ors; George Ernest Bray & Ors v. Commonwealth of Australia,* this had significant consequences. The court held that:

> [T]he Convention has not at any time formed part of Australian domestic law. . . .[I]t is well established that the provisions of an international treaty to which Australia is a party do not form part of Australian law unless those provisions have been validly incorporated into our municipal law by statute. Where such provisions have not been incorporated they cannot operate as a direct source of individual rights and obligations.

The court did acknowledge that the rules of legal interpretation allowed preference to be given to legal interpretations that accorded with the country's international obligations. However, the court hastened to say that it would not accord such a preference where the laws to be interpreted had been enacted before the international obligations had been assumed. This was the case of the Aboriginal Ordinance. The Ordinance was passed in 1918, long before Australia became party to the Genocide Convention in 1951.

The court could nonetheless have interpreted the provisions of the Aboriginal Ordinance in light of Australia's international obligations by referring to customary international law rather than by referring specifically to the Genocide Convention. After all, genocide was already forbidden under customary international law at the time that the Aboriginals Ordinance was enacted. The court, however, found difficulty here as well, this time based on problems inherent in the definition of genocide as a crime. According to the court, the transfer that the Aboriginals Ordinance authorized lacked the requisite mental element of "intent to destroy" the children's racial or ethnic group. Rather, the court held that the forcible transfers authorized by the Ordinance were intended "for the good and welfare" of the aboriginal population. The court based this interpretation on the conditions that prevailed at the time of the Ordinance's passage. At that time, the population of the aboriginals in the Northern Territory was rapidly decreasing due to disease and unsanitary conditions. The policies and measures adopted by the government of Australia were supposedly designed to rescue the aboriginal population from extinction.

The court did, however, admit that the measures adopted under the Aboriginals Ordinance were ill advised and mistaken, particularly by contemporary standards. It acknowledged that the measures led to the physical abuse, humiliation, dehumanization, and traumatization of generations of the aboriginal people. They also callously disregarded familial unity and cultural cohesion in the aboriginal community. They ultimately resulted not only in the cultural but also in the physical extinguishment of the group as a race. Nevertheless, according to the court, "a shift in view upon the justice or morality of those measures taken under an Ordinance which was repealed 40 years ago does not of itself point to the constitutional invalidity of that legislation and to the legal basis of the plaintiffs' claim." For all these reasons, the court dismissed the case.

Nevertheless, the case of *Alec Kruger & Ors; George Ernest Bray & Ors v. Commonwealth of Australia,* and others that followed, served to awaken national consciousness over the injustice done to the aborigines in Australia. At the level of the state legislatures, such cases led to the passage of motions acknowledging the inequity and cruelty of Australia's treatment of her aboriginal population and offering apologies for such treatment. For instance, the State Legislative Assembly of New South Wales passed a motion in 1997 that apologized "unreservedly" to the aboriginal people of Australia for the systematic separation of generations of Aboriginal children from their parents, families, and communities. It also acknowledged and regretted the assembly's role in enacting laws and endorsing policies of successive governments whereby "profound grief and loss have been inflicted upon Aboriginal Australians."

The Native American Experience
Similar to the case of the Australian Aborigines is the experience of Native Americans in the United States during the nineteenth century. The Removal Act of 1834 authorized the forcible removal of American Indians from desirable land to hostile environs. One of the results of the act came to be known as the "Trail of Tears," in the course of which aboriginal peoples were removed from Georgia to Oklahoma. Thousands of them died during the difficult march to their newly assigned territory. At the time, a U.S official asserted that, "[t]he American Indian is to become the Indian American," implying that the motive behind the forced transfer was to facilitate education, "civilization," and assimilation. Again, the charge of genocide is difficult to make in this case, since assimilation is not synonymous with physical destruction. As with the example of Australian Aborigines, the requisite mental element of "intent to destroy" the group as such, in whole or in part, was lacking. Therefore the transfers, though catastrophic in some instances, did not amount to genocide.

However, although the U.S. government's forcible transfers of Native Americans may not have qualified as genocide, they could qualify as crimes against humanity and subsumed under "deportation or forcible transfer of (a) population," according to the standards set forth by the International Criminal Court. This species of crime against humanity is defined as the "forced displacement of the persons concerned by expulsion or other coercive acts from the area in which they are lawfully present, without grounds permitted under international law." The other element that is needed to qualify the transfer as a crime against humanity is that the transfers must be carried out "as part of a widespread or systematic attack" directed against a civilian population. It would appear that this was the case with respect to the transfers forced upon Native Americans.

Forcible Transfer and Forced Labor
In his 1996 Nobel Prize–winning book *Fateless,* Imre Kertesz tells the story of Jewish boys from Hungary who were forcibly taken to Germany to work in labor and concentration camps. For instance, Georg Koves, the main character in the book, was described as a "laborer in training." He was only fourteen years of age when he and many other boys were snatched from buses and taken to Germany. Once there, they were subjected to unspeakably cruel and inhumane treat-

ment. Anyone who did not qualify to work, whether due to age, ill-health, or pregnancy, was killed in the gas chambers. Those who were not killed at the outset faced hunger and privation. Koves was so desperate for food that, in his words:

> [I]f I did not eat wood, iron, or stones, it was only because they were not chewable or digestible. For instance I did try to eat sand, and if I spotted some grass, I didn't hesitate for a moment. Unfortunately grass was difficult to find in the factory and in the camp (p. 120).

In spite of their deplorable state of health, Koves and the boys who shared his fate had to work. If any complained of being tired or hungry, they would have been subjected to beatings, kicks, and other forms of physical and psychological torture. Any who dared to complain of sickness were sent to the gas chambers. According to Koves, "Everyone works; don't get tired, don't get sick" (p. 62).

Kertesz's account of the treatment of the Hungarian boys by the Nazis amounted to genocide in several respects. Those who were to unable to work were actually and deliberately killed. Real physical and mental harm was inflicted on many of them. The deliberate reduction of food rations, leading to the boys' virtual starvation, also amounted to the "infliction of conditions of life calculated to bring about the destruction of their group," as invoked in the Genocide Convention.

Nevertheless, it is debatable whether the forcible transfer of Hungarian boys to Germany in and of itself amounted to genocide. This is so because the purpose of their transfer to Germany was not that they be absorbed into another group. Rather, the principal purpose of their transfer was to facilitate their contribution to Germany's war machine through forced labor. Indeed the inhumane and barbaric treatment that the German authorities subjected them to discounts any idea of any notion of their being absorbed or assimilated into any group in Germany.

Forcible Transfers, Genocide, and the Rights of Children
In condemning the forcible transfer of children as an act of genocide, the law is primarily concerned with protecting the larger group to which they belong. However, by such condemnation the law does indirectly protect children as a particularly vulnerable group. Children as such possess rights that are recognized and protected today under international human rights law. These rights are most concretely embodied in the 1989 UN Convention on the Rights of the Child.

Article 7 of the Convention provides that a child has "the right to know and be cared for by his or her parents" insofar as this is possible. In Article 9, the Convention further provides that "a child shall not be separated from his or her parents against their will, except when competent authorities subject to judicial review determine" that this should be done. The Convention assumes that, by protecting the parent-child custodial relationship, children are naturally guaranteed affection, as well as moral and material security—conditions that are vital to their physical, emotional, intellectual, and social development. Forcible transfer, by contrast, generally traumatizes children and naturally inhibits their normal physical, emotional, intellectual, and social development.

Article 8 of the Convention also provides that "the child is entitled to preserve his or her identity, including nationality, name, and family relations as recognized by law without unlawful interference." It is inhuman and deplorable to forcibly transfer children from their families, communities, and countries to groups, communities, or countries not of their choosing, even when this is done for allegedly altruistic motives, such as "civilizing them." The forcible transfer of children violates their right to liberty and security of the person as well as their freedom of movement and residence, and is also an affront to their human dignity.

SEE ALSO Almohads; Australia; Residential Schools; Trail of Tears

BIBLIOGRAPHY

Bassiouni, M. Cherif (1979). "International Law and the Holocaust," particularly Appendix A "Has the United States Committed Genocide Against the American Indian?" *California Western International Law Journal* 9:201–298.

Human Rights and Equal Opportunity Commission (2000). "Bring Them Home: The Report." Available from http://www.austlii.edu.au/au/special/rsjproject/rsjlibrary/hreoc/stolen/stolen19.html.

Kertesz, Imre (1996). *Fateless.* Evanston, Ill.: Northwestern University Press.

Kittichaisaree, Kriangsak (2001). *International Criminal Law.* Oxford: Oxford University Press.

Lemkin, Raphael (1944). *Axis Rule in Occupied Europe.* Washington, D.C.: Carnegie Endowment for International Peace Division of International Law.

Nsereko, Daniel D. Ntanda (2000). "Genocide: A Crime Against Mankind." In *Substantive and Procedural Aspects of International Criminal Law: The Experience of International and National Courts,* ed. Kirk Gabrielle McDonald and Olivia Swaak-Goldman. The Hague: Kluwer Law International.

"On the Occasion of National Sorry Day 26 May 1998: Personal Apologies and Parliamentary Speeches." Available from http://www.autlii.edu.au/au/special/rsjproject/rslibrary/parliamentary/sorry/index.html.

Schabas, William A. (2000). *Genocide in International Law.* Cambridge, U.K.: Cambridge University Press.

Daniel D. Ntanda Nsereko

Forensics

Forensics involves a multidisciplinary team of scientists, including medical doctors, anthropologists, physicists, and odontologists (scientists specializing in teeth), who carry out precise analysis of an event and evidence related to it. Their work is geared to providing a legal body with elements that serve to support or refute a testimony or document—a letter left behind by a victim, for example. When a scientific discipline is applied to a legal proceeding, it is called a forensic science. A forensic expert is someone who undertakes a scientific investigation that provides information, which is then used in the legal process. When a scientist provides scientific information on a case, the court considers him or her an expert witness. In most cases, this scientific information comes from the analysis of physical evidence, whether biological (a cadaver, skeletal remains, a bloodstain, saliva on an envelope) or nonbiological (projectiles, synthetic fibers, and other objects relevant to an investigation).

Physical evidence can be very important in the legal process. In contrast to witness testimony, it is difficult to manipulate physical evidence to benefit any party to a dispute, since the conclusions must be measurable, and based in a series of demonstrable steps accepted by a scientific community. In other words, scientific methods are important for the resolution of a case because they provide a degree of certainty greater than that of a testimony. A witness can be submitted to pressure, lie, become confused, or forget. Likewise, the certainty provided by physical evidence is greater than that of the content of a document, which can be true or false information. On the other hand, due to the complexity of forensic evidence, the people in the best position to alter evidence are the expert witnesses themselves. For this reason, the integrity of the expert witnesses is very important, as is the independence of the investigation. In an independent investigation, the scientist works free of any pressure to draw a particular conclusion and does not depend on either party to a dispute.

Although many disciplines contribute to legal problems, some are considered "traditional" and constitute the nucleus of what are called the forensic sciences. Historically, medicine was the scientific discipline par excellence in medical-legal investigations. The forensic disciplines used most frequently are forensic pathology, forensic odontology, toxicology, forensic

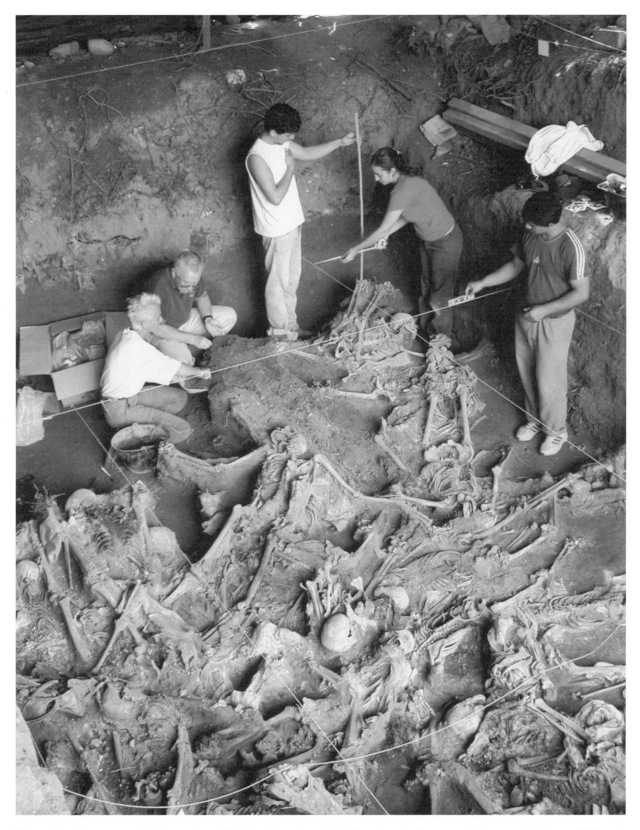

Exhumation of a mass grave in the province of Cordoba, Argentina, with bodies of people disappeared in the country between 1976 and 1977, during the last dictatorship in Argentina. [ARGENTINE FORENSIC ANTHROPOLOGY TEAM]

genetics, criminalistics, and forensic psychology. Disciplines relatively new to the legal context include archaeology and anthropology, involved in the recovery and analysis of skeletal remains and associated evidence; forensic taphonomy, or the study of changes in the body following death, and its interactions with the environment, including flora and fauna (entomology), which can indicate how long a person has been buried in a location; and forensic engineering, the analysis of buildings, which can establish the causes of a fire or an explosion.

"Criminalistics," or criminalistic sciences, are dedicated to the analysis of objects, fluids, or documents found in association with a crime scene, such as cadavers, blood, semen, fingerprints, documents, bullets, and firearms. This list can be much longer depending on the circumstances of a case. One could add forensic psychiatry, which plays an important role in determining the mental health of the accused, witnesses, and accusers, or the damage inflicted on the victim of a crime.

Physical evidence is usually studied in order to answer several key questions about a crime. A forensic doctor might study a cadaver to try to establish cause of death of an individual, while a forensic anthropologist would examine the skeletal remains. An odontologist studies dentition, the unique characteristics of an individual's teeth, to identify a body or to gain information from bite marks, for example. A chemist or a biologist might analyze a blood or semen sample to establish a person's genetic profile. This combination of disciplines contributes to a more complete analysis of the available evidence. Together, they can give a prosecutor objective information about identities and about both the cause and manner of a person's death. While the cause of a death might be "gunshot wound to the head," the manner of death, or how the person died, is a separate question. Was it the result of the action of another person (homicide), self-inflicted (suicide), or accidental? Another conclusion regarding manner of death includes "natural causes," for example, an illness. When there is simply not enough information to establish circumstances, the manner of death must be declared "undetermined."

In summary, a forensic investigation is always an interdisciplinary effort, to which specialists from many fields bring methods and techniques approved by their disciplinary communities to solve a legal case.

The Forensic Sciences and Political, Ethnic, or Religious Violence

During the twentieth century legal and political concepts such as genocide, war crimes, human rights violations, crimes against humanity, and violations of international law have become everyday terms for making sense of the use of violence, such as kidnapping, torture, extrajudicial execution, displacement of populations, concentration camps, and famines generated for political reasons.

Frequently, as violent processes come to their conclusions, and sometimes while they are still in progress, victims, affected communities, other parts of society, and/or the international community demand an investigation based on the rights to truth and justice. These investigations usually include a series of objectives:

1. To know what happened to the victims

2. To establish responsibilities: Who did what to whom?

3. To assign responsibilities and to bring those responsible to court

4. To establish measures, based on knowledge of the truth, to ensure that the events do not recur, and that they are not forgotten, and to make reparations to the people affected, so that society can begin the long process of reconstruction and eventual reconciliation with its recent past

Over the course of the twentieth century the objectives of different movements in search of truth and justice have varied from one country to the next, according to their unique histories, political circumstances, the balance of forces among parties to the conflicts, and the degree of cohesion of each society. Based on the aftermath of World War II, it is possible to elaborate a kind of typology of responses to periods of political violence: special investigative commissions, such as truth commissions, national and international tribunals, and total or partial amnesty laws, among others. In general, these processes have drawn increasingly on the forensic sciences to obtain objective, impartial, and concrete information about events under investigation.

Argentina

Argentina was governed by a military junta from 1976 until 1983. In 1984 a new, democratically elected president, Raúl Alfonsín, established Argentina's Truth Commission. After nine months of work, the Commission concluded that the country's armed and security forces had "disappeared" approximately nine thousand people—illegally detained them without providing their families with any information regarding their fates.

In 1988, at the request of the families and with the permission of the judge in charge of investigations, the Argentine Forensic Anthropology Team (*Equipo Argentino de Antropologia Forense* or EAAF) began work in Sector 134. Sector 134 is a rectangular area 12 by 24 meters situated at the rear of Avellaneda Cemetery, between the main graveyard and a city street. When the military took power in 1976, Sector 134 was placed under police guard. The high walls and a single metal gate concealed it from the eyes of curious passersby.

During the first three years of the military government, when thousands of people disappeared, people living across the back street observed military trucks and police vehicles entering and leaving Sector 134 through the gate, day and night. Isolated and abandoned for several years, it eventually became overgrown with weeds. Although many people suspected it contained the remains of *desaparecidos* (disappeared persons), Sector 134, like other places across the country, could not be investigated until 1984.

As in most of EAAF's investigations, work on the case followed four basic steps, described in greater detail below. In general, these steps are:

1. Historical research

2. Collection of antemortem data

3. Archaeological recovery of evidence

4. Laboratory analysis

The exact sequence of these steps can vary depending on each case. The historical research phase in particular tends to be ongoing, as additional sources of information become available. For example, the collection of antemortem data (information about the physical characteristics of individual victims) continues into the present.

Historical Research

The objective of this phase is to collect all information that can shed light on the case. It is compiled from surviving written records and by interviewing witnesses. The answers to an exhaustive set of questions help to develop strategies and hypotheses, which in turn structure the archaeological and analytic approaches to the case.

Despite official secrecy surrounding the repression, routine documents such as cemetery registers and death certificates related to Sector 134 showed that at least 220 people had been buried there during the junta years. Of these, 160 were described as unidentified young people, exhibiting gunshot wounds, whose bodies had been brought to the cemetery by police or military personnel. Most were buried between 1976 and 1978, at the peak of the repression. After 1978 burials continued, though at a slower rate, until 1982.

The repression in Argentina was organized in complex ways. Typically, a disappeared person was kidnapped by the military or security forces and taken to a clandestine detention center. At these centers, or "CDCs," most detainees were severely tortured. After days, weeks, or months, they were released, transferred to a legal prison, or extrajudicially executed. The bodies of persons permanently disappeared were either buried as *ningún nombre* (NN or anonymous persons) in municipal cemeteries, or were dumped from airplanes into the Argentine Sea. Often, a single prisoner would pass through several of the more than 350 CDCs that existed at the time. This fact makes tracing the painful journey of an individual *desaparecido* from the place of abduction to his or her grave a formidable problem. Still, through painstaking study of the documentary records and interviews with the few survivors, patterns began to emerge. Each death squad—much like an ordinary criminal organization—develops its own modus operandi. These journeys can be partially reconstructed to help fill in the gaps of information about individuals, and to help EAAF form hypotheses about the connection between particular CDCs and the cemeteries they may have used to dispose of bodies.

EAAF also collects information about members of unions and political, student, and guerrilla organizations, who were the regime's primary targets during those years. When the kidnappers made "sweeps" targeting a particular group, their members were likely to wind up in the same CDCs and, eventually, the same graves. Unfortunately, the same is often true of family members. In 1998 the work of analyzing the historical record was tremendously advanced when EAAF was finally given access to police records that had been previously unavailable to the public.

Collection of Antemortem Data

Historical investigation helps EAAF to decide which families to contact. With the help of presumed victims' relatives, EAAF can collect antemortem data—physical descriptions of the victim while still alive—through interviews with them and with family doctors and dentists. Antemortem data includes variable that can also be observed in the skeletal remains, such as age at death, sex, stature, and laterality (right- or left-handedness), as well as dental information, and any diseases or old injuries, particularly fractures. Today, genealogical information is especially important, since family members may eventually be asked for samples for DNA identification.

Archaeology

EAAF completed excavation of Sector 134 in March 1992, after exploring the entire area (432 square meters). They found a series of nineteen mass graves and eleven single burials. The mass graves were roughly oval-shaped, around 3 meters in diameter, and 2 to 3 meters in depth. The number of skeletons per grave ranged from ten to twenty-eight. Nearly all were buried without clothing. Personal effects were few: EAAF found wedding rings among the hand bones of two individuals and metal crosses associated with two others. EAAF also recovered two coins, one dated 1958 and the other 1976. The ballistic evidence consisted of more than three hundred projectiles, many of which were fragmented or deformed. No cartridge cases were found.

Laboratory Analysis

The exhumation of Sector 134 yielded a total of 324 skeletons—that is, 104 more than were indicated by the cemetery records. Approximately 77.8 percent of the skeletons were males. Most of the females belonged to younger age groups, comprising about one-third of the 21- through 45-year-old group, but only about one-tenth of the individuals over 60. This overall pattern reflects the fact that during the six-year period that Sector 134 was used as a burial ground, "ordinary" unidentified bodies (belonging mainly to elderly male indigents) were buried in the same mass graves as the desaparecidos, who were predominately young and often female.

EAAF found evidence of gunshot wounds to the head and/or chest in 178 (55%) of the skeletons, nearly all of which belonged to individuals who were under 50 years of age at the time of death. In contrast, such wounds were rare in the over-50 age group. Others who showed no signs of gunshot wounds could have also died violently, since it is known that a number of desaparecidos succumbed to the effects of physical torture (usually electrical) to which nearly all were subjected.

The skeletons exhumed from Sector 134 fell into two main groups. The first, smaller contingent consisted of elderly individuals, mostly male, who had died, as far as could be determined, of natural causes. They represented the ordinary NN population. The second, larger, and much younger group, almost one-fourth of whom were female, had died of gunshot wounds.

El Salvador

The El Mozote massacre was the largest killing of civilians reported during El Salvador's twelve-year Civil War (1980–1992). From December 6 to December 16, 1981, the Salvadoran Army conducted what it called Operation Rescue in the northeastern province of Morazán. It had two objectives: first, to force FMLN (*Frente Farabundo Martí para la Liberación Nacional*) guerrillas from the area and destroy their clandestine radio station, and second, to eliminate FMLN supporters among the civilian population. Spearheading the operation was the elite Atlacatl Battalion, a U.S.–trained and equipped counterinsurgency unit.

Reportedly, after a few encounters with the army, the guerrilla forces left the area. On December 9, as part of a "scorched earth" strategy, the army arrived in the hamlet of El Mozote, killed the villagers, destroyed their houses, burned their fields, and slaughtered their livestock. Over the next few days they repeated the same procedure in five other nearby hamlets. Some of the inhabitants of the outlying villages, alerted by the El Mozote massacre, managed to escape. Each night survivors returned to their villages under the cover of darkness to bury as many victims as possible in common graves where they were found. Of the survivors, most escaped across the Honduran border to United Nations (UN) refugee camps; others joined the FMLN or took refuge in other regions of El Salvador.

The outlying villages remained largely abandoned until 1989, when survivors began to return from Honduras. El Mozote itself remained almost deserted until several years later. The events, known as the Massacre of El Mozote, became the topic of intense debate in both El Salvador and the United States. At the time little information was available to the Salvadoran public regarding the nature of military operations in the countryside. There was no opposition press in the early 1980s, and such information as did exist was controlled by the armed forces. Only one local newspaper, *La Prensa Gráfica,* reported on Operation Rescue. In a story published on December 9, 1981, shortly after the operation began, the paper noted that, according to military sources, the area was ". . . under strict control of the army to avoid any regrettable or unpleasant act" and that access was denied to journalists and the International Committee of the Red Cross (ICRC). The FMLN's *Radio Venceremos* reported the massacre toward the end of December 1981.

The massacre became known to the international community on January 27, 1982, when three journalists from the *Washington Post* and the *New York Times* and a photojournalist walked into the area from Honduras. They interviewed survivors and took photographs, all of which were printed in their newspapers.

Reports of the El Mozote incident sparked conflict in the U.S. Congress, where the renewal of military aid to El Salvador was already the subject of controversy. Both the Salvadoran government and the U.S. State Department acknowledged that a military operation had occurred in the area, but insisted that what transpired in El Mozote had been a battle between the Salvadoran Army and the FMLN and no evidence of a "massacre" existed. Reports to the contrary were discounted as FMLN propaganda, and military aid was renewed.

Investigation of the Massacre

The refusal of both governments to support further investigations removed it from public attention in El Salvador and the United States for several years. Human rights groups, however, continued to press for investigation. In 1989, at the request of organizations from Morazán, the Human Rights Legal Office of the Archbishop of San Salvador, *Tutela Legal,* launched an investigation of the massacre. It found that about eight hundred villagers had been killed and over 40 percent of the victims were children under ten years of age. In October 1990 *Tutela Legal* helped several survivors of the massacre initiate a lawsuit against the army. To help build their case, *Tutela Legal* planned to conduct exhumations in El Mozote and requested forensic assistance from EAAF. In 1991 EAAF members made a preliminary trip to El Salvador, but the investigation was blocked by judicial officials who refused to grant permission for exhumations.

In early 1992, shortly after the Salvadoran government and the guerrilla army signed a peace agreement, *Tutela Legal* again invited EAAF to assist with its investigation. An EAAF member spent three months preparing and conducting a preliminary historical investigation. With the help of survivors, EAAF was able to locate some of the graves, gain an idea of the number of bodies in each, and compile lists of possible victims. EAAF members were named as expert witnesses in the El Mozote case. However, the Supreme Court and the local judge overseeing the case again denied permission for exhumations. Finally, in the fall of 1992, the UN Truth Commission for El Salvador paved the way for exhumations and appointed EAAF as technical consultants.

The forensic team was directed to conduct the excavation of Site 1 in the hamlet of El Mozote. The site consisted of the ruins of a small, one-room adobe building (4.3 x 6.4 meters) called *el convento,* which had stood next to the village church. Its walls had collapsed inward, leaving a meter-high mound of debris that included its charred roof beams. Removal of this debris revealed, lying on the floor, the commingled skeletons of 141 individuals, 134 of whom were under the age of 12. The adults consisted of six women and one elderly man. Fetal bones were found within the pelvic basin of one of the women. Along with remnants of clothing were dolls, marbles, toy cars, religious medals, crosses, and a few coins.

A total of 245 spent cartridge cases were recovered. Most were found in the southwest corner of the room,

indicating that the shooters were most likely standing close to this area. They were submitted to a U.S.–based archaeologist and ballistics expert. All the cartridges, with exception of one, were from 5.56-caliber bullets issued years before by the North Atlantic Treaty Organization (NATO). The ballistics expert determined that they had been fired from U.S.–manufactured M-16 automatic rifles. All of the cartridge cases bore the head stamps of the Lake City Arms Plant, located near Independence, Missouri, a U.S. Army provider. The firing pin impressions and ejection marks also indicated that at least twenty-four individual firearms were represented among the recovered cartridge cases. Various sources claimed that the Atlacatl Batallion was the only Salvadoran Army unit that possessed this type of rifle at the time of the massacre.

From within the building 263 bullet fragments were recovered. Most were concentrated in the northeast side of the room, opposite the corner where the cartridges were found. Most were embedded in the bones of the victims or in close relationship to them. In nine cases, bullets had penetrated the floor directly under gunshot wounds of the skull or thorax, showing that these victims were lying on the floor and the shooter was standing more or less directly over them. Although some of the children may have been shot outside and their bodies later dumped in the building, the recovered ballistic evidence demonstrated that the number of rounds fired was sufficient to account for all deaths.

After exhumation the skeletons were removed to a morgue in San Salvador for more detailed examination. At this stage additional forensic anthropologists, one forensic pathologist, and one forensic radiologist from the United States led the laboratory analysis of the remains. Osteological and dental age determination showed that the children ranged in age from birth to about 12 years, with a mean of 6.8 years. All the victims, including the seven adults, exhibited perimortem trauma typical of high-velocity gunshot wounds, postmortem crushing injuries, and exposure to fire.

The findings from Site 1 were among the principal bases for the UN Truth Commission's conclusion that the Salvadoran Army had committed a massacre in El Mozote and five nearby villages, which resulted in the deaths of at least five hundred persons and probably many more. The report also included the names of high-ranking officers in the armed forces of El Salvador who were responsible for the operation. The Commission's findings prompted the U.S. administration of president Bill Clinton to publicly rectify the U.S. State Department's previous position that the massacre had never occurred. In El Salvador the Atlacatl Battalion was officially disbanded, although many of its members were simply transferred to other army units.

During the 1992 mission the EAAF exhumed only one site in El Mozote, yet many other clandestine graves remained there and in the other five villages. Upon concluding its work in March 1993, the UN Truth Commission strongly urged that investigations be continued into wartime human rights violations, including the El Mozote massacre. However, a few days after the UN report was released, the Salvadoran legislature passed an amnesty law that not only barred prosecution of persons who committed human rights violations during the war, but which was interpreted at the time as preempting any further investigations (including exhumation) at El Mozote or of other similar cases.

Despite the amnesty, relatives of the victims of the El Mozote massacre and other incidents of human rights violations across El Salvador continued to demand further exhumations. Finally, in 2000, in a changed political climate, the judiciary approved the petition to resume exhumations on humanitarian grounds, though it ruled out any prosecution. EAAF committed itself to continuing to exhumations through 2004, in El Mozote and surrounding villages. The renewed project included training for local doctors and dentists from the Medical Legal Institute, so that they might eventually carry out similar work in other civil war cases. As in all of EAAF's investigations, the most immediate priority is to assist families in their long search for the truth about the fates of their loved ones. But in a broader context, the investigation's findings help clarify the historical record of one of the most contested events in Salvadoran history. Moreover, by gaining acceptance in the Salvadoran courts, forensic anthropological evidence may also contribute to strengthening democratic and judicial institutions by providing new tools to uphold the rule of law.

SEE ALSO Archaelogy; Evidence; Investigation; Mass Graves

BIBLIOGRAPHY

American Academy of Forensic Sciences. Available from http://www.aafs.org.

Argentine Forensic Anthropology Team (EAAF). Available from htp://www.eaaf.org.

Caddy, B. (2001). "Training and Education of the Forensic Professional for the New Millennium." Paper presented at the II Regional Course on Forensic Physics, Bariloche, Argentina.

Doretti, M., and L. Fondebrider (2001). "Science and Human Rights—Truth, Justice, Reparation and Reconciliation: A Long Way in Third World Countries." In Archaeologies of the Contemporary Past, ed. V. Buchli and L. Gavin. London: Routledge.

Doretti, M., and C. C. Snow (2003). "Forensic Anthropology and Human Rights: The Argentine Experience." In Hard Evidence. Case Studies in Forensic Anthropology, ed. D. W. Steadman. Upper Saddle River, N.J.: Prentice Hall.

Gutman, R., ed. (1999). Crimes of War: What the Public Should Know. New York: W.W. Norton.

Haglund, William D. (2002). "Recent Mass Graves: An Introduction." In Advances in Forensic Taphonomy, ed. William D. Haglund and M. Sorg. Boca Raton, Fla.: CRC Press.

"Human Remains–Forensic Sciences and Ethics" and "AI-Forensic Medicine and Ethics." Available from http://www.web.amnesty.org/ai.nsf/index/ACT750121999.

ICRC Project. "The Missing." Available from http://www.themissing.icrc.org.

James, S. J., and J. J. Norrdby, eds. (2003). Forensic Science, an Introduction to Scientifique and Investigative Techniques. Boca Raton, Fla.: CRC Press.

Kirshner, R. H., and K. E. Hannibal (1994). "The Application of the Forensic Sciences to Human Rights Investigations." Medicine and Law 13:451–460.

Physicians for Human Rights (PHR). Available from http://www.phrusa.org.

Snow, C., et al. (1984). "The Investigation of the Human Remains of the 'Disappeared' in Argentina." American Journal of Medicine and Pathology 5(4):297–299.

Steadman, D. W., and William D. Haglund (2001). "The Anthropologist/Archaeologist in International Human Rights Investigations." Paper presented at the Annual Meeting of the American Academy of Forensic Sciences, Seattle, Wash., February 19, 2001.

Stover, E., and G. Peress (1998). The Graves: Srebrenica & Vukovar. Zurich: Scalo.

Stover, E., and R. Shigekane (December 2002). "The Missing in the Aftermath of War: When Do the Needs of Victims' Families and International War Crimes Tribunals Clash?" Magazine of the ICRC 84.

UNITED NATIONS DOCUMENTS

Fondebrider, L., P. Bernardi, and M. Doretti (1993). Archaeological Report on Site 1 of El Mozote. New York: United Nations Truth Commission for El Salvador.

Guidelines for the Conduct of United Nations Inquiries into Allegations of Massacres (1995). UN document DPI/1710.

Manual for the Prevention of Extra-Legal, Arbitrary and Summary Executions (1991). UN document ST/CSDHA/12.

Scott, D. (1993). Firearm Identification of the El Mozote Execution Site. New York: United Nations Truth Commission for El Salvador.

Snow, C., R. Kirshner, and J. Fitzpatrick (1993). Laboratory Report on Site 1 of El Mozote. New York: United Nations Truth Commission for El Salvador.

Luis Fondebrider
Mercedes Doretti

France in Tropical Africa

France has been actively involved in the exploitation of goods, services, and labor in tropical Africa since the seventeenth century. Despite the public avowal of universal human rights within its national borders since the establishment of the First Republic in 1792, France's commitment to collective and individual rights in its African territories waxed and waned over the period of formal colonialism and varied by colony. The reestablishment of slavery by Emperor Napoleon I in 1804 was characteristic of this wayward policy and practice. French cultural, political, and development policies in colonial Africa were informed by the French Republican tradition, but shaped by administrative and economic exigencies that contradicted Republican values.

France regained its tiny colonial outposts in Senegal in 1817, following the Napoleonic Wars. This was part of an international agreement that included active participation in efforts to end the transatlantic slave trade and promote the production of "legitimate" commerce. Nevertheless, France returned to an African world that had been subject to the predations and insecurities of the slave trade for four centuries. France had been engaged in the transatlantic slave trade since 1644. French demand for slaves in the Caribbean colonies, particularly in Saint Domingue (later Haiti), contributed to the institutionalization of predation in precolonial Africa. Slaves of varying status were widespread in France's African colonies until 1848 when, under the Second Republic, France abolished slavery by reasserting the principle of the rights of man. Slaves, slavery, and servants remained central social and economic features of French colonies, however, well into the twentieth century.

With the beginning of aggressive colonial conquest in 1879, French administration extended over extensive areas of West and Central Africa, where domestic slavery and slave trading were widely practiced. The National Assembly, however, was reluctant to support the costs of expensive military campaigns in the African interior. Consequently, military leaders recruited African soldiers and auxiliaries, only some of whom received regular pay. While all military action entails human rights abuses, French colonial conquests involved some distinctive characteristics. France rewarded African soldiers and auxiliaries with a share of captured booty. French officers often distributed slaves, and thus participated in the persistence of slavery. Conquest also involved requisition of food stores, cattle, and labor. Even "peaceful" colonial missions of exploration, such as that of Paul Beloni de Challu in the Congo, involved the recruitment or impressment of an

Nineteenth-century artist's rendering of the arrival of the French army at Cotonou, on the West African coast, in 1851. As the French colonial thrust into the interior intensified, with African collaborators (such as the Senegalese soldiers shown here) and the threat of coercion, its abuses became rife, notably the taking of slaves. [ARCHIVO ICONOGRAFICO, S.A./CORBIS]

army of porters. For example, between 1896 and 1897, the Marchand expedition from Ubangi-Shari to the Upper Nile recruited some 3,000 porters.

The active military phase of colonialism in French West Africa (consisting of Senegal, Soudan [now Mali], Ivory Coast, Dahomey, Upper Volta [now Burkina Faso], Mauritania, and Niger) persisted into 1898. Military officers also found themselves charged with administering newly conquered territories, and many imposed forms of discipline that led to human rights abuses. In 1893, the civilian governor of the Sudan, Louis Alphonse Grodet, sought unsuccessfully to impose Republican values on his military administrators by prohibiting corporal punishment. Violence was an endemic part of this early phase in the establishment of colonial order. The capital of the Kingdom of Dahomey, Abomey, was burned to the ground and the king exiled in 1898. Because colonial administrators were so few in number relative to the size of the African population and the territories that they administered, officials had relatively little power outside their headquarters and could accomplish little without African collaborators and the threat of coercion.

Administrative coercion was enshrined in the establishment of *indigénat,* the decree empowering administrators with police powers, in 1887. Administrators could impose fines and prison sentences for a set of defined offenses dealing mostly with acts of disrespect or disorder toward colonial officials and official regulations without recourse to the courts or approval from superiors. Any French citizen or government official could summarily punish any African subject for a vast array of minor infractions, ranging from failing to pay taxes to neglecting to show administrators respect. Originally limited to sixteen identified offenses, the scope of these police functions increased over time. Each colony revised its own list of scheduled offenses. By 1907, the French Sudan listed twenty-four acts that were subject to the *indigénat,* and by 1918 the Ivory Coast had fifty-four. The fact that the *indigénat* was an arbitrary system of summary punishments that were only applied to African subjects (French citizens and assimilated Africans were excluded) and against which there was no appeal increased African resentment toward this aspect of the colonial legal system.

The establishment in 1895 of a federation of French West Africa with a governor-general based in Dakar was, in part, an effort to curtail the powers of the French military and to promote a civilian Republican agenda. In 1903 the rule of law was strengthened with the enactment of a new colonial legal code that provided an organized and hierarchical system of courts for both French citizens and African subjects. Although the West African federation was designed to tame the military, abuses persisted. In Fort Crampel in the military district of Chad in 1903, the French commander, nicknamed "the wild beast," celebrated Bastille Day by dynamiting an African accused of disobedience. Periodic revolts and resistance movements were harshly suppressed. Violent insurrections were crushed in northern Ivory Coast and Upper Volta, resulting in thousands of deaths.

In Madagascar and French Equatorial Africa—a federation of territories that included the former slave port of Libreville and the hinterlands annexed by the expeditions of Lieutenant Brazza (Gabon, Congo-Brazzaville, Central Africa, Chad)—the French presence was even fainter than in West Africa, and Republican traditions were more attenuated. In 1885 there were only thirty-six French officials in the Congo region, and perhaps one thousand African auxiliaries recruited locally and from West Africa. By 1904 the number of officials fell to thirty. Despite the paucity of administrators, military tactics were brutal. The suppression of the Madagascar revolt from 1896 to 1898, for instance, left as many as ninety thousand dead.

In the absence of a strong French administrative presence, the subdivisions of the colony adapted the neighboring Congo Free State's *regime domanial* model for economic development. Thus, monopolies over the "products of the soil," in particular rubber and ivory, were ceded to concession companies. The Société du Haut Ogooué acquired eleven million hectares, and the largest publicly traded company, the Compagnie des Sultanats du Haut-Oubangu, operated monopoly rights over 140,000 square kilometers. To make concessions profitable, concessionaires demanded forced labor. Although the French prohibited forced labor in principle, a poll tax was introduced in 1897 that effectively forced Africans to work by extracting resources and selling them to the company. During the early colonial period, sleeping sickness and other diseases preyed heavily on tired workers' immune systems, leading to a dramatic population decline. Concessionaires responded to this by increasing and elaborating new methods of coercion. On the Mpoko Concession, one of the few to declare a profit, forty European managers and 400 armed African guards shot on sight any African not collecting rubber. Between 1903 and 1905, the administration reported 1,500 murders. Most concession companies disappeared with the decline in easily accessible wild rubber during World War I, but a few persisted until 1935. The novelist André Gide brought international attention to the human rights abuses of French Equatorial Africa in his 1927 exposé, *Voyage au Congo* (Travel in the Congo). Major administrative reforms in 1906 and 1907 brought French Equatorial Africa into line with French West Africa, but the demand for tropical commodities led to new forms of human rights abuses in the region.

France's mobilization for World War I led to increased demands for military and domestic materials and African troops and porters. Aggressive recruitment of African *tirailleurs* (African riflemen) began in 1915 resulting in localized revolts. In addition to demanding troops, the French imposed a requirement that Africans produce maize, millet, rice, groundnuts, palm products, cotton, and rubber for the war effort. Already introduced in 1912, forced labor for public works was expanded dramatically during wartime mobilization. All French West Africans were subject to eight to twelve days of forced labor per year. In Equatorial Africa, Africans were subject to seven days per year in 1918, which was raised to fifteen days in 1925.

Following the war, the French introduced obligatory peacetime recruitment. The French drafted 14,000 men annually into *tirailleurs* regiments. In the process, they discovered that the majority of young men were not physically fit to serve. Many of the unfit were conscripted into a second tier of recruits for the purposes of public works, a poorly disguised form of *corvée* (forced) labor. Some 127,250 Africans were recruited in this way to work on the Congo-Océan railway in Equatorial Africa, and an annual average of 2,719 Africans were impressed into labor in French West Africa between 1928 and 1946. In the new French-mandated former German colonies of Togo and Cameroon, however, League of Nations treaties banned forced labor. The Permanent Mandates Commission stringently monitored the terms of labor in these two territories, but direct taxation that permitted payment in kind or in labor was permitted.

As France rebuilt its economy during the interwar period, it sought inexpensive raw materials. Africans were forced to cultivate commodities, especially cotton. Even before the war, Gabriel Angoulvant, who served as lieutenant governor of Ivory Coast, had raised cotton exports from zero in 1912 to 350 tons in 1916 by forcing every African subject to produce a certain amount of cotton for export. In 1924, when serving as West Africa's governor-general, Angoulvant proposed solving France's cotton deficit through what he called "the obligation to produce." Forced commodity production led to a food crisis in Ivory Coast, and to various forms of resistance, as well.

Conversely, the interwar period also saw the proliferation of African groups campaigning for human rights and the right to form labor unions. Some movements were inspired by trends back in France, such as the *Ligue pour la défense des droits de l'homme et du citoyen,* which founded branches in Dahomey and Togo, and Socialist Party committees. Others were mobilized by a new sense of rights and entitlements enshrined in the League of Nations charter and the Treaty of Versailles, and by the creation of an internationalized anti-colonial movement led by the Geneva-based International Labor Organization and the Moscow-based Communist International. Yet others were motivated by pan-African sentiments, expressed in such forums as the Pan-African Congresses organized by W. E. B du Bois (first held in Paris 1919); *The Crisis,* published by the NAACP, and *The Black Man,* published by the United Negro Improvement Association (both books were available throughout Africa). Also influential were the early Négritude writers such as Aimé Cesaire, Léopold Sedar Senghor, and Alioune Diop, who later established the journal *Présence Africaine.*

In France, the short-lived Popular Front government of Léon Blum between 1936 and 1938 led to the general reappraisal of colonial policy and to debate about "African human rights." Colonial Minister Maurius Moutet expressed his commitment to the extension of maximum social justice to the colonies and called for a review of colonial polices, including forced labor and commodity production. He also introduced major reforms, such as offering African women the right to choice in their marriages. With the approach of war in Europe, however, the Popular Front collapsed. Even after Germany conquered France, the Vichy government retained control over Algeria, French West Africa, Madagascar, and Togo, and reasserted that the role of colonies was to support the mother country through materiel and labor. Under the governorship of Félix Ebouey, Equatorial Africa and Cameroun sided with the Free French in opposition to Vichy collaborationists. In the territories it controlled, Vichy reestablished forced labor and obligatory commodity production, thus leading to a new phase of rights abuses. In Togo, villagers still narrate the tales of the excessive brutality that was deployed in the collection of oil palm kernels during World War II. A coup in Dakar in 1943, however, brought French West Africa into line with de Gaulle and the Free French.

As the tide of war changed, senior Free French officials met with political and trade union leaders at the Brazzaville Conference in 1944 to discuss postwar colonial policy. Delegates urged that both forced labor and the *indigénat* be replaced with guarantees of free labor and a unified penal code. In 1946, forced labor and the *indigénat* were abolished as part of a wider set of colonial reforms, including new development funds and rights for African political representation. Between 1958 and 1960, French tropical Africa became independent.

The legacy of the French colonial experience for postcolonial human rights regime is ambiguous. Despite the French government's commitment to human rights, its practices in Africa remained contradictory. Most states enshrined human rights in their constitutions during the immediate postcolonial period, but few respected them in practice. Regulation of labor also remains a chimera; Mauritania, for example, has abolished slavery by statute five times since independence in 1960. The post-1990 third wave of democratization in Africa has brought a reflourishing of African civil society and demands for constitutional protections of human rights.

SEE ALSO Algeria; King Leopold II and the Congo; Slavery, Historical; Sudan

BIBLIOGRAPHY

Asiwaju, Tony (1979). "Control through Coercion: A Study of the *Indigénat* Regime in French African Administration." *Bulletin de l'institut fondamental d'Afrique noire,* series B 41, 1:35–75.

Conklin, Alice (1997). *A Mission to Civilize: The Republican Idea of Empire in France and West Africa, 1895–1930.* Stanford, Calif.: Stanford University Press.

Conklin, Alice (1998). "Colonialism and Human Rights, A Contradiction in Terms? The Case of France and West Africa, 1895–1914." *The American Historical Review* 103(2):419–42.

Echenberg, Myron, and Jean Filipovich (1986) "African Military Labour and the Building of the Office du Niger Installations, 1925–50." *Journal of African History* 27 (3):533–551.

Gide, André (1927). *Voyage au Congo: Carnets de route.* Paris: Gallimard, 1995.

Klein, Martin (1998). *Slavery and Colonial Rule in French West Africa.* Cambridge: Cambridge University Press.

Lawrance, Benjamin (2004). "Refreshing Historical Documents of Civil Rights in Africa." *The Oriental Anthropologist* 4:34–59.

Suret-Canale, Jean (1971). *France in Tropical Africa, 1900–1945,* tran. Till Gottheiner, London: C. Hurst.

Benjamin Lawrance
Richard Roberts

Gas

Since ancient times, use of poison has been considered treacherous and, therefore, incompatible with honorable conduct in war. Yet, the history of mankind is blemished with numerous examples of combatants and civilians falling victim to various kinds of poisonous gases, which not only kill, but burn or paralyze the human body; singe lungs; cause blindness, malformations, cancer, and neuropsychiatric damage; or produce permanent genetic mutations, persistently affecting the health of the survivors' succeeding generations.

Use of Gas as a Method of Warfare

The history of the use of gas in the theater of war goes back to the fourth century BCE, when the belligerents in the Peloponnesian War created toxic fumes by igniting pitch and sulfur. However, it was not until the first large-scale use of poison gas by the German army in World War I (1914–1918) that the horrors of gassing were utterly unveiled. The gas attack was launched in April 1915 on the battlefields near Ypres, Belgium, and claimed as many as 5,000 lives and 10,000 casualties. By the end of the war, toxic chemicals, such as chlorine, mustard, and phosgene gases, had wounded more than one million soldiers and civilians and had resulted in nearly 100,000 ghastly deaths.

Use of Gas as a Means of Extermination

At the dawn of World War II (1939–1945), gassing ceased to serve only as a method of warfare. Instead, it developed into the means of extermination in the hands of the German Reich.

The Nazis began utilizing gas in September 1939, initially for the purposes of medical experiments, and later for a calculated slaughter of incurable and mentally ill patients, euphemistically referred to as euthanasia ("good death") program. The method of gassing then in use was the canalization of the exhaust of internal-combustion engines into rooms disguised as showers.

In August 1941 the killing of the sick with carbon monoxide gas was brought to an end. This did not, however, end the Reich's gassing scheme. In contrast, this was precisely the time when the Nazis began to use gas in the pursuit of Adolf Hitler's gruesome plan to exterminate Jews. In its initial stages, the gassing was performed by mobile killing units (*Einsatzgruppen*), which operated hermetically sealed trucks with engine exhaust channeled into the interior compartments. Although the gas vans took a heavy toll (nearly 700,000 victims), they were eventually deemed inefficient for the success of Hitler's Final Solution to what he termed the "Jewish problem." Consequently, in 1942 the Nazis replaced the mobile killing units and their vans with permanent gas chambers, each capable of holding hundreds of people at a time.

The chambers still employed engine exhaust as the killing gas, at first. Due to the frequent mechanical breakdowns of engines, however, in 1943 Commandant Rudolf Hess of the Auschwitz-Birkenau death camp ordered the replacement of carbon monoxide gas with hydrogen cyanide crystals (Zyklon B), which turn into lethal gas immediately upon contact with oxygen. The first experiment with Zyklon B, typically used as

Zyklon B consisted of wood pellets impregnated with liquid hydrocyanic acid. Upon contact with air, the pellets would release deadly hydrogen cyanide gas. In this 1979 photo, the walls of a gas chamber at the Majdanek concentration camp (near Lublin, Poland) are still stained by hydrogen cyanide.[NATHAN BENN/CORBIS]

a disinfectant, was conducted in September 1941 on Russian prisoners of war and inmates of the infirmary. Ultimately, Zyklon B proved the most effective technique of extermination. At the peak of its use, more than 12,000 Jews were being gassed each day at Auschwitz alone.

Use of Gas after World War II

Apart from the use of gas by Egypt against Yemen in the 1960s, the world was free of extensive gassing operations until 1983, when the Iraqi dictator Saddam Hussein launched a chemical campaign in the war against Iran (1980–1988). According to estimates, gases were deployed 195 times, killing or wounding 50,000 Iranians. In April 1987 Hussein turned the poison against his hated internal opponents, the Iraqi Kurds, as well. He launched at least forty gas assaults against the Kurdish population, the most dreadful of which occurred in 1988, between March 16 and March 19, in the town of Halabja. There, mustard gas and the nerve gases sarin and tabun killed 5,000 civilians.

Prohibition of Gas by International Law

The prohibition of poison is one of the oldest rules of the law of the armed conflict. Correspondingly, the use of poison gas, which causes unnecessary suffering and superfluous injury to combatants, and—as a weapon of mass destruction—indiscriminately affects civilian populations, stands in blatant violation of the most vital rules of international customary law applicable to the conduct of armed hostilities: the principles of distinction, military necessity, humanity, and dictates of public conscience.

Gassing has been prohibited since the nineteenth century by more than just customary law. Written agreements, the first being the 1874 Brussels Convention on the Law and Customs of War, and the 1899 Hague Declaration, ban the use of projectiles filled with gases. The landmark twentieth-century treaties include the 1907 Hague Convention IV Respecting the Law and Customs of War on Land (which reaffirmed the ban on poison); the 1925 Geneva Protocol for the Prohibition of the Use of Asphyxiating, Poisonous or Other Gases, and of Bacteriological Methods of Warfare (which constituted a desired response to the atrocities of World War I, but did not provide for any compliance mechanisms); the 1972 Convention on the Prohibition of the Development, Production, and Stockpiling of Bacteriological and Toxin Weapons; and, most important, the 1993 Convention on the Prohibition of Development, Production, Stockpiling, and Use of Chemical Weapons and on their Destruction.

Bringing Those Responsible to Justice

Under contemporary international criminal law, reflected in the 1998 Rome Statute of the International Criminal Court, the employment of asphyxiating, poisonous, or other gases during armed conflicts is deemed a war crime. The utilization of gases as a method of murder or extermination can be qualified as either a crime against humanity or a crime of genocide.

The first international judgment on the gassing of civilians was issued in the aftermath of World War II by the International Military Tribunal at Nuremberg, which convicted a number of major German war criminals for war crimes and crimes against humanity, committed, inter alia, through the use of gas. In the subsequent Nuremberg Proceedings, between 1946 and 1949, similar convictions were imposed upon the physicians who participated in the Nazi euthanasia program or mustard gas experiments (the Doctors Trial), and against SS administrators involved in the construction of gas chambers (*In Re Pohl and Others*). Finally, in a momentous trial known as the Zyklon B case, two German industrialists—Bruno Tesch and Karl Weinbacher of the Tesch and Stabenow company—were sentenced to death for supplying Zyklon B to the concentration camps. Significantly, the court rejected the defendants' contention that they lacked awareness that the toxic pellets were used for extermination, rather than for decontamination. In contrast, an analogous argument was accepted in the trial of executives from the I. G. Farben company, whose subsidiary firm—Degesch—was shipping Zyklon B to death camps along with Tesch and Stabenow. One of the most recent prosecutions occurred in 1963, when the national court of the Federal Republic of Germany convicted Robert Mulka, an adjutant to Hess and a supplier of Zyklon B to the Auschwitz gas chambers.

SEE ALSO Auschwitz; Einsatzgruppen; Ethiopia; Iraq; Kurds; War Crimes

BIBLIOGRAPHY

Center for Nonproliferation Studies (2004). "Chronology of State Use and Biological and Chemical Weapons Control." Available from http://cns.miis.edu/research/cbw/pastuse.htm.

During the investigations that preceded the Nuremberg Tribunal, U.S. and British prosecutors uncovered literally thousands of German documents and artifacts that proved the charges against the defendants. Here, a canister of Zyklon B, seized at the Mauthausen, Austria, concentration camp and later submitted as evidence. [CORBIS]

Goldblat, Jozef (1995). "The 1993 Chemical Weapons Convention: a Significant Step in the Process of Multilateral Disarmament." In *The Convention on the Prohibition and Elimination of Chemical Weapons: a Breakthrough in Multilateral Disarmament*, ed. Daniel Bardonnet. Boston: Martinus Nijhoff Publishers.

Gutman, Israel, ed. (1990). *Encyclopedia of the Holocaust*. New York: Macmillan Publishing Company.

Lippman, Matthew (1996). "Fifty Years after Auschwitz: Prosecutions of Nazi Death Camp Defendants." *Connecticut Journal of International Law* 11:199–278.

Organization for the Prohibition of Chemical Weapons (2002). "Background of Chemical Disarmament." Available from http://www.opcw.org/html/intro/chemdisarm_frameset.html.

Power, Samantha (2002). "Iraq: Human Rights and Chemical Weapons Use Aside." In *A Problem from Hell: America and the Age of Genocide*. New York: Basic Books.

Reitlinger, Gerald (1961). "The Gas Chambers." In *The Final Solution: the Attempt to Exterminate the Jews of Europe 1939–1945*. New York: A.S. Barnes & Co.

United States Holocaust Memorial Museum (2004). "Holocaust Learning Center." Available from http://www.ushmm.org/wlc/en.

Paulina Rudnicka

Geneva Conventions on the Protection of Victims of War

The Geneva Conventions are the essential basis of international humanitarian law applicable in armed conflicts. They evolved from rules of customary international law binding on the entire international community. In the second part of the nineteenth century, when the codification of international law started, most of these rules were included in international treaties, beginning with the 1864 Geneva Convention and the 1899 and 1907 Hague Conventions.

With contemporary wars continuing to produce disastrous effects, the Geneva Conventions signed on August 12, 1949, and two additional protocols adopted on June 8, 1977, are the most important treaties for the protection of victims of war. The treaties adopted include:

- The Geneva Convention for the Amelioration of the Condition of the Wounded and Sick in Armed Forces in the Field (Convention I)

- The Geneva Convention for the Amelioration of the Condition of the Wounded, Sick and Shipwrecked Members of Armed Forces at Sea (Convention II)

- The Geneva Convention Related to the Treatment of Prisoners of War (Convention III)

- The Geneva Convention Related to the Protection of Civilian Persons in Time of War (Convention IV)

- Protocol I Relating to the Protection of Victims of International Armed Conflicts

- Protocol II Relating to the Protection of Victims of Non-International Armed Conflicts

The 1949 Geneva Conventions are a rare example of quasi-universal treaties; by the end of April 2004 some 191 states were signatories to them. The states party to Protocols I and II number 161 and 156, respectively.

Historical Evolution

The effort to protect war victims is as old as conflicts themselves. Such efforts materialized in antiquity and the Middle Ages in all regions, civilizations, and religions. The first international treaty that was adopted aimed to protect soldiers wounded on the battlefield.

It came at the initiative of Henry Dunant, a young Swiss, who after the battle of Solferino, in 1859, witnessed firsthand the misery of forty thousand wounded and the inadequacy of the army health services. On his return to Geneva, Dunant published *A Memory of Solferino,* in which he proposed that warring parties conclude agreements in order to ensure assistance to the wounded and sick. He also proposed the creation of voluntary associations for the same purpose in each country, which later became the Red Cross societies. With the cooperation of four of his compatriots, in particular General Alfred Dufour, Dunant organized the first nongovernmental conference in 1863 to promote some of his ideas.

A year later the Swiss Federal Council invited twenty-five states to participate at a diplomatic conference; it adopted on August 22, 1864, the first Geneva Convention for the Amelioration of the Condition of the Wounded in Armies in the Field. After an unsuccessful attempt in 1868 to adapt the convention to maritime warfare, the International Peace Conference of 1899 in The Hague adopted the Convention for the Adaptation to Maritime Warfare of the Principles of the Geneva Convention, as did the later conference in 1907. The first 1864 Geneva Convention was revised in 1906 and again in 1929, when a new convention, related to the treatment of prisoners of war, was also adopted.

Important work, however, remained: a convention to ensure the protection of civilian populations. The International Committee of the Red Cross (ICRC) presented the draft of such a convention to the XVth International Red Cross Conference held in Tokyo in 1934, with the hope that the new convention would be adopted in 1940. The advent of World War II in September 1939 altered these plans. The ICRC's appeal to warring nations to apply the Tokyo draft on the basis of reciprocity met with no success. Civilians thus remained without appropriate legal protection during World War II.

Development of the Geneva Conventions was the main task of the postwar ICRC. The draft of these instruments was presented to the XVII International Red Cross Conference in Stockholm in 1948, and the ICRC's subsequent Diplomatic Conference, meeting in Geneva from April 21 to August 12, 1949, adopted the four Conventions.

If World War I provided the impetus for the revision and codification of the 1929 Conventions, and World War II that for the revision and new codification of rules in 1949, the nature of conflicts after 1945 required the development of new legal provisions. The rules elaborated in 1949 were not sufficient to ensure the protection of the victims in a growing number of civil wars and wars of national liberation. Technological developments in the means and methods of warfare also required new legislation.

After discussion at several Red Cross conferences—in Vienna (1965), Istanbul (1969), and Tehran (1973)—and the International Human Rights Conference in 1968, the Swiss Federal Council convened a diplomatic conference on the reaffirmation and development of international humanitarian law applicable in armed conflicts. After four sessions this conference adopted the two protocols of 1977.

Provisions Common to the Four Conventions and Protocol I

The Conventions and Protocols are applicable in the case of declared war or any other armed conflict arising between two or more parties from the beginning of such a situation, even if one of them does not recognize the state of war. They also apply to all cases of partial or total occupation, even if such occupation meets with no armed resistance. The application ceases at the general close of military operations. Protected persons benefit from the provisions until final release, repatriation, or settlement. The addition of Protocol I extended the provisions' application to wars of national liberation, that is, to the armed conflicts in which peoples are fighting against colonial domination and alien occupation, and against racist regimes in the exercise of their right of self-determination, as enshrined in the United Nations (UN) Charter and the Declaration on Principles of International Law Concerning Friendly Relations and Co-operation Among States in Accordance with the Charter of the United Nations.

The so-called Martens clause, which dates back to the 1899 and 1907 Hague Conventions, specifies that in cases not covered by the Conventions, Protocols, or other agreements, or in the case where these agreements have been denounced, civilians and combatants remain under the protection and authority of the principles of international law derived from established custom, the principles of humanity, and the dictates of public conscience.

The Conventions and Protocols are applied under the scrutiny of a protecting power, that is, one or more neutral states appointed to safeguard the interests of the parties to the conflict. The ICRC assists the parties in designating a protecting power. An organization that offers all guarantees of impartiality and efficacy may be designated to fulfill the duties incumbent on protecting powers.

The Conventions and Protocols include important provisions to sanction violations of the humanitarian rules. They include administrative and disciplinary sanctions as well as sanctions against "grave breaches" (i.e., war crimes) enumerated in the corresponding articles of each Convention and in the Protocols. Governments are required to enact legislation to provide effective penal sanctions for individuals committing or ordering any grave breaches. They must search for those persons alleged to have committed such acts or who have ordered their commission. Military commanders must prevent breaches, suppress them, and if necessary report them to the authorities. The principle of universality obliges a state either to summon the accused to its own courts or to extradite him or her to the state requesting extradition.

Protection of the Wounded, Sick, and Shipwrecked

The first and second Geneva Conventions include almost identical provisions on the protection of persons and property: the first applying to the armed forces on land, the second to armed forces at sea. Persons needing medical care and refraining from any act of hostility shall be respected and protected. Wounded, sick, and shipwrecked combatants who are captured become prisoners of war.

The Conventions and Protocols also ensure respect and protection for the medical and religious personnel of the parties to a conflict, whether military or civilian. Protocol I also provides that no one may be punished for performing medical procedures compatible with medical ethics, regardless of the beneficiaries of this activity. Conversely, no one may be compelled to carry out acts contrary to the rules of medical ethics.

Military or civilian medical establishments, units, and vehicles may not be attacked or damaged, or hindered in the exercise of their functions. They are protected, but such protection ceases if they commit acts harmful to the enemy after a warning setting a reasonable time limit has expired and after such a warning has gone unheeded. The Conventions and Protocol I also protect medical transportation.

A distinctive emblem, that is, a red cross or red crescent on a white background, must be displayed on the installations and mobile equipment of medical units, on medical transportation vehicles, on hospital ships, in hospital zones and localities, and on the person, clothing, and headgear of all medical and religious personnel. ICRC and their duly authorized personnel are permitted to use the emblem of the red cross on a white background at all times. Reprisals against protected persons and objects are strictly prohibited.

Protection of Prisoners of War

Any combatant who falls into enemy hands is a prisoner of war. The status of prisoners of war is governed jointly by Article 4 of the Third Convention, and Articles 43 and 44 of Protocol I. Article 43 provides the definition of armed forces as follows: forces, groups, and units under a command responsible to their Party to the conflict for the conduct of its subordinates, subject to an internal disciplinary system that, among other things, shall enforce compliance with the rules of international law applicable in armed conflicts.

A further obligation is for a combatant to distinguish him or herself from the civilian population by wearing a uniform or distinctive sign recognizable at a distance during military operations. Nevertheless, according to Article 44, paragraph 3, of Protocol I, in exceptional cases of a specific nature, a combatant may be released from this duty. However, in such situations, these combatants must distinguish themselves by carrying arms openly during the engagement and during any period when they are visible to the adversary while engaged in a military deployment preceding the launching of an attack in which they are to participate. This 1977 amendment arose in response to guerilla wars, where uniforms are often lacking. Spies and mercenaries are not entitled to the status of prisoner of war.

Prisoners of war fall into the hands of the enemy power and not the actual individuals who captured them. They must be treated humanely and they are protected by the rules of the Third Convention. As for potential sources of information, the prisoners are obliged to give only "surname, first name and rank, date of birth, and army regimental, personal or serial number, or failing this, equivalent information."

If captured in a combat zone, prisoners must be evacuated to camps situated outside the area of danger. The Convention regulates prisoners' living conditions, food, clothing, medical treatment, the type of work they may be required to do, relations with the outside world (in particular, correspondence with their families), and the right to receive individual parcels or shipments. The prisoners are "subject to the laws, regulations and orders in force in the armed forces of the detaining power." They may be submitted to penal and disciplinary sanctions. They may be put on trial for an offense committed prior to capture, notably for war crimes.

Seriously wounded or sick prisoners may be transported back home during a conflict, or released on parole, but they may not serve in the armed forces of their homeland subsequently. The detention of prisoners of war lasts in principle until the cessation of active hostilities, after which they "shall be released and repatriated without delay."

Protection of Civilian Populations and Civilian Objects

Few provisions of the Geneva Conventions deal with the general protection of the civilian population against the effect of hostilities. Before Protocol I most of the rules were included in the Hague Convention and customary rules of international law. Part IV of Protocol I addresses this issue in defining a civilian as "any person not belonging to the armed forces." In case of doubt, an individual is considered to be a civilian. The civilian population and individual civilians are protected against dangers arising from military operations. They shall not be the object of attack. The prohibition includes attacks launched indiscriminantly. Reprisals against civilians are also prohibited.

Similarly, a civilian object is anything that is not a "military objective" (i.e., objects that by their nature, location, purpose, or use make an effective contribution to military action and whose total or partial destruction, capture, or neutralization, in the circumstances existing at the time, offers a definite military advantage). Civilian objects shall not be the object of attack or reprisals. Special protection is provided to certain categories of civilian property:

- Cultural property, historical monuments, works of art, or places of worship that constitute the cultural and spiritual heritage of peoples

- Objects indispensable to the survival of the civilian population

- Natural environment, protected against widespread, long-term, and severe damage

- Works and installations containing dangerous forces, the release of which could cause severe losses among civilians

A special treaty—the 1954 Hague Convention for the Protection of Cultural Property in the Event of Armed Conflict and two additional protocols to it—supplement the protection outlined in the first item above. The Convention and Protocol also established protective zones: hospital and safety zones, neutralized zones, nondefended localities, and demilitarized zones.

General Protection Afforded by the Fourth Geneva Convention

Several provisions of the 1907 Hague Convention and the Fourth Geneva Convention concern the general protection of the civilian population against the effects of hostilities. As indicated in Article 4, the Fourth Convention concentrates on those who, at a given moment and in any manner whatsoever, find themselves, in case of a conflict or occupation, in the hands of a party to the conflict or occupying power of which they are not nationals. Part II of the Geneva Convention addresses the general protection of populations against certain consequences of war and covers "the whole of the population of the countries in conflict, without any adverse distinction based, in particular, on race, nationality, religion or political opinion, and [is] intended to alleviate the sufferings caused by war."

The 1977 Protocol significantly extends protection to specific categories: the wounded and sick; hospitals and hospital staff; land, sea, and air transportation; consignments of medical supplies, food, and clothing; protection of children, women, and families; provision of family news; and protection of refugees and stateless persons, including journalists.

Part III of the Fourth Geneva Convention deals with the two major categories of the civilian population: those who are in the territory of the enemy and those who are in occupied territory.

Section I includes common provisions for these two categories: Article 27 declares that

> Persons protected are entitled, in all circumstances, to respect for their persons, their honor, their family rights, their religious convictions and practices, and their manners and customs. They shall at all times be humanely treated, and shall be protected especially against all acts of violence or threats thereof and against insults and public curiosity.

Protection is granted without any adverse distinction. Special protection is granted to women. Protected persons will have the ability to make applications to the protecting powers, the ICRC, the National Red Cross or Red Crescent societies of the country where they reside, and any other organization that might assist them. Physical or moral coercion, pillage, and the taking of hostages are strictly prohibited.

Two additional sections of the Convention address the issues of aliens in the territory of a party to the conflict and the treatment of civilians in occupied territories. The rules concerning treatment of internees—outlined in Section IV—are very similar to those concerning the internment of prisoners of war.

Additional Protocol I, Article 75, was an important later provision. It specifies that persons who fall under the power of a party to a conflict and who do not benefit from more favorable treatment under the Convention and the Protocol shall be treated humanely in all circumstances and shall benefit from fundamental guarantees without discrimination of any kind.

Noninternational Armed Conflicts

The Geneva Conventions were designed for application during international armed conflict, as defined in Common Article 2. For the first time in 1949 the efforts of the ICRC and some states led to the adoption of the first provision of international law dealing with noninternational armed conflicts. This provision, Common Article 3, applies to all internal conflicts occurring in the territory of one of the parties to the Convention. Its scope of application is large, but the substantive, material protection it affords is limited to the minimum. The article specifies only the minimum humanitarian treatment to be provided to the victims of conflicts. It distinguishes two categories of protected persons: those taking no active part in the hostilities, including members of the armed forces who have laid down their arms, and those felled by sickness, wounds, detention, or any other cause. They shall in all circumstances be treated humanely, without any adverse distinction made on the basis of race, color, religion, sex, birth, wealth, or any other similar criteria.

The following acts with respect to protected persons are, and shall remain, prohibited at all times and in all places:

(a) Violence to life and person, in particular, murder of all kinds, mutilation, cruel treatment and torture.

(b) Taking of hostages.

(c) Outrages upon personal dignity, in particular, humiliating and degrading treatment.

(d) The passing of sentences and the carrying out of executions without previous judgment pronounced by a regularly constituted court affording all the judicial guarantees which are recognized as indispensable by civilized peoples.

The second category includes the wounded and sick who have to be collected and cared for.

Common Article 3 also provides that a humanitarian organization, such as the ICRC, may offer its services to the parties to a conflict and that these parties should further endeavor to bring into force, by special agreements, all or part of the Conventions' other provisions. In terms of the application of this article, it provides that such shall not affect the legal status of the parties to a conflict.

Common Article 3 was for several decades the only provision addressing internal conflicts and civil wars, including the wars of national liberation that took place in the 1960s. During the period following World War II the majority of the conflicts were noninternational. It was therefore quite obvious that improving the protection of the victims of these conflicts had to be the major objective of the new codification efforts occurring in the mid-1970s. It was only owing to the ICRC and a few delegations that Additional Protocol II was adopted during the very last session of the 1974 to 1977 Diplomatic Conference, albeit in reduced form.

Protocol II's purpose was to develop and supplement Article 3 without modifying its existing conditions of application. It was imperative to maintain the humanitarian minimum guaranteed by this article in all circumstances. Although Article 3's scope of application is very large, not providing a precise definition of conflict and leaving its determination to states or humanitarian organizations, the threshold of Protocol II is much higher. It applies only when a conflict takes "place on the territory of a High Contracting Party between its armed forces and dissident armed forces or other organized armed groups which, under responsible command, exercise such control over a part of its territory as to enable them to carry out sustained and concerted military operations and to implement this Protocol," internal disturbances and tensions, such as riots, isolated and sporadic acts of violence, and other acts of a similar violent nature being excluded.

Because the protection Protocol II affords is limited to conflicts of high intensity, the state parties at the 1974 to 1977 Diplomatic Conference were more generous with substantive provisions. If Article 3 contains the strict humanitarian minimum, Protocol II includes important articles on humane treatment: fundamental guarantees, and the special protection of children and individuals whose liberty has been restricted or who are being prosecuted. Basic protection based on the rules of Protocol I is provided to the wounded, sick, and shipwrecked and to the civilian population. There are, however, no provisions concerning the combatants or means and methods of combat. As of the end of April 2004, 156 states are parties to this second protocol, and it represents a great accomplishment of international humanitarian law.

SEE ALSO Hague Conventions of 1907; Humanitarian Law; International Law; War Crimes

BIBLIOGRAPHY

Basic Rules of the Geneva Conventions and Their Additional Protocols (1983). Geneva: International Committee of the Red Cross.

Boissier, Pierre (1985). History of the International Committee of the Red Cross: From Solferino to Tsushima. Geneva: Henry Dunant Institute.

Bothe, M., K. J. Partsch, and W. A. Solf (1982). New Rules for Victims of Armed Conflicts: Commentary on the Two 1977 Protocols Additional to the Geneva Conventions of 1949. The Hague: Martinus Nijhoff.

Bugnion, François (2000). The International Committee of the Red Cross and the Protection of War Victims. Geneva: International Committee of the Red Cross/Macmillan.

Cassese, Antonio (1984). "The Geneva Protocols of 1977 on the Humanitarian Law of Armed Conflict and Customary International Law." UCLA Pacific Basin Law Journal 3:55–118.

Commentary on the Additional Protocols of 8 June 1977 to the Geneva Conventions of 12 August 1949 (1987). Geneva: International Committee of the Red Cross.

Draper, G. I. A. D. (1958). The Red Cross Conventions (Commentary and Texts). London: Stevens & Sons.

Durand, André (1984). History of the International Committee of the Red Cross: From Sarajevo to Hiroshima. Geneva: Henry Dunant Institute.

Final Records of the Diplomatic Conference of Geneva of 1949 (1950). 4 volumes. Bern, Switzerland: Federal Political Department.

Fleck, Dieter, ed. (1995). The Handbook of Humanitarian Law of Armed Conflicts. Oxford: Oxford University Press.

Green, Leslie C. (2000). The Contemporary Law of Armed Conflicts, 2nd edition. Manchester, U.K.: Manchester University Press.

Kalshoven, Frits, and Liesbeth Zegveld (2001). Constraints on the Waging of War. An Introduction to International Humanitarian Law. Geneva: International Committee of the Red Cross.

Official Records of the Diplomatic Conference on the Reaffirmation and Development of International Humanitarian Law Applicable in Armed Conflicts, Geneva, 1974 to 1977 (1978). 17 volumes. Bern, Switzerland: Federal Political Department.

Pictet, Jean (1977). "Fresh Aspects of International Humanitarian Law." International Review of the Red Cross 17:339–401.

Pictet, Jean S., ed. (1952–1960). The Geneva Conventions of 12 August 1949: Commentary. 4 volumes. Geneva: International Committee of the Red Cross.

Solf Waldemar, A., and Roach J. Ashley (1987). Index to the International Humanitarian Law. Geneva: International Committee of the Red Cross.

Jiri Toman

Genghis Khan

[c. 1167–1227]
Mongol conqueror

The name of Genghis Khan (born Temüjin, son of Yisugei) is synonymous with bloodletting, barbarity, and wanton massacres in much of the Arab world, Europe, and the Americas. In Turkey and Central Asia, however, Genghis is not an uncommon name, and the legacy of his Turco-Mongol empire is viewed in a positive light. The globalization imposed by his Eurasian hordes in the thirteenth and fourteenth centuries roused strong reactions. Those biases remain present in the early twenty-first century.

Temüjin's harsh rise to power was the catalyst that resulted in the formation of the largest-ever contiguous land empire. He was born around 1167 on the banks of the Onan River, Mongolia, reputedly clutching a clot of blood in his right hand. He emerged first as the young son who fought for the survival of his destitute family, abandoned by their clan after the murder of his father, a minor chieftain. Then through ruthless determination, he was eventually accepted as tribal leader and thereafter as the supra-tribal ruler who unified the peoples of the Eurasian steppes. Finally in 1206 he was elected Genghis Khan, the supreme leader of the Turco-Mongol nomadic tribes and the world conqueror whose offspring accomplished spectacular feats, the outcome and influence of which are felt to this day. The relationship between Tibet and China was first defined by a Mongol ruler; the Sufi songs of Rūmī that resound around the world from California to Tokyo were nurtured under Mongol rule; the cultural and spiritual links between western Asia and the East were cemented under Mongol auspices. From Temüjin whose name once evoked derision, to Genghis Khan who cowed and riled the princes of Russia and Eastern Europe, and would awe emissaries from a fearful outside world, this Mongol emperor is more deserving of fame than of infamy. He was not only a world conqueror but also a world unifier.

The legacy of Genghis Khan and the Mongol hordes has been shrouded and obscured by the mythmakers of history and indeed by the propaganda of the Mongols themselves. Genghis Khan remains the epitome of evil and the Mongols are associated with barbarian rule and destruction. Their defenders are few and until recently their apologists rare.

Genghis Khan was a steppe ruler who transferred the cruel realities of steppe life to a sedentary urban environment. His initial raids into China c.1211 were in search of plunder and were intended to inspire awe, shock, and terror. His ferocious forage against the Islamic world c.1220 sought to avenge the wanton killing of his envoys by the Khwarazmshah. But even at this early stage, Genghis Khan was selective in his destruction and massacres. Craftsmen and artisans, poets and painters, and clerics and holy men of all faiths were spared the fate of their countrymen and taken to the increasingly cosmopolitan and luxurious Mongol camps. Genghis Khan, unlike steppe rulers before him, realized that the world outside the steppe would offer far

greater wealth tamed and harnessed rather than cowed and defeated. After the notoriety and horror of his initial attacks, there were few who would oppose him, and in the emerging *Pax Mongolica* he established the foundations of a great and prosperous empire. Unfortunately, it is the legacy of those early years that has endured and inspired many in more recent times, including such twentieth-century leaders as Joseph Stalin. They remember the blood and the fury and disregard the religious tolerance and nurturing of trade and cultural exchange. Genghis Khan was a harsh and mercilessly determined ruler. The empire he established through bloodshed and awe survived until his death in 1227, which strongly suggests that he gave his descendants more than just a taste for violence, rapine, and destruction.

SEE ALSO Mongol Conquests

BIBLIOGRAPHY

Bartold, W. (1977). *Turkestan Down to the Mongol Invasion.* London: Luzac & Co. Ltd.

Morgan, David (1986). *The Mongols.* Oxford, U.K.: Blackwell.

Onon, Urgunge (1993). *The Golden History of the Mongols.* London: Folio Society.

Ratchevsky, Paul (1991). *Genghis Khan: His Life and Legacy.* London: Blackwell.

Waley, Arthur (2002). *The Secret History of the Mongols.* New York: House of Stratus.

George Lane

Genocide

Few concepts carry the weight and power of the term *genocide*. The word's profound significance is bound to its unique role as a moral and legal marker of the very worst type of human behavior. Morally, genocide refers to acts of horrific violence such as mass murder, state terror, and other strategies of brutal repression. The term names an ethical boundary beyond which a government forfeits its legitimacy and society descends into barbarism. Legally, genocide refers to the intentional destruction of a group as such, a crime so severe that it demands immediate and total condemnation. As the United Nations Special Rapporteur on the subject stated, "Genocide is the ultimate crime and the gravest violation of human rights it is possible to commit."

The term *genocide* has a highly specific origin, rooted in two related sources: the invention of the word in 1943 by Polish jurist Raphael Lemkin; and its definition, several years later, as an international crime through the Convention for the Prevention and Punishment of the Crime of Genocide. The concept of genocide was a direct response to the Holocaust and the extraordinary destruction and brutality of World War II.

Lemkin created the term *genocide*, out of the Greek word *genos*, referring to race or tribe, and the Latin term *cide*, meaning murder. He defined genocide as a coordinated strategy to destroy a group of people, a process that could be accomplished through total annihilation as well as strategies that eliminate key elements of the group's basic existence, including language, culture, and economic infrastructure. Lemkin believed the Nazis' systematic eradication of various peoples represented an irreparable harm to global society and a special challenge to existing conceptions of criminal law. He created the concept as a means of mobilizing the international community to take strong, coordinated action to prevent the recurrence of such vicious, destructive violence.

The text of the Genocide Convention was approved by the General Assembly of the United Nations on December 9, 1948, and entered into force on January 12, 1951. The Convention defines genocide and obligates those states that accept the treaty to take serious actions to prevent its occurrence and punish those responsible. Article II of the Convention defines the crime as follows:

In the present Convention, genocide means any of the following acts committed with intent to destroy, in whole or in part, a national, ethnic, racial or religious group, as such:

(a) Killing members of the group;

(b) Causing serious bodily or mental harm to members of the group;

(c) Deliberately inflicting on the group conditions of life calculated to bring about its physical destruction in whole or in part;

(d) Imposing measures intended to prevent births within the group;

(e) Forcibly transferring children of the group to another group.

The Genocide Convention was the first of a series of international treaties that, taken together, form the modern system of fundamental rights and freedoms. While the brutal acts that define genocide were not new, the Convention's formal evocation of the crime as a foundational concept within the human rights system represented an act of great historic significance. The Convention remains the premier document for defining genocide and, by 2003, 135 nations had accepted its legal obligations. The Convention's definition has been reinforced through its repetition in relevant domestic legislation and in the statutes of the International Criminal Tribunal for the Former Yugoslavia (ICTY), the International Criminal Tribunal for Rwanda (ICTR), and the International Criminal Court (ICC).

The crime of genocide is widely accepted as a norm of *jus cogens* ("compelling" or "higher" law that transcends the limitations of individual national laws and which no country can violate with impunity). For this reason, genocide is prohibited even in those states that have not adopted the Convention, is not bound by statutes of limitations, and is subject to universal jurisdiction. In 1996 the International Court of Justice (ICJ) issued provisional measures in a case in which Bosnia and Herzegovina claimed that Yugoslavia was committing genocide. The ICJ also accepted jurisdiction over the merits of the case and stated clearly that the two countries were obligated to prevent and punish genocide, regardless of the nature of the conflict, the status of the new states, and key issues of territorial integrity.

The crime of genocide is composed of three essential elements: acts, intent, and victim group. There are five enumerated acts that are distinct in nature, yet unified as strategies. Three of these are aimed at destroying an existing group: killing, causing serious harm, and/or creating destructive conditions. The other two specified acts are aimed at ruining the possibility of the group's continued existence: preventing reproduction and the forcible removal of children. The issue of intent is complex, but is generally understood to limit claims of genocide to those cases where political violence is purposefully directed toward the destruction of a group. This political objective may be presented as official policy, or it may be expressed through the coordinated and systematic nature of state-sponsored terror. The issue of intent is one of the more contentious elements of the crime and is often discussed as a key limitation to successful prosecutions. The group victim requirement defines genocide as a unique crime that is directed not against individuals per se, but instead targets victims because of their membership in a national, ethnic, racial, or religious group. The definition is often criticized for its exclusion of political and social groups, for these, too, are often the targets of severe political violence.

Each element of the legal definition of genocide raises an array of troubling questions, many of which run counter to general moral understandings of the term. For example, one might have a case of genocide involving few casualties (as with the forced transfer of children) or a situation of extraordinary brutality that does not meet the definition (as with the mass murder of political opponents or others who are not targeted for their membership in one of the four protected groups). To address these issues, scholars have interpreted the crime to cover most forms of state-sponsored mass killing. Helen Fein, for instance, has suggested a "sociological definition," whereas Israel W. Charny calls for a "humanistic definition," and Leo Kuper suggests a broader understanding of the crime be developed, in order to address problems arising from the technical nature of the Convention's language. Others have suggested the need to create new terms. For instance, R. J. Rummel has coined the word *democide* to refer to all forms of mass state murder, and others have offered *auto-genocide* to deal with mass murder where both the perpetrators and victims are members of the same group.

Despite the existence of a global promise to prevent and punish genocide, the second half of the twentieth century presented many cases of extreme violence that could be termed genocide alongside limited international action. It was not until 1998 that the world witnessed the first international prosecution and conviction for genocide, in the *Akayesu case* at the International Criminal Tribunal for Rwanda. This historic decision was followed by a number of additional cases in the same court and at the International Criminal Tribunal for the Former Yugoslavia, allowing for the evolution of a new jurisprudence of genocide. These shifts have heightened an international commitment to understanding genocide as a crime of such severity that it can be prosecuted anywhere, regardless of ordinary jurisdictional limitations. Similarly, there is a growing concern for developing strategies and policy interventions that recognize the special status of victims of genocide and seek to address their social, economic, and political needs.

Genocide is iconic in its representation of the complex nature of modernity. The concept of genocide—from its genesis in the aftermath of the Holocaust to the present day—binds acts of unforgivable brutality to a global promise that extreme political violence will no longer be tolerated within an emerging international order premised on the protection of fundamental human rights.

SEE ALSO Convention on the Prevention and Punishment of Genocide; Explanation; Holocaust; International Court of Justice; International Criminal Tribunal for Rwanda; International Criminal Tribunal for the Former Yugoslavia; Lemkin, Raphael; Political Theory; Psychology of Perpetrators; Psychology of Survivors; Psychology of Victims; Sociology of Perpetrators; Sociology of Victims

BIBLIOGRAPHY

Bassiouni, M. Cherif, ed. (1999). *International Criminal Law.* Ardsley, N.Y.: Transnational Publishers.

Chalk, Frank, and Kurt Jonassohn (1990). *The History and Sociology of Genocide: Analyses and Case Studies.* New Haven, Conn.: Yale University Press.

Charny, Israel W. (1999). *Encyclopedia of Genocide.* Santa Barbara, Calif.: ABC-Clio.

Fein, Helen (1993). *Genocide: A Sociological Perspective.* London: Sage Publications.

Kuper, Leo (1981). *Genocide: Its Political Uses in the Twentieth Century.* New Haven, Conn.: Yale University Press.

Lemkin, Raphael (1944). *Axis Rule in Occupied Europe.* Washington, D.C.: Carnegie Endowment for International Peace.

Rummel, R. J. (1994). *Death by Government: Genocide and Mass Murder since 1900.* New Brunswick, N.J.: Transaction Publishers.

Schabas, William A. (2000). *Genocide in International Law.* Cambridge: Cambridge University Press.

Staub, Ervin (1989). *The Roots of Evil: The Psychological and Cultural Origins of Genocide and Other Forms of Group Violence.* Cambridge: Cambridge University Press.

Whitaker, Ben (1985). "Revised and updated report on the question of the prevention and punishment of the crime of genocide." Commission on Human Rights. United Nations. E/CN.4/Sub.2/1985/6 2 July 1985. Also available from http://www.preventgenocide.org/prevent/UNdocs/whitaker/.

Daniel Rothenberg

Germany

Nazism established itself in an extraordinarily short time as a major force in German politics and thereafter seized and consolidated its grip on power against all expectations. Humanity was to suffer appallingly as a consequence of the Nazis' success.

The Impact of World War I
Despite palpable tensions over the country's semi-absolutist constitution, early twentieth-century imperial Germany was among the more prosperous and dynamic of European societies. A vibrant literary and arts scene, a strengthening economy, and a relatively advanced welfare system gave grounds for influential citizens, such as the Jewish banker Max Warburg, to look to the future with optimism. States such as Prussia had sheltered and absorbed victims of foreign religious persecution for many generations and during its industrial revolution Germany attracted and successfully absorbed minorities from other parts of Europe. Jewish citizens had risen to prominence in the economy, among them Emil and Walther Rathenau of the electri-

The principal conspirators of the failed Munich Beer Hall uprising pose after their trial. They are, from left to right, Pernet, Weber, Frick, Kriebel, General Ludendorff, Adolf Hitler, Bruckner, Rohm, and Wagner.[HULTON-DEUTSCH COLLECTION/CORBIS]

cal engineering giant AEG; Paul Silverberg, the coal mining magnate; and, not without controversy, the banker Gerson von Bleichröder, who had worked closely with Chancellor Otto von Bismarck during the 1870s and 1880s.

However, imperial Germany had its darker side. Pressure groups, such as the Pan-German League, demanded an adventurous, imperialistic foreign policy and laced their message with anti-Semitic and anti-Slavonic racism. Demands for an overseas empire were expressed more widely in German society as business circles sought assured markets and public opinion looked to the prestige that overseas territories would bring. In order to deflect attention from demands for constitutional reform at home, the German government played to this imperialist gallery and pursued an aggressive foreign policy. This fateful strategy contributed to the outbreak of what became World War I in July and August 1914 and then, ultimately, to Germany's defeat in the fall of 1918.

The war itself saw Germany suffer millions of casualties, in common with all the main belligerents, but it also triggered misery on the home front. The demands of total war against an expanding and increasingly powerful enemy coalition stretched the economy to breaking point. Juveniles, the elderly, and women labored under grueling conditions to maximize war production, yet at the same time an Allied blockade and official ineptitude at home combined to create near famine conditions in the towns and cities. Malnutrition-related deaths soared; townspeople took to scavenging the countryside for food, with official connivance: Occasionally, trains were run for this very purpose, for want of any better policy. After the guns finally fell silent, in November 1918, a global influenza pandemic reaped as grim a harvest of souls in Germany as had many a great battle. Life, it appeared, had become very cheap.

The Inter-War Period

Defeat brought a curious, even contradictory, combination of hope, demoralization, and anger in equal mea-

encyclopedia of GENOCIDE *and* CRIMES AGAINST HUMANITY

sure. There was a near consensus that the old empire had failed and that the kaiser, William II, should abdicate, but it was less clear what should follow. After a brief attempt during October 1918 to establish a constitutional monarchy, comparable perhaps to Britain's, open revolution broke out and led to the proclamation of a provisional republic on November 9 of that year. Friedrich Ebert of the SPD (Social Democratic Party of Germany) formed a caretaker administration during the worst crisis to sweep Germany since the days of Napoleon. Most of the revolutionaries looked to the Marxist but staunchly parliamentarian SPD to establish a new social and political order. They also hoped to reach a tolerable peace with the victorious Allies. Public opinion generally anticipated a settlement on these lines. However, in the turmoil of defeat and revolution, the government had effectively lost control of day-to-day affairs, which made the fulfillment of these expectations unlikely.

Certainly, there were signs of hope. Industrialists and labor leaders reached a settlement of differences and, along with the civil service, collaborated in the successful demobilization of the war economy. Meanwhile, the army was extricated successfully from the former battle zones in France and Belgium, and, by January 1919, the process of constitutional reform was well on track. The resulting Weimar Republic saw the wholesale enfranchisement of women, a thoroughgoing commitment to social justice and welfare reform, and a significant democratization of the political process. As for the peace negotiations, an armistice came into effect on November 11, 1918, and the eventual Treaty of Versailles in June 1919 left the young German national state largely intact.

However, many did not see the situation as hopeful. Radicals on the political left and right bitterly resented the outcome of the revolution, which amounted to a compromise between the old imperial order and supporters of reform. Compromise could not satisfy extremists of any sort, and a series of armed uprisings, industrial strikes, and terrorist outrages followed. Some of Germany's brightest prospects, including the Catholic politician Matthias Erzberger and the Jewish industrialist-turned-statesman Walther Rathenau, were murdered, to the horror of mainstream public opinion. This unrest never threatened to topple the Republic, but it did have a significant, destructive impact on domestic and foreign perceptions of the new Germany. Furthermore, the country remained impoverished by the recent war. The currency began to devalue alarmingly, to the consternation of monied society, and devastating food shortages left many poorer Germans malnourished and prey to chronic disease or even premature death. The government lacked the necessary foreign currency reserves to meet its obligations, and agonized debates ensued over whether to pay a particular installment of reparations or to use the money to import wheat and keep the bakeries busy. Under these circumstances, the postwar reparations burden imposed on Germany turned public opinion against the Versailles Treaty.

At the January 1919 elections to establish a constituent assembly, voters had turned overwhelmingly to the republican parties. However, in subsequent parliamentary elections they began to shift toward parties that lamented the fall of the old empire, a time when Germany had stood proud among the world's nations, when there had been food on the table, and when money was worth what it seemed. More worrying, however, was the emergence on the right of a new breed of political extremism that advocated a witches, brew of social reform, national solidarity, and a racist program of retribution against Germany's alleged foreign and domestic enemies. These far-right demagogues claimed that the Treaty of Versailles (which they termed a "dictated" peace because there had been no open negotiations in 1919) had enslaved Germany to foreign Jewish capitalists who were growing rich on the toil of its ordinary, decent citizens.

Anti-Semitism was present in most European societies at the time, and not surprisingly these German extremists also vilified their country's own small, indigenous Jewish minority. Germany's Jews, it was argued, were treasonous and, working hand-in-glove with their co-religionists abroad, had undermined the war effort. Thereafter, the extremists claimed, Germany's Jews had sought to exploit the peace terms to deliver the country into foreign hands, caring little for the well-being of their homeland. Indeed, the accusation ran, Jews did not really have a homeland at all. These radicals named themselves National Socialists (*Nationalsozialisten*, abbreviated as Nazis) and called their party the National Socialist German Workers' Party (Nationalsozialistische Deutsch Arbeiterpartei, or NDAP). They advocated the solidarity and common good of the ethnic nation above class or other sectional interests. National Socialist ideologues, such as Dietrich Eckart, claimed that the Jews' allegedly treasonous behavior derived from inbred, racial characteristics that made their presence in Germany, let alone in any position of power, highly undesirable.

Up to this point, Nazism was only a fringe affair, its influence largely confined to Bavaria and, more particularly, its capital city, Munich. More significant criticism of the Republic and its institutions initially came from monarchist circles, but during 1923 a devastating series of crises brought the Weimar order and even the German state close to breaking point. The year began with a collapse in Franco-German relations. The French premier, Raymond Poincaré, accused Germany of deliberately defaulting on reparations. French troops invaded the industrial Ruhr District to extract payments in kind, by force if necessary. German opinion had always believed the reparations to be unpayable and regarded the French invasion of 1923 as a thinly-veiled imperialist adventure, for which the defaulted payments merely served as a pretext.

The people of the occupied territories of western Germany refused to cooperate with the invaders in any way. Instead, they effectively shut down economic activity in Germany's industrial heartland. The government supported this campaign of resistance with massive subsidies, but this only served to bankrupt public finances and, finally, destroy the ailing currency. The mark effectively became worthless, stripping middle-class Germans of all their savings. Soon enough the wider economic crisis precipitated mass unemployment in the towns and cities of the Ruhr. The district was ravaged by starvation for the second time in a generation, and hundreds of thousands of severely malnourished children had to be evacuated by train to farms in the east where, at least, there was food to be had.

Not surprisingly, political tensions exploded, destroying many of the compromises that had informed the German revolutionary settlement, fostering separatism in Bavaria and the Rhineland, and giving enormous encouragement to extremist groups of every kind. Communist-led strikes and uprisings broke out in central and northern Germany, whereas, in the conservative state of Bavaria, the far right gathered its forces. In November, Adolf Hitler's Nazis tried to launch a military coup from their stronghold in Munich and, although this putsch failed utterly, the Bavarian authorities were lenient: They only imposed a modest prison sentence on the Nazi leader. Hitler learned from his own mistakes. He resolved to exploit the Weimar constitution to seize power rather than attack the Republic head-on. This meant, from here on, that he would concentrate on fighting and winning elections.

In the fall of 1923, the liberal statesman Gustav Stresemann had dared to hope that these terrible events marked nothing worse than the growing pains of the young Republic. Weimar survived 1923, reached a revised settlement with the Allies over reparations in 1924 (the Dawes Plan), and finally became part of a European system of mutual security guarantees in 1925 (the Locarno Agreement). The economy recovered after a fashion, a stable currency was established, and important new social legislation was approved by parliament. However, the crisis of German democracy was only in remission, it was by no means cured. Simmering tensions persisted just below the surface. German democracy was in no condition to confront, let alone survive, another great crisis.

Even during the so-called golden years of 1925 to 1929, there were ominous danger signs. In 1925, the Social Democratic president, Friedrich Ebert, died. Presidential elections followed. The eventual victor was Field Marshal Paul von Hindenburg, who had served as commander in chief of the German armed forces during the latter part of the Great War. Despite his association with the former empire and with Germany's defeat in 1918, many voters saw in him a symbol of national unity, a man above the bickering of party politics, and a reminder of the country's former greatness. The Weimar constitution granted the president substantial powers, including the capacity under Article 48 to suspend parliament and sanction rule by decree. These powers were originally intended to permit a democratically minded president to ride out any future crisis, and they had been invoked during 1923 precisely for this reason, with the consent of the republican parties. Now, however, they were vested in a man who was prepared to uphold the law, but made no secret of his monarchist sympathies.

In addition, the 1924 parliamentary elections saw a remarkable growth in fringe parties that represented particular regions or particular interest groups, whether it be farming, small business, or people who had been cheated out of their savings. (This was even more marked during the 1928 elections.) Voters, it seemed, were losing faith in the larger parties, which invariably had to trade off one set of promises or commitments against another. Now, voters threw their support behind particular special-interest parties that would henceforward speak up directly and only for them. The Weimar constitution unintentionally encouraged such behavior, because the constitutional assembly had resolved in 1919 to let every vote count equally in elections. The objective had been fair representation for parties such as the Social Democrats, who had lost out in national elections during the imperial era through rigged constituency boundaries, and in many state elections through a property-based voter franchise.

Alongside the unanticipated plethora of fringe interests encamped in the Weimar parliament, deep political divisions now formed which ensured that no larger party had any hope of obtaining a majority on its own. A series of coalitions governed the country, not entirely without success, but the inevitable horse-trading and compromise that accompanies coalition government left the electorate cynical and dissatisfied. Industrial relations also became increasingly polarized, and in 1928 this situation culminated in a major crisis in the Ruhr District. Steel bosses refused to arbitrate during a fierce wages dispute and instead locked out their employees. It was clear that the Weimar Republic was no longer able to reconcile opposing social interests. As a result, powerful supporters of the old empire, who had been prepared in 1919 to tolerate the Republic, began to look toward a more authoritarian constitutional system, including, perhaps, a restoration of the monarchy.

In 1929 the German economy was already in decline, but in October the U.S. stock-market crash dealt it a hammer blow. Since 1924, Germany had been dependent on a generous flow of foreign credit, particularly from the United States, to pay reparations and even to fund domestic spending. Now, American loans dried up, and nervous overseas investors began to repatriate their capital. By 1931 the entire European banking and financial system had been compromised by the wider economic crisis. International trade had collapsed and domestic economies were sliding ever deeper into recession. Germany was particularly badly hit and by 1932 a third of the labor force had registered as unemployed; a further sixth had simply given up working. The dire poverty, hunger, and disease that had scourged Germany between 1915 and 1924 returned with a vengeance. Poverty-related crime soared, and in the towns and the countryside alike, there were noisy political demonstrations and even riots. Few had any real confidence that the Republic would, or could, address the crisis.

The Nazi Rise to Power
In early 1930, the last democratic coalition government collapsed, prompting the old elite to make its move. Military and business interests close to the president resorted to rule by decree (under Article 48) and resolved to hold early elections, in the expectation that voters were tiring of Weimar and would give the old guard another chance. Thereafter, they believed, the constitution could be looked at again, but the plotters got more than they bargained for. Hitler had been released from prison in 1924 and had reestablished the Nazi Party in the following spring. He made it plain to the paramilitary adventurers who had helped plan the November 1923 putsch that their violent days were over. Instead, he insisted that elections marked the surest way to power. The NSDAP had fared relatively poorly in the 1928 parliamentary elections, but in 1930 it achieved a breakthrough by winning almost a fifth of the votes cast. State and local elections across Germany gave similar results, confirming that the Nazis had become a major political force that no one could afford to ignore.

During the spring of 1932, Hitler ran a close second to von Hindenburg in fresh presidential elections, and his party triumphed in a new round of state polls. Finally, the NSDAP saw its vote double in July to over 37 percent in the national Reichstag elections.

How had this breakthrough been achieved, and which groups in German society responded most strongly to the appeal of Nazism? Historians once believed that the Nazis appealed to the marginalized, dispossessed middle classes of Protestant, small-town, and rural Germany. These were precisely the people who had abandoned mainstream politics in droves during the 1920s, turning instead to the special-interest splinter parties. These parties, however, had been unable to operate effectively during the Great Depression, leaving the middle classes open to the Nazis' xenophobic nationalism and promises of justice at home for the farmers and small businessmen of Germany.

More recent research does not deny the Nazis' appeal to these middle-class groups, but scholars now suggest that Hitler's party cast its net much more widely than had originally been assumed. Instead, these scholars argue, Hitler and the NSDAP appealed to almost all elements of German society with a message that promised national solidarity, economic reconstruction, and a just reward for hard work. The Nazis claimed to be the party for everyone: the professionals, the people of countryside, the industrial workers. Their racialism and aggressive foreign policy platform were no secret, but leading propagandists, such as Joseph Goebbels, played down these core Nazi beliefs, knowing them to be vote-losers. Nazi parliamentarians, such as Gregor Strasser, instead addressed the issues of the day, proposed daring solutions to the great economic crisis, and did their utmost to keep the appeal of Nazism general. Theorists have postulated that the Nazis pioneered many of the propaganda techniques of the modern political party, with parades, pageantry, and music all playing a crucial role. The Nazis adopted a militarist flavor that played well to German public opinion, selected and trained their public speakers with great care, and used emerging media such as film with devastating effect. No other party in Germany displayed comparable energy or had such a broad reach.

Above all, the success of the Nazi movement lay in its ability to recruit and mobilize an extensive army of activists who were willing to knock on doors, raise funds, convert friends and neighbors, and operate rudimentary welfare schemes for the party faithful. Meanwhile, the party recruited a cadre of young paramilitary volunteers, largely from the swollen ranks of unemployed workers. These were called Stormtroopers (*Sturmabteilung,* or SA), and they both attacked and intimidated political rivals on the left, while providing a highly visible public manifestation of militant Nazism. The uniformed SA was the mainstay of many a Nazi rally and parade and provided a constant reminder that the NSDAP was not simply another parliamentary party.

This almost unique ability to reunite the fractured elements of German society by creating a non-Marxist and strongly nationalist mass movement was quickly noticed by the conservative elite. It was struggling to rule the crisis-wracked country by decree, but General Kurt von Schleicher, who stood close to the president, was convinced that the monarchist right could harness and exploit the Nazis' huge and growing constituency to underpin a more authoritarian order with popular support. Accordingly, complex and initially fruitless negotiations opened between the monarchists and the Nazis. These talks dragged on through 1932, but Hitler's insistence that he head any such government as chancellor was unacceptable to the monarchists. At the turn of the year, however, President von Hindenburg was persuaded by his advisers, against his own better judgement, that Germany's only hope for a stable government would be a coalition government with Nazi participation, and thus a government with Hitler in charge. The Nazi leader was granted his wish on January 30, 1933.

Leading conservative politicians secured the majority of posts in Hitler's first cabinet and dared to hope that his inexperience in high office would render him their puppet. However, the new chancellor exploited the possibilities offered by Weimar's constitution up to and beyond the legal limits, and rapidly outflanked his coalition partners. He persuaded President von Hindenburg that extraordinary emergency powers under Article 48 were indispensable in dealing with an alleged communist threat to stability. When a Dutch communist, acting alone, committed an entirely fortuitous arson attack on the Reichstag, Hitler suddenly had a pretext for suspending civil liberties. He declared that Germany was under threat from Jewish-inspired global terrorism, against which the authorities had to act with all the means at their disposal.

New parliamentary elections were held in early March 1933 under anything but ideal circumstances, with Nazi stormtroopers prowling the streets. Political rivals were arrested and detained without charge in makeshift concentration camps, with no prospect of a fair trial. The media were increasingly subject to interference and censorship. Unsurprisingly, all of this resulted in Nazi gains at the polls. The NSDAP and its conservative allies won an overall majority in parliament, which effectively surrendered political power to

Hitler and his ministers through the Enabling Act of March 23, 1933. On August 2, 1934, President von Hindenburg died and Hitler swiftly proclaimed himself Head of State and Government, taking the title of Leader (Führer) and National Chancellor (*Reichskanzler*). Fragile reassurances were granted to the army chiefs that they would remain an independent pillar of the nation. In gratitude, they squandered this concession by swearing, along with their troops, a personal oath of loyalty to Hitler.

Hitler's Third Reich

Hitler's regime quickly tightened its grip on the country. A series of decrees were enacted, increasingly placing the Nazi regime above the law as it moved to persecute minorities, in particular the Jews, and to institutionalize the concentration camp system of which Dachau was the most notorious peacetime example. The regime incarcerated tens of thousands of individuals it deemed to be political, racial, or social enemies and, although most were eventually released, a significant minority were severely mistreated; some were even murdered. Soon enough, the courts were instructed to turn a blind eye to such outrages, and the way was opened potentially for a murderous eugenics program and, during the 1940s, genocide of an unprecedented ferocity.

The Nazis' racist ideals were now expounded overtly, and every means was mobilized to promote them throughout society. The educational system was nazified, and youth movements and organizations were dragooned or lured into the Hitler Youth and German Girls' League. The press quickly came to understand that self-censorship and the promotion of news and features friendly to the regime were the only practical way to ensure survival. Propaganda minister Goebbels masterfully exploited the radio and film industries, ensuring that the Nazi message was promoted through entertainment rather than blatant propaganda. Even news coverage of the early concentration camps was superficially reassuring. Newspaper features stressed that the dregs of humanity, hardened criminals, vagrants, and dangerous political radicals were being given a chance to redeem themselves through hard work in the outdoors and through firm but fair discipline. The most dangerous, irredeemable convicts, the public was reassured, were shot if they tried to escape.

Further aspects of the Nazis' early record proved relatively reassuring to the typical citizen. The blatant thuggery of the SA antagonized most Germans, but during June and July 1934, the stormtroopers were restrained and their leaders executed without trial on charges of homosexuality and corruption. Although il-

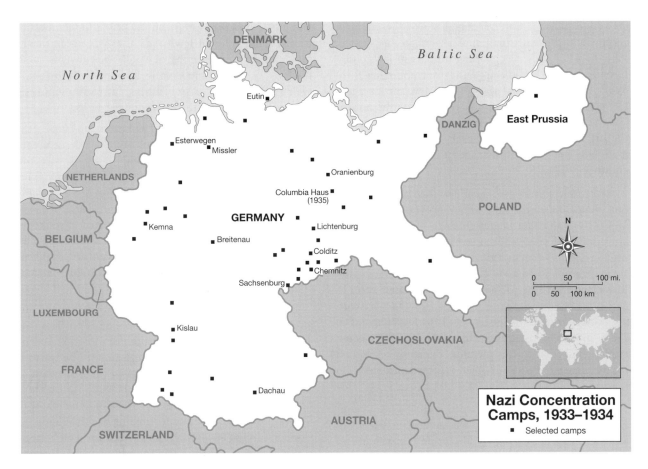

Positions of concentration camps in Germany. [XNR PRODUCTIONS/GALE GROUP]

legal, these executions met with public approval, and even the establishment refrained from protest. The Nazis, it reasoned, were cleaning out their own stables. Meanwhile, the government moved boldly and decisively to revive the economy, launching a series of job creation and vocational training programs.

By 1936 unemployment was virtually a thing of the past. The increasing availability of overtime and expanding employment opportunities for women, despite the Nazis' avowedly pro-natalist and antifeminist policies, meant that household incomes rose appreciably. Bitter years of abject poverty and political chaos were set aside. In simple but very important ways, the profoundly abnormal and immoral Nazi regime had reinstated a normal day-to-day existence for most of its subjects. Indeed, popular support proved sufficiently strong to enable even the most repressive dimensions of the Third Reich to operate relatively smoothly during peacetime. The SA rowdies were replaced by the more bureaucratic and infinitely more deadly *Schutzstaffel* (SS), under the command of Heinrich Himmler, which soon enough established control of all German police forces. However, Himmler's much-

feared Secret State Police, the Gestapo, was a relatively small organization that functioned largely through a flood of information, tip-offs, and outright denunciations that flowed in from the general public. The Nazi police state was a state in which the people policed themselves to a very significant degree.

Against this backdrop, anti-Jewish measures intensified only sporadically, and left even the Jews uncertain as to their future. Some hoped that the persecution would have its limits, even be quietly dropped once the government had finished playing to its anti-Semitic followers. However, careers in the public service were largely closed to Jews in 1933, and Jewish businesses were subjected to a boycott on April 1. In 1935, the Nuremberg Laws banned future intermarriage between Jews and Christians, although current marriages were grudgingly tolerated and the resulting offspring granted a tenuous security in an effort to avoid inflaming public opinion. The authorities began confiscating Jewish-owned businesses in 1937, under the so-called Aryanization program. Matters subsequently came to a head on November 9 and 10, 1938, when Goebbels staged a violent anti-Jewish pogrom. Kristallnacht

("Crystal Night"), was unleashed across Germany in response to the assassination of a German diplomat in Paris by a Polish Jew. A growing number of Jews chose to emigrate and, by the time that war approached, in 1939, some 280,000 of the 500,000 Jews in inter-war Germany had left the country. By the time the notorious Wannsee Conference in January 1942 confirmed the primacy of the SS in administering the Jews' ultimate fate, 360,000 had managed to emigrate from the country.

Anti-Jewish measures assumed their truly murderous, genocidal dimension with the coming of war in 1939. Germany had begun covertly rearming shortly after the Nazi takeover, and in 1935 Hitler publicly renounced the Versailles Treaty by reintroducing general conscription. In 1936, Germany remilitarized the Rhineland in further defiance of the Versailles and Locarno treaties, before seizing the foreign German-speaking territories of Austria and the Sudetenland in 1938. In early 1939 the Czech capital, Prague, was occupied and, finally, in September, demands on Poland for the return of former German territory escalated into a general European war.

Early on, Hitler had envisaged waging a war of conquest. Although some historians doubt the existence of any particular master plan or blueprint, it is widely recognized that the east, and particularly the Soviet Union, was perceived by the Nazis as ripe for conquest and colonization. Eastward expansion had informed German objectives even during World War I, but the Nazis linked it directly to their racialist agenda and vision of the world (*Weltanschauung*). The Bolshevik regime of the Soviet Union was regarded as a degenerate but deadly manifestation of the global Jewish conspiracy, and its destruction was considered vital for Germany's future security. Soviet functionaries and the Jews of Eastern Europe alike were therefore doomed to destruction as the Nazis sought both to conquer this alleged enemy and, simultaneously, to clear the territory for colonization. The destruction of Europe's Jews and the destruction of the Soviet Union came to be regarded by the Nazis as one and the same thing.

Poland's Jews had been subjected to a wave of atrocities beginning in September 1939. Now, in June 1941, persecution on a much greater scale ensued. East European Jews and other victims were rounded up and shot by special task forces (*Einsatzgruppen*) or by regular army units. The Babi Yar massacre outside Kiev saw the execution of almost 34,000 Jews and communist functionaries in just two days. Ghettos were established in Poland for the bulk of the remaining Jewish population, but scant rations were provided, and starvation and disease took their toll of the population. During late 1941, however, preparations began for the industrialized slaughter of Jews and other victims in newly built extermination camps, of which Auschwitz became the most notorious. Here alone, hundreds of thousands of Jews died in the gas chambers, on work details, or in a multitude of arbitrary, inhumane ways.

Germany's defeat in May 1945 came too late to prevent the slaughter. The survivors and their descendents have struggled ever since to come to terms with the enormity of these crimes, for which some of the surviving Nazi leaders were brought to account at the Nuremberg Trials. Germany, an erstwhile pillar and bedrock of occidental civilization, was devastated physically, emasculated politically, and so compromised morally that even during the later twentieth century, many of its citizens balked at taking any pride in German nationhood.

Germany's intellectuals have struggled to reconstruct a German identity and ethos that is not haunted and dominated by Hitler and the gas ovens of Auschwitz. Many have found their integration in the western Atlantic alliance and participation in the construction of a European Union in close partnership with their former enemy, France, a more ethically plausible way forward. This new Germany remains deeply allergic to war and foreign adventures, an attitude for which, ironically, it has recently been roundly criticized by its major postwar ally, the United States.

SEE ALSO Anti-Semitism; Auschwitz; Babi Yar; Concentration Camps; Einsatzgruppen; Extermination Centers; Gestapo; Ghetto; Goebbels, Joseph; Göring, Hermann; Heydrich, Reinhard; Himmler, Heinrich; Hitler, Adolf; Holocaust; Intent; Kristallnacht; Labor Camps, Nazi; Namibia (German South West Africa and South West Africa); Nuremberg Laws; Nuremberg Trials; SS; Streicher, Julius; Wannsee Conference

BIBLIOGRAPHY

Aly, Götz (1999). *"Final Solution": Nazi Population Policy and the Murder of the European Jews.* London: Oxford University Press.

Bankier, David (1992). *The Germans and the Final Solution. Public Opinion under Nazism.* Oxford: B. Blackwell.

Bessell, Richard, ed. (1987). *Life in the Third Reich.* New York: Oxford University Press.

Boemeke, Manfred, Gerald D. Feldman, and Elizabeth Glaser, eds. (1998). *The Treaty of Versailles: A Reassessment after 75 Years.* Cambridge: Cambridge University Press.

Bookbinder, Paul (1996). *Weimar Germany: The Republic of the Reasonable.* New York: St. Martins Press.

Bracher, Karl Dietrich (1973). *The German Dictatorship: The Origins, Structure, and Effects of National Socialism.* London: Penguin University Press.

Breitman, Richard (1991). *The Architect of Genocide: Himmler and the Final Solution.* London: Bodley Head.

Browning, Christopher (1992). *Ordinary Men: Reserve Police Battalion 101 and the Final Solution in Poland.* New York: HarperCollins.

Browning, Christopher (1992). *The Path to Genocide: Essays on Launching the Final Solution.* Cambridge, U.K.: Cambridge University Press.

Browning, Christopher (2000). *Nazi Policy, Jewish Workers, German Killers.* Cambridge, U.K.: Cambridge University Press.

Burin, Philippe (1994). *Hitler and the Jews: The Genesis of the Holocaust.* New York: Routledge, Chapman, and Hall.

Burleigh, Michael (1991). *The Racial State: Germany, 1933–1945.* Cambridge, U.K.: Cambridge University Press.

Burleigh, Michael (1994). *Death and Deliverance: 'Euthanasia' in Germany, 1900–1945.* Cambridge, U.K.: Cambridge University Press.

Burleigh, Michael (1997). *Ethics and Extermination: Reflections on Nazi Genocide.* Cambridge, U.K.: Cambridge University Press.

Burleigh, Michael (2001). *The Third Reich: A New History.* New York: Hill and Wang.

Crew, David (1998). *Germans on Welfare: From Weimar to Hitler.* Oxford: Oxford University Press.

Fischer, Conan (2002). *The Rise of the Nazis,* 2nd edition. Manchester, U.K.: Palgrave.

Fischer, Conan, ed. (1996). *The Rise of National Socialism and the Working Classes in Weimar Germany.* Providence, R.I.: Berghahn Books.

Friedlander, Henry (1995). *The Origins of Nazi Genocide: From Euthanasia to the Final Solution.* Chapel Hill: University of North Carolina Press.

Friedländer, Saul (1997). *Nazi Germany and the Jews: The Years of Persecution, 1933–1939.* New York: HarperCollins.

Fritzsche, Peter. *Germans into Nazis.* Cambridge, Mass.: Harvard University Press.

Gellately, Robert (1990). *The Gestapo and German Society: Enforcing Racial Policy, 1933–1945.* Oxford: Oxford University Press.

Gellately, Robert (2001). *Backing Hitler: Consent and Coercion in Nazi Germany.* Oxford: Oxford University Press.

Goldhagen, Daniel (1996). *Hitler's Willing Executioners.* New York: Knopf.

Hiden, John (1996). *Republican and Fascist Germany.* London: Longman.

Hildebrand, Klaus (1973). *The Foreign Policy of the Third Reich.* London: Batsford.

Hillberg, Raul (1983). *The Destruction of the European Jews,* 3rd edition. New Haven, Conn.: Yale University Press.

Hochstadt, Steve, ed. (2004). *Sources of the Holocaust.* Basingstoke, U.K.: Palgrave.

Kershaw, Ian (1999). *Hitler, 1889–1936: Hubris.* London: Allen Lane.

Kershaw, Ian (2000). *Hitler, 1936-1945: Nemesis.* London: Allen Lane.

Kershaw, Ian (2000). *The Nazi Dictatorship: Problems and Perspectives of Interpretation,* 4th edition. London: Arnold.

Kershaw, Ian, ed. (1990). *Weimar: Why did German Democracy Fail?* New York: St. Martins Press.

Lane, Barbara Miller, and Leila J Rupp, eds. (1978). *Nazi Ideology before 1933: A Documentation.* Austin: University of Texas Press.

Mommsen, Hans (1996). *The Rise and Fall of Weimar Democracy.* Chapel Hill: University of North Carolina Press.

Mühlberger, Detlef (2003). *The Social Bases of Nazism 1919–1933.* Cambridge: Cambridge University Press.

Nicholls, A. J. (2000). *Weimar and the Rise of Hitler,* 4th edition. New York: St. Martins Press.

Noakes, Jeremy, and Geoffrey Pridham, eds. (1983–1998). *Nazism, 1919–1945: A Documentary Reader,* 4 volumes. Exeter, U.K.: University of Exeter Press.

Overy, Richard J. (1994). *War and Economy in the Third Reich.* New York: Oxford University Press.

Overy, Richard J. (1996). *The Nazi Economic Recovery, 1932–1938,* 2nd edition. New York: Cambridge University Press.

Overy, Richard J. (1996). *The Penguin Historical Atlas of the Third Reich.* London: Penguin Books.

Peukert, Detlev (1991). *The Weimar Republic: The Crisis of Classical Modernity.* New York: Hill and Wang.

Rich, Norman (1973, 1974). *Hitler's War Aims,* 2 volumes. New York: Norton.

Roseman, Mark (2002). *Wannsee and the Final Solution.* New York: Metropolitan Books.

Schleunes, Karl A. (1970). *The Twisted Road to Auschwitz. Nazi Policy toward German Jews, 1933–1939.* Urbana: University of Illinois Press.

Stachura, Peter D. (1983). *Gregor Strasser and the Rise of Nazism.* London: Allen & Unwin.

Turner, Henry Ashby (1996). *Hitler's Thirty Days to Power: January 1933.* Reading, Mass.: Addison-Wesley.

Conan Fischer

Gestapo

Although the Gestapo certainly played a central role in Nazi genocide, its name is often misapplied to other SS and police organizations involved. To understand its actual role, one must understand its place in that larger complex, but especially the branch to which it belonged, the Security Police and SS Security Service (Sipo and SD).

The Gestapo routinely rounded up "undesirables." Here, Warsaw Jews are force-marched from the city for transport to concentration camps in the east, March 27, 1940. [BETTMANN/CORBIS]

As the Nazis took over Germany in 1933, they created separate security agencies of police detectives to fight political crime, that is, to prosecute their enemies. To build agencies that could infringe on civil liberties, they took advantage of fears about threats to national security, especially after the hysteria unleashed by the Reichstag fire, allegedly set by a communist terrorist.

Geheime Staatspolizei (Privy [Secret] State Police) was a traditional title for political police. The abbreviation GeStapo emerged innocently enough, only to become a symbol of police terror and genocide.

By 1936 Heinrich Himmler, head of the SS, had consolidated all such police into a unified national Gestapo. They had become veritably independent of all judicial and most normal governmental mechanisms of control. At the same time, he acquired command of all German state police to become Reichsführer SS and Chief of German Police. Himmler hoped to revolutionize them by fusion with his SS.

As part of this process, under Reinhard Heydrich he united three complementary agencies. While maintaining their separateness, they teamed the regular detectives, the *Kriminalpolizei* (Kripo), with the Gestapo, collectively called the Security Police (Sipo). To provide union with the SS, they added the SS Security Service (*Sicherheitsdienst,* SD) that had been created by Heydrich. Sipo and SD were to be the nerve center for identifying and eliminating any so-called threats to the national community.

The SD was an amorphous combination of academics, professionals, and young Nazis who wanted to shape future society, to provide ideological guidance for police work against alleged enemies of the people, to monitor and shape the public mood and advise the national leadership, and to monopolize domestic and foreign intelligence and counterespionage operations. Himmler and Heydrich planned to infuse Sipo with leaders and members of the SD; they also began to successfully recruit qualified detectives as SS/SD members. Although this two-way process never involved a majority of the detectives, it contributed significantly to mobilizing all involved for their future roles in genocide.

To enhance control, in 1939 Himmler and Heydrich created a special headquarters for Sipo and the SD—the Reich Security Main Office (*Reichssicherheitshauptamt,* or RSHA). Not only did RSHA become the command center for national security, it also extended its tentacles into all occupied territories where enemies and other peoples deemed unsuitable might undermine development of the "Thousand Year Reich." RSHA acquired authority for coordinating security efforts behind the lines.

Thus, although the Gestapo played a key role in Nazi genocide, it worked inseparably from its teammates in Sipo and SD. The RSHA coordinated with the Wehrmacht the operations of the Einsatzgruppen of Sipo and SD. Once areas were secured, RSHA morphed these forces into regional headquarters for its operations and the ongoing programs of "population management." Sipo and SD were the executive agencies for identification and extermination, organization of shooting teams, ghettoization, and assignment to labor and death camps. This involved them in the coordination of the uniformed German police and locally recruited police auxiliaries, both of whom played major roles in mass extermination. In the occupied west the Gestapo's Jewish experts worked under Sipo and SD commanders to locate, round up, and transport Jews and other victims to ghettos or concentration camps. In Allied countries they encouraged maximum collaboration.

Their Kripo colleagues had responsibility for rounding up and committing to the camps homosexuals, three-time criminal offenders, Romani, and anyone else who fell under the ever-broadening category of asocials. This authority resulted from the Nazi program of proactive crime prevention as opposed to reactive enforcement. Such logic involved them in the euthanasia program for exterminating the genetically unfit. Thus, Kripo acquired expertise in operating gas chambers. That, in turn, led to their involvement in developing some of the first death camps in Poland.

Neither branch of Sipo commanded either the early concentration camps or the slave labor and extermination camps that emerged with the Holocaust. They did, however, share primary responsibility for rounding up and determining the commitment and release of inmates. The much larger uniformed police force under Himmler, but outside Sipo and SD, supported them in all these operations, while another branch of the SS ran the camps.

Specifically in the evolution and execution of the Shoah, the Gestapo and SD played symbiotic roles from the beginning. Ostensibly, as police executive for domestic security, the Gestapo targeted legally defined enemies of the state. Of course, it also monitored and harassed all suspected enemies, and shut down their organizations. Its first targets were communists and socialists, but quickly liberal, conservative, and rival right-wing radical groups became suspect. Then any remaining non-Nazi professional or labor organizations came under scrutiny and attack. Among the vanguard of suspected enemies were Christian leaders whose sense of morality led them to publicly criticize the regime's programs. Catholic priests and organizations especially drew fire, but Jehovah's Witnesses were the first sect targeted for immediate elimination.

Freemasons and Jews had always ranked high on the Nazi lists of enemies. The Gestapo could break up lodges and Jewish organizations, but individuals had to be charged with specific crimes. Thus, the Gestapo originally devoted relatively limited energy to Jews. But the Nuremberg Laws of 1936, combined with an expanding body of legislation curbing Jewish economic and occupational activities, defined many otherwise normal human activities as crimes when performed by Jews. Thereafter, the police generated "statistical evidence of criminality" that allegedly proved the Jewish threat to public security. Policemen felt increasing pressure to prosecute/persecute this outgroup, whose very existence was perceived as a threat to law and order. Still, law enforcement could usually act only when a Jew broke the law.

By 1936 two other developments led the SD to acquire a growing interest in the "solution" of the "Jewish problem." Among its leading, highly educated officers, some with an ideological fixation on "scientific racism" had risen to prominence, and for them Jews ranked preeminently as the problem in achieving racial purity. Meanwhile, rivalry among Nazis made it clear to Himmler, Heydrich, and SD leaders that acquiring responsibility for solving the Jewish problem would win favor with Hitler. Consequently, the SD created a cadre of "experts on Jewry" who would apply so-called scientific methods of research to understand and solve the problem rationally. They claimed the right to a monopoly over such problem solving because of their superiority over conventional anti-Semites who in their counterproductive excesses were misguided by "mere superstition."

As a result, Heydrich created in 1937 a division of labor between the Gestapo and SD. The Gestapo prosecuted Jewish criminality, while the SD researched and monitored the problem, ensuring that its detectives had proper ideological-scientific insight. This lasted until the pogrom of Kristallnacht in November 1938. After the annexation of Austria in March 1938 greatly expanded the numbers of Jews in the Reich, Hitler's Jewish expert, Adolf Eichmann, developed a highly efficient office in Vienna to speed up the process of emigration, while thoroughly fleecing the victims. SD recommendations for also expelling Jews with Polish citizenship inadvertently precipitated the November pogrom, because it was the assassination of a German official by the son of such expelled immigrants that provided the pretext for the pogrom. The actions of radicals wreaked extensive economic damage with embarrassing international consequences. In response, to defuse radical dissatisfaction with the slowness of emigration and to solve the "Jewish problem." Heydrich was allowed to establish offices based on Eichmann's model throughout the entire Reich.

As the agency with police power, the Gestapo was better suited for such a responsibility, so Eichmann and his SD Jewish experts were transferred to the Gestapo. The SD retained only the mission of studying the Jewish problem. In this think-tank capacity, however, they sought to guide Nazi leadership and all police increasingly caught up in the evolution of the Final Solution. To maintain their position, they had to offer ever more radical and thorough solutions. Meanwhile, the joint involvement of Sipo and SD officers and personnel in the Einsatzgruppen, first in Poland and then on the Eastern Front, produced increasingly murderous responses. At every level, from Hitler down to the shooting teams, Sipo and SD helped initiate and further the decision to exterminate all Jews and eventually all other persons deemed unsuitable in the European population.

The most important question is not by whom and how all this was done, but the motivations of the perpetrators. Below the level of some ideologically motivated leaders and aside from a minority of rabid anti-Semites, the majority of the hundreds of thousands of perpetrators were "ordinary men" in most senses of that phrase. This applied to the professional police detectives in Kripo and the Gestapo. The availability and mobilization of such people for genocidal behavior remain key issues for research and debate.

SEE ALSO Barbie, Klaus; Germany; Göring, Hermann; Himmler, Heinrich; Holocaust

BIBLIOGRAPHY

Browder, George C. (1990). *Foundations of the Nazi Police State: The Formation of Sipo and SD.* Lexington: The University of Kentucky Press.

Browder, George C. (1996). *Hitler's Enforcers: The Gestapo and the SS Security Service in the Nazi Revolution.* New York: Oxford University Press.

Gellately, Robert (1990). *The Gestapo and German Society: Enforcing Racial Policy, 1933–1945.* Oxford, U.K.: Clarendon Press.

Johnson, Eric A. (1999). *Nazi Terror: The Gestapo, Jews, and Ordinary Germans.* New York: Basic Books.

Lozowick, Yaakov (2002). *Hitler's Bureaucrats: The Nazi Security Police and the Banality of Evil.* London: Continuum.

Paul, Gerhard, and Klaus-Michael Mallmann, eds. (1995). *Die Gestapo: Mythos und Realitaet.* Darmstadt, Germany: Wissenschaftliche Buchgesellschaft.

Paul, Gerhard, and Klaus-Michael Mallmann, eds. (2000). *Die Gestapo im Zweiten Weltkrieg: "Heimatfront" und besetztes Europa.* Darmstadt, Germany: Wissenschaftliche Buchgesellschaft.

Ruerop, Reinhard, ed. (1989). *Topography of Terror: Gestapo, SS and Reichssicherheitshauptamt on the Prinz-Albrecht-Terrain. A Documentation.* Berlin: Verlag Willmuth Arenhoevel.

George C. Browder

Ghetto

In the second half of the twentieth century the word *ghetto* in American culture was used to describe overpopulation and poverty in urban settings. Sections of cities, usually housing recent immigrants of African American or Latino origin, came to be referred to by this term. It communicated a kind of substandard living that could usually be ascribed to persistent discrimination against such communities, but also toward immigrants in general. In some instances, a sense of belonging and self-identification emerged from these negative connotations.

A sense of belonging evolved from the racial homogeneity and experience of shared persecution within the confines of the ghetto. African American or Latino ghettos do not always contain dilapidated buildings or deteriorating housing projects, but may signify home, places with an authentic racial identity or "soul" that yields a desire and yearning for life and the overpowering drive to rise above the immediate physical surroundings. This powerful image has been aptly captured in popular culture, especially literature. In the early twentieth century there were descriptions of a "negro ghetto" in Langston Hughes' plays and in his poem "The Heart of Harlem" (1945). In the latter Hughes captures the essence of this term:

The buildings in Harlem are brick and stone
And the streets are long and wide
But Harlem's much more than these alone
Harlem is what's inside.

This theme was echoed in the later work of other African American authors such as Countee Cullen, Claude McKay, Ralph Ellison, and Lorraine Hansberry. What links these writers is their reference to the mean streets of the ghetto, where life was hard but, despite poverty, crime, and rampant drug activity, dreams could be born that would transport people to a better way of life.

The derivation of the word *ghetto* is important. *The Oxford English Dictionary*, in seeking to trace its etymology, admits to a lack of clarity. There is tacit acceptance among scholars, however, that the word derives from the Italian verb *gettare* (to pour or to cast), a reference to the foundry existing in the city-state of Venice in the early 1500s. Nearly a hundred years later in Thomas Coryat's *Coryat's Crudities* (1611), the word first appeared in written form in the English language: "a place where the whole fraternity of the Jews dwelleth together, which is called the Ghetto."

From this passage it can be extrapolated that the early history of the word refers to a distinct section of a city, usually separated from the rest of the city by walls or gates. The people who lived within that walled section of the city were Jews. The connotation of negativity and discrimination followed the word from that point onward.

Origin of the Concept

The Jews who lived in Venice were mostly traders and moneylenders by profession. The presence of Jewish moneylenders played an important role in overcoming the religious prohibition, among both Christians and Jews, on collecting interest for loans made to members of one's own faith. As pointed out by Benjamin Ravid in 1992,

> The Jewish moneylenders not only helped to solve the socioeconomic problems of an increasingly urbanized society, but also made it less necessary for Christians to violate church law by lending money at interest to fellow Christians. Consequently the Venetian government periodically renewed charters allowing Jews to engage in money lending down to the end of the Republic in 1797.

The beliefs of the Jewish minorities in Venice across Italy and throughout Europe stood in stark opposition to the growing Christian Renaissance of the time. As a result, the incumbent powers in Venice and the city's population targeted the Jewish community. Laws were passed, notably *Calimani 1*, that required Jews to be grouped together to prevent free movement, especially at night. Another regulation, *Calimani 2,* required the Jewish population to wear a star-shaped yellow badge and yellow beret to differentiate them from the Christian majority. This public identification not only enabled the authorities to easily identify Jews, but it also attracted taunts and social cruelties. This discrimination was compounded by strict migration laws that prevented the Jewish population from growing through immigration.

The combination of social factors at play during that historical period and the creation of specific laws aimed at the Jewish community introduced the word *ghetto* into the lexicon. Discriminated against in mainstream society, Jewish traders and moneylenders were forced to remain together. The strict regulations requir-

In response to the 1943 uprising in the Warsaw ghetto, Nazi troops burned entire blocks of buildings. This was their principal line of attack against unexpected Jewish resistance.

ing them to live in a specific area of the city implied that they had to live within a section that could be easily monitored. The area near the foundry in Venice was ideal for such purposes. Persistent discrimination coupled with the passage of further laws identified this group to the authorities and the rest of the city's residents, making them subject to abuse. This provided additional motivation for Jews to live inside their own territory, where they were less likely to be subjected to derision.

Accounts of the time suggest that the ghetto itself did not necessarily signify a deterioration in living standards and status. Rather, for many Jews it represented the middle ground between unconditional acceptance and complete expulsion and exclusion. Residing within the ghetto allowed them to pursue their way of life and trade without interference. The ghetto appears to have been a place where Jewish culture and identify thrived.

Shades of Meaning

The word *ghetto* encompasses several strands of meaning that need to be identified and differentiated. At least three different connotations exist: (1) voluntary Jewish quarters; (2) quarters assigned to the Jews, either for their convenience or protection, or as an inducement for them to settle in a particular area; and (3) an area that was compulsorily Jewish and where no Christians were allowed to live.

These distinctions largely resulted from clerical pressures, social circumstances, and especially the edicts of the Nazi regime. Also important to understanding the meaning of the term is an examination of the environs in which the ghetto typically existed and the reaction of Jews when confronted with compulsory or optional living quarters.

There is little doubt that in the late medieval period many Jews, like modern immigrant groups of the twenty-first century, chose freely to live in close proximity to each other. This desire was often driven by the very practical needs of living a shared religious and social life that was significantly different from that of the rest of the population. This tendency was apparently reinforced in the eleventh and twelfth centuries when secular authorities in Germanic lands as well as *reconquista* Spain offered their Jewish populations specific quarters. It is important to note that the Jewish quarters at this stage were not compulsory nor were they used as a means of segregation. Rather, they were provided as an incentive for Jewish traders to conduct their trades within cities.

During this era there was regular contact between Jews and their Christian neighbors, despite the occasional recalcitrance of the Catholic Church, which frowned on such relations. This was captured in the stipulation adopted by the Third Lateran Council in 1179 discouraging Catholics from living among Jews. It was primarily this decree that led many European cities, including Venice, to pass legislation segregating Jews. As a result, Jewish quarters commonly were populated exclusively by Jews, with non-Jews, mainly Catholics, often prevented by law and emerging custom from living in these areas.

Developments in Venice

In Venice itself, Jews were allowed to settle anywhere within the city, with no concerted group settlement except for a brief period between 1382 and 1397. It was also common for Jews to settle on the mainland across the lagoon from Venice in Padua and Mestre, with the city of Venice allowing them to seek refuge there in the event of war. Within this context Jews fled to Venice from neighboring regions during the War of the League of Cambrai in 1509. When Venice successfully defended itself, acquiring the surrounding mainland territories, the refugees were ordered to return home. However, exceptions were made for Jews when city authorities realized the benefits of permitting this population to remain in Venice.

The principal reason for this decision was the potential revenue that might be collected from wealthy Jewish traders in a time of state penury caused by the expense of the recent war. The Jewish community's continued presence in the city would also assure the close proximity of moneylenders for the poor, whose numbers had risen sharply after the war. It was these circumstances that are reflected in the city charter of 1513, allowing Jews to live in the city and guaranteeing their freedom to continue moneylending activities there.

Role of the Church

The enlightened attitude of the Venetian government stood in sharp contrast to the views of civil society and the Church. The clergy regularly preached and incited hatred against the Jews, notably at Easter time when there were often calls for their expulsion from the city. The delicate balance between polity and the Church was overcome by a move on the part of the Venetian government in 1516 that sought to placate such sentiments and can be directly attributed to the growing use of the term ghetto. In a document passed by the Venetian Senate on March 29, the city government agreed to the Jews' continued presence in the city as moneylenders, but indicated that they could not dwell anywhere in the city and have freedom of movement day and night. Instead, the legislation stipulated that all Jews would be required to live on an island referred to as *ghetto nuovo* (the new ghetto). To guarantee that Jews lived within this area and remained confined within it at night, gates were erected at two locations. These gates were to be locked at sunset and only reopened the next morning at sunrise. Jews caught outside the gates during the hours between sunset and sunrise could be fined prohibitive amounts.

For the legislation to take effect, the Christians who lived within the area designated as the *ghetto nuovo* were required to vacate their homes. Landlords of properties within the newly formed ghetto were also allowed to charge their new Jewish tenants rents that were one-third higher than those paid by their former Christian tenants, with the increments exempt from any form of taxation.

Evolution of the Venetian Ghetto

The concept of ghetto that is understood in the contemporary world, although it reflects many aspects of current reality, may be traced back to the actions of the Venetian Senate in 1516. Many Jews initially resisted the stipulation that required them to leave their abodes and move to the newly gated area. In addition, while many of the Jews lived in close proximity to each other, they strongly objected to the idea of being segregated in the manner proposed by the Senate. However, because the Venetian government was adamant about its policy but did make some concessions in terms of the area's administration, the community gradually accepted the stricture. It was clearly preferable to being cast out of the city altogether and forced to trade from the mainland.

Records also reveal 1541 to be a significant date in distinguishing the Venetian ghetto from the radical concept of ghetto that the Nazis advanced nearly four hundred years later. That year a group of Levantine Jewish merchants visited the city and then approached the authorities, complaining that the existing ghetto was not large enough for them to both reside in and use for the storage of their merchandise. The Venetian government investigated the complaint and found it to be valid. Recognizing the value of the Jewish community in attracting trade to the city, it ordered that the ghetto be extended by appropriating a neighboring area that contained twenty dwellings. This amalgamation was accomplished by building a wall and a footbridge between the *ghetto vecchio* (old ghetto) and the *ghetto nuovo*. Thus unlike the Nazis, Venetian authorities did engage in a dialogue with the Jewish community and instigated measures to increase their comfort.

The Concept Spreads
The ghetto and the phenomenon of segregating Jewish populations were not confined to Venice alone. With the driving force being the pressure exerted by the Church on the regulation of the Jewish community and its interactions with Christians, the practice of restricting Jews to specific areas within cities became widespread. This trend was consolidated by the papal bull that Pope Paul IV issued shortly after his selection as pontiff in 1555. *Cum Nimis Absurdum* required all Jews, in papal states, to live on a single street and, if necessary, adjacent streets, with the area clearly separated from the living space of Christians and with a single entrance and exit. Thus, Jews in Rome were required to move into a designated quarter as a result of this edict, and subsequent reference to the area as a ghetto is contained in Pope Pius IV's papal bull of 1562, entitled *Dudum a Felicis.*

This trend was repeated across Italy, with similar activities reported in Tuscany and Florence (1571) and Sienna (1572). In each case the area that the Jews were

required to live in was referred to as a ghetto. The word also entered the lexicon of the Jewish community; it appears in Hebrew documents of the Jews of Padua. From 1582 onward this community engaged in similar discussions with the authorities, which resulted in the creation of a ghetto there in 1601 after Padua had gained its independence from Venice.

In Venice the use of the term rose steadily after the extension of the Jewish quarter in 1541. A second negotiation for additional space occurred in 1633 and it resulted in the designation of a third ghetto area called *ghetto nuovissimo*, also physically linked to the two earlier ghettos. However, this third ghetto area was not located on the site of the previous foundry. Thus, while the former two ghettos owed their names to the existence of foundries on the land prior to their redesignation as segregated places for Jews, the new ghetto had never been a foundry. It was simply referred to as a "ghetto" since it was the newest enclosed quarter for Jews. Thus, as pointed out by Ravid in 1992, "the term ghetto had come full circle in its city of origin: from an original specific usage as a foundry in Venice, to a generic usage in other cities designating a compulsory segregated, walled-in Jewish quarter with no relation to a foundry, and then to that generic usage also in Venice."

Although the first official ghetto evolved in Venice and can be directly linked to the Senate ruling of 1516, it would be incorrect to suggest that it represented the first segregation of Jews. Prior to that date, there had been quarters in cities that were populated primarily by Jews. An example is the Jewish quarter in Frankfurt established in 1462, predating the Venetian ghetto by more than fifty years. Thus, although the first ghetto was established in Venice in 1516, it was such only in a purely technical, linguistic sense. In a wider context, one that recognizes what a ghetto signifies, the concept of a compulsory, exclusive, enclosed Jewish quarter is arguably older than 1516 and may be traced to the Church's Third Lateran Council.

References in Literature
In terms of English literature, although William Shakespeare's *The Merchant of Venice* (1596) specifically refers to a Jewish moneylender who almost certainly would have lived in the ghetto, no mention is made of the word. The play does, however, portray the prejudice that existed toward Jews in the sentiments expressed against Shylock, the moneylender, but it is inaccurate in that no reference is made to the fact that Jews were required at that time to wear yellow stars and berets.

The first reference in the English language to ghetto, as mentioned earlier, appeared in the travelogue written by Thomas Coryat in 1611, *Coryat's Crudities*. The book details the author's travels, including a visit to Venice, and the word *ghetto* is used to describe the dwelling place for the "whole fraternity of the Jews."

While ghettos persisted for the next two centuries, the phenomenon was only sporadically represented in popular culture and writing. In 1870 some scholarship suggested that Western Europe's last ghetto, in Rome, had been abolished. Despite such a claim, it is clear that the practice remained widespread, in Russia and elsewhere around the world. The term *ghetto* also began to appear with greater frequency in the literature. It appeared in the work of literary critic Edward Dowden in his analysis of Percy Bysshe Shelley's poetry in the late nineteenth century. In two biographical studies of the same period, *Children of the Ghetto* and *Dreamers of the Ghetto* (1898), Israel Zangwill explores the idea of life in the ghetto.

With the steady rise in discrimination against Jews all over Europe as well as in the Ottoman Empire during the nineteenth century, it became common for many cities to designate Jewish quarters that were often referred to as ghettos. The word came to refer to any area that was densely populated with Jews, even when those places had no strictures that barred Jews from living in the rest of the city among the rest of the population. Eventually, the word lost its Jewish emphasis and simply referred to any densely populated area where a minority group lived. Most often, as in modern-day usage of the word, the rationale for the homogeneity was socioeconomic and cultural rather than legal, thus marking a significant departure from the term's original use in Venice when the law required that Jews be segregated into a ghetto.

The development of the word has resulted in a number of related phrases such as "out of the ghetto" and "ghetto mentality." These suggest that the ghetto is a place from which emancipation is necessary. Although it could be argued that the Jews confined to ghettos sought emancipation of this kind, the factors from which individuals living in modern-day ghettos seek a release are primarily socioeconomic rather than legal. Thus, getting out of the ghetto is a reference to acquiring enough wealth and influence not to have to live within its crowded confines. Similarly, ghetto mentality refers to the feeling of being under pressure or in a state of siege and reacting in a manner that is not otherwise considered rational.

Nonetheless, in the literature and other contexts the word *ghetto* has been mostly used in its classical Counter-Reformation sense, to refer to compulsory segregation in urban settings.

World War II

The crucial step in the evolution of the concept of ghetto to its modern-day meaning occurred during World War II, when the Nazis forced Jews into overcrowded and squalid quarters. Unlike earlier ghettos, Jews were simply grouped together in one specific place as a temporary haven on the planned road to total annihilation. With Adolf Hitler's rise to power in the 1930s, the idea of the ghetto reignited with a fury, exhibiting the worst manifestations of forcing a population to live within strict confines. The substandard living conditions introduced in the Nazi ghettos established and reinforced the concept of an archetypical ghetto as a place of severe hardship and misery. Nazi ideology with its theory of a superior Aryan race placed the minority Jewish population under direct threat, and ghettos became the means by which this population was segregated and then targeted for the fullest expression of Nazi aggression. German expansion eastward reestablished ghettos all over Europe. It is estimated that the Third Reich's conquests resulted in the creation of over three hundred ghettos in Poland, the Soviet Union, the Baltic States, Czechoslovakia, Romania, and Hungary.

The ghettos of World War II were extremely different from those of the Renaissance period. Although motivated by the same idea of segregation, the Nazi ghettos had a much more sinister purpose: the containment of a population that was soon to be exterminated. Nazi ghettos were demarcated from the rest of the urban landscape by the use of crude wooden fences, high brick walls, and, often, barbed wire.

Life in the Ghetto

Life inside the ghetto has varied tremendously at different points in history and in reaction to the pressures exerted on the community within its confines. In early Venetian times and in the aftermath of the papal bulls, ghettos became a place where Jews could maintain their own affairs and escape the discrimination they suffered in mainstream society. It was also a place where Jewish sociocultural and religious activity thrived, and a feeling of relative security might be experienced. In this era the ghetto had not yet become synonymous with overcrowding and dense overpopulation. As discussed above, when space was at a premium in the Venetian ghetto, Jewish leaders simply renegotiated with the Senate and secured additional areas to enlarge the original ghetto. There are also several accounts by authors and artists of the time, notably Leon Modena, Simone Luzzatto, and Sara Copia Sullam, that depict a society rich in culture and art within the Venetian ghetto.

What is clear is that life inside the ghetto in Venice was in sharp contrast to life in the Nazi ghettos throughout Europe, where existence was directly influenced by outside pressures. A significant factor in the level of Jewish self-expression and creativity during this period was not so much the circumstance that required Jews to live in the ghetto, but rather, "the nature of the outside environment and whether it offered an attractive supplement to traditional Jewish genres of intellectual activity" (Ravid, 1992). Thus, the conditions the Nazi regime imposed on Jews were reflected in the immense overcrowding and suffering of a people forced to live within the confines of a ghetto. In these circumstances daily life was extremely hard, often resulting in despair, as it was compounded by the knowledge that the ghetto was merely an interim stop on the road to annihilation by a regime that was intent on eradicating Jewish identity.

Thus, the meaning of the term *ghetto* has changed considerably over time. Although its connotations have always been negative, because of the underlying rationale of segregation, these were not necessarily present to the same degree when the word was first coined in Venice of the sixteenth century. The most negative connotation of the word clearly derives from the actions of the Nazis during World War II.

The Ghetto Uprising in Warsaw
Another aspect of the use of the word *ghetto* can be attributed to a specific incident that occurred during World War II, the ghetto uprising in Warsaw. It captured the public imagination worldwide as a struggle against immense odds. At the outbreak of World War II there were three million Jews in Poland, with as many as four hundred thousand living in Warsaw. The Nazis invaded Poland in September 1939, and by November of the following year they had established the Warsaw ghetto. It was surrounded by an eleven-mile wall, roughly ten to twenty feet high, topped with broken glass and barbed wire. With its original residents displaced elsewhere, some 140,000 Polish Jews were forced into this concentrated area. German soldiers were posted at the ghetto's exits; only those Jews working in war-related industries were allowed to leave and return. Jews from other parts of Poland were gradually moved in, and some estimate that at one time there were as many as half a million people living in the Warsaw ghetto. Nearly 63,000 Jews are estimated to have died from starvation, the cold, and disease during the life of this ghetto.

Conditions within the ghetto regularly resulted in death, and this, coupled with the news in July 1942 that a death camp existed in Treblinka some forty miles away, fueled actions of resistance. By early 1943 the residents of the ghetto began to fight back against their

Established by the Nazis in November 1940, the Warsaw ghetto is believed to have housed as many as a half-million Jews before the Third Reich began to implement its Final Solution. Behind the 11-mile wall shown in this wartime photo, squalid conditions prevailed, with disease and starvation rampant, and approximately 63,000 people died. [HULTON-DEUTSCH COLLECTION/CORBIS]

captors. Using a handful of pistols, grenades, and captured weapons, the fighters took on the might of their tormentors, perhaps strengthened by the fatalistic attitude that death in combat was preferable to their meek acceptance of the fate that awaited them at Treblinka and other concentration camps. Drawing the Nazis into a guerilla-style battle, the Jewish fighters achieved some success in skirmishes that mostly took place in narrow alleys and dark apartment passages. The period of resistance lasted a total of eighty-seven days.

The fighting reached a climax on April 19 when columns of approaching German troops, with tanks and armored vehicles, met with fierce resistance. They lost two hundred soldiers—either killed or wounded—and were forced to retreat. By April 23 the fighters issued a public appeal:

Poles, citizens, soldiers of freedom. . .we the slaves of the ghetto convey our heartfelt greetings to you. Every doorstep in the ghetto has become a stronghold and shall remain a fortress until the end. It is our fight for freedom, as well as yours; for our human dignity and national honor as well as yours. . . .

However, the resistance began to crumble as food and ammunition ran out. The Nazis squeezed the ghetto, setting fire to buildings and reducing most of it to rubble as they sought out every last perpetrator of resistance against their occupying forces. By May the Nazis has regained complete control of the ghetto. Nevertheless, the fierce struggle against impossible odds inspired many other struggles, and in a sense, the feeling of shared fraternity that accompanies the use of the word *ghetto* in modern parlance may be attributed, in part, to it.

SEE ALSO Catholic Church; Germany; Holocaust; Inquisition; Resistance

BIBLIOGRAPHY

Ainsztein, Reuben (1979). *The Warsaw Ghetto Revolt*. New York: Holocaust Library.

"Ancient Ghetto of Venice." Available from http://www.doge.it/ghetto/indexi.htm.

Grynberg, Michal (2002). *Words to Outlive Us: Voices from the Warsaw Ghetto*, trans. Philip Boehm. New York: Metropolitan Books.

"Jewish Virtual Library." Available from http://www.us-israel.org/jsource/vjw/Venice.html.

Ravid, Benjamin C. I. (1992). "From Geographical Reality to Historiographical Symbol: The Odyssey of the Word Ghetto." In *Essential Papers on Jewish Culture in Renaissance and Baroque Italy*, ed. David B. Ruderman. New York: New York University Press.

Stoop, Jürgen (1979). *The Jewish Quarter of Warsaw Is No More!* tran. Sybil Milton. New York: Pantheon Books.

University of Bordeaux website. Available from http://www-writing.montaigne.u-bordeaux.fr/univ/ghetto.htm.

Uris, Leon (1961). *Mila 18*. Garden City, N.Y: Doubleday.

Joshua Castellino

Goebbels, Joseph

[OCTOBER 29, 1897–MAY 1, 1945]
Nazi propagandist and close associate of Hitler

Joseph Goebbels was second only to Adolf Hitler as a propagandist of the Nazi movement. Small and sickly as a child, he was deemed ineligible for military service because of a clubfoot. His able and agile mind nonetheless led him to obtain a doctoral degree in German literature in 1921.

Goebbels joined the Nazi Party in 1924, entering a milieu where his talents were quickly recognized. Hitler appointed him as head of the Nazi Party in Berlin

in 1926. In that city the party was in chaos, but within a year, Goebbels had expelled a third of the membership, put those remaining to work in creating effective propaganda, and begun a weekly newspaper titled *Der Angriff* (The attack). He made Bernhard Weiss (whom he nicknamed "Idisor"), the Jewish deputy commissioner of the Berlin police, his particular target. Although support for the Nazi Party remained small, it was not long before all of Berlin was keenly aware of the Brownshirts' presence. As Goebbels said, "Making noise is an effective means of propaganda" (Bramsted, 1965, p. 22).

Soon after the Nazi takeover on January 30, 1933, Hitler named Goebbels Minister of People's Enlightenment and Propaganda, in charge of a new ministry made to order for him. This position gave him a major say in most matters relating to propaganda, but Hitler's habit of establishing jobs with overlapping responsibilities meant that Goebbels had to constantly contend with other Nazi leaders for power. During World War II Goebbels's influence gradually increased. His Total War speech in February 1943 was an attempt to mobilize mass support for the war effort after the defeat at Stalingrad, but also to increase his own power. As a propagandist, Goebbels followed Hitler's thinking. Propaganda was a collection of methods to be judged only on the basis of their effectiveness. Methods that worked were good; those that failed were bad. Academic theorizing was useless. Through natural ability and experience the skilled propagandist developed a feeling for what was effective and what was not. Propaganda had to be founded on a clear understanding of the audience. One could not persuade people of anything without taking existing attitudes and building on them.

Goebbels wanted Nazi propaganda to be easy to understand. It had to appeal to the emotions and repeat its message endlessly (but with variations in style). He favored holding to the truth as much as possible. However, Goebbels had no compunction about lying—although he thought it safer to selectively present or distort material rather than completely fabricate it.

Goebbels was a prime mover in the Nazis' anti-Semitic campaign. He regularly issued orders to intensify the campaign against the Jews. At the book burning in Berlin in May 1933, he announced the end of an "era of Jewish hyperintellectualism" (Reuth, 1993, pp. 182–183) and worked to eliminate Jews from German cultural life. He played a central role in the anti-Semitic violence of Kristallnacht (the night of broken glass) on November 9, 1938. He wanted Berlin to be one of the first major German cities to be "free of Jews."

Goebbels took a particular interest in film, especially the two vehement anti-Semitic films released in the fall of 1940: *Jud Suess* and *Der Ewige Jude* (The Eternal Jew). The former was a so-called historic film set in the eighteenth century that accused Jews of financial and sexual crimes, the latter a documentary-style film based largely on footage filmed after the German invasion of Poland. It compared Jews to rats and suggested that they were responsible for most of the world's ills.

In his final major anti-Semitic essay in January 1945, Goebbels wrote: "Humanity would sink into eternal darkness, it would fall into a dull and primitive state, were the Jews to win this war. They are the incarnation of that destructive force that in these terrible years has guided the enemy war leadership in a fight against all that we see as noble, beautiful and worth keeping" (p. 3). After Hitler committed suicide as the Russian siege of Berlin raged, Goebbels and his wife decided to also end their lives on May 1, 1945, to avoid capture, but only after administering a fatal dose of poison to their six children. To their way of thinking, death, even that of their children, was preferable to life under a government other than the Third Reich.

Although Goebbels did not succeed in persuading all Germans to be strongly anti-Semitic, his propaganda intensified existing attitudes and made it easier for Germans to believe that the persecution of the Jews was at least partially justified. The Holocaust would not have been possible in 1933. Ten years of unremitting anti-Semitic propaganda established the foundation on which the concentration camps were built.

SEE ALSO Advertising; Film as Propaganda; Propaganda

BIBLIOGRAPHY

Bramsted, E. K. (1965). *Goebbels and National Socialist Propaganda.* East Lansing: Michigan State University Press.

German Propaganda Archive. Translations of Goebbels's speeches and articles are available from http://www.calvin.edu/academic/cas/gpa.

Goebbels, Joseph (1945). *"Die Urheber des Unglücks der Welt." Das Reich* (January 21):1, 3.

Reuth, R. G. (1993). *Goebbels.* New York: Harcourt Brace.

Randall L. Bytwerk

Goldstone, Richard

[OCTOBER 26, 1938–]
South African jurist and advocate for international justice.

Widely recognized for his advocacy on behalf of international justice causes, particularly the establishment of the International Criminal Court, Richard J. Gold-

Joseph Goebbels, Hitler's Minister of Propaganda, c. 1940. A passionate advocate of Nazi policies, he stirred anti-Semitism and helped set the stage for the Final Solution. **[HULTON-DEUTSCH COLLECTION/CORBIS]**

stone can be credited for helping to instill greater respect for the rule of law within the post–cold war international legal order. During a career spanning over four decades, his significant contributions include striking down one of the apartheid regime's most pernicious laws, chairing a commission to investigate the causes of political violence in the run-up to South Africa's first democratic elections, serving as prosecutor for the International Criminal Tribunals for the former Yugoslavia and Rwanda (ICTY and ICTR), and helping to institutionalize the role of his country's first Constitutional Court.

Goldstone was born in Boksburg, South Africa, to Jewish parents, and grew up to be a politically active student leader at the University of Witwatersrand. After receiving his B.A. and LL.B. degrees (both cum laude), he was admitted to the Johannesburg Bar in 1963. He practiced as a commercial lawyer until his appointment to the Transvaal Provincial bench in 1980. Although only newly appointed, Goldstone wasted little time in ruling that police could not evict a black woman from her home in a white suburb unless they first provided

Richard Goldstone, chief United Nations prosecutor, addresses the audience regarding Bosnian Serbs' mass murder trial. [AP/ **WIDE WORLD PHOTOS**]

her with alternative shelter. This was a landmark ruling that effectively halted prosecutions of blacks under the apartheid regime's segregated housing laws.

In the mid-1980s, in an effort to suppress the rising number of violent anti-apartheid protests, the government adopted some of the harshest security laws of its rule. Under these draconian laws, tens of thousands of protestors were detained in jails and police stations across the country, where they were at risk of being tortured. While Goldstone could do little to free them, he soon became well known for his habit of personally visiting prisoners and detainees. In his view, this practice served to reassure not only the prisoners, but also the administration, that someone was taking an active interest in their well-being. By doing so, Goldstone became a notable exception in a time when few white judges within the apartheid regime enjoyed the trust and respect of the black majority.

From 1990 to 1994, due to his reputation as an impartial and unimpeachable judge, Goldstone became the obvious choice to lead an independent commission to investigate the causes of public violence and intimidation, whenever such actions threatened to disrupt the then-ongoing constitutional negotiations. Under his leadership, the commission conducted 503 inquiries and triggered the initiation of sixteen prosecutions for crimes such as murder, conspiracy to commit murder, illegal possession of firearms, and failure to testify before the commission. In November 1992, in what became one of its most important investigations, the commission exposed a secret military-intelligence cell within the South African Defense Force that was working to sabotage the political legitimacy of the African National Congress, while posing as a legitimate business corporation. Due to these and other revelations, President DeKlerk later was forced to dismiss sixteen intelligence officers.

Notwithstanding the importance of some of its revelations, Goldstone believes the commission's greatest achievement to be the contribution it made to reducing the violence that threatened South Africa's fragile constitutional negotiations. In his view, the commission's role was not so much to ferret out secrets as it was to smooth the way for democracy. This point is illustrated by Goldstone's claim that one of his proudest achievements is the agreement he facilitated between the police and African National Congress (ANC) that all but eliminated violence during protest marches. Indeed, it is generally recognized that the Goldstone Commission's efforts were instrumental in enabling South Africa to peacefully hold its first-ever democratic elections in 1994. Shortly thereafter, with the inauguration of President Nelson Mandela and the ANC government, the commission transferred its files to a newly established National Truth and Reconciliation Commission.

At about the same time that a new multiethnic democracy was taking hold in South Africa, the United Nations Security Council acted under Chapter VII of the UN Charter to establish the world's first ad hoc international criminal tribunal. It did so not to prosecute the architects of apartheid, as some had previously predicted, but in response to reports of deliberate acts of ethnic cleansing and systematic rape in the conflict that ensued the breakup of the multiethnic state of Yugoslavia. After initially proceeding quickly with the election of a number of international judges, the creation of the International Criminal Tribunal for the Former Yugoslavia later stalled over the appointment of a suitable prosecutor. After many months of delay and one failed attempt to appoint a prosecutor, President Mandela finally asked Goldstone to take the job. Goldstone agreed to a two-year term as prosecutor, on the assurance that his appointment to the new South African Constitutional Court be held in abeyance during this time.

From the beginning, Goldstone clearly appreciated the legal, political, and historic significance of ensuring the success of the first truly international criminal court with jurisdiction over genocide, crimes against humanity, and war crimes. Critics of the idea of international justice predicted that the ICTY would fail due to a lack of political will on the part of those who had created it, and pointed to the absence of any accused before it as evidence of its impotence. As a result, by the time the first trial finally got under way, it was clear that the court proceedings would be as much about the feasibility of the idea of an international criminal court as they were about culpability of the accused. This challenge was made more difficult by the fact that the first accused to be tried, Dusan Tadic, was viewed by some as being only a minor actor. This view apparently was not shared by the ICTY, which convicted him of willingly participating in crimes against humanity.

During his two years as prosecutor, Goldstone came to be seen as both jurist and international statesman. He frequently visited foreign capitals, where he met with politicians, diplomats, and UN officials to secure their support for the work of the ICTY. These efforts, together with his public lectures and media appearances, gradually breathed life and vigor into what some regarded as an empty political gesture on the part of the UN Security Council. Yet, even as the ICTY struggled into life, it confronted perhaps its greatest threat—the possibility of a general amnesty for the perpetrators it was created to try. The prospect of such a promise arose during the U.S.–brokered peace negotiations on a military base in Dayton, Ohio.

Some commentators warned that the peace process would fail without the inclusion of an amnesty agreement. Goldstone immediately responded by traveling to Washington, D.C., to urge the U.S. president and secretary of state to resist any such demands. Simultaneously, others at the tribunal made it known that such an amnesty would not be a legal basis for the ICTY to stop indicting those against whom it had evidence, and that the only the UN Security Council had the power to halt the ICTY's efforts. In the end, no amnesty was included in the peace agreement.

While the conflict still raged in the former Yugoslavia, another tragedy was unfolding in the heart of Africa. In April 1994, President Juvenal Habyarimana of Rwanda was killed when unknown assailants shot down the plane that was carrying him back from peace negotiations in Tanzania. Reports immediately began to emerge of large-scale killings being perpetrated against the country's Tutsi minority. The killings continued for almost four months, while the UN debated whether or not to call the massacres a genocide. In the

end, it was not the international community's intervention, but a military victory by the Tutsi-led Rwandan Patriotic Front, that ended the widespread and systematic killings. In what many regard as a belated and inadequate response, the UN Security Council again invoked Chapter VII of the UN Charter to establish yet another ad hoc international criminal tribunal, this time for Rwanda.

In an apparent attempt to ensure consistency between the two tribunals, the International Criminal Tribunal for Rwanda was made to share the same prosecutor and appeals chamber as the ICTY. As a result, Goldstone became an outspoken advocate on behalf of not only the two ad hoc tribunals, but also of a permanent international criminal court. In his view, the creation of ad hoc tribunals risked making international justice indefensibly selective unless these bodies were merely precursors to a permanent international criminal court.

Goldstone is the first to admit that the efforts of the ICTY and ICTR have not been flawless. For example, due to a seemingly endless refusal by North Atlantic Treaty Organisation forces operating in the former Yugoslavia to apprehend those whom the ICTY had indicted, the frustrated ICTY began holding ill-conceived Rule 61 indictment confirmation hearings, which effectively amounted to trials in absentia. Even without the problem of absent defendants, the Rwanda tribunal was plagued by a series of administrative missteps. Despite their shortcomings, the achievements and successes of the ad hoc tribunals, including the first-ever conviction of a former prime minister for genocide, paved the way for the adoption in 1998 of the Rome Statute, which established a permanent International Criminal Court (ICC). In this regard, it is also noteworthy that many of the precedents set by the ad hoc tribunals, particularly those regarding sexual violence and war crimes in internal conflict, are now codified in the ICC's statute.

After completing his two-year commitment as prosecutor for the ad hoc tribunals, Goldstone returned to South Africa to take up his seat on the still-nascent Constitutional Court. He served in that position for eight years, and participated in a number of precedent-setting decisions. Among these were decisions upholding the right of prisoners to vote, requiring the state not to extradite an accused without obtaining an assurance against the application of the death penalty, and overturning a state policy of not providing HIV treatment to pregnant mothers. He retired from the court in October 2003.

During his tenure on the Constitutional Court, Goldstone also participated in at least two international inquiries related to genocide and crimes against humanity. One of these was an international panel established in 1997 by the government of Argentina to monitor the inquiry into Nazi activities in that country since 1938. The inquiry was launched by the government in response to accusations that some of the Nazi gold looted from Jewish victims of the Holocaust might have been transferred to Argentina.

Two years later, Goldstone chaired the Independent International Commission on Kosovo, which investigated the events that led to NATO's military intervention in that region in March 1999. Established by the prime minister of Sweden, the commission was mandated to investigate and analyze the events that occurred in Kosovo in the decade since autonomy was withdrawn from it in 1989. After a yearlong investigation, one of the commission's primary conclusions was that the intervention was illegal but legitimate. According to the commission, "it was illegal because it did not receive prior approval from the United Nations Security Council. However, the . . . intervention was justified because all diplomatic avenues had been exhausted and because the intervention had the effect of liberating the majority population of Kosovo from a long period of oppression under Serbian rule."

SEE ALSO Arbour, Louise; Del Ponte, Carla; International Criminal Court; International Criminal Tribunal for Rwanda; International Criminal Tribunal for the Former Yugoslavia

BIBLIOGRAPHY

Goldstone, Richard J. (2000). *For Humanity: Reflections of a War Crimes Investigator.* New Haven, Conn.: Yale University Press.

Goldstone, Richard J. (2000). *Kosovo: An Assessment in the Context of International Law.* New York: Carnegenie . Council on Ethics and International Affairs.

Garth Meintjes

Göring, Hermann

[JANUARY 12, 1893–OCTOBER 15, 1946]
German commander of the Luftwaffe, Hitler associate

After brilliant service as a fighter pilot and squadron commander during World War I, Hermann Göring was one of the early supporters of Adolf Hitler and rose through the ranks of the Nazi Party to become one of the Führer's closest associates and partners in the murderous campaign against European Jews. Of aristocratic birth, Göring was highly intelligent, utterly egocentric, and cynical, and his decisive weakness proved ultimately to be his sybaritic lifestyle and self-aggrandizing approach to policy and administration. Placed in

charge of the Luftwaffe in 1935, he took on the challenge of the German economy the next year as commissioner of the Four Year Plan. Spearheading the confiscation of Jewish property, Göring had nominal oversight of the Jewish question as a whole at the time of the Kristallnacht riots against the Jews in 1938. He was also the leading promoter and organizer of Jewish emigration, centrally administered in an office he established in January 1939.

Notwithstanding these responsibilities, Göring's gradual estrangement from Hitler coincided with his yielding more and more authority over the Jewish issue to Heinrich Himmler, chief of Hitler's elite bodyguards, the Schutzstaffel (SS). With the outbreak of war in 1939, it was the latter who formulated German population policy in the east; Himmler's Reich police became the principal repressive arm of the state when it came to opponents of the regime, and his SS units began killing on a massive scale after the invasion of the Soviet Union in June 1941. Göring retained enough authority so that it was he who, on July 31 of that same year, signed an order charging Reich police chief Reinhard Heydrich with "making all necessary preparation with regard to organizational and financial matters for bringing about a complete solution of the Jewish question in the German sphere of influence in Europe." Heydrich operated under Himmler's command, however, and subsequent steps toward the deportation and murder of European Jewry fell unmistakably under the authority of the SS.

Having failed to successfully lead his Luftwaffe against Britain in 1940, and as a result of the political fallout from his inability to defend German skies from the menace of Allied bombing, Göring steadily slipped from favor, losing out to other paladins of the regime—Himmler, but also Joseph Goebbels, Hitler's propaganda minister; Martin Bormann, head of the Führer's chancellery; and Albert Speer, minister of armaments in charge of mobilizing the German economy for total war. At the end of the Nazi regime, Göring was dissolute, bitter, and diminished in stature, with much of his authority having eroded. Arrested by the Allies and sitting in the dock at Nuremberg, charged among other injustices with crimes against humanity for his role in the Holocaust, he soon became a leader among the defendants and stoutly defended the causes of Hitler and Nazism. Göring cheated the hangman by committing suicide on October 15, 1946, on the eve of his scheduled execution.

SEE ALSO Anti-Semitism; Germany; Gestapo

BIBLIOGRAPHY

Aly, Götz (1999). *"Final Solution" Nazi Population Policy and the Murder of the European Jews,* tran. Belinda Cooper and Allison Brown. London: Arnold.

Fest, Joachim (1970). *The Face of the Third Reich,* tran. Michael Bullock. New York: Pantheon Books.

Overy, Richard J. (1983). *Göring: The Iron Man.* London: Routledge and Kegan Paul.

Michael R. Marrus

Guatemala

In the early 1980s the Guatemalan army defeated a Marxist-led guerrilla movement by killing tens of thousands of Mayan Indians as suspected subversives. Remnants of various guerrilla organizations joined together in the Guatemalan National Revolutionary Union (URNG) and refused to stop fighting until they achieved peace with justice, that is, negotiated concessions. Only in 1996, and under much international pressure, did the Guatemalan government and the URNG formally end four decades of armed conflict. The army remains the most powerful institution in Guatemala. When active-duty or retired officers are prosecuted, activists, journalists, witnesses, and judicial personnel are besieged by anonymous threats and attacks, sending the deniable but unmistakable message that the army (or part of it) is willing to return Guatemala to the nightmarish political violence of earlier years. Under such conditions public support for human rights prosecutions has been limited. Yet to defer prosecution, until some distant future that may never arrive, risks perpetuating above-the-law status for the military. The dilemma raises key questions: Should human rights activists attempt to prosecute army officers for genocide and other crimes against humanity? Should the human rights movement insist on prosecution even if the defendants have the power to destroy Guatemala's tentative progress toward democracy?

In the October Revolution of 1944 schoolteachers, lawyers, and army officers overthrew the last of the liberal dictatorships that ran this Central American country like a giant hacienda. The elected governments of Juan José Arévalo (1945–1951) and Colonel Jacobo Arbenz Guzmán (1951–1954) abolished mandatory labor, encouraged workers to organize, and instituted land reform that led to the nationalization of United Fruit Company plantations. Because Arbenz had communist advisers, the Eisenhower administration in Washington decided to overthrow him. Through air strikes and a mock invasion staged by exiles, the Central Intelligence Agency (CIA) intimidated the Guatemalan army into abandoning Arbenz. Under the U.S.–selected Colonel Carlos Castillo Armas (1954–1957), the National Liberation Movement reversed the land reforms and many other achievements of the previous governments.

Insurgency and Counterinsurgency

Electoral fraud, political killings, and coups d'etat prevented the Guatemalan Left from competing in elections. In November 1960, 120 junior army officers tried to overthrow President Manuel Ydígoras (1958–1963) in order to, quoting from their manifesto, "install a regime of social justice in which wealth belongs to those who work and not to those who exploit." Several of the rebel officers went on to found the country's first Marxist guerrilla organizations. Resentful over its humiliation in 1954, the army was slow to welcome U.S. military advisers but, when it did in 1965, it soon exterminated the guerrillas' rural logistical base, which at this point consisted mainly of ladino (nonindigenous) peasants in eastern Guatemala.

In the 1970s surviving guerrilla cadre attracted new supporters among the indigenous Mayan peasants of the western highlands, who have been a subordinate caste since the Spanish Conquest and who represent approximately half the Guatemalan population. With the support of the Catholic Church, Protestant missions, and public schools, Mayas during this period began to regain control of many ladino-dominated municipal governments. They also started to demand equality for Mayan language and culture. Meanwhile, the left wing of the Catholic Church became a bridge for some Mayan communities to join the guerrilla movement, which by 1981 seemed to control much of the western highlands. Counterinsurgency violence peaked during the regimes of Generals Romeo Lucas García (1978–1982), Efraín Ríos Montt (1982–1983), and Oscar Mejía Victores (1983–1986). The Guatemalan army repeatedly butchered women, children, and elders as well as military-age men, even when they offered no resistance.

Under Mejía Victores the army allowed a new constitution to be drafted, which led to the resumption of elections and a civilian-led government. Under pressure from Europe, the United States, the United Nations (UN), and the Organization of American States, the government and army began negotiating with the URNG in 1990. Accords on refugee resettlement, indigenous rights, socioeconomic justice, and a truth commission culminated in the 1996 peace agreement, which is being monitored by the United Nations Mission to Guatemala (MINUGUA).

A forensic anthropologist cleans the remains of one of thirteen bodies found in a mass grave at a former army base in Chatalun, Guatemala, on December 19, 2000. About 5,000 Mayan Indians were rounded up by the Guatemalan army near Chatalun in December 1982. Of that number, 3,000 were reportedly killed and their bodies buried in several nearby locations. [AP/WIDE WORLD PHOTOS]

Two Truth Commissions: Did the Army Commit Genocide?

Like other Latin American militaries rejecting judicial accountability, the Guatemalan army has arranged broad amnesties for itself. The latest is the 1996 National Reconciliation Law, which extends amnesty to the guerrillas and is a condition to which URNG leaders agreed. Following protests from human rights organizations, the URNG obtained the government's commitment to a Commission for Historical Clarification (CEH). Because the CEH was prohibited from naming names or preparing cases for prosecution, the Catholic Church organized its own Recovery of Historical Memory (REHMI) commission. Led by Bishop Juan Gerardi, REMHI delivered its report in April 1998. Two nights later Gerardi was bludgeoned to death in his garage.

Several years of investigation were required to bring two army intelligence officers and a sergeant to trial for the murder. The "unknown men in civilian dress" who attack the army's critics have repeatedly been traced to the army's G-2 intelligence branch and to the presidential general staff, a security and intelligence operation that the peace accords sought to abolish, but which instead has continued to grow. Under international scrutiny death squad activity gradually diminished from the mid-1980s, to the point of almost disappearing in the mid-1990s, but since 1998 it has been on the rebound in response to the prosecutions of army officers. The trials of three military personnel for the murder of Gerardi, as well as of two generals and a colonel for the 1990 murder of the Guatemalan anthropologist Myrna Mack, were accompanied by threats and attacks against judges, prosecutors, and witnesses, with some killed and others forced into exile.

The amount of testimony compiled by REMHI and CEH is staggering and damning. The CEH was able to register a total of 42,275 victims, including 23,671 arbitrary executions and 6,159 forced disappearances, from which it estimates a total of more than 200,000 dead. According to its calculations, the Guatemalan state was responsible for 93 percent of the violations, and the guerrillas for another 3 percent, with responsibility for the remainder unclear. The CEH's most controversial finding was that the army committed genocide against the Mayas—a crime not covered by the 1996 amnesty because of Guatemala's obligations to the international genocide convention. Human rights groups hailed the genocide finding, but it was not accepted by President Alvaro Arzú (1996–2000), who signed the peace accord with the URNG. The Mayas suffered 83 percent of violations according to CEH calculations, but thousands of ladinos were also killed for supporting the guerrillas. If the army's intent in targeting victims was the elimination of a political group, the genocide convention does not apply.

According to the CEH's 1999 report, the army "defined a concept of internal enemy that went beyond guerrilla sympathizers, combatants or militants to include civilians from specific ethnic groups." Furthermore, "the reiteration of destructive acts, directed systematically against groups of the Mayan population" and including "the elimination of leaders and criminal acts against minors who could not possibly have been military targets, demonstrates that the only common denominator for all the victims was the fact that they belonged to a specific group and makes it evident that these acts were committed 'with intent to destroy, in whole or in part' these groups." From 1981 to 1983, the CEH concluded, the army committed genocide against four specific language groups that it suspected of particularly strong support for the guerrillas: the Ixil Mayas; the Q'anjob'al and Chuj Mayas; the K'iche' Mayas of Joyabaj, Zacualpa, and Chiché; and the Achi Mayas.

Human Rights Prosecutions and Backlashes
Prosecutions for war-related crimes in Guatemala have been few. Until 2000 virtually all convictions were of junior officers, enlisted men, and leaders of the civil patrols, a counterinsurgency militia into which the army conscripted hundreds of thousands of men, most of them Mayan. Since the army killed soldiers and civil patrollers who failed to carry out orders, many of the homicides documented in the REMHI and CEH reports were arguably committed under duress. Consequently, human rights groups have decided to focus on senior army officers as intellectual authors of the crimes. But such indictments are hard to prove in court, as demonstrated by the Gerardi case. Although three military men were found guilty of that crime, the convictions were soon overturned on appeal. Of the three senior officers tried for the murder of Mack, only one was convicted, and even this conviction has been overturned on appeal. As of late 2003, the cases were still pending.

Because the Guatemalan judicial system lacked independence until the 1990s, and is still antiquated and underfinanced, prosecutions depend heavily on the families and friends of victims and require much international support. Like other Guatemalan human rights organizations, the Archbishop's Office on Human Rights that coordinated the Gerardi prosecution receives most of its funding from Europe and the United States. Threatened judges, prosecutors, and witnesses have been able to obtain foreign asylum with the help of the Canadian and other embassies. Freedom of Information Act lawsuits in the United States have provided documentation. Unfortunately, international support makes the human rights movement vulnerable to nationalist backlashes. Public fear of postwar crime waves has repeatedly trumped support for human rights. In 1999 voters rejected constitutional amendments to remove the army from internal security and grant equality to Mayan culture. Mobs dissatisfied with ineffective police and judicial reforms have lynched more than 360 suspected criminals since 1996. Ex-members of the civil patrols, whom the CEH found responsible for 18 percent of human rights violations, have demanded compensation for the unpaid duty they performed for the army.

The leading symbol of opposition to the human rights movement is Ríos Montt, the evangelical Protestant military dictator who defeated the guerrillas in 1982 and 1983. Despite the REMHI and CEH reports, as well as dozens of exhumations of massacre victims, Ríos Montt and his populist party won the 1999 presidential election as champions of law and order. The victory enabled Ríos Montt to assume leadership of the Guatemalan congress just as 1992 Nobel peace laureate Rigoberta Menchú was trying to indict him for genocide (Ríos Montt claims no knowledge of the massacres). In the hope of repeating the Pinochet precedent—a Spanish court's indictment of ex-Chilean dictator Augusto Pinochet for kidnapping, torture, and murder—in March 2003 the Menchú Foundation persuaded a Spanish court to hear a torture case for twelve Spanish victims. In Guatemala the Legal Action Center for Human Rights is the legal representative for the Association for Justice and Reconciliation (AJR), composed of massacre survivors. More than a hundred witnesses have given testimonies, corroborated by exhumations at the sites of twenty-five massacres that cost an estimated 2,100 lives. If the cases against Ríos Montt, Lucas García, and six other former officials go to trial, these will be the first genocide indictments to be tried in any country where the crime was committed.

A constitutional ban on candidates involved in military coups prevented Ríos Montt from running for president in the 1990s. Then in July 2003 new constitutional court justices appointed by his party allowed him to run for president in the November election. Despite fears that Ríos Montt and his party would attract a massive Mayan vote, they finished third. Newly elected president Oscar Berger (2004–), a neoliberal businessman, has promised to reduce the army by nearly one-third. One reason that part of Guatemala's elite now supports neoliberal reform is that Guatemala has become a major shipment center for cocaine being transported from Colombia to the United States. Some army officers run protection rackets and the U.S. government has refused to certify Guatemala's compliance with drug enforcement. Under severe financial pressure from international lenders, the previous government agreed to a Commission to Investigate Illegal and Clandestine Security Forces (CICIACS). The new commission will be led by representatives of the UN, the Organization of American States, and Guatemalan citizenry. Now that Ríos Montt is no longer a congressman, he has lost his immunity from prosecution and is expected to face several indictments.

SEE ALSO Catholic Church; Death Squads; Forensics; Massacres; Ríos Montt, Efraín; Truth Commissions

BIBLIOGRAPHY

Archbishop's Office on Human Rights (Oficina de Derechos Humanos del Arzobispado de Guatemala, ODHAG) (1998). *Guatemala Nunca Más. Guatemala: Informe Proyecto Interdiocesano de Recuperación de la Memoria Histórica (REMHI)*. Also available from http://www.odhag.org.gt.

Carmack, Robert M., ed. (1988). *Harvest of Violence: Guatemala's Indians in the Counterinsurgency War*. Norman: University of Oklahoma Press.

Ball, Patrick, Paul Kobrak, and Herbert F. Spirer, eds. (1999). *State Violence in Guatemala, 1960–1996: A Quantitative Reflection*. Washington, D.C.: American Association for the Advancement of Science. Also available from http://www.shr.aaas.org/guatemala/ciidh/qr/english.

Commission for Historical Clarification (Comisión de Esclarecimiento Histórico, CEH) (1999). "Guatemala: Memoria del Silencio." Available from http://www.shr.aaas.org/guatemala/ceh.

Falla, Ricardo (1994). *Massacres in the Jungle: Ixcán, Guatemala, 1975–1982*. Boulder, Colo.: Westview Press.

Frank, Luisa, and Philip Wheaton (1984). *Indian Guatemala: Path to Liberation*. Washington, D.C.: Ecumenical Program for Interamerican Communication and Action (EPICA).

González, Matilde (2002). *Se Cambió el Tiempo: Conflicto y Poder en Territorio K'iche'*. Guatemala: Asociación para el Avance de las Ciencias Sociales en Guatemala (AVANCSO).

Green, Linda (1999). *Fear as a Way of Life*. New York: Columbia University Press.

Guatemalan Forensic Anthropology Foundation (Fundación de Antropología Forense de Guatemala, FAFG) (1997). *Las Masacres de Rabinal: Estudio Histórico Antropológico de las Masacres de Plan de Sánchez, Chichupac y Río Negro,* 2nd edition. Guatemala: FAFG.

Guatemalan Forensic Anthropology Foundation (Fundación de Antropología Forense de Guatemala, FAFG) (2001). *Informe Especial de la Fundación de Antropología Forense de Guatemala 1996–1999: Investigaciones antropológico forenses e históricas.* Guatemala: FAFG.

Handy, Jim (1984). *Gift of the Devil: A History of Guatemala*. Toronto: Between the Lines Press.

Jonas, Susanne (2000). *Of Centaurs and Doves: Guatemala's Peace Process*. Boulder, Colo.: Westview Press.

Kobrak, Paul (2003). *Huehuetenango: Historia de una guerra. Huehuetenango.* Guatemala: Centro de Estudios y Documentación de la Frontera Occidental de Guatemala (CEDFOG).

Le Bot, Yvon (1995). *La guerra en tierras mayas: Comunidad, violencia y modernidad en Guatemala*. Mexico, D.F.: Fondo de Cultura Económica.

Montejo, Victor (1987). *Testimony: Death of a Guatemalan Village*. Willimantic, Conn.: Curbstone Press.

Schirmer, Jennifer (1998). *The Guatemalan Military Project: A Violence Called Democracy*. Philadelphia: University of Pennsylvania Press.

Stoll, David (1993). *Between Two Armies in the Ixil Towns of Guatemala*. New York: Columbia University Press.

Wilkinson, Daniel (2002). *Silence on the Mountain: Stories of Terror, Betrayal and Forgetting in Guatemala*. Boston: Houghton Mifflin.

David Stoll

Gulag

Gulag is the generic term given to the system of forced labor camps that existed in the Soviet Union from the 1920s until the mid-1950s. These camps incarcerated millions of people and became an integral part of the Soviet economy's industrialization drive during the dictatorship of Joseph Stalin. The Gulag formed a central element in the Stalinist system of terror.

The word *Gulag* is an acronym from the Russian phrase *Glavnoe upravlenie lagerei* (Main Administration of Camps). This was the name of the administrative structure established in 1931 to oversee the camp network of the Soviet secret police. The precise subordination and nomenclature of the camps' administrative authority changed a number of times throughout its existence. Technically, therefore, the term Gulag was only the official name of the Soviet Union's forced labor

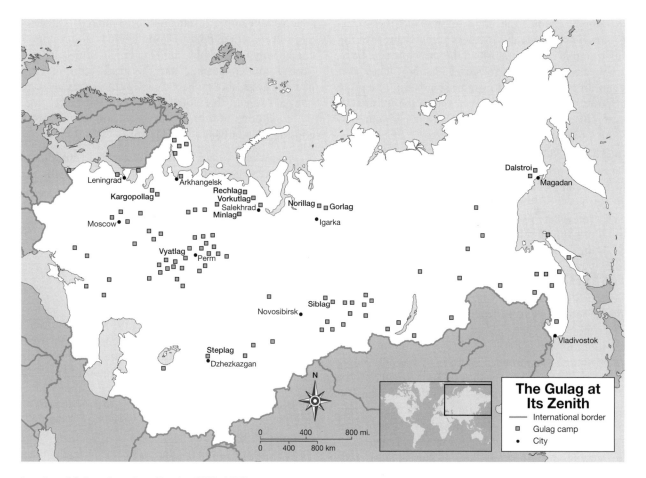

Location of Gulags throughout Russia, 1939–1953. [MAP BY XNR PRODUCTIONS. THE GALE GROUP.]

network for three years, until the first of these name changes occurred in 1934. Nonetheless, the acronym continued to be used as a generic term within the Soviet administration and beyond, eventually becoming widely known in the West through the title of Alexander Solzhenitsyn's celebrated three-volume work on the camp system, *Gulag Archipelago*.

Although the term *forced labor* was used in the Soviet Union, the more common official designation for the activity of the Gulag was "corrective labor." Understanding the nature of the Gulag requires an awareness of its distinct context. The Soviet Union was an ideologically based state, constructed in accordance with its interpretation of the central tenets of Marxism-Leninism. In terms of ideological justification, the Gulag camps were deemed superior to capitalist prison systems, with the ideological emphasis being on reeducating "criminals" through labor to become good citizens of the workers' state. In reality, labor far outweighed reeducation in the prisoners' experience.

The Gulag differed from straightforward conscripted slavery in that its victims were convicted of an offense and given a specific sentence. People did leave the Gulag at the end of their sentences, although many were re-sentenced on the completion of their initial term, and millions died before their release date was reached, either due to the harsh conditions of Gulag life or through execution. The Gulag camps were distinctly different also from Nazi concentration camps, in that they were not primarily places of extermination. Their primary purposes were economic and political rather than genocidal.

Origins

Almost immediately after the Russian revolution in October 1917, Lenin's communist regime began to imprison political opponents and, particularly once the civil war of 1918–1920 was under way, to execute individuals who were deemed to be "class enemies." Such repression of opponents was the norm throughout the 1920s as the communists tightened their grip on Soviet society and, following Lenin's death in 1924, Joseph Stalin gradually outmaneuvered his rivals for power and became the undisputed leader of the Soviet Union.

To some extent the repressions of the post-revolutionary years can be seen as the forerunner of the Gulag system. They established the principle that Soviet law was subordinate to Soviet ideology. They also began on a small scale to use prisoners for economic purposes. Nonetheless, it was not until the industrialization drive from 1929 onward that the phenomenon of the Gulag came into being.

The forced labor camp identified within official Soviet documents as the forerunner of the Gulag was on the Solovetsky Islands, situated in the White Sea in the far northwest of Russia. The Soviet secret police took over a monastery on these islands and turned it into a brutal prison camp for political prisoners. By the mid-1920s the prisoners at the Solovetsky camp began to be used as conscripted labor. Although forced labor had existed in Soviet Russia since its earliest days, and had been a feature of Tsarist Russia before that, the difference at Solovetsky from around 1925 onward was that the economic purpose of labor gradually shifted from providing for the camp's needs, to contributing to the wider national economy. Prisoners of the Solovetsky camp began working in the forestry industry in Karelia. A Politburo decision of June 1929, titled "On the Use of the Labor of Convicted Criminals," paved the way for growth. By the turn of the decade, the example of the Solovetsky camp had been followed elsewhere in northern Russia, in Siberia, and in the Far East, with tens of thousands of prisoners being set to work in forestry, road construction, the chemical industry, and paper production.

Development of the Gulag
The rapid rate of the Gulag's development from 1929 onward was driven by the Soviet Union's push to industrialize. By the end of the 1920s, Stalin's position of power was unchallenged, and he used his authority to decree measures designed to create a strong industrial base in a country hitherto overwhelmingly rural. According to Stalin, the Soviet Union had ten years in which to either catch up with the industrialized capitalist world or, as he put it, be crushed. The creation of a network of forced labor camps fitted into this picture in a number of ways.

Alongside the industrialization policy, the Communist Party sought the collectivization of agriculture. In line with the state's ideological stance, peasants were forced into collective farms. At the same time, *kulaks* (so-called rich peasants) were labeled class enemies and removed from their land. From 1931 onward, millions of such *kulaks* became available to the secret police to work in forced labor.

A key element of industrialization was the opening-up of vast areas of the country, whose natural resources had hitherto remained unexploited. These regions were often remote, uninhabited, undeveloped, climatically inhospitable, and lacking in infrastructure. Forced laborers seemed like the ideal solution: They had no choice about where they would work; they were not paid wages; they formed a mobile workforce; and the conditions in which they lived and worked were considered relatively unimportant.

Stalin saw forced labor as a means of building a number of prestigious projects, such as the White Sea Canal or the Moscow underground. In the case of the former, he deemed it a positive propaganda move to publicize the way in which the Soviet state allegedly rehabilitated its criminals through allowing them to contribute to the well-being of the workers' state. In later years, such propaganda was replaced by secrecy and silence, as the extent of the Gulag increased.

Backed by this correlation of forces, the Gulag system grew rapidly throughout the 1930s. Furthermore, the existence of a cohort of forced laborers was written into the Soviet Union's economic plans. Given that failure to meet the targets of the plan would often result in severe punishment for those deemed responsible, a continuing supply of forced laborers was required.

Number of Victims
The number of victims of the Gulag was for many years the subject of, at times, acrimonious historical debate. During the Cold War years, estimates by Western scholars appeared to some extent politicized, with those on the anti-Soviet right coming up with estimates significantly higher than those on the less anti-Soviet left. The difficulty was, of course, that no data were available from the Soviet Union, and so a diverse range of methods for estimating the number of forced laborers at different periods was employed. To generalize, the higher figures came from those using estimates based on the personal experiences of, for example, former prisoners or former employees of the Soviet state. The lower figures came from methodologies that sought to use official Soviet economic and demographic data in order to calculate the proportion of the population in the forced labor system. Serious estimates for the number of Gulag prisoners in the year 1941 ranged from just over three million to fifteen million.

At the end of the Soviet era (from 1989 onward) Russian, and later Western, scholars began to gain access to the archives of the Soviet secret police, where detailed records of the population of the forced labor camps were kept. It is unlikely that these figures were falsified to any great extent, as were the figures used by the authorities for setting targets in the Five Year Plans for the Soviet economy.

Interpretation of these statistics from the Soviet archives was complicated by the fact that a number of different forms of forced labor existed in the Soviet Union during the Stalin era. Under the control of the Soviet secret police there were the "normal" forced labor camps to which the word Gulag usually refers. In addition there were what the Soviet authorities termed "forced labor colonies." The principal difference between colonies and camps was that inmates in the former were serving sentences of less than three years. Otherwise the experience of prisoners in camps and colonies was little different. As well as camps and colonies, millions of Soviet citizens were placed in "labor settlements" where they were forced to work on state-designated tasks. Although the regimen in such settlements was usually less stringent than that in the camps and colonies, some of them were fenced off, and all were overseen by the Soviet authorities. Labor settlements had a higher proportion of women and children in them than did the camps and colonies.

Camps, colonies, and settlements were the main categories which could be deemed forced labor in Stalin's Soviet Union. Besides these, however, there were prisons and, during and after World War II, "verification and filtration camps" for returning Soviet prisoners of war.

From the archival data available it is now possible to fairly firmly establish the population of the Gulag's forced labor camps and colonies from 1930 to 1953. These data show that the quarter-million mark was reached in 1932, there were over half a million prisoners in 1934, and over a million by 1936. The two-million figure was surpassed briefly in 1941, before the demands and hardships of war saw the camps and colonies population decline to below one and a half million. In the postwar years, it rapidly rose again and reached its all-time peak of over two and a half million between 1950 and 1953. To these figures can be added well over a million people in "labor settlements" in the prewar years, and a further two and a half million in such settlements from 1950 to 1953.

The remaining key question is, how many individual prisoners suffered in the Gulag during the Stalin era? This figure is less easy to determine, not only because the annual totals from which the figures above are taken fail to account for prisoner movement within each year, but also because those totals include some of the same prisoners from one year to the next. To avoid such double-counting, it would be necessary to know the number of new prisoners entering the Gulag each year, and complete data are not available. The most credible estimate, based on the archival, is that approximately eighteen million people were at some point imprisoned in a Gulag labor camp or colony between 1934 and 1952. This figure, however, does not count the millions in forced labor settlements or the other forms of incarceration noted above.

Economic Role

As well as disputes over the number of prisoners, academics have also disagreed on whether the primary motivation behind the creation and continuation of the Gulag was economic or political. This is to some extent a misleading question, as the economic and the political overlapped. A role for forced labor in opening up previously unexploited areas and participating in public projects was deemed useful by the Soviet state, at the same time as political pressures—such as rising official paranoia that the Soviet project was being undermined by the 'enemy within'—meant that the isolation of millions of perceived "enemies of the people" could be seen to both protect the state and serve as an example to others.

Nonetheless, it is a fact that in Five Year Plans, the Soviet Ministry of the Interior was given production targets that relied on the continuation and expansion of the forced labor network. Given the potential penalties for failing to meet these targets, and given the relatively high death rates in the Gulag, it is clear that there were plan targets to be met that were based on a growing number of prisoners, and, therefore, those prisoners would have to be found. There was clearly, then, an economic motivation for finding sufficient "enemies of the people" to keep Gulag production in line with targets.

Prisoners in the Gulag worked in a variety of industries, and they were in demand across the economy, particularly during the labor shortages of the war years. In the early 1940s the Ministry of the Interior set up a number of forced labor administrations, organized by industry. These included administrations for industrial construction, mining, and the metallurgical industry, railway construction, the timber industry, and road construction.

Leaving aside for now all discussion of morality, arguments in favor of the economic benefits of forced labor in the Soviet Union during the Stalin years are simplistic. They portray the Gulag population as a mobile, cheap workforce easily replenished and able to develop inhospitable areas that were rich in natural resources. In fact, the economic benefits of using forced labor over free labor are difficult to identify. The Gulag certainly was not cheap to maintain, requiring an entire infrastructure of its own. The conflict between seeing the population of the Gulag on the one hand as prisoners to be punished and on the other hand as a valuable workforce was never reconciled, leading to unmotivated workers, weakened by poor living conditions and diet, and susceptible to a high death-rate.

In addition, it could be argued that the availability of such an easily identifiable workforce with no rights of its own led the authorities, and indeed Stalin personally, to indulge in projects with little intrinsic economic use. The much-publicized but economically useless White Sea Canal is but the best-known example of such a project, and many other long-disused railways and roads, not to mention now dead or dying industrial settlements, also testify to this tendency.

Life in the Gulag
The Gulag lasted in its mass form for more than two decades, and it was spread over the biggest state in the world. It is difficult therefore to generalize about living conditions, because they differed from camp to camp and year to year. Nonetheless, elements of the Gulag experience repeat themselves in the memoirs of its survivors.

Prisoners in the Gulag were dehumanized within the system. On arrest, or upon arrival at the camp, they were stripped of their clothes and made to wear standard prison garb. Their heads were shaved and they were given prisoner numbers. Contact with the outside world was denied to them, and their free relatives were denied information about the prisoners. A spouse or child would often not hear of a loved one again, and be left to wonder whether he had lived or died.

Rations in the camps were poor and were distributed according to the work performed by each inmate. Four categories of prisoner existed, based on fitness for work: the fitter the prisoner, the higher the rations. Workers were often organized into teams, so that collective responsibility for the ration given discouraged the inefficient worker.

Among the Gulag's prisoner population there was a division between "criminals" and "politicals." The distinction is not easy to make statistically, given that the harsh labor laws introduced during the industrialization drive made such things as lateness for work a criminal offense. Nonetheless, memoir materials, which were nearly always written by the politicals, tell of the brutality visited upon them by the criminals as well as by the guards.

Women usually made up under 10 percent of the Gulag population, though this rose to about 25 percent during World War II.

Terror and the Gulag
During the late 1930s, the Soviet Union suffered what has become known as the Great Terror, during which a significant proportion of the Soviet elite (Communist Party officials, military officers, industrial managers, and even the secret police) were purged by the regime. Some of these found themselves in the Gulag; many were summarily executed. Although the Gulag was a tool of the Stalinist terror, the two phenomena were not identical. At the lowest estimates, more than 750,000 victims of the Terror were executed without ever becoming part of the Gulag, although some estimates put this figure much higher. What is not in doubt is that, if the number of victims of the Stalinist repression who died in the Gulag is included, then somewhere between 3.5 and 7 million victims were killed by the Soviet regime. Such figures do not include the victims of the famine in Ukraine in the 1930s, nor the millions who died in World War II.

Periods in Gulag History
It is apparent that clear periods in the Gulag's history can be identified, such as the origins of the Gulag, the industrialization drive, and the Great Terror. Following on from these, other periods had particular features. From 1939 until the middle of 1941, the population of the camps grew rapidly. The Soviet Union's pact with Nazi Germany had given it control over new territories in East Europe, particularly in Poland, and the Soviet authorities there were only too ready to identify new class enemies to send eastward into the Gulag.

The outbreak of war in June 1941, when Germany invaded the Soviet Union, saw a rapid decrease in the number of prisoners, as most able-bodied men were called up for the front. During the war, conditions in the Gulag worsened to the point that death rates of 25 percent were occurring by 1942. The percentage of women in the camps increased, and the efforts of the workers, as of the country as a whole, were concentrated on the needs of war, particularly weapons production. What is perhaps remarkable is that the population of the Gulag stayed as high as it did during the war years, a period in which more Soviet citizens were incarcerated by their own state than were imprisoned by the enemy.

When the war ended, the Gulag population again rose rapidly, reaching its all-time peak in the early 1950s. Many returning Soviet prisoners of war were incarcerated in the camps, their capture by the Germans being taken as unwarranted surrender.

In the early 1950s the atmosphere in some of the camps began to change, and sporadic camp uprisings occurred. This small-scale shift gained momentum with the death of Stalin in March 1953. Within a few months of Stalin's death an amnesty was announced, though it was mainly the criminals, as opposed to the

Operations at the Gulag camps were conducted in secret, and much of the history of the camps located in Perm, Russia, deep within the Ural Mountains, will never be known. Perm-36 was perhaps the most brutal Gulag for political prisoners in the Soviet Union, and the last to close (in 1989). In this 1989 photo, prisoners at the Perm-36 camp. [P. PERRIN/CORBIS SYGMA]

politicals, who benefited from this. Nonetheless, the will to change was apparent by now in the highest echelons of the Communist Party, and over the next few years the Gulag as an instrument of mass incarceration and forced labor was gradually wound down. Khrushchev's "Secret Speech" in 1956, in which he went some way toward acknowledging the horrors of the Stalin years, gave the camp closures their final impetus.

Portraying the Gulag

The best-known chronicler of the Gulag's horrors is Alexander Solzhenitsyn, a former Gulag prisoner. In 1962 his short novel, *A Day in the Life of Ivan Denisovich*, appeared in a leading Soviet literary journal. Of course, all journals in the Soviet Union were controlled by the state. Nonetheless, 1962 was the height of the relative cultural thaw of the Khrushchev era, and so *Ivan Denisovich* was published. It caused a sensation, being the first work to deal directly and realistically with the taboo subject of life in the camps. By the time Solzhenitsyn's three-volume account of the horrors of the Gulag, *Gulag Archipelago*, was sent to the West and published in 1973, the hard line of the Brezhnev regime

meant that Solzhenitsyn himself was about to be exiled from the Soviet Union. It was not until 1989 that his work once more became openly available in Russia.

SEE ALSO Ukraine (Famine); Union of Soviet Socialist Republics

BIBLIOGRAPHY

Applebaum, Anne (2003). *Gulag: A History*. New York: Doubleday.

Bacon, Edwin (1995). *The Gulag at War: Stalin's Forced Labour System in the Light of the Archives*. New York: NYU Press.

Gregory, Paul, and Valery Lazarev, eds. (2003). *The Economics of Forced Labor: the Soviet Gulag*. Stanford, Calif.: Hoover Institute Press.

Solzhenitsyn, Alexander (1971). *A Day in the Life of Ivan Denisovitch*. New York: Farrar, Straus and Giroux.

Solzhenitsyn, Alexander (1973). *The Gulag Archipelago*. New York: Harper & Row.

Edwin Bacon

Gypsies see Romanis.

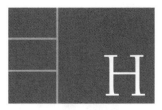

Hague Conventions of 1907

The codification of modern international humanitarian law began at the end of the nineteenth century. A peace conference was held at The Hague, Netherlands, in 1899, followed by a second conference, which met in the same city in 1907. The latter adopted a series of international conventions related to the peaceful settlement of international conflicts and the laws of war, which are known collectively as the Hague Conventions. Convention IV, which is the most relevant here, proclaimed the Laws and Customs of War on Land. Still in force, this Convention imposes upon the parties the obligation to issue instructions to their armed land forces in conformity with the Regulations annexed to the Convention. Each party to a conflict is responsible for all acts committed by individuals forming part of its armed forces, including militia and volunteer corps commanded by a person responsible, having a fixed distinctive emblem and carrying arms openly. A belligerent party who violates the provisions of the Regulations shall, if the case requires, be liable to pay compensation. On July 9, 2004, the International Court of Justice, in its advisory opinion on the Legal Consequences of the Construction of a Wall in the Occupied Palestinian Territory, referred to the 1907 Hague Convention IV as customary international law binding on all states in the twenty-first century.

General Principles

The main principle of Hague Convention IV, formulated in Article 22 of the Regulations, proclaims that the right of belligerents to adopt measures of injuring the enemy is not unlimited. Paragraph 8 of the preamble of the Convention must be added: It formulates the so-called Martens clause, which appeared for the first time in the Hague Convention of 1899 and according to which:

> In cases not included in the Regulations . . . the inhabitants and the belligerents remain under the protection and the rule of the principles of the law of nations, as they result from the usages established among civilized peoples, from the laws of humanity and the dictates of the public conscience.

It adds that certain provisions of the Regulations must be understood in this sense.

In different sections and chapters of the Convention, the following subjects are covered: the meaning and treatment of belligerents, prisoners of war, and the sick and wounded, as well as the means of injuring the enemy, the end of hostilities, and the military authority over occupied territories. Concerning the treatment of prisoners of war, the main principles affirm that while they are in the power of the hostile government they must be humanely treated, and all their personal belongings, except arms and military papers, remain their property. They may be interned and their labor can be used but must be paid and shall not be used in connection with the operations of war. Prisoners of war shall enjoy complete liberty in the exercise of their religion, on the sole condition that they comply with the measures of order issued by the military authorities. At the conclusion of peace, the repatriation of prisoners of war shall be carried out as quickly as possible.

The original 1907 Conventions remain a guiding force in international conflict resolution, human rights, and humanitarian law. Here, the inaugural session of the Hague Appeal for Peace Conference in the Riddersaal. [HULTON ARCHIVE/GETTY IMAGES]

A single article relates to the rules applicable to the sick and wounded: It only refers to the obligations inscribed in the 1864 Geneva Convention proposed by the International Committee of the Red Cross.

The section on hostilities forbids the employment of poison or poisoned weapons, killing or wounding treacherously individuals belonging to the hostile nation or army, killing or wounding an enemy who, having laid down his arms, or having no longer means of defense, has surrendered. It is also forbidden to declare that no quarter will be given, and to employ arms, projectiles, or material calculated to cause unnecessary suffering. The enemy's property shall not be destroyed or seized, unless such destruction or seizure is imperatively demanded by the necessities of war. It is forbidden to declare abolished, suspended, or inadmissible in a court of law the rights and actions of the nationals of the hostile party. A belligerent is likewise forbidden to compel the nationals of the hostile party to take part in the operations of war directed against their own

country, even if they were in the belligerent's service before the commencement of the war.

The attack or bombardment, by whatever means, of towns, villages, dwellings, or buildings that are undefended is prohibited. The officer in command of an attacking force must, before commencing a bombardment, except in cases of assault, do all in his or her power to warn the authorities. In sieges and bombardments all necessary steps must be taken to spare, as far as possible, buildings dedicated to religion, art, science, or charitable purposes, historic monuments, hospitals, and places where the sick and wounded are collected, provided they are not being used at the time for military purposes. It is, however, the duty of the besieged to indicate the presence of such buildings or places by distinctive and visible signs. In fact the emblem of the Red Cross is used for this purpose. The pillage of a town or place, even taken by assault, is prohibited.

Obtaining information about the enemy and the country plays an important role in armed conflicts. According to the Hague Conventions, ruses of war and the employment of measures necessary for obtaining such information are permissible. Specific provisions are devoted to espionage. A person can only be considered a spy when, acting clandestinely or on false pretenses, he or she obtains or endeavors to obtain information in the zone of operations of a belligerent, with the intention of communicating it to the hostile party. Soldiers not wearing a disguise, as well as civilians carrying out their mission openly, entrusted with the delivery of despatches, are not considered spies. A spy taken in the act shall not be punished without previous trial.

Military Occupation

Various sections also set rules on truce, capitulations, and armistices. A noteworthy section concerns the military authority over the territory of the hostile state. Such territory is considered occupied when it is actually placed under the established and exercised authority of the hostile army. The occupant shall take all the measures in his power to restore, and ensure, as far as possible, public order and safety, while respecting, unless absolutely prevented, the laws in force in the country. Family honor and rights, the lives of persons, and private property, as well as religious convictions and practices, must be respected and private property cannot be confiscated. Pillage is formally forbidden.

If the occupant collects the taxes, dues, and tolls imposed for the benefit of the state, he or she shall do so, as far as possible, in accordance with the rules of assessment and incidence in force, and shall in consequence be bound to defray the expenses of the administration of the occupied territory to the same extent as the legitimate government was so bound. If, in addition, the occupant levies other money contributions in the occupied territory, this shall only be for the needs of the army or of the administration of the territory in question and shall be effected as far as possible in accordance with the rules of assessment and incidence of the taxes in force. For every contribution a receipt shall be given to the contributors. No general penalty, pecuniary or otherwise, shall be inflicted upon the population on account of the acts of individuals for which they cannot be regarded as jointly and severally responsible. Requisitions in kind and services shall not be demanded from municipalities or inhabitants, except for the needs of the army of occupation and they shall be in proportion to the resources of the country. Such requisitions and services shall only be demanded on the authority of the commander in the locality occupied.

An army of occupation can only take possession of cash, funds, and realizable securities which are strictly the property of the state, as well as of depots of arms, means of transport, stores and supplies, and, generally, all movable property belonging to the state that may be used for military operations. All appliances adapted for the transmission of news, or for the transport of persons or things, all kinds of arms, or munitions of war may be seized when they belong to private individuals, but must be restored and compensation fixed when peace is made.

The occupying state shall be regarded only as administrator and usufructuary of public building, real estate, forests, and agricultural estates belonging to the hostile state and situated in the occupied country. It must safeguard the capital of these properties, and administer them in accordance with the rules of usufruct. The property of municipalities, that of institutions dedicated to religion, charity, and education, the arts and sciences, even when state property, shall be treated as private property. All seizure of, destruction or wilful damage done to, institutions of this character, historic monuments, works of art, and science, is forbidden, and should be made the subject of legal proceedings.

Conclusions

The 1907 Hague Conventions had the merit to formulate principles that were applicable during World War I and World War II. In 1949 its rules, which were generally adopted although often not respected, were further developed by the four Geneva Conventions on humanitarian law, themselves completed later by two Protocols adopted in Geneva in 1977. Breaches of all these rules could and should be sanctioned both by national and international jurisdictions.

SEE ALSO Geneva Conventions on the Protection of Victims of War; Humanitarian Law; International Law; War Crimes

BIBLIOGRAPHY

Best, Geoffrey Francis Andrew (1980). *Humanity in Warfare: The Modern History of theInternational Law of Armed Conflicts.* London: Weidenfeld and Nicolson.

Bordwell, Percy (1994). *The Law of War between Belligerents: A History and Commentary.* Littleton, Colo.: F. B. Rothman.

Bory, Francoise (1994). *Origin and Development of International Humanitarian Law.* Geneva: International Committee of the Red Cross.

Green, L.C. (2000). *The Contemporary Law of Armed Conflict,* 2nd edition. Yonkers, N.Y.: Juris.

Hull, William I. (1908). *The Two Hague Conferences and Their Contributions to International Law.* Boston: Published for the International School of Peace by Ginn.

International Committee of the Red Cross (1989). *International Law Concerning the Conduct of Hostilities: Collection of Hague Conventions and Some Other Treaties.* Geneva: Author.

Kalshoven, Fritz (1991). "State Responsibility for Warlike Acts of the Armed Forces—From Article 3 of Hague Convention IV to Article 91 of Additional Protocol I of 1977 and Beyond." *International and Comparative Law Quarterly* 40(827).

Pictet, Jean (1966). *The Principles of International Humanitarian Law.* Geneva: International Committee of the Red Cross.

Scott, James Brown (1909). *The Hague Peace Conferences of 1899 and 1907.* Baltimore: Johns Hopkins Press.

Alexandre Kiss

Harkis

In 2003 there were approximately 500,000 Harkis living in France. At present *Harkis* is a generic term referring to the Algerians who fought alongside the French army during the Algerian war from 1954 until 1962. They became Harkis for assorted reasons: for the regular pay, out of loyalty to a French army officer, to be on the side of the likely winners, to avenge a member of their family killed by the National Liberation Front (FLN), to obey their chief (*bachaga*), because they were Francophiles, or because, following the French army's tricks, they were perceived as traitors to their own people.

In 1962 French President Charles De Gaulle decided to quickly resolve the Algerian crisis: He ordered the French army to disarm the Harkis before departing and to prevent them from fleeing to France. After the ceasefire on March 19, 1962, tens of thousands of abandoned Harkis—some claim 150,000—were vengefully massacred by their victorious fellow countrymen.

From 1962 onwards the estimated 45,000 Harkis who had reached France were lodged either in Harki settlements near existing urban centers, such as Dreux, or in isolated hamlets in the rural south built for that purpose or in so-called temporary camps, such as Bias. Some of these camps had formerly housed refugees and political prisoners of various sorts. They were run in military fashion, with curfews, barbed wire, and watchtowers. Inside the Harkis had very few, if any, contacts with French natives. In 1974 more than 14,000 Harkis remained in such camps. All these emergency measures alienated the Harkis.

Some French viewed the Harkis' presence in France as a reminder of a war France had lost and of the failure of the Évian Agreements, which stipulated no reprisals would be taken against those who had supported France. The FLN fighters as well as some French nationals—especially those from the Left and the *porteurs de valises* (suitcase carriers), whose major activity was to smuggle the funds collected from Algerians in France for the FLN—regarded the Harkis as collaborators in French colonialism and traitors to their own people.

In 1975 the Harkis protested publicly for the first time against what they described as years of official amnesia, neglect, and marginalization by the French authorities. Since then the Harkis' offspring have sporadically and violently expressed their resentment toward France over such treatment, and have claimed they are owed a debt for their fathers' past loyalty. With regularity they have attempted to force France to publicly acknowledge its responsibility for the death of many Harkis after March 19, 1962. These actions culminated in their August 2001 lawsuit against the French government for crimes against humanity.

On September 25, 2001, the Harkis ceased to be "the archetype of official nonmemory" (Rosello, 1998, p. 170). President Jacques Chirac paid special tribute to the Harkis in a national ceremony and on December 5, 2002 inaugurated a memorial to the Algerian war. Its electronic message boards scroll the names of those 22,959 who died for France during the Algerian war—3,010 of whom were North Africans.

Over the years the French authorities have financed housing, education, and employment programs for the Harkis. The feeling that these positive measures of discrimination have had a negative side effect and resulted in the Harkis' ethnicization is shared by a significant number of Harkis and French academics.

SEE ALSO Algeria

BIBLIOGRAPHY

Cohen, W. B. (2000). "The Algerian War and French Memory." *Contemporary European History* 9(3):489–500.

Dine, P. (2000). "Memorial Boundaries and Textual Transgressions: The Narrative Politics of France's Algerian War." *Yearbook of European Studies* 15:71–82.

Rosello, M. (1998). *Declining the Stereotype–Ethnicity and Representations in French Cultures.* Hanover: University Press of New England.

Shepard, T. D. (2002). "Decolonizing France: Reimagining the Nation and Redefining the Republic at the End of Empire." Ph.D. diss. New Brunswick: State University of New Jersey.

Sutton, H. B. (1996). "Postcolonial Voices: Vindicating the Harkis." *Contemporary French Civilization* 231–239.

Tocqueville Connection (2000). "President Chirac Shocked by Remarks of Algerian Leader." Available from http://www.adetocqueville.com/cgi-binloc/getzip.cgi?0+3429.

Wihtol de Wenden, C. (1993). "The Harkis: A Community in the Making." In *French and Algerian Identities from Colonial Times to the Present: A Century of Interaction.* Edwin Millen Press.

Géraldine D. Enjelvin

Knights of the Ku Klux Klan stand in formation at a rally in Beckley, West Virginia, August 9, 1924. Though the influence of this white supremacist organization has decreased dramatically since the civil rights movement, its members continue to use hate speech to not only rally support, but also intimidate and silence their opposition. [CORBIS]

Hate Speech

Hate speech is a broad term that is used to identify a great variety of expressions. In general, however, it refers to words or symbols that are offensive, intimidating, or harassing, and/or that incite violence, hatred, or discrimination on the basis of a person's race, religion, gender, sexual orientation, or another distinguishing status. Although hate propaganda is seen as a major societal and political problem, in particular in those countries confronted with racial, ethnic, or religious tension, attempts to suppress hate speech are controversial. At the center of this controversy is the question about the extent to which hate speech restrictions may be reconciled with the right to freedom of expression.

Hate Speech and Freedom of Expression

The right to freedom of expression is an internationally recognized human right. However, freedom of expression is not absolute. Both national constitutions and international conventions allow restrictions on speech to safeguard other societal values. Among human rights lawyers and scholars there is a heated debate as to whether hate speech deserves free speech protection. Both sides offer powerful arguments. Those who favor some form of regulation emphasize the different kinds of harm caused by hate speech, to both the individual person and society as a whole. Expressions of hatred, it is often argued, inflict psychological or even physical injuries on members of the targeted group. These harms include "feelings of humiliation, isolation, and self-hatred" (Delgado, 1982, p. 137). A related rationale for suppressing racist expression is that it advocates discrimination and denies the right to equal protection and treatment. As a mechanism of subordination, it would reinforce the structural discrimination of socially marginal groups. Proponents of regulation also point at the silencing effect of hate speech. Racial or ethnic insults in a face-to-face situation would function as a "preemptive strike," inhibiting members of a targeted group from participating in the marketplace of ideas (Lawrence, 1990, p. 452).

Critics of regulation argue that hate speech laws are inefficient and even counterproductive. Eliminating racist speech "would not effectively address the underlying problem of racism itself, of which racist speech is a symptom" (Strossen, 1990, p. 494). Some authors have submitted that there is no empirical evidence from countries with strict antihate speech laws that censorship is an effective means of fostering tolerance. On the contrary, public proceedings in a court would only provide the offender with the opportunity to further disseminate his or her hateful message. Moreover, censorship would have the effect of making martyrs of those who are suppressed. Arguments against regulation also draw on the more indirect, negative side effects of censorship. For example, it is argued that outlawing speech is a "diversionary approach," which would make it easier for the government to avoid tackling less convenient and more expensive, but ultimately more effective, ways to combat discrimination (Strossen, 1990, p. 561). Another frequently heard argument is that the suppression of hate speech drives racist attitudes underground, which may result in explosions of racist violence at a later time. Finally, a more principled reason for protecting hate speech is that speech restrictions based on their content are unduly paternalistic and violate the principle of personal moral responsibility. According to this view, it is not for the government or the legislature to decide which ideas are false and which ideas people should be allowed to express or can be trusted to hear.

International and Domestic Norms

The last fifty years of the twentieth century witnessed many national and international initiatives to outlaw expressions usually qualified as hate speech. However, the existing hate speech regulations differ substantially in regard to the types of expressions prohibited and the sanctions involved. The oldest international agreement to outlaw a very specific example of hate speech is the Convention on the Prevention and Punishment of the Crime of Genocide. The Genocide Convention was adopted by the United Nations (UN) in 1948 in the aftermath of the Holocaust. Its Article 3 prohibits "direct and public incitement to commit genocide." In the 1960s the international concern with anti-Semitism, apartheid, and racial discrimination led to the development of the Convention on the Elimination of All Forms of Racial Discrimination (CERD).

CERD, adopted by the UN General Assembly on December 21, 1965, and to which 169 states are party, contains the most far-reaching international provisions on the suppression of hate speech. According to Article 4 of this Convention, "the dissemination of ideas based on racial superiority or hatred" and "incitement to ra-

cial discrimination" should be declared "punishable by law." The decision to punish the mere dissemination of ideas, without regard to additional requirements such as incitement or the likelihood of subsequent violence, was highly controversial. In order to render Article 4 more acceptable, its introductory paragraph declares that all measures should be enforced "with due regard to the principles embodied in the Universal Declaration of Human Rights," including the right to freedom of expression. The effect of this clause is still subject to debate.

The CERD monitoring body—the Committee on the Elimination of Racial Discrimination—has broadly interpreted Article 4, emphasizing in its General Recommendations VII and XV that the prohibition of dissemination of all ideas based on racial superiority or hatred is compatible with the right to freedom of expression. This view is not shared by several states, some of which have issued reservations or interpretive declarations limiting the impact of Article 4 on domestic free speech guarantees. Another important international provision, framed in more speech-protective language, is Article 20 of the 1966 International Covenant on Civil and Political Rights, which provides that "any advocacy of national, racial or religious hatred that constitutes incitement to discrimination, hostility or violence shall be prohibited by law."

In addition to and as a means of implementing these international standards, many countries have adopted laws limiting hate speech. As with the international agreements, these national laws envisage different kinds of expression. Some are rather broadly worded and encompass a great variety of offensive speech (e.g., the laws in France, Germany, Denmark, and the Netherlands); others are more narrowly tailored and require, for instance, incitement and/or the intention to incite hatred, or the likelihood of a breach of peace (e.g., the laws in Canada, Great Britain, and Belgium) (Coliver, 1992).

Striking a Balance

Those committing hate speech crimes have sometimes challenged their convictions under the right to freedom of expression. National and international courts have thus had to review the national norms dealing with hate propaganda and weigh the competing interests at stake. Despite the international agreements global consensus does not exist.

The United States occupies a unique position in the debate. In this country the balance has been largely drawn in favor of freedom of speech. The Supreme Court's usual interpretation of the First Amendment free speech guarantee leaves little room for hate speech regulations. Initially, the Court took a rather deferential stance toward legislation outlawing expressions of hatred. In the case of *Beauharnais v. People of the State of Illinois* (1952), it upheld a state law that made it a crime to distribute publications with racially or religiously defamatory content. Justice Felix Frankfurter, writing for the majority, analyzed the Illinois statute as prohibiting "group libel," a class of speech not within the area of constitutionally protected speech. Frankfurter conceded that strong arguments against hate speech restrictions exist, but he believed it to be "out of bounds for the judiciary to deny the legislature a choice of policy, provided it is not unrelated to the problem." Although this decision was never explicitly overruled, it has been thoroughly restricted by subsequent decisions limiting the constitutionality of libel laws in general.

An important step in this evolution was the Supreme Court's refusal to review a federal court's decision invalidating local town ordinances that prohibited the promotion and incitement of racial and religious hatred. One ordinance was designed to prevent a march of a neo-Nazi party in Skokie, Illinois, a town with a large Jewish community, including numerous survivors of the Holocaust. Arguments in favor of hate speech legislation have also drawn on the so-called "fighting words" doctrine. The Supreme Court has decided that fighting words—words "which by their very utterance, inflict injury or tend to incite an immediate breach of the peace"—are not protected by the First Amendment. Some scholars have argued that racist and discriminatory insults would clearly come within the ambit of this definition.

Nevertheless, reliance on the fighting words theory to justify hate speech laws was rendered ineffective by the Supreme Court's decision in *R.A.V. v. City of St. Paul* (1992). In this case the Court considered the conviction of white teenagers who had burned a cross on the property of a black family. The teenagers were prosecuted under a city ordinance that outlawed hate symbols, "which one knows or has reasonable grounds to know arouses anger, alarm, and resentment in others on the basis of race, color, religion, or gender." The majority ruled that the St. Paul ordinance drew impermissible content-based distinctions by outlawing fighting words, which injure on the basis of just a few categories, such as race and color. In the Court's view the First Amendment does not permit the imposition of special prohibitions on speakers "based on hostility—or favoritism—towards the underlying message expressed."

Critics of the U.S. approach have argued that its absolutist conception of freedom of speech refuses to rec-

ognize the competing values of liberty and equality at stake. In Europe the situation is quite different. If the U.S. Constitution could be said to reflect one perspective, the case law under the European Convention on Human Rights would surely represent the opposite side. One of the first European Convention cases to address hate speech regulations was *Glimmerveen and Hagenbeek v. The Netherlands* (1979). In this case the European Commission on Human Rights considered the convictions of two members of a right-wing political party for possessing leaflets inciting racial discrimination by urging the removal of all nonwhite immigrants from the Netherlands. The Commission declared the applications, based on the right to freedom of expression, inadmissible, relying primarily on Article 17 of the Convention, which prohibits the abuse of Convention rights. In the Commission's view, the applicant's discriminatory immigration policy was contrary to the text and the spirit of the Convention and likely to contribute to the destruction of the rights and freedoms of others.

The *Glimmerveen* case is illustrative of many subsequent decisions dealing with hate speech legislation. By declaring applications inadmissible on the basis of the "abuse of rights" doctrine, the bodies charged with enforcing the European Convention engage in a rather superficial examination of the circumstances of a case and the extent to which hate speech laws are compatible with the right to freedom of expression. This approach has been confirmed in several cases in which the European Court of Human Rights simply judged on the merits of the case. For example, in *Jersild v. Denmark* (1994), the Court stated, without further explanation, that "there can be no doubt" that racist remarks insulting to members of the targeted groups do not enjoy the protection of the right to freedom of expression. Although such a deferential attitude may be explained by the European experience with racist regimes in the first half of the twentieth century, it has been subject to criticism, even by those scholars who are generally sympathetic to some form of hate speech regulation.

Between these two extreme positions, courts in other countries have sought to arrive at a more balanced solution of the conflict caused by hate propaganda. The jurisprudence of the Canadian Supreme Court constitutes a good example of this. In *Regina v. Keegstra* (1990) it upheld a criminal statute prohibiting the communication of statements, other than in private conversation, that wilfully promote hatred against an identifiable group. The Court recognized that the provision interfered with the right to freedom of expression. But, according to the majority, such interference was justified, in regard to, among other things, the negative psychological results of hate propaganda, the importance of values such as equality and multiculturalism, the fact that the provision was narrowly tailored and that the accused was offered a number of defenses. For instance, the Crown had to prove a subjective intention to promote hatred and the likelihood of harm. After its careful analysis, the majority therefore concluded that the benefits of the challenged law outweighed its speech restrictive effects. However, in *R. v. Zundel* (1992), a case decided two years later, the Court struck down a much more broadly worded statute, which had been used to silence the author of anti-Semitic literature. In the majority's view the law, which prohibited the publication of false statements that cause or are likely to cause injury or mischief to a public interest, could "be abused so as to stifle a broad range of legitimate and valuable speech."

Which approach is preferable? The First Amendment and European Convention jurisprudence has the advantage of being clear in its commitment to either protect or not protect hate speech. The resolution of both systems can no doubt be explained and justified by the particular historical and philosophical backgrounds that characterize U.S. and European societies. The balancing approach, on the other hand, of which the case law of the Canadian Supreme Court is a good example, recognizes the harms resulting from both censoring and not censoring hate speech in terms of free speech and equality. It allows the courts to have regard for the different arguments advanced in favor of and against regulation.

SEE ALSO Incitement

BIBLIOGRAPHY
Brems, Eva (2002). "State Regulation of Xenophobia versus Individual Freedoms: The European View." *Journal of Human Rights* 1:481–500.

Coliver, Sandra (1992). "Hate Speech Laws: Do They Work?" In *Striking a Balance. Hate Speech, Freedom of Expression and Non-Discrimination*, ed. S. Coliver, K. Boyle, and F. D'Souza. Essex: International Centre against Censorship and Human Rights Centre, University of Essex.

Delgado, Richard (1982). "Words That Wound: A Tort Action for Racial Insults, Epithets, and Name-Calling." *Harvard Civil Rights-Civil Liberties Law Review* 17:133–181.

Dworkin, Ronald (1996). *Freedom's Law. The Moral Reading of the Constitution.* Oxford: Oxford University Press.

Gordon, Paul (1992). "Racist Violence: The Expression of Hate in Europe." *In Striking a Balance. Hate Speech, Freedom of Expression and Non-Discrimination*, ed. S. Coliver, K. Boyle, and F. D'Souza. Essex: International

Centre Against Censorship and Human Rights Centre, University of Essex. See Article 19.

Lawrence, Charles R. (1990). "If He Hollers Let Him Go: Regulating Racist Speech on Campus." *Duke Law Journal* 1990:431–483.

Matsuda, Mari J. (1989). "Public Response to Racist Speech: Considering the Victim's Story." *Michigan Law Review* 87:2320–2381.

McCrudden, Christopher (1995). "Freedom of Speech and Racial Equality." In *Pressing Problems in the Law. Volume 1. Criminal Justice & Human Rights*, ed. P. B. H. Birks. Oxford: Oxford University Press.

Partsch, Karl Josef (1992). "Racial Speech and Human Rights: Article 4 of the Convention on the Elimination of All Forms of Racial Discrimination." In *Striking a Balance. Hate Speech, Freedom of Expression and Non-Discrimination*, ed. S. Coliver, K. Boyle, and F. D'Souza. Essex: International Centre Against Censorship and Human Rights Centre, University of Essex.

Strossen, Nadine (1990). "Regulating Racist Speech on Campus: A Modest Proposal." *Duke Law Journal* 483–568.

Marc Bossuyt
Stefan Sottiaux

Herero

The Herero were traditional occupants of the temperate high plains of central Namibia. A Bantu people, they had moved south into this region from Angola, arriving about 1750. A series of nineteenth-century wars with the Nama, to the south, destabilized the entire region. Herero chiefs were autonomous, presiding over a decentralized tribal government, with extended families and their cattle herds spread over hundreds of miles. Germany first arrived in Africa in 1884, using the dubious private land claims of a businessman, Adolf Luderitz, as the legal basis for establishing a protectorate over a vast desert hinterland, making South West Africa its first African colony.

The first German treaties did not concern the Herero because they lived well-inland from the Atlantic Ocean. Chief Kamaherero negotiated a worthless agreement of protection with the British, who were unwilling to live up to its terms. Germans were everywhere in his country. It is, however, also clear that the Herero did negotiate *Schutzvertrags* (treaties of protection) in Okahandja and Omaruru in October 1885.

Germany had entered the race for African colonies long after its major European rivals. South West Africa was to be a model colony, showing the world what the new Germany, fresh from its victory in the Franco-Prussian War, was capable of. The brutality of the Herero War can be understood within the context of this need to perfect such a colonial ideal in order to establish modern Germany as the equal of other European powers. Indeed, evidence exists that the virulent racism characterizing the Holocaust was also partially formed there. Germany began experiments with sterilization on Herero prisoners of war in the name of the science of eugenics shortly after the turn of the century.

The Herero War

The Herero War of 1904 and 1905 killed at least 60,000 of the 80,000 Herero and resulted in the seizure of all their lands and cattle. The central region of South West Africa—now Namibia—was swept clean of black occupants, setting the stage for the creation of a white-dominated agricultural economy that has prevailed since. Although one can draw a number of meanings from the war, the central outcome in terms of land is clear: Germany terminated by conquest all Herero land rights in South West Africa. The details of the war are well known. Led by the aging Chief Samuel Maherero, offended by the increasing white occupation of their lands, and subjected to demeaning and inhuman treatment by colonists and traders, the Herero rose in revolt. Once the uprising was under way, the colonial administration refused all attempts to negotiate a resolution, instead adopting a policy of genocide to sweep the Herero off their lands.

German Genocide

Nothing in the origins of the Herero War is in any way unique to colonial practice. Other European powers forced African peoples off their lands in other colonial wars. What distinguishes the Herero War, and makes it an act of genocide, was a clearly announced military policy to destroy the Herero nation by killing all its members. This action seems to have developed in the upper echelons of the colonial hierarchy, born of acute frustration at the inability of troops to quickly win the war. The entire colonial enterprise was, in this group's view, endangered, and Germany's defeat in one of its colonies would be a disgrace in the eyes of its European competitors. Kaiser Willem II dispatched General Lothar von Trotha to take over control of the war from the discredited local administration. In a proclamation, issued at Osombo-Windimbe after church services on Sunday morning, October 2, 1904, he ordered all Herero men killed, and all their lands and cattle seized:

> I the great General of the German troops send this letter to the Herero people.
>
> The Herero are no longer German subjects. The Herero people must, however, leave the land. If the populace does not do this, I will force them with the cannon.
>
> Within the German borders every Herero, with or without a gun, with or without cattle, will be shot. I will no longer accept women and children, I will drive them back to their people, or I will let them be shot at.
>
> These are my words to the Herero people.
>
> The great General of the mighty German Kaiser.

[SAMUEL MAHERERO]

Herero Chief Samuel Maherero was a large, imposing and proud man, often appearing in a military uniform. The Herero were divided into nine tribes with a decentralized structure of leadership, and although no chief ruled above the others, Maherero was regarded as the "paramount" chief by German authorities.

Maherero was the son of Kamaharero, a great Herero warrior and cattle raider who maintained headquarters in Okahandja by the late 1860s. Maherero was educated in Lutheran mission schools. Upon his father's death in 1890, complex Herero rules of inheritance distributed most of his wealth and cattle to other relatives, but Maherero inherited the right to live in his father's house and, supported in wealthier relatives and relying on his education and connections with German missionaries, he soon rose to a position that enabled him to mediate between Herero culture and German rule. This enhanced his status and he became wealthy, although German administrators viewed Maherero somewhat derisively, as a cooperative chief fully under German control and, therefore, unlikely to lead a revolt.

Maherero's full role in the Herero War is still unknown, but he clearly came to resent Germany's colonial domination of his country, especially the loss of Native lands and cattle, the basis of the Herero's traditional culture. Acting with other chiefs, Maherero planned a secret uprising against German rule. The initial attacks were successful and resulted in the deaths of hundreds of German farmers; German women, children, and missionaries were spared. Maherero led the Herero forces during the conflict, but he was driven into the desert, together with most of his tribe. He reached Botswana, where he remained in exile until his death in 1923. He is buried with his father and grandfather in Okahanja. There the Herero people visit their former chiefs' graves every August on Herero Day.

There can be no doubt that genocide was the unambiguous intent of this action. Von Trotha personally read the proclamation to Herero prisoners and then proceeded to hang a number of warriors. After distributing copies of the document printed in the Herero language, he drove any remaining women and children into the Kalahari Desert.

Those Herero who fled were denied access to water holes, or their water supply was either poisoned or guarded, and they died. Few casualties of the war—several hundred at most—were due to military actions: Mass starvation over a period of months killed most Herero men, women, and children, and starvation and death occurred for several years afterward as stragglers tried to find their way across the Botswana border. Thousands of prisoners, most previously captured and held under inhuman conditions in prison camps where they were forced to work as slave laborers, also died. Their land was seized by the colonial state. To the extent that Germany needed to win the Herero War at all costs in order to protect its international position as a colonial power, the effort was successful. In the early twenty-first century central Namibia still functions as a model German colony. German colonial architecture remains evident in the cities, and a well-developed colonial infrastructure survived until South West Africa fell to invading British and South African forces in 1915, during World War I.

Herero Claims to Reparations

A few thousand Herero survived both genocide and exile only to face the imposition of apartheid by South Africa, which assumed the British mandate for South West Africa in 1919. Having taken refuge in northern Namibia, Angola, and Botswana, the Herero gradually returned to their traditional lands. Some labored as farmworkers, but others simply occupied unused desert land and rebuilt their herds. Namibian independence, in 1989, set the stage for the assertion of Herero claims for reparations, a legal claim that would have been impossible under apartheid.

In 1995 Herero Paramount Chief Kuaimi Riruako, on behalf of the Herero nation, demanded reparations of $600 million. In a related move, Chief Riruako filed a lawsuit against three German companies in the District of Columbia, asking for $2 billion in reparations, claiming that the companies had engaged in a "brutal alliance" with imperial Germany during the Herero War. Now numbering about 125,000, the Herero have persisted in pursuing their claim. The claim is based expressly on the belief that Herero War was an act of genocide, which links their claims to those of Jews and other European peoples seeking reparations for Nazi genocide later in the same century.

SEE ALSO Namibia (German South West Africa and South West Africa)

BIBLIOGRAPHY

Bley, Helmut (1971). *South West Africa under German Rule, 1894–1914.* London: Hugh Ridley.

Bridgeman, Jon M. (1981). *The Revolt of the Hereros.* Berkeley: University of California Press.

Drechler, Horst (1980). *Let Us Die Fighting: The Struggle of the Herero and Nama against German Imperialism, 1884–1915.* London: Zed Press

Gewald, Jan-Bart (1999). *Herero Heroes.* Athens: Ohio University Press.

Harring, Sidney L. (2002). "German Reparations to the Herero Nation: An Assertion of Herero Nationhood in the Path of Namibian Development." *West Virginia Law Review* (104):393–417.

Sidney L. Harring

Heydrich, Reinhard

[MARCH 7, 1904–JUNE 4, 1942]
SS officer and chief architect of the Final Solution

Tall, blonde, and blue-eyed, with chiseled features that reflected the Nazi "Nordic" ideal, Reinhard Heydrich was the second-most powerful person in the SS, subordinate only to Heinrich Himmler. He was intelligent and cynical, but not dogmatic. With ruthless ambition he managed the planning and execution of Hitler's Final Solution, the extermination of Europe's Jews during World War II.

Heydrich was born in Halle to an aristocratic family. Well educated and culturally sophisticated, he had displayed great promise as a violinist at a young age, but became a naval intelligence officer following his schooling. He was discharged from the navy in April 1931 and immediately joined the SS. Himmler entrusted him with the organization and leadership of the *Sicherheitsdienst* (Security Service or SD), the new intelligence branch of the SS.

Heydrich helped Himmler establish SS authority over the state police (Gestapo), first in Bavaria in 1933 and ultimately throughout the rest of Germany by the end of 1934. He played a key role in the brutal SS purge of the leadership of the SA, or *Sturmabteilung,* the military arm of the Nazi party, on June 30, 1934.

In June 1936 the SS unified all police forces in Germany under its authority. Himmler was named *Reichsführer-SS und Chef der deutschen Polizei* (Reichsführer-SS and Chief of the German Police). As *Chef der Sicherheitspolizei und des SD* (Chief of the Security Police and the SD), Heydrich became head of the Gestapo and Kripo (criminal police). He authorized the deportation of Jews from Austria after the Anschluss in March 1938 and had thousands of Jews arrested and transported to concentration camps during the Kristallnacht pogrom of November 9, 1938. Following the pogrom, Hermann Göring concentrated authority for Jewish emigration in the hands of the SS and authorized Heydrich to establish the *Reichszentrale für jüdische Auswanderung* (Reich Central Office for Jewish Emigration) in Berlin on January 24, 1939. This office facilitated the forced emigration of Jews throughout Germany using brutal methods perfected by his subordinate, Adolf Eichmann, in Austria.

The creation of the *Reichssicherheitshauptamt* (Reich Security Main Office or RSHA) under Heydrich's direction in 1939 formally unified state and party secret police agencies (the Gestapo and SD). He took charge of the Einsatzgruppen (action squads) that supervised the relocation of Polish Jews to squalid, overcrowded ghettos and their inhuman treatment there, as well as the establishment of *Judenräte* (Jewish Councils) beginning in September 1939. He was also instrumental in plans to concentrate Polish Jews on reservations in the East (the Nisko and Lublin plans) in 1939 and European Jews in Madagascar in 1940. For the brutality of his methods, Heydrich soon became known as "the hangman."

Heydrich's *Einsatzgruppen* undertook the mass murder of Russian Jews and Soviet officials during Germany's invasion of the Soviet Union. On July 31, 1941, Göring charged him with the task of devising a *Gesamtlösung* (total solution) to the Jewish question in Europe. Although the origins of the decision to systematically murder all of the Jews of Europe are still debated, Heydrich was responsible for drawing up the plans for the Final Solution. He revealed these plans to party and state officials at a meeting he convened at Wannsee in Berlin on January 20, 1942, to enlist their cooperation.

In September 1941 Heydrich was named Deputy Reich Protector of Bohemia and Moravia, and appointed Protector later that year. Attacked by Free Czech agents in an ambush near Prague on May, 27, 1941, he died of his wounds seven days later. In retaliation the SS destroyed the nearby Czech village of Lidice and killed its entire male population.

Heydrich's ruthless quest for power, perhaps more than his anti-Semitism, resulted in the murder of millions of Jews and other victims, and, ultimately, his own violent death.

SEE ALSO Gestapo; Germany; Kristallnacht; SS; Wannsee Conference

BIBLIOGRAPHY

Aronson, Shlomo (1971). *Reinhard Heydrich und die Frühgeschichte von Gestapo und SD*. Stuttgart: Deutsche Verlags-Anstalt.

Breitman, Richard (1991). *Architect of Genocide: Himmler and the Final Solution*. New York: Knopf.

Calic, Edouard (1985). *Reinhard Heydrich: The Chilling Story of the Man Who Masterminded the Nazi Death Camps*. New York: Morrow.

Deschner, Günther (1981). *Reinhard Heydrich: A Biography*. New York: Stein and Day.

Francis R. Nicosia

Himmler, Heinrich
[OCTOBER 7, 1900–MAY 23, 1945]
Father of the concentration camp

Heinrich Himmler has been labeled the "architect of genocide," the Nazi leader who more than any other encouraged and facilitated Adolf Hitler's decision to implement the Final Solution to the Jewish question, as well as other programs of ethnic cleansing that destroyed untold millions of lives during World War II. Few understood, embraced, and exalted the Führer's evil dreams as thoroughly as Himmler. For him they were a moral imperative.

Himmler was born the second son of a secondary-school teacher and one-time tutor to the Bavarian royal family. None of Himmler's scholarly biographers trace his hate-filled, phobic prejudices to his formative years. He no doubt absorbed conventional prejudices about minorities and outgroups, but nothing virulent. Germany's defeat in World War I transformed his conservative nationalism, like that of many future Nazis, into xenophobia, while conspiracy theories about Jews increasingly provided a scapegoat for national failure. His growing anti-Semitism fused with widely held ideas about racial purity versus degeneracy. His romantic nationalism evolved into a mystic vision of German regeneration through a combination of racial breeding and heroic struggle to colonize Slavic lands to the east. By 1924 he had abandoned Catholicism as inconsistent with his evolving views and added it to his conspiracy theories.

During this same period Himmler became a career Nazi as deputy to Gregor Strasser, head of the party's propaganda office, and his growing worldview received reinforcement. By 1926 he coordinated the propaganda of the SS, then a small paramilitary group with a bodyguard formation, and had become its deputy leader. That brought him into contact with Hitler. Impressed by Himmler's absolute loyalty, the Führer named him Reichsfuhrer SS. Himmler found his mission. He

Himmler preparing to address a crowd gathered at the town hall in Linz, Austria, in 1938, after the Nazis had invaded that country. Answerable only to Hitler, he soon became responsible for removing all undesirables from territories conquered by the Reich and ensuring an ethnically "pure" Aryan race.[HULTON-DEUTSCH COLLECTION/CORBIS]

dreamed of turning the SS into a racial and ideological elite, the highly trained police force of the Nazi movement, a state protection corps that would unquestioningly fulfill the Führer's will and advance their common goal of creating a homogeneous and disciplined society.

By the time the Nazis came to power in 1933, Himmler had built the SS into a power base in competition with Hitler's other paladins. He envisioned a fusion of Germany's police, as the internal defense force of the nation, with his SS. Although Hitler undoubtedly encouraged such dreams, Himmler had to compete with many rivals in the divide-and-control system that the Führer employed to keep any lieutenant from becoming powerful enough to threaten his preeminence or to set policy.

Himmler succeeded by early 1934 in gaining nominal control over all the separate political police, and by 1936 had consolidated them into a unified national Ge-

stapo. At the same time he acquired unified command of all German state police to become Reichsführer SS and Chief of German Police. As Hitler moved toward war, his phobias about domestic opposition had led him to favor Himmler's plans for an SS-police state as the most suitable means for domestic control. Soon Himmler was virtually independent from most normal state mechanisms of control, answerable almost exclusively to Hitler.

Himmler's SS-police state involved a tripartite wedding of SS, police, and concentration camps, all under his personal authority, with any legal appeals against them channeled through him. During the war his SS empire expanded further to become a veritable "state within a state," including the Waffen-SS military formations, a near monopoly of foreign and domestic intelligence operations, SS industries and social and cultural institutions, control over a vast reservoir of slave labor, the authority to resettle or exterminate millions, and the design and construction of the facilities needed for the expansion of the Nazi racial utopia into the occupied lands of the East.

The key to Himmler's powerful position was his dogged efforts to fulfill the Führer's every wish, especially in pursuit of a "racially pure" national community. To do so, he had to anticipate every evolution in Hitler's goals, and often encourage and facilitate their development toward ever more radical conclusions. Every step in the growth of Himmler's SS empire made it possible for Hitler to conceive of something more ambitious, and that in turn led to yet more opportunities for Himmler to add to his power.

Himmler and lieutenants like Reinhard Heydrich and Kurt Daluege developed police forces that eliminated opposition and proceeded to purge society of so-called undesirable elements, defined ideologically, religiously, culturally, socially, medically, and racially. The concentration camps would reeducate through incarceration all salvageable elements and forcefully employ or eliminate all others. At first this campaign of terror was to intended to encourage the emigration of such segments of the population as the Jews.

Heydrich's SS academics and Jewish experts in his Security Service (SD) outmaneuvered more radical Nazi anti-Semites by ostensibly studying the Jewish problem scientifically and proposing "rational" solutions. After the pogrom of November 1938 (Kristallnacht), when the actions of radicals wreaked extensive economic damage with embarrassing international consequences, Heydrich was allowed to establish model emigration centers throughout the entire Reich under Gestapo authority. It thus became the executive agency for handling the Jewish problem.

As Himmler developed the means to carry out solutions, Hitler gave him more authority for handling "population problems." Heydrich's *Kriminalpolizei* (regular detectives) facilitated Hitler's euthanasia program, combated homosexuality and prostitution, and dealt with the Romani problem. When the 1939 invasion of Poland greatly expanded such population management problems, Heydrich's Einsatzgruppen either exterminated any potential resistance leadership among Poles and Jews or consigned them to labor camps. Himmler became Commissar for the Strengthening of Germandom, responsible for removing all undesirables from areas incorporated into the Reich, absorbing any suitable people into the German gene pool, and resettling the ethnic Germans from Soviet territories. With the invasion of the Soviet Union in 1941 and the "racial war" that Hitler unleashed, Himmler's authority expanded to encompass most matters involved in building the future racial empire that would extend to the Urals. This rapidly came to include total extermi-

nation of the Jewish population in the East, and finally, by perhaps the fall of 1941, orders from Hitler to exterminate all Jews in Europe. With them would go most Romani and gradually all other peoples regarded as unsuitable human breeding stock in the occupied East.

Even after defeat became inevitable, Himmler could not turn against his Führer. Nevertheless, he increasingly allowed subordinates to pursue half-baked schemes for peace feelers with the Western Allies. He also approached Hitler as early as December 1942 with plans for trading Jews for foreign currency or other advantages. Although this contradicted their determination to exterminate all Jews, Hitler consented. Many convoluted maneuvers ensued with little benefit to any Jews. By late 1944 Himmler combined the two options, negotiating with the Allies for the release of some Jews, hoping to appear as the "responsible" leader. On April 28, 1945, when Hitler learned of Himmler's efforts to negotiate surrender, he ordered his arrest. Himmler survived but he was captured by the British and soon thereafter committed suicide.

Although most scholars agree that Hitler made the ultimate decisions to unleash first mass murder and finally genocide, and they concur on Himmler's responsibility for its execution, greater debate exists about Himmler's role in Hitler's decisions. Some argue, convincingly, that he and Heydrich presented far-reaching proposals or contingency plans as early as 1939. In the field their lieutenants and other Nazi and military regional authorities creatively exceeded their authority, thereby encouraging escalation. In particular, however, Himmler's SS empire consistently demonstrated that it had not only the organizational machinery for whatever Hitler conceived, but that it could also overcome the psychological barriers to the mobilization of the hundreds of thousands of perpetrators needed for the job.

SEE ALSO Einsatzgruppen; Gestapo; Heydrich, Reinhard; Hitler, Adolf; SS

BIBLIOGRAPHY

Ackermann, Josef (1970). *Heinrich Himmler als Ideologe.* Goettingen: Musterschmidt.

Bauer, Yehuda (1994). *Jews for Sale? Bartering for Jewish Lives.* New Haven, Conn.: Yale University Press.

Breitman, Richard (1991). *The Architect of Genocide: Himmler and the Final Solution.* New York: Alfred A. Knopf.

Breitmann, Richard (1995). "A Deal with the Nazi Dictatorship?: Himmler's Alleged Peace Emissaries in Autumn 1943." *Journal of Contemporary History* 30:411–430.

Breitmann, Richard (1999). "Plans for the Final Solution in Early 1941." In *The Holocaust in History: The Known, the*

Unknown, the Disputed, and the Reexamined, ed. Michael Berenbaum and Abraham J. Peek. Bloomington: University of Indiana Press.

Breitman, Richard (1999). "*Mein Kampf* and the Himmler Family: Two Generations React to Hitler's Ideas." *Holocaust and Genocide Studies* 13:90–97.

Smith, Bradley F. (1971). *Heinrich Himmler: A Nazi in the Making, 1900–1926*. Stanford, Calif.: Hoover Institution Press.

Witte, Peter, Michael Wildt, Martina Voigt, Dieter Pohl, Peter Klein, Christian Gerlach, Christoph Dieckmann, and Andrej Angrick, eds. (1999). *Der Dienstkalender Heinrich Himmlers 1941/42*. Hamburg: Hans Christians Verlag.

George C. Browder

Hiroshima

On August 6, 1945, a U.S. bomber, the *Enola Gay*, dropped an atomic bomb on Hiroshima, Japan. Three days later, a second atomic bomb destroyed the city of Nagasaki. Estimates of the number killed in both cities range as high as 210,000. Thousands more later succumbed to radiation disease. These two acts, authorized by President Harry S. Truman, raised profound ethical and legal issues.

The possibility of an atomic bomb had been revealed by Albert Einstein in a 1939 communication to President Franklin Roosevelt. Under the code name Manhattan Project, three bombs were built, and a test bomb was detonated at Alamogordo, New Mexico on June 16, 1945. Some Manhattan Project scientists urged a demonstration of the new weapon before its military use, but President Truman, advised by a high-level committee, ordered its use against Japan as soon as possible.

Truman's decision came at the end of a war of escalating brutality. The Japanese occupation of Nanking, China, in 1937, had been marked by extreme cruelty. Japan's surprise attack on Pearl Harbor; the wanton killing of U.S. prisoners by Japanese soldiers in the notorious 1942 "Bataan Death March"; and the ferocious Japanese resistance on Iwo Jima and Okinawa were all part of the context of the president's action. So, too, was the racist wartime propaganda, purveyed in editorials, songs, movies, and political cartoons, that had portrayed all Japanese as apes, vermin, and rats—subhuman creatures to whom the usual standards of ethical behavior did not apply.

Furthermore, throughout the twentieth century, new technologies—tanks, poison gas, aerial bombing, and rockets—had vastly increased war's destructive potential, including the mass killing of civilians. In World War II, German V-1 and V-2 rocket attacks on English

A spiraling cloud from the atomic bomb nicknamed "Little Boy" signals the destruction of Hiroshima, Japan, on August 6, 1945. Some 140,000 people, mostly civilians, were killed, with thousands more eventually perishing from the effects of radiation. [CORBIS]

cities had taken a heavy civilian toll. As the war became increasingly ferocious in 1944 and 1945, British and U.S. bombing raids on major German cities created firestorms that killed hundreds of thousands from blast, fire, and asphyxiation. The devastating February 1945 attack on the beautiful city of Dresden—a city of little military significance—epitomized the massive death and destruction caused by these raids. These were attacks deliberately calculated to produce indiscriminate devastation, to "break the morale" of the target population. In Japan, sixty-four cities endured massive air raids prior to Hiroshima, with casualties estimated at 300,000 killed and some 340,000 severely injured. A March 1945 raid on Tokyo killed an estimated 100,000. The deliberate targeting of civilians, and even the wholesale slaughter of tens of thousands in a single raid, in short, antedated the atomic bomb. The only thing new about the events of August 6–9, 1945 was the technology employed.

As Americans assessed the moral implications of the mass killing of civilians in World War II, culminating at Hiroshima and Nagasaki, the so-called "Just War" doctrine offered some benchmarks. From St. Augustine onward, theologians and ethicists had sought to place moral limits on war. The "Just War" doctrine holds, for example, that the means employed in war must not produce greater evil than the evil one seeks to eliminate. This doctrine also insisted that noncombatants, as well as wounded soldiers and prisoners, must be treated humanely. Pope John Paul II declared in 1995: "[T]he direct and voluntary killing of an innocent human being is always gravely immoral." By definition, this precludes deliberate attacks on civilian populations. As the Roman Catholic catechism sums up the doctrine: "Every act of war directed to the indiscriminate destruction of whole cities . . . is a crime against God and man." Other religious and ethical traditions express similar principles, declaring that even for a nation waging a legitimate war, the moral law remains in force. Having justice on one's side does not mean that victory by any means possible is ethically defensible.

Well before Hiroshima and Nagasaki, these principles had been swept aside as the concept of "total war" had become the Allies' guiding principle. Hiroshima and Nagasaki, by the magnitude and the instantaneous nature of the destruction, raised the question of ethical legitimacy in the starkest possible way. The "Just War" doctrine also holds, for example, that every possible means of a nonviolent resolution must be exhausted before the resort to war. By extension, this means that once a war is underway, each new step in the escalation of violence should be undertaken only after all possibility of ending the conflict has been explored. Much of the debate over Hiroshima and Nagasaki has focused on precisely this point: Did the American government exhaust all possible means for ending the war before destroying these two cities and snuffing out tens of thousands of human lives?

Many historians have concluded that the answer is no. Japan was a defeated nation in August 1945, its war-making capacity shattered. The Japanese government was divided, with influential figures seeking an exit from a hopeless war. The Japanese government had asked the Soviet Union to act as an intermediary in the surrender negotiations—a fact known to Washington since U.S. cryptologists had broken the Japanese diplomatic code. Many Japanese saw the survival of the Emperor as a key issue—a point the Americans conceded after the war, despite their demand for unconditional surrender. Further, the invasion of Japan, should the war have continued, was not scheduled until November 1, 1945—three months in the future.

Confronting these facts, many have questioned the morality of dropping two atomic bombs before all possibility of ending the war by negotiation had been explored. Of course, no one knows for certain that Japan's surrender could have been achieved through negotia-

A Bomb Dome (Genbaku Dome) Memorial in Hiroshima. For many, the skeletal remains of a building that survived the first nuclear attack pose a fundamental question: Was the U.S. decision to use this weapon a legitimate act of war, or does it qualify as a crime against humanity? [DAVID SAMUEL ROBBINS/ CORBIS]

tions. The point is that this option was never tried. The fact that Japan surrendered five days after the Nagasaki bombing, often cited by defenders of Truman's action, is irrelevant to the question of whether the war could have been ended by other means. From an ethical perspective, this is the crucial issue.

Truman always insisted that his sole consideration in ordering the use of the atomic bomb was to save American lives, but other factors may have been in play. At the February 1945 Yalta conference, and again at the Potsdam conference in June, Soviet premier Joseph Stalin had promised to enter the Pacific War within three months of Germany's surrender. Germany surrendered on May 7, 1945, and Moscow declared war on Japan on August 8. Some evidence suggests that Truman's decision was influenced by his desire to force Japan's surrender before Russia became a significant factor in the outcome. These speculations have a bearing on how one assesses the ethics of the Hiroshima bombing. The Nagasaki bombing raises further questions: Once Hiroshima had been destroyed, did the United States wait a sufficient time for the Japanese government to assimilate this terrible new reality before destroying a second city?

All these questions have shaped the discourse over how the atomic bombing of Hiroshima and Nagasaki should be viewed. Was it a legitimate act of war, or does it fall into the category of a crime against humanity? This debate arose in the earliest moments of the Atomic Age. President Truman, predictably, insisted that the bomb was justified, since it prevented the U.S. casualties that an invasion of Japan would have entailed. Many Americans, then and since, have agreed. But the alternative view has also found its supporters. Immediately after the Hiroshima bombing, for example, the future secretary of state, John Foster Dulles, then an official of the Federal Council of Churches, telegraphed Truman urging him, on moral grounds, not to drop a second atomic bomb. In *The Challenge of Peace* (1983), the American Roman Catholic bishops, addressing the larger ethical issues posed by the nuclear arms race, came close to condemning the Hiroshima and Nagasaki bombings as morally indefensible. In 1995 and again in 2003, proposals by the Smithsonian Institution to display the *Enola Gay* triggered further discussion of this question, which continues to trouble the nation's conscience, raising ethical issues of the gravest sort.

SEE ALSO Japan; Memoirs of Survivors; Memorials and Monuments; Memory; Nuclear Weapons; Photography of Victims; United States Foreign Policies Toward Genocide and Crimes Against Humanity; Weapons of Mass Destruction

BIBLIOGRAPHY

Alperovitz, Gar (1996). *The Decision to Use the Atomic Bomb*. New York: Vintage.

Boyer, Paul (1985). *By the Bomb's Early Light: American Thought and Culture at the Dawn of the Atomic Age*. New York: Pantheon Books; second ed. Chapel Hill, N.C.: University of North Carolina Press, 1995.

Boyer, Paul (1996). "Exotic Resonances: Hiroshima in American Memory." In *Hiroshima in History and Memory*, ed. Michael J. Hogan. Cambridge, U.K., and New York: Cambridge University Press.

Dower, John W. (1987). *War Without Mercy: Race and Power in the Pacific War*. New York: Pantheon Books.

National Conference of Catholic Bishops (1983). *The Challenge of Peace: God's Promise and Our Response*. Washington, D.C.: United States Catholic Conference.

Ramsey, Paul (1961). *War and the Christian Conscience: How Shall Modern War Be Conducted?* Durham, N.C.: Duke University Press.

Sherry, Michael S. (1987). *The Rise of American Air Power: The Creation of Armageddon*. New Haven, Conn.: Yale University Press.

Smith, Alice Kimball (1971). *A Peril and a Hope: The Scientists' Movement in America, 1945–1947*. Cambridge, Mass.: Harvard University Press.

Tucker, Robert W. (1960). *The Just War: A Study in Contemporary American Doctrine*. Baltimore, Md.: Johns Hopkins University Press.

Walzer, Michael (1992). *Just and Unjust Wars: A Moral Argument with Historical Illustrations*. New York: Basic Books.

Paul S. Boyer

Historical Injustices

History is replete with episodes of genocide, slavery, torture, forced conversions, and mass expulsions of peoples. For political, economic, religious, or ethnic reasons, states often abused or allowed the abuse of specific minorities or foreign populations. These events remain alive in memory and sometimes resurge as the foundation of modern conflicts. To a large extent, the existence and boundaries of all modern states are the result of past acts and omissions that would be unlawful today according to international law and most national constitutions and laws. The acts are also viewed in retrospect as morally wrong, even if they were not illegal at the time they were committed. Such acts and omissions are referred to as historical injustices.

Reparations Claims

Historical injustices are the subject of a growing number of legal and/or political claims to repair the harm they caused. In some instances, the consequences of the injustices persist into the present. As a consequence, states and societies throughout the world are being asked to account for historic abuses and provide redress to victims or their descendants. Unresolved injuries and losses from World War II, for example, have been addressed in recent years through litigation and negotiations. In Greece alone, more than sixty thousand cases were filed in the past decade concerning World War II abuses.

Some historical injustices involve events occurring a century or more ago. The United Nations Conference on Racism, held in Durban in 2001, debated the issue of reparations for the Atlantic slave trade and colonialism. In the United States, slave reparations have been claimed at least since the Emancipation Proclamation of 1865. Many descendants of slaves continue to seek redress and have brought lawsuits against individuals and companies for an accounting of their profits and assets acquired exploiting slave labor.

Abuses perpetrated against indigenous peoples represent perhaps the largest number of historical injustices. Many of these groups' demands are based on breaches of treaties entered into between a state and an indigenous group. In Canada, claims involve the relocation of the Inuit in the 1950s, and the sexual and physical abuse of aboriginal students in residential schools where they were sent after removal from their families. Native Hawaiians demand redress for the loss of their independence, lands, and culture. They have filed state law claims for back payment of ceded land trust revenues and to enjoin the negotiation, settlement, and execution of a release by trustees because of the overthrow of the government in 1893.

State Responses to Historical Injustice Claims

States and governments have responded in varying ways to the claims concerning historical injustices. Many heads of state or governments have issued formal apologies for past acts. Some claims, particularly those of indigenous groups, have led to the negotiated restitution of lands and resources. Australia returned 96,000 square miles of land in 1976 to Aborigines in partial compensation for land seized by white settlers. Canada also restored land to indigenous groups, after some thirteen years of negotiations. A recent agreement between Quebec and the Cree Nation gives the latter management of their natural resources and recognizes their full autonomy as a native nation. In the United States, as early as 1946 an Indian Claims Commission received jurisdiction to hear and resolve claims arising from the seizure of Indian lands and treaty breaches by the United States. The 1971 Alaska Native Claims Settlement Act granted indigenous Alaskans monetary relief as well as land. A 1990 federal law in the United States orders the restitution of human remains of Native Americans along with goods and funerary objects recovered from the original graves. New Zealand created a process for redressing wrongs committed in the late 1880s that involves returning lands and factories, fishing vessels, and fishing rights.

Compensation has also been forthcoming. In October 2000 Austria established a $380 million fund to compensate individuals forced into slave labor during World War II. Five U.S. Native-American groups successfully recovered monetary compensation, as did indigenous groups in Norway and Denmark. In 1995 the State of Florida paid $2.1 million in compensation for a race riot and massacre that occurred in 1923 in the town of Rosewood, Florida. In January 1998 Canada established a $245 million "healing fund" to provide compensation for the First Nation children who were taken from their families and transferred to residential schools.

Governments have rejected some claims. Japan has refused to offer an official apology or make reparations

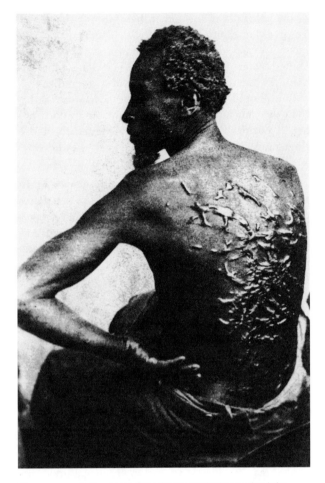

Slave owners in the antebellum South routinely practiced the most severe forms of corporal punishment. This c. 1862 photo (taken after the Civil War had started) shows the scars of one whipped slave. [CORBIS]

to World War II sex slaves, arguing that the acts were not illegal at the time and rejecting the assertion that the women were de facto slaves. The Australian government has denied reparations to members of the "Stolen Generations" of Aboriginal children taken from their families as part of a government assimilationist policy, despite recommendations to that effect contained in the government-commissioned official report on the matter.

Legal and Political Issues

Claims of historical injustice are considered moral rather than legal claims because either the law did not prohibit the acts at the time they were committed, there is some uncertainty about the state of the law, or there are procedural barriers to bringing a case. As a result of these problems, nearly all resolution of disputes over historical injustices, whether in the form of an apology, land, or money, has come about through negotiations or the political process rather than through the courts. To give one example, the U.S. 9th Circuit Court dismissed a case seeking reparations for slavery (Cato v. United States, 70 F3d 1103, 1105 [1995]), saying that damages due to enslavement and subsequent discrimination should be addressed to the legislature, rather than the judiciary. The court was unable to find "any legally cognizable basis" for recognizing the claim, distinguishing Native-American claims because the latter were based on treaties between nations.

Despite the lack of success in court, many lawsuits have been widely publicized and have led to negotiated or legislative settlements. Cases brought against insurance companies who failed to pay on policies owned by Holocaust victims led to the establishment of an International Commission on Holocaust Era Insurance Claims, formed by five of the major insurers. In February 2000 the commission announced that it would begin a two-year claims process to locate and satisfy unpaid Holocaust-era insurance policies. Similarly, a 1995 German–U.S. agreement concerning final benefits to certain U.S. nationals who were victims of National Socialist measures of persecution resulted from a lawsuit brought by an individual Holocaust victim.

Arguments For and Against Reparations for Historical Injustices

Reparations for historical injustices are supported for several reasons. First, some acts were illegal under national or international law at the time they were committed, but the victims have been unable to secure redress for political reasons, because evidence was concealed, or because procedural barriers have prevented them from presenting claims. In such circumstances, advocates argue that a lapse of time should not prevent reparation for harm caused by the illegal conduct. Second, states, communities, businesses, and individuals unjustly profited from many of the abuses, garnering wealth at the expense of the victims. Third, most examples of historical injustices have a compelling moral dimension because the events took place during or after the emergence of the concept of basic guarantees of human rights to which all persons are equally entitled. Redress is a symbol of moral condemnation of the abuses that occurred. Proponents argue that if human rights are truly inherent and universal, then they apply not only territorially, but also temporally and provide a basis to judge past practices. Advocates for redressing historical injustices also reject the notion that present generations have no responsibility for the past. They note that every individual is born into a society or culture that has emerged over time and that shapes each person, making the past part of the present and giving the society and individuals a historic

identity. On a practical level, un-righted wrongs fail to deter further harmful conduct and foster social resentment.

The most common objection to redress for historical injustices is that it involves retroactive application of the law. Nonretroactivity of law derives from the notion of fundamental fairness, the idea that individuals may legitimately rely on legal norms in force at the time they act:

> Elementary considerations of fairness dictate that individuals should have an opportunity to know what the law is and to conform their conduct accordingly; settled expectations should not be lightly disrupted. For that reason, the principle that the legal effect of conduct should ordinarily be assessed under the law that existed when the conduct took place has timeless and universal appeal (*Landgraf v. USI Film Products*, 511 US 244, 265 [1994]).

Nevertheless, reliance may not be legitimate if the rule is openly contested, in transition, or patently unjust.

Opponents also point to the long passage of time that clouds issues of causality and damage. They invoke the notion of personal responsibility to object to persons today paying for the acts of their predecessors, sometimes distant ancestors. In addition, opponents note that in many instances not only are living perpetrators absent, but there are no present-day victims of long-past violations. In some instances, opponents cite existing laws protecting human rights and affirmative action, calling these measures reparative in aim and effect. Some view reparations for historical injustices as the triumph of a victim psychology that blames everyone else for today's problems. They argue that when a community bases its communal identity almost entirely on the sentimental solidarity of remembered victimhood, it may give rise to recurring cycles of violence and turn victims into perpetrators.

International and national law can have retroactive effects, but is presumed to have prospective force. Most human rights treaty procedures, for example, permit complaints to be filed only for violations occurring after the treaty becomes legally binding for the state. The rule does allow a case to be filed, however, for a violation that began before the state was bound by the law if the wrong continues after the state becomes obliged to respect the treaty. Human rights law also requires nonretroactivity of criminal offenses, but this rule would not apply to resolving historical injustices through means other than prosecution. For property, international and national laws recognize that the unilateral acts of states may divest property owners of their previously acquired property, provided the taking is for a public purpose and nondiscriminatory, and accompanied by appropriate compensation.

It is not always clear that historical injustices involved acts that were legal at the time they were committed. If they were illegal, the law of reparations will apply. If the acts were lawful, the question of whether or not to ascribe retroactive effect to the law and condemn the acts involves a balancing of the equities, the strength of the claims, the need for reconciliation, and the practicalities of devising appropriate reparations between appropriate entities and persons. When considerable debate has arisen over the morality or legality of the acts, it may be more just to award reparations on the basis that reliance on the existing law was misplaced and unwarranted.

Experience thus far suggests that the resolution of claims which lack a legal foundation will take place through the political process. Many factors will affect the likelihood of reparations being afforded for past injustices and most of them are linked to the amount of time that has passed. First, it is more likely that reparations will be offered if the perpetrators are identifiable and still living. Second, the victims should be identifiable, with most still alive, or their immediate descendants present. The size of the group will certainly affect the amount, if not the fact of reparations. Third, demands for reparations will probably only succeed with political pressure and strong, cohesive support by the victims themselves. Perhaps most important, the substance of the claim must be one that presents a compelling human injustice which is well documented. The claim will be even stronger when there is continued harm and a causal connection between present harm and the past injustice.

Claims for historical injustices are pursued because redress can challenge assumptions underlying past and present social arrangements. They may involve restructuring the relationships that gave rise to the underlying grievance, addressing root problems leading to abuse and systemic oppression. This brings the notion of reparations close to the current idea of restorative justice as a potentially transformative social action. It also provides a reason why legislatures may be better suited to determine reparations. They are not bound by precedent and legal doctrine, but can fashion equitable remedies to avoid the creation of future historical injustices.

SEE ALSO Compensation; Reparations; Restitution

BIBLIOGRAPHY

Barkan, Elazar (2000). *The Guilt of Nations: Restitution and Negotiating Historical Injustices.* New York: Norton.

Brooks, Roy, ed. (1999). *When Sorry Isn't Enough: The Controversy over Apologies and Reparations for Human Injustice.* New York: NYU Press.

Robinson, Randall (2000). *The Debt: What America Owes to Blacks.* New York: Dutton.

Torpey, John (2003). *Politics and the Past: On Repairing Historical Injustices.* Lanham, Md.: Rowman & Littlefield Publishers.

Winbush, Raymond A., ed. (2003). *Should America Pay? Slavery and the Raging Debate on Reparations.* New York: Amistad Press.

Dinah L. Shelton

Historiography, Sources in

Suppressing, denying, or eliminating evidence of genocide is patently wrong. Morally and ethically, justice ought to mean the punishment of all culprits—political, religious, and media leaders from afar, and executioners in the killing fields alike—in proportion to their misdeeds. The duty of professionals assigned to study specific cases is to record legitimate, authentic documentation, not to prepare prosecutions or facilitate harmony. Meticulously and accurately—in the original language to prevent any misunderstandings and the potential loss of context in translation—reconstructing criminal events is their primary responsibility.

An expert analysis of personal testaments and written submissions by eyewitnesses to mass murders, particularly in terms of their inclusion in academic scholarship or journalistic publications, is highly problematic, especially in traditional cultures. Dilemmas concern the enormous risks inherent in identifying victims. Innocent people may be stigmatized, losing respect and dignity in their neighborhoods. Sensitivity and even self-imposed ethical boundaries—such as the scope of questioning—to determine authenticity are warranted. The brutally wounded suffer physical injuries and psychological troubles, having lost both close friends and relatives. Their pain endures, even if they survived without visible scars. To desensitize such traumatized people is a major challenge.

Nevertheless, even the most sympathetic researcher needs to probe for exact details, including time, place, scope of atrocities, names, and the severity of crimes. Interviews often involve deep memories of humiliation, for instance, those commonly associated with rape. They therefore remind subjects of personal shame, likely triggering immediate and or long-term psychological impact. These emotional circumstances may obscure the retrieval of imperative facts, or credible transcripts may be subsequently reversed during a judicial hearing, due to fears of a public loss of dignity or communal pressure. The creation of comprehensive archives with concrete evidence is crucial to determining the truth about perpetrators, and to bringing them to justice through a formal indictment.

An accurate, systematic, and balanced methodology is thus a necessity for responsible officials or human rights organizations. The advent of technology has provided some answers. The use of tape recorders, video cameras, websites, and the Internet in general allows the compilation of a multitude of resources and the classification of such accounts, while making them widely accessible. Another solution, after the violence has ended, is to treat the collection and assessment of information, and signed summations, as part of the healing process that collectives and individuals ought to face.

Rules to ensure consistency in analyzing evidence—especially in the most common form, oral history—have emerged gradually. They are not yet uniform, nor universally accepted, as so many individuals, organizations, and governments are involved. Conventional practices of qualitative analysis to evoke well-structured narratives of memories take psychological research theories on cognition into account. Oral and written data culled through methodologies employed in a plethora of academic pursuits enrich and make more sensitive mainstream thinking on how to best gain and assess relevant knowledge.

Any effort to reconstruct events related to genocide and crimes against humanity must incorporate input from segments of numerous traditional scientific authorities. Important disciplines include law, sociology, forensic and clinical psychology, medicine, pathology, social work, criminology, criminal justice, ethnography, cultural anthropology, gender studies, education, media and communications, history, political science, international relations, strategic and military studies, comparative literature, theology, philosophy, geography, demography, and economics. In addition, studies of racism, especially of anti-Semitism, coupled with the exploration of colonialism and the customs prevalent among particular urban or rural populations, are helpful. This comprehensive effort must be complemented by an analysis of the specific circumstances defining the lives of victims, such as Jews, Armenians, and any other affected groups, nations and tribes alike, in Africa, Asia, and Europe, and indigenous populations in Latin America and Oceania.

How killers and their cohorts reach the degree of hatred or vengeance necessary to commit crimes against humanity is another important query. The trials and tribulations of German and Jewish history, as obvious examples, are worthy of thorough exploration. Objective assessments of powerful social, economic, and political relationships in affected societies are necessary to understand, perhaps corroborate, although never justify, the circumstances attendant to a particular genocide, not the least of which is the context of the oral and written evidence provided by witnesses.

In sum, no one solution exists that perfectly addresses all the major dilemmas and boundaries faced by practitioners in the field on how to aptly translate the horrors of genocide into recognizable, perceptible terms and appropriate sources. Only a combination of standards, compassion, and common sense provides a flexible guideline. Exposing as many people as possible around the world to the visuals, graphics, and sounds inherent in genocide, thus educating them about such circumstances, may be the best measure to prevent future atrocities.

SEE ALSO Evidence; Historiography as a Written Form

BIBLIOGRAPHY

Daley, Peter M., ed. (2001). *Building History: The Shoah in Art, Memory, and Myth.* New York: Peter Lang.

Goldberg, David Theo and John Solomos (2002). *A Companion to Racial and Ethnic Studies.* Malden, Mass.: Blackwell.

Lorey, David E. and William H. Beezly, eds. (2002). *Genocide, Collective Violence, and Popular Memory: The Politics of Remembrance in the Twentieth Century.* Wilmington, Del.: SR Books.

Smith, Helmut Walser, ed. (2002). *The Holocaust and Other Genocides: History, Representation, Ethics.* Nashville, Tenn.: Vanderbilt University Press.

Itai Nartzizenfield Sneh

Historiography as a Written Form

Crimes against humanity and genocide may be seen as realities distinct from more normal human events, thus requiring a distinctive historiography. Cruelty carried to the point of genocide is abnormal in two ways: It violates moral norms that are central to many ethical and religious traditions, and the vast majority of people do not engage in such actions, or else feel guilt or discomfort if they do. Although continuity undoubtedly exists between normal, everyday human wrong-doing and genocide and crimes against humanity, these acts ought to occasion a special sense of revulsion, for by the deliberate intentions and actions of human beings, they lay waste to entire human worlds and leave ruin in their wake. The same can also be said of systematic and deliberate violations of human rights.

Large-scale atrocity raises peculiar difficulties for historians. First, it tends to wipe out those who know atrocity most intimately: the murdered many. Second, the historian's characteristically literal mode of representation (showing the past "as it actually was") risks representing the victims of atrocity not as human beings but as trodden upon objects. Third, historians face problems with regard to the assessment of atrocity. Characteristically, professional historians hold back from offering moral judgments concerning the events they describe. For example, it would generally be considered irrelevant and a sign of naiveté were a historian to make a negative moral judgment on that episode in the French Revolution whereby revolutionaries forced a group of two hundred alleged counterrevolutionaries, their hands tied behind their backs, onto boats, which they then sank in the Loire. To people concerned with discouraging atrocity in the present, such equanimity may seem misplaced, and yet the historian also has to treat readers as free persons capable of reaching moral judgments on their own.

These problems suggest that there are limits to what historians can do in confronting atrocity. In fact, confronting atrocity is not a task for historians alone, but also involves social scientists, jurists, philosophers, theologians, novelists, poets, and artists, as well as ordinary people. In their responses to atrocity, at least four different modes of approach may be found. One can think of these approaches as falling under the following headings: the investigation and reconstruction of what actually happened; the cultivation of memory and tradition; the creation of aesthetic forms; and ethical, philosophical, and religious reflection.

The historian's deepest emphasis is on investigation and reconstruction. (This is not the only task that historians engage in, but it is the most characteristic.) A classic example is Raul Hilberg's *The Destruction of the European Jews* (1961/2003). The historian is joined in the effort of investigation and reconstruction by two close allies, the journalist and the jurist. Each has a distinctive role to play. Hard-working and courageous journalists can bring genocide to light while there is still hope of limiting it. Jurists arrive when the action is over, bringing an element of justice to the scene and assembling a historical record. There is also the peculiarly hybrid institution of the "truth commission," such as the Argentine Commission on the Disappeared, which was established in 1983 and issued its report in 1986, and the South African Truth and Reconciliation Commission (TRC), which was established in 1995 and reported its findings in 2002. Such commissions might be regarded as semi- or quasi-judicial. They lack the punishment powers of a court, but they investigate

and report on abuses, as well as provide a forum for victims and their families to give their accounts of what happened, and some offer recommendations on the actions to be taken to prevent a recurrence. The South African TRC also offered amnesty in return for a sincere statement of confession accompanied by full disclosure of what had occurred.

The historian's task is more distanced than that of the journalist, jurist, or truth commissioner. More so than journalists, historians attempt to explore the wider historical context of atrocity. Unlike jurists, who have to make specific decisions regarding guilt or innocence, historians can be open-ended in approaching issues of moral and legal responsibility. Unlike jurists, historians do not have the power to punish. Finally, historians have more time to do their work than jurists, journalists, or truth commissioners, who are usually under pressure to arrive at their conclusions with some measure of speed.

However, confronting atrocity is not simply a matter of conducting an investigation and then writing up the results (or delivering a verdict). Legal and historical investigation may well establish the outlines of what happened, but it can hardly be expected to represent adequately, let alone repair, the hole that large-scale atrocity makes in the moral and human world. Confronting atrocity involves not just establishing what happened, but also coming to terms with what happened. Here is where memory and tradition, the creation of aesthetic forms, and ethical, theological, and religious reflection play their role. Indeed, the history of atrocity cannot be adequately written unless historians, too, take account of the breach that atrocity opens in the world.

Existentially considered, memory, and the testimony that memory generates, stand closest to the actual event of atrocity. When mass slaughter is intended, the survival of one eyewitness comes like a voice from another world, linking a horrible past experience to the present. The historian's word can never match the impact of a witness like Rivka Yoselewska, the sole survivor of a Nazi killing pit near Pinsk in Russia. Because victims' voices tend to be silenced in crimes against humanity and genocide, those voices tend to acquire a value of their own. Transcribed interviews, audiotapes, and videotapes are ways of preserving the testimonies of survivors. In relation to the Holocaust, the collection of such testimonies began in 1944 in Poland, under the auspices of the Central Jewish Historical Commission, and from the 1950s onward it continued on a larger scale at Yad Vashem and elsewhere. As evidence, these testimonies need to be regarded with caution, for eyewitness testimonies are often unreliable. However, the real aim of the continuing collection of testimonies is usually not to provide more evidence. Rather, it is to commemorate what happened and, in so doing, to reaffirm a communal (ethnic or religious) bond. Tradition and commemoration are not history, but to many people they offer a comfort and sense of meaning that history cannot.

Nonetheless, there are limits to the meaning that testimony offers. This is not only because most eyewitnesses of atrocity were themselves shot, gassed, or hacked to death, but also because the immediacy of the experience and the enormity of what happened may exceed what testimony can convey. In short, a special problem exists: speaking about the unspeakable. Here aesthetic forms—poetry, novels, painting, sculpture, architecture, film, and even comic books (e.g., Art Spiegelman's *Maus* [1986, 1991])—offer another way of confronting atrocity. Works like Anatoly Kuznetsov's *Babi Yar* (1970) and D. M. Thomas's *The White Hotel* (1981) tell stories that no historian could adequately verify, or imagine fantastic happenings in an attempt to speak the unspeakable. There is also a large genre of Holocaust memoirs, some of which take on, as with Primo Levi's *The Periodic Table* (1984), an aesthetic distance that makes them all the more powerful as meditations on genocide and humankind. Often the contemplation of mass atrocity leads to an art that is abstract, elliptical, fragmentary, or phantasmagorical, all in the interests of evoking an absence. Thus, one is moved by the only partly reconstructed Neue Synagogue in Berlin, its sanctuary left as a mere broken framework, and by the empty, interminably shunting trains of Claude Lanzmann's film *Shoah* (1985).

Mass atrocity also raises a philosophical/ theological/religious question that can and perhaps must be acknowledged by historians—as in the very title of Arno J. Mayer's *Why Did the Heavens Not Darken?: The "Final Solution" in History* (1988)—but can hardly be answered by them. The "why?" question evoked here has to do not with issues of causation (which historians are certainly capable of addressing), but with issues of ultimate meaning. The question might best be posed as: On what grounds and to what ultimate end did this evil occur? It is primarily political theorists, philosophers, and theologians who pose this question, whereas social scientists leave it aside (since "evil" is not a category that social science recognizes). Much of the work of the French philosopher Emmanuel Levinas, for example, can be seen as addressing such a question, as is also true of the German theologian Dietrich Bonhoeffer's *Letters and Papers from Prison* (1951), and it is arguably an impulse underlying the work of the French philosopher Jacques Derrida as

well. Closer to historians is Hannah Arendt's *Origins of Totalitarianism* (1951), which actually gives two different answers to the "Why did it happen?" question. One answer is of a type that historians routinely offer: It happened because of anti-Semitism and imperialism. The other answer is ultimate and excluded from "normal" historical and social science discourse: It arose out of radical evil (or out of banal evil, to evoke Arendt's later book, *Eichmann in Jerusalem: A Report on the Banality of Evil* [1963]).

It is also important to note that the ultimate question is not confined to works of philosophy of theology, but can be asked by ordinary people in ordinary circumstances. When in Tony Kushner's *Angels in America* (produced as a play in 1993 and as a film in 2003) one such ordinary person asks where God was when the horrors of the twentieth century occurred, precisely this question is being posed. Since *Angels in America* is about ordinary people getting on with their lives under difficult circumstances, this suggests that, contrary to the hypothesis of the present article, mass atrocity and ordinary life are not so far apart after all.

The historian's primary obligation is to serve as a skilled and disinterested investigator, attentive to the limits imposed on historical assertion by the limits of evidence, able to discern wishful thinking and outright lies among subsequent interpreters, and also attentive to the complexities of human motivation. But one must also note that to offer a reconstruction of past atrocity is to engage in an act that is partly aesthetic in character; that the historian's understanding of the event would be defective without some awareness of how atrocity might fit within wider ethical and human frameworks; and that the historian also needs to take account of the presence—or absence—of past atrocity within present-day memory and tradition. It is to be regretted that many of the atrocities of the twentieth century were long passed over in silence—whether because the surviving communities lacked resources and a voice (as often happened under colonialism), or because the events (as under Soviet communism) were for a long time successfully rationalized as necessary steps on the road to a better future, or because people were simply not interested in knowing.

SEE ALSO Explanation; Political Theory; Sociology of Perpetrators; Sociology of Victims

BIBLIOGRAPHY

Courtois, S., et al., eds. (1999). *The Black Book of Communism: Crimes, Terror, Repression*, trans. J. Murphy and M. Kramer. Cambridge, Mass.: Harvard University Press.

Douglas, L. (2001). *The Memory of Judgment: Making Law and History in the Trials of the Holocaust.* New Haven, Conn.: Yale University Press.

Friedlander, S., ed. (1992). *Probing the Limits of Representation: Nazism and the "Final Solution."* Cambridge, Mass.: Harvard University Press.

Glover, J. (1999). *Humanity: A Moral History of the Twentieth Century.* London: Jonathan Cape.

Hilberg, R. (2003). *The Destruction of the European Jews,* 3rd edition. 3 volumes. New Haven, Conn.: Yale University Press.

Osiel, M. (1997). *Mass Atrocity, Collective Memory, and the Law.* New Brunswick, N.J.: Transaction Press.

Allan Megill

Hitler, Adolf

[APRIL 20, 1889–APRIL 30, 1945]
German Führer, 1934 to 1945

Adolf Hitler's very first political document foreshadowed the Nazis' massive, ghastly genocide. In a letter dated September 16, 1919, the thirty-year-old lance corporal, then serving outside Munich in a political unit of the recently defeated German army, answered an inquiry about the Jews in postwar Germany by cautioning that they belonged to a deadly race scattered worldwide; national defensive measures against them, though needful and urgent, would be mere palliatives pending their "total removal." Five years later, in his self-mythicizing *Mein Kampf,* Hitler claimed that he came to his deadly anti-Semitism through observation and reflection while a day laborer in prewar Vienna. However, just as no day labor has ever been documented for the street artist in Vienna, no credible evidence of anti-Semitism is on record for Hitler before the German military defeat of 1918.

Outwardly seen, nothing in Hitler's distinctive early circumstances or upbringing predisposed him to mass-murder Jews. His father, Alois, was born to an unwed housemaid in Graz and, according to rumor, her Jewish employer; reportedly a skeptical Hitler attempted to disprove the rumor in 1930, but the effort backfired. In any case, his genocidal goal was set earlier. Alois grew up on a farm, and then made a career in the Austrian customs service, where he was reputedly bossy but liberal-minded. At age forty-seven, twice widowed with two young children in his charge, Alois married his twenty-five-year-old resident housekeeper and already pregnant mistress, Klara. She promptly bore him three children, all of whom perished in a diphtheria epidemic. Next came Adolf on April 20, 1889, and, after a five-year hiatus, a boy who died of the measles, then a girl who outlived Adolf. During the interlude following her tragic triple loss, Klara fretfully

Adolf Hitler in front of an SA parade in Berlin in honor of his birthday, April 20, 1938. [AP/WIDE WORLD PHOTOS]

overmothered Adolf, leaving him affectively bound to her for life with a sense of special election and protection. Alois died in 1903, having retired to Linz. There, Adolf started school at the top of his class and gradually slid to the bottom, finishing late with a certificate that left him few career prospects. After two years at home idling, he went to Vienna in late September 1907 hoping to train at the painting school of the Academy of Fine Arts. He flunked the entrance examination upon arrival, but was settling in anyway; however, his mother's suddenly worsening breast cancer brought him back to Linz.

Hitler's intense involvement the rest of that year with his mother's suffering and death at the hands of her kindly but inept Jewish doctor, Eduard Bloch, was the point of departure for his later genocidal animus against the stereotype he called "the Jew." Her cancer having metastasized to the lungs since, or even before, a mastectomy the previous January, Bloch duly pronounced it incurable. But Hitler persuaded Bloch that, if the patient was dying otherwise, a desperate remedy might as well be tried. Bloch obligingly packed iodoform onto her surgical wound almost daily for six-and-a-half weeks—a toxic, even lethal, regimen. She succumbed on December 21 after a prolonged agony. Just after her funeral, on Christmas Eve, Bloch collected the large balance due on his bill. Consciously Hitler felt only warm gratitude toward the hapless, compassionate doctor. However, all his later genocidal raging turned on three main themes, all dated 1907: the Jewish parasite (or cancer), the Jewish poison, and the Jewish profiteer.

Hitler's deadly hate for "the Jew," his take-off on Bloch, remained latent during his prewar years as a modest, self-taught view-painter in Vienna and later Munich, then his four years as a runner in a Bavarian regiment on the Western Front. He enjoyed good relations with Jewish comrades-in-arms including his last regimental adjutant, obtained for him an Iron Cross First Class in August 1918. His drastic turnabout dates from his gas poisoning near Wervicq in Flanders early on October 15, 1918. His eyes blindingly inflamed, Hitler suffered a nervous breakdown marked by depressive memories of his mother's death. Unlike several buddies gassed with him and treated topically close by the battlefield, Hitler was sent across Germany to Pomerania for psychiatric care. There Professor Edmund Forster, himself recently discharged from four years' service in Flanders, diagnosed Hitler's blindness as hysterical despite the regimental report that specified gas poisoning, perhaps because after some healing he relapsed into blindness at the news of the armistice on November 11. Through hypnosis, Forster called on Hitler to regain his eyesight by force of will because Germany needed him to triumph over her own disablement. He experienced Forster's therapy as a call from on high to save his mortally ailing Motherland. Within a year this summons took him into politics with the express aim of undoing Germany's defeat by removing the Jew from Germany and the world.

Hitler began by stressing the removal of Jews from Germany. Having infiltrated the small German Workers Party (soon to be renamed National Socialist German Workers Party) in September 1919 as an army spy, he fast became its star speaker, then its leader; spewing infectious rage in trenchant slogans and throaty accents, he blamed the parasitic, poisonous, profiteering Jew for Germany's defeat. Removing the Jew would reverse defeat—such was his key precept. Because the defeat had come from the west while German armies were triumphing in the east, this precept already hinted at a renewed eastward push. Hitler began calling outright for eastward expansion in the spring of 1921—sparingly for starters, but when he transformed himself from a local Bavarian agitator to a would-be national leader after a year in jail for his failed Beerhall Putsch of November 1923, he scaled back his rhetoric against the Jew and instead talked up a supposed German need for more land. Hitler's new victory formula ran: Re-

move the divisive, destructive element from the body politic to restore its inner strength for eastward conquest. Shortly after the Nazis' electoral leap forward in September 1930 he muffled his expansionism in turn to call simply for regaining outward strength. Finally he stressed the "national community," his middle term between removing the Jew and expanding eastward, as a cover term for both. The two diluted end terms registered no less effectively with his listeners, however blurrily. Together they were the long and short of Hitlerism, its single message. That message above all else fueled Hitler's rise to total personal power over Germany by the mid-1930s, the ground rule of his regime being that his word was law.

Meanwhile, in *Mein Kampf* (1925–1926) and especially in an unpublished untitled book (1928), Hitler theoretically reconciled those two end terms of his politics. Whereas other peoples compete for land and ultimately for world conquest, he argued, the Jew breaks this law of nature, being stateless, parasitic, egalitarian, and unwarriorlike; accordingly, nature mandates a "land grab" and a "Jew kill" both at once. The logic of this construction on its expansionist side was for Germany to ease Jews out, preferably to rival nations, so as to gain an edge in the struggle for the global reach needed to destroy the Jews altogether. It was emphatically not for Germany to kill Jews at home straightaway and thereby invite foreign reprisals, nor to push anti-Semitism abroad for the benefit of other peoples, let alone expend German resources ridding other nations of Jews. But logic could not always contain the animus against the Jew that took Hitler into politics in the first place. Thus he often called for destroying the Jew in Germany, or even abroad, before the expansionist battle was even joined. Mostly, though, he settled for ambiguities in his rhetoric such as "removing the Jew."

During his twelve-year dictatorship Hitler's policies betrayed the same tension between his hate for the Jew and its rational control for the sake of German expansion. Control predominated for roughly the first half of his rule, from the Havaara agreement of 1933 to the mission by Reichsbank President Schacht to London in late 1938, both aimed at facilitating Jewish emigration financially. Even the Nazis' internal discriminatory measures, including the much-publicized Jewish boycott of 1933 or Nuremberg Laws of 1935, served to induce Jews to emigrate voluntarily. Most such measures originated with lower authorities, though Hitler might intervene, as he did to prevent the crass marking of Jews or Jewish shops before 1941. However, he failed to curb the Reichskristallnacht pogrom of November 9, 1938, mounted by propaganda minister Joseph Goebbels, which besmirched the regime even in German eyes. Thereafter, Jews were officially murdered only out of sight. At the same time, Hitler's Jewish policies took an impolitic turn overall: he stopped Schacht from sealing a deal on Jewish emigration, switched to exporting anti-Semitism rather than Jews, and on January 30, 1939, prophesied to the Reichstag "the annihilation of the Jewish race in Europe" should war come. With this prophecy midway between easing Germany's Jews out and a world pogrom, hate definitively gained the ascendant.

By then it was evident that induced emigration was coming short: the Reich's Jew count was roughly cut in half by 1938, the Anschluss that March brought it back near its starting point. The absorption of the Sudetenland that fall, then the establishment of a protectorate over Bohemia and Moravia the following March, and especially the occupation and partial annexation of western Poland beginning in September 1939, ruled out the emigration option conclusively. There are signs that Hitler considered starting mass exterminations during the Polish war—that he could hardly uphold his expansionist logic against so many helpless Jews already within his reach. But the noise and smoke of battle needed to cover mass shootings dwindled too fast. Open killings risked provoking the United States and even, as Hitler saw it, the Soviet Union, not to mention arousing the Germans themselves, whose reactions he feared even while the Holocaust was an open secret. He scrapped his doctrinaire subordination of his Jewish to his expansionist policy once and for all with the invasion of the Soviet Union in June 1941, which enabled for mass executions of Jews in the guise of anti-partisan warfare. The exterminations were next mandated for all of German-controlled Europe and then only (reversing Hitler's original victory formula) for Germany itself.

A scholarly controversy developed in Germany in the 1970s between so-called "functionalists," who saw the Holocaust as having developed out of separate, often local, initiatives, and "intentionalists," who saw it as having been planned by Hitler from the first. The functionalist case is plausible insofar as Hitler did ordinarily allow events to take their course so long as they went his way. It remains that he aimed from his political beginnings to kill Jews even if he vacillated about which Jews to kill and when to kill them. In the end he used his war in the east as cover for his war on the Jews—his controlling political purpose. After first billing a Jew-purge in Germany as a means to German expansion, then implementing Jew-purges across Europe at the expense of German arms, he exited history in the resultant rubble and ashes, still enjoining Germans to keep the genocidal faith.

SEE ALSO Anti-Semitism; Germany; Gestapo; Himmler, Heinrich; Holocaust; Kristallnacht; Nuremberg Laws; United States Foreign Policies Toward Genocide and Crimes Against Humanity; Wannsee Conference

BIBLIOGRAPHY

Binion, R. (1979). *Hitler among the Germans,* 2nd edition. New York: Elsevier North Holland.

Jäckel, E. (1981). *Hitler's World View.* Cambridge, Mass.: Harvard University Press.

Jäckel, E., and A. Kuhn, eds. (1980). *Hitler: Sämtliche Aufzeichnungen 1905–1924.* Stuttgart: Deutsche Verlagsanstalt.

Lewis, D. (2003). *The Man Who Invented Hitler.* London: Headline.

Rudolph Binion

Holocaust

The term *Holocaust* refers to the Nazi German policy that sought the annihilation of European and North African Jews. It comes from the Greek, *holókauton*, meaning "burnt sacrifice." More rarely, the term is also used to describe Nazi German violence in general. The persecution and mass murder of Europe's Jewry evolved out of a shift from religious to racial or ethnic anti-Semitism during the Industrial Revolution and the rise of liberal capitalism and the nation state in Europe during the second half of the nineteenth century. Prominent in many countries, including Russia and France, the new blend of anti-Semitism combined traditional and modern elements and became especially popular among many of Germany's intellectuals and elites. With the growing importance of the workers' movement and Marxism, anti-Semitism increased further after the Russian October revolution of 1917. Anti-Jewish conspiracy theories emerged, particularly in the states that lost World War I, that were established as its consequence, or that suffered badly in the worldwide economic crisis of 1929 to 1939. Most right-wing, authoritarian regimes that came to power in Europe in the 1920s and 1930s were anti-Semitic. Many adopted anti-Jewish laws. Chief among these, however, was Germany after Hitler's rise to power in 1933.

From 1933 to 1939, National Socialist (i.e., Nazi) Germany pursued a policy of enforced emigration. Out of 700,000 Jews in Germany and Austria, two-thirds left these countries before World War II, mostly the younger and more wealthy. Immigration restrictions abroad and Nazi "fees" for emigration permits hampered this process. Jews were dismissed from civil service in 1933. They faced economic ruin and the gradual expropriation of their property. They were routinely harrassed, attacked by Nazi activists and youths, denied social services, and excluded from public education. Central as well as municipal institutions contributed to such policies. Sexual relations with non-Jews ("Aryans") were prohibited under the "Law for the Protection of the German Blood and Honor" in 1935. With the annexation of Austria in March 1938—where anti-Semitism was particularly widespread—and a nation-wide pogrom ("Kristallnacht," or Crystal Night) on November 9 and 10, 1938, the persecution of Jews was intensified. Nearly 30,000 Jews were temporarily imprisoned in concentration camps after Kristallnacht, during which more than 1,000 synagogues were destroyed and Jewish shops were looted. At least 91 Jews died in the pogrom, and hundreds more committed suicide.

Beginning in late 1938, the influence of the SS and the police under Heinrich Himmler grew increasingly influential in setting Germany's anti-Jewish policy, although SS and police never gained exclusive control over it. After Germany successfully invaded Poland in September 1939, more than 2.5 million Polish Jews came under German rule. By May 1941, Germany occupied another eight European countries, further increasing this number. Anti-Semitic regulations aimed at the isolation, deprivation, and humiliation of Jews throughout Germany's vastly expanded territory were gradually adopted. Jews were forced to wear identifying insignia, their access to means of communication and transportation was limited, and their food rations were reduced. Local German authorities in Poland individually ordered the creation of Jewish ghettos wherein Jews were permitted extremely few resources and were assigned one room (or less) per family. The overcrowding led to increased mortality and the spread of diseases.

Beginning in 1939, German authorities developed plans for the enforced resettlement of the Jews to specially designated territories, where it was expected that harsh living conditions and an adverse climate would lead to their slow destruction. The first of these territories were eastern Poland, then Madagascar; later on, northern Russia or Siberia were considered. These plans called for the inmates to be separated according to sexes and kept under German "police supervision." Initially intended as postwar projects, these plans indicated a radicalization of anti-Semitic thinking under the Nazi regime. They were never implemented in their original form, but they fit into a larger framework of Nazi schemes for restructuring, ethnic cleansing, and resettlement in Eastern Europe. From 1939 to 1941, the SS tried to settle several hundred thousands of ethnic Germans from Eastern Europe in Western Poland. To make room for these newcomers, nearly 500,000 local inhabitants—including up to 200,000 Jews—were deported to the German-occupied General Government of Poland. Such actions increased the war-related scarcity of housing, sanitation, employment and food, particularly as a large proportion of the ethnic Germans had to stay in camps for months or years. The occupational authorities diverted the resulting shortages to the Jews and intensified the search for other "solutions."

Mass Murder of Soviet Jews

The German war against the Soviet Union was planned as a war of extermination jointly by Hitler, the SS, and military and economic authorities. The attack aimed at destroying "world communism," forcing "racially inferior" Slavs to submit to German colonial rule, eliminating the USSR as a military power, improving Germany's strategic position, and achieving self-sufficiency in food and raw materials such as oil. Schemes for large-scale German settlements had little influence on the actual occupation policy. While the majority of the Soviet population was to remain alive to provide cheap labor for the Germans, large groups of them were to be killed. Tens of millions were intended to die of starvation, particularly those who lived in the cities and the populations of certain northern and central areas. Also slated for death were millions of "commissars," communists, intellectuals, state officials, and Jews. This violence was considered vital for the long-term German appropriation of Soviet resources, which, in the short run, were needed for the militarily critical supplies of German troops fighting on the eastern front. The violence would also allow Germany to control a vast territory with a much smaller number of occupation troops than would otherwise be needed. Soviet Jews became a special target, because the racially charged propaganda blamed them for having designed the communist system, and they were expected to put up a fierce resistance.

Germany's military leaders wished to assign special units of the SS and the police the job of securing part of Soviet rear areas, thus reducing the need for using army troops to handle this task. These units included a total of 3,000 men in four *Einsatzgruppen* (Operation Units), deployed by the Security Police and Security Service under Reinhard Heydrich; mobile Police Battalions, deployed by the Order Police under Kurt Daluege; and Waffen-SS Brigades. These units started mass killings in the rear immediately after the German attack on June 22, 1941, and during that year more than 90 percent of their victims were Jewish.

The total extermination of Soviet Jews was not officially ordered at the outset. Instead, the SS and police targetted only those men considered to belong to the "Jewish intelligentsia": a group that included state officials, teachers, and lawyers, and others of the professional class. Between late July and early October 1941, this target group was enlarged—in different areas at different times—first by including women and children, and then by annihilating entire Jewish communities. This expansion began in Lithuania and Latvia, where the local, non-German, anti-Soviet police and administrators cooperated in acts of persecution and violence. By the end of 1941, 800,000 Jews had been killed throughout the German-occupied Soviet territories. Most victims were marched to remote locations near their home towns or cities and shot at previously prepared mass graves.

Cooperation went especially smoothly between SS and police and the military, with army officers calling for mass executions or giving logistic and manpower support. Military and civil administrations handled the first measures, such as making the Jews wear yellow badges, concentrating them in ghettos or special districts, assigning them to forced labor, and seizing their assets. In territories under German military administration, such as northern and central Russia, eastern Byelorussia, and eastern Ukraine, nearly all the indigenous Jews had been killed by December 1941. Demand for Jewish forced labor was low because the urban centers were largely destroyed and the German occupiers pursued a general policy of de-industrialization. The drive to violence was aggravated by food and housing shortages. The destruction experienced in the western territories of Byelorussia and Ukraine (Polish territory until 1939) was less intense because the economies of these regions were more dependent on Jewish artisans. Here, the civil administrations were more apt to spare the Jews, and as many as 75 percent survived until 1942. Direct orders and inspections by Himmler, Heydrich, and Daluege coordinated the killing actions. Of particular importance was the chain of command that extended downward from Himmler to his regional plenipotentiaries, the Higher SS and Police Leaders. Yet local officers were given some autonomy as well. Massacres and the selection of target groups were based on continuous negotiations between regional and local SS and police, civil, and military authorities. In the spring of 1942, such negotiations resulted first in the extermination of those Jews deemed unable to work. The killings were stepped up in the second half of the year to a policy of almost total annihilation, and by March 1943, at least another 650,000 Jews (excluding eastern Galicia) were killed.

Toward a Continent-Wide Program of Annihilation

The killing of the Soviet Jews marked the beginning of the extermination. Mass killings soon took place in other areas as well. Eastern Galicia had been declared part of the General Government, and was ruled under a German civil administration. By the end of 1941, 70,000 Jews from this region were killed. In Serbia, which was under military occupation, the German army killed the entire adult male Jewish population—7,000 in all—as reprisals against partisan resistance in the fall of 1941. The women and children were murdered by the SS and Police in 1942. In Poland, food rationing was intentionally unequal, with Jews receiving less than their non-Jewish fellow citizens, and much less than Germans. More than 40,000 Jews died of starvation and diseases related to overcrowding in the ghetto of Warsaw in 1941. In the German-annexed Reichsgau Wartheland (in Western Poland) and in the General Government, the civil administrations together with SS and the police developed plans for extermination camps to kill a portion of the Jewish population. The first killing center went into operation in Chelmno, Wartheland, on December 8, 1941, and the second was opened in Belzec, in the General Government's territory, on March 17, 1942.

It is unclear how much of this policy was ordered by the German central government and how much might have resulted from local initiatives. There were several parallel developments in German anti-Jewish policy in the fall of 1941, and Nazi leaders issued a number of declarations of intent (of which there remain only fragmented records). Beginning in mid-1941, experiments in new mass killing techniques, including gassing, were carried out by different branches of the SS and the police and in several concentration camps. Under pressure from the SS and regional Nazi Party leaders, Hitler permitted the deportation of Jews from the German Reich into the East in September 1941. By December, 50,000 had been deported to Lodz, Minsk, Kaunas, and Riga. Six thousand of these deportees were killed in Kaunas and Riga in late November 1941, after which Himmler called a temporary halt to the mass murders. However, they were resumed in Lodz and Minsk in May 1942.

Hitler announced his intention to exterminate all European Jews during World War II in a meeting of Nazi Party leaders on December 12, 1941, after declaring war on the United States. On January 20, 1942, in a high-level meeting in Berlin with government and Nazi Party officials plus SS officers, Heydrich claimed responsibilty for "the solution to the Jewish question in Europe," and especially the definition of who was declared a "Jew" was discussed. He set out his plans for mass murder, which were probably still only vaguely developed at that time. In this meeting, called the Wannsee Conference, the governmental bureaucrats raised no objections to Heydrich's plans for the extermination of Europe's Jews, but they could not reach full agreement on how to proceed nor on a complete centralization of the measures against the Jews. Many scholars of the era argue that the extermination of European Jewry was ordered by Hitler no later than the autumn of 1941 (some saying that the order was issued early in the year), but others suggest that such a decision was not reached before December 1941 or in the spring of 1942. Some hold that the Holocaust simply "evolved," without the need for any explicit command decision issued by Hitler.

It has been argued that Himmler preferred using gas to kill Jews because he wanted to protect his firing squads in the east from mental stress. However, only a small proportion of the Soviet Jews were gassed in 1942 (in mobile gas vans). The majority, numbering some 500,000 in total, were shot. Killing techniques were never standardized. Only two of six major death camps (Auschwitz and Majdanek) employed prussic acid (also called Zyklon B) in gas chambers. In the Belzec, Sobibor, and Treblinka camps in the General Government, Jews were killed in stationary gas chambers into which engine exhaust fumes were vented. In Chelmno, the murders were performed in mobile gas vans. These killings differed from the mass murder of approximately 100,000 disabled patients. In that case, the patients were suffocated using bottled carbon monoxide, administered in stationary gas chambers or gas vans between September 1939 and August 1941. The killing of the disabled was organized by Hitler's chancellery in his capacity as the leader of the Nazi Party, known as the Kanzlei des Führers, or was carried out by regional civil administrations in annexed Western Poland, with the assistance of the SS. Personnel who had gained experience through participating in this "euthanasia" program (code named "T-4") were transferred to Belzec, Sobibor, and Treblinka in late 1941 and 1942.

In Poland, the mass killings were expanded and accelerated in 1942 in two stages, similar to the way the policies were pursued in the German-occupied Soviet territories. General Governor Hans Frank argued that a policy of extermination could reduce food problems, health risks, and black market activities. Jews deemed unfit for work in the districts of Lublin, Galicia, and Krakow were deported on trains to Belzec, beginning on March 17, 1942 and to Sobibor beginning on May 6, 1942, while other victims were rounded up and killed in mass shootings. The second phase of the mass killings in the region began in July, with the establishment of a third death camp at Treblinka, near Warsaw. Construction on the camp had started in May, and murders began there on July 22, 1942. At the same time, new and bigger gas chambers were installed in Belzec, with Sobibor and Treblinka following suit during September and October of that year. On Himmler's orders (and with the support of the head of the German Four-Year Planning Office, Hermann Göring), the demand for forced labor was largely ignored during the period from July to October 1942, and many Jewish workers summarily killed. Approximately 1.15 million Jews from the General Government were thus killed in the second half of 1942, and only 297,000 remained alive.

The deportations of French and Slovakian Jews to Auschwitz began in March 1942, although most of the first deportees were not killed upon arrival. Auschwitz had been founded in 1940 as a concentration camp, but by 1942 it was gradually being transformed into a death center. Large-scale gassings began in early May 1942—the first victims were Jews from German-annexed East Upper Silesia in Poland—and the extermination of prisoners reached full scale in July 1942, handling transports of Jews arriving from Poland and Western and Central Europe. Between 10 and 35 percent of the new arrivals were selected for forced labor, the rest were killed. The first two permanent, if improvised, gas chambers in the main camp of Auschwitz went into operation in May and on June 30, 1942. Planning for bigger gas chambers and crematoria to be built in the subcamp of Auschwitz-Birkenau began in August, but they only became operational in March 1943. More than half of all the Jews who were killed in the Holocaust died between March 1942 and March 1943.

Massive transports of Jews from Western and Central Europe began to arrive in Auschwitz in June 1942. Deportations of Jews from the Netherlands progressed smoothly, but in Belgium and France the deportees were primarily, if not exclusively, limited to foreign Jews (the authorities in these two states were reluctant to cooperate in the deportation of their own citizens). Many Jews from Germany, particularly the elderly, were sent at first to a "show" camp in the Czech town of Terezín (Theresienstadt), allegedly as a place for convenient long-term settlement, but most were later sent to Auschwitz to be killed. Deportations to Auschwitz continued throughout 1943, and the later transports included Greek and (beginning in autumn, 1943) Italian Jews. To a certain extent, the definition of "Jew" was kept vague. Outside of the eastern territories, however, Jews married to gentiles and so-called half-Jews were usually not murdered, even though they were required to register. Some German officials, and Hitler himself, objected to killing Jews of mixed heritage because they were afraid of protests by non-Jewish relatives.

The extermination of European Jews reached a new peak in the summer of 1944, after Germany invaded Hungary, and the new (but not yet fully fascist) Hungarian government fully cooperated in the deportation of 430,000 Jews to Auschwitz in only seven weeks, from May 15 to July 9. About 100,000 of the Hungarian Jews were selected for forced labor—they were assigned to work in the construction of factories for German fighter planes and other tasks. Another 80,000 Jews were exempted from deportation and consigned instead to the Hungarian Army's forced Labor Service. Deportations were temporarily stopped by the Hungarian leader, Admiral Miklos Horthy, on July 9. He balked at transporting the more "useful" urban Jews of Budapest. After Horthy was ousted from office by the fascist Arrow-Cross Party on October 15, 1944, the transports were resumed on a limited scale. In total, nearly 500,000 of Hungary's approximately 730,000 Jews were killed.

Deportation transports from outside the General Government and the Soviet Union were organized by the office for Jewish affairs (IV B 4) in the Head Office of Reich Security under Adolf Eichmann. Because they usually deployed only several hundred men for each occupied country, the security police and security service required the cooperation of the German military and civil administrators, foreign office occupation personnel, the local national police and administrations, and German and foreign railway authorities. As a result, deportations were not only based on complex bureaucratic procedures but depended also on negotiations at a political level.

By the fall of 1943, virtually all remaining Jews in German-ruled Central and Eastern Europe had been interned within the concentration camp system of the SS. In 1944, Himmler gave orders not to let prisoners fall into enemy hands during military retreats. In the last months of World War II, this led to murderous death marches, in which columns of concentration camp inmates were forced to walk hundreds of kilometers, on often circuitous routes, with few supplies, and under brutal treatment by their guards, by German Nazi Party organizations, by home defense units, and by individuals. Estimates of the mortality in these marches range from less than a third to half of the participants.

The Jewish Response

The Jewish response to this qualitatively new threat took various forms. These included traditional solutions, such as the payment of tributes, renewed spirituality, and emigration. This latter option proved to be the most effective response. Once World War II began, however, emigration was an option only open to a small minority, primarily young adults and single people, especially because of the stringent immigration restrictions imposed by potential recipient countries. For most people, other survival strategies were needed.

The German resolve to kill all Jews became clear only gradually so, at first, Jewish leaders attempted to make the members of their communities indispensable through employment in war-related industries. This strategy largely failed, due to the low demand for industrial labor in Poland and the German-occupied Soviet territories, where most of Europe's Jews lived. To meet the increasing demand for such labor in Germany after the intensification of war production in 1942, other sources, such as Soviet civilians, were given preference. The SS also increasingly turned to the principle of "selection" to counter Jewish labor schemes, separating Jewish workers from those not employed, and targeting the latter group to be killed first. Sometimes the organizers of the Holocaust gave priority to annihilation over any labor considerations, and many Jewish workers died of starvation and brutal treatment. With little access to arms, often isolated from non-Jewish resistance groups, and facing overwhelming German power, Jews turned to armed resistance only as a last resort, most prominently in the ghetto uprisings in Warsaw (April and May 1943) and Bialystok (August 1943), and through service in Soviet partisan units. Such uprisings usually could not rescue large groups. Instead, uprisings served as a final, symbolic signal of defiance and resistance.

Cooperation and Resistance of Non-Germans

A number of countries allied with or occupied by Germany, as well as non-German social groups and individuals, participated in the Holocaust, supported it, or (in the case of states) even ran their own extermination programs. Others resisted or obstructed German demands. In many places, however, Jews who could not claim citizenship were at a distinct disadvantage. This contributed to a considerable variation in the proportion of Jews killed during the Holocaust, with less than 1 percent mortality of Finland's Jews, 20 percent in Denmark, 25 percent in France, 40 percent in Belgium, 67 percent in Hungary, and more than 80 percent in the Netherlands.

Romania organized its own program of mass killings of Jews in 1941 and 1942, working in parallel with

When U.S. and British soldiers entered the Nazi concentration camps at liberation, they brought camera crews with them. These crews were the first to document the horrors of the camps. In this photo, taken April 17, 1945, U.S. soldiers walk across the grounds of the Nordhausen concentration camp, past row upon row of corpses. Nordhausen was a subcamp of the concentration camp Dora-Mittelbau.
[AP/WIDE WORLD PHOTOS]

the German Einsatzgruppen murders. At least 250,000 Jews living in, or deported to, the Romanian-occupied Soviet territories were massacred by Romanians or died of deprivation. However, Romania refused to allow the Jews from their mainland to be deported to German death camps in the fall of 1942. Although most of these Jews survived, they nonetheless suffered from persecution. Half of Croatia's 40,000 Jews were killed by their fellow, non-Jewish citizens in 1941; the rest were deported to Germany in 1942, where they were all killed. Approximately 30,000 Jews from Hungary were killed or died under the authority of Hungarian nationals in the army's forced Labor Service from 1941 to 1943, and during the chaotic Budapest ghetto violence between October 1944 and early 1945.

Germany demanded that all its European allies surrender their Jews in September 1942. The Slovak and Hungarian governments were eager to deport most of their Jews, with Slovakia complying in 1941 and 1942. Hungary refused at first, but began sending its own shipments in 1944. Finland, although a German ally, refused to deport its Jews, and Bulgaria vetoed deportations from its home territory. However, the Bulgarian government handed over the Jews who lived in the annexed territories of Macedonia and Thracia. Fascist Italy protected its Jews as well as those in Italian-occupied French, Yugoslav, Greek, and Albanian territories until September 1943. Then a new government took power in Italy and switched sides—German troops occupied most of the country. The fascist states of Spain and Portugal maintained neutrality, and diplomatically protected their Jewish subjects in the German sphere of influence. Some of their diplomats made limited attempts to rescue Hungarian Jews in 1944. Swiss and Swedish envoys did the same, but on a larger scale. Such options were unavailable in countries such as Poland and in the Soviet territories, which were denied any central government by the Germans.

The cooperation of administrators, elites, professional organizations, and individual citizens was crucial to the outcome of the Holocaust. It is difficult to accurately gauge popular attitudes toward the persecution and murder of Jews, because the Germans threatened harsh reprisals for anyone who helped Jews escape deportation or death in their occupied territories. In many countries, especially in Eastern Europe, local anti-Semitic propaganda, denunciations, and even manhunts made the survival of Jews nearly impossible. In the first weeks of the German attack on the USSR, a wave of bloody pogroms swept through the western Soviet territories from Latvia to Moldova. In many occupied countries, local police officers participated or were forced to participate in anti-Jewish measures and violence. Most of the guards in the four death camps in the General Government of Poland were actually Soviet auxiliaries, mostly Ukrainians, under German supervision. Lithuanian, Latvian, and Ukrainian police units under German command took part in the mass execution of Jews inside and outside their countries. Some local administrations created ghettos and many confiscated Jewish assets for redistribution to non-Jews.

In all European countries, including Germany, individuals and small groups made attempts to rescue Jews, especially in the Netherlands, Poland, and the Soviet Union, although these efforts were overshadowed by widespread administrative cooperation and popular anti-Semitism. A number of Jews escaped capture with the help of the clergy. The most prominent nongovernmental collective rescue action took place in German-occupied Denmark in October 1943. The German representatives in Denmark wanted to avoid a political confrontation, and non-Jewish citizens were able to help 7,200 Jews escape to Sweden by boat. Another 500 Danish Jews were nonetheless deported to the German Reich.

The readiness of foreign governments, civil administrators, and the general public to support anti-Jewish violence depended less on their attitude towards the Germans, than on domestic political considerations, and on their own attitudes regarding Jews. Local authorities, rather than German troops, seized Jewish property in most of these areas (the exception was in Poland) and sold it to finance their costs of war or German occupation, or used it to solve social and economic problems like housing, land scarcity, or a shortage of consumer goods. The deportation of Jews also facilitated the redistribution of professional positions and the building of new, allegedly more loyal elites. This helps to explain why Eastern European states such as Romania, Hungary, and Bulgaria were more willing to remove Jews from newly annexed territories. For some time, Lithuanian nationalists and the Hungarian government cooperated in the killing and deportation of Jews as a foreign policy strategy, in exchange for more political independence from the Germans. Conversely, protecting Jews earned the favor of the Anti-Hitler Coalition and the Vatican, which was important to Romania and Slovakia, and to Hungary before March and after July of 1944. During 1942, the United States, Great Britain, and the Soviet Union recognized Germany's comprehensive extermination program against the Jews and threatened punishment in a joint public declaration on December 17, of that year. However, they concentrated on achieving a military victory over Nazi Germany instead of mounting major rescue operations, in part to deny domestic anti-Semitic propaganda claims that the Allies were fighting to protect Jewish interests.

Consequences

Reliable statistics document that between 5.5 and 6.1 million Jews were killed in the Holocaust. Between 2.2 and 2.5 million of these deaths came from the Soviet Union, 1.9 million from Poland (both within the borders of 1945), 500,000 from "Greater Hungary" of 1944, 165,000 from Germany, 100,000 from the Netherlands, and 80,000 from France. Three million victims were killed by gassing, nearly two million were shot, the others were killed by other methods, died of starvation, exhaustion, forced labor, or the extreme living conditions imposed on them.

Among long-range consequences of the Holocaust was the loss of much of Europe's Jewish cultural heritage. This loss was further exacerbated by the postwar emigration of survivors to Israel and other countries. The Holocaust also led to the traumatization of generations of Europe's Jews, suffered not only by the survivors but also by many of their descendants. The Holocaust has been understood as an expression of a moral crisis either of European civilization, or the modern industrial society in general. Together with the enforced resettlements, population exchanges, and border adjustments during and after World War II, the Holocaust contributed to the emergence of ethnically and culturally far more homogeneous nation states after 1945.

Juridical trials and investigations against the perpetrators of the Holocaust took part in two phases, first during the immediate postwar era and then after 1957.

Initially seen as one crime among others (there was no separate treatment of the Holocaust among the thirteen Nuremberg Trials), a special awareness developed over time, and was evident in cases like the Einsatzgruppen and Auschwitz trials in West Germany (1957-58, 1963) and the Eichmann trial in Israel in 1961. Although nearly 100,000 persons were under investigation for Nazi violence in the two German states, an equal number in the Soviet Union, and many in the rest of Europe, few (except in the USSR under Stalin) received substantial punishment, and the trials raised doubts as to whether legal systems can adequately respond to modern mass violence, given a general lack of documentation and the division of labor and state-level participation of the crime. However, the trials did succeed in educating the public, and in the accumulation and dissemination of knowledge about the Holocaust. Further, they provided the opportunity for symbolic atonement.

Interpretations and Controversies

Increasingly, the Holocaust has been viewed as the most important result of World War II—it is even viewed by some to be the central event of the twentieth century, though both views are confined to North America and Western Europe. Several schools of interpretation have evolved. The "intentionalists" represent the dominant approach in teaching, arguing that the extermination of European Jewry was primarily based on Nazi ideology, Hitler's anti-Semitism, ordered by a central authority at a relatively early time, conducted within a hierarchical and homogenous system, and based on long-term, covert plans. Competing theorists, called "functionalists" or "structuralists," place less emphasis on ideology and central leadership. Instead, they suggest that the Holocaust emerged out of a political system that contained various, competing power centers with unclear or overlapping authority. They view the violence against Jews as arising out of a struggle among leaders for Hitler's favor or in anticipation of Hitler's will, which resulted in a radicalization of anti-Jewish policies. In such a view, the issuance of Holocaust orders from the central authority came late. Other scholars have pointed out the importance of a bureaucratic division of labor, or insisted that the Holocaust remains inexplicable.

Research in the 1990s and early 2000s has shown that broad intentionalist and structuralist interpretations are outdated, overly theoretical, and poorly documented. Newer studies have tried to combine elements of different approaches, acknowledging a variety of initiatives from outside the center, and offering multicausal explanations. Scholars try to link anti-Semitism with contemporary political issues such as ethnic cleansing, food policy, or the generation of political collaboration.

The research of specialists has remained widely detached from comparative genocide research, although the intentionalist understanding of the term "Holocaust" often serves as the model for the notion of genocide. Interconnections between the Holocaust and other mass violence in Nazi Germany remain a matter for further research. Major areas of debate include the question of the uniqueness of the Holocaust in comparison to other cases of mass violence; the decision-making process and the degree of centralization in the Holocaust; the explanatory weight put on ideology, state organization, or popular participation in Germany; the role of non-German cooperation; the motives of perpetrators and organizers (including economic motives); and the significance of Jewish armed resistance as opposed to other survival strategies.

SEE ALSO Concentration Camps; Einsatzgruppen; Extermination Centers; Germany; Ghetto; Jehovah's Witnesses; SS; Statistical Analysis; Wannsee Conference

BIBLIOGRAPHY

Ainsztein, Reuben (1974). *Jewish Resistance in Nazi-occupied Eastern Europe*. London: Elek.

Aly, Götz (1999). *"Final Solution:" Nazi Population Policy and the Murder of the European Jews*. London: Arnold and Oxford University Press.

Aly, Götz, and Susanne Heim (2003). *Architects of Annihilation: Auschwitz and the Logic of Destruction*. Princeton, N.J.: Princeton University Press.

Arad, Yitzhak (1987). *Belzec, Sobibor, Treblinka: The Operation Reinhard Death Camps*. Bloomington: Indiana University Press.

Arad, Yitshak et al., eds. (1999). *Documents on the Holocaust: Selected Sources on the Destruction of the Jews of Germany and Austria, Poland, and the Soviet Union*. Lincoln: Nebraska University Press and Yad Vashem.

Bankier, David (1992). *The Germans and the Final Solution: Public Opinion Under Nazism*. Oxford, U.K.: Basil Blackwell.

Benz, Wolfgang, ed. (1991). *Dimension des Völkermords: Die Zahl der jüdischen Opfer des Nationalsozialismus*. Munich, Germany: Oldenbourg.

Braham, Randolph (1994). *The Politics of Genocide: The Holocaust in Hungary*. New York: Columbia University Press.

Browning, Christopher (1993). *Ordinary Men: Reserve Police Battalion 101 and the Final Solution in Poland*. New York: HarperCollins.

Browning, Christopher, and Jürgen Matthäus. (2004). *The Origins of the Final Solution: The Evolution of Nazi Jewish Policy, September 1939–March 1942*. Lincoln: Nebraska University Press and Yad Vashem.

Burrin, Phillipe (1994). *Hitler and the Jews: The Genesis of the Holocaust*. London: Arnold.

Corni, Gustavo (2002). *Hitler's Ghettos: Voices from a Beleaguered Society, 1939–1944*. London: Arnold and Oxford University Press.

Friedländer, Saul (1997). *Nazi Germany and the Jews*, Vol I: *The Years of Persecution, 1933–1939*. New York: HarperCollins.

Gerlach, Christian (2001). *Krieg, Ernährung, Völkermord: Forschungen zur deutschen Vernichtungspolitik im Zweiten Weltkrieg*. 2nd ed., Zurich: Pendo.

Gutman, Israel, and Michael Berenbaum, eds. (1994). *Anatomy of the Auschwitz Death Camp*. Bloomington: Indiana University Press.

Herbert, Ulrich, ed. (2000). *National Socialist Extermination Policies: Contemporary German Perspectives and Controversies*. New York: Berghahn.

Hilberg, Raul (2003). *The Destruction of the European Jews*. 3rd edition, New Haven: Yale University Press.

Ioanid, Radu (2000). *The Holocaust in Romania: The Destruction of the Jews and Gypsies Under the Antonescu Regime, 1940–1944*. Chicago: Ivan R. Dee.

Laqueur, Walter (1980). *The Terrible Secret: Suppression of the Truth About Hitler's "Final Solution."* Boston: Little, Brown.

Safrian, Hans (1995). *Eichmann und seine Gehilfen*. 2nd edition. Frankfurt am Main, Germany: Fischer Taschenbuch.

Trunk, Isaiah (1972). *Judenrat: The Jewish Councils in Eastern Europe Under Nazi Occupation*. New York: Macmillan.

Yahil, Leni (1990). *The Holocaust: The Fate of European Jewry, 1932–1945*. New York: Oxford University Press.

Christian Gerlach

Homosexuals

The terms *homosexuality* and *homosexual* were coined by Karl Maria Kertbeny, a German-Hungarian journalist, in 1868 to describe sexual relations between individuals of the same sex. Such relations have existed throughout history and have often fallen under social scrutiny. Much of modern history has witnessed persistent discrimination against homosexuals, in some cases leading to persecution and crimes against humanity.

Image of Homosexuals in History

Attitudes toward homosexuality have fluctuated greatly over time. Examples of homosexuality can be found in religious texts dating back to the third and fourth century BCE, such as the Kama Sutra and other Eastern Tantric texts. This recognition of same-sex relations suggests that tolerance toward homosexuality has deep historical roots. In modern India homosexuality is tolerated as long as it does not interfere with the institution of marriage. The individuals who suffer discrimination are those who refuse to adhere to social

A plaque on Sheridan Square in New York City's West Village commemorating the Stonewall Riots. On June 27, 1969, police raided the nearby Stonewall Inn and a scuffle soon broke out with the bar's homosexual patrons: The violence continued for the next two nights. The event led many in this community, and others worldwide, to openly acknowledge their homosexuality and demand equality, it is regarded as a defining moment in the Gay Liberation movement. [KEVIN FLEMING/CORBIS]

pressures and instead lead openly homosexual lives. Although in China homosexuality is now legal, homosexuals suffered discrimination under the Qing government in 1740. The regulations that emerged were in response to homosexuality becoming an accepted way of life, one explored openly in literature of the time. The subsequent political reaction fueled a social intolerance that still exists in the early twenty-first century.

Western culture during the Greco-Roman period of history is laden with expressions of same-sex sexual desire. In general, society accepted such sexual activity as long as those involved adhered to accepted social conventions. This situation changed with the growing influence of Christianity, which referred to the story of Sodom in Genesis 18 and 19, and other biblical sources banning same-sex sexual behavior.

Between the fall of Rome and the beginning of the Renaissance, the rule of the Roman Catholic Church dominated Western views condemning homosexuality or any other sexual act not performed for the purpose of procreation. This era witnessed a significant increase in the persecution and execution of suspected "sodomites" (which included anyone who engaged in any act of sexual or social deviance). After the Protestant Reformation same-sex relations were still considered a sin and states began passing harsher statutes punishing sodomy as a crime. These convictions, primarily in Europe, reached their peak between 1750 and 1830, turning into social hysteria and leading to a relatively large number of arrests and executions.

Severe discrimination gave birth to a distinct identity based on sexual expression and desire. A new, more specific category of "homosexual" emerged during the Victorian era when a medical definition was assigned. The concurrent social discrimination paralleled an increase in self-identity and community awareness, as well as a desire by homosexuals to become socially recognized. Self-expression through literature blossomed during this era.

Discrimination against homosexuals in Europe and both North and South America took on a new and more virulent form from the late 1930s through the 1960s. In Germany the widespread acceptance that homosexuals had experienced under the Weimar Republic (especially in Berlin) was shattered during the Nazi regime. The Nazis employed a range of increasingly severe measures to repress homosexual conduct, including surveillance, registration, incarceration, medical experimentation, and, ultimately, extermination. Although female homosexual conduct was not expressly proscribed or as actively repressed by the state, lesbians suffered persecution as well. After World War II during the McCarthy era, homosexuals in the United States fell under increasingly severe pressures to conceal their identity. Those who refused risked alienation and, in many cases, loss of livelihood. Such social pressures gave rise to political and social organizations in both the United States and Europe throughout the 1950s and 1960s.

In the early twenty-first century a patchwork of laws and varying degrees of social acceptance exist throughout the world alongside mainstream television programs and other media forms that encourage social integration. These vastly different approaches reflect the great divergence of views about homosexuality and same-sex sexual conduct. In many parts of the world homosexuality is increasingly seen as a legitimate identity, with same-sex sexual behavior being a natural consequence of that identity. Among other groups, including major religious institutions, same-sex sexual attraction is seen as disordered and same-sex sexual conduct as a destructive aberration.

Legal Regulation: Prohibition and Protection

The legal position of homosexuals varies significantly from country to country—from constitutionally entrenched freedom, from discrimination on the basis of sexual orientation, to laws that make homosexual acts punishable by death. Even among countries where all individuals are guaranteed a standard of equal treatment, controversies remain over whether homosexuals

should be protected as such. One example is the continuing debate in the United States over hate crimes legislation and the inclusion of sexual orientation as grounds for that kind of criminal charge. Another example is the wide range of contemporary responses to same-sex marriages, partnerships, or civil unions.

Until very recently no legal protection on the basis of sexual orientation could be found at the international level. Although the horrors of World War II gave rise to significant advances in the protection of individuals and identifiable groups under international law, such protection did not extend to homosexuals. Notwithstanding the mass execution of homosexuals during World War II, there is virtually no mention of this victim group in the judgment of the International Military Tribunal at Nuremberg. Nor did homosexuals find protection in the 1948 UN Convention on the Prevention and Punishment of the Crime of Genocide, an instrument drafted on the heels of World War II and designed to protect groups from discriminatory annihilation. The continuing lack of protection for homosexuals as a group likely flowed, at least in part, from the belief that homosexuality is not intrinsic or fundamental to one's identity, but that it is simply a matter of aberrant behavior that could be justifiably regulated. Indeed for many years, the leading psychiatric diagnostic manual listed homosexuality as a mental illness, greatly influencing public opinion.

While international criminal law evolved little during the cold war, it gained renewed vigor following the establishment of the International Criminal Tribunals for the Former Yugoslavia (ICTY) and Rwanda (ICTR) in the mid-1990s. Despite the great strides in jurisprudence these institutions made, such developments did little to advance the legal protection of homosexuals. The Rome Statute of the International Criminal Court (ICC), adopted in 1998 and in many ways reflecting the culmination of international developments, fails to make any reference to sexual orientation. Indeed, the term *gender*, included as one of the grounds for the crime of persecution, is expressly defined as "the two sexes, male and female, within the context of society." The definition continues, "The term 'gender' does not indicate any meaning different from the above," in an apparent attempt to prevent the interpretation of gender from including sexual orientation (Rome Statute, Article 7[3]). Although the definition of persecution includes the residual phrase "or other grounds that are universally recognized as impermissible under international law," the use of "universal" could prevent the ICC from interpreting this phrase to include sexual orientation given the lack of consensus noted above.

Similarly, international human rights law has been slow to afford protection from discrimination on the basis of sexual orientation. The nondiscrimination provisions of the major human rights treaties make no mention of sexual orientation. Nevertheless, advances have been made through the jurisprudence of international human rights mechanisms. The earliest developments were grounded in the right to privacy, encompassing such matters as the decriminalization of same-sex sexual conduct, but failing to extend into public life.

Over time, however, the conceptual framework employed by human rights mechanisms has shifted from one grounded in privacy to one based on nondiscrimination. For example, the Human Rights Committee, the treaty body charged with monitoring implementation of the International Covenant on Civil and Political Rights, has found that "the reference to 'sex' in [the nondiscrimination provisions of the Covenant] is to be taken as including sexual orientation" (*Toonen v. Australia*, para. 8.7). While the Human Rights Committee ultimately grounded its decision in that case on the right to privacy, its reference to and interpretation of the nondiscrimination provision marked a significant turning point in the protection of homosexuals as such. Similar advances have been made among regional human rights mechanisms, particularly in Europe.

Even within the European human rights system, though, the scope of protection from discrimination remains limited. The European Court of Human Rights ultimately found that France's refusal to authorize the adoption of a child by a single gay man, a decision "based decisively on the latter's avowed homosexuality," was not discriminatory under Article 14 of the European Convention on Human Rights (*Fretté v. France*, para. 43).

Nonetheless, a clear trend exists within human rights law toward greater protection of homosexuals as a group. This trend is also reflected in the domestic sphere. For example, within the context of refugee law, domestic courts in many countries are increasingly granting asylum on the basis of persecution against homosexuals as a social group.

SEE ALSO Holocaust; Identification; Persecution

BIBLIOGRAPHY

Boswell, John (1980). *Christianity, Social Tolerance, and Homosexuality*. Chicago: University of Chicago Press.

Fone, Bryne (2000). *Homophobia: A History*. New York: Metropolitan Books.

Fretté v. France. Case No. 36515/97, European Court of Human Rights (February 2002).

Grau, Günter, ed. (1995). *Hidden Holocaust? Gay and Lesbian Persecution in Germany 1933–1945*. London: Cassell.

Human Rights Committee (1992). *Views on Toonen v. Australia*. Communication No. CCPR/C/50/D/488/1992.

Joseph, Sherry and Pawan Dhall (2000). " 'No Silence Please, We're Indians!'—Les-Bi-Gay Voices from India." In *Different Rainbows*, ed. By Peter Drucker. London: Millivres Ltd.

Ng, Vivien W. (1989). "Homosexuality and the State in Late Imperial China." In *Hidden from History: Reclaiming the Gay & Lesbian Past*, ed. Martin B. Duberman, Martha Vicinus, and George Chauncey, Jr. New York: Nal Books.

John Cerone
Jason Bricker

Huguenots

Huguenot was the popular term for French Protestants—the men and women who formed the French Reformed Church—from the mid-sixteenth through eighteenth centuries. The word's origins are unclear and contested. Opponents initially used it as a slur. Only gradually did *Huguenot* become the accepted designation for a French Calvinist. The Reformation had an early, forceful impact on France, and by the 1550s the Calvinist or Reformed tradition dominated. Reformed Protestantism, inspired by the Frenchman John Calvin and his ecclesiastical reorganization of the francophone city of Geneva, spread quickly throughout the realm. The growth of the Huguenot community provoked strong Catholic and monarchial reaction. Religious warfare erupted in 1562 and the turmoil devastated France for nearly forty years.

In addition to the clash of Catholic and Protestant armies, the assassination of individual political leaders and less calculated outbreaks of collective violence—deadly riots and vicious massacres—underscored the intense and bitter enmity surrounding these rivalries. The most famous incident was the Saint Bartholomew's Day Massacre of August 24, 1572. Huguenot nobles had gathered in Paris for the marriage of their leader Henry of Navarre to the king's sister. The king and queen mother seized the occasion to rid themselves of political and religious opponents. Zealous Parisian Catholics soon transformed the purge into carnage as they butchered thousands of Huguenots. The constant warfare and brutality did not cease until 1598 with the king's proclamation of the Edict of Nantes. The royal legislation established structures for promoting peaceful coexistence between Catholics and Protestants.

The Huguenots were never more than a minority. At their height during the 1560s they may have

Painting depicting the St. Bartholomew's Day Massacre in Paris, August 24, 1572. In the months that followed, similar massacres of Huguenots took place in Rouen, Orléans, Lyon, Bourges, Toulouse, Bordeaux, and other French cities and towns. The artist, François Dubois, was an eyewitness to the events in Paris and a Huguenot who survived the rampage. [THE PICTURE DESK]

amounted to 10 percent of the population. This initial growth did not survive the Saint Bartholomew's Massacre; afterwards Huguenot ranks thinned considerably. By the close of the sixteenth century they were no more than 7 to 8 percent of the French populace. Their strength further eroded in the seventeenth century. When Louis XIV finally revoked the Edict of Nantes in October 1685, the Huguenot community was 800,000 to 1 million persons.

The options for French Protestants after 1685 were limited and demanding. Some individuals were extraordinary in their resistance. For most, however, open defiance and the prospect of prison, the galleys, or execution were unattractive. The vast majority converted to Catholicism, if insincerely. About one-fifth of Huguenots—150,000 to 200,000—chose exile in the Swiss cities, various German states, the Netherlands, British Isles, and eventually North America, South Africa, Scandinavia, and Russia.

Many Huguenots who remained in France began to assemble secretly in the *désert* (wilderness), a moving biblical image that emphasized their tenacity. Women assumed an especially strong role. They led clandestine worship complete with prayers, scriptural readings, and the singing of psalms. Some women endured agonizing confinement. Those arrested at illicit religious assemblies were incarcerated in Catholic hospitals and nunneries. Women judged to have committed more serious offenses went to prison, where they often remained forgotten for decades. Finally, a few young women, and in time men, turned to prophesy, becoming anguished voices crying out to protest their oppression.

The prophesying movement spread and eventually turned violent as the more zealous adherents sought to wreak God's retribution on their Catholic oppressors. The murderous, protracted revolt of the Camisards—so designated for the simple white shirts that the insurgents wore—began in 1702. Protestants carried out acts of vengeance, such as murdering priests and burning churches. They also waged organized guerrilla warfare. Royal troops responded with further repression and reprisals. The fighting dragged on for eight years and led to the death of many Protestants and Catholics.

Although the active persecution of Huguenots gradually abated, the restoration of their civil status occurred only with the Edict of the Toleration in 1787 and the French Revolution two years later. In the end the ordeal of the désert became the heroic age for French Protestants. The memory of the eighteenth-century persecution and attending diaspora has eclipsed earlier struggles in shaping collective identity and goes to the very meaning of Huguenot.

SEE ALSO Catholic Church; Massacres; Persecution

BIBLIOGRAPHY

Diefendorf, B. (1991). *Beneath the Cross: Catholics and Huguenots in Sixteenth-Century Paris.* New York: Oxford University Press.

Mentzer, R. A., and A. Spicer, eds. (2002). *Society and Culture in the Huguenot World, 1559–1685.* Cambridge: Cambridge University Press.

Van Ruymbeke, B., and R. Sparks, eds. (2003). *Memory and Identity: Minority Survival among the Huguenots in France and the Atlantic Diaspora.* Columbia: University of South Carolina Press.

Raymond A. Mentzer

Humanitarian Intervention

The doctrine of humanitarian intervention in international law typically refers to the threat or use of force by a state, group of states, or international organization primarily for the purpose of protecting the nationals of a particular state from widespread deprivations of internationally recognized human rights, including genocide and crimes against humanity. Because the doctrine is not expressly recognized in the Charter of the United Nations (UN) as a permissible basis for using force, many states and scholars oppose its use, at least when exercised without authorization by the UN Security Council. Nevertheless, some states and scholars favor the use of the doctrine in extreme situations on the grounds that, in any just legal system, the value of preventing the loss of life and suffering must outweigh the value of normative constraints on the use of transnational force.

Humanitarian Intervention Prior to the UN Charter

Although he did not use the term *humanitarian intervention*, the great Dutch jurist Hugo Grotius (1583–1645) asserted in his treatise on the law of war and peace that resort to war was permissible to assist peoples who were resisting extreme tyranny. In developing this view, Grotius drew on earlier just war doctrines associated with Saint Augustine and Saint Thomas Aquinas. Grotius's position was adopted by many scholars throughout the nineteenth century. Moreover, state practice during the period reflected a belief in the doctrine of humanitarian intervention. Thus, during the 1800s European powers repeatedly intervened in areas under the control of the Ottoman Empire because, according to the interveners, such action was necessary to protect Christian minorities from Ottoman rule.

Throughout this period, however, there was no accepted prohibition on states' resort to the use of armed force in international law, so the concept of humanitarian intervention was not an exception to a general prohibition but, rather, a basis for explaining why an intervention was just. After the outbreak of World War I in 1914, states became increasingly interested in legally prohibiting the resort to war, out of a belief that international legal constraints could help prevent or at least contain warfare. This interest led first to an effort in 1919 to discourage warfare by creating the League of Nations (which promoted the use of arbitration to resolve disputes backed by the possibility of collective action against a recalcitrant state) and then to the outright renunciation of war as an instrument of national policy in the 1928 Kellogg–Briand Pact (a treaty that, as of 2004, remains in force with over sixty parties). These efforts, however, failed to prevent the outbreak of World War II, plunging the world once again into a lengthy and deadly conflict that only ended with the deployment of a terrible new type of weaponry, nuclear arms. Moreover, the conduct of the Axis powers during World War II demonstrated the potential for grave misuse of the doctrine of humanitarian intervention: Japan invaded Manchuria in 1931 claiming a right to protect the local population from anarchy; Italy invaded Ethiopia in 1935 claiming a need to abolish slavery; and Germany invaded Czechoslovakia in 1939 claiming, in part, a need to protect the Czech peoples.

States emerged from World War II even more committed to creating legal structures that would prevent the resort to war. The four powers that met at Dumbarton Oaks, Washington, D.C., in 1944 (China, the Soviet Union, the United States, and the United Kingdom) to begin drafting what would become the UN Charter were aware of the atrocities committed by Nazi Germany against its own nationals, but the four-power focus was broadly prohibiting the use of military force, and not allowing any exceptions to that prohibition for the protection of human rights. Although states meeting at San Francisco in 1945 to complete and adopt the UN Charter ultimately included in it some provisions on the recognition of and respect for human rights, the Charter remained heavily oriented toward preventing the resort to war, without any express language permitting humanitarian intervention.

French troops arriving in northern Rwanda as part of Operation Turquoise, a French-led UN peacekeeping mission, June 1994. Later media reports accused France of arming and supporting the Hutu-dominated government even after word of its atrocities and campaign of genocide reached the West. [PETER TURNLEY/CORBIS]

The UN Charter Paradigm

Article 2(4) of the UN Charter asserts that states "shall refrain in their international relations from the threat or use of force against the territorial integrity or political independence of any state, or in any other manner inconsistent with the Purposes of the United Nations." Although some scholars have argued that this language allows for humanitarian intervention if the purpose of the intervention is not to alter the boundaries of a state or to topple a government, the negotiating history of the text confirms that the drafters sought a broad prohibition.

The UN Charter, however, contains two exceptions to this broad prohibition. First, Article 51 of the Charter provides that "[n]othing in the present Charter shall impair the inherent right of individual or collective self-defense if an armed attack occurs against a Member of the United Nations, until the Security Council has taken measures necessary to maintain international peace and security." Second, the remaining articles in Chapter VII of the Charter envisage the Security Council making decisions to address a threat to

peace, including authorizing states to use armed force. The Security Council consists of fifteen member states, five of which are permanent members (China, France, Russia, the United Kingdom, and the United States) and the remaining ten are elected periodically by the General Assembly. For the Security Council to adopt any nonprocedural decision, the affirmative vote of nine members is required, including the affirmative vote or abstention of all five permanent members.

Thus, the basic UN Charter paradigm is that states are prohibited from using force against other states, but may do so when they are acting in self-defense against an armed attack or when authorized by the UN Security Council. The Security Council, in turn, is only empowered to act when there is a "threat to the peace," which was originally conceived as transnational threats. The doctrine of humanitarian intervention does not fit easily within this paradigm, since a state that uses force to protect the human rights of another state's nationals is not acting in self-defense against an armed attack and, in many instances, the deprivation of human rights may not entail a threat to transnational peace. At the

encyclopedia of GENOCIDE *and* CRIMES AGAINST HUMANITY

same time actual situations where the doctrine of humanitarian intervention is at issue often do not fall neatly into such categories. In situations of widespread deprivations of human rights, there may be foreign nationals threatened (thus allowing an intervening state to claim a right of self-defense to protect those nationals) and there may be collateral effects that arguably threaten transnational peace (thus allowing Security Council action), such as by flows of refugees across a border or by the agitation of related ethnic or religious groups in an adjacent state. In such situations it may be difficult to ascertain whether an intervention is purely humanitarian.

Even if an intervention is purely humanitarian, the practice of the Security Council reveals general acceptance that the Security Council may declare any situation a threat to the peace, even if its transnational effects appear minimal. As for purely humanitarian intervention without Security Council authorization, a minority of states and scholars have maintained either that the meaning of Article 2(4) must be interpreted to allow humanitarian intervention in extreme situations (since it cannot be that peoples in 1945 accepted the charter to the extent that it would protect a government engaged in murdering its people) or that such intervention should be regarded as legitimate even if not technically legal.

Humanitarian Intervention after the UN Charter
During the period of the cold war (1946–1989) the prospect of nuclear confrontation between East and West helped promote strong unity on the prohibition of the transnational use of force, thus tempering any enthusiasm for the doctrine of humanitarian intervention. At the same time, the East–West divide resulted in repeated deadlocks at the UN Security Council, with any one of the five permanent member nations having the power to veto a proposed action. As such, although many states might have supported efforts by the Security Council to authorize humanitarian intervention, the Security Council itself proved incapable of serving that function, thus fueling calls by a minority of scholars for greater latitude in allowing regional organizations or states acting alone to use force to protect human rights.

Despite those sentiments no authoritative state practice developed in support of a doctrine of humanitarian intervention. In several instances a state intervened in a manner that appeared to protect human rights, but the state typically would justify its intervention on the basis of self-defense, thus evincing doubt even on the intervener's part that humanitarian concerns alone were permissible legal base for acting (e.g., Tanzania's intervention in Uganda in 1979 against Idi

Amin). Moreover, the international community, through the voice of the UN General Assembly, usually would condemn such interventions as unlawful (e.g., Vietnam's intervention in Cambodia in 1978 against the Khmer Rouge).

The end of the cold war in 1989 allowed for a transformation of the Security Council as a collective security mechanism. In several instances during the 1990s the Security Council authorized a transnational use of force to address a threat to the peace that, at its heart, involved a widespread deprivation of human rights. Thus, in December 1992 the Security Council authorized a U.S.–led intervention in Somalia to end a civil conflict that threatened the lives of hundreds of thousands of Somalis (from violence or starvation). In June 1994 the Security Council authorized France's intervention in Rwanda to end a brutal civil conflict and genocide between the Tutsis and Hutus. The slowness with which the Security Council acted—some 800,000 Tutsis were killed prior to the intervention—led to sharp criticism that powerful states were not living up to their moral responsibilities in addressing such crises. In July 1994 the Security Council authorized a U.S.–led intervention in Haiti to reverse a military coup that had ousted the democratically elected president, Jean-Bertrande Aristide.

Nonetheless, the Security Council remained incapable, in certain circumstances, of reaching agreement on such intervention. During 1998 and 1999 many states feared that President Slobodan Milosevic of the Federal Republic of Yugoslavia (FRY) was about to unleash a wave of ethnic cleansing (and perhaps genocide) against ethnic Albanians living in the FRY province of Kosovo. Milosevic was widely regarded as the architect of genocide and crimes against humanity in Bosnia-Herzegovina in the early 1990s; the International Criminal Tribunal for the former Yugoslavia, located in The Hague, indicted him for such crimes in 2001. Russia and China, however, were unwilling to support a Security Council resolution expressly authorizing the use of force against the FRY to protect the Kosovar Albanians. Consequently, in March 1999 states of the North Atlantic Treaty Organization (NATO) collectively decided that the intervention was justified as a matter of international law and policy, leading to a ten-week bombing campaign against the FRY. Ultimately, Milosevic backed down and agreed to withdraw all FRY military and paramilitary personnel from Kosovo.

The Kosovo incident may support an emerging acceptance by states in the post-Cold War era of a doctrine of humanitarian intervention even without Security Council approval, since the Kosovo intervention was supported by the nineteen NATO states and many non-NATO states as well, was not condemned by the General Assembly, and was legally justified by several governments with reference to the doctrine of humanitarian intervention. At the same time many states (including Russia and China) opposed and condemned as unlawful the use of force against the FRY, whereas other states that supported the intervention (such as the United States) asserted that its legality turned on a variety of factors, including prior Security Council resolutions identifying the FRY's actions as a threat to the peace.

Criteria for Conducting Humanitarian Intervention

Various scholars have sought to delineate criteria that should govern the resort to humanitarian intervention. In the wake of the Kosovo incident one highly-respected group of experts—convened as the International Commission on Intervention and State Sovereignty (ICISS)—advanced in a 2001 report several criteria falling into four general categories.

First, the commission stated that there must be a just cause for the intervention, which can arise when there is serious and irreparable harm occurring (or likely to occur) to human beings. Specifically, the commission identified such harm as the "large scale loss of life, actual or apprehended, with genocidal intent or not, which is the product either of deliberate state action, or state neglect or inability to act, or a failed state situation." Such harm might also consist of "large scale 'ethnic cleansing', actual or apprehended, whether carried out by killing, forced expulsion, acts of terror or rape" (ICISS, 2001, p. 32).

Second, the commission advocated four precautionary principles as a means of ensuring that the intervention is undertaken properly. The primary purpose of the intervention must be to halt human suffering. All nonmilitary options for resolution of the crisis must first be explored. The scale, duration, and intensity of the intervention should be dictated by what is necessary to achieve the humanitarian objective. Finally, there must be a reasonable chance of success in halting the suffering, such that the consequences of action are not likely worse than those of inaction (ICISS, 2001, pp. 35–37).

Third, the commission urged that before embarking on such intervention, states must formally seek Security Council authorization. If Security Council authorization is not forthcoming, states should seek authorization from the General Assembly, regional, or subregional organizations. In the absence of such authority the commission did not declare humanitarian intervention to be unlawful, but noted that "in con-science-shocking situations crying out for action, . . . it is unrealistic to expect that concerned states will rule out other means and forms of action to meet the gravity and urgency of these situations" (ICISS, 2001, p. 55).

Finally, the commission proposed certain criteria to guide the military operation itself. The intervening military must have a clear and unambiguous mandate and the resources to support that mandate. When the intervention is conducted by several states, there must be a unified command, with clear channels of communication and chain of command. The intervening military must accept that there are limitations on the force to be used, since the objective is to protect the population of the state, not to completely defeat the state (at the same time the use of force cannot be limited to the protection of the intervening forces themselves). The intervening military must abide by precise rules of engagement that match its humanitarian objective, adhere to international humanitarian law, and coordinate their actions as much as possible with humanitarian organizations.

Criteria of this type provide useful guidance in the event that a state is considering a humanitarian intervention, but until such criteria are incorporated in a binding document and accepted by a wide variety of states, the legality of humanitarian intervention (at least in the absence of Security Council authorization) and the manner in which it is to be conducted will remain controversial.

SEE ALSO International Law; Prevention; United Nations

BIBLIOGRAPHY

Abiew, F. K. (1999). *The Evolution of the Doctrine and Practice of Humanitarian Intervention.* The Hague: Kluwer.

Chesterman, S. (2001). *Just War or Just Peace? Humanitarian Intervention and International Law.* New York: Oxford University Press.

Garrett, S. A. (1999). *Doing Good and Doing Well: An Examination of Humanitarian Intervention.* Westport, Conn.: Praeger.

Holzgrefe, J. L., and R. O. Keohane, eds. (2003). *Humanitarian Intervention: Ethical, Legal and Political Dilemmas.* Cambridge, U.K.: Cambridge University Press.

International Commission on Intervention and State Sovereignty (ICISS) (2001). *The Responsibility to Protect.* Ottawa: International Development Research Centre.

Murphy, S. D. (1996). *Humanitarian Intervention: The United Nations in an Evolving World Order.* Philadelphia: University of Pennsylvania Press.

Tesón, F. R. (1997). *Humanitarian Intervention: An Inquiry into Law and Morality,* 2nd edition. Irvington-on-Hudson, N.Y.: Transnational.

Wheeler, N. J. (2000). *Saving Strangers: Humanitarian Intervention in International Society.* Oxford, U.K.: Oxford University Press.

Sean D. Murphy

Humanitarian Law

International Humanitarian Law (IHL) is the *jus in bello,* or the law that regulates the conduct of armed conflicts. The International Committee of the Red Cross describes IHL as "the body of rules which, in wartime, protects people who are not or are no longer participating in the hostilities. Its central purpose is to limit and prevent human suffering in times of armed conflict. The rules are to be observed not only by governments and their armed forces, but also by armed opposition groups and any other parties to a conflict." Serious violations of this law are called war crimes.

Since World War II, the term *IHL* has also been used by scholars to include crimes against humanity insofar as that category of crimes has emerged from war crimes, even though it is now unrelated to war crimes and is applicable in times of war and peace; and genocide, insofar as that crime was originally a broader extension of crimes against humanity, which applies in times of war and peace.

IHL does not include the *jus ad bellum,* meaning the law applicable to the right or legitimacy to resort to war. Thus, "crimes against peace," as referred to in the International Military Tribunal Charter and the International Military Tribunal for the Far East Statute, and since the United Nations Charter's adoption known as aggression, are not part of IHL.

Framework

IHL's genesis dates back more than five thousand years to various civilizations that evolved humanitarian principles underlying the regulation of armed conflicts. In time, these humanitarian principles formed an interwoven fabric of norms and rules designed to prevent certain forms of harm from befalling civilian noncombatants and some categories of combatants such as the sick, wounded, shipwrecked, and prisoners, as well as persons covered by the Red Cross/Red Crescent emblems and those who provide medical and humanitarian assistance during armed conflicts. Eventually, the more serious breaches of these rules were criminalized.

IHL's normative development has never been part of a consistent or cohesive international legal policy. Instead, the law developed as a haphazard mixture of conventions, customs, general principles, and the writings of scholars. At first, the Hague conventions of 1899 and 1907 codified some of the customary princi-

ples and norms on which the state parties could agree. The Four Geneva Conventions of August 12, 1949, became a more comprehensive codification, later to be supplemented by two protocols in 1977.

Throughout history the tensions between humanitarian goals and military/political ones have been evident. Proponents of the former seek to expand the protections of persons and nonmilitary targets, to limit the use of force in general, and to restrict the use of certain weapons in particular. They have encountered resistance and opposition from those who press the concept of "military necessity" and seek to achieve victory through the fastest means and with the least costs, irrespective of the harm inflicted on the enemy. Humanitarian arguments alone have seldom been sufficient to induce states to limit the use of their might against their enemies, particularly against weaker ones who are incapable of inflicting reciprocal harm. Pragmatic and policy arguments, however, have greatly aided the development of IHL. Mutuality of interest and other considerations, such as economic costs and effectiveness, have combined with humanitarian ones to produce the existing body of norms and rules of conduct governing armed conflicts.

The Law of Armed Conflict Through the Ages

A historical review of the regulation of armed conflicts reveals that civilizations for more than five millennia have either prohibited or condemned unnecessary use of force against certain categories of persons and against certain targets. This historical process reveals the convergence and commonality of basic human values in diverse civilizations, in light of the fact that geographically separated groups have reached the same humanistic conclusions without, in some cases, any evidence of the migration of such ideas from one civilization to another. This convergence is embodied in the Preamble of the 1907 Hague Convention which indicates that such commonly shared values make up the "dictates of humanity" leading to the concept of "crimes against humanity."

The Chinese scholar Sun Tzu, in the fifth century BCE, asserted that in war it is important to "treat captives well, and care for them." He also wrote that a general should only attack the enemy's armies, "for the worst policy is to attack cities." The Chinese code of chivalry reveals that it is not the purpose of war to inflict unnecessary or excessive suffering on the enemy, nor is it useful. It was not until the late 1800s that Western civilization accepted the principle of prohibiting unnecessary human pain and suffering during wartime. This principle first appeared in the 1874 Brussels Declaration (Brussels Conference on the Laws and Cus-

Geneva headquarters of the International Committee of the Red Cross. The organization played a pivotal role in developing the four Geneva Conventions of August 12, 1949, for victims of war, still the core of modern international humanitarian law. [**VERNIER JEAN BERNARD/CORBIS SYGMA**]

toms of War) and was then included in the 1899 and 1907 Hague Conventions' Annexed Regulations. It is a basic principle of the 1949 Geneva Conventions and is considered to be part of customary international law. Like some other principles of IHL, namely, proportionality and discrimination, it is relative and subject in application to good judgment and good faith.

Parallel to the developments in China, and without evidence of the migration of Chinese ideas, the Indian civilization evidenced in the fourth century BCE the same values and policies. One of India's epic poems, *Ramayana,* reveals that it was expressly forbidden to use a mythical weapon that could obliterate an entire enemy nation because "such destruction en masse was forbidden by the ancient laws of war, even though [the enemy] was fighting an unjust war with an unrighteous objective." Another famous Hindu epic, the *Mahabharata,* which may date from as early as 200 BCE, similarly prohibits the use of hyperdestructive weapons. In the story, the mythical weapon called the *pasupathastra* was forbidden because its use was not conventional and Hindu teachings held that unconventional weapons were not moral.

Even though these tales are from mythological literature, they reflect social values. In the fourth century BCE, the Book of Manu developed norms based on these values. The Laws of Manu, as they were sometimes called, stated that "when a king fights his foes in battle, let him not strike with weapons concealed, nor with barbed, poisoned, or the points of which are blazed with fire . . . [because] these are the weapons of the wicked." The laws also prohibited weapons that caused unnecessary or excessive suffering. These included arrows with heated, poisoned, or hooked spikes and tips.

In ancient Greece, awareness existed that certain acts were contrary to traditional usages and principles spontaneously enforced by human conscience, thus establishing the applicability of customary law to armed conflicts. Herodotus recounts that as early as the fifth century BCE certain conduct was prohibited in Athens as "a transgression of the laws of men, and of the law of the human race generally, and not merely as a law applicable exclusively to the barbarians." In Homer's epic *The Odyssey,* the use of poisoned weapons was considered to be a grave violation to the way of the

encyclopedia of GENOCIDE *and* CRIMES AGAINST HUMANITY

gods. Once again, history records the recognition by a civilization that the "human race" has its laws.

Roman law evidenced these same values, probably inspired by the ancient Greeks. The Roman armies were more disciplined than those of any other ancient nation. They did not as a rule degenerate into indiscriminate slaughter and unrestrained devastation. They observed restrictions that others did not. This was the beginning of the notion of professionalism in armies that ripened in the nineteenth century to form a foundation for the modern law of armed conflict.

Such self-imposed restrictions were not universally respected. Ancient Greeks and Romans both applied the law of war only to civilized sovereign states, properly organized, and enjoying a regular constitution. Hence, barbarians and savage tribes were debarred from the benefits of these rules. The assumption was that such uncivilized combatants would not abide by the same rules. This assumption is reflected in the nineteenth-century law of armed conflict, namely, in the concept of mutuality of obligations.

Roman law also developed the terms *jus ad bellum* (the law governing the right to use armed force) and *jus in bello* (the law governing the conduct of hostilities), terms that continue to be used in contemporary international law. The Roman *jus belli*, or the law of war, served as a foundation for legal developments until the late 1800s.

The three monotheistic faiths of Judaism, Christianity, and Islam join in the affirmation of humanitarian principles. The second Book of Kings states:

> the King of Israel . . . said to Eli'sha, "My Father shall I slay them?". . . He answered, "You shall not slay them. Would you slay those whom you have taken captive with your sword and bow? Set bread and water before them that they may eat and drink and go to their master."

Another relevant text of the Old Testament is found in Deuteronomy, in which specific regulations for the conduct of sieges are spelled out:

> When thou shalt besiege a city a long time in making war against it to take it, thou shalt not destroy the trees thereof by wielding an axe against them; for thou mayest eat of them, but thou shalt not cut them down; for is the tree of the field man, that it should be besieged of thee? Only the trees of which thou knowest that they are not trees for food, them thou mayest destroy and cut down, that thou mayest build bulwarks against the city that makes war with thee, until it fall.

Traditional Jewish law in the Talmud also regulated the destruction of vegetation:

Josephus elaborates that this included not setting fire to their land or destroying beasts of labor. Maimonides flatly states that the destruction of fruit trees for the mere purpose of afflicting the civilian population is prohibited and, finally, we have the broad interpretation of Rabbi Ishmael that "not only are fruit trees but, by argument, from minor to major, stores of fruit itself may not be destroyed."

Jews honor the Sabbath and other holy days like Yom Kippur, when no warlike activities can be conducted; the same is true in Islam on the days of the Eid. In Medieval times, the Roman Catholic Church also specifically proscribed the conduct of war on particular days. The Archbishop of Arles proclaimed in 1035 that there was to be a "truce of God" from "vespers on Wednesday to sunrise on Monday."

The Islamic civilization had specific rules on the legitimacy of war and its conduct, based on the Koran and the Sunna, the tradition of the Prophet Muhammad, which are the two principal sources of the *Shari'a*, Islamic law. The Prophet Muhammad himself entered into a peace treaty with the Meccans, the treaty of Hudaibiya that provided for the protection of civilians.

Early Islamic values relating to warfare included the reduction of unnecessary or excessive suffering. The Koran enjoins on the victor the duty to feed captives. Also, Islamic legal treatises on the law of nations from the ninth century forbade the killing of women, children, elderly, blind, crippled, and the insane.

Since the Middle Ages, it has been primarily Western civilization that advanced the common values and shaped the principles, norms, and rules of conduct of what are now parts of IHL. The writings of Aristotle, Cicero, St. Augustine, and St. Thomas Aquinas set forth the philosophical premises for the conditions of legitimacy of war, the jus ad bellum, so as to distinguish between just and unjust war; but Western civilization also developed principles, norms, and rules of conduct limiting the means and harmful consequences of the conduct of war. St. Thomas Aquinas refers to these basic laws of humanity in the treatment of civilian noncombatants, the sick, wounded, and prisoners of war as follows, "these rules belong to the *jus gentium* which are deduced from natural law as conclusion principles." He called it "positive human law," not because it was codified, but because citizens of civilized nations had agreed to it.

As the laws of chivalry developed in medieval Western Europe, so did rules limiting the means and manner of conducting war. Heraldic courts developed a code of chivalry, enforced by the Christian princes

Flags of the International Red Cross and Red Crescent Movement fly at the societies' official museum, Geneva, Switzerland. The conventions on the protection of victims and conduct of war authored by their parent organization, the International Committee of the Red Cross, following World War II remain the core of international humanitarian law.[BARNABAS BOSSHART/CORBIS]

that regulated a knight's conduct in battle. The codes of chivalry prohibited the use of certain weapons, such as the cross-bow, whose use was forbidden by the Second Lateran Council of 1139.

National laws and military regulations followed the evolution of the law of armed conflict. Among early national regulations are those that Gustavus Adolphus of Sweden promulgated in 1621 in the *Articles of Military Laws to be Observed in the Wars.* They provided in the general article that "no Colonel or Captain shall command his soldiers to do any unlawful thing; which who so does, shall be punished according to the discretion of the judge." This was probably the first time that the rule of command responsibility was posited in a normative prescription. In the modern law of armed conflict it is a well-established principle.

In the United States, the first Articles of War, promulgated in 1775, contained explicit provisions for the punishment of officers who failed to keep good order among the troops. It also included a number of prescriptions for the protection of civilians, prisoners of war, and the sick and injured in the field. This provision was retained and strengthened in the Articles of War of 1806 and served as the basis for prosecutions arising out of the Civil War for conduct against the law of nations.

The most noteworthy national regulations are the United States Lieber Code of 1863, the 1880 *Oxford Manual,* the German General Staff *Kriegsbrauch im Landkriege* of 1902, and Great Britain's War Office *Manual of Military Law of 1929.* These are only some examples of national military regulations that preceded the "Law of Geneva."

Today most countries of the world have military or other legislation that includes either in whole or in part the norms of the four Geneva Conventions of August 12, 1949 and the two Additional Protocols of 1977. These conventions require the introduction of such norms in the national laws of the contracting parties, their dissemination, and training of military personnel to ensure compliance and to avoid claims of ignorance of the law.

Sources of Law and Legal Regimes

Assuming the broader meaning of IHL as encompassing all violations of the law of armed conflict, crimes against humanity, and genocide, it is necessary to distinguish between various legal regimes that pertain to the three subjects. They have not been brought together into a single legal regime, even though they all share the same goals and purposes of minimizing human harm and material damage.

The first legal regime is the customary international law applicable to the conduct of war, binding on all states. Its historical evolution described earlier ripened into the 1899 Hague Convention, which codified what the state parties considered the customary practices of states. That convention was amended in the 1907 Hague Convention No. IV on land warfare and its annexed regulations. Because the 1907 Convention and annexed regulations contained several broad principles that withstood the test of time, they are considered the foundation of customary international law applicable to armed conflicts. The four Geneva Conventions of August 12, 1949, which as of July 1, 2004, have been ratified by 192 states, are also deemed to reflect customary international law, as are parts of Protocol I (1977), which deals with conflicts of an international character (ratified by 161 states), and Protocol II (ratified by 156 states) relating to internal conflicts or civil wars. State parties and nonstate parties differ as to which provisions of these two protocols embody customary international law. Although it is thus clear that there is an overlap between the customary and conventional international law of armed conflict, there is a distinction between these two legal regimes that is confusing to nonexperts, particularly to those in the armed forces who have to apply these norms in the course of armed conflicts.

The Hague Conventions and the Geneva Conventions are often referred to as separate bodies of law because the main topic of regulation for each group differs to some extent. The Hague Conventions focus primarily on prohibited means of warfare, whereas the Geneva Conventions address the various categories of protected persons (civilians, sick, wounded, and prisoners of war). There is nonetheless considerable overlap in the so-called Law of the Hague and the Law of Geneva.

The regulation of armed conflict under customary or conventional international law is also divided on the basis of distinguishing conflicts of an international character from conflicts of a non-international character. The 1907 Hague Convention and its annexed regulations apply only to conflicts of an international character, that is conflicts between states. The Four Geneva Conventions of 1949 also generally apply to international conflicts, but they also establish a special regime for conflicts of a noninternational character. The latter are regulated by Article 3, which is identical in all four Geneva Conventions, and by Protocol II (1977), which deals exclusively with conflicts of a noninternational character. Common Article 3 of the Four Geneva Conventions of 1949 is also deemed part of customary international law, as are some parts of Additional Protocol II (1977). In addition, there are purely domestic conflicts that some experts argue should be included under Common Article 3 and Protocol II. Minor domestic or internal conflicts that do not rise to the threshold level of violence to be regulated by Common Article 3 or Protocol II are subject to another legal regime that is discussed later.

The existence of three sublegal regimes applicable to conflicts of an international and noninternational character and minor domestic or internal conflicts is incongruous insofar as the goals and purposes of all three regimes are the same, namely, the protection of certain persons and targets in times of violent conflict. Scholars have argued that there is no valid conceptual basis to distinguish between the same protections offered to the same persons and targets, depending on whether the conflict is legally defined as being of an international or a noninternational character or purely domestic or internal. The distinction, however, exists because it reflects the interests of governments who do not wish to give insurgents and combatants engaged in domestic conflicts with their government a legal status likely to give these groups political legitimacy. Governments usually argue that the resort to violence by domestic insurgent groups is in the nature of terrorism and thus deny them not only legitimacy, but the fundamental safeguards and protections contained in the regulation of armed conflict.

Under the 1949 Geneva Conventions, "grave breaches" include, inter alia, murder, torture, rape, mistreatment of prisoners of war and civilians, wanton and willful destruction of public and private property, destruction of cultural and religious monuments and objects, use of civilian and prison-of-war human shields, collective punishment of civilians and prisoners of war. Common Article 3 does not contain the same specificity, although scholars argue that the prohibitions are the same. Common Article 3 refers to transgressions of its prohibitions as "violations" and not as "grave breaches."

The 1949 Geneva Conventions and Protocol I (1977) establish certain consequences for "grave breaches," which include the duty for states to criminalize these violations in their domestic laws, to prosecute or extradite those who commit such violations, and to provide other states with judicial assistance in the investigation or prosecution of such "grave breaches." The Conventions also establish a basis for universal jurisdiction so that all state parties to the Geneva Conventions can prosecute such offenders, and removes statutes of limitation for such offenses. Common Article 3 of the 1949 Geneva Conventions and Protocol II (1977) do not contain the same explicit legal obligations. Scholars argue that the obligations to prevent and suppress "violations" of Common Article 3 and Protocol II (1977) should be treated in the same manner and with the same legal consequences as the "grave breaches" of the 1949 Conventions and Protocol I (1977); that is, as war crimes.

Contemporary doctrinal developments complement customary and conventional international law. In other words, the writings of scholars become the bridge between the different legal regimes of customary and conventional international law, the "Law of the Hague" and the "Law of Geneva" and between the subregimes of conflicts of an international character and conflicts of a noninternational character. This proposition is also bolstered by the fact that both conventional and customary international law are predicated on certain general principles enunciated in both the "Law of the Hague" and the "Law of Geneva," such as the principles of prohibiting the infliction of unnecessary human pain and suffering, proportionality, and discrimination in the use of force.

Prohibitions and restrictions on the use of certain weapons are deemed part of the customary law of armed conflict, but control of weaponry usually arises out of specific international conventions. Nonetheless, overarching principles contained in both customary and conventional international law prohibit the infliction of unnecessary human pain and suffering and require proportionality in the use of force.

The first efforts to proscribe weapons that cause unnecessary pain and suffering developed in 1868 in the St. Petersburg Declaration, which prohibits the use of explosive projectiles. The subsequent Brussels International Declaration Concerning the Laws and Customs of War (1874) states, "the only legitimate object which states should have in view during war is to weaken the enemy without inflicting upon him unnecessary suffering." Based on this principle, a 1925 protocol was adopted for the Prohibition of the Use of Asphyxiating, Poisonous, or Other Gases. A protocol prohibiting bacteriological methods of warfare followed, and later treaties addressed other weapons, culminating in the Anti-Personnel Mine Convention of 1997. In 1980 a major effort was undertaken in the Convention on Prohibi-

tions or Restrictions on the Use of Certain Conventional Weapons Which May be Deemed to Be Excessively Injurious or to Have Indiscriminate Effects. Four additional protocols have been adopted to ban or restrict Non-Detectable Fragments; the Use of Mines, Booby-Traps, and Other Devices; the Use of Incendiary Weapons; and Blinding Laser Weapons. The treaties clearly indicate continuity in the evolution of the basic principles mentioned earlier, and the efforts of the international community from 1868 to date in its pursuit of the humanization of armed conflicts. Governments argue that each and every one of the 73 conventions prohibiting or restricting the use of certain weapons is binding only on the states parties to the particular treaty. Yet, both customary international law and general principles of law also apply and are binding upon nonstate parties to these conventions.

Weapons of mass destruction, including chemical, biological, and nuclear weapons, which inflict unnecessary pain and suffering, also violate the principle of discrimination because these weapons cannot distinguish between combatants and noncombatants. The prohibition of chemical and biological weapons in the 1925 Protocol for the Prohibition of the Use in War of Asphyxiating, Poisonous, or Other Gases, and of Bacteriological Methods of Warfare and the 1993 Chemical Weapons Convention (which carries criminal consequences), reflect customary law principles, as does the 1972 Convention on the Prohibition of the Development, Production, and Stockpiling of Bacteriological (Biological) and Toxic Weapons and on Their Destruction. Notwithstanding the efforts of a majority of the state parties, the 1972 Biological Weapons Convention has not been amended to parallel the same level of prohibition and criminalization achieved by the 1993 Chemical Weapons Convention, because of the opposition of the United States government, which views such a regime as placing undo burdens on the American chemical and pharmaceutical industries. For similar but different political/military considerations, nuclear weapons have not so far been banned, even though they clearly, if used, violate the principle of discrimination between combatants and protected persons, and inflict unnecessary human pain and suffering on civilian populations. They also cause damage to the present and future environment and indiscriminately have an impact on future health. Thus, politics, more than rationality and humanitarian considerations, frequently impedes the development of international law.

An example illustrating the tension between international humanitarian law and the political/military interests of certain governments is the 1997 Convention on the Prohibition of the Use, Stockpiling, Production, and Transfer of Anti-Personnel Mines and on their Destruction. The states parties take the position that the prohibition of landmines that cannot be detonated or removed after the end of a conflict is necessary because they have proven to cause unnecessary human pain and suffering to innocent civilians long after the end of a conflict. Other governments, such as that of the United States, continue to claim that the use of landmines even without the ability to detonate or remove them after the end of a conflict is permissible. Clearly, the use of landmines violates the principle of discrimination between combatants and noncombatants, but proponents of their continued availability as a weapon argue that the principle of military necessity justifies the use of landmines without restrictions. Although military necessity may permit the use of mines in times of armed conflict, it is not a justification for not having mines that can be detonated after the end of the conflict, nor is it a justification for failing to require the state that placed these mines to remove them after the conflict's end.

The Expanded Meaning of Humanitarian Law
The expanded contemporary meaning of IHL includes crimes against humanity and genocide. There are two reasons for this inclusion, even though both of these crimes apply in peacetime as well as during war, in contrast to the law of armed conflict. Crimes against humanity originated in the work of the 1919 Commission on the Responsibility of the Authors of War and War Crimes, which was established after World War I by the preliminary Peace Conference in Paris. In that original conception, the notion of what was then called crimes against the laws of humanity was an extension of "war crimes" as defined in the 1907 Hague Convention and annexed regulations. The 1945 International Military Tribunal Charter, relying upon the 1919 Commission's concept, defined "crimes against humanity" as an international crime in Article 6(c). The Far East Tribunal followed suit in 1946. In both of these instruments, the connection to "war crimes" was necessary. Subsequently, that connection was removed, first by a 1950 report of the International Law Commission and then in the statutes of the ad hoc Tribunal for Rwanda and the International Criminal Court. The statute of the International Criminal Tribunal for the Former Yugoslavia preserves a connection between "crimes against humanity" and an armed conflict.

In 1948 the United Nations adopted the Convention on the Prevention and Punishment of the Crime of Genocide, which was intended to encompass "crimes against humanity." But the latter concept is broader and includes conduct not covered by the Genocide Convention. Genocide requires a specific intent to "eliminate in whole or in part" a "national, ethnic, or religious group," which excludes social and political groups, whereas crimes against humanity protects any group of persons against whom a state policy of persecution is directed and does not require a specific intent to eliminate the group in whole or in part.

Since the end of World War II, and with the establishment of the United Nations, a parallel development has taken place in the legal regime of international human rights law (HRL). Like IHL, HRL springs from the same commonly shared human values. Its norms and standards, however, apply in times of peace, but many of them also apply in times of war. For example, the right to life and the protection of physical integrity are protected under both IHL and HRL. Similarly, the protection of public and private property, cultural monuments and objects, and cultural heritage are equally protected under IHL and HRL. Other human rights may be curtailed in times of war or other national emergency. Thus there is an imperfect overlap between IHL and HRL.

Since the two legal regimes have different political constituencies, it is frequently argued by governments and military establishments that IHL should be kept separate and apart from HRL. Although that argument is methodologically appealing, it ignores the fact that HRL also applies in times of war, save for the human rights that may be suspended temporarily during wartime. If the aim is to protect persons and certain objects or property, then it makes little legal sense to have two superimposed and separate legal regimes whose ultimate goals and purposes, as well as specific protections are the same. A good example is the rights of victims to reparations and other forms of redress, which should not be distinguished on the basis of whether the violation occurs under IHL or HRL.

The inclusion within the meaning of IHL of violations of the law of armed conflict (whether they be called "war crimes" or "grave breaches" of the Geneva Conventions or "violations" of Common Article 3 of the Geneva Conventions and Protocol II), crimes against humanity, and genocide is conceptually justified from a humanistic perspective, namely, that of the protection of persons from certain depredations. For the same reason, HRL should also be integrated in a single legal regime. Suffice it to recall that torture is prohibited under HRL by the 1984 United Nations Convention Against Torture and Other Cruel, Inhuman, or Degrading Treatment, which criminalizes acts of torture. It is also prohibited under IHL by both conventional and customary international law, and is a "grave breach" of the Geneva Conventions, as well as a war crime. Other protections of life and physical integrity contained in IHL and HRL also evidence this conclusion. Since the goals and purposes of IHL and HRL are the protection of persons, it should make no difference whether the context is one of war or peace, or whether it is that of a conflict of an international or noninternational character, or a minor internal conflict.

The International Court of Justice, in an advisory opinion rendered in July 2004, held as follows: "the Court considers that the protection offered by human rights conventions does not cease in case of armed conflicts as regards the relationship between international humanitarian law and human rights law, some rights may be exclusively matters of international humanitarian law; others may be exclusively matters of human rights law; yet others may be matters of both these branches of international law." The International Court of Justice concluded that human rights law is the general applicable law and that international humanitarian law is the lex specialis.

SEE ALSO Crimes Against Humanity; Geneva Conventions on the Protection of Victims of War; Genocide; Hague Conventions of 1907; Human Rights

BIBLIOGRAPHY

Bassiouni, M. Cherif, ed. (1997). *International Criminal Law Conventions and Their Penal Provisions*. Irvington-on-Hudson, N.Y.: Transnational Publishers.

Bassiouni, M. Cherif, ed. (1999). "The Normative Framework of International Humanitarian Law: Overlaps, Gaps, and Ambiguities." In *International Criminal Law*, 2nd revised edition. Ardsley, N.Y.: Transnational Publishers.

Bassiouni, M. Cherif, ed. (2000). *A Manual on International Humanitarian Law and Arms Control Agreements*. Ardsley, N.Y.: Transnational Publishers.

Bassiouni, M. Cherif (2003). *Introduction to International Criminal Law*. Ardsley, NY : Transnational Publishers.

Best, Geoffrey (1980). *Humanity in Warfare*. New York: Columbia University Press.

Fleck, Dieter, ed. (1995). *The Handbook of Humanitarian Law in Armed Conflicts*. New York: Oxford University Press.

Green, Leslie. (2000). *The Contemporary Law of Armed Conflict*, 2nd edition. Yonkers, NY: Juris.

Howard, M., G. Andreopoulos, and M. Shulman (1994). *The Laws of War: Constraints on Warfare in the Western World*. New Haven, Conn.: Yale University Press.

Kalshoven, Frits (1987). *Constraints on the Waging of War*. Geneva: International Committee of the Red Cross.

Keen, Maurice H. (1965). *The Laws of War in the Middle Ages*. Toronto: University of Toronto Press.

Levie, Howard S. (1986). *The Code of International Armed Conflict*. New York : Oceana Publications.

Meron, Theodor (1989). *Human Rights and Humanitarian Norms as Customary Law*. New York: Oxford University Press.

Meron, Theodor, ed. (1984). *Human Rights in International Law: Legal and Policy Issues*. Oxford: Clarendon Press.

Schindler, Dietrich, and Jiří Toman (2004). *The Laws of Armed Conflicts: A Collection of Conventions, Resolutions, and Other Documents*, 4th revised edition. Leiden, Netherlands: Martinus Nijhoff.

M. Cherif Bassiouni

Human Rights

Human rights can mean different things to different people, but perhaps the best way of defining human rights is to refer to the body of international human rights law that has come into being over the past five decades. Today, there are literally thousands of ratifications to dozens of human rights treaties—coming out of every region of the world. Solemn declarations by political leaders and others reinforce this international legal regime, and there are numerous institutions that have been created to oversee its implementation. The most broadly based treaties are the International Covenant on Civil and Political Rights and the International Covenant on Economic, Social, and Cultural Rights— each of which has been ratified by approximately 150 countries. Regional human rights systems exist in Europe, Africa, and the Americas. Other more specialized treaties deal with human rights violations that center on racial discrimination, women, children, migrant workers, torture, minorities, and labor rights.

The United Nations (UN) Convention on the Prevention and Punishment of the Crime of Genocide (Genocide Convention) was adopted by the UN General Assembly on December 9, 1948, a day before its seminal adoption of the Universal Declaration of Human Rights. The Genocide Convention might be thought of as the first contemporary "human rights" convention, although earlier international treaties addressed concerns such as the slave trade, trafficking in women, and workers' rights.

Genocide is a particular form of mass killing, and it may be the ultimate human rights violation, since it is directed not only against individuals but against the communities to which those individuals belong. In addition, the Genocide Convention codified genocide as an international crime, and placed international legal obligations on states to prevent and punish that crime. This dual character—as human rights violation and international crime—renders genocide almost unique; only the international treatment of the crime of torture, which came about much later, is similar.

The Human Rights Content of the Genocide Convention

The Genocide Convention deals only with the most serious kinds of human rights violations, although its adoption in 1948 was a landmark in the evolution of protection for human rights. Today, however, conduct outlawed by the Genocide Convention is also effectively prohibited under later treaties, which do not contain the unique requirement of intent that characterizes the crime of genocide in the Genocide Convention. Thus, genocide would be prohibited today under international human rights law, even if the Genocide Convention did not exist.

The parallels between human rights as articulated in the Genocide Convention and more contemporary definitions of human rights are clear. As defined in Article 2 of the Genocide Convention, the crime of genocide takes in:

- "killing," which would be defined in human rights language as violation of the right to life

- "causing serious bodily or mental harm," which violates security of person and is also likely to constitute torture or inhuman or degrading treatment

- "inflicting on the group conditions of life calculated to bring about its physical destruction," which also constitutes arbitrary deprivation of life

- "preventing births within the group," which interferes with the rights to privacy and family

- "forcibly transferring children of the group to another group," which violates the rights to privacy and family, as well as the rights of the child

The right to life is obviously fundamental to all other human rights. At the same time, however, it is not an absolute concept, and it is only the "arbitrary" deprivation of life that is prohibited in the convention. For example, it is possible to imagine circumstances in which a state's killing of a person would be both morally and legally permissible, and some human rights treaties carefully codify such exceptions. Under Article 2 of the European Convention on Human Rights, for example, a government may execute a duly convicted prisoner (although a later amendment to this convention abolishes capital punishment). In addition, deadly force may be used if it is "absolutely necessary" to protect a person from unlawful violence, to effect a lawful arrest or prevent the escape of a lawfully held prisoner, or to quell a riot. Other treaties, such as the International Covenant on Civil and Political Rights (Civil and Political Covenant), simply prohibit arbitrary killing, implying that there are some circumstances in which the use of deadly force may not be arbitrary and therefore may be justifiable.

The failure of the USSR to sponsor or support the Universal Declaration of Human Rights in the decades following 1948 played a role in delegitimizing the communist regime and even contributed to its demise. Here, a man with a sledgehammer whacks at the Berlin wall (whose dismantling became a symbol of the cold war's end). [REUTERS NEWMEDIA INC./CORBIS]

There are many difficult concepts that lie at the edges of international formulations of the right to life: Does the right to life imply interventionist duties on the part of the state? Does the right to life affect the issues of abortion or suicide? Is capital punishment always prohibited? Under what specific conditions is the use of deadly force by law enforcement officials permissible? The provision (pertaining to the right to life) in the Genocide Convention, on the other hand, is relatively clear: Killing members of a group identified in the convention is prohibited. Because genocide, as formulated in the convention, also requires an "intent to destroy," genocidal killings are by definition committed deliberately, and attempts to destroy a group and its members cannot be justified under any of the exemptions from the crime of genocide enunciated in other treaties. Indeed, Article 6.3 of the Civil and Political Covenant specifically provides that the covenant cannot be interpreted as taking away from or lessening in any way the

A journalist/filmmaker has been allowed to set up inside Abu Ghraib and to film some of its operations on May 10, 2004—approximately two weeks after the infamous photographs of the U.S. abuse and torture of Iraqi prisoners had first come to light and provoked an international outcry. A May 2004 report of the International Red Cross cited estimates by U.S. Army intelligence officers that 70 to 90 percent of the prison's earlier inmates had been innocent civilians. [AP/**WIDE WORLD PHOTOS**]

obligations that states have assumed under the Genocide Convention.

Imposing "conditions of life" calculated to destroy a group also constitutes an arbitrary deprivation of life, even if that imposition is accomplished in an indirect manner. Deliberately starving a population or infecting it with a fatal disease violates international human rights norms; when these deeds are carried out for the purpose of destroying a group protected under the Genocide Convention, in whole or in part, they also constitute genocide.

"Security of person" protects individuals from treatment that might seriously injure them but not cause death. Such treatment is prohibited, whether it occurs while a person is in custody or under any other circumstances. Accordingly, all persons held in prisons or other detention facilities should be treated with respect, whether they have been convicted of a crime or only accused of one.

Domestic law (in many nations) usually prohibits the physical ill-treatment of any persons by government officials, and violation of this prohibition may result in compensation being paid to the victim or to dismissal of criminal charges. The international standard is not as all-encompassing, however, and the usual formulation prohibits only those acts that constitute "torture or inhuman or degrading treatment or punishment." There have been many attempts to shed light on these phrases in court cases, but there is no doubt that the "serious bodily or mental harm" that is prohibited under the Genocide Convention would be included within this broader international prohibition against ill-treatment.

"Rights to family and privacy" are also part of international human rights law, even though they may not be specifically protected under all domestic legal systems. The Civil and Political Covenant refers to the family as "the natural and fundamental group unit of society" and recognizes the right to marry and to found a family. Similar provisions may be found in the African, American, and European human rights conventions. The right to found or raise a family obviously includes the right to have children, and attempting to prevent births against the wishes of the parents would clearly violate international human rights norms.

The right to privacy is specifically articulated in many human rights treaties. It has a public sphere, wherein one's honor and reputation should be protected from the libelous or slanderous statements or actions of others, and a private sphere, which would entail noninterference by government in such matters as lifestyle and the decision to have children. As is the case with other human rights, however, the right to privacy may be restricted to accommodate other legitimate concerns of citizenries; only "arbitrary or unlawful" interference with privacy is prohibited under the Civil and Political Covenant. The regional human rights treaties are more specific, permitting the placement of restrictions on the right to privacy when those restrictions are necessary to protect, for example, national security, public safety, public health, public morals, or the rights and freedoms of others. It is inconceivable that attempts to prevent births within a national, ethnical, racial, or religious group (as prohibited by the Genocide Convention) would fall within one of these permitted restrictions.

The "rights of the child" are referred to in general terms in all of the major human rights treaties. More important, they are now guaranteed by the International Convention on the Rights of the Child (Child Convention), which as of 2003 had been ratified by every country in the world except Somalia and the United States. The basic principles underlying this convention are: (1) the best interests of a child should guide any governmental action that affects that child; and (2) a child's rights and responsibilities should evolve as the child's own capacities evolve with age and maturity.

Under Article 9 of the Child Convention, it is possible for a child to be separated from his or her parents against the parents' will, but only ". . . when competent authorities subject to judicial review determine, in accordance with applicable law and procedures, that such separation is necessary for the best interests of the child. Such determination may be necessary in a particular case, such as one involving abuse or neglect of the child by the parents, or one where the parents are living separately and a decision must be made as to the child's place of residence." Nothing in this formulation would justify transferring a child from one group to another group, as part of an effort to destroy the group from which the child is taken.

"Nondiscrimination" is at the heart of international human rights law, and the UN Charter itself states that human rights must be guaranteed to all, without distinction as to race, sex, language, or religion. Under human rights law, nondiscrimination is a separate norm, distinct from prohibitions against arbitrary killing or other ill treatment.

Under the Genocide Convention, however, discrimination and the attempt to destroy a group are implicitly linked. This linkage derives from the fact that it is not widespread killing per se that constitutes genocide—it is rather the attempt to destroy, in whole or in part, a national, ethnical, racial, or religious group. In contrast to the less restrictive characterizations of genocide that are part of international human rights norms, the Genocide Convention requires that three conditions must be obtained before an act rises to the level of the crime of genocide: [1] the commission of a prohibited act (killing, transferring children, imposing conditions of life, and so on) [2] with the intent of destroying a group [3] of a particular kind, that is, national, ethnical, racial, or religious. This restrictive formulation deliberately excludes from its scope the murder of political opponents and indiscriminate violence—although the widespread killing of individuals, whether or not the individuals belong to a particular group, surely violates contemporary human rights norms.

The prohibitions of the Genocide Convention are limited to acts calculated to destroy a group physically, and the convention fails to address issues of discrimination or cultural intolerance. Human rights norms have evolved to fill this gap, by recognizing special rights for certain kinds of minorities. Under Article 27 of the Civil and Political Covenant, for example, rights are granted to members of ethnic, linguistic, and religious minorities within states. In Europe, both linguistic and national minorities are protected by conventions and institutions created in the 1990s.

Modern formulations of minority rights include, among other things, the rights of minority group members to use their own language; to practice their own culture; to be educated in ways that will preserve and promote their distinct characteristics; and to participate effectively in the economic and political life of their society. In part, this broadening protection of minority rights is evidence that the mere prohibition of violence against minority groups is insufficient to protect them and to promote tolerance and diversity. But when these rights are respected, in spirit as well as letter, genocide is much less likely to occur.

Implementing Human Rights

Given the fact that the Genocide Convention was adopted in 1948, it is not surprising that it dealt only with the most heinous kinds of human rights abuses. Unfortunately, its early adoption also meant that a consensus could not be reached on how the convention might be implemented effectively—beyond the purely legal obligations imposed on states when they ratified it.

Today, human rights treaties generally have provisions that require the creation of institutions to oversee the implementation of those treaties. These institutions are usually composed of individual experts, rather than the diplomatic representatives of states, and their powers vary widely. Typically, human rights bodies are given the power (1) to periodically review and comment on reports submitted by state parties, in which the states describe how they are implementing the treaty in question and what problems they have encountered in doing so; (2) to receive, investigate, and determine the validity of allegations, made by individual victims or other state parties, that a state has violated its obligations under the treaty; (3) to investigate and report on the overall state of human rights in a particular country, outside the context of specific complaints; (4) [in the case of conventions on torture] to visit places of detention to ensure that ill-treatment is not occurring; (5) to interpret the treaty, often via the issuance of commentaries on specific rights or the scope of state obligations; and (6) to educate governments and the general public on the content of human rights law.

There are now three regional human rights courts. The European Court of Human Rights is the only permanent human rights body in the world, and every party to the European Convention on Human Rights is legally bound to obey the court's judgments. The judgments of the Inter-American Court of Human Rights are also legally binding (on parties to the American Convention on Human Rights), but acceptance of the court's jurisdiction by those parties is optional. The African Court on Human and Peoples' Rights was created in January 2004, although only a minority of African Union members has thus far accepted its jurisdiction.

Direct means of enforcing human rights treaties, such as the creation of bodies of experts and international tribunals, were unknown when the Genocide Convention was adopted in 1948, and the law that served as a model for the drafters of the convention was that of traditional international law between states. No specialized institution to oversee the convention was provided for, and signatory states are under no obligation to provide reports on their conduct to any international body. Although states are legally required under general international law to abide by their obligations under the convention (pursuant to the doctrine of *pacta sunt servanda* [promises must be kept]), there is no

forum automatically available to complainants that might hear complaints that a state is not fulfilling its obligations. In particular, individuals have no right under the Genocide Convention or customary international law to direct access to an international court or other body that could determine whether their rights have been violated.

Article 9 of the Genocide Convention does provide that disputes between the state parties, including disputes that have to do with the responsibility of a state for genocide that has been committed, or for allowing genocide to go unpunished, can be submitted to the International Court of Justice (ICJ) for resolution. Unfortunately, some states opted out of this provision by filing a reservation to the convention at the time they ratified it; the ICJ upheld this practice in a 1951 Advisory Opinion, even though the Convention does not specifically provide for it.

Despite the many instances of genocide and alleged genocide that have become apparent since 1948, only two petitions alleging a violation of the Geneva Convention have been submitted to the ICJ. Both grew out of the war in the former Yugoslavia in the 1990s, and they were filed against Serbia and Montenegro (by Croatia and Bosnia-Herzegovina). The omissions are only too obvious: Although Rwanda has been a party to the convention since 1975, it has not accepted Article 9 and thus could not be brought before the ICJ without the Rwandan government's special consent. Cambodia is a party to the convention and has accepted the court's jurisdiction, but no state was willing to challenge the conduct of the Khmer Rouge in the late 1970s by submitting a petition to the court, despite the efforts of many nongovernmental organizations to promote such an application.

Human Rights Crimes and Human Rights Violations

It is not uncommon to read references to human rights crimes in the press and other media, and many people view the newly created International Criminal Court (with headquarters in The Hague, Netherlands) as a human rights court. Such references are incorrect, however, and they blur a basic difference between (abrogations of) human rights per se and the international crime of genocide.

The protection of human rights is primarily an obligation of states or governments—those obligations stemming from international treaties and customary international law. While there are increasing efforts to impose moral or political obligations on corporations and other bodies in the private sphere to respect human rights, the obligation to promote and protect the human rights of individuals over whose lives these bodies hold sway legally falls on states.

Although there are a few exceptions, international human rights law does not generally impose criminal liability on those who may be the individual agents of human rights violations. Neither the policeman who seizes a banned publication, nor the magistrate who sends an accused person to prison after an unfair trial, nor the bureaucrat who discriminates against a religious group in making social welfare payments is committing a crime under international law, even though each of these acts might constitute a human rights violation on the part of the government that the individual agent represents. One of the only exceptions to this principle is the crime of torture, which has been specifically designated as an international crime under both global and regional antitorture treaties.

The other major exception, of course, is genocide. Article 1 of the Genocide Convention begins by affirming that genocide "is a crime under international law which they [the parties to the treaty] undertake to prevent and punish." Articles 5 and 6 specify that states will adopt laws to ensure "effective penalties" for persons guilty of genocide, and that persons accused of genocide will be tried by the state in which the genocide occurred (or by an international tribunal).

The distinctions between human rights violations and individual crimes may help to explain the absence of provision for enforcement machinery in the Genocide Convention. There was no international criminal court in 1948, and one would not come into force until more than fifty years later. Thus, because the criminal prosecutions called for under the convention could only be carried out by national authorities, the drafters may have felt that there was no need to create a new international oversight body.

Treaty formulations of the particularly heinous conduct called genocide have more common ground with the concept of a war crime or crime against humanity, rather than the typical human rights violation. For example, some types of conduct that take place within the context of an armed conflict are criminalized in the 1949 Geneva Conventions, and states must punish those who commit grave breaches of the laws of war. As was true for the Genocide Convention, the 1949 Geneva Conventions set up no new mechanisms to monitor the implementation of the provisions of the conventions, and enforcement was left to domestic law.

More direct international enforcement of international criminal norms was not achieved until 2002, when the Rome Statute of the International Criminal Court (ICC) entered into force. The Rome Statute con-

fers on the ICC jurisdiction over the crime of aggression, war crimes, crimes against humanity, and genocide. Human rights violations per se are not addressed under the ICC Statute, although the crimes it enumerates, if committed or tolerated by a government, would also constitute violations of a state's obligations under international human rights law.

Of course, the impact on victims is the same, whether, technically, they are victims of crime or of a human rights violation. But a verdict of genocide demands that there be an element of conscious intent (to destroy a protected group), which is absent from definitions of human rights obligations. The various international oversight bodies created to monitor the implementation of human rights treaties do not need to inquire into the motives of those responsible for alleged human rights violations. It is enough if government actions do violate international norms; those governments need not also intend to commit the violation.

This element of specific intent is what often leads lawyers and diplomats to contend with one another over whether a situation in which large numbers of people are being killed constitutes "genocide." The presence (or absence) of conscious intent in the human rights context is irrelevant, since "arbitrary" killings are prohibited no matter what their motivation(s). Every state is required to protect people under their jurisdiction from wholesale violations of the right to life, whether or not the deaths result from a discriminatory or genocidal motivation.

Conclusion

At the time it was adopted, the Genocide Convention was a milestone in international law, as it set limits on what a state was allowed to do within its own borders to its own citizens. Today, the international attention that is garnered by the internal affairs of states is familiar. The acts that constitute genocide are now illegal under a variety of domestic and international legal regimes.

At the same time, *genocide* remains an emotive word, as it evokes the horrors of the Nazi Holocaust and the end-of-century killings in Rwanda. Diplomats avoid its use, fearing the political consequences of identifying murderous events as genocide in instances in which they are unable or unwilling to stop the events. For opposite reasons, activists (oblivious to or wishing to reject genocide's actual definition in the Genocide Convention) attach the label of genocide to almost any killing of an identifiable group of people.

Legalistic and diplomatic debates over what constitutes genocide usually obscure the real question, which is—how the international community should react to widespread human rights violations or losses of life, whether or not the criminal actions meet the strict requirements of the Genocide Convention. Today, there is no concrete international law that permits the use of armed intervention in the prevention of serious human rights violations, although Rwanda and the Balkan wars have inspired a burst of scholarly and political commentary on this issue. Those who support intervention in extreme circumstances certainly believe that halting ongoing or imminent genocide justifies the use of force, but the limiting of intervention to genocide as it is defined in statutes may negate or nullify the principle of intervention. There is, as yet, no consensus on what criteria might justify intervention, who should authorize it, and by whom intervention might be carried out.

Despite its symbolic importance, genocide is now only one of many harms that international law seeks to prevent. Whether or not genocide was committed in Cambodia, Ethiopia, or the former Yugoslavia is less important than the fact that government-sponsored terror in these countries resulted in the deaths of millions of people. Rather than argue about what to call the killings, advocates should focus on how to prevent them and how to stop them if they recur. Protecting the lives of those at risk, for whatever reason—and continuing the daily task of promoting the human rights of tolerance, participation, and free expression—is more likely to accomplish the humanitarian goals of those who first sought to outlaw genocide.

SEE ALSO Humanitarian Law; International Law

BIBLIOGRAPHY

Buergenthal, Thomas, Dinah Shelton and David P. Stewart. (2002). *International Human Rights in a Nutshell*, 3rd edition. Minneapolis, Minn.: West.

Craven, Matthew (1998). *The International Covenant on Economic, Social, and Cultural Rights*. Oxford, U.K.: Clarendon Press.

Donnelly, Jack (2002). *Universal Human Rights in Theory and Practice*, 2nd edition. Ithaca, N.Y.: Cornell University Press.

Hannum, Hurst, ed. (2004). *Guide to International Human Rights Practice*, 4th edition. Ardsley, N.Y.: Transnational.

Holzgrefe, J. L. and Robert O. Keohane, eds. (2003). *Humanitarian Intervention: Ethical, Legal, and Political Dilemmas*. Cambridge: Cambridge University Press.

Ignatieff, Michael (2002). *Human Rights as Politics and Idolatry*. Princeton, N.J.: Princeton University Press.

International Commission on Intervention and State Sovereignty (2001). *The Responsibility to Protect*. Ottawa, Ontario: International Development Research Centre.

Megret, Frederic, and Philip Alston, eds. (2004). *The United Nations and Human Rights: A Critical Appraisal*. Oxford, U.K.: Oxford University Press.

Provost, René (2004). *International Human Rights and Humanitarian Law*. Cambridge: Cambridge University Press.

Risse, Thomas, et al., eds. (1999). *The Power of Human Rights: International Norms and Domestic Change*. Cambridge: Cambridge University Press.

United Nations High Commissioner for Human Rights. Available from http://www.unhchr.ch.

Weissbrodt, David, Joan Fitzpatrick, and Frank Newman (2001). *International Human Rights: Law, Policy, and Process*, 3rd edition. Cincinnati, Ohio: Anderson.

Hurst Hannum